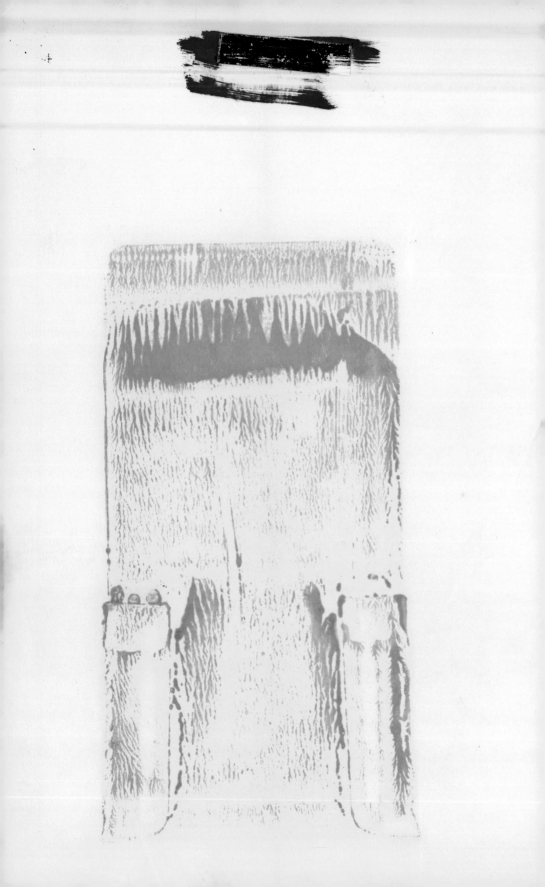

THE
WORLD
IN THE
TWENTIETH
CENTURY

GEOFFREY BRUUN

VICTOR S. MAMATEY

fifth edition

THE
WORLD *IN THE*
TWENTIETH
CENTURY

D. C. HEATH AND COMPANY
Lexington, Massachusetts

MAPS BY THEODORE R. MILLER

AND RAY GRANAI

PREFACE

A textbook on recent and contemporary times must surmount grave limitations. The events of earlier centuries have been evaluated by succeeding generations in the light of their unfolding consequences and may be judged with increasing finality and detachment. But for recent developments, for dramas still upon the stage, the historian can offer only a provisional analysis, a temporary verdict. Truth is the daughter of time.

To compensate for these admitted limitations, critics of the contemporary scene and its immediate antecedents may claim certain advantages. They are close enough to the events they describe to share the mood, the *mystique*, of those who participated in them. They address a receptive audience, curious to learn more fully how recent events shaped its problems and how they may affect its destiny. Finally, they have at their disposal a larger and better organized body of factual information than any previous generation enjoyed. Today the bureau of statistics has become the statesman's cave of oracles, and all students eager to grasp the significance of current developments must learn to interpret this "arithmetic of power." If, in the pages that follow, economic, geographic, and technological factors are frequently emphasized, and figures on population, income, production, and trade are repeatedly stressed, it is because such information offers the surest clues we possess to the forces that are shaping the world of today and will shape the world of tomorrow.

The interval that has elapsed since the original version of this text appeared in 1948 has provided a lengthened perspective and a new vantage ground from which to view the first half of the twentieth century. These intervening years have also added momentously to the content of twentieth-century world history. It has become necessary, as the century passed its midpoint and then its two-thirds mark, to increase the number of our chapters from fifty-three to sixty-eight, and to divide the expanded work into two approximately equal parts. The successive alterations and additions have, we trust, made the text more informative, more comprehensive, and better balanced. We have striven, however, to keep the general character of the work stable and to retain all major features that were commended in previous editions.

While taking account of events since the Fourth Edition was issued, and striving to place them in a historical perspective, we have had an opportunity to bring some earlier developments into what we hope is a clearer focus. We have also welcomed the chance to update our statistics as more recent tables became available, to add or substitute more up-to-date maps and charts, and to include new books in the chapter reading lists to supersede some of the older items. For this edition most of the illustrations have been replaced by newer pictures, and these are now distributed throughout the text instead of being concentrated in two groups, an arrangement that brings the illustrations into closer proximity with their subject matter.

The mounting importance which the Soviet Union, Eastern Europe, and the Near and Middle East have acquired in recent decades made an expanded and more authoritative treatment of these areas essential. This has been provided by Victor S. Mamatey, who also undertook Sections II and VIII. Geoffrey Bruun prepared Section IX and the chapters on the New World, while those on Western Europe, Africa, and farther Asia were divided. At all stages and in all details this latest revision has continued to be the product of a close, critical, and exceptionally harmonious partnership.

With the Fifth Edition, for the first time, *The World in the Twentieth Century: Before 1939* and *The World in the Twentieth Century: Since 1939* will be available as separate paperbound volumes. Their contents, however, will remain identical with Part One and Part Two of the complete text, which is issued, as hitherto, in a hardcover binding.

It is a pleasure to record our gratitude to Theodore R. Miller, who designed all the original maps, to Ray Granai, who prepared additional maps for the current edition, and to members of the College Division and the Art Department at D. C. Heath and Company, from whose advice, experience, and labor the work has profited immeasurably. There is not space to mention by name the many other friends and associates to whom we are indebted directly or indirectly, but to all of them we offer our deep and heartfelt thanks.

Geoffrey Bruun
Victor S. Mamatey

CONTENTS

PART ONE: TO 1939

vii

Contents ix

SECTION IV
Experiments in Government   227

PART TWO: SINCE 1939

LIST OF MAPS

LIST OF CHARTS AND GRAPHS

ILLUSTRATIONS

THE
WORLD
IN THE
TWENTIETH
CENTURY

PART ONE: TO 1939

Section I: THE CENTURY OF EUROPE'S APOGEE, 1815–1914

1

INTRODUCTION: THE HISTORICAL BACKGROUND

> *Better fifty years of Europe than a cycle of Cathay.*
> ALFRED TENNYSON

1. ORIGINS AND OPPORTUNITIES

TODAY, FOR THE FIRST TIME in the annals of mankind, all parts of the world are in communication, all peoples are members of an interdependent society. There is no nation so remote or isolated that it can remain untouched by events on other continents. This interdependence of the nations is a consequence of the hegemony established by the Europeans, for it was European conquest and technology that bridged the seas and knit the continents together. To understand how European civilization won such world-wide influence it will be helpful to recall briefly how it arose in Europe itself.

Europe is not, in a geographical sense, one of the major continents; it is a peninsula jutting westward from the Eurasian land mass. The earliest European civilizations were dependent and derivative, introduced by traders and colonists from the older civilizations that had arisen in the Nile and Euphrates valleys. The barbaric aborigines of those regions now known as Spain, France, and Britain were raised to civilized status by the Romans some two thousand years ago. When the Roman Empire declined, after the third century of the Christian era, all Europe, including Italy, seemed destined to lapse again into timeless barbarism. With the Moslem conquests of the seventh and eighth centuries the society of western Europe became an even more isolated and retarded society, little influenced by the more advanced civilizations of the Near East and farther Asia.

Yet vestiges of Roman and Greek culture survived and the church preserved the memory and the ideal of that unity of language, law, and custom which had held the Roman world together. For nearly one thousand years, the period of the Middle Ages, the peoples of Christian Europe had only the bond of religious faith to unite them. Politically and economically, society broke down, disintegrating into smaller and smaller

3

units until it became fragmentary and parochial. What little coherence remained was chiefly the product of a common faith and a common religious culture: Christendom was a community of the faithful. As trade and communications failed and towns decayed, the civilization of Roman times almost perished. The social unit became the hamlet or manor, where a few score or a few hundred families lived largely to themselves, raising their own supplies and depending upon an overlord and his armed retainers for administration and protection.

In this harsh era, poverty and hardship discouraged new experiments and daunted initiative. Society became and tended to remain static. Learning and even literacy were limited almost exclusively to the clergy. It was not lack of intelligence but lack of leisure and lack of opportunity which kept medieval communities backward. Even in the darkest centuries, between the sixth and the eleventh, some progress was achieved. Better methods of ploughing, of rotating crops, of harnessing horses and oxen, of constructing water and wind mills had been introduced before A.D. 1200. The canals, castles, and cathedrals constructed after that date all testify to the energy and will to collective activity which was developing in the later medieval period. But such collaboration suffered from rude practical limitations. It was limited by lack of political order, by absence of adequate means of transportation and communication, by deficiency of capital reserves for large-scale projects, and by confusion resulting from haphazard scales of measurement and inadequate tools. The localism, poverty, and social inertia, which overtook European society after the collapse of the Roman power, deepened for five centuries and then required another five centuries for growth and recovery.

No prophetic observer contemplating the frugal life, the backward economy, the chaotic political institutions of Europe in the year 1000 could have foreseen that before another thousand years had passed Europe would lead the world. Such an imperial destiny seemed much more likely to descend upon the peoples of Asia. During those centuries when Europe was a decentralized patchwork of minute, autonomous fragments, great empires arose and waned beyond the frontiers of Christendom. The eastern half of the Roman Empire survived the fall of the West, and Constantinople remained the capital of a sophisticated and luxurious civilization. Because the European peoples, isolated in their scattered parishes, ignored developments outside their narrow world, modern historians have too often treated European society during the Middle Ages as if it existed in a vacuum. This narrow view still influences the thought of many European peoples when they think about Europe and its cultural origins.

The contrast between the civilized East and the barbarous West during the European Middle Ages is not flattering to the West. By the eighth century the cities built by Roman engineers and masons had become heaps of plundered ruins where wolves roamed the deserted streets. Only the memory of a glorious past survived in the late Roman provinces from Spain to Britain. In A.D. 800 the victorious Frankish king, Charlemagne (771–814), was crowned emperor at Rome in a wistful attempt to revive the legendary greatness of the Roman era, but his empire dissolved after his death. The so-called Carolingian Renaissance proved a false dawn, and the backwardness of Europe at this time can be gauged by contrasting the barbaric court of this unlettered Frank with the splendor of Constantinople. At the Byzantine capital on the Bosporus a thousand ships came and went, and a hundred thousand artisans fashioned articles of luxury for the lavish court and the cultured, sophisticated aristocracy.

Even Constantinople in the ninth century, however, was eclipsed by the splendor of the Moslem capital at Bagdad. There a contemporary of Charlemagne, the caliph Harun al-Rashid (786–809), familiar to readers of the *Arabian Nights,* ruled a fabulous city of almost a million inhabitants. At the zenith of its glory the empire of Islam stretched like a threatening crescent from Syria to Spain, its horns closing upon Christian Europe. In Spain, which the Moslems conquered in the eighth century, a brilliant Moorish civilization flourished while the rest of Europe touched the nadir of its decline. But Saracen civilization, however brilliant, often proved impermanent. In the eleventh century the peoples of Europe opened a series of military campaigns against the Moslem world; and these crusades, which established temporary Christian kingdoms in the Holy Land, also drove back the Moslem power in Spain until Granada, the last stronghold of the Moors there, capitulated in the fifteenth century.

Meanwhile in the thirteenth century the Moslem court at Bagdad had been menaced by the advance of Mongol hordes from central Asia. Under Genghis Khan (1162–1227) and his successors, the Mongol empire extended from the Black to the Yellow Sea. The Mongol advance threatened to engulf the world of Islam and to inundate Europe. But the Europeans were learning from their contacts with these alien cultures and were profiting from their experience. The age of land empires reached its close by 1500; an era of sea empires was about to open. The European seaboard states, lying near the center of the world's land masses, were swept to world leadership on the tides of this new age.

2. THE AGRARIAN BASIS OF SOCIETY

Though only 3,800,000 square miles in area, Europe possessed exceptional natural advantages. The other continents, it is true, were much larger in extent. Africa (11,500,000 square miles) had three times the area of Europe. North and South America (16,420,000 square miles combined) and Asia (16,500,000 square miles) were over four times as large as Europe. But for the support of a dense human population a favorable climate and fertile soil are the most important factors and in these respects

THE CONTINENTS COMPARED

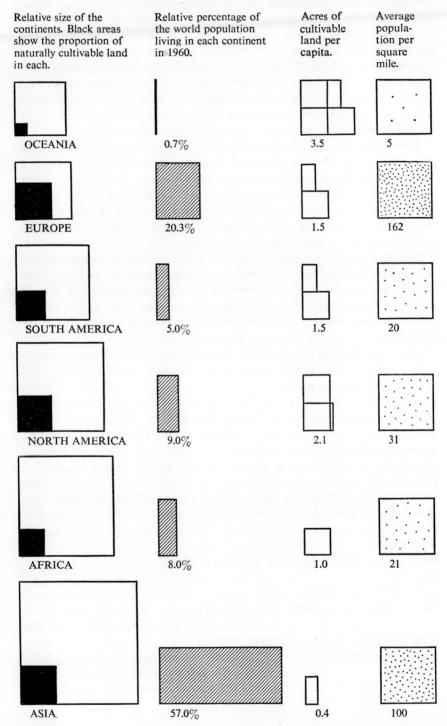

Relative size of the continents. Black areas show the proportion of naturally cultivable land in each.

Relative percentage of the world population living in each continent in 1960.

Acres of cultivable land per capita.

Average population per square mile.

OCEANIA — 0.7% — 3.5 — 5

EUROPE — 20.3% — 1.5 — 162

SOUTH AMERICA — 5.0% — 1.5 — 20

NORTH AMERICA — 9.0% — 2.1 — 31

AFRICA — 8.0% — 1.0 — 21

ASIA — 57.0% — 0.4 — 100

Europe surpassed any similar region. All of it (save the extreme north of European Russia) lay within the temperate belt, where the mean average temperatures ranged between 32° and 68° Fahrenheit. Almost all of it enjoyed an adequate rainfall, ranging between 20 and 60 inches annually. This rainfall, moreover, was reasonably well distributed throughout the year and fell gently; Europe did not suffer from excessive hurricanes, cyclones, or tornadoes, nor did the rain descend with such violence that it destroyed crops and swept away the topsoil. Finally, Europe possessed a larger proportion of *cultivable* land than any other continent, a point so vital it deserves special consideration.

All human life depends, in an ultimate sense, on plant life for its food. Even hunting and fishing tribes and meat-eating animals depend on vegetation indirectly. All great civilizations depend on staple agricultural crops, and for successful farming it is essential to have suitable land. This means land where four factors are found in combination: (1) Adequate rainfall, (2) a favorable temperature, (3) favorable topography or surface conditions, (4) fertile soil. Although the land area of the earth totals about 37 billion acres, only 7 per cent, or roughly 2.6 billion acres, enjoys this combination of natural advantages. These 2.6 billion acres are distributed around the globe, but some continents are more fortunate than others. Europe, though much smaller than Asia, Africa, or the Americas, was blessed by nature with more cultivable acres than any of the others.

Nearly 40 per cent of Europe's surface, roughly 1,400,000 square miles out of 3,800,000, was naturally suitable for cultivation. In this respect, Europe was some four times more fortunate than the next most favored region, North America, where 10 per cent of the land enjoyed the combination of advantages (rainfall, temperature, topography, soil) that encouraged farming. Asia came third, with 6 per cent of its vast area fitted by nature for successful cultivation. South America ranked fourth with 5 per cent; Africa and Oceania came last with only 3 per cent of their area naturally favored to the same extent.

It did not follow that, *because* a continent held land suitable for cultivation, this land would all be carefully cultivated. Nor did it follow that the people of the world would be distributed among the continents in the same proportions that the arable land was distributed. On the contrary, in A.D. 1500 the global population (approximately 450 million at that date) was very *unequally* distributed. Asia and Africa combined then held over four-fifths of the world's people but contained only one-third of the land naturally fitted for cultivation. Europe, the Americas, and Oceania together held less than one-fifth of the world's people but contained two-thirds of the land naturally fitted for cultivation. It is important to grasp the full significance of these facts. In the four centuries that followed (1500–1900) the world population increased almost

four-fold, and it also became more equally distributed as the table below
indicates.

	PER CENT OF THE WORLD'S PEOPLE IN 1500	PER CENT OF THE WORLD'S CULTIVABLE LAND	PER CENT OF THE WORLD'S PEOPLE IN 1900
Asia	60	24	57
Africa	22	9	8
Europe	13	35	25
North America	2	22	7
South America	2	8	2
Oceania	1(?)	2	1(?)

The significance of this table can be better appreciated if the *actual*
population of each continent at these dates is compared with its *ideal*
population — that is, with the number of inhabitants each continent
should have held if its share of the global population had been propor-
tioned to its share of the world's arable land.

	DISTRIBUTION OF GLOBAL POPULATION IN 1500		DISTRIBUTION OF GLOBAL POPULATION IN 1900	
	Actual	*Ideal*	*Actual*	*Ideal*
Asia	270 million	108 million	920 million	385 million
Africa	100 "	40 "	120 "	145 "
Europe	58 "	157 "	402 "	564 "
North America	9 "	100 "	110 "	354 "
South America	9 "	36 "	38 "	128 "
Oceania	4? "	9 "	4 "	32 "

It should be understood, of course, that the calculations on which
these charts are based can never be more than intelligent estimates, and
they do not tell the whole story. Good land may be neglected by peoples
who lack the knowledge and skill to farm it. Arid land, too dry to support
crops, may be transformed by irrigation. Nevertheless, the general conditions set forth here indicate the basic realities of world economy.

In an overcrowded continent such as Asia the masses had to toil desperately to survive. In 1500 there were two acres of cultivable land in
Asia and Africa for each inhabitant. In Europe at that date there were
fifteen acres of cultivable land for each inhabitant; in South America
there were over twenty acres, and in North America over sixty acres per
inhabitant. By 1900 the figures had changed but the situation of Asia
was even more severe. For the Asian population had increased until there
was less than one naturally cultivable acre for each inhabitant. In Europe
(although the population had multiplied seven-fold) there were still over
two acres per capita; in North America (where the population had multiplied twelve-fold) there were over three acres per capita; and in South

America (where the population had multiplied four-fold) there were about four acres per capita.

The most remarkable fact these charts illustrate is the exceptionally favorable condition of Europe. This small continent had more acres naturally suited for farming than any other continent. Nowhere else in the world was so much cultivable land concentrated in so small an area. This natural advantage, coupled with the fact that by 1500 the Europeans had become the most enterprising and adventurous people on the globe, helps to explain their rise to world dominance. Between 1500 and 1900 the population of Europe increased from between 50 and 60 million to over 400 million. But this represented only a part of the European achievement. During the same four centuries their mastery of the oceans enabled the Europeans to conquer and colonize the New World and also Australia and New Zealand. These regions, hitherto the most thinly populated continents of the globe, together contained one-third of the world's cultivable area. Added to the one-third the Europeans already possessed in Europe, these conquests gave them control of two-thirds of the world's naturally cultivable land. Furthermore, by 1900 they also had come to dominate half of Asia and almost all of Africa. Thus, by the close of the nineteenth century, nine-tenths of the world's cultivable area was controlled, directly or indirectly, by the Europeans and their descendants.

3. THE OCEANIC AGE

The geographical discoveries of the fifteenth century, especially the voyage of Columbus to America (1492) and of Vasco da Gama to India (1498), were bold feats of navigation. But they were epoch-making and opened a new age only because the peoples on the Atlantic seaboard of Europe were ready to exploit the new opportunities. Leif Ericson with his Vikings had visited America about A.D. 1000 and had founded nothing more substantial than a saga. In the five centuries between Leif and Columbus, however, a notable change transformed European society. The best proof of this change is the rise in population, testifying to a more adequate food supply and greater security of life and property. After A.D. 1200 there was a marked revival of town life and signs of quickening trade. In politics, the extension of royal power in Spain, Portugal, France, and England curbed the disruptive forces of feudalism and ushered in the national territorial state. The monarchs with the aid of the townsmen checked the warfare and depredations of the barons and created centralized governments strong and wealthy enough to undertake the conquest and colonization of empires overseas.

It seems strange at first thought that medieval European society, isolated, retarded, and landbound, could change in a few centuries and send its navigators forth to conquer the oceans. Four influences, however, geographical, religious, commercial, and technological, combined to foster this development. No equivalent area of the world has such a long and irregular coastline as Europe, with so many inland gulfs, natural harbors, and navigable rivers. The Europeans, like the ancient Greeks, learned to build and use boats because geography was their master. By A.D. 1100 they competed with the Moslem and Byzantine fleets for control of the Mediterranean. Their long religious strife with the Moslem empire became more acute after the Turks conquered Constantinople in 1453. Even before this date the rising population of Europe and the merchants in the reviving towns had come to covet a larger share of the commerce of Asia. The idea of outflanking "the Obstructive Turk" by sailing around Africa lured Portuguese seamen from c.1400 on. But to brave the Atlantic Ocean, and the strange people that might be met, better ships and arms were needed. The Europeans borrowed four inventions — the sternpost rudder, the fore-and-aft rig, the magnetic compass, and gunpowder — all developed earlier by the Chinese. From these combined techniques they produced the armed sailing ships that brought them the mastery of the oceans. History offers few better examples of how a machine (the sailing ship is fundamentally a machine operated by windpower) may alter the existing balance of power in favor of a people alert to seize the opportunity presented by technological advances.

The first European states to profit by the opening of the Oceanic Age were Spain and Portugal. Both were newly forged kingdoms, both had Atlantic harbors, in both the population responded readily to the twin urges of crusading ardor and commercial enterprise which impelled the early explorers. The sixteenth century was the great century of Iberian conquest, during which the Spaniards ferried tons of gold and silver from America and the Portuguese tons of spices (worth their weight in gold) from the East Indies. The future culture and language patterns of Central and South America and the destinies of millions of native peoples from the Philippines to Ceylon were largely decided in that significant century. Spain and Portugal led the van and set the tempo of expansion and conquest.

Ocean communications are tenuous threads upon which to string the jewels of a maritime empire, for if the thread is severed the jewels are likely to be lost. In the seventeenth century the Netherlanders, the French, and the English challenged Spain and Portugal for control of the sea. The Dutch took over most of the Portuguese posts and trading monopolies in the East. The British between 1600 and 1800 captured the trade of the Spanish and Portuguese colonies in Latin America, and after 1800 they helped these colonies to achieve political as well as economic emancipation from the control of Madrid and Lisbon. The French, who likewise entered the colonial race in the seventeenth century, established colonies in Canada, Louisiana, and the West Indies and acquired trading posts in India. But the wars of the eighteenth century swept most of these

French dependencies into the control of the British. The Spaniards under Philip II (1556–1598) and the French under Louis XIV (1643–1715) and Napoleon (1799–1814) learned the same bitter lesson — that even the most powerful state could not maintain a military hegemony in Europe and naval supremacy on the sea at the same time. By the opening of the nineteenth century Great Britain was the leading colonial, naval, and maritime power of the world, and the rapid mechanization of British industry was making her the leading industrial power also. Free from invasion and from the burden of a large military force, she diverted her energies to the sea and benefited prodigiously from the vast opportunities of the Oceanic Age. The insecurity, destruction, and indemnities which crippled her chief commercial competitors, Spain, Portugal, the Nether-lands, and France, as a result of European wars, redounded to the advan-tage of England. While European states exhausted themselves waging long campaigns to decide the fate of a few towns in Flanders, the English secured continental areas overseas.

Until 1750 colonial expansion was conditioned by two main factors: commercial profit and naval power. After the middle of the eighteenth century the British added a third element to the program of imperialism, the factory system. In the nineteenth century an overseas empire was to become the concrete expression of armed might, a territorial conquest financed by commercial profits, which produced raw materials for the mechanized industry of the mother country. The Industrial Revolution, gathering momentum in the late eighteenth century, transformed modern society, multiplied the products and profits of manufacture, and injected a new dynamism into the drama of imperial expansion. Colonies took on a new, a peremptory significance as sources of supply and as markets for factory output. Britain, the first state to feel the new industrial impulse powerfully, became in a few generations "the workshop of the world."

4. THE GREAT CENTURY OF EUROPEAN SUPREMACY: 1815–1914

How the Europeans won a commanding position in the world within four centuries is the central theme of modern history. It is impossible to understand the condition and the problems of the world today unless this phenomenal expansion of European influence, of Western civilization, is kept in mind. This expansion was stimulated, as already noted, by several developments working together. It will be helpful to list these develop-ments here and to see how they supplemented one another.

(1) The first factor that favored the Europeans was their possession in their own homeland of such an exceptionally large share of the world's cultivable land. This helped them to feed their rapidly rising population and improve their standards of living at the same time.

(2) The second factor that favored European expansion and leadership was control of the seas. The Europeans, with their superior ships and arms, could attack any people on another continent, but they could not themselves be attacked from overseas. Their control of the oceans and ocean-borne trade brought them great profits and also enabled them to conquer and colonize thinly populated regions. Between 1500 and 1900 they transported some 40 million settlers to the New World and also brought over 15 million Negroes from Africa to serve them there as slaves. Although the American colonies later severed their *political* ties with European countries, the New World was dominated by the Europeans and their descendants. With over 400 million people in Europe itself, and over 100 million of predominantly European descent living overseas, the Europeans comprised one-third of the global population by 1900. Four centuries earlier they had comprised only one-eighth.

(3) The third advantage the Europeans enjoyed was the extraordinary development they achieved in science and technology. More will be said about this later but its results must be mentioned briefly here. With steam power and electricity the peoples of the western world multiplied their manufactures, and speeded up transportation and communication. Machines also made the production and marketing of food cheaper and easier. Advances in medicine conquered many of the great plagues and prolonged life expectancy. With so many advantages, it is not surprising that by the nineteenth century European (or Western) civilization had become the first truly dominant and global civilization in history.

European influence reached its culmination in the hundred years between the Battle of Waterloo (1815) and the outbreak of the First World War (1914). This was Europe's "great century." Its population doubled, from approximately 200 to over 400 million. The European nations extended their colonial empires in Asia and divided up almost the whole of Africa. These conquests marked the final rewards of that control of the oceans which the Europeans had enjoyed for 400 years. The part that seapower played in promoting the rise of Europe cannot be overstressed. European supremacy depended on its naval and mercantile leadership — Europe dominated the globe because it became the greatest thalassocracy in history.

How complete European rule of the oceans had become by the nineteenth century is evident from the share of commerce and naval power the European states controlled. Two-thirds of all international trade, three-fourths of the merchant ships, and four-fifths of the warships of the world were in European hands. Yet by the close of the nineteenth century signs appeared that the supremacy of Europe would be challenged. By 1914 the rise of the United States and Japan marked the emergence of two great powers *outside* Europe. The fact that goods from American and Japanese factories began to compete with European manufactures in the world markets meant that the European monopoly of machine-made goods was at an end. Equally serious was the fact that the Americans and the Japanese constructed navies that could challenge the long-supreme naval forces of Europe. When the United States easily defeated Spain in 1898 the event did not seem highly significant for Spain was a second-class power. But when Japan defeated Russia in 1904–1905 the lesson was inescapable. For the first time in several centuries an Asian state had successfully challenged a European great power in war and worsted it.

Throughout the nineteenth century the European nations had avoided any long and exhausting wars among themselves. If they could have reconciled their interests and united their policies they might have faced the future with confidence, assured that the population, wealth, and resources of a united Europe would make them superior to any alliance of non-European countries. But the European nations chose instead to arm against one another and in 1914 they plunged into a four years' war. The outbreak of World War I in that year marked a turning point in world history.

2

THE CHARACTER OF WESTERN CULTURE

To regard all things and principles of things as inconstant modes or fashions has more and more become the tendency of modern thought.

WALTER PATER

1. SCIENCE AND TECHNOLOGY

ALTHOUGH MODERN EUROPEAN CIVILIZATION arose in Europe it spread to the Americas after 1500 and came in later centuries to influence all parts of the earth. A new name was needed for a culture that expanded so widely and it is customary to speak of it as Western Civilization. All civilizations have distinguishing features and the outstanding characteristic of Western Civilization was its science and technology. Never before had any people gained so much exact knowledge of nature as the modern Europeans amassed. Never before had any people developed such ingenious instruments of power and precision, or been so successful in harnessing the mysterious forces of nature and using these forces to drive their machines. The Europeans came to dominate the globe because they learned to control material forces and material things. But by their very triumphs they opened new vistas and made new discoveries that changed their civilization and their picture of the world. They were swept along irresistibly by the currents of their own material progress.

Any philosophy which teaches that the facts of the universe may be explained by the existence and nature of matter is known as a materialistic philosophy. A civilization in which people devote themselves too exclusively to material interests and values is described as a materialistic civilization. For the people of Europe and America the nineteenth century was an age of materialism. They were deeply impressed by the extraordinary progress of the natural sciences and by the rise in living standards which came with advances in technology and machine production. This materialistic philosophy persisted into the twentieth century, but what form it would assume, through what unifying concept it would express itself, was not immediately clear. If the answer were referred to the scientists and engineers, it appeared likely that some term such as

14

"dynamism" or "energism" would serve better than "materialism" to suggest the mood of twentieth-century civilization. Instead of matter, *force* or *energy* was proposed as the primal element, the ultimate reality of the cosmos. A brief survey of the more recent developments in physics may help to explain how this shift in emphasis came about.

The early years of the twentieth century saw a great number of scientific discoveries that altered the foundations upon which nineteenth-century physics had rested. Not since the speculations of Copernicus upset the Ptolemaic astronomy four centuries earlier had European man's conception of the physical world suffered such a rude reversal. The fundamentals of physical science in acceptance before 1900 were the Newtonian laws of motion and the twin principles of the conservation of mass and of the conservation of energy. Simply stated, these hypotheses taught that bodies in space, whether they were molecules or galaxies, moved in obedience to invariable formulas which could be expressed mathematically in terms of the mass of the bodies, their velocity, and the distance between them. Matter, the substance of which the universe was presumably composed, was regarded as indestructible. Its forms were classified by the chemists who distinguished ninety-two graduated elements, each element having constant, recognizable properties and a fixed atomic weight. Though matter might alter its form, the total mass remained constant, for not one atom could be created or lost. Through similar reasoning it was assumed that energy could be neither created nor annihilated, so that, whatever form it might take, the sum remained constant. It was assumed that matter (solid, liquid, or gaseous) formed the normal vehicle by which energy was conveyed and through which it manifested itself.

Such were the general concepts upon which physical science rested at the close of the nineteenth century. But already a series of destructive attacks had begun which endangered or modified all these major hypotheses. In 1895 the discovery of X rays by Wilhelm Konrad Roentgen opened the field of radioactivity with all its startling possibilities. The investigations of Pierre Curie (1859–1906), Marie Curie (1867–1934), Ernest Rutherford (1871–1937), and many other physicists revealed that certain forms of matter, high in the table of the elements, were disintegrating. The implications of this discovery were revolutionary because they indicated that matter might be transmuted into energy, thus challenging the law of the conservation of matter.

The atom itself had now become the problem child of physics, for it was not possible to conceive, as the Greeks had done, that this ultimate particle of matter was "solid, massy, hard, impenetrable." Instead, it had become a universe in itself with a structure which somewhat resembled a solar system. At its core was a small, heavy nucleus, about which a varying number of electrons revolved like planets or satellites around a sun. This nucleus carried positive charges of electricity, their potential balanced by the negative charges of the ambient electrons. The radiations given off by elements of very high atomic weight, as uranium and radium, were found to consist of alpha particles (the nuclei of helium atoms), beta particles (electrons moving at very high speeds), and gamma rays (radiations similar to X rays, one quantum or particle of which was named a photon). In their behavior and their effects these radiations seemed neither waves of energy nor particles of matter but something between the two. It was clear that the oversimple nineteenth-century theories about the nature of matter and energy required radical revision.

Concepts cautiously built up and tested through four centuries of physical experimentation were crumbling, and a newer system of physics and a newer mathematics were needed to supplant them. The most important advance in the development of new concepts came in 1905 when Albert Einstein offered his special Theory of Relativity. Time and space, he submitted, were not absolute, as Newton had suggested, but were both relative to the observer. In a universe in which nothing could be taken as immovable, all calculations of time and space were variable and would prove valid only for observers who worked under identical conditions. It now appeared that the mass of a body depended upon its rate of movement; a body which weighed one ton by conventional standards and scales might, if its velocity were increased until it approached the speed of light, become incalculably heavy.

Einstein's principle of relativity offered a clue to several other contradictions which had puzzled physicists and astronomers. But its most important practical application was his assumption, stated as early as 1905, that mass and energy would prove to be equivalent and that proof of this equivalence might be found in the behavior of radioactive elements. He computed that the amount of nuclear energy for a given mass could be expressed by the formula $E = mc^2$, using E to represent the energy, m the mass, and c the velocity of light. This innocent-appearing formula concealed an astounding possibility. Forty years after Einstein published his paper a group of physicists put the hypothesis on the equivalence of mass and energy to the test. The result was the atomic bomb.

The technological advances of the nineteenth and twentieth centuries multiplied prodigiously the power available for human needs among the Western nations. If a citizen of ancient Rome or Babylon could have visited the modern world, the change that would have most astonished him would have been the wide use of power-driven machinery. Even wind and water mills were little known in ancient times; their possibilities were not generally realized until the later Middle Ages. Steam engines, which wrought a prodigious revolution in manufacture and transportation, have been in use less than two centuries. The internal combustion engine, and electricity with all its many uses, have been developed for general public convenience in the last seventy years. Without the application of power for running the machines, the industrial development of the modern age and the marvels of mass production would have been impossible. The average Chinese workman, for example, with old-fashioned tools, could produce one-thirtieth as much as the average American workman. The Chinese might be more patient and industrious than the American but he lacked power-driven machines. Man's muscular energy, the first form of power he ever used, is still in many countries the form of energy he depends upon even for the heaviest tasks. Yet one pound of coal, efficiently burned in a machine, can liberate more energy than one strong man furnishes in an eight-hour day. The standard of living in every society bears a direct relation to the per capita energy available for productive purposes.

The technological advances of the nineteenth and twentieth centuries created new ingenious mechanical slaves to perform a hundred daily services. In the Western world science also prolonged human life by curbing disease and by assuring a more abundant food supply. Until the nineteenth century doctors fought diseases "in the dark"; they could not see or recognize the germs that slew nor could they discover how epidemics were spread. One by one the deadliest microbes were identified and combated, the great plagues curbed, the death toll cut. Three forms of strategy, three methods of defense were developed for this unremitting war. The first method was to check the spread of communicable diseases by more scrupulous quarantine regulations, by asepsis and antisepsis, and by the destruction of recognized plague-carriers such as rats, lice, and mosquitoes. A second means of defense was the development of exact tests which would detect a disease in its primary stages and so permit prompt quarantine and early treatment. A third method was the cultivation of serums and vaccines which would immunize human beings against the attack of specific bacteria.

To carry out these more stringent precautions doctors appealed to the lawmakers to declare vaccination against such diseases as smallpox compulsory, and invoked laws to govern the inspection of food markets and eating places, the pasteurization of city milk supplies, and decontamination of sewage. Improved hospitals, health clinics for the poor, and more rigid training for doctors and nurses also formed part of the campaign. Public health became an issue in all leading countries, and a declining mortality rate, especially in maternity cases and among children under one year of age, came to be recognized as an index of social, economic, and educational progress.

The war on disease could not by itself have doubled the population of the world in a century; this triumph of the modern age was also due to the reduction of famine. Food, the most persistent of human needs, was more plentifully produced and more economically distributed than ever before in history. The reasons for this advance were closely connected with the progress in science and technology, with the mechanization of agriculture and transportation, and with the invention of new techniques for raising and preserving food. The exploitation of neglected but fertile lands, notably the wheat-growing areas of the United States, Canada, and Russia, and the opening up of the sheep and cattle pastures of North America, Australia, and Argentina, greatly augmented the world food supply. The surplus from these thinly peopled regions helped to feed the congested cities of Europe.

Man was thus becoming less dependent upon the plant and animal world for everything save food. But the enjoyment of these new products of the technological revolution was denied to all save a minority of the earth's inhabitants by problems of trade, tariff, transport, distribution, and, above all, lack of purchasing power. Modern man had invented the machines to satisfy most of his material needs. The furniture for a new world society, with comfortable standards of living for all, was ready to come off the assembly lines. But man had not yet found the means to pay for that furniture or to share it equitably. The solution to this problem lay in the realm of human nature, and the sciences which dealt with man — anthropology, psychology, sociology — were the least exact and the slowest to advance. Because they were sciences of *classification* rather than sciences of *measurement* they did not yield results comparable to those brilliant mathematical generalizations by which the scientists extended their empire over the physical world.

2. ARCHITECTURE, ART, AND MUSIC

By the nineteenth century, science and technology were transforming the European and American way of life more swiftly than any society had ever been changed before. People, especially city people, accepted and enjoyed the *material* benefits of the new, machine-dominated age, the better health and the bodily comforts that modern science and technology brought them. But their *minds*, their *thinking*, remained rooted in the past. In other words, they welcomed the achievements of the scientists but they found it very difficult to believe that the universe was as soulless, as mechanical and materialistic, as scientific studies made it out to be. This split, this contradiction between the principles on which they acted and the principles in which they believed, forced modern people to live in two worlds simultaneously. In most of their activities they planned and acted *as if* the vast indifferent mechanical universe of science was real. But in their hearts, in their thoughts and feelings, they remained loyal to beliefs that their ancestors had cherished for thousands of years.

The fundamental conflict between the teachings of science and the inherited beliefs to which most people clung concerned the nature and importance of man himself. Scientific studies indicated that the universe, infinite in extent, had no concern for the fate of man, or for his dreams, hopes, and ambitions. All life on Earth was merely a chance development — "the superficial phenomena of arrested radiation on the outer crust of a cooling nebula." Man, however, from the beginning of history, had regarded himself as the center of things. The peoples of Europe had long accepted a religion that assured them the universe had been created by a benevolent God, with the Earth as its center, and that those who lived virtuously during their earthly existence would enjoy everlasting life after death. Not only the religion, but the art, architecture, literature, and music of European nations all reflected this belief in man's peculiar and supreme importance in the scheme of things. To understand modern art and literature, therefore, it is helpful to remember that artists and writers, like the religious teachers, remained primarily concerned with man and his importance. They could not accept the evidence, increasingly uncovered by the scientists, that in the universe as a whole man had virtually no importance or significance at all.

This inner conflict, this "schism of the soul" that beset modern man, was reflected in his activities. In architecture, the anarchic skylines of the spreading cities showed a strange blend of the old and the new. Structures that enshrined ancient traditions — churches, museums, libraries, colleges — might repeat the patterns of medieval Gothic cathedrals or the rectangular form and classical columns of Greek and Roman buildings. But "form follows function." New needs and new materials drove modern architects (often reluctantly) to strange and daring experiments. Skyscrapers, steel bridges, factories, ocean liners, evolved forms of their own. Such new "functional" architecture expressed the dynamic spirit of Western Civilization more truly than the nostalgic imitation of styles perfected by earlier cultures in earlier centuries.

In a similar fashion European painters and sculptors progressed from romanticism and idealism to realism and naturalism in the course of the nineteenth century. The saints and angels, gods and goddesses, which had pleased earlier generations, ceased to attract the new school of Realists who gained influence in the second half of the nineteenth century. "Show me an angel and I will paint one," scoffed the French painter Gustave Courbet (1819–1877), who preferred to sketch naturalistic nudes and unsentimentalized landscapes. Sculptors, too, broke away from the classic tradition that had inspired them to make modern statesmen look like Roman senators. But naturalism, the attempt to portray things as they are, resulted in much ugly and unimpressive art. Painters found less and less satisfaction in producing an exact likeness of what the eye beheld; a camera could do this. By 1900 a new artistic trend had developed which came to be called "nonobjective art." In the twentieth century many painters and sculptors preferred to create strange geometric canvases, arrangements of contrasting colors, and contorted shapes and figures that resembled no outward model. These artists appeared to be in revolt against the increasingly mechanized world around them. They retreated into themselves and drew on their own dreams and fantasies for inspiration.

This conflict between art and reality affected music also. In the later nineteenth century the most dynamic and influential composer was Richard Wagner, a romantic artist who borrowed the themes for his operas from Norse and Christian mythology. With the twentieth century, though traditional music remained popular, new experimental schools arose that broke with tradition. Some composers even abandoned accepted tone scales and harmonies to improvise strange clashing compositions that often sounded harsh and discordant.

3. LITERATURE, PHILOSOPHY, AND EDUCATION

Modern Western literature reflected most clearly of all the arts the cleavage between man's inherited concepts of himself and "the frigid theories of a generalizing age." Around 1860 the spirit of realism invaded the newer novels and dramas. Poetry yielded to prose. The time when a Dante or a Milton could compose majestic epics to "justify the ways of God to man" had passed. The great writers of the later nineteenth century — Henrik Ibsen (1828–1906), Count Leo Tolstoy (1828–1910), Émile Zola (1840–1902), Thomas Hardy (1840–1928), and others — were concerned with the problem of how to justify the ways of man to man. The human individual, with his struggles, his hopes, and his dreams, remained the central and absorbing theme for the writers. But modern man was becoming increasingly uncertain of himself,

> I, a stranger and afraid
> In a world I never made.

The sense of his desolate and incommunicable singularity turned man's thought upon himself. The study of inner thoughts and feelings became an absorbing passion; psychology flourished; art turned introspective; and uprooted millions became members of "the lonely crowd." All these changes were mirrored in the newer literature.

As the nineteenth century closed and the twentieth century opened, philosophy, religion, and education likewise gave evidence of the "crisis of conscience" that afflicted Western man. Human vanity had suffered a severe blow when the Copernican system replaced the Ptolemaic, and the Earth, instead of being the center of the universe, became no more than the satellite of one among a billion billion suns. But science dealt a crueler blow to man's ideal of himself when Charles Darwin published his theory of biological evolution. Instead of being a special creation, a little lower than the angels, man learned that he was only an unusually intelligent animal, related to the anthropoid apes. It is hardly surprising that most people distrusted the scientists who continued to deal such merciless blows to man's exalted concept of himself and his importance.

Rapid changes in their fundamental beliefs leave people with a sense of doubt and bewilderment. For thousands of years, philosophers, from Socrates to Kant, had warned that there is no certainty, that man cannot grasp any ultimate unchanging truth behind the flux of things; "All that we know is, nothing can be known." Modern philosophers, no less perplexed than common men by the rapid discoveries of science, tried to formulate new general principles of knowledge. If truth, as some skeptics affirmed, was only "the most convenient form of error," it was apparent none the less that some truths were more useful than others. Some ideas, some theories, worked better when put to a practical test. This conclusion provided a basis for the philosophy known as pragmatism taught by the American philosopher William James (1842–1910). Pragmatism, however, offered no final or ultimate truth to which mankind might cling. Nor could the scientists provide a solid foundation on which to rely. Even the most fundamental principles of science might become outmoded tomorrow and be discarded in favor of new hypotheses.

In an age when new scientific discoveries challenged many old beliefs, should children be taught the old or the new truths? This problem of what to teach in the schools became a hotly debated question throughout the Western world. Until the eighteenth century education had been closely allied to religion. Children were taught that "the powers that be are ordained of God," and that good citizens should obey the moral commands of God, revealed through religion, and the civil laws proclaimed by the government. With the rise of democracy, however, the authority of a government came to rest "on the consent of the governed." The authority behind the laws became the will of the majority — that is, law and government came to be based on a human and secular instead of a divine and transcendental authority. Education likewise was "secularized." It was taken out of the hands of the clergy and entrusted to laymen. In countries where the church and state were separated, instruction in religion was left to the churches and children received no religious instruction in the schools.

Yet because tradition was strong, the subjects taught in the schools remained largely the old "traditional" subjects. Ancient languages (Latin and Greek), and "humane" learning (literature, history, philosophy) received more attention than the new sciences. This emphasis on "the humanities" and neglect of "the sciences" continued into the twentieth century. Here, too, the cleavage in modern culture could be discerned. For the humanities in general stressed man's worth and importance, while modern science and mathematics, with their chill impersonal conclusions, emphasized man's insignificance and conflicted with his exalted opinion of himself.

It was natural and understandable that people preferred to hold fast to their older, more comforting beliefs, and their inherited superstitions.

The methods and progress of science might indicate that the cosmos was a vast impersonal mechanism oblivious of man. But most people (while accepting the material benefits of science) clung to the religious faith of their ancestors. Few of them tried to reconcile in a logical manner the miracles and mysteries of religion with the laws and principles of science. They chose instead "to trust the soul's invincible surmise."

3

EUROPE IN THE AGE OF TECHNOLOGY

The Roman civilisation was built upon cheap and degraded human beings; modern civilisation is being rebuilt upon cheap mechanical power.

H. G. WELLS

1. THE NEW SOCIAL FORCES

UNTIL SCIENCE and technology wrought their radical and dynamic changes in methods of production, transportation, and communications, the broad masses of working people maintained, at best, a subsistence existence. By toiling with the sweat of their brow they were able to produce barely enough food, clothing, and shelter to survive. Even social elites living off the toil of the masses in relative abundance were not spared the effects of periodic famines. The Industrial Revolution, by substituting power-driven machinery for human hands, draft animals, sails, and wings of windmills, opened the prospect of an age of plenty and relative leisure, not only for social elites but also for the broad masses of workingmen. And, indeed, by mid-twentieth century, some two hundred years after its beginning in England, the Industrial Revolution has largely fulfilled its promise — at least in highly industrialized western countries.

The forty-hour working week, which has become standard in the industrial countries of Western Europe and North America, leaves the industrial worker ample leisure. The high wages which he receives provide abundantly for food, clothing, and shelter. They even leave him a surplus from which to buy a variety of creature comforts which in past ages would have been regarded as unbelievable luxuries even by the richest of men. The Industrial Revolution has created aggregates of wealth in comparison with which the wealth of the Pharaohs of Egypt, of Roman Caesars, and of the feudal lords of medieval Europe, was piddling. Moreover, the horn of plenty is not about to be exhausted. Not even in the industrial West has the Industrial Revolution reached its peak. New sources of energy, such as nuclear energy, are being discovered. New methods of production are being invented, which substitute elaborate,

automatized machinery not only for human hands but for human brains.
New methods are being introduced, which make transportation and communications steadily swifter, cheaper, and more efficient. All of these
discoveries promise to reduce further the time and strain of man's daily
work.

Naturally, such great changes in production, transportation, and communications have not been achieved without great — and sometimes painful — social changes. Before the Industrial Revolution the main source of
wealth in Europe was land. The class which controlled the land, the
landed nobility, was Europe's social elite. The class which tilled the land,
the peasantry, was its working class. In between these two classes there
grew up, from the late Middle Ages, the classes of merchants and artisans.
They provided the nuclei of the new industrial classes, the industrial
capitalists and the industrial laborers. In time, however, as industry
expanded and needed a new supply of labor, the peasantry provided the
bulk of the industrial working class. And many noblemen sought to
recover their declining fortunes by marrying into or entering the class of
industrial capitalists.

The industrial capitalists, commanding frequently very great wealth,
were aggressive, confident, and — as *nouveaux riches* frequently are —
socially selfish. They tended to identify the interests of the nations of
which they were a part with their own. The bourgeois revolutionaries of
France pleaded eloquently for the Rights of Man and Citizen, but were
careful to exclude the workers from the right to vote in the Constitution
of 1791 and to deny them the right to form protective unions in the Le
Chapelier Law of the same year. Similarly, the English liberals tended
to identify the interests of British industry with the interests of the whole
British nation. The Combination Acts of 1799 denied the British workers
the right to form unions, and the celebrated Reform Bill of 1832 excluded
them from the right to vote. Both the French bourgeoisie and the British
middle class, while determined to break the monopoly of political power
enjoyed by the landed nobility, were not anxious themselves to share it
with the working class.

The lot of the industrial workers was initially hard. The transformation of rural peasants into urban industrial workers was a painful one.
It involved bewildering changes in social patterns and way of life. In
the closely-knit society of the village every man had a well-defined place.
Family and neighborly relations were close. In time of distress the peasant
could count on the help of his neighbors and often on that of his landlord
who frequently had a paternal feeling for his tenants. In the atomized
society of the city every man stood alone. In time of difficulty he could
seldom count on the help of his neighbors or his employer. In the city
the uprooted peasant was lost and demoralized. The transformation into
a worker frequently meant for him a step downward before it became
a step upward. The early industrial working class, consisting of hetero-

geneous elements, lacked a corporate consciousness. Unorganized, it was often ruthlessly exploited by get-rich-quick employers.

The plight of the industrial workingmen inspired dynamic social movements. The leaders of these movements were generally not workingmen but intellectuals, members themselves of the propertied classes, who were moved by the misery of the workers and took up the cudgels for them. Some of these social reformers, like those associated with the British Fabian Society, demanded merely greater social justice for the laborers. Others, like Marx and Engels, demanded a radical transformation of society by revolution, if necessary, which would abolish the capitalist system altogether and transfer ownership of means of production and distribution from private into public hands.

While the intellectual sympathizers no doubt helped the cause of the workingmen by publicizing their plight, it was the workers themselves who did most to improve their lot. In the city, where life was more varied than in the village, their horizons broadened, they became literate and articulate in expressing their needs, and they developed a corporate feeling and organized into protective unions. Gradually, they were also able to make their weight felt in politics. The state, which at the beginning of the nineteenth century leaned heavily in favor of capital, at the end of the century moved toward a more neutral position of arbiter between capital and labor. Beginning with Bismarck's Germany in the 1880's, the states of Western Europe adopted social welfare legislation designed to protect the laborers from the inequities of the industrial system.

As the workingmen won a secure place in the western society, they began to feel that they belonged to it and that they had a stake in its preservation. The emancipation of the working class stimulated not only the democratization of the European society but also European nationalism. At mid-nineteenth century Marx, angered at the indifference of the "bourgeois" state toward the working class, said that the workingman had no fatherland, only a "birthplace." Whether this was true at the time or not, it was certainly not true in the First World War when the European workers generally rallied to the defense of their native countries and fought as stoutly as members of other classes.

Since the First World War the attitude of capital and labor to one another appears to have changed in the western countries. Both have discovered a large area of common interest between them. The capitalists have discovered that the workers are also customers, and that prosperous workers are better customers than poor ones. The workers have discovered that they prosper when business and industry prosper. By mid-twentieth century the once-bitter conflict between capital and labor had been moderated in the western countries by a compromise acceptable to both parties.

2. THE MODERN STATE

Thomas Hobbes, the seventeenth-century English political writer, called the modern state "the Leviathan" — so large and powerful it appeared to him. Yet, compared to the European states as they emerged in the nineteenth century, the power and resources of their predecessors in the seventeenth century were relatively limited. In the seventeenth century European governments filled only a limited number of functions: collection of taxes, supervision of economy, administration of justice, conduct of foreign and colonial affairs, and organization of national defense. The Industrial Revolution and the growth of democracy in the eighteenth and nineteenth centuries resulted in a singular increase in power and resources of European states. European governments entered into a range of activities which would have astonished Hobbes: operation of posts and telegraphs; control or actual management of railroads; supervision of banking and finance; administration of a variety of social services, such as workers' accident and sickness insurance programs, old-age pension funds, hospitals and health institutions, and research institutes; inspection of mines and factories; supervision of education or actual operation of public school systems; subsidizing libraries, museums, theaters, and art galleries; etc. The assumption of all these additional functions led to a great proliferation of bureaucracy — a trend which in the twentieth century has reached in some European countries absurd proportions.

The advance of democracy resulted in the extension of the rights of citizens, but also of their duties. In the seventeenth century noblemen were largely exempt from taxation, but in return assumed a large proportion of the burden of military service. In the nineteenth century the burden of taxation was more equally distributed, but on the other hand universal military service was introduced. While individual rights were extended, the control of the citizens by various organs of the state was increased. Formation of national police forces reduced lawlessness and banditry, but also the possibility of uprisings and revolutions against unpopular and oppressive governments. Above all, however, the ninteenth-century European states differed from their predecessors in the extent of their military power.

The general economic expansion resulting from the Industrial Revolution greatly increased the revenue of European governments. The increase in revenue and the introduction of universal military service made it possible to pass from small professional armies to large citizens' armies. After completing their period of compulsory military training, the citizen soldiers were transferred to the reserves and subject to call for periodic summer exercises or — in time of war — for active service again. The concept of "nation in arms," resorted to by French revolutionaries only as an extreme measure, thus became a permanent feature of national defense in all European countries. Only Britain, thanks to her insular position and command of the seas, dispensed with a large national army.

The advance in technology resulted in improving the quality of weapons, and factory production increased their output. The substitution of the rifle for the old-fashioned musket and the introduction of the machine gun vastly increased the firepower of armies. The American Civil War revealed the advantages of railroad transportation and of telegraph communications to armies. The railroad made possible quick concentration of large bodies of troops and their proper supplying with munitions, food, and necessities of war. The telegraph and the telephone made possible close coordination of the movements of armies over vast areas. Simultaneous attacks could now be carried out on widely separated fronts. At the same time the substitution of the steam-driven, iron-clad warships for the old timber sailing vessels revolutionized naval warfare. The introduction of the submarine added a new dimension to it.

As armies grew in numbers and increased in efficiency, better planning of their activities became necessary. The spectacular victories of Prussia in the wars of German unification, which were largely due to careful planning by the Prussian General Staff, until then the only organization of its kind, convinced other European states of the advantages of maintaining permanent general staffs. Following the Prussian model, the European general staffs planned in peacetime the campaigns of future wars. The capacity of European countries to inflict deep wounds on one another greatly increased.

The great military power of the European states gave them a particular advantage in dealing with the non-European peoples, who had not yet developed modern industry, modern organization, and modern armies. Frequently, a mere show of force, for instance, the dispatch of the grey, iron ships of the British navy to Shanghai or Alexandria, was sufficient to secure the compliance of the non-European peoples with the wishes of the European governments. With a minimum of effort and expense the European nations were able to conquer or occupy vast areas of Asia and Africa and to impose their rule on populations frequently much larger than their own.

3. THE NEW IMPERIALISM

In a previous chapter it was explained how in the sixteenth century Europe reached out and progressively imposed its influence on large portions of the world. Colonies represented rich prizes, and the race for them created intense rivalry among European powers. Colonies augmented the wealth and power of European states and thus affected the European balance of power. Struggle for colonies became inextricably tied up with the struggle for power in Europe.

Spain and Portugal, the pioneers of colonization, evaded conflict over colonies by a simple partition of the world beyond Europe into two broad spheres: the Western Hemisphere was to be Spanish and the Eastern Hemisphere Portuguese. In the seventeenth century, however, the "Iberian monopoly" of colonies ended. France and England established footholds in North America. The Dutch carried their struggle for independence from Spain (1568–1648) beyond the seas. By the middle of the seventeenth century the Dutch not only won independence but carved out for themselves a rich colonial empire — mainly at the expense of Portugal, then tied to Spain in a personal union under the Hapsburg dynasty (1580–1640).

For a brief period the Dutch Republic enjoyed the position of the leading naval power of Europe. In this position of eminence, however, it was soon challenged by England, under the farseeing Puritan leader, Oliver Cromwell. He understood well the importance to England of sea power and colonies. In a series of three naval and colonial wars (1651–1674) the English weakened the Dutch while strengthening their own hold on the American coast by capturing New Netherland (New York). At the same time England waged a war against Spain (1656–1659) and by seizing Jamaica established a foothold in the Caribbean. The Glorious Revolution (1688), by bringing the Dutch leader, William of Orange, to the throne of England, ended Anglo-Dutch rivalry and opened a long period of Anglo-French rivalry.

In four wars with France (1689–1763) England developed an effective strategy which ultimately assured her of victory over France: by continental alliances she tied down the French on the Continent, while she herself attacked them on the high seas and in America. In the eighteenth century the Anglo-French conflict was extended to India, where the decline of the Mogul empire permitted both the French and the British to make a bid for empire. The Anglo-French wars thus partook of the nature of world wars, with theaters of operations in Europe, America, and India as well as on the high seas. Britain's able strategy and superior naval power brought spectacular results. By 1763 the French empire in America and India collapsed and Britain emerged as the leading naval and colonial power in the world. The attempt of France to exploit British embarrassment over the American Revolution (1775–1783) was a failure. Britain, indeed, lost the thirteen American colonies but the hope of the French to recover their American empire was dashed.

For over a century the British position in the colonial world appeared unassailable. The preponderance of British naval power was such that no change in colonial relationships could be effected without British cooperation or, at least, acquiescence. The link between the struggle for a European balance of power and colonial rivalries was broken. In the non-European world Britain imposed a *Pax Britannica*. The French Revolutionary wars and the Napoleonic wars, as well as the mid-nineteenth century wars, remained purely European wars. The British navy prevented their spreading beyond the seas. Britain exploited this situation to strengthen her position in the colonial world. From Holland, a helpless satellite of Revolutionary France, she seized Ceylon and Cape Colony and declined to restore them at the Congress of Vienna simply to honor "legitimacy." The French occupation of Spain and Portugal during the Napoleonic wars isolated these countries from their colonial empires. This gave Britain an opportunity to break the Spanish and Portuguese overseas connections, and so hasten the hour when the colonies would win independence. However, unlike Spain and Portugal, Britain did not take advantage of her naval preponderance to exclude other nations from trading with the British empire. British tariffs were moderate and after 1847 abolished altogether. Goods flowed freely to and from British possessions. The British free-trade policy contributed to the rise of a world economy. Its nerve center was London but it contributed to the prosperity of other nations too.

Toward the end of the nineteenth century the British position in the colonial world became less secure. For a variety of reasons there was a virulent revival of colonial imperialism after 1870. The United States and Germany caught up to and surpassed Britain in industrial development. France, Japan, Austria, Italy, and Belgium, though trailing behind Britain, also developed considerable industry. None of these newer industrial nations reciprocated Britain's free-trade policy, while they squeezed her out of many of her traditional markets. A sharp competition developed among the industrial nations not only for markets but also for raw materials, which their growing industries demanded in ever greater quantities. Colonies were necessary, imperialists argued, to provide new markets and to assure a steady flow of raw materials. As the industrial development particularly of the United States, Germany, and France reached a high level, they accumulated, like Britain before them, considerable surplus capital. The underdeveloped, non-industrialized areas of the world needed capital to develop their resources and offered opportunities for profitable investment. But such "backward" areas often lacked sufficient political stability to guarantee the safety of loans. It was justified, imperialists felt, for great powers to establish colonial control over such areas to protect their investment. And once an area was acquired as a colony, strategic considerations often made it expedient to bring adjoining regions under control too. This was all the more tempting because the great disparity in military power between advanced, industrialized countries and the backward, non-industrialized peoples made it feasible with very little military effort. Other factors which motivated the "new imperialism" of the late nineteenth century were considerations of prestige (possession of colonies was a status symbol to the great powers) and a missionary zeal (often a mere smokescreen for imperialism but often enough a sincere desire to bring to the non-European peoples not only the revelations of Christianity but also the advantages of the western civilization).

The most promising area for colonization at this time was the "Dark Continent" of Africa. In the 1870's only a few parts of Africa had been claimed by colonial powers: in the north, Algeria by France, in the south, Cape Colony by Britain; and all along the coasts numerous trading posts had been established by France, Britain, Spain, and Portugal. The hinterland of Africa was then largely unknown. For some time intrepid explorers had been venturing inland along the jungle rivers of Africa. There was, however, little popular interest in their efforts until the highly publicized exploration of Henry Stanley, sent in 1871 by an American newspaper as a sales promotion stunt to find Dr. David Livingstone, a Scottish medical missionary and explorer. In 1876 the foundation of the International Association for the Exploration and Civilization of Africa, under the auspices of King Leopold II of Belgium, inaugurated frenzied exploration and concession-hunting in Africa, as a result of which the Dark Continent was not only thoroughly explored but also partitioned among the European powers in less than twenty years. Other areas partitioned by the European powers during this period of imperialism were southeast Asia (Burma, Indochina, and Malaya) and the Pacific Islands. The Ottoman, Persian, and Chinese empires, though not brought under direct colonial rule, were subjected to a variety of imperialist controls. Latin America was protected from the attention of the imperialist powers by the Monroe Doctrine, sternly upheld by the United States. But in 1898 the United States itself became a colonial power when it acquired the remnants of the Spanish empire in the Caribbean and the Philippines and annexed Hawaii. In various parts of Latin America also it exercised indirect imperialist controls.

As in the seventeenth and eighteenth centuries, the competitive race for colonies in the nineteenth century affected the balance of power in Europe. Colonial rivalries presented an increasing threat to the peace of Europe and of the world.

4

GREAT BRITAIN

The weary titan staggers beneath the too vast orb of its fate.
JOSEPH CHAMBERLAIN

1. RESOURCES: THE PROBLEM OF SUPPLY

NATURE ENDOWED GREAT BRITAIN with many of the advantages which
helped to make it a leading power. As an island people the British were
relatively secure from invasion and could dispense with a large army if
they maintained a strong navy. Good harbors and a position near the
center of the world's land masses were primary assets in the Oceanic Age.
The moist but healthy climate, law-abiding population, and liberal political institutions permitted a steady expansion of the national energy and
the national initiative. Spared the march of foreign armies and (save in
the seventeenth century) the destruction of civil war, modern Britain
grew stronger and richer with each generation.

In the eighteenth century these and other advantages made Britain the
first country to profit by the Industrial Revolution. In England the rise
of the factory system was favored by conditions that could be matched
nowhere else. The capital required for experiment and for the construction of costly machinery had been accumulated in the hands of enterprising men. A supply of cheap labor became available opportunely
because the enclosure movement in agriculture drove many farm hands
and free tenants to the city. The wars of the French Revolution (1792–
1815) kept Britain's rivals, especially France, occupied and blockaded
during a critical quarter of a century, leaving British manufacturers a
monopoly of ocean trade and the world for a market. Finally, iron to
build machines and coal to run the steam engines were both available in
England. The annual production of these two essentials rose prodigiously
in the nineteenth century. The coal output rose thirty-fold, the iron output twenty-fold between 1800 and 1914. One notable result of the mechanization of British industry and the rise of the factory system was a
phenomenal expansion of the manufacturing cities. In 1800 nine out of
ten people in England lived in the country or in small villages. By 1914

this ratio had almost been reversed: seven people out of ten lived in urban communities. This inevitable increase in the urban population is an index of industrialization, and it will be noted in other states as the methods of machine production spread to the Continent. In England one result of this overwhelming migration to the cities was the decline of agriculture. The island kingdom had been largely self-sustaining in 1800 but as it became the workshop of the world the population learned to rely more and more extensively upon imported food. Here again statistics tell the story vividly as a few figures will illustrate.

By 1914, when World War I commenced, the British were importing annually some 300,000,000 bushels of wheat, oats, and barley, 1,000,000,000 pounds of dairy products, 1,000,000,000 pounds of beef, 2,000,000,000 pounds of ham, pork, and mutton, 3,000,000,000 pounds of sugar. There is no need to extend the list to make the lesson clear. England, like a vast city, lived on the food delivered daily. Some of the imports came from nearby sources, from Ireland, Denmark, Holland; but most of it had to be shipped thousands of miles across the oceans, from Australia, the Argentine Republic, Canada, and the United States. Every working day of the year, 33,000,000 pounds of wheat, 10,000,000 pounds of sugar, 3,000,000 pounds of dairy foods, 1,000,000 pounds of tea, and many other items of food had to be landed safely on British docks. The average Englishman accepted this unparalleled achievement in transportation as a matter of fact. Yet it was a startling thought that he could enjoy his five o'clock tea, muffin, and marmalade for a few pennies although the ingredients might have come half way around the world. Those who paused to ponder the problem could hardly fail to realize how vulnerable Britain would become if a hostile power disrupted the sea lanes and cut off this daily stream of sea-borne supplies.

To feed 35,000,000 people, largely on imported food, was a problem difficult enough, but to feed the factory machines which consumed raw materials not by the pound but by the shipload was a staggering task. British textile mills required 1,000,000 tons of cotton annually, imported chiefly from the United States. The cloth produced for markets all over the world was valued at $500,000,000. In 1914, 50,000 tons of rubber (largely from the East Indies), 100,000 tons of copper, 20,000 tons of nickel (mostly from Canada), were annual requirements of British industry. The total import and export trade of Great Britain was worth seven billion dollars a year when the First World War disrupted international economy.

To transport this great overseas trade Britain possessed a mercantile marine rated (1914) at over 18,000,000 tons, almost one-half the mercantile ocean tonnage of the world. These ships did not serve British needs alone; they conveyed goods for many nations and their operations were linked with the services provided by British bankers, insurance brokers, and commercial agents in all parts of the world. From their vast network of financial, maritime, mail, cable, and passenger services, as well as from their great investments of capital in foreign countries, British firms derived an invisible income which helped to equalize the trade balance of the nation. This added income from services was important because the cost of imports, including food, outran the value of exports. In 1913 this deficit in the trade balance rose to half-a-billion dollars.

By concentrating their activities upon the rewards of trade, industry, and finance, the British had grown wealthy and powerful. But they had also grown vulnerable. With three out of four wage earners dependent upon industry, commerce, shipping, or mining, it was evident that any serious disruption of the delicate balance of world trade would bring them swift and critical losses. When electricity, or "white coal," began to replace the steam engine, when oil and gasoline afforded new sources of fuel and energy, British coal miners by the hundred thousand were thrown out of work. When other nations — France, Germany, Italy, Russia, the United States, and Japan — developed their own factory machines, British industrial prosperity was shaken. Because business was expanding every-where the *total value* of British trade continued to increase but the British *share* of world trade was falling.

Even in peacetime, therefore, Britain at the opening of the twentieth century faced the danger of an economic decline. If war or foreign block-ade halted the shuttling of the ships, symbol of British greatness, the nation might be paralyzed and impoverished in a few months. The sup-plies of food and materials on hand were seldom sufficient for more than a season. Prolonged interruption of trade would mean hunger for millions of the population and idle factories starved for raw stuffs. To safeguard the nation against such a contingency was a primary duty of the govern-ment, a responsibility which dominated the calculations of all leading British statesmen.

2. DEFENSE: FROM SPLENDID ISOLATION TO THE TRIPLE ENTENTE

Throughout the nineteenth century Britain "ruled the waves." On all the oceans the ships of other nations dipped their ensigns in acknowledge-ment of her might. Naval squadrons had only a limited range of effec-tiveness; like a beam of light a battleship lost power the farther it moved from its base. But British bases dotted all the oceans and they possessed added value because many of them were strategically located where the lines of maritime commerce converged at geographical bottlenecks. The map on pages 34–35 reveals why control of such points as Gibraltar, Suez, Aden, and Singapore enabled the British to police the world commerce routes, and why supplementary stations such as Halifax, Bermuda, Cape Town (at the southern tip of Africa), the Falkland Islands (at the south-ern point of South America), and a score of lesser stations permitted the

British ships to remain at sea and perform their vital service of protecting British maritime interests.

To assure this naval supremacy the British found it advisable after 1889 to adopt the principle of the "two-power standard." New navies were in process of construction and the British decided that their security demanded the maintenance of a fleet equal to any two other navies of the world combined. It had been relatively easy to maintain this preponderance during the halcyon days of the mid-nineteenth century. By 1900, however, naval competition had become a tense and critical problem. The French, the Russians, the Americans, the Italians, and the Japa-

WORLD EMPIRES, 1914

nese began to construct impressive fleets. But the threat which most alarmed the British was the German naval program. A German law of 1898 outlined plans for a powerful high seas fleet and a second law of 1900 defined the aims still more clearly and ominously. Unless checked, Germany would soon possess a navy which approached that of Britain in strength. As the German forces could all be concentrated in the North Sea, whereas the British squadrons were normally dispersed throughout the world, this situation might easily result in relative German superiority in the waters around the British Isles.

The Lords of the Admiralty decided that Britain must maintain the

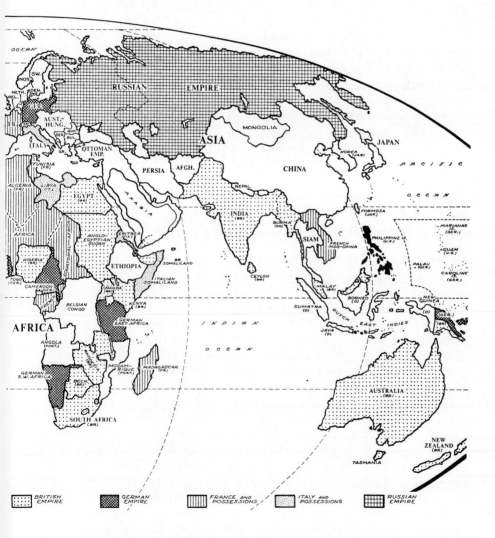

two-power standard even if this meant building two warships for every one laid down in German shipyards. They also adopted plans for a new type of superbattleship. The first model, the *Dreadnought*, launched in 1906, was so heavily gunned and armored that it made all existing capital ships second rate. This achievement proved, ironically, not a gain but a setback for the British, for it opened a new phase in naval construction. All first line ships had to be replaced, and Britain's rivals began to build a new fleet of dreadnoughts from an even start. The Germans voted new and extravagant naval appropriations; British attempts to reach an agreement with them on naval limitation had no success. By 1908 the British government in a state of near panic was laying the keels of eight new dreadnoughts and was designing still larger and more expensive craft, the superdreadnoughts.

The jealousy engendered by this naval race was intensified, especially in Britain, by Anglo-German trade rivalry. By 1900 German steel production had risen to double the British; by 1914 it had trebled it. The value of German foreign trade climbed to two-thirds the British total, and some German wares outsold British products even in British markets. The psychological effects of such a trade war will be considered later in connection with subsequent trade crises. In this case there can be little doubt that after 1900 the combination of naval and business rivalry helped to increase Anglo-German distrust. In the 1890's the two countries had been on fairly friendly terms and proposals for an alliance were discussed in Berlin and in London. But after 1900 an estrangement grew and became official. The death of Queen Victoria (1901) brought a change of mood in court circles, for her son and successor, Edward VII (1901–1910), disliked his nephew, Kaiser William II, and showed a marked preference for the French. At the height of power Britain had avoided entangling alliances and maintained a position of "splendid isolation." But the balance was shifting and as the twentieth century opened Britain stood at the parting of the ways. The choices made by British diplomats between 1901 and 1904 had profound implications. They were motivated by, and helped in turn to hasten, a change in European and world affairs. The twentieth century was to be marked by vaster changes, more cataclysmic wars, and more destructive revolutions than any the nineteenth had witnessed.

There were two main reasons why the British decision to abandon a policy of isolation had far-reaching implications. Except for the brief Crimean War (1854–56) when the British and French checked Russian designs against Turkey, Britain avoided a clash with any great power from 1815 to 1914. By remaining neutral when France defeated Austria (1859), when Prussia defeated Austria (1866), and when Prussia defeated France (1870–71), Britain helped to keep these wars from spreading. Because all these wars remained "limited" conflicts, and were soon over, they did not cause extensive destruction nor impair Europe's prosperity and world leadership. When, after 1904, the British forsook the role of a powerful but independent neutral and began to support one group of European states against another, they forfeited their freedom of action and their "stabilizing" role. As no other great European power was in a position to assume this role, any subsequent conflict was likely to spread until it involved all Europe. This was the first reason why the change in British policy had grave significance.

The second reason why Britain's involvement in the European competition for power had portentous implications was that Britain possessed a worldwide empire. This empire, at the opening of the twentieth century, included approximately one-fourth of the land area and one-fourth of the population of the globe. If Britain became involved in a European war the war could no longer be limited to Europe. Nor (since it would take some time for the British to muster their far-flung resources) was it likely that such a war would be short, local, and limited in its destructiveness as European conflicts had been during the nineteenth century.

The first proof that the British were preparing to abandon their policy of isolation came in 1902. A treaty between Great Britain and Japan, negotiated in that year, safeguarded British interests in the Far East. It also gave the British a means of exerting pressure on Russia. If the Russians threatened India the danger that Japan (encouraged from London) might attack Vladivostok would make the Tsar's advisers think twice before they challenged Britain. But the Anglo-Japanese accord offered the British still another advantage. It permitted them to recall some of their warships from the Pacific and station them in home waters to meet the growing threat of the German navy. British statesmen thought in global terms.

The statesmen of the other five great powers of Europe — Germany, Austria, Italy, France, and Russia — still thought primarily in terms of Europe. At the opening of the twentieth century these five powers were ranged in two competing systems of alliances. Since 1882 Germany, Austria-Hungary, and Italy had been linked in a Triple Alliance. Since 1894 France and Russia had formed close ties and concluded military accords. Peace in Europe depended on the preservation of a balance between these two opposed groups, and the balance had become precarious because of Germany's rapidly increasing strength. If the British decided to join one side or the other, which side should they favor? Until 1898 their traditional enmity toward France and distrust of Russia made it seem probable they might support Germany and Austria. But between 1898 and 1904 their attitude changed rapidly. Alarm over the growth of German trade and particularly the growth of the German navy moved the British to seek a closer understanding with France.

The death in 1901 of Queen Victoria, who had German sympathies, and the succession of Edward VII, who favored the French, played some part in this change of mood. But the basic motive was national defense.

In London the need to strengthen the home fleet made an accord with France seem advisable. In Paris the astute foreign minister, Théophile Delcassé, favored a Franco-British understanding. In 1904 he achieved his wish. The British, still too hesitant to conclude a treaty of alliance, accepted instead an accord that was termed an *Entente Cordiale*, a "cordial agreement." Several colonial disputes that had caused friction were adjusted and the accord simplified British naval problems. Britain no longer needed to outmatch the French fleet in the Mediterranean and the German fleet in the North Sea simultaneously — it could reduce its Mediterranean squadrons to reinforce its North Sea defenses. By 1906 French and British experts discussed (in secret) the military aid Britain might send France if war came, and by 1911 the new distribution of Anglo-French naval forces had been made and secretly agreed upon. Officially, Britain was still "uncommitted." No formal treaty, no definite alliance, had been concluded. But the British secretary of state for foreign affairs, Sir Edward Grey, noted as early as 1906 in a private memorandum that:

If there is war between France and Germany it will be very difficult to keep out of it . . . On the other hand the prospect of a European War and of our being involved in it is horrible.

In 1907 the British strengthened their accord with France by concluding an *entente* with France's ally Russia. Thus a Triple Entente (France, Russia, Britain) came into existence to match the Triple Alliance (Germany, Austria-Hungary, Italy). To the diplomats who organized these two opposing *blocs*, the alliances seemed a means of preserving peace by maintaining a balance of forces. But by ranging three of the great European powers against the other three these diplomats made it almost certain that, if war came, it would involve all Europe. "Peace," as one observer recorded realistically, "is at the mercy of an accident."

3. POLITICAL AND SOCIAL PROBLEMS: LAISSEZ-FAIRE AND SOCIAL JUSTICE

In the seventeenth and eighteenth centuries, when most of the European states were still ruled by absolute monarchs, the British people evolved a parliamentary form of government. Their kings became "constitutional monarchs" with strictly limited powers, and the real authority passed to a committee or cabinet of ministers. As this cabinet came to be responsible to the party which held a majority of seats in the House of Commons, and the members of the House were chosen by a vote of the electors, the statesmen who ruled England exercised powers delegated to them by the people or at least by that portion of the populace which enjoyed the right to vote. Britain was the first great European country to develop a working system of representative government, with a ministry responsible not to the monarch but to an elected assembly. As a consequence of its success the experiment, studied and imitated in many parts of the modern world, earned for the government at Westminster the proud title "Mother of Parliaments."

During the nineteenth century the British steadily enlarged their system of political democracy. Successive reform bills redistributing seats in parliament and extending the franchise were passed in 1832, 1867, and 1884–1885, so that by the close of the century four out of five adult men had the right to vote. This extension of the franchise made parliament more responsive to the wishes of the common people, and both political parties, the Liberals (or Whigs) and the Conservatives (or Tories), learned to formulate programs which would attract popular support.

Plans to assure a richer life and wider opportunities for members of the lower classes thus became important issues in all election campaigns. Broadly considered, there were two major methods whereby the status of the worker might be improved. One was to assure him a more adequate wage so that he could live more comfortably. The alternative was to reduce the cost of living so that he could buy more with the wage he received. In general, the Conservative Party, which represented the landowners with their agricultural interests, the Church of England, and some members of the wealthier classes, favored the first course. The Conservatives took a paternal attitude toward most social problems. They were willing to have the government regulate wages, hours, and working conditions, to assure a fair wage, and to check the exploitation of labor. But they were opposed to the trade unions and labor unions which the workers organized on their own initiative in order to extract better terms from their employers.

The Liberals in general were likewise unfriendly toward the unions. But they were even more strongly opposed to government regulation of business. They argued that Britain had grown rich and powerful under a laissez-faire policy, that workers and employers ought to be left free to settle terms among themselves, and that free trade, which allowed foodstuffs to enter England without hindrance, assured the worker the lowest possible world price on his bread. This, the Liberals submitted, was the surest way to promote the workers' welfare. These political arguments stemmed from economic conditions. Many Liberals were members of the new industrial classes, factory owners, businessmen, traders, or ship owners. What they desired was cheap food for the workers and the command of foreign markets. Trade is a reciprocal affair. Unless agrarian countries could sell their produce to England and thereby establish credits, they could not pay for British factory wares. The Liberals were not willing to protect British farmers by taxing importations of wheat; the Corn Laws which had protected agriculturists were repealed in 1846.

The business classes, knowing England was far ahead of all rivals, favored a free-trade policy, and for a century commerce flowed in and out of English ports without tariff checks. Such a laissez-faire policy, with free trade, optimists averred, would draw the nations of the world together, permitting each people to produce whatever crops or manufactures they found most profitable. Tariff discrimination and tariff barriers, on the other hand, not only constricted the natural arteries of trade but bred hostility and war. This laissez-faire philosophy, under which England prospered in the nineteenth century, persisted into the twentieth when conditions changed. The British people did not bring themselves to abandon it until after the First World War.

In foreign as well as domestic policies the Liberals and Conservatives held divergent views. The Conservatives were less afraid of war than the Liberals, who dreaded a disruption of their trade; and Conservative cabinets were likely to be more imperialistic than Liberal regimes. The Conservatives believed that the government should make its power respected by subject peoples and by rival nations. This imperial policy led the Conservatives to oppose home rule for the Irish and helped to involve Britain in a bitter war with the Boer republics of South Africa. The embattled Boer farmers held out from 1899 to 1902 and inflicted some stinging defeats upon their mighty adversary. The conflict brought home to the British their unpopularity, their unpreparedness, and their imperial responsibilities. They realized that a policy which exposed troops to defeat in Africa, at a time when discontented workers were striking at home, was a policy of conflicts and contradictions. When the resistance of the Boers was finally broken, the much criticized Conservative government promised South Africa self-rule within a few years, voted millions of pounds to restore the ruined farms, and then turned to placate the working classes at home.

It was time to heed the demands of the workers for they were preparing for political action. The conflict between capital and labor in Britain had taken a new turn after 1900. During the Boer War the unions suffered a sharp reverse when the Tory-minded House of Lords ruled that labor unions might be held legally and financially responsible for losses caused an employer through a strike (Taff Vale Decision, 1901). This ruling placed in jeopardy all the union funds, accumulated penny by penny from the workers' wages. Many workingmen had given scant attention to politics, believing that under a laissez-faire regime they could best improve their lot by dealing directly with their employers. After the Taff Vale Decision an increasing number came to feel that they had made a mistake in neglecting politics, that they should strive to elect more representatives to parliament and fight for their rights and their class interests by introducing remedial legislation. One result of this change in attitude was the rapid growth of a third party in British politics, the Labor Party. In the elections of 1906 the new group won twenty-nine seats.

The demand for social legislation and the need for a more powerful army and navy made it necessary for the government to raise a larger national revenue. The Liberals and the Conservatives differed on the wisest method of raising it. Joseph Chamberlain, a Liberal who had joined the Conservative Party, advocated a closer federation of the states of the empire with "imperial preference" for goods produced within the limits of Britain and the Dominions, and a tariff on foreign products entering British ports. A protective tariff would increase the national revenue and help British industries to compete against foreign rivals. Chamberlain's opponents were quick to point out that import duties would raise the price of many commodities favored by the British consumer and that the poor would feel the rise more sharply than the rich. The proposal for imperial preference and import duties aroused heated debates and was rejected.

In the election of 1906 the Conservatives were beaten and the Liberals assumed office. For the next eight years a Liberal-Labor combination controlled parliament and pressed a double program: to promote the welfare of the working classes and to arm Great Britain against the growing threat of war. The two aims were often in conflict, for both involved heavy expenditures and one or the other had to be curtailed. As the Liberals were the free trade party they could not well resort to a tariff and had to increase the revenue by additional taxation. In drafting new fiscal measures the question most difficult to settle was the *incidence* of the proposed taxation, that is, the manner in which it should bear upon the various classes.

With the support of the Labor members of Parliament and the Irish Nationalists (a group seeking home rule for Ireland) the Liberals could count upon 514 seats to 156 for the Conservatives. This strong majority made it certain that far-reaching reforms would be attempted. Under prime ministers Sir Henry Campbell-Bannerman (1905–1908) and Herbert Asquith (1908–1916) the Liberal cabinet attacked the social questions which had grown acute during the previous decade of Conservative rule. Although government interference in matters of hours, wages, health, and employment rules meant a frank abandonment of laissez-faire ideals in domestic politics, the Liberals prepared to abandon some of their ancient principles in return for Labor support. The prompt enactment of a Trade Disputes Bill (1906) made peaceful picketing legal and nullified the effect of the Taff Vale Decision by declaring that a union was not liable for damages resulting from illegal acts of its members. A Workingmen's Compensation Act, passed the same year, decreed that employers must compensate workers for injuries incurred at their trade. An Old Age Pension Law (1909) promised annuities for all citizens over seventy whose annual income was less than £31 10s. Stricter provisions to safeguard the health of the young followed, a Trade Boards Act created commissions to judge wage rates and investigate sweatshop conditions, and government employment agencies freely assisted able-bodied workers to find occupations suited to their skill. The climax to the ambitious program of reform came with the National Insurance Act of 1911, which planned to institute medical supervision and sickness insurance for the working population of the British Isles and to provide unemployment insurance for over 2,000,000 workers whose type of work exposed them to frequent lapses of employment. Funds for these services were to be created from contributions made by employees, employers, and the state.

To administer these Acts would clearly impose a heavy responsibility and a heavy expense upon the government. The social services and naval expansion together caused a sharp increase in the budget. To meet it the energetic Chancellor of the Exchequer, David Lloyd George, proposed (1909) to increase taxation on estates and incomes. His "war budget" in the fight against poverty was aimed at the rich; it taxed private parks, game preserves, and other "idle" land and established special levies on various forms of unearned income. Producers and consumers were spared, while idle possessors of wealth, and those who received large incomes without making an adequate economic return to society, were adjudged fair objects of taxation. All luxuries were likewise subject to taxes, from the rich man's automobile to the poor man's beer.

When the House of Lords, where the Conservatives were still entrenched, rejected the Lloyd George budget, the Liberals appealed to the nation and were returned to office with a reduced majority (1910). Insisting that the upper chamber was thwarting the expressed will of the people, the Liberals prepared to curtail its powers. As an institution the House of Lords seemed anomalous; its 620 members were made up of the peers of England, sixteen Scottish noblemen, twenty-eight Irish peers, and twenty-six bishops or archbishops of the Anglican Church. In addition there were four "Law Lords" (later seven) who decided legal cases referred to the House of Lords as a final court of appeal. To change the status of this chamber was equivalent to a constitutional amendment. As drawn up by the Liberals the Act embodying the proposed reform provided that the Lords should not veto money bills; that, despite their opposition, other measures would become law two years after their first introduction into the Commons if three successive sessions of the Commons approved them; and that a general election must be held at least once in five years. When the Lords rejected this Act, Asquith appealed to the electorate for the second time within a year (November, 1910). Once more the Liberals were returned to power, and Asquith threatened to ask the king, George V (1910–1935), to create enough new peers of Liberal persuasion to assure a majority for the bill. As in 1832, when they were faced by the same dilemma, the Lords yielded and the Parliament Act of 1911 was passed abridging their ancient prerogatives.

The outbreak of World War I in 1914 put a temporary halt to social experiments and ended the eight-year period of Liberal reforms. This was especially tragic for the Irish nationalists, whose hopes of winning home rule once more miscarried. Ireland, which had been the object of the earliest British expansion, remained for centuries an unreconciled and unassimilable conquest. After the loss of the American colonies the British granted Ireland a local parliament (1782), but the privilege was cancelled in 1801 when Britain was struggling against Napoleon and a French invasion of Ireland was a persistent danger. Throughout the nineteenth century Irish discontent led to persistent strife, with famine and emigration so reducing the population of that "most distressful country" that the total fell over a million between 1800 and 1914.

An evil fate seemed to attend all efforts to solve the Anglo-Irish problem. The great Liberal leader, William Ewart Gladstone (1809–1898), introduced a bill for Irish home rule in 1886 but was defeated in parliament. His second Home Rule Bill (1893) passed the Commons but was rejected in the House of Lords. Nothing less than home rule, however, would pacify the Irish Nationalists who were not satisfied merely to see Ireland represented in the British parliament. Their eighty members in the House of Commons kept up a constant agitation for a new home rule bill, and in 1912 the Liberal cabinet of Herbert Asquith introduced a measure providing for a parliament at Dublin. But the Irish people themselves were divided on the issue of independence. Fierce opposition developed in Ulster where the population, predominantly Protestant and distrustful of a settlement which would make them a minority in a Catholic state, threatened to resort to civil war. By 1913 an army of 100,000 Ulstermen was training openly and the Home Rule Bill was amended to exclude Ulster from its provisions indefinitely. This unresolved conflict was destined to grow more acute during World War I and culminated after 1918 in a savage struggle which will be discussed later (see pp. 253–254).

5

GERMANY

The course remains the same: full speed ahead!
WILLIAM II

1. RESOURCES: THE PROBLEMS OF ORGANIZATION

A CENTURY AGO "the Germanies" were still a loosely linked aggregation of two-score large and small states. In the Middle Ages most of the lands that were later to form the Austrian and the German empires were included in the Holy Roman Empire, but this loose political structure was weakened by conflicts between the emperors and the medieval popes. The emperors were "elected" by leading German princes and prelates, but after 1438 the title was always conferred on a member of the Hapsburg family and this gave the empire a vague dynastic authority. The Thirty Years' War (1618–1648) weakened the empire further because the component states gained a semi-independent status, and by the eighteenth century Voltaire could declare, derisively, that the Holy Roman Empire was neither holy, nor Roman, nor an empire. Napoleon weakened this "First Reich" still further by his victories over the Hapsburg forces, and the Emperor Francis II changed his title to Francis I, Emperor of Austria. After Napoleon's fall the diplomats who met at Vienna in 1814–1815 substituted a "Germanic Confederation" for the defunct empire, but Austria still retained the leadership and exercised a shadowy authority over the new organization.

During the eighteenth and nineteenth centuries, Brandenburg-Prussia became the strongest and most militant state of north Germany, and in the 1860's it successfully challenged the Hapsburg leadership. After defeating Austria in 1866, Prussia, under Bismarck's vigorous direction, linked most of the German states into a North German Confederation (1867) and enlarged this league into a German Empire (1871) with the Prussian king, William I, as German Emperor. This new empire did not include the Austrian dominions. Headed by a Hohenzollern instead of a Hapsburg ruler, and dominated by Prussia instead of Austria, the German Empire was a new organization, the "Second Reich." It was better integrated and more uniform than the polyglot Holy Roman Empire, the

Germanic Confederation, or the Austrian Empire could ever become, for the German Empire, proclaimed in 1871, had a population predominantly German in speech, tradition, and sentiment.

It is important to note that the Germans, as a great nation, with a centralized government and territorial unity, did not win their place as a great power until 1871. Spain, Portugal, France, and England had achieved political unity under national monarchies four centuries earlier, and this integration proved a valuable asset to them in their European contests and their fight for empires overseas. The Germans were left behind in the colonial race.

The long delay in achieving genuine political unity affected the character and destiny of the Germans in two important respects. (1) Lacking national unity and naval resources, the Germans were too disorganized and too deeply involved in local affairs to compete for overseas colonies. (2) Because Prussia, the most militant and bureaucratic of the German states, took the lead in the work of unification, many Germans before 1871, and almost all of them after that date, were disposed to overvalue the "state" and its role in human affairs. They venerated the state as a power in itself, free from the moral obligations which restrain the individual; and they accepted the idea that the citizen and the group must be subordinate and submissive. These conclusions seemed justifiable because their own experience had shown that too much individualism or "particularism" kept a nation impotent. As a consequence they placed undue importance upon unity and discipline.

Once political union was theirs the Germans realized that they had all the resources of a great, a very great, power. Their population was intelligent, frugal, and industrious. It had doubled in a century and by 1914 it reached a total of 67,000,000. They held rich deposits of coal and iron, indispensable for an industrial state, and they could acquire the latest machinery from Britain without waiting generations to develop it. With unification, their businessmen acquired a large central European market. They hastened to expand their factories, equip laboratories, train technologists, and promote the coordination of science and manufacture which, within a few decades, made Germany the most aggressive industrial nation of the world. Between 1870 and 1914 the output of its industries increased tenfold and the value of its foreign trade increased 250 per cent.

Partly to weld the state together, and partly to encourage business expansion, the government planned an excellent system of internal transport and communication, joining roads, railways, and canals. Harbor facilities were rapidly improved and after 1900 German mercantile and naval tonnage was surpassed only by that of Great Britain. In all parts of the world consumers learned to appreciate the quality of Germany's products; her salesmen even invaded the British Isles, which offered an open market because of the British free-trade policy. The industry of the

workers, the skill of the technicians trained in special schools, the resources and natural advantages exploited with foresight and decision by
the bankers and businessmen of Berlin, Bremen, Essen, and other centers,
made Germany by 1914 the most successful and dynamic of the European
states. Between 1880 and 1914 the British share of international trade
fell from 23 to 17 per cent, while the German share rose from 9 to 12 per
cent. Many Englishmen felt that their relative loss had been Germany's
gain. But trade rivalry alone would not have made a war between Britain
and Germany a growing threat; the United States increased its share of
world trade from 10 to 15 per cent in this period without exciting British
antagonism. It was not German power alone that excited mistrust but
the use the leaders of Germany might make of that power. Their purposes
seemed to be darkly foreshadowed by their program of armaments.

All the neighbors of Germany watched her rising production, wealth,
and energy with envy and alarm. They saw much to admire but more to
fear in her spirit and method. Teutonic order and efficiency, the union
of science with industry, high standards of education, particularly technological training, the variety of manufactures, the patience and perti-
nacity of salesmen, the enterprise of German bankers, and the alertness
of consular agents in detecting new and promising fields of business —
all these set a standard not easy to match. Germany was forging irresistibly ahead, and forging ahead by invading areas and markets which
the businessmen of other nations had marked out for themselves. Not
only in Europe but in Asia, in Africa, and in Latin America, German trade
gains often meant a loss of orders for British, French, Belgian, Dutch,
Swiss, Swedish, and American manufacturers. This rivalry in the economic sphere aroused tension and antagonism. The Germans were only
one of the competitor nations, but their success, their aggressiveness, the
rapid pace they set, and the new methods and techniques they perfected,
focused upon them the resentment of less energetic rivals.

For years German chemists led the world in the production of new
materials and the discovery of substitutes for old ones. German firms
flooded the world with synthetic drugs, fabrics, plastics, and metal alloys
which in many cases proved both superior to and cheaper than natural
products. One of their outstanding triumphs in the field of industrial
chemistry was the development of synthetic dyes; a second was the production of synthetic nitrates. Before the twentieth century over 95 per
cent of the world's nitrate supply had come from deposits in Chile, but
the Germans perfected a formula for "fixing" the nitrogen which constitutes four-fifths of the atmosphere. By 1914 their chemical plants were
producing 12,000 tons of nitrates a year, a valuable addition to the
national economy because nitrates are equally indispensable for fertilizers
and for explosives. This domestic supply, rapidly augmented, helped to
carry Germany through the First World War, when German imports from
Chile were cut off by the British blockade.

Thus German ingenuity and systematic organization helped to solve problems of supply, created new resources, and rendered the industry of the country less dependent upon imports. Moreover, German chemists and engineers tapped new sources of power and production and opened wider fields for exploitation. Although Germans had lagged behind other peoples at the opening of the Oceanic Age when the world was first revealed to Europeans, German chemists and physicists led the way in the modern attack upon matter and laid bare veins of wealth which rivaled the treasures of the Indies. Unfortunately, as their former feeling of inferiority was replaced by pride and self-confidence, the Germans grew increasingly arrogant and tactless. They wanted "a place in the sun," and they excited the envy, the fear, and the hostility of their neighbors by the methods they adopted to attain it.

2. DEFENSE AND EXPANSION: WELTPOLITIK AND ENCIRCLEMENT

Had German progress been confined to the arts of peace, opponents might have accepted the competition with less alarm, but the Germans, in the decades before 1914, became the most powerful and most efficiently militarized nation on the Continent. Their veneration for the state, their hardy respect for military virtues, and their acceptance of war as a necessary process in the forging of nations made them militaristic. German national pride had been born of the battlefield; the War of Liberation against Napoleon in 1813–1814 had stirred the flame; a war with Denmark (1864) brought the border duchies of Schleswig and Holstein under Prussian control; a war with Austria (1866) settled the issue whether Vienna or Berlin was to be the capital and focal center of the Reich; and a war with France (1870–1871) brought Alsace and Lorraine and a billion dollar indemnity to the victors. As a dramatic touch, the King of Prussia was proclaimed German Emperor in the palace of Louis XIV at Versailles (January 18, 1871), a few days before Paris surrendered to the German army. These associations not only intensified the national spirit, they made the army and the state one in German thought. In the long interval of peace from 1871 to 1914 the power of the military caste did not decrease; compulsory military service initiated all German youths into the service of the state; industry was developed with a view to war needs as well as profits; roads were built to facilitate the movements of troops and guns as well as goods; and the spirit of military organization and discipline reached into all departments of life. Germany was the Sparta of the modern European world.

Otto von Bismarck, the architect of unification and first chancellor of the new German Reich after 1871, desired a period of peace in which to consolidate the national government he had helped to construct. Until his retirement in 1890 he managed to maintain fairly amicable relations with Austria, Russia, Italy, and Great Britain. By astute and realistic diplomacy he built up an intricate system of alliances which left France isolated and therefore enfeebled. For Bismarck was haunted by a "nightmare of coalitions." He feared that the French would seek revenge for their humiliation in 1870–1871 and his premonition was ultimately vindicated. After he resigned control German diplomacy suffered a long series of reverses. The first setback came when France and Russia concluded a military alliance in 1894. Then, as recorded in the preceding chapter, France and Britain arrived at an entente or friendly understanding in 1904. Finally France, Russia, and Britain united to form the Triple Entente in 1907.

German statesmen became alarmed as they realized that their country might find itself "encircled" if war developed. To match the armaments of the three entente powers, Germany could rely only upon the aid of Austria-Hungary. Italy was also a nominal ally of Germany and Austria, but this Triple Alliance, though it had been formed in 1882 and renewed at intervals, was unstable. At Berlin the leaders realized that the Italians could not be depended upon for serious military aid, especially in a war against Great Britain. Germany and Austria-Hungary, the Central Powers of Europe, would have to stand or fall together.

The apprehension at Berlin over the mounting threat of war can be read in the successive army bills submitted to the Reichstag. When France and Russia became allies in 1894, the German army was raised from 487,000 to 557,000 men, a move which convinced the French and Russians in turn of the need to strengthen their alliance. When France and Britain established their entente in 1904, the German standing army was further increased to 605,000. With each successive crisis in international affairs, from 1908 to 1914, their forces climbed steadily — to 617,000 (1910), 631,000 (1911), 666,000 (1912), and 820,000 (1913). The German high command, which retained control over millions of reservists as well as over the soldiers in service, was an arrogant and independent organization, free from the control of the electors and their representatives in the Reichstag. In theory the high command was subject to the orders of the emperor, but this meant that the real decisions lay with the military cabinet which advised the kaiser on army affairs. In these circles a preponderant influence was exercised by the Junkers, members of the landed nobility and particularly of the aristocracy of eastern Prussia. The firm monopoly the Junkers retained over the German army may be judged by the fact that before 1914 thirty out of thirty-two commanding generals and thirty-seven out of forty-four lieutenant generals were of noble birth. In the lower grades, skill, character, and length of service might assure promotion, but for the highest posts aristocratic lineage was almost essential.

As the diplomatic skies darkened after 1900, the general staff accepted the realities of the international situation and drew up plans for a war on

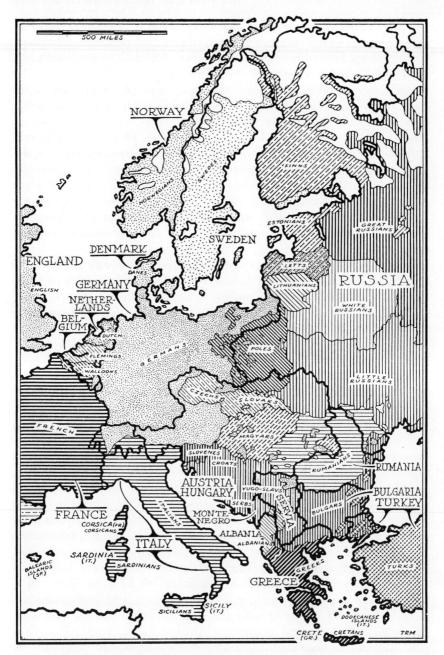

NATIONAL AND POLITICAL BOUNDARIES IN MIDDLE EUROPE, 1914

two fronts. Since Germany had no strong natural frontiers to serve as defense barriers, German strategists anticipated that fighting would prove costly and the battle lines fluid and tenuous. Freedom of movement and the ability to maneuver rapidly would thus offer major advantages. To magnify their striking power and make full strategic use of their inside lines, the Germans completed a network of railways which would enable them to shuttle their forces from the French to the Russian front as needed. They were hopeful that, if war came, they could hold one opponent in check while defeating the other independently and swiftly. They recognized, however, that their most implacable enemy might prove to be *time*, and they prepared to open hostilities with a crushing campaign which would bring speedy victory. For a prolonged war, especially if Germany were blockaded, would ruin trade, deplete resources, and might ultimately reduce the people to defeat through malnutrition and exhaustion.

Despite subsidies and tariffs maintained to encourage and protect agriculture, Germany had ceased to be self-sufficient in the matter of food. As the nation became highly industrialized and the urban population increased, it found itself, like Great Britain, dependent upon imports. By 1914 half the working population was engaged in industry or trade; one-third lived in cities of 20,000 or more; and only one worker in four was left for agriculture. This increasing dependence upon trade was of course one reason why Germany built a navy and sought colonies. But the gamble was a gigantic one because in war Germany's ocean trade, her ships, and her colonies would be hostages of fortune. Her imports, which by 1914 were worth almost $3,000,000,000 annually, were certain to suffer if the sea routes were blockaded. After 1907 it had become increasingly probable that the sea routes *would* be blockaded, for German diplomacy failed to dissolve the accord growing between France, Russia, and Britain. Overseas investments, the colonies in Africa, the treaty ports in China, the island bases in the Pacific Ocean (belated acquisitions of the young but lusty German imperialism) would all be severed from the Reich when hostilities commenced. The entente nations could then take over these isolated outposts at leisure. War, for Germany, therefore promised to prove a risky venture, certain to involve heavy fighting in Europe, destruction of trade, loss of colonies, and the likelihood of a long blockade. But these hard probabilities, instead of persuading the Germans to avoid war, convinced the high command that the war must be made short, sharp, and decisive.

In Europe the area of greatest tension was the Balkan peninsula. A succession of diplomatic crises from 1908 to 1914 brought the central empires into sharp competition with Russia for the control of the lesser Balkan states. German businessmen from the 1880's onward had appreciated the commercial possibilities of the Near East. Great Britain, which enjoyed almost half the Turkish foreign trade, was not at first unduly alarmed by German penetration, but after 1900 a graver note of warning was sounded in London. It was evident that German influence in the Turkish Empire and in Persia (modern Iran) was growing rapidly. The Germans had even proceeded so far as to plan a new railway line linking Berlin to Constantinople and running thence to Basra on the Persian Gulf.

The key point in this strategy of expansion was Constantinople. If the Germans obtained the mastery at this "crossroads of empire," it would mean a signal reverse for Britain and a major defeat for Russia. For Constantinople guarded the only exit Russia possessed to the warm seas. A trade depot at Basra, with shipping lines to follow, would bring the Germans to the gates of India and of Turkestan. Russia and Britain, themselves frequent rivals in the Near East, were moved to adjust their differences and to join forces against the menace. The entente of 1907 set boundaries for the British and Russian spheres of influence in Persia, and Russia recognized the preponderant position of the British in Afghanistan. France, which had maintained trade connections with the Levant since the time of the crusades, was likewise alarmed by the German drive. It was evident that old Europe had become too narrow a field for the expanding forces generated by modern industry and that the Balkan area was the most permeable region and therefore the one most likely to soften under the increasing pressure. This made it also the region in which an open conflict was most likely to develop.

3. POLITICAL AND SOCIAL ISSUES: THE STATE, THE CHURCH,
   AND THE SOCIALISTS

The new Germany, consolidated in 1871, had a government that was parliamentary in appearance but authoritarian in spirit and practice. The Germans did not have a long history of evolving parliamentary precedents like the British, nor semi-autonomous bodies for local self-government like the English county, parish, and borough, where aspirants for public office could learn the art of politics. Nor had the Germans passed through a century of alternating revolution and reaction, like the French after 1789, whereby various forms of government might be tried out and the virtues or failings of each demonstrated. As a consequence the Germans lacked wide experience in managing their political affairs and were more familiar with the advantages of energetic bureaucratic rule than with the party system, popular assemblies, and the ballot. Since the teaching of history influences the attitude of every people toward different methods of administration, it should be kept in mind that for Central Europeans "election" brought to memory the mode of choosing the Holy Roman Emperors, whose lack of authority and inability to unite their realms had spelled division and war for centuries. The Polish Diet, which "elected" the kings of Poland but granted them no funds or authority to govern, seemed a further example of the weakness of assemblies, an example emphasized by the disintegration and dismemberment of Poland in the eighteenth century. Parliamentary rule had been further discredited for the Germans by the fiasco of 1848–1849, when the Assembly of Frankfort attempted and failed signally to frame a constitutional union for the German states.

In 1862, when William I of Prussia appointed Otto von Bismarck his chancellor, the Prussian Diet (Parliament) opposed the heavy military outlay that the king and Bismarck believed necessary. William, declaring that he ruled by the grace of God and no one else, refused to yield. Bismarck stood firm beside his royal master and defied the Diet. "Not by speeches and majority votes are the great questions of the day decided," he insisted, " — that was the mistake of 1848 and 1849 — but by blood and iron." Though hated and denounced by many liberals, the "Iron Chancellor" supported the Prussian minister of war, Albrecht von Roon, and the chief of staff, Helmuth von Moltke, in building up the Prussian army. When the well-trained Prussian divisions defeated Austria in 1866 the Diet applauded the result, voted approval of the "unconstitutional" methods Bismarck and his colleagues had pursued, and congratulated them. In other words the Diet reversed itself, conceding that the autocratic ministers had been right and the elected representatives of the people had been wrong — a concession hardly calculated to increase the nation's respect for its parliament. The further implication, that a policy — even an arbitrary and unconstitutional policy — was right if it led to a German victory, set a pragmatic (and Machiavellian) precedent for later German governments.

The efficiency of the Prussian conscript armies, which brought the Austrians to terms in seven weeks (1866) and the French in six months (1870–1871), seemed a practical vindication of the Prussian system. The "unification" of Germany became in a sense the "Prussianization" of Germany. The extraordinary economic expansion which followed the political unification of 1871 seemed proof that the bureaucrats in control knew their business. Most Germans were therefore disposed to leave problems of administration to the rulers who had shown themselves expert in these matters. It had long been the practice of the Prussian kings and their ministers to draw army officers from the nobility and civil servants from the upper bourgeoisie. The high standards of loyalty, efficiency, and honesty which characterized most Prussian officials, and the conscientious toil of an army of obedient and industrious clerks, offered a further clue to Prussian influence. In politics, as in most affairs, those who are willing to assume laborious tasks and perform them consistently accrete power by imperceptible degrees. The Prussians (often with the aid of patriotic Germans from other states who joined the Prussian service) led the van in all phases of unification. They fought the French under Napoleon (1806 and 1813–1814); they worked to organize the states in a common customs union (the *Zollverein*) between 1819 and 1844; and they assumed direction and responsibility in the critical years from 1860 to 1870. When Bismarck became chancellor of the new empire, Prussian standards and methods were already admired and imitated throughout the Reich.

The ideal of authoritarian bureaucracy differed from the ideal of responsible government and democratic control which had gained ground in Britain, France, and the United States in the nineteenth century. The new Germany occupied a middle position, geographically and politically. It lay between the western democracies, Britain and France, and the dynastic absolutism of Austria-Hungary and Russia. After 1871 the German government was a compromise between autocratic and popular rule. The Reichstag, a popularly elected chamber with 382 deputies, represented the people, but although the population of the electoral districts shifted, the conservative rural constituencies kept the same number of representatives as urban districts with five or even ten times the number of voters. The states composing the new empire were represented in an upper chamber, the Bundesrat, the members of which were nominated, not elected. As Prussia held seventeen of the fifty-eight votes in the Bundesrat and could control several others, the indissoluble union of states was very largely under Prussian control.

In yet another respect the government remained authoritarian rather than parliamentarian in its functioning. The head of the cabinet, who was known as the chancellor, was nominated by the King of Prussia in his role as German Emperor and was not necessarily acceptable to a majority of the Reichstag. As the chancellor usually named the associate ministers to head the various departments of state, he preserved an almost dictatorial control over the administration. In parliamentary regimes, the essential control which the representatives of the people exercise over the cabinet depends on their control of money appropriations. In France and Britain the representatives of the people could repudiate and overthrow a cabinet at any time by refusing it a vote of confidence. In the new German constitution these controls did not function effectively. The chancellor could and sometimes did ignore the opposition of a majority in the assembly, for he could retain his office as long as the monarch supported him. Freedom to criticize the government, freedom of speech and of the press, which in France was often carried to extremes under the Third Republic, were restrained in Germany. The government maintained a strict supervision over the journals and over all public organizations. An efficient police system preserved order, the highly centralized army instilled a sense of discipline into the young men, and the regimentation which ruled the army and the bureaucracy made itself felt in every field of German national activity.

As citizens, the Germans proved themselves docile, law-abiding, and respectful of authority. The rapid rise and bold bid for power of the new empire inspired them with a fervent patriotism which easily became chauvinism. It would seem that these people, modest and unaggressive as individuals, found compensation for their own restraint and frustration by exalting the state. They applauded their leaders when the latter asserted the claims of Germany to a larger influence in international affairs, and the leaders gratified them by frequent displays of undiplomatic truculence and sword-rattling. Such exhibitions of pride and power earned for Kaiser William II (grandson of William I) a reputation for aggressiveness which made him appear to contemporaries as the "War Lord of Europe." Unfortunately Europe was too small a field for German ambitions. The economic and military aggrandizement of the Reich, sustained by the ardent efforts of industrialists, chemists, engineers, bankers, diplomats, and soldiers, pushed the empire by 1914 into a grandiose policy of *Weltpolitik* or global politics.

One factor in the phenomenal rise of German industrial power, a very significant factor, was the high performance and relatively low wages of the German worker. The need of the state for soldiers, technicians, clerks, and factory hands, as well as farmers, was foreseen and provided for in the school training program. The worker accepted his role and discharged his duties in remarkably faithful fashion. The average income in Germany in 1900 was only two-thirds that in Great Britain, although German products were in many respects superior in quality and in workmanship. It was inevitable that in time German workers would grow critical of a system which denied them a richer reward for their labor. The dissemination of socialist doctrines and the rise of a Socialist Party after 1900 gravely alarmed Germany's conservative leaders.

As early as 1880 the alert and realistic Bismarck had foreseen the danger that working class voters might be affected by socialist ideas. He decided to combat the threat by a comprehensive scheme of social insurance which would attach the working classes more firmly to the state. Twenty years before the British government turned to similar measures, he sponsored a Sickness Insurance Law (1883), an Accident Insurance Law (1884), and an Old Age and Invalidity Insurance Law (1889). The funds for the first law were contributed by the workers and the employers; for the second, by the employers; and for the third by workers, employers, and state. These acts, by relieving the worker and his family of the ever-present fear of sickness and swift destitution, and by assuring the aged against misery and want, removed much of the insecurity and hardship from their lives. These reforms made the workers grateful toward the "paternalistic" state which instituted and supervised this protection.

Bismarck's program of social legislation recognized the truth of the Dutch proverb that to make a man a conservative you must give him something to conserve. The rootless, propertyless urban classes, if they had nothing to lose, would have been more susceptible to the enticements of revolutionaries who promised them a better life under a new order. But the insurance to which they had contributed gave them a stake in the future. Like holders of national bonds, the workers acquired an interest and a motive for defending the existing imperial regime. As the state guaranteed them the benefits of their accumulating policies and promised them a retirement annuity when they were too old to work, they had less reason to become revolutionaries and more reason to hope that the existing government would remain stable.

Bismarck distrusted the populace and regarded socialists and communists as dangerous agitators who might destroy the empire which he had consolidated. In 1878 he introduced a law suppressing public meetings, journals, and the collection of funds for socialistic or communistic causes. After 1890, however, when the Iron Chancellor was forced to resign by the new emperor, William II,[1] this law against the socialists was allowed to lapse. William was determined to play a leading part in matters of policy, and the chancellors who followed Bismarck were less independent and masterful men. The earnest but inexpert Leo von Caprivi (1890–1894) was succeeded by the aged and courtly Prince Hohenlohe (1894–1900). Then came the adroit but somewhat irresolute Count Bernhard von Bülow (1900–1909) and the conscientious but colorless Theobald von Bethmann Hollweg (1909–1917).

William II's erratic moves confused and weakened the policies of his ministers, and his government met with increasing difficulties and reverses in domestic and foreign affairs. The treatment of the socialists affords a striking example of this confusion. Craving popularity and eager to win the workers, William and his ministers approved a number of concessions between 1890 and 1911. Working hours were limited by law; factory conditions were improved; workers' committees (formed to negotiate with employers) received recognition; a department of labor was created; accident, sickness, and old age insurance were broadened and increased; and the entire field of security legislation was embraced in a single act, the Imperial Insurance Code of 1911. Had it been possible to placate the lower classes by paternal legislation, these concessions should have met the situation.

Democracy was on the march, however, and the German people, seeing the greater political liberty enjoyed by the French, the British, and the Americans, demanded a larger share in their own government. The Socialist Party, able to come into the open after 1890, grew rapidly and, as often happens in such cases, became more moderate in its aims as it increased in numbers. In 1912 it elected 110 members, the largest single group in the Reichstag. The socialists drew their chief support from the cities. They were opposed by the militarists because they sought to reduce army appropriations, by the wealthy because they favored inheritance and income taxes, by the landowners because they wished to lower the

---

[1] William I died in 1888; his son Frederick, who succeeded him, died within a few months, and William's grandson, William II (1888–1918) became king of Prussia and German Emperor.

tariff on farm produce and import cheaper food, and by the employer class generally because they demanded better pay for servants, laborers, and factory hands. But although the Social Democrats received over one-third of the votes cast in the election of 1912 and dominated the Reichstag with the aid of liberal allies, they could not control the ministers. In 1913 the Reichstag passed a vote of lack of confidence in the government, but the chancellor, von Bethmann-Hollweg, did not resign, for he regarded himself as the appointee of the emperor and responsible to him. Thus political crises, which in England would have overturned the cabinet and forced an election, passed in Germany with a few heated debates and resolutions of protest. These conditions made it possible to argue that Germany was not a democracy, that the power of decision lay with the kaiser and his advisers and the people could not control this ruling group.

6

FRANCE

One must be deliberately blind not to realize that the [German] lust for power, the impact of which makes Europe tremble each day, has fixed as its policy the extermination of France.

GEORGES CLEMENCEAU[1]

1. RESOURCES: THE PROBLEM OF POPULATION

THE "FAIR LAND OF FRANCE," as the old chroniclers named it, contains some of the richest farms, orchards, and vineyards of Europe. To these gifts Nature has added a moderate climate, moist in the north and sunny in the south. These advantages help to explain why France leads in the production of rare wines and why the French are the foremost bread consumers among the nations. With a population not too densely concentrated (approximately 230 to the square mile) and large areas that repay cultivation, the French people remained largely self-sufficient in the matter of food. In this they preserved an advantage lost in the twentieth century by the British, Italians, and Germans who became increasingly dependent upon imported supplies.

The natural richness of the land also helped to explain why relatively few Frenchmen emigrated, why so many remained attached to the soil, and why even city workers, still farmers at heart, often kept a small vegetable garden (sometimes no more than a few square yards in extent) where they could smoke their pipes in the evening while weeding the lettuce beds. Before 1914 there were still two Frenchmen on the land for one in a factory or shop. The millions of sturdy, independent farm proprietors formed a powerful stabilizing class, for as property owners and taxpayers they were disposed to be conservative in politics and conventional in their thinking.

In addition to its agricultural wealth and productivity France entered the twentieth century with well developed industries. She ranked fourth in the total of her foreign trade in 1900, third in her output of textiles, and

---

[1] Georges Clemenceau, *L'Homme libre*, May 21, 1913.

third in iron production. Her artisans, long noted for their skill in creating luxury goods, specialized in fine fabrics of cotton, silk, and wool, exquisite laces, perfumes, leather work, glass, porcelain, and jewelry. Since the seventeenth century, when Louis XIV made Versailles the model of elegant life, France had set the fashion for international society. High among the assets of the nation were the profits derived from the tourist trade, for millions of visitors came each year to view the historic chateaux and cathedrals, to shop, to visit the beaches and watering places, and to assist, by their payments for these services, in preserving for France the favorable balance of trade which enabled her to accumulate gold reserves.

A further asset which the French acquired was the second largest colonial empire in the world. French overseas territories in Africa and Asia ranked next to those of Great Britain in area and population. This extensive list of protectorates and colonies had been acquired in a few generations. Until the nineteenth century the history of French colonial enterprise had been a story of heroic exploration and settlement followed by disheartening reverses and forfeitures. Attempts to found permanent colonies and establish spheres of control in Canada, in Louisiana, in the West Indies, in Egypt, in India, even in Australia, had all been frustrated in the end by superior British sea power. But a new and more progressive chapter in overseas expansion opened for the French in 1830 when they sent a punitive expedition to occupy Algiers. Cautiously but inexorably French imperialism was pushed outward until by 1914 its conquests included 4,000,000 square miles of African and Asian territories, with a colonial population somewhat larger than the 40,000,000 total of France itself.

Relatively few Frenchmen, however, aside from soldiers and administrators, left France for the colonies. Although they were proud to establish order, build roads and hospitals, garrison and govern their protectorates in other continents, they did not feel impelled to emigrate overseas as freely as the Spaniards and Portuguese, the British, Italians, Germans, and Scandinavian people did. Settlers from all European countries emigrated to the United States in the nineteenth century but so few Frenchmen came that France ranked twentieth in its contribution. Some French colonists went to Indochina, and more to French North Africa, but they remained a minority among the indigenous millions there. This planting of European minorities in alien continents, minorities too small to dominate or displace the native populations, was a policy that created serious problems for France in the twentieth century (see Chaps. 53 and 66).

Many thoughtful Frenchmen doubted the value of possessions overseas and opposed the imperial urge which led to such conquests. Their huge African domains, divided into five administrative divisions — Morocco, Algeria, Tunisia, French West Africa, and French Equatorial Africa —

had been costly to conquer and remained costly to administer. The second great *bloc* of French protectorates lay in southeastern Asia, comprising the (nominally) Chinese provinces of Cochin China, Cambodia, Tonkin, Annam, and Laos, a combined area larger than France itself, with a population over 20,000,000. To subdue this empire required many minor military campaigns, expensive to the French taxpayer in their totality. To hold these distant regions demanded the presence of armed forces and the maintenance of a powerful navy.

Anti-imperialists stressed these facts. They pointed out that colonial trade did not justify such expansion of territory because it formed only a small fraction of French external trade. As France had no problems arising from excess home population, and the colonies were in general unsuited to settlement by Europeans, they would never form reserves of manpower, and to train Asians and Africans as soldiers might ultimately threaten white supremacy. Thus the French taxpayer, upon whom the burden of defending the empire ultimately fell, derived no adequate return. The risks implicit in the imperialistic gamble, and the international rivalries and wars which might develop from it, provided anti-imperialists with further arguments against the retention, or at least the extension, of the empire. These risks and rivalries were real and threatening. The Third Republic came close to war with Italy, with Great Britain, and with Germany in turn, as disputes over African territories grew sharp; and the value of the claims involved did not warrant the cost and losses of a major war.

Cautious citizens doubted the wisdom of scattering part of their forces on distant continents when France might have to face at any moment an attack from across the Rhine or across the Alps. The rising population of Germany threatened in time to become double that of France; the population of Italy, Russia, and Great Britain was also increasing. But the population of France remained stationary, and this alone seemed sufficient reason for keeping Frenchmen at home. Frenchmen could not ignore this growing numerical weakness; its implications for the future influenced their consideration of all important political issues; and they realized that their own country, with the smallest population among the great powers, might be reduced in time to a secondary place in the concert of the nations. For all the French assets — gold, wheat, machinery, coal, iron, shipping, colonies — could not preserve French potential if manpower failed. Rather, these advantages would become responsibilities because they would excite the envy of more aggressive and prolific peoples. Already by 1914 thousands of Italian, Spanish, Belgian, and other foreign workers crossed into France annually to fill vacancies in field and factory. As the French birth rate, lowest among the European nations, continued to decline, the manpower problem grew more urgent.

2. DEFENSE AND EXPANSION: REVANCHE AND THE SEARCH FOR ALLIES

The Franco-Prussian War of 1870–1871 made Germany an empire and France a republic. Bismarck favored the republican form of government for France for the same reason he opposed it in Germany: he believed democracies and republics were more subject to internal division and proved inept in war because the executive power was divided and dispersed. The fate of France after 1870 seemed to offer some justification for this argument. Royalists and republicans wrestled for control, internal divisions discouraged plans for a war of revenge, and a succession of political scandals discredited the republican regime. The instability of the French cabinets made it difficult for the country to pursue a consistent foreign policy or to secure support, for other governments could not readily negotiate or make binding agreements with a ministry which might be out of office before the ink on the agreement was dry.

As a result, France for a quarter of a century after 1870 had a diminished prestige and influence in the concert of Europe. This isolation made it impossible for the French to feel secure; and as German industrial and military might continued to grow, the French likewise maintained a conscript army, spent increasing sums on armaments, and pressed their diplomatic campaign for an alliance of states to curb the preponderant power of the Reich. The first successes in this campaign came after Bismarck's retirement, when the system of alliances built up by the great chancellor began to disintegrate. The Three Emperors' League binding Germany, Austria, and Russia had already dissolved (1887), but Bismarck had maintained the Dual Alliance of Germany and Austria-Hungary, the Triple Alliance of Germany, Austria-Hungary, and Italy, and a new Reinsurance Treaty with Russia promising neutrality by the other party if either Germany or Russia were attacked. In 1890 this treaty was allowed to lapse, and four years later Russian military and diplomatic officials agreed to an accord with France. International politics make strange bedfellows; republican France, most radical of the European regimes, concluded a pact of military support with tsarist Russia, most reactionary of the great powers. This accord of 1894, casual and tentative at first, was strengthened with chains of gold in the years that followed, for the French government authorized loans to Russia for railways, arsenals, guns, and battleships, loans which by 1914 had passed 12,000,000,000 francs. The German high command saw in this Franco-Russian alliance the certainty of a two-front war unless the alliance could be dissolved. It was this pact which first aroused the German fear of encirclement, but the kaiser's advisers long clung to the illusion that they could break it up by a policy which combined bluff, bargaining, and blunt threats.

The French Foreign Office found an agreement with Great Britain more difficult to achieve. Fortunately for their plans, the instability of French cabinet rule was less apparent after 1900, and foreign policy was ably handled for seven years (1898–1905) by a cool-headed and determined minister, Théophile Delcassé. Bismarck, before his death in the same year that Delcassé took office, foresaw the danger of anti-German coalitions which would encircle the Reich. Delcassé, more than any other statesman, was responsible for their creation. The first task that faced him was to smooth over a grave crisis in Anglo-French relations which developed when both powers claimed the Upper Nile region (the Fashoda Affair, 1898). The French were obliged to withdraw; but instead of being angered by this reverse, Delcassé deliberately courted British friendship. The two countries were rivals in the Levant, in Egypt, in Madagascar, and in the Far East, but compromises and concessions so reduced the tension that by 1904 an accord became possible. Unwilling to make a formal treaty of alliance, which would require parliamentary approval, the British cabinet preferred a friendly understanding, an entente as already explained (see p. 38). This entente rendered possible the concentration of the British fleet in the North Sea, promised France and her colonies safety from German naval attack, and adjusted Anglo-French colonial disputes.

After 1904 the new balance of power took rapid form. It became the purpose of French diplomacy to draw Britain and Russia together and the purpose was rapidly achieved. The defeat of Russia in the Russo-Japanese War of 1904–1905 was the critical event that speeded the new alignment, for it proved to the British that their fear of Russian strength had been exaggerated and it gave the German-Austrian-Italian combination, the Triple Alliance, a stronger position because Russia could not risk another war for the time being. At Berlin this advantageous turn of events was fully appreciated — too fully, perhaps, for it made Germany truculent. Russia, in grave difficulties, was half persuaded into an alliance with Germany, and the French poured out further loans to hold their wavering ally. To the French, German diplomats hinted broadly that Delcassé and his policy of encirclement had become a threat to peace and he must be dismissed.

Delcassé accordingly resigned (June, 1905) but the German imperialists were not placated. They had watched with jealous eyes the steady increase of French influence in the nominally independent north African Sultanate of Morocco, and they feared that German trade there would suffer if Morocco became a French protectorate. To assuage German protests a conference of the interested powers was convoked at Algeciras (January-March, 1906). The independence and territorial integrity of Morocco were solemnly affirmed, with equal opportunity promised in the Sultanate for the trade of all nations. The French, however, were allowed limited police powers in certain areas, and they continued to expand their influence. As a result the Germans complained that once again they had been thwarted. Since their dream of colonial expansion required a powerful high seas fleet, they increased their naval program. At the same time they renewed the Triple Alliance ties (June, 1906), and William II sought to weaken France by flattering Nicholas II of Russia and proposing a Russo-German agreement.

The British, alarmed at the German expansion and more so at the German naval threat, decided that it was time to redress the balance of power. With French diplomats eagerly watching the negotiations, the British and Russian governments established an entente in 1907, adjusting a number of disputes that had caused Anglo-Russian friction in Persia (Iran), Afghanistan, and other areas in Asia. The French statesman Georges Clemenceau, who was premier in these critical years, was delighted to see a Triple Entente (Britain, France, Russia) taking shape as a counterweight to the Triple Alliance. The policy that Delcassé had sponsored progressed even though the Germans had helped to force him out of office because of his distrust of Germany.

By 1907, therefore, France not only became stronger through the assurance of Russian support and the virtual assurance of British support, but French diplomats also had the satisfaction of weakening their opponents. With British agreement they appeased Italy and Spain by recognizing that these two Mediterranean powers were entitled to territory in North Africa. These Franco-British efforts to reconcile the Italians and Spaniards were important, for they made it less likely that Italy would aid Germany and Austria in a war against France or that the Spaniards would try to close the Straits of Gibraltar against French or British ships if war came. The Mediterranean was the British "life-line" to India and Australia, while for the French it was the essential route to their North African Empire from which they counted on importing minerals, extra food, and Algerian troops to help them defend France itself.

Yet even with strong allies and the ocean routes open to them the French did not feel secure. "For France the danger of invasion is very real," Clemenceau declared in 1908. "We know that on the morrow of the outbreak of war between Germany and England, the German armies will invade France by way of Belgium, and that Germany will seek in France an indemnity for the losses they are likely to suffer on the sea at the hands of the English." Clemenceau was a realist. He knew that France could not count with certainty on British aid, despite warm speeches celebrating the friendship of the two nations, for the understanding between them had not been reduced to a binding treaty. The two governments had agreed that, if war came, the British fleet would protect the north and west coasts of France while the French fleet was to be largely concentrated in the Mediterranean Sea. If, however, the British failed to fulfill these terms, long sections of the French coastline would be vulnerable to German attack. The Russians, on whom the French could count more definitely, might prove doubtful allies for another reason. The tsar's government, weakened by internal strains, might fail to survive under strong German attacks.

It was on land that the French expected the war to develop and on land that they believed it would reach a decision. Memories of the invasion of 1870, the siege of Paris, the humiliation of defeat, and the loss of Alsace and Lorraine kept alive in French hearts a conflict of sentiments. Fear of war mingled with and checked the desire for revenge against the Prussians. Few Frenchmen would have maintained that revenge or even the recovery of the lost provinces was worth the certain horrors and losses of a modern armed conflict. Frenchmen, Germans, Russians, Italians, and Englishmen all responded to patriotic appeals when they thought their country was menaced or insulted, but no one save a few intriguers and irresponsible hotheads wanted war. The growing tension, the bulging military budgets, the conscript armies forever expanding, the dreadnoughts and superdreadnoughts, these were all elements in a dark drama, motivated by vast forces beyond any statesman's understanding, any diplomat's control. Distrust bred suspicion, suspicion begot fear, fear became panic. Darkening each diplomatic parley, hovering over every conference table, hung the nightmare vision of the waiting cannon, the gray battleships, the marshaled men, all the inexorable machinery of the nation-in-arms. Everyone realized that this machinery required no more than a word to set it in motion, and once started it could not be arrested. As already explained, the Germans, fearful of encirclement, raised their effectives from 487,000 to 820,000 men in the twenty years before 1914. The sharpest rise came on the eve of the conflict, a rise from 623,000 to 820,000 between 1911 and 1913. The French countered by extending their period of military training to three years and by establishing a reserve of 750,000.

Fear, it has been said, is a poor counselor. The French, because of their sense of insecurity, had worked to build a system of alliances which, opposed to the Triple Alliance, created a precarious equilibrium among the European powers. This balance, the diplomats insisted, was the surest guarantee of peace because each nation would seek to restrain its allies and none would thoughtlessly invoke a war which it stood an even chance of losing. A war, moreover, whether won or lost, was certain to prove burdensome, bloody, and unpredictable. Some militarists even averred with sincerity that the better armed the nations became and the more terrible the weapons science provided, the less risk there was of actual conflict because all sane people would shrink from it and insist upon arbitration. This line of reasoning may have been sound logically but it proved unsound psychologically. The growing threat of hostilities induced a war mentality, a fatalistic sense that something so steadily foreseen and provided for must be inevitable. The balance of power which the diplomats so carefully built up to preserve peace became a mechanism of interlocking parts, so that when the crisis came the powers were dragged one after another into the catastrophe which each had labored to avert and each had prayed it might avoid.

3. POLITICAL AND SOCIAL QUESTIONS: THE ARMY, THE CHURCH, AND THE SOCIALISTS

The Third French Republic was proclaimed on September 4, 1870, after the Second Empire collapsed in defeat and Napoleon III surrendered to the invading Prussians at Sedan. For five months the "Government of National Defense" fought against the armies which had overthrown the empire in five weeks, but the war was already lost; the heroic and belated resistance prolonged it but could not reverse the verdict; and besieged Paris was driven to capitulate in January, 1871. A French National Assembly which met at Bordeaux on February 12 agreed to an armistice two weeks later. In the peace treaty, signed May 12, France ceded Alsace and most of Lorraine and undertook to pay a billion dollar indemnity.

Like the German Republic of 1919, the Third French Republic was founded in an hour of national humiliation and its first official act was the acceptance of a harsh treaty. Launched in this inauspicious fashion, the new ship of state tacked back and forth uncertainly for several years. Republicans and Royalists, Radicals, Liberals, Clericals, and Conservatives, with a dozen minor groups, fused with or fought one another as they strove to form a *bloc* which would give them control. In the outcome the moderate Republicans achieved a leading position with the support of the middle classes. A "Law on the Organization of the Public Powers," passed in January and February, 1875, gave the new regime a constitutional basis. Popular sentiment was still so divided, however, that the critical amendment introducing the word *republic* was carried in the National Assembly by only one vote, 353 to 352. Not until 1879 were the Republicans confident of their supremacy. In that year they won a majority in the Senate as well as in the Chamber of Deputies. Marshal Mac-Mahon, a president with royalist sympathies, who had been installed in 1873, attempted to impose his own choice of ministers upon the chambers, creating a series of crises from 1877 to 1879. Failing in his attempts, he resigned in the latter year before his seven-year term was done. As the constitutional laws provided that the presidential office should be filled by a nominee elected by a majority of the deputies and senators voting together, the Republicans replaced him by Jules Grévy, a man who enjoyed their confidence.

The internal history of the Third Republic proved a drama which lacked grandeur. Partly because the journals were free and acrid in their criticism, the political leaders moved in a tarnished setting darkened by party passions and sordid scheming. There were mock-heroic *coups* that failed and unheroic compromises that succeeded, and the parliamentary sessions were punctuated by a series of crises and scandals. To other nations it appeared that the political life of France was not healthy and that ominous undercurrents fed by tides of suspicion and prejudice threatened the stability of the state.

In reality, despite the cabinet crises, the political scandals, the vituperative journals, and acrid electoral campaigns, France preserved a remarkable *administrative* and *social* stability. Although the cabinet ministers might change frequently, and weeks might intervene between the overthrow of one cabinet and the foundation of its successor, the government departments continued to function with remarkable efficiency. For behind each temporary minister stood a permanent *secrétaire général* and a corps of experienced civil servants who kept each branch of the administration functioning and assured a considerable continuity of policy. This centralized bureaucratic machine, organized by Napoleon, survived with little change under successive French regimes, but the important part it played in governing France was often overlooked by foreign observers. A second factor that gave the French nation stability and belied the apparently erratic and unpredictable surface currents was the solidity and durability of its social structure. The classes — bourgeoisie, workers, and peasants — preserved their status and traditions with remarkable tenacity. There was little shifting of families from one class to another. This lack of social mobility helped to keep French society stable, but it also fostered a rigidity of outlook, a conservatism, that sometimes verged on stagnation.

Of the many unsettled issues that stirred popular feeling in France after 1871 three proved serious enough to rock the Republic. The first of these centered about the handsome and popular general, Georges Boulanger. Named minister of war in 1886, Boulanger achieved exceptional popularity by demanding military reforms, more comforts for the army recruits, and a firm, if not defiant, attitude toward Germany. Fifteen years had passed since the humiliation of 1871, but Frenchmen were not reconciled to the loss of Alsace and Lorraine. Many of them dreamed of *revanche*, of a successful campaign under a brilliant leader who would restore French military prestige. But Boulanger, despite the hysterical enthusiasm of his followers, was no Napoleon. He did not dare to seize power by a *coup d'état*, and after three years *Boulangisme* lost vigor and ceased to be a threat. When the Senate investigated his activities, Boulanger fled from France, his followers repudiated him, and in 1891 he committed suicide.

The second affair which threatened to discredit and possibly wreck the Republic was the Panama scandal. The great engineer and humanitarian, Ferdinand de Lesseps, who had constructed the Suez Canal, headed a company to cut through the Isthmus of Panama. The project proved more difficult and expensive than the promoters anticipated and the company finally went bankrupt in 1889. When indignant investors learned that part of the funds had been used to bribe journalists not to reveal the deficits, and that members of the Chamber of Deputies had also accepted loans and favors from the harassed company under conditions which suggested a blend of bribery and extortion, public anger reached a dangerous pitch. Enemies of the Republic seized upon the case as proof that a regime controlled by the middle class and administered by republican politicians could not be trusted and would be open to graft and corruption. The Panama scandal forced several politicians from public life and shook the confidence of the electors, but the Republic survived.

The third crisis, *the Affair* as it came to be known because it overshadowed the others, was the Dreyfus case. In 1894 a Jewish army officer, Alfred Dreyfus, was sentenced to life imprisonment by a French military court. The charge was treasonable communication with the agents of a foreign power. Convinced that Dreyfus had been arbitrarily condemned, a group of socialists and radical republicans attacked the arrogant army staff, which refused to lift the veil of secrecy that obscured the case or to grant Dreyfus a new trial. By 1898 France was tragically divided over the bitterly fought issue. The famous novelist, Émile Zola, publicly accused members of the French high command of shielding the real traitor, a Major Esterhazy. For his audacity, Zola was sentenced to a year's imprisonment and fled abroad; but "truth was on the march" as he had affirmed. In 1899 Dreyfus was brought back from his five years on Devil's Island, tried by a second court martial, and again found guilty; but President Émile Loubet pardoned him and he was finally exonerated by the Supreme Court in 1906. The case against him had been built upon error, forgery, anti-Semitic prejudice, and arbitrary injustice. But the fact that stood out most clearly was the arrogance of the army command, which had persisted in its error as if it were above public criticism and independent of the civil government and civilian control.

Those who had believed Dreyfus guilty included militarists, royalists, and many clericals, and they were discredited by the outcome of *the Affair*. In 1900 the people showed their revulsion of sentiment by sweeping into office a number of republican and socialist deputies whom they had denounced a few years earlier for daring to doubt Dreyfus's guilt. The left-wing parties, now securely in control, formed a radical coalition pledged to purge the army of royalist influence and to secularize the schools. The reorganization of the army was carried through resolutely and effectively, but in their program of secularization the republicans opened anew the unresolved controversy between church and state.

From its first years the Third Republic had been disturbed by the opposition between clericals and anticlericals. Most ardent republicans favored a complete separation of church and state, and the Primary Education Law of 1882 made no provision for religious instruction in the public schools. Many monarchists were earnest Catholics, and the republican leaders, recalling the conflict between the First French Republic of 1792 and the church, and the historic alliance of the altar and the throne which had persisted for centuries in France, viewed clericalism as a force hostile to the republican regime. For a few years after 1890 the clerical question seemed nearer a solution. Church and state had many common aims, especially in the colonies, where Catholic missionaries and civil and military officials often worked side by side to extend civilization. In 1891 and 1892 the papal encyclicals *Rerum novarum* and *Inter innumeras*, issued by Pope Leo XIII, instructed French Catholics that it was proper to accept new governments when these became established and were endorsed by the people. The result was a rally of many Catholics to the support of the Republic, while many republicans found much to admire in the wise admonitions the pope offered on social questions and on the strife between capital and labor. Unhappily, these improved relations were again disturbed by the bitterness of the Dreyfus affair.

By 1901 anticlerical sentiment had grown so strong in France that the numerous schools conducted by religious orders were closed by government decree and the orders suppressed (the Associations Law). In 1904 the French government recalled its ambassador to the Vatican, and in 1905 it promulgated a decree separating church and state and terminating the Concordat of 1801 which had regulated the appointment and salaries of ecclesiastics. The property of the church was claimed by the state, which allowed private corporations to take over the maintenance of churches. Protestant and Jewish congregations, which had likewise been under state supervision and subsidy since the early nineteenth century, were also disassociated from the state.

The parties of the left, dominant in the Chamber of Deputies after 1900, thus asserted the supremacy of the Republic over the army and the church. To do so, the republicans of the Center leaned upon the socialist groups, but fear of socialism and of working class movements made the middle classes cautious. The real balance of power rested with the moderate republicans who spoke for the property holders of France. It was not only the great industrialists, bankers, and owners of country estates who kept the government firm in its defense of private property; it was farmers who owned a few acres apiece (a numerous class), the *rentiers* who had purchased government or business bonds and lived on the interest, the small tradesmen and shopkeepers, and the professional groups to whom a hard-earned diploma and its rewards represented a form of investment. All these groups possessed private wealth of one form or another, and they stood together against revolutionary proposals and threats of confiscation. The Third Republic remained in essence a bourgeois republic; it failed to accept real responsibility for the fate of the landless country laborers or the proletarians of the factory towns.

The radical republicans had long chided the moderates for their failure to introduce a frank program of social reform. In earlier, more ardent days, before they achieved power, many republican deputies advocated an income tax, government ownership of mines, banks, and railways, the abolition of the senate, the substitution of a citizen militia for the professional army. But when these "radicals" won power after 1900 they failed signally to attack existing evils. It was the Socialist Party, brilliantly led by Jean Jaurès, which took over their program, heartened the workers, fought the vast outlay for arms and the loans to autocratic Russia, and offered the hand of friendship to German workers. The socialists also directed their attacks against the concentration of wealth in too few hands, against the great industrialists and bankers, and against the bourgeois control of the state. But their demands for a more generous program of benefits for the masses had little effect. No far-reaching measures of social insurance such as Bismarck sponsored in Germany, no heavy income or inheritance taxes such as Lloyd George wrote into the British budget in 1909, were enacted in France.

It is not surprising, therefore, that French workingmen who sought to better their lot had little faith in the promises of the politicians. Some put their trust in the program of social justice offered by the church, especially after the encyclical of Pope Leo XIII, "On the Condition of Labor," appeared in 1891. Other workers joined cooperative societies or formed labor unions. When sober protests and moderate leaders failed to obtain benefits for them, many discontented workers drifted into the ranks of the syndicalists. The *syndicats* were labor organizations which sought to organize all the employees in an industry, so that all transportation workers, or all coal miners, might be called out on strike simultaneously. The ultimate ambition of the syndicalist leaders was to unite all the *syndicats* into a *Confédération Générale du Travail,* a general confederation of labor. The executive committee of this C.G.T. could then dictate to the government under threat of a nation-wide strike. Labor appeared at last to be fashioning a weapon with which it could coerce the ruling classes and extort concessions for "the disinherited."

Yet when the weapon was employed it failed to achieve its purpose. Strikes of seamen, miners, electricians, wine-growers, and even government postal employees were attempted between 1906 and 1909, but they were all frustrated by punitive measures or broken up by the action of the police or the army. An attempt by the C.G.T. to call a general strike (1909) ended in failure. The following year a strike of the railway workers was broken by the proclamation of martial law, and engineers and switchmen, who struck as union members, were commanded to don their military uniforms and ordered back to their posts as soldiers.

When loyalty to his union and loyalty to the army conflicted in a Frenchman's mind, he found that patriotism was stronger than class solidarity. The years of military training which all able-bodied male citizens received at an impressionable age conditioned them to obey the call of country and exerted a conservative, disciplinary influence on their characters. As the danger of war increased, it became manifest that class strife within France and strikes which paralyzed industry weakened the nation and encouraged its foreign foes. The war mood was a major obstacle to social reform; this fact helps to explain why the socialists advocated international arbitration, a reduction of military service and armaments, and the repudiation of imperialistic aims. But the army was the shield of the Republic, and socialist overtures to Germany or criticism of French armaments seemed to ardent French chauvinists to tend toward treason. When war came in 1914 a hotheaded patriot assassinated Jean Jaurès, the socialist deputy and journalist, because he had often pleaded for the reduction of armaments and a more friendly attitude toward the Germans.

At the test of war, the socialist dream that national antagonisms might be softened by an alliance of the working classes of all nations broke down. Nationalism triumphed over class loyalty. In the German Reichstag and the French Chamber of Deputies members of the socialist groups forgot their earlier resolutions to stand firm in support of a Socialist International. Almost without exception they voted for war and endorsed the war measures of their respective governments. In other words, when Nationalism and Socialism clashed, Nationalism proved the stronger impulse. No outstanding leader had yet found a way, in 1914, to *unite* these two drives.

7

ITALY

Italy's geographical situation is particularly unfavorable.
PROTEST TO THE LEAGUE OF NATIONS, 1927

1. RESOURCES: THE PROBLEM OF SHORTAGES

IN ROMAN TIMES Italy had been mistress of the Mediterranean world. In the Renaissance era the flame of Italian genius made the politics, arts, and letters of Italy models for all Europe. For two thousand years Rome had been a focal point of Western civilization as the city of the Caesars and the city of the popes. Modern Italians are proud to remember that twice their country achieved a primacy among the nations and that it has long been the home of the classical tradition, sharing with Greece the honor of being the first European center to achieve high culture.

A tradition of leadership is not easy to maintain. After the fifteenth century Italy fell behind the more progressive maritime states of the north. The shift of commercial routes from the Mediterranean to the Atlantic, and the political disunion which persisted in the peninsula, partly account for the decline. Still preserving "the fatal gift of beauty" Italy seemed, in the seventeenth and eighteenth centuries, to enter a long twilight after a golden day. This impression of a land where time had paused, where the sunlight was gentle to the fading palaces and majestic ruins, has doubtless been intensified by the painters. But the economic decay was real enough, for Venice, Genoa, and Florence lost their banking and trading wealth to Lisbon, Amsterdam, and London. Not even the *Risorgimento,* the political and national revival of the nineteenth century which forged Italy into a single kingdom, nor the coming of the Machine Age with smoking factories and surplus goods, could bring back the economic leadership Italy had once enjoyed.

Yet the people did not lack vitality. Between 1800 and 1914 the population doubled, rising from some 18,000,000 to 36,000,000. Unfortunately this proof of vigor was not an unmixed blessing because the national food supply remained insufficient. The major part of Italy is mountainous terrain, the rainfall is generally inadequate, and although some areas are

70

suited to grape and olive culture there are not sufficient forest regions, grazing lands, or wheat fields. These facts are reflected throughout the countryside in the substitution of stone for wood as building material, in the gray hue of the treeless sections during the dry season, and in the relative scarcity of dairy cattle, the vegetation being in general more suitable for goats. To compensate for a deficiency in cereals, the Italians (who consume almost as much wheat per head as the French) have become dependent upon imported grain; in 1913 they had to purchase 66,000,000 bushels of wheat abroad to supplement the 214,000,000 bushels produced in the country. Foodstuffs, it is important to note, then formed half the annual imports. This involved a serious strain upon the national economy because such imports had to be paid for, and Italy suffered from an adverse trade balance. Even in average years the value of the imports was almost double that of exports.

Had Italy become highly industrialized, she might have paid for imported foodstuffs in manufactures and services. Great Britain, with a population approximately the same and a smaller area, had grown powerful and wealthy through industry while neglecting agriculture. Unfortunately nature had denied Italy most of the requisites of industry as she had denied her most of the essentials of agriculture. Industrialization has three basic requisites: natural resources, capital, and labor. Of these essentials Italy was almost completely deficient in the first, highly deficient in the second, and rich only in the third. She lacked the sinews of modern industry, coal, iron, and minerals, all of which had to be imported, causing a heavy drain on her financial resources. Thus imports of coal, coming chiefly from England, accounted for one-fourth of the annual deficit. Nor was it any great advantage to her when oil began to displace coal, for she was deficient in this fuel too. It was only the development of hydroelectric energy which promised to alleviate her fuel shortage. The rivers and cataracts of the peninsula promised an estimated 6,000,000 horsepower, but only one-fourth of this had been developed before the First World War. Another obstacle to industrialization was the lack of ready capital and of sufficient managerial skills. Italy's middle class was relatively small and consisted principally of government employees, professional men, and intellectuals. Nevertheless, in spite of severe handicaps a start in industrialization was made. A good network of railways was built, connecting Italy to the rest of Europe and facilitating trade. This was no mean achievement in view of the ruggedness of Italy's terrain. Shipping was also developed, and Genoa vied with Marseilles for the place of the first port in the Mediterranean. Milan outstripped Lyons as a center of the silk industry. Even when the silk industry declined as a result of the competition of synthetic fabrics, Milan retained importance as a cotton and textile center. Turin, the capital of Piedmont, in which, before unification, Cavour laid the basis of a sound economy to serve the rest of Italy as a model, became an important center of metallurgical and machine industries. Italian workmanship won worldwide respect. The genius which had so long inspired this gifted and beauty-loving people to produce exquisite paintings, statuary, cameos, jewelry, and glassware, also inspired machinists and designers to create articles of striking perfection, from delicate precision instruments on the one hand to expensive automobiles on the other.

Yet this economic progress, though gratifying to Italy, was unimpressive when measured by the scale of progress achieved at the same time by other western nations. Before 1914 Italy's steel production was less than that of the Grand Duchy of Luxemburg, and her exports less than those of Belgium. What saved Italy from financial ruin was tourism and emigration. The beauty of Italy, her moderate, Mediterranean climate, and the ruins and monuments of her glorious past annually attracted thousands of tourists who brought and spent foreign currencies. On the other hand, the lack of opportunity, low wages, and chronic unemployment drove many laborers into emigration. Some were seasonal migrants, seeking employment in France, Switzerland, or Germany for a part of the year; but several hundred thousand left annually to find permanent homes in the United States or in South America. This exodus was psychologically a painful loss to the nation. There was, however, one compensation. Most of the expatriates sent back remittances to help support their relatives in Italy, and this influx of foreign credit was an important national asset. Foreign currency, whether left by tourists or sent by emigrants, helped redress the trade balance and augment the purchasing power of the *lira,* the Italian monetary unit.

2. DEFENSE AND EXPANSION: ITALIA IRREDENTA AND THE COLONIAL EMPIRE

When the Middle Ages drew to an end in the fourteenth century, the Italian peninsula was divided, like most of Europe, into minute political fragments. Some eighty principalities, duchies, counties, republics, communes, and city-states filled the region from the Po Valley to Sicily. By A.D. 1500, however, these fragments had been fused into a dozen major political units or areas. This rapid progress was acclaimed by Niccolò Machiavelli (1469–1527), who besought the Italians to become a strong and united nation. But the drive toward political unification was arrested and separatism continued until the nineteenth century. The "Kingdom of Italy" created by Napoleon embraced only one-third of the country and collapsed with his overthrow. The Congress of Vienna re-divided Italy into eight units. Once again she became — in the words of Metternich — only a "geographic expression." Repeatedly Austrian military intervention frustrated daring revolts led by Mazzini, Garibaldi, and other apostles of the *Risorgimento.* The Italians appeared unable to carry out the proud motto of King Charles Albert of Piedmont-Sardinia, "Italy will do it herself." Cavour, a realistic statesman and as shrewd a diplomat as lived in his day, recognized that Italy would need foreign help to defeat Austria — the main obstacle to unification. In 1858 at Plombières he struck the famous bargain with Napoleon III whereby Piedmont promised to surrender Nice (the birthplace of Garibaldi) and Savoy (the original home of the dynasty) in return for French military help. The defeat of Austria by French and Italian armies in 1859 opened the way to unification. The Italian states — Piedmont-Sardinia, Lombardy, Parma, Modena, the Romagna, Tuscany, and the Kingdom of the Two Sicilies — were linked into a new Kingdom of Italy under the House of Savoy. Venetia did not come in until 1866, surrendered by Austria after the Austro-Prussian War, and Rome was not occupied until 1870, when the French garrison, maintained there for the protection of the pope, was withdrawn to fight in the Franco-Prussian War. On September 20 Italian troops bombarded and occupied the Eternal City despite the protests of Pope Pius IX. Neither he nor his successors would recognize the annexation of the city or accept monetary compensation for its loss, and for almost sixty years the "Roman Question" embarrassed the Italian government. (See Chap. 24.)

As in the case of the Germans, national unification stirred the Italians to a high pitch of patriotic exaltation. The entire nation became infected with a passionate pride in the past and fervent faith in the future. In their enthusiasm the Italians expected to see their country immediately assume the rank of a European great power, to liberate the "unredeemed" Italians still under the Hapsburg yoke, to claim the heritage of the former Venetian empire on the eastern shore of the Adriatic Sea, and to acquire a colonial empire overseas — the rightful attribute of a European power. But the Italian government, conscious of the economic debility of the country, was more cautious. It had assumed the debts of the constituent states, and this fiscal burden, combined with the adverse trade balance, crippled the national finances. Italy did not have the means to build the indispensable instruments of a policy of force — a powerful army and navy. Politicians might demagogically stir up public sentiment, mobs might demonstrate in the streets, but the government was in no position to exert much influence in the councils of Europe. At the first great diplomatic gathering after Italian unification, the Congress of Berlin, which met in 1878 to deal with the perennial Near Eastern Question, the Italian delegation acted almost timidly. It returned with "hands clean but empty." Moreover, it failed to prevent Germany and Britain from pledging Tunisia to France.

Yet if Italy were to build a colonial empire, the acquisition of Tunis was the logical point of departure. It lay close to Italy, across a narrow strait, almost within sight of Sicily. It contained the site of Carthage, Rome's ancient enemy, and it had been a part of the Roman Empire for centuries. In modern times Italian commercial enterprise had been active there, and the largest number of Europeans living there were Italians. When France occupied it in 1881, Italian opinion was understandably aroused. But since Germany and Britain backed France, Italy was helpless. The crisis brought forcibly home to the Italians their diplomatic isolation. In the following year the Italian government joined Germany and Austria in a Triple Alliance, which assured Italy of support against France if the two powers clashed in Africa. The secret agreement ended Italy's isolation, but the price was considerable. Since the struggle for unification Italy's relations with Germany had been cordial, but Austria was still regarded by most Italians as their "historical" enemy. Entering into an alliance with Austria necessitated adjourning, if not completely abandoning, the claims to the "unredeemed" Italians in Trent and Trieste and to lands across the Adriatic Sea which Venice had once controlled. However, agreement with Austria, a Catholic power with traditionally close ties to the Holy See, would prevent the government of Vienna from trying to embarrass Italy by reopening the Roman Question.

Blocked from expansion in Europe, Italy looked all the more longingly to Africa, then being rapidly partitioned among the more prosperous European powers. Nationalist opinion urged the government to hurry up lest Italy be left out of the scramble. Francesco Crispi, premier from 1887 to 1891 and again from 1893 to 1896, decided to abandon the cautious policy of maneuvering and resort to force. He pressed Italian claims to Eritrea and Somaliland in eastern Africa. In between these coastal acquisitions lay the mountainous, ancient, Christian empire of Ethiopia. In 1889 Italy negotiated a treaty with Menelik, the Ethiopian ruler, which gave her an excuse to claim a protectorate over Ethiopia. Despite a desperate financial situation at home, and despite the frowns of France, which sent arms and military instructors to Ethiopia, Crispi dispatched an expeditionary force to subjugate the country (1895). After several reverses the Italian force of 25,000 men was completely crushed at Adowa (March 1, 1896). This humiliating defeat at the hands of a primitive people made Bismarck's caustic quip, "Italy has such a great appetite, but such poor teeth," appear almost as a dry statement of fact. Crispi fell from power, and for fifteen years Italy abandoned colonial adventures.

Once again Italian diplomacy reverted to cautious maneuvering to protect the country's interest. The fluid state of European diplomacy called for extreme caution. The Bismarckian system was disintegrating and the Triple Entente was in the making. In the battle of giants Italy must not be caught on the losing side. Although the course might win Italy a reputation for duplicity and unreliability, weakness compelled her to pursue a policy of two irons in the fire. In 1902 Italy adhered again to the Triple Alliance, but at the same time entered into a secret agreement with France which practically repudiated the Triple Alliance. In return France dropped her objections to Italy's acquisition of Turkey's last possessions in Africa — Tripoli and Cyrenaica. Her partners in the Triple

Alliance, as well as Britain, had agreed long before to her seizure of the Turkish provinces. Not until the second Moroccan crisis in 1911 did Prime Minister Giovanni Giolitti moved to claim the territory. On September 28, 1911, prodded by a revived nationalist opinion, he dispatched an ultimatum to Turkey. The Turkish government rejected the ultimatum, and Italian troops landed at Tripoli and occupied the coastal towns. In November Italy formally annexed the territory, though a small Turko-Arab force in the interior kept up a stout resistance for another year. A naval demonstration off the Dardanelles and occupation of the Dodecanese Islands was necessary before the stubborn Turks bowed to the inevitable and recognized the loss of Tripoli and Cyrenaica (Treaty of Lausanne, October 18, 1912). At last Italy had a colony — presently renamed "Libya" — near at hand. Libya possessed few known resources and was costly to pacify and administer. Nevertheless, Italian patriots were gratified in heart though depleted in pocket.

The outbreak of the First World War caught Italy unprepared. Her realistic statesmen, well aware of the limitations of her strength, were determined that if she should enter the conflict it must be on the winning side, and that she must receive maximum compensation for her sacrifices. Pursuing a policy of "sacred egoism," Italy declined to join her partners of the Triple Alliance in the conflict, on the technical grounds that Austria had failed to consult her before declaring war on Serbia, as she was supposed to under the terms of the alliance treaty. For ten months Italy maintained a watchful neutrality and negotiated with both parties at war to guarantee her interests. It was not until May, 1915, that she made the plunge into the war — on the Allied side.

3. POLITICAL AND SOCIAL QUESTIONS: THE STATE, THE CHURCH, AND THE SOCIALISTS

Upon unification Italy became formally a constitutional monarchy. As in England, the King reigned but did not rule. His powers were exercised by the Prime Minister and cabinet. The *Statuto* or Constitution — adopted in Piedmont in 1848 and extended to the Italian Kingdom in 1861 — provided for a legislature of two houses, the Chamber of Deputies and the Senate, resembling those of the Third French Republic. The administration — also originally Piedmontese — was patterned on the centralist system of France. The franchise, at first quite limited (600,000 voters), was progressively extended to virtual manhood suffrage (8,500,000 voters in 1912). The *forms* of democratic government thus made rapid advances in Italy, as in all leading European states during these years. But it takes more than the adoption of a democratic constitution to create a democracy that really functions. Democratic formulas failed to function effectively in Italy because cultural, social, economic, and political conditions did not favor the growth of democracy.

Behind the façade of a unitary, centralized state a great deal of localism

and regionalism survived after unification. The aphorism, "We have made
Italy, now we must make Italians," uttered after unification, contained a
great deal of truth. Many Italians felt as Neapolitans, Venetians, Sicilians,
or Piedmontese first and as Italians second, if at all. Moreover, the differences between the North and the South were very pronounced. While
in the North socio-economic conditions approximated those of Central
Europe, in the South they were as primitive as any in Eastern Europe
or some parts of Asia. In 1870 it was estimated that for Italy as a whole
illiteracy averaged 70 per cent, but in the South it exceeded 90 per cent.
While in the North peasant proprietorship of the land prevailed, in the
South land was owned by the nobility in large tracts (*latifundia*) and the
peasant tenants and farm laborers were reduced to a virtual serfdom.
Industry, when it developed in Italy, tended to center in the North, while
the South remained almost exclusively agrarian. All Italian governments
before unification were oppressive, but the Bourbon government of Naples
and Sicily won the dubious distinction of being the worst in Europe, not
excluding the Ottoman Empire.

Class distinctions were sharply defined before unification and continued
to be pronounced afterwards. Three-quarters of the Italian people were
peasants and workers. Traditionally, they regarded all governments as
capricious and tyrannical masters, which had to be endured like floods,
earthquakes, cholera, or other visitations of God, but could be of no possible assistance to them. And, unfortunately, the middle and upper class
oligarchy which ruled Italy often justified this image. It paid eloquent
lip service to Mazzinian idealism but retained of the Mazzinian program
only an intense nationalism, and that it debauched by rank chauvinism
and xenophobia. Socially it was selfish and irresponsible. Mercantile
interests were carefully protected, but the social welfare of the people
was woefully neglected. Taxation was heavy and socially unjust. The
vast exodus of emigrants was symptomatic of the social ills of Italy.
Another index was the outbreak and steady increase of agrarian and
industrial strikes and violence. In 1891 the Italian Socialist Party was
founded. In Parliament its influence remained insignificant until the elections of 1913. But it had a growing influence over workers and intellectuals in spite of the sharp competition of anarchists and syndicalists, who
spurned political compromises and sought by direct revolutionary action
to destroy the "bourgeois state." In 1900 the assassination of the innocu-
ous King Humbert by an anarchist dramatized the situation. Strikes and
violence were repressed by the government with a harshness and vindic-
tiveness that further alienated the masses from the state.

At the same time political life, monopolized by the middle and upper
classes, was uninspiring. Official pressure, trickery, and bribery were used
on a wide scale to influence elections. Maladministration of finances,
shockingly revealed by the collapse of the *Banca Romana* in 1893, marred
the record of almost all the cabinets. In Parliament secret deals between

opposing party leaders, political jobbery, and a scramble for patronage brought the entire constitutional system into discredit. Political parties, apart from the Republicans and later the Socialists, were primarily political machines without any program except to perpetuate their bosses in power.

The great political bosses, Depretis, Crispi, and Giolitti, whether in or out of office, largely dictated politics from 1876 to the outbreak of the First World War. The notable policies of Depretis were motivated by his anger at France for seizing Tunis. It was he who led Italy into the Triple Alliance, started colonial expansion in east Africa, and launched a tariff war with France which proved detrimental to the agrarian interest of Italy. Crispi, a temperamental Sicilian, repressed social unrest with an iron hand and provoked a serious crisis between Italy and the Church. In 1871 the Italian Parliament had voted The Law of Guaranties defining relations between the State and the Church. It provided notably for granting the pope full sovereign powers in the Vatican and the payment of an annual subsidy out of the Italian treasury equivalent to the pope's former income from his lost territories. But Pope Pius IX refused the proposed settlement, continued to regard himself as a "prisoner," and struck back at the State by forbidding Italian Catholics to vote or to hold public office (*Non expedit*). In 1887 Crispi opened negotiations with the Holy See on the basis of The Law of Guaranties, and when they failed he launched a vigorous anticlerical policy which resulted in abolition of ecclesiastical tithes and of compulsory religious instruction in schools. In 1889 relations between the State and the Church became so tense that the pope considered leaving Italy and placing himself under foreign protection.

Giolitti, who succeeded Crispi after the Ethiopian fiasco of 1896, moved to ease the quarrel by relaxing the anticlerical measures. The pope, in turn, partly rescinded the *Non expedit,* permitting Catholics to enter public life and to form a Catholic party. But full reconciliation of the State by the Church had to wait until the fascist regime was established after World War I. Giolitti was also conciliatory toward labor. During his ministries rudimentary social legislation was passed, more energy was shown in combatting illiteracy, and electoral reforms were undertaken. But social agitation continued unabated. Like his predecessors, Giolitti was not above trying to divert public opinion from domestic ills by foreign adventures. But unlike his predecessors, he was more successful at it: he brought the Tripolitan War to a successful conclusion.

The social and political ills of Italy were by no means exceptional. They were present in some degree everywhere in Europe on the eve of the First World War. But in Italy they were more extreme. It is therefore not surprising that their symptoms, the twin forces of nationalism and socialism, took on a more rabid form in Italy than in the rest of Europe.

8

IMPERIAL RUSSIA

From the Nile to the Neva, the Elbe to Cathay,
From the Volga to the Euphrates,
The Ganges to the Danube,
There is the Russian realm.[1]

TIUTCHEV

1. RESOURCES: THE PROBLEMS OF SPACE AND EFFECTIVE EXPLOITATION

THE LARGEST compact land empire in the nineteenth century was Imperial Russia. It covered an area of about 8,300,000 square miles, or about one-sixth of the land surface of the earth. It had grown out of a modest nucleus, the Duchy of Muscovy, with an area of only 748,000 square miles. Growth has been the most astonishing feature of Russian history, growth not only in size but also in population; it is estimated that the population of Russia grew from some 10,000,000 in 1700, to 37,000,000 in 1800, and to 132,000,000 in 1900.

Within her vast expanse Russia contained riches which in the nineteenth century were only half suspected: large tracts of arable land and forests, rich deposits of coal, iron, oil, and minerals of all sorts. The development of these rich resources, however, was long delayed by the general backwardness of the country. The riches were scattered over a wide area, and Russia lacked an adequate system of transportation. It was not until after the Crimean War (1853–1856), which strikingly revealed this weakness from a military point of view, that the Russian government made a serious effort to master the problem of space by developing railway transportation. The progress then made was considerable. In 1856 Russia had only 660 miles of railroads in operation; by 1912 she had 40,000 miles of railways. The most ambitious venture in railroad-building was the construction between 1892 and 1905 of the famous Trans-Siberian line, a single track railroad that linked Moscow and Vladivostok, separated by a distance of 5500 miles. Though relatively rapid, the railroad building

[1] Waclaw Lednicki, "Panslavism" in Feliks Gross (ed.), *European Ideologies* (New York: Philosophical Library, 1948).

program still fell far short of the need. In the United States over 220,000 miles of railroad were built at about the same time to service an area less than half that of Russia. For transportation of bulk goods Russia still had to rely to a large extent on rivers and canals.

Other obstacles in the way of industrialization were lack of labor and of capital. It was not until after the liberation of the serfs in 1861 that an adequate pool of free and mobile labor was developed. Even then Russia continued to suffer from lack of skilled laborers, engineers, and managers. This was partly overcome by employment of foreigners, principally Germans. To overcome the other handicap, lack of capital, Russia also had recourse to foreign help. Foreign capital long shied away from Russia because of the chaotic state of her finances. It was not until 1897 that the gold standard was introduced and the currency stabilized. This important measure was the achievement of the famous Minister of Finance, Sergei Witte — an unusual type of a Russian, a self-made man and one fully conversant with problems of modern finance. Thanks to his efforts, German, British, and above all French capital began to pour into the country. The flow of French capital, however, was not inspired by economic reasons alone. In 1894 France and Russia concluded a military alliance, and for military reasons the French government was anxious to see Russia strengthen her economy in the event of a showdown with Germany. France made direct governmental loans to Russia and assisted her in floating loans in the private money markets of Paris. But the principal supplier of goods and the principal customer of Russia remained Germany. In 1913 nearly half of Russia's imports came from Germany and more than one-third of her exports went to that country.

With the aid of foreign advisers and foreign capital Russia began to develop her resources at a remarkable rate: iron in the Urals, coal in the Donets basin, oil at Baku in the Caucasus region, cotton in the steppes of Central Asia. Factories appeared in the outskirts of St. Petersburg, Moscow, Warsaw, Lodz, and other Russian cities. The ports of Odessa, Riga, and Vladivostok hummed with activity. In the production of cotton goods she held the fourth place, after England, the United States, and Germany, and was able to compete successfully with England, for instance, in Persia. In the production of oil she held the second place, and only the United States surpassed the Russian output in oil. Though important, Russia's industrialization was not proportionate to her needs and even less to her potentialities. Nor was it a healthy and sturdy growth. Russia's industries were developed under the paternal guidance of the Russian government behind a protective wall of tariffs. Industries were assisted by government contracts, subsidies, tax exemptions, and preferential railroad rates. They were inefficient, and the cost of their products remained high. Their profits were made possible, in part, by the low wages and wretched working conditions of Russian laborers.

Industrialization in Russia largely bypassed the rural population, which before the First World War constituted about three-quarters of Russia's population. Because of their low purchasing power, the needs of the peasants — apart from such items as sugar, salt, alcohol, and kerosene — were still supplied by domestic production through strolling vendors, or at fairs as in medieval Western Europe. Nor were Russia's industries able to supply fully the market that existed in Russia. Russia had to import coal, chemicals, metalware, machinery, armaments, textiles, and manufactures of all sorts. Her exports were primarily agrarian products: cereals, flax, hemp, dairy products, timber, furs, and leather. Her solvency depended on "his excellency the harvest," as Minister of Finance Kokovtsev aptly put it. Even in years of bumper crops Russia's trade balance was unfavorable, and she had to have continuous recourse to foreign loans. Paradoxically, although Imperial Russia possessed in Central and Eastern Asia a vast colonial empire, her economy was and remained until the fall of the monarchy semi-colonial.

2. DEFENSE AND EXPANSION: SLAVDOM AND THE SEARCH FOR OUTLETS TO WARM SEAS

The geography of Russia creates special problems of defense. The Duchy of Muscovy lay in the center of the Russian plain, a plateau nowhere exceeding 1500 feet above sea level. It was open to invasion on all sides. This meant, on the other hand, that no natural barriers stood in the way of its expansion. Much of Russian history has been a story of repelling devastating invasions and of reaching out to strike at Russia's enemies. When, in the fifteenth century, the Duchy of Muscovy shook off the "Tartar yoke" — Mongol rule which for two centuries and a half isolated Russia from Europe — it found itself hemmed in by hostile neighbors. Most Russians still lived under foreign rule. The great figures of Russian history are associated with the persistent Russian effort to break through the circle of enemies, to "gather in the Russian lands" still under foreign rule, and to reach the great sea routes which would permit Russia to enter into free contact with the rest of Europe. Ivan the Terrible (1530–1584) battered down the remainders of the Mongol Empire, the Khanates of Kazan and Astrakhan. This opened the way for Russian expansion in the east into Siberia, and in the southeast to the Caspian Sea and Persia. However, in his efforts to break through in the west, Ivan was less fortunate. There hostile and powerful neighbors blocked Russia from contact with Western Europe: in the northeast Lutheran Sweden, in the west Catholic Poland, and in the south Moslem Turkey and its Crimean Tartar tributaries. Russia had only one tenuous link with the West, a sea route opened during Ivan's reign by intrepid English and Dutch sailors around the dangerous northern bend of Scandinavia and through the icy White Sea to Archangel. The usefulness of Archangel was limited by the fact that the harbor froze over for four months out of twelve. Russia needed a warm seaport.

It was not until the beginning of the eighteenth century that Peter the Great (1682–1725) crushed Sweden and opened a coveted "window to Europe" through the Baltic Sea. He attached so great an importance to this outlet that he presently transferred Russia's capital from ancient Moscow to St. Petersburg, newly founded in the marshy estuary of the Neva River. In the second half of the eighteenth century Catherine the Great (1762–1796) followed up by defeating Turkey and winning an outlet to the Black Sea. Russia now had access to two warm seas, but they were inland seas and egress from them was controlled by foreign powers. Catherine also practically completed the task of "gathering in Russian lands." She eliminated hostile Poland by partition and annexed over half of the dismembered kingdom. For better or for worse, Russia was now one of Europe's great powers.

The defeat or elimination of Sweden and Poland brought Russia into closer contact with the powers of the West: Prussia, Austria, France, and Britain. In 1812 Napoleon invaded Russia in a supreme effort to crush her. By extraordinary exertions, however, Russia not only hurled back the Napoleonic Grand Army but led a successful crusade to rid Europe of the Napoleonic tyranny. It was Russian soldiers who stormed Montmartre and snuffed out the last resistance of Napoleonic France in 1814. This prodigious feat raised Imperial Russia to the peak of her prestige, but also deepened suspicions of her in the West. Great Britain now came forth as her main antagonist. Much of the diplomatic history of nine-teenth-century Europe is filled with episodes of the "struggle of the whale and the bear," the Anglo-Russian duel for power. The advantage in the contest generally lay with Britain. Industrialization gave her resources and power out of proportion to her modest size and numbers. Controlling the seas, she could fight distant wars at points of her own choosing where numbers would not necessarily decide the issue. Russia, on the other hand, had only the advantage of numbers. Her army was large but cumbersome; after 1874 it was recruited on the basis of universal military service. Its officers were usually brave but technically poorly trained. Its recruits were mostly illiterate peasants, astonishing in their capacity for physical hardship and admirable in their stoical courage in the face of danger. Like warriors of old, Russian soldiers — in times past as well as present — have considered it the soldier's right to loot and rape. The presence or passage of Russian troops outside Russia left civilians terror-stricken. This characteristic has done much to create in the minds of Westerners a picture of Russia as a land of brutish barbarians, and has cancelled much good will toward Russia as an ally.

The least adequate branches of the Imperial Russian army were the transport, supply, and the medical services. They were primitive, inefficient, and corrupt. Space, which proved of such advantage in the Napole-

onic invasion, was a disadvantage in offensive wars. In 1812 it permitted
the Russian army to retreat almost indefinitely while it forced Napoleon
to over-extend his lines of supply. But Russia was unable to transport
and supply her own army adequately on distant battlefields. In the
Crimean War the Russians had greater difficulty supplying their army in
the Crimea (that is, on Russian soil) than did the British and French in
supplying troops far removed from their home bases.

The principal bone of contention between Russia and Britain was the
perennial Near Eastern Question and more specifically the control of the
Straits of the Bosporus and the Dardanelles, connecting the Black Sea
and the Mediterranean. To block Russia's efforts to gain control of the
Straits, England championed the "territorial integrity" of the decaying
Ottoman Empire. Russia countered by championing the cause of the
Greek Orthodox Christians in the Ottoman Empire. The idea, inciden-
tally, was not Russian but that of the Balkan Slavs, who had held legitimate grievances against Turkish rule and appealed to the "Big Russian
Brother" for help as early as the seventeenth century. To liberate the
Ottoman Christians and to restore the Byzantine cross on the dome of
St. Sophia in Constantinople became Russia's ideological objective. While
the officials in charge of Russian foreign policy were sober and realistic
men, more concerned with Russia's political and strategic interests than
with the plight of the Balkan Slavs and the cause of Greek Orthodoxy,
there were Russians who believed sincerely in Russia's liberating mission.
The Slavophil Khomyakov cried:

> And the domes of ancient Sophia
> In the new Byzantium
> Once more Christ's altar will enshrine!
> Fall down before it, Russian Tsar
> And rise as Tsar of all Slavs![2]

Four times in the eighteenth century and four times in the nineteenth
century the Russians lunged southward around the Black Sea into the
Balkans and the Caucasus in an effort to wrest the control of the Straits
from Turkey. In the Russo-Turkish War of 1877–1878 they came within
sight of Constantinople, but the threat of war with Britain made them
desist. They contented themselves with imposing on Turkey the humiliating Treaty of San Stefano (March 3, 1878). Its main feature was the
creation of a large Bulgaria, which the Russians hoped would serve as
their advance post in the Balkans. Britain objected to the treaty and prepared to go to war ("We don't want to fight, but by jingo, if we do, we've
got the men, we've got the ships, we've got the money too.") until Bismarck offered his services as "honest broker" and induced Russia to submit
the question to an international conference. At the Congress of Berlin

[2] Michael Boro Petrovich, *The Emergence of Russian Panslavism, 1856–1870* (New
York: Columbia University Press, 1956), p. 279.

(June 13–July 13, 1878) Russia's diplomacy was expertly foiled by Disraeli, eagerly seconded by the Austrians. Austria was compensated by the right to occupy, though not to annex, the Turkish provinces of Bosnia and Herzegovina. In a private arrangement with Turkey, Britain compensated herself for her defense of Ottoman "integrity" by the right to occupy the island of Cyprus. The Russians left the Congress deeply disgruntled at being deprived of the fruits of their victory after a costly war. They were further offended when the Bulgars were not inclined to accept Russian domination in place of Turkish, and insisted on genuine independence. Incensed over Bulgar "ingratitude" Tsar Alexander III declared: "The Slavs must now serve us and not we them" — as if the Slavs had ever been anything else but a tool of the Russian policy of expansion.

The point of Russia's expansive energy then shifted to Central Asia. Here, too, Britain successfully blocked her by 1885. The Franco-Russian Alliance of 1894, by covering her European front, permitted Russia to exert increasing pressure in the Far East. In 1896 Russia secured from China the right to construct a section of the Trans-Siberian Railroad across northern Manchuria. Later she secured a lease on the Liaotung Peninsula in the Yellow Sea and the right to link her bases there, Port Arthur and Dairen, by railway to the Trans-Siberian. During the Boxer Rebellion Russia occupied Manchuria and exercised a strong influence in Korea. Once again Britain moved to block her. In 1902 the British concluded an alliance with Japan, which was threatened by Russian activities in Korea. In February, 1904, after vainly seeking an accommodation with Russia, the Japanese struck without warning at the Russian fleet at Port Arthur.

In the Russo-Japanese War which followed, Japan astonished the world. A newcomer among the powers, barely out of oriental seclusion, she defeated Russia, an old military power, both on land and sea. In the Treaty of Portsmouth (September 5, 1905), in part mediated by President Theodore Roosevelt, Russia ceded to Japan the northern half of Sakhalin Island, her lease to the Liaotung Peninsula, and the South Manchurian Railway. Russia also renounced all claims to Korea, leaving it thus to Japanese annexation four years later. She retained, however, the control of the section of the Trans-Siberian Railway crossing Manchuria and a degree of influence in the northern part of that Chinese province.

Checked in the Far East, the Russians reverted to their old battleground, the Balkans. Their defeat at the hands of the Japanese facilitated an agreement with Britain, which had no interest in seeing Japan grow too powerful. On August 31, 1907, the famous Anglo-Russian Convention was signed, which became the basis of Anglo-Russian cooperation until the First World War. It eliminated old points of friction between the two powers in Persia (which was divided into three spheres of influence: north — Russian, south — British, and a middle buffer zone), in Afghanistan (where Russia recognized the supremacy of British interests), and in Tibet (toward which both powers agreed to maintain a hands-off policy). The convention did not deal with the old Anglo-Russian bone of contention, the Straits Question, because both powers at the time were out of favor at Constantinople, where German influence had become supreme.

Having composed her differences with her old antagonist, Britain, Russia's Foreign Minister Alexander Izvolsky set out on a tour of European capitals to secure the powers' consent to the opening of the Straits to Russian warships. The time seemed propitious for this venture because confusion reigned at Constantinople as a result of the Young Turk Revolution. In September, 1908, Izvolsky met the Austrian Foreign Minister, Alois Aehrenthal, at Buchlau in Moravia. The Buchlau conference resulted in an informal agreement, according to which Russia would not oppose Austrian annexation of Bosnia-Herzegovina and Austria would not oppose opening of the Straits to Russian warships. An international conference was to confirm these modifications of the Treaty of Berlin. On October 6, while Izvolsky was visiting in the western capitals, Austria went ahead and declared the annexation of the provinces without international sanction. A first-rate international crisis broke out. Serbia and Montenegro, which had hoped to annex the two Slav-inhabited provinces, violently protested, and nationalist opinion in Russia took up the cudgels for them. Izvolsky was instructed to disavow the agreement with Austria. This he did, pretending to have been duped. Russia insisted that Austria submit the Bosnian Question to the approval of an international conference. Germany backed up Austria in her refusal. France, on the other hand, was not prepared to go to war over this question and failed to back up Russia. Faced with a possibility of fighting Germany and Austria alone, Russia backed down. Though the Bosnian Crisis was thus exorcised, the humiliation rankled in Russia, and even more in Serbia and Montenegro.

The military and diplomatic defeats suffered at the hands of Japan and Austria induced the Russian government to make an earnest effort to improve Russia's armed forces. The army was reorganized and re-equipped, transport improved, and many arsenals and bases established. But the effort was far from completed when the outbreak of the First World War forced Imperial Russia into her last test of strength.

3. POLITICS AND SOCIETY: AUTOCRACY, THE PEASANTRY, AND THE REVOLUTIONARIES

As conceived by its founder, Peter the Great, Imperial Russia was a military-bureaucratic state. Peter was influenced in his concept of the State less by French political ideas, then in vogue in continental Europe, than by Prussian concepts. The State stood above all, including the Tsar, who was less a "divine-right monarch," like Louis XIV, than the "first

Nicholas II and the Russian royal family (Wide World Photos).

Russian ships sunk at Port Arthur during the Russo-Japanese War (Brown Brothers).

Burial of victims of the Russian Revolution, St. Petersburg, 1905 (Brown Brothers).

servant of the State," like the Hohenzollern kings of Prussia. The Tsar
had autocratic powers but he was conscience-bound to exercise them, not
for his own pleasure nor for the benefit of any particular class, but in the
interest of the State alone. Characteristic of this belief was Peter's famous
order of the day on the eve of the fateful battle of Poltava (1709) with
Sweden: "Do not think of Peter, all that matters is that Russia remain
alive." Peter was unsparing of his energy in working to transform Russia
from a semi-oriental despotism into a European great power, and he
demanded that all his subjects work with equal diligence. All noblemen
were obliged to serve the State, either in the bureaucracy or in the armed
forces. Peasants, whether they belonged to the State, Church, or noblemen, had to provide recruits for the army, pay taxes, and furnish physical
labor for State enterprises. The few merchants and townsmen — a negligible quantity in Russia's social scheme — paid taxes and had on demand to
furnish service. All State functions were classified according to a Table
of Ranks, with analogous ranks for civil and military officers. Both wore
distinctive uniforms. The upper ranks were reserved to noblemen, but
ambitious and competent commoners sometimes gained promotion into
the upper ranks whereby they automatically became hereditary noblemen.
Privilege was tied to service. Formally, the Table of Ranks remained in
force until 1917. The system, however, changed considerably during the
two centuries of its existence in Imperial Russia.

The strong rule of Peter the Great was followed by weak reigns of
frivolous women and minor children. During this time the nobility succeeded in gradually limiting their obligations to the State until, under
the Charter of the Nobility issued by Catherine the Great in 1785, they
were freed from obligatory service to the State altogether. This broke
the tie between privilege and service. By tradition Russian noblemen
continued to fill the "prestige" offices in government service — high military, bureaucratic, and diplomatic posts — but as a whole they became
increasingly idle, exclusive, and socially parasitic. When a privileged class
ceases to pay for its privileges with commensurate service it is likely to
decay and to produce from its own ranks its bitterest critics. The "repent-
ant nobleman" was not a specifically Russian type — France had its Mira-
beau and Hungary was to have its Count Károlyi — but the number of
noblemen-turned-revolutionaries in Russia was really extraordinary.
Bakunin and Kropotkin may be mentioned — to cite but two well-known
names. The cause of this phenomenon was undoubtedly the fact that in
Russia social contrasts were more glaring than elsewhere. At the same
time that Catherine the Great freed noblemen, she allowed the peasants
to be degraded to a position hardly distinguishable from that of slaves.
Paradoxically, in the Middle Ages when West European peasants were in
bondage, Russian peasants were free. On the other hand, in modern
times, when Western Europe was astir with ideas of the dignity and
equality of all men, the Russian peasants were reduced to a particularly

degrading bondage. This is a striking illustration of the observation often made that Russia always marches at a counterpace with the West. The peasant question created great tensions in Russia, and in one form or another it continued to plague the Imperial regime until the regime collapsed in 1917.

In the nineteenth century a political threat to the autocracy was added to the grave social problem in Russia. The echoes of the French Revolution were heard in Russia, though faintly and belatedly. A small group of men, mostly aristocratic officers who served in the Russian army in Western Europe during the Napoleonic Wars, began to dream of limiting or abolishing the autocracy. The sudden death of the Emperor Alexander I (1801–1825) in December of 1825 and the uncertainty as to which one of his two brothers, Constantine or Nicholas, was to succeed him, afforded these men an opportunity to try to realize their dream. With the cry "Constantine and a Constitution," they fomented a mutiny in some regiments of the garrison in St. Petersburg. The ostensible objective of this "Decembrist Revolt" was to promote the succession of Constantine, but its real aim was to secure a constitution. It thus represented the first attempt at a political revolution in Russia, even though the "Decembrists" used the old-fashioned technique of a palace revolution to try to attain their objective.

The Decembrist Revolt was speedily put down, and severe repression followed. The Emperor Nicholas I (1825–1855) was a convinced conservative and a determined foe of liberalism both at home and abroad. Abroad he assiduously promoted monarchical solidarity against revolutionary threats. In 1849, when the Hungarian Revolution threatened the throne of his fellow-monarch, the Emperor Francis Joseph of Austria, he sent the Russian army into Hungary to help in repressing the revolution. At home he combatted liberal ideology by promoting an official conservative ideology. Against the motto of the French Revolution, "Liberty, Equality, Fraternity," he set the slogans "Autocracy, Orthodoxy, Nationalism" — "One Tsar, One God, One Nation." Under the direction of the "Third Section" of His Majesty's Chancellery, political police ferreted out and punished revolutionaries, real or imaginary, and heavy-handed censors scanned the press and literature and suppressed the slightest expression of liberal thought. Outwardly the autocracy presented a picture of strength and solidity, but inwardly it was decaying.

The humiliating defeat in the Crimean War revealed the internal weaknesses of Imperial Russia. Tsar Alexander II (1855–1881) recognized the imperative need of reforms. Police surveillance and censorship were relaxed. The most pressing problem of Russia was the peasant question. During the preceding reign of Nicholas I no less than 712 distinct peasant uprisings had been officially recorded. In 1861 serfdom was abolished and the peasants emancipated. The Emancipation of Serfs, however, failed to satisfy the peasants, who protested against the terms of the simultaneous solution of the land question. They found the amount of land allotted to them too small and the "redemption dues" which they had to pay for it too high. Moreover, though free in law they were still not quite free in practice, because the title to the land allotted them was not vested in individual peasants but in the ancient village communes (*mir*) as a whole, and the peasants could not withdraw from the communes without forfeiting their land. The abolition of serfdom was followed by wholesale reforms in local and municipal government, the judiciary, education, and the armed forces. No political reform, however, was undertaken at this time. Alexander II was a strongly conservative statesman. While realistic enough to accept — and even urge — the necessity of reforms, he had no intention of sharing his autocratic powers with a parliament. He remained the "Autocrat of All the Russias." Liberal thinkers in Russia, who had hoped that he would "crown the edifice" of reform by granting a constitution, were bitterly disappointed. The demand for "land and freedom" was increasingly voiced by the opposition, the principal spokesmen of which were a new element in the Russian society, the *intelligentsia*.

By the time of the great reforms the Russian nobility had already sunk into deep decay. Until industrialization late in the nineteenth century there was no true middle class in Russia in the western sense. The void in leadership was filled by this new social elite, the *intelligentsia*, whose hallmark was not possession of wealth but education. The phenomenon was again not specifically Russian: it was taking place all over Eastern Europe at the time. In our days it is appearing in the liberated colonial world, where the former colonial masters, as well as the native chiefs, sheiks, and rajahs, are being replaced by young native leaders whose badge is a university diploma — usually from a western university. The Russian intellectuals embraced with fervor the liberal, secular, and scientific concepts that animated western intellectuals at the time. Socialism with its pretentious claims to solve all the ills of mankind by one neat stroke, particularly attracted them. Comparing Russian conditions with their ideals, they became critical of the autocracy, of the socio-economic conditions, and even of the cultural and moral values of Russia.

At the same time, Tsar Alexander II, alarmed by revolution in Poland in 1863 and an attempt on his life in 1866, became disillusioned with reform, which instead of relieving tensions seemed to increase them. Gradually, his government returned to the reactionary methods of the reign of the Emperor Nicholas I. Once again the censor suppressed all expressions of criticism in the press and literature and policemen stalked members of the opposition and harassed the national and religious minorities. In this atmosphere of disillusionment and frustration the Russian revolutionary movement was born. Mild enough in its beginnings, it grew progressively more violent as the government became more oppressive. In the 1870's a bitter underground war broke out between the police and the revolu-

tionaries. The assassination of hated officials, arrests, exile, and executions marked this war of terror. In 1881 the Tsar Liberator fell victim to
a terrorist's bomb. Ruthless repression then wiped out overt terrorism
but did not allay the revolutionary threat. Industrialization added fuel
to the revolutionary movement.

As in Western Europe, the progress of industry gave rise to a middle
class, anxious to assert itself politically, and to a labor class which demanded better social conditions. After 1900 peasant riots and labor strikes
broke out with increasing frequency. The defeats of the Russo-Japanese
War gave impetus to the Revolution of 1905–1906. A stupid blunder on
the part of the government precipitated revolutionary outbreaks. On
"Bloody Sunday" (January 22, 1905) troops fired on a peaceful crowd
bearing a petition to Tsar Nicholas II (1894–1917) at the Winter Palace
in St. Petersburg. The bloodshed fused the various elements of opposition: the middle-class liberals who demanded a constitution, the laborers
who demanded social justice, and the peasants who demanded land. In
the border areas, inhabited by the oppressed national minorities — Finns,
Estonians, Latvians, Lithuanians, Poles, Jews, Armenians, Georgians,
Tartars — the revolt took the form of a nationalist as well as social upheaval. Strikes, riots, peasant revolts, mutinies in the armed forces culminated in October, 1905, in a general strike, in which the professional
classes joined the workers and together brought the economic life of the
country to a standstill.

The October strike forced the government to capitulate. On October
30 the Tsar issued the famous October Manifesto which, taken at its face
value, was a promise to transform Russia from an autocracy into a constitutional monarchy. It guaranteed civil rights, promised universal suffrage,
and stipulated the rights of the Duma, a national assembly, with which
the government was prepared to share power. The Manifesto divided
the ranks of the opposition. The workers continued to agitate for social
changes, the peasants for land redistribution, but the middle class was
satisfied with the promise of a constitution and frightened by the threat
of social revolution. The revolutionary movement of 1905 lacked cohesion
and unified leadership. The Soviets (i.e., councils) of workers and intellectuals, which appeared in St. Petersburg and Moscow during the October strike, proved to be only harbingers of things to come in 1917. Having
split the ranks of the opposition, the government took courage again and
drowned the last revolts in blood.

Russia's experiment in constitutional government was not a happy one.
Social, economic, and psychologic conditions did not favor it. The October Manifesto permitted the formation of Russian political parties or their
emergence into the open from a shadowy illegality. They ranged from
extreme left to extreme right. On the extreme left was the Social Democratic Party ("SD's"), founded theoretically in 1898 but actually at a
congress in London in 1903 where it at once split into a radical "Bolshevik"

(majority) wing of orthodox Marxists and a more moderate "Menshevik" (minority) wing. Both addressed themselves to the rising industrial proletariat. Next was the Social Revolutionary Party ("SR's"), founded at about the same time, which tied on to the older Russian revolutionary tradition and addressed itself to the peasants. Left-of-center liberals were represented in the Constitutional Democratic Party ("Cadets"), which sought to go beyond the October Manifesto and introduce full democracy in Russia. Right-of-center liberals were represented in the Octobrist Party, which accepted fully the October Manifesto. The conservatives were represented in the Party of Monarchists-Constitutionalists and the Party of Rightful Order, supported by the Union of the Russian People (the "Black Hundreds") — Europe's first fascist organization. All of the Russian parties, being new, of necessity lacked experience in democracy.

Prime Minister Peter A. Stolypin (1906–1911), a conservative but energetic and able statesman, was willing to cooperate with the Duma — provided he could find one which would be docile and amenable to the wishes of the government. The first two Dumas that were elected, however, proved anything but docile and were dissolved after brief sessions. Only when Stolypin succeeded in obtaining a conservative "landowners'" Duma, by outrageously manipulating electoral laws and disfranchising whole segments of the population, was this "parliament" permitted to live out its legal existence. To strengthen the position of the government, Stolypin on one hand cracked down mercilessly on the socialist and intellectual critics of the government, and on the other tried to win back by concessions the loyalty of the peasants — still the largest segment of the population. The remainder of the "redemption dues" was waived, and the peasants were permitted to withdraw from the village communes and keep possession of their land. The purpose of Stolypin's agrarian reforms was to create in this way a class of independent, self-respecting farmers, whom ownership of property would make socially conservative and impervious to socialist agitation. The experiment was not without success but was far from completed when Russia was plunged into the First World War.

THE HAPSBURG AND OTTOMAN EMPIRES

The Turkish and Austrian Empires are condemned to death. The instrument of their death is in the hands of the Slavs.

JOSEPH MAZZINI, *Lettere Slave*

1. PROBLEMS OF MULTINATIONAL EMPIRES IN THE AGE OF NATIONALISM

ON THE POLITICAL MAP of Europe drawn by the Congress of Vienna in 1815 Central and Eastern Europe appeared quite simple compared to Western Europe. Along fairly straight, long lines there met only three states: Russia, Austria, and Turkey. Under this apparent simplicity, however, was hidden a great complexity. All three of these states were multinational empires. They comprised a great variety of peoples who spoke many different languages, had different historical origins, were of different religions, and had attained greatly varying levels of cultural, social and economic development. The fate of the Russian Empire has been discussed in the previous chapter. Of the three multinational empires it alone has survived up to present times, although much changed by a great revolution at the end of the First World War. The other two, the Hapsburg and the Ottoman Empires, have disappeared from the political map of Europe.

In the age of modern nationalism and technology multinational empires became an anachronism. Modern nationalism has acted both as an integrating and as a disintegrating force in politics. In the case of Germany and Italy, which had been divided by Europe's feudal history into a large number of petty kingdoms, duchies, and principalities, nationalism acted as an integrating force. It unified the Germans and Italians into national states. In the case of Austria and Turkey, which were haphazard products of feudalism and imperialism, nationalism acted as a disintegrating force. It broke these states up into their national components.

But it was not only the abstract force of nationalism that broke up the empires of Austria and Turkey. In the age of modern technology they

90

were greatly handicapped by their heterogeneous nature. Modern government calls for ever greater centralization and standardization. In Austria and Turkey the stubborn insistence of their component peoples on their historical "states' rights," or provincial and communal privileges, made reform and modernization extremely difficult. The administration of Austria and Turkey remained antiquated and inefficient, and in the case of Turkey also extremely corrupt. The problem of defense in a modern state necessitates a centralized command, standardization of weapons, and a relatively high educational level on the part of its soldiers. The efficiency of the Austrian and Turkish armies was greatly impaired by lack of standardization, the babel of the many tongues which their soldiers spoke, and the low educational level of many recruits. Reminiscing about his days as adviser to the Ottoman army, the great Prussian strategist Helmuth von Moltke wrote: "The reform (of the Ottoman army) consisted chiefly in externals, names, and trappings. The army was built on the European plan, with Russian tunics, a French code, Belgian guns, Turkish turbans, Hungarian saddles, English sabres, drill sergeants of every nation." Describing summer maneuvers of the Austrian army, an anonymous observer noted that while he was speaking to an Austrian officer, a cavalry patrol rode up "and the leader . . . reported something in Czech. The captain, not conversant with the language . . . questioned him in German but could get no other answer but '*Nerozumím*' (I do not understand). While the captain was giving orders to a lieutenant to go reconnoitering . . . a second patrol . . . arrived. The excited leader spoke very rapidly and sonorously in Magyar. Every question of the captain was answered monotonously with '*Nem tudom*' (I do not understand) . . . Then a panting sergeant . . . gabbled most furiously in Polish and to the captain's eager query, 'Can you not speak German?' he had but one answer: '*Neznam*' (I do not understand)."[1]

Business and industry flourish best in countries which have fairly uniform laws, standards, and practices. These conditions were lacking in the Austrian and Turkish Empires. But the greatest weakness of both empires was that their statesmen had failed to develop a satisfactory relationship among their many peoples. They lacked any sense of solidarity with one another. In fact, they often cordially hated each other. The Slavs, notably, but by no means solely, felt oppressed in Austria and Turkey because of their nationality, religion, or social class. The fact that many of the disaffected peoples of Austria and Turkey had kinsmen or coreligionists across the border made the two empires extremely vulnerable to irredentist propaganda of their hostile neighbors. In the First World War the antiquated and fragile structure of Austria and Turkey broke down, and each of their peoples went its own way.

[1] Arthur J. May, *The Hapsburg Monarchy, 1867–1914* (Cambridge, Mass.: Harvard University Press, 1951), p. 491.

2. AUSTRIA: PROPPING UP THE "RAMSHACKLE EMPIRE"

In 1914 the Hapsburg Empire was territorially the largest state of Europe after Russia. It was a natural geographic unit with well-defined natural borders: in the southwest the Alps, in the northwest the Bohemian mountains, in the northeast and east the Carpathian arch, and in the south the Danube, the Sava, the Balkan Mountains, and the Adriatic Sea. The Danube, which traversed it, provided a convenient water route to Germany in the west and into the Balkans in the southeast. The Moldau and the Elbe linked it to Hamburg, and railways led to its own thriving ports in the Adriatic, Trieste and Fiume. The Hapsburg Monarchy was in an excellent position to trade with all of Europe. Its natural resources were considerable: the plains of Hungary were one of the richest granaries of Europe; the forests of the Alps and Carpathians provided abundant timber; in Silesia there were rich deposits of coal; in Galicia oil; in Transylvania minerals; the numerous streams had a high potential of hydro-electric energy. Its population of fifty-one million was industrious and, at least in the western portions of the empire, possessed a level of education and technical skill sufficient to manage modern industry. Bohemia, with its giant Škoda armament plant, with large textile and shoe industries, with famous breweries and glassworks, with numerous sugar factories, was one of the most important industrial regions of Europe. Yet the Hapsburg Monarchy was a weak and ill-compacted political entity. Like Italy, it was a land of heavy emigration — commonly an index of poor social conditions. Lloyd George's caustic characterization of Austria as a "ramshackle empire" contained an element of truth. The main reasons for this were its peculiar historical origin and its multinational character.

The Hapsburg Monarchy was a product of singularly fortuitous circumstances. In 1526 the great Ottoman Sultan, Suleiman the Magnificent, invaded Hungary and on the plain of Mohács near the Danube crushed the Hungarian feudal levies that opposed him. Louis Jagellon, King of Hungary and of Bohemia, perished in the fray. The frightened Estates of Bohemia and Hungary hastened to elect to their vacant thrones Louis' brother-in-law, Ferdinand Hapsburg, Archduke of Austria and brother of Charles V, Holy Roman Emperor and King of Spain. Thus, unlike the neighboring Russian and Ottoman Empires, the Hapsburg Monarchy came into existence not by expansion and conquest on the part of any one of its many nationalities, but by free association of the peoples of Hungary, Bohemia, and Austria. Later the Hapsburgs increased their possessions by war and diplomacy. By the end of the seventeenth century Hungary and Transylvania were cleared of the Turks, and the Hapsburg realm stretched eastward to the Carpathians and southeastward to the Sava and the Danube. In the eighteenth century most of Silesia was lost to Prussia, but the loss was compensated for by the acquisition of Bukovina from Turkey and of Galicia through the partitions of Poland. In the

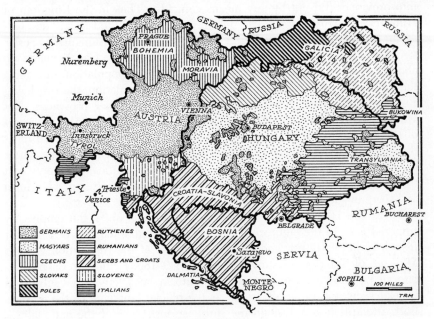

AUSTRIA-HUNGARY, 1914

nineteenth century the Hapsburgs made new gains. At the Congress of Vienna they acquired the Italian states of Lombardy and Venetia, as well as the former Venetian possessions across the Adriatic, Istria and Dalmatia. The unification of Italy deprived them of Venetia and Lombardy, but the loss was partially compensated for by the occupation of Bosnia and Herzegovina, authorized by the Congress of Berlin in 1878. The empire thus created had geographic unity but little cultural or historical unity. It was a patchwork of heterogeneous provinces and a medley of polyglot peoples.

The population of the empire consisted of eleven nationalities in all (Germans, Magyars, Czechs, Slovaks, Poles, Ruthenes, Serbs, Croats, Slovenes, Rumanians, and Italians). Numerically, all were minorities. In 1910 the most numerous and advanced of the empire's peoples, the Germans, constituted only 23.9 per cent of the population, and the Magyars, next in importance, 20.2 per cent. Moreover, the empire's peoples had attained very different levels of cultural, social, and economic development. By 1914 the Germans and the Czechs in Austria and Bohemia, which had been parts of the Holy Roman Empire and of the Germanic Confederation and had participated in the general cultural and economic revival of the German world in the nineteenth century, had attained general standards as high as any people in Europe. At the same time the Rumanians of Transylvania and Bukovina and the Serbs of Bosnia and Herzegovina, for instance, remained quite primitive. Moreover, the lines of nationality and the historical divisions of the empire into provinces did not by any means coincide. Thus in the Kingdom of Hungary, the Hungarians (i.e., the Magyars) constituted barely one half of the population, the rest being Slovaks, Ruthenes, Rumanians, Serbs, Croats, and Germans; in the Kingdom of Bohemia the Czechs made up about two-thirds and the Germans one-third of the population; in Galicia the Poles amounted to about three-fifths of the population, the rest being Ruthenes and Jews. Similar situations existed in other provinces. Yet Hungarians, Czechs, and Poles demanded as the price of their support of the empire not only autonomy for themselves but the right to run as they pleased the whole of Hungary, the whole of Bohemia, or the whole of Galicia, as the case might be. The demand for political autonomy and the insistence on historical "states' rights" made any attempt at reform and reorganization of the empire very difficult.

Twice the Hapsburgs attempted to reform and unify the empire by Imperial *fiat*. In the eighteenth century the enlightened despot Emperor Joseph II (1780–1790), and after the collapse of the Revolution of 1848 Minister of Interior Alexander Bach (1849–1860) who exercised dictatorial powers, tried to promulgate uniform laws, create a centralized bureaucracy, and impose German as the official language of the empire. Both attempts failed through the stubborn insistence of the nationalities on their historical "states' rights" and their jealousy of one another. The Hapsburg Monarchy was never integrated into a uniform and harmonious whole. It remained a dynastic empire, in which the Hapsburgs ruled under different titles in each of its units. It was held together not by the solidarity of its peoples with one another but by their feudal loyalty toward the Hapsburg dynasty. In return for their loyalty they expected the dynasty to act as impartial arbiter of their differences. The Hapsburgs solved the difficult problem of ruling their ill-compacted empire by a subtle policy of divide and rule. They played the nationalities against one another and kept the reins of government firmly in hand. "My peoples are strangers to one another, and so much the better," said the Emperor Francis Joseph (1848–1916). "I place Hungarians in Italy, Italians in Hungary, each guards his neighbor. They do not understand each other and they detest each other. From antipathies is born order and from their reciprocal hates general peace."[2] The policy worked as long as the Hapsburgs did not identify themselves definitely with the national interest of any one of their peoples.

Even the French Revolution, which maligned monarchs and exalted nations, failed to shatter the multinational Hapsburg Monarchy. More dangerous was the Revolution of 1848. It shook the empire to its foundation. But even then the leading Czech political spokesman František Palacký declared: "If Austria did not exist, it would be necessary to create her, in the interest of humanity itself." Unfortunately, in 1866, stunned by a humiliating defeat at the hands of Prussia and the loss of

[2] *Ibid.*, p. 487.

Venetia to Italy, the Hapsburgs determined to try a new course, which proved fateful. Unable either to impose a centralist solution or to find a federalist one, they accepted a policy which proposed to appease the strongest of the nationalities and disregard the displeasure of the others. In 1867 the famous Austro-Hungarian Compromise or *Ausgleich* was concluded, which transformed the empire into the "Dual" Austro-Hungarian Monarchy. It was in effect an alliance between the Magyars of Hungary and the Germans of Austria against the rest of the nationalities. By abandoning their pretended role of impartial arbiters among the nationalities and by siding with one group of them against the rest, the Hapsburgs deprived the empire of its *raison d'être* and doomed it. The Slavs, Italians, and Rumanians were alienated. In 1848 Palacký thought that the empire was a necessity; now, disillusioned, he exclaimed: "Before Austria was, we were, and when Austria no longer is, we still shall be." The division of the peoples of the empire into "ruling" and "subject" nationalities generally linked political inferiority to social inferiority. Most of the subject peoples had no upper or middle class. They were almost exclusively nations of peasants and workers, and were treated as despised helots. This was particularly true in Hungary. In this situation irredentisms throve; the Italians began to look across the border to Italy, the Serbs to Serbia, the Rumanians to Rumania, and the Ruthenes to Russia. The Poles looked to the Poles of Russia and Germany and hoped to reunite with them in a restored, independent Poland. The Slovenes, Croats, and Serbs began to consider the desirability of uniting with their kinsmen in Serbia and Montenegro in a common Yugoslav state. The Czechs and Slovaks, who had no kinsmen across the border, became fatuously Russophil.

Even some groups among the ruling nationalities were affected by irredentism. This was notably the case of the German Bohemians (styled after the First World War Sudeten Germans). The German Bohemians and the Czech Bohemians heartily hated each other. They had in common only one belief, namely, that Vienna was perfidious. While the Czechs execrated the Emperor Francis Joseph for going back on his promise to have himself crowned King of Bohemia and to give them a status in Bohemia analogous to that of the Magyars in Hungary, the Germans of Bohemia lived in eternal dread of a possible deal between Vienna and the Czechs at their expense. The German Bohemians therefore tended to lean outside of the empire, toward Germany. Contrary to a common belief, it was not Russia that first appealed to the Austrian Slavs, but the Austrian Slavs to Russia. Before 1914 Pan-Germanism in Germany and Pan-Slavism in Russia had little broad, popular support, but both throve in the Hapsburg Empire because of the inability of its statesmen to adjust satisfactorily relations among its nationalities.

The *Ausgleich* provided for some common agencies for the two halves of the empire: the Delegations of the parliaments at Vienna and Buda-

pest and joint ministries of Foreign Affairs, War, and Finance. Otherwise,
however, it left the internal organization of Austria and Hungary to
their respective governments to determine. Theoretically, constitutional
government existed in both countries. But in Hungary it was vitiated
by an electoral system which disfranchised the broad masses of the
people, and by a policy which sought to assimilate forcefully the non-
Magyar nationalities and transform Hungary, in which the Magyars
constituted barely one-half of the population, into a national Magyar
state. In Austria the old Hapsburg policy of divide and rule continued,
and the jealousy of the nationalities facilitated it. Count Taaffe, Prime
Minister between 1879 and 1893, boasted that he governed by "keeping
all the nationalities in a state of uniform, nicely tempered discontent."[3]
The parliament at Vienna, elected after 1907 on the basis of universal
manhood suffrage, became notorious for its forensic — and physical —
battles and for its carping and singularly unconstructive criticism, fili-
bustering, and incapacity to act. The Austro-Hungarian Monarchy faced
many pressing social and economic problems — and solved some of them
successfully — but the unsolved nationality question overshadowed them
all; like a pall, it hung over all phases of life.

The internal quarrel of Austria's nationalities was increasingly reflected
in her foreign policy, and indirectly became one of the major causes of
the First World War. The unification of Germany and Italy by 1870 had
excluded Austria from these areas where she had traditionally exerted an
influence. In the nineteenth century it was axiomatic for European statesmen to believe that a great power must continuously expand. Theoretically, Austria could seek compensation for her losses in Germany and
Italy by engaging, like other European powers, in colonial expansion.
But of all European statesmen the Austrian leaders were the most "continental," that is, absorbed in the continental game of balance of power
and ignorant of the non-European world. The possibility of colonial
expansion never seems to have been seriously entertained in Vienna.
Instead, Vienna revived its long-forgotten ambitions to expand in the
Balkans, the ultimate objective of which was to gain an outlet on the
Aegean Sea at Salonika.

Austria was launched on a course of foreign policy by Count Julius
Andrássy, Foreign Minister from 1871 to 1879, a course from which she
deviated little until the First World War. A Magyar magnate who had
fought in the Hungarian Revolution of 1848, Andrássy hated Russia for
having helped the Hapsburgs to crush that revolution. Austria, he determined, "should offer her hand to Germany and show her fist to Russia."
Such a conception of Austrian policy was unfortunate, not only because
it increased tensions among her nationalities, but also because it gratu-
itously sowed trouble between Russia and Germany, which at the time
were on friendly terms. With both German and Slav elements in the pop-

[3] *Ibid.*, p. 487.

ulation, it was obviously best for Austria to work for amicable cooperation between Russia and Germany, while maintaining independence of both. Austria's natural allies should have been France and Britain — France to balance the pressure of Germany and Italy, Britain to balance the pressure of Russia in the Balkans. Association with the western liberal powers might also have helped to create a climate in Austria propitious for a liberal solution of the nationality question. But, guided by his hatred of Russia abroad and his fear of the Slavs at home, Andrássy proceeded to force Austria, an empire over one-half Slav, into the absurd role of a champion of anti-Slavism abroad. Though he acquiesced in Bismarck's Three Emperors' League, he proceeded to sabotage it by reviving Austria's Balkan ambitions. His cooperation with Disraeli at the Congress of Berlin in 1878 gained for the empire the control of Bosnia and Herzegovina without firing a shot. But the policy was fraught with dangers for the empire. It angered Russia, which had been many times Austria's ally and never her enemy (except briefly and reluctantly during the Napoleonic Wars). It also alienated the Balkan Slavs, who had once looked to Austria for support but now came to regard her as a jackal snatching the fruits of their victory.

In 1879 Andrássy consummated his efforts by concluding the Dual Alliance with Germany which gave up Austria's freedom of action abroad for Germany's support of the dualist system at home. Andrássy's successors continued his policy in the main. Aehrenthal's baiting of Russia and Serbia during the Bosnian Annexation Crisis — successfully brought off thanks to Germany's backing — gave the Germans and Magyars a fine sense of virility and humiliated the Slavs. The declaration of war on Serbia in 1914 was also motivated by internal political considerations. A short victorious war to wipe out Serbia, the supposed source of Yugoslav agitation at home, was just the medicine needed. But wars are more easily started than won. The little war with Serbia spread into a great world conflagration in which Austria's ramshackle structure broke down, permitting the nationalities to go each its own way.

3. TURKEY: THE "SICK MAN" ON THE BOSPORUS

The Ottoman Empire began in extremely modest circumstances as a feudal domain of a small Turkish tribe, the Osmanli, in western Asia Minor in the thirteenth century. It spread, however, with extraordinary dynamism, at first expanding westward at the expense of the decaying Byzantine Empire. In the 1350's the Turks crossed the Dardanelles, bypassed Constantinople whose formidable walls were still too much of a challenge for them, and swept into the Balkans. After destroying the Slav states of Serbia and Bulgaria, they tightened their vise on the Byzantine Empire, reducing it gradually to the city of Constantinople, a small frontage, and a few islands. In 1453 they laid siege to the Imperial city and captured it by using artillery on an unprecedented scale to breach its walls. Under the name of Istanbul the ancient city of the Emperor Constantine became the capital of the Ottoman Empire, which was to endure until 1918. The expansion westward was followed by expansion eastward at the expense of other Turkish tribes and of the Kurds and Arabs. In 1516–1517 Sultan Selim the Grim conquered Syria, Palestine, and Egypt. From a shadowy descendant of the Abbasside Caliphs of Bagdad residing at Cairo he took the venerable title of Caliph or Successor (i.e., to the Prophet Mohammed) and gave it new luster.

The Ottoman Empire reached the peak of its power under Selim's son Suleiman (1520–1566), known to the Westerners as the "Magnificent" and to his own people as *El Kanuni* (the Lawgiver). Suleiman was a cultured and sophisticated gentleman of the Renaissance Age and an easy match — both as a warrior and as a statesman — for any of his famous contemporaries, Charles V of Spain and Germany, Henry VIII of England, Francis I of France, or Ivan the Terrible of Russia. Under him Turkish soldiers laid siege to Vienna, the Hapsburg capital in the heart of Europe (1529), and Turkish sailors fought with Portuguese navigators in the Indian Ocean for the control of the lucrative Eastern trade. In both ventures the Turks were unsuccessful, but nevertheless they held sway over an empire which stretched from Algiers to the Persian Gulf and from the steppes of southern Russia to the cataracts of the Nile.

At its best the Ottoman Empire was a prosperous and well-governed state. It had a well-trained civil service and an incomparable professional army. Until 1632 both were recruited by the "blood tax," by drafts of youths from the conquered Christian provinces who were rigorously trained for their tasks in palace schools at Constantinople. The bulk of the Ottoman armed forces consisted of feudal levies of Moslems who were awarded land in the conquered territories and in return owed military service. The Ottoman Empire was a multinational empire in which the Turks constituted a minority of the population. Until the rise of modern nationalism this mattered little, for the population was divided on the basis of religion and not of nationality. The Ottoman government used in ruling its polyglot subjects a combination of the millet system and regional autonomy. The millet system, introduced from Egypt by Mohammed the Conqueror (1451–1481), grouped subjects by religion, which had the advantage of divorcing law and government from territory. Since in the Moslem view the source of law is divine, members of each religious group — wherever they lived — had to be ruled in accordance with the precepts of their religion. Thus the most numerous Christian community in the empire, the Greek Orthodox, was placed under the jurisdiction of the Patriarch of Constantinople, the Armenians under the Armenian Catholicos, the Jews under a rabbinical board, etc. In 1535 Suleiman the Magnificent placed the Catholics under the protection of the King of France with whom he was in alliance, an alliance motivated by their common enmity toward the Hapsburgs. This concession by Suleiman was the first of the later disastrous "capitulations." During its period of strength the Ottoman Empire was religiously very tolerant, but the non-Moslem *rayah* (which means literally cattle) were always clearly marked as second-rate subjects; they had to pay special taxes, wear distinct costumes, and were denied such attributes of free men as the right to bear arms and ride horses. Considerable regional autonomy was granted to outlying provinces, such as the Barbary States, Egypt, and the Crimean Khanate.

In the seventeenth century the Turkish Empire began to stagnate. In 1683 it bestirred itself to its last great military effort in Europe. The objective of the campaign was the capture of Vienna. On September 12, 1683, under the walls of Vienna, a relieving force of Poles and Germans led by the valiant King of Poland, John Sobieski, defeated and routed the Ottoman army. The great Ottoman retreat from Europe had begun: it was to end only in 1913.

The power vacuum created by the Ottoman decline opened the perennial Near Eastern Question, which was to keep Europe's diplomats busy from the Peace of Karlowitz (1699), when the first humiliating treaty was imposed on the Ottoman Empire by a concert of European powers, to the Peace of Sèvres (1920), when it was completely dismembered by them. Turkey represented a rich strategic prize because it controlled the crossroads of three continents, Asia, Africa, and Europe. A great power in control of it could mount an offensive against any of the three continents. Napoleon thought of this when he invaded Egypt. His Egyptian adventure failed because of lack of sea power, but it prepared the ground for Mohammed Ali, an Albanian adventurer originally in Turkish service, to launch Egypt on its way to virtual independence and modernization. The Ottoman Empire became an object of intense rivalry among the imperialist powers of Europe.

On the eve of the Crimean War Tsar Nicholas I proposed to partition Turkey. "We have," he said to the British Ambassador, "on our hands a sick man — a very sick man. It will be, I tell you frankly, a great misfortune, if one of these days he should slip away from us, especially before all necessary arrangements are made." Encouraged by Ottoman weakness, first Austria and later Russia attacked the empire and lopped off provinces in the name of protecting the oppressed Ottoman Christians. The plight of the Christians was real enough, for during the "Sick Man" era the Ottoman Empire was one of the worst-governed states in the world. The Christians, notably the Armenians, frequently became victims of Moslem bigotry and Turkish xenophobia. The western powers — in the eighteenth century mainly France and in the nineteenth century mainly Britain — fearing Russian expansion into the Mediterranean, adopted the posture of protectors of Ottoman "territorial integrity," but

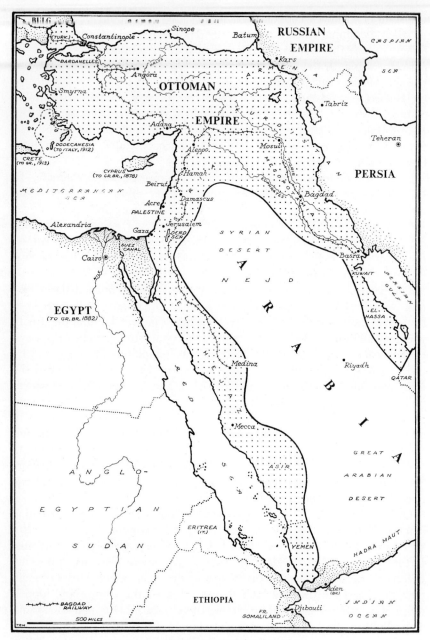

THE OTTOMAN EMPIRE, 1914

were not averse, on occasion, to helping themselves to Ottoman territory too. France seized Algeria in 1830 and Tunisia in 1881. England took Aden in 1839, Cyprus in 1878, Egypt in 1882, and extended her "protection" to the sheikdoms along the coasts of southern Arabia and the Persian Gulf. In the 1890's Germany entered the scene, but her immediate objectives were economic. Twice Kaiser William II visited the Sultan — the first Christian monarch ever to do so. In 1899 he raised the hackles of every British, French, and Russian diplomat by proclaiming himself in a speech in Damascus the friend of "the 300,000,000 Moslems . . . dispersed throughout the East."

The population of the Ottoman Empire was desperately poor, but Turkey still represented a rich economic prize. She raised cotton, had many minerals, and was believed to be rich in oil. The opening of the Suez Canal in 1869 revived the Mediterranean as a great avenue of commerce. The Ottoman Empire needed foreign capital and foreign skills to build its railroads and canals and develop its resources. Bankers and concession hunters flocked to Constantinople and to autonomous Egypt, and, exploiting Turkish and Egyptian lack of capital, ignorance of finance and industry, and the venality of their officials, systematically despoiled them. The great powers assisted these adventurers by extracting from the Ottoman government "capitulations," that is, treaties exempting their subjects from Ottoman jurisdiction and according their businessmen a variety of privileges. In 1875 Turkey and in 1876 Egypt declared bankruptcy. Thereafter they fell economically completely into the hands of European money lenders. Ultimately, the administration of their public debt, customs, foreign trade, banking, railroads, telegraphs, and most modern industrial establishments was in the hands of foreigners.

Economic despoliation and political humiliation provoked a reform movement (*Tanzimat*) in the Ottoman Empire. The reformists were small groups of men, at first mostly officials who had spent some time in Europe on diplomatic missions, later western-trained intellectuals, and finally the "armed intellectuals" — young officers trained in German-organized military schools in which, quite incidentally to acquiring technical training, they imbibed western ideas and began to question the Ottoman system. In harmony with the western political thinking of the day the reformists thought that the way to save and rejuvenate the empire was by adopting a liberal constitution. In 1876, amidst the diplomatic crisis preceding the Russo-Turkish War of 1877–1878, Midhat Pasha, the Grand Old Man of Turkish liberalism and a competent administrator, succeeded in persuading the young Sultan Abdul Hamid II (1876–1909) to grant a constitution. It declared that all subjects of the Sultan were equal, regardless of race and religion, guaranteed the conventional civil liberties, and provided for the usual cabinet and elected parliament.

Abdul Hamid had acquiesced in the constitution mainly because he hoped that it would allay foreign intervention. When it failed in this purpose and Russia declared war, he dismissed Midhat, quietly adjourned parliament, and ignored the constitution. There followed thirty years of most pernicious tyranny which won the Sultan the epithets "Abdul the Damned" and the "Red Sultan." Midhat was strangled in jail, and other liberals were arrested or forced into exile. Exiles abroad and conspirators at home formed secret societies with the common objective of restoring the constitution. In 1907 at a congress in Paris they were fused into the "Society of Union and Progress" whose members soon became known as "Young Turks." In July of 1908 the Society of Union and Progress, assured of armed support by the Third Army Corps, launched the Young Turk Revolution in Salonika. The wily Sultan saved himself temporarily by pretending to have been misled by bad ministers and restored the constitution of 1876 on July 24. For a few weeks there was wild rejoicing and fraternization among the nationalities. "Under the same blue sky we are all equal; we glory in being Ottomans," declared Enver Pasha, a leading Young Turk. But it is easier to proclaim a constitution than to translate its principles into action.

The Young Turks, schooled in the religiously tolerant West, were prepared to forget about religious differences, but they were strong nationalists. They insisted on "Ottomanization," that is, on Turkification of the non-Turkish peoples of the empire. This policy failed to win the non-Moslem people, such as the Greeks, Macedonians, and Armenians, who wanted not equality in the Ottoman Empire but complete national freedom outside of it. The policy, moreover, alienated the non-Turkish Moslems, such as the Albanians and Arabs, who lost their privileged status as Moslems under it and in addition were expected to surrender also their nationality. The Young Turk government was also plagued by a series of disasters abroad. In 1908 Austria profited from the confusion in Constantinople to annex Bosnia and Herzegovina, and Bulgaria, which previously nominally recognized the suzerainty of the Sultan, declared its complete independence. In 1911 Italy seized Tripoli. In 1912 the Balkan states of Bulgaria, Serbia, Montenegro, and Greece declared war on Turkey, to liberate their "unredeemed" kinsmen, and decisively defeated her (First Balkan War). They presently quarreled and fought over the division of the spoils (Second Balkan War). Under the Peace of Constantinople (September 29, 1913) Turkey recovered some losses from Bulgaria, but her rule in Europe, except for Constantinople and a small strip of land west of it, was ended.

The Young Turks clung to power in spite of foreign disaster, Albanian revolt, and Arab unrest. An attempt at counter-revolution in April, 1909, was repressed. Abdul Hamid, who sided with it, was deposed and replaced with his brother, Mohammed V, a weak and helpless man – a perfect tool in the hands of the dictatorial triumvirate of Young Turks: Enver Pasha, Talaat Bey, and Jemal Pasha. Of the liberal Young Turk program little remained except a rank Turkish chauvinism. Soon the Young Turks renewed the repressive police methods of Abdul Hamid. In foreign policy they reverted to his preference for Germany – after a brief honeymoon with England, the home of liberalism, in the early, hopeful days of the revolution. When the First World War broke out the Sick Man on the Bosporus was ready for his burial.

10

THE SMALLER STATES OF EUROPE

The day of small nations has passed away: the day of Empires has come.
JOSEPH CHAMBERLAIN (1904)

1. THE LIMITED AUTONOMY OF SMALL STATES

SIX GREAT POWERS — Britain, Germany, France, Russia, Italy, and Austria-Hungary — dominated Europe in 1900. In a sense it might be said that these six great powers *were* Europe. Over four-fifths of the population, territory, wealth, foreign trade, and armed might of the Continent was vested in them. The principle that all European states were "sovereign" and equal, inherited from the days when such nations as Switzerland, Sweden, or Holland could defeat and repel the armies of the Holy Roman Emperor, the King of Spain, or the King of France, was in 1900 a diplomatic fiction.

The development of industry and technology increased greatly the disparity in military power between great and small nations. The independence of small states did not depend any more on their ability to fend off all comers but on the operation of the European balance of power. Fortunately for the small nations, this operated to limit not only their independence but also that of the great powers. With the exception of Britain, which thanks to her insular position and naval power could not be overrun and completely defeated, none of the European great powers could defend itself, without allies, against all comers. After 1900, as Great Britain's leadership in naval and industrial power diminished, even the British found it expedient to limit their "splendid isolation" and seek allies. The fear and jealousy of the great powers toward one another provided some guarantee of freedom for the small powers. No great nation would willingly allow an opponent to extend its boundaries by absorbing small neighboring states.

The independence of all European states was *relative*, not absolute. There were, of course, significant differences in the measure of their freedom. The relationship between the small and the great powers may be summed up in the oft-cited Roman adage *Quod licet Jovi non licet bovi*

(what is lawful to Jupiter is not lawful to the ox). What was permitted
to a great power was not permitted to a small one. The diplomatic freedom of the small states was in fact, though not in theory, severely limited.
Moreover, the status of the small nations was not uniform or fixed for
all time. The relationship of the great powers to each other and to the
small states continually changed, as the balance of power was not a static
but a dynamic reality. It might shift abruptly or imperceptibly, but it
shifted continually in response to every pulse of European life.

Generally speaking, there were three categories of small European
states. The first group was that of "buffers." The classic example of the
buffer state was Switzerland. Its status as a neutral was internationally
guaranteed from the Congress of Vienna onward. It was surrounded by
four great powers – Germany, Austria, Italy, and France. Their pressures
on Switzerland cancelled each other, permitting the Swiss to enjoy an
internal autonomy as great as that of any other nation. In some respects
Swiss autonomy was greater, because, having accepted the status of a
neutral, the Swiss did not have to make as many adjustments in internal
policy to accommodate exigencies of external policy as did the powers
with an active diplomacy. For instance, Switzerland did not have to curb
the socialists and revolutionary groups to please an autocratic ally, as did
neighboring France. Traditionally, Switzerland was the haven of political
exiles of all sorts, whose activities the Swiss observed with a complacent
indifference. A position analogous to that of Switzerland was that of
Belgium. In 1914 the German violation of Belgian neutrality (guaranteed
internationally since 1839) provoked instant British retaliation. Similar to
the status of Switzerland and Belgium, though less secure, was that of
Holland and Denmark. They had no guarantees of neutrality, but they
too trusted to the jealousy of the great powers to guard their independence.

The second category of small nations included those living on the northwestern and southeastern periphery of Europe: the Scandinavian and
Iberian states. Long established and accepted, lying off the main highways of European history, looking more outward to the Atlantic than
inward to Europe, their independence was also secure – at least in time
of peace. In time of war they had to tread warily and accept many humiliating impositions on their freedom by the main belligerents. But, for that
matter, so did all small neutrals because the great powers were ruthless
and devoid of principle when engaged in mortal combat.

The third category of small states were the inchoate nations of the
Balkans. Barely emerging out of Turkish bondage at the opening of the
twentieth century, they did not as yet have a well-defined and generally
accepted status. Economically weak and politically unstable, they maintained their independence only with difficulty by accepting the undignified status of clients or satellites of one or another of the great powers,
which meddled outrageously in their internal affairs. It was not until
after the First World War, during a temporary eclipse of German and

Russian military power, that the Balkan states attained a measure of internal stability and external independence.

While the small nations did not directly determine the political destinies of Europe, their contributions to European arts, sciences, and thought — the real glory of Europe — were often impressive. At least the more responsible of great European statesmen recognized that the preservation of the small nations of Europe was necessary not only for the sake of European stability but also for the sake of European civilization.

2. SPAIN AND PORTUGAL

For Spain the twentieth century held a tragic ordeal in store. Before the century opened, war with the United States stripped this once dominant colonial power of almost the last outposts of empire remaining to it. Cuba, Puerto Rico, the Philippine Islands, and Guam passed under American protection after a brief and decisive conflict (1898). In European affairs Spain had come to play a minor part, although it possessed a population of twenty million in 1914 and an area of 196,000 square miles, only slightly less than that of France. But lethargy and bureaucratic inefficiency, economic backwardness, lack of vigor and initiative, widespread poverty in the agrarian sections, illiteracy, and political unrest paralyzed or distracted the energy of the people. In the sixteenth century, the "golden century" of Spain, the shadow of Spanish power had overhung Europe and the enterprise of Spanish colonizers had brought a new world within the orbit of European civilization. Modern Spain, however, failed to maintain this ascendancy or to fill the role in world affairs which the traditions, the genius, and the valor of the Spaniards had won for them in the fifteenth and sixteenth centuries.

Economic backwardness and financial insolvency were major factors in retarding the development of Spain. In 1914 her foreign trade was less than that of Sweden or Denmark, amounting in fact to only one-half that of Argentina, once a Spanish colony. Capital was urgently needed to develop mines, factories, and communication systems and to generate hydroelectric power to operate them. Enlightened leadership was likewise needed to reform the schools, to procure credit for new enterprises, to improve public health and sanitation. A farsighted land policy was needed to raise the living standards of the rural population, to break up the great estates, and to end for the peasantry and sheepherders conditions that verged on peonage. Spain lacked the class which in France had come to form one of the most stable elements in the nation, the millions of independent farmers with a few acres of their own to make them responsible men of property. But it had taken a revolution to transform France from the old regime to the new; and reform in Spain, however instituted, was certain to prove revolutionary in its effects. Whether the needed reforms, agrarian, social, economic, and political, could be carried through without the confusion and suffering of a civil war the twentieth century was to reveal.

The Spanish government, like Spain itself, remained confused, tradition-bound, and weakened by dissension. Throughout most of the nineteenth century Spain suffered from recurrent civil war. The fierce national resistance against Napoleon (1808–1814) ended with the restoration of the Spanish Bourbon line in the person of Ferdinand VII (1814–1833). His conservatism provoked several unsuccessful revolts, and his decision to revoke the Salic Law and leave the throne to his daughter Isabella II (1833–1868) exposed Spain to further disorders. Isabella's cousin Don Carlos disputed her right to rule (Carlist Wars, 1833–1839), and although she resisted his attacks further strife and intrigue continued until she was forced to abdicate in 1868. After six years of experiment and disorder, army leaders proclaimed Isabella's son, Alfonso XII (1874–1885), who restored order and granted a constitution. After his early death his widow Maria Christina assumed the regency for a posthumous son, Alfonso XIII (1886–1931).

Socialist and anarchist doctrines, that spread among European workers in the later nineteenth century, injected a further element of discord into Spanish affairs. The Spanish-American War of 1898 revealed the weakness and inefficiency of the government, and attempts to expand Spanish influence in Morocco overstrained the national finances. By 1914 poverty, inefficiency, and inequality had brought Spain close to revolution, but as a neutral in World War I the nation found ready markets for its exports and enjoyed a moderate prosperity. The return of peace brought economic hardships and deepening discontent. Mounting tensions during the 1920's ended in a revolution that overthrew the monarchy in 1931 and led to a tragic civil war. (See Chap. 36.)

Unlike Spain, Portugal retained into the twentieth century a considerable overseas empire, including the Azores, Madeira, and Cape Verde Islands; Goa, Damão, and Diu in India; Macao in China; part of Timor in the East Indies; and Angola and Mozambique in Africa. These possessions held a native population greater than the 5,000,000 Portuguese in Europe, and their combined area (1914) was almost one hundred times larger than Portugal itself, a state of only 35,582 square miles. Portugal, like Spain, suffered a severe depletion of manpower in the sixteenth and seventeenth centuries, when Latin America received an estimated 3,000,000 immigrants from the Iberian peninsula. As late as 1750 the Spanish and Portuguese population in the New World was increasing twice as fast as the total for all other European settlements together. Brazil was lost to Portugal in the early decades of the nineteenth century, and the great migration of 1815–1914, which carried 50,000,000 Europeans across the Atlantic, further depleted the Spanish and Portuguese home population.

The Portuguese lacked the naval or military power to defend their far-scattered ports and colonies, retaining them in the past three centuries largely through British aid. If these overseas possessions of Portugal had passed to a first-class power they might have proved a danger to nearby British holdings; so the British were satisfied to leave them in Portuguese control because this helped to assure Portuguese neutrality. The Anglo-Portuguese friendship was of old standing, for it dated from the mid-seventeenth century when the English helped the Portuguese to separate from Spain (1640–1658) and to establish themselves as an independent kingdom once again. In 1703 a closer alliance was negotiated between the two kingdoms, strengthened by a tariff agreement (Methuen Treaty) which opened Portugal to British woolen goods in return for a reduction of the duty on Portuguese wines entering England. To the British the use of the Portuguese harbors in peace and in war offered important advantages.

Like Spain, modern Portugal suffered from misgovernment, administrative inefficiency, impoverishment, and illiteracy. Civil war rent the country from 1828 to 1834 and disorders and ministerial crises punctuated the next twenty years. The reigns of Peter V (1853–1861) and Louis I (1861–1889) proved calmer, but under Carlos I (1889–1908) discontent increased until he was assassinated in 1908. He was succeeded by his equally extravagant son Manoel II (1908–1910). In 1910 a revolution dethroned Manoel and substituted a republican regime.

The new republic found itself beset with economic problems. The Portuguese had failed to share in or to benefit greatly from the economic advances that transformed most of the Western European countries in the later nineteenth century. Although the republican government sought to stabilize the finances the new currency it introduced steadily depreciated. Strikes and labor troubles reduced output, but World War I helped Portugal financially as it did Spain. Wartime demands, and loans from Britain, aided the government at Lisbon, and in 1916 Portugal entered the war against Germany. As a reward the Portuguese received a minor portion of German territory in Africa and a small share of German reparation payments. But the republican regime established in 1910 proved increasingly corrupt and inefficient and was finally overthrown by a military revolt in 1926. Two years later a professor of economics, Antonio de Oliveira Salazar, became minister of finance in the bankrupt and tottering republican government. By firm financial policies he succeeded in balancing the budget and strengthened the government until it became a veiled dictatorship. A soldier, General Antonio Oscar de Fragoso Carmona, acted as president (1928–1951), but the "strong man" of the regime was the quiet disciplinarian, Salazar. His authoritarian rule brought Portuguese workers greater security but they were forbidden to strike and their incomes remained among the lowest in Europe.

3. THE NETHERLANDS AND BELGIUM

The peoples and provinces which now form Belgium and the Dutch Netherlands came very close, historically, to merging into a great power. In the fifteenth century the House of Burgundy controlled most of the area between the crystallizing kingdom of France and the long disunified Germanies, but the attempt of Charles the Bold (1467–1477) to make himself king of this middle and disputed area failed with his death. The Netherlands passed by marriage to the Spanish Hapsburgs and were ruled from Madrid until they revolted against Philip II. The seven northern provinces — Holland, Zeeland, Utrecht, Gelderland, Groningen, Friesland, and Overyssel — proclaimed their independence of Spain in 1581 and became a prosperous sovereign state, but the southern and western provinces submitted to Spain and became the Spanish (and after 1713) the Austrian Netherlands. In 1815 the Congress of Vienna united both sections as the Kingdom of the Netherlands but the Belgians broke away in 1831 and were recognized as a separate kingdom by the powers in 1839.

Had the Kingdom of the United Netherlands remained a unit it might almost have ranked as a great power by the opening of the twentieth century. Although the combined population was still moderately small — about 12,000,000 in 1900 — and the area limited (Netherlands, 12,712 square miles; Belgium, 11,775), the wealth, industry, and colonial possessions of these two states were impressive. The Netherlands overseas empire included a population six times and an area sixty times those of Holland itself. Belgium likewise ruled territories in other continents, chiefly in Africa, with a population double and an area eighty times those of the home state. The density of population in Holland and Belgium, especially in Belgium, was almost the highest in Europe, and the standards of living and per capita wealth were likewise high.

The Netherlanders, after repudiating the rule of Philip II of Spain in 1581, established a republican federation, and the Netherlands did not become a monarchy until 1815. In the century that followed (1815–1914) the population tripled, rising from two to six million. The good fortune of the Dutch in avoiding wars and any serious internal disturbances throughout this century increased their prosperity. They expanded the area of their homeland by constructing new dikes to hold back the North Sea. They increased their agricultural output by scientific farming and their foreign trade by shrewd business methods. Although their overseas empire had shrunk (they lost the Cape of Good Hope and Ceylon to Britain during the Napoleonic Wars) they extended their control of the Netherlands East Indies and drew a large income from the mines, forests, and plantations there.

The spread of democracy in Europe during the nineteenth century brought slow and gradual changes in the Netherlands. William I (1815–1840) guarded his royal authority jealously, but William II (1840–1849) granted a more liberal constitution. After 1848 the ministers became responsible to parliament (States General) the lower chamber of which was chosen by a limited electorate. Later reforms extended the suffrage until by 1917 almost all citizens had the right to vote. William III (1849–1890) was followed by his daughter Wilhelmina whose long reign lasted from 1890 to 1948. As the Grand Duchy of Luxemburg, which had been attached to the Kingdom of the Netherlands in 1815, could not be ruled by a woman, it became independent with its neutrality guaranteed by the great powers.

The Belgians differed from the Dutch in several significant respects. Approximately half of them spoke Walloon, a French dialect; the other half spoke Flemish, a low German dialect akin to Dutch. Almost the entire Belgian population remained Roman Catholic, whereas in the Netherlands the Protestants outnumbered the Catholics. The two states also differed in their economic development: Belgium became one of the most highly industrialized regions of Europe while the Netherlands maintained a more equal balance between industry and agriculture. The Belgian population, like the Dutch, increased rapidly in the nineteenth century, rising from three million in 1800 to nearly eight million in 1914. In politics the Belgians gained responsible government more rapidly than the Dutch, enjoyed a higher average income, and a more equal distribution of wealth.

4. SWITZERLAND

Switzerland differs from the Netherlands and Belgium in that it has no sea coast and no colonies. Nevertheless the Swiss succeeded in achieving a remarkable degree of prosperity, based upon their intelligent use of local resources and the expansion of their industries and trade. Circumspect in diplomacy, vigilant in defense, self-respecting and industrious, they entered the twentieth century with a hundred years of peaceful development behind them. The factors that strengthened the bonds of cohesion in most national states were absent in Switzerland, for it did not have the unity of language, uniformity of custom, and centralized administration that distinguished most European countries. Its twenty-two cantons were twenty-two sovereign units, joined voluntarily by a loose federal tie. The population of Switzerland rose from less than two million in 1800 to nearly four million in 1914. Slightly more than half the inhabitants professed the Protestant faith, slightly less than half were Roman Catholic. There was no single or official language, for a majority of the inhabitants in sixteen cantons spoke German; in five French was the accepted tongue; in one, Italian; and a small minority spoke a dialect known as Romansh. Yet despite these disparate influences and local liberties, the Swiss communities maintained a singular firmness and unanimity in preserving their federation. The mountain barriers which divided the cantons from one another also helped to preserve Switzerland from attack by its four great neighbors, Germany, France, Austria, and Italy. That Geneva was chosen as headquarters by the convention which founded the international Red Cross movement in 1863, and that it became the seat of the League of Nations after 1919, was a tribute to the strict neutrality and broad outlook the Swiss preserved in world affairs.

The liberty-loving Swiss preserved their republican institutions after 1815 when republics were out of fashion in Europe. But they found it advisable, after a brief civil war in 1847, to remodel their government by partly imitating that of the United States. Each of the cantons sent two delegates to a federal council or chamber (corresponding to the American Senate) while members of the co-equal national council (or House of Representatives) were elected by popular suffrage. But the Swiss did not elect a president in the American fashion. They entrusted the executive authority to a council of seven, chosen by the legislators of the two houses, and the chairman of this council acted as chief of state and minister for foreign affairs. In 1874 a revision of the constitution set up a Federal Supreme Court, and after 1898 a federal code of law was gradually worked out. These moves tended to increase the power of the central government but each canton retained a large measure of control over its local affairs.

5. THE SCANDINAVIAN COUNTRIES

Denmark, Norway, and Sweden represent another grouping of states which have been closely linked in the past. Had historical trends permitted, the three might today form one unified and powerful state. The crowns of Denmark and Norway were united from 1381 to 1814. Sweden in the seventeenth century almost established a Scandinavian hegemony. But the eighteenth and nineteenth centuries brought political divergence and national autonomy instead of cohesion among these three neighbors. The Norwegian kingdom, detached from Denmark and joined to Sweden in 1814, seceded in 1905. All three, while developing representative institutions and adopting democratic reforms, remained constitutional monarchies. Sweden, the most highly industrialized, produced 7.4 per cent of the world's iron ore in 1913 and took an early lead in developing the great resources of hydroelectric power. Norway, though likewise favored with abundant waterfalls for such power, remained industrially undeveloped, partly because the energies of the people were engaged on the sea, where the tonnage of their shipping ranked fifth in 1914 among the merchant marines of the world. Sea fishing was also an important occupation and source of gain; the Norwegian catch of cod and herring placed the nation eighth among the world's powers in marketing this commodity before 1914. But Norwegian shipping and fishing suffered heavily during the years of blockade from 1914 to 1918.

Denmark, the only one of the three kingdoms which claimed any considerable territory overseas, retained title to Iceland and Greenland and to the Virgin Islands in the West Indies. The last named were sold to the United States in 1917 for $25,000,000; and the protection of Iceland and Greenland rested in reality with the British or the American navy. For Denmark had no navy equal to the task of protecting its empire or its merchant shipping. Its area, 16,575 square miles, made it much the smallest of the three states. As a flat peninsula and islands, lacking mountains and waterfalls, large forests, or great mineral wealth, it could not match the metallurgical industry of Sweden or the lumber trade of Norway. In compensation, the Danes produced an abundance of farm and dairy commodities which found a market in Germany and England in normal times.

The high level of culture and education maintained in Norway, Denmark, and Sweden gave these nations an influence out of proportion to their numbers in the literary, artistic, and musical developments of the nineteenth and twentieth centuries. The sculptor, Albert Bertel Thorwaldsen (1770–1844), the literary critic, Georg Brandes (1842–1927), and the writer, Hans Christian Andersen (1805–1875), were Danes. The composer, Edvard Grieg (1843–1907), the dramatist, Henrik Ibsen (1828–1906), and the novelist, Sigrid Undset (1882–1949), were born in Norway; and the dramatist August Strindberg (1849–1912) and the engineer and philanthropist Alfred Nobel (1833–1896) were Swedish.

6. THE BALKAN STATES

The Balkan states emerged in the nineteenth century out of the decaying body of the Ottoman Empire. The expansion of the Ottoman Empire into Europe in the fourteenth and fifteenth centuries (see pages 97–99) had isolated the Balkan peoples — the Greeks, Bulgars, Serbs, Albanians, and Rumanians — from Christian Europe and attached them to the Moslem Near East. Five hundred years of Turkish rule, however, failed either to Turkify or (with the exception of the Albanians, some Serbs in Bosnia, and a scattering of Bulgars) to Moslemize them. The Greek Orthodox Church, to which the overwhelming majority of the Balkan peoples remained faithful, kept alive in them a sense of a destiny separate from that of the Moslem peoples of the Near East. At the end of the eighteenth century and the beginning of the nineteenth, under the influence of the ideas of the French Revolution, the Balkan peoples awakened to a modern sense of nationality. The extremely unenlightened and oppressive Turkish rule stirred in them a deep longing for freedom. During the course of the nineteenth century one by one they rose to shake off the Turkish yoke.

There were altogether five stages in the struggle of the Balkan peoples for emancipation from Turkish rule. The first four were connected with the four Russo-Turkish wars of the nineteenth century (1806–1812, 1828–1829, 1853–1856, 1877–1878). The fifth one was represented by the Balkan Wars (1912–1913). The rise of the Balkan states was inextricably linked with the various phases of the Near Eastern Question in the nineteenth century. The uprisings of the subject peoples of the Ottoman Empire and the harsh Turkish attempts to suppress them invariably resulted in great-power intervention in the Balkan imbroglio.

The Austrian Empire, which in the eighteenth century had led the way in expelling the Turks from Europe, stood pointedly aloof from the struggle for freedom waged by the Balkan peoples in the nineteenth century. Prince Metternich, Austrian minister for foreign affairs from 1809 to 1848, a native of western Germany rather than of Austria, took little interest in the traditional Austrian Eastern policy. Moreover, he primly disapproved of all revolutions, for he was respectful of the divine rights of monarchs, even those of the Moslem Sultan and Caliph. "It matters not much," he wrote after the outbreak of the Greek War of Independence, "if over there beyond our frontiers three or four hundred thousand people get hung, strangled, and impaled." This Austrian indifference to the Near Eastern Question in the nineteenth century left the field free to Russia.

The liberation of the Balkan peoples was incidental to the main purpose of Russia in the Balkans, which was to secure control of Constantinople and the Straits. Russia failed to attain this objective because of the hostility of Britain and France, which feared Russian expansion into the Mediterranean. But the Russo-Turkish wars loosened the Turkish bonds on the Balkan peoples and facilitated their liberation. Moreover, even though France and Britain long opposed the dismemberment of the Ottoman Empire, they too, on occasion, assisted the Balkan peoples in their emancipation, in response to prodding of liberal opinion at home or to offset Russian intervention in Ottoman internal affairs. While it was the Balkan peoples themselves who took the initiative to attain freedom, this would have been long delayed, if not impossible, without the help of the great powers.

The first Russo-Turkish war of the nineteenth century (1806–1812) was of great assistance to the Serbs who were the first Balkan people to rise against the Turkish rule. In 1804, amidst the Napoleonic wars, a Serbian leader, Kara (Black) George, raised the banner of revolt, and thanks to the preoccupation of the Turks with the war with Russia he almost succeeded in establishing Serbian independence. But the imminence of the Napoleonic invasion of Russia in 1812 forced the Russians to withdraw abruptly from the war. In spite of a promise of clemency for the Serbian insurgents, extorted by the Russians in the Peace of Bucharest (1812), the Turks drowned the Serbian revolt in blood.

In 1815 another Serbian leader, Miloš Obrenović, led a more successful revolt. The Napoleonic wars were by then over, and Russia was free to remind the Sultan of his forgotten promises made in the Treaty of Bucharest. The Turks found it expedient to appease the rebellious Serbs with a grant of autonomy and recognition of Miloš Obrenović as hereditary Prince of Serbia (1817). A tragedy, however, marred this success. When Kara George returned from Austrian exile to take part in the second revolt he was murdered by partisans of Miloš Obrenović. Thus began the famous blood feud between the Karageorgević and Obrenović dynasties, which alternated on the Serbian throne, supported now by Russia and now by Austria, until the final extermination of the Obrenović family and establishment of Russian influence in Serbia in 1903.

The second Russo-Turkish war of the century (1828–1829) resulted in international recognition of Greek, Serb, and Rumanian autonomy. In 1821 the Greeks raised the banner of revolt. Enthusiastic liberals throughout Europe and America greeted with admiration the war for freedom of the modern Hellenes. The death of the romantic English poet, Lord Byron, while assisting the Greek insurgents, set a seal of romantic approbation on their cause. A century ago, when all educated people had been grounded in classical history, the Greek rebels wore the guise of Athenians defying the might of Persia. In 1827, prodded by enthusiastic "Philhellenes," Britain, France, and Russia carried out a naval demonstration in behalf of the Greek cause. It resulted in an accidental battle in the bay of Navarino and the destruction of the Turkish fleet. In the following year Russia declared war on Turkey, and a French force, with British approval, cleared the Turks from the Peloponnese. In the Peace of Adrianople (1829) Russia extorted from the Turks recognition of the autonomy of Greece, Serbia, and the "Danubian Principalities" of Wallachia and Moldavia inhabited by the Rumanians. Fearing lest autonomous Greece become dependent on Russia, the British moved to secure complete independence for it (Protocol of London, 1830).

The newborn state, inspired by classical tradition, chose at first the republican form of government. In the Age of Metternich, however, republics were frowned upon, and Greece soon discarded the republic for a monarchy. As the first "King of the Hellenes," the great powers chose and Greece accepted a youthful and romantic Philhellene, the Bavarian Prince Otto of Wittelsbach (1832–1862). The grant of independence, however, did not solve the Greek problem, for the new kingdom included less than half the Greek people. The majority of them still remained in Turkish bondage. The agitation of Greece in behalf of these "unredeemed" brethren continued to add fuel to the Near Eastern Question.

The third Russo-Turkish war of the century, the Crimean War (1853–1856), resulted, through Franco-British intervention, in the defeat of Russia. The Balkan peoples, nevertheless, profited from the war. In the

Peace of Paris (1856) the powers placed the subject peoples of the Ottoman Empire under their joint protection. In 1859, with the encouragement of Napoleon III and the grudging consent of the other powers and of Turkey, Wallachia and Moldavia were united into a single state called Rumania. By threatening the Turks with an appeal to the powers, the Serbs were able to induce the Turks to evacuate their last garrisons from Serbia by 1867.

The fourth and final Russo-Turkish war of the century (1877–1878) resulted in the liberation of the Bulgars. In 1875 a revolt broke out in the provinces of Bosnia and Herzegovina which spread in the following year to Bulgaria. Russian intervention duly followed, and in the Peace of San Stefano (March 3, 1878) Russia obtained the creation of a large autonomous Bulgarian principality. It comprised not only present-day Bulgaria but also Thrace and Macedonia. Little of the Ottoman Empire in Europe remained except Constantinople, the Straits area, and Albania. Alarmed lest the large Bulgarian principality become an advance post of Russian expansion toward the Mediterranean, Britain and Austria protested. Under the threat of war, they induced Russia to submit the question to the judgment of the Concert of Europe at the Congress of Berlin (June–July, 1878).

Unfortunately, at the Congress of Berlin the powers were less concerned with obtaining a just and durable solution to the Near Eastern Question than with their own immediate and very narrowly conceived interests. With complete indifference to the wishes of the peoples whose fate they decided, the powers used Ottoman territory simply as small change in the game of compensations — a corollary of the balance of power. Since Russia had advanced in Bessarabia and the Caucasus, Austria demanded and obtained "compensation" in Bosnia-Herzegovina, Britain in Cyprus, and France in Tunisia. Only Bismarck refrained from demanding compensation for Germany, observing wisely that the "whole of the Balkans was not worth the bones of a single Pomeranian grenadier." Unfortunately, his successors were not so wise. By the end of the century Germany was deeply involved in the Near Eastern Question, vying with other powers to obtain concessions, and dreaming of building a railroad which would link up the Middle East to Middle Europe, from the North Sea to the Persian Gulf.

As for Bulgaria, the Peace of Berlin (July 13, 1878) provided for the return of Macedonia and Thrace to Turkish rule (or misrule). The rest of Bulgaria was divided into two units, Bulgaria proper and Eastern Rumelia, both to be nominally tributary principalities of the Ottoman Empire but actually to be Russian protectorates. In 1885, when the two principalities united despite Russian opposition, Russian influence in Bulgaria collapsed. Paradoxically, Russia, which had done so much to create Bulgaria, then became its most bitter enemy. Austria and Britain, on the other hand, which had done their best to prevent the creation of

Bulgaria, then came forth as its great and gracious friends. In 1908, amidst the confusion attending the Young Turk Revolution, Bulgaria repudiated its last formal ties to Turkey and affirmed its complete independence.

The independence of Rumania, Serbia, and Montenegro had been recognized in the Treaty of Berlin. This, however, changed little in their actual status. They had most of the trappings of independence before, and did not gain its substance afterwards. They remained satellites of the great powers, which played them off against each other and exploited them for their own ends. In this unsavory game the great powers were aided by the many irredentas created — sometimes deliberately — by the Treaty of Berlin. There were still large numbers of Bulgars, Serbs, and Greeks under Turkish rule. Macedonia, which contained fragments of every Balkan nationality, was the worst trouble spot. But Bosnia and Dobrudja were scarcely less irksome. The agitation of the Balkan peoples in behalf of their "unredeemed" brethren and the meddling of the great powers in the situation created dangerous threats not only to the peace of the Balkans but of Europe generally.

In 1912 Greece, Bulgaria, Serbia, and Montenegro, in defiance of a solemn warning from the great powers, declared war on Turkey in an effort to liberate their "unredeemed" kinsmen from the Turkish yoke. To the general surprise and the great discomfiture of Germany and Austria, which had backed Turkey, the Balkan allies speedily defeated the Turks and drove them out of Europe (with the exception of Constantinople and the Straits area). Great-power relations were at this point too strained to permit united action against the Balkan states. In spite of their earlier warning, the great powers acquiesced in the new situation, and contented themselves with arbitrating the territorial claims of the Balkan states. At the peace conference in London, Austria and Italy, which were determined to block Serbia and Montenegro from gaining access to the Adriatic Sea, persuaded the great powers to create a new Balkan state: Albania. Serbia then demanded "compensation" in Macedonia. This greatly offended Bulgaria, which had hoped to recover the frontiers of the Peace of San Stefano. In the end the great powers imposed a compromise solution, which left everyone dissatisfied.

Within a month of the conclusion of the Peace of London (May 30, 1913), ending the First Balkan War, Bulgaria attacked Serbia and Greece, provoking the Second Balkan War. In this conflict Serbia, Greece, Montenegro, Rumania, and Turkey joined and speedily defeated Bulgaria. On August 10, 1913, the Balkan states concluded the Peace of Bucharest — this time without the dubious benefit of great-power ministrations. Bulgaria was deprived of much territory. Surprisingly, the settlement proved durable. With the exception of minor rectifications of Bulgarian borders in 1919 — to the further detriment of Bulgaria — the inter-Balkan frontiers have remained stable ever since.

The Balkan Wars of 1912–1913 completed the emancipation of the Balkan peoples from Turkish rule and reintegrated them into Europe. They remained, however, poor and retarded. The Albanians, the last liberated and most primitive of the Balkan peoples, had not gone beyond the tribal stage in their socio-economic development. Economically, the Balkan countries were agrarian nations, virtually without modern industry. Socially, they were mainly peasant nations. Peasant proprietorship of the land prevailed everywhere except in Rumania where it was owned by a rich and irresponsible nobility. Only Greece had a substantial merchant class.

Politically, the Balkan states were, in theory at least, constitutional monarchies — as was then the fashion in Europe. Eventually, all the Balkan principalities promoted themselves to the dignity of kingdoms. With the exception of Serbia and Montenegro, they were all ruled by foreign dynasties: the Hohenzollern-Sigmaringen dynasty (German) in Rumania, the Saxe-Coburg (German) in Bulgaria, and the Holstein-Glucksburg (Danish) in Greece (after 1863). Without roots in their adopted countries, these foreign monarchs were ill-prepared to rule their turbulent subjects. In practice the Balkan states were crude dictatorships, run sometimes by the monarchs themselves but more often by powerful ministers. Their long association with the Near East left them with a heritage of low and brutal standards. Murder of political opponents, crude intrigue, and unashamed bribery were standard political practices. The Balkans needed a long period of peace and stability to catch up to Europe in their development. But this they were not to gain soon.

The liberation of the Balkan peoples from Turkish rule did not complete their emancipation; there remained Balkan peoples under Austrian rule. Summing up the results of the Balkan Wars, the Serbian Prime Minister, Nikola Pašić, indicated the future course of events: "The first round is won, and now for the second round — against Austria."

11

NEWCOMERS ON THE WORLD STAGE

Until a few decades ago it was believed that European civilization was the monopoly of its owner, or at most, that a few purely technical externals might be copied by others.[1]

1. THE UNITED STATES

THROUGHOUT THE NINETEENTH CENTURY the supremacy of Europe and its dominant position in the world appeared self-evident to most Europeans. They were disposed to attribute their leadership to some innate and peculiar virtue they alone possessed. "Only a few nations, and those of European origin, advance," Walter Bagehot wrote in 1872. The probability that the offspring, the overseas colonies founded by European nations, might in time become more powerful than their motherlands, failed to impress itself upon the Europeans. The possibility that non-European peoples might adopt European weapons and techniques and become a threat to European domination likewise seemed to them an eventuality too improbable to merit serious concern. Yet by the close of the nineteenth century there was convincing evidence available that the supremacy of Europe would be challenged and perhaps overthrown in the twentieth century. This chapter will discuss the rapid rise of new powers, *outside* Europe, that appeared on the world stage so swiftly their rise took the complacent European nations by surprise. Of these new powers the most successful and dynamic was the United States of America.

Nowhere in history is there a story of nation-building so remarkable as the epic of the United States. For a handful of colonists to invade a continent, expand their dominion, and increase their number until in three and a half centuries they formed a united nation of one hundred and eighty million is an unparalleled achievement. These transplanted Europeans carried overseas the forms of an ancient culture, adapted historic ideals and techniques to the problems of a novel environment,

[1] *The Rape of Europe*, Luis Díez del Corral (New York: The Macmillan Company, 1959), p. 299.

117

improvised as the need arose new formulas, new tactics, new devices. At times they experimented audaciously. They dared, for example, to adopt a republican form of government, to set up a democratic regime of a type never previously maintained with success in a broad and expanding empire. They not only "brought forth on this continent a new nation," they so governed and developed the nation that it became a leading world power, while its citizens acquired a greater measure of political liberty and material welfare than any other empire of equal size had ever conferred upon so many millions of men.

It is estimated that 50,000,000 emigrants left Europe between 1815 and 1914, and that three-fourths were attracted to the United States. To land-hungry farmers the chance to acquire their own farms was an irresistible lure. To political refugees the New World offered a haven. To the ambitious, the myriad opportunities, the system of free enterprise, the rewards awaiting men with vision made the United States the "Land of Promise." But for native-born Americans above all others the mystery and magnificence of that half-void continent waiting to be conquered formed a perpetual heritage and challenge.

The result was that saga of westward expansion which is the most distinctive theme of American history. The republic was the achievement of pioneers. In the century and a half from the founding of Plymouth to the War of Independence the English colonists conquered the wilderness at a rate of ten square miles a day. After 1783 the young United States, born with a giant's energy and a giant's appetite, expanded its frontiers for the next hundred and fifty years at the rate of fifty square miles a day. Its restless sons were forever on the move, forever heading into uncharted areas, inventing new tactics, testing new techniques, raising a cabin in the clearing or a trading post by the stream, only to abandon them abruptly and move on when other settlers followed on their heels. They learned skills as they needed them, trail making, trapping, hunting, and planting. They built log houses in the woodlands and sod houses on the plains. They followed the ruts of the covered wagons to Oregon and California. They knew the epic of portage and prairie camp and mountain pass. Then at a critical turning point the railway arrived, bringing a revolution in land transport. Ten thousand settlements lost in the immensity of the great central plains were linked by the magic rails, and soon the silver filaments threaded the mazes of the Rocky Mountains to guide a host of pioneers to the Pacific shores.

Then, in a generation (1890–1910), the frontier passed. Its boisterous influence, which had dominated the rise of American democracy and inspired the virile, self-confident, and often lawless individuality of the range, was curbed by newer forces. With the opening of the twentieth century the United States entered a more disciplined era. Agriculture, which had been the primary source of income hitherto, yielded place to industry and commerce. Urban population overtook and finally surpassed

THE SHIFT FROM AGRICULTURE TO OTHER OCCUPATIONS

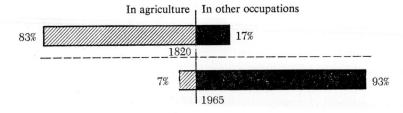

In agriculture | In other occupations

83%   17%

1820

7%   93%

1965

the total of the rural districts. The millions of arriving immigrants, who had poured out onto the farm lands while the richer areas were still unclaimed and unworked, tended after 1900 to settle in the cities, seeking employment in factories, in construction work, in the mining and metallurgical trades. These changes came so swiftly that they created a number of problems which had been unprovided for because few of them had been foreseen.

The crisis caused by this readjustment, the methods adopted to meet this rapid industrialization and urbanization, wove new patterns of American life. After 1900 the citizens of the United States found themselves facing several problems which most European peoples had been coping with for generations. Of these problems the most significant formed the triad already met in earlier chapters: the problem of resources, the problem of defense, and the problem of social justice. Before the twentieth century the favorable conditions in the New World had made these problems much less acute for Americans than they had long proved for Europeans.

In the march of progress modern America left behind much that was lovable and picturesque — the little red schoolhouse, the old oaken bucket, the open fireplace, the village blacksmith, hay rides and sleigh rides, the old gray mare, and the old swimming hole. As substitutes, America acquired brick schools a block in area, hot and cold running water, central heating, train, bus, and automobile transportation, chain stores, telephones, motion pictures, and radios. Even farming, the most ancient craft, was transformed by machinery for ploughing, reaping, threshing, milling, milking, cotton picking. The total effect was a wider diffusion of education, improvements in hygiene and public health, more comfortable standards of living, and an extraordinary reduction in physical toil.

The continental United States contained regions of rich soil, a varied topography, a rainfall that was adequate and dependable over extensive areas, and climatic zones that ranged from severe through temperate to semitropical conditions. These natural advantages enabled the American people to cultivate within their own borders almost all the commodities required for an abundant and variegated diet. The average American commanded ten times the food supply of the average Asian, and his food was not only more plentiful but better balanced and more palatable.

The natural wealth of the New World seemed so inexhaustible that the American people were overreckless in exploiting it. Never in history was a continent plundered so impetuously. By the end of the nineteenth century some of the penalties of waste and wanton destruction were already apparent. In 1871 a Commissioner of Fisheries was appointed to save the coastal fishing grounds from exhaustion. Twenty years later the Department of Agriculture moved to create a national forest reserve, before lumbering, land clearance, and bush fires should destroy the forests beyond recovery. By 1900 the federal government had accepted the grave responsibility of calculating the nation's reserves and resources and measuring them against its future needs. Plans for a national survey, for a national reclamation service, and for the preservation of essential resources in the public domain were pressed by farsighted legislators who recognized the wastefulness of unregulated exploitation.

Because exhausting wars, except for the War between the States, were spared Americans until the twentieth century, they could afford the luxury of an unobtrusive government. They could dispense with military conscription and allot to education the funds which less isolated nations dedicated to defense. Largely for this reason their laws were less exigent, their taxes remained lower, their personal liberty was greater, and their freedom flowered in a manner that European countries could not equal. Furthermore, because the resources of the new land seemed more than adequate for the needs of the young nation, there was no good reason to fear an unfavorable trade balance, no need to mortgage the future by asking for too much foreign aid, monetary, military, or technical. American sovereignty was more nearly absolute and unhampered than that of any other important nation. This wide independence and relative immunity to foreign interference was important. It provided the living space and the atmosphere in which the democracy of the New World developed.

American democracy could be threatened, however, by internal as well as by external developments. As the nineteenth century advanced a new aristocracy, an aristocracy of money, rose to leadership in the business world and dominated American society. In the era of business expansion which followed the War between the States, the conflicting demands of capital and labor, which had already split European classes asunder, became a lively issue in politics. Popular orators argued that the rise of vast personal fortunes, the exercise of monopolies, and the creation of business trusts and corporations would concentrate too much power in the hands of a small ruling group, a plutocracy. Equality of economic opportunity, a foundation stone of American democracy, appeared to be threatened by such concentration of wealth. The question thus arose whether it was not the duty of Congress to prevent by positive legislation undue accumulation of economic power by small private groups.

POPULATION GROWTH OF THE UNITED STATES, 1790-1960

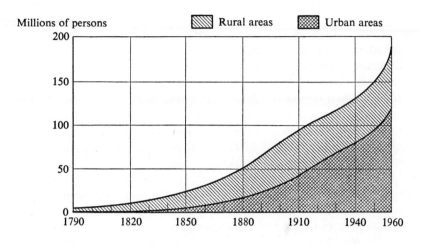

The first important legislative attempts to limit the power of "big business" were the Interstate Commerce Act (1887) which sought to bring the railways under federal control, and the Sherman Antitrust Act (1890) which declared contracts, combinations, and trusts illegal if they could be shown to be conspiracies in restraint of trade. The enforcement of these Acts depended upon the courts, and as they were called in question by many adverse court decisions the efforts to limit or dissolve the trusts were only partly effective. A supplement to the Sherman Act, known as the Clayton Antitrust Act, was adopted in 1914. It was designed to restrict still more specifically the practice of price discrimination, to forbid exclusive business agreements which violated the principle of free competition, and to hinder the formation of too many interlocking directorates, a device whereby the real control of several corporations might be held by a few key men.

2. AMERICAN FOREIGN AFFAIRS

The expansion of American economic life in the last decades of the nineteenth century, especially the growth of industry, enabled the United States to overtake Great Britain and Germany and to become the greatest economic power in the world. But nine-tenths of American production was absorbed by the home market, where more than a hundred million consumers with the highest living standard in the world constituted a coast to coast market. This relative self-sufficiency of the United States partially obscured its growing strength. Many Americans, because they were self-centered and preoccupied with local problems, failed to foresee the important role which their country would soon be called upon to play in world affairs. Only after the surge of frontier expansion and settlement had dwindled did the people of the United States turn their gaze across the oceans. They were surprised to discover that by then they had already acquired commitments in other continents.

Until the twentieth century the United States had suffered little from the wars in Europe, Asia, or Africa. As the dominant power of the New World and guardian of the Americas, it was satisfied to warn all foreign nations not to interfere aggressively in the affairs of the Latin American republics. In 1889 it sought to establish its responsibilities for the defense of this hemisphere more definitely, and formed plans for a permanent league of all the American republics. Since the United States could not fail to exercise preponderance in such an association, the proposal did not thrive. The Argentine Republic in particular was opposed to it, resisting the plans for a common code of international law for the Americas, a coordination of Pan-American highways and railways, and the integration of currency and customs rates. But although the move for a genuine Pan-American league failed at this time, it had one positive result. A diplomatic council was established, pledged to meet from time to time for the discussion of common hemisphere problems. With this tentative measure of consolidation the friends of Pan-American solidarity had temporarily to rest content. In fact, for a decade and more inter-American relations deteriorated. The activity of United States forces in the Caribbean, the Spanish-American War of 1898, and the energetic acquisition of the Canal Zone at Panama alienated and alarmed many Latin Americans, who looked with apprehension at the exuberant power of the "Colossus of the North."

A further indication that the United States had taken the road to expansion in the late nineteenth century was the annexation (1898) of the Hawaiian Islands. Three years earlier the United States had intervened in a dispute between Great Britain and Venezuela and checked British designs against this South American state by insisting upon arbitration. But if the United States was to defend the Latin American republics and extend its protection to islands in the mid-Pacific, a strong navy was essential. Ardent patriots and expansionists therefore urged Congress to vote an ambitious program of naval construction to support the more active role that the United States was expected to play in world politics. The outbreak of a revolt in Cuba (1895), which was repressed with great severity by the Spanish authorities there, roused sympathy for the insurgents. In 1898 the unsettled Cuban question led to a war between the United States and Spain. This brief conflict ended the same year in a swift and signal defeat for the Spanish forces. A United States fleet destroyed the Spanish squadron at Manila Bay in the Philippines without the loss of a single American life. A few weeks later a second Spanish squadron was destroyed in Cuban waters. Peace was concluded in August, 1898, Spain ceding to the United States the Philippines, Puerto Rico, and Guam. For the Cubans the war brought independence from Spanish rule, and the United States assumed responsibility for the protection of Cuban liberty by the Platt Amendment (1901) which was incorporated in the Cuban constitution.

The Spanish-American War proclaimed to the world that the United States had become a naval power, with responsibilities which only a great naval power could successfully fulfill. The maintenance of advanced bases in the Pacific, the protection of the Central and South American coasts, and the patrolling of Alaskan waters called for an expanded naval policy. Commitments so far flung could be met only by dividing the American fleet and stationing part in Atlantic, part in Pacific waters. The long voyage around Cape Horn made it difficult to reinforce the reserves in either ocean, and if an emergency arose one section of the fleet might be shattered before the other could arrive to support it. The surest way to strengthen American naval defense was to link the east and west coast bases by a waterway that would accommodate battleships and this meant the construction of an interoceanic canal across the Isthmus of Panama.

In the 1880's a French company had undertaken to build a Panama Canal, but the venture collapsed in scandal and bankruptcy. The Suez Canal, which linked the Mediterranean to the Red Sea in 1869, had been financed by an international syndicate, but the United States could not remain indifferent if foreign governments built a canal across Panama or Nicaragua. Theodore Roosevelt, who became President of the United States in 1901 when President McKinley was assassinated, personified the new, confident, expansionist mood stirring the American people. He was not a man to delay in a matter of importance, nor was he easily daunted by technical, diplomatic, or financial obstacles. When the Republic of Colombia negotiated, and then failed to ratify, an agreement authorizing the United States government to construct a canal at Panama, the project was threatened with indefinite delay. But a convenient revolt broke out in Panama province and Panama seceded from the Republic of Colombia (1903). The State Department at Washington promptly recognized the *de facto* government, which in return immediately ratified the desired canal concession. An accord had already been reached between the United States and Great Britain in 1901, and the property and privileges of the defunct French company were purchased by the United States in 1902. After years of battle against tropical diseases, landslides, labor problems, and technical difficulties, the canal was completed in 1914.

The people of the United States did not realize, when the twentieth century opened, that their period of isolation was over. They still believed they could avoid entanglement in the conflicts of the Old World and the struggle for spheres of influence in Asia and Africa. In reality, however, they had developed economic connections with Europe through their trade and had acquired an interest in Asian affairs by their conquest of the Philippines. After 1914 the American people learned that their wealth and influence condemned them to play a part in world affairs. They accepted their new international responsibilities reluctantly; they even sought to evade them; but as the twentieth century advanced they found it impossible to return to a policy of isolation.

3. THE BRITISH SELF-GOVERNING DOMINIONS

The phenomenal growth of the United States had its parallels (on a lesser scale) in the growth of the British overseas dominions. In the half-century before 1914, Canada, Australia, New Zealand, and South Africa acquired the right of self-government but remained a part of the British Empire. Within that period of fifty years (1864–1914) the total white population of these four British colonies quadrupled, rising from four to sixteen million. For comparison, one may note that between 1864 and 1914 the population of Great Britain rose much more slowly, from some twenty-four to forty million. This difference in the rate of population growth was profoundly significant for the future of Great Britain and of Europe. If maintained, it meant that sometime in the second half of the twentieth century the combined (white) population in the British dominions would come to exceed that of Great Britain itself.

That the dominions would continue to grow in wealth and population appeared almost certain for all of them possessed great natural resources. Their total area exceeded seven million square miles, more than eighty times the area of Great Britain. All of them had extensive areas available for farming or grazing, untapped mineral resources, rivers capable of generating hydroelectric power, and natural ports and harbors to facilitate ocean trade. The opportunities they offered attracted immigrants who helped to expand their population and develop their economy, and their future appeared to offer prospects of rapid and uninterrupted growth.

On closer examination, however, each of the four dominions — Canada, Australia, New Zealand, and South Africa — could be seen to possess problems and limitations peculiar to itself. None enjoyed in equal measure the exceptional combination of advantages that had hastened the rise of the United States to the position of a great power. This fact soon becomes apparent when the four dominions are considered individually.

French Canada did not come under English control until the Seven Years' War (1756–1763). Although English-speaking immigrants and their descendants came in time to outnumber the French *Canadiens*, the population remained divided into two main streams, with the French and

English languages enjoying legal equality. The French Canadians also preserved their Catholic faith, whereas a majority of the English-speaking inhabitants were Protestants. Differences in language, religion, character, and tradition tended to hold the two groups apart so that Canada has sometimes been described as one country but two nations.

In its total area (nearly four million square miles) Canada exceeded the United States and its dependencies. Much of this vast dominion, however, had a climate too severe or a surface too rugged for settlement. Above the fiftieth degree of North Latitude a broad belt of coniferous forest stretched from Labrador to British Columbia. Above the sixtieth degree this forest gave way to tundra and mountain flora, and above the Arctic Circle the Canadian coastline bordered the Polar Sea with its frozen islands and frozen wastes. The most habitable area of Canada was the territory that lay within a few hundred miles of the United States border. But the great natural resources of the remainder — minerals, oil, gas, timber — could be exploited and the rivers could provide electric power.

In 1867 the British North America Act, passed by the British Parliament, recognized Canada as a self-governing Dominion. Each province retained control of its local affairs but national problems were to be handled by a Senate, the members of which were appointed, and a House of Commons composed of representatives elected by the people. A governor-general acted as constitutional head of the state and represented the British sovereign, but as in Great Britain a cabinet of ministers responsible to the parliament exercised the essential executive functions. This experiment in colonial self-government worked so satisfactorily that it provided a model for later British colonies as they emerged into nationhood.

Australia, an "island continent" almost three million square miles in area, did not come under British control until the nineteenth century. The first British settlement (a penal colony) was established in 1788, but later free colonists arrived and began to explore the hinterland. Sheep-raising proved easy and profitable, and the discovery of gold about 1850 attracted a fresh stream of immigrants. The native peoples of Australia, few and primitive, offered no serious problem, and by 1900 the white population exceeded three and a half million. In that year the five states or provinces on the mainland, together with the island of Tasmania, united to form the Commonwealth of Australia. Like Canada, this new British Dominion acquired its own responsible government, with a two-chamber legislature and a governor-general who represented the British monarch.

The islands of New Zealand, twelve hundred miles southeast of Australia, did not come under British control until 1840. In area they were only one-thirtieth as large as Australia, but they enjoyed greater natural advantages. Unlike Australia, the interior of which lacks an adequate rainfall and is largely desert, New Zealand enjoys a plentiful rainfall on both its North and South Island. Vegetation is plentiful except on the loftier mountain peaks, numerous rivers provide electric power, and sheepraising, crops, and mineral resources enriched the settlers. For ten years (1854–1864) the hostile Maori tribes resisted the Europeans but were finally conciliated and later received voting rights. In 1907, when the population was approaching one million, New Zealand became the third self-governing Dominion within the British Empire. Its people had already distinguished themselves by adopting farsighted laws on social welfare. Old age pensions were established in 1898 and legislation providing for the care, protection, and education of children followed in 1907.

The Union of South Africa, the fourth self-governing Dominion of the British Empire in 1914, had a more troubled past and a more threatening future than Canada, Australia, or New Zealand. A settlement at Capetown, founded by the Dutch in 1652, passed into British control in 1806. Thirty years later, many of the Dutch farmers (Boers), who were dissatisfied with British rule, moved into the interior (the "Great Trek") where they set up independent communities — the Orange Free State and the Transvaal Republic. The discovery of gold and diamonds in South Africa brought an influx of new colonists after 1886 and strained the relations between the Boers and the British. The Boer War (1899–1902) ended in victory for the British, who attempted to soften the resentment of the Boers by promising them self-government. In 1909 the Cape Colony, Natal, the Orange Free State, and the Transvaal Republic were joined in a federation as the Union of South Africa.

Like Canada, South Africa included the descendants of two distinct European nations. The Boers, who preserved their customs and language (they spoke a form of Dutch known as Afrikaans), equaled in influence the English-speaking colonists. The white population of the Union, which totaled one and one-quarter million in 1909, was outnumbered nearly four to one by the non-whites: the native Africans, Asians, and Coloured (people of mixed blood). As both whites and non-whites increased at approximately the same rate, the whites remained very much in the minority. They were determined, however, to preserve the control of the government in their own hands and to keep the non-whites in a position of social and economic inferiority. This policy was later to meet increasing opposition from the repressed majority (see Chaps. 30, 58, and 66).

4. THE EMERGENCE OF JAPAN

The last of the newcomers on the world stage who will be discussed here were the Japanese. Their rapid development in the second half of the nineteenth century had profound significance, for they were the first *non-European* nation of modern times to rise to the position of a great power. The transformation and modernization of Japan proved that an Asian people could adopt and apply modern Western methods and techniques within a few generations. Asia held more than half the global population. If its millions of people learned to make and use the machines and weapons of the Europeans, they might challenge the European domination of the globe.

Unlike the Chinese, who were reluctant to accept European techniques and machinery, the Japanese deliberately remade their society, adopting Western science and technology and even the form of Western legal, financial, and political institutions. This policy of imitation and adaptation followed the historic visits (1853–1854) of a United States naval expedition under Commodore Matthew Calbraith Perry whereby the Japanese government was persuaded to approve the Treaty of Kanagawa and to open two ports to American trade. Similar treaties with Great Britain, Russia, and the Netherlands followed within three years. A realistic group of Japanese statesmen, recognizing the inevitable, undertook the extraordinary task of remaking a hitherto isolated Oriental state into a modern world power. With the accession of the young and able Emperor Mutsuhito in 1867 the feudal warlords surrendered their power to the Mikado, and the shogun, a sort of prime minister who had been the power behind the throne, resigned. Attempts to seal the ports once more and to expel all foreigners (a policy supported by a powerful section of the people) were abandoned, and Japan began a period of rapid industrialization on the Western plan. The reign of Mutsuhito from 1868 when he established the capital at Tokyo to his death in 1912 is known as the Meiji Period.

The people of Europe were at first skeptical and somewhat amused when they learned how seriously the Japanese were studying Western ways. But the Japanese knew that their existence as an independent nation was at stake. They chose the best models and followed them faithfully: their navy was copied from the British, their army built on Prussian formulas, their constitution combined British and German elements but leaned toward authoritarianism, their schools owed much to American educational plans, their law courts adopted French and German modes of procedure. Specialists in the natural sciences, in architecture and engineering, in mining, manufacturing, shipbuilding, in every field from history to horticulture, were invited to Japan to give instruction, and Japanese students were sent abroad to observe and to learn. While in China seven-eighths of the people remained illiterate, in Japan a system of compulsory education, planned as early as 1872, was expanded until all boys and girls received elementary schooling and the abler students were encouraged to attend high school and college.

The world was first awakened to the astonishing progress made in Japan during the Meiji Period by the outcome of the Russo-Japanese War of 1904–1905. In a sudden attack the Japanese laid siege to Port

Arthur, shutting up the Russian Far Eastern fleet, defeated the Russians in a series of military and naval engagements, and then wisely made peace before the strain of war could exhaust their newly developed strength. Although Japanese patriots believed the war gains inadequate, victory brought control of Korea, where economic exploitation had already prepared the way, and won half of Sakhalin Island; while Manchuria, evacuated by the Russians and restored to China, became a field for later penetration. The island of Formosa (Taiwan), which the Japanese won in a short war with China in 1895, had given them an important base off the coast between Shanghai and Hong Kong; but Korea, which they formally annexed in 1910, gave them a bridgehead on the mainland. Their preparations for the establishment of a New Order in the Orient under Japanese leadership were completed. All they awaited was a favorable moment to expand.

Section II: WORLD WAR I: 1914–1918

12

THE WAR ON LAND AND SEA, 1914–1916

Modern wars in the life of nations are the same things as examinations in civil life, namely proofs of fitness . . . All politics is economic politics, or war pre-paredness.

WALTER RATHENAU

1. THE ALIGNMENT OF POWERS

ON A SUNDAY MORNING, June 28, 1914, in the colorful little town of Sara-jevo in Bosnia, a young Bosnian Serb, Gavrilo Princip, assassinated the Archduke Francis Ferdinand and his wife. The Archduke was a nephew of and the heir apparent to the Emperor Francis Joseph of Austria. This act of violence set off a chain reaction of events which moved inexorably, like a plot in a Sophoclean tragedy, toward war. Although the complicity of the Serbian government in the crime was uncertain, the Austrian government determined to use the murder as an excuse to crush Serbia in the hope of solving in this way Austria's internal Yugoslav problem. Although the Austrian statesmen wished to keep the conflict limited to Austria and Serbia, the Austrian declaration of war on Serbia on July 28 put in operation Europe's system of interlocking alliances. The "July Crisis" of 1914 became another test of strength between the Triple Alliance and the Triple Entente.

As in the Bosnian Crisis six years before, Russia backed up Serbia, and Germany backed up Austria. Unlike the Bosnian Crisis, however, during the July Crisis France backed Russia. On July 29 the Russian government ordered the general mobilization of the Russian armed forces. In the psychological climate then existing in Europe general mobilization was regarded as a point of no return, a measure equivalent to a declaration of war. Russia's preparations were aimed against Austria, but Germany was pledged to support Austria. It had long been a part of German mili-tary thinking that Germany must offset Russia's numbers by her speed. Once the German generals were convinced that war was inevitable, they determined that Germany must take the initiative. On July 31 the Ger-man government declared a "state of threatening danger of war." On the same day it sent Russia a twelve-hour ultimatum, demanding that she cease military preparations at once, and a more polite inquiry to France, requesting that she state what her attitude would be in the event of a German-Russian war. Russia failed to reply within the time limit of the ultimatum, whereupon Germany declared war on her (July 31). On August 1 France replied that she would be guided by her interest. Germany interpreted the reply — correctly — to mean that France would come to the support of Russia, and on August 3 declared war on France.

German plans for a Franco-German war called for a flank attack on France through the flat lands of Belgium rather than a frontal attack across the hilly and heavily fortified Franco-German border. On the eve of the declaration of war on France, Germany asked Belgium to permit passage of German troops across Belgian territory. Belgium, however, faithful to her obligations as a neutral, refused. Thereupon Germany invaded her, pleading — in the words of the German Chancellor Bethmann-Hollweg — that "necessity knows no law." The violation of Belgian neutrality by Germany raised the question of the attitude of Great Britain, which until August 2 had kept her hands free. Britain was pledged to protect Belgian neutrality, and on August 4 she declared war on Germany. When the British Ambassador informed Bethmann-Hollweg of the British decision, the German Chancellor lamented that Britain was going to war merely for the sake of a "scrap of paper." In his agitation Bethmann-Hollweg missed the point. Britain was indeed in the habit of honoring scraps of paper bearing her signature, but above all it had traditionally been British policy to prevent any European great power from seizing the low countries lying across the Channel from Britain.

Britain's declaration of war brought into the conflict the far-flung British Empire and a little later (August 23, 1914) also her Far Eastern ally, Japan. Thus in a matter of days an obscure conflict in an obscure part of Europe, the Balkans, spread by interlocking alliances into a world war.

The belligerent camps became known as the Allies and the Central Powers, respectively. At the beginning of the hostilities the Allies comprised Great Britain and the British Empire, France, Russia, Japan, Belgium, Serbia, and Montenegro. On September 4 France, Britain, and Russia signed the Pact of London, whereby they entered into a formal alliance and pledged themselves not to discuss or conclude peace separately. The Central Powers were Germany and Austria-Hungary, Italy having deserted her allies on August 3. Germany and Austria were bound together by the Dual Alliance, originally concluded in 1879 and periodically renewed after that date.

From the beginning of the hostilities both belligerent groups sought new allies. In this scramble for new recruits the Allies were more successful than the Central Powers. While only Turkey and Bulgaria joined the Central Alliance in 1914 and 1915 respectively, the Allies were joined in

1915 by Italy, in 1916 by Portugal and Rumania, and in 1917 by Greece, the United States, many Latin American countries, and China.

The First World War was the largest and most intensive conflict in history up to its time. A democratic age called for a war of whole nations, not only governments and professional armies. There were precedents in modern history for the concept of the "nation-in-arms," notably the French Revolutionary Wars and the American Civil War, but they were limited to single nations. In the First World War all the major powers of the world and many smaller nations harnessed every human and material resource at their command for a grim test of strength. Factory, shop, farm, and government bureau became battlefields almost as much as the military fronts themselves. All parties to the conflict were grimly determined to win a total victory and staked everything they had on it.

In this desperate and reckless gamble, which was to sap the strength of Europe severely, both warring groups had certain advantages and disadvantages. The Allies had on their side overwhelming numbers and greater resources. It is estimated that in all the years of fighting the Allies called into service over 42,000,000 men. Their great naval superiority assured them of access to non-European resources, in addition to their own. Both advantages, however, were brought to bear only gradually. Mobilization of overseas manpower and supplies was slow. As late as the summer of 1918 the Allied victory appeared in doubt. But the morale of the Allied peoples was sustained through repeated adversities by the knowledge that they had more men and resources to draw on than their adversaries. Time, they felt, was on their side.

On the other hand, the Allies suffered from the fact that they were dispersed in a wide circle around the enemy. They had difficulty communicating with each other, coordinating their moves, and shifting their forces from one front to another, according to the needs of the moment. They depended largely on sea transportation for communicating with one another, and the Central Powers could interfere with Allied shipping by means of submarines. The Allies long suffered also from lack of unity of command. It was not until November, 1917, that they formed the Allied Supreme War Council at Versailles and empowered it to coordinate their moves on all fronts. And they did not achieve unity of tactical command on the Western Front until April, 1918.

The principal assets of the Central Powers were the advantage of "inner lines" and better unity of command. Unlike the Allies, the Central Powers were contiguous. They depended for transportation on a good system of railroads, with which the adversary could not interfere, the range of airplanes then being very limited. They could, therefore, more easily shift troops and supplies from one front to another, according to the need of the moment. While in the Allied team none of the powers clearly dominated the rest, Germany towered over her allies and largely dominated them. The Central Powers never created a central military clearing house analogous to the Allied Supreme War Council, but the redoubtable German General Staff provided most of the planning for Germany's allies. Thanks to better transportation and coordination, the Central Powers held the military initiative through most of the war. Their armies fought largely in enemy territory. With minor exceptions, Germany was spared the horrors of fighting on her soil.

As against these assets, the Central Powers suffered from isolation from the non-European world. As the Allied powers multiplied, they were able to forge a complete ring around the Central Powers. The position of the Central Powers was increasingly that of a beleaguered fortress. They were dependent on their own manpower and supplies and on those of the conquered countries. The Central Powers were able to muster an estimated total of 22,850,000 men — only about half as many as the Allies. Yet they gave a very creditable military performance. It took the combined resources of the mighty empires of Britain, France, Russia, Japan, and the United States, and over four years of heavy fighting to bring them to their knees.

2. THE STRUGGLE ON LAND

The German preparations for an offensive war had been drafted as early as 1893 when the Bismarckian system broke down, Russia drifted into the arms of France, and Germany faced the prospect of a "two-front" war — a contingency which Bismarck had dreaded but always managed to exorcise by skillful diplomacy. The German plans were constantly modified until they took form in 1905 as the Schlieffen Plan.

Count Alfred von Schlieffen, German chief of staff from 1891 to 1906, drew on Prussian military experience to prepare his plan. Like Prussia in the Seven Years' War (1756–1763), Germany in the First World War faced a coalition of powers superior in numbers and resources. In a prolonged conflict time would work against her, because the German reserves would ultimately be used up while those of the Triple Entente increased. On the other hand, Germany, like Prussia, enjoyed the advantage of "inner lines." This would permit the Germans to concentrate their armies more quickly at any point of the vast perimeter of conflict. If they were to win the war they would have to act swiftly and defeat their enemies piecemeal by concentrating superior forces against one opponent at a time. Assuming that the French could mobilize faster than the Russians, Schlieffen proposed to attack France first, while inferior forces held the Russians at bay.

On August 3, 1914, in accord with the Schlieffen Plan, German divisions began rolling relentlessly through Belgium, Luxemburg, and northern France in a vast movement intended to swing five German armies on five concentric arcs, the largest of which would sweep beyond Paris before it

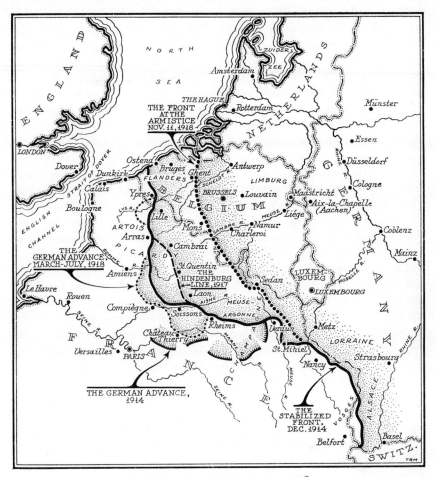

THE WESTERN FRONT, 1914–1918

curved toward the east. If the plan succeeded the French forces, out-flanked and caught like ripe grain inside the sweep of a scythe, were to be destroyed or captured, and France eliminated from the war in a few weeks. Then the German army would wheel around and deal with Russia. After a month of fighting the Germans were still on schedule and almost within sight of Paris. Uneasiness prevailed in the French capital as the government was evacuated to Bordeaux. The German command was so confident of victory that it withdrew a number of units from the Western Front and sent them to the east where the Russians showed unexpected aggressiveness.

At the crucial moment, however, the French army, supported by the small Belgian army and the British Expeditionary Force, resolutely counterattacked. The ensuing Battle of the Marne (September 5–12) changed the whole character of the war in the west. The Germans were held up, and on September 9 they began to fall back to the Aisne River where they entrenched themselves. Before winter the extended front had become a fortified system of trenches, stretching in parallel, zigzag lines from the North Sea to the border of Switzerland. The war of movement had come to an end, and the war of position had begun. Although the French suffered heavy casualties and lost their most important industrial regions, they were not eliminated from the war. A stalemate developed in the west which was not broken until four years later, after the arrival of the Americans.

Meanwhile, the Germans were more successful in the east, against the Russians who had invaded East Prussia in response to French appeals to create a diversion in Germany's rear. In the Battles of Tannenberg (August 25–31) and the Mazurian Lakes (September 6–15) they dealt the Russians stunning blows and sent them reeling out of Germany. The twin battles were the most clear-cut victories won by any army in the First World War. The doughty old commander of the German armies in the east, Field Marshal Paul von Hindenburg, became an idol of the German people, although he was not primarily responsible for either the planning or the direction of the battles. Although badly mauled by the Germans, the Russians were successful in their operations against the Austrians. By late winter they drove the Austrians out of most of Galicia. The Russian sacrifice in East Prussia was also not in vain; it influenced the course of the Battle of the Marne in the west.

The stalemate in the west led both warring camps to turn their attention to the east in 1915. In the Allied councils there began a long-drawn debate between "Easterners" and "West Fronters." The Easterners felt that in view of the stalemate in the west the Allies should seek a solution elsewhere, preferably in the Eastern Mediterranean. The West Fronters believed that the war would be and could be won only on the Western Front. As was almost inevitable in coalition warfare, the outcome of the debate was no clear-cut, definite decision in favor of either of the two schools of strategy but a series of compromises. The first compromise produced the ill-fated Gallipoli campaign against Turkey. The Ottoman Empire had joined the Central Powers in October, 1914, and established two fronts: in Palestine, facing the Suez Canal, and in the Caucasus, facing the Russians.

After bungling a naval attempt to crash through the Dardanelles in March, 1915, the Allies landed a motley force of British, Australian, and French colonial troops at the entry of the Strait in April. The ensuing engagements proved to be the most bloody in the First World War in proportion to the number of the troops involved. The Turks, under the command of Mustafa Kemal Pasha, the future dictator of Turkey, defended themselves with admirable courage and tenacity. At the close of 1915, having made little progress and having suffered fearful losses, the Allies abandoned the campaign. The troops evacuated from Gallipoli

Dogfight between French and German planes (Culver Pictures).

Automobiles used to convey French soldiers to the Verdun sector during World War I (International News Photo).

The British Grand Fleet in review at Spithead, July, 1914 (Radio Times Hulton Picture Library).

were sent to Salonika, where, together with motley reinforcements of French, British, Serbian, Russian, Italian, and Greek troops, they opened in 1916 the Macedonian Front — another segment in the circle of fronts hemming in the Central Powers.

The Gallipoli campaign resulted in great loss of prestige to the Allies in the Balkans and the Near East. They had hoped to isolate Turkey, open the Straits, and win new allies in the Balkans; instead, Bulgaria joined the Central Powers, Serbia was crushed, Greece remained prudently neutral, and the Straits remained closed to the Allies, with fateful results for Russia. Nor was this the only humiliation suffered by the Allies in 1915. The Russians, although severely hampered by a shortage of guns, ammunition, clothing, and food, hoped to knock out Austria in 1915 in conjunction with Italy, with whom the Allies were then negotiating in London (see p. 160). But when the Italians entered the war in May, their offensive against Austria bogged down in the difficult Alpine terrain. By then the Russians were in serious trouble.

The Central Powers also decided to force a decision in the east in 1915. Unable to eliminate France, the Germans turned their offensive power against Russia. They took over from the bungling Austrians the direction of operations against the Russians. In May the Austro-German armies broke through the Russian lines and proceeded to roll back the whole Russian Front in Poland. They advanced continuously through the summer until September when the Russians managed to stabilize the front along a line running from west of Riga in Latvia south to the Rumanian border. Although the Germans failed in their objective of encircling and destroying the Russian army, they inflicted fearful losses on it. It never quite recovered from the demoralization of the great retreat from Poland. But even in defeat the Russian army represented a formidable obstacle to victory of the Central Powers. It held down considerably more than half of the Austro-German forces.

The stabilization of the Eastern Front freed the Germans and Austrians for the long-delayed punishment of little Serbia. In October the Germans and Austrians, joined in war at this point by the Bulgarians (see p. 160), attacked Serbia from the west, north, and east and overran the country. Owing to a reversal in Greek internal politics (see p. 160), the Allies were unable to come to Serbia's rescue. Left to their own devices, the Serbian government and army, nevertheless, refused to surrender. With unique courage, they retreated fighting clear out of the country and across the desolate Albanian mountains to the Adriatic Sea. Their battered but undaunted remnants were evacuated on Allied ships to the island of Corfu. The Serbian government maintained headquarters there until the end of the war, and the Serbian army was sent to fight again on the Macedonian Front. The elimination of Serbia opened a direct link between Berlin and Constantinople. At last the dream of German expansionists of joining Middle Europe to the Middle East under German hegemony appeared to be realized. And the elimination of Serbia did not exhaust the catalog of Allied defeats in 1915. In October a small British-Indian force pushed up the Mesopotamian valley from Basra in an attempt to capture Bagdad. In December it was surrounded by the Turks at Kut-el-Amara and, after a heroic defense, it was forced to capitulate in April, 1916.

Meanwhile, the stalemate in the west continued. Early hopes of ending the war "before the leaves fell" — as the Emperor William promised the German soldiers in 1914 — had long evaporated. Trench warfare baffled the generals on both sides. They yearned to resume mobile warfare and seek a quick decision, but no one knew how to break the deadlock. New offensive weapons and techniques were tried, but none could overcome the effectiveness of defensive ones, notably the deadly effectiveness of the machine gun. In 1915 the Germans used poison gas, and in 1916 the British introduced "tanks." Ultimately, tanks were to end the seeming impregnability of trenches, but the First World War was over before this new weapon was perfected and its full potentialities realized. Meanwhile, the struggle in the west degenerated into a dreary war of attrition, in which generalship meant little; only numbers, matériel, and the physical and moral stamina of the frontline soldiers counted.

The generals could think of no other way of breaking the deadlock except to concentrate more men and more guns in a given area in the hope of punching a hole in the enemy's lines and breaking through into open country. The most costly and futile of such attempts were made in 1916. From February until July the Germans assaulted the French fortress city of Verdun; and from July until November rains and mud stopped them, the British, supported by the French, attacked the German positions on the Somme River. It is estimated that casualties in these inconclusive battles amounted on the Allied side to 950,000 and on the German side to 785,000 men. By the end of 1916 the lines in the west were much as they had been a year earlier, but neither Allied nor German military morale quite recovered from the inconclusive carnage. In December the Liberal cabinet of Herbert Asquith in Great Britain gave way to a coalition cabinet formed by Lloyd George. In France there was also a reshuffle of the cabinet and the high command. Aristide Briand became Premier, and General Nivelle replaced General Joffre in command of the French army.

In the east the Central Powers were successful in 1916 as they had been in 1915. In June the Russian army, under General Brusilov, attacked and broke through the Austrian lines. Once again, however, the Germans rescued their luckless ally. German troops, partly brought up from the Western Front, were rushed into the breach and by the end of July stopped the Russian advance. The Russian offensive relieved the pressure on Verdun, but its cost in casualties was formidable (about a million men). Together with previous severe casualties, this was too heavy a drain for the Russians to bear, even with their traditional indifference to human losses. The Russian army sank into a state of torpor from which it never recovered.

At this moment the Rumanians made up their minds to intervene on the Allied side (see p. 160). On August 28 the Rumanian army invaded Transylvania. The province had been stripped of Austrian troops, and at first the Rumanians advanced rapidly. But the retaliation of the Central Powers was swift, while the promised Allied help to Rumania failed to materialize. An Austro-German force counterattacked in Transylvania, and a German-Bulgar force invaded Rumania from Bulgaria. Threatened with encirclement and destruction, the Rumanian army was forced to evacuate not only Transylvania but also Wallachia, with its rich stores of wheat and oil. Bucharest, the capital of Rumania, fell on December 6, and the government fled to Jassy in Moldavia. In January of 1917 the Rumanians managed, with Russian reinforcements, to stabilize their lines along the Seret River.

At this moment of triumph the Central Powers proposed to the Allies a peace parley. The idea had originated with the Austrians. On November 21, 1916, the venerable Emperor Francis Joseph of Austria died. His youthful successor, the Emperor Charles, had from the first no liking for the war which was not of his making. The Austrians proposed to their allies to combine an offer to negotiate with a statement of their peace terms. But the Germans were reluctant to limit their freedom of action by revealing their aims at a moment when the Central Powers were fighting everywhere on enemy soil. Nevertheless, the strangling effect of the Allied blockade and the blood-letting of Verdun and the Somme inclined them to give the idea of a peace parley a try. Accordingly, on December 12, the four governments of the Central Alliance issued separate but similar statements in which, after boastfully recounting their feats, they invited the Allies to enter into peace negotiations. For opposite reasons, the Allies were reluctant to negotiate. At the moment their armies were almost everywhere on the defensive, but they were confident that time worked for them. In a joint note on December 29 the Allies haughtily dismissed the boasts of victory on the part of their opponents as representing only "a superficial and passing situation" and rejected their peace offer as "empty and insincere."

The Germans then realized that the Allies would not negotiate as long as they could hope to swing the balance in their favor by drawing on their overseas reservoirs of strength. The Allied power most capable of mobilizing overseas manpower and resources was Britain. At the beginning of the war, when the Germans hoped to win by swift blows against their enemies on land, they tended to discount Britain. However, as victory eluded them and the war continued without a solution in sight, the Germans re-appraised Britain's role in the war. As long as Britain could pour men and supplies to the fronts in France, Italy, Macedonia,

Palestine, and Mesopotamia, victory would continue to elude the Central Powers. The destruction of British sea power, the German leaders decided in January of 1917, was the key to victory.

3. THE STRUGGLE ON THE SEAS

At the beginning of the First World War the British determined to use against Germany the same strategy which served them so well against France in the wars of the eighteenth century and in their struggle against Napoleon. They expected to limit their participation in land warfare to symbolic proportions — until the war's "Waterloo." Then they would appear in strength to have a decisive voice in the postwar settlement. Meanwhile, they would provide loans and ship food and arms to their continental allies, while they themselves conducted the war at sea. The exhaustion of the continental allies by 1916 forced them to modify this strategy. They were obliged to adopt universal military service (January, 1916) and take a larger part in land warfare than they had originally anticipated. But at sea they carried out their original strategy with brilliance and success. Assisted by the French navy, the British set about seizing or blockading all German ships, halting German sea-borne commerce, and occupying German colonies.

The outbreak of the war caught several German warships in distant seas. Like a pack of relentless hounds trailing foxes, British, French, and (after August 23) Japanese warships hunted them down and either destroyed them or drove them off the seas.

Two German cruisers, the *Goeben* and the *Breslau*, trapped in the Mediterranean, fled to Turkish waters where they added decisive weight to the arguments of German diplomats seeking to persuade Turkey to join the Central Powers (cf. p. 159). Five German warships, stationed in the German possessions in the Pacific and in China, made for home around Cape Horn and the Atlantic. On their way they terrorized isolated British and French stations, and off the coast of Chile they destroyed an inferior British naval force. The British reacted with vigor. On December 8, 1914, a British force intercepted and sank four out of the five German ships near the Falkland Islands off the coast of Argentina. The remaining ship was hunted down later and blown up by her own crew after a brief career as a raider. Two more German surface raiders harassed Allied shipping in the Indian Ocean until one was hunted down and sunk and the other was chased and forced to seek refuge in a jungle river in Africa.

These defeats of Germany on the high seas doomed the German colonial empire. Japanese, Australian, and New Zealand forces overran German possessions in the Pacific (Marshall Islands, Marianas, Carolines, Palau, Samoa, New Guinea, and the Bismarck Archipelago). The

Japanese, joined by a British force, expelled the Germans from the Shantung province in China. British, French, and South African forces overran Togoland, the Cameroons, and German Southwest Africa. Only in German East Africa (Tanganyika) did a German force hold out by bold action and skillful maneuvering until after the armistice.

Meanwhile, the British Grand Fleet, a mighty armada consisting of twenty dreadnoughts and assorted battle cruisers, cruisers, destroyers, and other craft, stationed in British home waters, had little opportunity to show its prowess. Its opponent, the German High Seas Fleet, consisting of thirteen dreadnoughts and assorted craft, refused to emerge from its home base at Kiel. Though smaller in tonnage, it was equal to the British fleet in equipment and organization. It was not an unworthy opponent. But as long as the Germans hoped to win the war on land, they hesitated to risk the High Seas Fleet in an open engagement. It was not until May 31, 1916, that under Admiral Scheer it emerged in strength from Kiel to clash directly with the British Grand Fleet under Admiral Jellicoe in a major action. The ensuing two-day Battle of Jutland (Battle of Skagerrak in German terminology) has been adjudged a draw. The Germans inflicted on the British twice the losses in tonnage and casualties that they themselves suffered and then escaped back to port. In marksmanship, maneuvering, and night fighting they outmatched their foes. But the British remained in control of the seas, and the Germans did not venture to repeat the challenge.

While there were few classical naval battles in the First World War, with fleets drawn up in battle array, firing broadsides at each other, naval warfare played a great — perhaps decisive — role. Naval supremacy gave the Allied powers three marked advantages which increased as the war lengthened: access to the resources of the world, the opportunity to influence neutral nations with maritime interests, and the power to blockade the Central Powers.

The fate of the German colonies provided a stern lesson for all neutrals with colonial possessions. Italy's course of action was influenced, in part, by fear of Allied naval power (see p. 160). Spain and Portugal, which — unlike Italy — did not adjoin the Central Powers, were even more respectful of Allied sea power. While Spain traded exclusively with the Allies but remained neutral, Portugal joined the Allies in 1916. The Netherlands, which possessed a rich colonial empire, was exposed to Allied naval pressure on sea and to German military pressure on land. In these circumstances, the Dutch maintained a judicious neutrality. Similar prudence determined the policy of Denmark which was in an analogous position by virtue of adjoining Germany and possessing Iceland and Greenland.

The position of the Scandinavian neutrals, Sweden and Norway, was different. Neither possessed colonies or adjoined Germany. But both were subjected to naval pressure, Sweden mainly on the part of Germany, Norway on the part of the Allies. In these circumstances, while both

THE SUBMARINE BLOCKADE IN WORLD WAR I

countries remained neutral, Sweden traded principally with Germany and Norway with the Allies.

The British navy kept the North Sea and the Channel under ceaseless observation and effectively blockaded Germany. Only an occasional German raider managed to slip through the British patrols to carry out hit-and-run raids against the British coast or to harass Allied shipping. Mines and shore batteries kept the British ships from approaching close to the German coasts, and it was not safe for them to penetrate the Baltic Sea. For by widening the Kiel Canal, a project completed by 1914, the Germans were able to move their largest warcraft from the North Sea to the Baltic Sea without going around the Danish peninsula. This permitted them to blockade the Baltic and prevent Russia from receiving much-needed supplies through this most direct and, in peacetime, most important route of Russian sea trade.

In the Mediterranean Sea the French and (after May 25, 1915) the Italian navies performed an analogous function. They blockaded Austria and Turkey. Turkey, in turn, blocked the sea route through the Straits to Russia. Thus the Central Powers maintained an inner blockade while the Allies maintained an outer blockade. This proved fateful to Russia, but it proved equally disastrous to the Central Powers.

Except with their neutral neighbors, German and Austrian foreign trade practically ceased after the outbreak of war. This brought a severe economic loss and a critical shortage of many materials essential for war production, as well as a restriction of food imports. The shortages were only partially alleviated by Germany's conquests, for even the richest regions of Europe were dependent on the import of essential commodities from overseas. The advance of the German armies across Belgium and northern France brought valuable mines and industrial plants under German control, but these regions were densely populated and added little to the food supply. The Polish, Serbian, and Rumanian territories occupied by the Austro-German armies did yield some assets — potato, beet, and cereal crops, wheat, cattle, pigs, sheep, and oil. But the beleaguered peoples of the Central Powers still lacked certain essentials, fats in particular. The inadequacy of their diet reduced their efficiency, health, and morale. Devitalization of the human machines proved as serious a handicap as the shortage of rubber, copper, mercury, and other materials, lack of which finally stalled the German industries and the German armies.

Threatened with economic strangulation, the Germans decided to strike back at the Allies by instituting a counter-blockade. The Germans could not enforce this counter-blockade in the traditional manner with surface vessels, so they determined to resort to a relatively new weapon, the submarine boat. On February 4, 1915, the German government issued an announcement defining a war zone around the British Isles and along the coasts of France. In this zone, the announcement warned, after February 18 German submarines would sink all ships, possibly without warning. The German submarine warfare involved Germany in a protracted controversy with the United States, which ultimately led to the American intervention in the First World War.

13

THE WAR ON LAND AND SEA, 1917–1918

No fair-minded neutral . . . can doubt our right to defend ourselves against this war of starvation, which is contrary to international law.

THEOBALD VON BETHMANN-HOLLWEG (1916)

The present German submarine warfare is a warfare against mankind.

WOODROW WILSON (1917)

1. THE AMERICAN INTERVENTION

THE OUTBREAK of the First World War in Europe caught most Americans completely by surprise. Since his inauguration in 1913 President Wilson had been engaged in promoting a program of internal reforms, the "New Freedom," and gave scanty attention to foreign affairs. His reaction to the outbreak of war in Europe, like that of most Americans, was that Europe's conflicts were none of America's business. On August 4 he issued a proclamation of neutrality and offered the belligerents his "good offices" to mediate the conflict. The belligerents politely declined the offer, and Wilson exhorted the Americans to remain "neutral in fact as well as in name" and "impartial in thought as well as in action." Defense of neutral rights and efforts to induce the belligerents to come to terms became the guiding principles of his policy, which he pursued with great tenacity for two years and a half.

While the Americans did not expect to be participants in the war, they observed it with increasingly passionate interest. The propaganda of the belligerents, emotional attachment to this or that European country, as well as economic interest led many Americans to take sides in the conflict. But the greatest passion was undoubtedly aroused by the Allied blockade and German submarine warfare, both of which encroached on the freedom of seas, the right, historically claimed by the United States, to send ships to any sea in time of war or peace and to trade with neutrals or belligerents.

In October, 1914, the United States government appealed to the belligerents to respect the Declaration of London, which had been adopted by a naval conference of ten nations in London in 1909. The declaration

144

defined the rights and duties of both neutrals and belligerents in naval warfare. The Central Powers readily agreed to respect the declaration, since they were weaker in naval power than their opponents. The Allies, on the other hand, refused to accept it, since this would cancel to some degree their advantage in possessing superior sea power. In February, 1915, the Germans resorted to submarine warfare. They did not deny that it violated the Declaration of London, but justified it on the ground that the Allied blockade violated it too. Legally, they had a good case, but psychologically it was a poor one. The Allied blockade caused no direct loss of human life, while the German submarine warfare did. The slow starvation of millions of German and Austrian children could not compete in dramatic appeal with the sudden and violent death of a few thousand seamen and passengers torpedoed by German submarines.

The United States, while continuing to press the Allied governments to accept the Declaration of London, protested vigorously against the German intention to wage submarine warfare. In a stiff note on February 10, 1915, Washington informed Berlin that it would hold it to a "strict accountability" for "property endangered or lives lost" through submarine warfare. The sinking of the first American ship, the *Gulflight*, on May 1, and of the British ocean liner *Lusitania* on May 7, brought the United States and Germany to the verge of war. On the *Lusitania* 1198 lives, including 139 Americans, were lost. American public opinion was outraged. The revelation that the ship carried a part-cargo of small arms and ammunition failed to appease its wrath.

There was, however, a lack of unity in American public opinion and dissension in the government at Washington concerning the best policy to follow. On June 8 Secretary of State William Jennings Bryan, a pacifist-at-all-costs, resigned rather than affix his signature to a note of protest which, if rejected by the Germans, would logically lead to a declaration of war. This encouraged the German government to believe that it could get away with the sinking of the *Lusitania*. But Bryan's successor, Robert Lansing, pressed strongly for satisfaction in the matter. The German Ambassador in Washington, Count Johann von Bernstorff, was alive to the danger of the situation and succeeded in persuading his government to back down. On September 1, 1915, after much legalistic quibbling, the German government promised that no passenger ships would be sunk in the future without warning and without giving the crew and passengers time to take to the boats. The submarine crisis then abated for some time.

At the same time as he defended neutral rights, Wilson sought, through public speeches and secret negotiations, to bring the belligerents to terms. In 1915 and in 1916 he sent his confidential adviser, "Colonel" Edward M. House, to Europe to sound out the belligerents. But both public speeches and confidential negotiations failed to elicit a favorable response from the warring nations.

The American people were more deeply impressed by Wilson's peace efforts than were the belligerents. In November, 1916, he was reelected, by a narrow margin, largely on the slogan "He kept us out of war." Wilson took this as an encouragement to further peace efforts. On December 18, a week after the peace proposal of the Central Powers (see p. 139), he appealed in a note to all belligerents to state their war aims in the hope that the differences dividing them might prove to be not as irreconcilable as they appeared. In their reply on December 26 the Central Powers refused to state their war aims but suggested a direct exchange of views with the Allies. In their joint reply on January 10, 1917, the Allies refused to negotiate but stated their war aims (see p. 161). Wilson followed up with an address to the Senate on January 22, in which he urged the belligerents to accept a "peace without victory" and reiterated the terms on which the United States would be willing to mediate and guarantee peace. At the end of January Colonel House succeeded in eliciting a confidential statement of Germany's terms. But, by this time, Germany was not interested in negotiating on these or any other terms.

On January 8 the German leaders had made the fateful decision to renew unrestricted submarine warfare. In making this decision, which constituted a repudiation of their pledge given after the sinking of the *Lusitania,* the Germans took a calculated risk. They knew that it would probably provoke war with the United States. But they calculated that if German submarines could sink 600,000 tons of Allied shipping a month, the British would be on their knees in six months — long before the Americans could mobilize their great resources and come to the rescue of Britain. To divert the Americans further the German Foreign Secretary Zimmermann instructed the German Minister in Mexico City to seek an offensive alliance with Mexico and Japan. In the event of American intervention Mexico was to help itself to the "lost" territories in the American Southwest. The efficient British Intelligence Service intercepted and decoded the message. But the British government shrewdly awaited a psychologically propitious moment before revealing it to Washington.

On January 31 the German government acknowledged Wilson's Peace without Victory address with a tongue-in-cheek expression of appreciation of his good intentions. With supreme tactlessness, in the same note Berlin informed Washington of its intention to resume unrestricted submarine warfare. Wilson, offended and disheartened, retaliated by breaking off diplomatic relations with Germany on February 3.

The resumption of unrestricted submarine warfare deeply affected American public opinion. As long as the Allies appeared able to take care of themselves, most Americans were content to remain neutral. The initial success of the submarine campaign in 1917, however, opened the prospect of the defeat of Britain, whose fleet had stood for a century like a protective shield between the Old and the New Worlds. American public opinion began to rally to the need of intervention. The ranks of the interventionists were greatly strengthened by the publication on

March 1 of the Zimmermann note. The fall of the Russian monarchy on March 15 removed a great psychological obstacle to American intervention on the Allied side. With the apparent transformation of Russia from an autocracy into a liberal democracy it could be said that all the Allies stood for freedom, whereas the Central Powers stood for tyranny.

In these circumstances Wilson summoned Congress into special session to recommend a declaration of war on Germany. Addressing Congress on April 2, he skillfully justified war by defining it as both a defensive measure necessary to protect America's rights and a disinterested crusade to "make the world safe for democracy." He distinguished carefully between the German people, for whom he professed friendship, and the German government, which alone he held responsible for the conflict. Similarly, wishing to separate Germany from her allies, he refrained from recommending a declaration of war on Austria, Bulgaria, and Turkey. The declaration of war on Germany was approved in the Senate by a vote of 82 to 6 on April 4, and in the House of Representatives by a vote of 373 to 50 on April 6. On the same day, April 6, the President signed the war resolution, and the United States formally entered the First World War on the side of the Allies.

Soon after, Austria and Turkey, out of solidarity with Germany, decided to break off diplomatic relations with the United States. Bulgaria alone of the Central Powers continued normal relations with the United States, while at war with the Allies.

2. THE RUSSIAN REVOLUTION, 1917

When the First World War broke out the majority of the Russian people rallied around the Tsar and the government in support of the war. They believed it to be a just war of defense against aggression on the part of Germany and Austria, the historical enemies of the Slavs. A few socialists, it is true, spoke up against the war, but they appeared insignificant because their organizations had been broken up and their leaders imprisoned or exiled. In the Duma the opposition parties proclaimed a political truce and formed with the pro-government parties a Sacred Union for the duration of the war. However, the autocratic government, suspicious of any spontaneity on the part of the population, failed to harness the enthusiasm of the Russian people for the war. The Duma was indefinitely prorogued, and the government alone assumed the responsibility for the conduct of the war.

Had the war been short and victorious, no doubt the Russian monarchy would have emerged from it strengthened. But the war proved to be long and arduous. None of the belligerents had anticipated this. But while the more advanced nations of Western Europe rapidly adjusted to the strains of war, the antiquated and inefficient structure of Imperial

Russia, like that of Austria and Turkey, disintegrated under them.

The summary, unselective mobilization of all able-bodied men resulted in oversupplying the army with manpower and depriving industry and agriculture of essential labor. Millions of soldiers never saw the front but still had to be fed and clothed from the diminishing stocks of food and clothing. Railroad transportation, inefficient even at its best, broke down under the strain of hauling troops and supplies to and from the fronts. A runaway inflation developed as a result of the disappearance of consumers' goods from the markets. Food and fuel shortages developed in the cities as a result of the shortage of labor, the breakdown in transportation, and the reluctance of the peasants to sell their produce for the worthless, inflated currency. The plight of the cities was aggravated by a flood of refugees from Poland, after the great retreat of the Russian army in 1915.

The Russian masses were used to hardships and would have perhaps endured the privations of war without complaint had the war been victorious. But that was hardly the case. After the catastrophe of the army in 1915 the earlier enthusiasm for the war evaporated, and the opposition to the government revived. To restore confidence in the army and ultimate victory the Emperor Nicholas assumed personal command of the army in September, 1915, and thus also personal responsibility for its further defeats. His departure from the capital (renamed Petrograd in 1914) to the front, left the responsibility of making urgent decisions in the hands of the Empress Alexandra, a neurotic, religiously exalted German princess, who was completely out of touch with Russian realities. She was under the influence of an adventurer, Gregory Rasputin, an ignorant and cunning peasant, who meddled ineptly in the affairs of state. In 1916 a group of noblemen assassinated him to save the monarchy from the "dark forces," dragging it down into an abyss. Ugly rumors of incompetence and treason in high places circulated widely. In the winter of 1916–1917 disaffection became general.

On March 8, 1917, the "March Revolution" began with a spontaneous outbreak of bread riots in Petrograd. The riots presently assumed menacing proportions as workers went on strike, and soldiers of the swollen, idle garrison of the capital mutinied rather than fire into the rioting mobs, as ordered. On March 15 the Emperor, held up by railroad workers at a provincial railway station while trying to regain the capital, abdicated in favor of his brother, Grand Duke Michael. In view of the revolutionary situation in Petrograd Grand Duke Michael declined the throne and handed over power to a provisional government. The Romanov monarchy had come to an end. But revolution was not over in Russia; it was only beginning.

From the beginning of the revolution there emerged two centers of power which sought to fill the vacuum left by the fall of the autocracy: the Provisional Government, composed of the leaders of the former opposi-

A scene from the Russian Revolution of 1917 ("The Recording Eye," by Helmut & Alison Gersheim. G. P. Putnam Co.).

Returning American troops parade under the Arch of Freedom during celebration of the Armistice in New York City, November, 1919.

tion parties in the Duma, and the Soviet of the Workers' and Soldiers' Deputies, composed of elected or self-appointed representatives of the workers and soldiers in Petrograd. While the Provisional Government was representative of the liberal middle-class, capitalist, and land-owning interests, the Petrograd Soviet was representative of the radical, socialist, working-class elements. A tenuous liaison was maintained between the two bodies by Alexander Kerensky, originally the only socialist in the cabinet. Although the Petrograd Soviet had jurisdiction nominally only in the capital, it sought to elbow the Provisional Government out of the way and assumed the prerogatives of a national government.

It is now generally agreed that the Provisional Government could have saved itself and a liberal parliamentary regime in Russia only by instantly concluding a separate peace and concentrating on internal consolidation. But the members of the Provisional Government had vehemently criticized the fallen regime for incompetence and lack of vigor in prosecuting the war, and now felt impelled to show that they could do better than the Tsar. The Provisional Government assured the Allies that Russia would continue in the war until a "victorious end." It deferred consideration of the question of the form of government for Russia and of land reform until the convocation, at some unspecified future date, of a constitutent assembly. But it lived up to its liberal billings by decreeing an amnesty for all political offenders against the old regime. It guaranteed also civil rights and the rights of national and religious minorities.

Soon political exiles began to return to Russia. Among them was V. I. Lenin, the leader of the Bolsheviks, who returned from Switzerland — via Germany, with the assistance of the German government, which hoped that he would undermine Russia's war effort. In this it was not disappointed. Lenin's program called for an immediate conclusion of peace — a separate peace if necessary; immediate seizure of land by the peasants; workers' control of industry; and the transfer of all power to the Soviets.

Meanwhile, the Provisional Government made preparations for Russia's last military effort. On June 29 the Russian army, already undermined by revolution, launched an offensive against the Austrians. After a brief initial success the offensive collapsed, and the army disintegrated as a fighting force. The discredit which defeat brought to the Provisional Government encouraged the Bolsheviks to make their first attempt to overthrow the government in July. In September the commander in chief of the army, General Kornilov, on whom the conservatives pinned their hopes, marched on the capital. Both attempts were beaten off, but the Provisional Government, buffeted between the political left and right, steadily weakened. On November 6–7 the Bolsheviks, now much stronger than in July, overthrew the Provisional Government by an armed coup in Petrograd (the "November Revolution").

The Bolshevik government ("Council of the People's Commissars"), organized under the presidency of Lenin, proceeded at once to implement

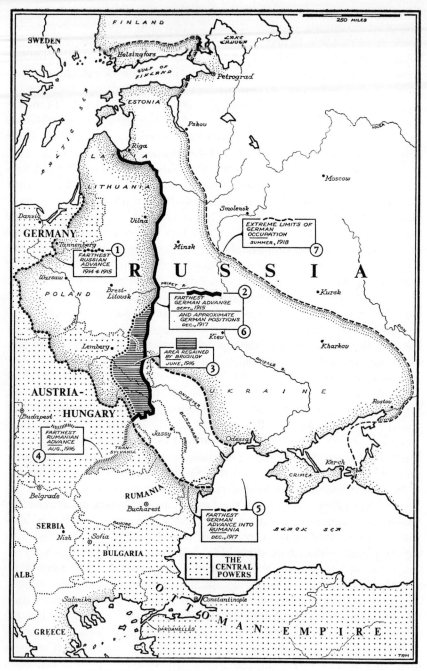

EASTERN FRONT, WORLD WAR I

his program. The most pressing problem was to restore peace in order to satisfy the war-weary Russian masses and to give the Bolsheviks an opportunity to consolidate their as-yet-insecure rule in Russia. On November 7 the Bolshevik government issued the "Decree of Peace," and two weeks later the Bolshevik Commissar of Foreign Affairs, Leon Trotsky, addressed a note to all belligerents, summoning them to enter into immediate peace negotiations on the basis of "no annexations, no indemnities, and the self-determination of peoples." The Central Powers agreed to negotiate, and on December 5 they granted Russia an armistice. The western Allies ignored the Bolshevik summons for the same reasons that they had rejected the peace proposal of the Central Powers a year earlier.

On December 22, 1917, a peace conference opened between the Central Powers and Russia at Brest-Litovsk. It soon transpired that the Central Powers, despite their acceptance of the Bolshevik peace formula, intended to deprive Russia of all her borderlands inhabited by non-Russian nationalities. The Bolsheviks at first balked, but then yielded when the Central Powers denounced the armistice and resumed their advance into Russia. On March 3, 1918, the crestfallen Bolsheviks signed the humiliating Peace of Brest-Litovsk. It deprived Russia of Finland, the Baltic provinces, Poland, White Russia, the Ukraine, and Transcaucasia, reducing her thus to about the size she had been before the conquests of Peter the Great. Peace in the east freed the Germans to unleash their full fury against the Allies in the west.

3. THE TRIUMPH OF THE WESTERN ALLIES

In 1917 the situation of the western Allies appeared anything but hopeful. In April the German submarines sank 875,000 tons of Allied shipping, which exceeded the Germans' own expectations and the Allied ability to replace the lost tonnage. The French attempt under General Nivelle to break through on the Western Front in April resulted in failure, appalling casualties, and widespread mutinies in the French army. Nivelle's successor, General Pétain, succeeded by firmness and patience in pacifying the troops, but thereafter the French army limited itself to defensive operations. "Wait for the Americans!" became its motto. The army crisis provoked a series of cabinet crises. In November, Georges Clemenceau, the "Tiger" of France, assumed the offices of premier and minister of war with the motto *"Je fais la guerre."* He ruthlessly stamped out all signs of defeatism and resolutely set about leading France to a victory of arms.

The collapse of the Russian army in the summer permitted the Austrians and Germans to withdraw troops quietly from the Eastern Front and prepare for a decisive push against Italy in the fall. On October 24 they launched a powerful attack along the Isonzo River, and broke through the Italian lines at Caporetto. The demoralized Italians fell back

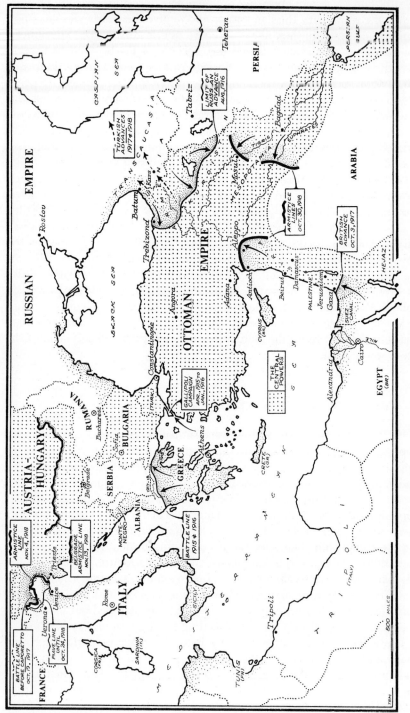

THE MEDITERRANEAN AND NEAR EAST FRONTS, WORLD WAR I

in a disorderly rout almost to the gates of Venice. Fortunately for the Italians, the Germans and Austrians were surprised by the extent of their victory and were unprepared to exploit it fully. Heavy fighting continued until Christmas, but the Italians, reinforced by French and British troops rushed in from France, managed to hold the line along the Piave River. The rout from Caporetto (vividly described by Ernest Hemingway in his famous novel *Farewell to Arms*) affected very adversely Italian political and military morale. In a reshuffle of the cabinet and the high command Vittorio Orlando became premier and General Díaz commander-in-chief of the army. Díaz proved to be an extremely battle-shy commander; for a year, until the final days of the war, he refused to undertake any offensive operations. To boost Italian morale the United States declared war on Austria-Hungary on December 6. However, for the moment, no American troops were available for service on the Italian Front.

By the end of 1917 only the British among the Allies appeared to have energy left. In the fall they conducted the dismal Battle of the Passchendaele Ridge, which exacted very heavy casualties but failed to alter the balance on the Western Front. From their defeats the Allies at last derived a lesson: on November 27 they formed the Supreme War Council to coordinate their efforts.

While unsuccessful on the Western Front, the British were successful in the east. In Palestine they broke through the Turkish lines and on December 8 marched into Jerusalem – the first time the Holy City had seen Christian troops since the crusades. What was more important was the fact that the British mastered the situation on the seas. In May, with the help of the United States navy, they adopted the convoy system of sending ships in escorted groups, which slowed down the swifter vessels but offered better protection to all. To hem in the German submarines the Allies laid a mine barrage across the North Sea from the Orkney Islands to Norway and across the Channel from England to France. They developed new methods of detecting and destroying submarines, notably depth bombs and the use of hydroplanes for scouting. At the same time shipbuilding, especially in American shipyards, was pushed to the limit. As a result of all these methods the Allies succeeded by the end of 1917 in reversing in their favor the ratio of losses to replacements in shipping. The Germans were able to replace losses in submarines too, but submarine warfare had clearly failed in its purpose of cutting off the Allies from their overseas reservoirs of strength.

In these circumstances, the Germans reverted in 1918 to their original strategy of seeking a decision on land. The Central Powers were no less weary of the war than the Allies. But they heeded the advice of General Erich Ludendorff, Hindenburg's nominal subordinate but actually the brain of the German High Command, that one more drive, a *Friedenssturm* in the west, would bring them victory and peace. The withdrawal of Russia from the war permitted the Germans to build up a numerical preponderance on the Western Front of about 2,500,000 men to 2,000,000 Allied troops. Would the Americans come to France in time to reverse the balance and rescue the Allies? "That, and that only, was the decisive question," Hindenburg later recorded. "I believed that I could answer it in the negative." "In the autumn of 1917," Lloyd George later recorded, "[American] reinforcement was arriving with what seemed to be disconcerting and perplexing slowness. Both the French and ourselves were apprehensive lest, if it were not speeded up, it should arrive too late to save the Allied front from collapse."

After the American declaration of war the American people generally assumed that the United States would limit its participation in the war to naval activity and economic help to the Allies. However, in April, 1917, British and French war missions arrived in Washington to present their needs. General Joffre of the French mission appealed for 500,000 American troops to help the Allies on the Western Front. The United States agreed to send an American Expeditionary Force under General John J. Pershing to France. The existing American army (11,327 officers and 208,338 men), while adequate for the defense of the United States, was insufficient for service on the Western Front. On May 18 Congress passed the Selective Service Act to raise a national army.

The decision to raise an American mass army for service overseas created extremely complex logistical problems. It involved training, equipping, and transporting across the ocean close to 2,000,000 men. It further involved supplying this expeditionary force and providing at the same time extensive economic aid to the Allies. This was a mighty challenge. American organizing genius rose to the challenge and ultimately mastered the problems. But it took time, and the need of the Allies was urgent. Invoking broad war powers conferred on him by Congress, the President created a General Munitions Board, a Railroad War Board, a United Shipping Board, and a Food Administration to coordinate the national economic resources. To provide funds Congress voted a $4,000,000,000 federal appropriation for defense and authorized a $7,000,000,000 war bond drive. While the navy was able to take an early part in convoying ships to and from Europe, more than a year elapsed before the army was in a position to assume a proportionate burden alongside the Allied armies on the Western Front.

On March 21, 1918, the Germans unleashed the first of their four great offensives of 1918. The first blow fell upon the British lines at St.-Quentin, parted them, and carried the Germans ahead some forty miles through the breach before French reserves, generously poured in, helped to check the German advance. The hope of Ludendorff had been to separate the British and French armies and to roll the British back to the sea. Two weeks later the Germans struck again, and again they tore a hole in the British lines. But lack of reserves prevented their exploiting the situation fully. During the crisis, on April 14, the Allies agreed to name the French commander-in-chief, the able and cool-headed strategist, Ferdinand Foch, as Allied generalissimo. At the same time the Allies pressed Pershing to permit the American units, as they arrived in France, to be fed as reinforcements into the depleted French and British divisions. But Pershing refused because he had his heart set on creating an independent American army.

The third German blow fell upon the French on May 27, and carried the Germans to the Marne only some thirty-seven miles from Paris. They seemed about to realize the decision which escaped them in 1914. For the Allies these were desperate days. Only the appearance at last of the Americans at the front nerved them for the ordeal. On June 1 the Americans, battle-green but eager to fight, joined in the defense of Château-Thierry on the Marne. On July 15 the Germans launched their last desperate offensive. The ensuing Second Battle of the Marne (July 15–August 7) was recognized by both sides as the climactic battle of the war. If the Germans won it French resistance and the Allied front in France would probably collapse. But even though the Germans succeeded in crossing the Marne they made little headway against strong French and American resistance. On July 18 Foch ordered a counterattack. It proved so successful that six days later he confidently informed the Allied generals that the time had come "to abandon the general defensive attitude forced on us until now by numerical inferiority and pass to the offensive." In the Allied offensive, which began on August 8 and continued relentlessly until the armistice, the American army progressively took over the worst burden of fighting. Under its blows German morale began to crumble. On September 29 Ludendorff, almost in panic, advised the German government to seek peace.

Scenting victory, the Allies now attacked on all fronts. In Macedonia the Allies attacked on September 15 and broke through the Bulgarian lines. In Palestine the British, aided by the Arabs in revolt, attacked on September 18 and steadily drove the Turks northward. In Italy the timorous General Díaz at last yielded to the exhortations of the Allies and attacked the tottering Austrians on October 24. The first among the Central Powers to give up were the Bulgarians. On September 30 they signed an armistice and stepped out of the war. Next went the Turks on October 30, and the Austrians on November 3. Five days later a German armistice commission was received by Marshal Foch at his headquarters at Compiègne and after three days of discussions signed an armistice dictated by him. At 11 A.M. on November 11, 1918, the terrible First World War came to an end.

14

THE WAR OF FINANCE, DIPLOMACY, AND PROPAGANDA

England and France have not the same views with regard to peace that we have by any means. When the war is over we can force them to our way of thinking, because by that time they will . . . be financially in our hands.[1]

WOODROW WILSON

1. ECONOMIC WARFARE

NONE OF THE BELLIGERENTS in the First World War had made any economic preparations for the war because they all believed that the war would be short. Indeed, it was frequently asserted before 1914 that a modern war could not last more than a few months because the expense of equipping and maintaining mass armies would soon bankrupt the wealthiest state. The war lasted unexpectedly long, but the principal belligerents proved amazingly able to find unsuspected reserves with which to finance the steadily mounting costs of war. The ultimate sum directly expended by all the powers engaged in the war has been reckoned at $186,000,000,000. Of this total the Central Powers spent approximately $63,000,000,000 and the Allied Powers $123,000,000,000. These figures indicate that the Allies spent almost twice as much as their opponents. They could do so because their aggregate wealth greatly exceeded that of the Central Powers.

Throughout the war Great Britain, and to a smaller extent France, sought to maintain "business as usual" in order to pay with exports for the imports needed for their war economies. Outgoing ships bore cotton goods, woolens, cutlery, leatherware, porcelain, perfumes, Scotch whisky, champagne, cognac, and anything the two countries could produce and spare to sell in order to pay for ships, services, food, raw materials, manufactures, and munitions purchased in all parts of the globe. But the demands of war economy far exceeded their ability to pay with exports. Almost immediately after the outbreak of the war both countries were

---

[1] Ray Stannard Baker, *Woodrow Wilson: Life and Letters* (New York: Doubleday & Co., 1927–1939, VII, 180).

156

forced to draw on their reserves of gold and to convert their assets abroad into available exchange in order to pay for essential imports.

In 1914 Great Britain had invested in foreign countries about $17,440,-000,000 and France about $7,390,000,000. Of these amounts Britain had invested about $10,000,000,000 in North and South America but France only about $1,600,000,000. While Britain found it easy enough to convert much of her foreign assets, almost half of the French foreign investments were tied up in the Russian and Turkish Empires and could not be liquidated. As early as 1915 the British and French assets dwindled so much that they had to seek loans, principally in the United States. After some vacillation the United States government authorized American bankers to extend to the Allies funds with which to pay for imports of American goods. By the time of the American declaration of war these loans amounted to about $500,000,000. After the United States entered the war, the federal government took over from private bankers, and by the end of the hostilities had extended to the Allies about $7,000,000,000 in credits. This was a sum equal to five times the public debt of the United States in 1916, the last year of peace. As a result of the liquidation of British and French assets in the United States and the extension of American loans to the Allies, the United States, which had been a debtor nation until 1914, became the principal creditor nation in the world. Although the Allied nations were glad to obtain American credits during the war, they resented their financial dependence on the United States after the war.

The Central Powers also tried to continue their international trade after the outbreak of the war, but because of the Allied blockade they were largely unsuccessful. German foreign trade, which before the war had reached $5,000,000,000 and had ranked second only to that of Great Britain ($7,000,000,000), dwindled to an insignificant exchange with Germany's neutral neighbors. Owing to their superior financial resources, the Allies were able to interfere even with this small trade by means of a practice known as "preclusive buying." This consisted in paying higher prices, even extravagant prices, for rare minerals, drugs, and other items; even if such purchases could not be removed or used by the Allies they might be destroyed to keep them from reaching the Central Powers.

Nations which normally traded with the Central Powers were forced, whether they liked it or not, to transfer their commerce to the Allies. The superior financial resources of the Allies, combined with their superior sea power, gave them a great influence over the neutrals. By 1917 the American economy was so geared to exporting to the Allied countries that a sudden interruption of this flow of goods would have caused serious economic dislocations in the United States. With each shipment rerouted by the war to London or Cherbourg from its original destination to Hamburg or Trieste, whether it was American cotton, Chilean nitrates, Bolivian tin, Argentine beef, Spanish minerals, or Persian oil, the country producing the cargo became more and more definitely an economic belligerent, although it might maintain technically the status of a neutral. Profits thus combined with sentiment and considerations of their own security to draw the neutral nations into the Allied camp.

2. WAR AIMS

At the outset of the war none of the belligerents had any defined aim except to win. The Allied Powers felt threatened by German power and were determined to destroy it. Germany, on the other hand, felt hemmed in and threatened by the Allied Powers, and was determined to break out of the encirclement imposed on her. But as the war progressed, the belligerents defined, each for itself, their particular aims. These more concrete war aims were generally old historical ambitions and hopes for gains, the prospect of which had been opened by the war.

Austria, which began the war, had at the outset no other aim than to crush Serbia — the supposed source of her internal difficulties. The Austrian leaders had no plans with regard to Serbia after they had crushed her, except to think vaguely of partitioning her; they could not very well annex her, for that would only increase Austria's internal difficulties. Serbia, on the other hand, full of confidence after her initial success in repelling the Austrian attack, announced in December, 1914, that it was her aim to unite not only all the Serbs but also all the Yugoslavs in a common state.

Russia had originally no aim beyond the protection of Serbia. Turkish neutrality at the beginning of the war prevented the Russians from advancing their historical aim of controlling the Straits of the Bosporus and the Dardanelles. Casting about for an aim, the Russian leaders thought of Poland. On August 14 Russia staked out a claim to Poland in a manifesto of the Grand Duke Nicholas, the commander-in-chief, which announced that it was Russia's intention to reunite Poland "under the scepter of the Emperor of Russia . . . free in its religion, language, and autonomy."

Germany had originally no definite plans for expansion, but as her armies made conquests, the German leaders contemplated annexations in both the west and the east. In the west they toyed with the idea of keeping Belgium and portions of northern France. In the east they intended to satellize Poland. A joint manifesto of the German and Austrian emperors on November 5, 1916, announced their intention to create out of conquered Russian Poland "an autonomous state, having the form of an hereditary, constitutional monarchy." But it was understood between Vienna and Berlin that the Polish state would be a German satrapy. The military collapse of Russia in 1917 opened prospects of further extending German power in the east. Under the Peace of Brest-

Litovsk (March 3, 1918) the Baltic Provinces, White Russia, the Ukraine, and Transcaucasia were detached from Russia, and German officers busied themselves with setting them up as German satellites.

France hoped from the beginning of the war to recover the lost provinces of Alsace and Lorraine, although she had not entered the war to conquer them. Beyond that, France hoped to assure her security by reducing Germany in size; she wished to detach and erect as a buffer state, German territory west of the Rhine. But her inauspicious military situation long made these aims only fond dreams. It was not until February, 1917, that she obtained a guarantee of these aims, and then only from Russia, which was on the eve of revolution.

Britain entered the war determined to restore Belgium and to destroy the German fleet. She was also resolved to deprive Germany of colonies which had served as justification for the creation of the German navy. Beyond that Britain hoped to see guarantees that after the war the rule of law would prevail in international relations.[2]

Japan entered the war for the sole purpose of making territorial gains while the European powers were too busy to interfere. After her conquest of the German possessions in the Pacific, Japan withdrew for all practical purposes from the war until the collapse of Russia and the Allied intervention in Siberia offered her new opportunities for adventure by fishing in the troubled Russian waters.

Turkey joined the Central Powers in war in October, 1914, in the hope of recovering her losses to the Allied Powers. Her entry into the war removed the reason for Russia's restraint with regard to the Straits. On March 4, 1915, as the western Allies prepared for the Gallipoli campaign (see p. 136), the Russian government demanded of them that the Straits and adjoining territory be included in the Russian Empire. The Russian demand opened a virtual Pandora's box. It led to the conclusion of the notorious Allied "secret treaties" providing for the dismemberment of the Ottoman Empire. On March 12, 1915, Britain yielded to the Russian demand with a readiness that was surprising in view of her historical opposition to the Russian control of the Straits. France gave in more grudgingly on April 10, 1915, and demanded compensation. Russia agreed that the western Allies were entitled to compensation, but insisted on a second payment in Armenia. On April 26, 1916, the three allies signed a secret treaty providing for a division among themselves of the Asian provinces of Turkey as well as of substantial portions of Turkey itself. Later, in the St. Jean de Maurienne agreements (April 19–21, 1917), Italy was allotted a sphere of influence in southwestern Turkey.

Italy, in fact, was able to obtain compensation at the expense of both Turkey and Austria. Being a neutral at the beginning of the war, she was in the advantageous position of being courted by both parties at war

[2] The ideas of Sir Edward Grey on this subject, of which Wilson learned through Colonel House, led the President to espouse the idea of a league of nations.

and of being able to exact a stiff price for her support. She could thus define her war aims in advance and obtain advance guarantees of them. On April 26, 1915, Italy signed with the Allies the secret Treaty of London which promised her the Austrian provinces of Southern Tyrol (High Adige), Trieste, Istria, and Dalmatia as well as a share of Turkey. This program went far beyond securing *Italia irredenta*. It was, in fact, designed to give Italy absolute security by putting her northern border on the Brenner Pass and giving her the complete control of the Adriatic in the east.

The decaying Hapsburg empire served the Allies as a sort of fund from which to pay new recruits for their cause. In the summer of 1915 the Allies promised Bulgaria Serbian Macedonia in order to induce her to join them in war and help relieve the pressure on them at Gallipoli. To reconcile Serbia to this sacrifice, they promised her compensation at the expense of Austria (August 18, 1915). Serbia was to be permitted to complete the unification of the Serbs, but not of the Yugoslavs, by incorporating Bosnia and Herzegovina and a strip of southern Hungary. She was also to receive an outlet to the Adriatic Sea in southern Dalmatia. Bulgaria, however, declined the Allied offer and joined the Central Powers (September 6, 1915), which guaranteed to her not only Serbian Macedonia but also portions of Greek Macedonia and Thrace and of Rumanian Dobrudja — if Greece and Rumania joined the Allies, as then seemed likely.

Rumania, like Italy, was able to obtain advance guarantees of her war aims. In the secret Treaty of Bucharest (August 17, 1917) the Allies promised Rumania not only Transylvania, Bukovina, and the Banat, to which she had a reasonable ethnic claim, but also a wide band of the purely Magyar plain of Hungary. The Allies made also generous promises of other nations' territory to Greece (Thrace, the Aegean archipelago, and Cyprus). But because of an internal quarrel between the partisans of the pro-Allied Prime Minister Eleutherios Venizelos and the pro-German King Constantine, Greece missed the opportunity. The Allies ultimately broke the impasse between Venizelos and King Constantine by landing troops in Greece and deposing the King, but they did not renew their offer. Greece formally entered the war on the Allied side in July, 1917, without an advance guarantee of her war aims.

The United States entered the war without a preliminary agreement with the Allies and without any territorial ambitions in mind. President Wilson never tired of pointing out: "We seek no indemnities for ourselves, no material compensation for the sacrifices we shall freely make." The principal American war aim was the freedom of the seas. Beyond that, the Americans hoped to see a settlement which would guarantee a millennium of peace under the aegis of the League of Nations. President Wilson's peace terms, it soon turned out, were hardly in harmony with the Allied war aims.

3. PEACE PROGRAMS AND PROPAGANDA

From the beginning of the war both belligerent groups resorted to propaganda on an unprecedented scale. The purpose of this propaganda was threefold: to sustain their own morale, to subvert that of the adversary, and to sway the neutrals in their favor. In all belligerent countries government information bureaus were opened, which sought to funnel desirable information into the press. In most belligerent countries censors scanned the press and the mails, and withheld from the citizens information which their governments considered undesirable. Most belligerents maintained also information services in the countries of their allies and in key neutral countries. Switzerland, wedged between the two groups of belligerents, became the scene of particularly intense propaganda and intelligence activities. At the fronts, by means of runners, rifle grenades, rockets, and airplanes, the belligerents inundated each other's trenches with leaflets in an effort to sow defeatism and dissension in each other's ranks.

Before the American intervention and the Russian Revolution, however, this propaganda had no ideological content; the European belligerents did not seek to subvert each other's form of government. This propaganda claimed simply that both groups of belligerents were fighting a "defensive war" and for a "just and durable peace." If that had been the case, the belligerents should not have had any difficulty in coming to terms and speedily ending the war. But, as has been seen in the preceding pages, both groups harbored secret plans of annexation. They were, therefore, rather embarrassed when President Wilson, in an effort to bring them to terms, called on them in December, 1916, to state publicly their war aims.

The Central Powers declined the suggestion. The Allied Powers also at first demurred, but on the advice of Walter Hines Page, the strongly Anglophile United States Ambassador in London, they reconsidered. On January 10, 1917, they stated their war aims, cleverly wrapped in the garb of a comprehensive program of liberation of oppressed peoples, in complete harmony with Wilson's principle of national self-determination (see p. 172). Although self-determination had not been a motive of Allied policy toward Austria and Turkey, the ethnic principle could be used, by stretching the term a bit, to justify the amputations the Allies proposed to perform on the Hapsburg empire, but hardly the vivisections they intended for the Ottoman Empire. Nevertheless, the Allies gained, for the moment, a considerable propaganda advantage over the Central Powers, who by refusing to divulge publicly their aims left themselves open to suspicion of harboring sinister intentions.

The outbreak of the Russian Revolution and the American declaration of war in 1917 intensified and complicated propaganda warfare. While Russia continued to fight alongside the Allies, the Russian revolutionaries began to detach themselves from the Allied cause and address themselves almost impartially to both groups of belligerents. When America joined the Allies, President Wilson continued to maintain the posture of an impartial arbiter. By consistently using the term "Allied and Associate Powers" (the "associate" power being the United States), he emphasized that the United States did not identify itself completely with Allied aims. Both the Russian revolutionaries and President Wilson subjected Europe to blasts of ideological propaganda, addressed over the heads of governments directly to the belligerent peoples and delivered with great moral earnestness. While one spoke of a "peace without annexations or contributions on the basis of self-determination of peoples," the other spoke of a "peace without victory" and "government by consent of the governed."

The Russian withdrawal from the war after the Bolshevik Revolution in November, 1917, further complicated the situation. The Bolsheviks solemnly renounced the imperialist aims of Tsarist Russia, accorded the minority peoples of the Russian Empire the right of self-determination, and invited the belligerents to negotiate peace on the basis of their formula — no annexations, no contributions, and self-determination of peoples. The formula was unacceptable to either the Allies or the Central Powers. Nevertheless, the Central Powers agreed to negotiate on its basis, because they wanted at all costs to get Russia out of the war, in order to concentrate their forces against the western Allies and knock them out before the Americans could come to their rescue. For opposite reasons the Allies refused to negotiate. To embarrass them the Bolsheviks then published the Allied secret treaties. They hoped to provide in this way proof before world opinion that the Allied governments wanted to continue the war solely for the purpose of achieving imperialistic aims. This put the Allies in an unenviable position, for after three and a half years of fighting the peoples of Europe, including the Allied nations, were weary to death of the war and in no mood to fight for imperialistic ambitions.

At this juncture President Wilson stepped in and announced the famous Fourteen Points peace program (January 8, 1918). The Fourteen Points was a liberal program, but hardly an "idealistic" one. It was intended less to provide a basis for peace than a justification for continuing war. In this immediate purpose it succeeded, but at the cost of causing many difficulties later. The Allies, who had not been consulted in its formulation, readily acquiesced in it at the time, because it extricated them from a difficult position. But they had mental reservations about it, and when the time came to implement it they raised objections to it. The Central Powers rejected the Fourteen Points at the time they were announced, but remembered them later — when defeat stared them in the face. Moreover, by imposing on Russia the harsh Peace of Brest-Litovsk (March 3, 1918), they dissipated the moral advantage which they had gained by agreeing to negotiate with the Russians. They could have worked out a plausible case for the Brest-Litovsk amputations by justifying them with the principle of self-determination — the Russian minorities *really* wanted to leave the Russian Empire — but Germany had no intention of according them self-determination. Moreover, the principle of self-determination was anathema to Germany's allies, Austria and Turkey, who were themselves oppressors of national minorities and thus very vulnerable to it. So the Central Powers claimed annexations from Russia by right of conquest, which exposed them to the charge of imperialism. Wilson could therefore declare with justice on April 6, 1918: "I am ready, ready still, ready even now to discuss a fair and just and honest peace at any time that it is sincerely proposed. . . . But the answer, when I proposed such a peace, came from the German commanders in Russia, and I cannot mistake the meaning of the answer." "There is, therefore, but one response possible from us: Force, Force to the utmost, Force without stint or limit. . . ."

In battles of propaganda with such prophets as Wilson or Lenin the leaders of the Central Powers were hopelessly outclassed. The ultimate defeat of the Central Powers was greatly aided by the breakdown of morale on their home fronts, resulting, in part, from Wilsonian and Bolshevik propaganda.

15

POLITICAL, SOCIAL, AND ECONOMIC RESULTS
OF THE WAR

*The Czech, Hungarian, and German bourgeois, who only yesterday cringed
before the Hapsburgs . . . now shout: "Long live Wilson!" To assist this swin-
dler's trick, American capital promises you bread; we, however, tell you . . . :
American, French, and English capital is just as much an enemy of the working
class as German capital.*[1]

LENIN

1. WAR CASUALTIES AND WAR COSTS

WHEN THE ORDER to cease fire halted the First World War on November
11, 1918, a stunned humanity prepared to audit the costs of four years of
mass destruction. This stocktaking required time. Some estimates are
even yet in debate, but the loss of life and the official expenditures have
been summarized in round numbers. Eight million dead and twenty
million wounded proved that modern war had become systematic mass
murder. Through four and a quarter years of fighting, men had died at
the rate of six to seven thousand a day. In three particulars the military
figures of the First World War surpassed all previous known records: the
proportion of the male population called to the colors was higher than in
any previous national wars for which computations were available; the
absolute total of men mobilized, a total probably in excess of sixty million,
was without precedent in history; and the ratio of dead and wounded, in
proportion to the total number engaged, had risen sharply. The casualties
represented nearly 40 per cent of the combatants, even if we assume that
some names figured on the casualty lists more than once. For the chief
belligerents the casualty figures stood approximately as follows:[2]

[1] Manifesto to the workers of Austria-Hungary, November 3, 1918.

[2] W. L. Langer (editor), *An Encyclopaedia of World History* (Boston: Houghton
Mifflin Company, 1940), p. 960.

	DEAD	WOUNDED
Germany	1,808,000	4,247,000
Russia	1,700,000	4,950,000
France	1,385,000	3,044,000
Austria-Hungary	1,200,000	3,620,000
Great Britain	947,000	2,122,000
Italy	460,000	947,000
Turkey	325,000	400,000
United States	115,000	206,000
	7,940,000	19,536,000

In proportion to population France had endured the heaviest sacrifices. Even the reacquisition of Alsace-Lorraine could not replace numerically the French lives blotted out in the four years' slaughter. For Americans to form an idea of this drain on French manpower, which was to sap fatally the *élan vital* of France, it is necessary to translate these losses into proportional estimates based upon the population of the United States in 1945. A comparable tragedy for America would mean 5,000,000 servicemen dead and 11,000,000 wounded, a total in excess of all the men in the armed services of the United States in World War II.

France was not the only European nation seriously reduced by the disaster of war. Germany suffered a larger total of war dead, although in proportion to the population of the Reich the percentage was lighter. For Austria-Hungary the burden was almost as high as for Germany. Russian estimates acknowledged a list of slain almost as high as the German total and very probably higher had complete statistics been available.

Twentieth-century warfare proved costly in money as well as in lives. In twenty years of warfare against the French, from 1793 to 1814, the British national debt increased eightfold. But in the four years from 1914 to 1918 British indebtedness, domestic and foreign, rose from $3,000,000,000 to $35,000,000,000. These figures suggest that war had grown ten times as costly in the course of a century, but as population, production, and living costs had all risen in the same period comparisons are not easily made. For all the belligerents of World War I the official direct expense has been calculated at $186,000,000,000. The indirect cost was almost as great. The loss in property cannot be easily measured. The labor and energy diverted to nonproductive or actively destructive purposes deprived humanity of a wealth of durable goods and services which might have been provided with the same effort.

The First World War gave the generation which lived through it a deep traumatic experience, as the large pacifist literature produced after the war by the veterans of trenches testifies. The novel of Remarque *All Quiet on the Western Front* is a good example, and an eloquent testimony of the agony of these brave men. The loss of nerve on the part of the ruling elites of France and Britain on the eve of the Second World War is largely explainable by the memory they had of the carnage in the First World War, in which they had provided brave and energetic leadership and lost proportionately more men than the lower classes. The confident, prosperous, and optimistic Europe of the prewar era was gone. Instead there emerged an impoverished and deeply troubled Europe. The contemporaries were not clearly aware of it, but the First World War had ended the primacy of Europe in the world.

2. TRIUMPH OF DEMOCRACY — REALITIES AND APPEARANCES

The question which the distressing figures on the costs and casualties of the First World War inevitably bring to mind is whether these terrible sacrifices served any just or reasonable purpose. The question may perhaps be best answered by comparing the results of the war with its objectives. President Wilson believed that the main objective of the war was to "make the world safe for democracy," because "a steadfast concert for peace could never be maintained except by a partnership of democratic nations." His faith was shared by many, not only in the Allied countries, but — according to the testimony, for instance, of Count Julius Andrássy, the last Austro-Hungarian Foreign Minister — also in the Central Powers. Reminiscing on the final phases of the war, Count Andrássy wrote: "Demagogues and some naïve souls asked whether it was not revolting treachery to continue the war if Wilson declared, in the name of the great American Republic, that the war was not conducted against nations, but against the autocratic system which caused the war and which the people did not wish to tolerate any longer anyhow. . . . Anyone who did not believe the promises of the American President was mercilessly stamped as an agitator for war. Wilson, 'the enemy,' was more popular than the own statesmen of the people."

If, indeed, as Wilson believed, the main issue of the war was struggle of freedom against tyranny, then the sacrifices of the war were not in vain. The war advanced the cause of democracy, although it did not secure it for all time. That would be the task of the peacemakers. Before 1914 all European countries were governed, whether by custom or by law, by social elites drawn largely from the upper and middle classes. Even in the democratic countries of Western Europe the lower classes tended by tradition to defer to their "betters" in politics. During the war the masses were called upon to make unprecedented sacrifices and realized their importance. After the war they demanded governments more responsive to their needs. The war thus hastened the democratization of European society.

But the demand for freedom was not the only force stimulated by the war. It stimulated also a demand for social justice and the nationalism of the masses. Could social justice be assured and national aspirations be satisfied under the old nineteenth-century, laissez-faire form of democracy? In Western Europe, where the roots of representative government were deep and the art of government by judicious compromises was well understood, few doubted that they could. The western democracies had withstood the supreme test of war successfully, and — though they were impoverished and weakened by war — they would surely find the wisdom and statesmanship necessary to solve their postwar problems without violence and within the framework of existing governments. In Central and Eastern Europe, however, the answer was less certain.

The defeat of Russia and the Central Powers resulted in chaos throughout their former empires. The question was what kind of governments would arise on the ruins of their former autocratic regimes: democratic governments, some new form of authoritarian governments, or Bolshevik rule as in Russia? The fall of the Russian monarchy and the destruction of the liberal Provisional Government by the Bolsheviks have already been reviewed in the preceding pages. But the issue in Russia was far from decided. At the time of the western armistices Russia was in the throes of a terrible civil war between the Bolsheviks and the White forces. It will be discussed in the following pages. The Bolsheviks regarded as the main issue of the war, not struggle of freedom against tyranny, but struggle of socialism against capitalism. Parliamentary democracy was to them simply an extension of capitalism in the field of politics. Therefore, they regarded the destruction of democracy as necessary, not only in Russia but also in other countries. Even while engaged in a life-and-death struggle with the Whites at home, they sought to promote social revolutions abroad. Whom would the peoples of Central and Eastern Europe heed: Wilson, Lenin, or perhaps some local leader as yet unknown seeking to promote some new form of authoritarian government? As the war ended, that was the great issue in Central and Eastern Europe. Its outcome depended, to a large extent, on the wisdom and statesmanship of the peacemakers, then gathering in Paris.

3. THE FALL OF THE GERMAN MONARCHY AND THE RISE OF THE GERMAN REPUBLIC

In Germany events seemed to be following the Russian pattern. The German people had fought bravely for the glory of the Fatherland, socialist workers fighting as stoutly as Prussian Junkers or Ruhr industrialists. However, when Germany faced defeat and humiliation instead of glory and conquest promised by the German rulers, the German people, usually so obedient and respectful of authority, revolted. The signal for the revolution was given by the sailors of the German navy. On October 28, 1918, they mutinied against a senseless order to the fleet to steam out of the Kiel Harbor and engage the British navy in a last *beau geste* battle.

The revolt presently spread to other German ports and cities where the sailors and soldiers were joined by workers in forming soviets on the Russian model.

Matters were then taken in hand by the German socialists Friedrich Ebert and Philipp Scheidemann. The socialists had originally supported the war as a legitimate defense of the Fatherland against the Russian autocracy. But after the Russian Revolution they increasingly questioned whether war was justified. On November 9, 1918, they proclaimed the German Republic. The Emperor William, frightened by revolution, fled to Holland. His flight was followed by the collapse of the other German monarchies. The ruling classes, though strongly disapproving of the republic, acquiesced in the events for the moment in the hope that the new republican government could obtain better terms from the Allies than they themselves could. On the same ground the generals of the defeated army persuaded the inexperienced socialist leaders to assume the onus of negotiating the armistice with the Allies. Later this permitted the generals to claim that the army had not surrendered but had been "stabbed in the back" by the socialists, Jews, and other slackers.

While the monarchists on the extreme political right, although unreconciled to the republic, lay low, the government was attacked by the Spartacists (i.e., communists) on the extreme left. In January, 1919, the Spartacists precipitated a revolt in Berlin in order to topple the government and prevent it from holding elections for a constituent assembly, which was to decide Germany's future form of government in a democratic way. With an assist from the generals and the remnants of the Imperial army the revolt was crushed. The danger to the republic was for the moment exorcised. But whether it would ultimately survive depended largely on the generosity and understanding of the peacemakers at Paris.

While defeat brought Germany humiliation, confusion, and misery, in the multinational Austrian and Turkish Empires it resulted in complete dissolution — events which will be discussed in the following pages. On the other hand, developments in Bulgaria, a homogeneous, national state, were analogous to those of Germany. The defeat toppled the unpopular King Ferdinand. He fled abroad, but the attempt to proclaim a republic was defeated with the aid of German troops. The throne was saved for Ferdinand's son, Boris. However, a new government was formed by the agrarian leader Alexander Stambolisky, who had been imprisoned during the war for his outspoken criticism of King Ferdinand and his steadfast opposition to the war. Stambolisky earnestly endeavored to introduce democracy in Bulgaria. But, like the socialist leaders in Germany, he had to assume the ungrateful task of concluding peace after a lost war. Whether he would succeed in promoting democracy in Bulgaria depended largely on the terms accorded to him by the Allies at the peace conference.

4. THE RUSSIAN REVOLUTION AND CIVIL WAR, 1918–1920

When the Bolsheviks seized power by a *coup d'état* in Petrograd on November 7, 1917, they encountered little overt opposition to their rule in Russia. Except for some resistance in Moscow, the country followed passively the lead of the capital, just as it had in the March Revolution. This, however, did not mean that a majority of the population actively supported the Bolshevik regime, but only that most Russians were too weary of strife and confusion to care for the moment who ruled Russia.

Opposition to the Bolshevik government began to form almost at once. It came into the open after the conclusion of the humiliating Peace of Brest-Litovsk (March 3, 1918) which outraged Russian patriotic opinion. Not only conservatives but also the Social Revolutionaries denounced the Bolsheviks as cowards or pro-German traitors. In the spring of 1918 "White" armies began to form in the peripheral regions of Russia, over which the Bolshevik government had imperfect or no control. Russia's withdrawal from the war also outraged the Allies, who regarded the Bolsheviks as pro-German or as German agents pure and simple. They encouraged the Whites to rise and promised to aid them by military intervention. Feeling itself menaced from within and without, the Bolshevik government prepared to defend itself by forming political police (the notorious "Cheka") under Felix Dzerzynski, a madcap Polish nobleman and fanatical Bolshevik, and the "Red Army" under Leon Trotsky, a brilliant intellectual and able organizer.

The Civil War between the "Reds" and the "Whites" broke out in May, 1918, and raged until the end of 1920. Unlike the March and November Revolutions of 1917, which were accomplished without much loss of human life, the Civil War was marred by a ghastly slaughter of opponents. Like the French Jacobins in 1793 the Russian Bolsheviks used terror as a deliberate instrument of policy. The Whites retaliated in kind. Genocide as a method of disposing of opposition is a tragic Russian contribution to twentieth-century political practice; the fascists and the nazis were mere imitators of the Bolsheviks, albeit eager ones.

Militarily, the Reds had the advantages of a single command and of "inner lines." They were able to repel the White armies piecemeal, as they converged in an uncoordinated fashion on Moscow (to which the Bolsheviks transferred the capital in March, 1918) from all directions: from the south the army of General Denikin and the Don Cossacks supported by the Allies (after the Germans withdrew from the war, the French landed troops in the Ukraine and the British in the Caucasus); from the east the forces of Admiral Kolchak and the Czechoslovaks[3] sup-

[3] The "Czechoslovak Legion" in Russia was a body of about 50,000 Czech and Slovak troops, organized by the Russians from volunteers and Austro-Hungarian prisoners of war originally to combat against the Central Powers. It was, in fact, the successful

ported by the Allies (in August, 1918, American and Japanese troops landed at Vladivostok, but did not move far from their base); from the north the forces of General Miller and the Allies (in the spring and summer of 1918 British, French, and American forces landed at the ports of Archangel and Murmansk); from the Baltic region General Yudenich's army and Baltic forces; and from the west the Poles (April–October, 1920). Politically, the Reds had the advantages of a single government and a single program. The Whites, on the other hand, had neither a single government nor a single program. They consisted of very heterogeneous elements, ranging from Social Revolutionaries on the far left to monarchists on the far right. They were unable to agree on a program, and dissipated their strength fighting each other. The principal White government was that of Admiral Kolchak in Siberia, which was recognized by the Allies. Kolchak was a competent naval officer and distinguished arctic explorer but an extremely inept politician. He wasted his effort combatting the left-wing opponents of the Bolsheviks more eagerly than the Bolsheviks themselves. Allied recognition of his government was probably more of a hindrance to him than a help, for Allied policy toward the Russian Revolution was inept and confused in the extreme.

The Allies never agreed among themselves on their aims in Russia. President Wilson consented to intervention only with extreme reluctance, and then only as a military measure (to guard military stores which had been shipped to Russian ports from passing into the hands of the Germans, and in Vladivostok to keep an eye on the Japanese, of whose purposes the Americans were extremely suspicious). He was strenuously opposed to political intervention, that is, to an Allied attempt to overthrow the Bolshevik government or to help the Russians to overthrow it. As early as September, 1918, when victory over Germany came in sight, he disassociated the United States from the Allied intervention in Russia. Allied support of the Whites proved to be a kiss of death to them, for militarily it was utterly ineffectual and politically it exposed them to the charge of being "lackeys of the Western imperialists," bent on dismembering Russia. The Reds, who started out in the Civil War with the stigma of pro-German traitors, managed (after the German withdrawal from the war) not only to shake off this handicap but to don the patriotic mantle of defenders of Russia's national heritage against greedy foreigners and their native henchmen. By harnessing the dynamic forces of socialism and Russian nationalism, the Bolsheviks succeeded not only in winning the Civil War but also in restoring, to a large extent, the multinational Russian Empire. This provided them with a large base, from which to attack in the years to come non-communist regimes in Europe and Asia.

resistance of the Czechoslovaks to an attempt by the Bolshevik government to disarm them in May, 1918, and the ease with which they seized the Trans-Siberian Railway, that encouraged the Whites to rise and the Allies to intervene.

5. THE BREAKUP OF THE HAPSBURG EMPIRE AND THE RISE OF THE SUCCESSOR STATES

When General Weber of the Austrian army signed the armistice agreement on November 3, 1918, he was performing a hollow legal ceremony, for the Austrian Empire was no more. Austria precipitated the war to save herself from disintegration. Instead, the war hastened her dissolution.

When the war came the ruling nationalities of Austria were jubilant that the moment of reckoning with the troublesome Slavs was finally at hand. The Slavs, on the other hand, appeared cowed. Yugoslav and Czechoslovak soldiers responded to the mobilization orders obediently, though sullenly, and marched off to fight for the Emperor as in wars of old. Their politicians hastened to profess their loyalty to the Emperor and then adopted a cautious wait-and-see attitude. The Poles, on the other hand, showed more genuine enthusiasm for the war against Russia, traditional enemy of the Poles. Galicia became the center of a movement for Polish unification under the Hapsburg dynasty. Joseph Pilsudski, a Russian Pole, organized a volunteer Polish Legion to fight alongside the Austrians against the Russian oppressors. Similarly the Austrian socialists, who normally opposed war as a matter of party dogma, were quite willing to fight Russia — the bastion of reaction and enemy of socialism. As for the Italians and Rumanians in Austria-Hungary, they had little reason to stir as long as Italy and Rumania remained neutral. There was, therefore, little indication at the beginning of the war that Austria might disintegrate during its course.

Indeed, had the war been short and victorious, the Austrian monarchy might have come out of it strengthened. But the war proved long and arduous. The Austrian army was repeatedly defeated and suffered terrible casualties. The complicated administration and weak economy of Austria were ill adapted to a total war and progressively broke down. By 1917 the population of the empire faced starvation. The outbreak of the Russian Revolution and the American declaration of war emboldened the opposition and quickened the disintegration. Revolution might have broken out in 1917, but the power of Germany, looming behind the weak Austrian government, deterred would-be revolutionaries and encouraged loyal elements.

However, groups of exiles abroad were hard at work from the early days of the war trying to bring about Austria's defeat and dissolution. In 1915 a Yugoslav National Committee was founded in London under the presidency of Ante Trumbić, a former Reichsrat deputy. In the same year a Czechoslovak National Council was organized in Paris by Thomas G. Masaryk, a distinguished Czech scholar and Reichsrat deputy. Finally, in 1917 the Polish National Committee in Paris was established by Roman Dmowski, a member of the Russian Duma. All of these organizations sought to commit the Allies to a policy of dismembering the multinational Austrian Empire and replacing it with national states.

This had originally not been the intention of the Allies. Austria had been a part of Europe's balance-of-power system for four centuries and most Allied statesmen regarded her preservation as essential to European stability. While western statesmen feared that the void created by her disappearance would be filled with Russian satellites, Russian statesmen feared lest it be filled with western-oriented democracies. However, as the war progressed the Allies were forced to consider, first the diminution and ultimately the complete dismemberment of the Austrian Empire. First, they acquiesced when Russia staked out a claim to Poland. Then, to reward or compensate Italy, Serbia, and Rumania, they proposed to detach the peripheral provinces, Trent, Istria, Dalmatia, Bosnia-Herzegovina, Transylvania, the Banat, and Bukovina. Finally, casting about for a way to make their aims palatable to Wilson, they included in their statement of war aims on January 10, 1917, "the liberation of Italians, of Slavs, of Rumanians, and of Czechoslovaks from foreign domination" (see p. 161).

This blanket statement implied that the Allies intended to dismember Austria completely. It frightened the Austrian statesmen and led them to put out numerous peace feelers. These, in turn, aroused a hope in the Allies to detach Austria from Germany. In secret negotiations, which stretched from March, 1917, to April, 1918, the French, the British, and the Americans, each in turn, tried to induce Vienna to conclude a separate peace on the basis of preserving Austria essentially unimpaired. Indeed, they went even further: they held out to Austria the prospect of union with Poland, Rumania, and Serbia, as well as of parts of Germany in a great Central European Confederation under the Hapsburg dynasty if she would forsake the German alliance and agree to fill the role of a "counterpoise" to Germany and (after the Bolshevik Revolution) to Russia. The negotiations ultimately broke down because of the reluctance of Italy to give up the gains promised to her in the Treaty of London, and, above all, because Vienna would not and could not betray its powerful ally. The Allies then reluctantly turned to the alternate policy of dismembering Austria, and gave official recognition to the Polish, Czechoslovak, and Yugoslav movements for independence.

On October 4, 1918, Austria offered to surrender on the basis of the Fourteen Points. Point Ten of this program envisaged giving the Austrian nationalities "the freest opportunity of autonomous development" but not complete independence. To implement this demand the Emperor Charles issued on October 16 a manifesto announcing the federalization of the Austrian half of the empire. Because of violent opposition of the Magyars, Hungary was not included in the manifesto, and this weakened it. But even if Hungary had been included, it is doubtful whether the manifesto could, at this late date, save Austria. On October 19 Wilson declined the Austrian offer to surrender on the basis of the Fourteen Points, on the ground that since the issuance of this program he had committed himself to support Czechoslovak and Yugoslav independence. On October 27 Vienna bowed to the inevitable and asked for an armistice without any condition. This became the signal for the dissolution of the empire. It was accomplished by an internal revolution but with remarkably little bloodshed in a few days. The Allies did not occupy Austria-Hungary (except some peripheral areas) and did not assist in the revolution. It was unnecessary, for the collapse of Russia in the previous year and the imminent collapse of Germany had removed the principal obstacles to the freedom of the Austrian peoples.

The "Successor States" of Austria-Hungary invariably established democratic governments and looked not to Russia but to the Allies for help and guidance. Count Károlyi, leader of the new Hungarian Republic, expressed these states' hope in a pathetic appeal to Wilson: "Mr. President, we appeal to your feeling . . . come to the assistance of the young Hungarian democracy!" The President was willing, even eager, to respond to this appeal. In his address to Congress on Armistice Day he recommended that the peoples of the Central empires be given economic aid, for "hunger . . . breeds madness." But more than economic assistance was needed if democracy were to survive in Central Europe: the situation demanded statesmanship and long-term guidance. For this the President would need, among other things, support of Congress and of the American people. In congressional elections on November 5 the Democratic Party — Wilson's party — lost both houses of Congress. This augured ill for the role of the President as peacemaker and mentor of democracy in Europe.

6. THE DISSOLUTION OF THE OTTOMAN EMPIRE AND THE ARAB PROBLEM

Turkey entered the war to save herself and like Austria she thereby signed her death warrant. The Ottoman Empire had once sprawled over large portions of Asia, Europe, and Africa, but by 1914 had been reduced to its Asian possessions. The Young Turk leaders dreamed of restoring it to its former glory. In December, 1914, the Sultan and Caliph proclaimed the "Djihad" or Holy War in defense of Islam and called on the Moslems of the Russian, British, and French empires to rise. The Moslem subjects of Britain, France, and Russia might have risen if the Turks had been able to carry the war into enemy territory. But the Turkish armed forces could, at best, hold the enemy at bay. This they did successfully enough at Gallipoli, at Kut al-Amarah, and in Armenia until 1916. Ultimately, however, the structure of the Turkish Empire began to crack under the strain of war and the Allies were able to invade the country. The Russians advanced deep into Armenia in 1916, and the British advanced in Mesopotamia and Palestine in 1917.

The Allies, moreover, were able to exploit the disaffection of the non-Turkish minorities. The Russians stirred up the Armenians and the British the Arabs. The outbreak of the Russian Revolution relieved the Turks of Russian pressure, but the British became ever more menacing.

As early as 1915 the British entered into relations with the Arab chieftains ibn-Saud and Husein. Ibn-Saud, a Wahabi warrior, controlled the desert of Nejd in the central plateau of Arabia. Sherif Husein of Mecca — a scion of the proud clan of Hashim, which claimed descent from the Prophet — controlled Hejaz on the Red Sea. For British gold ibn-Saud agreed to ignore the Djihad (December, 1915), and husbanded his forces for a postwar showdown with his Arab rivals. For British money and arms and for British recognition — with certain reservations — of the independence of Arabia, Husein agreed to raise the banner of Arab revolt against the Turks (Husein-MacMahon correspondence, July–November, 1915). The Arab revolt broke out in Hejaz in June of 1916. In 1917 an Arab force under Husein's son Faisal joined the British forces under General Allenby in Palestine, and materially contributed to the ultimate Turkish defeat.

With the Turkish defeat in 1918 Turkish rule over the Arabs came definitely to an end. But the Arab hope of achieving freedom did not materialize because in the meantime the Allies had entered into secret compacts to partition the Arab lands. In the Anglo-Russian-French agreement of April 26, 1916, Russia agreed to the partition of Arabia between France and Britain as compensation for the Russian claim to Constantinople, the Straits area, and Armenia (see p. 159). France and Britain followed this up on May 9, 1916, by concluding an agreement, known after its authors as the Sykes-Picot Treaty, which defined their respective shares of Arabia. France was to control two areas in Syria (the coastal area directly and the inland area indirectly), and Britain two areas in Mesopotamia (the southern area directly and the northern area indirectly). Palestine was to be internationalized. Peninsular Arabia, which was then regarded as a complete waste (oil was discovered there only later), was not affected.

The Sykes-Picot Treaty did not violate the letter of Britain's promise to Sherif Husein, but it certainly violated its spirit. The relations of the Allies with the Arabs were further complicated by the Balfour Declaration of November 2, 1917, which promised the Jewish Zionists "the establishment in Palestine of a national home for the Jewish people." The renunciation of the Russian claims to Turkish territory by the Bolshevik government and its publication of the secret treaties in November, 1917, embarrassed the Allies, not only before the Arabs but before world opinion in general. The secret treaties put their candor and honesty in doubt. Thanks largely to the timely issuance of the Fourteen Points, which assured the non-Turkish peoples of the Ottoman Empire of "an absolutely unmolested opportunity of autonomous development" (Point Twelve), the Allies were able to allay Arab suspicions and stare down world opinion — for the moment. But at the Paris Peace Conference the Ottoman heritage proved to be one of the most difficult problems with which the Allies had to cope.

Section III: THE SEARCH FOR INTERNATIONAL

STABILITY

16

THE PROBLEMS OF PEACEMAKING

The atmosphere of Vae victis *is not a good one in which to frame a treaty of lasting peace.*[1]

LORD ROBERT CECIL

1. THE WAR GUILT THESIS

THE PRIMARY MISCONCEPTION which dominated the thought of many millions of people in 1919 was the belief that a few wicked men in high places had planned the war. This has been well described as the "conspiracy theory" of war causation. It assumed that certain statesmen, diplomats, and militarists, in collusion with a handful of financiers and industrialists, had plotted the great tragedy. In the course of the fighting, the persistent and effective propaganda of the Allied publicists fastened the dire responsibility for the catastrophe upon the Kaiser, the German and Austrian military leaders, and German industrial magnates. Arrogant, irresponsible, and avid for power, these men, it was widely believed, had plunged the world into war to further their own selfish interests.

It has been said that in a war truth is the first casualty. The Allied blockade, which isolated the Central Powers, made it difficult for them to justify their position to the world because their enemies controlled the main instruments of communication between the continents, the ships, mails, and undersea cables. After four years of fighting, the judgment reiterated by the Allied governments — that German and Austrian leaders were responsible for the war — had been accepted by the Allied nations and by most people in neutral countries as well. It was easier to accept this "devil theory" of war, to blame it on a handful of power-mad militarists in Berlin and Vienna, than to face the somber truth. World War I had rolled up such a colossal death toll and caused such immeasurable destruction that the victors wanted to purge themselves of any responsibility for the holocaust. The Allied governments assured their peoples, and their peoples willingly agreed, that they had fought only to defend

---

[1] Lord Robert Cecil, *A Great Experiment* (New York: Oxford University Press, 1941), p. 71.

themselves against a savage and unwarranted attack. The blame, not only for starting the conflict, but for its savagery, for the introduction of poison gas and submarine warfare, was placed almost exclusively on the shoulders of Kaiser William II, his generals, and his advisers.

Such a judgment inevitably raised the question: How could a few malign men come to hold such arbitrary power over the fate of millions? To this question, also, the peoples of the democratic countries believed that they knew the answer, and this was their second misconception. They insisted that the fault lay in the fact that Germany and Austria-Hungary, as conservative monarchies, were subject to autocratic rule. Lacking true democratic traditions and institutions, the peoples of central Europe had been unable to control the army staff and the imperial advisers who shaped the policy of the state. Their governments had been undemocratic and therefore irresponsible. War had come when the autocrats and militarists who planned it considered the moment ripe for the execution of their satanic plans of conquest. In other words, wars were caused by autocrats and militarists who prepared them through secret pacts and understandings.

Against the possibility of such premeditated violence the peace-loving nations, which meant to people in the Allied countries the democratic nations in particular, had of necessity taken some protective measures. But their expenditure for armaments before 1914 proved insufficient. It had required years of effort in the midst of war for them to arm, equip, and train the forces needed to assure victory. The belief that democratic governments always desired peace led to the third major misconception, that if there were no irresponsible autocrats in the world there would be no wars. Woodrow Wilson summarized this deep faith in the peaceful intentions of the common man and of popular governments when he issued his ringing declaration that the world must be made "safe for democracy."

Wilson, like millions of his admirers, was deeply and fervently convinced that the world was about to enter a new, more generous, more peaceful, and more democratic era. "The day of conquest and aggrandizement," he proclaimed, "is gone by. So is also the day of secret covenants entered into in the interests of particular governments and likely at some unlooked-for moment to disturb the peace of the world." This was the fourth major misconception. The victors in the First World War were themselves bound by secret commitments which they hesitated to avow, and the peace treaties which terminated the war were drawn up in secret. Conquest and aggrandizement, like militarism, are relative terms. To the defeated nations and to some neutral peoples the democracies appeared militaristic because they had won the war, and their annexation of German colonies by force of arms appeared indistinguishable from conquest and aggrandizement. The world had changed less than the idealists wanted to believe.

To safeguard peace in the future and make World War I truly a "war to end war" numerous proposals were offered for the creation of a league of democratic states, the citizens of which would form their governments by self-determination and live at peace with their neighbors, adjusting any disputes by frank and open methods. It was hoped that hatred of war would prove strong enough to persuade all nations, or a controlling majority, to modify their pretensions to absolute sovereignty to the extent of promising to submit all international controversies to a world court and to abide by its decisions. This faith that a world league of states and a world court could preserve peace was the fifth misconception or miscalculation prevalent in 1919.

Idealistic programs can be dangerous when they excite hopes which cannot be realized, for a mood of popular exaltation is certain in such a case to be followed by a sense of disillusionment and betrayal. When the misconceptions of 1919 are summarized, it becomes easy to understand why the war was certain to be followed by disappointment and cynicism. But to understand and interpret a period the student of history must recognize the faiths which inspired the people living in it. At the height of the war effort millions of people did accept the assertion that a few evil and ambitious leaders had plotted the war; they sincerely believed that such misuse of power could occur only in an autocratic regime; they were assured that a democratic nation was a peace-loving nation, that once secret diplomacy and militarism were curbed, war would be curbed also, and that a League of Nations would preserve peace on earth. In the exaltation of a great common struggle, millions of Americans, Englishmen, Frenchmen, and Italians, as well as citizens of the lesser Allied and neutral nations, caught an apocalyptic vision of a world remade. The war, hateful and costly though it proved to be, inspired something like the ardor and expectation of a crusade. The noble intention to build a better world steeled the Allied nations to hold on until victory was certain. The endorsement of their effort and their ideal by the people of the United States was a verdict and a vindication. The encouragement which American aid brought to their faltering morale was as important as the reinforcements which the United States forwarded to second their military efforts.

From 1914 to 1917 the United States stood outside the war as the most powerful neutral nation. It was also the greatest democratic nation in the world, a land of freedom and opportunity to which people in other lands looked with respect and envy. The rich and powerful American Republic had formed no entangling alliances and needed none because it was safe from attack. These facts, which placed it above the struggle that racked Europe after 1914, enabled the American people to judge the war justly and objectively. Or so at least it seemed to the rest of the nations, belligerents and neutrals. When, in 1917, the President and Congress of the United States decided to enter the war on the side of the Allies, it meant that they had decided which parties in the struggle were in the right and which were in the wrong. Because the United States had come to symbolize the spirit of freedom and democracy, the American decision to aid the Allies seemed a historical vindication of their cause and a historical verdict rendered against the Central Powers. By identifying the cause of America and its associates with the cause of democracy, justice, and *peace* Woodrow Wilson confirmed and crowned the arguments built up for three years by the Allied propagandists. World War I was "a war to end war."

The subject peoples of Austria-Hungary and even the German socialists and liberals were influenced by the proposals for a fairer world order. They came to hope that if they repudiated the governments which had led them into war they might be welcomed into the society of free peoples and be permitted to assist in organizing the League of Nations. By 1918 the faith had become general that a covenant might be drawn up which would assure peace and justice among nations. It was a doctrinaire faith, overwritten with phrases and formulas, a too generous and too credulous belief that political instruments and institutions in and by themselves could remold humanity. But it was, while the mood endured, a living faith. It brought a surge of hope to the European peoples who were stunned and stricken by the war, starved for food, submerged in political chaos by the collapse of the Russian, Austrian, and German imperial regimes. Democratic government and the principle of self-determination appeared a panacea for all their problems, and they had been encouraged to believe that in repudiating their wartime leaders they would escape the penalties of defeat. This miscalculation, which deceived millions in central Europe with a false hope, added to the postwar bitterness, but the Allied spokesmen had intended no deliberate deceit. The new, struggling, democratic regimes which appeared in central Europe after 1918 were aided and encouraged by the victor powers. The United States in particular offered generous financial and material aid. The real tragedy lay in the fact that no change in government, no new political tenets or formulas, could resolve the problems of Europe. Economic pressures, class conflicts, national ambitions had been intensified by the war and could not be assuaged.

2. THE VICTORS' PEACE

"The policies of reality and of idealism are at grips," a French journal announced at the opening of January, 1919. Two weeks later the Paris Peace Conference met for its first plenary session. Woodrow Wilson had come to Paris in person as leading delegate for the United States. Knowing the ideals which had stirred the masses in all the belligerent countries, ideals to which he had given such eloquent expression, he was determined to see the hopes of humanity enshrined in a just settlement. Pitted against him as exponents of the "policies of reality" were Georges Clemenceau and David Lloyd George. The seventy-eight year old French statesman had helped to defend Paris against the Prussians in 1870 and had lived to become president of the French council of ministers in the critical days of 1917 and 1918. Shrewd, cynical, and disillusioned, Clemenceau sought but one main guarantee from the peace: security for France against a future German attack. The mercurial Welshman, Lloyd George, like Clemenceau the wartime premier of his country, had steered Britain through what he later described as a "blood-stained stagger to victory." A parliamentary master tactician, a brilliant debater, a resourceful diplomat, he proved to be Wilson's most formidable opponent. The British people re-elected him in December, 1918, and sent him to Paris to defend their interests, to "hang the Kaiser," and to make Germany pay for the war. Thus Lloyd George came to the conference with a definite mandate and the assurance that he had popular support at home. Clemenceau likewise knew that the French Chamber of Deputies stood behind him, for they voted confidence in his leadership by 398 to 93 on December 29. In contrast, Wilson could no longer feel assured that the United States Congress would support him, for the congressional election of November, 1918, had given the Republican Party and Wilson's opponents control of the Senate and the House of Representatives. Before he set sail former President Theodore Roosevelt offered a prophetic word of warning: "Our Allies and our enemies and Mr. Wilson himself should all understand that Mr. Wilson has no authority to speak for the American people at this time."

Wilson, Lloyd George, and Clemenceau, with the advice of specialists in all fields with whom they could consult, were the architects of the Treaty of Versailles. The Italian prime minister, Vittorio Emanuele Orlando, took but a minor part in the discussions leading to the Treaty of Versailles, for Italy's main quarrel had been with Austria, not with Germany. Similarly, the Japanese delegates were interested primarily in those discussions which concerned the disposal of German colonies in the Pacific. The remainder of the Allied and Associated Powers shared in the discussions only when their interests were directly involved; their delegates met with the Big Three on rare occasions and then by invitation. Much of the preliminary work was done and some sections of the treaty drafted by the fifty-eight committees and commissions of experts, but all sections were subject to revision by Wilson, Lloyd George, and Clemenceau.

These three statesmen who framed the Peace of Versailles have been severely criticized for its deficiencies. The criticism is legitimate in that they accepted the responsibility of making peace. It may be that they were too exclusive in their attitude; war concentrates authority and it is not easy to pass at once to the more leisurely dispersion of power that is

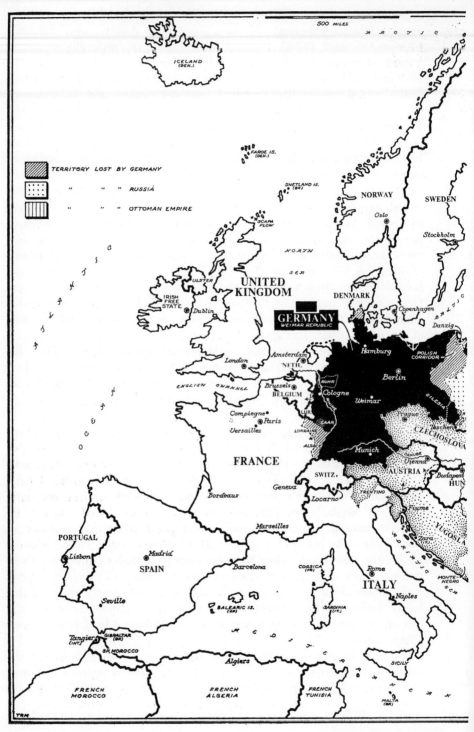

TERRITORIAL CHANGES

RESULTING FROM WORLD WAR I

usual in peacetime. It is only just to these leaders to realize the sense of urgency that drove them on and the limitations and difficulties under which they worked. No three human beings, however thoughtfully they labored, could have solved the complex and multiple issues that were referred to the Big Three day after day. They themselves did not realize how final many of the rapidly phrased decisions would prove to be. They thought their work was provisory and assumed that a peace congress would follow the peace conference and review the preparatory draft. A further point to note in their defense is that they were not free agents. Each was bound to interpret and as far as possible to execute the will expressed by a majority in their respective legislatures. They also knew the exalted hopes and expectations which had stirred the masses and they knew these hopes could not be fully realized. But they dared not disavow either the idealistic aims of the humanitarians or the more selfish program of the nationalists among their fellow countrymen lest a revolt of the electorate deprive them of their mandate. They were the prisoners of their own wartime propaganda.

At every step contrary considerations made a decision difficult. Over-generous terms to the defeated nations were certain to rouse criticism from the people in the victorious countries. Overhard terms might drive the Germans, Austrians, and Hungarians into an alliance with Soviet Russia. All the statesmen in Paris were harassed by petitioners and critics, misled by rumors and misrepresentations, exhausted by debates, pressed for time. Inevitably the Big Three compromised, condoned, countermanded, and sometimes conceded terms which they intended to review but forgot as new and more pressing problems arose. After three or four months the need to end the uncertainty by proclaiming some sort of settlement, however hasty, to the waiting world, forced them to con-clude their draft, and some of the sections were thrown together almost as swiftly as a newspaper going to press.

The Covenant of the League of Nations, composed by Wilson and his colleagues on the League Commission, was attached to the treaty as a preamble or introduction. This was a grave mistake. The League of Nations, if it was to win the respect of all peoples and function as an impartial world organization, should have worn the aspect of impartiality, of universality, from the outset. To incorporate its charter in the peace treaty, to associate it directly with a severe punitive peace, made the League appear to many people an agency of the victors, an instrument invented to help them to preserve their gains and enforce their demands.

The authority and privacy with which the Big Three settled the peace terms was maintained to the last, despite the petition of "suitors and suppliants" for a closer share in the discussions. Even the delegates of the minor Allied and Associated Powers were left in uncertainty regard-ing some clauses in the treaty draft, and the defeated Germans waited in ignorance of their fate until the last moment. Then the government of the recently formed German Republic was instructed to send delegates to Paris to learn the terms on which they might obtain peace.

The haste, the compromises, the provisory nature of the Versailles treaty, constituted a major weakness in later years when it was under attack. There can be little question that the proceedings were summary, many of the decisions curt and arbitrary, and the mode of ratification dictatorial. When, on May 6, 1919, the delegates of the Allied and Associated Powers were called to a plenary session to endorse the terms offered Germany, many of them had seen only a short summary of the 80,000 word document. Only six plenary sessions of the Peace Conference were called between January and June, 1919, and the proceedings at each were formal and almost void of discussion. Despite the wartime denunciations of the evils of secret diplomacy, the condition of the world did not permit open sessions at which all the tangled questions might have been argued. All sovereign states were (theoretically) equal in their rights and privileges. But the realities of the situation overrode theories. With Germany defeated and disarmed, Austria-Hungary dissolved, Russia in revolution and chaos, Italy enfeebled, and Japan remote from European affairs, there were only three powers which remained dominant. The peace was shaped by the representatives of France, Britain, and the United States because these three powers were in a position to do so, and no others were in a position to oppose them.

3. IDEALS AND REALITIES

The settlements imposed upon the defeated states — Germany, Austria, Hungary, Turkey, and Bulgaria — pleased few critics and were destined to provoke years of controversy. This was unavoidable because they were the result of compromises and were shaped in a period of stress, confusion, and bitterness. Many people came to believe that it was the defects in the treaties of 1919–1920 which sowed the seeds for a second world war twenty years later. It would, of course, be more just to say that the treaties were imperfect because they were a compromise between the ideal world society desired by dreamers and the practical, often selfish, demands of over fifty independent sovereign states.

Woodrow Wilson's Fourteen Points summarized the hopes of the idealists. In judging this program it is well to keep in mind the circumstances under which it was planned and issued (see pp. 162–163). It was conceived as a rejoinder to the Bolsheviks of Russia who seized power in November, 1917, broke with the Allies, and called for concluding an immediate peace on the basis of "no annexations, no indemnities, and the self-determination of peoples." It was announced in January, 1918, at a time when the Allied military fortunes had reached their lowest ebb. It was therefore moderate and in some respects deliberately vague. At the time, the Central Powers rejected it; the Bolsheviks ignored it and concluded a separate peace at Brest-Litovsk (March, 1918); and the western Allies, who had not been consulted in its formulation, acquiesced in it only with certain reservations.

When the Paris Peace Conference met a full year after the announcement of the Fourteen Points, the situation had completely changed. The Allies had won a resounding victory; Germany and Bulgaria had been defeated; the Austrian and Turkish empires had completely dissolved; and Russia had fallen prey to a terrible civil war, in which the Allies intervened on the side of the Whites against the Bolsheviks. Since it remained in doubt who really represented Russia, whether the Whites or the Reds, Russia could not be represented at the conference, and the settlement of the whole range of East European problems affecting Russia had to be postponed. In their armistice overtures of October, 1918, the Germans, who had rejected the Fourteen Points ten months earlier, suddenly remembered them and offered to surrender on their basis in the hope that this would protect them from Allied revenge. Under American pressure, and noting that the Fourteen Points contained no specific provision which would impede them in carrying out their plans with regard to Germany, the western Allies then endorsed them and agreed to the surrender of Germany on their basis.

In the completely altered circumstances after the war the vague formulas of the Fourteen Points proved a completely inadequate guide to solve the host of complex and detailed problems which the peacemakers faced. Therefore, while some points of the program were carried out, others had to be abandoned. The fate of the general points of the program may be cited as illustrative of the difficulties of carrying it out. Wilson's first point, "Open covenants, openly arrived at," was disregarded by most of the committees which drew up the peace terms. The deliberations of the Big Three, the labor of the special commissions, and the compromises arranged among the delegates were all pursued in an atmosphere of reticence if not of complete secrecy. It is difficult, however, to see how the diplomats could have proceeded in any other manner without defeating their own intentions. Diplomacy and war both deal with the disputes arising among nations. The maneuvers of the diplomats, like the campaigns of the generals, often depend for their success upon the concealment of objectives, upon actions concerted secretly in advance, upon surprise moves and strategic withdrawals. The idealists were naive in thinking that the war had changed the world of human nature.

The second of the Fourteen Points, "Freedom of the Seas," was set aside before the conference met, largely out of deference to British objections. In fairness to the British, however, it may be recalled that since World War II, out of which the United States has emerged as the largest naval power in the world in command of all the important sea routes, the Americans have ceased to insist on their historic policy of freedom of the seas. Point three, the removal of economic barriers, remained an unfulfilled hope, for the treaties confirmed the existence of many new states in Europe and tariff frontiers were extended instead of being reduced. The fourth point, adequate guarantees of disarmament, was enforced upon the vanquished nations but not carried out by the victors. Strict measures of disarmament were drawn up for Germany, Austria, Hungary, Bulgaria, and Turkey. These provisions, severe and specific as they were, failed in the outcome to lower European military expenditures or to prevent a renewal of the armament race some years later. The details of this failure are discussed in chapters 35 and 36.

The fifth point, an impartial adjustment of colonial claims, was defined, before the conference met, as applying only to claims created by the war, that is, to the former German colonies and the Arab possessions of the Ottoman empire, which became "mandates" of the League of Nations. In theory the mandates were to be "schools in nationhood" for the former colonial peoples under mandatory powers, which were Britain, France, and Japan. In practice their lot greatly varied as the policies of the mandatory powers were not uniform. Britain carried out the principle of mandates honestly enough, France less successfully, and Japan ignored it altogether. Points six through thirteen dealt with various territorial issues and are discussed in the next chapter.

Point fourteen proposed the establishment of a League of Nations. To Wilson and his supporters it was the most important of all. As chairman of the commission on this League, Wilson helped to draft the covenant and he was eager to see the new experiment launched and its covenant made a fundamental section of all the peace treaties. For he believed the League would prove a court of appeal and a rectifying instrument whereby any errors or injustices implicit in the hastily drawn treaties might later be amended. This hope proved too sanguine. The League, erected by the victors and enshrined in the "victor's peace," served to maintain the imbalance of that peace rather than to resolve international tensions.

Within a few years it became apparent that the doctrinaire spirit of the League covenant made it an unrealistic document. The views which Wilson and his admirers upheld were couched in admirable phrases but they too often proved inapplicable when pressed down on the obdurate facts. Suggestions for settlements on "clearly recognizable lines of nationality" had a simple and persuasive logic as principles. But the ethnographic patterns of Central and Eastern Europe were hopelessly confused, and no clearly recognizable lines of nationality could be found in many disputed areas. When applied, the formulas of the idealist lost much of their magic.

These formulas, moreover, had a further limitation: they were conceived too exclusively in political terms and they ignored economic realities. Thus, the liberation of the peoples of the Danube Valley turned the late Hapsburg empire into a patchwork of small states. This created new political frontiers, with attendant tolls and tariff barriers that restricted the flow of trade in an area where communication was already difficult and inadequate. An economic federation of the Danubian states might have solved national grievances, but the inchoate nations of the region regaled in their newly found freedom and resisted such suggestions. And the peacemakers were too preoccupied with other problems to try to coerce them.

Finally, the principles upon which the League of Nations and the peace treaties were nominally founded were weakened by the fact that they were honored when it suited the makers of the peace to honor them but ignored by them when it did not. To right an ancient wrong by confirming the independence of Poland was idealistic but it may have been dubious statesmanship. Germany and Russia, unrepresented at the Paris Conference, could not be expected to endorse its decrees willingly nor to respect them when a revision of the treaty became possible. In the chaos attendant on the defeat of Russia and Germany the Poles had carved out for themselves a large, independent, but vulnerable homeland. The peacemakers confirmed it in the name of self-determination. But the Irish, who had been in rebellion against British control during the war and demanded home rule, were not permitted to present their case to the conference; and the Egyptian government, which likewise demanded independence, asked for it in vain. There were no clear principles which would resolve all cases, and by pretending to discover and apply such principles the treaty-makers exposed themselves to the charge that, when it suited them, they betrayed the ideals for which the war had been fought.

17

POLITICAL SETTLEMENTS, 1919–1924

We shall seek only peace, which we intend to make just, solid, so that those who come after us may be spared the abominations of the past.
G. CLEMENCEAU, Address to the French Senate, September 17, 1918

1. THE TREATY OF VERSAILLES

GERMANY HAD SURRENDERED to the Allies on the basis of the Fourteen Points program in the hope that it would protect her from Allied revenge. To be sure, none of the points of this program specifically assured Germany of immunity against losses. In fact, some of them demanded righting of historical wrongs committed by Germany or before her by Prussia. But in introducing the Fourteen Points, Wilson gave Germany general assurances against a Carthaginian peace: "We have no jealousy of German greatness, and there is nothing in this program that impairs it. . . . We do not wish to injure her or to block in any way her legitimate influence or power." Unfortunately for Germany, the vagueness of the Fourteen Points permitted a wide margin of interpretation; what appeared as a "just peace" to the Allied peacemakers did not appear so to the Germans.

The return to French control of the "lost provinces" of Alsace and Lorraine was justified by point eight of the Fourteen Points as righting a wrong done to France by Prussia in 1871. Actually, the German claim to the provinces was older than the French, and the bulk of their population was German-speaking — although, the French claimed, French in sentiment. Their loss, although not sanctioned by a plebiscite, was accepted by the Germans without undue resentment — for the moment at least. But the assignment of three small districts, Moresnet, Eupen, and Malmédy, to Belgium, which had a vague historical claim to them and a better economic one, stung German pride. They were likewise irritated when the Allied peacemakers reopened the question of Schleswig-Holstein. Denmark, from whom Prussia seized the provinces in 1864, had not participated in the First World War and when first offered the provinces by the Allies, declined them. In the end the Danes accepted only a portion of northern Schleswig after a free and honest plebiscite held in the province indicated that some of its population wished to rejoin Denmark.

While in the west the peacemakers undid the wrongs committed by Bismarck, in the east they undertook to undo even older wrongs, committed by Frederick the Great against Poland in the eighteenth century. Point thirteen of the Fourteen Points called for the restoration of an independent Polish state "which should include the territories inhabited by indisputably Polish populations, which should be assured a free and secure access to the sea." Poland had emerged without any direct Allied assistance at the time of the armistice, and was recognized at the peace conference as an Allied nation. The Poles showed an enormous appetite for territory. Not only did they demand the restoration of the pre-Partition Poland of the eighteenth century — which, it is well to recall, was a multinational empire in which the Poles were a minority — but raised historical claims even older. Moreover, where history did not favor them but ethnography did, quite inconsistently they raised ethnical claims as well. The Allied peacemakers fixed the western border of Poland roughly where it had been in the eighteenth century. This left minorities on both sides, rather more Germans in Poland than Poles in Germany, which was inevitable in view of the ethnographically mixed nature of the German-Polish borderland. The French backed even the most exaggerated Polish claims, but thanks to British and American resistance the peacemakers rejected the Polish demand for an outright cession of East Prussia.[1] Unfortunately, it was isolated from the main body of Germany by the Polish "corridor" to the sea, as it had been in the eighteenth century. The port of Danzig at the estuary of the Vistula River was a natural Polish economic outlet but overwhelmingly German in population. The peacemakers resolved this difficulty by setting Danzig up as a free city under a League of Nations commissioner. A somewhat similar status was given to Memel, another old German port city at the estuary of the Niemen River, which served as an economic outlet for Lithuania.[2] In Upper Silesia, a territory rich in coal and iron and with a mixed German-Polish population, the peace treaty provided for a plebiscite. It was held in 1920 and resulted in the partition of the area in a manner which left both sides dissatisfied.

As for the borders with Germany's other eastern neighbors, Czechoslovakia and Austria, the peace treaty provided for the retention of the old German frontier with Austria-Hungary, with one minor exception in

[1] The Allies permitted plebiscites in two border districts of East Prussia, which were held in 1920. They resulted in overwhelming victories for Germany and the populations were permitted to remain in Germany.

[2] In 1923 the Lithuanians engineered a coup in the city and seized it. But they were obliged by the Allies to sign the "Memel Statute" providing for the autonomy of the city.

Silesia in favor of Czechoslovakia. For the moment, the Germans raised no objection, but in later years they were to question this settlement.

While the Germans accepted their losses in the west — for the moment at least — with resignation, they were outraged by their losses in the east. The isolation of East Prussia particularly rankled. By agreement with Poland the Germans obtained the right of free transit across the Polish Corridor to East Prussia, but the province was difficult to defend. However, it was not so much practical inconveniences — irritating though they were — as subtle psychological influences that fed German resentment. The Germans had for a long time considered Central Europe as their special preserve and resented western interference in it. They regarded the non-German peoples of the region as inferior *Düngervölker* (dung people) whose destiny it was only to "fertilize" the soil of the region. The Allied, particularly French, tendency to side with the Poles and other peoples of the area against them, appeared to the Germans as a deplorable and unwise breach of solidarity among *Herrenvölker* (master nations) standing face to face with barbarians. In 1925 the German government voluntarily acknowledged and guaranteed the frontiers fixed by the Versailles Treaty between Germany and Belgium and Germany and France, but all German governments steadfastly refused to extend this guarantee to the frontiers of Germany in the east.

One mutilation of territory which the Germans would have found most difficult to endure, they were spared. At the peace table the French demanded the cession of the left bank of the Rhine so that a Rhine Republic might be formed to serve as a buffer between Germany and France. The idea of erecting a buffer between the two ancient foes had merit; it would have fortified peace. But it lacked equity since it was to be created out of German territory alone. Had France been willing to contribute territory to the buffer, at least Alsace-Lorraine, it might very well have won the support of Wilson and Lloyd George. As it was, however, they fought the proposal vigorously; it would, they insisted, create a new irredentist problem more threatening to European harmony than Alsace-Lorraine had been. In the outcome, the French were persuaded, most reluctantly, to accept a compromise. The left bank of the Rhine and the bridgeheads on the right bank were to be occupied by Allied forces for fifteen years. The Saar Valley was to be detached and administered by a League of Nations commissioner for the same period, after which a plebiscite was to decide its fate.[3] The motive for this last provision was economic rather than political. During its retreat from France in 1918, the German army had systematically flooded French mines and destroyed factories. The Saar coal reserves were equal to those of the whole of France, and the mines were to be open to French exploitation while they put their own in operation again.

[3] In 1935 a plebiscite was held in the Saar territory, which resulted in favor of its return to Germany. This was actually done.

French military advisers had urged the creation of a Rhine Republic because they believed such a barrier indispensable if France with 40,000,000 people was to be safe from Germany with 65,000,000. In 1919 the fear expressed by the French that they would be attacked by a revived Germany appeared excessive to most British and American observers. Henry White, a member of the United States delegation, commented on the French dread of the future. "It is impossible," he wrote from Paris in March, 1919, "to comprehend the extraordinary obsession felt in this country lest Germany within the next few years repeat the actions which she took in 1914." To dispel this "extraordinary obsession" Germany was disarmed. The German army was reduced to 100,000 men and was deprived of heavy artillery and military aircraft. A belt extending thirty miles beyond the Rhine was demilitarized. The German navy was reduced to six warships, with other units in proportion. To satisfy further the French demand for security the British and American delegates proposed a treaty of mutual aid. Great Britain and the United States were to come to the rescue of France if she ever became a victim of German aggression again. Wilson approved the accord, but when the United States Senate rejected the Treaty of Versailles it went by the board. The British, on the ground that the American rejection nullified the agreement, likewise backed out of their promise. The French not unnaturally came to feel that they had surrendered a substantial barrier for a paper promise and had emerged with neither. When the passing years proved the French dread of Germany to be well founded, Frenchmen looked back with increased bitterness to this betrayal, or at least desertion, by their allies.

All the former German colonies, treaty ports, trade concessions in backward countries, foreign investments, merchant ships, undersea cables, and even patents registered in enemy states which the victor powers had been able to seize during hostilities were confiscated without compensation. The German lease on Kiaochow and economic privileges in Shantung as well as the German title to a number of Pacific islands north of the equator were assigned to Japan. German Pacific islands south of the equator were transferred to Australia, with the exception of German Samoa which went to New Zealand. The Union of South Africa acquired German South West Africa. Great Britain took over German East Africa and divided with France the Cameroon and Togoland territories which the Reich had held in 1914.

In all, Germany ceded 25,000 square miles of territory in Europe, with a population of some 6,000,000; and 1,000,000 square miles overseas, with 12,000,000 inhabitants. But this loss of land and population was only part of the German forfeiture. By the famous "War Guilt Clause" (Article 231) of the Treaty of Versailles, Germany was obliged to acknowledge the responsibility for "all the loss and damage" suffered by the Allies "as a consequence of the war imposed upon them by the aggression of Germany and her allies."

Regardless of the merits of the war-guilt thesis, it was not unreasonable for the Allies to demand some compensation for war losses because the war in the west had been fought almost exclusively on Allied soil. Northern France, the most industrialized part of the country, as well as portions of Belgium had been frightfully devastated. The British had not suffered much destruction but had lost a huge amount of shipping upon which they, as an island nation, depended for life. Germany, meanwhile, had not only escaped unscathed by the war but had greatly expanded and improved her industrial plant. Had the Allies forgone all reparation, they and not Germany would have been the losers in the war — as, indeed, in the end proved to be the case, because of the German refusal to pay reparations. At first, however, the Germans were not unwilling to make some amends. They proposed that their colonies and other property seized during the war be assessed at a reasonable valuation, and the total credited to Germany as reparations paid. But the Allies rejected this proposal. A special Reparations Commission was created which worked until 1921 to compile a bill to Germany. Its work will be discussed in the following chapter.

When the Allies presented the completed draft treaty to the Germans in May, 1919, Count Brockdorff-Rantzau, the German Foreign Minister, after vainly protesting against it indignantly refused to sign it and returned home to Berlin. A brief government crisis followed, as no responsible German politician wanted to assume the ungrateful task of signing the humiliating treaty. Eventually, however, the German government bowed to the inevitable and sent two obscure functionaries to sign the Allied "dictate" on June 28, 1919 — five years to the day after the assassination of the Austrian Archduke — in the Hall of Mirrors in the palace of Versailles.

Wilson, Lloyd George, and Orlando then departed for home, and the work of the peace conference was taken over by a second-echelon team, the Council of Foreign Ministers. It, in turn, was superseded at the end of 1919 by the Conference of Ambassadors. The task of these two bodies was to finish the large amount of work left undone by the Big Three, notably the drafting of the treaties with Germany's allies. In the Conference of Ambassadors the United States maintained only an "observer" because by that time further American participation in the peace conference was put in doubt by the rejection of the Treaty of Versailles by the United States Senate.

2. THE TREATIES WITH AUSTRIA, BULGARIA, AND HUNGARY

When the Paris Peace Conference met in January, 1919, the Austro-Hungarian Empire was no more. It had disintegrated by an internal revolution into its national components in the days immediately preceding and following the armistice. Italy claimed *Italia irredenta* as well as the other Austrian lands promised to her by the Treaty of London in 1915, Rumania proceeded to occupy the lands promised to her in the Treaty of Bucharest in 1916; the Poles of Galicia joined with the German and Russian Poles in a new Polish state; the Serbs, Croats, and Slovenes joined with Serbia and Montenegro in a new Yugoslav kingdom under the Serbian dynasty; and the Czechs of Bohemia joined with the Slovaks of Hungary in the new Czechoslovak Republic. Similarly, Austria and Hungary repudiated their ties to the defunct Hapsburg empire. On November 1, 1918, Hungary seceded from the empire and on November 16 the Hungarian National Council proclaimed an independent Hungarian Republic under the liberal leader Count Károlyi. On November 12 the Austrian National Assembly proclaimed a "German Austrian Republic" under the socialist leader Karl Renner. The German Austrians claimed the right of national self-determination and announced their intention to effect an *Anschluss*, or union, with the Germans of Germany, in the same way as the Austrian Poles, Italians, Yugoslavs, and Rumanians had united with their kinsmen across the borders of the former Hapsburg empire. By the time the peace conference met, the "Successor States" of Austria-Hungary were already well entrenched. The peacemakers were thus faced with a *fait accompli*, which they had to recognize because of Allied wartime commitments.

The Allies had sanctioned the dismemberment of Austria-Hungary already during the war. With Italy and Rumania they concluded the treaties mentioned above. After the fall of the Russian monarchy they gave official recognition to the Polish movement for unity and independence, and in the final months of the war they gave it to the Yugoslav and Czechoslovak movements. At the peace conference, therefore, the question of whether to "save" or "destroy" the Hapsburg empire never arose; it had long been settled in favor of dismemberment. The task of the peace conference was simply to arbitrate the frontiers between the Successor States and to apportion among them the financial obligations of Austria-Hungary.

The delimitation of new frontiers was not an easy task because of the overlapping historical and ethnical claims of the Successor States. When disputes arose, the Allied peacemakers generally favored "allied" nations against "enemy" nations. The recognition of Czechoslovakia, Yugoslavia, and Poland as Allied nations was more than a legal fiction. It gave them a great advantage in territorial disputes. They were able to send delegations to Paris to plead their case. Austria and Hungary, on the other hand, were denied admission to the peace conference. In vain they protested that they, too, were "new states," the same as Czechoslovakia, Yugoslavia, or Poland, and that they should not be held responsible any more than these states for the sins of the defunct Hapsburg empire. The peacemakers rejected this thesis and treated them as simple continuations of the Austrian Empire and the Kingdom of Hungary, respectively, shorn of provinces. Peace terms were dictated to them, the same as to Germany.

More difficult to resolve for the peacemakers were disputes among Allied nations. Such disputes had arisen between Italy and Yugoslavia over the control of the eastern shore of the Adriatic Sea; between Czechoslovakia and Poland over the possession of the coal-rich district of Teschen in Silesia; and between Yugoslavia and Rumania over the possession of the Banat. While the questions of Teschen and the Banat were eventually settled by compromise, the Adriatic Question defied solution. Italy sought an early settlement of her claims on the basis of the Treaty of London but encountered the vigorous opposition of President Wilson. The controversy envenomed the atmosphere of the conference perhaps more than any other question. At one point Wilson appealed over the head of Orlando to the Italian people to support him against their own Prime Minister. Orlando indignantly withdrew from the conference and returned only when the Italian people resoundingly backed him against the American President. In the end the conference reached an impasse over the Adriatic Question and was forced to leave its solution to bilateral Italo-Yugoslav negotiations. It was settled — perhaps adjourned would be a better term — by two treaties. The Treaty of Rapallo (December 12, 1920) confirmed Italy in possession of Istria and the east Adriatic islands but not of Dalmatia, with the exception of the port of Zara. The Treaty of Rome (January 27, 1924) divided the hotly disputed port of Fiume, rendering it useless to both parties. These treaties failed unfortunately to exorcise the Adriatic Question. It continued to trouble relations between Italy and Yugoslavia throughout the *inter-bellum* period. Yugoslavia could not remain indifferent to the harsh treatment accorded the Yugoslav minority in Italy. Italy, on the other hand, felt deeply dissatisfied with the failure to realize her war aims. Although one of the victorious powers in the First World War, she was driven by this dissatisfaction to make common cause with revisionist Germany.

The peacemakers were less partial in apportioning financial burdens than in distributing territory. Ability to pay was their guiding principle in distributing the burden of paying the financial obligations of Austria-Hungary. Theoretically, Allied nations were not supposed to pay reparations. Nevertheless, the Successor States, whether they belonged to the Allied camp or not, were obliged to pay them, camouflaged in the case of Allied nations as war debts and "liberation fees." In fact, the heaviest burden was placed on Czechoslovakia, an Allied nation, because of her ability to pay; she had inherited 82 per cent of all the industries of the Austrian Empire.

Like the peace treaty with Germany, the peace treaties with Germany's allies were signed in various palaces in the suburbs of Paris and bear their names. Of Germany's allies, peace was first concluded with Austria, in the château of St.-Germain on September 10, 1919. Because of the opposition of France, Italy, and Czechoslovakia, Austria was forbidden in the Treaty of St.-Germain to unite with Germany. She was obliged to drop the modifying "German" from her name and to assume obligations to refrain from acts that might "compromise" her independence. The Austrian army was limited to 30,000 men and she was obliged to pay reparations. Paradoxically, while the other Successor States reveled in their newly found independence, Austria was distressed by hers. The viability of Austria, a small, mountainous country, would have been difficult in any circumstances. But with a substantial number of her citizens questioning the value of independence, her survival as an independent nation appeared doubtful. Throughout the *inter-bellum* period, the Austrians oscillated between a desire to restore the Hapsburgs and a desire for *Anschluss* with Germany. In 1938 Austria fell easy prey to the revisionist expansionism of Hitler's Germany.

After Austria, peace was next concluded with Bulgaria. The Bulgarians, too, paid the penalty of siding with the losers in the war. In the Treaty of Neuilly (November 27, 1919) Bulgaria was obliged to cede some border districts to Yugoslavia, but what was worse, she also had to cede Western Thrace to Greece which deprived her of access to the Aegean Sea. The Bulgarian army was reduced to 20,000 men and the impoverished little country was obliged to assume a heavy burden of reparations.

The signing of peace with Hungary was delayed by internal turmoil: the fall of the liberal republic of Károlyi, a short-lived Bolshevik regime, the White Terror, and Rumanian occupation (see p. 233). The peacemakers took a dim view of the turbulence in Hungary, particularly of the Bolshevik experiment, and their terms to Hungary were very harsh. While they had heeded the Czechoslovak plea not to disturb the ancient historical borders of the Kingdom of Bohemia vis-à-vis Germany and Austria, even though this left some 3,000,000 Germans in Czechoslovakia, they ignored an analogous Hungarian plea not to disturb the equally ancient historical borders of Hungary. Under the Treaty of Trianon (June 4, 1920) Hungary lost three-quarters of her territory and two-thirds of her population, not only the non-Magyar periphery of the country but also broad strips of the purely Magyar plain of Hungary. The Hungarian army was limited to 35,000 men and Hungary was obliged to assume the burden of reparations.

The Treaties of Neuilly and Trianon deeply offended the patriotism of the Bulgarians and Hungarians. Their incessant agitation for revision of the treaties troubled the peace of Central and Southeastern Europe in the interwar period and their dissatisfaction drove them into the arms of revisionist Germany and Italy.

3. THE TREATIES WITH TURKEY: SÈVRES AND LAUSANNE

One of the most difficult tasks which the peacemakers faced was to dispose of the heritage of the Ottoman Empire. When Turkey surrendered on October 30, 1918, the Allies occupied Constantinople and the Straits area. The British and their Arab allies had already occupied Palestine, Syria, and Mesopotamia. Soon after the armistice the French landed troops in Syria and in southeastern Turkey and the Italians in southwestern Turkey, both intent on claiming their shares of the Ottoman Empire which had been promised to them in the secret treaties.

For a variety of reasons, however, it proved impossible to carry out the secret treaties completely. The United States, which was not a party to them, opposed them. Russia, which had sought them under the tsarist regime, had exposed and denounced them when the Soviet government came into power. Britain likewise was prepared to renounce them, but not to abandon the gains guaranteed her in them. On the contrary Lloyd George felt that in view of the preponderant role of the British in the defeat of Turkey they deserved more than had been agreed upon in the Sykes-Picot Treaty. Specifically, he wanted the oil-rich district of Mosul, which had been promised to France, and Palestine, which it had been agreed would be internationalized. Clemenceau at first resisted the British demand but ultimately yielded in return for a promise of a substantial cut in the Mosul oil for France. There remained the need to secure the approval of President Wilson for this scheme. Wilson, however, insisted on consulting the Arabs before making a decision. On his insistence Emir Faisal, the commander of the Arab army in Syria and son of Sherif Husein, was invited to present the Arab case before the conference. Faisal pleaded for recognition of Arab independence and suggested that the Allies send a committee of inquiry to Arabia to ascertain the wishes of the Arabs in this matter. Wilson liked the suggestion and on his insistence it was decided to send an inter-Allied commission to the Arab lands. The French, who were bitterly opposed to Arab nationalism, never appointed their delegates to the commission. The British, who were cool to the suggestion, appointed theirs but did not send them. In the end, therefore, only Americans were represented on the commission.

The King-Crane Commission, as it became known from its principal delegates, after a visit to the Near East recommended the establishment of short-term mandates for Syria (including Palestine) and Iraq. As mandatory powers it suggested the United States for Syria and Britain for Iraq. Should the United States be unavailable, it recommended that Britain assume a mandate also for Syria, but strongly advised against the selection of France because of the alleged hostility of the Syrian population to her. However, the recommendations of the King-Crane Commission as well as proposals that the United States take a mandate to Armenia and assume the task of policing the Straits area were never adopted because after its rejection of the Versailles Treaty the United States bowed out of the Near Eastern settlement.

France and Britain were then free to adopt a solution more to their liking. At the conference of Allied prime ministers at San Remo in April, 1920, Lloyd George's original proposal for British mandates in Iraq and Palestine and a French mandate in Syria as well as a cut of the Mosul oil was adopted. In March, in an effort to forestall this decision a Syrian General Congress declared the independence of Syria and elected Faisal King of Syria. A meeting of Iraqi leaders took a similar step for Iraq, choosing Faisal's brother, Abdullah, as the future monarch of the country. The Allies, however, disregarded these moves. As a result, a revolt broke out in Iraq in June, 1920, which took the British several months of heavy fighting to suppress. In July the French, fearing that the Iraqi revolt might spread to Syria, attacked the forces of King Faisal and drove him out of the country. The suppression of the Arab movement by force, coming after the high-blown wartime promises, caused bitter disappointment to the Arabs. While the French relied on force in dealing with the Syrian Arabs, the British, with their long experience in colonial rule, realized that they could not long rule an intensely antagonistic people by force. Therefore they decided upon a policy of conciliation. In March of 1921 at a conference of British officials connected with Arab affairs, presided over by Winston Churchill, then Colonial Secretary, it was decided to offer the throne of Iraq to Faisal and to promise the country early independence. It was further decided to partition Palestine along the Jordan River, and to set up the independent kingdom of Transjordan in the eastern half to provide a throne for Abdullah.

Meanwhile, the Allies signed with Turkey the Peace of Sèvres on August 10, 1920. It provided for the cession of the Arab lands of the former Ottoman Empire to the Allies, who were to be free to dispose of them; the internationalization of the Straits and demilitarization of the adjoining area; the recognition of the independence of Armenia, whose borders were to be determined by President Wilson; the cession of the Dodecanese islands and of Rhodes to Italy; the cession of the Smyrna area and of Eastern Thrace as well as of a number of Aegean islands to Greece; the control of Turkish finances by Allied commissioners; the restoration of the humiliating capitulations (abolished by Turkey in 1914); and the reduction of the Turkish army to 50,000 men. The Sultan's government, under the threat of Allied naval guns at Constantinople, was helpless and accepted this treaty. But at Ankara, on the bleak plateau of Anatolia far from the reach of Allied naval guns, a nationalist government was formed under the leadership of Mustafa Kemal Pasha, the hero of Gallipoli, which denounced the weak Sultan's government and defied the Allies to enforce the treaty. It adopted as its program a "National Pact" which renounced any claim to non-Turkish territory but insisted

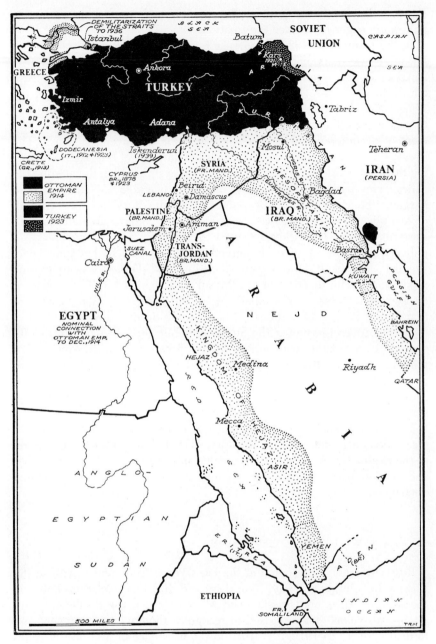

On the map:

DEMILITARIZATION OF THE STRAITS TO 1936

Istanbul

BLACK SEA

Batum

SOVIET UNION

CASPIAN

GREECE

Ankara

Kars 1921

A R M E N I A

SEA

TURKEY

Izmir

K U R D I S T A N

Tabriz

Antalya

Adana

Iskenderun (1939)

Mosul

Teheran

DODECANESIA (IT., 1912 & 1923)

SYRIA (FR. MAND.)

TIGRIS R.

IRAN (PERSIA)

CRETE (GR., 1913)

CYPRUS BR., 1878 & 1923

Beirut

M E S O P O T A M I A

Bagdad

OTTOMAN EMPIRE 1914

LEBANON

Damascus

EUPHRATES R.

TURKEY 1923

PALESTINE (BR. MAND.)

Amman

IRAQ (BR. MAND.)

Jerusalem

TRANS-JORDAN (BR. MAND.)

A R

Basra

Cairo

SUEZ CANAL

KÜWAIT

PERSIAN GULF

EGYPT
NOMINAL CONNECTION WITH OTTOMAN EMP. TO DEC., 1914

N E J D

Riyadh

BAHREIN

NILE R.

A

KINGDOM

HEJAZ

Medina

QATAR

RED SEA

B

I

OF HEJAZ

A N G L O -

Mecca

ASIR

E G Y P T I A N

ERITREA (IT.)

YEMEN

ADEN (BR.)

S U D A N

ETHIOPIA

FR. SOMALILAND

INDIAN OCEAN

500 MILES

T.R.M.

DISMEMBERMENT OF THE OTTOMAN EMPIRE

on the preservation of the integrity of the territory "inhabited by an Ottoman Moslem majority" (i.e., by Turks and Kurds) and on the abolition of the capitulatory regime. This put the Allies in a quandary because by 1920 they had few forces left in the Near East, and in view of the war weariness of the Allied peoples it was impossible to bring in troops from

Europe. But in Greece, under the ambitious Venizelos, they found a policeman eager to enforce the treaty.

In the summer of 1920 the Greeks began a push from Smyrna inland but after two years of fighting failed to capture the nationalist capital at Ankara. In the summer of 1922 the Turks mounted a strong offensive which drove the Greeks into the sea (September, 1922). In October the Allies concluded an armistice with the nationalist government and agreed to set aside the Treaty of Sèvres and to renegotiate the Near Eastern settlement at a conference which met at Lausanne in November, 1922. The Treaty of Lausanne (July 24, 1923) was the only one of the treaties following the First World War which was negotiated rather than dictated by the Allies. The Turks made the most of their advantage and drove a hard bargain. They renounced any claim to Arab territory but recovered all of Anatolia. Greece was forced to surrender the Smyrna area and most of Eastern Thrace. The Allies accepted the partition and disappearance of unhappy Armenia (previously agreed upon between Turkey and Soviet Russia). The capitulations were abolished and Turkey was to pay no reparations. The disposal of the Mosul area, which the Turks claimed on the ground that it was inhabited by the Kurds, was left to arbitration by the League of Nations.[4] In a separate Straits convention Turkey recovered sovereignty over the Straits area but agreed to keep it demilitarized. In a separate convention Greece agreed to a forced exchange of minorities. While this settled an old and vexing problem between the two countries once and for all, it established an unhappy precedent. The brutal practice of moving populations to conform to new political borders was imitated on a mass scale after the Second World War.

The Near Eastern settlements have proved the most enduring of all the settlements effected after the First World War. With the exception of the rise of Israel, the divisions created in the Arab world by the Allies and the new borders agreed upon at Lausanne for Turkey have remained unchanged.

4. PEACE WITH THE SOVIET UNION

Russia was not represented at the Paris Peace Conference because the Russian Revolution and Civil War disrupted diplomatic relations between the western Allies and Russia. The Allies regarded the Bolsheviks with intense suspicion. They refused to recognize the Soviet government and to deal with it. In 1919, it is true, on the insistence of Wilson the Allies invited both the Reds and the Whites to meet in a conference in the Prinkipo islands to decide, among other things, on Russian representation

---

[4] In 1925, under British pressure, the League of Nations awarded Mosul to Iraq, which so outraged the Turks that they presently concluded a friendship pact with Soviet Russia.

at the Paris Peace Conference. The Reds expressed their readiness to meet the Whites, but the Whites, then still confident of victory in the Civil War, refused to meet their adversaries. In consequence the Allies deferred consideration of the Russian peace settlement until the end of the Civil War and the emergence of a government controlling all of Russia. They did not regret too much the Russian absence from the peace conference because it facilitated their work – although it limited their purview. While the Allies waited for "the dust to settle" in Russia, the situation in Eastern Europe slipped completely out of their hands. In the end the Russian peace settlement was not effected through the Paris Peace Conference but by direct and separate negotiations of the Soviet government with its neighbors.

Most of the European neighbors of Soviet Russia had been wholly or in part portions of the Russian empire. In November, 1917, the Soviet government issued a Declaration of the Rights of the Peoples of Russia which expressly granted the non-Russian minorities of the Russian empire the right of secession. This, however, proved to be merely a tactical move designed to prove at the forthcoming Brest-Litovsk peace conference that the Soviets had implemented the right of national self-determination, which they loudly proclaimed should be the basis of peace. However, when Finland, the Baltic provinces, White Russia, the Ukraine, and the Transcaucasian provinces availed themselves of the right of secession and declared their independence, the Soviet government tried to interfere on the ground that their governments did not represent the toiling masses but only reactionary, bourgeois elements. By fomenting insurrections of local Bolsheviks and, in some instances, by outright intervention of the Red Army, the Soviet government tried to prevent the border peoples from seceding from the Russian empire. Nor did it always respect the provisions of the Treaty of Brest-Litovsk (March 4, 1918), which enjoined it to evacuate the border territories. As a result, a very complex situation developed: the Russian Civil War was reproduced in each of the border states with both Soviets and Germans intervening. In fact, what saved the border states from Soviet annexation was the rivalry between Soviet and German imperialism. The Germans invariably met the Soviet attempts to create puppet governments in the border states by sending in troops and creating puppet regimes of their own. However, under the Compiègne armistice (November 11, 1918) the Germans were obliged to withdraw from the border states of Russia. The power vacuum left by the German withdrawal from the region was soon filled by native armies, Russian White forces, and scattered and feeble Allied forces, all united by their opposition to Soviet Russia.

Of Russia's border states the most important army was possessed by Poland. When the Red Army conquered the Ukraine in 1919, a nationalist Ukrainian leader, Petliura, fled to Poland and appealed for Polish help. The Polish leader, Marshal Pilsudski, an intense nationalist, dreamed of restoring the old Polish-Lithuanian empire stretching "from sea to sea," from the Baltic to the Black Sea. In December, 1919, the Allied peace-makers attempted to fix a border between Russia and Poland by decreeing the so called "Curzon Line."[5] But both the Poles and the Russians ignored it. After coming to an agreement with Petliura on setting up a Polish-Ukrainian federation, the Poles invaded the Ukraine in May, 1920. The Soviets, in turn, launched an offensive against Poland which brought the Red Army to the gates of Warsaw by August. Consternation reigned in the western capitals over this militant advance of communism into the heart of Europe. French supplies and a military mission under General Weygand were rushed to assist the Poles in repelling the invasion. By extreme exertions the Poles succeeded in reversing the tide, driving the Red Army out of Poland, and invading Russia. By October, the Soviet government, weary of war and anxious to turn to pressing tasks of recon-struction, sued for an armistice. By the Treaty of Riga (March 18, 1921) peace was restored between the two countries. The line of the farthest Polish military advance became the new Polish-Russian frontier, which endured until the collapse of Poland in 1939. Although it fell short of the frontier of 1772, which the Poles had hoped to attain, it left considerable Russian populations in White Russia and western Ukraine on the Polish side.

At about the same time exhaustion induced Soviet Russia to abandon plans for the reconquest of the Baltic states. By a series of treaties the Soviet government made peace with and recognized the independence of Estonia (Dorpat, February 2, 1920), Lithuania (Moscow, July 12, 1920), Latvia (Riga, August 11, 1920), and Finland (Dorpat, October 14, 1920). Meanwhile, the Red Army had reconquered Georgia, Azerbaijan, and part of Armenia. On March 16, 1921, Soviet Russia concluded a treaty with nationalist Turkey by which the old adversaries, now driven into each other's arms by the Allied hostility to both of them, made peace and agreed upon a new border with partitioned Armenia. The Soviet govern-ment, however, refused to recognize the loss of Bessarabia, which Rumania had seized in 1918 with German encouragement. The Allies ruled in favor of Rumania, but the Soviets refused to recognize the verdict and the question remained unsolved throughout the inter-war period.[6]

Although the peace settlements with Soviet Russia were not dictated but freely negotiated and accepted by both parties, they had the ear-marks of stopgaps. An air of impermanence hovered over them even more than over the dictated settlements in the west. Few observers felt sure that Russia, once she put her house in order and recovered military strength, would not try to make good her losses from the First World War.

[5] The Curzon Line was almost identical with the present, post-World War II, Russo-Polish border.
[6] In 1940, profiting from the general preoccupation with the fall of France, Russia reclaimed Bessarabia by a threat of war on Rumania.

18

THE ECONOMIC SETTLEMENTS

The time has now come for a heavy reckoning of the accounts. You have asked for peace. We are prepared to offer you peace.
GEORGES CLEMENCEAU, to the German Delegates, May 7, 1919

1. THE REPARATIONS BILL

IN THE MIDST of the First World War President Wilson affirmed that the democracies, when victory crowned their efforts, would not seek to impose any "punitive damages" upon their defeated foes. David Lloyd George, wartime prime minister of Great Britain, asserted that the British for their part did not favor the infliction of a war indemnity. These unmercenary avowals, however, were wartime statements. The complete collapse of the Central Powers put the unselfishness of the Allied nations to a crucial test for it left the victors in a position to demand extensive compensations. The British, French, Belgian, and Italian people, many of whom had suffered losses through the air raids and submarine toll or more directly through the wastage of the battlefield, insisted that reparations must be collected. It should be remembered that all the people in the Allied and Associated nations had been studiously indoctrinated with the argument that the leaders of the Central Powers had plotted the war and waged it with the deliberate intention of destroying their neighbors. The German and Austro-Hungarian people might be less to blame, but they had supported their leaders in waging an aggressive war and for this they deserved punishment. In these circumstances and on the basis of these premises, to demand reparations appeared logical and just.

The Allied governments therefore sought a formula which would reconcile their earlier assertion that they sought no military indemnities with the later decision that they could and should collect reparations. They solved the contradiction by stipulating at the time of the armistice that the defeated nations must make compensation "for all damage done to the civilian population of the Allies and their property by the aggression of Germany by land, by sea, or from the air." This qualification left them at liberty to assess Germany and her allies an indefinite sum calculated

on the value of civilian property destroyed through enemy action during
four years of war. In effect it was equivalent to substituting the phrase
"reparations for civilian damages" for the phrase "military indemnity."

The Allied peoples believed reparations justified not only as a reasonable compensation for wanton damage but as a warning to any nation
which might be disposed to wage aggressive war in the future. It was
thought advisable to impress upon the Germans in particular but also
upon the Austrians, Hungarians, Bulgarians, and Turks, the fact that
nations which allowed their governments to violate humane principles
and international obligations would be brought to justice by an international verdict supported by all peace-loving peoples. Such a lesson, it
was hoped, would provide a salutary deterrent to any nation that might
develop aggressive inclinations at a later date.

In the case of the Germans such reasoning proved faulty. The war
itself had already cost them heavily. If additional penalties and sacrifices
could have counteracted the will for militarism and conquest, the terms
of the "Carthaginian Peace" should have done so, for these terms were
heavy and they were intended to remind the offenders of their misdeeds
and to keep reminding them for decades to come. But unfortunately the
corrective effect of the penalties miscarried. The Germans considered
the penalties undeserved and therefore unjust. The whole German nation
felt humiliated and embittered. So deeply did they resent the accusation
of guilt, which they were forced to acknowledge before the world, that
the determination to reverse the verdict of 1918 became a national aspira-
tion. After the first mood of defeat and discouragement ebbed, the German people came to the conclusion that their mistake lay, not in having
waged a war, but in having lost it. From that point a number, especially
of younger Germans, went on to the conclusion that the way to reverse
the ignominious verdict of Versailles was to wage a second war and
win it.

The post-war mood of the German people was not so much a logical
and conscious reaction to events as a psychological and subconscious
rebellion. The sense of mortification, the indignation burning in German
hearts, prepared the nation for a sudden upsurge of chauvinism. Leaders
with the temerity to stimulate and capitalize upon this defiant and recal-
citrant mood were certain to appear at the appropriate moment. Such a
reaction might have been forecast in 1919. The French did in fact foresee
and fear it. But this did not prevent the Allied governments from delud-
ing themselves that they might collect reparations from a presumably
docile Germany until 1980. The German nation which had made the
war was to pay for it throughout the remainder of the century, unless
Germany rebelled.

There seemed good reason to believe in 1919 that the German nation
could pay substantial reparations for damage done. How much it could
pay the more cautious economists hesitated to predict. Some optimistic

statisticians estimated the total at one hundred billion dollars; some set it even higher. Accordingly, the various commissions appointed to collect claims for civilians' injuries inflated their lists, adding charges for property destroyed by fire, shells, air raids, and ship losses, for mines flooded, bridges blown up, farms gutted, orchards slashed, and cattle slain. The sum quickly rose to astronomical figures. Some items not easy to justify under the head of civilian damages were inserted none the less as pensions for soldiers and their dependents; and the loans contracted by Belgium as well as the military expenditures of the Belgian government from 1914 to 1918 were also included. To complete the reparations bill on these extended lines demanded much listing and itemizing, and the compilation seemed likely to take considerable time. In the interim the Germans and their allies were ordered to commence payments in the form of tangible assets.

Protests that Germany was ruined by war and in no condition to meet heavy charges were weighed by the Allied economists. They found that the German government had expended the equivalent of forty billion dollars in waging war and that nearly two million Germans had perished as war casualties. The health of the nation had been reduced because war economy and the Allied blockade had caused a shortage of essential foods, especially fats, and a deficiency of many raw materials. Before 1914 the wealth of Germany had been rising rapidly because of the highly efficient industrial development. But the armistice and treaty terms deprived Germany of two-fifths of her coal and nearly two-thirds of her iron ore supply, a serious blow to an industrial nation. The treaty also detached one-tenth of the German factories and confiscated the German colonies, foreign investments, commercial concessions, and all merchant ships over 1600 tons. It was possible, however, for Germany to commence some forms of payment immediately, and the nation was ordered to surrender gold and goods to the value of five billion dollars before May 1, 1921. As an initial payment, 250,000 farm animals — horses, cattle, sheep, swine, and goats — were to be transshipped; some millions of tons of coal; up to half the existing reserves of drugs and chemicals; building materials of all types; locomotives, coaches, and freight cars; industrial machinery, minerals, fertilizer — the list was long and could be lengthened indefinitely. The Allied claims, it appeared, would be limited only by the capacity and willingness of the defeated nations to produce and turn over the materials demanded.

The total reparations bill had not yet been completed when the peace treaty was laid before the delegates of the German Republic in Paris on May 7, 1919. Failure to mention a specific sum at this time was a tactical, or at least a psychological, error. It left the Germans apprehensive but still hopeful that they might clear off the burden of reparations quickly, as France had cleared off the billion dollar indemnity imposed by the victorious Prussians in 1871. When, two years after Versailles, the Germans finally learned the national mortgage they had assumed in signing the treaty, they were appalled and indignant at the total. After much preliminary debate, the Allied experts had reached a compromise on the calculation of German wealth, the maximum annual payments which might be expected, the mode of transfer, and the final sum with interest charges. In April, 1921, they announced the total: it had been fixed at approximately thirty-one billion dollars. This did not represent an exact accounting; many items were so confused, many lists so detailed, that they had resisted analysis; but the members of the Commission finally compromised among suggested totals and announced the sum indicated.

A schedule of payments had likewise been prepared by the Commission on Reparations. It called for payment of the first billion dollars within twenty-five days. If the Germans failed to pay, the Treaty of Versailles provided for penalties, including possible occupation of territory in addition to that already held for military security, the seizure of state property, the diversion of taxes, customs revenue, and other assets of the Reich, and a charge against public utilities and other property owned by the component states and municipalities. The possibility of further assessments and even further increases in the total was not ruled out, and military pressure by the Allied armies of occupation was to be a reserve weapon that would be applied if the Germans failed to meet their obligations under the treaty. Unforeseen developments had already been covered by a blanket clause of the treaty which declared that "all matters relating to the occupation and not provided for by the present Treaty shall be regulated by subsequent agreements, which Germany hereby undertakes to observe." The delegates of the Weimar Republic who signed at Versailles had no logical authority thus to promise in advance that subsequent governments would observe the terms of agreements which had not yet been devised. It is not altogether surprising that German youths, reading the Treaty of Versailles in later years, came to think of the Weimar regime as a weak and shameful administration which had mortgaged the rights and liberties of the nation throughout future generations.

2. INTERGOVERNMENTAL DEBTS

To the nations that had suffered from a German invasion, especially to the French, the payment of reparations appeared simple justice and they looked upon the settlement with the rigidity of a creditor who had been awarded damages against a criminal and evasive defendant. World War I, which the French believed they had done nothing to cause, cost their government an estimated twenty-six billion dollars. The devastation wrought in the invaded areas added to this a twenty-billion-dollar bill for reconstruction. The Allies, recognizing that the French Republic had borne an excessive share of the common effort and the common destruction, agreed to allot to France 52 per cent of the expected payments from Germany. By the same arrangement, negotiated in 1920, the British Empire was to receive 22 per cent, Italy 10 per cent, Belgium 8 per cent, and the remaining Allied and Associated powers 8 per cent among them. As the Belgians felt and usually voted with the French on the reparations issue, the two shared a 60 per cent equity in the expected payments. They were, quite understandably, the most urgently aroused and the most insistent upon reprisals when the payments fell into arrears and the Germans defaulted.

The question of international debts was one of the most involved problems intensified by the war. It had two sides: the reparations account with all its bitter implications, and the question of intergovernmental loans covering all the credits advanced to one another by the Allied powers. These two phases of international finance had no direct relation to one another, but despite their separate origins they tended to become opposite sides of the same coin, and a swiftly depreciating coin at that. War in the twentieth century had proved so ruinously expensive that the financial reserves of Russia, France, Italy, and Great Britain had become exhausted and by 1917 the United States was the chief source of credit. After the fighting ceased in 1918 the United States continued to make advances to foreign states, largely to aid the program of postwar reconstruction. By 1924 the total obligations owed to the United States by other governments totaled over twelve billion dollars. Britain, which owed about four and one-half billion of this total, was the leading debtor. But Britain was also a creditor; France alone owed her almost seven billion dollars. Other countries in turn owed France an even larger sum, although most of these debts had become mere figures in a ledger. Like the billions of francs which the French had advanced to the imperial government of Russia before its collapse, these loans were uncollectible and some had been frankly repudiated.

The British government proposed that the situation might be clarified by an all-round cancellation. The British were primarily interested in a return to normal trading relations because their prosperity largely depended on a healthy international trade and they feared that a debt deadlock might delay the trade revival. But the proposal for cancellation was unacceptable to the United States. This government had no equivalent debts outstanding to match the twelve billion dollars in credits owed to it, and the loss incurred through wiping out the debts would have fallen too largely upon the American taxpayer.

Consequently all the debtor nations (except Soviet Russia) worked out agreements between 1921 and 1930 for refunding and repaying their debts, agreements which brought some order into the bookkeeping but did not assure the execution of the terms arranged. As the chief creditor nation the United States took the lead, concluding over a dozen funding agreements between 1922 and 1926. It was obvious that, regardless of the amounts involved, some states were in a better position to pay than others. The American negotiators made allowance for this fact and sought to adjust the ultimate burden to the debtors' capacity to pay. Interest rates were scaled down and the period for repayment extended to sixty-two years, but the principals, both on wartime loans to Allies and on postwar loans for reconstruction, were maintained and added together. The settlement with Britain involved the largest total, amounting to four billion six hundred million dollars, at 3.3 per cent interest. The French debt came next, being funded at roughly four billion dollars, but for France the average interest rate was cut to 1.8 per cent. Italy received an especially low rate of 0.4 per cent on a funded debt of about two billion dollars. These three accounts comprised 92 per cent of the total of twelve billion dollars in funded debts owed to the United States by Allied or neutral or ex-enemy countries.

As payments and interest soon fell in arrears, the sums owed or in default grew steadily. The British government, which received the least generous concessions in the refunding, made the most earnest efforts to meet its annual assessment and repaid a larger share of its debts than France or Italy. But the problem of repayment was increased by the refusal of the United States to accept payment in goods. American producers were alarmed lest foreign nations, needing United States dollars to pay their debts to the United States treasury, would pour floods of low-priced merchandise into the American market. To prevent such competition, Congress was urged to protect the American standard of

WORLD WAR I DEBT OWED U. S. AS OF JUNE 30, 1960

COUNTRY	INDEBTEDNESS			TOTAL	TOTAL PAYMENTS
	PRINCIPAL		INTEREST		
	DUE AND UNPAID	UNMATURED	DUE AND UNPAID		
Armenia	$11,959,917	. . . .	$24,401,099	$36,361,017	. . . .
Austria	18,919,470	$7,061,010	44,058	26,024,539	$862,668
Belgium	152,900,000	247,780,000	227,639,077	628,319,077	52,191,273
Cuba	. . . .	. . . .	. . . .	. . . .	12,286,751
Czechoslovakia	63,496,108	101,745,000	78,643,514	243,884,623	20,134,092
Estonia	5,212,012	11,254,000	16,613,637	33,079,650	1,248,432
Finland	. . . .	5,926,989	180,765	6,107,755	13,103,903
France	1,658,739,454	2,204,910,545	2,129,808,804	5,993,458,804	486,075,891
Great Britain	1,352,000,000	3,016,000,000	4,326,159,301	8,694,159,301	2,024,854,297
Greece	21,016,000	10,500,000	11,895,135	43,411,135	4,127,056
Hungary	563,545	1,345,015	1,827,930	3,736,490	556,919
Italy	586,000,000	1,418,900,000	171,857,159	2,176,757,159	100,829,880
Latvia	2,145,064	4,734,000	6,823,785	13,702,850	761,549
Liberia	. . . .	. . . .	. . . .	. . . .	36,471
Lithuania	1,896,305	4,301,377	6,100,104	12,297,786	1,237,956
Nicaragua	. . . .	. . . .	. . . .	. . . .	168,575
Poland	62,489,000	143,568,000	207,925,124	413,982,124	22,646,297
Rumania	25,037,560	38,823,000	38,263,452	102,124,012	4,791,007
Russia	192,601,297	. . . .	399,928,913	592,530,210	8,750,311
Yugoslavia	18,584,000	43,041,000	10,091,093	71,716,093	2,588,771
Total	$4,173,559,735	$7,259,889,938	$7,658,202,959	$19,091,652,632	$2,757,252,107

Source: *The World Almanac*, 1961, p. 788. (Published by the *New York World-Telegram and The Sun*, New York: 1961.) The totals include some omitted figures.

living by raising the protective tariffs, and the Fordney-McCumber Tariff Act of 1922 established the highest rates hitherto tolerated in American history. Unable to ship in sufficient goods or obtain dollars by other means the debtor countries made part payment in gold and silver, but the limited amount of bullion in the world and the fact that more than half the monetary gold accumulated in the United States made this method impracticable also.

The stand taken by the United States on debt collection decided the British attitude. When Congress made it clear that the debts must be honored, the British negotiated with their debtors in turn, for Britain was likewise a creditor country with some ten billion dollars outstanding. This was more than twice the sum Britain owed the United States, but nine-tenths of the British advances were never collected. To their debtors the British explained that they would base their scale for refunding on the scale set by the United States and if the United States canceled debts Britain would do the same. This was a shrewd policy because the British knew that their debtors would almost certainly default, whereas they themselves took their own debt more seriously. After 1930 a general cessation of payments, or universal default, brought into effect something which resembled the original British plan for all-round cancellation. But by that time Great Britain had paid out nearly one-quarter of a billion more to the United States than the British treasury had received from German reparations and loan repayments combined. The United States was not the only country that "took a loss" when intergovernmental debts proved uncollectible.

The British reaction to the American stand was adroit but somewhat embarrassing to the United States. For the British repeated that Britain would assess her debtors in proportion to American demands and would reduce the obligations other Allied nations owed in London as soon as the United States reduced the obligations Britain owed in Washington. In effect, this threw the onus of exacting payment upon the American people, and Uncle Sam began to appear in hostile sections of the European journals as Uncle Shylock. The United States government persisted in its refusal to cancel the debts outright, although some of its foreign loans were refunded at a lower rate of interest and the period for repayment extended. The debtor nations, moreover, found a further argument to justify or attempt to justify a delay in their repayments. It was almost inevitable that, as Germany fell behind on the scheduled reparations transfers, the French and British would insist they could not pay the United States until the Germans paid them. The Germans were thus disposed to see the United States as the ultimate beneficiary and therefore as the ultimate assessor forcing indemnities from them. Despite the idealism and generosity of the American war effort, the vanquished as well as the victor nations, envious of the extraordinary American prosperity of the 1920's, came to see the United States as an opulent power too greedy to forgive battle-racked and impoverished peoples their unequal burden of debt. For the American people the debt controversy was a long lesson in disillusionment which increased their inclination after 1919 to avoid any new entanglement in European quarrels.

3. GERMANY IN DEFAULT

The hardening stand of the United States on the debt question incited the British, French, Belgians, and Italians to adopt a harsher attitude toward Germany. In April, 1921, the Reparations Commission announced that the total which the Germans must pay over the years would be at least thirty-one billion dollars. The immediate effect of this drastic assessment was a depreciation of German currency, a fall in revenue, and a partial default on the preliminary reparations payments already due. In 1922 the mark (the German monetary unit) continued to decline on the international exchange, and Germany again failed to furnish the stipulated payments in cash, coal, materials, and labor. On January 9, 1923, the Reparations Commission formally announced that Germany was again in default. Thereupon, French and Belgian troops marched into the Ruhr Valley, the most highly industrialized section of Germany, to enforce the methods of direct action or "sanctions" which the Versailles Treaty had prescribed to cover such an eventuality.

Disarmed and demilitarized, the Germans could not fight back actively but they resisted by a passive strike. Business halted in the occupied areas; the mood of noncooperation stiffened throughout all Germany; in the months of enervating deadlock that followed, credit collapsed in a bottomless sea of inflation and the mark depreciated until it became valueless. All Europe felt the dislocation, the economic life of the Continent was threatened with chaos, and even the French franc lost 25 per cent of its value. Pressure had not solved the problem. At the close of 1923, therefore, the Reparations Commission appointed committees to consider a new program. Accepted in 1924, and known as the "Dawes Plan" because of the active participation of the American delegate, Charles Gates Dawes, in devising it, the new plan offered a way out of the impasse. The German currency was to be stabilized, German industry was to be revitalized (with the aid of a two hundred million dollar foreign loan), and the reparations payments were to be reduced temporarily to a quarter of a billion dollars a year. Under this schedule the Germans paid nearly two billion dollars in the next five years and the French and Belgian forces were withdrawn from the Ruhr Valley.

Under the Dawes Plan German industry and economic life made a surprising recovery, aided by the fact that American loans were available to finance the recovery and speed the wheels of production. In 1928 a further modification was introduced, named for another American, Owen D. Young. The total which Germany still owed on reparations was scaled down to the sum of some twenty-nine billion dollars and payments on it were calculated to run for fifty-nine years. With the ratification of this pact the last Allied forces of occupation were withdrawn from the Rhineland (1930) and the German government continued payments to the extent of six hundred and eighty-five million dollars. Within two years, however, the whole issue had passed into history, for the great depression that began in 1929 so dislocated world economy and international finance that on June 21, 1931, President Herbert Hoover proposed a moratorium on international debts. A year later, at Lausanne, representatives of the Allied powers finally accepted the truth that the reparations claims against Germany would never be realized. They proposed a drastic scaling down in the schedule of payments, so drastic that it would have amounted to a practical cancellation of reparations and war debts alike. But once again the United States declined to admit any legal connection between the two types of indebtedness. Germany, however, made no more payments on account of reparations, and after 1931 the British, French, Italian, and other governments made only token payments or none at all on their funded obligations. Finland was the only exception and continued to pay the United States the annual sum agreed upon when it accepted financial aid after separating from Russia in 1917.

Thus reparations and intergovernmental debts, which had been carried as a sort of elastic, marginal item, impressive but unreal, in the budgets of the powers, were written off as bad debts. The records indicated that the Germans had paid over six billion dollars on reparations up to September 1, 1924, and an additional two billion six hundred million between this date and June 30, 1931, a grand total of nearly nine billion dollars. This did not represent a really crushing burden for a great power; after 1933 the German government found it possible to spend larger appropriations for military and naval rearmament. But because of the passions aroused the whole question remained clouded and confused. Even the actual amounts paid were variously estimated as debtor or creditor restated them in terms of shifting currencies and set arbitrary values on the payments in kind and in services.

The major problem in the whole tangle, a problem never very clear to the average citizen in New York or London, was not whether Germany could or even would pay, but *how* she was to pay. It was quite possible to set aside a portion of the annual German budget, especially as a demilitarized Germany had no armament expenses, and a part of the national revenue from the state railways or from tariff dues or internal taxes might have been transferred to the account of reparations. But to *transfer* such amounts out of Germany to the receiving nations was another matter: for this purpose it was necessary to establish credits abroad. Germany could not pay in gold, for her gold reserves were exhausted.

The British and French did not wish to accept German manufactures as payment because this glutted markets which they preferred to supply themselves. Payment in kind instead of in coin often proved no blessing to the receiver; while the Germans, for instance, built ships for Britain to replace the tonnage lost in the war, the British shipyard workers were standing idle and claiming unemployment insurance. When French industries received coal from Germany as partial reparations dues, the British coal mines which had previously helped to supply French needs were shut down. This dilemma continued to embarrass the experts, for Germany could make really substantial payments only in goods and labor, or by selling German products in the world markets and then transferring the profits thus gained to the reparations account. Either way, German wares reached consumers who might otherwise have bought French or British products.

The Germans, with their workers active and their factories humming, kept abreast of modern methods, improved their machinery, and coordinated their industries. To undersell their opponents they were compelled to become more efficient, and they introduced new processes, new synthetic chemicals, new inventions to speed production. In addition they rationalized the management of their great industries into trusts and combines, grouping interdependent factories under the direction of efficiency experts and coordinating production by the creation of supertrusts and international cartels.

The legend that Germany was crushed and crippled after World War I by the extortion of a ruinous tribute is thus seen to have little real truth. It overlooks the fact that the democratic powers, while striving to collect reparations for a decade, were also helping Germany to recover her place in world economy and to rebuild her industries. This aid, it is true, was not always official or even intentional. It was very largely financial aid, advanced in the form of loans negotiated through the great investment brokers of New York, London, Paris, and other capitals. But the *effect* was to subsidize a vast expansion of German industry. The first five years of peace (1919–1924), with defeat, political disorder, the occupation of the Ruhr Valley, and the ruinous inflation, brought much suffering to the Germans; but this was not in general the result of military occupation or reparations, it was the consequence of economic exhaustion and the loss of the war. The second five years (1924–1929) offered a more cheerful picture. Foreign funds to the extraordinary amount of nearly eight billion dollars flowed into Germany, of which about two and one-half billion came from American investors. Approximately two dollars went into Germany for each one that came out in cash as part of the reparations schedule, a fact which makes a fair estimate of the financial situation still more difficult to achieve. After 1931 Germany not only ceased to pay reparations but defaulted on most of the private loans which had been floated by German municipalities, public utilities, industries, and banks. In these transactions American investors were again the heaviest losers, but as the United States was the richest country in the world they could best afford the loss.

4. PAYMENT DEFERRED

In the final analysis, therefore, it would appear that the United States government not only failed to collect on the loans made to its Allies during World War I; it advanced, and again failed to collect on, large sums lent to a number of European governments after the war. Furthermore, in addition to an official loan of two hundred million dollars advanced to the Reichsbank under the Dawes Plan of 1924, American citizens bought German bonds to the total of two and one-half billion dollars after 1924, and most of this sum likewise they never recovered, although it helped to finance the recovery of Germany and prepared the way for rapid German rearmament in the 1930's. This situation appears so illogical and has been so widely criticized by many American commentators that it needs more careful study.

After 1922, as already explained, the war loans and other intergovernmental debts then outstanding were adjusted by a series of agreements negotiated by the United States with its various debtors. By 1930 subsequent arrangements had scaled down the anticipated payments because few of the debtors had met the schedule of annual payments, and some nations were already in default on agreements which still had half a century to run. Collectively, the intergovernmental debts owed to the United States would have amounted to some twenty-two billion dollars by 1933 if accounts had been strictly kept. Actually, unpaid principal and interest piled up in the ledgers, but only about one-tenth of the over-all total, or roughly two billion dollars, was ever repaid. Thus some twenty billion dollars in principal and accumulated interest might still be considered as due the United States when payments ceased. French and British observers could point out, however, that the total of unpaid German reparations was even larger, for they estimated it at twenty-five billion dollars. It was thus possible to argue that the German failure to pay left the United States the loser. But this was an oversimplification of the issue. The United States was not the only creditor unpaid. Great Britain failed to collect on loans and credits of some ten billion dollars which had been advanced to associates during and after the war and were later repudiated. France, in addition to the enormous property losses suffered during four years of campaigning and enemy occupation, had also to write off as uncollectible some seven billion dollars lent to her associates and allies.

Private investors in Britain and France and in all the wealthier centers of Europe also lost on loans advanced to speed German expansion in the 1920's. The Germans urgently needed credit and capital to develop new plants, purchase raw material, and exploit their resources, and they offered attractive terms and high interest rates to float bonds on the international money markets. Many Americans had money to invest in the prosperous decade after 1919, and of eight billion dollars borrowed by the Germans nearly one-third came from the United States. Thus a circular system of exchange grew up, whereby American investors, through international financiers, lent billions of dollars to German enterprises, the German government transferred millions of dollars to the French, British, Italian, and Belgian governments as reparations, and the French, British, Italian, and Belgian governments turned a part, but only a part, of the reparations thus obtained back to the United States government to reduce the interallied debts. Out of all these intricate transactions and the bitter arguments they inspired, one fact emerges quite clearly. By 1933 the total of intergovernmental debts and of reparations demands still outstanding was between fifty and sixty billion dollars. But they had become paper obligations, owed back and forth among the nations, and they would never be repaid.

19

THE ATTEMPT AT INTERNATIONAL ORGANIZATION

I can predict with absolute certainty that within another generation there will be another world war if the nations of the world do not concert the method to prevent it.

WOODROW WILSON

1. SEARCH FOR AN INTERNATIONAL ORDER

THE IDEA THAT ALL the states or nations of the world should be united in one empire, a society of states, or an international federation, is almost as old as the earliest records of civilization. From the most ancient eras successful conquerors dreamed of universal dominion, and ambitious law-givers strove to make one code supreme throughout the world of men. Egyptian, Babylonian, Persian, and Chinese dynasts called themselves lords of the world in their day. The Roman Empire, in the first centuries of the Christian era, brought a remarkable degree of uniformity in legislation, custom, and culture to the Mediterranean world and left behind a powerful tradition of universal sovereignty and the memory of the *Pax Romana* or Roman peace. Then Rome declined, the European section of the once mighty empire was split into barbarian kingdoms, and the Roman provinces in Africa and Asia were conquered in the seventh century by the followers of Mohammed. For a thousand years, from the fifth to the fifteenth century, western Europe or Christendom, though shattered into feudal fragments, remained united in spirit by the ties of a common religious faith. But after the fifteenth century the rise of national territorial states, the separation of the Protestant denominations from the Catholic Church, and the dissolution of that shadowy political conception, the Holy Roman Empire, left Europe permanently divided. There was no tribunal to which all princes would turn, no international court with the authority to intervene and arbitrate the recurrent controversies which drove the sovereign states to frequent war.

Projects for the establishment of an international court or league were proposed by many eminent thinkers. In the seventeenth century the Duke of Sully, minister of Henry IV of France, formulated a "Grand Design," and the scholar Émeric Crucé urged that human society was in

215

reality one body and that no part of it could suffer without the whole feeling the affliction. In the eighteenth century the Abbé de Saint Pierre and the philosopher Immanuel Kant drafted projects for perpetual peace. In the nineteenth century a host of writers devised a variety of intelligent plans. But none solved in workable fashion the fundamental problem of state sovereignty *vs.* league authority or explained how a national government could pledge itself to accept the decision of an international court yet remain the supreme and sovereign judge of its own actions.

The penalty for this condition of international anarchy was the succession of general wars which darkened European history every few decades. Each major conflict from the sixteenth century on was followed by a mood of horror and remorse and inspired the creation of diplomatic machinery which was intended to avert by frequent conferences, compromise, and arbitration the outbreak of further disastrous conflicts. These various efforts, endorsed sincerely enough by their framers while the dead still lay unburied on the battlefields, never crystallized into an enduring tribunal, and the plans to summon regular international conferences were always abandoned after a few years. The last ambitious attempt of this kind was undertaken a century before the First World War broke out. When the Napoleonic Wars with their mounting casualties culminated in the defeat of France, the Quadruple Alliance of the victorious powers, Britain, Russia, Austria, and Prussia, was set up as the foundation for a Confederation of Europe. After three years the defeated power, France, was admitted to membership. But Great Britain had already begun to draw away, and the Confederation, which lacked any permanent meeting place, any formal structure, any body of officers or recognized secretariat, ceased to be an instrument of diplomacy and became only a convenient idea. In theory there was a "Concert of Europe" throughout the nineteenth century. But the relative tranquillity of the era was primarily due to the balance of power favored by Great Britain, and to the release of European tensions through expansion overseas and the opening up of the world. The dawn of the twentieth century found a Confederation of Europe no nearer reality than before.

By 1900 the exploitable regions of the earth had been very largely preempted and national rivalries in Europe were intensified yearly by the rivalries of the imperialist powers in their overlapping colonial spheres. The rise of armament budgets and the growing tension convinced many lovers of peace that there was an urgent need for some sort of cooperative action. In 1899 a peace conference, called at the suggestion of Tsar Nicholas II of Russia, met at The Hague. The delegates drew up a formula for the arbitration of disputes among sovereign states and proposed that a permanent court of international justice be established to hear appeals and render decisions. In 1907 a second Hague Peace Conference was convened. But no real progress was achieved in the crucial issue, the limitation of armaments, and the states would not agree in advance to submit their quarrels to the Permanent Court and promise to abide by its decisions. Despite some well-meant gestures and minor concessions, despite the earnest efforts of the peace societies and other public groups which favored disarmament, the Hague Conferences had no real influence upon the foreign or domestic policies of the great powers. The crisis of 1914 found Europe without any peace machinery adequate to avert or even to delay the appeal to arms.

Four years of anguish and eight million war dead brought the nations once more to the conviction that a permanent international body to preserve peace was essential if civilization was to be preserved. Pondering the waste and tragedy of war as the campaigns racked Europe, people everywhere persuaded themselves that the tragedy might easily have been averted, that a World Court, with the prestige and the jurisdiction to arbitrate the Austro-Serb quarrel, would have made a general war inexcusable and unnecessary. Leaders stood forth in all the democratic countries to expound this belated truth — Lord Robert Cecil for Great Britain, General Jan Christiaan Smuts of South Africa for the British Dominions, Léon Bourgeois for France, Woodrow Wilson for the United States. These eloquent proponents for a league to preserve peace secured a large and inspired following in 1917 and 1918, and the faith that a real and honest attempt would be made after the war to organize such a league heartened the Allied nations in their crusade for victory. When the Paris Peace Conference assembled in January, 1919, all four of the above mentioned statesmen were elected to a "Commission on the League." The commission was entrusted with the task of drafting a constitution for the Association of Nations which Woodrow Wilson had listed among his Fourteen Points.

2. FORMATION OF THE LEAGUE OF NATIONS

The form proposed for the League of Nations was designed to make it a sort of superstate with machinery capable of discharging the three normal functions of a government: executive, legislative, and judicial. The paramount purpose was to promote peace and security among the nations. At the plenary session of the Peace Conference, which met on January 25, 1919, a resolution was adopted declaring that:

It is essential to the maintenance of the world settlement, which the Associated Nations are now met to establish, that a League of Nations be created to promote international cooperation, to insure the fulfillment of accepted international obligations, and to provide safeguards against war.

The chief organs of the League were to be two legislative chambers, to be known as the Assembly and the Council. All member states were accorded one vote in the Assembly, great powers and small nations ranking alike in this respect. The Council, as first planned, was to consist of nine members. Five of these were to be permanent members and would represent the five great powers, the United States, Great Britain, France, Italy, and Japan. The four nonpermanent members were to be chosen by the Assembly. Later the number of the nonpermanent members was raised to six and finally to nine. The Assembly and the Council were declared competent to debate any question which concerned world peace.

The judicial functions of the League were to be entrusted to a Permanent Court of International Justice, a World Court. This body was organized with eleven (later fifteen) judges, elected for a nine-year term by the Assembly and the Council. Ratified in 1921, the Court was duly installed in 1922, taking its seat not at Geneva, where the other League organs and commissions assembled, but at The Hague. It was provided that any national governments involved in a dispute might appeal their case to the Court by mutual accord, and it was hoped that many states would bind themselves in advance to ask such arbitration before resorting to war and would promise to accept the decision resulting from such "compulsory arbitration."

The executive powers of the League were the powers most likely to infringe upon the authority of the sovereign states. They were left weak and nebulous. There was no prince or president, no cabinet under the direction of a chairman or prime minister as in parliamentary regimes, no executive committee with a clear mandate or definite delegated powers. A permanent secretariat or bureaucracy, headed by a Secretary General who also acted as secretary for the Council and the Assembly meetings, preserved the records and provided a rather tenuous line of continuity between sessions. Responsibility in specific fields was delegated to committees on economic affairs, labor, mandates, and minorities. The investigations and recommendations of these committees were supposed to furnish information upon which the Assembly and the Council might take action, but it was easier to compile a body of data on a critical question than to secure any positive result when the chambers met. The Council, as the smaller body with the weightier prestige, showed the more determined front, but the Assembly, where the smaller nations most in need of protection could unite their protests, gained more confidence as the years passed. Both chambers were inhibited by the knowledge that their enthusiasm or indignation, their debates and their resolutions, would prove echoes in a desert of silence unless a majority of the national governments translated them into positive policies.

The League remained primarily a consultative body, a debating society. It could recommend a course of action to the member states but it possessed no effective coercive powers to enforce respect for its decisions. If, despite League protests, a war came, and nations took up arms in violation of their pledges and in defiance of League admonishment, the

Council might invite member states to apply an economic boycott against an aggressor. The Council might even recommend armed reprisal against the offender. But the appropriate measures of restraint, economic or military, could be applied only by the governments of individual states. The League itself possessed no weapons, no armed force, and a French proposal to place an international police corps at its disposal was voted down. The weight of a League decision was dependent upon the strength of public opinion in enlightened nations, and when public opinion was ill-informed, confused, or divided (as is commonly the case when international crises arise) the League lacked the authority to intervene with force and effect. Even if a strongly worded vote of censure condemning a belligerent state were passed by the Assembly and the Council, no means existed for bringing pressure against the troublemaker except through a joint boycott imposed by other members. In theory, this mode of concerted action appeared promising, but when attempts were made to apply it no effective, coordinated boycott could be achieved. The solid front desired could never be established because nonmembers were generally uncooperative, some member states were evasive, and some were in open or secret sympathy with the aggressor. Nevertheless even when the League appeared to fail most impotently, it left a residual judgment in the minds of sober men everywhere, a judgment which identified and condemned those nations which showed aggressive impulses.

It is easy, after a quarter of a century, to point out the defects that weakened the League of Nations. It was cumbrous in organization, slow and formal in deliberation, unprepared (because seldom in session) to cope with a sudden crisis, unprovided with instruments to check aggression when aggression commenced. The financial resources of this august body were severely restricted, and its annual budget of some seven million dollars was less than that of leading American universities. Yet all these limitations, which might have been repaired in time, did not cripple the League in fundamental fashion. The real defect of the League as a confederation of sovereign states was the fact that it never was a truly international, independent, world-embracing organization. It never achieved the prestige and standing of a supranational parliament, it never won the active support of all the leading world states, it never attained the neutral and universal character which its founders envisaged for it.

The first and heaviest blow it suffered was dealt by the nation which had seemed its warmest friend. When Woodrow Wilson asked the United States Senate to approve the Treaty of Versailles, which included the League Covenant, the Senate rejected both. His faith in the people still firm, Wilson carried his appeal to the nation, but the election of 1920 sustained his opponents, and the Congress finally voted for a separate peace with Germany in 1921. This repudiation by the American people, who had led the crusade to "make the world safe for democracy" and then abandoned the one organ which seemed a guarantee of peace and justice, crippled the League permanently. Responsibility for this unhappy outcome to ardent hopes was shared by Wilson, his opponents, and the sovereign people of the United States.

Thus, from the outset, the United States was absent from the circle of the League, gravely impairing the usefulness of this international organization. But there were other gaps almost as distressing. In the early years two other great powers, Germany and Russia, were also absent. An association of nations which included no more than four of the seven great powers could be called a "world league" in name only. It is true that the number of great powers within the League was increased to five in 1926 when Germany received a permanent seat on the Council, and this event marked the high tide of League achievements. To estimate how much the League accomplished it will be helpful to strike a balance by measuring its successes against its failures.

3. ACHIEVEMENTS AND FAILURES OF THE LEAGUE

League arbitration was not always vain. In a score of disputes between secondary states the committees at Geneva found a workable solution. In several cases action by the League not only averted hostilities, it even halted open warfare after the fighting had commenced. The tale of such successes makes more encouraging reading than the list of antagonisms unhealed and ruptures which could not be averted.

In 1921–1922 a dispute between Sweden and Finland, both of which claimed possession of the Aaland Islands, was submitted to the League for decision. The verdict, which granted the islanders autonomy under Finnish sovereignty, moderated the controversy. In 1925 border clashes almost brought on a war between Greece and Bulgaria, but arbitration under League auspices assured a peaceful settlement. In 1932 an incipient war between Peru and Colombia was resolved peaceably through League mediation. Several controversial claims arising from the Versailles settlement, confided to the League for adjustment, were likewise arbitrated with success. Under League supervision a plebiscite was held in Upper Silesia in 1921 to resolve the border separating Germany and Poland. A majority of the inhabitants wished the territory in dispute to remain within the German Reich. The League Council recommended a partition of the region which awarded Poland a somewhat more generous share than the vote seemed to justify but which did settle a most acrid dispute without violence and laid down a line of demarcation in a troubled area. A second difficult assignment for which the League should receive honor was its fifteen-year supervision of the Saar Valley. In accordance with the provisions of the Versailles Treaty the League conducted a plebiscite in 1935. The results indicated that 90 per cent of the inhabitants desired the reincorporation of the territory in Germany, and the League thereupon approved the reunion of this important mining and industrial area in the Reich. These five cases are examples of patient negotiation and responsible statesmanship. The publicity and clamor that accompanied many appeals to the League were often an embarrassment; some of the most effective work accomplished by the League diplomats was successful because it did not reach the headlines of the newspapers. Every sane settlement of an international dispute is likely to be a compromise, and governments find it easier to withdraw extreme claims if the spotlight has been turned elsewhere. Public excitement, especially when deliberately fanned by governments as part of their offensive, can create an atmosphere so tense and stormy that a calm analysis of the questions at issue becomes impossible.

Some of the soundest and most constructive tasks attempted by League commissions seldom attracted popular attention. Financial aid to the insolvent Austrian republic, advice and assistance to several eastern European nations in combating typhus, improvement in the status of natives in backward regions and obscure protectorates — these and other services were undramatic and passed with little general notice. Yet the existence of a Commission on Mandates with responsibility for scrutinizing conditions in Togoland or Samoa marked an important change in the attitude of the European states toward the treatment of submerged peoples and the exploitation of colonial areas. The League did not possess a police force that could intervene to prevent injustice, but it could appeal to the enlightened opinion of civilized people in the advanced countries. In Europe and America intelligent and humane citizens read the League reports and besought their governments to introduce corrective measures to benefit forgotten peoples caught in the net of the rival imperialisms.

Perhaps the greatest ultimate benefits conferred by the League resulted from its studies on human welfare. Year after year its investigators compiled carefully tested and remarkably objective statistics on the effects of famine, of deficiency diseases, of epidemics, of vaccines and preventive medicine, of vice, slavery, the drug traffic, labor conditions, and many other social problems affecting the welfare of mankind. Many of the evils uncovered were of such a nature that they could be curbed only through international cooperation. Though the League possessed very limited funds its agents performed invaluable services in collecting information and coordinating the findings of national and international charitable organizations, in quickening the consciences of civilized peoples, and in making available the facts and figures upon which campaigns for a better and healthier world could be based. For the first indispensable step to all social reform is the compilation of fair and accurate data on the conditions to be remedied. The League of Nations Year Book and other reference works which published trustworthy figures on tax rates, living standards, incomes, vital statistics, literacy, armament budgets, and a hundred equally significant facts, provided an arsenal of useful information. Legislators, reformers, journalists, and lecturers could draw upon the international guides when preparing campaigns or criticizing abuses.

The promotion of intellectual cooperation among the thinkers and artists of all nations was a further aim of the League sponsors. To link culture to culture and class to class through the exchange of scholars, lecturers, scientists, and artists; to hasten the translation of important books; to encourage exchanges in research; and to broaden the channels of international travel and communication were all worthy purposes and all gained strength through League enterprise.

Finally, it is just to note the role played by the International Labor Office, an agency of the League created for the improvement of relations between employers and employees and for the promotion of remedial measures to reduce class tension and class rivalry. Modern society was not only threatened by the devastation of war between nations, it was endangered by the prospect of war within nations, war that could turn one class against another. To find a solution to class antagonisms and so reduce the risk of civil conflicts was a vital function of any organization that was intended to assure peace by collective action. This truth was likewise clear to the idealists who framed the League of Nations.

The failures of the League of Nations were more dramatic than its successes and outweighed them. One serious limitation that reduced its strength and effectiveness has been mentioned already: the United States never became a member. There were other abstentions or resignations almost equally crippling, with the result that the League never included more than five of the seven great powers at one time. Its history may be divided into two seven year periods and two three year periods. From 1919 to 1926 only four great powers had representatives on the League Council — Britain, France, Italy, and Japan. The admission of Germany in 1926 raised the total to five, and for the next seven years (1926–1933) the League came closest to being a global organization. In 1933, however, Japan and Germany withdrew, leaving Britain, France, and Italy the only great powers on the Council. The admission of Soviet Russia in 1934 restored the total to four, but the withdrawal of Italy in 1937 reduced it to three again. In 1940 Russia was expelled, leaving Britain and France the only great powers still in attendance.

A further source of weakness for the League arose from the distrust non-European peoples felt toward it. The Japanese proposed in 1919 that the League protocol should recognize the equality of races but the drafting commission rejected this suggestion. This decision emphasized the Europocentric bias of the League and two-thirds of the world's population felt that the whites regarded them as inferiors. The peoples of Asia and Africa, especially those living in colonies, protectorates, or mandates administered by European powers, did not feel confident that the League would listen to their complaints with impartiality, and doubted that it would heed them at all.

Within Europe those nations disposed from the first to distrust the League as an instrument of the victor powers found some reasons to justify their misgivings. They noted that it was reluctant to criticize any action of its leading members. It hesitated to criticize the French, who insisted upon maintaining the most powerful army in Europe although the Central Powers were disarmed and helpless. It failed to curb Poland (a satellite of France) when the Poles detached Memel from Lithuania in 1920 or when they seized additional territory from Russia in 1921. It failed to enforce arbitration upon the Italians when they shelled Corfu in 1923 and exacted an indemnity from the Greeks in retaliation for a border incident. When it was a matter of enforcing the Versailles terms against the vanquished, however, the League was accused of too much zeal by some critics. Austria, reduced to a third-rate power by the treaty, would normally have merged in a political or at least an economic alliance with Germany. But this choice was forbidden lest Germany grow too strong. The unsound economic condition of the new Austria made a common customs union with Germany a reasonable plan, but neither appeals to the principle of self-determination nor the economic chaos in Austria persuaded the French to permit the *Anschluss* or union proposed. Recourse to the League was vain: as late as 1931 the Court of International Justice declared such a merger contrary to the Treaty of Versailles, a ruling which affronted German patriots.

In the critical tests of the 1930's the League failed each time it sought to check the aggressive moves of a great power. It failed to arrest the Japanese invasion of Manchuria and northern China which commenced in 1931. It failed to halt the Italian invasion and annexation of Ethiopia in 1935 although the Ethiopian government, like the Chinese, appealed repeatedly to Geneva for protection and arbitration. It failed during the desperate Spanish civil war of 1936–1939 to prevent the Germans and Italians from sending thousands of technicians, airmen, and whole divisions of infantry to aid the insurgents, while the Russians supported the Republican government. It failed to prevent German infiltration and occupation of Danzig, although the Free City was under its direct protection. Finally it failed to avert the German attack upon Poland which opened World War II in 1939.

Yet the blame for these failures does not properly belong to the League as an organ. The members of the Council, the delegates to the Assembly, the personnel of the secretariat strove earnestly, despite weakened authority and waning prestige, to uphold its rules and maintain its functions. The fault lay with the statesmen of the leading states, with the public in the advanced nations, who lost faith in the League as an organization. To flout the League became a popular gesture with German, Japanese, and Italian politicians who wished to arouse nationalist enthusiasm by appealing to the chauvinist emotions of their constituents. The League itself did not cease to function: it simply failed to affect the course of events. When the Japanese pushed into Manchuria, the Council adopted a judicious report on the Far Eastern situation and condemned the Japanese government on the charge of military aggression. But the rebuke did not halt the Japanese. When the Italians invaded Ethiopia, the League members agreed to invoke an economic blockade of Italy to restrain the Fascist plan of conquest. Italy was particularly vulnerable to blockade; the withholding of oil alone might have stalled the Italian drives. But the economic sanctions were too lightly enforced to prove effective. These tests, and these successive proofs that the League could judge a situation, could bring in a verdict, but could not enforce it or persuade an effective majority of the national states to enforce it, were milestones on the road to the Second World War.

4. DISARMAMENT: THE CRITICAL TEST

When the Germans, in deep humiliation, accepted the Versailles Treaty in 1919, they particularly resented the conditions that all but abolished their armed forces and left them defenseless. The chairman of the conference, the French statesman Georges Clemenceau, assured them that German disarmament was to be the first step in a world-wide reduction and limitation of armed forces. By 1926 the commission the victors had appointed to supervise the disarmament of Germany reported that the program had been carried out in almost all respects. Thus the assurance that Clemenceau had offered was put to the test. During World War I the Allied governments had asserted that Germany had been responsible for the arms race that preceded the outbreak of hostilities. But when Germany had been defeated and disarmed, Britain, France, Italy and other nations did not welcome the opportunity to disarm likewise. On the contrary, though the League of Nations included a disarmament commission created to speed the general reduction of military forces its activities produced few effective results. The Germans protested with some justice that the British and French failure to disarm proved that Britain and France were insincere and that their claim that German militarism had caused the arms race before 1914 was demonstrably untrue. When, in 1933, Germany resigned from the League, the German government cited this failure of the victors to disarm as the reason for its repudiation of the League.

Public opinion still respected the high ideals upon which the League was founded, and delegates at the sessions did not cease to warn against the increase of armaments and to deplore the growth of aggression and the disregard of treaties. But horror of war is a relative passion; it was strong among the lesser nations which were predestined victims of aggression, and weak among the ambitious nations conscious of power and eager for expansion. Cynics pointed out with some truth that the states which remained within the League were either second and third class countries which could not afford to wage a war or satiated powers which had ample areas in which to expand. The three great powers left in the League after 1937 were not moved wholly by moral considerations in denouncing war. All of them for one reason or another preferred to see a balance of power in Europe and the world, and they made the League an instrument by which violent change might be discredited, denouncing from its forum those restless and hungry nations which threatened world equilibrium or coveted their neighbors' lands. Britain, France, and the Soviet Union could afford to support a policy which "froze" existing frontiers and prohibited further conquest, for they were, as their critics pointed out, "satiated" powers. Taken together, the three empires comprised almost half the land area of the earth.

The fact that the three "have not" powers, Japan, Germany, and Italy, all gave offense to the more peaceful members, were all charged with aggressive and militaristic actions, and all resigned in resentment, suggests a grave defect in the League as an instrument of peace. The German, Italian, and Japanese imperialists insisted that their nations, too, were entitled to large colonial empires, to "living space," or *Lebensraum*, as the German expansionists termed it. The idealists who supported the League believed that it might become a mechanism for assuring peaceful change in the world, for lowering obstructive tariffs, opening up neglected areas, and assuring all nations a fair share in world trade and raw materials. But world trade fell sharply after the depression of 1929 and each nation sought selfishly to safeguard its own share. This sharper economic nationalism which drove the powers toward a policy of self-sufficiency, added to the bitterness of the "have not" states. It is important to understand how the dissatisfied imperialists in Berlin, Rome, or Tokyo viewed the League in order to understand why it failed to hold their support. To the Germans it never outgrew its early association with the Versailles pact, it never achieved a truly independent or international status in their eyes. The Italians likewise, who felt that they had been cheated in the peace settlement of 1919, never regarded it with enthusiasm. In all parts of the world there were many people with similar views, people to whom the League never appeared the detached, impartial tribunal they might have trusted, but merely a complicated piece of diplomatic machinery constructed by the statesmen who framed the Versailles Treaty and controlled by them as a device for protecting their conquests. This was not a just estimate of the League; it was not even a logical estimate, but it was an estimate widely advertised by its foes.

As an experiment in collective security the League of Nations failed. But the list of its failures is not perhaps the most significant part of the record. It was not a wholly abortive experiment. Its successes, and it had many minor successes, were too readily forgotten. Even its missteps and frustrations had their value, for errors provide a warning. The League

sessions helped to set a precedent and a pattern for international cooperation which future generations might recognize more clearly and rate more
highly than contemporary observers did. Its failures became a part of
history but its successes held the clue to a better international order.

Section IV: EXPERIMENTS IN GOVERNMENT

20

DEMOCRACY ON TRIAL

Genuine democracy must be economic and social as well as political.

T. G. MASARYK

1. WANING OF THE LIBERAL IDEAL

THE FIRST WORLD WAR dealt a deathblow to many cherished tenets of liberalism, both political and economic. Basic to the concept of freedom of the nineteenth-century liberals was the belief — aptly summed up by Jefferson — that the government which governed least, governed best. Governments, the nineteenth-century liberals believed, should confine their activities to the maintenance of law and order and to the conduct of foreign affairs. Free enterprise at home and free trade abroad were the liberal ideals. These were, it should be noted, only ideals, never a reality; even the most liberal governments did not by any means confine themselves to the role of policeman, judge, and guardian of foreign interests. They shaped economic and social policies, even if only in the role of regulators or arbiters and not of organizers or participants. And except for Great Britain, no nation practiced free trade. But the liberals hoped that even this modest role of governments would diminish in time because they thought that the historical trend was toward ever greater freedom. The world, they hopefully believed, was moving, haltingly perhaps but steadily, toward the day when poverty, ignorance, and oppression would vanish everywhere and the whole of mankind would be prosperous, civilized, and free. Toward the end of the nineteenth century, it is true, some liberals, typified by the British statesman Joseph Chamberlain (see p. 41), questioned whether this was indeed the trend and, if it was, whether it was a desirable one, but by and large liberals still held to this optimistic faith until the First World War rudely shattered it.

The outbreak of the war disrupted international trade and forced the warring nations to rely heavily on their own resources. It thus reversed the prewar trend toward growing economic interdependence of nations, and stimulated a neomercantilist tendency toward autarky, or national economic self-sufficiency. Driven by fear of defeat and by hope of victory

229

the belligerent governments were forced to enter into a variety of activities previously never engaged in by any government. To mobilize their resources and to organize them for victory the belligerent nations created a variety of war boards and devised intricate and detailed controls to regulate every phase of national life. The key controls were those affecting production and consumption; war production boards determined what should be produced, in what quantities, and how it should be distributed. The normal operation of the law of demand and supply was completely suspended. Competition, regarded in peacetime as a healthy stimulus to efficiency in production, was discarded as wasteful and emphasis was placed on coordination of production. Priorities were established and industries were allotted raw materials, told what to produce, and given production quotas. Wages and prices were fixed. The finished products, carefully rationed, were allocated to the armies and the civilian population. In Germany, where war controls and planning were most highly developed, they were frankly and appropriately called "war socialism." War socialism, that is government control and direction of all national resources and productive forces, made of the First World War a total war and prolonged it for four years and a half — a development which in 1914 no one would have thought possible. This prodigious achievement made a deep impression. It led to the logical question: If such a great effort could be made for a destructive purpose in war, why not also make it for a constructive purpose in peace? People got used to the various new services provided by the state during the war and insisted that they be continued in peacetime. The old faith of liberals in the superior virtue of governments which governed least and in economic laissez-faire was undermined. Security and stability rather than freedom became the great demands of the day.

After the war, the nostalgic yearning for a "return to normalcy" led to the abandonment of the wartime controls and planning. For a few fleeting years the liberal hope persisted of a world united politically under the League of Nations and economically by a free world economy, but it remained only a hope and never became a reality. Paradoxically, while crying against government "regimentation," public opinion everywhere insisted at the same time that governments "do something" about the many postwar problems. While lip service was paid to the necessity of freeing international trade from the many restrictions placed on it during the war, tariffs were generally raised and the wartime tendency toward economic self-sufficiency continued. Among the major powers, Great Britain alone made a gallant struggle against the rising tide of neomercantilism. In order to maintain the firmness and free convertibility of the pound, the British financed their postwar reconstruction by heavy taxation rather than by inflation of their currency, as most other nations did. In order to recover their prewar position as the greatest trading nation in the world, the British tenaciously maintained their free-trade policy against mounting competition. During the war, when the British were unable to supply their old customers, these turned to other sources of supply or developed their own industries. The United States and Japan greatly expanded their production and took over many traditional British markets. The Latin-American countries, the British Dominions, and even India developed industries and after the war sought to protect them by adopting tariffs. Britain thus found many of her old markets closed to her, even in her own dominions.

The World Depression finally routed the liberal forces, both political and economic. Economic controls, reminiscent of the wartime regulations, were introduced nearly everywhere to save nations from economic collapse and to cushion the hardships of unemployment and bankruptcy. As all nations retrenched, even the British surrendered to the general tide of economic nationalism. In 1931 they were forced to abandon the gold standard, and in 1932 they abandoned free trade and adopted protective tariffs. The World Economic Conference, which met in London in 1933, largely under British prodding, was a complete failure. All countries preferred to seek national solutions to the vexing problems of the depression. Economic nationalism had prevailed everywhere over economic laissez-faire.

2. ECLIPSE OF DEMOCRACY

It has been seen in Chapter 15 that the victory of the western Allies in 1918 was followed by a triumph of parliamentary democracy everywhere in Europe. The conservative autocratic empires of Europe had collapsed and on their ruins there arose new democratic regimes. This was natural; nothing succeeds like success. Since the victorious powers were liberal parliamentary democracies and the defeated powers conservative monarchies, it was logical to conclude that parliamentary democracy was a superior system to conservative monarchy. The outcome of the war seemed to prove that parliamentary democracy assured not only political freedom but military prowess as well. That the western nations were also advanced industrial and maritime powers was overlooked, because Germany was an industrial and maritime power too — yet she had lost the war. On the part of the defeated nations there was also an element of opportunism in the haste with which they scrambled to join the ranks of democratic nations. By embracing democracy they hoped to secure better terms from the victorious democratic powers.

However, the triumph of liberal parliamentary democracy after the First World War proved short-lived and the pendulum began to swing the other way almost at once. Parliamentary democracy did not prove to be the panacea that many expected it to be. This system was designed to remain in equilibrium because it operated through a balance of power.

As developed in England, parliamentary democracy was in principle most immediately responsible to the people because a cabinet was obligated to resign at any time if it failed to obtain a vote of confidence from the House of Commons, and the resignation of a cabinet was the signal for a general election. Thus the electors might be consulted at frequent intervals, or whenever there was reason to doubt whether the ministers in office had the confidence of the majority of the people. Under this form, true parliamentary government could never be despotic or dictatorial, for a cabinet which promulgated unpopular or tyrannous decrees would be overthrown. A people endowed with habits of self-restraint and trained in the art and technique of parliamentary rule could make the system work remarkably well. But in a country where factional strife was too bitter and the populace tended to divide uncompromisingly on many issues, a feud-ridden parliament might reflect all too faithfully the disunity of the nation. If the level of political morality were low, the prevalence of corruption at the polls and the venality of the deputies might destroy the faith in the patriotism and capacity of a parliament. Though the form of democratic rule remained, the promise of equal justice under law might be vitiated and the political group in power might retain its control through a vast, half-acknowledged conspiracy rather than through enlightened and independent plebiscites.

The responsibility of self-government was apparently too severe for some peoples who had not come of age politically. In the countries of Central and Eastern Europe, where parliamentary government was first adopted after the First World War, it often failed to function properly. The new, inexperienced democratic leaders in these countries frequently exhausted themselves in debates over constitutional and ideological principles and in party battles and failed to come to grips with the pressing postwar economic and social problems. In these circumstances, parliamentary democracy became identified in the eyes of the masses with endless and abstruse talk, party wrangling, and failure to act — in short, with weakness and confusion. It is not surprising, therefore, that many men began to rediscover the virtues of strong, authoritarian regimes which could "shut up the babblers" and deal resolutely with postwar problems. Many of the defeated nations, moreover, were disappointed when adoption of democracy failed to secure for them lenient terms from the democratic peacemakers. An underlying principle of the Paris peace settlement was national self-determination, which implied non-interference in internal affairs of other nations. The peacemakers appeared not to care much what form of government the defeated nations adopted, as long as they accepted and carried out the peace terms. Since the humiliating peace terms came from the hands of democratic statesmen, democracy became identified in the minds of the defeated nations with them.

The earliest and in the long run the most damaging failure of democracy occurred in Russia. Bolshevism, which followed the short-lived liberal regime, was the most complete negation of the liberal tenets of parliamentary democracy. For the moment, however, bolshevism was too insecurely established in Russia to be a serious threat to democracy elsewhere. A greater immediate threat to democracy was the rise of new dictatorial regimes which came to be known generally as fascist.

Hungary was a good weather vane of postwar political trends in Europe. In rapid succession Hungary experimented with democracy, bolshevism, and fascism. The liberal regime of Count Károlyi collapsed as early as March, 1919, when the Allies ordered the Hungarian government to withdraw its troops not only from the non-Magyar periphery of the country but from a band of purely Magyar territory as well. Outraged by the Allied order, the Hungarian people turned from democracy to bolshevism. The Károlyi government was followed by the Bolshevik regime of Béla Kun, which proposed to defend Hungarian territorial integrity with arms in hand. "We placed our trust," declared Alexander Garbai, the President of the Hungarian Soviet Republic, "in the intention of the Allies to aim at a just peace. Our trust is entirely destroyed by this new ukase [i.e., the Allied note]. . . . The new policy for us must be to look to the East for that which the West has denied us." But the East, that is Soviet Russia, was then in no position to help Hungary. The Bolshevik regime in Hungary remained isolated. It collapsed after only five months, giving way to the "white" regime of Admiral Nicholas Horthy — the first successful fascist government in Europe.

In 1922 the parliamentary system collapsed in Italy. It was followed by the rise of the fascist state which provided the classical model for fascism everywhere. In the following years the democratic governments of Central and Eastern Europe gave way, one by one, to fascist or semi-fascist regimes while the western democracies looked on indifferently. By the time of the arrival of the World Depression, democracy in Central and Eastern Europe was in full retreat. When the parliamentary system collapsed in Germany in 1933, the retreat turned into a rout. Parliamentary democracy in Central and Eastern Europe could have been saved only if the western nations had from the beginning made an effort to save it, comparable to the military, political, and economic effort made by the United States in behalf of democracy in Europe after the Second World War. The reason why they failed to make such an effort was that after the First World War there was present no clear, imminent military threat to them — unlike after the Second World War when the threat of Nazi Germany was followed almost immediately by the threat of Soviet Russia. In the 1920's both Germany and Russia were militarily too weak to present serious threats to the western nations. And in the 1930's when they effected a military comeback, the violent hostility of Nazi Germany and Soviet Russia to each other made it look more likely that they would attack each other before they turned on the western nations. The two threats thus appeared to cancel each other.

In these circumstances the western nations failed to see that they had a stake in the preservation of democracy in Central and Eastern Europe. The United States, disillusioned with the "betrayal" of its ideals at Paris, repudiated the settlement and withdrew into a sulky isolation. In the following years, in so far as the Americans showed any interest in the European developments, it was only to shake their heads in disapproval and mutter "We told you so." The American recriminations were generally justified but they were hardly helpful. As for Britain and France, they were too weakened by the war, disunited in purpose, and absorbed in their own difficult problems to do much about the situation. The noble ideal of Woodrow Wilson of making the world safe for democracy went up in smoke. Following the Second World War another opportunity to realize it did not present itself. The question has been rather whether democracy can survive in its old strongholds along the Atlantic seacoast.

3. RISE OF THE TOTALITARIAN STATES

The totalitarian systems arose out of the debris of parliamentary democracy in Central and Eastern Europe by exploiting the social and nationalist fears and hatreds fomented by the war. Philosophically they had their roots in various intellectual currents of the nineteenth century. Some of their roots were common and some separate. As in any political, social, and economic system (the parliamentary-democratic system included) there were wide discrepancies between theory and practice in the totalitarian systems. Like other systems, the totalitarian systems did not remain static but evolved with the passage of time; a valid observation made about them at one time might not be valid at another. In theory the main totalitarian systems — bolshevism, fascism, and naziism — diverged on many points; their symbolism and rationale varied greatly. But in practice they had more similarities than dissimilarities. It is their practice which interests us here more than their theory.

For different reasons, Soviet Russia, Nazi Germany, and Fascist Italy claimed to represent impartially the interests of all their citizens and assumed the responsibility for their welfare. Soviet Russia even claimed to have abolished classes and to have inaugurated a classless society. In practice, they all subordinated the interests of their citizens to the interests of the state. The monolithic, all-powerful state was the principal creation and characteristic of all totalitarian systems. Ultimate powers were vested in a "leader" (*Vozhd, Duce, Führer*). The State was the absolute master, not the servant, of the citizens. Laws were for the citizens to obey, but not for the State when they clashed with its interests. The people had no individual rights, even if, as in Soviet Russia, civic rights were formally guaranteed by a liberal constitution. All of the totalitarian states assumed the right to direct the energies and control the property of their citizens, even if, as in Germany and Italy, private property and the capitalist system were not abolished. All of the totalitarian states were economic autarchies.

The totalitarian systems were exclusive and were intolerant of opposition. All of them believed that their cause was sacred and that any means which advanced it was justified. All of them were one-party states, in which the opposition was destroyed, often by an unprecedented and barbaric use of violence, torture, and genocide. Since they all claimed to hold exclusively the truth, they all demanded of their citizens an absolute and unquestioning acceptance of their official philosophies, which were all-inclusive. To inculcate these philosophies in their citizens, they plied them with propaganda in an unprecedented fashion and isolated them from the knowledge of other systems by exercising a rigid censorship of all media of communication. The totalitarian states were jealous of any organizations, such as churches, which claimed — and thus split — the loyalty of their citizens. Fascist Italy, for tactical reasons, came to an understanding with the Roman Catholic Church in 1929, under which, in return for recognition of its exclusive position in Italy, the Church agreed to support the fascist state. In Nazi Germany, whose official philosophy was neopagan, the churches were harassed and persecuted. In Soviet Russia, whose official philosophy was materialistic and atheistic, the churches were intensely persecuted until the Second World War, when the state and churches arrived at an unofficial modus vivendi which accorded the churches a grudging tolerance in return for a grovelling support of the soviet state.

The totalitarian states were invariably very nationalistic and xenophobic. Partly for ideological reasons and partly for reasons of political expediency (to deflect the discontent of their people) the totalitarian governments encouraged, overtly or covertly, a pernicious hatred of foreign nations and of alien or minority groups in their own midst. Germany and Italy professed a solidarity for one another, which the events of the Second World War proved more apparent than real. But both were intensely hostile toward Soviet Russia, although they owed much in their systems to Bolshevik experience. All three felt a mixture of fear, envy, and hatred for the western democracies. They considered the existence of democracy a threat to their internal stability; they were envious of the wealth of the western nations; and they felt a grievance against the Paris peace settlement, which had been largely the handiwork of the western powers. "Capitalist imperialists," "judeo-plutocracies," "decadent democracies," "democratic perfidy" were some of the epithets hurled by their propaganda against the western nations. The totalitarian states were revisionist, expansionist, and militaristic. Their rise weakened the Paris peace settlement and ultimately brought upon Europe and the world the Second World War in which the nazi and fascist systems were destroyed but out of which the communist system emerged stronger than ever.

21

THE UNITED STATES

You cannot extend the mastery of the government over the daily life of a people without somewhere making it master of people's souls and thoughts.

HERBERT HOOVER

1. RETURN TO NORMALCY

BY THE EARLY YEARS of the twentieth century the growth of "Big Business" had become a threat to the priniciple of free enterprise in the United States. By organizing powerful trusts, and by linking up a number of firms through interlocking directorates, a few enterprising financiers might secure extraordinary influence. It seemed possible that, by bold manipulations, a small group of men might obtain a monopoly over the production of essential commodities or public services. A single aggressive company, if it could buy out or ruin its competitors, might achieve virtual control in its field and translate such control into a monopoly. If this happened — if a "sugar trust" came to dominate the refining and marketing of sugar, or an "oil trust" could monopolize the production, manufacture and sale of petroleum products — the benefits of free competitive enterprise might be lost.

This fear of the evils of "Big Business" was often exaggerated, but it was not without foundation. In some fields a large corporation had an indisputable advantage over small rivals because the large corporation could centralize and coordinate its activities more efficiently, could influence market prices, and sometimes bring pressure to bear on state legislators. The belief spread that trusts often operated to the disadvantage of the consumer and the "little man." It seemed to many Americans that financial leaders were acquiring so much power that they could evade or defy the authority of the political leaders elected by the people. If "Big Business" became too powerful and independent it might undermine the processes of democratic government.

Theodore Roosevelt, who served as President from 1901 to 1909, won wide popularity among the people by his attempts to curb the trusts and assert the authority of the federal government to regulate business. His successor, William Howard Taft (1909–1913), proved less popular, largely because he abandoned Roosevelt's "trust-busting" program and favored "Big Business" by approving a rise in tariff rates to "protect" American manufacturers from foreign competition. In 1913 the Republicans were defeated and the Democrats elected Woodrow Wilson. In his Inaugural Address Wilson promised to regulate the trusts, reduce the tariff, reform the banking system, free laborers from unnecessary restrictions, and encourage farmers by improving the efficiency of agriculture through the aid of science.

The reform program that Wilson and his "Progressive" supporters advocated was carried forward with energy. But the outbreak of World War I in Europe in 1914 and the entry of the United States in 1917 turned the attention of the American people to foreign affairs. When the war ended in 1918, the problems of peacemaking claimed Wilson's attention. His fight to obtain American approval of the Versailles Treaty and the League of Nations ended in his defeat. The Republican Party, which had regained control of Congress in 1918, won the election of 1920 and elected Warren Gamaliel Harding President.

Harding declared that what the American people wanted was to "return to normalcy." Their "crusade" to make the world "safe for democracy" had ended in disillusionment, and "Wilsonian idealism," in domestic as well as in foreign affairs, had lost much of its earlier appeal. Under Republican leadership the nation turned its back on the rest of the world and resumed a policy of "isolationism." The postwar decade (1919–1929) was for the American people a decade of unparalleled prosperity. Selfishly absorbed in their own activities they exploited their wealth and pursued material profit. Their rising standard of living, the rapidity with which they applied new inventions and techniques to exploit their resources and enrich their lives, made them the envy of less fortunate nations.

Their material achievements in the years from 1919 to 1929 filled the American people with a mood of pride and self-confidence. Yet it was not a *sturdy* mood. All the proof of power, the nimble machines that gave each American citizen the services of a score of energy slaves, the soaring skyscrapers, the soaring incomes, failed to equip the citizens of the United States with the faith and hardihood to meet an economic reverse with firmness. The collapse of the overinflated stock market in 1929 produced a financial panic that unsettled the nerves of the nation. American despondency magnified the mood of depression that spread around the globe. If the American people could not have a resolute confidence in that machine civilization which had bestowed on them its richest blessings, what confidence could less fortunate nations be expected to display?

2. FROM PROSPERITY TO DEPRESSION

When world trade declined suddenly after 1929, falling over 60 per cent in a few years, economists sought anxiously to analyze the causes of this depression. It seemed dangerous to proceed until business leaders and statesmen had learned how to avert further dislocations so shattering to international prosperity. When no simple or satisfactory explanation could be found and no expedients, however drastic, seemed to arrest the decline, the general disquietude increased. There was more grimness than humor in the reply offered by one economic expert when he was asked how long a business depression could last. The Roman Empire, he reminded his hearers, sank into a depression which lasted a thousand years. Western civilization was undoubtedly ailing but there was no good reason to conclude that the malady would prove fatal. Its most disturbing manifestation was the sense of insecurity which gnawed at the hearts of people everywhere. In some countries of Europe it was to drive them to remedies more desperate than the disease.

When the first shock of the panic passed and people began to appraise the situation more calmly it became clear that the prosperity of the years before 1929 had been increasingly artificial. Greed for high profits had driven many industrialists to overexpand their plants and investments. Many nations, like the United States, eager to sell their excess manufactures abroad, had attempted at the same time to wall in the home market with tariffs and keep it for themselves. This endeavor to sell more than they bought led the American people to lend prospective purchasers the money wherewith they might buy goods "Made in U.S.A." Without such loans many foreigners could not have obtained the international exchange to pay for their purchases.

Investors with capital accumulating on their hands turned it over to investment brokers who advised them where they might obtain high returns. State governments, municipalities, and corporations which needed credit urgently offered the most tempting rates of interest. One field of rapid expansion was postwar Germany, and under the prevailing system of international credit the Germans by 1929 had borrowed $5,000,-000,000 from their neighbors, in part to discharge reparations but also for the construction of new factories, workers' homes, superhighways, and other national improvements. The rapid expansion of business inspired by the necessity of replacing property destroyed in the First World War created a false impression of market demands and consumption in the decade 1919–1929. The sudden acceleration of business and the mounting paper profits of investors made millions greedy, and greed helped them to believe that the prosperity would prove permanent and the expansion of trade and manufacture would persist indefinitely. People did not ask themselves soberly whether the Germans, for example, would be able and willing to pay back their borrowings if their economy suffered

NEW YORK STOCK QUOTATIONS, 1911-1960

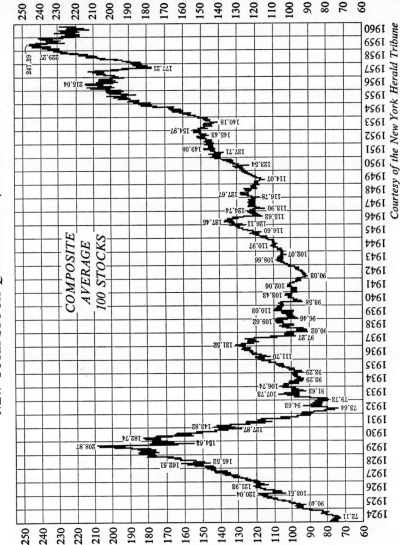

The fluctuations of the New York Stock Market in the twentieth century reflected the variations in American business prosperity. The increasing role the United States played in the global economy made New York the financial center of the world. Changes in business activity there produced immediate reactions on other continents. The New York Stock Market became a barometer of world economic prospects, and prices quoted in New York were closely studied in London, Paris, Berlin, Capetown, Melbourne, and Tokyo.

a setback nor whether American firms could meet their overextended obligations if supply overtook demand and production slowed down instead of increasing yearly as calculated.

On the stock exchange the quotations on favored stocks doubled and sometimes doubled again. These runaway market quotations gave millions the illusion of wealth, but real wealth had not increased at the rate which the climbing stock citations suggested. If all the stockholders and investors had sought to transmute their paper profits into tangible assets they would have found there was neither gold nor goods in existence to exchange for their supposed fortune. When this discrepancy became apparent to a growing number of investors and they began to convert their stocks into more real and substantial forms of wealth, values began to fall because there were more sellers than buyers. When stocks began to fall, investors all over the country tried to unload all at once and the fall became a plunge. Consumers who had thought themselves rich and spent accordingly suddenly ceased to buy. Mounting unemployment from business failures further curtailed the purchasing power of the home market, and production languished while the panic increased. Finally, when American investors no longer poured their money into foreign bonds with high interest rates, foreign firms were no longer able to obtain funds and canceled their orders for American goods. American business activity suffered an additional relapse from these delayed blows. In every country bound up with the economy of the Western world this chain of events was producing business dislocation and depression in varied forms but all increasingly acute.

Normal trade is exchange for mutual advantage. In their zeal for profit too many industrialists and investors had failed to consider sufficiently the one-sidedness of their transactions. While seeking opportunities for foreign expansion they had allowed their most important markets to contract. Thus in all countries agriculture lagged behind the general march toward prosperity and in America it was evident that the farmer's purchasing power was deficient because of his declining share of the national income. City workers, too, even the industrial workers whose efforts helped to produce the wealth of the machine age, found that their wages failed to overtake the rising cost of living. Accordingly the large agrarian and industrial classes, numerically the major market for the nation's mass output, could not absorb an adequate share of the goods their industry brought into existence. Yet even when they could not afford to pay for the commodities which they needed, wage earners were solicited through campaigns of high pressure advertising to buy on credit. This "time payment" program provided a further example of the insecure economy of the "boom" period. When depression struck the country and cut the national income in half, it left millions of purchasers burdened with monthly payments which they had assumed because they expected their incomes to soar instead of to sink.

The "prosperity" of the 1920's therefore concealed an ill-balanced give-and-take, a lopsided distribution of purchasing power. The machinery of production was going ahead full speed and industrial plants expanded. To feed men and machines the output of basic commodities — wheat, sugar, coffee, wool, rubber, tin — was also increasing swiftly. With improved machines and the rationalization of industry more automobiles, textiles, plastics, and electrical devices were produced yearly and produced at a profit. But this profit was not evenly distributed; in some fields the producers had a near-monopoly and held prices up through trusts or cartels. The ultimate effect of such artificial price levels was to deny the consumer manufactured wares he would gladly have bought at a lower cost. Thus many products of industry were too dear for wide mass consumption. But a second trend was also killing the mass market: machines were replacing men. In Europe industrial production continued to rise after 1926 but industrial employment fell. All over the world the workers, especially those who produced basic commodities, found prices rising faster than wages and they lost their purchasing power.

By 1928 some commodity stockpiles (tin, for example) were literally a surplus on the market, and when prices collapsed in 1929 the crash was blamed in part upon such overproduction. Producers of basic commodities were urged to "manufacture a shortage" by restricting their output or, if necessary, by burning millions of pounds of coffee or bushels of wheat. Obviously something was out of gear in an economic system which required the use of such wasteful remedies. To speak of a surplus, of overproduction, of excess supplies of wheat or wool in a world where millions were hungry and ill-clothed, was illogical. It seemed apparent that the system of distribution, not the system of production, was at fault.

Many critics explained the depression by blaming it on "the fluctuations of the business cycle." This did not help very much because the business cycle itself was not clearly understood. In earlier centuries "good times" and "bad times" were commonly blamed upon some local development and a business depression attributed to a poor crop, a plague, or a destructive fire. The first "global" depression that may be readily distinguished was that of 1857. This followed the wide business expansion of the early 1850's; it revealed the "cyclical fluctuation" in all its phases — expansion, recession, contraction, and revival. Thereafter economic crises became more world embracing as global economy became more closely knit. The causes and control of depressions and the misery they brought to millions were studied with grave attention. For such crises were the darkest threat (war excepted) which democratic governments and the democratic way of life had to conquer.

The problem of business fluctuations proved so complex that no explanation offered a clear analysis or suggested a sure method of control. Theorists related them to the sun-spot cycle, to an excess of savings, to an excess of production, to greed for profits, to the progress of mechanical invention which substituted machines for men (technological unemployment), and to a myriad other causes. But no theory seemed clear or sufficient. The Great Depression spread panic among the peoples most affected because it implied that the forces shaping modern civilization were beyond man's control or comprehension. The economic cycle which ran from overexpansion to collapse, through reviving production to expansion, overproduction, and collapse again, ought to be harnessed and stabilized by foresight and careful planning. But in countries where free business enterprise was cherished the governments did not have the authority to enforce long-range economic aims. Furthermore, plans which miscarried might make a critical situation worse.

3. THE NEW DEAL

The laissez-faire or "let-alone" policy favored by the Republican Party satisfied most Americans during the "prosperity decade," 1919–1929. But when the stock market crash of 1929 ended the "boom" and brought economic confusion and unemployment, a growing demand arose that the government "do something" to relieve the distress. The financiers and business leaders, who had increased production while multiplying their profits, were applauded as long as their methods appeared to promise continued expansion and a rising standard of living. The depression changed this admiration to anger and contempt. When banks failed, factories closed, and millions of workers lost their jobs, people wanted to know why blind and selfish business leaders had been left free to pursue a course that led to economic collapse and unemployment. The laissez-faire policy of the government, it was felt, had betrayed the welfare of the American people into the hands of greedy and reckless speculators. Through selfishness or stupidity, these business tycoons had wrecked the prosperity they were supposed to safeguard.

If bankers and businessmen could not be trusted, to whom should the nation turn for leadership in its hour of confusion? President Herbert Hoover (1929–1933) believed that the American economy was essentially sound and that it would recover from the Depression under a system of free enterprise. He was in favor of the creation of a Reconstruction Finance Corporation through which the federal government made loans to banks, railroads, and ailing industries to help them to survive. But he vetoed more radical plans which progressive politicians urged upon him, plans that would "put the government in business" by authorizing it to use public funds to feed the hungry, create jobs, fix prices, and build dams to furnish cheaper electricity. Too much government interference in economic activities, Hoover believed, would weaken and ultimately destroy the spirit of free business enterprise upon which American liberty and prosperity had been founded.

Unfortunately for Hoover, the Depression deepened, unemployment increased, and the national economy appeared incapable of recovering by itself. By 1933, after three years of confusion and hardship, a mood of despair had spread throughout the nation. The conviction that the government should adopt more forceful and radical measures to speed recovery led millions to desert the Republican Party and look to the Democratic Party for more dynamic leadership.

When the election of 1932 approached the Democrats nominated for President the resourceful and popular governor of New York State, Franklin Delano Roosevelt. In addition to great personal charm and political talents, Roosevelt possessed a further appeal to the imagination of the electors. Stricken by poliomyelitis in 1921, in the middle of a promising career, he had overcome this crippling disability and success-fully re-entered political life. This triumph of courage and will power made him a symbol of hope to a nation half-paralyzed by economic depression. He promised that, if elected, he would adopt forceful and far-reaching measures to help the unemployed and restore the nation's prosperity. Hoover warned the American people that the expedients suggested by the Democrats were dangerous. "Our opponents," he insisted, "are proposing changes and so-called new deals which would destroy the very foundations of our American system . . ." The voters refused to take alarm: they wanted action. In the election of 1932 the Democrats defeated Hoover by 472 electoral votes to 59. This popular landslide gave Roosevelt his chance to introduce his promised "New Deal" for the "forgotten man."

The reforms that Roosevelt and his advisers introduced appeared so radical to some conservative thinkers that they described them as a revolution. This was an exaggeration. Roosevelt's New Deal legislation was approved by the Congress, and although the Supreme Court rejected some measures as unconstitutional, most of these enactments were recast in a form the Court could approve. In reality, much of the New Deal legislation was overdue. By the 1930's the United States, like most Euro-pean countries, had become highly industrialized. The simpler political patterns, the "horse-and-buggy" methods of the nineteenth century, no longer sufficed. The demand for a stronger, more highly centralized government, with authority to regulate business, reduce abuses, protect the workers from exploitation and promote their interests, aroused all the leading nations in the twentieth century. After World War I this demand became irresistible. In some countries (Russia, Italy, Germany) the social discontent led to the creation of dictatorships. In others, where democracy was more strongly rooted (Britain, France, the United States) the trend toward stricter government control led to orderly changes adopted by popular consent. In all cases, however, these changes gave the national governments greater power to supervise and regulate the social and economic activities of the citizens. Society, in the twentieth century, has been increasingly *regimented* by government decree.

One aim of the New Deal legislation was to bring all business enter-prises — banks, corporations, public utilities, transportation systems, investment houses — under stricter federal control. A second aim was to protect the factory and office worker, the farmer, the small store-keeper, the home owner, from the destitution which threatened him as the business depression spread. Relief and rehabilitation for ten million unemployed, federal loans to the banks to safeguard savings, financial aid to farmers threatened with foreclosure, and a civil works program to create jobs were some of the measures adopted by the Democratic Con-gress which convened in 1933. By 1935 government plans to take perma-nent care of the indigent and the aged had been embodied in the Social Security Act. With federal contributions, the state governments were to promise $15 a month to aged residents over sixty-five, who were in need; to provide unemployment insurance in the form of payments for a limited period to workers deprived of occupation; and to create a fund which would enable qualified registered workers to retire at sixty-five with a pension of $10 to $15 a month.

These relief measures, federal loans, and contributions to old age and unemployment funds rapidly increased the federal debt. Between 1932 and 1939 it doubled, rising from approximately $20,000,000,000 to $40,-000,000,000. New taxes were introduced which struck at corporation profits, increased the income tax and surtax, and placed luxuries and amusements under tribute. These measures suggested that the New Deal leaders considered it expedient not only to curb and regulate "big business" but to redistribute the national income by collecting revenue from the wealthy through surtaxes and other levies and raising the income of the poor by a system of pensions. These changes in policy, so rapidly extended after 1932, indicated a swing toward social and economic control in the United States. The concept of the "weak state" which made its authority felt as little as possible had played its part in American life and been discarded. Federal inspectors, a federal police (the Federal Bureau of Investigation), federal taxes and security regulations were reaching into all parts of the country. Many employers and businessmen complained that they were handicapped by the demand to fill out inter-minable form sheets, by the visits of government inspectors, by the con-trol exercised over raw materials, by the processing taxes, and by social security rules. They hoped that when the economic crisis which com-menced in 1929 had abated, federal control would be relaxed. But a large proportion of small farmers, city workers in mill and office, mem-bers of the lower middle class, and the businessman with a small inde-pendent firm or store approved of the New Deal. Roosevelt was re-elected in 1936 and in 1940 by imposing majorities, and thus became the first American president to serve a third term. After 1937, however, the increasing danger of war turned the attention of the people to foreign as well as domestic affairs. The measures proposed and the multiplied powers requested by the federal government, in bridging the economic crisis, were prolonged and extended into a broad program of national defense. This organization of economic, military, and naval forces for the protection of the United States can be discussed more logically in connection with foreign affairs.

4. THE UNITED STATES AND WORLD AFFAIRS

Before the United States entered World War I in 1917 few observers realized the vastness of its power and resources. The rapidity with which millions of American soldiers were trained, equipped, and transported across the Atlantic, made it clear that the United States had become a leading world power. Success in war, however, did not make the American people eager for territory or inspire them to further conquests. At the Paris Peace Conference President Wilson claimed no territorial compensations. The American armies were demobilized as rapidly as possible and some of the American battleships dismantled. After proving, in a burst of energy, that they could play a leading part in world affairs, the American people chose, after 1918, to revert to a policy of isolation.

It was not possible, however, for the United States to ignore world problems altogether. When World War I closed, Britain and America possessed the two mightiest navies on the oceans, with the Japanese fleet ranking third. It appeared possible that the three powers might become involved in a naval race, a race in which the Americans, with their enormous resources, could afford to outbuild their rivals. Such a race for naval supremacy was certain to prove costly, however, and the desire to avoid it moved the United States government to propose an international agreement by which the leading naval powers would voluntarily limit their fleets to a fixed ratio.

The terms of the agreement were worked out at a conference which met in Washington in 1921 and 1922. As a result of the parley a measure of stability was restored in the Far East. Japan returned Kiaochow to China. The territorial integrity and independence of China were reaffirmed in a Nine-Power Treaty, with China, the United States, Britain, France, Italy, Belgium, The Netherlands, Portugal, and Japan as signatories. A ten-year naval holiday was decreed during which no capital ships were to be laid down, and a total capital ship tonnage of 525,000 tons was set for the United States and Britain, with a limit of 325,000 tons for Japan and 175,000 each for France and Italy. This 5:5:3 ratio, as it came to be termed, offended Japanese pride but helped to postpone the intense naval rivalry and building race which had appeared unavoidable.

The relaxation of warlike preparations and the reduction of naval expenditure were welcomed by the American people. A change of mood

had come over the nation with the close of the war. Disillusionment at
the outcome of foreign ventures, distrust in the terms of the peace settlements, suspicion and cynicism toward the League of Nations, and resentment over the nonpayment of the war debts turned many Americans
against new undertakings in distant countries. They argued that if the
United States guarded American interests but avoided entangling alliances and wars on other continents, it would be unnecessary to maintain
a conscript army or a large and expensive navy. The rewards of imperialism and participation in global responsibilities had ceased to seem
attractive. National self-sufficiency appeared the sane and preferable
ideal. Reversing the trend of the previous twenty years, the United States
after 1918 swung back to a course of cautious isolationism and left the
other continents to settle their own quarrels.

This postwar mood remained strong for over a decade and helps to
explain why the American people were almost indifferent when the
Japanese renewed their penetration of China. In 1931 Japanese forces
opened a carefully timed offensive, a military campaign which was in
reality an undeclared war. Within a few months they had occupied
southern Manchuria and intervened at Shanghai. Conversations were
opened between London and Washington on the need for joint Anglo-
American action but no action was taken. The League of Nations, of
which the United States was not a member, was more resolute in criticizing the Japanese. After investigation it adopted the Lytton Report which
condemned the Japanese attacks; but it failed to halt these attacks. Manchuria, proclaimed an autonomous state with the title of Manchukuo,
became in actuality a satellite under Japanese rule. To the expansionists
at Tokyo, the militarists and industrialists who fostered Japanese imperialism, the hesitancy at Washington and the helplessness of the League
were taken as proof that a bold course of action would assure Japanese
domination over all East Asia.

Had the United States taken a firmer stand against Japanese expansion
in Manchuria and China in 1930 and 1931, the balance of power in the
Pacific area might have been altered. The war which came ten years
later might have been averted; or, if it had proved inevitable, the American forces would have held stronger positions. But in 1930 the American
people were in an isolationist mood. They were absorbed in the domestic
crisis resulting from the economic depression, in the spreading unemployment, the falling prices and falling income, and the business failures.
They wanted tax reductions and government aid at the same time, a
program which could most readily be achieved by reducing "unnecessary" expenses such as battleships. At the same time, American diplomats
wanted to demonstrate American faith in disarmament for the benefit of
foreign nations. The result of all these pressures may be read in the
concessions made to Japan and to Britain when the Washington Naval
Treaty was revised at the London Naval Conference of 1930. The "holiday" on capital ships was extended to 1936, and the ratio on naval tonnage

was extended to include several other types of warships besides the giant battleships. Moreover, in balancing up the tonnage for these lesser categories, the British-American-Japanese ratio of 5:5:3 was revised to favor Japan. In small-gun cruisers and destroyers the Japanese were permitted seven-tenths of the parity ratio maintained by Britain and the United States. In submarines Japan and the United States were to be equal.

These real concessions might well have assuaged Japanese pride and cancelled Japanese doubts regarding American intentions. For although the naval limitation treaties allowed Britain and America a 10:6 or 10:7 superiority over Japan in absolute tonnage, it must be remembered that the British and American navies were distributed throughout vast reaches of ocean, in the Atlantic and the Pacific, and had almost illimitable reaches of coastline to safeguard. The Japanese navy, entirely concentrated in the Orient, could maintain an almost unassailable supremacy in Far Eastern waters. This supremacy was further assured by the concessions of 1930, which raised Japanese light cruiser strength. But as an additional gesture of reassurance to demonstrate that America had no aggressive intentions, the United States renewed the pledges on Pacific bases which had been incorporated in the Washington Naval Treaty of 1922. These pledges prohibited the construction or expansion of naval bases or fortifications in the Pacific islands. Japan was thus freed from the fear that the United States might strengthen Guam or fortify the Aleutian Islands in a manner to threaten Japanese mastery in Japanese home waters.

The London Naval Treaties proved to the world that the people of the United States, moved by a variety of motives, were prepared to take long strides toward disarmament. In the Atlantic as well as the Pacific American naval strength was cut, for the American heavy cruiser program was reduced while the British won permission to raise their cruiser strength if they deemed it necessary. In the capitals of the world, in London and Paris, in Berlin, Rome, and Tokyo, the American naval limitation, the American hesitation to oppose Japanese moves in China, and the American neutrality laws which followed shortly, all appeared to proclaim the same truth: the United States would defend the Americas but it would not be drawn into the wars of Asia or of Europe. This was, as subsequent history showed, a false assumption. But it was not, in the light of American policies from 1919 to 1939, an implausible assumption. To understand the course which the United States government followed in this twenty-year period, it is important to realize that a majority of the American people throughout these years not only *wanted* to stay out of foreign wars but believed it was *possible* to stay out of foreign wars. In their desire to avoid foreign commitments and foreign entanglements they were isolationists. It was only when American involvement in World War II was recognized as unavoidable that the word *isolationist* became a term of reproach.

22

GREAT BRITAIN

Sir, we must beware of needless innovation, especially when guided by logic.
WINSTON CHURCHILL

1. THE BRITISH ECONOMIC DILEMMA

THE BRITISH PEOPLE found it difficult after 1918 to restore their prewar prosperity. Disrupted trade, declining industries, ruined markets, increased foreign (especially American) competition, and heavy taxation made the economic future dark. A return of international stability and the revival of world trade promised Britain the surest hope for economic recovery, for British power rested upon the income drawn from commerce and manufacture. If British commerce declined, British influence among the nations would decline with it. Great Britain, as a geographic unit, was the least self-sufficient of the world powers, and the British economic dilemma could be summed up in three words: export or die.

World War I imposed a staggering burden on the British budget. The public debt, which stood at about £650,000,000 in 1913, rose so rapidly during the war and postwar years that by 1933 it had increased tenfold to £6,613,000,000. The taxpayer carried an excessive share in the cost of imperial defense, for the navy policed the oceans, protected the empire, and safeguarded many small nations which would otherwise have been vulnerable to attack. Defense, however, was only one item in an expanding budget. The social services — especially sickness, accident, old age, and unemployment insurance — which had been introduced during the Liberal reform era of 1906–1914, required an increasing share of the national revenue when postwar depression grew severe in 1921. A "dole" of twenty shillings a week to unemployed men and eighteen shillings to women forced a rise in the tax rate when the total of registered unemployed passed one million.

Successive cabinets strove without success to solve the grim problem. In 1922 the wartime prime minister, David Lloyd George, was succeeded by a Conservative, Andrew Bonar Law, who resigned the premiership in 1923 to another Conservative, Stanley Baldwin. A general election at the close of that year brought in the first Labor cabinet under Ramsay MacDonald; but before the close of 1924 it was swept out in another general election which opened five years of Conservative rule under the second Baldwin ministry.

In 1926 the mounting discontent of the miners and transport workers and the persistence of unemployment induced a general strike which severely dislocated business for a week. The following year the Conservatives responded by declaring all strikes and lockouts would be held illegal if they endangered the public welfare and the national safety. The financial situation, already strained, became desperate with the world depression which commenced in 1929, and by 1931 it was evident that drastic changes must be made to balance the budget. National and imperial defense expenditures, a dole for 2,000,000 unemployed, relief for the coal mining companies, subsidies for the merchant marine, and carrying charges on public and intergovernmental debts had overtaxed the exchequer. The Labor cabinet, recalled to power in 1929, was in a quandary. It was essential to increase the revenue and to cut expenditures. But the Liberal supporters of the government, with their laissez-faire ideals, refused to sanction a tariff on imports; the Laborites fought any reduction in the government aid for the poorer classes; and the imposition of higher taxes on the wealthy and the business interests threatened to discourage and depress empire trade.

This painful economic crisis split the second Labor ministry of 1929–31. But instead of resigning, MacDonald remained to head a National Coalition government with Conservative, Liberal, and Labor members. This coalition cabinet promptly abandoned the gold standard, with the result that the pound sterling fell from $4.86 to $3.50 in terms of dollar exchange. The government likewise forsook the venerable tradition of free trade (1932) and passed a tariff on imports, while launching a campaign to "Buy British" and negotiating agreements with the Dominions to maintain "imperial preference" in their trading policies. A slow business recovery and the achievement of a balanced budget appeared to justify the course adopted. MacDonald continued to head the cabinet until 1935, but he and those who served with him were expelled from the Labor Party and the cabinet was in reality dominated by the Conservatives or Tories. The abandonment of free trade and laissez-faire principles had left the Liberal Party an impotent minority, and the desertion of MacDonald had split and dismayed the Labor group. General elections in 1931 and 1933, however, gave the coalition government the assurance that the nation was satisfied with its firmer policies.

It was highly significant that the British preserved their parliamentary system intact and made only moderate adjustments to meet the economic confusion and international challenge which shattered many other governments in the years 1919–1939. Even the unexpected abdication of Edward VIII, who succeeded his father George V in 1936 and resigned the same year, failed to disrupt the sober routine of parliamentary rule. This vitality and resilience, in a government which to many foreigners appeared cumbrous and old-fashioned, was not easily to be explained. British administrative methods often impressed the British themselves as time-consuming and unsystematic. British politicians "muddled through" from one dubious compromise to another, and each succeeding generation agreed that things were in a bad way. Yet the British people had sur-mounted crisis after crisis while neighbor states were plunged into defeat or dislocated by revolution. Hostile critics ascribed the prosperity and prestige of Great Britain to an unexampled series of fortunate accidents. Admirers preferred to credit the growth of the empire and the expansion of British influence to the virtues of British character and the moderation of British methods. Whatever the explanation might be, the British empire at the close of the nineteenth century had become "the world's most successful experiment in international organization." It remained to be seen if the talent the British had developed for muddling through would enable them to meet the challenges of the dynamic twentieth century.

2. BRITISH POLITICAL GENIUS

In their long political development the British had shown a decided preference for evolution rather than revolution. Especially after the civil war and rebellions of the seventeenth century they avoided violent domes-tic strife. In the nineteenth century responsible government and democ-racy advanced by constitutional steps, and instead of the sporadic revolu-tions and new regimes which punctuated French history after 1789 the British adopted a series of legislative measures. The reform bills of 1832, 1867, 1884–1885, and the Parliament Act of 1911 transformed an oligarchy into a working democracy. The progressive steps were taken cautiously and followed no fixed plan or ideological formula. This same reluctance to put too much trust in logic or to constrict the growth of society by insisting upon an excessive uniformity marked British democratic reforms in the twentieth century. The electors showed themselves more respon-sive to arguments based upon appeals to custom or to practical experience than to arguments supported by axioms and syllogisms.

In 1918, as the war to make the world "safe for democracy" was ending, the British parliament adopted a bill to establish universal manhood suffrage throughout the United Kingdom. The bill also decreed one elec-tion day for the entire kingdom and all but ended the practice of plural voting which had permitted certain electors to vote in more than one constituency. But the most significant provision in this Reform Bill of 1918 was the extension of the franchise to every woman over thirty if she or her husband was qualified to vote in local elections. The question of woman suffrage had excited a lively controversy before 1914. While some women were content to work quietly and patiently to influence parliament, others adopted more spectacular methods to call attention to their grievances, shouting their demands from the visitors' gallery in the House of Commons, pouring acid in mail boxes, or going on hunger strikes when they were arrested for disturbing the peace. During the four years of World War I women proved their ability to take over much of the men's work in office, industry, and agriculture, and this made it appear more anomalous than ever to deny them legal equality in a democratic country. In 1919 an Act of Parliament decreed that women should enjoy legal equality with men and should not be disqualified because of their sex from holding public office or entering a profession. Full equality in the exercise of the franchise was not established until 1928, when the Representation of the People Act declared that all electors, men or women, must be twenty-one years of age or older, and must have complied with certain residence qualifications in order to vote.

Equality before the law did not bring genuine equality of opportunity to the women of Great Britain. More powerful than any act of parliament was the constricting effect of custom, which still disposed people in all ranks to resist a change of status or privilege. In the schools, the professions, and the business world, women were still handicapped by the traditional assumption that men were the superior sex. This almost unanimous opinion, as prevalent among the women as among the men, delayed the emancipation of women. They lacked the fuller measure of freedom and self-confidence attained by their sisters in the Scandinavian countries, in the self-governing Dominions, and in the United States. The fact that there were almost two million more women than men in the United Kingdom (1931) reduced the prospects of marriage for a sizable feminine minority and made the conventional argument that a woman's place was in the home a somewhat ironical platitude for the surplus homemakers.

British conservatism, which provided the chief clue to an understanding of the British character, puzzled foreign observers. They noted in most English people what appeared to be an irrational preference for the traditional method, a preference which often blinded them to suggested improvements or newer techniques. The retention of pounds, shillings, and pence, and the refusal to adopt the decimal system of accounting was an example of this attitude. The preservation of outmoded rituals at the royal receptions, the procedure in the older colleges, the law courts, and the sessions of parliament, reflected still more strongly the British respect for historic precedent. The accumulated body of customs inherited from the past seemed a safe guide to the nation, and glittering generalities were distrusted. This cautious attitude had been eloquently defined and defended by the great parliamentary orator, Edmund Burke, at the end of the eighteenth century. "All your sophisters," he protested, "cannot produce anything better adapted to preserve a rational and manly freedom than the course that we have pursued, who have chosen our nature rather than our speculations, our breasts rather than our inventions, for the great conservatories and magazines of our rights and privileges."

The most paradoxical feature of British conservatism was the fact that this custom-ridden people, who "muddled through" their difficulties and remained so lacking in system that they possessed no written constitution, had nevertheless established a remarkable degree of law and order over one-fourth of the world. This nation so rigid and archaic in its respect for ancient rituals had developed the most popular, most flexible, and most variegated methods of responsible government in political annals. This cautious people so slow to change had preserved the stability of their state in an age of conflict that shattered most contemporary governments. As a system of international cooperation the British Empire-Commonwealth had no parallel. Never before in history had half a billion people of diverse creeds and races been governed and protected by such a small handful of soldiers and administrators as the personnel of the British imperial services. As administrators the British remained most noteworthy for their restraint, and few ruling groups in history had been less corrupted by power. If the test of political genius was the ability to promote peace and security, to protect individuals and minorities from persecution, to enforce respect for law and for human rights without recourse to cruel and unusual punishments or unnecessary bloodshed, then the British might claim to be the most successful administrators the world had known.

The British administration of their vast and variegated empire had not, however, been a record of unbroken success. The loss of the Thirteen American Colonies in the eighteenth century was one proof of this. The Boer War (1899–1902) aroused widespread criticism of British imperialism. But the most persistent example of British mismanagement of a conquered people was the fate of the Irish. The demand of the Irish for independence caused repeated disorders until it reached a climax in the twentieth century. How the British reacted when their colonial peoples became strong enough to manage their own affairs deserves separate consideration.

3. THE LOOSENING OF IMPERIAL TIES

When World War I ended in 1918 the outstanding victor appeared to be Great Britain. In Asia Minor, the dismemberment of the Ottoman Empire left Palestine, Transjordania, and Iraq — three of its segments — to be transformed into British mandates. In Africa, what had been German East Africa, together with a large share of Togoland and the Cameroons, became British mandates also, while German Southwest

Africa passed to the Union of South Africa. In the Pacific, German New Guinea and some smaller islands went to Australia, and German Samoan possessions to New Zealand. As a further result of the war the German navy was eliminated and German ocean commerce crippled. The greater share of the 20,000 miles of undersea cables surrendered by the Germans passed into British control, so that London in 1919 was still the chief center of world communications.

On closer inspection, however, it was evident that these British gains were offset by serious debits. It was true that the territories nominally included in the empire had expanded until they exceeded 13,000,000 square miles, one-fourth of the land area of the earth. But the political ties which held the British Empire together seemed to be dissolving. The Indian Nationalists had increased their demand for independence. In Egypt, which had been proclaimed a British protectorate in 1914 after thirty years of British occupation, a clamorous group of Nationalists were likewise demanding sovereign rights, and Egypt became an independent kingdom in 1922. British forces, however, continued to occupy the hinterland, the Anglo-Egyptian Sudan, and to protect the Suez Canal. In Palestine a bitter feud between the Jewish immigrants and the Moslem population made the problem of maintaining order a difficult and thankless one for the British forces. In the Arab state of Iraq, where a constitutional regime was established by 1924, the people declared themselves ready for self-government, and in 1932 Iraq entered the League of Nations as a sovereign state. It seemed as if the British were schooling their subject peoples to secede, or at least urging them to achieve self-rule and sovereignty.

Another problem in self-government nearer home, the most ancient and envenomed problem in British imperial relations, also found a partial solution after 1919. This was the Irish Question. For centuries the attempts of the British to dominate Ireland had bred revolts and reprisals. True to their conviction that England's extremity was Ireland's opportunity, a group of Irish Nationalists staged an unsuccessful rebellion in 1916 when British fortunes were at their lowest in World War I. Though the revolt was crushed it left the country in a condition approaching civil war, and after 1919 the Sinn Fein Party was strong enough to insist upon home rule. The Irish Free State became a self-governing Dominion in the British Commonwealth (1922). Northern Ireland (Ulster) was not included. The people of Ulster established their own parliament (1921) but continued to send thirteen members to the historic British parliament at Westminster. The constitution of the new Dominion declared Ireland (Eire) a "sovereign, independent, democratic state." No Governor-General was accepted as representative of the British crown; a president, elected by direct vote of the people, appointed the prime minister, who was known as head of the government. Although the Irish Free State was still associated for some purposes with the British Commonwealth of Nations, the Free State government appointed its own diplomatic representatives to foreign capitals and did not feel itself bound to follow the British lead in foreign policy. In 1939, for example, it did not join the other units of the Commonwealth in the war with Germany.

The emergence of the self-governing Dominions as equal and independent partners in the British Commonwealth marked a new and startling experiment in statecraft. It was, however, a logical step in keeping with a century or more of British practice. The Dominion of Canada had been federated and had acquired a national parliament in 1867; the Commonwealth of Australia had achieved federal unity in 1901; New Zealand became a Dominion in 1907; and the Union of South Africa was formally proclaimed in 1910. The political relationship that linked these self-governing Dominions to Great Britain and to one another thus became a matter for legal speculation because there was no exact precedent which covered it. When the Irish Free State was established in 1922, the independent attitude of the Irish made this question of Dominion status an issue requiring definition. In South Africa, as in Ireland, a powerful political group urged complete political independence of Britain; and in Canada, Australia, and New Zealand there were national-minded citizens who criticized the ambiguous imperial bond.

The question of Dominion status was therefore clarified at a conference which assembled in London in 1926. The rise of the empire had been so largely a spontaneous and unplanned growth that the British and Dominion premiers who debated the issue were themselves uncertain how best to define the numerous and complicated ties which held the imperial structure together. But they agreed on one common conviction. The chief strength of the empire lay in the voluntary and reciprocal attraction of its members and no attempt to link it more firmly or explicitly by legal formulas or coercive measures would make it stronger. Rather, they thought, a further dissolution of political bonds was in order, and they offered a new definition to describe the political status of Great Britain and the self-governing Dominions. "They are autonomous communities within the British Empire, equal in status, in no way subordinate one to another in any aspect of their domestic or external affairs, though united by a common allegiance to the Crown and fully associated as members of the British Commonwealth of Nations." The logical corollary of this declaration followed five years later (1931) when the British parliament passed the Statute of Westminster. The most important article declared that "no Act of Parliament of the United Kingdom passed after the commencement of this Act shall extend, or be deemed to extend, to a Dominion . . . unless . . .the Dominion has requested, and consented to, the enactment thereof."

23

THE FRENCH REPUBLIC
1919–1939

The heart of the French bourgeois is on the left but his pocket book is on the right.

ANDRÉ SIEGFRIED

1. VICTORY WITHOUT SECURITY

THE FRENCH PEOPLE emerged from World War I to face what their aged but indomitable premier, Georges Clemenceau, termed "the grandeur and misery of victory." They had won back the provinces of Alsace and Lorraine, lost to Germany in the Franco-Prussian War of 1870–1871, but they had paid a terrible price. The total population of France in 1914 had been 39,800,000. The total population in 1919, with Alsace and Lorraine reannexed, was only 38,700,000. A declining birth rate, civilian casualties, and 1,385,000 war dead had crippled France in its most vulnerable asset, its population. In addition to the war dead, one million disabled veterans — one out of forty inhabitants, often hideously disfigured, mutilated, truncated, or blinded men — daily reminded the French people of the terrible price of their victory. Few, indeed, were the French families which had not lost one or several members in the war. And what made these painful personal losses a national calamity was the fact that the war dead and disabled were mostly young men between the ages of twenty and forty — a group which in any nation is the most energetic and productive element. Official efforts to raise the birth rate by paying a government bonus for each child failed to check the decline, and the added charge was a burden for a nation already paying pensions to a million disabled veterans. While other nations made up rapidly their war losses and increased their populations, the population of France increased only very slowly. Alongside such growing giants as the United States (population: 105,710,000 in 1920 and 131,669,000 in 1940) or the Soviet Union (population: 147,000,000 in 1926 and 170,000,000 in 1939), France, once the most populous *Grande Nation* of Europe, with her virtually static population of about 40,000,000 sank to the position of a minor nation.

The demographic problem of France had an adverse effect on all phases of French life.

The war had left the survivors debilitated. The whole French life between the two World Wars was marked by a curiously escapist quality, a nostalgic yearning for *la belle époque* — the good old days before 1914 — and a reluctance to face squarely the somber future, to stray off the beaten path, to experiment, to explore, or simply to rethink the problems of France in the light of the given situation. Even the vaunted French cultural life had not escaped the debilitating effect of the war. While aesthetical and intellectual standards continued high, French culture was marked by an excessive concern for form, which often hid a trivial content, and an effort to impress or shock rather than to delight or enlighten. In the more mundane world of economics there was a clear decline; with a static population there was little incentive to economic expansion. The French building industry, for instance, after reconstructing the devastated areas in the north, came to a complete standstill. With little increase in population there was no demand for new housing. With a population consisting largely of older people well set in their ways (the average age of the French population was the highest in Europe) there was little incentive to innovation in business and industry. To the casual visitor France presented a picture of a pleasantly antiquated country steeped in slothful habits and slowly sinking into decay. This was a superficial impression; actually, France had considerable reserves of energy but they needed to be mobilized and channelized. This was difficult to do because French leadership was mediocre. The great public figures of France were invariably older men who had arrived before 1914. Individually, they were often brilliant men — intelligent, erudite, eloquent, on the whole honest and hard-working — yet quaintly parochial, old-fashioned, and completely bewildered by the postwar problems for which their experience had not prepared them. With the national self-centeredness of members of old and long successful nations, they drew exclusively on past French experience for methods to deal with the problems which now confronted France. When these failed they had no new solutions to offer.

The overwhelming desire of the French people after the war was for stability and security: economic and social stability and security at home and a stable and secure peace abroad. As in all other countries, French domestic and foreign policies were inextricably tied together, but because of the basic military weakness of France after the war the solution of French domestic problems depended to a larger degree on the successful solution of foreign problems than was the case elsewhere. The United States, for instance, protected from potential enemies by two oceans, could better afford an attitude of aloofness in foreign affairs than France, separated from hostile and revisionist Germany only by the Rhine River. To secure herself against German revenge France had insisted first on a stern peace with Germany and then on its strict fulfillment. France hoped to keep Germany disarmed and weak indefinitely — or at least until France recovered her strength. But her former allies, Britain, Italy, and the United States, soon disassociated themselves from the policy of strict fulfillment of the Paris peace treaties. When France assumed the burden of enforcing the treaties alone they often accused her of seeking to establish French "hegemony" over Europe.

Superficially, the postwar policy of France indeed resembled her policy in the seventeenth and eighteenth centuries when she sought to dominate Europe. Abandoned by her western allies, France reverted to her old policy of seeking eastern allies by concluding alliance treaties with Poland (1921), Czechoslovakia (1924), Rumania (1926), and Yugloslavia (1927). The function of France's eastern allies was to act as a *barrière à l'est* (eastern barrier) against the German *Drang nach Osten* and a *cordon sanitaire* (quarantine belt) against Soviet-communist westward infiltration. But there was an essential difference between French postwar policy and their policy in the palmy days of Richelieu, Mazarin, and Louis XIV. The postwar French alliances were strictly defensive in purpose. They were motivated by the common interest of France and the new nations of Central and Eastern Europe in maintaining the *status quo* established by the Paris peace treaties. Moreover, the French policy of alliances did not exclude a policy of collective security. Haunted by the specter of another war, France eagerly signed the Locarno Treaty (1925) and the Pact of Paris (1928), both based on collective security. In the end, however, neither alliances nor collective security proved of any avail; with the rise of the totalitarian powers collective security collapsed. When Germany and Soviet Russia effected a military comeback the small eastern allies proved more of a liability to France than an asset. The chimera of a stable peace continued to elude the French people.

At the same time France failed to attain internal stability. The heavy cost of armaments, of paying her huge war debts, of reconstruction, and of providing increasing social services exceeded French financial resources. When Germany defaulted on the payment of reparations and Soviet Russia steadfastly refused to pay the Tsarist debts, the only way that France could meet her financial obligations was to allow her currency to be depreciated. This inflationary policy inevitably created many inequities which, in turn, provoked great political and social tensions and troubled the internal tranquillity of France throughout the inter-war period.

2. POLITICAL PARTIES AND FACTIONS

The Third Republic survived the war and emerged seemingly even strengthened. Victory augmented the prestige of the Republic and gave it respectability. The overwhelming majority of the French people, even the bulk of the Catholic clergy, accepted it as permanent. The old battles in defense of the Republic and against clerical influence quieted down. Nevertheless, the war by weakening the French people had also undermined the Republic. But the damage did not show up until the 1930's when France faced the twin challenge of depression and totalitarianism.

Soon after victory French political life returned to "normal." The old unedifying practices — the devious *couloir* politics, personal vendettas, scurrilous newspaper attacks, and whiffs of scandal — again marred the reputation of France. The old divisions among the French people — between the Left and the Right, clericals and anti-clericals, socialists and anti-socialists, the bourgeoisie, workers, and peasants — which had been "papered over" during the war, soon reappeared, and some new ones were added. All were faithfully reflected in the parties in the National Assembly. The old aphorism, "One Frenchman — intelligence; two Frenchmen — debate; three Frenchmen — anarchy," contained a grain of truth. The two-party system had never appealed to the French. The deep class divisions and the French penchant for intellectualism in politics, the passion for debate, and doctrinaire hairsplitting had resulted in the rise of a plethora of political parties.

The French political spectrum after the war changed only little from what it had been before the war. On the extreme Right there were still the royalists, reduced to a few diehards who had in their hearts given up any hope of restoring the monarchy but kept up the opposition to the Republic "for the sake of principle." On the extreme Left there appeared a new party: the French Communist Party. It originated in 1920 when the French Socialist Party split and the radical Left wing seceded and adhered to the Communist International in Moscow. In the Center were the republican parties of various hues, from conservative and nationalist to progressive and liberal. A key position among the republican parties was held by the Radical Socialist Party. It was neither radical nor socialist but a middle-of-the-road party, somewhat in the nature of the British Liberal Party. In keeping with French tradition the Radical Socialists *talked* radically but usually *acted* moderately. They leaned now to the Right and now the Left, but remained usually the keystone of the coalitions of republican parties which governed France in the inter-war years.

No single party had a majority in the all-powerful Chamber of Deputies. Cabinets, therefore, had to be supported by coalitions or blocs of parties. Before forming a cabinet, the parties bargained and agreed on a program and the distribution of posts in the cabinet. When the program was accomplished — and often before — the blocs broke up, and new ones had to be formed. Generally, the passage of each piece of important legislation required the formation of a new bloc — and, consequently, of a new cabinet — because the member parties of the bloc might agree, for instance, on foreign policy but not on social policy. This led to an extraordinary turnover in French cabinets. Between 1870 and 1939 the French set up eighty-eight ministries, four times as many as the British formed during the same seventy-year period. However, under the French system the fall of a cabinet was not usually followed, as in England, by a general election. The Chamber of Deputies normally served out its full four-year term, and the same personalities generally reappeared in successive cabinets. A change of cabinet frequently meant simply a reorganization of the governing team but not a drastic change in policy. While cabinets changed often, there were only five major changes in coalitions in France between 1919 and 1938 — the same number as in Britain. There was more continuity in the French cabinet system than met the eye; nevertheless, the system of "revolving-door" cabinets had its inconveniences. It forced the French politicians to waste an inordinate amount of their time and effort on the mere "game" of politics; it encouraged evasion of responsibility; and it made it difficult to plan and implement a long-range policy.

In the first election after the war, in November, 1919, the old coalition of republicans, which had under the leadership of Clemenceau secured victory and signed the peace, split into a Right *Bloc National* and a Left *Cartel des Gauches*. The *Bloc National* carried the elections and its successive cabinets remained in power until 1924. The soul of the *Bloc National* after Clemenceau's retirement in 1920 was Raymond Poincaré, the wartime president of France. Poincaré's main policies were the reconstruction of the devastated areas in the north of France and the strict enforcement of the Treaty of Versailles. The reconstruction of the former war zone was carried out with commendable energy. In the process of rebuilding their factories and mines the French modernized them, which led some overenthusiastic observers, like the British historian Toynbee, to hail the "new technique" and the "new spirit" of France. This proved premature; French technology and economic organization remained generally antiquated. When Germany defaulted on the payment of the reparations Poincaré sternly invoked the Treaty of Versailles, and in 1923 French and Belgian troops occupied the hub of German heavy industry, the district of the Ruhr. The policy, however, proved a complete failure. The Germans expertly sabotaged the French and Belgian effort to collect reparations in kind, even though it aggravated their own economic plight. Moreover, the occupation of the Ruhr provoked strong criticism of France in the United States and Britain.

Disgruntled by the failure of Poincaré's foreign policy and by the sharp rise in the cost of living, the French people turned the *Bloc National* out and brought the *Cartel des Gauches* into power in the election of 1924. The Foreign Minister in the new government was Aristide Briand, a man who believed in the necessity of reconciliation between France and

Germany and in a more friendly attitude toward Soviet Russia. In 1924 France recognized *de jure* the Soviet Union. Without abandoning the policy of eastern alliances, Briand proposed to complement it with a policy of collective security. Almost simultaneously a conciliatory states- man, Gustav Stresemann, became foreign minister of Germany (see p. 278). In 1925 France and Germany concluded the Locarno agreements, which brought a great relaxation of international tensions. The principal agreement provided for a mutual guarantee on the part of France and Belgium on the one hand and of Germany on the other of the inviolability of the Franco-German and Belgo-German borders. The agreement was given the character of a collective security arrangement by guarantees of two outsiders, Britain and Italy, who pledged themselves to come to the rescue of the victim, should one or the other of the two parties to the agreement violate it. Since Germany refused to extend a similar guar- antee to her eastern neighbors, Poland and Czechoslovakia, France re- affirmed her pledges to them. The French and Belgian troops were with- drawn from the Ruhr, but Allied troops maintained a token occupation of the left bank of the Rhine until 1930.

The deteriorating financial situation of France ended the rule of the *Cartel des Gauches* and brought Poincaré back to power in 1926 to "save" the franc. Since the war the franc had steadily declined until it dropped from a prewar level of 19.3 cents to two cents in 1926. France seemed to be heading for the catastrophic type of inflation which had wrecked German credit three years earlier. To meet the crisis Poincaré formed a *Union Nationale* ministry in which sat six former prime ministers. By introducing drastic economies and new taxes and by balancing the budget, the new government stabilized the franc by 1928 at 3.92 cents. This was a far cry from its prewar level. In effect, four-fifths of the existing paper debts of the government and the people had been repudiated. The *rentier* class, which lived chiefly on the income derived from financial invest- ments, suffered severely by this proceeding. But the national credit was re-established, a sinking fund created to redeem the standing debt, and the sanctity of private property reaffirmed.

In foreign policy Poincaré made no attempt to return to the policy of strict enforcement of the Treaty of Versailles. Briand, who was retained as Foreign Minister, continued his policy of conciliation. In 1928, as a result of his efforts and those of the United States Secretary of State, Frank B. Kellogg, representatives of fifteen nations signed the Pact of Paris. The pact condemned "recourse to war for the solution of interna- tional controversies," and the signatory powers renounced war "as an instrument of national policy." Unfortunately, the pact provided for no sanctions against violators. In the 1930's when the totalitarian powers challenged by force the *status quo* established by the Paris peace treaties, the Pact of Paris proved a dead letter.

3. FRENCH DEMOCRACY IN CRISIS

The World Depression which began in 1929 brought to the fore the long-neglected social question in France. Unlike Germany or Great Britain, France had not enacted any extensive social legislation before the war, and the war had stimulated the growth and dispersals of French industries. Since the old industries had been concentrated in the north they had come under German occupation; with government encouragement and aid, industries were established in other parts of France. After the war they continued to grow because of the pent-up demand for industrial goods and the careful, protectionist policy of France. The growth of industry resulted in the further growth of the industrial proletariat. In the 1920's the relative prosperity and the almost total absence of unemployment softened the social question. Apart from extending the benefits of the Workingmen's Compensation Act of 1898 to agricultural laborers in 1922, no social legislation was enacted. The acute labor shortage assured reasonable wages. To relieve the labor shortage and augment the depleted population of France, the government encouraged immigration. Since at this time the United States was closing its gates to immigrants, much of the immigrant labor from Central Europe and Italy was diverted into the mines, factories, and farms of France. By 1939 10 per cent of the population was foreign-born. This was to create many difficult problems of adjustment — so familiar to the Americans but new and bewildering to the French, an old and inbred people. The foreign laborers were often ruthlessly exploited, and when unemployment developed during the depression they were the first ones to lose their jobs. Consequently, they tended to radicalism and added to the social restlessness that swept over France during the 1930's.

The depression came later to France and never affected her as acutely as the more industrialized countries: the United States, Germany, Great Britain, and Japan. But owing to peculiarly French conditions, social tensions were more explosive in France than in other industrial countries. Relations between capital and labor in France were marked by a singular lack of good will. The rigid class structure and intense class antagonism created an unbridgeable chasm between them and they regarded each other with an open and unremitting hostility. Owing in part to the lack of a mass market in France and in part to the concentration of much of French industry on production of luxury commodities, the French employers never learned the lesson of Henry Ford that laborers were also customers and that prosperous laborers were better customers than poor ones. In the absence of a mass market, most French industry was organized on a low-turnover and high-profit basis. Since the luxury industries produced primarily for export, French employers had little interest in raising the wages of their workers. A worker in the perfume industry, if his wages were raised, would probably not buy more perfume. Nor would a Renault or Citroën automobile worker, unlike his Detroit counterpart, buy an automobile, because until after World War II motor cars were not a means of mass transportation anywhere in Europe but only a diversion and status symbol of the rich. In these circumstances, French employers seldom had a direct interest in the prosperity of their workers. During the depression they often ruthlessly exploited unemployment to knock down wages. On the other hand, French workers never understood that only a prosperous business could pay good wages; the "filthy rich" could always pay, they believed.

Since they were barely on speaking terms, both capital and labor preferred political action to direct bargaining to gain their ends. The control of the great wealth in France was concentrated in an extraordinarily restricted, exclusive, hereditary oligarchy. The notorious "Two Hundred Families" were not an invention of marxist propaganda; they existed and through the control of the Bank of France (a private institution established by Napoleon) they dictated fiscal policy and could interpose an effective veto over legislation by withholding credits from the government. Many a cabinet was brought down by these arrogant oligarchs. The workingmen were organized in two large labor organizations: *Confédération Générale du Travail* (socialist) and *Confédération Générale du Travail Unitaire* (communist). Although large, both organizations were ineffective in securing gains for labor. The French workers readily heeded a call to march in a street demonstration and brawled bravely with the police, but they were too undisciplined to carry out a prolonged strike. In spite of its revolutionary tradition and penchant for violence, the French labor movement was essentially weak. It depended on the socialist and communist parties to fight its battles — on the floor of the National Assembly.

Standing between capital and labor, and suspicious of both, was the mass of small bourgeois and peasant proprietors. They provided the support of the republican parties of the Center which had governed France since the turn of the century. But with the advent of the depression the Center began to crumble and the extreme Right and Left grew. French democracy entered into a deep crisis. While the royalists had been noisy but harmless there now appeared alongside them more resolute enemies of the Republic: a variety of fascist and semi-fascist groups (*Jeunesses Patriotes, Croix du Feu, Solidarité Française*, and the *Cagoulards*). On the extreme Left the communists increased their strength.

In 1929 Poincaré resigned on account of ill health, and with his demise from politics the *Union Nationale* coalition dissolved. In the next seven years France was governed by a succession of cabinets based on rapidly shifting blocs with little or no inner cohesion. In 1930 a left-wing coalition passed the first important piece of social legislation in the century, the National Workingmen's Insurance Law, under which workers were to be insured against sickness, old age, and death. Workers, employers, and the state were to contribute to the cost of this social service. Its administration added heavily to the financial burdens of France, which at this time were again threatening the stability of the franc, and it failed to appease social unrest. A political scandal in 1933 (the Stavisky case), which involved leading politicians in questionable deals, angered the population and provided the fascist groups with their first opportunity to attack the Republic. In February of 1934 a violent riot broke out in Paris, in which seventeen persons were killed and many more wounded by the police. For a while, there was acute fear of a fascist uprising. The cabinet of Édouard Daladier hastily resigned and a Center coalition cabinet took charge. Tranquillity was restored but not public confidence. A majority of the people were becoming critical of all parties and scornful of the politicians – an ominous sign in a democracy.

While French democracy drifted, the nazis came to power in Germany. Hitler's intention to tear up the Treaty of Versailles was hardly a secret, and this presented a serious threat to France and the eastern neighbors of Germany. It was suggested by some that France and her allies in Eastern Europe wage a preventive war against Germany, but the idea was resolutely rejected since French military thinking was entirely defensive. Fascinated by the war of position in 1914–1918, the French generals put their trust completely in the Maginot Line, the elaborate system of fortifications, built and continuously perfected along the German border. When it became apparent that France would do nothing to check the rise of Nazi Germany, Poland turned around and concluded a ten-year non-aggression pact with Germany (January, 1934), which largely nullified the Franco-Polish alliance. The system of French eastern alliances had begun to crumble. To check the disarray among their eastern allies Foreign Minister Barthou set out on a grand tour of the European capitals in the hope of building an alliance system against Germany (April–June, 1934). But his efforts were cut short by the bullets of a Macedonian revolutionary, who killed him along with King Alexander of Yugoslavia, on a visit of state to France (October, 1934).

When Germany announced its intention to introduce conscription and build a large army in violation of the Treaty of Versailles (March, 1935), France hastened to conclude an alliance treaty with Soviet Russia (May, 1935). On instructions from Moscow, equally disturbed by German rearmament, the French communists reversed their previous policy of opposition to all "bourgeois" parties and approached the left-wing parties with a view to forming a Popular Front to defend the Republic against the nazi-fascist threat at home and abroad. When Hitler reoccupied the demilitarized zone in the Rhineland (March, 1936) in violation not only of the Versailles *Diktat* but also of the Locarno agreements freely entered into by Germany, the French government again failed to act. Belgium, frightened of German aggressiveness and despairing of French passivity, hastily abrogated the Franco-Belgian military alliance, concluded in 1920, and withdrew into prudent neutrality. On the wave of dissatisfaction with the government's internal and external policies, the Popular Front parties won a resounding electoral victory and formed an all-Left cabinet, composed of socialists and Radical Socialists under the presidency of the socialist leader Léon Blum (June, 1936). The communists did not enter the cabinet, but pledged themselves to support it.

The Popular Front government at once carried out many social reforms, such as a forty-hour working week, vacations with pay for workers, and compulsory arbitration of labor disputes. The government determined further to curb the power of the financial oligarchy by nationalizing the Bank of France and the munitions industry. Social reform was long over-due in France, but the tragedy was that it came at the wrong time. France was exposed to threats on all sides: the Italians had completed the con-quest of Ethiopia and were free to act in Europe again; the Germans had refortified the Rhineland and were feverishly rearming; and the Belgians had reaffirmed their neutrality, making it necessary to extend the Maginot Line to cover the Belgian borders. The southern frontier was likewise jeopardized, for the outbreak of Civil War in Spain (July, 1936) and the German and Italian aid given to the insurgent leader, Francisco Franco, made it probable that if the Spanish Nationalists won the Civil War Spain would ally itself with Germany and Italy.

All of these policies made it imperative for France to strengthen her defenses and national unity. Yet the Popular Front policies had the opposite effect: French production fell off as a result of the forty-hour week, paid vacations, and a rash of strikes, which involved as many as 300,000 workers. It was natural that the French workers wanted to profit from the arrival of the first pro-labor government in French history to recover some of their losses, but the strikes proved disastrous to the de-fense of France. The Popular Front policies outraged the wealthy classes of France. The slogan, "Rather Hitler than Blum," expressed accurately their feeling. Political and social relations became envenomed as they had not been since the days of the Dreyfus affair. The wealthy classes were determined to bring Blum down, reverse the Popular Front policies, and end the alliance with Soviet Russia. An ominous hint of the tension and bitterness which tinctured the rift was the discovery of a conspiracy to overthrow the Republic by an armed *coup* and to set up a fascist or authoritarian government, allied to the Axis powers. When Blum de-manded emergency fiscal powers to save the franc, the Senate, where the financial groups were entrenched, refused them and he was forced to resign (June, 1937). He tried again for a few weeks in 1938 to form a new Popular Front government, but was again defeated.

The schism within French political life made it impossible for the French government to speak with any authority in international affairs. Increasingly France deferred to Britain, which came forward as the most resolute of the *status quo* powers. The British made it quite clear that they would fight if France were a victim of unprovoked aggression. In July, 1938, King George V made a visit of state to Paris, which reaffirmed the Franco-British *Entente Cordiale*. But British support had a price; Britain made it clear that she would not fight if France went to war to rescue her eastern allies. Leading British statesmen were convinced that if Germany were given a free hand in the east, she would attack Soviet Russia before turning on the western powers. In this situation France looked on helplessly as Hitler swallowed up Austria (March, 1938), whose independence had been guaranteed in the Treaty of St.-Germain largely at the insistence of France. The complete degradation of France as a great power came when Premier Daladier, feebly trailing behind Prime Minister Chamberlain, abjectly agreed at the Munich Conference (September, 1938) to Hitler's demand, made under a threat of war, to dismember France's most faithful ally, Czechoslovakia. The Munich Conference, to which Soviet delegates were not invited, nullified the anemic Franco-Soviet accord of 1935. It demonstrated also that France would not stand by her eastern allies who scurried to come to terms, as best they could, with Hitler's Germany, which, like Bismarck's Germany some seventy years earlier, had emerged as the leading power of the European continent. France was left without a single friend on the continent. From the proud victor of 1918 France had descended by 1938 to a second-rate power, patronized by her only friend left, Great Britain, and despised by her enemies.

Despite the humiliation it imposed on France, the Munich agreement was welcomed with delirious joy by the French people because it had averted war. Blum expressed the feeling of most Frenchmen when he said on hearing of the Munich accord: "I feel a cowardly relief." Daladier, much to his surprise, enjoyed an immense, albeit short, popularity. Nevertheless, "for the sake of the principle," the socialists abstained from voting for and the communists voted against the Munich agreement in the National Assembly. This forced Daladier, originally a left-wing Radical Socialist who had energetically suppressed the fascist riots in 1934, to turn to the Right for support. But the price of that support was the revocation of recent concessions made to French labor by the Popular Front government. The Daladier government announced that the promise of a forty-hour week could not be kept, a move justified by the need to build up armaments more swiftly, but a move which embittered the laboring classes. The labor organizations called a series of strikes, and while Europe drifted toward war the French continued to weaken their financial, productive, and military efforts by a strike deadlock and frequent disorders.

The blame for this sacrifice of national efficiency was laid upon the Left. Turning still more definitely against the socialists and communists, Daladier asked the Chamber of Deputies for semi-dictatorial powers.

Labor leaders were arrested, strikers threatened with military penalties, while the leading armament makers were encouraged by government orders and the assurances of a fair profit. By the spring of 1939, the Daladier cabinet had been granted power to rule by decree with no fixed limit on the use made of this extraordinary authority. By dictatorial methods a measure of order had been restored, but it was clear that France was adopting some of the methods of the totalitarian regimes in order to strengthen the nation against such regimes, an ironic and tragic illustration of the corrupting influence of tyranny. In foreign affairs, Daladier followed docilely the lead of Britain through all the preliminaries of the Second World War. And when Britain decided upon war, France disconsolately followed suit.

24

ITALY

For Fascism the State is an absolute before which individuals and groups are relative.

BENITO MUSSOLINI

1. THE COLLAPSE OF PARLIAMENTARY GOVERNMENT

THE DYNAMISM of the twin forces of nationalism and socialism, released by the war, was more clearly evident in Italy than in other countries. Italian nationalism was deeply frustrated by the results of the war. Italy had entered the war on the basis of a precise contract with the Allies, the secret Treaty of London of April 26, 1915, which promised Italy certain exactly defined territories. At the Paris Peace Conference, however, owing to the opposition of President Wilson the Treaty of London was not carried out. Italy received most but not all the territories which had been promised to her by the Allies. Specifically, she received southern Tyrol (High Adige), Trentino, Trieste, Gorizia, Istria, and the Dalmatian Islands (but not Dalmatia itself, with the exception of the port of Zara). Frustrated in Dalmatia, the Italian nationalists seized on a rather petty objective: the port of Fiume, which had not been promised to Italy in the Treaty of London. In September, 1919, a band of nationalists led by Gabriele D'Annunzio, a distinguished poet and irresponsible adventurer, seized Fiume and held it for fourteen months in defiance of Allied injunctions and despite an official Italian disavowal of the adventure. The ensuing fracas was wholly disproportionate to the importance of the issue. The inhabitants of the city were in the majority Italian but the surrounding countryside was solidly Yugoslav. The port had been an economic outlet for Hungary just as Trieste had been an outlet for Austria; both were completely worthless to Italy which had abundant outlets to the sea. Deprived of their Central European hinterland both Fiume and Trieste declined in economic importance. But to inflamed nationalists economics were unimportant.

The Treaty of London had promised Italy also a share of the Ottoman Empire, but owing to the rise of nationalist Turkey, Italy was unable to collect it. She did, however, hold on to the Dodecanese Islands and to Rhodes, which were inhabited in the main by Greeks and had been promised by the Allies to Greece. This was to provoke a quarrel between Italy and Greece in the Aegean analogous to the quarrel between Italy and Yugoslavia in the Adriatic. Altogether, the Italian gains amounted to 9,000 square miles of territory with 1,600,000 inhabitants. This was not inconsiderable, but to the Italians, looking at the far greater gains made by Britain and France, it seemed a pitiful reward for their contribution to the Allied victory. They had always felt like poor relatives among the "rich" western allies, and, just as the Germans developed a deep sense of grievance against the Versailles "dictate," so the Italians were deeply aggrieved by what they termed their "mutilated" (i.e., incomplete) victory. Internally, this resulted in discrediting parliamentary government in Italy for having, through weakness and indecision, permitted these reverses. Externally, it resulted in Italy's joining the ranks of revisionist powers, in spite of the fact that she had been one of the victors in the First World War.

In addition to the mutilated victory, parliamentary government in Italy was discredited by its inability to solve mounting postwar economic and social problems. Italy was a poor country and its finances were precarious at best. The war had seriously strained its limited economic resources, and the cost of postwar reconstruction and of pensions to disabled veterans and war widows added heavily to the financial burdens of the country. Since the government was unable to balance the budget the value of the *lira* steadily sank. Owing to overpopulation, scanty resources, and intense class antagonism, Italy always had had a grave social problem. After the war it was aggravated by mounting unemployment as the burdened economy proved unable to absorb the demobilized soldiers into the national labor force. The problem was further aggravated by the fact that Italy's traditional safety valve of social discontent, emigration, was shut at this time by adoption of immigration restrictions in the United States and many Latin-American countries. In this situation even the most energetic and honest government would have been hard put to find a solution, and parliamentary government in Italy had never been very strong or particularly honest.

In June, 1920, Giovanni Giolitti, the great compromiser and parliamentary tactician, returned to power on a wave of discontent with the external and internal policies of the government. It was felt that if any of the parliamentary politicians of standing could make the moribund Italian parliamentary system work it was Giolitti. In the years before the war he had appeased social unrest by a policy of extending suffrage and of maintaining a prudent neutrality in social conflicts. He had opposed Italy's intervention in the war and was therefore not blamed for the mutilated victory. When he returned to power in 1920 his policy was again one of conciliation. He proposed to settle the quarrels of Italy with her neighbors and to adopt a hands-off policy in social conflicts. But the situation was much more explosive than before, for the war had greatly stimulated the forces of nationalism and socialism, and they appeared determined to destroy each other. While the nationalist parties were indifferent to the social problem, the socialist parties[1] ignored Italian nationalist ambitions. To gain their ends the socialist parties encouraged strikes. However, to an even higher degree than the French workers, the Italian workers lacked the economic reserves and discipline necessary to carry out prolonged, orderly strikes, which could really hurt capital. The "bony hand of hunger" always brought them back to work after a few days. In their frustration and helplessness they often resorted to violence and destruction of property, which alienated them from liberal elements who might have otherwise sympathized with them.

As the specter of a violent social revolution hovered over the country, there appeared a prophet who promised to reconcile the seemingly irreconcilable forces of nationalism and socialism: Benito Mussolini. Mussolini (1883–1945) appeared qualified for the role. A son of a village blacksmith and anarchist (he was christened Benito in honor of the Mexican revolutionary Benito Juárez), he gained an education by his own efforts, and first won attention as the radical, internationalist editor of the socialist organ, *Avanti.* During the war he left the Socialist Party and became a strong nationalist and interventionist. Wounded in active service, he was discharged from the army and re-entered politics as the editor of his own journal, *Il Popolo d'Italia* (The People of Italy). His acumen had convinced him that nationalism and socialism were the two most powerful trends of the age but that in conflict nationalism would prove stronger than socialism. He planned to unite elements in each which had the greatest popular appeal. When he helped to organize a new political party after the war, he meditated calling it by a name that would suggest "nationalism" and "socialism" in conjunction, but as the older Socialist Party had repudiated him he let his followers take the title of *Fascisti.* The name derived from the Italian word *fascio,* which meant literally "bundle" and figuratively "a bundle of rods and an ax" — the imperial emblem of ancient Rome. The name suggested to the Italians national unity and imperial strength.

However, it was in divining that the country demanded not a policy of conciliation but action that Mussolini proved a far shrewder politician than the veteran politician Giolitti. Claiming that the postwar labor strikes and discontent in Italy were leading to communism, the Fascisti posed as saviors of society. The government and the police, they insisted, were too weak and timid to grapple with the communist threat. Bands

[1] In 1921, the Italian Socialist Party, like socialist parties everywhere in Europe at that time, split into the Communist Party, which owed allegiance to Moscow, and the Socialist Party, which — though specifically Italian — was also wedded, in doctrine at least, to Marxian internationalism.

of fascist toughs, the *fasci di combattimento,* recruited principally among war veterans, opened a violent campaign against socialist and communist groups, broke up their meetings, assaulted their leaders, and wrecked their headquarters. In the first election held under universal manhood suffrage in May, 1921, the Giolitti coalition was toppled. The socialists gained 107 seats in the Chamber of Deputies (a sharp decline from their previous strength of 160), the fascists thirty-five, and the communists eighteen. This did not reflect the true strength of the two extremist parties. Their strength was not in numbers but in their readiness to act. While politicians engaged in forensic mock battles on the floor of parliament, communist and fascist bands engaged in real battles on the streets of nearly every town. Scores were killed in these brawls, but Mussolini's Black Shirts apparently had more courage and fewer scruples than their opponents and struck back more murderously. Their party, with headquarters at Milan, soon dominated northern Italy.

In October, 1922, the fascists felt strong enough to attempt to overthrow the government by force. Mussolini announced that they would "march on Rome." The inert government then bestirred itself to declare martial law. But unexpectedly the King, the ineffectual Victor Emmanuel III (1900–1946), who had always contented himself with the role of a constitutional monarch, on the advice of military men who sympathized with the fascists, refused to approve the government's decree on martial law. The cabinet then resigned, and the King invited Mussolini to form the succeeding one.

2. THE FASCIST STATE

The seizure of power by the fascists was not openly illegal. Mussolini formed a cabinet under a mandate from the King, and the Chamber of Deputies approved it by a vote of 306 to 116. A majority of the Italian people appeared to welcome the fascist "revolution" as a promise of firmer government and a stricter political morality. However, from its first years the fascist state was based on force. The Black Shirt militia and the agents of security police O.V.R.A. (*Opera volontaria repressione antifascista*) subjected the opposition to brutal persecution. By kidnapping, beating, dosing with castor oil, and sometimes by murder, the fascists established a reputation of gangsterism which they never outlived. The most infamous example of their methods of intimidation occurred in 1924. Although they secured two-thirds of the popular vote in the elections of that year, victory did not make them generous toward the liberal and socialist minority groups. The opposition, however, was not yet wholly intimidated, and a socialist deputy, Giacomo Matteotti, denounced the fascists with vigor, insisting that he could produce evidence which would convict some of the leaders of venality and violence. A few days after making these charges, Matteotti was kidnapped and murdered by fascist partisans. This act of terrorism produced, as Mussolini admitted, "a profound moral oscillation" and led the opposition groups to withdraw from the parliament in protest. But the fascists clung to power and survived the storm although it was common knowledge that high officials in the regime had approved the measures to silence Matteotti.

Mussolini frequently proclaimed his contempt for parliamentarism and for what he stigmatized as "plutodemocracy," but he hesitated to destroy entirely the organs of representative government. Instead, he brought them under his control or so weakened them that they lacked force enough to oppose "the Party." He left Victor Emmanuel on the throne although he would have preferred a republican state, and he took for himself the position of head of the government. The Senate, the members of which were appointed, was gradually packed with prominent citizens who favored his leadership. The Chamber of Deputies was rendered obedient by a new election law (1923) which reduced the numerous small parties and assured one-party dominance by decreeing that the party which led in the elections (provided it secured at least one-fourth of the ballots cast) would be allotted two-thirds of the seats in the chamber. With its official influence, ruthless methods, and strong organization the Fascist Party could hardly fail to win under such an arrangement. The parliament became a debating society which listened to eulogies of Mussolini and voted its appreciation, but it ceased to exercise any real influence over the ministers. The principle of cabinet responsibility and legislative representation had been nullified.

Mussolini was not satisfied when he had paralyzed parliamentary initiative and rendered the deputies of the nation impotent. He also destroyed what vigor and independence the council of ministers might have retained by assuming eight of the fifteen portfolios himself and he treated the ministers who served under him as secretaries of administrative departments rather than as executive officers. The real policy-making organ of the regime was a new creation, a Grand Council of some thirty members, but it was a body responsible in no direct manner to the King or to the people. The leading fascist dignitaries who sat on the Grand Council might be considered the actual governing organ of the state, with Mussolini as chairman of the board. The state had become a dictatorship in fact and spirit even though the shells of parliamentary government, the cabinet, the Senate, and the Chamber of Deputies, continued to exist. These, too, however, were further modified after 1928.

The rights and liberties of the citizen, which liberal laws and democratic government had been specially devised to protect, withered as the fascist sun rose high. Freedom of speech became a mockery when an unguarded word might bring a visit from fascist *squadristi*. Freedom of the press was revoked on the ground that the official censors knew best what news the people should hear. Workers lost the right to strike or to bargain collectively, and businessmen found their transactions regulated by government ordinances and by tariff, currency, and priority rules. The economic problems which beset the people were not solved by fascist methods, but this was not for lack of official interest. Though Mussolini denounced the communists for their heresy in stressing economic pressures as the dominant forces in society, he himself gave a major part of his time to the economic dilemma which faced the Italians. "Political power creates wealth," he declared. He had been granted political power and he had to meet the challenge of a paucity of resources.

The most original contribution which the fascists made to statecraft was the concept of the "Corporate State." Mussolini condemned political parties — whether they were organized, as was conventional in Continental Europe, on the basis of social class, region, religion, or nationality — on the ground that they divided and weakened a nation by fostering class, regional, religious, or national strife. He condemned also the conventional division of countries into electoral districts on the ground that this fostered a spirit of localism in politics. Yet he felt that political parties were necessary because they could mobilize the energies of the nation as no other organization could. To solve the dilemma which this presented, he proposed that each nation should have only one political party. Furthermore, while he condemned class, region, religion, or nationality as a specious basis of political organization, he conceded that the great *corporate* interests of a nation were valid interests and should be given representation. By this he meant that all citizens who were dependent on the same general field of activity — upon manufacture, for instance, or agriculture, or transportation — had more essential interests in common than all citizens of the same class, living in the same region, or belonging to the same religion or ethnic group. The fascists therefore encouraged the formation of thirteen syndicates, corporate bodies established to regulate and to represent all branches of national activity from agriculture to the arts and learned professions. In 1929 these syndicates were instructed to submit eight hundred names to the Fascist Grand Council. This list, supplemented by two hundred names from other sources, was then reduced by the Council to four hundred, and these carefully selected members became the deputies designated for the next parliament. Those Italians who enjoyed the franchise were permitted to exercise it in a plebiscite, to approve or reject the prescribed list of four hundred names. Very few voters had the temerity to cast a negative ballot.

Although the new syndicates were nominally independent units, in practice they provided the machinery through which the head of the government planned to control production, prices, and working conditions. All labor unions had been dissolved, laborers had lost the right to strike, and many critics saw in fascism merely the dictatorship of big business. But it was more than that, and the bankers and industrialists of Italy who had applauded Mussolini's denunciation of communism, found that they as well as the workers had acquired a master. Industry and agriculture were regimented. Stern orders went forth from Il Duce's offices in the Palazzo Venezia at Rome to speed production, and the output of electric power, automobiles, steamships, silk, and other indices of economic activity rose rapidly. New roads, improved communications, impressive buildings, and grandiose public parades and party spectacles advertised the program to revive the nation's prosperity and prestige. A loan of $100,000,000 from New York bankers helped to stabilize the currency but the national credit remained precarious. The heavy outlay for armaments oppressed the taxpayers, and the rising population kept the problem of an adequate food supply acute. To increase the crops and encourage larger families at the same time the government offered rewards to farmers and to the parents of five or more children, a resort to state aid which did not relieve the taxpayers.

When the years of relative prosperity from 1922 to 1929 were followed by the World Depression in the latter year, the fascist boast that a corporative state could solve the crises which ruined millions in a democratic society was put to the test. The Italian treasury poured out credits, supported ailing industries, tightened the controls over the syndicates, subsidized programs of public works. By 1934 the syndicates had been reshaped into nine main departments of economic activity with over a thousand subsidiary guilds, combines, and labor units. At the head stood a National Council of Corporations of some eight hundred members, which by 1936 supplanted the now powerless popular assembly, the Chamber of Deputies. Thus, under the stress of economic pressure and a world crisis, the relics of parliamentary government were further transformed and the corporative organization of society extended. But the results of this transition had still to be tested. The Italian people had little chance to judge the efficiency of the new system because public criticism was restricted. Accurate information was so scarce that even government officials were unaware of the true strength of army divisions or the number of aircraft fit for service, and the population had to rest content with outbursts of oratory, vehement and vague, and official communiqués from the government press. Foreign observers were disposed to agree that Mussolini had infused new energy into the administration, but they regarded his reorganization of the government as primarily a series of changes to consolidate his control. They questioned whether the new machinery or the new men had improved the position of Italy as a great power or solved the economic deficiencies which made an adventurous foreign policy an extravagance for Italy and major war a desperate gamble.

3. THE FASCIST FOREIGN POLICY

Mussolini insisted that will counted for more than wealth, and that fascists must learn to live dangerously. He poured contempt upon the parliamentary politicians who had taken the Italian people into the First World War, for which they were unprepared, and a peace in which they were outwitted. Had the Italian delegates at the Paris Peace Conference only dared to pound the conference table with their fists, he implied, the effete diplomats of the decadent democracies would have cowered in fear. Fascist foreign policy was aggressively nationalist and openly revisionist. One of Mussolini's pet hatreds was the League of Nations, a product of the Paris peace treaties and a guardian of the *status quo* established by them. He encouraged the small revisionist nations of Central and Eastern Europe, Austria, Hungary, and Bulgaria, in their agitation for the revision of the treaties. Nevertheless, while France and Britain still dominated European diplomacy in the 1920's, Mussolini was prudent enough not to defy them or break with the League. Thus when the Italian members of an international commission appointed to delimit the Greek-Albanian border were assassinated (1923), presumably by Greeks, Mussolini showed his fist. The Italian navy was dispatched to bombard and occupy the Greek island of Corfu. But after only a month Italy yielded to the pressure of the League and of Britain and France and evacuated the island. Mussolini settled Italy's protracted quarrel with Yugoslavia over Fiume peacefully by treaty (1924). Italy's various quarrels with Greece were also adjourned, if not settled, by conclusion of a Greek-Italian treaty of friendship (1927). The price which Yugoslavia and Greece paid for these settlements was their recognition of a virtual protectorate established by Italy over Albania (1926).

The greatest success of fascist diplomacy in the 1920's was the settlement of the "Roman Question," which had troubled Italy since the Italian troops occupied Rome in 1870 (see p. 73). In 1919 Pope Benedict XV (1914–1922) lifted the long ban on participation of Catholics in Italian political life. In consequence, a Catholic party, the Populist Party, was founded under the leadership of Don Luigi Sturzo. Basing itself in social matters on the encyclical *Rerum novarum* issued in 1891 by "the workingman's pope" Leo XIII, it gained rapid strength. When the fascists came to power in 1922 their arbitrary acts brought them into frequent conflict with the Church. The fascist monopolization of political power resulted in the destruction of all competing political parties, including the Populist Party. But there was a real desire on both sides to find a solution to the long disagreement. The fascist state desired the moral support of the Catholic Church to which the overwhelming majority of the Italians belonged, and the Catholic Church approved of the energy with which the fascists suppressed the "godless" marxist parties. In 1929 the fascist state and the papacy reached an accord which was embodied in the Lateran treaty. It followed closely the lines of the Law of Guarantees, the original settlement proposed by Italy to the papacy in 1871. A small area of about 109 acres in the heart of Rome, the City of the Vatican, was declared a sovereign state under the temporal authority of the pope. As compensation for the territory and revenue which had been taken by the Italian kingdom in 1860–1870, the papacy accepted an indemnity of 1,750,000,000 lire, to be paid partly in bonds and partly in cash. This treaty was supplemented by a concordat to define the position of the Catholic Church in the Italian state, but despite the care with which the stipulations were drawn all causes of friction were not ended. The educational policies of the government, the militaristic stand which it frequently assumed, and the theories of state supremacy advocated by many fascist spokesmen drew repeated rebukes from the Holy See.

Mussolini's favorite idea for a substitute for the despised League of Nations, in which small nations exercised a measure of influence, was the formation of a four-power directory consisting of Britain, France, Germany, and Italy, which — like the post-Napoleonic Quadruple Alliance — would dictate the policies of Europe. For this reason he agreed to the Locarno treaties of 1925 (see p. 260), although they were concluded in strict accordance with the League Covenant and their purpose was to fortify the *status quo* established by the Paris peace treaties. Mussolini's idea was actually realized in an emasculated form in the Four-Power Pact (1933). It remained, however, ineffective, as the rise of Hitler to power in Germany affected adversely the relations among the four western powers.

The relations between Nazi Germany and Fascist Italy were at first not especially friendly. The first personal meeting of Hitler and Mussolini (1934) left them both cool. The reason for this was the clash of the interests of Germany and Italy in Central Europe. By the Rome Protocols (March, 1934) Mussolini tied Austria and Hungary to Italy. The original purpose of the protocols was to outflank the eastern allies of France — Czechoslovakia, Yugoslavia, and Rumania — organized in the Little Entente. But the first test of the protocols came not from France and the Little Entente but from Germany. In July, 1934, the nazis tried to seize power in Austria by a *coup* (see p. 316). The attempt failed largely because of the energetic action of Mussolini who mobilized troops and sent them to the Brenner Pass on the Austrian border. In 1935, however, to divert Italian public opinion from the insoluble economic problems at home and to put to use the large Italian army and navy before they became obsolete, Mussolini launched Italy on a reckless career of foreign adventure and empire-building in Ethiopia, Spain, and Albania. These ventures, which are summarized in subsequent chapters, cost Italy dearly in blood and treasure but brought few tangible economic or political advantages. The hostility of Great Britain and to a smaller extent of France to these ventures and to Mussolini's grandiose claim to the Mediterranean as *"mare nostrum"* (our sea) forced Italy into the arms of Germany. Italy demonstratively withdrew from the League of Nations and formed with Germany the Rome-Berlin Axis (October, 1936). This compact, like the compact of Dr. Faustus with the devil, brought Italy short-term advantages and long-term disaster. The first price Italy paid for it was the abandonment of Austria to Germany (March, 1938). The appearance of the mighty German army on the Brenner Pass in place of the negligible Austrian one limited severely Italy's freedom of action. It made Italy's intervention in the Second World War on the side of Germany logical, although not inevitable. This fateful decision (June, 1940) was made by Mussolini personally against the urgent counsels of his sanest advisers. The Second World War, in which Italy became a prominent battlefield, brought the country to defeat and dishonor and the dictator himself to death before an Italian firing squad in 1945.

25

GERMANY

The great masses of the people will more easily fall victim to a great lie than a small one.

ADOLF HITLER

1. THE WEIMAR REPUBLIC

THE GERMAN DEMOCRATIC republic, born in defeat in 1918–1919, endured for fourteen years. It was burdened from the outset with the stigma of surrender and with the dishonor of acknowledging German war guilt and signing away German territory. Few Germans became deeply devoted to its inglorious annals or regretted its demise. In 1933 it was supplanted by the Third Reich, an aggressive totalitarian regime dominated by the National Socialist Party and by the party leader (Führer), Adolf Hitler.

The flight of Kaiser William II in the last week of World War I left Germany without a government. The leaders of the Social Democratic Party announced that Germany would become a democratic republic and called for the election of a National Assembly to draft a constitution. To emphasize the changed spirit and the peaceful intentions of the "new Germany" the assembly met, not in Berlin but in Weimar, a city associated with the fame of Goethe and Schiller and a center of German culture. The constitution adopted there in 1919 provided that Germany should be a federal republic.

Division and disunion plagued the "Weimar Republic" from the first. The German socialists were not a united party in 1918. A majority of their representatives, led by Friedrich Ebert and Philip Scheidemann, favored a cautious and progressive program for the socialization of industry. A second group, the Independent Social Democrats, favored the immediate creation of a socialist state, but they wanted to achieve this without violence. A third, more radical group, the Spartacists, demanded a "dictatorship of the proletariat" such as the Russian communists had recently established. They tried to seize power by a revolt but were defeated in January, 1919.

The German people, despite their defeat and disillusionment, were not ready for communism. Most of them supported the "Majority Socialists," who won 165 seats; the Center Party (Catholic), which gained 88 seats; or the German Democratic Party (bourgeois), which followed closely with 75 seats. The remaining seats were divided among a small group of reactionaries on the extreme right and a small group of radicals on the extreme left.

The assembly elected Friedrich Ebert President of the provisional government and Schneidemann prime minister. The first major crisis the new regime had to face was the question of accepting or rejecting the severe peace terms the Allied governments offered in May, 1919. The Scheidemann cabinet resigned in protest, but a new cabinet, led by Gustav Bauer, yielded, and the assembly voted, 237 to 138, to accept the *Friedensdiktat*, the "dictated peace." Patriotic Germans never forgot the humiliation and the penalties the Weimar assembly accepted by this surrender, and the Weimar Republic was weakened from the start by the accusation that it had "betrayed" Germany. The charge was unjust, for the Allied governments threatened to continue the wartime blockade and inflict further penalties on the prostrate German nation if the peace terms were not accepted.

From 1919 to 1924 the Weimar Republic had to cope with the problem of reparations payments, the French and Belgian occupation of the Ruhr Valley (1923), and the uncontrolled inflation that made the German currency valueless. But after 1924 Germany steadily recovered its economic strength. When President Ebert, who had been a saddle maker in his early years, died in 1925, the Germans elected Field Marshal Paul von Hindenburg as his successor. This choice of their most popular military leader of World War I suggested that hatred of militarism and "Prussianism" was already fading and that the basic character of the German people had not changed.

The second five years of the Weimar Republic, 1924 to 1929, restored German confidence. By 1929 the industrial output of Germany exceeded that of Britain, France, Russia, or Italy and was exceeded only by that of the United States. German merchant shipping almost equaled its prewar total. The foreign markets lost during the war and the wartime blockade had largely been recaptured, and the value of German exports exceeded the value of German imports.

Germany also improved her foreign relations during the years 1924–1929. Gustav Stresemann, who served as foreign minister of the Weimar Republic from 1923 to 1929, believed that it would be wise to conciliate rather than to oppose and antagonize the Allied powers that had won the war. His negotiations with the French foreign minister, Aristide Briand, produced the Locarno treaties, whereby France and Germany agreed to respect the new frontiers established between them in 1919. This evidence that the Germans had "reformed" won them admission to the

League of Nations (1926). Stresemann's final achievement before his death in 1929 was to win easier reparations terms and a promise that the Allied occupation forces in Germany would be withdrawn in 1930.

This era of good feeling reached its high point in 1928, when Briand and the United States Secretary of State Frank Kellogg prepared their anti-war pact (see p. 260). Germany promptly joined with other nations in accepting this proposal to "renounce war as an instrument of national policy." Unfortunately, the World Depression, which commenced at the close of 1929, brought economic distress to all the leading nations and sharpened international rivalries. With business declining and unemployment spreading, the "spirit of Locarno" was rapidly replaced by a mood of bitterness and suspicion. German resentment over the "Friedensdiktat" of 1919, which had softened during the years 1924–1929, flamed up again. The result was a renewed sense of wrong and indignation that inflamed German hearts and favored the rise of Adolf Hitler and his National Socialist (Nazi) Party.

2. RISE OF THE NATIONAL SOCIALIST STATE

Until 1930 Hitler's name was almost unknown even in Germany. Born an Austrian citizen in 1889, the son of a customs official, he was a moody and emotional child with artistic yearnings. In 1914 he volunteered for service in the German army and survived the war as a corporal. At once ambitious and introspective, he knew the bitterness and frustration of the "little people" and it was in the beer halls and lodging houses of Vienna and Munich that he first discovered his extraordinary talent. He had been born with the gift of oratory and he learned how to rouse his depressed listeners to a pitch of hysterical enthusiasm by his raucous tirades. Humiliation is the harsh stepmother of ambition, and all Germany, frustrated and resentful, was a theater prepared for his harangues. The audience, however, required over ten years of preparation before it was in the mood to accept Hitler. His early efforts as a political agitator were mere sound and fury. In 1923 he joined with the autocratic general, Erich Ludendorff, and others, in organizing a futile revolt in Munich which was dubbed the "Beer Hall Putsch" by the contemptuous authorities who crushed it. Hitler was sentenced to five years imprisonment but was released after less than one. While shut up he strung together his aims and ideas in *Mein Kampf* (*My Battle*), a book which became a bible for his followers.

Like Mussolini in Italy, Hitler had divined the powerful appeal which lay in a blend of nationalist and socialist propaganda. He joined and soon became a leading spirit in a small group of agitators who called themselves the National Socialist German Workers Party, better known to history as the National Socialists or Nazis. The most dangerous element in the nazi propaganda was its savage, insistent appeal to national pride.

The Germans yearned more intensely than most of them realized to re-
trieve their lost prestige and vindicate themselves before the world. They
believed that an injustice had been done them; that the legend of German
war guilt was a hypocritical formula invented by the democracies to
excuse Allied extortions and conquests. In dark hours even peaceful
Germans doubted if they would ever receive fair treatment unless they
rearmed and demanded it. The abortive Beer Hall Putsch was only one
of several half-desperate reactions in 1923 to the arrogance of the French,
who had marched into the Ruhr Valley to collect on defaulted reparations. With the Dawes Plan the following year and a slow return of
German economic prosperity in the years 1924–1929, the fulminations of
Hitler and other demagogues attracted less attention and the Nazi Party
barely held together. But the economic depression of 1929 and the cancellation of further American loans produced an immediate effect in
Germany. National indignation flamed up strongly, the spreading unemployment and hardship were blamed upon reparations, the ten-year-
old Versailles *Diktat* became once more the charter of all German woes,
and the National Socialist group in the Reichstag rose from 12 to 107
deputies in the election of 1930.

A wave of patriotic fervor was welding the German people into an
embattled nation. The socialists still had 143 seats in the Reichstag, and
the communists 77, but the defiant slogans of the nazis were winning
new supporters daily. In the presidential election of 1932 the aged Field
Marshal Paul von Hindenburg was re-elected, but Hitler ran second and
received over 11,000,000 votes. The nazis were becoming so powerful
and so ruthless that they intimidated the rival parties. They had built up
a party organization which disposed of large "contributions" and they
had become a state within the state through their troops and district
leaders. Like the Italian fascists they gathered their own uniformed police
force and action squads to guard nazi meetings, to break up counter
demonstrations, and to extend the party organization and control. The
individual liberty and freedom of speech assured by the Weimar constitution made it difficult for the nerveless government of the republic to
check these developments.

Thus Hitler's ascent to power was marked by many incidents of violence, coercion, bloodshed, and buffoonery, some of which must forever
remain obscure. By 1933 the nazis were the most powerful party in the
Reichstag, and Hindenburg appointed Hitler chancellor. But the nazis
were not ready to stop short with parliamentary control under the Weimar
constitution; they wanted a new regime which would assure the dictatorship of the party and a division of the spoils of victory. Hitler's first act
was to decree a new election. The nazi Storm Troopers attacked opposing
parties, broke up their meetings, and wrecked their headquarters and
printing presses. A conveniently timed fire which destroyed the Reichstag
building was immediately blamed upon the communists. Although the

new election (March, 1933) gave the nazis less than half the votes, they dissolved or absorbed the remaining parties and rushed through a bill granting Hitler dictatorial powers for four years.

A revolutionary government, or crisis regime, is always provisory. This is likely to make the men who head it nervous in the face of opposition and arbitrary in the use of their power. The ruthlessness with which Hitler was prepared to exercise his control was demonstrated to Germany and the world in 1934. In June he crushed an alleged plot against his regime by hundreds of summary executions, the victims being shot down without trial. A month later Hindenburg died and Hitler assumed the supreme executive power. The Weimar constitution of 1919 had ceased to have any meaning. The new government was endorsed by a popular plebiscite announced as 88 per cent favorable. There is no good reason to doubt that a majority of the German people were enthusiastically in favor of Hitler's rule. The quickened national pride, the promise of justice for the "little man," the program of public works, the reduction of unemployment, even the authoritarian spirit of the party and the revival of military uniforms and disciplines were apparently welcome to most Germans. A mystical exaltation, a blind faith in the Führer and in the destiny of the race, seduced the people into a trance of irresponsibility in which they joyfully surrendered all vital decisions affecting their destiny to the chiefs of the nazi hierarchy.

The triumph of the German National Socialists in 1933 dismayed and astonished people in the democratic countries, for it was a repudiation of popular government, a victory of totalitarian over liberal principles and ideals. The totalitarian ideal has been succinctly summarized as: "Everything for the State; nothing against the State; nothing outside the State." How profoundly this philosophy could transform every department of the national life the revolution in Germany soon demonstrated.

The National Socialist Party was declared to be the only official party; all others were dissolved and the formation of independent political groups was forbidden. As members of the Nazi Party had come to form a majority of the Reichstag and nazis were assigned to all important posts in the cabinet and the administration, it became clear that in Germany, as in Italy and Russia, one party, a well disciplined minority group, was to rule. This arbitrary centralizing tendency also led Hitler to annul the relics of local independence and particularism which the German states still preserved. The Reichsrat, a body somewhat resembling the United States Senate, to which each of the seventeen component German states sent delegates, was abolished, and administrative officers (*Statthalter*) were appointed to govern each state under orders from Berlin. Thus Germany became a unitary national despotism rather than a federal union.

The personal liberty of the citizens was severely curtailed. Nothing illustrates more sharply the divergence between the liberal democratic state and the totalitarian state than the question of individual rights.

Since the seventeenth century the idea had gained increasing acceptance in European society that the power of the government in the national states should be restricted in the interest of individual liberty. The totalitarian thinkers reversed this view and insisted that individual liberty must be restricted in the interest of the state. Under the nazi regime the deciding principle in law was: What benefits the German nation? People's courts were set up to try all offenses against the nation. The vigilance of the police, the secrecy of the trials, and the severity of the sentences created a reign of terror against which few dared to protest because criticism was so easily represented as hostility to the Party and the Leader. Those suspected of antisocial or of anti-nazi activities might be arrested at any time without warning and transported to a concentration camp, a danger to which all citizens were exposed once the traditional legal safeguards of personal liberty had been abrogated. The civilized world was slow to learn and slower to comprehend the inhuman cruelty and systematic extermination practiced in the work camps, and the details which later became available appeared incredible. Throughout the twelve years of nazi rule, and especially after the outbreak of World War II in 1939, victims who had incurred the ill will of the officials were worked, tortured, starved, poisoned, gassed, or strangled to death, not by the hundreds or by the thousands but by the *millions*. The total can never be accurately estimated.

The most tragic victims of this official terrorism were the 600,000 German Jews. Before 1933 the nazis had made antisemitism an article of their creed but after Hitler came to power the persecution became official. Dismissed from all government services, driven out of business and professional life, deprived of the status of citizens, thousands of Jewish families abandoned their homes and property and fled from Germany. Others, unable to flee, became impoverished, and a large proportion, including young children, were herded to the concentration camps. The motives which inspired the nazis thus to make antisemitism an official policy were a fusion of prejudice and calculation. They needed scapegoats on whom to lay the blame for anything that went wrong. They needed wealth and property to award to party members, and the Jews were active in German business and professional life. It was unwise to blame the French, the British, or even the Russian government too loudly for the defeat and impotence of Germany after 1918, but the nazis could vent their fury by vague references to a conspiracy of world Jewry to defame and destroy the German race. Although the Jews of Germany had contributed their share to the military effort of 1914–1918, Hitler popularized the fantasy that the collapse of 1918 had come because Jews and communists spread defeatism, that the German people had not been vanquished in a fair fight but had been "stabbed in the back." Such propaganda inevitably marked the Jews and communists out for reprisals as German nationalism revived.

Germany's President Paul von Hindenburg, with Chancellor Adolph Hitler and Herman Goering, Premier of Prussia, July, 1934.

Roll call of German troops (British Combine).

Nazi book burning in Germany during the thirties (Wide World Photos).

In fine, the nazis rose to power as a party of protest. They were anti-liberal, anti-clerical, anti-communist, anti-semite. They denounced the great banks and corporations which ruined the "little man" of business, the profiteers who had grown fat on war contracts and currency fluctuations, the alien immigrants who wished to intermarry and contaminate the strain of the "master race." When the nazis won control, the full fury of this terrible, irrational, manufactured hate fell most forcibly upon the groups that were most recognizable, defenseless, and profitable to plunder. But Jews were by no means the only victims. If figures were available, they would show how many million people of other faiths also died in the concentration camps of the nazis.

3. THE REVIVAL OF MILITARISM

The National Socialists abandoned the liberal theories of laissez-faire economy and free business enterprise, substituting instead an intricate system of economic nationalism. The ideal which was held out to the people was *Autarkie* or economic self-sufficiency. Germans were exhorted to increase production and to renounce or find substitutes for foreign commodities which could not be produced at home. All foreign trade was regulated by export and import licenses. Gold and currency could not be taken out of the country nor foreign currency purchased except through official channels. Within the Reich strict rules for the allotment of steel, coal, electric power, petroleum, and other essentials of industry brought all manufacturing trusts under state supervision. As in Soviet Russia, where a state planning commission was coordinating all aspects of economic life, so in Germany a board of economic experts strove to make the nation strong and self-sufficient so that it might survive the strains of peace or war. In 1936 the Nazi economists introduced a Four-Year Plan to regulate all economic life in the interests of *Autarkie*.

Unlike the Russian communists, however, the nazis did not nationalize the land, organize state farms, or collectivize the major industries. On the contrary, the number of small, privately managed farms was increased, and peasant families were encouraged to settle on them as hereditary occupants. There was much exaltation of the mystic affinity of "blood and soil" and the vital relation between the soul of a people and the land they ploughed. But the practical effect of the nazi agrarian decrees was to produce specific crops and tie the farmer to his task. By similar methods, the workers in the mines and factories were regimented and lost the privilege of striking or even of changing their occupation at will. The employer became the "leader" of the group he employed. His main responsibility was to fill the quota which the government economists demanded of him. In the first years of the nazi revolution the spur of national enthusiasm and the stimulus of rearmament brought a swift rise in business activity and production, and Hitler was given credit for a program that had conquered the depression.

There was some basis for this claim though it is questionable whether the improvement in output could justly be credited to Hitler or his preachments. Unemployment declined sharply in Germany after 1932. A vast program of public works, roads, fortifications, military equipment, and, to a lesser extent, of consumers' goods, created the appearance of unusual prosperity. But the national debt increased rapidly, the currency was maintained by rigid "pegging," and the armament outlay was underwritten by compulsory loans from the people. These obligatory contributions to nazi funds and charities, the rising cost of living, and the state regulation of wages left the average German no better off than before. The employers were assured a more adequate supply of man power, for no one was permitted to be idle and no workdays were now lost through strikes or lockouts. Like the workers, the employers found that they had forfeited their independence, they were heavily taxed, and they could not change their formulas or expand their plants without official approval. Some of the great financiers and industrialists, who had helped to finance Hitler's rise, now found that they had become the prisoners of his success.

The dominant impulse in Hitler's complex character was the will to power; he had no intention of becoming a tool of the German industrialists, the generals, or the nazi inner circle. Although he was prepared to reward the industrial magnates with government orders, subsidies, and monopolies, he was not genuinely solicitous for the material welfare or economic prospects of the German people or German business. His romantic and egocentric thoughts turned perpetually to new intrigues, to force and conquest, and to mastery over ever larger bodies of men for the intoxication which cajoling and coercing these millions brought him. Despite his talk of a Reich which would endure for a thousand years his triumphs all had a quality of the theatrical, they were intense but insubstantial, they left him under an added compulsion to surpass himself. These defects of his character were communicated to the regime. It was more predatory than constructive; it ruined its enemies to enrich its adherents; it was under a compulsion to expand, to feed on new converts, to transform neighbor states into prostrate provinces. The militant spirit of the National Socialist command did not evaporate when they reached the position of a governing clique in Germany; rather, from their new elevation they looked abroad for new areas and new adversaries.

From their first campaign speeches, the nazis had protested that Germany was denied adequate "living space." Maps showing the wide areas under the British, French, and Soviet Russian flags, with the relatively minute territory controlled by Germany as a contrast, formed a telling item in the arsenal of propaganda. Hitler made envious references to the minerals of the Urals, the wheat fields of the Ukraine, and the oil wells of the Caucasus. Such greed for possessions and supplies suggests the material advantages which the nazis anticipated from a war of conquest. The German factories after 1935 were purposely integrated for war production, the people were indoctrinated with the idea that Germany must take by force the areas and supplies to which the nation was entitled, and the army was organized for an aggressive strategy of lightning strokes or *Blitzkrieg*. Hermann Göring, second in command in the hierarchy and supervisor of the heavy industries, declared that the slogan of the German people must be "Guns before butter." The consequences of such preparations and such propaganda were a rapid rise in tension and the multiplication of international crises after 1935. "Germany," declared the British statesman Winston Churchill, "must soon either expand or explode."

The peace terms imposed by the victorious Allies after 1918 stripped the Reich of defenses and arms, and so long as these terms remained in force the Germans lacked the capacity to launch an aggressive war. The Rhineland, the area nearest the French frontier, was demilitarized; the navy was reduced to a few ships; the army was limited to 100,000 men; the manufacture or maintenance of military aircraft was forbidden. Although some feeble efforts were made to evade these limitations (German pilots trained in engineless gliders and a few bands of military-minded youths drilled in secret) Germany remained a third-class power in a military sense until after 1930. The fact that the nazis were then able, in less than ten years, to make Germany the most powerful armed nation in the world showed their will, energy, and gift for organization. But these virtues would have wrought no miracle by themselves. It was possible for Germany to regain the military hegemony of Europe in a decade because Germany was the leading industrial state of the Continent. The steps in the transformation from a peace to a war footing were surprisingly logical once the plan to rearm had been set in motion. The only grave danger was that neighbor nations most directly threatened might unite for a "preventive war" before rearmament was sufficiently advanced to safeguard the Reich.

The nazis had already violated the implicit terms of the Versailles treaty before they won power in 1933. Their Storm Troops, organized in military formations with weapons and uniforms, were a private army. In 1932 the wavering government of the Weimar Republic removed its ban against these units, a ban it had never seriously attempted to enforce. By the following years the Brown Shirt forces had expanded into a more or less organized militia of some 3,000,000 men. This army of the party was viewed with disfavor and apprehension by the officers of the small professional army who resisted suggestions that the two forces should be merged. In March, 1935, Hitler announced the reintroduction of compulsory military service, thus making all German youths of military age subject to regular army training.

At the same time (March, 1935) he denounced the Versailles treaty, declaring that the German people would no longer be bound by its humiliating limitations which had been imposed by force. Although the government leaders of Britain, France, and Italy took hurried counsel, none offered effective protest to the defiant action of the German chancellor. Hitler had calculated very astutely the differences of opinion between London and Paris and between Paris and Rome, and he did not fear that the powers would combine for joint action. To placate British alarm and alienate Britain from France, he agreed to a Naval Limitation Treaty (June, 1935) whereby German total naval tonnage was to be held to 35 per cent of that of the British Commonwealth. Eight months later, he made another sudden move in his program of rearmament. On March 7, 1936, he ordered German forces to reoccupy the demilitarized Rhineland. The French, British, and American forces which had kept a watch on the Rhine after World War I had been withdrawn since 1930, and once again Hitler's bold and defiant move to strengthen Germany for war met with no effective opposition.

With the formation of the Rome-Berlin Axis the following October the discomfiture of France was almost complete. If they acted in concert, Germany and Italy could attack the French Republic on two frontiers. Germany was rapidly constructing the most powerful air force in the world; her mechanized divisions were reported to possess unprecedented mobility and firing power; and Europe trembled once more before the threats of a war lord at Berlin. The outbreak of a civil war in Spain at the close of 1936 furnished an opportunity for German airmen and engineers to test out their new weapons by helping the insurgent forces. In 1938 the occupation of Austria was accomplished by German tank detachments which raced to Vienna in an unopposed invasion. The military balance had changed with almost bewildering rapidity and all the neighbors of the Reich were suddenly aware that Germany was armed and arrogant and that no fortifications could make a frontier invulnerable.

Once the Reich was rearmed and refortified, Hitler became more indifferent to foreign opinion. He was ready to risk war, he knew the British and French were desperately anxious to avoid it, and he used this knowledge to drive a ruthless bargain. In 1938, at Munich, he extorted cessions which ruined the Czechoslovakian Republic, ended the threat of the Czech armies, and brought the Czech armament factories and resources within his reach. The union of Italy and Germany in a full political and military alliance (May, 1939) gave Germany an ally for war, although that ally was the weakest of the great powers. More important was the negotiation of a commercial pact and a non-aggression treaty at Moscow which assured Russian neutrality (August 23, 1939). Hitler had now completed his political and military plans, and Germany was ready for a test of strength which, with or without war, might reverse the decision of World War I and make Germany supreme. One week after the conclusion of the Moscow accord World War II opened with the march of German armies into Poland (see p. 424).

26

THE SOVIET UNION: FORMATION

The Communists disdain to conceal their views and aims. They openly declare that their ends can be attained only by the forcible overthrow of all existing social conditions.

THE COMMUNIST MANIFESTO (1848)

1. WAR COMMUNISM, 1917–1921

"WE SHALL NOW proceed to construct the socialist order." With these casual words in the All-Russian Congress of Soviets on the morrow of the Bolshevik *coup d'état* of November 6–7, 1917, Lenin launched the Soviet state. A word may be in order at this point about this extraordinary man, for he possessed unusual qualities of leadership: intelligence, daring, ruthlessness, confidence in his judgment, and an unshakable faith in the justice and ultimate success of his cause. Vladimir Ilyich Ulyanov (1870–1924), better known under his revolutionary name Lenin, like most prominent socialist leaders, was not of proletarian origin. His father was a Tsarist official who had risen in the Table of Ranks to the position of a nobleman. Lenin was brought up in comfortable and very harmonious circumstances — at least until the age of sixteen, when his father died. In the following year an even starker tragedy struck the family; his elder brother Alexander was arrested for his part in an unsuccessful attempt on the life of Tsar Alexander III, tried, and executed. From this time dated Lenin's black, implacable hatred of Tsarism. After completing the study of law in St. Petersburg he became a convert to marxism and a professional revolutionary. For his revolutionary activity he was exiled to Siberia. Upon completion of his sentence in 1900, he went to western Europe where he lived, studied, wrote, and incessantly plotted — with the exception of a brief return to Russia during the Revolution of 1905 — until the March Revolution of 1917.

Upon his return to Russia in April, 1917, Lenin set out at once to seize power by capturing the Soviets — "All power to the Soviets!" (see Chapter 13, Section 2). After the first unsuccessful Bolshevik uprising in July, 1917, while hiding from the Provisional Government, he prepared a blue-

print for the foundation of the Soviet state.[1] Lenin had little confidence
in the readiness of the Russian people to accept socialism — at least, his
version of it — voluntarily. Therefore it would be necessary for the Bolsheviks to seize power by force. When this was accomplished, he expected
that there would follow a long transitional period, during which the working class — as represented by the "Bolshevik Party" and it, in turn, as directed by himself — would exercise a "dictatorship of the proletariat." All
means of production, that is, land, mines, and factories, as well as all means
of distribution, that is, business firms, transportation, and communications,
would be "socialized." During this "socialist" stage the principle "from
each according to his ability, to each according to his work" would prevail. Lenin firmly believed that the Russian Revolution was only the first
step toward the World Revolution which would result in the destruction
of the capitalist system and the rise of socialism everywhere. When that
hopeful moment arrived the dictatorship of the proletariat would become
superfluous and the state would "wither away." Then it would be possible to pass from *socialism* to *communism* — the final stage of man's development. When communism was established, then the noble principle
"from each according to his ability, to each according to his need" would
be applied.

Lenin did not expect this utopia to be realized overnight. When they
came to power in November, 1917, he and his associates faced the more
mundane and pressing problems of entrenching themselves and of governing a huge empire, disorganized by war and revolution. They tackled
these tasks with their characteristic energy and realism. The early state
of Bolshevik rule, which coincided with the Civil War (see Chapter 15,
Section 4), is known as the period of "War Communism" (1917–1921).
During this period there poured forth from the Bolshevik headquarters
at the Smolny Institute and (after the removal of the capital to Moscow
in March, 1918) in the Kremlin a torrent of decrees and directives, which
affected every phase of Russian life. The first step of the Bolsheviks was
to organize the Soviet government by creating the Soviet or Council of
People's Commissars (*Sovnarkom*). Lenin became its Chairman or
premier, Trotsky the Commissar of Foreign Affairs, and Stalin the Commissar of Nationalities. Its first ukase was the famous Peace Decree
(November 8, 1917). Peace, of course, could not be unilaterally *decreed*,
certainly not by a defeated nation, which Russia was in 1917, but had to be
negotiated and *concluded* with the Central Powers. This was not accomplished until March, 1918, by the disastrous Peace of Brest-Litovsk. When
announced, however, the Peace Decree served the purpose of impressing
on the war-weary Russian masses that the Bolsheviks were serious about
carrying out Lenin's program of "Peace, Land, and Bread."

The other portions of the program were implemented in a similarly

---

[1] It was later published in pamphlet form under the title *State and Revolution.*

demagogic way. The Land Decree, issued also on November 8, 1917, authorized the peasants to seize the land immediately and partition it without compensation to the landowners. In February, 1918, when the government felt more secure in power, the Land Decree was supplemented with one nationalizing the land, although no attempt was made to implement this decree for the moment. Later, during the Civil War the government imposed on the peasants a food levy. They were ordered to surrender their entire food surplus. When they proved reluctant to do it troops were sent into the villages to collect food forcibly. In November, 1917, the government decreed workers' control of factories, but in June, 1918, factories were nationalized. An eight-hour day was decreed, but later compulsory labor service was instituted. Strikes were forbidden and labor unions brought under Bolshevik control.

The government attempted to fix prices and wages but without success because a runaway inflation reduced the currency to worthlessness. Complete social security was promised to the workers but it was a long time before this promise could be carried out. Other decrees nationalized banks, privately owned railroads, and the merchant marine. The stock market was closed, and transactions in stocks and bonds as well as payment of interest and dividends were forbidden. Inheritance was abolished. The national debt, both domestic and foreign, was repudiated. The government assumed a monopoly of foreign trade. All titles and the coveted bureaucratic and military ranks were abolished. Army officers became simply "commanders." Civil and criminal courts were replaced with "people's courts," designed to administer "class justice." What was left of the old police force was disbanded, and a "workers' militia" took its place. New security police, the *Cheka* (see p. 169), were organized, and soon became more dreaded than the former Tsarist security police, the *Okhrana,* which had been disbanded by the Provisional Government. Church and state were completely separated. Religious freedom was proclaimed, but the exercise of this freedom was severely hampered by the nationalization of all church property, including objects used in religious services, such as chalices, vestments, etc. It is not surprising, therefore, that during the Civil War the churchmen invariably sided with the Whites against the "godless" Bolsheviks. In retaliation, the government brutally persecuted them. Martyrs among the clergy were legion. Registry of births, deaths, and marriages became the exclusive function of the state. Men and women were declared equal. Divorce was legalized, and divorce proceedings made simple and inexpensive. On February 7, 1918, the Gregorian calendar used in the west replaced the Julian calendar, which had fallen thirteen days behind. The alphabet was simplified.

To give a veneer of legality to these revolutionary changes the Bolshevik government had them confirmed by the All-Russian Congress of Soviets. This loose body, elected in an irregular fashion, was packed with Bolsheviks, who manipulated it as they pleased. There remained the question of what to do about the Constituent Assembly. Convocation of a constituent assembly had been the dream of generations of Russian revolutionaries. Just before its downfall, the Provisional Government set November 25, 1917, as the date for elections to the Constituent Assembly. Before coming to power the Bolsheviks had been the loudest in demanding its convocation, but once in power they lost interest in it, as it might dispute their authority. Nevertheless, feeling still uncertain of their hold on power, they felt impelled to go ahead with the elections. Lenin regarded democracy as a particularly pernicious bourgeois subterfuge, designed to give the masses the illusion of controlling political power, while they were in reality controlled and exploited by economic power, safe in the hands of the capitalists. But he was prepared to tolerate a modest amount of democratic window-dressing, provided it did not disturb the Bolshevik monopoly of power. The results of the elections, however, indicated that the Constituent Assembly would not be a willing tool of the Bolsheviks. The Bolshevik Party had scored only 25 per cent of the votes while its hated rival, the Social Revolutionary Party, gained 58 per cent. This doomed the Constituent Assembly. There was room for other parties in Russia, Lenin once remarked, "only in jail." When the Constituent Assembly met on January 18, 1918, the Bolshevik delegates introduced a resolution suggesting that the Assembly hand over its mandate to the Congress of Soviets and disband. When the resolution was voted down, the Constituent Assembly was dissolved and dispersed by force. That ended the only freely elected and fully representative body Russia ever had, and with its disappearance went the last legal opposition to the Bolshevik monopoly of power.

To cover the nakedness of their dictatorship with a cloak of legality the Bolsheviks adopted in July, 1918, a constitution. It was prefaced with a "Declaration of the Rights of the Toiling and Exploited Peoples" and formally established the "Russian Socialist Federated Soviet Republic" (R.S.F.S.R.). It codified the existing system of soviets — local, cantonal, district, provincial, regional, and the All-Russian Congress of Soviets — into the legal structure of the state. The All-Russian Congress of Soviets, which was the supreme legislative body of the state, elected an All-Russian Central Executive Committee, and it in turn appointed the Council of People's Commissars, which was the supreme executive organ of the state. The constitution did not mention the Communist Party,[2] which nevertheless constituted the real state. Its organization roughly paralleled the organization of the Soviet state. The top personnel of the state and the party was largely identical. Analogous to the All-Russian Congress of Soviets were the Communist Party Congresses. They elected a Central Committee which remained in permanent session. The party bureaucracy consisted of a Secretariat and an Organization Bureau (*Orgbureau*). The

[2] The Bolshevik Party officially adopted the name "Russian Communist Party (Bolshevik)" at its Seventh Congress in 1918.

party hierarchy was topped off with the Political Bureau (*Politbureau*) consisting usually of seven top Bolsheviks. Before 1917 the Bolshevik Party was a small, well-disciplined group of professional revolutionaries. After 1917 Lenin, fearing the influx of opportunists and careerists into the party, tried to maintain its monolithic nature by insisting on stringent conditions of admission. These conditions called for sponsorship of a candidate by accredited members of the party and a long probationary period. Sponsorship was not easily secured because if the candidate proved unworthy this reflected on the sponsors. To weed out the weak and unworthy the party was periodically purged. As a result, the Communist Party, unlike the Nazi Party in Germany and the Fascist Party in Italy, never became a mass party but always remained a small elite group of dedicated communists. It averaged only from 1 to 2 per cent of the population of Soviet Russia. This small elite effectively controlled the vast Soviet empire. As Stalin put it: "Not one important political organizational question in our state institution is decided without the direction of the Central Committee of the Party."

2. THE NEW ECONOMIC POLICY

By the end of 1920 the Civil War in European Russia was over. It had been more destructive than the World War, which it followed, for it affected the whole territory of the Russian empire. A large number of cities lay in rubble and villages in ashes. Industry and agriculture were disorganized and at a virtual standstill. The population was decimated and starving. When the first census after the war was taken in 1926 it was found that the population numbered only 147,000,000. According to the normal rate of growth, it should have been 175,000,000. That left a deficiency of 28,000,000 people. War losses, sickness, starvation, flight into exile, and breakup of families accounted for this frightful toll. The Bolsheviks had won the Civil War, but there was general disaffection in the country.

On March 1, 1921, the sailors at the Baltic naval base of Kronstadt mutinied and demanded that the government ease the harsh policies of War Communism, permit free election of the Soviets, and restore civil rights. A mutiny of the Cossacks, the hated servants of the old regime, or of the conservative Moslem tribes in eastern Russia, the Caucasus, or Central Asia would not have surprised the Bolsheviks, but the sailors had been the shock troops of the revolution, the most loyal of the loyal, the bravest of the brave. In communist mythology they held a place equivalent to crusaders in Christian lore. The mutiny of the Kronstadt sailors was suppressed by force but the Bolsheviks were deeply troubled. A change of policy was imperative.

At the Tenth Communist Party Congress in Moscow in March, 1921,

Lenin announced a "New Economic Policy" (NEP), which ushered in a new period in Soviet history, lasting until 1928. There were to be no political concessions, such as demanded by the Kronstadt sailors, but in the realm of economics, the Bolsheviks having failed "to take the citadel of capitalism by a frontal attack," there was to be "an organized retreat." The government would retain the control of the "commanding heights" of the economy, that is, of heavy industry, big business, banks, foreign trade, etc., but in small industry and enterprises a limited amount of private enterprise would be permitted. In agriculture the policy of forced food levies was to be discontinued. The peasants were to pay a tax in kind, but they were to be free to dispose of any surplus they might have in an open market at prices subject only to the law of demand and supply. This change of policy was followed in 1924 by a fiscal reform which replaced the worthless, inflated currency with a new, gold-based issue, which remained stable. NEP was hailed abroad as a return to saner economic methods and irrefutable proof that communist economic methods could not work. This view, events were to prove, showed wishful thinking. NEP was only a partial and *temporary* return to capitalist methods of production to get the wheels of Russian economy moving again — a case of *reculer pour mieux sauter,* of stepping back in order to leap forward better.

Before the results of NEP were felt, however, the accumulated effects of war, revolution, and Bolshevik mismanagement resulted in widespread famine, notably in the Volga region. The Soviet government was at first reluctant to admit its inability to cope with the situation and declined offers of foreign relief agencies to bring aid to the stricken area. But in 1922 the situation reached catastrophic proportions and the government permitted Herbert Hoover and others to organize relief for the starving population of the Volga region, which undoubtedly saved millions of Russian lives. The remarkable recuperative powers of Russia had long been observed by students of Russian affairs. Once again Russia astounded the world with the speed of her recovery. Not only was the famine brought under control, but stimulated by the "predatory profit motive" agriculture and industry rapidly revived. In the villages there emerged a class of prosperous peasants (*kulaks*) and in the cities a class of thriving businessmen (*Nepmen*) — prosperous and thriving, at least, by Russian standards. By the end of the NEP period prewar levels of production had been more or less regained.

During the NEP period the "Union of Socialist Soviet Republics" (U.S.S.R.) was established. By the end of the Civil War the Soviet government had recovered the Ukraine, White Russia, and the Transcaucasian republics. To accommodate these non-Russian peoples it was decided not to annex them to the Russian Socialist Federated Soviet Republic but to form a union of four republics. In January, 1924, a Union Constitution was adopted which hailed the establishment of U.S.S.R. as a "decisive step" toward the formation of a "World Soviet Socialist Republic." The Union Constitution followed closely the constitution of R.S.F.S.R. In theory it allowed considerable autonomy to the constituent republics, but in practice they were firmly tied to Moscow by the Communist Party.

In social and cultural matters the NEP period was one of wild experimentation. The Russian Revolution was not limited to politics and economics alone, but extended to manners and morals as well. There was a widespread revolt, in the cities at least, against accepted standards of "bourgeois morality." The facility of divorce has already been noted. Abortions were legalized and performed free of charge in government clinics. In the revolt against the past, many Russians rejected wholesale all of Russian cultural and national heritage. "History began in 1917," declared an ardent young Bolshevik. Revered figures of the Russian past were dragged in the mud. Russian history was reinterpreted in accordance with the precepts of dialectical materialism. The impressive Russian artistic achievement of the pre-revolutionary era was frequently dismissed as mere "bourgeois" art. Brave but not especially successful attempts were made to create a distinct "proletarian" art. In education there was a revolt against discipline and traditional subjects and experimentation along lines suggested by the American educational philosopher John Dewey. The quality of higher education generally suffered during this period, but primary education was greatly expanded and improved.

During the last decades of the old regime an earnest effort had been made, not so much by the government as by the Zemstvo assemblies and private organizations, to reduce illiteracy. Still, in 1917 about 60 per cent of the Russian people were illiterate. An illiterate and ignorant peasant was virtually impervious to propaganda. The Bolsheviks were determined to correct this situation, both because they were sincere believers in "enlightenment" and because they wanted to control the minds of the Russian people. Education and indoctrination were in fact virtually synonymous to them. Despite the lack of teachers and school facilities, they energetically tackled the problem of illiteracy and claimed to have reduced it by 1939 to 19 per cent. The minority peoples were encouraged to develop their national cultures, as a reaction to the former policy of Russification. In the case of some primitive Siberian tribes who had no literary culture, Soviet linguists invented alphabets and devised grammars for them. The Bolsheviks also encouraged popular adult education. Libraries, museums, art galleries were opened in every large community. When radio and motion pictures were developed, the Bolsheviks eagerly seized on these media of mass communication for purposes of propaganda and enlightenment.

In the matter of criticism and freedom of expression the policy of the Soviet government was an ambivalent one. It was well aware of the stultifying effect of censorship under the Imperial government. Yet it was determined to control the thought of the Soviet citizens. To solve this dilemma the government encouraged what it called "self-criticism," that is criticism of concrete and practical shortcomings of Soviet life. But the basic philosophy of the regime (marxism), its basic foreign and domestic policies, and its highest personalities were rigorously exempt from all criticism. Within these limits the Soviet artist during the NEP period was given a fair degree of freedom to experiment and criticize. Some writers, such as the Ukrainian humorist Zoschenko, ventured to criticize life under the Soviets with a poignancy reminiscent of Gogol's satires of life under the Tsars. The iconoclastic mood and experimentation in Russian intellectual life during the NEP period attracted and impressed avant-garde artists from the west. "I have seen the future — and it works," reported the American journalist and writer, Lincoln Steffens, after a visit to Soviet Russia.

3. THE STRUGGLE FOR LENIN'S SUCCESSION

In 1922 Lenin suffered a paralytic stroke and was forced to limit his participation in party and government activities. Even before his death in January, 1924, the struggle for his succession began. Like most tyrannies, the Bolshevik dictatorship suffered from the lack of any orderly way to select the successor to the dictator. The struggle partook of the nature of a backstage, interparty fight, reminiscent of the confused and unscrupulous contests of the Italian *condottieri* in the Renaissance period. Alliances and counter-alliances were made. The ground on which the struggle was waged continuously shifted from the Politbureau, to the Central Committee, to Party Congresses, and back again. The struggle soon narrowed to two principal contestants: Trotsky and Stalin. Leon Davidovich Bronstein (1879–1940), better known under his revolutionary name Trotsky, was a brilliant and cosmopolitan intellectual and flamboyant orator of middle-class Jewish origin. He had come to public attention for the first time during the Revolution of 1905. In the Revolution of 1917 he played a role second only to that of Lenin. Joseph Vissarionovich Djugashvili (1879–1953), better known under his revolutionary name Stalin, was a man of humble Georgian origin. Originally he was destined for an ecclesiastical career, but after his expulsion from an Orthodox seminary he became a professional revolutionary. He repeatedly suffered imprisonment and exile in Siberia. An undistinguished orator, with a grating foreign accent,[3] he was a good organizer and bold man of action. In the Revolution of 1917 he played an important but unspectacular part. In 1922 he was appointed to the then obscure post of Secretary General of the Communist Party, which he built up into the most important one in Russia by using his power of appointment to fill the key party and

[3] The Georgians of the Caucasus region are unrelated ethnically or linguistically to the Russians.

government posts with his followers. At the time of the death of Lenin, although virtually unknown abroad, Stalin was the most influential man in Russia.

The contestants raised several issues, but the one which overshadowed them all was the question of "permanent revolution" versus "socialism in one country." Trotsky insisted that socialism in Russia could not be safe as long as Russia remained surrounded with hostile capitalist countries. The first task of the Russian communists, therefore, was to "broaden the base of socialism," that is, to foment revolutions abroad. Stalin, on the other hand, insisted that it was possible to build socialism in Russia alone, and that in view of the failure of the revolutionary movement abroad this was the task to which the Russian communists should first address themselves. The quarrel between Trotsky and Stalin was thus over tactics or priorities rather than over goals. Stalin by no means renounced world revolution as an ultimate goal. At the Fourteenth Party Congress in 1925 Stalin's thesis, supported by Zinoviev and Kamenev, carried the day. However, Zinoviev and Kamenev then joined hands with Trotsky to stop Stalin. By opposing what was accepted party policy, Trotsky, Zinoviev, and Kamenev committed a breach of party discipline — a very serious offense in Bolshevik eyes. They were expelled from the party. Zinoviev and Kamenev recanted and were eventually readmitted to the party. But Trotsky persisted in his opposition to Stalin's policy, and in 1929 he was expelled from the Soviet Union.[4] Although sporadic opposition to Stalin continued for some time, he was in the main free to turn to the task of implementing his policy of building socialism in Russia alone.

[4] Trotsky ultimately found refuge in Mexico. From there he continued his campaign against Stalin, whom he accused of "betraying" the revolution. He was assassinated in 1940. The assassin denied at his trial that he was a Soviet agent. But upon his release from prison in 1960, he promptly headed for Communist Czechoslovakia.

27

THE SOVIET UNION: GROWTH OF POWER

Communism is Soviet power plus electrification.

LENIN

1. PLANNING THE ECONOMY

THE ATTAINMENT of prewar levels of industrial production by 1927, gratifying though it was to the Russians, meant that Soviet Russia had fallen
far behind the capitalist industrial nations, for these had not stood still
since 1914 but had greatly broadened their industrial base. If Soviet
Russia wanted to survive in a hostile capitalist world, she had to catch
up to and surpass the capitalist countries in industrial production. This
was the rationale of the forced industrialization of Soviet Russia, which
began in 1928 and has — except for the interruption of World War II —
continued ever since.

Economic planning was not wholly new in Soviet Russia. As early as
1920 a State Planning Commission (*Gosplan*) had been created. It
"planned" the Soviet economy throughout the NEP period by means of
annual "control figures." What was new, however, was the projected rate
and range of industrial expansion. On October 1, 1928, the Soviet government put in operation a plan which called for an increase in industrial
production of 236 per cent at the cost of about $32,500,000,000. The plan,
which was to be completed in the incredibly short space of time of five
years, was known as the Five-Year Plan. During the course of its execution the government decided to speed it up, and in 1932 announced that
the First Five-Year Plan had been completed in four and one-quarter
years. The First Five-Year Plan was immediately succeeded by the
Second Five-Year Plan (1933–1937), and in turn by the Third Five-Year
Plan (1938–1942), which was still uncompleted when the German armies
invaded Russia in June, 1941. After the war economic planning was immediately resumed with the Fourth Five-Year Plan (1946–1950).

Industrialization has three basic requisites: raw materials, labor, and
capital. The Soviet Union is probably the most richly endowed country
on earth in natural resources. Soviet surveyors and scientists calculated
that Russia possessed one-fifth of the world's coal deposits, one-fourth of

the timber lands, one-half the reserves of oil and iron ore, and a plentiful supply of various minerals which are indispensable to modern industry. Soviet Russia had also an abundant pool of labor, although she was deficient in skilled labor, engineers, scientists, and technicians. A large portion of more than one million Russians who had fled abroad during the Revolution were professional and skilled men. Since then the deficiency had been only partially made up by training new cadres of professional and skilled personnel. The Soviet government therefore had to resort to the assistance of foreign specialists. In response to offers of generous pay a crowd of German, American, British, French, and other engineers and technicians flocked to Russia to assist in building up her industries.

Soviet Russia was quite deficient in capital. Unlike the Imperial government, the Soviet government could not borrow capital abroad, since the repudiation of the Tsarist debts had ruined Russia's credit. But even if foreign loans could have been secured they would inevitably have had strings attached, and the Soviet government wished to be free of obligations to the capitalist countries. Soviet leaders therefore decided that Russia had to pull herself up by her own bootstraps. They hoped to finance industrialization by a variety of methods. The obvious methods, taxation and floating of internal loans, were both used, but fell short of producing enough capital.

Great effort was made to increase the productivity of the workers in the hope of reinvesting the profits thus made into industrial expansion. The productivity of Russian workers had always been low in comparison with that of western workers. To remedy this situation the government used the old carrot-and-stick method of giving generous rewards for success and stern punishment for failure. The rewards were of both a psychological and a material nature. Successful workers were awarded medals and titles, such as "Hero of Socialist Labor," and wages paid for skilled work were, by Russian standards, high. The wage differential in Russia had always been rather wide, and during the Five-Year Plans the difference in wages for skilled work and unskilled work became steadily wider until it exceeded considerably that prevailing in the western countries. Extra food, clothing, and housing — at pegged prices — were the emoluments of superior skill. Acquisition of skills was encouraged and facilitated by organization of night schools, factory instruction, free lectures, and reading rooms. Introduction of piecework and speedup methods (*Stakhanovism*) — both frowned upon by western labor leaders as particularly vicious methods of exploiting laborers — offered possibilities of earning higher wages. On the other hand, labor discipline was tightened up. The authority of managers and foremen was strengthened, and labor unions became less organizations to protect the workers than to discipline them. Absenteeism, negligence ("wrecking"), and willful negligence ("sabotage") could be punished by sentences up to twenty years at hard labor, and theft or destruction of state property by death.

The Five-Year Plans laid emphasis on the development of heavy industry to produce fuels and power (coal, oil, electricity) and production goods (machines, tractors, trucks, etc.) Light industries designed to produce consumer goods were neglected and production of consumer goods was curtailed in order to save on raw materials and labor. Officially, only the natural increment in the production of consumers' goods after 1928 was to be diverted into industrial expansion. Theoretically, therefore, no lowering of living standards would result; they would merely remain static. Actually, however, production of consumers' goods, notably during the First Five-Year Plan, was cut to a spartan minimum, resulting in a drastic lowering of living standards. Food and clothing were extremely scarce and rationed until 1935. Housing and household goods were also in extremely short supply. The fortitude with which the Soviet people endured these hardships is a testimony to their extraordinary stamina.

While the Soviet government found ways of financing industrial expansion without resort to foreign loans, it still needed foreign currencies with which to pay the army of foreign specialists in Russia and to purchase a multitude of expensive machinery ("machines to produce machines"), precision tools, as well as certain rare raw materials abroad. To do this the Soviet government was obliged to increase exports. Traditionally, Russia had exported agricultural products and industrial raw materials. To increase the export of these items, however, presented difficulties since Russia now needed industrial raw materials herself and she had no appreciable surplus of agricultural products for export. The large surpluses of grain, which Russia exported before 1914, were produced on the great estates. With the partition of the estates among the peasants in 1917–1918 the surpluses declined, even though agricultural production in 1927 had attained substantially the same level as in 1913. The explanation of this paradox lay partly in the increase in population and partly in the psychology of the Russian peasants. Centuries of ruthless exploitation had disinclined the Russian peasants to produce large surpluses for sale. Long and bitter experience had taught them that it did not pay, because any sign of affluence had always been an invitation to the tax-collector to come and rob them of any wealth they might accumulate above a subsistence level. Their experience under the Soviets, notably during the forced food levies in 1918–1921, did little to dispel this pessimistic belief. They aimed, therefore, at self-sufficiency. They produced only enough food to feed themselves and a small surplus, from the sale of which they financed the purchase of the modest necessities which they could not produce themselves (salt, sugar, kerosene, etc.). In years of good crops they ate better, but they had little incentive to accumulate wealth. Even the much-abused kulak was, by any other than Russian standards, a very modest fellow; it has been estimated that the value of the possessions, other than land, of the average kulak amounted to only about $400.

RELATIVE POPULATION OF SEVEN GREAT POWERS, 1938

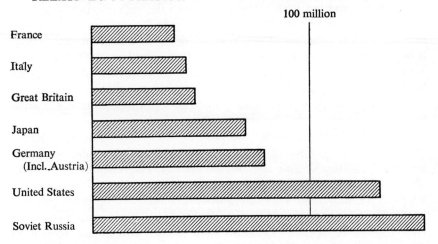

100 million

France

Italy

Great Britain

Japan

Germany
(Incl. Austria)

United States

Soviet Russia

The Bolsheviks had always regarded small-scale, private farming only as a temporary expedient, both because it was inefficient and because it was "capitalistic." They had experimented — not too successfully — with large, state-operated farms (*sovkhoz*). The necessity to increase exports moved them to carry out their long-deferred intention to socialize agriculture. In 1928 the Soviet government took steps to oblige the peasants to pool their land, tools, and livestock into larger units, the collective farms (*kolkhoz*), which could be operated by modern, mechanical methods. The purpose of the collectivization of agriculture, which was an integral part of the First Five-Year Plan, was to socialize ownership of land and to raise the amount of exportable surpluses of grain. The Plan envisaged collectivization of only 20 per cent of the farms but the eager commissars in charge of the operation exceeded this goal by far. The bewildered and angry peasants, especially in the fertile Ukraine, resisted collectivization both actively and passively. It was often necessary to send troops into the villages to make the peasants comply with the government orders. Thousands, perhaps millions, of peasants were deported into penal labor camps operated by the police all over the Soviet empire. In 1930, upon alarming news that the peasants were slaughtering their livestock and destroying their seed grain, Stalin called a temporary halt to the orgy of collectivization with a famous article, "Dizzy with Success." However, after some overeager commissars were shot as scapegoats, the drive was resumed and by 1938 95 per cent of the farms were collectivized. In 1936 the government, already certain of success, made a small concession to the individualism of the peasants: each family was permitted to retain about half an acre to raise vegetables, poultry, and a few animals for its own use.

While a severe famine raged in 1931–1932 in the Ukraine, the Soviet government exported grain. Moreover, since the collectivization of agriculture coincided with the World Depression and a world slump in prices of farm products, the Soviet government "dumped" the grain, that is, sold it below the prices on the world market. This caused much ill will toward Soviet Russia abroad and incredible hardships at home. But the Soviet leaders were determined to carry out their economic plans at all costs.

The Five-Year Plans were accompanied by a frenzied propaganda drive to make them succeed. The press, radio, and motion pictures were harnessed to the task of "selling" the plans to the public. Public buildings and thoroughfares were covered with posters, streamers, and bandroles bearing suggestive slogans and clichés, such as "Five-in-Four" (i.e., fulfill the Five-Year Plan in four years). Like whirling dervishes sent out to whip up the fanaticism of Moslem troops, communist "agitators" set out for the factories and villages to urge the workers and peasants to produce with "Bolshevik tempo." Factories were pressed to compete with each other in production, and production figures were tabulated and displayed like results of sports events. By use of military metaphors (e.g., industrial "front," agricultural "front") the communist propagandists created an atmosphere of emergency, as in war.

After the completion of each of the Five-Year Plans the Soviet government claimed that they had been a complete success, in fact that their goals had been "over-fulfilled." According to Soviet statistics, gross industrial production (measured in rubles at their value in 1927–1928) rose from 15,700,000,000 in 1927 to 95,500,000,000 in 1937 and 185,000,000,000 in 1942. The showpieces of this achievement, proudly exhibited to foreign visitors, were the *Dnieprostroy* (the largest dam and hydroelectric plant in Europe), a large tractor factory at Stalingrad, automobile plants at Moscow and Gorky (Nizhny Novgorod), a new steel town, Magnitogorsk (the "Soviet Pittsburgh") in the Urals, as well as thousands of lesser plants. Foreign economists, after subjecting the Soviet statistics to careful scrutiny (no other statistics were available), disagreed on the extent of the Soviet industrial expansion. Some critics also pointed out that the cost of the Soviet products was exorbitant and the quality extremely shoddy. The Soviet government, recognizing that cost was high and that quality had often been sacrificed for the sake of quantity, sought to remedy the situation by increasing the productivity of labor and (in the Third Five-Year Plan) devising qualitative as well as quantitative norms. In agricultural production Soviet statistics were less boastful and there seems to be little doubt that achievement fell short of the goals set. Although Soviet statistics were silent on the cost of industrialization and collectivization in human suffering, neutral observers estimated that from 1928 to 1941 probably 10,000,000 Soviet citizens died from famine, forced labor, imprisonment, or execution. No one, of course, ventured to estimate the heartbreaks and misery of those citizens who lived through

Russia's "Iron Age." Whatever the material and human cost, however, few doubted that Russia, largely an agrarian country in 1917, had become by 1941 a respectable industrial power, second only to the United States.

2. TRANSFORMATION OF THE SOVIET SOCIETY

The industrialization and collectivization of Soviet Russia was a revolution scarcely less violent and dramatic than the Revolution of 1917. Millions of people were uprooted and forced to change their way of life; there was a vast migration of people from the rural districts to the cities and from western to eastern Russia, where many of the new industrial plants had developed. The urban population increased from 26,000,000 in 1926 to 55,000,000 in 1939. In 1926, 77.5 per cent of the population was engaged in agriculture and 10 per cent in industry. By 1939 agricultural population had declined to 55 per cent and industrial population had risen to 25 per cent. Such an upheaval, combined with growing international tension in the 1930's, provoked much unrest even in the ranks of the Communist Party. In 1934 Sergei M. Kirov, a close associate of Stalin and party boss of Leningrad, was assassinated by a party member. Stalin, who was already showing signs of paranoia — illusions of grandeur and persecution mania — then unleashed a savage purge of the party and government apparatus, which rolled on relentlessly until 1939. High or humble, revered companions of Lenin or lowly party hacks, high government officials and army officers or lowly clerks and subalterns, no one was safe from summary arrest and imprisonment by NKVD agents.[1] Most of the victims of the purge were tried in secret and sentenced to varying terms of penal labor or quietly executed.

Three carefully staged public trials of the "Old Bolsheviks" were held to which foreign diplomats and newspapermen were admitted. These were astounded to hear the accused eagerly "confess" to conspiracy with foreign powers, plots against Stalin, and other heinous crimes. In 1936 the so-called "Left Deviation" (i.e., opposition), including Zinoviev and Kamenev, who had had the bad judgment to side with Trotsky against Stalin in the struggle for Lenin's succession, were tried and executed. In 1937 another batch of Old Bolsheviks was tried and shot. In 1938 the so-called "Right Deviation," including Bukharin and Rykov, who had opposed Stalin's harsh policy toward the peasants, were tried and executed. In 1937 the world was startled by the announcement that Marshal Michael N. Tukhachevsky and seven high officers of the Red Army had been tried by a secret military tribunal on charges of espionage and high treason and forthwith shot. The purge ended, ironically, by "purging the purgers,"

---

[1] In 1924 the Cheka was dissolved and its functions transferred to the GPU, which in turn became the OGPU, NKVD, MVD, and MGB. But *plus ça change plus c'est la même chose* — the more it changed the more it remained the same thing.

namely the police force; two top policemen, the sinister Henry Yagoda and the unspeakable Nicholas Yezhov, were tried and "liquidated."

The motives of the great purge are still obscure but the results of it became clear at once. Stalin emerged as a despot and complete master of Russia, infinitely stronger than Lenin or any of the Tsars after Peter the Great. Lenin had been treated with deference but not servility. Stalin became an object of a "cult of personality," a center of fawning public adulation such as had not been seen in the civilized world since the days of Byzantium. All of Russia was covered with statues and pictures of the "Leader" (Vozhd), often lit up day and night, like ikons of old.

Ironically, at this time the Leader chose to grant Russia a more democratic constitution. In 1936 the Union Constitution was replaced with a new "Stalinian" constitution which has provided the legal framework of the Soviet Union to this day. In introducing it Stalin affirmed that the exploiting classes in Soviet Russia had been abolished and that the Soviet society had become a classless one. Consequently the various restrictions existing in the earlier constitutions were unnecessary. Unlike the constitution of 1924, the new constitution made voting direct, equal, and by secret ballot. All citizens, male and female, over eighteen had the right to vote. Supreme power was vested in the Supreme Soviet, a bicameral legislature consisting of the Soviet of the Union and the Soviet of Nationalities, both elected for four years. The former chamber was to represent the people of the Soviet Union as a whole, and the latter chamber the constituent republics and autonomous nationality areas. The Supreme Soviet elected a Presidium, whose chairman was the formal head of the Soviet state, and appointed the Soviet or Council of People's Commissars (i.e., cabinet). The "Declaration of the Rights of the Toiling and Exploited Peoples" in the constitution of 1918 gave way to a statement of "Fundamental Rights and Duties of Citizens," which guaranteed the conventional civil rights (Art. 125) as well as "freedom of religious worship and of anti-religious propaganda" (Art. 124). The rights to own and to inherit private property were also guaranteed (Art. 10). The constituent republics, which were guaranteed the right of secession (Art. 17), hastened to change their constitutions to comport with the Stalinian constitution of the union.

On the face of it, the Stalinian constitution was a good, liberal constitution. Unfortunately, it remained largely window-dressing because of the one-party system and lack of judicial review. The Supreme Soviet met once a year for a brief session to vote en bloc, to approve by a show of hands decrees already issued by the Council of People's Commissars, and to hear eulogies of the Soviet leaders and the Communist Party. Unlike the constitution of 1918, the new constitution recognized explicitly the unique position of the Communist Party in Soviet Russia (Art. 126). On the other hand, the new constitution de-emphasized the earlier internationalism by dropping the reference to the "World Soviet Socialist Republic."

In public life the relative freedom which had existed in the early years of the Soviet regime gave way at this time to a robot-like discipline. Artists were not only deprived of all freedom of expression but were coerced into following the new official doctrine of "socialist realism," which turned the Russian arts, once full of vitality, into a bleak desert. Perhaps because of the dullness of the contemporary art, there was a revival of interest in the classical Russian art of the nineteenth century. The Russians rediscovered their past. St. Vladimir, St. Alexander Nevsky, Ivan the Terrible became heroes again, and Peter the Great was hailed as "the first Bolshevik." The minorities were not deprived of their cultural autonomy, but there was a new accent on the achievement of the Great Russians, reminiscent of the Great Russian chauvinism in Tsarist Russia. In education, discipline and traditional subjects were restored. The emphasis was on the sciences, that is, on the training of the scientists, engineers, and technicians needed in the technological development of Russia. In the armed forces ranks, medals, and resplendent uniforms were restored. Despite official affirmations that the Soviet society had become a "classless" one, its stratification into three distinct classes — workers, peasants, and the "intelligentsia" (i.e., managers, professionals, and white-collar workers) — became more pronounced. In manners and morals the earlier laxity gave way to a Puritan rectitude and Victorian prudery; abortion became illegal and divorce extremely difficult and there was a new emphasis on the importance of the family. Revolutionary fervor was giving way to a desire for stability. As World War II approached there were indications that the Russian Revolution had run its course, and that the Soviet people were settling down to more conventional ways.

3. THE SOVIET UNION AND WORLD AFFAIRS

The part played by the Soviet Union in world affairs in the inter-war period was relatively unimportant. Its military weakness in the 1920's and its concentration on internal development in the 1930's precluded an active Soviet part in international affairs. The Bolsheviks were originally ardent marxian internationalists who lived only for the day when the World Revolution would sweep the "imperialist-capitalist" powers away. They had an aversion to conventional diplomacy and were vastly ignorant of it — "What, are we going to have foreign relations?" Lenin exclaimed when he was first confronted with the problem of organizing a Soviet foreign office. Nevertheless, the Bolsheviks had fallen heir to a great empire and the Germans forcefully reminded them that it was still at war with the Central Powers. Therefore, the Soviet government, while awaiting the World Revolution, organized a People's Commissariat of Foreign Affairs (*Narkomindiel*) to deal with the problems arising out of the war. Upon taking charge of the Narkomindiel, Trotsky said, "I will issue some

revolutionary proclamations to the peoples and then close up the joint."
Diplomacy by revolutionary proclamations resulted in the fiasco of the
Peace of Brest-Litovsk, and Trotsky hastened to hand over the Narkomindiel to an old Tsarist professional diplomat but a dedicated Bolshevik,
George V. Chicherin (1918–1930), who in turn was succeeded by his
assistant, Maxim Litvinov (1930–1939). But the Bolsheviks had not given
up their belief in the imminence of the World Revolution, and to assist its
arrival they created (March, 1919) in Moscow the Third (Communist)
International (*Comintern*) under the leadership of an experienced revolutionary, Gregory Zinoviev.

The Narkomindiel and the Comintern often worked at cross-purposes.
While Chicherin sought to win recognition of the Soviet government and
normalize its relations with foreign governments, Zinoviev sought to overthrow them by fomenting internal revolutions against them. When this
discrepancy was pointed out to the Soviet government, it would invariably
disclaim any responsibility for the activities of the Comintern, insisting
that it was a private organization whose headquarters happened to be in
Moscow. But foreign governments were not easily taken in by this subterfuge and the activities of the Comintern interfered with those of the
Narkomindiel until Stalin's thesis of "socialism in one country" prevailed
and the activities of the Comintern were subordinated to the policies of
the Narkomindiel.

In 1922 the western powers invited the Soviet government to a conference at Genoa where they indicated their readiness to establish normal
relations with Soviet Russia, provided the Soviet government would
recognize the debts of the Tsarist and Provisional governments
($13,000,000,000). Chicherin expressed readiness to discuss the debts,
but submitted a counter-demand, a bill for the damages caused by the
Allied interventionist forces in Russia which exceeded the Allied claims
($60,000,000,000). Nothing came of the conference, although during its
course Chicherin slipped off with Walther Rathenau of Germany to
Rapallo and concluded a Soviet-German treaty of friendship. The Treaty
of Rapallo (April, 1922) was based on the community of interests which
existed between the two outcasts of the Versailles system. It became the
cornerstone of Soviet policy for the next ten years. The western powers
were disturbed by this "Unholy Alliance" between revisionist Germany
and Soviet Russia and sought to break it up, on one hand by recognizing
Soviet Russia (1924) and on the other by conciliating Germany (the
Locarno treaties, 1925). But, despite some fears on the part of the Soviet
leaders, Germany did not betray them. The Rapallo treaty was renewed
(1926) and the Soviet-German cooperation continued. It was most fruit-
ful in the economic and military fields. Once again, as before the war,
Russia became one of Germany's best customers. The Soviet government
permitted the Germans secretly to build airplanes and tanks (both forbidden to them under the Treaty of Versailles) in Russia and to train both

German and Soviet soldiers in the use of them. Soviet staff officers were trained in the German War College in Berlin. Ironically, one of its Soviet alumni, Marshal Zhukov, became the captor of Berlin in 1945.

The coming of the nazis to power in Germany in 1933 ended Soviet-German cooperation and Soviet Russia began to seek the friendship of the western nations. In 1934 she entered the League of Nations, which previously her spokesmen had scathingly denounced as "the Holy Alliance of the bourgeoisie for the suppression of the proletarian revolution." Now no more eloquent a spokesman of collective security and the sanctity of treaties under the League could be found than Maxim Litvinov. In 1935 the Soviet government concluded military alliances with France and her protégé, Czechoslovakia. Simultaneously, it moved to ease tensions with Japan by liquidating its interests in the Chinese Eastern Railway and pulling out of Manchuria. Foreign communists were instructed to form "popular fronts" with the "bourgeois" parties against fascist and nazi aggression.

A great deal of suspicion, however, still prevailed between Soviet Russia and France (see p. 264). The savage purge of the Soviet high command in 1937 inculcated doubts in the minds of the French generals of the value of Soviet Russia as a military ally. When the French and British prime ministers met with Hitler and Mussolini in the Munich Conference (September, 1938) to decide the fate of Czechoslovakia, Soviet Russia — a guarantor, like France, of Czechoslovak independence — was not invited to attend. Rightly or wrongly, this convinced the Soviet leaders that France and Britain were trying to divert the aggressiveness of Germany eastward, toward the Soviet Union. In a foreign policy statement to the Eighteenth Congress of the Communist Party in March, 1939, Stalin obliquely warned the western statesmen ("the warmongers who are accustomed to have others pull their chestnuts out of the fire for them") that the game of "let's you and him fight" could be played both ways. The dismissal of Litvinov, the eloquent advocate of collective security, and his replacement in May with Vyacheslav Molotov, a dour Old Bolshevik, was another indication that a change in Soviet policy was imminent.

When it became Poland's turn to be swallowed up by Hitler, both Germany and the western powers approached Soviet Russia. Germany sought a guarantee of Soviet neutrality during her imminent attack on Poland. In return she offered Russia a generous share of Poland and a free hand against the Baltic states. The western powers sought a Soviet guarantee of Poland against German attack, but in return were not prepared to offer any territory. In these circumstances the Soviet leaders decided to accept the German offer. On August 23, 1939, the deal between the supposedly implacable enemies was sealed. It astonished the world. Churchill found Soviet policy "a riddle wrapped in a mystery inside an enigma." As the western powers went to war with Germany ten days later, the Soviet leaders felt a deep satisfaction at having avoided war by diverting the aggressiveness of Nazi Germany westward. They expected the conflict in the west to be a long-drawn-out stalemate, as in World War I, at the end of which they might intervene and impose on the exhausted combatants a Soviet peace. Before long, however, they were to find out, as the western powers had found out after the Munich agreement, that the advantages of deals with Hitler were very ephemeral.

28

THE BORDERLAND OF GERMANY AND RUSSIA

We National Socialists . . . terminate the endless German drive to the south and west of Europe, and direct our gaze to the lands in the east.

ADOLF HITLER, *Mein Kampf*

1. CHARACTERISTICS OF EAST CENTRAL EUROPE

THE AREA OF EUROPE between Germany and Russia and between the Baltic and the Black seas — which will be called here East Central Europe —was a borderland not only in the political but also in the cultural sense. Germanic and Slavic, Roman Catholic, Greek Orthodox, and Protestant influences, all mingled in it. It had little cultural or political unity. The defeat of Russia and of the Central Powers in World War I permitted the rise of several new "national" states in the area: Finland, Estonia, Latvia, Lithuania, Poland, Czechoslovakia, Austria, Hungary, and Greater Rumania.

Seemingly, this triumph of national self-determination in the area of East Central Europe should have solved the vexing problems arising out of the discontent of the former subject nationalities and their ceaseless agitation for freedom. Actually, the dissolution of the Austrian and Russian multinational empires and the curtailment of Germany solved the nationalistic problems of the area only partially. As a result of the various peace settlements the total number of persons living under alien and oppressive governments greatly decreased, but the number of national minorities actually increased as the area became crisscrossed with new national boundaries. Over the centuries the ethnic composition of East Central Europe had become so mixed that it proved impossible to create in it perfectly homogeneous national states, except by the brutal expedient — used by Turkey and Greece, and Bulgaria and Greece after World War I — of forced exchanges of minorities. All of the states of East Central Europe were saddled with resentful national minorities, a source of internal weakness and external friction. The suggestion to solve the problem of national minorities by federalization was generally rejected for fear that federalism would lead to disintegration. Instead, the new states of East Central Europe invariably followed the French model and established centralized, bureaucratic governments.

Compared to the older states of Western Europe, the new states of East Central Europe were poor, underdeveloped, and predominantly agrarian nations. With the exception of Austria and the western (Czech) half of Czechoslovakia, they had few industries and urban centers. But the existing cities, especially the capital cities — such as Budapest, Vienna, Prague, Warsaw, and Bucharest — were lavishly modernized and very elegant. In most of the states of East Central Europe there survived a decayed nobility, which was often of foreign origin. The middle class, except in Austria and western Czechoslovakia, was small and very different in composition from the middle classes in Western Europe. Formally styled *intelligentsia,* as in Russia, it consisted almost exclusively of government officials and professional men. Businessmen were mostly Jews and foreigners, and both were excluded from national life. Xenophobia and anti-Semitism were universal in East Central Europe. As was true with the middle class the industrial working class in East Central Europe was relatively limited; the broad masses of East Central Europe were peasants, often illiterate, tradition-bound, and invariably poor. In every state of East Central Europe parliamentary democracy was introduced after World War I, although political, social, and economic conditions in the area did not favor the development of democracy. The new democratic regimes were assailed at once by undemocratic forces from the political Left and Right.

In the confused postwar years communism, with its utopian and demagogic appeals, gained a considerable hold over the masses in East Central Europe. In Hungary, it has been seen, the communists temporarily seized power. However, by opposing nationalism — in harmony with the internationalist program of world revolution pursued at the time by the Communist International — the communists committed a tactical error which led to their defeat. Conservative elements, by identifying themselves with nationalism, were able to mobilize public opinion and the communists were generally suppressed. Frequently non-communist left-wing and moderate parties, and parliamentary democracy itself, became victims of the "Red hunt." Among the non-communist groups, the largest following was commanded by agrarian parties which were strongly nationalistic. Although agrarian politicians liked to speak glowingly of international peasant solidarity and the necessity to organize a "Green International," these suggestions fell on deaf ears. But while nationalistic, the agrarian parties were — at least in the 1920's — democratic and socially progressive. Their great aims were land reform and peasant democracy. However, land reform, when attempted, almost invariably resulted in the decline of agricultural production and the rise of food prices, which provoked resentment on the part of the urban classes and discredited the agrarian program. The economic depression of the 1930's hit the agrarian countries of East Central Europe very hard, and parliamentary democracy generally gave way to authoritarian regimes of one type or another. The agrarian parties were either destroyed along with other parties or saved themselves by abandoning their political and social program and by emphasizing their nationalism. Hungary proved to be an early weather vane of the trend.

The tragedy of the agrarian parties was that they tended to regard land reform as a sort of panacea. Actually, the solution of the economic and social problems of the agrarian countries of East Central Europe did not lie in land reform alone but in a combination of reforms and policies: re-education of the tradition-bound peasantry, diversification and greater mechanization of agriculture, improvement of transportation and of food-processing methods (notably canning and refrigeration), cheaper credit, better balance between agriculture and industry, and better economic and political cooperation among the states of the area. These were manifestly Herculean tasks which could hardly be accomplished in the short space of time allowed the countries of East Central Europe between the world wars — unless by the drastic methods adopted for the same purpose in Soviet Russia.

2. FINLAND, ESTONIA, LATVIA, LITHUANIA

The best developed of the successor states of the Russian Empire was Finland. Prior to Russian occupation in 1809, Finland had been for centuries attached to Sweden. In 1917 many of the Finnish landowners and businessmen were still Swedish-speaking (about 10 per cent of the population). Thanks to many contacts with the Scandinavian countries and Germany, the Finns had attained generally higher social, economic, and cultural standards than the Russians.[1] Enjoying autonomy in the Russian Empire, including the right to elect a Diet, the Finns were also better acquainted with the parliamentary system than the Russians.

Although a fairly large country (147,000 square miles), Finland supported a small population (3,081,000). Only the southern portion of the country was suitable for agriculture, in which two-thirds of the population were engaged. The central part of the country was a region of innumerable lakes and forests, the latter providing the basis for Finland's principal industry — the timber industry. The far north was mostly an inhospitable tundra.

After a turbulent period of civil war and foreign intervention, Finland adopted a democratic constitution (1919) and carried out a land reform

---

[1] In more recent times the Finns have won the distinction of being probably the "best-read" nation in the world — if the fact that Finland publishes per capita more books annually, both titles and volumes, than any other country is an indication.

which resulted in partition of the estates of the gentry and the creation of some 100,000 new farms. Whereas before 1917 most Finnish peasants were tenants or farm laborers, after the completion of the land reform about one-third of the families in Finland owned land. Thanks to the intelligence, thrift, and industry of the Finnish farmers, and to the popularity of cooperatives, the partition of the estates did not bring a decline in the production of foodstuffs — as was often the case in other parts of East Central Europe. Altogether, Finland made heartening progress in the period between the world wars and gave proof that a small country — if left alone by the great powers — could solve its problems successfully.

The birth and development of Estonia, Latvia, and Lithuania on the southeast shore of the Baltic Sea had many analogies with those of Finland. They, too, arose out of the Russian Empire as a by-product of the Russian Revolution. With a combined area of 64,000 square miles, they were, even in the aggregate, smaller than Finland, but they were more populous (5,000,000). Like Finland, all of the Baltic states adopted democratic, republican constitutions and carried out radical land reforms. The expropriation and partition of the estates in the Baltic states was justified, not only on social but also on nationalistic grounds. The landowners belonged to alien groups (German in Estonia and Latvia, Polish in Lithuania) and had long been regarded as oppressors of the Baltic peoples. The trade of the Baltic states, previously directed to Russia, was reoriented to Germany and England. Their exports were mainly foodstuffs (especially dairy products) and lumber.

Democratic government, which throve in Finland, failed in the Baltic republics. Inexperience with the democratic process, the presence of large and hostile national minorities, and the threat of communism led to the downfall of democracy (in Lithuania in 1926 and in Latvia and Estonia in 1934) and the establishment of authoritarian regimes. Nevertheless, the Baltic republics made considerable social, economic, and cultural progress during their short existence as independent nations.

3. POLAND

To the southwest of the Baltic states lay Poland. In World War I Poland had been a battlefield, and four years of conflict left the country frightfully ravaged. The war was followed by two years of turbulence and military adventure which delayed the pressing tasks of reconstruction. The Poles, moreover, faced a complicated task of unification. Their country had been the prey, not of one but of three empires, the Russian, Austrian, and German. Three different legal codes, administrative bureaucracies, railroad and communication systems had to be welded into one. Not only external trade but the entire internal economy had to be reorganized.

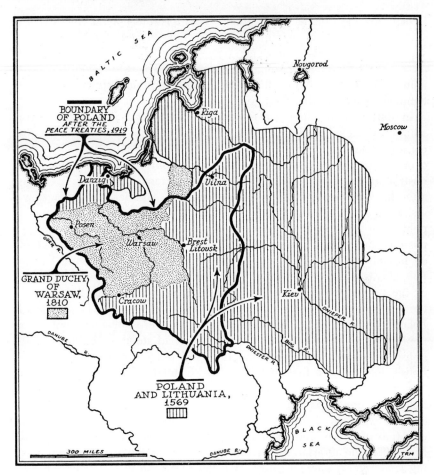

THE FLUID FRONTIERS OF POLAND

The struggle for liberation had produced two rival leaders: Roman Dmowski, who had worked for Polish independence in the framework of the Allied victory, and Joseph Pilsudski, who had fought for Polish freedom on the side of the Central Powers. In 1917, however, when the Central Powers were slow in implementing their promises to Poland, which they then occupied, Pilsudski broke with them and was imprisoned until the end of the war. A conflict between Dmowski and Pilsudski was averted by Ignacy Paderewski, who was not only a great pianist but also a skillful statesman. In January, 1919, Paderewski formed a cabinet of National Union in which Pilsudski assumed the functions of provisional president and Dmowski was appointed Poland's delegate to the Paris Peace Conference. While Dmowski negotiated with the Allies, Pilsudski, acting on the principle that possession is nine-tenths of the law, antici-pated their decisions by a series of military moves against Germany,

Czechoslovakia, Russia, and Lithuania. As a result, Poland emerged substantially larger than it might otherwise have become, with an area of some 150,000 square miles and a population of 26,473,000. However, almost one-third of the population consisted of resentful minorities (Germans, Ukrainians, White Russians, Lithuanians, and Jews) who contributed to the instability of Poland.

In 1921 Poland adopted a republican, democratic, and centralist constitution modeled on that of France. As in the eighteenth century, Polish constitutional life after the war was vitiated by factionalism (there were over eighty parties) intense party strife, conflicts of personalities, and obstructionism on the part of the abused national minorities. Ten days after his election, the first elected president, Gabriel Narutowicz, was assassinated. While the Polish politicians concentrated on the "game" of politics, pressing economic and social problems were neglected. Despite possession of considerable mineral wealth (coal and iron in Silesia and oil in Galicia) and of nascent industries in Warsaw, Lodz, and Poznań, Poland was still overwhelmingly an agrarian country. Sixty-eight per cent of the population was engaged in agriculture. As in the Baltic states, the land question was the central problem in Poland. The landowners in Poland, unlike those of the Baltic countries, were not aliens but Polish noblemen. In the nineteenth century they had stood at the head of the Polish nationalist movement and they still played an important role in Polish public life, a fact that made it difficult to expropriate their land. Nevertheless, in December, 1925, amidst much confusion and strife, the Polish parliament passed a land law providing for the distribution annually for ten years of some 500,000 acres of land to the peasants. But the adoption of a law and its implementation are two different things. In May, 1926, the agrarian leader, Vincent Witos, took office, intent on pressing land reform energetically. Two days later he was overthrown by a military *coup d'état* led by Marshal Pilsudski.

From then until his death in 1935 Pilsudski was Poland's military dictator. He held the office of Minister of War continuously and sometimes assumed the office of premier, but more often he ruled through his trusted associates, of whom President Mościcki was one. The constitution was amended and in 1935 replaced with a frankly authoritarian one. When Pilsudski became dictator in 1926 the land law was not repealed, but it was only halfheartedly enforced, and in 1939 the land question was still unresolved.

After Pilsudski's death in 1935 no single successor emerged to take his place. The country was governed, until its destruction in 1939, by a group of Pilsudski's associates (the "rule of colonels"), with the Minister of War, Marshal Śmigly-Rydz, acting as chairman of the board and the Foreign Minister, Colonel Joseph Beck, as the moving spirit of the group.

4. CZECHOSLOVAKIA, AUSTRIA, AND HUNGARY

The Danubian states of Austria, Hungary, and Czechoslovakia had constituted the original core of the Hapsburg monarchy and were also its principal heirs. The traditions of the monarchy were carried on most closely in Czechoslovakia, a medium-sized state of 54,207 square miles with a population of 13,370,000 (1921). Like Austria-Hungary, Czechoslovakia was a composite, multinational state. It consisted of the provinces of the former Kingdom of Bohemia (Bohemia, Moravia, and Silesia) and the Slovak and Ruthene districts of former Hungary. Theoretically, the Czechoslovaks, who constituted 65 per cent of the population, were the carriers of the idea of the Czechoslovak state, while the rest of the inhabitants (Germans, Magyars, Ruthenes, Jews, and Poles) were regarded as minorities. But the Czechoslovaks were themselves a composite people, consisting of 6,805,000 Czechs and 1,955,000 Slovaks. Both were Slavic peoples, closely related by race and language, but separated by profound social, economic, and cultural differences. The Czechs, inhabiting the heavily industrialized Bohemian provinces, were a thoroughly western people with a numerous middle class and an industrial working class. The Slovaks, inhabiting the poor and mountainous province of Slovakia, were mostly a peasant people. In practice, the Czechs alone, together with a few Slovaks willing to accept the Czech outlook and policies, ruled Czechoslovakia.

Czechoslovakia adopted a republican, democratic, and centralist constitution, closely modeled on that of France (1920). Thanks to the enlightened leadership of the President-Liberator, Thomas G. Masaryk, and the moderation and good sense of the Czech politicians, the constitution functioned reasonably well and remained in force until the collapse of the republic. Earlier (1919) a moderate Land Law had been adopted which provided for the expropriation and partition of the large estates with compensation to the landowners — mostly German and Magyar noblemen. But the measure did not have the same importance in Czechoslovakia as in the other states of East Central Europe since Czechoslovakia was not primarily an agrarian state. She had inherited 82 per cent of the industries of the whole Austrian Empire. Since the partition of the empire had deprived these industries of their traditional markets the task of finding new markets for them was difficult. The economic problems of Czechoslovakia were therefore as much industrial as they were agrarian. The principal trading partner of Czechoslovakia was Germany with whom her relations were, until the rise of Hitler to power, perfectly polite, if not especially cordial. Thanks to a better balance between agriculture and industry, Czechoslovakia — compared to her neighbors — enjoyed relative prosperity.

The central problem of Czechoslovakia was not economic but political. The national minorities and many Slovaks were either indifferent or positively hostile to the republic. Of the national minorities the most dangerous to the security of the Czechoslovak state were the so-called Sudeten Germans. They numbered 3,120,000 (1921) and lived in compact masses along the German and Austrian borders. The Czechs and the Sudeten Germans had struggled for the control of Bohemia for centuries (see p. 95). After 1918, when the Sudeten Germans ceased to be one of the ruling nationalities of Austria-Hungary (not of Germany to which they had not belonged!) and became a national minority, the struggle sharpened. Czechoslovakia signed the minority treaties, which had been imposed on the nations of East Central Europe at the Paris Peace Conference, and implemented them honestly but unimaginatively. The Sudeten Germans had some specific grievances against Czech rule, but these were subordinate to the basic issue between them and the Czechs which was whether Bohemia was going to be a German or Slavic land. On this issue neither party would admit compromise. There could be between them only a temporary modus vivendi. In the 1920's some of the Sudeten German parties (notably the Agrarians and Social Democrats) were "activist," that is they cooperated with the Czechoslovak government as a temporary expedient. But when Hitler rose to power in Germany, a pro-nazi "Sudeten German Party" was formed under Konrad Henlein in Czechoslovakia. The activist Sudeten German parties then dissolved and their members joined Henlein's party.

During the great Czechoslovak crisis of 1938 the Sudeten German Party eagerly offered itself to Hitler for the role of a Trojan horse to batter down Czechoslovak resistance. It declined concessions offered to it by the Czechoslovak government, for it was confident that Hitler would succeed in breaking up Czechoslovakia. Events were to prove the Sudeten German expectation correct and the Czech faith in their alliances unwarranted. Therefore the question became, from a Czechoslovak point of view, whether they would go down fighting or submit without a struggle. (It is psychologically all-important for a new nation to show a readiness to strike a blow for its own freedom.) Ultimately, the decision rested in the hands of President Eduard Beneš (1935–1938, 1939–1948), Masaryk's successor and close associate. Unlike Pašić, who in a somewhat analogous situation in 1914 did not hesitate to plunge Serbia and Europe into war, Beneš chose to submit, thus inaugurating a pattern of personal and national behavior which he and his people were to repeat ten years later. At the time, the western peoples, much relieved that the danger of war had been averted, hastened to reassure the Czechs of their "superior courage" shown in submitting to live and fight another day, but ultimately the Czech surrender brought them dishonor and discredit.

Austria emerged from the First World War a much diminished (32,369 square miles) and very unhappy country. After the turbulent and chaotic period following the dissolution of the empire, Austria adopted a republican, democratic, and federal constitution on the Swiss model, which provided for considerable autonomy to the eight provinces of Austria (1920). Vienna, the handsome capital of the former empire and then of the small republic, was one of the autonomous provinces. With a population of 2,000,000 out of the total Austrian population of 6,500,000, Vienna was too large for the republic and a burden on its economy. Considerable antagonism existed between the capital and the countryside, emphasized by the political alignment of the country. Vienna was a strong bastion of the Social Democrats, whereas in the country the clerical (Catholic) Christian Socialists and nationalists predominated. A threat of civil war hovered over the country as the Social Democrats organized a private army, the *Schutzbund,* and the clericals and nationalists responded by organizing the armed *Heimwehr.* One vexation at least Austria was spared: the presence of fretful national minorities. She was predominantly a German-speaking country. On the other hand, islands of "unredeemed" Austrians had arisen in Italy, Hungary, and Czechoslovakia. And Austria herself was regarded by many Germans, as well as Austrians, as an "unredeemed" German land which would have to "return" some day to the German fatherland.

The economic life of Austria, deprived of her empire, was precarious in the extreme. The swollen bureaucracy, banks, central offices of business firms, and numerous industries in Vienna had all been designed to service an empire, not a small republic. Austria had been the center as well as the playground of the empire. Since the vast forests of Austria were game preserves of the Imperial family and the nobility, with only a small amount of arable land owned by the peasants, there was a demand for a land reform. The Austrian peasants were literate, hard-working, and efficient farmers. They gradually raised the production of foodstuffs but never sufficiently to feed the country. Nevertheless, with determination, Austria (as she was to prove after World War II) could solve her economic problems. But many Austrians felt that since the Allies had prevented their merger (*Anschluss*) with Germany in 1919 (see p. 196), it was an Allied responsibility to solve their economic problems. The lack of will to determine their own destiny was in fact the central Austrian problem. They oscillated between a desire for the *Anschluss* and for the restoration of the Hapsburgs and the empire, but appeared to care little about maintaining their own independence.

Of the former Allied powers France had a stake in the preservation of Austrian independence and took the lead in providing financial aid to Austria. In 1931, when the Austrian government announced that it had concluded an agreement with Germany to form a customs union, France and Czechoslovakia vigorously protested. To bring pressure to bear on the Austrian government to desist from the project France withheld credits from it. This maneuver resulted in failure of a major Austrian bank, the Credit Anstalt, which pulled down with it many other banks, not only in Austria but in the neighboring countries as well. A severe economic crisis followed, during which a supposed economic expert, Engelbert Dollfuss, a conservative Christian Socialist, took over the government.

The rise of Hitler to power in Germany in 1933, and his destruction of the German socialists and harassment of the German Catholics, disillusioned many Austrians about the benefits of the *Anschluss*. On the other hand, many Austrians rallied to the nazi cause. Chancellor Dollfuss determined to defend Austrian independence by leaning not on distant, democratic France but on nearby fascist Italy. He proposed to replace the democratic constitution of 1920 with a corporate one. As a preliminary step he dissolved political parties. When the Social Democrats resisted their dissolution, they were bloodily suppressed (February, 1934). The nazis then tried to overthrow the government and pave the way for the *Anschluss,* but they were in turn suppressed (July, 1934). However, a band of nazis managed to penetrate the Chancellery and to assassinate Dollfuss. Italian mobilization probably prevented German intervention and for a time saved Austria (see p. 275). An associate of Dollfuss, Kurt Schuschnigg, carried on his policies; but the German-Italian rapprochement in 1936 removed the protecting hand of Italy from Austria. The result was inevitable. In March, 1938, after a violent propaganda barrage and a display of force, Hitler took over his native land without firing a shot. The *Anschluss* had become a fact.

Hungary, after a turbulent period of revolution and counter-revolution (see p. 233), adopted a monarchical constitution (1920). The constitution preserved the trappings of parliamentary democracy but vitiated its principles by providing for a very limited suffrage. In practice Hungary was governed by an oligarchy of great magnates and upper-middle-class politicians. Nicholas Horthy, an admiral in the former Austro-Hungarian navy and commander of the White forces during the Civil War, assumed the office of Regent. The restoration of monarchy encouraged the former Emperor Charles to attempt to recover his Hungarian throne. Twice (March and October, 1921) he returned to Hungary, but both times Czechoslovakia and Yugoslavia mobilized and threatened to invade the country to prevent his restoration. He was forced to return into exile and Horthy continued as Regent. This put Hungary in the anomalous position of being a kingdom without a king ruled by an admiral without a navy.

Hungary was a rich agricultural country and a land of large estates. In a population of slightly over 7,000,000 some 3,000,000 were landless peasants. During the revolution a start had been made toward partition of the estates, but the victory of the counter-revolutionary forces undid this work. The great Magyar magnates were once again in the saddle and the peasants bowed and scraped before them, as in older days.

The whole energy of the Hungarian nation was directed toward undoing the Treaty of Trianon, which had reduced Hungary to a small country (35,000 square miles) and left some 3,200,000 Magyars outside of her borders. So long as Hungary remained isolated, however, there was little hope of revising the treaty. Then, in 1927, Italy took Hungary under her protective wing, and in return the rulers of Hungary assiduously aped fascism. In the 1930's a rabble-rousing, Jew-baiting fascist movement (the "Arrow Cross") arose under the leadership of Ferencz Szálasi. Its adherents looked to Germany rather than to Italy for support and antagonized the land-owning conservatives of Hungary by raising the land question. In 1938 Szálasi and some of his associates were imprisoned and the "Arrow Cross" movement ostensibly stamped out.

In foreign affairs Hungary continued to cooperate with both Germany and Italy, for which she was rewarded in 1938–1941 by the restoration of some of the territories lost in 1919 to her hated rivals, Czechoslovakia, Rumania, and Yugoslavia. But the association with the Axis powers dragged Hungary into World War II on their side and ultimately to defeat and terrible punishment.

5. RUMANIA

Although the long association of the old Rumanian provinces of Wallachia, Moldavia, and Dobrudja with the Ottoman Empire gave them a strongly Balkan flavor, they were not, geographically, part of the Balkan peninsula. After World War I they constituted only a part of the "Greater Rumania" which emerged from the peace settlement. Greater Rumania was twice as large (122,280 square miles) and had a population (18,000,000) three times as large as the smaller Rumania of 1914. Such rapid expansion was not an unmitigated blessing for it created difficult problems of unification. Rumania, like Poland, was the heir to three empires: the "Old Kingdom" (Wallachia, Moldavia, and Dobrudja) forty years after the declaration of its independence (1878) still bore the imprint of the long Turkish rule; Transylvania, Bukovina, and the Banat were stamped with the civilizing influence of·the Hapsburg empire; and Bessarabia had the slothful air of a neglected province of Imperial Russia. It was no mean task to weld these disparate units into a cohesive state. The unifying force in Rumania was Rumanian nationalism. The Rumanians, unlike the Czechoslovaks or Yugoslavs, were a homogeneous people who proudly claimed to be descendants of the Romans. Although their culture derived from Byzantine, Slavic, and Ottoman sources, their language belonged to the Romance family of languages, and they assiduously cultivated relations with their "Latin sisters," France and Italy.

The territorial expansion of Rumania also intensified its foreign problems. Soviet Russia and Hungary resented very bitterly their loss of

territory to Rumania, and Bulgaria still smarted over the earlier loss of
Dobrudja. Acquisition of new territory saddled Rumania with numerous
fretful minorities (Magyars, Ukrainians, Germans, Bulgarians, Jews, and
a scattering of smaller groups), amounting to 30 per cent of the population. Some of these groups, particularly the Magyars and Germans, were
notably disgruntled and looked abroad for aid. They considered themselves superior to the Rumanians and showed undisguised contempt for
the vaunted "Latin civilization" of Rumania.

Of all the countries of East Central Europe, Rumania was the most
richly endowed in natural resources. She had some of the best farm land
in Europe, abundant timber lands, and a rich storehouse of minerals (oil,
coal, iron, copper, lead, antimony, gold, and salt). But save for the
exploitation of oil, industry was little developed and Rumania was largely
an agrarian country. Before the First World War land was owned by
noblemen, who were Rumanian in the Old Kingdom, Rumanian and
Russian in Bessarabia, and Magyar in Transylvania and the Banat. The
condition of the peasants in all parts of Rumania was very poor — perhaps
even worse than in Imperial Russia. The outbreak of the Russian Revolution in 1917 frightened the Rumanian government and King Ferdinand
(1914–1927) promised the Rumanian peasants a new deal. A fairly radical land reform program was carried out (1919–1921), but the question
of compensation to the landowners provoked a bitter and protracted
quarrel between Rumania and Hungary. Hungary laid before the League
of Nations the case of the Magyar landowners of Transylvania and the
Banat, who had availed themselves of a provision in the Treaty of Trianon
permitting them to choose Hungarian citizenship and to emigrate to
Hungary (the "optant claims," 1923–1930).

Political corruption, which was fairly common in East Central Europe,
attained truly monumental proportions in Rumania. Theoretically, Rumania was a constitutional monarchy, but in practice she was a crude
dictatorship. In 1923 a new constitution was adopted which provided for
universal suffrage, but this remained a mockery since the party in power
always "won" the elections. Until his death in 1927, Ionel Brătianu, the
principal engineer of Rumanian unification and the leader of the Liberal
Party — a rather conservative party which favored big business and industry — was prime minister and virtual ruler of Rumania. After Brătianu,
Juliu Maniu, the leader of the United Peasant Party, came to power. A
Transylvanian and a former member of the parliament of Budapest, Maniu
was a man of integrity who tried to rule honestly, but, as was characteristic of the frustrated leaders of the minorities in old Hungary, he was
the most intractable of politicians.

In 1927 King Ferdinand I died and was succeeded by King Michael,
who was only six years old. Michael's father, the former Heir Presumptive
Carol, had renounced his rights in 1925 and gone to live in exile with his
famous red-haired mistress Magda Lupescu. However, the regency of

Carol's brother, Prince Nicholas, proved unsatisfactory, and in 1930 Maniu determined to bring Carol back. He stipulated as the condition of Carol's restoration that he leave his mistress abroad and effect a reconciliation with his wife, Queen Hellen, of the Greek royal family. Carol agreed, but after returning to Rumania he refused to carry out his part of the bargain. Maniu was dismissed, and Lupescu brought back to Bucharest, where she became the center of an unashamed camarilla.

As a ruler Carol II (1930–1940) was not content to play the role of a constitutional monarch but sought to be the effective master of the state. To this end he played off parties and party leaders one against another, and the country saw a long procession of short-lived cabinets, dependent on the favor of the king. As in other parts of East Central Europe, a virulent fascist movement appeared in Rumania (the "Iron Guard") under the leadership of Corneliu Codreanu. King Carol at first favored it, but later it annoyed him with its rabble-rousing and anti-Semitism; he suppressed it, and Codreanu and his associates were shot "while trying to escape from prison." In 1938, on the pretext of curbing party strife which had reached dangerous extremes, Carol suppressed all parties and replaced the democratic constitution with an authoritarian one. He appeared at last to have realized his ideal of a royal dictatorship, but his triumph was short-lived. The outbreak of World War II put Rumania in a very difficult position. King Carol, who tried to stave off disaster by keeping a foot in each belligerent camp, ultimately fell between them. Rumania was forced to pay ransom to both groups: to cede Bessarabia to Soviet Russia and half of Transylvania to Germany's ally, Hungary (June–August, 1940). On the wave of indignation which swept over the Rumanian people at this humiliation King Carol was driven from the country (September, 1940).

6. EAST CENTRAL EUROPE IN INTERNATIONAL AFFAIRS

The foreign policy of Finland and the Baltic states was determined by the fact that they lived completely in the shadow of Soviet Russia, from which they had separated themselves. The only possible counterweight to Soviet pressure on them was Germany. Until the rise of Hitler, Germany was on fairly friendly terms with Soviet Russia, but when Hitler came to power Germany began to press her revisionist claims and took an interest in the German minorities in the east. The German-Lithuanian quarrel over Memel (see p. 190) was reopened and the Baltic German minorities in Latvia and Estonia became restive. In these circumstances the Baltic states avoided association with any major power of Europe and pursued a policy of cautious neutrality.

Poland, a much more substantial factor than the Baltic states, had no such hesitations. She concluded an alliance with France (1921), aimed against both Germany and Soviet Russia, and an alliance with Rumania (1921) against Soviet Russia. But the Polish efforts to line up the Baltic states against Soviet Russia failed because of the bitter and prolonged quarrel between Poland and Lithuania over Vilna — the former Lithuanian capital — which the Poles seized in 1920. On the other hand, Poland declined to join the Little Entente, a league formed by Czechoslovakia, Rumania, and Yugoslavia (1920–1921) to check the persistent efforts of Hungary to obtain a revision of the Treaty of Trianon. Poland had no quarrel with Hungary but did have one with Czechoslovakia over the Teschen question (see p. 195). So the Poles put their trust in a Franco-Polish alliance, a dangerous course because it helped to provoke a Soviet-German rapprochement (Rapallo agreement, 1922) and to keep Russia and Germany on friendly terms.

Since the purpose of the Little Entente was to maintain the *status quo* established by the Paris peace treaties, France — the principal guardian of the treaties — looked on it with favor. She concluded alliance treaties with its members — Czechoslovakia (1924), Rumania (1926), and Yugoslavia (1927) — and extended military and financial aid to them. France also took an active interest in the preservation of Austrian independence and subsidized that country. As a result of all these commitments, France exercised in the 1920's a preponderant influence in East Central Europe. French influence in this area was first challenged by Italy. As France was the champion of the *status quo* nations, Italy began to support the revisionist nations in the area. By taking Hungary (1927) and Austria (1930) under her protection, Italy outflanked the French alliance system along the Danube. By the Rome Protocols (1934) the Italian system was extended to the economic field.

The rivalry of France and Italy in East Central Europe increased the tensions among its nations. The situation was further complicated when Germany and Soviet Russia recovered military strength and influence in the 1930's. In the confused contest of great powers the small nations of East Central Europe were reduced to helpless pawns. They felt no solidarity with one another, and each sought salvation in its own way. Poland — whose foreign policy was directed from 1932 until 1939 by a cool gambler, Colonel Joseph Beck — tried to save herself by the dangerous game of playing off the great powers one against another. She concluded a non-aggression pact with Soviet Russia (1932). When Hitler came to power in Germany, he concluded a non-aggression pact with Poland (1934). The Soviet-Polish and German-Polish non-aggression pacts violated the spirit if not the letter of the Franco-Polish alliance without ultimately providing any real security for the Poles.

Unlike Poland, Czechoslovakia remained staunchly loyal to France and followed the French example of concluding an alliance with Soviet Russia (1935). But the value of her alliances with France and Soviet Russia was dubious for Czechoslovakia had no common border with either of these two powers. Austria, as already noted, sought salvation by placing herself under Italian protection, which won her a temporary reprieve from annexation by Germany (1934). But the Italo-German rapprochement (1936) doomed her and in March, 1938, Austria was annexed by Germany.

The annexation of Austria gravely weakened the strategic position of Czechoslovakia which had always been precarious (see map, p. 311). At the Munich Conference (September, 1938) Czechoslovakia was mutilated and later (March, 1939) obliterated altogether. Poland profited from the concentration of world opinion on the Austrian and Czechoslovak crises to settle her old quarrels with Lithuania and Czechoslovakia. By peremptory ultimata she extorted from Lithuania recognition of the loss of Vilna (March, 1938) and from Czechoslovakia the cession of the Teschen area (October, 1938). Hungary also shared in the dismemberment of Czechoslovakia.

Poland's triumphs were short-lived, however, for she was the next target of Germany's aggression. Belatedly, Great Britain, which since World War I had steadfastly refused to commit herself in East Central Europe, moved to block further German expansion in the area. She offered Poland an unsolicited, unilateral guarantee of her independence (March, 1939). But only Soviet Russia was in a position to give effective help to Poland. In the negotiations that developed in the spring of 1939 between Britain and France on the one hand and Soviet Russia on the other, the Russians insisted on the right to station troops in Poland and the Baltic states as a condition of their cooperation against Germany. This the Poles adamantly refused to agree to, fearing that once the Russians entered Poland they would never leave — until Poland was communized. The fate of the Baltic states in 1940 and of Poland herself after World War II bore out these suspicions. The terrible dilemma of Poland and the other states of East Central Europe was summed up in the words of Marshal Smigly-Rycz: "With Germany we risk losing our liberty, with Russia our soul." In these circumstances, Russia came to terms with Germany. In the famous Nazi-Soviet pact (August 23, 1939) the two powers agreed to partition Poland. Germany also gave Soviet Russia a free hand in Estonia and Latvia. Assured of Soviet neutrality, Germany then attacked Poland, thus precipitating World War II. As the war engulfed Europe, Poland and the rest of the nations of East Central Europe were easily picked off from east and west by the resurgent imperialism of Germany and Soviet Russia.

29

SOUTHEASTERN EUROPE

One cannot understand southeastern Europe without remembering that nations are not identical with States.[1]

STOYAN PRIBICHEVICH

1. CHARACTERISTICS OF SOUTHEASTERN EUROPE

THE AREA OF SOUTHEASTERN Europe, comprising the Balkan peninsula, was more homogeneous in its cultural, social, economic, and political development than East Central Europe. The dominant cultural influences in Southeastern Europe were Byzantine and Ottoman, and in more recent times Italian and French. A large majority of the Balkan peoples belonged to the Greek Orthodox Church, while the Catholic element was small and Protestants virtually nonexistent. On the other hand, there were Moslem minorities in all the Balkan states, and in Albania the Moslems constituted a majority of the population. Although the peoples of Southeastern Europe had been liberated from foreign domination earlier than the peoples of East Central Europe, after World War I they still bore a heavy imprint of Turkish rule. Corruption was universal and generally accepted as an inevitable way of life, and cultural standards were substantially lower in Southeastern Europe than in East Central Europe.

Socially, the Balkan nations were almost entirely nations of peasants. They had no aristocracy because the landowners under the Ottoman rule had been Moslems who had been removed after the collapse of the Ottoman control. Ownership of the land had largely passed into the hands of the peasants. The middle class — or *intelligentsia* — was even more sparse in the Balkans than in East Central Europe, and, with the exception of Greece, a seafaring and trading nation, there were few merchants. Industry was undeveloped, agriculture primitive, cities few in number and without modern conveniences, transportation and communications most inadequate. Modernization of agriculture and the development of

[1] *World Without End, The Saga of Southeastern Europe,* Reynal and Hitchcock (New York, 1939), p. 169.

industry were even more pressing necessities in Southeastern Europe than in East Central Europe.

The Balkan states, which all had been constitutional monarchies – the fashionable form of government in Europe in the nineteenth century when they were founded – adopted new, democratic constitutions after World War I in harmony with the trend of the times. Seemingly, the absence of aristocracy and of pronounced social contrasts should have made the development of democracy in Southeastern Europe easier than in East Central Europe, where a feudal influence was more pronounced. Actually, this did not prove to be the case. The weight of Turkish political traditions, the meddling of the military in politics, the unbridled nationalism, and the low educational level of the peasants – all militated against development of democracy. After experimenting with democratic governments in the 1920's, all the Balkan nations ended up with dictatorial regimes in the 1930's.

2. THE STATES OF SOUTHEASTERN EUROPE

The largest and most populous state in the Balkans was Yugoslavia. It was formed in 1918 by uniting, under the Serbian Karadjordjević dynasty, the kingdoms of Serbia and Montenegro and the Yugoslav provinces of the Hapsburg empire. It had an area of 96,134 square miles and a population of 12,300,000. Its natural resources were not inconsiderable; it possessed excellent farm land along the Danube and the Sava rivers, abundant timberlands, and many minerals (copper, lead, mercury, bauxite, chromite, magnesite, and silver). However, it lacked coal and iron, a lack that helps to explain why industry developed slowly and the Yugoslav economy remained predominantly agrarian. In 1938 there were only thirty-eight establishments employing more than 1000 persons.

In the "Old Kingdom" of Serbia the Moslem landowners had been liquidated at the time of its emancipation from Ottoman rule in the nineteenth century. There remained, however, a landowning class in the more recently acquired provinces: Macedonia, Bosnia, and the former provinces of Hungary. These landowners were expropriated under a land law adopted in 1919 and Yugoslavia became, like the other Balkan nations, a land of peasant proprietors. In spite of inefficient and antiquated farming methods, the Yugoslav peasants produced enough wheat, corn, and fodder for export as well as domestic needs. Yugoslavia's most pressing problem was not economic but political.

Like Czechoslovakia, Yugoslavia was a composite multinational state. The Yugoslav people consisted of the Serbs, Croats, and Slovenes, among whom there were profound historical, cultural, social, and political differences. Although the Serbs and Croats shared a common language, they were sharply divided by religion and culture. The Serbs were Orthodox believers and their culture derived from eastern Byzantine and Ottoman sources, while the Croats were Catholics and their culture derived from western Latin and Germanic traditions. On the other hand, the Croats and Slovenes shared a common religion and culture, but were separated by a language barrier, for the Slovenes spoke a distinct tongue. In addition to the three branches of the Yugoslav people, Yugoslavia contained numerous national minorities (Magyars, Albanians, Macedonians, and a scattering of Germans, Italians, and other groups). The Bosnian Moslems, although Yugoslav in race and language, also had to be reckoned a minority because Islam is not only a religion but a distinctive way of life. Altogether the national and religious minorities amounted to 24 per cent of the population. While the relationship between the minorities and the Yugoslav state was by no means harmonious, minority problems were overshadowed by a more critical issue, the unsatisfactory state of Serbo-Croat relations.

As a concession to Croat and Slovene particularism, Yugoslavia was officially styled (until 1929) the "Kingdom of the Serbs, Croats, and Slovenes," but this was a purely formal concession. The Croats and Slovenes had proposed federalism as the best formula for accommodating the national, religious, and regional differences among the various peoples of Yugoslavia. But King Alexander (regent 1914–1921, king 1921–1934) and Prime Minister Pašić resisted this demand because of their fear — not altogether unwarranted — that federalism would lead to the disintegration of Yugoslavia.

In 1921 a centralist, albeit democratic, constitution was adopted, which left the Croats in particular deeply dissatisfied. Since the Croats refused to cooperate with the government, the Serbs alone — with some cooperation from the Slovenes — ruled Yugoslavia. The growing Serbo-Croat tension reached a climax in 1928, when the spokesman of the Croat opposition, Stepan Radić, leader of the Croat Peasant Party, was shot down in parliament in Belgrade. The Croats thereafter withdrew from parliament and would have nothing to do with the Belgrade government. After vainly trying to effect a compromise, King Alexander suspended the constitution, dissolved parliament, and proclaimed a royal dictatorship (1929). In 1931 a limited constitutional regime was restored, but Serbo-Croat relations remained tense. They were not improved by the assassination of King Alexander in Marseilles (1934), a crime in which several Croat émigrés were implicated. Prince Paul, acting as regent for the young King Peter (1934–1945), continued most of Alexander's policies. It was not until the very eve of World War II (August, 1939) that a Serbo-Croat settlement along federalist lines was reached. It came, however, too late to appease the old and bitter quarrel and to prepare Yugoslavia for the ordeal of war.

Bulgaria emerged from the war defeated and further diminished (to 42,000 square miles). The dream nurtured by Bulgarian nationalists of restoring the Great Bulgaria of the Peace of San Stefano (1878) had again been frustrated. This reverse left the Bulgars with a bitter feeling of frustration and they refused to regard the Peace of Neuilly as permanent. Their attitude was comparable to that of the Hungarians who refused to accept the Peace of Trianon. Memories of their defeat and humiliation were kept alive among the Bulgarians by thousands of refugees from Macedonia and Thrace, to whom Bulgaria offered haven but whom she could not effectively absorb. In this situation extremist movements throve. A strong communist group and a Macedonian revolutionary party kept the country in turmoil and the Greek and Yugoslav frontiers alive with incidents. The obsession of the Bulgars with the question of their boundaries caused them to neglect their internal development.

Bulgaria was a strictly agrarian country, producing surpluses of tobacco, grain, and corn, which she exported. In return, she imported manufactures, for her own industries were insignificant. The Bulgars offered a classical example of a peasant people and they were extraordinarily homogeneous, both socially and nationally. There was no aristocracy, only a small middle class, and few minority groups. In 1919, on the wave of anti-war feeling, Alexander Stambolisky, an Agrarian leader who had bitterly opposed Bulgaria's entry into the war on the side of the Central Powers, came to power. Stambolisky was an ardent apostle of peasant democracy and of international peasant solidarity (the "Green International"). But his policy of reconciliation with the neighbors of Bulgaria, which implied the abandonment of her territorial claims, provoked the wrath of Bulgarian nationalists and Macedonian revolutionaries. In 1923 he was overthrown by a coup and shortly afterwards murdered.

For some years Bulgaria wallowed in terror and counter-terror. Gradually, however, King Boris (1918–1943), a quiet, devious, and enigmatic man, gained control. All parties were dissolved, the Internal Macedonian Revolutionary Organization and its allies in the army suppressed, and the authority of the government restored (1934). Later (1938) a "National Socialist" movement, modeled on that of Germany, was also suppressed and relations with Bulgaria's neighbors were stabilized. But the dream of restoring Greater Bulgaria led the Bulgars to ally themselves with Germany once more in World War II, with the result that they were again defeated and humiliated.

Albania had been established as a principality by the Great Powers in 1913 (see p. 115), but was organized as a nation only after World War I. The Albanians proudly claimed to be the oldest people of Europe (they are supposedly descendants of the Illyrians of classical times), but they were also its most primitive people. Under Ottoman rule the socio-political organization of the Albanians was tribal rather than national. Although they were liberated from Turkish rule in 1913, World War I broke out before they could organize a national government. During the war Albania was overrun by armies of both belligerent groups, and after the war Italian, Greek, and Yugoslav troops remained in the country. Greece and Yugoslavia laid claim to portions of Albanian territory, while Italy sought to establish an influence over the whole country. In 1918 a National Assembly met in Tirana and chose a government. By guerrilla warfare and by playing Italy, Greece, and Yugoslavia off against one another, the Albanians gradually freed themselves from foreign occupation. But it was not until 1926 that the original 1913 borders of Albania were internationally confirmed.

The leading figure of Albanian politics was Ahmed Zogu, leader of an important Moslem clan. His rise to absolute power was briefly checked in 1924 by a Harvard-trained bishop, Fan Noli, leader of the Albanian Orthodox community. But with the aid of the Yugoslavs Ahmed Zogu soon returned to power. In 1925 he became president and three years later proclaimed himself king.

Although indebted to the Yugoslavs, King Zog I (1928–1939) began to lean on Italy because she was willing to provide the financial aid and technicians necessary to develop the country. Albania was a very poor country and its economy remained half-pastoral, half-agrarian, and wholly primitive. Only the malaria-infested coastal plain was suited for farming, while the interior of the country was covered with rugged, barren mountains. By the Treaty of Tirana (1927) Italy established a virtual protectorate, and under Italian guidance roads were built (Albania was the only European country without a single railroad), communications developed, and the rudiments of a modern administration established. But the Albanians paid for this modest progress with their freedom. On the eve of World War II Italy formally annexed the country (April, 1939).

Greece emerged from the war somewhat enlarged (51,000 square miles), but her gains fell far short of the Greek dream of restoring the Byzantine Empire, with Constantinople as its capital, and with possessions on both sides of the Aegean Sea. Although very successful at the Paris Peace Conference thanks to the extraordinary diplomatic skill of Prime Minister Venizelos, Greece was driven by her ambitions into further adventures. Venizelos was turned out of office and King Constantine, who had been forced by the Allies to abdicate in 1917 (see p. 160), was restored to the throne (1920). After plunging Greece into a war with Nationalist Turkey, in which the Greeks were ignominiously beaten (see p. 200), King Constantine was forced to abdicate for the second time (1922). His son, George II, reigned briefly and then the monarchy collapsed (1923). A republic was proclaimed (1924) and a democratic constitution modeled on that of France adopted.

The main problem facing the subsequent republican administrations in Greece was the problem of resettling some 1,400,000 Greek refugees from Turkey, Bulgaria, and Russia. Greece was a desperately poor country with few natural resources; only about 25 per cent of the land was arable, the rest being barren mountains. Greece produced surpluses of "Turkish" tobacco, olives, and raisins which she exported, but she was deficient in the production of cereals, which she had to import. A substantial part of the Greek national income derived from trade, shipping, tourism, and remittances from overseas Greeks. Thanks to generous loans, arranged by the League of Nations, Greece succeeded in absorbing her refugees. They were resettled mainly in northern Greece and Macedonia, and in Thrace, from which by agreement with Bulgaria and Turkey the Slav Macedonians and Moslem Turks had been removed. The refugees were at first a crushing burden on Greece, but they later proved a boon. They brought in many new skills and industries and augmented the Greek population to over 7,000,000. Despite her poverty, Greece was a more advanced country and enjoyed higher standards than her Balkan neighbors.

Greek politics had always had a mercurial quality, swinging wildly and unpredictably from one extreme to another. There were many political parties but two were dominant: the republican Venizelist Liberal Party, and the royalist Populist Party. From 1924 until 1932 a coalition clustering around the Liberal Party dominated the political scene. Then the Populists came to power and in 1935 restored the monarchy under George II. In 1936 General Metaxas carried out a *coup d'état*, abolishing the constitutional regime (but not the monarchy), and establishing a fascist dictatorship. It endured until World War II. Despite her old democratic tradition and greater political experience, Greece thus followed the general trend in the Balkans toward dictatorial systems.

3. SOUTHEASTERN EUROPE IN INTERNATIONAL AFFAIRS

After World War I the Balkans, traditionally the powder keg of European politics, were relatively quiescent. There were, to be sure, many "border incidents," notably between Bulgaria and Greece and between Bulgaria and Yugoslavia, and the usual squabbles over minority rights; but there were no major conflicts involving the great powers and threatening the peace of Europe. One reason for this was that those great powers which, before 1914, had meddled most persistently in Balkan affairs were unable to do so after the war. The Austrian Empire was gone altogether, and Russia and Germany were too weak militarily in the 1920's to exercise an important influence. In their absence the influence of Italy, which had been relatively small before the war, grew considerably. For the Greeks and Yugoslavs, Italy had taken the place of Austria as the power which most frequently harassed them. Italy had territorial quarrels with both Yugoslavia and Greece. These disputes were adjourned by treaties concluded with Yugoslavia in 1924 and with Greece in 1928, but Italo-Yugoslav and Italo-Greek relations remained unsatisfactory.

In 1920–1921 Yugoslavia joined Czechoslovakia and Rumania in the Little Entente to keep Hungarian revisionism in check. In 1927 she concluded an alliance with France. Italy bitterly resented the extension of French influence into Southeastern Europe and she countered it by extending her protection to Albania (1927) and to the revisionist nations, Hungary (1927), Austria (1930), and Bulgaria (1930). To check the growing Italian influence in the Balkans, and to cope with the World Depression, the Balkan nations and Turkey held a conference in Athens in 1930, initiated by Venizelos of Greece. Bulgaria attended the conference but made the revision of her borders the price of her cooperation with her neighbors. This proved unacceptable to them. In 1934, after protracted negotiations, Turkey, Greece, Rumania, and Yugoslavia concluded the Balkan Pact, which provided for the maintenance of the *status quo* in the Balkans and for economic cooperation among the adhering nations. Bulgarian absence from the Balkan Pact weakened it, and inevitably it became an instrument to check Bulgarian revisionism, just as the Little Entente was primarily an instrument to check Hungarian revisionism. Nevertheless, in spite of Bulgarian reluctance to cooperate with her neighbors, the enigmatic King Boris made peace overtures to Yugoslavia and Greece. In the following years Bulgaria concluded a friendship pact with Yugoslavia (1937) and an agreement with Greece (1938).

In the 1930's Germany made a dramatic reappearance on the Balkan scene. Drawing on her experience during the Allied blockade in World War I, Nazi Germany revived the *Mitteleuropa* schemes, designed to convert the whole of Eastern Europe into a German economic sphere. In 1934 Germany launched a vigorous economic offensive in the Balkans, partly to cope with the problems of the World Depression and partly to obtain the raw materials for her rearmament. The Balkan nations did not at first feel menaced by the German economic offensive; on the contrary they welcomed it as an alternative to the Italian pressure and also because it seemed to promise a solution for their economic problems. Germany offered to buy up their agricultural surpluses and industrial raw materials at prices substantially above world prices. She could not pay cash for them, but offered seemingly advantageous trade clearing agreements; she would pay for her imports with exports of industrial goods. This seemed fair enough, and Balkan politicians rejoiced as they built up huge credits in Berlin, but their joy was soon dampened when it turned out that the German commodity which they desired most, namely armaments, was unavailable because Germany needed it herself for her own rearmament. Instead of guns and munitions, the Balkan nations were often forced to content themselves with aspirin, toothpaste, and mouth organs.

The swift growth of German power and the commensurate decline of French power caused uneasiness in the Balkans. This mounting apprehension turned to panic when the Western powers sacrificed Czechoslovakia at the Munich Conference. The belated British efforts to rally the Balkan nations in the spring of 1939 proved quite futile. Greece and

Rumania, to whom Britain offered unilateral guarantees of independence, did not even dare to acknowledge them. As Germany swiftly re-established her influence in East Central Europe, the Balkan nations outbid one another in their scramble to come to terms with her.

30

THE CHANGING BRITISH COMMONWEALTH

No Act of Parliament of the United Kingdom passed after the commencement of this Act shall extend, . . . to a Dominion . . . unless . . . that Dominion has requested, and consented to, the enactment thereof.

STATUTE OF WESTMINSTER (1931)

1. THE SLACKENING OF IMPERIAL TIES

IN THE FIRST QUARTER of the twentieth century the British Empire attained its zenith. By 1900 its total area had reached twelve million square miles and its population totalled four hundred million people. By 1920 this area had increased to more than thirteen million square miles with a population approaching five hundred million. More than one-fifth of the land area of the globe and more than one-fourth of the global population had been gathered within this world-wide Empire. With all its dominions, colonies, and protectorates it was the largest empire in recorded history.

Yet by 1920 the world-wide influence of Great Britain (like that of Europe itself) was already undermined. New forces had developed that checked further British expansion and weakened the ties holding the British Empire together. It was an empire that had been built up and was still dominated by an active minority; only one-eighth of its population (some sixty million out of half a billion) were of European descent. When the Asians and Africans under British rule felt the stirrings of an independent spirit and acquired a determination to rule themselves, they were certain to challenge British control. Even before World War I, criticism and discontent in India provided a warning that the pressure for independence would grow (see pp. 366–367). In the self-governing Dominions likewise, the inhabitants had come to resent the term "colonials" and wished to control their own affairs more completely.

That the strains and pressures within the Empire would increase was apparent to far-seeing statesmen before 1914. But World War I delayed and postponed the necessary readjustments. When Britain entered the war against Germany the dominions and colonies supported her loyally, raising and dispatching military forces to aid the Motherland and speeding the production of war supplies. These efforts, however, made the Canadians, Australians, New Zealanders, and South Africans more conscious of their strength and resources and more determined to assert their individuality. The war propaganda sponsored by the Allied governments, especially Woodrow Wilson's emphasis on the right of "self-determination" for all nations, increased the desire for independence that was already stirring subject peoples everywhere. Self-determination was a dangerous doctrine to propagate in a world where one-third of the population was subject to the control, more or less direct, of European powers. If the belief became widely established that every people had the right to independence, that every nation should aspire to govern itself, the colonial empires the Europeans had conquered in Asia and Africa were almost certain to break up.

No serious revolts disturbed the British Empire during World War I. There was, however, a short and tragic outbreak in Ireland, where a small group of Irish patriots attempted to stir up a rebellion in 1916. Although many Irishmen had long demanded independence, few were yet ready to spring to arms, and the "Easter Rebellion" of 1916 was suppressed after a week of fighting. The severity of the British, who shot several of the captured Irish leaders, strengthened instead of intimidating the *Sinn Fein* party; its members proclaimed Ireland a republic in 1919 and elected Eamon de Valera president. Although the British arrested him and other *Sinn Fein* leaders, the struggle grew fiercer, and was marked on both sides by savage raids, murders, and reprisals. In 1920 the British Parliament passed a Government of Ireland Act; the six counties of Northern Ireland accepted it, but the twenty-six counties of Southern Ireland chose independence (1922) as the Irish Free State. All ties between the Free State and Great Britain were gradually dissolved, and the Irish Free State finally became the independent Irish Republic. Northern Ireland remained within the Empire, with twelve members to represent it in the British House of Commons.

One indication that the self-governing Dominions within the British Empire were achieving nationhood was their admission to the League of Nations as independent countries. When the League took form in 1919–1920, Canada, Australia, New Zealand, and the Union of South Africa sent representatives to the League Assembly as if they were sovereign states. India, also, although the Indians did not control their own government, became a member of the League, and the newly proclaimed Irish Free State was admitted in 1923. Among the Dominions, Canada took the lead (1920) in announcing that it would assume some other prerogatives of a sovereign state by maintaining its own diplomatic representatives in foreign capitals and negotiating treaties with foreign countries.

The need to clarify the changing relations between Great Britain and her colonies was officially recognized in 1926. Since 1907 the self-

AREA AND POPULATION OF GREAT BRITAIN
COMPARED TO THAT OF THE BRITISH
EMPIRE-COMMONWEALTH, 1939

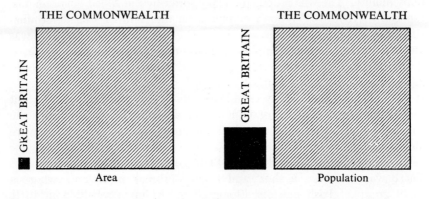

governing colonies had been termed "Dominions," and the "Colonial Conferences" whereby the British and colonial governments adjusted their differences became known as "Imperial Conferences." At the first Imperial Conference (1923) that followed World War I the question of closer economic ties was discussed but little progress made. A further conference (1926) took up the problem of clarifying the status of the Dominions and adopted the following definition:

They are autonomous Communities within the British Empire, equal in status, in no way subordinate one to another in any respect of their domestic or foreign affairs, though united by a common allegiance to the Crown, and freely associated as members of the British Commonwealth of Nations.

Five years later the diminishing authority of the British monarch and Parliament over the Dominions was defined even more explicitly. With the consent and approval of the Dominion governments, the British Parliament adopted an act known as the Statute of Westminster (1931). Article 4 of this Statute affirmed that:

No Act of Parliament of the United Kingdom, passed after the commencement of this Act shall extend, or be deemed to extend, to a Dominion as part of the law of that Dominion, unless it is expressly declared in that Act that that Dominion has requested, and consented to, the enactment thereof . . .

This voluntary loosening of imperial ties showed that British statesmen could yield with good grace when conditions demanded this. In two instances (the Thirteen American Colonies and Ireland), when they attempted to hold their dependencies by force, they lost them. By yielding tactfully and in time to the demand of their Dominions for self-determination they avoided any sharp conflict and preserved the Commonwealth from strains that might have disrupted it completely. Yet the formula by which four Dominions gained equal status with the Motherland, and became joint partners in the Commonwealth, reduced the relative importance of Great Britain. Thenceforth, if the British Empire-Commonwealth continued to act as a unit in world affairs, its unity would depend on the strength of sentiment and of concerted interests, not on a centralized authority exercised from London.

In Canada, Australia, and New Zealand, where the people were almost exclusively of European (and largely of British) descent, the ties of sentiment might prove strong and enduring. South Africa, where half the whites (the Boers) had no deep love for Britain, might in time secede as the Irish did when they won the opportunity. India, which was still struggling for self-determination in 1931, could not be counted upon to support the Commonwealth once it became independent. These considerations made it clear that by the second quarter of the twentieth century the British Empire was ceasing to be an empire in any strict sense and was becoming instead a league or alliance of states from which any of the major members might separate at will.

2. CANADA

In the twenty-five years between 1914 and 1939 the Dominion of Canada took its place among the important and progressive states of the world. Though long overshadowed by the phenomenal growth of the United States, Canada actually increased its population at a much faster pace than its great neighbor to the south. Between 1800 and 1914, when the population of the United States rose tenfold, from roughly ten to one hundred million, the population of Canada increased twentyfold, from some four hundred thousand to almost eight million. Between 1914 and 1939 the rate of growth in the two countries became more equal. While the American population rose 30 per cent, from 100 to 130 million, that of Canada rose 40 per cent, roughly from eight to eleven million.

The population of Canada was more exclusively of European (particularly British) ancestry than was the population of the American Republic. Less than 1 per cent of the Canadian people were of African or Asian descent, against 10 per cent in the continental United States. Emigrants from the British Isles and their descendants accounted for almost half the Canadian population; colonists from France and their descendants (the *Canadiens*) comprised one-third; and the remainder, less than 20 per cent, were almost all of German, Russian, Dutch, Italian, or Scandinavian extraction.

In the earlier colonial period the fur trade and the fishing off Newfoundland were valuable sources of revenue. In the nineteenth century farming, lumbering, and mining gained importance. Despite the arctic or subarctic climate of northern Canada and the rocky and mountainous terrain of many areas, Canada includes half-a-million square miles of cultivable land, which, if fully developed, could support ten times its present population. By 1939 the value of the farm output reached two billion dollars. As forests cover one-third of the country, lumber (especially pulpwood) was available for use and export. Mining increased in importance with the development of iron resources; coal, petroleum, and natural gas in quantity promised unlimited energy. Canada also had extensive resources for the development of hydroelectric power. These facilities, rapidly explored and developed in the twentieth century, led to an expansion of industry. By 1939 manufacturing surpassed agriculture in the value of its output and employed a larger proportion of the population.

With the expansion of industry the Canadian population tended to concentrate in the cities, the largest of which were Montreal, Toronto, Vancouver, and Winnipeg. In 1914 the rural population still outnumbered the town dwellers; by 1930 the two groups were approximately even; but by 1939 the urban population definitely outnumbered the rural population.

The Canadians preserved their determination to remain politically and economically independent. Although they relaxed their political ties with Great Britain they had no intention of drifting under the domination of the United States. To preserve a balance was not easy, however. Despite their efforts to preserve close trade with Britain, the United States, as a nearer and larger market, absorbed a growing share of their exports. At successive imperial conferences, plans were formulated to increase trade *within* the British Commonwealth by adopting preferential tariffs. Canadians were ready to sell their products to Britain but less eager to purchase British products in return. By 1939 Canadian exports to the United Kingdom had three times the value of British exports to Canada, thus creating a balance unfavorable to Britain. On the other hand, Canada's exports to, and imports from, the United States exceeded the value of its trade with Britain. For the United States, Canada had become the leading foreign market, but the goods Canada sold there did not equal in value the goods it imported from the United States.

Canadians wanted American products, especially manufactured goods, but they also wanted to guard their own developing industries which they protected by import tariffs. To cross this tariff wall, American manufacturers sometimes opened separate factories in Canada, factories that employed Canadian workers and were subject to Canadian regulations. This helped to advance Canadian prosperity but it also represented a threat because it introduced more American capital into Canada. By 1939 the United States had invested more than ten billion dollars in foreign countries, and more than one-third of this sum(nearly four billion dollars) was invested in Canada.

3. AUSTRALIA AND NEW ZEALAND

By 1900 the population of Australia had reached three and a half million, by 1914 it was four and a half million, and by 1939 seven million. Thus the Commonwealth of Australia doubled its population in thirty-nine years, a rate of growth three times as fast as that of the world as a whole during the same interval. Its neighboring Dominion of New Zealand likewise doubled its population between 1900 and 1939, from about 750 thousand to one and one-half million. In Canada and the Union of South Africa, the white population also doubled during the same years.

It was a matter of urgent importance to Australia and New Zealand that they acquire a larger population. For they lay off the southeast coast of Asia, only a few thousand miles from densely peopled lands where a billion Chinese, Japanese, Indians, and Indonesians struggled to keep alive with insufficient living space. In these Asian countries as a group the population exceeded 160 to the square mile and in New Zealand less than fifteen. As the population of Asia began to expand rapidly in the twentieth century, and better communications drew all regions of the earth into closer contact, the danger increased that the hungry multitudes of Asia would turn envious eyes on sparsely peopled areas and demand to share them.

As the Australians and New Zealanders wished to preserve their British traditions and culture they encouraged immigrants from the British Isles and from European countries but excluded Asians and Africans. They also sought to maintain a high birth rate by providing government payments to families for each child. The aged and incapacitated, the sick and the unemployed also received financial aid. In New Zealand a Social Security Act passed in 1938 provided for medical care for the sick and for free treatment by physicians and hospitals for expectant mothers. This concern for the health and welfare of the citizens helped to reduce the death rate in Australia and New Zealand to less than 10 per thousand by 1939, a rate lower than that of the United States or any European country except the Netherlands.

To pay for these social services the governments of Australia and New Zealand imposed heavy income taxes but the citizens could afford them because their income remained high. Statistics compiled for the League of Nations indicated that in 1939 the per capita income in Australia and New Zealand was the highest in the world, with the United States ranking third. In comparison with an average per capita income equivalent to $560 a year, enjoyed by Australians and New Zealanders, the inhabitants of China, India, and Indonesia had per capita incomes that averaged $25 a year, or less than one-twentieth as large. Such striking disparity had its dangers, for it has been said that "race hatred is founded on international covetousness." If Australia and New Zealand had lain unclaimed one century longer, the Japanese might have colonized them.

So long as the British navy controlled the oceans Australia and New Zealand were secure from invasion. But an awareness of their vulnerability moved the Australians to establish a naval squadron in 1911 which cooperated with the British Royal Navy. The New Zealanders adopted a Naval Defense Act in 1913 to provide a similar force which was placed at the disposal of the British government. The Canadians, who felt confident that the American navy would protect them if the British navy could not, showed less zeal to help Britain police the seas. This was understandable because Canada held no distant dependencies to defend; its offshore islands in the polar seas were too ice-bound to be easily attacked.

Australia and New Zealand, on the other hand, both acquired dependencies distant from their shores. In 1906 Australia took over the administration of the Territory of Papua on the island of New Guinea. After World War I it received a further segment of the island (formerly German New Guinea) as a mandate, together with some adjacent islands. In 1933 Australia claimed a large portion of the Antarctic Continent, an ill-defined portion, almost as vast as Australia itself, but this claim was not recognized by the United States and some other powers. New Zealand likewise asserted a claim to some Antarctic territory, and to a number of islands in the southwest Pacific. These included the Cook, Kermadec, and Union islands, and Western Samoa.

In 1927 the seat of the Australian government and parliament was transferred to Canberra, a new city established (like Washington, D. C.) in a special district, the Australian Capital Territory. This territory, some 900 square miles in area, lies in the southeast corner of Australia in the most densely settled area. The insufficient rainfall in the central and western portions of Australia has retarded settlement there (save on the coast) and these portions, which comprise two-thirds of the island, support only one-seventh of the population.

Australia and New Zealand maintained close economic ties with Great Britain, shipping more than half their exports to and receiving over half their imports from the mother country before World War II.

4. SOUTH AFRICA

In the Union of South Africa the descendants of the original Dutch settlers and the more recent British colonists faced problems that differed from those of the Canadians, Australians, and New Zealanders. As indicated earlier (see p. 126) the whites in South Africa remained a minority, outnumbered about four to one by people of non-European or of mixed blood. The Bantu, the native Africans, comprised over two-thirds of the total population, but most of them lived in extreme poverty. This lowered the average (or per capita) income in South Africa to $186 a year (one-third that of the Australians and New Zealanders). The actual income of the non-whites was much lower for the largest share of the wealth went to the white minority.

The South Africans supported Britain in World War I but preferred to direct their major efforts against the German protectorates in Africa. After the war they received the former German territory of Southwest Africa as a mandate under the League of Nations, a territory considerably larger than Texas. South West Africa was very sparsely populated, with less than two inhabitants to the square mile in 1939, whereas the Union of South Africa had over twenty inhabitants to the square mile at that date. Furthermore, control of this territory brought an additional three hundred thousand Africans under the administration of the South African government but added only thirty thousand whites.

South Africa produced its own food supplies and began to develop its own manufacturing plants in the twentieth century. The most vital factor in its economy, however, remained its gold and diamond fields. It furnished one-third of the world's gold supply and more than half of the world's new diamonds, the shipment of these precious commodities making up two-thirds of South African exports. In the 1920's Great Britain provided over half the imports and absorbed three-fourths of the exports of the Union, but after 1933 heavy American purchases of gold deflected part of the South African output to the United States with which South Africa had hitherto had little commerce.

A Defense Act adopted in 1912 provided that all male citizens between seventeen and sixty would be liable for military service in wartime. Half the male citizens of European descent were expected to undergo some military training between seventeen and twenty-five, and the remainder received instruction in rifle practice. As no equivalent emphasis was placed on naval defense, it is possible that the training and arming of the whites in peacetime was motivated in part by the fear of native insurrections.

The four British self-governing Dominions, Canada, Australia, New Zealand, and South Africa together embraced over seven million square miles, roughly one-eighth of the land area of the globe. Their total population by 1939 had reached some thirty million, of which some twenty-two million were of European descent. Although it was true that considerable portions of Canada, Australia, and South Africa were almost uninhabitable, it is clear nonetheless that these Dominions were very thinly populated. They comprised 13 per cent of the world's land area but supported less than 2 per cent of the global population. For the world the average population was close to forty inhabitants per square mile of land. For these British Dominions as a whole it was about four to the square mile. The people in the Dominions enjoyed ten times as much "living space" as the people of the world at large. These superior resources, together with their energy, initiative, foresight, and good government, helped to explain why the (white) citizens of the Dominions enjoyed an average income that was ten times as high as that available to the peoples of Asia or the native Africans. The good fortune and enterprise of the Europeans, especially the English, in controlling the oceans during a critical period of world history, had enabled them to occupy vast and almost empty areas of the globe and hold them for the benefit of a relatively small number of European colonists. But could these Dominions preserve themselves in a new era, when a "population explosion" was overtaxing the resources of Africa and Asia?

31

LATIN AMERICA

The only thing the world needs to fear is poverty.
EZEQUIEL PADILLA

1. PERENNIAL PROBLEMS OF THE LATIN AMERICAN PEOPLES

THE HISTORY of Middle and South America has always differed sharply from that of North America. Before the white man came, the area that now comprises the United States and Canada was very sparsely populated. In 1500 the Indians of the New World apparently numbered between fifteen and twenty million, with all but one million living in Middle or South America. There the most notable cultures of the New World had developed, and it was by overthrowing the rule of the Aztecs and the Incas that the Spaniards made themselves masters of a rich colonial empire, while the Portuguese claimed and colonized Brazil.

It is important to note that, although the Indian population of Middle and South America declined after the conquest, it was not exterminated. For some two centuries (1550–1750) the number of inhabitants in these areas apparently remained fairly stable at about twelve million. The Spanish and Portuguese conquerors and colonists remained a minority, outnumbered by the Indians, the Negroes imported from Africa, and the people of mixed blood (mestizos).

During these same centuries the population of North America is likewise believed to have remained fairly constant at about one million. As the white settlers there (chiefly English and French) and their Negro slaves increased, the number of Indians declined. In the later eighteenth century the population of the New World began to rise rapidly, but it rose much more sharply in North America than in Middle and South America. In 1750 Latin America supported over ten times the population of North America; by 1850 they were drawing even; by 1900 North America (the United States and Canada) was ahead, with some eighty million to sixty million. With the twentieth century, however, the trend reversed itself. Now it became the turn of the Latin American peoples to catch up. By 1939 they had almost done so, with 132 million to 142 million. By the midcentury they were even, and thereafter the Latin Americans led.

Thus, in the second quarter of the twentieth century the Americas were divided into two halves, which may be distinguished as the Anglo-Saxon bloc and the Latin American bloc. These two halves were approximately equal in numbers and area, but they were equal in little else. Their differences were much more striking than their similarities, for politically, culturally, socially, and economically they presented contrasts.

Politically, Latin America differed from Anglo-Saxon America in three important respects. First, during the colonial period, Spain and Portugal had allowed the Latin Americans almost no opportunity to learn the art of self-government, whereas the people of the United States and Canada had gradually learned to handle their own affairs. Secondly, and partly for this reason, most of the Latin American republics had a turbulent history of wars, revolutions, *coups d'état*, and dictatorships, whereas the United States and Canada had prospered under remarkably stable institutions. Third, many Latin American republics engaged in wars that wasted resources and strengthened the military cliques, while the United States and Canada remained largely free from exhausting wars for over a century (the exception being the War between the States, 1861–1865).

Culturally, the Latin Americans tended to remain true to an older, humanistic tradition, and to their Catholic faith. They were not greatly interested in commercial and industrial pursuits, in technology, in mechanical inventions, in natural science. They were less fitted to compete in the modern business world than the North Americans, and they lacked the initiative, the capital, and the training to exploit their natural resources. These differences in cultural attitudes also distinguished the modern Spaniards and Portuguese in comparison with the British. Like many Spaniards and Portuguese, most Latin Americans remained illiterate and distrustful of foreigners.

Socially, the Latin Americans tended to remain divided, as they had in colonial times, into a small "master class" of wealthy and influential families and a peon class of poor whites, Indians, Negroes, and mestizos. There was no powerful middle class of merchants, bankers, and businessmen. Army officers, government officials, plantation owners, professional men, and the higher clergy enjoyed a dominant position. The great majority of the people constituted the hewers of wood and drawers of water. Yet even the poorest and most humble inherited some of the stoic dignity, the grave courtesy, and good manners of the Spaniard. It should not be forgotten, however, that the composition of the classes varied from region to region. In the Caribbean islands and northern Brazil the Negroes outnumbered the Indians and whites. In Ecuador in 1939 less than 10 per cent of the population was estimated as white; the remainder were of Indian or of mixed blood with only 2 per cent Negroes. In the Argentine Republic, where the Indian population had never been large, and few Negroes were imported, the population was "overwhelmingly European in origin."

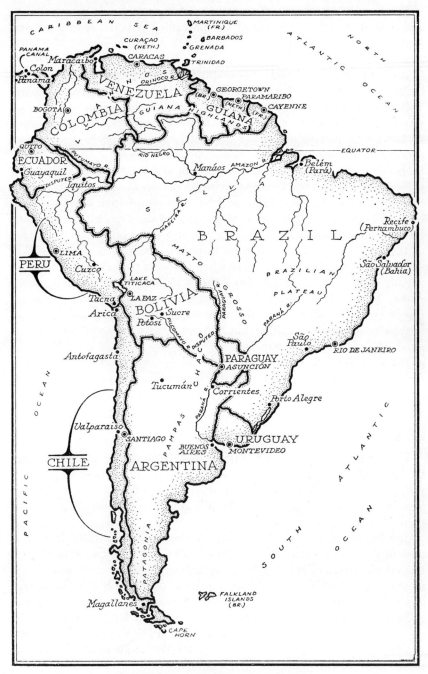

THE SOUTH AMERICAN REPUBLICS

The economic problems of most Latin American republics were acute and difficult to solve, because of the prevailing poverty, ignorance, and disease. Lacking the capital to develop their natural resources, the Latin Americans became dependent on foreign capital, and much of the profit from their mines, railroads, telegraph lines, power plants, farms, and factories was drained off in the form of dividends and interest on loans. This "economic vassalage" transformed millions of people into "bond-servants," often without their knowledge or consent. In some cases dictators who had seized power granted foreign syndicates extravagant concessions in return for arms. Sometimes, too, the economy of a repub-lic became dependent on a single product and a decline in the market price could mean ruin. Uruguay, with 95 per cent of its exports limited to animal products, provided a striking example of such overspecializa-tion. In Bolivia, tin ore made up 90 per cent of the export trade for years. In Costa Rica, Guatemala, and Salvador coffee sales provided 75 per cent of the exports. Chile, which once furnished nine-tenths of the world's supply of nitrates, suffered acutely when chemists perfected a method for making nitrates synthetically from the limitless nitrogen of the atmos-phere. Venezuela, which was found to have the third richest petroleum resources in the world and also enormous iron deposits, proved more fortunate and grew wealthy, but the wealth was concentrated in the hands of a small ruling group.

These and other differences made all generalizations about Latin America subject to qualifications. Each republic had problems peculiar to itself, as a study of the individual states will demonstrate.

2. MIDDLE AMERICAN STATES

The lands that lie between the Isthmus of Tehuantepec and the Isthmus of Panama are often referred to collectively as Central America. A more suitable term, which includes Central America and also Mexico and the islands of the Caribbean Sea, is Middle America, and this term will be used here.

The largest of the Middle American states, and the third largest in area of the Latin American republics is Mexico. Its population in 1939 totaled nineteen million, of which approximately one-seventh were listed as pure white and six-sevenths as Indians or of mixed blood. Long eco-nomically retarded and impoverished, Mexico entered the twentieth century with two pressing problems: the need for land reform and the need to escape the exactions of foreign-owned corporations which were exploiting the resources of the country for the profit of alien investors rather than for the benefit of the Mexicans.

The land question rose out of the hacienda system which had been introduced by the Spanish conquerors three centuries earlier. By the end of the nineteenth century a few families had come to own most of the arable land throughout whole provinces, and a majority of the rural workers were in a state of peonage. Their food was inadequate, their hours of labor excessive, and their homes miserable windowless huts of one or two rooms floored with earth. The rising ferment within the country broke into revolution in 1911. General Don Porfirio Diaz, who had maintained a firm rule since 1876, was overthrown and exiled, and Mexico entered a decade of turmoil.

The revolutionary slogan, "Land and Liberty," was realized slowly in the midst of confusion and civil war. A new constitution, adopted in 1917 and modified in 1929 and 1933, provided for a Chamber of Deputies of 170 members elected for three years and a Senate of fifty-eight members elected for six years. There were two senators from each of the twenty-eight states of the republic and two from the Federal District surrounding Mexico City. The president of the republic was elected by direct popular vote for a term of six years. The political edifice constructed after 1911 was less important than the social and economic changes. Lands confiscated by the government were allotted to the village assemblies for distribution as family holdings. The rural village became the real administrative unit, and in recognizing this fact the revolution brought about a partial return to the communal society of the Aztecs, known as *ejido*. The new agrarian laws which turned private estates over to the people constituted the essence of the revolution, for some two million families comprising half the Mexican people received individual allotments of land. The rapid increase of the population (a 17 per cent rise between 1930 and 1940) suggested that living conditions had definitely improved. There was also a vital artistic renaissance, especially in painting, which suggested that the latent energy and talent of these long submerged people would astonish more advanced nations.

The second great problem, the question of foreign investments and foreign control of resources, was resolved in part through confiscation, repudiation, or refunding. The external debt of the republic had been in default since 1914 and amounted to about $235,000,000 in 1939. On one-fifth of the debt, held by investors in the United States, the Mexican government made a settlement; another fifth, owed to British bondholders, remained in default; and three-fifths, owed to German citizens or corporations, was repudiated. British and other foreign investors also held 97 per cent of the mining properties of the republic. As Mexico produced 40 per cent of the world's silver, and silver and gold together constituted one-fourth of the nation's exports, this alien ownership deprived the Mexicans of the management and profit of their most lucrative natural resources. It was not surprising, therefore, that the government sought to terminate this era of foreign financial control. In 1937 the main railway lines were declared national property; the railway bonds, half of which were held in London, remained in default. A year later, after negotiations had failed, the Mexican government appropriated the oil properties

which had been developed at considerable cost by three foreign companies. The Mexicans were determined to regain the control and enjoyment of their own resources

In all the Latin American republics the size, the power, and the wealth
of the United States excited misgivings. This fear of the "Colossus of the
North" increased after 1898 when the United States defeated Spain and
helped Cuba and Puerto Rico to become free of Spanish rule. It soon
appeared, however, that these Caribbean islands had only exchanged one
alien control for another. The United States kept Puerto Rico and maintained military forces in Cuba. Five years later (1903) the United States
encouraged the province of Panama to secede from Colombia, and the
new republic promptly gave its protector authority to construct the
Panama Canal across the isthmus.

Although the United States opposed intervention by any other great
power in the affairs of Middle America, it frequently interfered itself in
the early years of the twentieth century. Between 1912 and 1919 American soldiers entered nearly all the republics of Middle America when local
disorders created a threat to the life or property of United States citizens.
Nicaragua (1912), Mexico, Haiti, and the Dominican Republic (1914),
Honduras and Puerto Rico (1919) all endured the landing of American
marines on their shores, and sometimes these military forces remained for
years.

As the United States had also secured a powerful economic influence
over the Middle American countries their inhabitants feared that they
might lose their sovereignty and become outlying dependencies of their
great neighbor to the north. As early as 1902 an Argentine statesman, Luis
Maria Drago, had proposed that no foreign power should use armed force
or occupy the territory of a sovereign American state in order to compel
the payment of public debts. The Hague Convention of 1907 approved
this Drago Doctrine but only after some modifications. Armed force was
to be used only as a last resort after efforts to settle disputes by arbitration had failed.

After 1933, under the administration of Franklin D. Roosevelt, relations
between the United States and the Latin American republics improved.
At a conference of American nations held in Montevideo (1933) the
United States renounced the use of armed intervention in their affairs
and the following year withdrew its military forces from Haiti. This gave
more force and harmony to the Pan American Union, a loose organization
of the twenty-one American republics which had been slowly taking form.
When the delegates of the Union met at Buenos Aires in 1936, they
agreed that all the republics should hold common consultations whenever
the peace of the New World was threatened. Two years later at Lima,
the Union approved a resolution that declared every independent American state enjoyed absolute sovereignty and that all would defend themselves against foreign aggression or intervention. These agreements, in

which the United States joined, reduced the fears of the Latin American peoples and made them less suspicious toward the United States.

3. THE ANDEAN REGION

The geography and climate of Latin America helped to explain why the Spanish colonies split up into twenty republics. Like North America, Middle and South America have high mountain ranges on the west coast. From Panama to the Straits of Magellan the Andes stretch like a mighty barrier, four thousand miles in length. They are loftier than the Rocky Mountains and more difficult to cross, for no rivers comparable to the Columbia and Colorado cut through them to the Pacific and few of the passes are lower than twelve thousand feet above sea level. Three-fourths of South America lies in the tropics, and the vast rain forest of the Amazon basin — the largest expanse of virgin forest on the globe — adds to the difficulties of communication. These conditions explain why the population is largely concentrated in more or less isolated pockets, separated by almost empty regions of lofty upland or low-lying tracts of almost impenetrable forest.

Four countries — Colombia, Ecuador, Peru, and Chile — span the west coast of South America. With these Bolivia may be included, for although it has no seacoast it too is transected and dominated by the Andes. These five mountainous republics have a total area of nearly two million square miles, roughly half that of the United States and its outlying possessions, and their combined population in 1939 was about twenty-five million. The composition of this population varied greatly. In Ecuador, which lies (as its name suggests) on the equator, less than one-tenth of the people were classed as white; in Chile the great majority were of European origin.

The Andean countries also differed sharply in their wealth and stage of development. In most of them agriculture remained the major activity and income was depressingly low. The stage of development and modernization could be estimated most readily by the amount of mechanical energy that each country had succeeded in harnessing from fuel and water power. In Colombia, Ecuador, Peru, and Bolivia the supply of mechanical energy per capita was equivalent to that available in 180 kilograms (about 400 pounds) of coal. In Chile, where half the people were urban and the energy consumption ten times as high, the per capita income was strikingly superior. By 1939 annual income per capita in Chile had reached $180, whereas in Ecuador it was only $44, less than one-fourth as high.

For comparison, one may note that the average income per capita for the world as a whole was calculated at $120 in 1939; consequently all the Andean nations except the Chileans were considerably below that average. In this they shared the fate of the Africans and Asians. For one-fourth of the global population — the 550 million inhabitants of the United States, Europe, and the British dominions — enjoyed about $180 billion out of an estimated global income of $260 billion, an average of $328 per capita. The remaining 1600 million people of the world shared about $80 billion among them, an average of $50 per capita. The Latin Americans as a whole received about $85 per capita, and were therefore twice as well off as the Asians and Africans who received only $40 per capita on the average. But the Latin Americans had their wealthy neighbors to excite their envy, for the people of the United States enjoyed an income of more than $500 per capita in 1939.

4. ARGENTINA, URUGUAY, AND VENEZUELA

These three republics will be discussed together because of their economic progress. In 1939 the per capita income in these countries already exceeded that of their neighbors and it was rising much faster. Within another ten years all three were to secure a per capita income four times as high as that of the Latin American peoples as a whole. An examination of the resources, methods, and advantages these nations utilized to advance their well-being suggests where the clues to Latin American progress may be found.

The Argentine Republic, with an area of roughly one million square miles and a population of some twelve million in 1939, already possessed many advantages. The climate was healthy and not excessively hot; the Rio de la Plata and its tributaries provided access to the interior; the low-lying plains were suitable for wheat farming and the pampas for cattle grazing; and the Argentine population, almost entirely of European descent, was literate and progressive. Facing the Atlantic, Argentina could ship its wheat and meat to Europe and receive in exchange the manufactured goods it needed. But it had also begun to develop industries of its own — by 1939 their output was worth one-third as much as the products of the farms and cattle ranges. Buenos Aires, the Argentine capital, with a population of two million, was the largest city of South America.

Uruguay, with 72,000 square miles and two million people, was in many respects a small replica of Argentina. But it was more exclusively devoted to stock raising; in 1939 it had eighteen million sheep, eight million cattle, and over half a million horses. Only 7 per cent of the total area was reserved for agriculture. Animals and animal products comprised 95 per cent of Uruguayan exports; manufactured goods had to be imported, for lack of coal, oil, and hydroelectric power retarded the development of industry. Nevertheless the per capita consumption of energy was two-thirds that of Argentina and Venezuela in 1939, and much higher than that of all the Andean states except Chile. A favorable balance of trade furnished a twelve million dollar surplus, and the Uruguayans enjoyed free education, old age pensions, and medical care for the poor, for expectant mothers, and for children.

Venezuela differed from Argentina and Uruguay in climate, resources, and racial strains. It lay in the tropics with its southernmost point almost touching the equator, and part of the interior was so inaccessible it resisted exploration. The population, over three million in 1939, combined several strains, and although estimates varied, the great majority (over 90 per cent) were considered to be of Indian, Negro, or mixed blood. Until the twentieth century Venezuela remained a poor and retarded country, but the discovery of oil around Lake Maracaibo improved the national economy. By 1939 it ranked third among the countries of the world as a source of petroleum. This raised the national income, but the profits were not widely distributed and did little to benefit a majority of the people who remained poor and illiterate. In other words, although the *national* income climbed, most Venezuelans had a lower standard of living, less education, and a shorter life expectancy than the inhabitants of Argentina and Uruguay. Their birth rate in 1939 was more than double that of the Uruguayans, but their death rate was also more than double.

A rise in national income was not sufficient in itself to solve the problems of the Latin American countries. As the case of Venezuela showed, an equitable distribution of that income was also important, as well as adequate facilities for education, sanitation, and public welfare. Almost all the Latin American republics possessed natural resources sufficient to assure a high standard of living for their people. What most of them lacked was the skill, the capital, and the machinery to exploit those resources effectively and distribute the benefits equitably.

5. THE UNITED STATES OF BRAZIL

The Republic of Brazil is the largest and most populous of the Latin American states. In 1939 it included almost half the area and population of South America. Its area of more than three and a quarter million square miles exceeded that of the continental United States. By 1939 the population of Brazil had reached forty million, twice that of Mexico, the second largest Latin American nation. Most Brazilians spoke a modified form of Portuguese, but groups of Italian, German, and Slavic immigrants, especially in southern Brazil, preserved their own languages and customs. The composition of the population combined several strains, some three-fifths being officially classified as white, the remaining two-fifths as Negroes, mulattoes, or Indians. All the larger cities and the bulk of the Brazilian people were found along the Atlantic coast. Although the area around Rio de Janeiro held more than 250 inhabitants to the square mile in 1939, the great rain forest of the Amazon valley was almost empty, with less than two inhabitants per square mile.

Brazil in 1939 had great resources but a low standard of living. Per capita income, estimated at $50 a year, was little more than half that of Latin America as a whole. Per capita energy consumption was less than one-sixtieth that of the United States. Dependable statistics on the birth rate and death rate were unobtainable but both were unquestionably high. Two-thirds of the people were illiterate. Millions of Brazilians labored on great agricultural estates under conditions that were little better than peonage.

In the small inland state of Paraguay on the southern border of Brazil income was somewhat better but the government was burdened by heavy internal and external debts. A war with Bolivia (1932–1935) doubled the area of Paraguay to about 150,000 square miles with a population (1939) of one million. There were few Negroes in Paraguay, the people being of mixed Indian and European descent, with Spanish and Guarani (an Indian speech) the prevailing languages.

Brazil and Paraguay combined held half the population of South America, and the harsh conditions there also prevailed in more or less acute form in almost all the Latin American states. These conditions were a threat to the peace of the Americas for two reasons. First, the contrast between the high standard of living in the United States and Canada and the low standard of living in most of Latin America could not fail to excite disturbing comparisons. Secondly, the North Americans were growing relatively richer while the Latin Americans were growing relatively poorer. In 1939 the per capita income in North America was approximately six times larger than that in Latin America and this disparity was *increasing*. Within ten years it was to be ten times larger. One reason for this growing discrepancy was that in North America income was rising more rapidly than population whereas in Latin America population was rising more rapidly than income.

If these trends continued unchecked, it was easy to foresee that Latin America would become an explosive area, seething with discontent. It is difficult for impoverished people not to envy rich and extravagant neighbors. In their resentment the Latin Americans would find it easy to believe that the North Americans were exploiting them — plundering their resources, refusing them a fair price for their crops, making high profits from the capital they had invested in mines, oil wells, and plantations while paying minimum wages to the Latin American laborers who worked in these enterprises. When such convictions gripped a Latin American nation, anger against the "foreign imperialists" might move them to confiscate foreign-owned property in order to operate mines, railways, factories, and plantations for their own profit. This had happened in Mexico after the revolution of 1911. As the prospect of poverty and population pressure became more acute it was likely to happen in other Latin American countries. But would such a policy ease the poverty and solve the complex problems that beset Latin America?

Section V: ASIA AND THE COLONIAL WORLD

32

THE NEAR AND MIDDLE EAST AND AFRICA

Two-thirds of mankind live in a global poorhouse, one of the worst of which is the Middle East.[1]

EMIL LENGYEL

1. PROBLEMS OF THE AREA

THE NEAR AND MIDDLE EAST[2] lies in the center of the world's greatest arid belt, which stretches from the Atlantic Ocean through North Africa and Southwest and Central Asia to the confines of China. Owing to limited rainfall or its complete absence, much of the area of the Near and Middle East is covered with bleak deserts and barren mountains, which were denuded of forests centuries ago. Settled life is possible only along the seacoasts, in the valleys of great rivers (the Nile and the Tigris-Euphrates) and on high mountain plateaux. Other areas can support only a dispersed population of nomads, who roam the semi-deserts with their flocks of sheep and goats. Finally, some areas are total deserts and are devoid of population altogether. Until the discovery of oil in the Near and Middle East in the twentieth century, it possessed no very valuable resource; its importance lay in its geographic location at the crossroads of three continents: Europe, Asia, and Africa. The principal trade and strategic routes of the Old World traversed it. In addition to agriculture, trade provided employment and sometimes considerable wealth. The discovery of all-water routes to India and the Far East in the fifteenth and sixteenth centuries caused the economic and strategic importance of the Near and Middle East to decline, but the opening of the Suez Canal in 1869 once again revived it.

[1] *World Without End, The Middle East* (New York: John Day, 1953), p. 3.

[2] Until World War I the term "Near East" was generally used in reference to the lands facing the Eastern Mediterranean, including the Balkans, and the term "Middle East" in reference to the lands facing the Persian Gulf and the Arabian Sea. Since then the term "Middle East" has increasingly been used to refer to both areas, but excluding the Balkans. To prevent confusion both terms will be used in conjunction in the following narrative.

In ancient times the Near and Middle East was the heart of the civilization of the Old World. Three of the surviving great religions and philosophies of the world — Judaism, Christianity, and Islam — were born there. In modern times, however, the Near and Middle East became the meeting ground of the hostile civilizations of the West and East. In the nineteenth century it became the battleground of the rivaling imperialisms of the West, notably Russian and British. In the front line of this conflict stood the lands called sometimes the "Northern Tier" of the Near and Middle East: Turkey, Iran, and Afghanistan.

2. TURKEY, IRAN, AND AFGHANISTAN

The Turkey which emerged from World War I was a diminished but still fair-sized country (about 244,000 square miles). Moreover, it was much more homogeneous in population and culture than the former Ottoman Empire. Under the leadership of Mustafa Kemal Pasha (1881–1938), the only successful Turkish general in World War I, the Turks resolutely turned their backs on their Imperial Ottoman past and set about transforming Turkey into a modern national state on the western model. Sultan Mohammed VI, who had completely discredited himself by agreeing to the humiliating Peace of Sèvres, was deposed (1922), and Turkey was proclaimed a republic (1923). Kemal was strongly influenced by western liberal, rationalist, and secular thought. He was an ardent Turkish nationalist and apparently also a sincere believer in democracy. But unlike many reformers in Asia, he wisely recognized that Turkey was socially, culturally, and politically unprepared for parliamentary democracy. In 1923 Turkey adopted a conventional western liberal constitution, but this remained a promise for the future because only one party, the People's Republican Party, was permitted. Until his death, Kemal exercised dictatorial powers and he used them with an energy and harshness reminiscent of Peter the Great of Russia to reform every phase of Turkish life.

Kemal regarded Islam as an obstacle to the modernization of Turkey. He determined to break the close ties between the State and Church existing in Turkey — and in all Islamic lands — and to transform the country into a purely secular state. The Caliphate was abolished (1924) and the legal system based on the Islamic Sacred Law was replaced with one based on secular codes inspired by European codes (1926). The influence of the conservative Moslem clergy was curbed and the fanatical dervish orders were suppressed. Polygamy was abolished and civil marriage made compulsory. The wearing of the fez by men was forbidden and the use of the veil by women discouraged. All men were ordered to assume family names in the western fashion. For Kemal the National Assembly chose the name Atatürk (Father of the Turks). The Moslem calendar was replaced with the Christian (Gregorian) one, and Sunday rather than Friday became the official day of rest in the week. The western Latin alphabet replaced the Arabic one, and the Turkish official and literary language was purified of Arabic and Persian words, which had made it incomprehensible to the uneducated Turk. A great emphasis was placed on developing a western-style, secular system of education. Primary education was made compulsory, and an earnest effort was made to wipe out illiteracy.

Economic problems also received the close attention of Kemal. The Turkish economy was essentially an agrarian one. Land was owned in small lots by the peasants, who were the backbone of the Turkish nation. The government was well aware of this and aided the peasants with price supports, easy credit, and advice on farming methods. The government was interested also in the development of industry, but the industrialization of Turkey was hampered by lack of capital and of a native commercial and managerial class. In the Ottoman Empire business had been almost exclusively in the hands of the minorities (Greeks, Jews, and Armenians) or of foreigners. The Turks preferred government or military service and farming. Foreign capital and enterprise were neither welcome nor readily available. Remembering the humiliating capitulations and Ottoman economic servitude to foreign nations, Kemal pursued a policy of expropriation and nationalization of foreign-owned business firms in Turkey. In the absence of native private capital and business enterprise, the government decided itself to enter the field of economic enterprise. In 1934 it adopted, on the Soviet model, a five-year plan of industrialization, designed to develop Turkey's mineral wealth (copper, chrome, coal, and iron) and the production of basic consumers' goods (textiles, shoes, paper, etc.). Some progress was made, but the over-all results were not comparable to those in Soviet Russia. Agriculture and production of industrial raw materials remained the essential Turkish economic activities. Like the Balkan countries, Turkey signed in 1936 a clearing agreement with Germany who speedily became Turkey's best customer. When Kemal Atatürk died in 1938, Turkey had become a modernized and rejuvenated nation and by far the strongest country in the Near and Middle East.

The development of Turkey's eastern neighbor and ancient rival, Iran (Persia), ran along somewhat similar lines. Like Turkey, Iran had been an object of intense rivalry between Russia and Britain. In 1907, in the famous Anglo-Russian Convention, Iran was divided into spheres of influence. During World War I, although Iran had declared her neutrality, she was occupied by Russian and British forces, which operated from her territory against Turkey. Both occupants organized Iranian forces (the Russian-trained Persian Cossacks and the British-trained South Persia Rifles), the authority of the government of Ahmed Shah (1909–1925) was shattered, and the country sank into anarchy. During the Russian

Revolution the Russian forces were withdrawn and the British became dominant in the whole country. After the war, they prevented the admission of an Iranian peace delegation to the Paris Peace Conference and imposed on Iran a treaty which reduced her practically to a British protectorate (August, 1919). This highhanded treatment provoked a strong nationalist reaction in Iran. The Majlis (parliament) refused to ratify the treaty, and after British evacuation of Iran a nationalist force under the command of Reza Pahlavi marched on Teheran and overthrew the government (February, 1921). The discredited Ahmed Shah was packed off into exile and Reza Pahlavi became dictator.

Like Kemal Atatürk, Reza Pahlavi (1877–1944) was a soldier. He had risen from the ranks in the Russian-trained Persian Cossacks. Upon becoming dictator, he thought of following the Turkish example and proclaiming a republic. But the abolition of the Caliphate in Turkey in 1924 and Kemal's anti-clerical policy stirred up the powerful Iranian Moslem clergy and provoked an anti-republican reaction in Iran. Instead of proclaiming a republic, Reza Pahlavi deposed Ahmed Shah and proclaimed himself shah (1925). Iran had been a constitutional monarchy since 1906. The constitution of 1906 was not disturbed, but it remained pure window dressing. Reza Shah (1925–1941) was for all practical purposes an absolute monarch, but like Kemal he was a reformer. He hired an American financial adviser, Dr. A. C. Millspaugh, to put the Iranian finances in order and work out a program of reforms (1922–1927). An effort was made to improve public sanitation and education and to develop the resources of the country, but it was notably less successful than in Turkey.

The most important resource of Iran was oil. It had been developed already before the war by the British-owned Anglo-Persian Oil Company, but Iran derived little benefit from the oil industry. Under the terms of the original concession the Iranian government received 16 per cent of the company's net profits. Oil is a commodity, the price of which is subject to wide fluctuations. The royalties of the Iranian government consequently also greatly varied. During the depression they fell below 300,000 pounds annually. At the same time the company paid three times as much in corporate taxes to the British government, which moreover received as the principal shareholder in the company (51 per cent) large dividends. In 1932 the Iranian government cancelled the concession. After an acrimonious dispute, which the British government placed before the League of Nations, a new concession was negotiated which guaranteed the Iranian government an annual minimum of 750,000 pounds in royalties and 225,000 pounds in taxes (1933).

Thanks in part to the oil revenue, Reza Shah organized a small but efficient army with which he restored the authority of the government in the distant provinces and over the unruly nomads. Iran is a large country (628,000 square miles) with a rugged terrain. The ability of the government to impose its authority over distant provinces was improved by the construction, at great cost, of the Trans-Iranian Railway. It was completed in 1938 and stretched from the Caspian Sea to the Persian Gulf. But most reforms designed to improve agriculture and develop industry were failures owing to the dishonesty and incompetence of officials and the generally low standards in the country. Unlike Turkey, land in Iran was owned by a small, sophisticated, and socially irresponsible class of absentee landowners who kept the peasants in virtual bondage. Another obstacle to reform was the bigoted, diehard clergy. Reza Shah, who unlike Kemal had failed to create a group of dedicated associates and a political party, did not dare to move against either of these powerful groups. Iran remained a weak, backward country, whose existence depended — as before the war — on the balance of power between Britain and Soviet Russia.

Iran's eastern neighbor was the mountainous and primitive country of Afghanistan. Since the Anglo-Russian Convention of 1907 Britain exercised a preponderant influence in the country. After the war the Afghans became restive and clashes between them and the British Indian Army occurred. Although Britain was perfectly able to deal with the Afghan forces, she was at the time retrenching and decided to give the Afghans their freedom. In 1919 she formally recognized Afghan independence and discontinued her subsidies to the Afghan government. Like Turkey and Iran, Afghanistan produced a reformer after the war, Emir Amanullah (1919–1929). In 1923 he proclaimed a constitution and launched a program of well-meant but erratic reforms which provoked the wrath of the bigoted Moslem clergy and of the warlike tribesmen. In 1929 Amanullah was forced to abdicate, and under his successor the country reverted to its time-honored stagnant ways.

In foreign relations Turkey, Iran, and Afghanistan leaned in the postwar period toward Soviet Russia. This was a natural reaction to the growth of British power in the Near and Middle East. It also appeared justified by the attitude of the Bolsheviks who had forsworn imperialism and renounced all the concessions and privileges which had been extorted from Asian countries by the Tsarist government. In 1921 all three countries signed treaties with Soviet Russia, pledging respect for each other's sovereignty. An era of relatively good relations between Soviet Russia and her southern neighbors followed. In December, 1925, one day after the League of Nations awarded the oil-rich Mosul district to Iraq (see p. 200), Britain's protégé, the disgruntled Turks signed a friendship pact with Soviet Russia. Soviet-Turkish friendship, however, did not prevent Kemal Atatürk from ruthlessly suppressing the Turkish communists.

As Italy's aggressiveness grew in the Mediterranean in the 1930's, Turkey began to seek closer relations with her neighbors to the west and to the east. In 1934 she entered into the Balkan Pact with Greece, Rumania, and Yugoslavia, and in 1937 she entered into the analogous Saadabad Pact with Iran, Afghanistan, and Iraq. Meanwhile, in 1936, Turkey obtained at the Montreux Conference of the signatories to the Straits Convention of 1923 (see p. 200) the right to refortify the Straits area. This reflected the concern of the western powers as well as of Russia with the growing aggressiveness of Italy and Germany. At the same time it paved the way for a reconciliation between Turkey and the western powers. As the clouds of war drew over Europe, France became more inclined to yield to Turkey in the matter of her border with Syria. The Treaty of Lausanne had awarded the district of Alexandretta (Hatay), in which the Turks claimed to have a majority, to Syria — a mandate of France. In 1938 France consented to a complicated condominium over Hatay and a year later yielded it outright to Turkey. In return Turkey signed mutual assistance pacts with Britain and France (May–June, 1939). But when World War II broke out, Turkey launched on a policy of cautious and cagey neutrality, which exasperated both groups of belligerents but which probably prevented the extension of the war into the Near and Middle East.

3. ARABIA

The defeat and disintegration of the Ottoman Empire resulted in freeing the Arabs from Turkish rule, but the policy of the victorious Allies did not favor their unification. The Allies created several Arab states, which were divided by rather artificial borders designed not to mark any natural divisions between them (although these existed) but rather to establish a balance between French and British interests. This caused a bitter disappointment among Arab nationalists who had hoped for a united Arab state comprising all of Arabia. Some of them had even dreamed about restoring the great Arabic Empire stretching from the Atlantic to the Indian Ocean. The broad strata of the Arab people — the poor peasants, nomads, and (in the cities) petty tradesmen and artisans — had as yet little national consciousness, but they were often religiously fanatic and socially discontented. Both sentiments could easily be turned against the West. The Arab potentates and social elite — the "effendi class" of government officials, army officers, landowners, and tribal chiefs — found the divisions in the Arabic world really to their advantage. But the ideal of Arabic unity was popular and they paid lip service to it. To blame the western powers not only for the divisions among the Arabs but also for the wretched economic and social conditions prevailing in the Arab states was, the effendis found out, the easiest way to divert the discontent of the Arab masses, whom they ruthlessly oppressed and exploited.

Economically, the Arab countries were mainly agrarian and pastoral states. Owing to a water shortage, the amount of arable land was very limited. It was generally owned by small groups of conservative and socially irresponsible landowners, who kept the peasant tenants in veritable bondage. Industry grew slowly. The most important industry was the oil industry. It held the promise of great wealth, which if invested in improvements might go far toward balancing the water shortage and dearth of other resources. In 1927 oil was found near Kirkuk in the Mosul district of Iraq, in 1931 in Bahrain, and in 1938 in Saudi Arabia. The Arab oil industry was really not developed until after World War II, but the companies paid generous advances on future royalties to the Arab potentates. Unfortunately, most of this wealth was foolishly and irresponsibly squandered. The Arab states remained undeveloped and desperately poor.

The real leaders of Arab nationalism were the rising generations of Arab intellectuals, many of whom were trained in the West or in western schools in the Near and Middle East (e.g., the American University in Beirut). Fed on western ideas of nationalism and democracy, they found the dependence of the Arab states on the western powers intolerable. The West was represented in the Arab countries almost exclusively by France and Britain. Italy and Germany tried in the 1930's to establish an influence in the Near and Middle East, but not with much success. France and Britain were rivals in the Near and Middle East, but they were not enemies. This saved the Arab states from the tensions and dangers, experienced by the Balkan peoples in the nineteenth century, of belonging to two rival blocs of powers. Although the Arab states were dependent on France and Britain, their relationship to them greatly varied

In northern Arabia the French mandate of Syria was inhabited in the main by Arabs, but they were divided into a large number of mutually antagonistic Moslem and Christian sects. Of whatever religion or sect, however, the Syrian Arabs were generally hostile to French rule. They felt that France had stolen their freedom after their liberation from the Turks — a liberation to which France had contributed little. French administration, although infinitely superior to the corrupt and inefficient Ottoman rule, often provoked greater resentment than the latter. Bureaucratic centralism, inherent in the French system, left very little to local initiative. Encountering increasing difficulties in ruling Syria, France resorted to force and an unashamed policy of divide and rule. The district of Lebanon, which had a precarious Christian majority, was separated from Syria and treated as a separate state. The rest of Syria was divided into four autonomous states. The mutual antagonism of the religious communities was encouraged.

In 1925 the warlike Druze mountaineers rose in rebellion which spread through Syria. The revolt was put down after two years of heavy fighting, during the course of which Damascus was twice bombarded and shelled. In 1928 France inaugurated a policy of reconciliation by summoning constituent assemblies in both Syria and Lebanon. But it was not until 1936 that France succeeded in coming to terms with the two countries along the lines of the Anglo-Iraqi Treaty of 1930 (see below). Franco-Syrian and Franco-Lebanese treaties were signed which provided for ending the French mandate in three years and for an alliance of twenty-five years. During this time France was to have the right to maintain troops in Syria and Lebanon and to equip and train their armies. But the cession of the district of Alexandretta to Turkey without Syrian consent and the outbreak of World War II in 1939 put the whole arrangement in doubt.

The British generally showed greater skill in ruling the Arabs. Their system was less rigid, and though jurisdictionally often vague, it was better adapted to local circumstances. From their long experience in dealing with colonial peoples they had learned that the easiest way of controlling them was by ruling them indirectly, through a native elite and a native ruler, "assisted" by British military and political advisers. By this arrangement — formally an alliance and practically a protectorate — they had long controlled the Arab states along the coasts of the Arabian Sea and the Persian Gulf: Aden, Hadramaut, Oman, Trucial Coast, Qatar, and Kuwait. Now they proposed to extend their control to other portions of Arabia by using various members of the Hashimite dynasty. In Hejaz, along the coast of the Red Sea, they recognized King Husein. In Iraq, along the Tigris and Euphrates, they installed Husein's son Faisal, and in Transjordan another son, Abdullah (see p. 198). Hejaz was independent, Iraq was a mandate, and Transjordan was a part of the Palestinian mandate. The British were anxious to end their mandatory responsibilities and to enter into the more convenient alliance-protectorate arrangement — provided they could secure guarantees of their economic and military interests. This they succeeded in doing with Transjordan informally as early as 1923 and formally in 1928. Transjordan was a poor desert kingdom with a population of less than one million, consisting mainly of Bedouin nomads. Emir Abdullah was thankful for the British subsidies and military and technical assistance, and, until after World War II, relations between Britain and Transjordan were very cordial.

With Iraq the British found it more difficult to come to an agreement. Iraq (ancient Mesopotamia) was a much larger (172,000 square miles) and populous (about 3,500,000, almost half of which were minorities) country. It possessed arable land and oil. Iraqi politics were chronically unstable and marked by sudden shifts and outbursts of violence. After the suppression of the Iraqi revolt of 1920, the Anglo-Iraqi relations were never cordial. Nevertheless, after much hard bargaining, Britain succeeded in coming to an agreement with Iraq in 1930, which provided a prototype for her relations with Egypt as well as for French relations with Syria and Lebanon. The Anglo-Iraqi Treaty of 1930 provided for an alliance of twenty-five years and the right of Britain to maintain a number of bases in Iraq and to train and equip its army. Two years later Iraq was admitted to the League of Nations and the British mandate ended.

Of three Hashimite rulers, Husein proved the most intractable ally. A haughty man, he alienated other Arabs by his pretensions (he proclaimed himself Caliph after the Turks abolished the Caliphate in Constantinople) and the British by insisting that they carry out in Palestine their wartime promises to the Arabs. Moreover, he was an incompetent administrator who resisted westernization and — worst of all — neglected his armed forces. When he refused to accept further British assistance and a formal alliance in 1923, the British decided to shift their support to his great rival, ibn-Saud, the Wahabi warrior who had been engaged for some time in building an empire in central Arabia (Nejd). In 1924–1925, after the British had removed their protecting hand from Hejaz, ibn-Saud conquered it and proclaimed himself King of Nejd and Hejaz (1926). The British hastened to recognize the conquest (1927), but Saudi Arabia declined British subsidies and advisers. A shrewd statesman, ibn-Saud (1880–1953) preferred to rely for technical guidance and assistance on private individuals and private business firms. In 1932 he granted a concession to the Arabian-American Oil Company. Although the company did not find oil until 1938 and did not exploit it commercially until after World War II, it advanced money to the Saudi government. Between Hejaz and Aden on the coast of the Red Sea lay Yemen. A theocratic state, ruled by a religious imam, it maintained complete aloofness from Britain and its Arab neighbors.

With one Arab country, Palestine, the British failed dismally to work out a satisfactory relationship. By making contradictory promises to the Jewish Zionists and the Arab nationalists during World War I (see p. 174), the British created in Palestine a situation, the consequences of which were to plague them and the world even after their departure from the country in 1948. They had grossly underestimated the dynamism of Jewish Zionism and Arab nationalism. Instead of living peacefully together, as the British supposed they would, the Jews determined to transform Palestine into a national Jewish state. The Arabs were equally determined to keep it an Arab national state. Riots between Jewish immigrants and the Arab population broke out as early as 1921. In 1929 the conflict took on menacing proportions and resulted in many deaths. In 1936, after the persecution of the Jews in Germany stimulated their emigration to Palestine, a savage guerrilla warfare broke out, which lasted until the outbreak of World War II. Caught between the irreconcilable forces of Jewish Zionism and Arab nationalism, the British vacillated. They sent several Royal Commissions to Palestine to investigate conditions and propose solutions; they published White Papers; and they summoned round-table conferences. But they could not find a solution, for a solution presupposed a readiness to compromise and the Jewish Zionists and Arab nationalists, driven by a religious and nationalist fanaticism, regarded their respective causes as sacred and any compromise as treason. In the end, the British, who had originally enjoyed the good will of the Jews and the Arabs, incurred the wrath of both — not only in Palestine but elsewhere. When World War II broke out, the Jews, who regarded Nazi Germany as their principal enemy, suspended their struggle for a Jewish Palestine for the duration of the hostilities and rallied to the Allied cause. The Arabs, on the other hand, had no reason to dislike the Germans and many reasons to distrust the Allies. They generally welcomed the war as a God-given opportunity to shake off the French and British yoke.

4. NORTH AND CENTRAL AFRICA

The most populous and important Arab country, Egypt, lay not in Arabia but in Africa. Modern Egypt was established by Mehmet Ali (1769–1849), an Albanian adventurer and Ottoman officer who made himself hereditary governor (Khedive) of Egypt during the Napoleonic wars. Thanks to the reforms of Mehmet Ali and his successors, Egypt was more advanced in her cultural, social, and economic development than any other Arab country. Egypt was the cultural center of the Arabic world, and the Arabic language as spoken and written by educated Egyptians became standard modern Arabic. The economy of Egypt was based on agriculture. Since time immemorial the Nile valley has been one of the most intensely cultivated areas in the world. Thanks to the fertility of its alluvial soil, hot climate, and controlled irrigation, two or three good crops a year could be raised in Egypt. In ancient times Egypt used to be the granary of the Mediterranean world, but in the nineteenth century the introduction of cotton culture resulted in decline of food production. The consequent rise in food prices and the phenomenal increase in population (from an estimated 2,500,000 in 1798 to 12,750,000 in 1917 and 15,920,000 in 1937) depressed the living standard of the Egyptian population to a pitifully low level. While cotton brought handsome but uncertain profits to the Egyptian landlords, it made the Egyptian economy dependent on the fluctuations of the world market.

Ambitious building and financial improvidence brought about Egyptian bankruptcy, Anglo-French financial control (1876), and finally British occupation (1881). Egypt, however, remained an Ottoman dependency until Turkey's entry into World War I when Britain proclaimed a protectorate over her (December, 1914). During the war Egypt was the base of British operations against Turkey in Palestine. The presence of large numbers of British troops, forced labor conscription, economic dislocations attendant on war, and Allied propaganda which promised freedom to the Arabs, all stimulated the desire of the Egyptians for independence. After the war when the British arrested and deported a group of Egyptian nationalists proposing to go to the Paris Peace Conference to plead the cause of Egyptian independence, an uprising broke out which the British suppressed with military force. Realizing their growing unpopularity in Egypt, the British proclaimed Egyptian independence in 1922, but continued to occupy the country until they could obtain guarantees of their economic and military interests, especially the control of the Suez Canal. King Fuad (1917–1936) might have conceded the British demands, but the nationalists insisted on unconditional independence. In 1923 Egypt became a constitutional monarchy, and the nationalist Wafd Party — whether in or out of power — ceaselessly agitated for British withdrawal. In 1936, at last, an agreement was concluded between Britain and Egypt on the model of the Anglo-Iraqi Treaty of 1930. The Anglo-Egyptian Treaty transformed the protectorate into an alliance for twenty-five years. British officials were withdrawn from Egypt and British forces remained only in the canal zone.

Agreement was also reached concerning joint Anglo-Egyptian control of Sudan — a vital question to Egypt, for he who controls Sudan controls the distribution of the Nile waters on which Egypt depends for survival. Sudan is a vast land, intermediary between Arabic North Africa and Negro Central Africa. Because of its position athwart the sources of the Nile, Egyptian rulers since time immemorial have sought to control it. In 1823–1828 the forces of Mehmet Ali conquered it, but it was lost when the famous "Mad Mahdi" (Mohammed Ahmed of Dongola) at the head of an army of fanatical dervishes wiped out the Egyptian garrisons (1883–1885). When the French showed their intention of annexing it, the British decided to forestall them. In 1896–1898 Lord Kitchener at the head of an Anglo-Egyptian army recovered it. At Fashoda he encountered a French expedition, and the ensuing dispute almost precipitated an Anglo-French war (1898).

To the west of Egypt, along the Mediterranean coast, lie the lands which the Arabs call Magreb and Europeans once called the Barbary (i.e., Berber) states of Tripoli, Tunis, Algeria, and Morocco. They had been provinces of the Roman, Byzantine, Arabic, and (with the exception of Morocco) Ottoman empires. In the nineteenth and twentieth centuries they became European colonies. With the exception of isolated areas in the Atlas Mountains where the indigenous Berber population survives, North Africa is predominantly Arabic in language and culture. In 1830 France began the conquest of Algeria. Its pacification was not completed until the 1880's, but already in 1848 — in harmony with the French centralist system — Algeria was declared an integral part of metropolitan France. However, with the exception of small, select groups of "evolved" (i.e., Europeanized) natives, the Algerians were not given the rights of French citizenship. In 1881 France annexed Tunisia, provoking a crisis with Italy, and in 1906 Morocco, provoking a great international crisis with Germany. In Tunisia and Morocco France decided to follow the British example and establish protectorates. The native rulers of Tunisia and Morocco were not deposed, like the ruler of Algeria. But the bureaucratic centralism of the French colonial administration did not permit any loose, ill-defined, but mutually satisfactory relationship such as the British were able to establish. The rulers of Tunisia and Morocco were relegated to purely ornamental functions, and French officials ran the show down to the village level. By international agreement France reserved a strip of northern Morocco to Spanish control, and Tangier became a free port. Theoretically, however, all three units remained domains of the Sultan of Morocco residing at Rabat.

After World War I an uprising of the Riffs broke out in Spanish Morocco and spread to French Morocco. It was suppressed only with great difficulty in 1926. Similarly, the pacification of Tripoli and Cyrenaica, which had become the Italian colony of Libya in 1911, was not completed until 1930. While tribal resistance to European rule was suppressed, the foundations of a new nationalist resistance were being laid. Its leaders were young men, trained in western schools where they had imbibed western democratic and nationalist ideas. They were also affected by the Arabic revival in the Near and Middle East. Although the French economic development of North Africa was impressive, it invariably favored the European settlers. The masses of the Arab and Berber natives remained desperately poor. Their social discontent gave the North African nationalist movement a mass basis, but it did not become a potent force until after World War II.

South of the Atlas Mountains lies the great Sahara desert, peopled only very thinly by Berber (Tuareg) nomads. In the nineteenth century it had little known value, but France conquered it to consolidate her colonies to the north and the south of it into a solid block.

South of the Sahara lay "Dark" tropical Africa, inhabited by Negro tribes. This was the last region in the world to be claimed by European colonial expansion. In 1800 Africa on maps was a narrow coastline surrounding a great white blank. It was known principally as an apparently inexhaustible reservoir of slaves for the plantations of America and the slave markets of the Near and Middle East. Then intrepid explorers — Mungo Park, Heinrich Barth, David Livingstone, Henry Stanley, and others — plunged into the vast, unknown hinterland of Africa and traced its rivers, mountains, and lakes on the maps. The well-publicized search of Stanley for Livingstone in 1871 awakened the European powers to the economic value of Africa. There followed a feverish race to claim African territory, which resulted in its complete partition among European powers by 1890. Britain, France, Germany, Belgium, Portugal, Spain, and Italy engaged in this "Great African Hunt." Explorers were followed by soldiers, traders, missionaries, and doctors. European capital and enterprise and African natives impressed into European service as laborers began to develop the rich resources of tropical Africa: timber, rubber, coffee, cocoa, palm oil, diamonds, gold, copper, and many other minerals and commodities. Roads and railroads were built, mines and factories opened, telephone and telegraph lines extended, and modern, handsome

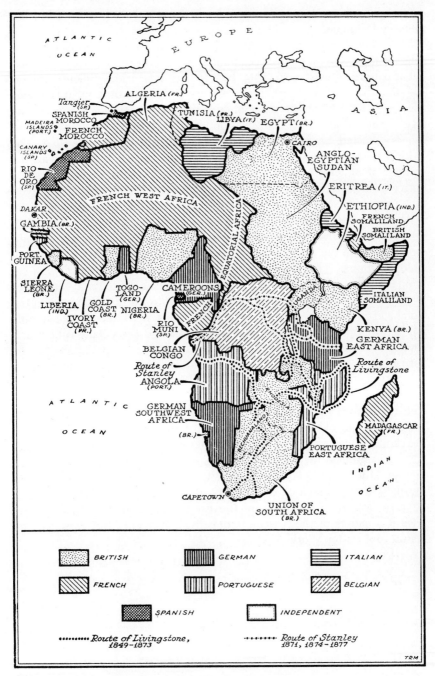

ATLANTIC
OCEAN

EUROPE

ASIA

Tangier
(SP.)
ALGERIA (FR.)
SPANISH
MOROCCO
TUNISIA (FR.)
LIBYA (IT.)
EGYPT (BR.)
*Madeira
Islands
(Port.)*
FRENCH
MOROCCO
CAIRO
ANGLO-
EGYPTIAN
SUDAN
*Canary
Islands
(SP.)*
RIO
DE
ORO
(SP.)
FRENCH WEST AFRICA
ERITREA (IT.)
ETHIOPIA (IND.)
FRENCH
SOMALILAND
BRITISH
SOMALILAND
Dakar
GAMBIA (BR.)
EQUATORIAL AFRICA
PORT.
GUINEA
SIERRA
LEONE
(BR.)
TOGO-
LAND
(GER.)
CAMEROONS
(GER.)
ITALIAN
SOMALILAND
LIBERIA
(IND.)
GOLD
COAST
(BR.)
NIGERIA
(BR.)
IVORY
COAST
(FR.)
RIO
MUNI
(SP.)
UGANDA
KENYA (BR.)
FRENCH
GERMAN
EAST AFRICA
BELGIAN
CONGO
*Route of
Stanley*
*Route of
Livingstone*
ANGOLA
(PORT.)
ATLANTIC
OCEAN
GERMAN
SOUTHWEST
AFRICA
MADAGASCAR
(FR.)
(BR.)
BECHUANALAND
PORTUGUESE
EAST AFRICA
INDIAN
OCEAN
CAPETOWN
UNION OF
SOUTH AFRICA
(BR.)

	BRITISH		GERMAN		ITALIAN
	FRENCH		PORTUGUESE		BELGIAN
	SPANISH		INDEPENDENT		

•••••••• *Route of Livingstone,*
1849–1873
•••••••• *Route of Stanley*
1871, 1874–1877

TRM

THE PARTITIONING OF AFRICA TO 1914

cities built where only a few decades before there was nothing but impenetrable jungle.

The African natives were quite bewildered by the European social relationships and capitalist economics, which disrupted their familiar tribal pattern of existence. They had, for instance, some difficulty understanding the European aversion to slavery and the institution, at the same time, of forced labor service. Some of them became demoralized in the fetid slums that mushroomed around the gleaming new cities, but others adjusted to the new way of life with remarkable rapidity. The British, who never liked to rule a colonial area directly and without the consent of at least a segment of the population, soon began to train a native elite to act as a buffer between them and the mass of the natives. Pursuing a different principle, namely the principle of French cultural assimilation, the French also trained a small native elite. Not infrequently, an "evolved" (i.e., thoroughly Gallicized) native would be promoted through the ranks of the French colonial administration to responsible positions. The German and Italian colonial experience was too limited to be of importance. Of greater interest was the colonial experience of the Belgians, who took over in 1908 the control of the Congo from the Congo Free State (a private company). They performed a remarkable job in developing the rich resources of the Congo (especially rubber and copper and uranium ore), ended the scandalous exploitation of the natives, and did much to improve their social and economic welfare. But they held firmly to the principle that the natives were fit for physical labor only. As a matter of policy they sought to prevent the rise of an educated native elite. The Portuguese, who had substantial holdings in Africa, held to old-fashioned, mercantilist colonial methods and lacked the capital necessary to develop the resources of their possessions. Neither did they do much for the social and material welfare of the natives. But they greatly encouraged the work of Catholic missionaries who brought the natives the solace of Christianity and its promise of a better hereafter. It was from the ranks of the Europeanized natives that were to arise the leaders of the African nationalist movements, but these did not mature until after World War II.

33

INDIA, SOUTHEAST ASIA, AND THE PACIFIC ISLANDS

An Indonesian who does not believe in magic is no Indonesian.

A. D. A. DE KAT ANGELINO

1. INDIA

BRITISH INFLUENCE in India grew and expanded from the seventeenth to the twentieth century. In 1876 Queen Victoria added the distinction "Empress of India" to her other titles and it became the custom to regard the Indian empire as "the brightest jewel in the British crown." By most Englishmen the subjugation of India was not considered conquest or oppression but a civilizing task, a responsibility willingly undertaken. Imperialism had two faces. It might be viewed as merciless exploitation of the weak by the strong or as a duty accepted by the strong and competent to govern and protect retarded and incompetent peoples.

The power which the trained British official exercised in India has been described as "bewildered omnipotence." His role might be compared to that of Mark Twain's Connecticut Yankee at King Arthur's court. Rudyard Kipling in a famous poem bade the British "take up the white man's burden" and serve their captives' need. Idealistic young officials saw themselves as heralds from the future who could bring modern civilization to millions of Asian peoples living in poverty, ignorance, and superstition. To lead a retarded people from the dark ages to the light of civilization appealed to the missionary impulse which most Europeans shared.

In striving to modernize India, the British assumed a task in some ways comparable to that of the national monarchs in Europe at the close of the Middle Ages. The sections made subject to British law corresponded to the disparate segments of a royal domain. The Indian States, ruled by local rajahs and maharajahs, were like baronies of semi-independent vassals whose fiefs had not yet been assimilated. Like the national monarchs the British extended their control through four invaluable instruments of government: they commanded the armed forces of India, the "King's Army;" they established and maintained a standard currency, the "King's coinage;" they developed and administered the main systems of transportation, the "King's highway;" they controlled foreign policy no Indian state was permitted to form treaties with its neighbors or with any foreign power save through British mediation.

To placate the Indian princes for their lost prerogatives the British left them almost autonomous rights within their own hereditary domains. Some of these rulers agreed to make an annual contribution for the common defense of India and for other services but some did not. The British (again like the early national monarchs) raised a revenue from various monopolies and won the support and contributions of the small but energetic business class. The townsmen composed less than 10 per cent of the Indian population, and they needed legal protection in a land of arbitrary despots, uncertain taxes and tariffs, and feudal restrictions. Craftsmen, tradesmen, shopkeepers, moneylenders, professional men of all vocations, who had property or positions or privileges to safeguard, came to rely upon the British law to protect their vulnerable assets. Property needs protection, and men of wealth buy that protection, as they buy any other commodity, where they can obtain it most cheaply and efficiently. Medieval European merchants demonstrated this when they voted subsidies to the king and urged him to extend the royal courts. In the archaic society of India, British supervision of justice created a hierarchy of courts with final appeal to the Privy Council in England. It has been charged that this system brought justice in the sense of legality for existing customs rather than justice in the sense of equity as it is understood in democratic countries. Naturally, those classes which benefited from traditional customs desired to see those customs sanctioned and upheld. The magistrates who presided in the law courts of India, whether they were British or Indian born, understood that their duty was to apply the law. If some of the statutes worked injustice it was the function of the legislator, not of the judge, to reform them.

Many Indian Nationalists affirmed that British rule meant a progressive impoverishment for their country despite the real advantages of peace and order that it brought. They insisted that India in the seventeenth century had been the leading agricultural country of Asia and the industrial workshop of the world and that British conquest and policies in the eighteenth and nineteenth centuries had reduced Indian prosperity. Complete independence, they believed, with taxes and tariffs adjusted to benefit India instead of Great Britain, would restore the economic leadership the Indian empire had lost. The Nationalists also argued that the peasants were even worse off under British rule than in the seventeenth century. The usurers, who held millions of them in a thralldom of debt which might accumulate through generations, had been fortified in their prerogatives by the decisions of the courts; they were both moneylenders and landlords, and the interest which they exacted was "justified" as rent. It was not surprising that the landlord class, the independent peasants who were fortunate enough to own their own farms, the townsmen of middle class status, and the princes in their glittering courts, valued British protection. They feared that a weakening of the British control might bring an agrarian revolution or a communistic upheaval with confiscation of private property.

The Indian quest for unity was confused and retarded by the complex schisms, vertical and horizontal, which split society. The states of the princes were half-autonomous territorial units, feudal bastions which had still to be reduced. In addition to this vertical segmentation there were weakening horizontal rifts and strata that would not fuse. The caste system, the timeless customs which relegated certain functions and forms of labor to specified groups and classes, made economic, social, and political equality an almost meaningless concept in India. Despite the introduction of modern machinery and transportation, social evolution could not be unduly hastened. To suppose that India might traverse in three or four decades the long stages of development which in Europe required three or four centuries, was to misread the tenacity of the Indians and their resistance to change. The Indian peoples had defended their preferences and clung to their ways of life for thousands of years despite successive conquests by more energetic northern invaders. It was possible to impose a veneer of Western educational methods, jurisprudence, military drill, and factory routine upon acquiescent millions. But tradition remained strong. The Indian who absorbed a Western education was not better fitted thereby for a happy life within his natural milieu. On the contrary, he often became Europeanized and was isolated from his kindred. British schooling made many Indian intellectuals of the twentieth century cultural exiles, wanderers between the Eastern and the Western worlds. This also was part of the British heritage to India.

By the opening of the twentieth century many leaders of the Indian people had become highly critical of the British control and administration. They demanded self-government, and some of them insisted that India should expel the British and seek complete independence. During World War I the unrest in India gathered strength but there was little violence. This was partly due to the influence of Mohandas K. Gandhi, an ascetic Hindu lawyer known to his followers as the Mahatma or saintly one. After the war ended in 1918, however, Gandhi urged the need for prompt concessions to Indian demands. The British government had promised (1917) that institutions leading to complete self-government would be introduced progressively, but they delayed any positive action. In 1919 a tragic incident at Amritsar, the "Amritsar Massacre," in which a British commander ordered his troops to fire upon an unarmed gathering of Hindus, killing nearly four hundred, aroused deep indignation.

The British sought to mollify the increasing opposition by passing, later in 1919, the Government of India Act. This set up a dual system of administration (the Dyarchy), whereby the British Governor-General was to divide his power with an Indian Legislature. Provincial legislative councils were likewise to advise the provincial governors, and Indians were to be admitted to the higher as well as the lower ranks of the civil service. Led by Gandhi, the Indian National Congress rejected this compromise as inadequate (1920) and Gandhi preached a campaign of civil disobedience. Despite his pleas to his followers to limit the movement to nonresistance, there was widespread disorder. Gandhi was arrested in March, 1922, and sentenced to six years' imprisonment.

A deepening sense of grievance and a growing spirit of solidarity made the Nationalist movement increasingly powerful. Hindus made their own salt from sea water to avoid the government revenue tax, boycotted the liquor stores to evade the tax on spirits, and even refused to pay the assessments on land. In the cities the industrial workers, a radical element, were organizing and might in time provide a serious revolutionary threat. All classes suffered from the world-wide economic depression which began in 1929. The Indian National Congress now demanded full Dominion status, and when this was not definitely promised, the Congress declared itself in favor of complete independence. Recognizing the need to yield, the British government called a Round Table Conference in 1931 and again in 1932, inviting Indian leaders to attend. The suggestions made were embodied in a new Government of India Act passed in 1935 and put into operation in 1937. One motive for this concession was the disastrous fall in government revenue resulting from the campaign of civil disobedience and the economic depression.

The new experiment provided for the formation of a federation of Governor's Provinces, Chief Commissioner's Provinces, and such Indian States still under local rulers as might join. Government was to be vested in a Governor-General (representing the King-Emperor in London), a Council of State, and a Legislative Assembly. Some members of the Council and the Assembly were to be elected, some appointed. A Council of Ministers, or cabinet, responsible to the legislature, was to assist the Governor-General. The legislature was to have power (subject to certain restrictions) to make laws for all persons within British India, all British subjects in other parts of India, and all Indian subjects of the King-Emperor in any part of the world.

In its form and wording this Act seemed to make India, or at least the British-ruled provinces of India, a self-governing Dominion. But this was a superficial and European reading of a situation too complex to be well understood even in India itself. There were four major conditions peculiar to the country which made the attainment of a true national status and real political autonomy a difficult goal to achieve. The obstacles to national unity and effective self-government for India might be conveniently summarized under four heads.

The first obstacle was lack of social homogeneity. India was not one country or one nation, it was a subcontinent. Its population had risen from over two hundred million in 1900 to nearly three hundred million in 1939. The peoples of India ranged from the highly civilized to the totally primitive and revealed a diversity of racial strains from Aryan to Negroid. There were seven recognized language groups or categories; these were further divided into at least twenty-four subdivisions, and the subdivisions included scores of local dialects. Although some degree of literacy was claimed for one Indian out of eight, less than one in one hundred had a knowledge of English. Religious differences further segregated the population into rival groups of Hindus, Moslems, Sikhs, Parsees, Buddhists, and Christians, not to name the multitudinous minor sects. Religion was a vital concern in India; rioting between rival sects, especially between Hindus and Moslems, was a frequent cause of disorder. The Moslems, who formed almost one-fourth of the total population, insisted that if India became independent they must be granted their own self-governing area to be known as Pakistan. Among the Hindus the persistence of strict caste rules, which separated the classes so rigidly that intermarriage or even communication between some of them was forbidden, created a perplexing barrier to democracy or social unity. It was clear that the peoples of India did not possess, and could scarcely hope to achieve, that racial, linguistic, and cultural unity which distinguished the strong, self-governing nation-states of the European world.

The second great obstacle to union and autonomy was the administrative disjunction. To plan, as many Indian Nationalists did, to impose swift political centralization on a society rent by social and religious cleavages, was unrealistic. It was, in fact, a European conception transported by doctrinaire minds to an Oriental setting. India had never possessed an efficient centralized administrative system that could serve as a pattern, and to create a workable unified administration swiftly would tax the greatest lawgiver. Although the British had maintained order, peace, and protection in the peninsula for over a century, they had brought little symmetry or uniformity to India as a whole. Two types of states existed: those which made up British India and were subject to British rule, and the Indian States, or semiautonomous provinces, the rulers of which were sovereigns "allied" to Great Britain by treaty. British India, the more important section, covered a little more than half the area of the peninsula, but it was the more prosperous portion and included three-fourths of the population. It comprised seventeen provinces, some with local legislatures but most of them split into divisions run by commissioners. These divisions were further subdivided into districts under a local British official who was magistrate, tax collector, and deputy commissioner. The districts were the real units of administration. Thus British India was politically atomized. All real authority rested with a handful of trained and competent British officials, who had wide discretionary powers. The prestige which the British won as alien conquerors, a sort of supercaste, had given them a rare advantage in their supervision of Indian affairs. A sudden transition to self-government and the withdrawal of the British ruling hierarchy might open the way to chaos unless it were carried through with caution and dexterity.

A third obstacle to unity and independence was lack of education. The vast majority of the Indian peoples had never been trained to exercise or even to understand the principles of British law or the responsibilities of self-government. Nine-tenths of the population, over 250,000,000 people, lived in rural areas, many under extremely primitive and isolated conditions. Divided by caste, blood, religion, language, and occupation, as well as by political differences, the Indians had much to master in the field of social integration and cooperation. They had been conditioned by centuries of habit to evade, to endure, or to flatter their conquerors, but the masses had never learned to participate in their own government. They could not soon acquire initiative and experience or adapt themselves in a few years to Western ideals of individualism and democracy.

A fourth obstacle that hindered political consolidation was the attitude of most of the independent princes. These rulers were despots, many of them enlightened despots and some quasiconstitutional despots, but despots none the less by force of immemorial tradition. They were reluctant to associate or combine their hereditary states with the parliamentary regimes which the British provinces slowly developed. Without including the Indian States no unification of all India was possible. Up to 1939 fifty of these States had rejected the invitation to adhere to the federation proposed in the Government of India Act of 1935. Until at least half of them joined the federation, the Act could not become operative. Thus, in a sense, the network of conservative native states, the rulers of which were in general loyal to Britain, were forts of resistance stretched across India. No revolutionary wave could sweep the peninsula from end to end until these "blockhouses" were reduced or amalgamated.

One further problem that complicated Indian affairs was the question of foreign capital investments. British financial and manufacturing interests suffered after the Indian legislature won the right to lay import duties upon British goods. British businessmen had invested a sum equal to five billion dollars in India, and were reluctant to withdraw from the largest foreign market any one nation ever controlled. Regardless of political ties, these economic connections continued to exercise a powerful influence over Anglo-Indian relations. Most of the public utilities, power stations, railways, posts, telephone and telegraph lines, banks, shipyards, and ordnance works functioned under British control or state management. Aircraft manufacture, automobile assembly plants, farm machinery, chemicals, metallurgy, and machine-tool industries were partly nationalized. But so long as the capital essential to such developments, the shipping, the control of raw materials, and the professional personnel remained at the disposal of the British or of Indian industrialists loyal to British rule, the tie with Great Britain would remain strong. Even if the political

A canal market in Bangkok, Thailand (United Nations).

Gandhi at the second Indian Conference, London, 1921 (Kemsley Picture Service).

*A Malayan farmer transplanting
rice shoots* (British Information
Service).

A Ceylonese farmer taking his rice crop to market (United Nations).

ties were to be dissolved, it seemed probable that Anglo-Indian collaboration on other planes would continue to prove useful and profitable to both peoples.

2. BURMA, MALAYA, INDOCHINA, AND THAILAND

To the east of India, across the Bay of Bengal, lay a second large peninsula with a smaller population and a more irregular coastline. During the nineteenth century all this area except the kingdom of Thailand (Siam) came under the control of the Europeans. The British annexed Burma and Malaya while the French secured Indochina.

To safeguard the frontier of India and expand their influence eastward, the British fought three Burmese wars (1824–26, 1852, 1885), until they had added Burma to their Indian empire. Its area, about 260,000 square miles, was equal to that of Texas. Its population increased rapidly under British rule, reaching ten million by 1900 and sixteen million by 1939. This last figure gave Burma an average of sixty inhabitants per square mile.

Burma was thus less densely populated than India but the people possessed greater homogeneity. Three-fifths of them were Burmans; the remainder were classed as Indians, Karens, Shans, and other minorities. Buddhism was the dominant, almost the exclusive, religious faith, claiming seven-eighths of the people, but society was not subdivided into rigid castes as in India. Thus Burma, with one widely used language, one prevailing religion, and a fairly homogeneous populace, might be transformed into a unified nation-state more readily than the Indian empire with its many languages, faiths, castes, and political fragments. The British administrators, after extending their influence through war and diplomacy as in India, brought the ancient kingdom of Burma and the adjacent Shan states under the rule of a governor and district commissioners. The result was a consolidation of the existing class structure which perpetuated the status of the various groups. Although there was a legislature for British Burma, with two chambers, actually a small number of European officials formed the core of the administration. There was a small middle class of merchants and property owners largely made up of Chinese and Indians, and the native Burmans formed the large submerged class of peasants, laborers, and servants. Primary education remained in the care of the Buddhist monks who maintained a school in each village, while higher education was fostered by a university and by government schools.

British Malaya (the Straits Settlements, Federated and Unfederated Malay States, and some scattered islands) comprised altogether some 50,000 square miles of territory in southeastern Asia, with a population of five million. The Straits Settlements were so named because Singapore guarded the most important strait on the sea route between India and China; it was, in fact, one of the half-dozen vital "bottlenecks" in the oceanic trade of the world. This colony was administered by a British Governor who was also High Commissioner for the Malay States and for Brunei in Borneo and British Agent for North Borneo and Sarawak.

French Indochina before 1939 consisted of the colony of Cochin-China, with four protectorates, Annam, Cambodia, Tonkin, and Laos. This territory had been conquered and organized by the French in less than a century. The total population was about 25,000,000 and the total area was estimated at 281,174 square miles. Thus in southeastern Asia the French had come to control a region one-fourth larger than France itself, with a population two-thirds as numerous. In French Indochina, however, as in India and Burma, demands for self-government grew stronger with each passing year.

Thailand (or Siam) was the only independent state remaining as a sovereign autonomous principality in southeast Asia. The name of the state was changed to Thailand by decree in 1939, but the traditional name, Siam, remained in common use. The area of Siam was about 200,000 square miles and the population 15,000,000. After 1932 the government was changed from an absolute to a constitutional monarchy with an elected parliament. As an Asian state enjoying political autonomy, Siam offered a contrast by which to measure the benefits or ills of the European-ruled colonies which bordered it. It survived the march of rival imperialisms in Asia largely because neither the French nor the British would allow the other to annex it. But although it was still autonomous in theory, it was strongly influenced by conditions in the neighboring states of Burma, Indochina, and Malaya, and its economy and welfare were contingent upon its trade relations with the great powers. Its industry, commerce, mining, lumbering, and even small trade were predominantly under the direction of foreigners. Seven-eighths of the population lived by agriculture, lumbering, or other labor on the land, as in similar Asian countries. It was significant, however, that the living conditions and the average wages of laborers were in general higher in Siam than in Burma or Indochina.

3. THE NETHERLANDS EAST INDIES

In the seventeenth century the Netherlanders were the most daring navigators and colonizers in the world, and a rich portion of the maritime empire they then acquired remained in their control. With their talent for seafaring, trade, and administration, they made their colonies productive and drew extraordinary dividends from them. Their island empire in the East Indies, 735,000 square miles in extent, was a living testimony to their shrewdness, tenacity, and business acumen. The population, increasing at a rate of a million a year, was approximately seventy million in 1939, two-thirds of it concentrated in the islands of Java and Sumatra. Although this Netherlands empire had only one-third the area of India and included only one-fourth the population of the British Asian empire, the import and export trade was equal in value to half that of India in 1939. Furthermore the surplus value of Indonesian exports over imports for that year was reckoned at $100,000,000, while the surplus value of exports from British India over imports was only $50,000,000.

The chief products of the Netherlands Indies were rubber, petroleum, vegetable oils, tin, sugar, and tea. These six items had come by 1939 to comprise 90 per cent of the exports. The islands proved well suited to a productive economy for the soil was fertile and the rainfall adequate, so that the population could sustain itself without difficulty. Valuable natural resources, especially mineral and oil reserves, awaited modern modes of exploitation to yield enormous profits. The labor supply was provided by the tractable and industrious native population.

The twentieth century brought unrest and demands for more independence even from this carefully guarded society, but the Netherlanders, like the British in India, were reluctant to bestow self-government. The discontent of the Indonesians was partly economic, for the Netherlanders long sought to supply all the manufactured goods required by the colonial peoples from factories in the home country, and discouraged the construction of industrial plants in the islands. This subordination of their economic life was resented by Indonesian patriots as discrimination, and they compared the wages and standards of living in the Netherlands with their own. In the islands a monthly wage of $10 was considered reasonable by the employers.

It was not easy for the peoples of the Netherlands East Indies to combine for any collective action. They inhabited islands which stretch for nearly three thousand miles along the equator, the most important being Sumatra, Java, Celebes, most of Borneo, and half of Timor and New Guinea. After 1916 the Netherlands government granted the people a share in the administration with an advisory council to represent their interests. But the National Indonesian Party continued to agitate for independence although the Indonesians lacked political experience and geographic unity. The ocean and high mountains separated the provinces and divided the islands. Some regions were almost unexplored and the inhabitants in some areas extremely primitive. There was no simple solution for the language problem, for although Dutch was the official speech, Portuguese was spoken by a minority; Malay, a common language throughout the East Indies, was a general medium; while most of the natives conversed in Javanese or in local dialects.

Like the British and French in their Asian empires, the Netherlanders failed to introduce a system of schooling well adapted to the culture, the interests, and the mentality of the peoples they ruled. Concern for the

peace, health, and prosperity of their protectorates remained the dominating concern of the European administrators; they sought to preserve
social conditions rather than reform them. Netherlands officials in general
conceived it to be their duty to ratify the position held by an alien (predominantly Chinese) business class in Indonesia; to protect the monopoly
of the plantation-owning, trading, and industrial (European) group; and
to leave the Indonesian majority to the status of cultivators, artisans, and
servants. Such a system of social organization was not really a political
government at all. It was economic in function and discriminatory in fact.
The administrators controlled the colony as if it were primarily a factory
organized for production rather than a society existing for the development and happiness of the individuals composing it.

4. THE PHILIPPINES AND HAWAII

When the United States formally acquired the Philippine Islands from
Spain in 1898, it took over the responsibility of defending a commonwealth of more than seven thousand islands with a total area slightly
larger than New Zealand and about equal to that of Arizona. Most
of these islands were dots in the ocean. Fewer than five hundred had
an area of more than one square mile, and only ten or eleven were important. The total population increased rapidly under American protection,
exceeding sixteen million by 1939, the great majority being native born.
Between four and five million spoke English, another half million Spanish,
and the remainder the various local patois. In 1937 Tagalog, a Malayan
dialect, was declared to be the official language but during the transitional period before independence was achieved the teaching of English
was compulsory in the free, secular, coeducational schools. About one-
half the Filipinos over ten years of age were literate, and four-fifths were
followers of the Roman Catholic religion.

When the Filipino people revolted against Spanish rule in 1896 their
leader, Emilio Aguinaldo, accepted American aid. But he wished complete independence for the islands, and after the defeat of the Spaniards
he opposed American occupation from 1899 until his capture in 1901.
The following year the United States Congress established a bicameral
legislature for the commonwealth but retained the power to veto its acts.
The removal of tariff restrictions and quota limits on trade with the United
States provided a market for sugar, tobacco, and other island crops. A
desire for complete independence remained strong among the Filipinos,
although commissions of investigation sent out by the United States
government reported that they were not yet equal to the problems of
self-rule or the burdens of self-defense.

After 1929, however, the American attitude and sentiment toward
Philippine independence underwent a change. American economic pene-

tration of the islands had made less progress than had been anticipated, the free entrance of island crops, notably sugar and tobacco, competed with the produce of American farmers, and the cost of defending possessions in Asian waters added greatly to the naval budget. A plan to set up a transitional regime, leading to independence after twelve years, passed the United States Congress in 1934. Under the provisions of this Tydings-McDuffie Act the Filipinos adopted their own constitution in 1935, choosing Manuel Quezon as their first president. A Popular Party continued to agitate for immediate independence, but Quezon's Nationalist Party held its leadership. The United States continued to supervise defense, foreign relations, finance, and justice, with the understanding that the period of tutelage would terminate in 1946 with full autonomy for the Filipinos. The Act of 1934, however, though it promised the Filipinos their independence as "a separate and self-governing nation," provided that the United States might maintain naval reservations and fueling stations in the islands after granting them independence.

In contrast to the Philippines, the islands of the Hawaiian archipelago with nearly half a million inhabitants gradually tightened their political bonds with the United States. Formally annexed in 1898 and granted the privileges enjoyed by American states through an Act of Congress in 1924, the Territory of Hawaii sent one delegate to the Congress at Washington. There was increasing agitation for full statehood. The important strategic role which Pearl Harbor came to play in American Pacific defense plans and the fact that one-third of the population in Hawaii was Japanese or of Japanese descent, made the question of bestowing statehood upon this important Territory a complicated one that was not resolved until after World War II.

5. THE PACIFIC ISLANDS

All the land areas of the earth, if united, would approximately fill the 55,000,000 square miles of the Pacific Ocean. This watery hemisphere, with its minute and multitudinous islands, became an ocean of destiny in the twentieth century. The problems of defense and expansion which induced the government of the United States to acquire the Aleutian Islands, Hawaii, and the Philippines before 1900, likewise persuaded alert statesmen in Australia and New Zealand to urge wider British annexation of islands still unclaimed, while French, German, and Japanese imperialists were also raising flags on unconsidered atolls and pressing claims to lonely archipelagoes.

Sovereignty was often difficult to maintain on scattered groups of islets; and as continuous occupation was impossible on most of the South Pacific reefs and atolls because few of them will adequately support even a small population, it became the custom in the twentieth century to allot the

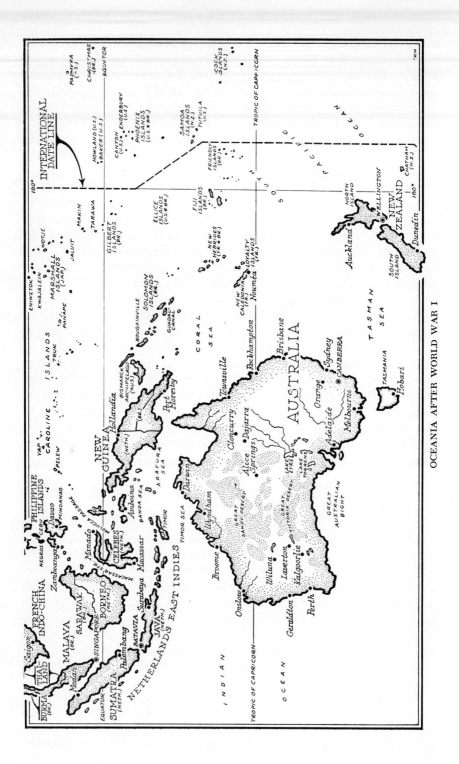

OCEANIA AFTER WORLD WAR I

different powers fields of ocean lying between specified degrees of latitude and longitude. Thus, almost without their knowledge, isolated island peoples, who had seldom seen Europeans except for visiting whalers or missionaries, found themselves swept into the sphere of influence of a government located on the other side of the world. The process of demarcation and annexation was hastened by the events of World War I. By 1919 few islands in the vast expanse remained unappropriated.

In Oceania, half of New Guinea, with New Britain and New Ireland, became an Australian mandate after World War I. Samoa was mandated to New Zealand. The Fiji, Tonga, Solomon, and Gilbert Islands went to Great Britain with other scattered possessions. In general the equator formed the northern limit of the British area of supervision. North of the equator lay the Japanese mandates, which embraced the Caroline Islands, Yap, the Marianas, and the Marshall Islands. Only a study of the map can make evident how intermeshed the Japanese and American lines of communication became with the extension of Japanese influence. The American stepping stones from Hawaii to the Philippines, especially Midway, Wake, and Guam, lay directly across the Japanese routes of advance.

It is not difficult to understand why the people of Australia and New Zealand came to respect American naval strength as their first line of defense against a possible southward thrust by Japan. At the Washington Naval Conference of 1921–1922 (see p. 245) the United States, Britain, France, and Japan agreed not to change the existing situation or expand their influence further. Each of the four powers promised the others that it would "respect their rights in relation to their insular possessions and insular colonies in the region of the Pacific Ocean." At the same time the United States, Britain, and Japan agreed not to increase their naval bases and fortifications in the western Pacific. The Japanese resented these restrictions and felt that the United States and Britain wanted to limit Japanese expansion. This was true. The British allowed their alliance with Japan (formed in 1902) to lapse, a move that pleased the Americans, Australians, and New Zealanders. These changes reflected a new balance of power in the Pacific — the white nations were lining up to oppose the designs of the Japanese to extend their empire in Asia and the adjacent seas. The Pacific Ocean, with its innumerable islands, had become an area of tension.

34

CHINA AND JAPAN

To most Americans the vast and teeming lands of the Orient are still terrae incognitae.

New York Times, *editorial (May 12, 1945)*

1. CHINA: THE LAND AND THE PEOPLE

TODAY CHINA, as a communist nation on the march, inspires a growing fear, and very well it might, for it is the largest nation-state in the world in point of population. By 1965, China had a population of 750,000,000, and it was growing at a rate of 2 per cent, or 15,000,000 annually.[1] If China maintains that rate of growth, her population should pass the billion mark well before the end of the present century. Harnessed to the fulfillment of a common purpose by the totalitarian doctrine of communism, this mass of humanity is bound to affect the course of history profoundly.

The student who wishes to gain some general idea of East Asia might note some comparisons between China and the United States. They have approximately the same area. Greater China has an area of 3,750,000 square miles, which is a little more than the aggregate area of the United States and its overseas possessions (3,628,130). Both lie in approximately the same latitudes. Both have a neighbor to the north, a neighbor with sparsely settled provinces stretching toward the Arctic; and both have tropical areas, peninsulas, and islands to the south, for Burma, Siam, Indochina, Malaya, and Indonesia may be roughly likened to Mexico, Central America, and the Caribbean Islands. Both the United States and China face the rising sun with a long, bulging, eastern coastline with numerous ports, and in both the population is heavily concentrated in the eastern section, with sparsely populated, semiarid regions commencing between one and two thousand miles inland. Still farther inland both have high mountain ranges to the west and the south. But there the comparisons end. China has no Far West, no second coastline beyond the mountains, with growing ports, timbered ranges, rich fruit-

[1] *The Statesman's Yearbook, 1965–66* (New York: 1965), p. 878.

lands, fisheries, factories, and shipyards like those which stretch from Washington to California.

Throughout their long history the Chinese have lived with the knowledge that they had a desert behind them thinly peopled by barbarian tribes against whom early emperors constructed the Great Wall. This oft-cited example of China's spirit of isolation is one of the greatest engineering ventures of all times. Built by a prodigious use of human labor, the massive Great Wall stretches from the Yellow Sea 1500 miles inland. In front of the Chinese lay the widest of the world's oceans, which, so far as the Chinese knew, had no other shore. Thus Chinese civilization developed according to its own intrinsic patterns, flourishing on the fertile stretch between two deserts, the desert of the hinterland and the desert of the sea.

Today China is undergoing a radical political, social, and industrial revolution on the Soviet model, which is rapidly changing her traditional way of life. But until the twentieth century, Chinese civilization, the Chinese character, and the Chinese way of life remained remarkably stable. The Chinese possessed their own pictographic and ideographic records 3500 years ago and had developed an advanced culture before 1000 B.C. They possessed also, in rudimentary form, such modern inventions as printing, paper, and gunpowder long before the Europeans. Their subtle poetry and philosophy; their exquisite masterpieces of painting, sculpture, and metalwork; their marvelously colored silks and brocades; their tasteful work in ceramics and lacquer; and their delicate and arresting architecture have won for the Chinese an honored place among the most highly gifted peoples of history. The Chinese character commanded respect because of their realism, adherence to the golden mean, cheerfulness in adversity, and resiliency. In religion they were tolerant and philosophical. While the upper classes professed Confucianism (which is really an ethical code rather than a religion), the lower classes adhered to Buddhism and Taoism. The great Chinese sage Confucius (551–479 B.C.) extolled respect for parents above all virtues. The Chinese of all classes worshipped their ancestors and regarded duty to the family as standing above all duties. China had no hereditary aristocracy, but owing to strong family loyalties many families retained a position of pre-eminence over long generations. Since time immemorial the Celestial Empire — as China was sometimes called — was a hereditary monarchy. It was ruled by an emperor who was styled the "Son of Heaven." He was believed to rule by a "mandate of heaven." Under the emperor was a hierarchy of officials (mandarins), chosen by competitive exams in the Chinese classics. Scholastic ability was believed to be the best test of fitness for public office. Writers, scholars, and philosophers enjoyed a social standing second to none.

Until recently the great bulk of the Chinese people were engaged in agriculture. They lived in tiny villages and worked their family farms, which seldom exceeded five acres, in a garden-like fashion. An owner of ten to fifteen acres was reckoned a rich landowner. He did not work his land himself, for he could afford hired labor. The alluvial plains on the lower reaches of the great Chinese rivers — Hoangho, Yangtze, and Si — are very fertile. In the south the tropical climate permits raising of two crops annually. As pressure of population increased, the Chinese people migrated westward up the river valleys and into the hills of western China, which they denuded of forests and terraced, often up to the very summits. Terracing was necessary to make the fields level, for the staple crop of China was rice and it has to be inundated for some time during its growth. Another important crop was tea. Cities were numerous and colorful, with their massive walls, towered gates, and characteristic "pie-crust" roofs. The townsmen included artisans and merchants, both working in family-operated shops and both organized into guilds, as in medieval Europe.

Chinese civilization and the Chinese monarchy exercised an influence beyond China proper, that is the water basins of the great Chinese rivers, which comprise only about 1,500,000 square miles of the total area of Greater China. Beyond China proper, stretching to the Himalaya and Altay mountains, lay the sparsely inhabited outlying provinces of China. In the southwest on the high Himalayan plateau lay Tibet, a land of monks and nomad herdsmen ruled by the Dalai Lama at Lhasa, a god incarnate, who recognized the political suzerainty of the Chinese emperor. In the west, astride the ancient "Silk Road" to Europe, lay Sinkiang (Chinese Turkestan), a land of bleak deserts and towering mountains through which roamed fierce Turkic-Moslem nomads. In the north, separated from China proper by the Gobi desert, lay Mongolia. It was inhabited by Mongol herdsmen who were descendants of the warriors of Genghis Khan. Finally, in the northeast lay Manchuria, the land of the Manchus, who had given China her last dynasty. Unlike other outlying provinces, Manchuria contained good farmland, abundant timber lands, and rich deposits of coal, iron ore, and oil. But until the end of the nineteenth century it was closed to Chinese immigrants to prevent friction with the Manchu tribesmen.

The relationship of the outlying provinces to China varied. When the Chinese monarchy was strong it asserted its authority over them; when it was weak they asserted their independence of it. In the thirteenth century the Mongols and in the seventeenth century the Manchus overran China and imposed their rule on the Chinese. But thanks to their large numbers and their superior civilization, each time the Chinese "conquered their conquerors" by assimilating them. At different times in the long Chinese history the Chinese monarchy asserted its authority also over Burma, Siam, Indochina, and Korea. And all over East Asia Chinese civilization exercised an influence comparable to the influence exercised by Roman civilization over the Mediterranean world. Isolated from the

Western world, the Chinese long regarded their country as the center of the universe (hence China's name *Chungkuo,* meaning Middle or Central Kingdom) and their civilization as the highest ever attained. This self-centered and self-satisfied concept was rudely shaken by the arrival of the Europeans in East Asia.

2. CHINA IN REVOLUTION

Western influence came to China late. In the sixteenth century the Portuguese established themselves at Macao, and individual Jesuit missionaries were received at the Chinese court. In the eighteenth century western merchants were permitted to trade at Canton. But owing to her relative unity, isolation, and inaccessibility, China escaped western imperialist penetration until the nineteenth century. Then by the First Opium War (1839–1842) the British forcefully "opened up" China to western influence. By the Treaty of Nanking (1842) Britain secured Hongkong and extraterritorial rights in Shanghai and four other "treaty ports" and — to add insult to injury — exacted an "indemnity" for the aggression she had committed against China. The Treaty of Nanking established a precedent for a long line of "unequal treaties" imposed on China by European powers. Under the rules of European imperialist diplomacy a concession granted to one power had to be followed by a round of "compensations" to the other powers in order to maintain a balance of power in the area. Russia, France, Japan, and Germany joined Britain in seeking concessions in China. Like tearing the leaves of an artichoke, they seized one Chinese port and province after another. Only the United States stood aloof from this undignified scramble and vainly pleaded for the preservation of Chinese territorial integrity and the maintenance of an "Open Door," that is, the right of all nations to trade with China on equal terms (1899). By the end of the century, China had lost control over Burma, Siam, Indochina, Korea, Formosa, many provinces of China proper, and all her principal ports.

The humiliations inflicted on China caused rebellion and mounting restlessness; but unlike the Japanese, who in an analogous situation rapidly came to the conclusion that the only way to stop the western imperialists was by modernizing Japan, the conservative and tradition-bound Chinese were slow to accept this lesson. In 1900 members of a patriotic society, called the Boxers by westerners, attacked the western embassies in Peking. The siege was relieved by an international expedition, and further humiliations followed. During the Boxer Uprising the Russians occupied Manchuria and refused to evacuate it afterwards. The Chinese government was helpless to do anything about it, but Japan, which had an eye on the province herself, challenged Russia. The quarrel led to the Russo-Japanese War (1904–1905) and the defeat of Russia. However, Russian defeat did not mean Chinese victory, for the result of the war was to divide the rich province into Russian and Japanese spheres of interest.

The complete helplessness of the Manchu government caused it to lose face in the eyes of the Chinese people. In 1911 a revolution broke out which led to the dethronement of the boy emperor Pu-yi and the proclamation of the Chinese Republic under Dr. Sun Yat-sen (1867–1925), an Americanized Chinese revolutionary from Canton (1912). But while the Manchu dynasty had clearly lost the mandate of heaven to rule, the republican government had not acquired it. Republican and democratic concepts were beyond the comprehension of most Chinese people. Sun Yat-sen was soon forced to step aside and an old imperial general, Yuan Shi-kai, assumed the presidency. He proposed to restore the monarchy with himself as emperor, but death prevented him from carrying out his plan (1916). The central government in Peking, whether monarchical or republican, had in any event little control over the country. The Chinese empire had disintegrated into a number of shifting states. Encouraged by the British and the Russians, Tibet, Sinkiang, and Mongolia had asserted their independence. In China proper a number of the old imperial governors had set themselves up as independent war lords and paid scanty attention to the decrees of the Peking government. Like feudal dukes in medieval Europe, they organized private armies in their fiefs, collected taxes, administered justice, and made war on one another and occasionally on the Peking government. China was not united again under a single government until 1949 – by the communists. The outbreak of World War I lessened the pressure of the European imperialist powers on China, but increased that of Japan. The Japanese took over the German concession in Shantung and made on China the notorious Twenty-one Demands (see p. 386). Seeking American protection against Japan, China followed the example of the United States and declared war on Germany (August, 1917). But she contributed little to the Allied war effort and was cavalierly treated at the Paris Peace Conference. The Allies refused to act against Japan and return the Shantung concession to China, and the Chinese delegates demonstratively left Paris without signing the Treaty of Versailles.

The anger of the Chinese nationalists against the Allied peacemakers pushed them into the arms of Soviet Russia. The Bolsheviks, acting on Lenin's dictum that the road to Paris and London led through Peking and Bombay, renounced all the privileges secured from Asian peoples by the Tsarist government and presented themselves as victims of European imperialism – the same as colonial peoples. The exclusion of the Soviet government from the Paris Peace Conference and the Allied intervention in Russia gave some plausibility to this posture. The Russian Revolution had also internal repercussions in China. The western imperialist nations had brought the modern industrial age to China. In the coastal areas, where they were active, railways, telephones, telegraphs, and machine

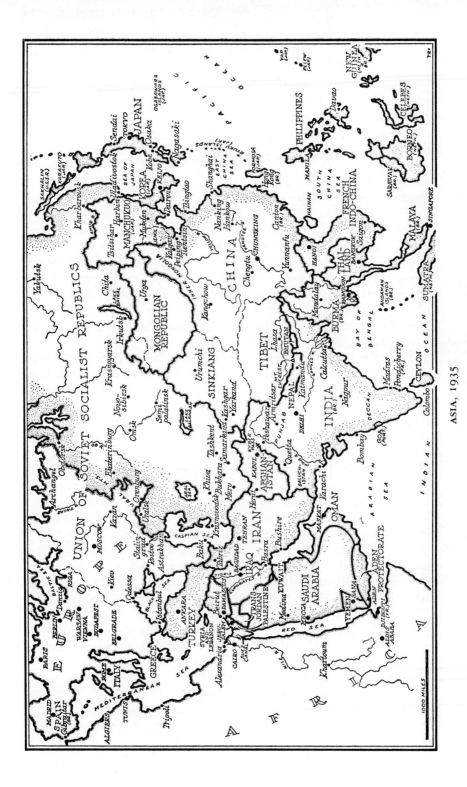

ASIA, 1935

industry appeared alongside the old Chinese handicraft industries. Small but growing Chinese industrial capitalist and working classes were born. Stimulated by the Russian Revolution, a small but energetic Chinese communist party appeared, which proceeded to organize the industrial proletariat. But by far the most important Chinese revolutionary party was Sun Yat-sen's Kuomintang party, based in his native city of Canton in the south. Its program was nationalist rather than socialist. It was based on the "Three Principles of the People" (nationalism, democracy, and social progress). But their common enmity to the western powers created a bond between the Kuomintang and communist parties. Sun Yat-sen received a Russian Comintern agent, Michael Borodin, as adviser on party organization and techniques to seize power and admitted the Chinese communists into the Kuomintang (1924). His brother-in-law and chief lieutenant, General Chiang Kai-shek, an able officer trained in Japan, visited Moscow to study Russian military and political tactics. Upon his return, he organized with the aid of Soviet and German military instructors the Whampoa Military Academy for training of Kuomintang officers (1924). Before an attempt to seize power could be made, Sun Yat-sen died (1925). He was presently enshrined, like Lenin, and passed into Chinese revolutionary mythology.

In the following year Chiang Kai-shek marched north from Canton with the Kuomintang army to make his bid for power. He was barred from Peking by the Japanese, but at Nanking he established the Chinese Nationalist government (1927). It was eventually recognized by most foreign powers and at least outwardly by China's war lords. Meanwhile, the right-wing conservative elements in the Kuomintang party became increasingly disquieted by the activities of the communists and urged Chiang to get rid of them. Shortly after the establishment of the Nanking government, Chiang, fearing a coup within a coup, turned against his communist allies and bloodily suppressed them. Soviet advisers left China, and the debacle of the Soviet China policy figured prominently in the battles of Trotsky and Stalin for Lenin's succession (see p. 295).

Some of the surviving Chinese communist leaders, notably Mao Tse-tung and Chu Teh, withdrew to the southeastern province of Kiangsi and, completely unassisted by the Russian communists, established a Chinese Soviet Republic (1931). But they were soon dislodged from Kiangsi by the Nationalist forces and effected the famous "Long March," an orderly anabasis over thousands of miles of China's back yard to the northwestern province of Shensi where they re-established the Chinese Soviet Republic (1934–1935). The Chinese communists were left completely to their own devices by the Russian communists. Stalin was apparently guided by considerations of Russian national security more than by world revolutionary idealism. Believing Chiang's Nationalist government to be the only force capable of organizing China against Japan, he supported it fully until 1945.

The Chinese and Russian communists differed in basic tactics. Analyzing the reason for the earlier failure of the Chinese communists, Mao Tse-tung came to the conclusion that it was because they had addressed their appeals to the small Chinese industrial proletariat in the treaty ports instead of to the broad masses of Chinese peasants all over China. For a marxist this view was a great heresy. Marx had postulated and Lenin reaffirmed that the industrial proletariat was the sole and only possible banner carrier of true proletarian revolutions. The unorthodox tactics of the Chinese communists and the apparent lack of support they received from Soviet Russia convinced many Chinese and foreign observers (including several American State Department officials) that there was an essential difference between the Russian and Chinese communists and that the latter were merely "agrarian reformers." Consequently they urged Chiang to desist from attacking the communists and to form a common front with them to resist the Japanese. In 1936, while on an inspection tour in the northwest, Chiang was kidnapped by one of his own generals, the former war lord in Manchuria, Chang Hsueh-liang, who was in charge of operations against the communists. He too urged on Chiang an agreement with the communists. Whether Chiang agreed to it in principle is not clear, but he was forced to agree to it in fact by the outbreak of full-scale war between China and Japan (1937). An uneasy and oft-broken truce prevailed between the nationalists and communists until 1945. Against the Japanese Chiang adopted a Fabian tactic of retreat, trading space for time, but he refused to compromise with them. The Japanese army, owing to its great superiority in organization and equipment, was able to capture Chinese cities at will, but it was unable to break China's resistance. The war between China and Japan was merged into World War II, in which the Sino-Japanese conflict was subordinated to the strategic exigencies of the two great coalitions at war (see Chapter 44).

3. JAPAN

The astonishing rise of Japan in two short generations from a medieval, feudal monarchy to a modern military and industrial power has already been reviewed (see Chapter 11). Modernization of Japan, however, brought problems; by creating new opportunities, it stimulated a phenomenal growth of the Japanese population. Between 1852 and 1910 the population of Japan grew from 27,000,000 to 49,600,000, and was to grow to 72,500,000 by 1940. At the same time the area and resources of Japan increased only slightly. The area of Japan proper was only 147,707 square miles, less than the size of California, and much of it was covered by unproductive mountains. The logical answer to this dilemma appeared to be expansion.

The outbreak of World War I provided a new opportunity for expanding. By joining the Allies, Japan with a minimum of effort and no risk collected the German possessions in the Pacific and in China. At the same time the war stimulated a demand for Japanese goods, led to great industrial expansion, and brought considerable prosperity to her population. As the war lengthened, the Japanese looked around for further gains. China, left unguarded by the preoccupation of the European powers with the war, seemed to be the logical victim. In 1916 Japan presented the government at Peking with the notorious Twenty-one Demands, which would have reduced China to a Japanese puppet. The United States, to which the Chinese appealed for protection, was hampered from taking a strong stand against Japan by its preparations for the war. It obtained an adjournment of the Japanese demands on China, but in return it recognized their "special interests" in China (Lansing-Ishii notes, November, 1917). At the Paris Peace Conference the United States tried to curb the Japanese taste for expansion both in China and in Siberia (under the guise of Allied intervention against the Bolsheviks), but the European Allies were not anxious to pull chestnuts out of the fire for China, and the problem remained unsettled. At the Washington Naval Conference in 1922, however, the United States succeeded in pressuring Japan to adhere to the Nine-Power Pact, which subscribed to the well-known principles of American China policy: Open Door and respect for Chinese territorial integrity. At the same time Japan had to agree to an inferior naval position in relation to the United States and Great Britain. These restraints gave the Japanese militarists a feeling of frustration not unlike that of Italy after the war. Everywhere Japan turned, it seemed to them, she was blocked by the western powers, particularly the United States. They bitterly assailed their own government for its supposed failure to "stand up" to the western powers.

As a new great power and the only oriental one at that, Japan was extraordinarily sensitive to real or imagined slights by the older western powers. Japanese chauvinists often saw in tactless statements or acts, born of western ignorance of the Orient, deliberate and studied insults; and in what were only normal maneuvers of great power diplomacy, sinister plots of the "white" nations to deny Japan her rightful place among the powers. The passage by the United States Congress in 1924 of the Immigration Law confirmed the Japanese in their suspicions that the United States policy toward Japan was based on racial considerations. By limiting European immigrants but excluding completely Japanese immigrants, it seemed to imply that the latter were inferior and less desirable than the former. This created much resentment in Japan. While the general American public was hardly aware of it, the American-Japanese relations, which before the war had been very cordial, sharply deteriorated after the war. The growing bitterness and frustration of the Japanese was to have dire results for the Japanese relations with the western powers and for parliamentary democracy in Japan.

Although since 1889 Japan had been formally a constitutional monarchy, it was actually ruled by an oligarchy of elder statesmen and generals in the name of the emperor. After World War I democracy was popular in Japan and there were genuine impulses to make it more real. Emperor Hirohito (1926–   ), an unobtrusive little man, was willing enough to play the role of a constitutional monarch. The militarists were impressed with the victory of the western democracies over their foes in the war, which proved to them the superiority of democracy over the German system. The big monopolistic business interests of Japan, which had grown rich and powerful during the war, favored parliamentary democracy because they could bend it to their ends by unashamed bribery. But the arrival of the World Depression brought a reversal in Japanese opinion. By 1930 the Japanese population had grown to 64,500,000, almost half of which made a living from trade and industry. Like Britain, Japan had to trade or die. However, as nations began to retrench, many of them adopted restrictions on imports of Japanese goods, and this caused severe hardship to Japan. The militarists and expansionists became once again vocal. The feudal-minded officer caste, which despised both business and democracy, accused the parliamentary government of weakness and corruption. Fanatical young officers organized secret patriotic societies and launched a campaign of violence, murder, and intimidation against the parliamentary politicians.

In 1931, without governmental sanction, the military attacked in Manchuria. When the Japanese government and the League of Nations failed to check this act of insubordination and aggression, the military adventurers knew no more restraint. They launched Japan on a career of aggression and military adventure which was to lead her into World War II on the side of Nazi Germany and Fascist Italy. This will be discussed in a subsequent chapter. Here suffice it to say that at home in Japan all political parties were suppressed by 1940 and a military dictatorship established. No single dictator appeared, as in Italy and Germany, but rather — in harmony with Japanese tradition — Japan was ruled by an oligarchy of senior officers in the name of the emperor. Austere, dutiful, fervently patriotic, but strangely parochial and ignorant of the outside world, these military oligarchs took Japan into World War II, in which she was defeated and humiliated.

Section VI: THE FAILURE OF COLLECTIVE

SECURITY

35

ECONOMIC INSECURITY AND THE GREAT DEPRESSION

. . . Mankind is tending more and more to regulate the whole of its social life . . .
KARL MANNHEIM

1. ECONOMIC INTERDEPENDENCE OF THE MODERN WORLD

IN MODERN TIMES the methods by which civilized peoples obtain food and goods and services have grown more involved and more complex with each passing year. In a primitive society a tribe or even a single family may manage to support itself with little or no outside aid. During the Middle Ages the inhabitants of many European hamlets raised their own food, made and mended their own tools, tanned their own leather, fashioned their own shoes and harness, and wove their own cloth. People who meet their own simple needs from their own limited local resources are said to be economically self-sufficient. Even in the Middle Ages, however, dwellers in remote isolated villages obtained a few articles they could not produce themselves by buying them from travelling merchants. Or they might journey to a town a few miles away and purchase goods at a fair. Thus they were not exclusively dependent on their own labor.

The Age of Discovery, at the close of the Middle Ages, opened the oceans of the world to European ships and made it possible for Europe to obtain goods from distant continents. Later, with the Industrial Revolution, the Europeans learned to produce quantities of manufactured goods cheaply, and to sell what they did not need in exchange for raw materials, tropical products, and additional food. During the nineteenth century *international* trade — trade between countries and between continents — increased at a rapid rate. By 1900 the total value of such commerce was ten times as great as it had been in 1800. By 1913 it was twenty times as great; and by 1929 (despite the disruption of World War I) it was over thirty times as valuable as it had been in 1800. In other words, almost all nations in the nineteenth and twentieth centuries became increasingly dependent on *foreign* markets, on selling goods to and buying goods from countries in other parts of the world.

WORLD INDUSTRIAL OUTPUT AND WORLD TRADE, 1921-1937

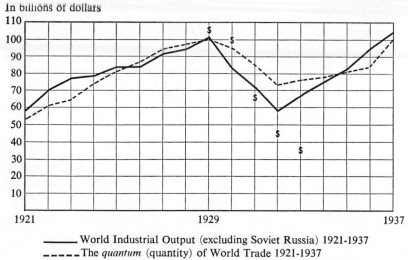

_____ World Industrial Output (excluding Soviet Russia) 1921-1937
_ _ _ _ _The *quantum* (quantity) of World Trade 1921-1937
$ Fall in *value* of World Trade measured in gold dollars 1929-1933

As the value of this international trade increased the peoples of the world became more dependent on one another. Countries that possessed a surplus of some commodities sought to exchange that surplus for goods they wanted but lacked the means to produce for themselves. International trade brought the nations of the world into closer contact. It made them more dependent on one another, and made it more important that they *cooperate* in supplying one another's needs for the benefit of all. The American economist, Henry George, summed up this situation very simply in three words. He said: *civilization is cooperation.*

The fact that, by the twentieth century, the world had come to resemble one vast market helps to explain its rapid progress and development. It helps to explain why goods were produced more abundantly and distributed more widely than ever before, why standards of living rose, and the global population increased at an astonishing rate. Unfortunately, however, the increase in food and manufactured goods, the increase in wealth and prosperity, was not equally distributed. Some nations, that possessed or achieved unusual advantages, that developed more effective machines and techniques, grew wealthy. Other nations, less favored by nature, less efficient, less resourceful or less industrious, remained poor. Just as in individual countries, a small minority of the inhabitants might be exceptionally wealthy and might preserve and enlarge their family fortunes, while the majority remained relatively poor, so among the nations of the world a few achieved a high standard of wealth while the majority subsisted on very much lower incomes.

Some countries and continents enjoyed a much larger share of world trade than others, and the countries with a large foreign trade were the wealthy countries where income and living standards were high. Before World War I, for example, Europe, with about one-fourth of the world's people, monopolized nearly 60 per cent of the world's international trade. This was more than twice as much as the Europeans would have controlled if the international trade of each continent had been proportional to its population. After World War I the European share declined to less than half the world total while that of North America (the United States and Canada) rose. By 1926 the North Americans claimed one-fifth of the international trade of the globe, nearly three times as much as their numbers would have entitled them to if this trade had been divided in proportion to population. But their good luck was due in part to the destruction and dislocation Europe had suffered during the war. After 1926 the Europeans recovered some of the trade they had lost, while the share the North Americans had obtained declined.

These facts suggest several points concerning international trade which it is important to remember. In *theory* the universal exchange of goods seems deceptively simple. If every people produced those goods which their resources and skills best fitted them to produce, and all nations were willing and able to exchange goods freely, the whole world would benefit and its peoples would become more and more cooperative and interdependent. To some extent this is what has come about in modern times. But the growth of international trade has been slowed and hampered by three difficulties that proved very hard to overcome. It is impossible to understand the strains and tensions of the modern world unless these obstacles to trade, and their causes, are taken into account.

The first difficulty is that the peoples whose need is greatest buy the least. For trade is an *exchange* and very poor people with low incomes have little surplus to offer for things they lack. In 1926, for instance, Asia, Africa, and South America together held over three-quarters of the world population but enjoyed only one-quarter of its international trade. A second difficulty is that a rich nation that could afford to buy the surplus a poor nation offers frequently refuses to do so. Some Asian countries that need and want to buy machines or medicines from the United States may have cotton or rice to offer in exchange. But American farmers also raise cotton and rice. To protect them, the United States may refuse to buy cotton or rice from Asia although it is cheaper than their own. This may mean that American consumers pay higher prices for their home-grown rice or cotton than they need to do, and the Asian people, who want to buy goods from the United States, are unable to buy them. Tariff barriers and other obstacles that nations impose on the free exchange of goods obstruct international trade. Governments do not regulate their trade in the way that will be best for humanity as a whole. They do not always regulate it in the way that would be most advantageous for their own people as a whole. Sometimes they impose import duties on a commodity in a way that inflicts a hardship on foreigners and on most of their own people, but enables a small number of their own people to obtain a higher price for their products. It must be kept in mind, however, that by producing a commodity within its own frontiers, even if it could buy an ample supply more cheaply abroad, a nation preserves one important advantage. Its supply of that commodity cannot be cut off by a blockade or a war.

In a world of competing states every nation seeks to protect itself. It wants other countries to become dependent on it but it does not want to become dependent on them. This situation creates a paradox. For while international trade makes nations more *interdependent*, they try to regulate their imports and exports in such a way that they will be more *independent*. The basic wish of every nation is to be secure and prosperous but these selfish goals are unattainable. In the world of the twentieth century no country is secure from attack and prosperous countries excite the envy of the impoverished majority. This is one reason why the modern age has been called "the Age of Anxiety," but there are other reasons also for the strains and tensions that afflict modern society.

2. THE SENSE OF INSECURITY

As noted in earlier chapters, there were already serious strains in European society before 1914. The First World War grew out of these unresolved conflicts, but the fighting solved no fundamental problem and intensified national antagonisms. As a result the European peoples gained no lasting sense of security from the peace settlement of 1919. Rather, in comparison with the years before 1914, the postwar era seemed threatening and chaotic, and men began to look back to the relative calm of the preceding century as to a golden yesterday. A mood of pessimism and cynicism, of fatalism and futility, spread through the Western world. The discontent and disillusionment, the fear and insecurity and mounting violence offered a marked contrast to the more orderly methods, the respect for legal forms, contracts, and treaties, which had distinguished the leading nations in the nineteenth century. Even the optimistic faith in progress which had inspired civilized peoples before 1914 lost its earlier intensity. It is important to seek the causes, some of which have already been foreshadowed, which help to account for this change of temper in modern society.

The first unsettling factor to note was the rapid and irreversible increase in the number of city dwellers, especially the urban proletariat. Within half a century all the industrialized nations found that a city population had grown up within their borders which outmatched, outvoted, and outnumbered the once dominant rural and agricultural classes. In Britain,

Germany, Belgium, France, the United States, and to a lesser degree in the remaining European countries, the generation which came of age about 1920 was a generation largely born and bred in the cities, shaped and dominated by city patterns and city ideals. The resulting change in the character of the average twentieth-century citizen born after 1900 is not easy to analyze or to describe. Yet there was a change, a real and disturbing change, in the mentality and the expectations of this modern generation. It might, perhaps, be summed up by saying that the young people had more superficial self-confidence but less genuine self-reliance than their predecessors.

This was understandable. The sense of security which makes people feel habitually calm and at ease is based upon emotional rather than intellectual certainties. For millions of people the transition to city life tended to weaken the two most fundamental "frames" within which men had oriented themselves and learned to feel at home: the immemorial framework of the family group and the framework of the native village or community. City families were in general smaller than rural families and were often severed from the older generation. They lived in more transient fashion, in rented and often restricted quarters. They had fewer permanent possessions than rural families but more diverse interests. The individuals who composed a city family depended less on one another and less on their immediate neighbors than had been common in village communities. It has frequently been said that modern city dwellers are "rootless," and the charge is just in the sense that millions of city people feel no personal or intimate ties binding them to their block or precinct. They have no bonds comparable to those which attach a man to the fields he has ploughed for years or the villager to the church spire in the shade of which his ancestors are buried.

Children who grew up in a rural environment shared more intimately in family responsibilities, joined early in the common labors, and learned their capacity and their worth. But city children were often a financial burden throughout school years. As members of large classes and neighborhood groups they were submerged in numbers. When they went to work they were likely to pass their days at a mechanical routine with little chance to feel or express their individuality because, to the industry or corporation which they served, they were impersonal and replaceable automatons. Many large firms, recognizing these defects, sought to promote group activities among their employees, to enlist their loyalty by stressing the mutuality of the business relationship, and to reward their fidelity by the distribution of shares or bonuses. But the impersonality of modern business and industrial methods continued to frustrate the individual. In the city environment it was less easy for a human being to develop those tendrils that attach him to his world and give him the sense of security which comes to those who are known and needed by their fellows. City adolescents reflected this difficulty in achieving emotional adjustment. They learned to be alert and brisk and knowing in manner but they often remained inwardly unsure. The strain and the dissatisfaction that made modern life a burden for millions led to an alarming increase in mental ailments and in juvenile delinquency. Mental and emotional ills incapacitated more people than any other maladies.

To these psychological hazards of modern life there was added, especially after 1929, a deepening sense of economic insecurity. In earlier times, the man in business for himself, the farmer, carpenter, storekeeper, or general practitioner, did not worry about dismissal because he was his own employer. A poor crop or a business recession might mean some lean years but not sudden unemployment and imminent privation. The factory or office worker, however, who had nothing but his job, lived in fear that his job might fail. This fear lay behind the various government measures, adopted more and more widely in the twentieth century, which promised the working classes some form of insurance against the risks of sickness, accident, disability, and unemployment. The rise in savings accounts, insurance policies, and government social security funds all reflected the need of the workers to lay up some reserve against disaster, or have their government do it for them.

Unfortunately, savings deposited with the banks or the government were not always safe. Bank failures, inflation, ruinous taxes, revolution, or war might destroy the financial security of a whole class or nation. World War 1 proved to millions of Europeans, who had been subsisting on fixed incomes or annuities, that currency could depreciate and prices soar. The German people learned the full tragedy of inflation after 1920 when their currency depreciated until it became literally worthless. Millions of families watched their wealth, insurance policies, mortgages, pensions, or investments turn to valueless paper. In France the franc lost four-fifths of its prewar value, falling from twenty cents to four. Finally, even the British pound, monetary unit of the world for a century, fluctuated and fell from the gold standard. The impact of these forfeitures shook the confidence of the disinherited classes. Throughout all the industrialized states many people found their jobs dependent upon vast economic forces they could not comprehend and their savings dependent upon financial fluctuations which they could not control. To the young who faced the world after 1920 the old and stable values which their parents had trusted seemed less sure. This was not their misconception; they were living in a disreputable age in which the honor of nations, the sanctity of contracts, and the equity promised by the law were often and brazenly betrayed. Such conditions breed fear even in nations which are spared them. The impoverished classes of central Europe, the fugitives from Russia who had been dispossessed by the revolution, the French families that lost their men in the war and their savings in the peace, the British who were fighting to hold their threatened leadership in world trade, all felt the prevalent mood of economic insecurity.

A third factor in the general disquiet was the unhinging of international exchange rates. Here sharp national antagonisms added to the bitterness that is always incited by forfeited investments and repudiated debts. In the economic competition after 1920 few nations admitted themselves at fault but all accused their rivals of cheating. The Germans blamed the Treaty of Versailles and the Reparations Bill for the collapse of their currency. The French blamed the German failure to meet reparations payments in full for the fall of the franc. The British blamed a disordered world exchange for their dislocated trade and proposed a cancellation of war debts all around. When the United States, which would suffer the heaviest loss from such a course, declined the suggestion, all debtor states criticized the American government. In reality, the war debts and reparations quarrel was no more than a superficial issue in a much graver problem. World production, agricultural and industrial, had been speeded up and world population doubled in a century. But no adequate machinery had been developed to assure the industrialized countries an equitable share of raw materials or an equitable approach to world markets, with the result that the rival powers fought with tariffs and cartels and currency rules for the trade of a shrinking planet. Nor had any machinery been devised to assure an equitable distribution of wealth, and the maldistribution of purchasing power created needy and depressed classes and famine stricken peoples.

Before its first quarter had ended, the twentieth century revealed itself as a century of deeper violences and sharper vicissitudes than the nineteenth had been. The difference could not be blamed upon any check in material progress and prosperity. In spite of the loss and destruction of World War I the peoples of Europe in 1925 had higher living standards, greater wealth, and a longer life expectancy than they had ever known. But their mood, their methods of government, their political morality had declined since the halcyon years of the long peace, 1871–1914.

If material prosperity and the progress of science could have assured a stable society, the United States should have held a secure and tranquil population. America led the world in the parade of inventions, discoveries, and technological achievements wherewith science has enriched the life of man. The years 1900–1939 brought a 73 per cent gain in the American population, multiplied 4000 automobiles into 4,000,000, equipped 23,000,000 homes in the land with electric light, popularized the motion picture and radio, developed the airplane and other mechanical wonders, and raised the standard of living, of leisure, of income, and of education to levels unimagined a few generations earlier.

Such achievements might well have filled the American people with a mood of sturdy self-confidence. They did breed a mood of confidence between 1920 and 1929, but it was not a sturdy mood. All the proof of power, the nimble machines which gave each American the services of a score of energy-slaves, failed to equip the citizens of the United States with the faith to meet an economic reverse with firmness. The stock market collapse of 1929 induced a panic which unsettled the nerves of the nation, and American despondency magnified the wave of depression already traversing the globe. If the American people could not have a resolute confidence in that machine age which had bestowed upon them its richest blessings, what confidence could less fortunate nations be expected to display?

3. THE GREAT DEPRESSION

In 1929 a panic on the New York Stock Exchange heralded a worldwide decline of business activities. International trade and industrial production dropped sharply. Wages shrank, unemployment rose, and widespread misery proved that something was wrong with the economic system. The whole world felt the impact of this economic dislocation but some countries suffered more acutely than others.

The effects of the Great Depression in the United States have already been described (see Chapter 21). Here an attempt will be made to estimate its influence on the world as a whole. This is a difficult task because values and currencies fluctuated sharply and accurate statistics are unavailable for many regions. Even when dependable calculations on production and consumption were compiled, and on prices, wages, and unemployment, such figures did not tell the whole story. There is no yardstick for measuring human misery, no formula for computing what the loss of a job, increasing privation, and the necessity of asking for public relief may mean to a man and his family. Still less is it possible to estimate what the shrinkage of international trade meant to inarticulate millions in Asia, Africa, and Latin America, who found they could not sell their crops and raw materials in the declining world markets.

For the nations that felt its effects most severely the Great Depression had the qualities of a nightmare. Some malign irresistible force seemed to have seized control and all efforts to arrest the decline appeared futile. Banks collapsed, factories closed down, millions of workers were discharged from their jobs. The disaster had struck without warning. No one could explain clearly what had gone wrong; no one could foretell how much worse conditions might become. These uncertainties produced a sense of helplessness and despair. The Great Depression left an indelible memory behind, particularly among the people of the United States. Fears that a similar economic collapse might overtake the world again still haunt millions of people even yet. It is important, therefore, to judge the Great Depression calmly in the perspective of history. It was a great misfortune, but it was neither so ominous nor so mysterious as some of the legends told about it suggest.

What people in America and Europe noted most inescapably about the Depression was the reduction of their incomes. In addition to millions of wage earners who were thrown out of work entirely, millions more became part-time laborers. Even those who kept full-time jobs often had to accept a reduction in wages. In the United States the per capita income fell from about $700 in 1929 to some $400 in 1933. Most of the European people suffered in similar fashion. Only Soviet Russia, which had almost isolated itself from the rest of the world, escaped the effects of the Depression. But the Russian people, especially in the Ukraine, suffered severely for several years after 1929 from other causes. The forcible attempt to establish collective farms brought misery and death to millions of Russian farmers (see Chapter 27).

A second effect of the Depression which filled many people with apprehension was that international trade and manufacturing shrank rapidly. In 1929 the estimated value of United States imports and exports had reached almost ten billion dollars. By 1933 the value had dropped to three billion. Furthermore, American industrial output was cut in half. The world as a whole, however, weathered the storm somewhat better. Although prices dropped sharply and the "dollar value" of international trade fell more than 60 per cent, the actual decline in the cargoes shipped was about 25 per cent. World industrial output likewise suffered less sharply than that of the United States, falling about one-third in four years.

It is important to realize that statistics on the decline of national income, of industrial production, and of international trade provided a gloomier picture from 1929 to 1933 than the actual world conditions warranted. The majority of the world's workers did not make their living from industry or trade; they supported themselves through agriculture. If the world *food supply* had dropped 60 or 50 or even 25 per cent between 1929 and 1933, mankind would have faced a much greater tragedy. It is true that the market prices paid for agricultural produce dropped. But in the world as a whole the number of acres cultivated and the amount of food produced actually *increased* during the years of the Depression. In 1933 the world acreage devoted to wheat, rice, rye, maize, barley, and oats was larger than in 1929. Other crops, such as potatoes and sugar, that furnish calories for human consumption likewise rose. As six out of seven human beings depend on cereals for most of their nourishment this gain in agricultural production was a matter of the utmost importance.

To humanity as a whole, therefore, the Great Depression brought hardships but it did not bring acute disaster. There was no sharp rise in deaths from starvation and disease. On the contrary, the world death-rate *declined* in the 1930's, and life expectancy continued to rise. These encouraging trends may be seen in the statistical tables compiled by the League of Nations. But these tables also reveal certain *negative* effects in the 1930's for which the Depression was almost certainly responsible. Although the world population continued to increase, and the deathrate continued to drop, there was a perceptible decline in the world birth rate in the 1930's. When people feel increasingly insecure and view the future with deepened apprehension, they are less likely to marry and less eager to have children whom they may find it impossible to support. During the period of the Great Depression and for some years afterwards the world birthrate averaged about one-tenth lower than it had during the "prosperous" 1920's.

A decline of one-tenth in the birthrate may not seem very significant. It meant that during the 1930's there were about three less births per year for each thousand people than there would have been if the birthrate of the preceding decade had continued unchanged. By 1930 the global population had reached two billion, so a drop of three per thousand in the birthrate meant some six million fewer babies were born in a year. It meant that, between 1930 and 1940, approximately 550 million babies were born into the world instead of perhaps 600 million that might have been born if there had been no Depression. Fifty million human beings is a total greater than all the soldiers and civilians killed in both world wars.

When the Great Depression is judged by its effect on the birthrate it takes on the shape of a massive calamity. It is possible to argue, of course, that the decline in the birthrate after 1929 was not due to the Depression at all but to other factors. But no other factors appear to provide a more adequate explanation. If the statistics that are available may be trusted, the global birthrate fell steadily between 1930 and 1935, when the Depression made its effects felt most acutely, remained low until after 1940, and then began to *rise* again in the midst of World War II. In other words, the Depression seems to have had a more unfortunate effect on the birthrate than the turmoil of a world war did.

4. PROGRAMS FOR ECONOMIC RECOVERY

The dislocation of trade and industry, the falling prices, and the rising unemployment that came with the Depression forced statesmen and economists to seek remedies. But the experts could not agree in their diagnoses of what was wrong or what measures would prove most effective in restoring prosperity. Each nation sought to improve its own condition and some of the selfish measures adopted by individual governments made world conditions worse. Why this was so becomes clearer when the programs followed by the leading states are examined.

On June 20, 1931, President Herbert Hoover proposed a moratorium, a suspension of payments on intergovernmental debts for one year. But the Depression had grown too serious and involved for any simple remedy, and Hoover's proposal failed to arrest the decline. The spread of financial confusion, constricting the flow of world trade upon which Great Britain depended for prosperity, forced the British government to abandon the gold standard in September, 1931. The pound sterling immediately fell 20 to 30 per cent in value. For the British this result was not entirely a loss, for their debts could now be paid in devaluated pounds; and the reduction in wages made British manufactures relatively cheaper and therefore more welcome on the international market. Eighteen months later (April, 1933) the United States likewise abandoned the gold standard, although the major share of the world gold reserve was in this country. Soon the currencies of all the leading nations were unhinged from any fixed value, and the unpredictable fluctuations of the dollar, pound, franc, mark, or lira added a further hazard to discourage businessmen from the risks of international commerce. Without fixed policies, respect for contracts, and a stable unit of money with which to reckon costs and prices, traders could not negotiate or bankers calculate the prospects of a project or the worth of securities.

All these factors, which were at once causes and effects, increased the disastrous fall in world commerce after 1929. For that year the total international trade within Europe exceeded $11,000,000,000 (1929 dollar value). Trade between European and non-European countries reached $15,000,000,000. Five years later foreign trade within Europe had shrunk to $4,000,000,000 (1929 dollar value), and European trade with the rest of the world to $5,000,000,000. So sharp a reduction in the value of international transactions could not fail to bring ruin or unemployment to millions. The economic prosperity of all the leading nations was very largely dependent upon the profits of manufacture, transportation, banking, and insurance, and upon the dividends from money invested in these lucrative activities. The Depression had repercussions which struck at all classes, for with factories idle the output of the mines, the crops from the fields, and the cargoes from distant quarters of the earth all declined.

In countries like Germany and Italy, where the average income of the workers and their per capita wealth were about half that enjoyed by Englishmen or Frenchmen of equivalent station, the loss and hardship were naturally more pressing. Social unrest impelled all governments to experiment with panaceas which promised to bring temporary relief to a critical situation. The widespread suffering, the mood of bewilderment and anger that stirred the masses, and the demand from the destitute and the unemployed that their leaders find a remedy, must be kept in mind by the student who wishes to understand this clamorous decade 1929–1939. The grandiose national programs, the inflation of the currencies, the mad chauvinism preached by European leaders, were in part dictated by the exigencies of the Depression. It was almost inevitable that politicians who could not conquer the economic ills should distract the attention of discontented and angry electors by seeking some minority as a scapegoat for the general misery, or by pointing abroad at some foreign rival as the cause of national frustration. It is important to note, too, that in countries which had no long discipline in the methods of democratic self-government, there was a general readiness to look to the government or to a strong and dictatorial leader for a solution to the crisis. In countries where democracy was more firmly rooted and free economic enterprise had flourished more sturdily the individual citizens recognized that recovery must depend very largely upon their own energy and their own constructive efforts.

None of the many plans proposed by statesmen and economists to stimulate the return of world prosperity by conferences, proclamations, cancellation of debt payments, or manipulation of currency rates, produced the result desired. In every state, therefore, the leaders turned to measures which might aid in solving their local problems and bring about recuperation in their national economy. The world was too large and complex for legislators to prescribe a program for world recovery, even if they could have agreed upon one; and although the rapidity with which the Depression spread from continent to continent proved that all trading nations were interdependent, they were not cooperative but competitive in their policies. It was therefore of little use to plan measures or promulgate rules for international application, because no real agreement or control or enforcement was possible in a world where each nation-state might adopt a course that weakened its neighbors and nullified any general program for world recovery.

Nations which contained within their political frontiers the raw materials most vital for their economic well-being were fortunate. The United States possessed varied and abundant resources and the population formed a domestic market which could absorb the output of the mills and the farms. The British Empire-Commonwealth, with colonies and possessions and self-governing Dominions in every clime and continent, could likewise plan to revive its economic life within a framework of "imperial preference." Soviet Russia, where all foreign trade was a monopoly of the state, had its own economic program, its own resources, and its own industrial, agrarian, and social needs to satisfy. Self-sufficient states, especially the United States and Soviet Russia, might restore order within their own borders and meet their own needs even if the rest of the world drifted into economic anarchy. But many countries were largely dependent upon one or two products which they must sell in the world market, on coffee or tin or nitrates which they produced in abundance but could not consume themselves. For industrialized states, such as Germany and Japan, which had highly developed manufactures to produce and sell, the dislocation of trade and the division of the world into jealously guarded preserves caused increasing difficulty. The ingenuity of their chemists might produce synthetic substitutes for some of the raw materials which they could no longer import. But unless they could achieve complete self-sufficiency (and very few countries could find all the commodities needed within their borders) these states had to export in order to pay for imports, and they could not export to areas which some other power had sealed against them by raising an insurmountable tariff wall.

When their attempts at economic penetration were frustrated, businessmen could hardly fail to remind themselves that the situation might be improved if their government could secure control over the area they desired to exploit. Nations which lacked large colonial empires were easily persuaded that this lack exposed them to undue restrictions and hardships. In Rome, Berlin, and Tokyo the industrialists, the statesmen, and the militarists all recognized that a war of conquest might offer the most obvious solution to their immediate problems. That such a program might prove costly and tragic in its ultimate effects they understood; but they were realists, the pressure of events and the clamor of the people compelled them to offer some positive program, and they craved power. A bold armament campaign might mean increased taxes but it also meant that the government would have large sums of money to spend. Expanded orders for weapons and equipment would assure activity in the heavy industries. By calling additional classes of conscripts for army training, the government could reduce unemployment and provide itself with trained and obedient soldiers who would break a strike or repress internal disorders. Whether a war came or not, military preparedness was the most persuasive argument a dominant party or dictatorial clique could invoke to justify the arbitrary acts, extraordinary expenditures, and illegal usurpation of power practiced by all the totalitarian dictatorships.

It was recognized by thoughtful men everywhere that the "planned recovery" instituted by the German, Japanese, and Italian governments as a means of escaping from the Depression was a threat to peace. The existence of a powerful army is in itself a powerful argument for using it. Armament programs, moreover, are always competitive, and even in the less militaristic countries some part of the revenue voted for economic recovery was turned to increased production of arms. As unemployment declined and armaments mounted, it began to seem as if preparation for war was the most certain cure for an economic Depression. This grim enigma led one writer to ask the disturbing question: "Is modern industry, then, a sick giant which can rouse itself only to kill?"

36

THE RESORT TO AGGRESSION

It is a fact that, without declaration of war, a large area of what was indisputably Chinese territory has been forcibly seized and occupied by the armed forces of Japan . . .

LYTTON COMMISSION REPORT TO THE LEAGUE OF NATIONS (1932)

1. THE FAILURE TO DISARM

CHAPTER 35 DESCRIBED how the leading powers, emerging from the debilitating effects of the world-wide Depression, sought individually to mend their national economies. In every state expenditures for national defense played some part in the official plans to strengthen ailing industries. The years after 1933 brought a revival of militarism, and the armament race was soon more desperate and costly than that which had preceded the outbreak of World War I in 1914. Two motives have been stressed as hastening this fateful development: first, the need to stimulate business and reduce unemployment, if necessary by placing large government orders for weapons and war material; and second, the belief of chauvinists and expansionists that the possession of military, naval, and air power would win advantages and secure spheres of influence for a vigorous nation and enable it to expand.

It will be recalled that the League of Nations was empowered to invite proposals which might lead to a measure of general disarmament. The failure to disarm or to limit armed forces by general agreement after World War I must be attributed to the persistence of international distrust. No nation was willing to reduce its strength in really substantial fashion. The proposals submitted in discussion were always formulated in such a way that they would leave the nation sponsoring them no weaker, relatively, than it had been. This was understandable and logical. The men at the head of a modern state, and especially the naval and military experts whom they consult on questions of national security, have the defense of the state as their highest responsibility. They cannot dutifully approve a step which may expose to increased danger of attack and invasion the nation they are appointed to defend. It is possible, of course, in countries where a cabinet of civilians shapes the national policy that the military and naval advisers may be overruled and the armed forces reduced despite their protest. This is less likely to occur in a country where the general staff dominates the civilian government, a fact which explains why proposals for mutual disarmament made to a government in which the military men are in control have little chance of acceptance.

In war, deception is a primary element of strategy, and in preparing for war concealment is a customary expedient. This applies not only to secret weapons but to the size and nature of the armed forces. All nations fear that their potential enemies may be stronger than they seem and that their acknowledged forces are only a screen for much larger reserves. Armed forces vary in training and quality, and it is easy to deceive a neighbor and to disguise the degree of a nation's military preparation. A sports association or shooting club may train its members in route marches and rifle practice. A flying club, such as young Germans organized for glider experiments, may train war pilots. New automobile highways and railway lines may be constructed to accord with plans secretly approved by the War Department. In industrial plants the possibilities for coordinating peace and war production are unlimited. Machines for making tin cans may be set to produce shell cases; bombs and baby carriages may be manufactured with equal ease; standardized alarm clocks are timing mechanisms; lenses and telescopes make range finders; nitrates for fertilizers or for explosives may come from the same chemical plants. The one obvious fact which cannot be disguised or ignored, however, is the *industrialization* of modern warfare. Without factories to supply them, men cannot fight a major military campaign.

Thus the military strength of an industrial nation is very difficult to gauge or limit. On the other hand, the regulation of naval armaments can be much more easily achieved, for a battleship takes years to build, it cannot be disguised, and it has no peacetime purpose. Because of these facts and because many experts began to question the value of large battleships in an age of air power, a measure of naval limitation was attained after World War I. The Washington Naval Treaty of 1922 inaugurated a ten-year holiday in the construction of capital ships, and this provision was later extended to 1936. But an attempt made in 1930 to induce the five leading naval powers, Great Britain, the United States, Japan, France, and Italy, to limit their categories of cruisers, destroyers, and submarines brought no general agreement. The French feared to weaken their communications with North Africa, and they refused to accept parity with Italy because they had Atlantic and North Sea ports as well as a Mediterranean coastline to defend. The British, burdened by taxes for the support of the unemployed and weakened by loss of trade, agreed reluctantly to reduce their estimated needs in cruisers and destroyers, and Japan and the United States likewise accepted a limited program of construction. This reduction partly explains why, when war came after 1939, the British were to find themselves desperately short of armed vessels to escort their merchant convoys. The great age of British naval supremacy, when the Royal Navy was equal to any two other fleets in the world, had passed. Yet it is not certain that economic pressure really compelled the reduction in strength which the British accepted, and it is not easy to judge whether this measure of disarmament helped the cause of peace. The candid acknowledgment from London that Britain was limiting its first line of defense left the Japanese more powerful in the Pacific and caused Italy to grow more truculent in the Mediterranean Sea. The Germans likewise speeded up their naval program in defiance of the restrictions laid upon them by the Versailles Treaty.

By 1933, however, the Versailles Treaty had become almost a dead letter and a new pattern of power was taking shape. The Anglo-French victory in 1918 had made Britain relatively secure at sea and the French army dominant in Europe. Both states therefore sought to limit armaments at that level and preserve a pattern of power which confirmed their leadership. The pattern endured about ten years. When the Germans protested that only the defeated nations had disarmed and demanded that France and her allies reduce their military forces in some equivalent manner, the refusal of the French made them seem arrogant and militaristic. The Germans pressed their advantage, urging that either France must disarm or Germany must be permitted to rearm. A world conference on disarmament, finally summoned by the League of Nations in 1932, accomplished nothing effective. In the midst of the great economic Depression the burden of expenditure for defense seemed to most nations more insupportable than ever, but although the conference prolonged its meetings into the following year no agreement resulted. The world armament bill was already one-third higher than it had been in 1914, and for the next six years it was to rise inexorably until it burst into the crescendo of World War II.

2.   THE MARCH OF AGGRESSION: THE JAPANESE IN CHINA

The argument urged by many pacifists, that armaments did not pay, seemed to be belied by the success of the more aggressive powers, especially after 1931. In the Far East, Japan demonstrated to the world that a weaker neighbor might be invaded with impunity and that conquests could be made a source of profit. The motives which inspired the Japanese to invade Manchuria have been noted already (see p. 387). After September, 1931, Japanese troops moved deeper and deeper into this province, widening the area of conquest, until in 1932 the militarists at Tokyo judged the moment ripe to set up a puppet government and proclaim the "independent" state of Manchukuo. Japanese advisers controlled the puppet government of Manchukuo. From this base the Japanese armies continued their penetration southward, with the evident intention of detaching further Chinese provinces from the rule of the republican government at Nanking.

For the weak and defenseless nations of the world the fate of China provided a grim warning. China was a member of the League of Nations and had a clear case. If the sanctity of treaties and the principles of collective security were worth anything, China should have been safe from attack. The Nine Power Treaty of 1922, which had been ratified by Japan and eight other nations, guaranteed the territorial integrity and the political independence of the Chinese Republic. In January, 1932, the United States secretary of state notified all signatories of the Nine Power pact that any change of status brought about by armed force and in defiance of existing treaties would not be recognized by the United States. The British government, however, failed to support the American stand promptly and vigorously, and the Japanese were not deterred. The Chinese could offer no strong military opposition but they proclaimed a boycott of Japanese manufactures. The Japanese retaliated by a destructive bombardment of Shanghai and landed troops there to occupy the port. On the plea that Japan had "resorted to war" the Chinese government appealed formally to the League of Nations and invited the League Council to review the dispute.

The League dispatched a commission to investigate the causes of the Sino-Japanese clash, but even the presence of officials from Geneva did not halt the desultory fighting in Manchuria and North China. Unfortunately neither the United States nor the Soviet Union was a member of the League, a lack which limited the effectiveness of any policy which the League might adopt. Even Great Britain did not offer strong or consistent support to the Chinese plea for aid. But among many of the minor peoples sentiment ran so strongly in favor of China, and Japanese arrogance was so uncompromising, that the Council adopted the Lytton Report, which criticized the Japanese for their aggressive tactics but recommended a settlement that would have left Japanese influence supreme in the disputed area. The Chinese, losing hope that the League would aid them in any effective manner, made the best they could of a confusing situation and allowed the Japanese possession of most of the territory north of the Great Wall. It was evident that the League had suffered one more defeat. The Japanese government dealt it still another by announcing its intention to resign in 1933. In carrying out this decision, the Japanese did not offer to return the Pacific islands which they had received in 1919 under mandate from the League. No one seriously expected that they would do so, because all the powers had transformed their mandates into virtual protectorates by that time.

It was still possible for friendly powers to aid China indirectly with loans, supplies, and ammunition if they had the will to do so. But here likewise the almost hopeless inferiority of a weaker state was made clear. With a pretense of scrupulous neutrality, the British government announced that it would not permit British firms to supply arms to either Japan or China, an embargo which embarrassed the Japanese little because they had the ships to import and the factories to construct implements of war whereas the Chinese were almost wholly dependent upon the arms they could purchase abroad. Lacking large modern industrial plants, and deprived of the mines of Manchuria, the Chinese could not hope to equip an army that might match the well trained and well armed Japanese divisions. The Chinese suffered a further handicap in that the Japanese navy could enforce an unofficial blockade of all Chinese ports, but the Chinese had no battleships to halt the flow of scrap iron from the United States which helped feed the Japanese armament works. As the peoples of the world observed the unequal struggle waged by the Chinese, their faith in the League as an instrument of international justice fell still lower. The Chinese delegate at Geneva reminded other League members that China had asked repeatedly for the protection promised it under the Covenant; and he concluded with the grave warning that "the absence of any effective action by the League has encouraged those who all along have been proclaiming the belief that might is right." Successful aggression elsewhere, and the failure to halt the Japanese in the early stages of their advance into China, would persuade them that all China would soon be theirs.

Such was, indeed, the conclusion which the Japanese leaders reached by 1933. Once they were firmly installed in Manchukuo their agents began to expel the personnel, capital, and influence of all European groups and to replace or confiscate foreign investments for the benefit of Japanese business firms. Military conquest and political protection were only stages of consolidation whereby their economic hegemony could be rendered secure. After numerous "incidents" and considerable friction the Russian Soviet government was persuaded to sell its half share in the Chinese Eastern Railway to the new state of Manchukuo, and by 1936 the Japanese had won a position of almost exclusive mastery over an area of North China twice the size of Texas, with a population of 40,000,000. Such rapid penetration and assimilation of new provinces made it seem a fair surmise that they would be able to extend their control over the remainder of the country within a few years and make it the central portion of their "Co-Prosperity Sphere," as they liked to style their proposed Asiatic empire.

In execution, however, their plan encountered checks which slowed it down and ultimately reversed it. For ten years after 1931 their armies in China waged successive campaigns until they had subdued ten provinces and brought the four largest cities under their rule. As in Manchuria, they attempted to mask their direction of affairs. After Nanking, the Chinese capital, fell to their armies they established a puppet "Chinese"

Government forces loyal to General Franco attempt to break rebel supply lines in northern Spain during the Spanish Civil War, (Wide World Photos).

An Italian mule train brings supplies to the Italian army in Ethiopia, 1935 (Acme).

Hitler and Mussolini meet in Berlin in October, 1937, shortly before Japan joined the Rome-Berlin Axis (Acme).

government. But the legitimate government moved to Chungking and kept up a heroic resistance. With the outbreak of World War II in 1939 the Chinese struggle for survival was merged into the larger global conflict. The history of the Sino-Japanese War after 1939 will therefore be described in a later chapter where it forms part of the Japanese bid for hegemony in the western Pacific, a gigantic gamble which culminated and collapsed between 1941 and 1945.

3. THE MARCH OF AGGRESSION: THE ITALIANS IN ETHIOPIA

It is not easy for the student of history to recapture the lost mood of millions of peace-lovers who saw the steady drift towards a general war after 1933 but were powerless to check it. The fiasco of the Disarmament Conference and the failure to halt Japanese aggression in China excited earnest discussion and the governments of the leading nations were embarrassed by a wave of sharp criticism. There was, however, a deep irony in the international situation which pacifists did not readily appreciate, for the more frankly a people admitted its devotion to peace the more surely an aggressive nation might hope to extort blackmail by the threat of war. In 1934–1935, for instance, a "peace ballot" was circulated in Great Britain as an unofficial test of public opinion. Nearly 12,000,000 citizens voted. Nine out of ten approved of active participation in the League of Nations, favored the reduction of armaments, and endorsed economic pressure against aggressor states. Only seven in ten, however, supported the use of military measures against an aggressor. Although the British cabinet and parliament weighed the results of this ballot thoughtfully, it is not easy to judge how strongly the vote may have influenced British foreign policy. Some critics insisted that it advertised the divided hopes and wishful thinking of the democratic peoples, but in truth their hopes and aims were less divided than they seemed. In a world in which military aggression still occurred, civilized people were seeking to mobilize public opinion against it and to find effective measures short of war that would deter a government from warlike actions. Nevertheless the fact that the British people so clearly wished to avoid war encouraged militarists in Germany, Italy, and Japan to disregard and even to defy British opposition.

The year 1935–1936 brought further reverses to the League which practically ended its prestige and usefulness as an instrument for collective security. The new aggressor and troublemaker was the Italian fascist government. The Italians had long been dissatisfied with their modest colonial empire and envious of the larger and more profitable dominions ruled by Britain and France. Since the later nineteenth century they had regarded Ethiopia (Abyssinia) as an area of African territory reserved for Italian exploitation, but their attempt to conquer it had met with military defeat in 1896. Ethiopia survived into the twentieth century as an autonomous state under a hereditary monarch and in 1923 was admitted to the League of Nations. As no other region of Africa remained free of European domination the Italian government waited for a favorable opportunity to undertake its conquest. From 1932 onwards it was commonly known that plans for an Ethiopian war had been drawn up by the Italian high command. In 1934 the predictable "border incidents" developed at points where Italian Eritrea and Somaliland joined the Ethiopian frontier. It was evident that Italy was preparing excuses which might serve when the moment came for armed intervention. In January, 1935, the Ethiopian government appealed to the League of Nations. The League was solicited to use its "friendly right" of inquiry to investigate the causes of disagreement which threatened to involve two members, Italy and Ethiopia, in hostilities. The League noted the appeal but postponed action on it.

In March Ethiopia appealed a second time, the delegates citing Article 15 of the League Covenant which prescribed the course to be adopted when peace was directly threatened. Once more the League delayed action. The German government had just announced the reintroduction of military conscription, forbidden Germany by the Treaty of Versailles, and European statesmen were preoccupied with this new step toward war. So the months passed and a third and a fourth Ethiopian appeal fell upon deaf ears, while the Italians completed their preparations and opened the fighting with a large-scale invasion of Ethiopia. When thus directly challenged by events, the League voted that sanctions must be applied against Italy to restrain the attack. Only economic sanctions were invoked, however. Oil, the most indispensable article needed by the Italian war machine, was not placed upon the embargo list nor was the Italian line of communications through the Suez Canal severed. Thus, although they suffered some hardship from the restriction of imports, the Italians were able to continue the war. They entered the Ethiopian capital in May, 1936. Thereafter resistance rapidly collapsed. An aggressive military policy had succeeded once again.

4. THE MARCH OF AGGRESSION: CIVIL WAR IN SPAIN

The tragedy of China and the assault on Ethiopia befell countries outside the limits of Europe. The Western nations might read about, discuss, and deprecate these events, but most of them, however genuine their concern, considered China and Ethiopia as remote, half-civilized countries where disorder and warfare were perhaps inevitable. But with the year 1936 war came to a European state, war in its most desperate and corrosive form, between people of the same speech and blood. The civil conflict which flamed up in Spain was too close to be ignored. Its horrors were reported by journalists who witnessed them and by volunteers who served in the opposing armies.

Spanish society had been disordered and Spanish economy moribund before 1914. The First World War brought a measure of prosperity, for the warring powers needed Spanish minerals and raw products; but after 1919 this trade languished. The heavy taxes, the general incompetence of the administration, and the archaic methods of holding and working the land inspired deep discontent. Revolution was averted from year to year by every expedient known to harassed monarchs, but in 1931 a swift upheaval finally unseated Alfonso XIII and replaced the ancient Spanish monarchy by a republic. For five years the new regime strove to extend reforms, distributing the land among the peasants and broadening the basis of education and political liberty. The Spanish people, however, were tragically divided between the old way and the new. Pride, passion, and the hardy individualism characteristic of the Iberian native stock made it difficult to mold society to a disputed pattern. The anticlerical policies proclaimed by the republicans profoundly disturbed millions of believers, for Spain was a country in which the Catholic faith was firmly rooted.

On winning power in 1931 the republicans adopted a new constitution which provided for a unicameral parliament elected by universal suffrage, and a cabinet responsible to the parliament. Decrees proclaiming the separation of church and state, confiscation of church property for national purposes, and secularization of the schools, advertised the anticlerical spirit of the government. Additional measures were voted but not firmly enforced, aiming at the division of large estates among the landless farmers and the nationalization of public utilities.

From the first, however, the republicans were confused and divided by contradictions in their policies and conflicts within their ranks. Some of them were thinking of a revolution similar to the French Revolution of 1789, a series of reforms that would destroy the relics of feudal land tenure, create a class of free tenant farmers, liberate the middle class, encourage business initiative by intelligent legislation, and strip the church and the monastic orders of their wealth and influence. But the Spanish revolt of 1931 was motivated by modern trends as well as by historic traditions. In Barcelona and other industrialized cities a relatively small but well organized body of workers had formed labor unions and studied the writings of Karl Marx. They regarded themselves as brothers-in-arms with the Russian communists, heralds of the latest revolution, which was to establish the classless society in all countries.

The French Revolution had been a bourgeois struggle for power whereas the Russian Revolution was a proletarian struggle for power. Thus eighteenth and twentieth century ideals confused the Spaniards and merged incomprehensively in a pattern of violence. Few foreigners understood the deep issues in dispute. Fewer still were familiar with the fierce regional pride of the Spaniards, many of whom had never renounced their ancient provincial liberties and sense of local independence. Differences of dialect, dress, and custom still disposed millions of the Iberian peoples to think of themselves first as Basques or Catalans and only secondly as Spaniards. Spain was not in the twentieth century a homogeneous nation with one speech, one uniform set of laws, one system of education, such as Britain, France, and Germany had become.

A civil war is always a national tragedy; but when issues are deeply confused and deliberately misrepresented, the tragedy is certain to grow more bitter. Without foreign interference the Spaniards might possibly have worked out a compromise solution and erected a stable government. But a divided country is always a weakened country, and the European powers, already preparing for a general war, were jealous and fearful. Control of Spanish mines, harbors, and airfields was a tempting prize, for Spain would make a useful ally in a European war. The military leaders at Rome and Berlin, who were knitting the Italo-German Pact of Steel (the "Axis" of 1936), appreciated the value of Spain. If they helped to set up a regime there which would be indebted to Germany and Italy for support, they would have won an initial move in the far-reaching strategy of conquest they meditated.

Many Spanish republicans, by 1936, while still loyal to the Revolution, were disappointed by the vicissitudes of policy and the divided aims of their leaders. On the other hand, many wealthy landowners and capitalists and many army officers were deeply resentful of the republican program and ready to support a move to restore the monarchy. With German and Italian factories ready to supply guns and planes to these reactionaries it was easy for them to open a sudden attack in July, 1936, which threw the republican regime on the defensive. Assuming the title of Nationalists, the insurgents named General Francisco Franco "Chief of the Spanish State" and pressed a fierce and pitiless attack upon the key centers of republican resistance. Germany and Italy promptly recognized Franco's government; Britain and France sponsored a policy of nonintervention and refused to authorize aid to either side; and Soviet Russia shipped food and arms to the republicans when possible. With a strong Spanish force, some Moorish troops from Morocco, 100,000 Italian soldiers, and German technical advisers and airmen, Franco won the advantage at the cost of bitter and prolonged fighting. When his forces captured Barcelona in January, 1939, Britain and France reluctantly recognized his government, and the fall of Madrid a month later ended the Spanish Republic. The civil war had been waged with a relentlessness and ferocity that appalled civilized peoples. It cost 700,000 lives, caused incalculable property damage, and left millions ruined and hundreds of thousands in exile or in Franco's concentration camps. The national life of the Spanish people was poisoned, and the memory of the countless betrayals, reprisals, and assassinations was a heritage to darken the years.

Once again the pleas of the pacifists and the paper projects of fact-finding commissions had been mocked by the realistic aggressors who were ready for war and not afraid to risk it. The democratic powers had sought to isolate the struggle, but the Anglo-French policy of nonintervention had broken down and the success of Franco and the Nationalists was celebrated in Rome and Berlin as a victory for the Axis. The well-timed strategy whereby Rome and Berlin alternated their moves, so that the attention of their opponents might be confused and divided, was producing dramatic successes. The Italian dictator, Benito Mussolini, tacitly abandoned Austria to German designs and in return the German government recognized the Italian claim to Ethiopia. By the close of 1936 the Rome-Berlin Axis had come into effective play, and Germany and Japan had likewise concluded an agreement for mutual accord. By 1937 the three militant and authoritarian states, Germany, Italy, and Japan, were linked for the promotion of their varied aims and common advantage.

The only choice left to the democratic powers appeared to be for them to draw together likewise, arm themselves rapidly, and oppose force with force. The world had seen the futility of protests that were not backed up by guns and the willingness to use them. China, Ethiopia, and Spain were proof that aggressive governments which did not fear public criticism or diplomatic rebukes could and would ignore the protests of irresolute and pacifistic nations. Yet the peaceful peoples still sought to evade this truth, and their leaders, when they proposed appropriations for increased armaments, were defied by complacent legislators immersed in local affairs. Each successive crisis excited a momentary apprehension, a flurry of suggestions, and a stiffening of mind among the democratic nations. Then, as the tension eased, the peoples strove to ignore recent implications and reverted to more optimistic hopes. Throughout the fateful years after 1933 Hitler's cynical assertion that it was difficult to deceive people, but easy to help them deceive themselves, received almost daily confirmation. Faith in the possibility of achieving collective security through honest and patient diplomacy, and hope for the ultimate triumph of right reason, persisted in millions of hearts until the last hours of the twenty-year truce of 1919–1939.

37

THE ROAD TO THE SECOND WORLD WAR

I believe it is peace for our time.
NEVILLE CHAMBERLAIN, SEPTEMBER 30, 1938

1. THE FUTILITY OF APPEASEMENT

AFTER 1936 THE ARMED threat offered by the totalitarian powers was the dominant force shaping European history. By that year the German government had repudiated the reparations, walked out of the League of Nations, reintroduced conscription, marched troops into the demilitarized Rhineland, and launched a gigantic rearmament program. In short, the Treaty of Versailles, the League of Nations, and the rule of law in international relations had been all but destroyed. The law of the mailed fist had once again become the supreme law governing the relations of nations. And the mailed fist was wielded by the totalitarian nations, the principal one of which was Germany. It was known that the Germans were creating the most powerful air force in the world and that they had hundreds of thousands of men at work constructing a defensive line along the Franco-German frontier. German industry had been coordinated for the production of arms and German economy directed toward the accumulation of reserves and imports which would enable the nation to survive a naval blockade.

To strengthen her hand, Germany concluded a pact with Italy (October 21, 1936), which Mussolini dubbed the Rome-Berlin "Axis," around which — he said — the policies of Europe would henceforth revolve. A month later, Germany concluded with Japan an "Anti-Comintern" pact (November 25, 1936), which was ostensibly aimed against the international communist movement but which — it later transpired — contained a secret protocol providing for German and Japanese military cooperation against Soviet Russia. The principal revisionist powers were thus arrayed in a Rome-Berlin-Tokyo Axis.

It was obvious that the aggressiveness of the Axis powers could be stopped only by united action of the other European powers: France, Britain, and Soviet Russia. But they showed little inclination to do so.

For different reasons they had acquiesced in each violation of the Treaty of Versailles and remained divided on the means to check future aggressions of the Axis powers. The principal guardian of the Treaty of Versailles had been France. In 1923 the French had marched into the Ruhr district of Germany to enforce the Treaty of Versailles. However, apart from the fact that the attempt had been a failure which only won for France the resentment of Germany and censure of her former allies, it was one thing to coerce Germany in the 1920's when she was disarmed and quite another in the 1930's when she had become strong. An attempt to coerce Germany after 1936 risked full-scale war. And France, increasingly rent by internal dissension, had no stomach for war alone with Germany. France had a particularly vivid memory of the carnage and destruction of World War I and she wished nothing from Germany but security, that is, the maintenance of the *status quo*. It seemed absurd to Frenchmen to plunge into war in which they would surely be further weakened and could gain nothing but the restoration of the *status quo* — that is, provided they had won the war. In 1935 France contracted an alliance with Soviet Russia. But apart from the fact that French opinion was divided on the wisdom of allying France with communist Russia, this was a defensive arrangement. Soviet Russia was at the time involved in her internal development. In spite of her fulsome lip service to collective security, she was little inclined to go to war to uphold the Treaty of Versailles, which she had not signed and which in fact she had always severely condemned.

As for Great Britain, she had the same painful memory of the slaughter of World War I but did not feel the same enthusiasm for the Treaty of Versailles as France. British opinion was sensitive to the propaganda of the "have not" powers. The accusation that the world's colonial spheres were most unequally divided, that the Treaty of Versailles was a vindictive document, that the war-guilt clause was a hypocritical and one-sided indictment of Germany, that the extortion of reparations inflicted a galling injustice on the defeated, and that the principle of self-determination was applied where it suited the victors and ignored where it did not, influenced a wide audience in Britain — as, incidentally, it did also in the United States. "Justice," one Englishman sententiously affirmed, "is no less justice because it is demanded by a dictator." The British might have been less inclined to be "fair" to Germany had they felt as threatened by the German resurgence as France. But Hitler shrewdly sweetened his repudiation of the clauses of the Treaty of Versailles concerning German disarmament by concluding a bilateral Anglo-German naval agreement (1935) which provided that the German navy (including submarines) was not to exceed 35 per cent of the British navy. Hitler also gave Britain general assurances against raising the colonial question. Relations among nations, no less than relations among individuals, are governed in part by the sentiment expressed in the old English adage: "It all depends on whose ox is being gored." So, France, Soviet Russia, and Great Britain, like timid bathers who hesitate to step into cold water, continued to procrastinate about coming to grips with Axis aggressiveness, with polite little nods at each other: "After you, Sir."

The policy of appeasement of the Axis aggressors was born of the debility of France, the moral uncertainty of Britain, and the distrust existing between France and Britain on one hand and Soviet Russia on the other. The grave defect of the policy of appeasement was the fact that it left France, Britain, and Russia weakened in morale, in prestige, and in allies, and that each concession magnified the prestige and the bargaining power of their opponents. As the arrogance and appetite of the aggressive states grew sharper, the timidity and irresolution of their opponents increased. Thomas Mann, one of the greatest German writers of the age, observed that until 1938 the Germans held a moral advantage because they were united in the conviction that they had wrongs to right. It was not until the spring of 1939, after a series of diplomatic disasters, that Britain recognized the futility of appeasement and acquired a deep conviction of being morally in the right. She proceeded then with great energy to organize a grand alliance to stop Hitler. But by then it was well nigh too late. The policy of appeasement probably hastened rather than delayed the outbreak of World War II.

2. THE ANNEXATION OF AUSTRIA AND THE DISMEMBERMENT OF CZECHOSLOVAKIA

By 1936 Hitler had rid Germany of the "shackles" of the hated Versailles *Diktat*. The aim of all German governments since 1918 had been attained. Germany had become a respected and powerful nation again. What would be the future course of German policy? Why or against whom did she continue to build up her armed forces? Today we know the answer. Thanks to the capture of the German archives by the Allied armies at the end of World War II, German prewar policy can be reconstructed with accuracy. On November 5, 1937, Hitler summoned his minister of war, his foreign minister, and the three chiefs of the German armed services and said that he intended to annex Austria and Czechoslovakia in the near future. When his astounded subordinates observed that this might provoke a European war, he admitted the possibility but did not think it likely. The key to the situation was Britain. She would not move, he was confident, because she was not interested in Central Europe. Without Britain, France would not move, and without France neither would Russia.

Hitler's plans for aggression against Austria and Czechoslovakia were at the time of course unknown outside the narrow circle of his close associates. But German war preparations were no secret. In his famous tract *Mein Kampf,* written in 1924 while in jail at Lansberg after the failure of the Beer Hall Putsch, Hitler had given a clear enough picture of his foreign policy aims. He had rejected both the Bismarckian *Ostpolitik* (that is, a policy of alliances with Germany's eastern neighbors: the Russian and Austrian empires) and the Wilhelmian *Weltpolitik* (that is, the policy of colonial expansion buttressed by a strong navy) and reached back centuries in German history to the policy of eastern expansion of the Holy Roman Empire. "We National Socialists," he wrote in *Mein Kampf,* "consciously draw a line through the foreign-policy trend of our pre-War period. We take up at the halting place of six hundred years ago. We terminate the endless German drive to the south and west of Europe, and direct our gaze toward the lands in the east. We finally terminate the colonial and trade policy of the pre-War period, and proceed to the territorial policy of the future." By "territorial policy" Hitler meant the acquisition of *Lebensraum* (living space) in Eastern Europe to solve "the discrepancy between [German] population and area." At the time few paid attention to Hitler's dreams of expansion, either in Germany or abroad, for Germany was too preoccupied by the pressing problems of the day to dream of expansion. Moreover, Hitler's views were not typical of the Germans who were mostly western oriented. They revealed rather Hitler's Austrian background. It was during his unhappy and frustrated youth in Imperial Vienna, where he was forced to rub shoulders with the dozen Hapsburg nationalities, that he developed his frenzied hatred of the Jews and Slavs and his preoccupation with Eastern Europe. After coming to power in Germany and until 1938, he was too preoccupied with ridding Germany of the "bonds" of Versailles to give much of an indication of his future course, although there was, to be sure, his violent polemic with communism. There was also his earlier, unsuccessful attempt to seize Austria by an internal coup (1934).

In 1938 Hitler returned to the task of subjecting Austria with greater assurance. The unhappy Austrian Chancellor, Kurt Schuschnigg, was summoned by Hitler to Berchtesgaden (February 11). He was subjected to crude threats and pressured into agreeing to accept an Austrian nazi, Artur Seyss-Inquart, into the cabinet and to amnesty all nazi offenders against the Austrian government. Encouraged by a menacing speech by Hitler, in which he proclaimed himself protector of the ten million Germans living outside of Germany (February 20), the Austrian nazis staged violent demonstrations in favor of *Anschluss* with Germany. As disorders grew, Schuschnigg in desperation called for a plebiscite of the Austrian people on the question of *Anschluss* (March 9). A plebiscite might reveal that many Austrians were not anxious to "return to the German fatherland." To forestall it, Hitler ordered troops to the Austrian borders and submitted a peremptory ultimatum to the Austrian government demanding the postponement of the plebiscite and the resignation of Schuschnigg. To prevent bloodshed Schuschnigg yielded. His successor, Seyss-Inquart,

appointed on Hitler's demand, invited the German troops to enter Austria
(March 12). Two days later Hitler returned to his native land and staged
a triumphal entry into Vienna. The plebiscite was held a few weeks
later, after thorough nazi preparations, and resulted in a predictable overwhelming approval of the *Anschluss*. As Hitler had anticipated, none of
the European powers intervened to save Austria. Italy, which in 1934
had acted most energetically to prevent the *Anschluss*, had become a
member of the Rome-Berlin Axis (1937) and remained aloof. France,
which in 1919 had insisted on Austrian independence, would not act without Britain. And Britain was uninterested. The inactivity of the western
powers could be excused on many grounds. Austria was, after all, a
German-speaking land; she had wanted to join Germany in 1919; the
treaties which had prevented her union with Germany were by 1938
largely a dead letter.

The turn of Czechoslovakia was next. On April 21, 1938, Hitler gave
orders to prepare operation "Green," the military plan for the seizure of
Czechoslovakia. For the moment he set no date for its execution, because
he thought that he could break up Czechoslovakia by political means,
without resort to force. The German propaganda machine — ably directed
by Hitler's propaganda chief, the sinister, clubfooted Dr. Goebbels —
began a systematic campaign of vilification against Czechoslovakia.
Ostensibly the campaign demanded relief for the supposedly oppressed
Sudeten German minority in Czechoslovakia. The Sudeten Germans
became a willing tool of German policy and launched a campaign of
disruption, analogous to that of the Austrian nazis in Austria (see p. 314).
But Czechoslovakia was not as helpless as Austria. Apart from a strong
system of fortifications along her frontier with Germany and a well-
equipped army of thirty-five divisions, her international position appeared
to be much stronger than that of Austria. In addition to the peace treaties
of 1919, she had other guarantees of her independence, namely, alliance
treaties with France and Soviet Russia, drafted — it seemed — for precisely
such a contingency as had arisen in 1938. The Czechoslovak crisis, therefore, unlike the Austrian crisis, became from the first a great international crisis involving the major powers of Europe. As Hitler had anticipated the key position in the crisis was held by Britain, because France
would not act without Britain, nor Soviet Russia without France.

The conduct of British foreign policy was in the hands of Prime Minister Chamberlain, a courageous and honest but somewhat old-fashioned
and insular British statesman (1937–1940). Remembering the charge
often made against Sir Edward Grey that he could have prevented the
outbreak of World War I had he made Britain's position clear in 1914,
Chamberlain was determined not to let war come through British inactivity or equivocation. From March, 1938, he made Britain's position
clear: she would fight if France were attacked without provocation but
would not fight if France were involved in war to save Czechoslovakia.

In May the nervous Czechoslovak government, on false reports of German troop movements along its borders, ordered the general mobilization of the Czechoslovak army. France and Russia approved the measure. The Sudeten Germans toned down their agitation and Germany appeared to be checked. Hitler was outraged by Czechoslovak defiance, the show of French and Soviet solidarity, and because he was accused of an act that he intended but had not yet committed. On May 31 he informed his war chiefs that he intended to "smash" Czechoslovakia by force, and set a date for the execution of operation "Green": October 1, 1938. As the summer months wore on, the crisis deepened and tensions mounted. The crisis came to a head after an intemperate speech by Hitler at Nuremberg on September 12, full of threats, angry abuse against President Beneš of Czechoslovakia, and a demand for self-determination for the Sudeten Germans. On the following day, the French cabinet, unable to reach a decision on whether to fight Germany, appealed for British support. Chamberlain then developed a feverish activity. Since he was determined to keep Britain out of the conflict and since he knew that if France intervened Britain would sooner or later be involved too, he decided to sacrifice Czechoslovakia ("a far-off country of which we know little") and thus to extricate France from her obligations to the Czechoslovaks. He had already sent to Prague Lord Runciman, a man with a record of appeasement going back to the First World War when he advocated a negotiated peace with Germany. Runciman's mission, ostensibly to "mediate" between the Czechs and the Sudeten Germans, was actually to prepare the ground for Czechoslovakia's dismemberment. Meanwhile, Chamberlain set out to negotiate with Hitler personally and three times flew to Germany for personal conferences with the Führer. At Berchtesgaden on September 15, Hitler insisted that areas of Czechoslovakia in which Germans predominated must be ceded to the Reich. After deliberation the British and French cabinets "advised" the Czechoslovak government to yield. Faced with the alternative of fighting alone — or possibly with only the suspect assistance of Soviet Russia — Prague yielded (September 21). Chamberlain then hastened back to Germany with the Czechoslovak consent for another conference with Hitler (Godesberg, September 21–23). But the German leader had increased his demands to include immediate occupation of the areas claimed and a plebiscite in further portions of the state. Polish and Hungarian claims on Czechoslovakia were also to be satisfied. An honest man, Chamberlain was angered by Hitler's blackmailing tactics and returned to London without an agreement. The British and French governments made preparations to support Czechoslovakia and Soviet Russia affirmed her will to oppose Germany. A number of German generals, frightened of the prospect of a general European war for which they did not believe Germany to be ready, began to plot to remove Hitler. In Rome fascist leaders warned Mussolini that Italy was not equipped to enter a major war as an ally of Germany. Europe appeared to be on the verge of war. But the last cards had not been played. From Washington President Roosevelt addressed messages to Hitler, Benes, Chamberlain, Daladier, and Mussolini (September 26) and another one to Hitler alone (September 27) urging a conference as the last expedient for averting war. Chamberlain and Daladier pressed Mussolini to use his influence with Hitler to arrange one more meeting. Hitler agreed, arriving at Munich on September 29, and was joined by Chamberlain, Daladier, and Mussolini. The Soviet government was not invited to participate, a significant omission which strengthened the position of Germany. The Czechoslovak government likewise was absent while the fate of Czechoslovakia was settled.

In the conference the western leaders yielded to Hitler on all essential points. German troops were to march into the ceded areas and take possession within ten days. The occupation was to be supervised by an international commission and in disputed areas plebiscites were to be held. Polish and Hungarian claims were likewise to be adjusted. In a futile attempt to disguise the completeness of their surrender, Chamberlain and Daladier insisted that rump Czechoslovakia be given a joint four-power guarantee of her independence and integrity. This guarantee proved of little value. No plebiscites were held and no international commission was formed. Poland claimed her share of Czechoslovakia under an ultimatum, and Hungary's claim was arbitrated by Germany and Italy alone. When all claims were adjusted, Czechoslovakia had lost about one-fourth of her territory and over one-third of her population (including 1,161,000 Czechs and Slovaks). On German insistence, her new borders were deliberately drawn so as to render her strategically undefensible and economically unviable — and thus prepare her for complete liquidation at a later date.

The Munich agreement acquired in later years an odium which greatly embarrassed Englishmen and Frenchmen, but at the time it was very popular with the French and British population. From September 23 to September 29 the peoples of Europe had waited from hour to hour for the sound of the first bombing planes. News that a last-minute parley had been called at Munich seemed an almost miraculous reprieve, and word that an accord had been signed at midnight was greeted with delirious joy and relief when the confirmation was broadcast on September 30. Daladier, returning gloomily from Munich, expected to be lynched by the French population for forfeiting "the honor of France" — normally a concept dear to the hearts of Frenchmen — by betraying a small but loyal ally. Instead, he was frenziedly acclaimed and for the first time in his political career enjoyed real popularity. Chamberlain was likewise enthusiastically acclaimed in London. Acknowledging the cheers of a crowd, he characterized the Munich agreement as "peace with honor" and thought that it was "peace for our time." From Washington President Roosevelt congratulated him in a terse telegram: "Good work!" But a

A reception following the signing of the four-power peace pact at Munich. Left to right: Herman Goering, Adolph Hitler, his interpreter, Benito Mussolini, Edouard Daladier, Neville Chamberlain, and the French ambassador to Berlin (Wide World Photos).

Chamberlain returning from Munich, September, 1938 (Acme).

German motorized units invading Poland, September, 1939 (Brown Brothers).

more worldly-wise British statesman, Winston Churchill, then in political eclipse because of his staunch opposition to appeasement, commented gloomily and prophetically: "We have lost our honor and we shall have war."

The Munich agreement had preserved peace at an ominous price for France and Britain: it left them without a friend on the European continent. The smaller nations, realizing that French and British guarantees were no longer effective, scrambled to come to terms with Hitler while they still could. Worse still, Soviet Russia was alienated; her leaders became convinced that Munich was a conspiracy of the western powers to divert the expansive energy of Germany eastward against the Soviet Union. Although the Soviet government would no doubt have participated in the conference had it been invited to Munich, later — when Munich became synonymous with cowardice and treachery in the eyes of most Europeans — it congratulated itself on its absence. Soviet propaganda made considerable political capital out of the fact that Soviet Russia alone among the major European powers was not associated with the dubious policy of Munich. In Germany the Munich agreement consolidated Hitler's position. The opposition of the generals melted away before the genius of Hitler who had once again won a great victory without firing a shot. The respite from war, which Munich had secured, worked to the advantage of Germany because the rate of her armament was increasing faster at the time than that of France and Britain — as they were to find out to their great detriment on the field of battle.

3. THE PRELIMINARIES OF WAR

The euphoria produced by Munich proved very short-lived. Hitler did not regard Munich as a definite settlement but only as the first stage toward the complete liquidation of Czechoslovakia. "That fellow [Chamberlain] has spoiled my entry into Prague," he complained upon returning to Berlin from Munich. He desired all of the provinces of Bohemia and Moravia (western Czechoslovakia) with their great industrial complex which would contribute importantly to the German war potential. In the poor eastern provinces of Slovakia and Ruthenia he was not interested. Already on December 17 he issued orders for the plans to occupy "Czechia."

Unhappy, truncated Czechoslovakia tried as well as she could to adjust to her new position of living on German sufferance. The Czechs and Slovaks made some rather grotesque attempts to adjust to the nazi *Weltanschauung*. President Beneš, associated with Czechoslovakia's former pro-western orientation, resigned and went into exile (October 5). His successor became Emil Hácha, an aged, non-political, former Austro-Hungarian bureaucrat and later justice of the Czechoslovak supreme

court. To remove the complaint of Czech oppression of the other nationalities the constitution was amended to transform the former unitary state
into a Czech-Slovak-Ruthene federation. This arrangement facilitated
the German plans to bring about the disintegration of the rump state.
In March, 1939, nazi agents encouraged the Slovaks to agitate for complete independence and the central government in Prague to suppress
the separatist movement. The ensuing disorders provided Hitler with an
excuse to intervene. He summoned to Berlin Mrg. Joseph Tiso, the
provincial prime minister of Slovakia, and President Hácha. Msrg. Tiso
was told to declare Slovak independence or face partition of Slovakia
between Poland and Hungary. President Hácha was forced to sign a
document placing Bohemia and Moravia under German "protection." In
consequence, the provinces, which were at once occupied by German
troops, became a "protectorate" of the German Reich (March 15, 1939).
Slovakia, on the other hand became nominally an independent state and
actually a *Schutzstaat* of Germany. And Ruthenia was left to Hungarian
occupation.

The western powers, which had at Munich solemnly guaranteed rump
Czechoslovakia, uttered only pious protests. Hitler's arrogance and contempt for his opponents then knew no bounds. Without even allowing
the world a decent time to forget the cynical liquidation of Czechoslovakia, he seized the port-city of Memel from Lithuania (March 23) and
demanded the surrender of Danzig and other concessions from Poland.
Not to be completely outdone by Hitler, Mussolini hastened to occupy
and annex Albania (April 7). Again Britain did not move, although this
constituted a violation of the Anglo-Italian agreement, signed in April
and ratified only in November, 1938. But that was the last "peaceful"
conquest of the Axis powers. The cynicism and arrogance of the Axis
dictators shocked Britain into a realization of the utter futility of appeasement. The liquidation of Czechoslovakia, in violation not of any provision
of the Versailles *Diktat* but of a pledge freely given by Hitler at Munich,
disillusioned those who had believed that he was only an avenger of the
injustices of Versailles and a protector of oppressed German minorities.
Prime Minister Chamberlain, with the cold anger of an honest man who
had been foully deceived, now became the most determined opponent
of Hitler. A virtual revolution took place in British diplomacy. Since
World War I Britain had refused to commit herself in Central and Eastern
Europe and rather deprecated the French eastern alliances. Munich had
dislocated these alliances, and now Britain took the initiative to rebuild
them. The French leaders, who had never had the same confidence in
Hitler's sincerity as the British statesmen and consequently were not
especially shocked by his perfidy, resignedly tagged along behind their
British colleagues.

Britain and France offered unilateral, unsolicited guarantees of independence and integrity to Poland (March 31) and — after the

Italian aggression in Albania — to Rumania and Greece (April 13). The Rumanian and Greek governments were so fearful of Hitler that they did not dare to acknowledge the gesture, but the Polish government was more plucky. Colonel Beck, the Polish foreign minister, hastened to London where he concluded a preliminary pact with Britain (April 6). The Franco-Polish alliance of 1921, which was theoretically still in force but had practically lapsed, was reaffirmed. Next Britain and France moved to cover their Near Eastern flank by making overtures to Turkey. Turkey responded and concluded a mutual assistance pact with Britain (May 12) in case of war or aggression in the "Mediterranean area" (i.e., by Italy). But because of her quarrel with France over the Syrian district of Alexandretta (Hatay) (see p. 356), Turkey delayed in concluding an analogous pact with France until after the settlement of this issue (June 23).

Hitler's reaction to the British and French moves was first to order the preparation of operation "White," the plan of attack on Poland (April 11). Next he denounced the Polish-German non-aggression pact of 1934 and the Anglo-German naval agreement of 1935 (April 28). Finally, the Rome-Berlin Axis was transformed into a formal Italo-German military alliance (the "Pact of Steel," May 22). Discussing his plans of attack on Poland with his war chiefs on May 23, Hitler showed that he was aware that Britain and France meant business this time. But he was not unduly alarmed, for he had another iron in the fire. To reassure his generals that Germany would not face a two-front war as in 1914, he hinted to them that he was negotiating with Soviet Russia.

The Soviet-German negotiations had developed in April, originally out of discussions for a trade agreement. At the same time the Soviet government was negotiating with the western powers. Its price was the same in both cases: a sphere of influence from the Baltic to the Balkans. But there was an important difference in what the western powers and Germany wanted from Soviet Russia. The former wanted Soviet participation in the event of war with Germany, while the latter wanted only Soviet neutrality while the German army finished off Poland and dealt with the western powers. Both were reluctant to pay the Soviet price. Germany had long had important interests in the Baltic and was counting on the Balkans to supply her with food and raw materials in the event of a naval blockade. The western powers could not very well surrender the Baltic and Balkan peoples to communist Russia to keep them out of the clutches of Nazi Germany. The negotiations were spun out during the summer months, with a great deal of bluffing and maneuvering on all sides. The western leaders, who were rightly suspicious of Soviet intentions, underestimated the value of Soviet military assistance. Since the purge of the Soviet high command in 1937 the efficiency of the Red Army was generally held in low esteem. The Germans, on the other hand, were anxious to launch the Polish campaign before the autumn rains turned the bleak plain of Poland into a quagmire. In these circumstances the Germans succeeded in outbidding the western powers for Soviet support. They determined to sacrifice the Baltic states and a share of Poland to Russia, but not the Balkans. On this basis the famous Nazi-Soviet (Ribbentrop-Molotov) pact was signed in Moscow on August 23, 1939. Ostensibly it was a simple and respectable non-aggression pact for ten years. But a secret protocol provided for the partition of Poland and a free hand for Russia against the Baltic states.

The Nazi-Soviet pact produced consternation in the western world. After years of acrid nazi-communist polemics, it seemed an incredible diplomatic and ideological monstrosity. By extinguishing the hope of Soviet military assistance it caused also some faint hearts in France. The French people, on whom the brunt of land fighting would fall in the event of war with Germany, had not forgotten that it was a Russian offensive which turned the tide in the Battle of the Marne in 1914. But having no other friend left, France had to follow the initiative of Britain. And in Britain the Nazi-Soviet pact, if anything, strengthened the resolve not to truckle to the dictators any more. On the morrow of its signing, the Anglo-Polish alliance was signed. As Germany prepared to attack Poland, the nazi propaganda machine rose to its usual crescendo of vituperation against Poland and threats to the western powers, but the Polish crisis proved an anticlimax compared to the Czechoslovak crisis of the year before. Resignedly, almost fatalistically, Europe marched to war. On September 1, 1939, the German *Wehrmacht* crossed the Polish border. Some frantic, last-minute efforts were made to induce Britain to acquiesce in this act of aggression, but she would have none of it. On September 3 Britain resolutely declared war on Germany and France somewhat disconsolately followed suit. The Second World War had begun.

4. A CRITICAL MOMENT IN WORLD HISTORY

The year 1939, like the year 1914, was one of the definitive dates in European and world history. It has been chosen as a logical dividing line, breaking into two parts this account of the world in the twentieth century. The fact that the conflicts of 1914–1918 and 1939–1945 were called "world wars" emphasizes the merging of European with global history. In 1914 the center of gravity, the balance of world power, still lay in Europe, where six of the eight great powers were concentrated. In 1939 there were only seven great powers, for Austria-Hungary had disintegrated in 1918. Two of the seven (Italy and France) were relatively weaker in 1939, whereas two powers outside Europe (the United States and Japan) had gained greatly in strength and prestige. Furthermore, as events were to demonstrate, the Soviet Union was much stronger and better organized in 1939 than tsarist Russia had been in 1914, and Russia was the least "European" of the European powers.

These shifts reflected the declining importance of western Europe in world affairs. This decline became so manifest by the close of World War II that a new balance of world power proved unavoidable. The Europeans had weakened their position of world leadership by their exhausting struggle of 1914–1918. In the suicidal conflict of 1939–1945 they weakened themselves further and forfeited their leadership. The years after 1939 saw three powers outside western Europe press into the world arena to claim a share of the hegemony the western Europeans were relinquishing. Of these three claimants, Japan was speedily eliminated, leaving the United States and Soviet Russia to emerge after World War II as the two superpowers on the world stage.

In the lengthening perspective of world history the year 1939 is coming to appear a more critical turning-point than 1914. It is true that 1914 marked the close of an era, the era of almost undisputed western European ascendancy. The twenty years' armistice between the world wars (1919–1939) now is taking on the appearance of an indecisive interlude. The most fateful developments of those twenty years were not the insubstantial dreams of peace embodied in the Covenant of the League of Nations and in the Kellogg-Briand proposal to renounce war as an instrument of national policy. Nor was the rise of dictators like Mussolini and Hitler, whose sword-rattling and aggression brought on a new war, the most important development of the interlude between 1919 and 1939. In terms of world history, the critical change in those years was the rapid exploitation of American and Soviet resources. The United States and Soviet Russia were the only great powers with populations exceeding a hundred million; the only great powers with unified territories continental in extent; the only great powers with the immediate resources, energy, and capacity to become superpowers. The indices of production in the United States and Russia during these years provided a surer clue to the shape of things to come than did the internal struggles of Europe. This was not readily apparent at the time; it was to become more evident during the war years from 1939 to 1945; and in the years after 1945 it was to announce itself inescapably to a startled world.

PART TWO: SINCE 1939

Section VII: WORLD WAR II: 1939–1945

38

INTRODUCTION: CONTEMPORARY CIVILIZATION

With each advance in our knowledge of nature, science adds to the already immense power that the social order exerts over human welfare. With each increment in power, the problem of directing its use toward beneficial ends becomes more complex, the consequences of failure more disastrous, and the time for decision more brief. What was once merely a gap now threatens to become a discontinuity which may disrupt the history of man.

REPORT OF THE AMERICAN ASSOCIATION FOR THE
ADVANCEMENT OF SCIENCE, 1960

1. "ENERGY IS CAPACITY FOR PERFORMING WORK"

IN THE TWENTIETH CENTURY men learned with each decade how to mine more metals, draw more coal, petroleum, and natural gas from the earth, develop more electrical energy, raise larger crops of food, and build more powerful and intricate machines. This outburst of productive energy was so prodigious that, like a mountain viewed close at hand, it overshadowed all else, and an observer found no easy way to judge or compare his own time with earlier ages. Modern civilization is a machine-dominated civilization. The capacity to harness natural energy and produce material goods and weapons has become the chief index of a nation's wealth and power. Yet only a few specialists, a handful of scientists and technologists, understand how the machinery of production operates. These experts, sometimes called technocrats, form an indispensable group in an industrialized society. The nations that possess the most powerful machines, that have harnessed energy most successfully, and produced goods and arms most efficiently, are the nations that command most respect and claim a leading place in world affairs. Such nations, however, have become increasingly dependent on the scientists, technologists, engineers, and research teams that build and supervise the instruments of power and precision on which the national welfare depends.

In more primitive eras the human race had depended entirely on the energy provided by the muscles of men and later of domesticated animals. Man, "the animal that uses tools," discovered in prehistoric times how to fashion instruments that enabled him to apply his muscle power more

429

PERCENT OF GLOBAL POPULATION AND GLOBAL ENERGY PRODUCTION IN SEVEN REGIONS OF THE WORLD (1963)[1.]

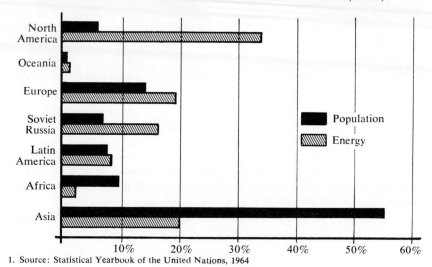

1. Source: Statistical Yearbook of the United Nations, 1964

effectively. The sling, the bow and arrow, paddles for propelling a boat, and wheels under a wagon were such instruments. So long, however, as the only form of energy used was *animate* energy – that provided by men or animals – the human race progressed very slowly. The spectacular advances came when man learned to draw upon and apply some of the measureless sources of *inanimate* energy – wind and water power and chemical energy from combustion. Windmills and waterwheels, the sailing ship, gunpowder, and the steam engine were applications of *inanimate* energy that wrought radical changes in human society. In the late nineteenth century further inventions – the internal combustion engine and the generation of electricity – made energy cheaper and more available; and in the twentieth century a new and cataclysmic form of power, nuclear (or atomic) energy, was discovered.

By the middle of the twentieth century nine-tenths of the energy men used in their work was drawn from inanimate sources, predominantly from coal, petroleum, natural gas, and water power. To produce this sum of energy from human muscles would have required forty-two billion men (seventeen times the world population in 1950) working forty hours a week throughout the year. In other words, by the middle of the twentieth century each human being had the equivalent of seventeen "slaves" working for him – or would have had if this vast fund of mechanical energy had been equally apportioned among the peoples of the world.

Actually, the amount of energy developed in different continents varied widely. An inhabitant of North America had more than twenty times the amount of energy that was available to the average inhabitant of Asia,

Africa, and Latin America. It is important to note that the per capita income of the 160 million North Americans was likewise about twenty times the per capita income of the 1600 million people living in Asia, Africa, and Latin America. In other words, a people's standard of living depended very largely on the amount of energy they developed and made available to drive their machines. Without energy to operate them, machines were useless; without machines people still had to depend on human and animal power as they had done in primitive times and societies.

In an economic sense, the most remarkable development of the twentieth century was the increase in the total energy available to speed the world's work. Between 1900 and 1965 the world population doubled but the output of energy increased twenty-fold. This greater supply of energy helped to explain why more goods were produced and the standard of living improved. As men could apply this increased energy to destructive as well as constructive purposes it also helped to explain why the wars of the twentieth century became increasingly violent and lethal.

Because modern civilization had become dependent on machines that required energy to run them the conquest and harnessing of more energy each year was essential to the march of progress. The world food supply barely kept pace with the growth of the world population and the world population was rapidly increasing. A time was approaching when the food supply would have to be augmented, when more of the earth's desert areas would have to be made cultivable by irrigation. Perhaps it might prove possible to pump in billions of gallons of sea water from which the salt had been removed. Perhaps additional food could be "synthesized" in factories by chemical methods. Whatever the solutions, it appeared certain that vast supplies of energy would be indispensable. The heat in volcanoes, the rise and fall of the tide, controlled nuclear reactions, the sun's rays were all potential sources of energy. How they might be harnessed and applied economically enough to serve man's need was a problem for technicians and engineers to solve. Would modern scientists prove equal to the tasks that faced them?

2. THE REIGN OF SCIENCE

The twentieth century brought so many advances in scientific research and exploration that even scientists could not follow them all and had to specialize in one or two fields. Although science and mathematics were taught in the schools most people made little serious endeavor to understand the complex nature of scientific experiments, problems, and theories. Efforts to "popularize" scientific knowledge, to describe the significance of scientific advances for "the man in the street," had only a limited success. The average citizen regarded science as something too alien and mysterious to comprehend. As already noted earlier, in Chapter 2, most people accepted unthinkingly the benefits and conveniences provided for them by science and technology — the "wonder drugs" that saved millions from death, the automatic elevators and refrigerators, the airplanes, radios, television sets, and dial telephones. But although millions of adults and children learned the simple procedures by which the new devices could be used, very few understood their intricate mechanism or could repair them when they broke down. One result of this has been emphasized already. As mechanization spread more and more widely, mankind became increasingly dependent upon the specialized knowledge and skills of a small minority of scientists and specialists. A small group of highly trained experts, a "priesthood of science," became extraordinarily important and influential in modern society.

It was nothing new in history for a small group to possess extraordinary influence. Human beings have always known they were subject to mysterious powers that they did not comprehend, and they have always depended on leaders who claimed to understand how these forces worked. Primitive tribes believed their magicians and medicine men knew spells that would persuade the ruling spirits to send rain or cure the sick. More civilized peoples accepted the teaching of religious prophets who explained that man was powerless in the hands of inscrutable gods, but that he must strive to obey their commands as best he could. Later still the concept of a single God, who was just and benevolent, spread throughout a large part of the world. In recent centuries the European peoples and their descendants overseas came to believe that misery, disease and poverty were not unavoidable misfortunes ordained by the will of God. They came to feel that these evils were largely the consequences of human ignorance and folly. By using their intelligence, by study and experiment, by improving methods of government and promoting social justice, they hoped that poverty, disease, and war might be abolished. This optimistic dream captured the imagination of many European thinkers in the eighteenth century, and faith in human progress remained strong in the nineteenth century. In the twentieth century the hope that disease could be curbed, and that better methods of production could provide a richer and more abundant life for mankind was vindicated in an astonishing fashion. Never before had so many people escaped fatal illnesses and survived to old age. Never before had life been richer or more interesting. Never before had so many shared so much.

Yet despite this unparalleled material progress the peoples who benefited most by it grew less optimistic, less hopeful, in the twentieth century. By the middle of the century their faith in progress and in themselves had been seriously shaken. They had passed from an "age of optimism" to an "age of anxiety." Why was this?

The main reason for the "loss of confidence" in the twentieth century was that man found he was his own worst enemy. After 1914 a succession of profoundly disturbing events demonstrated that he was still very far from controlling his own destiny or mastering his own passions. Two world wars, hitherto unmatched in their scope and destructiveness, and an economic Depression that severely dislocated trade and industry, afflicted humanity despite all the efforts that "men of good will" could make to avert them. After World War I the patient progress whereby Western nations had developed democratic governments, and established laws and institutions to safeguard the rights and liberties of the individual, suffered a sharp setback. In Italy and Germany parliamentary government gave way to totalitarian dictatorships. In Russia, where a limited representative system was just beginning to operate in 1914, it was replaced after the Revolution of 1917 by a Communist dictatorship. These despotic governments resorted to merciless methods of repression, organizing secret police forces to hunt down and destroy any individuals who dared to resist or criticize the regime. The victims were "liquidated," sometimes without a trial and without a trace. In Germany, on the pretense of "purifying" the nation and ridding it of alien elements, millions of Jews, and other innocent people, were herded into concentration camps and destroyed by working and starving them to death, or by asphyxiating them in gas chambers.

The leaders and their subordinates who perpetrated these unbelievable "crimes against humanity" used scientific methods and devices and sometimes invoked perverted scientific arguments to defend themselves and their policies. The radio made it easier for a dictator to play upon popular passions and shape public opinion; tanks and machine guns made it simpler for his police and army to repress insurrections. Against a ruthless government that controlled the armed forces and the systems of transportation and communication a revolt by unarmed and unorganized civilians was suicide.

In war, too, the people living in large urban centers became increasingly vulnerable to the devices and weapons the scientists perfected. At the close of World War II whole cities were destroyed by a single nuclear bomb. In the years after 1945 newer bombs a thousands times more powerful were developed, and giant rockets constructed to carry them to targets thousands of miles away. It had become possible, if another war came, for one country to wipe out half the population of another country in a few hours or days. Worse yet, the radioactive "fall-out" from many great nuclear explosions might spread around the world and decimate mankind.

Thus the "reign of science," which had promised humanity the opportunity to assure health, plenty, and a longer life span for all peoples, produced instead a "reign of terror" in which humanity faced the possibility that it might be destroyed by its own passions and its own weapons. The swift succession of baleful developments in the first half of the twentieth century left many thoughtful people disillusioned about "science" and "progress" and despondent about the future of civilization. They came to feel that man's inventions had outrun his control and that humanity was headed for disaster. This dark and fatalistic mood obscured the more encouraging victories the scientists continued to win. The astounding triumphs achieved in science and technology provided a bright contrast to the dark forebodings of the pessimists. These triumphs constituted the chief glory of the modern age and should have filled humanity with pride and hope. ✕

In physics tireless research teams continued to investigate the electrons and other particles that composed the atom until over thirty of these particles had been identified. The new science of electronics produced fresh marvels yearly, from the radio and television sets in common use, to electron microscopes, electronic computing machines, radar and radio-telescopes. With these and other "tools of precision" scientists probed the secrets of matter and energy, from atoms to galaxies. They found ways to detect the wave length of X rays, so accurate that this "atomic clock" would vary less than one second in a million years. They learned to calculate the age of rocks by the degree to which radioactive elements in them had "decayed," and the age of bones and other fossils by the amount of radioactive carbon they contained.

In the years after World War II the surface of the earth, the ocean currents, the atmosphere and the weather were studied more thoroughly than ever before and all the leading nations joined in an "International Geophysical Year" of study (1957–58). Observation posts were established at the North Pole and on the desolate plateau at the South Pole. A British expedition climbed to the top of Mount Everest in 1952; an American team reached the deepest abyss in the floor of the ocean in 1960.

The most spectacular feats were the launching of scores of rocket vehicles which sent back radio reports about the moon and the nearer planets. The Russians opened the era of space exploration with three dramatic feats. They launched a satellite into orbit around the earth in 1957; two years later they sent a camera-bearing missile to photograph the hidden side of the moon and transmit pictures back to earth; and by 1961 the Russian astronaut, Major Yuri Gagarin, had circled the earth and returned safely. These achievements were soon outstripped by both Russian and American teams. American space vehicles, though usually less massive than Soviet space craft, carried more sophisticated instruments and transmitted a variety of accurate, scientific data. These successes encouraged the hope that human beings might reach and explore the moon within a few years.

Meanwhile, advances of far greater importance for the welfare of mankind were made at less expense and with less propaganda in biology, medicine, nutrition, and the conquest of disease. Under the United Nations a World Health Organization was formed to curb the most common plagues. This campaign against disease was fought on so many fronts and in so many forms there is space here to describe only two or three of them.

Since prehistoric times one of the most prevalent ailments afflicting the inhabitants of tropical and subtropical regions had been malaria. It is probable that throughout history malaria has killed or disabled more people than any other disease. In 1945 two-thirds of the global population was still exposed to its ravages; it was killing two to three million people a year and undermining the health of hundreds of millions more. Malaria is spread by the bite of anopheline mosquitoes and it is possible to curb these carriers with DDT and other insecticides. Victims of the infection can be helped by quinine, atabrine, and newer drugs. Within twenty years (1945–1965) malaria was eradicated from areas containing half a billion people, and reduced in areas where three-fourths of a billion lived. In other words, of the two-thirds of the global population hitherto exposed to this disease, more than half were freed or partly freed from its menace. It was hoped that a resolute world-wide campaign might eliminate malaria almost entirely, for where there are no victims of the disease the mosquitoes cannot pick up the parasites and transmit them. But the scientists had to race against time, because in a few years the mosquitoes could develop a resistance to the insecticides used to destroy them. Among one-tenth of the world's population (roughly 300 million people) malaria was still prevalent in 1965.

The progress of medical knowledge and practice in the twentieth century also brought striking reductions in the deathrate from typhus, typhoid, and paratyphoid epidemics, and curbed the ravages of tuberculosis, cholera, and the plague. Diseases particularly dangerous in childhood — diarrhea, measles, scarlet fever, diphtheria, and whooping cough — declined steadily in the advanced countries. Methods for immunizing children and adults against poliomyelitis were developed in the 1950's.

The most notable gains in the battle against disease were achieved by reducing infant mortality. A child's first year of life is the most hazardous and millions of babies die annually from causes that could be eliminated by better medical care. The World Health Organization, with the assistance of national governments, set out to educate the local medical authorities and the mothers in the better care of infants. Statistics for the whole world are unavailable; but of some seventy countries and colonies for which figures could be listed it was found that, on the average, the infant mortality rate was cut in half in fifteen years. Where one-tenth of the babies had died in their first year in 1948, by 1963 only one in twenty-five died during those first critical twelve months. Applied to the world as a whole, where over 100 million babies were born annually, such a reduction of infant mortality would mean the saving of 6 million lives a year. It would also mean that each year 6 million mothers were spared the anguish of watching a child die when its life had scarcely begun.

This reduction in the death rate, not only of infants but of children and adults, largely accounted for the phenomenal rise in the global population under the "reign of science" (see graphs, pp. 446 and 448). Improved medical care, better sanitation and nutrition, not only assured people a longer life expectancy; it brought them more vigorous health, freeing hundreds of millions from "the weariness, the fever, and the fret" of painful and wasting diseases. This alleviation of misery, made possible by the labor of obscure, hardworking men and women all over the world, who compiled statistics, investigated epidemics, and distributed instructions, serums, and medicaments, deserved more acclaim than it received. It was far more significant, though less dramatic, than the labor of scientists who devised rockets capable of carrying a nuclear bomb to a target on another continent. "Peace hath her victories no less renowned than war."

3. RELIGION AS A CONSERVATIVE FORCE

In 1964, when the global population was over 3 billion, the five leading religions of the world embraced nearly three-fourths of mankind. These leading faiths, listed according to the approximate membership ascribed to each, were as follows: [1]

			Roman Catholic	590 million
Christian	960 million	{	Protestant	227 "
			Eastern Orthodox	143 "
Moslem	465	"		
Hindu	409	"		
Confucian	358	"		
Buddhist	165	"		
	2,357	"		

The Taoist, Shintoist, and Jewish faiths accounted for another 130 million, and some 750 million belonged to various primitive groups, or to none.

A common characteristic to note about the faiths named above is that all are old and some exceedingly ancient. Islam dates from the seventh century after Christ, Christianity from the first century. Confucius and Gautama (the Buddha) are believed to have lived in the sixth century B.C. Hinduism is so old it may have had its commencement in the late Stone Age. The Taoist and Jewish canons are older than Christianity, and although the term "Shinto" was first recorded in the eighth century after Christ the practices it referred to were many centuries older. Nothing better illustrates the durability of a firmly established religion than the fact that the great majority of people in the twentieth century, whether their belief is deep or superficial, accept religions that are on the average between two and three thousand years old.

A continuing religion is a *conservative* force in two senses of that word.

[1] Source, Encyclopaedia Britannica Book of the Year, 1966.

It perpetuates long-established precepts and principles of conduct, usually preserving them in the form of a recorded doctrine. Its tenets are generally regarded by those who accept them as embodying truths of divine or transcendental origin and validity. The task of safeguarding and perpetuating these truths is commonly entrusted to a select group, a priesthood. But a firmly established religion is also conservative in that it trains those reared in it to follow the same pattern of belief and conduct which their ancestors followed. The hold which a religion exercises over successive generations is less a matter of reason and logic than of emotion and tradition. In this it somewhat resembles a "mother tongue" learned in childhood. Every religion impresses on its followers a "way of life" and stresses certain moral rules and obligations. One of these admonitions, known as the golden rule, occurs in the teaching of all leading religions although the manner of phrasing it varies. In the Bible it is most simply expressed in the form, "As ye would that men should do to you, do ye also to them likewise."

When the cultural interests and economic activities of a society change, the time-honored religious beliefs of the people sometimes appear to be a barrier to progress. Rigid unimaginative adherence to an established custom, or a too-literal interpretation of an ancient precept, may delay the acceptance of better methods and sounder customs. "The letter killeth, but the spirit giveth life." In India today strict followers of the Jain sect carry their respect for animal life to such extremes that they may refuse to boil water to kill the germs in it. In Russia, before the Revolution, an ignorant peasant who was told to boil his contaminated drinking water replied that "If God had intended men to drink boiled water He would have heated the rivers."

A blind conservatism, a dogged resistance to any change, particularly when such opposition assumes the guise of religious piety, is difficult to overcome. In Russia, where the Orthodox Church had long supported the despotic government of the tsars, the communist leaders who seized power in 1917 attempted to abolish the church altogether. They recalled the statement of Karl Marx that religion is the opiate of the people. It had helped, Marx believed, to keep the masses enslaved by teaching them that humble submission to their masters was the will of God. But the communists found that millions of Russians clung to their religious beliefs despite all discouragement. In other Christian countries Russian communism was denounced as a godless creed because the revolutionary leaders closed many of the Russian churches. Wherever communism spread in the twentieth century it found established religious institutions, the Roman Catholic Church in particular, among its most resolute opponents. For the communists insisted that loyalty to the Communist Party and obedience to the Communist State outweighed all other duties. But religious people believed that their first duty was to obey their conscience and the commandments of their religion.

4. LITERATURE AS A MIRROR OF SOCIETY

In the opening year of the twentieth century the philosopher George Santayana passed a harsh judgment on contemporary Western literature. The capacity to see life steadily and see it whole, he declared, had been denied to the present age. What moral strength he could discern in contemporary writing seemed to him "a blind and miscellaneous vehemence," and the poetry of the period was "the poetry of barbarism." Fifteen years later the German philosopher Oswald Spengler, in a work translated as *The Decline of the West*, announced that Western civilization had reached its sunset. In the deepening twilight of Western man's decline no creative art on the grand scale could be expected of him. What passed for art in the twentieth century, Spengler wrote, was "impotence and falsehood." Spengler argued that each civilization was a unique organic entity but that all (unless destroyed earlier) completed their life cycle in about one thousand years.

A similar conviction that entire societies, rather than "national states or city-states, or any other political communities," were the "intelligible fields of historical study" inspired the erudite British scholar, Arnold Joseph Toynbee. In his twelve volume work, *A Study of History* (1934–1961), Toynbee attempted to dissect and interpret the character and fate of more than twenty societies or civilizations. Like Spengler he concluded that European (or Western) civilization was breaking down, but he did not entirely rule out the possibility that it might renew itself by some sort of religious regeneration. Other "prophets of doom" called attention to more specific and more imminent dangers. They warned that science was hurling mankind down an unknown road; that the revolt of the non-European peoples would put an end to Western supremacy; or that the human race would be destroyed or plunged back into barbarism by nuclear war.

Every age has its Jeremiahs. Western writers of the twentieth century had good reasons for deciding that the times were out of joint. The society in which they lived was changing so rapidly that they found it difficult to keep their bearings. By 1900 both Europe and the bourgeois class found their supremacy threatened and began to slip from the pinnacle of power. Perceptive writers sensed this disintegration of the bourgeois synthesis. Thomas Mann in Germany, John Galsworthy and Bernard Shaw in England, Jules Romains (Louis Farigoule) in France, Theodore Dreiser, Sinclair Lewis, and Scott Fitzgerald in the United States, all reflected in different ways their dissatisfaction with the acquisitive society in which they lived. After World War I the note of discontent, of disillusionment, in Western literature grew more pronounced. Some of the most talented American writers, including Thomas Stearns Eliot and Ernest Hemingway, left the United States for Europe, in the hope of finding a more congenial intellectual atmosphere. But almost all writers of the period were "exiles" in a deeper sense because modern man was himself a rootless being, an exile from his own past. Like the hero of Joseph Conrad's novel, *Lord Jim,* he was still wedded to "a shadowy ideal of conduct," but he was an enigma to himself, "excessively romantic" and "inscrutable at heart." Like Lord Jim, modern man seemed destined to pass away "under a cloud," leaving no one certain what it was he sought. "We ought to know," Conrad concluded, driving home the moral. "He is one of us — "

It is not surprising that a subjective note, an absorption with the inner self, became the dominant characteristic of much twentieth-century Western literature. Sigmund Freud and other eminent psychologists had emphasized the importance of dreams and fantasies as clues to man's subconscious drives and illogical compulsions. Writers became psychologists, exploring the secret thoughts and impulses of the characters they described. Some, like the Irish writer James Joyce, invented an elaborate symbolism and adopted an eccentric allusive style in their efforts to suggest the "stream of consciousness" that flows, turbulent and dreamlike, behind the conventional masks that people present to the world.

The search for a worthy cause, a movement to which they might dedicate themselves, drew some writers to communism and led them to idealize it. A number of Russian authors and journalists celebrated the promise and achievements of communist society with vigor and eloquence. But the censorship imposed on art and literature in Russia, and the official insistence that artists and writers must follow the "Party Line," denounce bourgeois fallacies, and avoid criticism of Soviet aims and practices, weighed heavily on independent thinkers. Boris Pasternak, one of the greatest Russian writers of the twentieth century, was expelled from the Soviet writers' guild because the spirit of his novel, *Doctor Zhivago,* was "the spirit of nonacceptance of the socialist revolution."

The most remarkable limitation of Western literature in the first half of the twentieth century was its failure to celebrate in adequate fashion the proudest achievement of the age, the progress of science and technology. Architects attempted to develop a "functional" style, painters and sculptors sometimes introduced elements of machinery and even of mathematics into their abstractions. But few of the great literary leaders tried to come to terms with science. The Irish poet and novelist Lawrence Durrell pretended to invoke scientific relativity ("Three sides of space and one of time") as a pattern for a four-volume work, but the device had little relation to the literary value of his remarkable "Alexandria Quartet." The English novelist Charles Percy Snow, in a series of novels, "Strangers and Brothers," endeavored to link "the two cultures," that of the sciences and that of the humanities, but the estrangement between them remained unhealed. Mr. Snow recognized that "Science has had a devitalizing effect upon all the contemporary arts." For serious writers the realization that they could not assimilate, could not interpret, could not even understand the most dynamic and significant development of the age was a humiliating experience. Their predicament arose from the fact that for the writer "the proper study of mankind is man," his personal hopes and fears, his search for happiness, for dignity, for moral values. But science, by making man a part of nature, threatened to reduce him to a soulless mechanism, life to a chemical formula, and morality to social statistics. "In nature there are neither rewards nor punishments; there are only consequences."

39

BACKGROUND OF CONFLICT

Perhaps there is no more fatal combination in politics than the deductive method worked by passion.

JOHN MORLEY

1. ECONOMIC COMPETITION

THE WORLD DEPRESSION forced all governments to face severe economic problems. Ailing industries, declining exports, and unemployment reduced revenues at a critical time when demands for government assistance were increasing. Income shrank while unpaid debts expanded as the interest on them accumulated. In those countries that had a stable currency debtors urged that debts be cancelled or scaled down. Creditors, on the other hand, wanted to be paid in full. How could this situation be solved in a way that would relieve the economic paralysis, quicken trade, and raise exports?

The solution most widely adopted by national governments was to devalue their currency. In 1931 the British decided to abandon the gold standard and the pound sterling declined almost one-third in relation to stable currencies. Many other governments followed the British example and by the end of 1932 thirty-five countries had abandoned the gold standard. Among those that still adhered to it the most important was the United States.

Why did so many countries deliberately reduce the value of their national currency? The answer is that they expected to benefit at home and abroad. An Englishman who owed £1000, or roughly $5000, could now pay it off in "devalued" pounds for the equivalent of £700, or $3500. To reduce the pound about one-third was in a sense to cancel one-third of the debts the people and the government owed. This meant of course that those who were not in debt, but had money loaned or invested, suffered a loss. The pounds they had loaned were worth nearly $5 but the pounds they would receive back would be worth only $3.40. Wage earners on a fixed salary might still take home the same *number* of pounds as before but in reality they too would suffer a reduction of nearly one-third in their real income.

441

This reduction in wages and salaries was part of the recovery plan. For British manufactures could now be produced more cheaply and so could compete more successfully in the world market. Countries that remained on a gold standard found that their goods were too highly priced to sell abroad. In 1933 the United States abandoned the gold standard and in 1934 the dollar was revalued at roughly three-fifths of its former worth.

Most governments also adopted other methods to encourage exports, restrict imports, and keep their wealth at home. Many of them raised their import duties. Some negotiated barter agreements, exchanging coal for wheat or machinery for sugar. Some tried to become self-sufficient. Some, like Britain, that had large overseas possessions, made exchange agreements with their colonies to keep their trade within the empire. The total effect of these individual remedies and restrictions was probably harmful and delayed the revival of international trade. It intensified the economic competition between states, stirred up resentments that led to reprisals, and increased the jealousy and rivalry nations felt toward one another.

In a world where national rivalries were already dangerously intense the tightening of the economic contest increased the mood of suspicion and hostility. It has been said that "if goods don't cross frontiers, armies will." Throughout the 1930's the hardships resulting from the World Depression, and the difficulties created by fluctuating currencies, unreasonable tariffs, bilateral trade pacts, and other obstacles to free trade all combined to sharpen the spirit of jealousy and antagonism.

2. "HAVE" AND "HAVE-NOT" POWERS

Three leading nations, the Germans, Italians, and Japanese, grew increasingly bitter because they believed they had been treated unjustly. They compared the large land areas over which the British, French, Russian, and American flags flew, with the small land areas controlled by Germany, Italy, and Japan. The disproportion was indeed remarkable. In 1930 Britain, France, Russia, and the United States together with their possessions occupied some thirty million square miles of territory. This was more than half the total land area of the globe. In striking contrast, Italy, Germany, and Japan held a little more than one million square miles. Of the seven great powers, four appeared to be "Have" nations with abundant territories and resources to draw upon, while the remaining three were "Have-not" nations, cramped and confined within narrow frontiers and denied the chance to expand.

When the question was narrowed down to a comparison between Britain and France and the "Have-not" countries, Italy, Germany, and Japan, the disproportion became even more striking. The home population of Britain and France totaled less than 90 million, yet these two European states had incorporated 19 million square miles, one-third of the land area of the globe, into their overseas empires. By contrast, the home population of Italy, Germany, and Japan totaled 180 million (double the Anglo-French figure), but the combined empires of these three powers amounted to only *one-fiftieth* of the global land area. Yet when the Italians asked for colonies after World War I, the British and French gave their late ally a niggardly and ungracious answer. Germany was left no overseas possession whatever after the war. The Japanese, though they gained some islands in the Pacific and the small German claims in China after World War I, found the French and British opposed to their further expansion.

When the Have-not nations compared the average income of their people with that of British and French citizens their indignation increased. The 90 million inhabitants of Britain and France together enjoyed an income equivalent to 33 billion dollars, a per capita average of $375 a year. The 180 million people living in Italy, Germany, and Japan together earned approximately the same total, but because of their greater numbers their per capita income averaged only $193 a year. It was easy for them to believe that the reason the British and French had an income almost double their own could be explained by the fact that the British and French had large empires.

This line of reasoning is suggested here, not because it was sound, but because it was such persuasive nonsense it captivated millions of unthinking people. An old proverb declares that "figures can be made to prove anything," and a modern wit has added the warning that "figures don't lie, but liars can figure." When studied dispassionately, the income statistics for various nations showed that the possession of a large empire did not guarantee wealth, nor the lack of an empire condemn a nation to poverty. The factors involved were much too numerous and complex to be dismissed by such an over-simplified explanation.

Numerous examples were available to demonstrate that the mere possession of territory does not assure a good income. In the 1930's, for example, the Russian population was about 170 million, and the Russians held some eight million square miles of territory. The population of the United States and its possessions was then about 140 million and the area under the Stars and Stripes less than four million square miles. The Americans controlled only half as much land as the Russians, but they were far more wealthy. It is difficult to estimate the per capita income of the Russians because Soviet statistics were deceptive and incomplete, but it is probable that the average American worker received an income five to ten times larger than that of the average Russian worker. An even more striking illustration was provided by the United States and China. The Chinese Republic held slightly more territory than the United States and had a population over three times as large. Yet the annual national income of China was only one-tenth, and the per capita income only one-thirtieth that in the United States.

In Europe itself the economic condition of neighboring states contradicted the argument that a colonial empire was essential to assure the prosperity of a nation. The British people, it is true, enjoyed the highest per capita income of any European state, and Britain possessed the largest empire in the world. But the per capita income of the Swedes was almost equal to that of the British and Sweden had no colonies. The Germans, who had lost all their colonies in World War I, ranked fifth in Europe in per capita income, while the French, with a colonial empire twenty-five times the area of France, ranked tenth. Finally, it might be noted that the Italians, who acquired a colonial empire ten times the size of Italy, remained one of the poorest European nations, while their Swiss neighbors, with no colonies or even a seaport, had a per capita income over three times as large.

If the chauvinists in Have-not countries who urged their governments to conquer more territory had paused to study statistics they might have realized how difficult it is to decide what factors contribute most effectively to a nation's wealth. In the 1930's the two countries where people enjoyed the highest average incomes in the world were New Zealand and Australia. Both had land resources more than ample for their small populations. Third came the United States which also had ample land. From these examples one might conclude that to have plenty of land available was essential for any people who wanted to maintain a high standard of living.

Yet this conclusion seemed to be reversed when attention was directed to Europe. The seven countries there with the highest per capita income were, in order, Britain, Sweden, Switzerland, Norway, Germany, the Netherlands, and Denmark. What did these states have in common that might explain their prosperity? Only two of them — Britain and Germany — were great powers. Britain had a vast empire and had been on the winning side in a recent war. Germany had lost the war and possessed no colonies. Both, however, had extensive industries and a large foreign trade. Did industry and trade explain high incomes? The answer seemed to be that they did throw some light on the problem.

Further study strengthened this conclusion. Compared to other European peoples, these seven favored nations all stood near the top of the list in per capita consumption of mechanical energy and in per capita value of their exports and imports. A large energy consumption, a flourishing trade, and a high income apparently went together. But there were other clues even more revealing. These seven countries also led Europe in their low death rates and low infant mortality rates, and consequently in the life expectancy of their citizens. They were likewise near the top of the list in education, in the low percentage of illiterates among their populations. Finally, it was significant that of these seven nations all but Britain and Germany had managed to maintain peace, internal and external, for nearly a century.

These facts might have persuaded thoughtful people that the surest way to promote the welfare of a country was to develop healthy, law-abiding, literate, and industrious citizens, intelligent and enterprising enough to adopt modern machinery and techniques, to avoid revolutions, and if possible to stay out of wars.

Unfortunately, the Italians, Germans, and Japanese chose to ignore these lessons and to believe that they could get ahead faster by military expansion. They listened to leaders who assured them that the Have nations had gained their enviable position by war, and that only by war could the Have-not nations win equal advantages. The argument was not wholly false: throughout history successful wars played a part in the building of great empires. But even a militarist as brilliant as Napoleon had been brought to realize "the total inability of force to organize any-thing." By the twentieth century wars had grown so costly and destructive that to provoke one was a desperate gamble. This fact, however, did not deter the Italians, Germans, and Japanese. Throughout the 1930's their leaders became increasingly belligerent and aggressive.

3. POPULATION PRESSURES

It was the misfortune of the Italians, Germans, and Japanese that their nations had not been able to enter the race for colonial territory until almost all areas suitable for human habitation had become unavailable. Italy and Germany did not achieve national unity until the second half of the nineteenth century, and Japan did not abandon its isolation until the same period. All three claimed that their home countries were over-crowded and that they needed "living room" for their surplus population. This demand was not altogether unreasonable. Four Have powers, Britain, Russia, the United States, and (to a lesser degree) France, all controlled sparsely populated areas. These areas were fitted to support much larger populations than they contained. Why, then, did not the "land hungry" Italians, Germans, and Japanese leave their overcrowded homelands and migrate to other regions where there was more "living space" available?

One answer is that millions of them did. In the half-century between 1880 and 1930 nearly ten million Italians left their homeland, an average of almost one-fifth of a million a year. The great majority went to the New World, and although some returned, most remained and became citizens of the United States, Canada, or the Latin American countries. The money these expatriates sent back helped to support the relatives they left behind. By 1930, however, this stream of Italian emigration was shrinking. From 1931 to 1940 it averaged about 22,000 annually, roughly one-tenth of what it had been. Thus some two million Italians remained

EMIGRATION FROM EUROPE TO OTHER CONTINENTS, 1860-1960

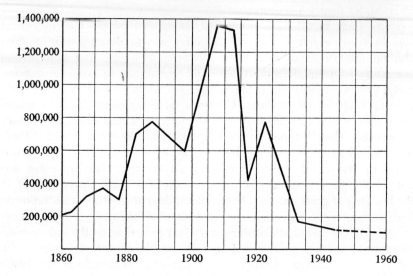

in Italy in the 1930's who would have left if emigration had continued at the 1880–1930 level. These two million people increased the population pressure in Italy.

Emigration from Germany likewise fell off sharply in the 1930's. Between 1880 and 1930 two million Germans sought new homes overseas, most of them in the United States. This was an average of 40,000 a year. After 1930 this emigration fell to some 12,000 a year, and Hitler urged thousands who had left to "return to the Fatherland." Had earlier trends continued, between a quarter and half-a-million Germans would have left Germany in the 1930's who remained there instead. This may not seem very significant in a population of seventy million. But most emigrants are young people, especially young men, who are restless and ambitious. For the countries of the Old World, emigration had been a safety valve. Among the two to three million Germans and Italians who remained home in the 1930's, as a result of the drop in emigration, a large proportion were restless young men seeking opportunities to make something of their lives. Both Hitler and Mussolini knew how to inflame and use such ardent youths in their programs for nationalist aggrandizement.

It would be a mistake, however, to suppose that the decline in emigration *accounted* for the rise of fascism in Italy and nazism in Germany. Great Britain, which was more densely populated than either of these countries, suffered a similar check in emigration in the 1930's without disturbance. Between 1880 and 1930 nearly twelve million British people emigrated, an annual average of nearly a quarter of a million. This exodus dwindled after 1930 to 25,000 a year, a steeper decline than either Italy or Germany sustained.

Why did the tide of European emigration drop from a peak of over eleven million in the decade 1900–1910 to about one and one-half million for the decade 1930–1940? There were several contributing causes of which three were particularly significant. The first cause to note was that after World War I the United States restricted immigration sharply. Between 1880 and 1920 the influx had averaged 600,000 a year. During the 1920's this declined to 400,000, and in the 1930's to some 50,000 a year. Not only did American immigration laws become stricter, they became more discriminatory. They set up a quota system whereby the annual total was limited to 150,000, and the number to be accepted from each country was fixed in advance. New World states were exempted from these provisions, but the new quota system made it difficult for Europeans, especially those born in the south and east of Europe, to enter the United States. Immigration from Asia and Africa was limited still more strictly and only 17,000 applicants were admitted from those continents in the 1930's.

A second reason for the fall in emigration, especially from Europe, was the continued decline of the European birth rate, especially after the onset of the Great Depression in 1929. A third reason was that the Soviet Government made it difficult for Russians to leave, and the Italian and German governments sought to keep young men at home to build up their armies.

Many Europeans, denied entrance to the United States, elected to settle in one of the British dominions or in Latin America. The British dominions, however, like the United States, virtually excluded Asians and Africans. This discrimination angered the Japanese in particular. Japan was one of the most densely populated countries in the world, and the argument that the Japanese people needed more living space had considerable justification.

The fact that the United States and the British dominions excluded orientals helped to increase world tension. There were only six major areas of the globe that had notably favorable climates — Europe, North America, the southeastern segment of South America, south and south central Africa, New Zealand and eastern Australia, and eastern Asia. Of these all but the last were held by the Europeans or their descendants. Yet the people of predominantly European blood constituted less than one-third of the global population, and the non-Europeans were multiplying more rapidly. In the heavily settled regions of south and east Asia and adjacent islands over a billion people occupied two and one-half million square miles. This meant that nearly half of the world's population was concentrated on less than one-twentieth of its land surface, at a density of 400 inhabitants to the square mile. For contrast one might note that North America, with approximately the same total of *cultivable* acres

WORLD POPULATION GROWTH

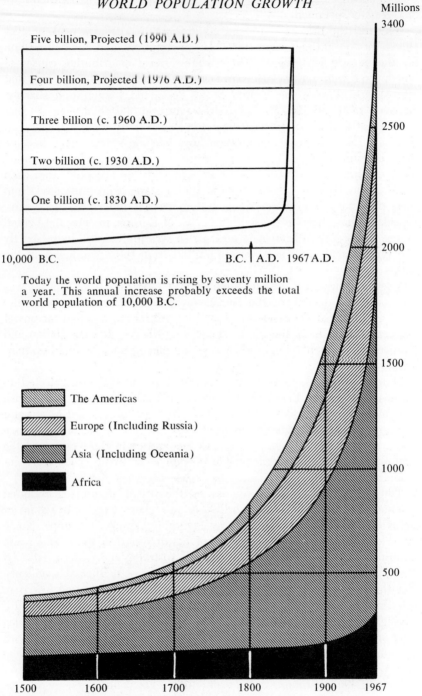

Millions

Five billion, Projected (1990 A.D.)

Four billion, Projected (1976 A.D.)

Three billion (c. 1960 A.D.)

Two billion (c. 1930 A.D.)

One billion (c. 1830 A.D.)

10,000 B.C.   B.C. | A.D. 1967 A.D.

Today the world population is rising by seventy million
a year. This annual increase probably exceeds the total
world population of 10,000 B.C.

The Americas

Europe (Including Russia)

Asia (Including Oceania)

Africa

3400

2500

2000

1500

1000

500

1500   1600   1700   1800   1900   1967

as Asia, supported only one-sixth as many people in the 1930's, and had an average of only 22 inhabitants to the square mile. Even more striking was the contrast between Asia and Australia. Australia and New Zealand together held less than ten million people in the 1930's, and averaged less than four people to the square mile.

Australia and New Zealand combined contained one-tenth as much cultivable land as Asia. But whereas in Asia there was about half an acre of cultivable ground per inhabitant, Australia and New Zealand had seven acres of cultivable ground per inhabitant. It is not surprising that the Japanese in particular envied such good fortune and resented the barriers that excluded them from sharing it. Of the three aggressive Have-not powers, Italy, Germany, and Japan, Japan had the most valid claim to greater living space. Less than one-sixth of the surface of the volcanic Japanese islands was cultivable. As a group the Australians and New Zealanders had fifteen times as much cultivable land per capita as most Asians and forty times as much as the Japanese. Yet Australia and New Zealand, like the United States and Canada, excluded Asians by strict immigration laws. The Asians had no means (save war) by which they could break through the implacable barriers erected against them. There was no global law of eminent domain, no provision for compulsory purchase or compulsory surrender, whereby hungry millions could take over empty cropland to save themselves from starvation. This situation had ominous implications for the future and loomed like a dark cloud in the background of world events.

4. TOTALITARIANISM VERSUS DEMOCRACY

The First World War was widely represented as a struggle between democratic nations (Britain, France, the United States) and autocratic regimes (Germany, Austria-Hungary) which had begun the conflict. The belief that it was "a war to end war" steeled the people in the Allied countries to make the sacrifices that carried them to victory. Until 1917 the fact that Russia, most autocratic of European powers, was in the Allied camp weakened the argument that the Allies were all champions of democracy. But the overthrow of tsardom and the entrance of the United States into the war in that year gave a semblance of justification to the argument that the Allied and Associated Powers had fought their way to victory "to make the world safe for democracy."

The post-war years brought disillusionment. The Russian Revolution destroyed tsarist despotism but substituted a more ruthless and efficient communist dictatorship. The Italians, dissatisfied with their inept parliamentary monarchy, which had mismanaged the war and failed to vindicate Italian claims at the peace table, allowed a vigorous Fascist Party headed by Benito Mussolini to gain control in 1922. The Germans, embittered by defeat, gave Adolf Hitler and his National Socialists sufficient support that he was able to establish a dictatorship after 1933. These events were serious reverses for the cause of democracy.

The Communist, Fascist, and National Socialist governments, though they differed in their ideologies and their aims, had several significant features in common. They were all "totalitarian" regimes, highly centralized governments controlled by a single disciplined group that allowed no other political groups or parties to share in the government or even to exist. All resorted to the use of secret police, attacked their opponents ruthlessly, and adopted measures to censor the press, silence agitators, and place all citizens, their lives, their liberties, and their wealth at the mercy of the state. The democratic ideal, "government of the people, by the people, for the people," was supplanted by a system that might be described as government of the party, by the party, to promote the program of the party.

The two most powerful forces in Europe in the years after World War I were socialism and nationalism. Before 1914 most socialists had been internationalists, criticizing war, militarism, and the acquisition of colonies. Mussolini, a former socialist himself, realized that if the appeal of the quest for social justice could be fused with the patriotic urge for national strength and aggrandizement, the union of these two powerful forces might well prove an irresistible combination. When the Italian Fascist Party was taking shape the term "national socialism" was considered. Almost simultaneously in Germany Hitler and his colleagues hit upon, and retained, the same label. In Russia the communists placed less emphasis on nationalism and stressed the international aspects of their "Marxian" revolution. But pride in Russia as a country and a culture that differed from the decadent Western European nations continued to inspire the Russian people.

Communist, fascist, and nazi spokesmen all denounced democratic government as a corrupt, inefficient, and hypocritical form of rule. To the communists democracy was a façade for bourgeois control. To the fascists it was pluto-democracy, the rule of selfish money-loving groups. To the nazis democratic nations appeared soft, timorous, and divided. The Have nations wanted peace because they had become swollen with their spoils and feared that hardier, more courageous, more resolute peoples would force a redistribution of land and wealth. The conviction that the democratic peoples were afraid to fight (a belief fostered by the Anglo-French policy of appeasing the dictators) led Mussolini and Hitler into more and more aggressive moves.

The defenders of totalitarianism argued that unity is strength and that firm unanimous support of their government would make a people strong. "Political power creates wealth," Mussolini exhorted the Italians. Hitler assured the Germans they had not been defeated in 1918 — they had been betrayed by a cowardly and treacherous minority in their midst. United behind him, he insisted, the Germans would be unbeatable. They were a master race, and to achieve perfect union and unanimity they must expel or exterminate all non-German elements. The result of this fanatical thinking was the ghastly concentration camps where non-Aryans were imprisoned, starved, over-worked, and finally murdered by the millions.

Observers in democratic countries watched the emergence of totalitarian regimes with wonderment and confusion. It appeared incredible that any enlightened people of the twentieth century could *voluntarily* renounce the benefits and safeguards of democracy. That the Russians should exchange one form of despotism for another was not wholly incomprehensible: they had never enjoyed self-rule. That the Japanese should come increasingly under the domination of militarists might be accounted for by the fact that they were, despite their adoption of western technology and institutions, an Asian people. But that the Italians and Germans, after achieving parliamentary democracy, could accept dictators and support them, shook the faith in progress, in parliamentary institutions, and in popular government that had grown steadily stronger throughout the modern age of liberalism. The ideological rifts between the differing concepts and ideals of government increased the international tensions that preceded and hastened World War II.

40

THE WAR IN THE EAST AND THE WEST, 1939–1941

"I have struck this instrument [assistance from Russia] *from the hands of the Western Powers. Now we can strike at the heart of Poland. To the best of our knowledge the military road is free.*

HITLER TO HIS GENERALS, AUGUST 22, 1939

1. THE MECHANIZATION OF WARFARE

THE GERMAN GENERALS had put to good use the "Twenty-years Armistice" since 1918. They brooded over their defeat in 1918 and studied its causes carefully. The principal cause of the German defeat in 1918 had been the costly stalemate in World War I, which permitted the Allies to mobilize their superior manpower and resources and overwhelm the Germans. The German strategists therefore determined that in the next war there must not be a new stalemate, but that their new opponents — who were likely to be their old ones — must be overwhelmed by a *Blitzkrieg* (lightning war) before they could bring their superior economic and manpower potential to bear again. In searching for weapons and tactics with which they could carry out a swift war of movement, the German strategists fastened onto the tank and the airplane. Both had been used in World War I, but not effectively. Tanks had been used solely as a screen for infantry attacks, not as an independent weapon. Airplanes, apart from reconnaissance, had little practical value. The dramatic "dogfights" of such famed air "aces" of World War I as Manfred von Richthofen, René Fonck, Billy Bishop, or Eddie Rickenbacker gave a nostalgic touch of sportsmanship and chivalry to the drab war of trenches. Bombing by hand-dropped bombs from airplanes and Zeppelins achieved a certain psychological effect. But neither use of air power had any noticeable effect on the outcome of the hostilities.

After the war, military specialists of many nations worked on improving the armor, range, and speed of tanks and airplanes and sought new methods for their use. But it was German soldiers, scientists, and engineers who thought about and experimented with tanks and airplanes most consistently. By 1939 the Germans had organized several independent

Panzer (armored) divisions, the function of which was to pierce the enemy's front, like a battering ram, and to wreak havoc deep in his rear. By 1939 they had also built up an efficient, independent *Luftwaffe* (air force), carefully trained to give close cooperation to ground forces.

Meanwhile, the generals of the western powers were more inclined to put their trust in the methods of 1918. They did not, it is true, wholly neglect tanks and airplanes. The organization of special armored divisions using tanks as an independent weapon was suggested, among others, by an obscure French Lieutenant-Colonel, Charles de Gaulle by name. Most French generals, however, continued to think of tanks as weapons suited best for the support of infantry because they believed in stationary war. They were fascinated by the seeming impregnability of the trenches in 1914–1918. Therefore they concentrated on perfecting trench warfare by building elaborate, permanent "trenches" of concrete and steel – the famous Maginot Line along the Franco-German border.

This elaborate system of fortifications was a broad belt of defensive escarpments and underground passages that stretched from the Swiss to the Belgian border. It ranged from twenty-five to one hundred miles in depth, contained some twenty-thousand gun emplacements, and included stores of ammunition, food, and other supplies, as well as underground living quarters for the defenders. The billions of francs poured into the Maginot defenses could have provided France with planes, tanks, and mechanized divisions stronger than those of Germany. But devoted as they were to a static system of defense these billions were largely wasted. For the Maginot Line grew narrower as it approached the border between France and Belgium, and it ended at Sedan. From Sedan to Dunkirk on the English Channel the Franco-Belgian frontier was defended by a shallow trench but little more.

After 1936, when the Germans began to construct a parallel defense line, the West Wall, the concept of a locked, impassible frontier limited French military thought. British military planners, on the other hand, gave considerable attention to the changes that air power was likely to introduce into warfare. British aircraft designers kept apace of their German counterparts. However, the official policy of appeasement held aircraft production to a minimum. In the United States the generals and admirals were reluctant to admit that control of the skies might decide future wars.

2. THE CAMPAIGNS IN EASTERN EUROPE

The drawback of the French defensive strategy was that it left the initiative to the Germans. The Germans first used this advantage to dispose of Poland, completely unhindered by the Western Allies. Leaving only a screening force of conventional troops to man the defenses of the West Wall, the Germans concentrated forty-four divisions (out of the sixty-six which they then had), six armored and six motorized divisions, and virtually their whole air force for the Polish campaign. The Polish army was large enough (twenty-two divisions including one division and seven independent brigades of cavalry) and well enough equipped for the type of warfare that prevailed on the Eastern front in 1914–1918. But it was woefully unprepared for modern mechanized warfare. The German *Blitzkrieg* against Poland, which began at dawn on September 1, 1939, proved to be a "campaign from the book." The weather was what newspapermen later came to call "Hitler weather" — dry and sunny, perfect for the operations of airplanes and tanks. Converging on Poland from East Prussia and Slovakia as well as from Germany, the German *Wehrmacht* overwhelmed the Polish army and won a military decision in ten days. Most of the small Polish air force was destroyed on the ground the first day of the campaign. The *Panzer* divisions cut through the Polish forces at will and isolated them for later disarming. By September 15 organized Polish resistance collapsed. The Polish government fled to Rumania and France where it was reorganized as a government-in-exile under President Rackiewicz and Prime Minister General Sikorski. Only Warsaw heroically held out until the end of the month. Meanwhile, on September 17, Soviet troops invaded Poland from the east on the specious grounds of protecting the Ukrainian and White Russian minorities in Poland, actually to collect the Soviet share of Polish booty promised to them in the Nazi-Soviet pact of August 23. The bewildered Poles fleeing eastward at first thought that the Red Army advancing westward was coming to their rescue. They were speedily disillusioned; they were taken prisoner and deported to camps in Siberia.

On September 29 the German and Soviet governments partitioned Poland, the Germans taking some 73,000 square miles of territory with about 22,000,000 people and the Russians 77,000 square miles of territory with a population of 13,000,000. The Soviet government annexed its share of Poland to the White Russian and Ukrainian constituent republics of the Soviet Union respectively. The German government annexed outright those portions of Poland which Germany held in 1918 and set up the rest as a "Government General" under the Austrian nazi Seyss-Inquart as governor.

The Soviet government then moved to claim the rest of the booty promised to it in the Nazi-Soviet pact of August 23. From helpless Estonia, Latvia, and Lithuania it extorted the right to establish military and naval bases on their territory (September–October, 1939). At the same time the Soviet government demanded bases and territorial concessions also from Turkey and Finland, which had not been a part of the Nazi-Soviet deal. The Turks firmly rejected the Soviet demand. Turkey had treaties of mutual assistance with the western powers, which assured her of their support. Fearing complications if it tried to coerce Turkey, the Soviet government did not insist. But when Finland refused its demand, the

Murmansk

NORWAY
OCCUPIED BY
GERMANY

Narvik

FINLAND

SWEDEN

Oslo

Helsinki

Leningrad

NORTH

Stockholm

Reval
ESTONIA

SOVIET

Smolensk

DENMARK
OCCUPIED BY
GERMANY

SEA

Copenhagen

MEMEL-
LAND

Riga
LATVIA

B A L T I C   S E A

LITHUANIA
Kaunas

Vilna

EAST
PRUSSIA

BIALYSTOK
DIST.

UNION

NETH.

Berlin

GREATER

Warsaw

P   O   L   A   N   D

Kiev

BELG.

GERMANY

EUPEN
LUX.

CROATIE

ALSACE

SUDETEN-
LAND

Prague
BOHEMIA

MORAVIA

LEMBERG
DIST.

FRANCE

SLOVAKIA

Vienna

AUSTRIA

SWITZ.

Budapest

HUNGARY

TRANSYLVANIA

BESSARABIA

ITALY

CORSICA
(FR.)

Rome

CROATIA

GER.
RES.

Belgrade

(YUGOSLAVIA)

SERBIA

RUMANIA

Bucharest

A D R I A T I C   S E A

MONTE-
NEGRO
(IT. PROT.)

ALBANIA
(TO ITALY)

Sofia

BULGARIA

Istanbul

TURKEY

GREECE

TRM

AXIS AND SOVIET EXPANSION, 1938–1941

Soviet government decided to use force to secure Finnish compliance. On November 30, 1939, the Soviet army attacked Finland in the north, center, and south. The Finns, under the command of Baron Gustav Mannerheim, a former Imperial Russian officer and adjutant of Tsar Nicholas II who had fought and defeated the Bolsheviks with German aid in 1918, put up a heroic resistance. The Soviet commanders were discomfited by several humiliating defeats, which confirmed the world in the opinion then generally held that the Soviet army was worthless.

The Soviet act of aggression against Finland provoked great indignation in the west. Soviet Russia was expelled from the League of Nations, and the western Allies began to gather an expeditionary force to go to Finland's rescue. But neutral Norway and Sweden refused to grant the force free transit, and the Baltic Sea was guarded by the German navy. Left to her own devices, little Finland could not resist mighty Russia indefinitely. When the Red Army breached the fortified Mannerheim Line on the Karelian Isthmus, the Finns sued for peace and the "Winter War" came to a close. Under the treaty of peace signed in Moscow on March 12, 1940, the Finns ceded to Soviet Russia an area of over 16,000 square miles with a population of about 450,000 — territory which included the city of Viipuri (Vyborg) and a naval base at Hanko (Hangö).

The Allied plan of intervention in the Soviet-Finnish conflict shows how little the western leaders thought of Soviet military power at the time. Had the plan gone through, Soviet Russia would have been forced into an open alliance with Germany and World War II would have taken a course which it is difficult to imagine. There was also suppressed indignation over the Soviet attack on Finland in Germany, which had helped the Finns to freedom in 1918. But the German government maintained a strictly "correct" attitude toward Russia during the conflict because it still needed Soviet neutrality and supplies while it settled scores with the western powers.

3. THE CAMPAIGNS IN WESTERN EUROPE

Hitler was now impatient to turn on the western Allies at once. But his generals felt that Germany was far from prepared for a major campaign in the west, especially with winter approaching. The British and French declarations of war had filled the whole German people with evil foreboding. There were no stirring scenes of patriotism and enthusiasm for the war in Berlin in 1939, as there had been in 1914, even though the immediate campaign against the despised Poles was popular. Even Hermann Göring, Hitler's successor-designate and commander of the *Luftwaffe*, was moved to exclaim after the British ambassador delivered the British declaration of war to Hitler: "If we lose this war, then Heaven have mercy on us." But Hitler brooked no opposition or restraint. On

October 9 he issued orders for the preparation of operation "Yellow," the plan of attack on the Netherlands and Belgium, which was to give Germany a large area on the Channel coast as a base for naval and aerial operations against Britain, preliminary to the grand assault on the western Allies in France. As the date of execution of his plan he set November 12. But his generals, fearful of the coming conflict in the west, stalled and again plotted his removal. After an ugly, angry scene with the commander in chief of the army, Hitler postponed the operation. The Allies, feeling smugly safe behind the Maginot Line, also did not stir. The period of inactivity which resulted, was dubbed by the Germans *Sitzkrieg* (sitting war) and by American war correspondents, disgruntled by lack of news copy, "phony war." But both sides continued to arm feverishly, and the Germans, at least, continued to plan.

In January, 1940, the plans for operation "Yellow" fell by accident into Belgian hands and had to be recast completely. Meanwhile, Hitler's attention was drawn to an operation suggested by the naval command, namely, to seize Denmark and Norway as bases for submarine operations against the British navy. It was approved by Hitler on March 1 and received the code name "Exercise Weser." Naval warfare took the same form in World War II as it had in World War I. Immediately after declaring war on Germany, the British navy blockaded the German coast. The French navy meanwhile kept an eye on Italy, which had not yet entered the war. The German navy in 1939 was much more modest than it had been in 1914. The submarine fleet consisted of only fifty-seven U-boats, of which only twenty-six were suitable for Atlantic operations, but thereafter the submarine fleet grew rapidly. The Germans endeavored to effect a counter-blockade of Britain and France by mines and submarines. On September 4, one day after the British and French declarations of war, a German U-boat sank the British liner *Athenia* without warning, causing a loss of over one hundred lives. Air raids and a new type of "magnetic" mine inflicted heavy destruction on British shipping, forcing the merchant vessels to crowd into the western harbors which were at the time beyond the range of German bombers. The British navy countered the German move by multiplying their sea and air patrols, tightening the blockade, scrutinizing all neutral shipping, sowing mines in German harbors, and bombing their port installations. In December three British cruisers chased a German battleship *Graf Spee* into the harbor of Montevideo. When the Uruguayan government asked it to leave, it was scuttled by its crew. On February 17, 1940, the British seized a German ship, which served as a prison for Allied seamen, in Norwegian coastal waters. Despite protests from the Norwegian government, the British and French announced (April 8) that they had mined Norwegian coastal waters to halt the transit of German vessels which had been eluding the Allied blockade. On the following day the Germans launched "Exercise Weser."

The German army invaded and occupied Denmark, which offered no resistance. German naval units attacked Norwegian ports, while hundreds of paratroops floated down on their airfields. Oslo, Bergen, Trondheim, Stavanger, and Narvik were occupied in surprise invasions, but after their momentary consternation the Norwegians rallied courageously. The Allied expeditionary force, originally destined for Finland, was rushed to aid them, and Trondheim, Bergen, and Narvik were temporarily recovered. Prime Minister Chamberlain was of the opinion that this time "Hitler had missed the bus." Unfortunately for the Allies, the Germans maintained a complete superiority in the air. This enabled them to pour troops at will into any vital point. German troops advanced steadily north and by June 8 extinguished the last Norwegian resistance and forced the Allies to evacuate Narvik. The King of Norway, Haakon VII, escaped with his ministers to London, where he set up a government-in-exile. In Norway the German occupants set up a puppet government under a pro-nazi politician Vidkun Quisling, whose name became speedily synonymous with perfidy and treason. All parties, except Quisling's *Nasjonal Samling*, were abolished and for five years Norway passed into the darkness of totalitarianism.

The Allies had sustained one more humiliating defeat. About the only consolation they could derive from it was that during the struggle for Norway the British inflicted severe losses on the German navy (four cruisers and several destroyers and troopships). Although both suffered about equal losses, the small German navy could less well afford them — a belief borne out a few months later when Britain herself was threatened with invasion. Nevertheless, the British government had suffered a grievous loss of prestige, and Chamberlain was forced to resign. On May 10 Winston Churchill formed a National government consisting of Conservatives and Laborites, which promised to infuse Britain's war effort with greater vigor. Previously (March 20) the cabinet of French Premier Daladier had given way to one formed by Paul Reynaud, who enjoyed a reputation for great energy. It was high time for these changes, for on the same day that Churchill assumed power the Germans launched operation "Yellow." The battle in the west had begun.

The Germans had assembled for it a mighty host of 135 conventional, ten armored, and four motorized divisions and two air fleets (1500 fighters and 3500 bombers). Opposing them, apart from the small, ill-equipped, and unprepared Dutch army and the more substantial and well-equipped Belgian army, were the Allied armies consisting of ninety-five French and ten British divisions. Part of the French strength, however, was tied up in manning the Maginot Line and guarding the Alpine passes against a possible Italian attack. In total armored strength the Allies were equal to the Germans (about 2450 tanks on both sides). But only a portion of their armor (four divisions) had been recently organized into independent mobile units. The rest was distributed in brigade, battalion, and regimental strength all along the front to support the infantry. In air

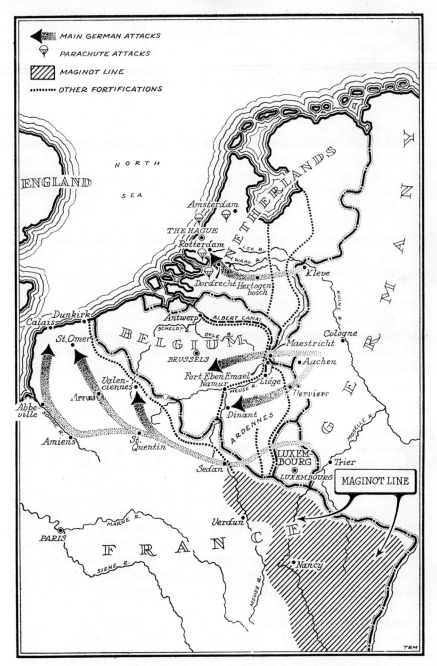

GERMAN INVASION OF THE LOW COUNTRIES AND FRANCE, 1940

power the Allies were quite inferior to the Germans (1000 French and 700 British planes in France). The Allied generals firmly expected the Germans to repeat the Schlieffen plan of 1914 and invade France through the flatlands of Belgium. Therefore they decided to anticipate the Germans by marching into Belgium as soon as the German violation of Belgian neutrality permitted it. But the Germans had decided to follow not the invasion route of 1914 but the more difficult but unexpected invasion route of 1870. The revised plans for operation "Yellow" called for sending inferior forces into the Low Countries and concentrating their armored and motorized divisions for a powerful blow against the Allied lines at a point where the German, French, and Belgian frontiers meet.

When, on May 10, the Germans hurled their divisions against the west, little Luxemburg put up no resistance and the resistance of neutral Holland collapsed in five days. Queen Wilhelmina and the Dutch government fled to London. On May 13 the main German force, spearheaded by the *Panzer* divisions and supported closely by the *Luftwaffe*, broke through the Allied lines in the Ardennes Forest to Sedan, just where the Maginot Line ended. The public learned then for the first time that this famous line, in which the French put an almost mystical faith, covered only the Franco-German but not the Franco-Belgian borders. Meanwhile, the whole British expeditionary force and three French armies marched north into Belgium — and thereby walked into a German trap. After the main German force broke through at Sedan, there was nothing much to stop its advance down the Somme valley toward the sea. The Germans exploited the advantage fully. One French armored division, which tried to intercept them, ran out of gasoline and was defeated. Another one under de Gaulle, which engaged them farther west, was brushed aside, and on May 20 the German spearheads reached the English Channel at Abbeville, isolating the Allied armies in Belgium from the Allied armies in France. Panic broke out in Allied councils. The Allied commander in chief, General Maurice Gamelin, was replaced with General Maxime Weygand. The new commander, after surveying the situation, ordered the Allied armies in Belgium to attack south to break through the thin German spearhead separating them from the forces in France. Simultaneously, he moved north to aid the breakthrough by attacking the Germans. However, his attack was beaten off and Lord Gort, the commander of the British expeditionary force, disregarded his orders. This was to provoke bitter French recriminations, but in the light of subsequent events the British decision was probably correct. The Battle of France had already been lost; the thing to do was to prepare for the coming Battle of Britain. Lord Gort feared lest the Germans, who had reached the Channel and turned north, cut off his egress to the sea. On May 28 the King of Belgium, Leopold III, ordered the Belgian army to surrender. For this the Belgian government, which had fled to France and was later to go to London, declared him deposed. On the same day the British began to pull out of Belgium by way of the Dunkirk beaches. By June 4 a motley armada of ships, from liners to tugboats, had succeeded in evacuating to Britain some 220,000 British and 112,000 French soldiers.

The public in Britain was unaware of the extent of the catastrophe. The press even hailed the "Miracle of Dunkirk" as a victory. But Churchill soberly reminded the country that "wars are not won by evacuations." Indeed, the evacuated army had left behind all its heavy equipment and some 600,000 soldiers, mostly French, who were captured by the Germans or had been killed. If the Germans had had a plan and attempted to invade Britain immediately after Dunkirk, they might very well have succeeded. Instead, however, they regrouped to carry out operation "Red," the conquest of France herself. General Weygand tried to throw up a defense line north of Paris, but it caved in at the first German touch (June 5). The French army had been organized for and conditioned to a stationary war and the fluid war of movement, imposed on it by the Germans, bewildered it. Above all, it lacked anti-tank guns, without which it was completely helpless against the German *Panzers*. The government evacuated Paris, which was declared an open city and left undefended, and when the Germans entered it on June 13 they found it largely deserted. The population had panicked and fled by the thousands, clogging up the roads to the south and impeding the movements of the army trying to throw up a new defense line along the Loire River. On June 10 Italy declared war on France and attacked in the Alps and along the Riviera. With the lack of vision characteristic of many continental statesmen, Mussolini assumed that the approaching fall of France meant the end of the war. His transparent intention to share in the spoils before the war was over provoked President Roosevelt to break the silence imposed on him by American neutrality and brand the act "a stab in the back." The second line of defense on the Loire proved no more effective than the first. The government, which had moved to Bordeaux, began to discuss surrender. In a desperate effort to persuade the French government to continue the struggle, if need be from North Africa, Churchill flew to Bordeaux. To move his French colleagues he made a startling proposal: complete fusion of the British and French empires until final victory. But to the French statesmen, who regarded France as the heart of the anti-German coalition, to move to Africa appeared absurd and Churchillian rhetoric a counsel of despair. With the fall of France, they were firmly convinced, the war would be over. An era of *Pax Germanica* was about to begin and the best course for France was to try to accommodate herself to it.

On June 16 Reynaud resigned and the aged Marshal Henri Philippe Pétain assumed power. He was the Hero of Verdun in 1916, but in the 1930's he allowed himself to be used as a front man by various fascist movements. His first official act was to appeal to Hitler for peace. On June

21, 1940, in the same old railway command car of Marshal Foch at Compiègne in which the Germans had signed the armistice terms on November 11, 1918, the French delegation faced Hitler. On the following day the second Compiègne armistice was signed. After the ceremony Hitler ordered the destruction of the monument commemorating the first Compiègne armistice; the scores were now even. A separate settlement was signed with Italy on June 24. For the moment France had ceased to be a great power. Half the country, including Paris, was to be occupied by the Germans, who seized control of the entire Atlantic coast as far as the Spanish border. All naval, military, and air forces of the Third Republic were to be demobilized. The French fleet was to return to French ports and be demobilized, and French war matériel in occupied France was to be surrendered.

The fall of France was not merely a defeat administered to a democracy; it was a defeat for the principle of democracy itself. The leading politicians of France had been discredited, and the parliament itself lost confidence in its capacity to direct the affairs of the humiliated nation. Two weeks after the armistice the French Senate and Chamber of Deputies, quietly purged of its most militantly republican and democratic members, approved almost unanimously a motion to endow the Pétain ministry with the powers of an authoritarian dictatorship. The Third French Republic, which was born in the turbulence of defeat in 1870, came to an end in the turbulence of defeat in 1940, after seventy years of existence marked by much strife but also by solid achievement. France was officially designated "The French State" and Marshal Pétain "Chief of State." No French government ruling under the shadow of German demands, helpless to defy Hitler, and driven to an unheroic policy of evasion, procrastination, and subterfuge to ward off heavier exactions, could have played its part with dignity in these dark years. Pétain inherited a heavy mandate, but it cannot be said that he discharged it intelligently. Behind the respectable façade of the Hero of Verdun there slipped into the saddle a motley crew of royalists, fascists, and opportunists who had been undermining the Third Republic for years. At the head of this unsavory cohort, which preached the necessity of French "collaboration" with Germany in the New Order, stood Pierre Laval, an opportunist politician who had begun his political career before World War I as a violent anti-war socialist but gradually moved over to the right until he became identified with the French appeasers of Hitler and Mussolini. As the strength of the Marshal declined, Laval, as premier, became virtual master of the French government, which moved its seat to Vichy, a resort town in central France.

But not all Frenchmen were ready to collaborate with Hitler or were content to "wait and see." On June 17, as the French government prepared to surrender, a British airplane carried off to London General de Gaulle, the unheeded prophet of mechanized warfare. On the day after

Hitler dances at the French offer of surrender, June, 1940 (British Combine).

Some of the five or six million victims of German concentration camps (Wide World Photos).

Churchill inspecting German bomb damage to the Houses of Parliament, May, 1941
(Wide World Photos).

the armistice, in a stirring address over the London radio exhorting his compatriots to resistance, he declared: "France has lost a battle but not the war." Gradually there grew up about him a Free French Committee and Free French forces which proposed to lead France to redemption.

4. BRITAIN'S FINEST HOUR

The French withdrawal from and the Italian entry into the war deprived Britain of the assistance of the French navy and added to her burdens that of blockading Italy and of keeping the Mediterranean open to her bases in the Near and Middle East, India, and the Far East. And this at a time when — as was generally assumed — the Germans would attempt to invade Britain soon. In these circumstances the fate of the French fleet became of paramount importance to Britain. The armistice had provided for its return to French ports to be disarmed. But the British had little confidence in the Vichy government's keeping French warships out of German hands. If the French fleet were added to the German fleet, it could tip the balance against Britain in an invasion attempt. With a ruthlessness born of their determination to survive, the British decided that this must not happen. On the morning of July 3, British forces boarded French naval units in Britain and Alexandria and gave the French crews the choice of joining the Free French or of being interned. At the same time a British squadron appeared off Mers-el-Kebir, the French naval base in Algeria, and summoned the French ships there to sail either to Britain to join the Free French or to a neutral port for internment. The French commander refused, whereupon the British opened fire and sank three battleships, one aircraft carrier, and two destroyers. Over a thousand French seamen perished in the fray. The Vichy government was outraged by this action of its recent ally and broke off relations with London. But Britain felt safer.

As a matter of fact, the drastic British measure was probably unnecessary, for the Germans had no plan for the immediate invasion of Britain. Like most continental Europeans, the Germans assumed that the fall of France meant the end of the war, and had given no thought to what would happen afterwards. It was not until July 14 that Hitler gave orders for the preparations of operation "Sea Lion," the invasion of Britain, which was to be launched some time in August. But even then he hoped to "come to terms" with Britain, for two days later he made her an official offer of peace; if Britain would recognize German supremacy over the continent of Europe, he would "guarantee" her supremacy everywhere else. Britain ignored the offer, which astonished and angered Hitler. It is well to remember that he was an Austrian German and his thinking was wholly continental. He had no violent prejudice against the British, an "Anglo-Saxon" (i.e., Germanic) people, and coveted no British or colonial territory. Sea power, colonies, world trade meant nothing to him. The objective of his policy, it has been seen, was acquisition of living space in Eastern Europe (see p. 417).

In thinking that he could come to terms with Britain, Hitler misjudged British policy and character. After the fall of France, the British felt more threatened than they had been since Napoleon prepared to invade Britain in 1804. Just as then, however, Britain was not fighting for survival alone. She could have had peace, without loss and possibly with gain, for the asking. She was fighting to see Europe free — and divided — in short, for the restoration of a balance of power on the continent. As long as she had a fleet, an air force, and the will to fight, there would be no peace. Churchill expressed accurately the mood and resolution of the British people when he said in a broadcast on June 17: "What has happened in France makes no difference to our actions and purpose. . . . We shall defend our island home, and with the British Empire we shall fight on unconquerable until the curse of Hitler is lifted from the brows of mankind."

So the Germans were forced to proceed with preparations for operation "Sea Lion." On closer look, however, both the navy and army chiefs became extremely doubtful as to the feasibility of the operation. Only Göring was confident that his *Luftwaffe* could easily knock the Royal Air Force out of the skies. It was therefore decided (July 31) to begin by "softening up" Britain by aerial attacks, and the invasion was postponed to the middle of September. On August 8 the great aerial Battle of Britain began. At first the *Luftwaffe* struck at harbors and channel shipping; later it extended its raids to industrial installations, and finally concentrated on the densely populated area of London in an effort to break down the morale of the British people and make them sue for peace. To the great discomfiture of the Germans, the Royal Air Force put up a stout resistance. With a courage that won the admiration of the world RAF fighter pilots went up in their Spitfires and Hurricanes time and time again to intercept and beat back the waves of the *Luftwaffe* bombers. At the same time RAF bomber pilots took off to bomb port installations and concentrations of shipping on the continental side of the Channel and to make raids on German cities. As the German losses in planes began to exceed their rate of replacement, and as it became apparent that the *Luftwaffe* was unable to gain the mastery of the air over Britain, Hitler lost interest in operation "Sea Lion." First he delayed it, and on September 15 he put it off indefinitely. The raids continued until the autumnal fog laid a protective cover over England when they gradually tapered off. The Battle of Britain had been won. The raids affected only southeast England, as the range of the small and medium German bombers was limited, and the industrial Midlands and western and northern Britain were largely unaffected. Yet the cost was high. By December 31, 1940, over 20,000 civilians had been killed, and one home out of every five was destroyed or damaged by the explosive or incendiary bombs. The assaults, which never wholly ceased, were intensified again in the spring of 1941. By then, however, methods of interception had steadily improved, the population had learned to take safer cover, and the fire hazard had been reduced. The British people suffered the depressing effect of the nightly blackout, the air raid warnings, and the constant tension to the end of the war. The last year of the struggle was to bring still more dreadful forms of flying death, rocket bombs hurtling from heavens, but there was no panic and the courage of the population never faltered. After London had been bombed eighty-two out of eighty-five nights running, a motion to consider peace, introduced in Parliament in December, 1940, was voted down 341 to 4. The British people are not easily bullied into submission.

5. THE UNITED STATES AND THE EUROPEAN WAR

When World War II broke out in Europe, President Roosevelt was obliged under the Neutrality Act of 1935 (enlarged in 1936 and 1937) officially to proclaim American neutrality and halt the export of arms and munitions to the belligerents (September 5, 1939). Other American exports to the belligerents were subject to the "cash-and-carry" provision; that is, the belligerents had to pay for them in cash and carry them to Europe in their own ships. American citizens were forbidden to travel on belligerent ships and to make loans to warring nations. The Neutrality Act had been designed by isolationist senators and congressmen, who dominated Congress, to prevent the rise of circumstances such as had led to the involvement of the United States in World War I. But from the beginning pressures arose to modify the Neutrality Act.

As in World War I, because of their ancestral ties to European countries and because of the principles involved, groups of Americans passionately took sides with one or the other group of belligerents. President Roosevelt was personally sympathetic to the western democracies, as his much-criticized (by isolationists) "quarantine-the-aggressors" speech of 1937 showed. On the other hand, during the Czechoslovak crisis of 1938 he added his considerable prestige to the counsels of appeasement of Hitler. At any rate, he was enjoined by law to pursue a policy of neutrality. American military experts, both official and unofficial, while not underestimating the efficiency of the German army, were agreed that the Allies could take care of themselves and would probably win the war. If they admitted the need for American intervention at all, it would not be until some very distant point in the war. There was, therefore, little feeling that American security was directly endangered by the European war. The great bulk of the American people were content to observe the war from the side lines. The depression was still keenly felt in the United States in 1939, with business in a slump and unemployment high. The demand of the belligerents for American goods promised to mitigate these conditions if the Neutrality Act was liberalized. In consequence, in November, 1939, Congress repealed the embargo on arms and munitions to the belligerents and extended the "cash-and-carry" provision to them. This undoubtedly favored the western powers, as they controlled the Atlantic Ocean and were the only belligerents who could avail themselves of the opportunity to buy arms and munitions in the United States. However, remembering how rapidly their assets dwindled in the United States in World War I, Britain and France were in no hurry to place orders for American munitions and arms — until the German assault in the west in May, 1940.

The startling collapse of France and the expected invasion of Britain made the European war appear suddenly close to Americans and created a concern for American security. At the same time, the aggressiveness of Japan, which profited from the preoccupation of the European powers with the war to extend its influence in the Pacific, caused a concern for American interests in that area. In these circumstances, Congress passed an act to create a "two-ocean navy" (July, 1940) and the Selective Service Act, which — for the first time in peacetime American history — proposed to draft American youths for compulsory military service (September, 1940).

The Battle of Britain stirred a deep sympathy in the United States for Britain, but it did not increase the American desire to be involved in the European war, as the chances for the British to survive appeared to most Americans at the time slight. On July 10, 1940, when President Roosevelt requested of Congress a new appropriation for national defense, he said nothing about support of Britain, but reaffirmed his determination to keep the country out of war: "That we are opposed to war is well known not only to every American, but to every government in the world. We will not use our arms in a war of aggression; we will not send our men to take part in European wars." In 1940 President Roosevelt was seeking an unprecedented third term against the Republican presidential candidate Wendell L. Willkie and was particularly sensitive to isolationist criticism. When, after the fall of France, the British government asked to purchase a number of superannuated World War I American destroyers to replenish its overextended navy, American isolationists insisted that the United States keep the destroyers to defend the Western Hemisphere. The United States government managed to satisfy both demands by a deft deal whereby it exchanged fifty overage destroyers for ninety-nine-year leases on eight naval and air bases in the British possessions in the Western Hemisphere (September, 1940).

As Britain proved her ability to hold out, American willingness "to bet on a British victory" increased. By the beginning of 1941, Britain's assets in the United States had greatly dwindled, while her need for American arms, munitions, and food had greatly increased. Because of the "cash-

and-carry" provision of the Neutrality Act it appeared that she would not be able to purchase her needs in the United States. Churchill made an eloquent appeal to the United States to give Britain "the tools to finish the job" of defeating Axis tyranny. On March 11, 1941, Congress passed the famous Lend-Lease Act, under which any country whose defense the President deemed vital to the defense of the United States "became eligible to receive any defense articles by sale, transfer, exchange, lease, or loan." The United States had become, in the words of President Roosevelt, "the great arsenal of democracy." The Lend-Lease Act reassured all embattled or threatened democracies that they might turn to the United States for aid. It also reassured American manufacturers that if they accepted orders from Britain or other states and expanded their plants to meet the demand for war material, they would be reimbursed because the federal government stood behind the transaction. The Act also made it possible for ships of Great Britain and her allied governments-in-exile to seek repairs in American docks, it provided for the pooling of defense information, and it permitted the immediate transfer to Britain of food and arms for which there was urgent need. By the spring of 1941 the food shortage in England had grown so acute that when the first shipments of cheese, eggs, and evaporated milk sent under Lend-Lease arrived in May, the nation had only a few weeks' reserve rations on hand.

The United States brought further relief to Britain by assuming during 1941 much of the burden of defense in the Atlantic. It established bases in Greenland (April), relieved the British garrison in Iceland (July), and assumed the protection of convoys as far as Ireland (September). When a submarine sank the American destroyer *Reuben James,* with the loss of seventy-six of her crew (October 30, 1941), President Roosevelt ordered naval commanders to "shoot at sight" on Axis submarines. The United States thus entered into an undeclared naval war with Germany. The summer of 1941 marked a turning point in the war for embattled Britons in another way. They were not alone any more, for the insensate policy of Hitler had forced Soviet Russia into the war.

41

INVOLVEMENT OF SOVIET RUSSIA AND THE
UNITED STATES, 1941–1943

The war against Russia will be such that it cannot be conducted in a knightly fashion. This struggle is a struggle of ideologies and racial differences and will have to be waged with unprecedented, unmerciful, and unrelenting harshness.
ADOLF HITLER TO HIS GENERALS, MARCH 17, 1941

1. NAZI-SOVIET RELATIONS

AFTER COLLECTING the rewards of the Nazi-Soviet pact of 1939, the Soviet leaders sat back to watch the struggle of Germany against France and Britain. Like the Americans, they expected it to be a repetition of the long war of attrition in the west in 1914–1918; when the combatants were exhausted, Soviet Russia might intervene and impose on Europe a *Pax Sovietica*. Meanwhile, under the terms of the German-Soviet trade agreement of August 19, 1939, the Soviet government furnished Germany large quantities of wheat, oil, and minerals, becoming thus, in a sense, the "arsenal of dictatorships," just as the United States became the "arsenal of democracy." The Soviet government also gave loyal diplomatic support to Germany by expelling from Moscow the envoys of the countries which Germany had overrun and by recognizing the puppet governments which Germany had set up.

The unexpectedly rapid collapse of France startled the Soviet leaders because it left Russia alone on the continent with a powerful Germany. While the attention of the world was focused on the final phases of the struggle in the west, the Soviet government moved quickly to consolidate its position in the east. On June 15, 1940, the Red Army occupied in force the Baltic republics, in which it already held bases. Under the watchful eyes of Soviet commissars elections were then held. The newly elected pro-communist governments at once "requested admission" to the Soviet Union. Their request was graciously granted, and in August, after twenty years of independence, Lithuania, Latvia, and Estonia became the fourteenth, fifteenth, and sixteenth republics respectively of the Soviet

Union. At the same time (June 26) the Soviet government extorted by an ultimatum addressed to the Rumanian government the retrocession of the province of Bessarabia and part of Bukovina.

The Soviet government had not consulted the German government before making these moves. Hitler was angered particularly by the Soviet encroachment in Rumania, on which Germany counted for filling a substantial part of her needs in oil and wheat. He decided to forestall any further Soviet moves in Rumania. First, Rumania was made to disgorge half of Transylvania to Hungary and a portion of Dobrudja to Bulgaria, which held a higher place in the hierarchy of German satellites. Then the German government "guaranteed" the rest of Rumania, that is, put a "no trespassing" sign on it. These humiliations brought about the downfall of King Carol, who abdicated and fled abroad. A frankly fascist regime was organized by General Ion Antonescu under Carol's son, King Michael (1940–1947), which permitted the Germans to send in troops to "protect" the Ploesti oil fields (October, 1940). Russia was thus blocked from access to the Balkans. However, at the same time an Italian blunder opened them to the British.

Mussolini was disgruntled with the little that Italy had received of the French spoils, and he often complained that Hitler did not consult him. In October, 1940, he decided to have a little adventure of his own. Without consulting Berlin and without any provocation, he declared war on Greece. The Italian army invaded Greece from Albania, the Italian air force bombarded her cities, and the Italian navy attacked her shipping. The pro-Axis dictator of Greece, General Metaxas, was forced to accept British assistance. British Imperial troops from the British Middle Eastern Command in Egypt occupied Crete and three squadrons of RAF landed in Greece. The Greek army, however, proved perfectly capable of taking care of itself. Not only did it succeed in containing the Italian invaders, but in a difficult winter campaign hurled them back and invaded Albania in its turn. After so many setbacks, the Allied peoples were cheered by the spectacle of a strutting dictator getting his just deserts — even though it was at the hands of another, though less obnoxious, dictator.

The foothold gained by the British in Greece disquieted Hitler. Raging against the ineptitude of his Italian partner, he ordered the preparation of operation "Marita," the invasion of the Balkans, to be undertaken in the spring of 1941. Before undertaking this operation, Hitler wished to ascertain the attitude of Russia. On his summons, the Soviet Foreign Commissar Molotov arrived in Berlin for discussions (November 12–14). During the conversations, which were interrupted by a British air raid sending the Soviet and nazi dignitaries scurrying for the safety of an air-raid shelter, Hitler suggested that Russia join the Axis Tripartite Pact of 1940. In the inevitable discussion of spoils, Hitler reserved the Balkans for Germany and Italy and suggested that Russia seek compensation farther east, in Iran and Afghanistan. This would — as Hitler hoped and the

Soviets wished to avoid — embroil Russia with Britain. Hitler's proposals exceeded Molotov's instructions, and he returned to Moscow without committing his government. A little later the Soviet government submitted a counterproposal, which had many precedents in the relations of Imperial Russia with the Austrian empire and with Napoleon, namely, a division of the Balkans into spheres of influence: the western Balkans (Yugoslavia) were to be German and the eastern Balkans (Bulgaria and the Straits) Russian. To this proposal Hitler never replied. Instead, on December 18, 1940, he ordered the preparation of operation "Barbarossa," the invasion of Russia. Preparations for the invasion were to be completed by May 15 before the end of war with Britain. Thus Hitler, like Napoleon in 1812, frustrated by Britain's resistance, turned to the east for a solution. Napoleon's fate apparently did not impress him. The conquest of Russia and the annexation and colonization of the rich wheat fields of the Ukraine and of the oil of the Caucasus had always been his ultimate aim. The Nazi-Soviet pact of 1939, like Napoleon's agreement with Tsar Alexander I at Tilsit in 1807, was only a tactical, temporary departure from his plans.

The decision to attack Russia added a reason to secure the right wing of the German army by sweeping the British out of the Balkans. To prepare for this preliminary step, the Balkan nations were strongly urged to join the Rome-Berlin-Tokyo alliance. Rumania, Hungary, and Slovakia had already done so in November, 1940. Bulgaria adhered to it on March 1, 1941. On the same day German troops entered Bulgarian territory and took up stations along the Greek and Yugoslav borders. Yugoslavia, after much soul-searching, adhered to the pact on March 24. Three days later, however, the Yugoslav government was overthrown by a military coup. The Serbs — but not the Croats or Slovenes — were strongly pro-Allied and anti-German. They had fought heroically on the Allied side in World War I and had a strong tradition of independence. The world applauded their gesture of defiance. Even Soviet Russia, which viewed Hitler's extension of power into the Balkans with misgivings, encouraged the Yugoslavs by signing a non-aggression pact with them (April 5). But Russia was not prepared to support Yugoslavia militarily, and Britain, which no doubt would have been willing, was in no position to help. As a result, German punishment was swift and effective.

On April 6, without bothering about the formality of declaring war, the Germans, supported by the Hungarians, Bulgarians, and Italians, struck with a savage fury at Yugoslavia and Greece. Yugoslav resistance collapsed in twelve and Greek in seventeen days. King Peter II of Yugoslavia and King George II of Greece and their governments fled abroad. British Imperial troops, which had landed in Greece proper on March 27, hastily withdrew to Crete after suffering severe losses. Yugoslavia was partitioned among Germany, Italy, Hungary, and Bulgaria. Only an "independent" Croatia, ruled by a fanatically anti-Serb and pro-Axis politician, Ante Pavelić, remained. Greece was deprived of Thrace and Macedonia to permit the realization of the old Bulgar dream of a Greater Bulgaria. Once again Bulgaria tied her fate to that of Germany, and once again she was to go down in defeat with Germany. Turkey, which was bound by the Balkan pact of 1934 and by her mutual assistance pact with Britain of 1939 to come to the assistance of Britain, Yugoslavia, and Greece, remained prudently neutral during the fray and in June concluded a friendship pact with Germany. To occupy Yugoslavia and Greece, however, did not mean to conquer them. Both were rugged, mountainous countries, with old traditions of guerrilla warfare. Soon Yugoslav and Greek guerrilla forces began to harass the occupants.

Meanwhile, in the middle of May, the Germans launched an airborne attack on Crete. During a week of savage fighting they suffered severe losses but drove the British off the island and sank several British naval units. This clearcut victory of air power over sea power made a deep impression; if it could be done in Crete, perhaps it could be done – on a larger scale – in Britain. The Germans were also in a position to seize the strategic Near and Middle East either by a bold leap from Crete or by reinforcing the Axis forces in Libya (see p. 476). However, having cleaned up their Balkan wing, they turned to the main business of invading Russia.

2. GERMANY AND RUSSIA AT WAR

At four A.M., June 22, 1941, the German *Panzers* lumbered across the Soviet border under a protective umbrella of the German *Luftwaffe*. At the same hour, the German foreign minister informed the astonished Soviet ambassador in Berlin that Germany was at war with Russia. No Soviet provocation preceded the invasion. A few hours later, speaking over the London radio, Prime Minister Churchill offered Russia an alliance, and on July 13 Britain and Russia concluded a mutual assistance pact, which was later transformed into a formal Anglo-Soviet alliance valid for twenty years (May 26, 1942). The Soviet government hastened to re-establish relations with the governments-in-exile in London, whose envoys it had previously unceremoniously expelled from Moscow. In November, 1941, after a visit to Moscow of President Roosevelt's confidential adviser, Harry Hopkins, the United States pledged Lend-Lease assistance to Russia. However, Britain was too hard pressed herself to give much assistance to Russia, and American aid, because of the inaccessibility of Russia and the involvement of the United States itself in war, did not arrive in Russia in appreciable quantities until 1943.

For three years Russia took on the brunt of German military power largely alone. She was to pay dearly for disassociating herself from the western powers in 1939 and encouraging Hitler to attack them. In her struggle with Germany Russia enjoyed one advantage: Japanese neutrality. On April 13, 1941, the Japanese foreign minister, after a visit to

Berlin during which he received no inkling of the German intention to invade Russia in two months, stopped off in Moscow and concluded with the Soviet government a non-aggression pact valid for five years. Despite a great show of outward solidarity, the members of the Rome-Berlin-Tokyo alliance felt little real confidence in one another. Each followed its own interests without regard for the others. While Japan remained neutral toward Russia, Germany's European allies and satellites all hastened to declare war on her. The Finnish, Rumanian, and Hungarian armies supported the German *Wehrmacht* from the beginning. Later, contingents of "volunteers" from Italy, Spain, Vichy France, Holland, Norway, Slovakia, Croatia, and all of occupied Europe arrived. Like Napoleon's Grand Army in 1812, which invaded Russia exactly 129 years and one day before the Germans, Hitler's armies in Russia came from all of Europe. The German propaganda, which represented the German-Soviet war as an all-European crusade against communist Russia, had a certain basis in fact.

The organization of so vast a host could not be completely concealed. The Soviet government had ample warnings of the German war preparations from its own intelligence services as well as from the western powers. But it tended to discount them as alarmist rumors and — on the part of the western powers — as a pious wish to see Germany and Russia embroiled. It was completely surprised by the German attack. The German plan was to annihilate the Soviet army in a few swift blows and to seize the great Russian cities: Leningrad, Moscow, and Kiev. After that, the Germans expected, the Soviet government would surrender and disintegrate. At first, their campaign proceeded "according to plan" — to use the characteristic phrase of the German war communiqués. German armored divisions penetrated Russia and encircled in great pincers movements whole Soviet army units, leaving them to later destruction by conventional forces. City after city fell, millions of Soviet soldiers were captured or killed, and vast quantities of war supplies were lost. But while surprised by the German attack, Russia was not unprepared for war; in fact, for twenty years the energies of the Soviet people had centered on war preparedness. After initial chaos, the Soviet government moved energetically to organize its defenses. Adopting a "scorched earth" policy, it ordered the removal or destruction of all factories and supplies before the advance of the Germans. Despite heavy losses, the Soviet army retreated in good order. It had many natural advantages for defense: the vastness of Russia, poor roads, and a climate characterized by short, hot summers, separated from long, rigorous winters by periods of thaw in the spring and rains in the fall, when military operations had to be suspended.

By September 8, the Germans reached Leningrad in the north and invested it. Hitler attached great psychological importance to the capture of the City of Lenin — the "cradle of Bolshevism." But the siege, marked by great heroism and harrowing suffering on the part of the defenders,

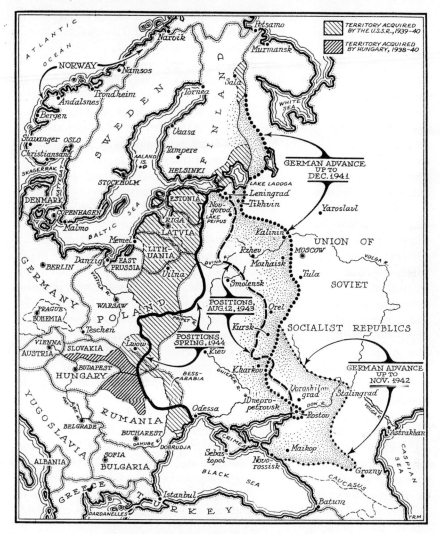

GERMAN INVASION OF RUSSIA, 1941–1944

dragged on for over two years. Leningrad, with a population of nearly 3.5 million in 1941, lost a million civilians; but the city was never taken. In the south, when Kiev, the "Mother of Russian cities," fell to the Germans on October 18, Hitler boasted, prematurely, that the enemy had been crushed and would never rise again. By the end of November, the invaders had driven to the suburbs of Moscow. The Soviet government bureaus and the foreign diplomats were transferred to Kuibyshev (Samara), over 500 miles east of Moscow on the Volga River. When the German offensive approached within 25 miles of Moscow, some of its population of 4 million fled, and looting broke out in the half-deserted sections of the city, which appeared doomed. But Stalin and his associates were still in the Kremlin, planning a counteroffensive. Marshal Timoshenko, an old Civil War general in command of the defenses, was replaced with General George Zhukov, one of the crop of younger commanders trained in Germany. On December 6 Zhukov hurled fresh units from the independent Soviet Far Eastern Command into the battle. Soviet units all along the front went into an offensive and the German lines wavered and fell back. Panic developed in the German headquarters, but Hitler assumed operational command (he had been Supreme Commander in Chief right along) and prevented the retreat from turning into a rout by draconic stand-or-die orders. The Germans withdrew into "hedgehog" positions — armed camps bristling with defenses in all directions.

The severe winter took a heavy toll from the Germans, who had expected to defeat the Russians before winter and were unprepared for a winter campaign. At the same time, they had to cope with increasing guerrilla activities. When they first entered Russia, the civilian population, especially the non-Russian population in the recently annexed regions, was not unfriendly. If Hitler had come to Russia as a liberator instead of as a conqueror, he might very well have rallied much of the Soviet population against their communist government. However, like Napoleon in 1812, he preferred to rely on military means alone to defeat Russia. As commissioner of the occupied regions, he appointed the nazi "ideolog," Alfred Rosenberg, a Baltic German and former Russian subject who as a student at the University of Moscow had witnessed the Russian Revolution. Rosenberg hated not only communism but everything Russian and instituted many harsh and humiliating policies which alienated the Russian population. Thus, Russian historical and cultural monuments — old churches, monasteries, palaces, or the homes of Leo Tolstoy and Peter Tchaikovsky — were systematically and deliberately desecrated. At the same time, the Soviet government adopted clever and ruthless policies to prevent defections. In the occupied regions the Communist Party maintained an underground organization, which directed the resistance against the Germans. To prevent fraternization communist agents committed deliberate outrages against the Germans, provoking them to brutal reprisals against the population — taking and shooting of hostages, burning of villages, deportations to concentration camps, or forced labor in Germany. The Soviet government also toned down its marxian, international propaganda and increased its Russian, nationalist propaganda. It even resurrected the old tools of Russian nationalism and imperialism: the Russian Orthodox Church and Pan-Slavism. Stalin received Orthodox bishops in the Kremlin and made peace with the Church in return for its support of the war. A Pan-Slav Committee in Moscow broadcast to the Central European and Balkan Slavs, urging them to rise against the Germans. As a result of German shortsightedness and Soviet cleverness, the Russian people rallied to the defense of the "Soviet fatherland."

In the spring of 1942 the German army reorganized for a new offensive, whose objective was to complete the conquest of the Ukraine and to seize the Caucasus region as far as the Volga. After that the Germans would be able to turn north or south, and from the east outflank Moscow or the lands of the Near and Middle East. Churning through the dust of southern Russia, the German armored and motorized units reached Stalingrad on the right (western) bank of the Volga by August 23. The conventional tactic for the Soviet army to adopt would have been to retire to the left (eastern) bank of the Volga and form a defensive line based on the river, but this would have cut the Soviet supply of oil coming in tankers across the Caspian Sea and up the Volga. There was also a psychological factor, in that the city bore the name of Stalin and its fall would have diminished the prestige of the dictator. On his hold-or-die orders, the Soviet army, strengthened by the local population, clung to the city. The battle of Stalingrad — the Verdun of World War II — got under way. As days, weeks, and months went by, the battle increased in intensity. At first the Germans and Russians fought over quarters of the city, then over streets, and finally in fierce man-to-man combats over individual houses, floors, and rooms. The city was reduced to a pile of rubble. As winter approached, the German generals advised retreat, but Hitler, who had already proclaimed Russia broken and defeated, would not hear of it — not even when the Soviet army mounted an offensive to the north and the south of Stalingrad, broke through the German lines, and encircled the German Sixth Army in front of the city (November, 1942). The inevitable result of Hitler's folly came on February 1, 1943, when Marshal von Paulus, twenty-four German and satellite generals, and 91,000 Axis troops (of the original 330,000 trapped by the Soviet army) surrendered. This catastrophe broke the offensive power of the German army. From this time on, the initiative on the Eastern front was safely in the hands of the Soviet army. At the same time the western Allies were liquidating another German pincer reaching out to the lands of the Near and Middle East through the deserts of North Africa.

3. THE BATTLE OF THE MEDITERRANEAN

The battle for the control of the Mediterranean did not develop until after the Italian entry into the war in June, 1940. From Italy the Axis forces could — and at times did — cut the Imperial lifeline between Britain and her bases in the Near and Middle East, India, and the Far East. On the other hand, from the much-battered island fortress of Malta Britain could harass the convoys supplying the Axis forces in Libya. Moreover, Britain by closing the Suez Canal isolated the Italian empire in east Africa.

In September, 1940, with the ultimate objective of reopening the Canal, the Italians mounted an offensive against the British in Egypt. In November the British under General Wavell vigorously counterattacked and turned the Italian invasion into a rout. Two months later the British reached Benghazi, 500 miles to the west. At the same time, they proceeded to liquidate the Italian colonies in east Africa. Two small British columns, one setting out from the Sudan and another from Kenya, converged on Ethiopia. In May, 1941, after forced marches over very difficult terrain, they joined to overwhelm the numerically superior Italian forces and marched triumphantly into Addis Ababa. Mussolini's proud east African empire had collapsed. This disgrace of Italian arms in Africa and their simultaneous defeat at the hands of the Greeks in Albania led Hitler to intervene in the situation. A specially trained *Afrikakorps* under the audacious master of tank warfare, General Erwin Rommel, was dispatched to Libya to stiffen up the Italians. Hitler considered also an attack on Gibraltar through Spain, but the price demanded by General Franco — all of French Morocco and part of Algeria — seemed too steep to Hitler. Spain remained neutral, and Franco, alone among the fascist dictators, safely survived the war.

In the spring of 1941 the situation took an ominous turn for Britain. In April, concurrently with the German invasion of the Balkans, Rommel opened up an offensive in Libya and drove the British — weakened by dispatch of troops to Crete and Greece — back to Egypt. The Islamic peoples between the Nile and the Caspian Sea stirred, waiting for Britain to falter so they could revolt against her tutelage. Egypt refused to declare war on the Axis despite the invasion of its territory by German and Italian troops. In Syria the representatives of the Vichy French regime were ready to collaborate with Axis forces if they appeared. Turkey remained studiously neutral, but in June concluded a friendship pact with Germany and began to ship valuable copper and chrome to supply German needs. Iran was thick with Axis agents and only waited for Axis forces to appear to join them openly. In Iraq a pro-Axis leader precipitated a revolt against the pro-British government on May 2. If Hitler had decided to seize the Near and Middle East, this was the most propitious moment. By a bold leap from Crete or by reinforcing the Axis forces in Libya, he could have probably seized the Suez Canal and gained a firm foothold in the area. But he was anxious to get on with the invasion of Russia and refused to divert sufficient forces for action in the eastern Mediterranean.

The British, on the other hand, acted with vigor. Small British forces from Palestine and Jordan rushed across the desert to quell the revolt in Iraq (May). Other British forces, supported by detachments of Free French, moved into Syria and ended the Vichy rule there (June–July). By agreement with the Soviet government, British and Soviet forces occupied Iran (August). The pro-German Reza Shah was deported to South Africa and replaced by his son Mohammed Reza (1941–   ). Through these energetic steps Britain reaffirmed her control of the Near and Middle East. But the main test of her strength was yet to come with the Axis forces in Libya.

In the winter of 1941–42, Hitler yielded to the plea of his Italian ally and strengthened his forces in North Africa. German submarines and aircraft were diverted to the Mediterranean to protect communications with the famous *Afrikakorps* commanded by General Erwin Rommel. In May, 1942, Rommel launched a drive from Libya that reached El Alamein, only sixty miles from Alexandria. With other German armies approaching Stalingrad, and the Japanese sweeping the Pacific, the tide of Axis success was full. Hitler dreamed of simultaneous drives south through the Caucasus and north from Egypt. Mussolini had already sent to Africa the white charger on which he planned a triumphal entry into Cairo.

By 1942, however, the United States had been drawn into the war, and the weight of American industrial and military might began to turn the tide against the Axis. Largely because of American supplies and shipping, the British built up their Eighth Army in Egypt for a decisive counterstroke against Rommel's forces in the fall of 1942. Their reinforced divisions were entrusted to General Bernard Montgomery, a meticulous planner and a cagey commander, who struck only when he was confident his line of supplies was secure and his preparations complete.

On October 23, 1942, the Eighth Army leaped forward from El Alamein in a mechanized drive which expelled the Axis forces from Egypt in two weeks. Meanwhile, Rommel had gone to Berlin to plead for men and supplies for his depleted forces. When he returned to Libya, he found his *Afrikakorps* in full flight. The British offensive from Egypt was synchronized with an Anglo-American expedition commanded by General Dwight D. Eisenhower, which disembarked in French Morocco and Algeria (November 8). This gigantic amphibious operation (code-named "Torch"), which required 850 ships, was preceded by secret negotiations with the French commanders in North Africa and resulted in the speedy capture of Casablanca, Oran, and Algiers. Except at Casablanca, the French offered no resistance. The Germans promptly retaliated by moving into unoccupied France. They also attempted to seize the French warships interned at Toulon, but the ships were scuttled by their crews. Belatedly, the Germans poured thousands of airborne reinforcements into Tunis and Tripoli in an effort to hold back the closing jaws of the twin Allied drives. They succeeded only in delaying the ultimate Anglo-American victory in North Africa. The British and the Americans had hoped to wind up the campaign by January or February, 1943. However, the British Eighth Army, which had raced a thousand miles west from El Alamein to Tripoli between October 23 and January 24, was suddenly held up by the Mareth Line in southern Tunisia, originally built by the French to protect the colony against the Italians. The Americans, coming from the west, were sharply checked in February by a skillful and stubborn German defense in the Kasserine Pass on the western fringes of Tunisia. But the Allied strength grew steadily, thanks to their command of the seas and the air, while the Axis strength steadily weakened, owing to their inability to convoy troops and supplies safely to Africa. The Americans broke into Tunisia in the middle of March and the British at the end of the month, and they linked forces on April 8. The Axis rear guard was crowded toward the tip of the Tunisian headland and captured in the early days of May. The British entered Tunis on May 7, while the Americans and their French allies captured Bizerte. The last units of the broken Axis army, cut off from escape by the Allied sea and air supremacy, gave themselves up on May 13.

Mussolini had dreamed for twenty years of recreating a "Roman Empire" which would span the Mediterranean. By an irony of fate, his last African cohorts capitulated near the site of ancient Carthage which the Romans had destroyed in 146 B.C. The Italian attempts to hold Italian Somaliland, Eritrea, Ethiopia, and Libya — a territory ten times the size of Italy with a population of 15,000,000 — cost the Axis armies an estimated 950,000 military casualties. Of these, 150,000 were taken prisoner in the final week of the Tunisian campaign, May 6–13, 1943. The Allied victory in North Africa reopened to Allied ships the Mediterranean lifeline to Egypt and the East and exposed "the soft underbelly of Europe" — to use a colorful Churchillian phrase — to Allied attack.

4. JAPANESE-AMERICAN RELATIONS

The outbreak of war in Europe in 1939 changed the balance of power in the Far East. The European powers with possessions in the Pacific — Britain, France, and the Netherlands — were all belligerents and had to devote their major energies and forces to the conflict in Europe. The great neutrals, the United States and Russia, both had interests in the Pacific and were free to act. But both were in an isolationist mood and seemingly indifferent to Pacific developments, which left only one strong power, Japan, ready to fill the vacuum of power. Just as in 1914, the Japanese militarists regarded the European war as a "golden opportunity" to bring under their control new lands to provide raw materials for Japan's expanding industries, new markets for her expanding production, and new homes for her expanding population. After 1931 and especially after 1937, Japan increased her influence in China. In October, 1938, amidst the excitement caused by the Munich crisis in Europe, Japan seized Canton, the last important port held by Nationalist China. At the same time, the Japanese seized Hankow, which had become the seat of the Nationalist government after the fall of Nanking. But the leader of the Nationalist government, General Chiang Kai-shek, refused to surrender. Trading space for time, the Chinese government withdrew to Chungking on the upper Yangtze. Cut off from the sea, it opened China's "back door," by building, with a prodigious use of human labor, the famous Burma Road, leading from Kunming in southwestern China across the towering Himalaya ranges to Lashio, a railhead in northern Burma.

The "China Incident" — as the Japanese euphemistically referred to their conquest of China — was far from over when the outbreak of war in Europe presented them with opportunities too tempting to pass up. The fall of France and of the Netherlands in 1940 left French Indochina and the Dutch East Indies to shift for themselves. The British position in the Far East was likewise weakened by the necessity to prepare for a possible German invasion. British forces were withdrawn from Shanghai and North China posts, British naval units were recalled to danger points nearer home, and — as a gesture of appeasement toward Japan — the British closed the Burma Road. In 1937 Japan had adhered to the nazi-sponsored Anti-Comintern pact. This, however, was voided, much to Japan's dismay, by the Nazi-Soviet pact of 1939. In September, 1940, Japan concluded the Tripartite pact with Germany and Italy, and extorted from the helpless Vichy government the right to establish bases in northern Indochina.

Resistance to the new Japanese policy came from an unexpected quarter — the United States, which, to be sure, had been shaking an indignant finger over Japanese activities in China ever since the Japanese invasion of Manchuria in 1931 but had never done anything about them. On September 22, 1940, the United States government put an embargo on exports of scrap and steel, on which Japan depended for a substantial part of her need. Japan paused but by no means renounced her plans to create an "East Asia Co-Prosperity Sphere" under her aegis. In April, 1941, Japan concluded a non-aggression pact with Russia to free herself for action against the possessions of the weakened European powers. The German invasion of Russia two months later, of which the Japanese had no advance notice, surprised the Japanese leaders but did not displease them. They declined the German suggestion to join in the war against Russia, being confident that Germany could defeat Russia alone. They thought that with no effort they could then collect the Soviet Far Eastern possessions, which they had coveted for a long time. Meanwhile, the German-Soviet war made it doubly sure that they could turn south without fear of being attacked by Russia in the north.

In July, 1941, the Japanese occupied southern Indochina. Again the United States government retaliated by "freezing" all Japanese assets in the United States. The British and Dutch governments adopted the same measure. This was a serious blow to Japan since it had the effect of cutting her off from her sources of oil, rubber, tin, and other raw materials, without which the Japanese economy and war machine would soon come to a halt. Japan was presented with a difficult choice: she could obtain these indispensable commodities either by yielding to the United States or by conquering their sources in defiance of the United States. Since March, 1941, the Japanese had been carrying on "informal conversations" with Washington for a settlement. Like the Russians in the negotiations preceding the outbreak of the Russo-Japanese war of 1904-1905, the Japanese proposed a deal to the Americans: "a joint overlordship by Japan and the United States of the Pacific area." However, this proposal was firmly rejected by the American leaders who insisted on the old principles of American Far Eastern policy: return to the *status quo* of 1931 and "open door," i.e., equality of commercial opportunity in China for all. By August the negotiations had reached an impasse.

On September 6, 1941, an "Imperial Conference," presided over by the Emperor Hirohito and attended by the high military and political dignitaries of Japan, met in Tokyo to consider the situation. Counsels were divided: Prime Minister Prince Konoye and the emperor favored continuation of negotiations with Washington. The minister of navy, on which the brunt of fighting would fall in the event of war, also favored negotiations, but the minister of war, General Tojo, firmly opposed all concessions to the United States. In the end, it was decided to present Japan's "minimum demands," and if Washington rejected them Japan would go to war. The demands included: immediate revocation of the economic sanctions adopted against Japan; a free hand in China; and a free hand in Indochina until the conclusion of peace, after which the Japanese might relinquish it. The possibility of by-passing the United States and attacking only the British and Dutch possessions was apparently not considered, for it would have left the Japanese forces operating in the South Pacific at the mercy of an American attack in the rear from the Philippines. The Japanese leaders were thinking in politico-military terms and assumed the same type of thinking from their American adversaries. In this they showed a parochial ignorance of the American system. If they had attacked the British and Dutch possessions, the United States government would certainly have protested and adopted additional economic sanctions but it could not declare war on Japan without the approval of the American people. And in the psychological climate then existing in the United States it is highly unlikely that Congress would have authorized war, because, lacking an overt act of aggression against American territory, it would have appeared to the American people only as a war to rescue the British, Dutch, and French colonial empires.

Konoye was given until October to secure American approval of Japan's minimum demands. He plunged into negotiations with Washington, proposing even to come to the United States to negotiate with President Roosevelt in person. Nothing came of the suggestion, because when the Japanese demands were submitted to Washington they were rejected out of hand. Thereupon Konoye resigned, and General Tojo formed a cabinet with a mandate to make war (October 17). Negotiations with Washington were continued as a smokescreen for the Japanese war preparations.

At the end of November a number of Japanese naval and aerial task forces slipped out of port and quietly sailed for American, British, and Dutch possessions in the Pacific.

5. THE UNITED STATES AND JAPAN AT WAR

On the morning of December 7, 1941, a Japanese task force arrived, miraculously undetected, off Hawaii, dumped its deadly load on the United States Pacific Fleet assembled at Pearl Harbor, and retired unmolested. Owing to total surprise, the Japanese attack had a devastating effect. Of the eighty-eight American naval craft in the harbor eighteen (including five battleships and three cruisers) were sunk and many were damaged. Lined up on nearby airfields, 117 aircraft were destroyed. Over 2000 persons were killed and many were injured. This sudden stroke crippled almost half the United States Navy and paralyzed American striking power in the Pacific temporarily.

Sometime before, the American intelligence services had succeeded in breaking the Japanese diplomatic code, which permitted them to eavesdrop on messages exchanged between Tokyo and the Japanese embassy in Washington. From these messages American leaders knew that the Japanese were about to strike, but did not know where. The revelation of this fact after the war provoked a bitter historical controversy. Led by the eminent Charles Beard some American historians, as well as the American commanders disgraced at Pearl Harbor, affirmed that President Roosevelt deliberately goaded Japan into war, and that the Pacific fleet was deliberately kept at Pearl Harbor as bait to tempt the Japanese to commit an act of aggression so monstrous it would shock the American people out of isolationism and force them to face the grim realities of war. Other eminent American historians have rejected this theory. They have pointed out that in the negotiations with Japan the Roosevelt administration followed only the old principles of United States Far Eastern policy, the "open door" principle of 1899 and the "Hoover-Stimson doctrine" of 1931 — non-recognition of territories acquired by acts of aggression — (see p. 407). As for its failure to disperse or alert the fleet, they have pointed out that the administration leaders did not know the exact intentions of the Japanese, and that at worst they showed lack of imagination in not anticipating that the Japanese would have the audacity — and the folly — to attack the United States. Be that as it may, the attack on Pearl Harbor surprised and shocked the American people and united them in a grim and angry resolve to settle scores with the Japanese.

On December 8 Congress declared war on Japan but, for the moment, not on Germany or Italy. The initiative for a German-American war came from Hitler, who was well informed about American industrial might but whose views of the American people were distorted by his racist beliefs.

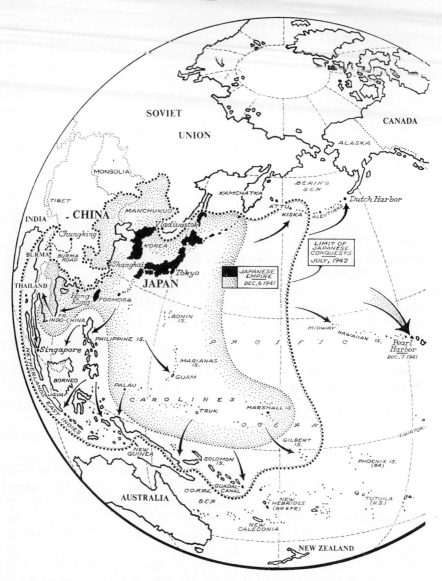

JAPANESE OFFENSIVE IN THE PACIFIC TO 1942

Had he refrained from declaring war on the United States, as Japan had refrained from declaring war on Soviet Russia, it is very possible that two separate wars, one in the Pacific and one in Europe, would have developed. But Hitler was angered by the undeclared naval war existing between the United States and Germany since September, 1941, when the United States navy assumed the task of convoying supply ships to Britain, and on December 11 Germany and Italy, followed by their satellites, declared war on the United States. Congress reciprocated the declaration on the same day. Britain and the various governments-in-exile in London declared war on Japan on December 8. On the other hand, China declared war on Germany, and many Latin American countries declared war on all members of the Axis. Only Russia remained neutral toward Japan until the final days of the war. Thus the week of Pearl Harbor saw World War II become for the first time a truly global conflict, with a European and a Pacific theater of operations. However, before the United States could make its weight felt in either theater of operations, it was necessary that it get its vast production machine in high gear. Meanwhile, for many months the Axis powers held the initiative.

In the six months after their attack on Pearl Harbor the Japanese conquered the sources of rubber, oil, tin, quinine, and other products of the East Indies which they had coveted. In rapid succession they overwhelmed the famous bastions of Southeast Asia — Hongkong, Manila, and Singapore. Allied naval units were shattered in the Battle of the Java Sea at the end of February; and by March, Malaya, Burma, Java, and Timor had fallen. In the Philippines the small American force under the command of General Douglas MacArthur, and later of General Jonathan Wainwright, retreated to the Bataan Peninsula and the island fortress of Corregidor, and after a heroic siege of six months surrendered (May). In the Central Pacific Guam and Wake islands had fallen in the early days of the war, and in the Northern Pacific three islands in the Aleutian chain were seized by the Japanese in June. The threat to Australia and India was acute. The fall of Burma closed the Burma Road to China, which was once again isolated from her allies except by long and tenuous air routes. But in May Allied naval and air power halted Japanese plans against Australia by their victory in the Battle of the Coral Sea, and in June the United States Navy repelled a Japanese naval force near Midway Island. Thailand (Siam), the only independent state in Southeast Asia, joined Japan in a treaty of alliance (December 21, 1941). But the Japanese propaganda of "Asia for the Asiatics" failed to excite a revolt in India or to win the cooperation of many Chinese. The oriental peoples whom the Japanese "liberated" from European colonialism soon found that they had only changed masters and that the new master was in many ways more demanding than the old one. The Japanese propaganda which sought to incite a "revolt of Asia" against European colonialism did not bear fruit until after the war.

In July the Japanese sought to extend their control to the Solomon Islands, New Hebrides, and New Caledonia at the northeastern and eastern approaches to Australia, which was the main base of Allied operations in the Southwest Pacific. This would have cut the most direct sea route from the United States to Australia, and General MacArthur, the Allied commander in the Southwest Pacific, determined to check the move. In August American marines were landed on Guadalcanal Island in the

Solomons. Months of difficult jungle fighting followed before the Ameri-cans gained control of the islands, but that control would have been lost again if the Japanese had kept their earlier naval superiority. In three naval engagements (August, October and November, 1942) the Japanese lost twenty-eight ships, including warcraft and transports. Of the three-day engagement in November, Admiral William F. Halsey wrote,

This battle was a decisive American victory by any standard. It was also the third great turning point of the war in the Pacific. Midway stopped the Japanese advance in the Central Pacific; Coral Sea stopped it in the South-west Pacific; Guadalcanal stopped it in the South Pacific . . .[1]

The period of Japanese expansion in the Pacific theater was over, and the period of Allied counter-offensive was at hand.

[1] Fleet Admiral William F. Halsey and J. Bryan III, *Admiral Halsey's Story* (New York, 1947).

42

RESOURCES AND PRODUCTION OF THE ALLIED POWERS

The final phase of "The Wizard War" was, of course, the radar developments and inventions required for our counter-attack upon Germany.[1]

WINSTON S. CHURCHILL

If the Führer hears about it he'll ask "How much time will you need? Six months?" And then, if we haven't got the atom bomb in six months, all hell will break loose.[2]

HEAD OF THE GERMAN ARMY WEAPONS DEPARTMENT

1. SCIENCE AND WAR

THROUGHOUT HISTORY the element of surprise has played an important part in warfare, and one form of surprise is the introduction of new weapons. Each invention, however, that has given those who first adopted it a military advantage, has been matched sooner or later by defense measures that restored the balance. In modern times the competition to develop new weapons and counter-weapons has become a desperate race. The arms that even the most advanced nation assembles are rendered obsolete within a few years — sometimes within a few months — by still newer and more astonishing advances made by its opponents. In the twentieth century victory and defeat have come to depend as much upon the scientists as upon the soldiers. The ancient truth that "the price of liberty is eternal vigilance" has taken on a new and deeper meaning. It is not only the sentry, guarding the ramparts in wartime, who must remain alert to every move, every ruse of the enemy. There is a second frontier, secret, mysterious, and vulnerable, where an enemy may make an unexpected advance and win an overwhelming advantage. This is the nebulous and ever-shifting frontier of scientific research and technological invention.

[1] Winston S. Churchill, *The Second World War*, 6 volumes (Boston: Houghton Mifflin Company, 1948–1953), II, pp. 396–97.

[2] Robert Jungk, *Brighter Than a Thousand Suns* (New York: Harcourt, Brace and Company, 1958), p. 165.

In World War II the relentless contest waged by the scientists on both sides was fittingly described by Winston Churchill as "The Wizard War." The race to perfect new and secret devices, while guessing in advance what the enemy was preparing and devising effective counter-measures, kept German, British, and American scientists working at a frenzied pace. The story of this battle of the laboratories was as significant as the naval and military campaigns, and equally important to the outcome of the war.

One of the first disconcerting "surprises" of World War II was the German use of magnetic mines. These underwater hazards, scattered outside British harbors, exploded when the metal hull of a ship passed near them. The British countered them by "demagnetizing" their ships with an electric cable around their hulls. A second German invention was the projection of radio beams to guide their night bombers over English cities. British inventors found a way to "bend" the beams, and four-fifths of the German bombs fell outside the target areas. On one occasion German planes went so far astray they bombed Dublin in neutral Ireland. The British, on their part, had surprises for the Germans. Their development of radar (RAdio Directing And Ranging) enabled them to "see" German planes through fog and darkness. British fighter planes and anti-aircraft batteries took an increasing toll of German air raiders as radar detection methods improved.

For naval warfare the British developed sonar (SOund Navigation And Ranging) which greatly aided them in detecting German submarines. Its effectiveness helped the Anglo-American naval forces to maintain their sea supremacy, as explained later in this chapter. Another invention that depended on the "echo" reflected back by radio waves was the proximity fuse, perfected by the Americans. This device, carried in a shell or rocket, exploded the missile when it came within destructive range of its target.

The Germans placed great hopes in their unmanned rocket bombs, by which they hoped to damage London and other English cities so heavily that the British would be forced to yield. No effective defense was found against these swift and deadly missiles. Fortunately for the British, the Germans did not have them ready until late in the war, and before they could be manufactured in large numbers the Anglo-American forces liberated France and captured the rocket launching sites. The Germans also developed jet-propelled fighter planes late in the war — too late to enable them to regain air supremacy. Had their rockets and jet-planes been perfected a few years earlier the Allies might have paid a much heavier price for survival.

All the new inventions introduced during World War II were eclipsed by the last and most terrible — the atomic bomb. Because allied scientists, with the wealth and resources of the United States to draw upon, produced this "ultimate" weapon first, it has been largely forgotten that up to 1939 the Germans were ahead in nuclear science. The allied scientists believed they were racing against time and that Germany might be the first power to produce and use atom bombs. Actually, German scientists made only limited progress in nuclear experiments between 1939 and 1945. Hitler failed to encourage their efforts by granting them the necessary supplies. Unlike the American government, he did not have two billion dollars to gamble on a highly uncertain venture. But if the war had been delayed a few years, or if German science had advanced a little more rapidly, how different the outcome might have been! Nothing could illustrate more clearly that in modern warfare the most critical developments may occur, not on the battlefield, but in the laboratory.

2. PRODUCTION AND TRANSPORTATION

When the Soviet Union and the United States entered the general conflict in 1941, World War II became in the literal sense a world war because the population and resources of all the continents were involved. As in World War I the two groups of contestants seemed grossly unequal at first glance. The Axis powers controlled about 3,000,000 square miles of territory and a population of 500,000,000, whereas the United Nations with their empires dominated 40,000,000 square miles and 1,500,000,000 people. For industrial needs — and industry, as already noted, is indispensable in twentieth century warfare — the United Nations possessed more than twice the coal and iron resources and twenty-five times the petroleum output of the totalitarian states.

Clearly, if the United Nations could mobilize their superior resources in men, money, and materials, the Axis empires were doomed. On the other hand, if the Germans, Italians, and Japanese could cut off Russia from Britain and Britain from her empire and from the United States, they might dispose of Russia first, then defeat the British by blockade and starvation, and finally confront the United States. Such was the general aim of Axis global strategy. It grew clearer with the conquest of Norway and France, the isolation of Britain from Europe. It explained the drives on Suez and Singapore, vital "bottlenecks" in main routes of ocean transportation. It motivated the U-boat war on Allied shipping. The effort to seize supplies essential to themselves, while denying them to their opponents, sent the Germans lunging to the Caucasus and the Japanese to the East Indies.

In the First World War it was said that the Allies floated to victory on a sea of oil. In the Second World War the statement was scarcely an exaggeration. Oil provides the most dramatic example of the part a single commodity may play in deciding modern strategy. Mechanized warfare requires thousands upon thousands of jeeps, trucks, tractors, self-propelled guns, tanks, and planes, and these in turn demand oil and gasoline. So consuming was the need for liquid fuel in World War II that one-half the cargoes shipped to the American Expeditionary forces abroad consisted of petroleum or petroleum products. Despite the U-boat war on tankers this stream of oil continued to flow. Had it been interrupted, the armies of the Allied nations would have been immobilized, their battle fleets impotent, their planes grounded. There was no real danger of such a paralyzing possibility so long as ocean routes remained open and the ships could sail, for the Allied nations monopolized 85 per cent of the world's oil output. The Germans and Italians, on the other hand, found oil production a crucial problem. The Rumanian and Caucasion supply was inadequate; the Persian fields they failed to reach. To supplement their limited reserves they utilized a process for extracting oil from coal, but in the end bombing raids shattered their refineries and extraction plants. To the Italians, who lacked even coal and refining plants, the shortage of oil was crippling, and it kept their ships in port on more than one critical occasion.

The Japanese met the problem of oil requirements more successfully: they seized British Malaya and the Netherlands East Indies which produced about 4 per cent of the world's oil total. Furthermore, the Japanese area of conquest also produced nine-tenths of the world supply of natural rubber, and the loss of this commodity handicapped the Allies. The sudden acute shortage which faced the United States, hitherto the world's heaviest rubber consumer, forced the government to develop synthetic rubber as a substitute. By the end of the war the chemists had met the challenge and United States home production of rubber exceeded prewar imports. With similar ingenuity the chemists met the demand for drug substitutes for such specifics as quinine, nine-tenths of which had likewise come from the East Indies. The shortage of tin, half of which had been mined in Malaya before the war, embarrassed the Allies to the end of hostilities, but they found alternatives.

The United States was the storehouse and arsenal of the Allied nations, and Germany was the industrial core of Axis productive effort. As late as 1942 it was estimated that the Allied countries controlled perhaps 60 per cent of world output of manufactured goods against 40 per cent for the Axis. But the German factories were slowly starved for essential materials; they were bombed with mounting devastation; they were crippled by the lack of skilled manpower. As a result the balance of war potential, already adverse, shifted steadily against the Germans. Supplies from Spain, Switzerland, and Sweden, supplies which no Allied naval blockade could intercept, were cut down when the Anglo-American Blockade Committee used its superior financial resources to purchase key products it could not otherwise withhold from the Reich. Prices on some essentials, such as ball bearings, cutting tools, platinum, and tungsten were quoted at ten to one hundred times their peacetime level until the Germans lost purchasing power in this unacknowledged auction.

The problem of transportation, so acute in the first years of the war, was conquered by mass output. So extraordinary was the American achievement in shipbuilding that by 1945 the United States and Britain possessed more merchant shipping (despite losses) than the whole world had claimed in 1939. The construction period for freighters was reduced from thirty weeks to seven, and standardized ships were built in sections and put together like cars on an assembly line. Between 1939 and 1945 American shipyards manufactured over 5,000 cargo ships, one of which was built in *four days*. Without this bridge of boats the armies could not have moved. Over 26,000,000 tons of equipment were ferried to Britain and 50,000,000 tons of war material to the armies in Europe. The weight of war material per fighting man had increased sixfold since World War I. New machinery, prefabricated barracks, landing ships, bulldozers, and a score of other devices made the Service of Supply a gigantic and sometimes a wasteful operation. The Americans fought "a millionaire's war."

In peacetime the United States had formed the largest single uniform market in the world, and this vast body of consumers had stimulated the rise of organizations equipped to produce a standard product for the millions. This practice in mass production was invaluable in wartime; it enabled the United States to produce $186,000,000,000 worth of military supplies by doubling its industrial output in five years. The varied weapons and accoutrements required, the enormous rise in output, the experienced personnel demanded, the rehearsals in pilot plants, all created problems which could be met only because American business efficiency had developed machinery for solving them. It is difficult to conceive the meshing and synchronizing of a million minds and a million gears in one coordinated enterprise. A modern military campaign is the most awesome example of mass activity the world has ever known and it must function without a hitch or the schedule may be dislocated. When it is remembered that these elaborate undertakings must be planned with secrecy and carried into execution despite every obstacle and destructive measure an alert and ruthless enemy can interpose, the responsibility which the commanders must assume appears almost insupportable.

3. MASTERY OF THE SEA AND AIR

In World War I the destruction of allied ships by German submarines dismayed the British more profoundly than any other threat to their security. In World War II this menace might have proved decisive if the Germans had exploited it to the full. Hitler, however, thought in military terms and underrated the importance of naval communications. By the summer of 1940 the Germans had conquered ports from Norway to the Bay of Biscay, and could also base their submarines on Italian harbors. But they lacked sufficient sea-going U-Boats to make the best use of their opportunity. How critical a more determined submarine offensive might have proved for the allies is clear from the losses they suffered in 1942.

In 1939 the world's merchant ships totaled eighty million tons, of which one-fourth was controlled by Germany, Italy, and Japan. This did not mean, however, that the remaining sixty million tons was all available for British wartime needs. Although many Norwegian, Danish, Dutch, Belgian, and French ships escaped when the Germans conquered these nations, some of their merchant vessels fell into enemy hands or were destroyed. The war efforts of the allies placed an unprecedented strain on ocean shipping resources. Those resources (as they stood in 1939) were seriously depleted by enemy activities, which destroyed over twenty-

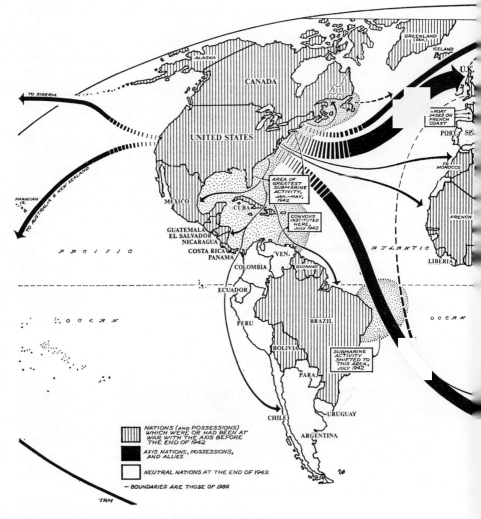

SEA ROUTES OF LEND LEASE

one million tons of merchant shipping. It is not surprising that Winston Churchill confessed after the war that the depletion of allied shipping gave him greater anxiety than any other threat the Germans offered.

In 1942 over six million tons of allied merchant shipping (chiefly British) was destroyed by enemy action. The Germans lost one submarine for each sixty thousand tons sunk and had some 400 U-Boats available at the end of the year. By tremendous efforts, the shipyards in allied countries, mainly in America, speeded up construction of new ships. At the opening of 1943 the rate of construction had caught up with the rate of destruction. But to hold the balance even was not enough. The gigantic

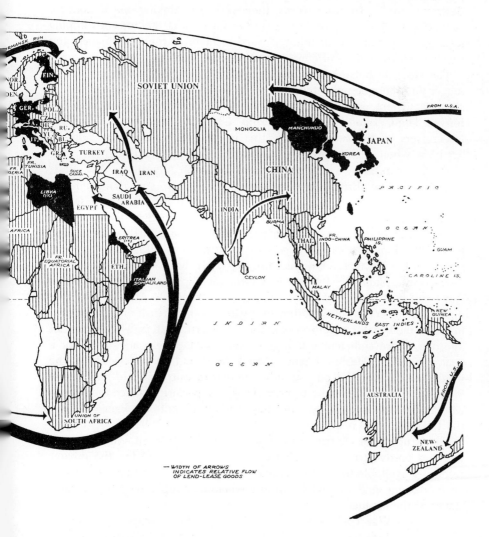

— WIDTH OF ARROWS
INDICATES RELATIVE FLOW
OF LEND-LEASE GOODS

landing operations anticipated by the Anglo-American strategists — in North Africa, Italy, France, and in the Pacific theater — would mean that great military expeditions must be transported and supplied by an uninterrupted flow of ocean shipping.

Four-fifths of the allied merchant ships lost during the war were sunk in the Atlantic, or in Arctic waters as they carried supplies to Murmansk and to Archangel. The essential problem the British and Americans faced was therefore to curb the German U-Boat menace. This they began to achieve by the spring of 1943. In May their losses fell to less than 200,000 tons, about one-third the monthly average they had suffered the previous year. At the same time they raised the total of submarines destroyed to 41. In other words, they were now sinking one U-Boat for each 4500 tons of shipping lost instead of for each 60,000 tons of shipping lost. The sea war had definitely turned in favor of the allied navies and thenceforth their lines of communication were relatively safe.

The struggle between the *surface* warships of the belligerents was a longer and more complicated drama. As in World War I, German battleships in distant oceans were speedily hunted down by superior British forces. The German "pocket battleship" *Graf Spee* was attacked by British cruisers off the coast of Argentina in December, 1939, and sunk by her crew when defeat appeared inevitable. The mighty *Bismarck*, pride of the German navy, which made a foray into the Atlantic in May, 1941, sank the largest British battle cruiser, the *Hood*, and damaged the *Prince of Wales*. But before the *Bismarck* could return to port it was intercepted by a British squadron and sunk. The destruction of the *Bismarck* made the British feel safer in the Atlantic, and they dispatched two battleships, *Prince of Wales* and *Repulse*, to Singapore to keep watch on the Japanese. On December 10, 1941, both warships were sunk by Japanese planes, just three days after the Japanese had shattered an American fleet in Pearl Harbor. The need to keep the Atlantic sea lanes open and to secure the Mediterranean forced the British and Americans to retain their major naval forces in these western theaters. They could not afford to spare sufficient warships to halt the Japanese advance. For a year after Pearl Harbor Japan enjoyed naval and air superiority in the southwest Pacific. But only an allied defeat in Europe could have made it possible for the Japanese to preserve that superiority. Once the Americans and British were free to turn their full attention to the Pacific theater the Japanese were doomed.

The struggle for control of the seas was matched by an equally relentless and costly struggle for control of the skies. There too the greater resources available to the British and Americans enabled them to achieve an increasing, and ultimately an overwhelming, superiority in the later stages of the conflict.

In World War I air power was still in its infancy and played only a minor role. With the Second World War the air force took its place with the army and the navy as the third department of national defense. Armies and navies could no longer move in safety if they lost command of the skies, and strategy suddenly became a series of problems in three dimensions. A totally new method of outflanking an enemy and of attacking his rear revolutionized the rules of warfare, for paratroops might now be dropped at any point in the enemy's territory and enemy forces might be overwhelmed by "vertical envelopment." Superior naval strength was no longer sufficient to guarantee islands against invasion, warships became dangerously vulnerable to aerial bombs and torpedoes, beleaguered garrisons and marching columns could be reinforced and supplied by aerial transport, and civilians living within the widening range of enemy bombing planes were now in the zone of battle.

To outbuild the Axis powers in aircraft and obtain control of the skies over Europe was essential for the defeat of Germany. But the German aircraft plants had a long start and had standardized their designs before the war opened. Their assembly lines were in full operation. In comparison, United States factories were producing only a few hundred combat planes in 1939. As late as 1941, American firms could construct only 2400 planes to meet urgent British needs. But plans for real mass production had been drawn and the results, when they came, literally darkened the skies. By the close of 1942 the United States production rate was 5400 planes a month; six months later it had climbed to 7500 a month, and in 1944 it passed 9000. When the year 1945 opened, American factories had produced 250,000 aircraft in four years and British factories 100,000. Russian plane production had likewise risen phenomenally although exact figures were not available. The Allies were assured of ultimate dominion in the air. To convey the planes to their field of action in record time and maintain a global air transport service, the United States Air Transport Command was established, with airfields, radio beacons, and weather stations functioning around the globe.

To Germany this rise in Allied air power brought a terrible retaliation for the ruthless bombing which the *Luftwaffe* had inflicted on Rotterdam and London. German air raids brought death to 60,000 British civilians in the course of the war, but British and American sorties killed 500,000 people in Germany. Against the steel plants, airplane factories, and U-Boat pens this bombing did not prove very effective. But the synthetic nitrogen plants, munitions works, and especially the oil refineries were crippled by repeated raids. The result was evident by 1944 when the *Luftwaffe* ceased to be a major threat. There were other results, some unintentional but all destructive to the German war effort and the German morale. One-fifth of the dwelling space in German cities was wrecked; 7,500,000 people were made homeless; transportation was seriously deranged. The long ordeal of heavier and heavier raids undoubtedly speeded the material and moral collapse of the German people.

In this long air war the British and American fliers destroyed 55,000

German planes and dropped 2,500,000 tons of bombs over the Reich. Their own losses in planes exceeded 40,000, and in personnel, 158,000. These casualties were shared about equally between the United States air force and the British air force. The sacrifices were heavy but they won results that were essential to Allied victory and they saved the ground forces months of fighting that would have taken a much higher toll in lives. The destruction of German air supremacy over Europe made the invasion of Europe possible, it prepared the way for the Soviet sweep to victory, and it paralyzed the German armies waiting to hurl back the Allies when they invaded Italy and Normandy. The bombing of factories, chemical plants, ammunition depots, railway junctions, and bridges slowed down German industry and ultimately grounded the *Luftwaffe* and all but immobilized the *Wehrmacht*. With their magnificent railway and highway system severed, and petroleum reserves exhausted or destroyed, the German war machine stalled.

Air superiority also brought the Allies advantages of another sort: it enabled them to anticipate new German weapons and outrace the German scientists. Aerial photographs, checked against reports from secret agents within the Reich, betrayed vital German centers of research and experiment to the British and American intelligence officers. The leading schools for aeronautics and ballistics, the rocket assembly plants and the launching platforms for the robot bombs, the laboratories where German specialists in nuclear physics were working to release atomic energy — all suffered from sudden and shattering raids. Spared the resulting loss of time, material, and personnel, the Germans might have perfected rocket missiles that could reach New York or have won the race to produce the atomic bomb.

4. INTER-ALLIED COOPERATION

The foundations of inter-Allied cooperation were laid even before the entry of the United States into the war. The most outstanding example of it was the Lend-Lease operation, authorized by Congress in March, 1941. By 1946 the United States had advanced to its allies nearly fifty billion dollars' worth of arms, munitions, vehicles, ships, food, fuel, clothing, and services of all sorts. The Lend-Lease agreements proved to be preponderantly a one-way traffic, from the United States to its allies, but not exclusively so. The British Empire, which was the largest beneficiary of Lend-Lease aid (over 60 per cent), also reciprocated generously by providing bases, food, fuel, quarters, transportation, and a variety of services to the American troops overseas. Russia, the next largest beneficiary (over 20 per cent), provided little in return in the way of goods and services, but paid for the aid received in the most painful way, in human lives and suffering, by resisting the brunt of German aggressive power for three years.

Political cooperation among the Allies was also strengthened, before the entry of the United States into the war, by the Atlantic Charter, issued on August 14, 1941. This accord was a result of the first wartime meeting of President Roosevelt and Prime Minister Churchill off Newfoundland.

LEND-LEASE AID EXTENDED BY THE UNITED STATES TO
THIRTY-EIGHT NATIONS; TO JULY 31, 1946[3]

AMERICAN REPUBLICS		OTHER GOVERNMENTS	
Bolivia	$5,633,989.02	Belgium	$148,394,457.76
Brazil	332,545,226.45	British Empire, including	
Chile	21,817,478.16	Australia, New Zealand,	
Colombia	7,809,732.58	India, South Africa	31,267,240,530.63
Costa Rica	155,022.73	China	1,548,794,965.99
Cuba	5,739,133.33	Czechoslovakia	413,398.78
Dominican		Egypt (paid fully in cash)	1,019,169.14
Republic	1,610,590.38	Ethiopia	5,151,163.25
Ecuador	7,063,079.96	France and possessions	3,207,608,188.75
Guatemala	1,819,403.19	Greece	75,475,880.30
Haiti	1,449,096.40	Iceland	4,795,027.90
Honduras	372,358.11	Iran	4,797,092.50
Mexico	36,287,010.67	Iraq (paid fully in cash)	4,144.14
Nicaragua	872,841.73	Liberia	6,408,240.13
Panama	83,555.92	Netherlands and possessions	230,127,717.63
Paraguay	1,933,302.00	Norway	51,524,124.36
Peru	18,525,771.19	Poland	16,934,163.60
Salvador	892,353.28	U.S.S.R.	11,260,343,603.02
Uruguay	7,148,610.13	Saudi Arabia	17,417,878.70
Venezuela	4,336,079.35	Turkey	26,640,031.50
Total	$456,094,634.58	Yugoslavia	32,026,355.58

Total charge to foreign
governments $48,361,210,768.24

Aid not charged to foreign governments (including lost shipments, administrative costs, and Lend-Lease aid diverted to United States forces) 2,578,827,000.00

Total Lend-Lease aid $50,940,037,768.24

[3] Credit: *The New York Times*, October 19, 1946.

Reminiscent of Wilson's Fourteen Points, though less concrete, the charter expressed under eight headings the ideals and aims of the United States and Great Britain in the war. The first and foremost principle was renunciation of "aggrandizement, territorial or other." This typical expression of American idealism harmonized well enough with Britain's aims, but hardly with those of Russia, which nevertheless adhered to the Atlantic Charter on September 27, 1941.

The Atlantic Charter secured for the Allies a great and immediate propaganda advantage. Later, when it turned out that Russia had by no means renounced plans for aggrandizement and the western powers yielded to Soviet demands for territory, there were recriminations and charges of hypocrisy and bad faith. When the United States entered World War II, it concluded — just as in World War I — no conventional alliances with any of its associates. But it took the initiative in the formation of the United Nations, a loose association of twenty-six nations, joined in war against the Rome-Berlin-Tokyo alliance. This association was based on the United Nations Declaration, signed on January 1, 1942, in Washington, which restated the principles of the Atlantic Charter. In basing the relationship of the United States to its allies on broad, general principles, rather than on hard and fast politico-military agreements, President Roosevelt was guided by considerations of internal American politics. To the American people war was an evil, justified only in self-defense or for the sake of upholding moral principles. Any frank definition of political and military policy, in harmony with the famous dictum of Clausewitz that war was but a continuation of diplomacy by other means, was to the Americans anathema. This made it necessary to represent the issues of the war as a clear-cut choice between right and wrong, when in fact they often involved the problem of choosing among evils. The American press, in a patriotism perhaps exaggerated, contributed to the gross over-simplification of the issues and forces at war. Journalists tended to present America's allies as wholly blameless and admirable, and her adversaries as wholly evil and despicable. While the press showed a commendable self-discipline in suppressing — without the necessity of formal censorship — information which might give aid and comfort to the enemy, it also withheld from the American public information unfavorable to the Allies for fear that it might disillusion the American people and weaken their war effort. This resulted, among other things, in obscuring for the American people the fact that Soviet Russia was not only a brave and valuable ally in war, but also a potentially dangerous rival after the war.

Military cooperation between the United States and Great Britain was assured by the creation of the Combined British-American Chiefs of Staff in Washington during Prime Minister Churchill's visit to the American capital immediately after Pearl Harbor. Thanks to a common language, and a community of cultural and political interests, the solidity and harmony of the Anglo-American military partnership was perhaps without precedent in coalition warfare. Divergences of view between American and British members in inter-Allied councils did arise, but they were generally settled without acrimony or ill-feeling. Once a joint decision was reached it was carried out by both British and American members of the team with the utmost energy.

In sharp distinction to the harmony of the Anglo-American military partnership, military cooperation between the western Allies and Russia was very limited and marked with ambiguities and suspicion. Historically, Russia had always maintained an exclusive attitude. This trait was intensified in Soviet Russia by communist indoctrination and by a morbid suspicion of the hostile capitalist world. Russia neither sought nor accepted intimate relations with the western Allies. Military liaison between Russia and the western Allies was handled by the regular military, air, and naval attachés in Moscow, London, and Washington. The Red Army was not represented on the Combined British-American Chiefs of Staff in Washington and never admitted any western officers into the inner circles of its High Command. Toward the end of 1943 a special American military mission was dispatched to Russia. Its chief, General John Deane, arrived in the Soviet Union full of enthusiasm for promoting inter-Allied cooperation but he was speedily disillusioned. Soviet officers were taught to think, like Germans and Japanese, in politico-military terms. General Deane's political innocence and eagerness to help puzzled and embarrassed them. In December, 1944, General Deane reported to Washington: "We never make a request or proposal to the Soviets that is not viewed with suspicion. They simply cannot understand giving without taking, and as a result even our giving is viewed with suspicion. Gratitude cannot be banked on in the Soviet Union. Each transaction is complete in itself without regard to past favors."[4]

Except for one ceremonial visit, General Deane was not even admitted to the Soviet High Command or the battle front, let alone consulted on operations. He was confined to Moscow and relegated to the functions of military mailman between the Soviet and United States commands, and expediter of Lend-Lease shipments to Russia. Later in the war Soviet officers were admitted to the headquarters of General Eisenhower in Europe. But they neither offered nor solicited advice. Apart from urging speedy establishment of a Second Front in western Europe and increased Lend-Lease shipments to Russia, they contented themselves with watching and reporting home on what was going on in the Anglo-American camp.

A certain degree of military and political cooperation was achieved between the western Allies and Russia only at the "summit," the carefully staged wartime conferences of Churchill, Roosevelt, and Stalin.

[4] John R. Deane, *The Strange Alliance* (New York: The Viking Press, Inc., 1947), pp. 84–5. Quoted with the permission of the Publisher.

43

THE ALLIED COUNTEROFFENSIVE
1943–1944

We, the United Nations, demand from the Nazi, Fascist, and Japanese tyrannies unconditional surrender. By this we mean that their will power to resist must be completely broken, and that they must yield themselves to our justice and mercy.

WINSTON CHURCHILL, JUNE 30, 1943

1. THE ALLIED STRATEGY

GLOBAL WAR CALLED for grave political and military decisions which only the heads of state could make. Thanks to the rapid development of air transportation, Allied leaders, accompanied by their political and military staffs, met frequently in personal conferences to plan the strategy of the war. A week after the Pearl Harbor blow, Prime Minister Churchill was in Washington to confer with President Roosevelt. In accordance with a recommendation made already in September, 1941, by the United States Joint Chiefs of Staff for the eventuality of war with Germany and Japan, it was decided to give priority to operations in Europe over those in the Pacific. This "Hitler first" strategy was based on the belief that Germany was a more powerful and dangerous enemy than Japan. Although it was assailed by a substantial body of opinion in the United States (the "Pacific firsters") and questioned by some United States naval officers, it prevailed until the final defeat of Germany. In discussing possible operations in the European theater, Churchill submitted a plan for an Anglo-American invasion of North Africa.

This proposal was to inaugurate a long-drawn debate in Allied councils, reminiscent of the debate between the "West fronters" and "Easterners" in World War I (see p. 136). The Americans and the British usually found themselves on opposing sides in the debate. Prime Minister Churchill and General George C. Marshall, the chairman of the United States Joint Chiefs of Staff, became the principal contestants in the verbal jousting, while President Roosevelt assumed the role of a benevolent arbiter. In discussing the best way of assailing the Nazi-dominated "Fortress Europe," Churchill, who had been an ardent "Easterner" in World War I, urged an invasion of Europe by the southern and southeastern approaches from the Mediterranean. On the other hand, General Marshall, who had been an officer on the staff of General Pershing — a stout "West fronter" — in World War I, pressed for an immediate cross-Channel invasion of France.

The two proposed strategies reflected different aims as well as differences in historical experience between Britain and the United States. The strength of Britain was relatively limited and was moreover dispersed to guard her far-flung empire. In continental warfare the British have always suffered a numerical disadvantage. Consequently, they could hope to win only by maneuver, not by mass. They have shown a consistent predilection for "peninsular" campaigns, that is, for selecting narrow, inaccessible theaters of hostilities which denied their adversaries the elbow room necessary to deploy their superior numbers. The United States, on the other hand, enjoyed in both World Wars a great numerical and material superiority. Consequently, American generals favored a "frontal assault" on Germany, for they were confident that they could beat her in a square fight. They tended to regard British strategy as oversubtle and British readiness, for instance, to divert forces to support Balkan guerrillas, as a waste of time and men. They felt the thing to do was to build up the Allied forces in Britain and then hit Germany with all they had by the shortest route possible, that is, across the Channel.

Another point on which the British and Americans differed was in their attitude to the war in the Pacific. While the British were by no means indifferent to the conflict in the Pacific, their first concern was naturally with the more imminent threat in Europe. On the other hand, the Americans, while not seeking to reverse the "Hitler first" strategy, were naturally deeply concerned with the war in the Pacific, for the winning of which they had assumed primary responsibility. Another issue on which the British and Americans differed was that the British sought to coordinate political and military strategy in the sense of the famous dictum of Clausewitz that war is but a continuation of diplomacy by other means. The Americans tended to frown on such efforts as proposals "to sacrifice American lives for the sake of political advantages." In accordance with the American doctrine of strict separation of the military and political spheres, war was regarded as the business of soldiers and diplomacy as the business of diplomats. The two should not mix. When the soldiers delivered victory, then — and then alone — would it be time for the diplomats to step in. This doctrine was admirable in many ways, but it was hardly realistic. Wars, after all, are not international tournaments to prove whose army is better; all wars are in fact waged for political and economic advantages, although these may take different forms.

However, while the American generals were completely apolitical, they

were not unmindful of American security. In fact, they weighed all strategic decisions with cold realism exclusively in the light of their bearing
on American security. Thus, they proposed the "Hitler first" strategy not
to please the British, but because they regarded the establishment of
Anglo-American influence in Western Europe as vital to American security. On the other hand, they then did not regard Central and Eastern
Europe and the Near and Middle East as important to American security.
Therefore, they did not object to the extension of Soviet influence into
these areas — especially if this were to be the price of Soviet cooperation
in the Pacific war, which they earnestly desired and continuously pressed
American diplomats to secure. On this point the Americans sharply
clashed with the British, who regarded the Near and Middle East and
Southeastern — if not all of Central and Eastern — Europe as vital to
British interests. This basic divergence of view was never fully reconciled
but only patched up in a series of uneasy compromises.

The first Allied conference in Washington in December, 1941, ended
with a tentative approval of the British proposal to invade North Africa.
However, in April, 1942, General Marshall worked out a plan (code-
named "Sledgehammer") for a cross-Channel invasion of France in 1942,
with the limited objective of establishing an Allied beachhead on the
continent and relieving the German pressure on the Russians. With the
approval of President Roosevelt, he then flew to London to secure British
approval of the plan. This, however, they absolutely refused to give.

General Marshall was motivated by fear lest the Germans knock out
the Russians in 1942. In May, on the invitation of President Roosevelt, the
Soviet Foreign Commissar Molotov flew to London and Washington and
back to London before returning home. After his departure, a communiqué announced that in London he had signed a twenty-year Anglo-
Soviet alliance (May 26, 1942) and in Washington a new Lend-Lease
agreement. The communiqué added ambiguously that "a full understanding" had been reached "with regard to the urgent task of creating a
second front in Europe in 1942." Later, it transpired that the promise to
open a second front in Europe in 1942 had been given to Molotov by
President Roosevelt, and that Churchill, faced with a *fait accompli*, had
concurred in it only very reluctantly and with many explicit reservations.
In July General Marshall flew to London to try again to secure British
approval for operation "Sledgehammer." However, Churchill, while admitting the ultimate necessity of a cross-Channel invasion, was adamant
in his opposition to it in 1942, for he feared that it would result in disaster. After much wrangling, he appealed over Marshall's head to President Roosevelt, who yielded on July 25 and issued a directive to postpone operation "Sledgehammer" in favor of operation "Torch" (invasion
of North Africa). Churchill undertook to go to Moscow to explain the

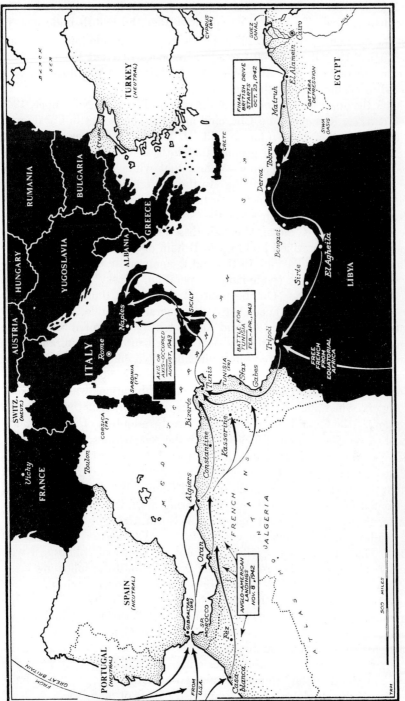

ALLIED OPERATIONS IN THE MEDITERRANEAN AREA, 1942–1943

change in plans to Stalin. Their meeting in August was reported to be less than cordial. To prove their point further the British undertook to test the German "Atlantic Wall" defenses by a commando raid on Dieppe on August 19. Of the 5000 Canadians who carried out the raid, 3369 became casualties. The Americans were sobered but the Russians continued to grumble about the lack of a second front.

After the successful launching of operation "Torch" in November, 1942 (see p. 477), Roosevelt and Churchill and their staffs met in Casablanca to concert further plans (January 14–24, 1943). Stalin was invited but declined to attend on the ground that he was too busy directing the operations of the Soviet army — a hint that while he was fighting the western leaders were only talking. In the conference Churchill proposed that after the completion of the destruction of the Axis forces in North Africa the Allies should strike at the "soft underbelly of Europe" by an invasion of Italy. General Marshall dissented on the ground that this would weaken the Allied build-up in Britain and delay attending to the Allied needs in the Pacific. In the end a compromise was agreed upon: to invade only Sicily (code-named operation "Husky") to secure the Mediterranean lifeline. On the political side, much time was taken up by composing the differences between General de Gaulle, supported by Britain, and General Henri Giraud, supported by the United States. The Americans had been angered by de Gaulle's hauteur and intransigence and put up Giraud, a brave but politically naive officer, as a competitor to de Gaulle to head the administration of French North Africa. Later (June 4), a "French Committee of National Liberation" was established in Algiers, which included both de Gaulle and Giraud. Another important decision of the Casablanca conference was the adoption of the "unconditional surrender" formula for peace with the Axis nations. After the war, with the wisdom of hindsight, many criticized this formula as having contributed to the over-weakening of Germany and Japan and the subsequent extension of Soviet power in Europe and China. But at the time it was welcomed in the Allied nations with roaring approval.

After the completion of the conquest of North Africa in May, the western leaders met for another conference in Washington (May 12–28, 1943). Since Russia was by that time out of danger of collapse, it was decided to postpone the cross-Channel invasion until the following year. Its "target date" was to be May 1, 1944. Churchill once again proposed an invasion of Italy after the completion of operation "Husky" and also suggested several possibilities for invading the Balkans, all of which raised the hackles of the American generals. In the end, General Eisenhower in North Africa was given ambiguous orders "to plan such operations in exploitation of 'Husky' as are best calculated to eliminate Italy from the war," but whether Italy should be invaded or not was reserved to a later decision of the Anglo-American Combined Chiefs of Staff.

2. THE INVASION OF ITALY

On July 10, 1943, operation "Husky" was launched by British and American forces under the command of General Sir Harold Alexander. While paratroops established beachheads, amphibious forces landed at several points in Sicily. After initial fumbling, the campaign progressed well and by August 16 the conquest of Sicily was completed. The Allied success so daunted the Italian people that on July 25 Mussolini was overthrown in a surprise move, and Marshal Pietro Badoglio assumed his place as head of the government. A demand for peace spread throughout the country; and the Germans, realizing that their ally might defect, transformed their divisions in Italy into an army of occupation and seized all strategic centers. Italy sank from the role of Axis partner to the role of a prostrate state like France, a state that would have to be "liberated."

The obvious desire of the Italian people to get out of the war led Churchill to press again for the invasion of Italy in order to help her to extricate herself from the strangling embrace of her German partner. The question was thrashed out at the Quebec conference of the Allied leaders, at which China was represented but to which Russia again refused to send delegates (August 11–24, 1943). Churchill's proposal was approved, and on August 18 General Eisenhower was given orders to prepare the invasion of Italy. On the political side, the Quebec conference approved Allied recognition of the French Committee of National Liberation in Algiers as a *de facto* government of the "French overseas territories which acknowledge its authority."

On September 2 British and American forces leaped the Strait of Messina to the toe of Italy. A week later, a second Allied force, made up chiefly of American units, fought its way ashore at Salerno. Within a month the foot of Italy was cleared and Naples fell on October 1. But then the campaign bogged down, as General Marshall had feared, and became a profitless drain on the Allies, as Rommel's campaign in Africa had been on the Axis. The Apennine peninsula, with its backbone of mountains and river valleys to the west and east, provided an endless series of natural defense lines. Hitler, faithful to his principle never to retreat voluntarily, gave orders to hold Italy at all cost. Skillfully exploiting the Italian terrain, the Germans held up the Allied advance for months at the historic abbey of Monte Cassino, between Naples and Rome. In an effort to outflank the Germans, a new beachhead was established north of their lines at Anzio below Rome (January 22, 1944), but six months of savage fighting, with heavy casualties, ensued before the Eternal City was liberated on June 4.

For the Italian people the situation of their country in 1943 and 1944 was confusing and tragic. The government of Marshal Badoglio concluded an armistice with the Allies one day after their landing in Italy (September 3, 1943). The terms, which were kept secret, provided that the Italians with the status of "co-belligerents" would assist the Allies, permit their forces to occupy strategic areas, surrender the Italian fleet, and accept temporary Allied control over their national finances, censorship, communications, and transport. However, Badoglio could not enforce the agreement because his influence did not extend to the regions where the Germans still held control. Mussolini, who had been imprisoned after his fall in July, was rescued by a daring German commando raid in September, 1943, and proclaimed a "Fascist Republic" in northern Italy. Thus two regimes, one dominated by the Germans and one subservient to the Allies, claimed the divided loyalties of the Italian people. In the long struggle from September, 1943, to May, 1945, Italians served on both sides, but the major fighting to liberate Italy was done by the American, British, French, Polish, Brazilian, and other units which composed the Allied expeditionary force. The Germans fought stubbornly, falling back from one prepared line to the next, and only when Germany itself collapsed did their resistance in Italy cease.

3. THE RUSSIAN WESTWARD DRIVE

While the Germans temporarily checked the western Allies in Italy, they lost the initiative to the Russians in 1943. At the beginning of that year, they still occupied regions which had held 30 per cent of the Soviet population before the war, produced 20 per cent of their oil, contained 40 per cent of their coal reserves and their machine tool industry, and 50 per cent of their richest wheat fields, livestock, and farm lands. But the Soviet government took energetic steps to keep production going in the areas still under its control. Many factories were dismantled before the advance of the Germans and reassembled in the Urals and beyond, in Siberia, where much of the refugee population was resettled. Moreover, by 1943, American and British Lend-Lease supplies began to arrive in substantial quantities by way of Murmansk and Archangel in the north, Vladivostok in the east, and Iran in the southeast. Canned meats, butter, fats, powdered eggs, and dehydrated milk, potatoes, fruits, and vegetables helped to keep the Soviet population from starvation. What was even more important, substantial quantities of war matériel arrived. By the end of the war in Europe, Soviet Russia had received from the western Allies 6800 tanks, 13,300 airplanes, 1000 locomotives, 406,000 motor vehicles, 150,000 yards of cloth for uniforms, 11,000,000 pairs of boots and shoes, and scores of other supplies. The tanks, locomotives, and motor vehicles gave the Soviet army what it most sorely lacked — mobility. While the battle of Stalingrad was fought in the main with Soviet-made weapons, the great Soviet offensives which soon followed would have been severely handicapped without American vehicles. Ironically, it was on American wheels that the Russians rolled into Berlin in 1945.

The turning point in the war in Russia came in February, 1943. Almost daily the guns of the Kremlin shook Moscow with their succession of victory salutes. The remnants of the German Sixth Army trapped at Stalingrad surrendered on February 1, Kursk was retaken on February 8, Belgorod, February 9, Rostov, February 14, and Kharkov, February 16. By the opening of March, the Axis losses in killed or captured were 500,000 for the previous ninety days, an average of over 5000 a day. Like a mortally wounded beast, the German *Wehrmacht* could no longer charge any great distance, but could still strike locally. Kharkov was wrested from the Russians once again (March 15) and Belgorod reoccupied a week later. But exhaustion was descending upon both combatants after the winter's incredible work, and the morass of mud that marks the Russian spring chained their feet. For three months (April–July, 1943) there was a breathing spell, while both sides gathered strength for summer offensives. The Germans made plans for large-scale drives to mark their third summer in Russia, but for the first time the Russians had the initiative in summer fighting and they kept it. By October, 1943, they had reached the Dnieper and in November, when the summer offensive ended, they entered Kiev, 650 miles west of Stalingrad. Almost without letup a winter offensive followed, which saw Soviet troops across the pre-1939 borders of Poland in January, 1944, and of Rumania in March. By May, the pocket of Germans in the Crimea, previously bypassed, had been wiped out and essentially all pre-1939 Soviet territory freed.

This opened several new courses to the Soviet government: it could withdraw from the war, without loss of face, and let the western Allies fend for themselves; it could halt operations and wait for the outcome of the struggle in the west; or it could continue to recover the territories secured by agreement with Hitler in 1939 and, further, to carve a sphere of Soviet influence in Central and Eastern Europe — possibly even to crush Hitler and realize the fond dream of Lenin of a Soviet Germany. The third course commended itself most to the Soviet leaders — provided they could secure assurances from the western Allies that they would not let the Soviet army fight Germany alone indefinitely while they contented themselves with aerial and naval warfare and minor peninsular campaigns on the periphery of Hitler's "Fortress Europe."

In 1943, as the Soviet military position improved, their relations with the western powers deteriorated. The principal reasons for this were the continued absence of a second front and the troublesome question of Poland. As the Soviet army seized the initiative, German propaganda began to lay a heavy stress on the theme: Germany — shield of Europe against the spread of Bolshevism. In April, the Germans announced, with much fanfare and feigned horror, the "accidental" discovery of mass graves of some 10,000 to 12,000 Polish officers in the Katyn Forest near Smolensk, and alleged that they had been murdered by the Soviet police. When the Polish government-in-exile in London indignantly requested the International Red Cross to conduct an "impartial investigation," the Soviet government broke off relations with it on the ground that it had accepted the "slanderous" German version of the crime.[1] Beyond this incident, there loomed the questions of Polish-Soviet borders and of Soviet influence in Eastern Europe in general. To counter the German efforts to exploit the general fear of the spread of Bolshevism, the Soviet government announced in May the dissolution of the Communist International, which had directed the international communist movement since 1919. Events were to prove that this measure meant little; the Communist movement simply went underground for the time being. But at the time the manifestations of a resurgence of Great Russian nationalism convinced many men in the west that as a result of the war Russia had undergone a basic transformation and that it had renounced communism as an export commodity.

The western leaders were determined, in any event, to keep the good will of Russia, for they, too, like the Soviet leaders, wished to bring the war in Europe to its logical conclusion — the destruction of Hitler and nazism. The Americans, moreover, were extremely desirous of securing Soviet help in the war against Japan. President Roosevelt, who set great store by personal diplomacy, proposed a personal meeting to Stalin in May, 1943, but the simultaneous information that the western Allies were postponing the invasion of France until 1944 wrecked the possibility. However, in October, 1943, Secretary of State Cordell Hull and Foreign Secretary Anthony Eden traveled to Moscow to explore the Soviet attitude and lay the ground for a Big Three meeting. They gave the Soviet leaders solemn assurances that the western Allies would invade France in the spring of 1944. In return, they received unsolicited assurances that Russia would join in the war against Japan after the destruction of Germany — the first indication of Soviet interest in the Pacific war. The Moscow conference (October 19–30, 1943) created two new inter-Allied agencies: the European Advisory Council in London, charged with working out the terms of surrender for Germany and her satellites and with delimiting occupation zones, and the Advisory Council for Italy in Naples, charged with supervising the complex Italian situation. At the conclusion of the Moscow conference a joint communiqué was issued, together with declarations regarding Italy and restoration of Austrian independence.

The Moscow conference was followed by a first meeting of the Big Three at Teheran (November 28–December 2, 1943). Churchill, Roosevelt, and Stalin again exchanged assurances of an Anglo-American invasion of France and of Soviet participation in the war against Japan. Concerning Poland, they agreed that Russia should have substantially the

---

[1] Testimony gathered after the war by the United States Congress and other agencies clearly points to the Soviet responsibility for the grisly crime.

American dive-bombers en-
route to an attack on a Japanese base in the Pacific
(Official Navy Photograph).

American supply convoy
climbing a stretch of the
Burma Road, headed for
the China front east of
Kunming (Imperial War
Museum).

Hiroshima after the dropping of the atomic bomb, August, 1945 (Alan Band Associates).

borders secured by agreement with Hitler in 1939, and that Poland should be "compensated" for her losses of territory in the east to Russia at the expense of Germany in the west. In bland disregard of the principles of the Atlantic Charter also, they discussed various ways of dismembering Germany. The conference was important not so much for the results obtained as for establishing cordial relations among the Big Three. This, however, was achieved at the expense of Anglo-American solidarity. In an effort to impress Stalin with his sincerity and to allay any suspicion that the western leaders were "ganging up" on him, President Roosevelt tended to assume the role of a benevolent arbiter, as in the Churchill-Marshall debates, and sided as often with Stalin as he did with Churchill. This left the onus of defending the common western interests largely up to Churchill. Thus, Churchill's proposal to divert forces earmarked for a southern invasion of France, and instead invade the Balkans at the head of the Adriatic Sea, with the ultimate aim of seizing Vienna and possibly Budapest and establishing western influence in the Danubian valley, was vetoed jointly by Stalin and Roosevelt. Following the conference, a joint communiqué was issued as well as a declaration assuring Iran of Allied respect for its territorial integrity and sovereignty.

The Teheran conference was billed as one dealing with the war in Europe alone, for Russia was not yet at war with Japan. China was therefore not represented at Teheran. But on their way to Teheran the western leaders conferred with Chiang Kai-shek at Cairo (November 22–25, 1943) to concert their plans against Japan. "It is their purpose that Japan shall be stripped of all the islands in the Pacific which she has seized or occupied since the beginning of the First World War in 1914, and that all the territories Japan had stolen from the Chinese, such as Manchuria, Formosa, and the Pescadores, shall be restored to the Republic of China. . . . In due course, Korea shall become free and independent," announced a subsequent communiqué. On their return trip, the western leaders invited to Cairo the president of Turkey, Ismet Inönü (December 4–6, 1943), but failed in their effort to induce him to abandon Turkish neutrality and join the Allies.

4. THE AMERICAN OFFENSIVE IN THE PACIFIC

The Cairo communiqué indicated that the Allies were determined to force Japan to surrender unconditionally and to strip her of all of her territorial gains since the Sino-Japanese war of 1894–1895. Since Japan was not likely to surrender of her own volition, it was necessary for the Allies to destroy the Japanese armed forces completely, invade Japan, and occupy it bodily. This created very special strategic problems for which there was no precedent in the history of warfare since, like Britain, Japan was an island empire. Britain has been conquered twice, by Caesar in

55–54 B.C. and by William the Conqueror in A.D. 1066, but in both instances the conquerors encountered no naval opposition. Moreover, they were able to attack Britain from a close base, the continent of Europe. By contrast, Japan, which liked to boast that she had never been conquered, was a first-rate naval power. Moreover, in view of the previous Japanese conquest of the Asian mainland, Japan could be attacked only from very distant bases, the Hawaiian Islands and Australia, 3800 to 3900 miles away.

The struggle against Japan was eminently a naval and aerial war. The American navy, supported by its air and fighting arms, was the senior service in the Pacific. The war with Japan was also a predominantly American effort; only in the China-Burma-India theater did it partake of the nature of an inter-Allied effort. In the final phases of the struggle Britain joined energetically in Southeast Asia and Russia in Manchuria, but in the great battles in the vast expanses of the Pacific, which determined the outcome of the war, the United States fought alone. This had one advantage: the planning in the Pacific was done largely by the United States Joint Chiefs of Staff alone and was free of the inevitable bickering of coalition warfare and the adjustments in strategy necessary to suit different national purposes. The war in the Pacific was won by characteristically American means: superior technology and organization. But the American generals and admirals showed themselves also brilliant and original strategists.

The United States Navy recovered from the crippling blow at Pearl Harbor with amazing speed. The value of the battleship had been questioned even before the war by some experts who thought these costly vessels too vulnerable in the air age. The lesson of Pearl Harbor and the sinking of the British battleship *Prince of Wales* and the battle cruiser *Repulse* by Japanese land-based bombers off Malaya (December, 1941) raised further doubts regarding the worth of capital ships. The United States completed only ten battleships and two battle cruisers in the four years from 1941 to 1944 but commissioned six heavy cruisers and twenty-seven light cruisers. On the other hand, the aircraft carrier attained a new eminence. It was around these "floating airfields" that the new naval task forces were built. In the naval battles in the Pacific the United States and Japanese fleets seldom approached near enough to each other to exchange broadsides. Rather, they attacked each other, sometimes over a distance of fifty or more miles, by carrier-based aircraft carrying bombs and torpedoes. Aircraft carriers also served as escorts for convoys. On December 7, 1941, the United States possessed only seven first-line aircraft carriers, and in less than a year combat losses cut the number to three. This emergency was met by rushing to completion and converting available craft, with such success that by the end of the war seventeen new full-sized carriers were ready for duty, along with nine light carriers converted from cruiser hulls and 114 escort carriers. This expansion called for a rapid increase in aircraft, especially fighters. In 1941 new planes built for the navy totaled 3638; in 1944 the number was 30,070. The cost was enormous, an average of some $4,000,000,000 a year for naval aviation, but the results proved worth it. The construction of submarines rose sharply from eleven in 1941 to seventy-seven in 1944. Submarines not only retained but enhanced their importance in the Pacific war.

Japan, as an island empire, depended upon the daily arrival and departure of the myriad of ships which maintained its economic life. In 1939 the Japanese merchant marine ranked third among the great powers, being exceeded only by those of Great Britain and the United States — 6,000,000 tons of shipping of over 500 tons gross weight. Although during the war the Japanese built or captured an additional 4,100,000 tons, the need to import additional supplies for the war effort and to transport troops and supplies to the Japanese armies on the mainland and in the islands, overtaxed the merchant marine. The real crisis in shipping, however, was caused by American aircraft and submarines which inflicted crippling losses. In 1942 they sank 134 Japanese vessels, in 1943, 284, and in 1944, 492. For the seven war months of 1945 the number declined to 132, not for lack of hunters but for lack of quarry. Of the total of 8,900,000 tons of Japanese shipping sunk, 54.7 per cent was accounted for by American submarines. In addition they sank one battleship, four carriers, four escort carriers, three heavy and nine light cruisers, forty-three destroyers, twenty-three submarines, and 189 minor combatant vessels and auxiliaries. Of all the United States armed services, the "silent service" made the largest single contribution to the defeat of Japan.

A phenomenal development in the American navy was the program, dictated by the tactics of amphibious warfare, for landing craft. From tiny rafts to 300-foot transports that landed tanks and infantry, the freakish procession grew. Some had shallow bottoms and bows like a drawbridge; some plunged through the waves like a tugboat and climbed the shore like a tank. In 1941 the navy had only 123 vessels classed as landing craft; by 1945 the total was 54,206. Wartime expansion affected all naval categories. In 1944 the size of the fleet almost doubled within twelve months, while the manpower, which totaled 13,149 officers and 206,959 enlisted personnel in 1941, had risen to 43,140 officers and 461,376 enlisted personnel in 1944. After the war the Japanese complained that they had been defeated by machines, not by men. This was in a sense true, but it took men to devise and build the machines and then to operate them.

Both men and machines were used boldly and imaginatively to defeat Japan. The conventional idea of a battle front as a line of demarcation separating distinct areas held by opposing forces had little meaning in the Pacific. The shadow of Japanese power did not spread like an eclipse across the western Pacific; it would be nearer the fact to picture the Japanese expansion as the rapid spread of a vine. The shipping lines

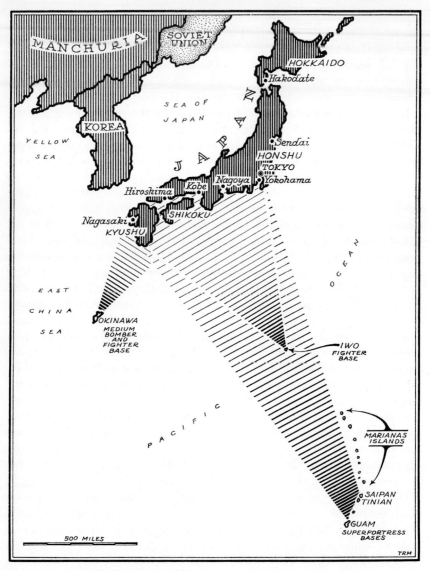

UNITED STATES AIR POWER IN THE PACIFIC, 1944–1945

were the long, sinuous stalks; and ports and islands were holds where the
tendrils could seek a grip, strike root if possible, and then spread again.
However, if the main stalks were cut, the whole vine would wither, and
this was the idea which governed American strategy. From west to east
the vines of Japanese expansion toward the Indonesian islands followed
the coast of Asia, from China through Indochina and Malaya; in the
center a shorter vine wound through the Ryukyu Islands, Formosa, and
the Philippines; and in the east the most tenuous vine leaped through the

Bonin, Mariana, and Caroline Islands (with branches to the Marshall and Gilbert Islands in the east) to New Guinea and the Solomon Islands.

In contemplating how to defeat Japan, the American generals and admirals decided not to try to flush the Japanese systematically out of every island, from south to north, but to adopt what became known as the "island-hopping" strategy. In essence it proposed to leave the Japanese in the Dutch Indies undisturbed and to select as targets small islands to the north. These were seized by winning local air supremacy with carrier-based fighters and rushing in landing forces. The islands were then transformed into airfields. And the maneuver was repeated from these advanced bases. The strategy was initially slow and costly, for the Japanese garrisons in the islands fought to the last man and the Japanese navy boldly engaged the American navy. The year 1943 was largely spent in neutralizing the Japanese in New Guinea and in winning a foothold in the Bismarck Archipelago immediately to the north. But as the Americans gained strength and skill by constant repetition, they were able to speed up their advance by these "leapfrog" tactics. Thousands of Japanese were left behind on scattered archipelagoes, to "wither on the vine," as American task forces broke through to seize bases nearer Japan.

In November, 1943, the Americans seized selected islands in the Gilbert group, in January, 1944, in the Marshalls, and in June in the Marianas. By October, they were ready to risk a leap to the Philippines and, on October 20, the troops of General MacArthur landed on Leyte. The Japanese made an all-out effort to halt the invasion of the Philippines, for they knew that if the Americans succeeded in gaining control of these islands they would be able completely to cut the Japanese lines of communication to the Dutch East Indies. According to Admiral Soemu Foyoda, the Japanese naval command felt that "there would be no sense in saving the fleet at the expense of the loss of the Philippines." Without the oil and other products of the Dutch Indies, the Japanese fleet would be helpless and Japanese industries crippled. Between October 22 and 27 the Japanese navy fought the American navy in an intricate series of engagements known as the Second Battle of the Philippine Sea. The Japanese gamble failed; they lost two battleships, four carriers, six heavy cruisers, three light cruisers, and probably nine destroyers. Although a remnant of the fleet managed to extricate itself from the battle, the Japanese navy never recovered from the blow. In the islands the costly struggle went on for months, but aided by Filipino guerrillas the Americans gained the upper hand.

The next step was to carry the war to the Japanese islands. But this, the American generals and admirals felt, should await the defeat of Germany and a joint American-British-Russian effort.

44

THE TRIUMPH OF THE ALLIES
1944–1945

Our enormous material superiority gave us an unchallengeable advantage over our foes . . . More important even than the weapons, however, was the indomitable fighting spirit of the men of the Allied nations who wielded them.

GENERAL DWIGHT D. EISENHOWER

Japan was beaten in the first part of 1945. That was when your submarines and naval aircraft cut off our supplies from the south.

ADMIRAL ZENISHIRO HOSHIMA

1. THE SOVIET CONQUEST OF EASTERN EUROPE

IN THE SPRING of 1944, while the western Allies feverishly prepared to invade France, the Soviet army carried its offensives beyond the Soviet borders. By July, it had swept up to the Vistula River. On August 1, in anticipation of the Soviet entry into Warsaw and in response to Soviet broadcasts exhorting the Poles to revolt, the Polish underground forces in Warsaw rose against the Germans. However, the Soviet army halted in Praga, a suburb of Warsaw on the eastern bank of the Vistula, and made no attempt to relieve the Polish insurrectionists. The pleas of Polish exiled leaders and of western statesmen were equally ineffective. British and American airplanes, which flew all the way from Britain to drop supplies to the beleaguered Warsaw insurrectionists, were refused permission to land in Soviet-held territory and when they strayed there they were shot at. The Soviet government explained its attitude by the strategic decision of the Soviet High Command not to advance beyond the Vistula for the moment. But it seems apparent that this decision was influenced by political considerations. The leadership of the Polish underground was non-communist, and the Soviet government had already recognized a pro-communist government at Lublin and was not anxious to help its "bourgeois" competitors in Warsaw. Meanwhile, the Germans took savage reprisals in Warsaw. The city, already heavily damaged in 1939, was reduced to rubble. After two months of fighting, the insurrection was crushed (October 2). Similar was the fate of the Slovak uprising, which broke out against the Germans and the pro-German Slovak government of Monsignor Tiso on August 24. There, too, the Soviet army halted and allowed the Germans in October to crush the uprising, the leadership of which was not communist.

While pausing on its central front in Poland along the Vistula, the Soviet army began to straighten out its flanks by offensives in the Baltic and the Balkans. Germany's eastern satellites were ready to jump to the side of the victorious allies; the question for them was only one of timing the switch meticulously with the arrival of Allied troops in force so as to escape the fate of Italy — of being torn and trampled between the great combatants, both equally indifferent to their fate. On August 25 hard-pressed Finland requested an armistice, which was signed in Moscow on September 19. But the German troops trapped in Finland resisted disarming and were not subdued by Finnish and Soviet troops until December. On September 22 Soviet troops captured Tallin, the capital of Estonia, and on October 13 Riga, the capital of Latvia. Meanwhile, Rumania managed deftly to pass to the Allied side. On August 25 King Michael, who had been secretly negotiating with the Allies, arrested the pro-nazi dictator General Antonescu and requested an armistice, which was signed in Moscow on August 30. The Soviet and Rumanian forces speedily disarmed the feeble German forces in Rumania. The defection of Rumania permitted the Soviet army to advance rapidly to the Danube and Bulgaria in the south and across the Carpathian Mountains toward Hungary in the west. Bulgaria, whose peasantry was traditionally Russophil, was the only one of the German satellites which had not declared war on Soviet Russia but only on the western Allies. For some time Bulgarian representatives had been secretly negotiating for a surrender with the British Middle Eastern Command in Cairo, but owing to fear of German reprisals and the absence of any Allied troops in the Balkans to protect them, they delayed too long. On September 5 the Soviet government unceremoniously declared war on Bulgaria, and the Soviet army on the Danube invaded the country. Instead of signing an armistice with the western Allies at Cairo, Bulgaria was forced to sign one with Russia at Moscow (October 28). One more Balkan country thus passed under Soviet influence. Both Rumania and Bulgaria agreed to help the Allies with their armies and were given the status of co-belligerents, like Badoglio's Italy.

The situation in Yugoslavia and Greece was different because they were not German satellites but Allied occupied countries with duly recognized governments in exile in Allied territory. In both countries substantial guerrilla forces had arisen shortly after their occupation in 1941, which had harassed the German occupants quite effectively. At one point there were more German divisions engaged in fighting the Balkan guerrillas than the western Allies in Italy. Unfortunately, both the Greek and Yugoslav resistance forces broke up into communist and nationalist factions, which often fought each other as ardently as they fought the Germans. The British and later the Americans, on the premise that whoever fought the Germans was deserving of help, parachuted military missions and supplies to both groups impartially — at least at first. Later, they tended to give greater support to the communists, who managed by attending more diligently to their propaganda at home and abroad to create the impression that they were fighting the Germans more resolutely than their nationalist competitors. Russia gave no help to either group until the actual arrival of the Soviet army in the Balkans in 1944. On October 21, after effecting a junction with the Soviet army, the Yugoslav communist partisans seized Belgrade. Yugoslavia thus appeared to be passing under Soviet influence.

Next came the turn of Hungary. Coming from Rumania, Slovakia, and Yugoslavia, Soviet forces converged on Budapest. On October 15 the Hungarian regent, Admiral Horthy, who had been secretly negotiating with the Allies, denounced the German alliance and ordered the Hungarian army to cease fighting the Allies. But the Germans, who had anticipated the Hungarian defection, seized Budapest, arrested and deported Horthy to Germany, and threw up a defense line along the Danube. While the Germans set up a puppet government under the Hungarian fascist leader Ferencz Szálasi in Budapest, the Russians set up another puppet government under General Béla Miklós at Debreczen. Unhappy Hungary suffered the same fate as Italy; she was cut in twain and Hungarian soldiers were forced to fight on both sides. The siege of Budapest, which began in November, did not end until February 13, 1945. It left the handsome Danubian capital a shambles.

By the fall of 1944 Soviet forces had conquered Eastern Europe up to a Warsaw-Budapest-Belgrade line and were poised to attack Germany herself. Meanwhile, the western Allies had liberated France and Belgium and were ready to invade Germany from the west.

2. THE INVASION OF FRANCE

On D-Day, June 6, 1944, the western Allies launched operation "Overlord," the invasion of France. An Allied amphibian force under the supreme command of General Eisenhower crossed the English Channel and assailed the Normandy beaches. Throughout the preceding night paratroops had been dropped behind the coastal defenses; 600 warships buried German posts and pillboxes under a barrage of shells; and 10,000 Allied aircraft patrolled the skies. This naval and air supremacy made it possible for the military forces, transported in 4000 ships, to reach shore and establish beachheads within a few hours. Deployment proceeded rapidly while the defenders were still confused by the naval and aerial bombardment. German reconnaissance airplanes were unable to patrol the Channel; and

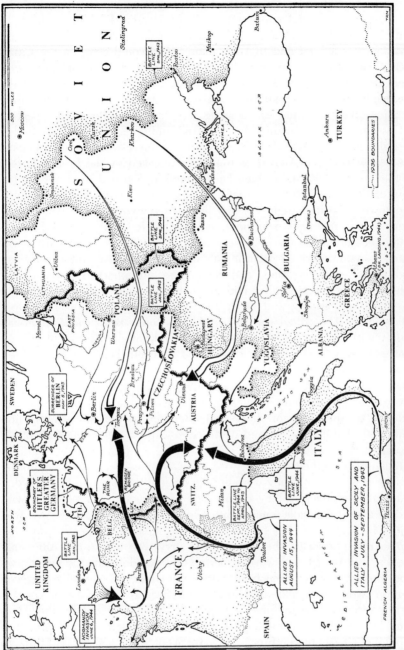

ALLIED AND SOVIET ADVANCES IN EUROPE, 1943–1945

lacking information on the size and movements of the invading armada, the German commander in the west, Field Marshal Karl von Rundstedt, and his subordinate, General Rommel, at first thought that the Normandy invasion was a feint and that the main blow would come in the Calais area. They were, moreover, hamstrung by standing orders not to commit their mobile reserve without approval from Hitler's headquarters on the Eastern front. The Germans were, therefore, slow in reacting to the Allied invasion, and the initial Allied losses were much smaller than expected.

Despite adverse weather the gigantic amphibian operation unfolded steadily. All bridges and railroads by which the German reinforcements could arrive were blasted from the air or wrecked by the French Forces of the Interior (F.F.I.), which had trained and armed in secret for the hour of liberation. Knowing that all major French ports would be mined and fortified, Allied engineers had improvised two special harbors, constructed in a few days from pontoons, pierheads, causeways, and breakwaters floated across the Channel and moored in place. One harbor was scarcely open before an Atlantic gale destroyed it but the other survived and tanks, guns, supplies, and men were disembarked in unceasing columns. Twenty pipe lines laid under the Channel carried gasoline to the tanks and trucks, and as the battle front advanced the fuel pipes followed it. The Allied command, able to equip British and American troops with effective weapons in almost unlimited quantity, improved their efficiency, speeded their drives, and reduced their battle casualties. The extraordinary effectiveness of the medical services provided maximum advantages for the wounded. Critical cases were treated in the battle zone by auxiliary surgical groups; blood plasma and new drugs reduced the problems of shock and infection; and plastic surgery and improved therapy saved and restored a higher percentage of battle casualties than in any previous war.

Rallying from their early surprise, the Germans struck back vigorously and for over a month they were able to confine the Allies to the crowded beaches. The lovely rolling countryside of Normandy, crisscrossed with hedges and stone walls fencing in apple orchards and pastures, was well suited for defense. Had the Germans had sufficient reserves and their former air superiority, they might have very well hurled the Allies into the sea. But their forces were dispersed and tied down by too many tasks from France to Russia and from Norway to Greece. Hitler, like a greedy glutton, would not relinquish any of his prey for the sake of concentrating strong German forces against the Allies. Gradually, the Allies extended their toehold in Normandy in width, though not in depth. The capture of Cherbourg on June 27 gave them control of a major port through which they could pour in men and supplies. On July 9 the pent-up strength of the Allies burst through the German ring between Caen and St.-Lô, and the Allied forces fanned out into open country. The heavily armored American Third Army, under General George S. Patton,

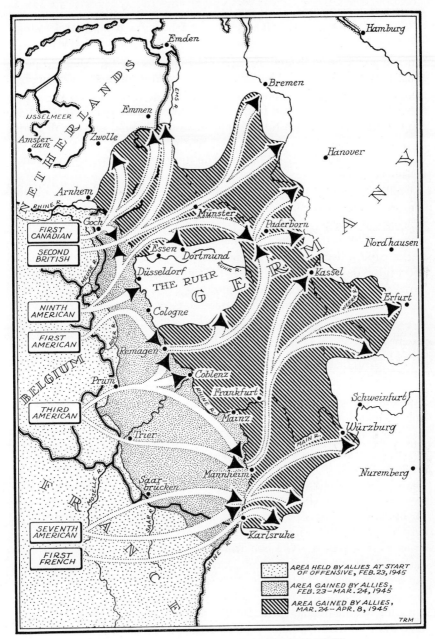

THE INVASION OF GERMANY FROM THE WEST

raced first westward to sweep the Germans out of Brittany, then turned
in its tracks and rolled eastward toward Paris. On August 15 a second
amphibious invasion in the south of France (operation "Anvil") placed
the American Seventh and French First Armies on the Mediterranean
coast between Nice and Marseilles. Encountering little German opposition, they raced up the Rhone valley. The Allied advances eastward from
the Atlantic and northward from the Mediterranean threatened to cut off
the German forces in western France. Leaving behind only small forces
to deny the Allies the use of the Atlantic ports as long as possible, the
Germans hurriedly fell back, harassed on their retreat home by the French
resistance forces.

Unlike in Italy, where the Allied invading forces found the population
confused and apathetic, in France the Allies received an enthusiastic
welcome and eager cooperation from the population. On the night of
August 19–20, as the Allies approached Paris, the French resistance forces
in the capital, led by the Paris police force, rose against the Germans.
After three days of confused street fighting, the German commandant of
Paris, who had at his command mostly service troops, decided to disregard Hitler's direct orders "to defend Paris to the last, destroy all
bridges over the Seine, and devastate the city," and handed Paris, virtually intact, to the F.F.I. command. On the following day, August 24, the
Allies marched in, acclaimed with frenzied joy by the population.

General Montgomery then proposed to General Eisenhower the controversial "big thrust" strategy. His idea was to concentrate all Allied
armor in one sector for a powerful thrust through Belgium toward the
Ruhr, which he assured the commander in chief would end the war before the end of the year. Eisenhower agreed that the main direction of
the Allied advance should be through Belgium, but largely because of the
jealousy of the British and American generals he determined on the
"broad front" strategy of simultaneous advances of all armies, which
gave all generals a chance to reap some glory. Thrusting north, the British liberated Brussels on September 3 and seized Antwerp (but not its
harbor) on the following day. By September 12 American armored columns were across the German frontier near Eupen. On the same day
the forces of "Overlord" and of "Anvil" effected a junction near Dijon,
and a continuous front from the Netherlands to Switzerland was created.
But then the German resistance stiffened. A daring Allied attempt to outflank the German lines through the flat Dutch territory to the north
(operation "Market Garden") failed. A British airborne division dropped
across the Rhine near Arnhem was two-thirds destroyed (September 17–
26). It became evident that the Germans had rallied and would fight
fiercely for their homeland, and that the "fluid front" of the summer, so
favorable to Allied initiative, had hardened. "After Normandy our
strategy became unstitched," Field Marshal Montgomery recorded in his
memoirs. "There was no plan; and we moved by disconnected jerks."

From the Netherlands to Switzerland the Allies now had seven armies, the Canadian First, the British Second, then the American Ninth, First, Third, and Seventh, and the French First, hammering at the German West Wall. From D-Day to the middle of September 2,200,000 troops, 450,000 vehicles, and 4,000,000 tons of supplies had been poured into France. But after the hard summer campaigning, when they covered 400–500 miles, the Allied troops were exhausted. And according to Eisenhower, "the life-blood of supply was running perilously thin through the forward extremities of the Army." It seemed best to rest, reinforce, and regroup the Allied armies, and to reorganize their lines of supply and communication. As the Allied advance came to a halt at the end of September, a sense of disappointment swept over the Allied peoples, who had been led to expect by the speedy liberation of France and Belgium that the war would be over by Christmas.

Defeat had dimmed Hitler's prestige, and led the conspirators who had been plotting against him since 1938 to try to assassinate him and seize power. On July 20, 1944, one of the conspirators, Colonel Count Claus von Stauffenberg, left a bomb in Hitler's headquarters at Rastenburg in East Prussia while the Führer was conferring with his staff. The explosion killed four of the twenty-four persons present at the conference and wounded many more, but by incredible luck Hitler escaped with minor burns. At the same time, by a most improbable series of coincidences, the elaborate arrangements of the conspirators to seize control of the armed forces from the War Ministry in Berlin failed. Within hours Hitler was in charge of the situation, and terrible vengeance followed. Scores of high-ranking officers and officials were executed after summary trials before specially constituted "People's courts." Others, including the brilliant Field Marshal Erwin Rommel, were given the choice of taking poison to save their families. Rommel's death was announced as resulting from his wounds, and Hitler decreed national mourning for the hero whose name would be "forever linked with the heroic battles in North Africa."

The July 20th plot was a conspiracy by aristocratic, conservative elements ("blueblooded swine" Hitler called them). The conservative conspirators realized that Hitler was dragging Germany into an abyss and wanted to conclude peace while Germany still had some bargaining power left. But they were divided as to whether to conclude a separate peace with Russia and continue the war against the western Allies or the other way around. The failure of the plot strengthened the control of Hitler and of the Nazi bitter-enders over the crumbling German empire.

The rapid fall of German prestige persuaded Hitler to risk his dwindling reserves in a desperate offensive, an attempt to split the Allied armies in Belgium. Field Marshal von Rundstedt opened the drive, with all the advantages of tactical surprise, on December 16. Within a week the unprepared American and British forces in the Luxemburg sector had been hurled back to the Meuse. The situation was tense, but General Eisenhower refused to be disconcerted. Rallying divisions on both sides of the "Bulge" to squeeze the German salient, he succeeded in stabilizing the lines before the end of the month. When the year 1945 opened the American, British, and French forces in the west, with detachments from the British dominions and units of Polish and other soldiers from occupied states, and the Soviet armies in the east, were ready for the finale. The assault on Germany was to be fully coordinated and relentless. From the Rhine, from the Danube, and from the Vistula the invading armies were to press the Reich in a vast combined operation. From the skies the American air forces and the Royal Air Force, with a maximum strength of 14,000 bombers protected by 12,000 fighters, would deal the final blow to German transportation and supply.

3. THE YALTA CONFERENCE

With victory in Europe in sight, political problems began to outweigh strategic considerations in the thinking of the Allied statesmen. The advance of the Soviet army into Eastern and Central Europe greatly disturbed Churchill. Reports of rape, murder, and mayhem, perpetrated by Soviet soldiers in the time-honored tradition of Russian armies on the people whom they "liberated," began to crop up in the west. What was even more ominous was that in the wake of the Soviet army native communists were emerging everywhere and seizing power. As early as August 5, Churchill called at Eisenhower's headquarters and sought to persuade him to divert the Allied divisions in Italy, earmarked for the southern invasion of France, for an invasion of the Balkans at the head of the Adriatic Sea, in an effort to head off the Soviet advance into Central Europe. But "Ike said no, continued saying no all afternoon and ended by saying no in every form of the English language."[1] Next, Churchill took up the matter with Roosevelt at the second Quebec conference (September 11–17, 1944), and also proposed that they make joint representations to Stalin. But the President was still concerned more with the actual menace of nazism than with the potential menace of communism. At Quebec he, and at his suggestion Churchill, approved the famous "Morgenthau Plan" for "converting Germany into a country primarily agricultural and pastoral in its character."

In October, therefore, Churchill set out alone to Moscow in an effort to strike a bargain with Stalin. He made an unusual proposal to the Soviet dictator, namely, a "division of responsibility" (a euphemism for spheres of influence) based on percentages: Rumania 90 per cent Soviet and 10 per cent western; Bulgaria 75 per cent Soviet and 25 per cent western; Greece 90 per cent western and 10 per cent Soviet; Yugoslavia 50 per cent Soviet and 50 per cent western; and Hungary 50 per cent

[1] Captain Harry Butcher, *My Three Years with Eisenhower* (New York: Simon & Schuster, 1946), p. 634.

Soviet and 50 per cent western. Moreover, he brought up again the possibility of a western invasion of the Balkans. Surprisingly, Stalin, who at Teheran had opposed a western invasion of the Balkans, this time approved both schemes without any hesitation. Possibly, he foresaw that it was too late for the western Allies to mount an offensive into the Danubian region, and without British and American soldiers in Central and Eastern Europe to enforce the division of responsibility it would be ineffective. Indeed, this was what subsequently happened. Upon returning home, Churchill pried from the reluctant American generals an allocation of necessary landing craft, but was advised by his own generals that the invasion could not be mounted before February, 1945. In December he abandoned the project.

The only advantage that Churchill salvaged from his agreement with Stalin was to establish British influence in Greece. In October, with Soviet concurrence, British soldiers were landed in Greece to forestall an attempt by the Greek communists to seize Athens, as the Yugoslav communists had seized Belgrade. In December, civil war broke out between the Greek communists and nationalists, in which the British were involved. In January, 1945, after severe fighting in Athens, during which the city suffered heavy damage and the British over 2000 casualties, Churchill arranged a truce with the communists, which assured the capital to the nationalists. In the countryside, however, the civil war was to go on for years.

Meanwhile, President Roosevelt, freed from domestic concerns by his electoral victory in November, felt ready for another Big Three meeting. While he seemed apathetic to the affairs of Central and Eastern Europe, he was deeply concerned over the affairs of China, which were then not going auspiciously for the Allies. Until their respective entry into the war, both the United States and Russia had furnished aid to China. Thereafter, however, China was totally cut off from her allies by the Japanese seizure of Burma. Fortunately for the Chinese Nationalist government, the Japanese were preoccupied with their expansion into the South Pacific and suspended operations in China, except for an annual "rice-bowl campaign," a foray into the rice-bearing provinces of central China to collect the rice crop. At the Anglo-American war conference in Washington in May, 1942, the President approved a project to relieve China the boldness of which was characteristically American. Since China could not be approached by land or by sea, the Americans proposed to approach it by air. In consequence, the "Hump Lift," delivery of aid to China from airfields in northeastern India over the towering Himalaya ranges in southwestern China, was inaugurated. An American air squadron, the "Flying Tigers" (later the Fourteenth Air Force) under General Claire Chennault was sent to assist the Chinese army. An American general, Joseph W. Stilwell, assumed command of the vast China-Burma-India theater and became Chiang Kai-shek's chief of staff.

General Stilwell believed that the Chinese army, if properly trained and equipped, could play an important role in the Pacific war. But it would need massive assistance, and this could be delivered only by land. In consequence, while the Chinese army assisted by picked American commandos ("Merrill's Marauders") sought to clear the Japanese from northern Burma, an American army engineering unit began to build the Ledo Road in northeastern India to link up with the Burma Road. The operation was eventually successful; in February, 1945, the first truck convoy reached China. Meanwhile, however, the Japanese resumed in 1944 their operations against China and drove the nationalists out of the rice-bearing provinces in the east into the poor Chinese hinterland in the west. This increased pressure on Chiang Kai-shek's government to accept a "united front" against Japan with the Chinese communists, which the latter had proposed right along. The Soviet government, which had supported Chiang Kai-shek's government and had given no aid to the Chinese communists, began to echo these suggestions. General Stilwell, with the single-minded concentration on military victory and unconcern for political consequences characteristic of American soldiers, also urged cooperation with and aid to the Chinese communists until Chiang Kai-shek, angered by his importuning, requested his recall (October, 1944). His successor, General Albert C. Wedemeyer, and the United States ambassador in China, Patrick Hurley, continued to urge conciliation but not with much success. Although the nationalists and communists went through the motions of negotiating, both were convinced that the United States would win the war against Japan alone and both were anxious to husband their forces for a postwar showdown over the control of China. This then was the Chinese situation when the Big Three met for the second time at Yalta in the Crimea (February 4–11, 1945), after a brief preliminary meeting of the western leaders at Malta.

President Roosevelt arrived at Yalta determined to secure three basic objectives: a firm commitment on the Soviet entry into the war in the Pacific; permission for American bombers to use bases in eastern Siberia; and continued Soviet support for the Chinese Nationalist government. He was generally successful. Stalin gave him a firm assurance of joining in the war against Japan two or three months after the end of the war with Germany, but he demanded a price for it, namely, the restoration of "the former rights of Russia violated by the treacherous attack of Japan in 1904" (i.e., southern Sakhalin, the Kurile Islands, lease of Dairen and Port Arthur, operation of the Manchurian railways, and maintenance of the *status quo* in Outer Mongolia). With some minor modifications, the President agreed to these Soviet "rights" — rights which had been obtained by the Tsarist government by particularly ruthless imperialist diplomacy and which the Soviet government had specifically renounced in the Soviet-Chinese Treaty of 1924. Roosevelt made his acceptance conditional on the concurrence of Chiang Kai-shek — concurrence which he agreed to obtain. Stalin promised to provide bases for American bombers in eastern Siberia after the Soviet entry into war with Japan. He also pledged continued support for the Chinese Nationalist government.

In the discussions of Far Eastern problems Roosevelt and Stalin were the principal bargainers; Churchill readily concurred in their agreements when it was made clear that Britain's former rights in Asia, including Hong Kong, would be restored. On the other hand, in the discussion of European affairs Churchill and Stalin were the principal bargainers, with Roosevelt assuming the position of an honest broker. With regard to Germany the Big Three approved the occupation zones worked out by the European Advisory Council, the allotment of an occupation zone to France (to be carved out of the British and American zones), and the formation of an Allied Control Council. The Big Three further reserved to themselves the right to dismember, disarm, and demilitarize Germany as well as to exact reparations from her. But since they were unable to agree on the modalities of implementing these resolutions, they referred them to special commissions for later action. With regard to Poland and Yugoslavia, they agreed to advise broadening their *de facto* communist government by inclusion of democratic elements. In a "Declaration on Liberated Europe" they assured other occupied European peoples that they would assist them in creating "democratic institutions of their own choice," in accordance with the principles of the Atlantic Charter. Another happy augury to smaller nations was the proposal to summon the United Nations for a conference in San Francisco in April to draft a charter and form a permanent organization.

After the war the Yalta agreements (part of which was only then revealed) came under violent criticism in the western nations. At the time, however, they did not appear to be an unfair bargain. The difficulty arose later when the unity of the Big Three, on the continuation of which their implementation was postulated, broke down.

4. THE DESTRUCTION OF GERMANY

As 1945, the "Year of Decision," opened, the fate of Germany was sealed. Yet Hitler, fatuously trusting that the British-American-Soviet coalition would break up before the defeat of Germany, refused to surrender and insisted on fighting to the last, both in the west and the east. The German people were united behind him by fear — fear of invasion by the "Russian hordes" and fear of "pastoralization" by the western Allies under the widely publicized Morgenthau Plan. There were no peace resolutions or serious defections in Germany at the end of World War II, as had happened toward the end of World War I.

The final act of the European war was opened by Soviet armies on January 12, 1945. Crashing across the Vistula, they captured Warsaw,

Cracow, and Tarnów. Other Russian spearheads drove to the Baltic shores across East Prussia. From the Vistula the Germans fell back to the Oder, striving to make a stand that would preserve the war industries of Silesia, but the Russians gave them no rest. By the end of February the Soviet armies had swept 170 miles from East Prussia to the lower Vistula, and 350 miles from the upper Vistula to the Oder. In March the methodical Marshal Zhukov secured Königsberg on his right and Breslau on his left, freeing his flanks for a final drive on Berlin. Further south, in the Danubian valley, after the fall of Budapest on February 13, Marshal Rodion Y. Malinovsky resumed the Soviet drive toward Vienna.

Meanwhile, on February 8, the western Allies launched their offensive with a powerful drive into Holland. The Germans fell back toward the Rhine, behind which they hoped to make a strong stand. But on March 8, exactly a month after opening their drive, the Allies managed to cross the Rhine over a bridge at Remagen, which the Germans — usually so thorough — in their haste had forgotten to blow up. In the north the British raced toward Bremen and Hamburg, in the south the Americans and French drove toward Munich, while in the center the Americans seized Essen and then drove toward the Elbe. On April 11, after an incredible advance of fifty-seven miles in a single day, advance units of the American Ninth Army reached the Elbe at Magdeburg and established a bridgehead across it on the following day. Only fifty-three miles separated them from Berlin. "At that time," wrote the American field commander General Omar N. Bradley, "we could probably have pushed on to Berlin had we been willing to take the casualties Berlin would have cost us. Zhukov had not yet crossed the Oder and Berlin lay almost midway between our forces."[2] Since March, Churchill had been bombarding Washington and General Eisenhower's headquarters with urgent pleas for the Americans to make the extra effort necessary to seize Berlin. But the American generals, believing — correctly — that Churchill was not thinking of military victory but of the postwar balance of power, felt that it was not their task to secure political advantages. "As soldiers we looked naively on this British inclination to complicate the war with political foresight and nonmilitary objectives,"[3] observed General Bradley. On General Eisenhower's orders the American army halted along the Elbe and awaited the Soviet army which reached the river at Torgau on April 26. Berlin, a valuable political pawn, was thus deliberately thrown away by the western Allies.

Ten days earlier, Marshal Zhukov's forces had penetrated the German defenses on the Oder and had reached the eastern outskirts of Berlin on the 20th. The shattered, half-leveled city was shelled and burned anew as the Soviet forces battled the defenders from block to block. Hitler, aban-

---

[2] General Omar N. Bradley, A Soldier's Story (New York: Henry Holt, 1951), p. 537.
[3] Ibid., p. 536.

doned by many of his close followers, directed the desperate resistance from an underground shelter in the chancellery until April 30. Then he appointed Admiral Karl Dönitz his successor and committed suicide rather than surrender. The last German resistance in the city collapsed on May 2. For a week, Soviet soldiers, drunk with victory, looted the gutted city, still obscured with clouds of smoke. Admiral Dönitz as well as Heinrich Himmler, representing another faction of the defeated government, sought to parley with the Allies, but the Allied governments knew that the National Socialist regime was in dissolution and insisted upon unconditional surrender. Many German field commanders were already ordering their men to lay down their arms.

In Italy the Allied armies had driven the Germans back to the Po River by the end of April. The German-sustained regime of Mussolini collapsed while Berlin was burning, and the Italian dictator, captured by anti-fascist partisans as he fled toward Switzerland, was shot on April 28. The German troops in Italy, whose commander had been in touch with the United States secret service, capitulated on May 1. Their line of retreat to Germany had been threatened since April 12, when the Russians captured Vienna and pushed up the Danube valley toward Linz, while the Americans and French pushed down the Danube toward Salzburg.

Before the end of German resistance, the western Allies threw away another, though minor, political prize: Prague. On May 5 the American Third Army crossed the Czechoslovak border. Encountering little resistance, it headed for Prague, the population of which rose against the Germans on the same day. But the Soviet High Command, wishing to reserve the honor of liberating Prague to Soviet arms, protested at once to General Eisenhower, who yielded and ordered the American army to halt at Pilsen, some fifty-five miles from Prague. This left the Prague insurrectionists in a quandary. The American army, under orders, would not move from Pilsen, and the Soviet army was still some seventy miles away from Prague and encountering stiff German resistance. Ironically, Prague was saved by Russians, but not Red ones. It was the remnants of the German-recruited "Russian Army of Liberation" under the former Soviet general Andrey A. Vlassov, who in a last-minute attempt to redeem themselves turned on their German masters in Prague and defeated them. The Soviet army did not reach Prague until one day after the armistice.

On May 7, in General Eisenhower's headquarters at Rheims, representatives of the German army signed the instruments of unconditional surrender, but the Soviet government, conscious of the prestige that would accrue to the army which received the German surrender, insisted on a repetition of the ceremony before its representatives in Berlin on May 8. At one minute after midnight, May 8, the hostilities in Europe officially came to an end.

The unconditional surrender of Germany created a legal vacuum. The government of Admiral Dönitz was dissolved and the Allied Control

Council, consisting of the commanders of the Allied occupation armies, assumed the task of ruling Germany, as provided by the Yalta agreements. The German people were so stunned by their complete defeat that for some time they were incapable of any initiative. They showed the same docility toward the Allied authorities as they had shown toward Hitler's government. On June 1, as provided at Yalta, the Soviet army admitted the western Allies to Berlin, which, like Germany, was divided into four occupation zones and ruled by an Allied "Kommandatura." There remained, however, the problem of determining the long-range Allied policy toward Germany, which had been discussed but not settled at Yalta. Therefore, another (the last) Big Three conference met at Potsdam (July 17–August 2, 1945). Its personnel had partly changed. On April 12, exhausted by twelve years in office during troublous times of depression and war, President Roosevelt died and was succeeded by his last vice-president, Harry S. Truman. Amidst the conference (July 26) Churchill's magnificent war term was ended by elections in Britain which brought the British Labor Party and Clement R. Attlee to power. Of the original Big Three only Stalin remained.

The Potsdam conference approved steps to deprive Germany of her ability to wage war by dismantling her war industries, by war reparations, by denazification, and by the trial of war criminals, and it defined the exact authority of the Allied Control Council. It further authorized the expulsion of some 6,500,000 Germans from the countries of Central and Eastern Europe, the Soviet occupation of part of East Prussia, and the Polish occupation of East Germany up to the Oder-Neisse line. These provisions, however, as indeed all the Allied wartime agreements, were subject to final confirmation by a general peace conference. No one at that time suspected that because of the breakdown of Allied unity no general peace conference would meet, and that the Allied wartime agreements, meant as temporary arrangements, would largely provide a permanent framework for the postwar world.

To the peaceful and moderate elements among the German people the Potsdam conference held out hope that democratic ideals and efforts at honest and responsible self-government would be respected, and that freedom of speech, press, and religion would be guaranteed insofar as military security and order permitted.

5. THE COLLAPSE OF JAPAN

In a report to the Yalta conference the United States Joint Chiefs of Staff estimated that the war in the Pacific could be brought to a conclusion eighteen months after the end of the war in Europe. They calculated that it would take four to six months to redeploy the Allied forces from Europe to the Pacific and one year to conquer the Japanese islands. Events were to prove this estimate too cautious, but it was based on sound reasoning. In the Pacific islands the Japanese had fought to the last man. It was not unreasonable to expect that they would fight with equal valor in defense of their home islands. A nightmarish vision of a bloodbath, of 70,000,000 Japanese fighting to the last to defend Japan, deeply affected American military thinking. It was at the bottom of the persistent pressure of American military men on the American political representatives to secure Soviet assistance in the war with Japan. The Soviet army could greatly reduce the cost of the conquest of the Japanese islands. In April, 1945, the Soviet government denounced its nonaggression pact with Japan, which would not have expired for one more year. No one in the United States at the time expressed any great indignation over this Soviet repudiation of an international treaty. The breach fitted American war plans.

In making their estimate of the Pacific war the United States Joint Chiefs of Staff did not, of course, take into account the effect of atomic bombs, since these had not been completed and tested at the time. However, even before the use of this formidable weapon, the Japanese power of resistance had been weakened more than the Allies suspected. As early as April 18, 1942, six carrier-based American bombers carried out a surprise raid on Tokyo. The purpose of this raid was primarily psychological: to remind the Japanese at home that they were not immune from the war and to bolster the American domestic morale. In November, 1944, however, long-range B-29 bombers based on Saipan inaugurated systematic bombing of Japan, to which the crowded Japanese cities with their flimsy housing were particularly vulnerable. To get closer to Japan, American troops were landed on Iwo Jima (750 miles from Japan) in February, 1945, and on Okinawa (only 325 miles from Japan) in April, 1945. This made it possible, even without use of bases in eastern Siberia, to subject all of Japan to intensive bombardment. But the Japanese exacted a stiff price for the two islands: 19,938 American casualties, including 4198 dead, on Iwo Jima, and 34,568, including 11,260 dead, on Okinawa. This tended to confirm the fears of the American commanders of the probable high cost of taking the Japanese islands. Eventually, from island and carrier bases, American bombers dumped 29,400 tons of bombs on Japanese industrial areas and 104,000 tons on urban areas. In the final months of the war, with the Japanese fleet crippled and its air force swept out of the skies, the United States fleet moved into coastal waters and shelled factories and dockyards with its heavy guns and then moved away unscathed, meeting no serious opposition. Plans for a landing in Japan (operations "Olympic" and "Coronet") were energetically pushed. Over three thousand ships and a million men were to be available for a double invasion, supported by naval forces and thousands of bombers.

The operations never took place. By July, Japan was ready to surrender. On the 13th the Japanese government appealed to the Soviet leaders, then preparing to go to the Potsdam conference, to mediate peace. On the first day of the Potsdam conference President Truman received a report that on the previous day (July 16) the first atomic bomb had been successfully exploded on the Alamagordo proving grounds in the New Mexican desert. This put in his hands a new weapon with which to coerce Japan. On July 26 he, Churchill, and Chiang Kai-shek (Stalin abstained because Russia had not yet declared war on Japan) addressed a stern summons from Potsdam to the Japanese government to surrender or face destruction. The Japanese government rejected the ultimatum because of the uncertainty about Allied intentions with regard to the Japanese emperor. President Truman then authorized the use of atomic bombs. On August 6 a B-29 super-fortress dropped an atomic bomb on Hiroshima, destroying three-fifths of this Japanese city and killing 78,150 people. Events then moved in rapid succession.

Three months to a day after the end of the war with Germany, Russia declared war on Japan and the Soviet army opened a drive into Manchuria (August 8). A second atomic bomb was dropped on Nagasaki, leveling most of the city with a heavy toll in lives (August 9). The Japanese government appealed for peace on condition that the Allies respect the prerogatives of the emperor (August 10). The Allies replied noncommittally: "From the moment of the surrender the authority of the emperor and the Japanese government to rule the state shall be subject to the Supreme Commander of the Allied Powers" (August 11). The Emperor Hirohito accepted this declaration and ordered a "cease fire" (August 14). American troops landed in Japan (August 28) and occupied the country without encountering any resistance. The Japanese overseas forces surrendered piecemeal to the nearest Allied armies: In Manchuria to the Soviet army under Marshal Alexander M. Vasilevsky; in China to the Chinese army under General Chiang Kai-shek; and in Southeast Asia to British forces under Admiral Lord Louis Mountbatten. The final ceremony of surrender took place on board the U.S.S. *Missouri* in Tokyo Bay (September 2). Six years and one day after its opening by Hitler's invasion of Poland, World War II came to an end.

45

POLITICAL, SOCIAL, AND ECONOMIC RESULTS
OF THE WAR

In absolute figures, the wars of the twentieth century have probably caused more deaths than any wars of the past.[1]

1. WAR COSTS AND WAR CASUALTIES

When the fighting ceased, it became possible to compile figures that would represent approximately the loss of life and destruction of property caused by World War II, but the estimates can never be complete or exact. The total outlay made by the belligerent governments for armaments and war materials was calculated at more than $1,000 billion. Nearly one-third of this total represented the outlay of the United States, which came to $317 billion. The Soviet Union spent the equivalent of $192 billion and Great Britain, $120 billion. The outlay for Germany was calculated at roughly $273 billion, for Italy, $94 billion, and for Japan, $56 billion. The sacrifices made by the Chinese in gold and blood during their prolonged resistance to the Japanese could not be estimated.

This list of official war expenditures did not include the losses caused by the destruction of civilian property, and figures on such losses are hard to establish. Damage to civilian property in Great Britain, largely through air raids, exceeded $5 billion. But Britain fared well in comparison with Russia, where the clashing armies in their advances and retreats, the war of the partisans behind the German lines, and the wholesale reprisals of the invaders caused destruction estimated at $128 billion. Property damage suffered by Germany possibly reached $75 billion; and the total for other European countries afflicted by the war may have exceeded $150 billion.

[1] Raymond Aron, *The Century of Total War* (New York, Doubleday, 1954), p. 75.

The number of men killed in action in World War II has been estimated in round figures at more than 15 million. The deadliness of the ferocious struggle waged on the Eastern European front is attested by the mortality lists. Russian casualties were by far the highest among the Allied nations and German casualties among the Axis powers.

BATTLE DEATHS IN WORLD WAR II

AXIS POWERS & ASSOCIATES		ALLIED POWERS & ASSOCIATES	
Germany (including Austria)	3,500,000	U.S.S.R.	7,500,000
Japan	1,219,000	China	2,200,000
Rumania	300,000	British Commonwealth	544,596
Hungary	140,000	Yugoslavia	410,000
Finland	82,000	United States	291,557
Italy	77,494	France	210,671
Bulgaria	30,000	Greece	73,700
Slovakia	27,000	Belgium	7,760
		Netherlands	6,238
		Norway	1,000

No sure method has been found for computing how many civilian victims perished in air raids, how many were caught in the tides of battle, how many died as a result of disease, exposure and malnutrition caused by the conflict. Although the total for non-military casualties has been set tentatively at 12 million, it is probably higher if it is taken to include the millions who perished in the Axis concentration areas and extermination camps. Total casualties, military and non-military, for World War II, may have reached 30 million, and the injured may have exceeded 35 million. A substantial proportion of the civilian casualties resulted from the bombing from the air. Both groups of belligerents engaged not only in "strategic" bombing, designed to destroy the adversary's production and transportation facilities but — despite the Geneva convention which forbade the bombing of "open" cities — in "psychological" bombing, designed to break the adversary's morale. Pursuing the latter objective, the Germans bombed Rotterdam, Coventry, and the densely populated areas of eastern London. The Allies then felt justified in retaliating in kind. Thus in July and August, 1943, for three solid weeks, the Americans by day and the British by night, bombed Hamburg, leaving the great port in rubble and killing thousands of its inhabitants. In the final phases of the war, when the Allies attained almost complete air supremacy, they selected German cities for destruction by a single blow — single raids of over a thousand planes dropping monstrous "block-busting" bombs. But the outstanding example of psychological bombing was the destruction of Hiroshima and Nagasaki with atom bombs.

In addition to bombing, the ancient companions of war, starvation and disease, took a heavy toll. In China, in Europe, and in all parts of the world where people lived in want and squalor and fear, the scarcity of food, lack of drugs and medical care and preventive medicine caused a sharp rise in the rate of disease. It required several years to complete a statistical picture of conditions in the war-ravaged countries and to compute the actual cost of life. It must be borne in mind that the destruction of files and records, the changes in government, the dispersion and replacement of personnel, disrupted the archival labor upon which population statistics are built. Wherever the tides of war swirled and shifted, millions of people, soldiers and civilians, disappeared. Even on the army lists the number of dead was often exceeded by the number recorded as missing. Among civilians the list of displaced or missing persons grew each year. The transfer, whether forced or voluntary, of millions of workers from one area to another, the exodus from bombed cities and conquered provinces, the growth of secret and unidentifiable groups of partisans, the deserters from the armed forces and from labor battalions and factories, the escaped prisoners of war, all helped to create an unparalleled problem of homeless and displaced persons. Only years of patient search can establish the fate of millions who disappeared without trace or record, and the final tally can never be complete.

No feature of this prolonged mass tragedy so shocked the conscience of the world as the horrors perpetrated in the Axis prison camps. From 1933, when the National Socialists seized power, they had systematically confined not only thousands of known opponents but also other thousands deemed "politically unreliable" in concentration centers under conditions which became more brutal each year. Rumors of calculated cruelty, torture, and starvation which the guards inflicted upon the victims in these camps had appalled the civilized peoples of Europe and America before 1939. Hitler's insensate denunciation of the Jews, which excited his followers to a fanatical anti-semitism, drove many of the most brilliant artists and scientists of Germany to other lands. Within Germany the persecution of Jews, communists, and any unfortunate minority suspected of opposition to the National Socialist regime, filled the camps.

The outbreak of war, and especially the occupation of foreign countries by the Germans, intensified the regime of terror. The dreaded *Gestapo* (Secret State Police) operated so arbitrarily that no German and no foreigner in the sphere of German influence could feel safe from arrest, for the legal safeguards and the ideals of justice common to all civilized states had been cast aside by the nazis. Right was defined in 1936 as "what is in the interests of the German people." Prisoners who could be charged with no specific crime might still be confined if the court considered them punishable "according to the underlying idea of a penal code or according to healthy public sentiment." From all parts of occupied Europe prisoners were dispatched to the concentration camps where millions disappeared without a trace. Only after the conquest of

Germany by the Allied armies did the world learn the manner of their death. The worst camps had become mass extermination centers, where only the hardiest prisoners, who could endure the starvation, forced labor, beatings, and disease, had a chance of survival. Certain groups, such as "race polluters" (which included not only the large Jewish community but also the small gypsy community) as well as other "undesirables" (men and women too weak or too sick to work) were marked for prompt extermination. When conventional methods of execution, hanging and shooting, proved inadequate the prison camp authorities experimented with poisoning, inoculations, and finally fixed on asphyxiation in gas chambers. Efficient extermination plants were built in which the victims of nazi fanaticism were dispatched in batches of several hundred a day. Their bodies were cremated, after their hair was shorn to make mattresses and their gold fillings extracted, which with the gold jewelry taken from the victims of the nazis added several tons of gold to the reserves of the German National Bank.

This appalling tragedy was duplicated in most of the neighboring countries that the Germans occupied. Evidence assembled after the war indicated that nearly two million Jews from Austria, Hungary, Rumania, Czechoslovakia, Yugoslavia, Greece, France, Belgium, and the Netherlands died or were put to death in the German prison camps. Another million or more from occupied Russia, Lithuania, and Latvia shared the same fate. But the heaviest and most nearly incredible toll was taken in conquered Poland, where nearly three million Jews disappeared. Altogether, it is possible that almost six million European Jews met death under the nazi regime.

This horrifying evidence of the savagery that remains latent in civilized communities is the darkest blot in the annals of recent European history. Nor can the responsibility for these millions of murders be laid upon Hitler or upon the nazis exclusively. All who shared and perpetuated irrational prejudices against the Jews, and all who failed to aid the victims of Hitler's policies, incurred some small share of the blame. A physicist at the University of Berlin, who later helped the United States develop the atomic bomb, has described how German scholars and scientists reacted to the nazi program of removing "undesirables."

The German learned societies did not raise their voices in protest against these early dismissals. . . . It seemed much more important at that moment to fight for the established rights of those who had tenure, and this could be done much more successfully, so they thought, if they made concessions on minor points. In a sense, the German government kept its word with respect to those who had tenure. It is true that before long most professors who were considered "undesirable" were retired; but they were given pensions adequate for their maintenance. And these pensions were faithfully paid to them until the very day they were put into concentration camps, beyond which time it did not seem practicable to pay them pensions. Later many of these professors were put to death, but this was no longer, strictly speaking, an academic matter with which the learned societies needed to concern themselves.[2]

In countries where the citizens were courageous and ingenious enough to resist nazi pressure the Jews suffered much less severely. The small Jewish community in Italy — about 47,000 — apparently remained as numerous after the war as before it. In the Netherlands there were some 16,000 Jews before 1939 and 14,000 after 1945. The Danes boasted, not without reason, that they helped their small minority of some 6000 Jews to hide or escape and that virtually none of them fell into the hands of the Germans. These exceptions suggest that, if all the European peoples (including the Germans) had preserved an equal sense of courage and humanity, the monstrous purge that Hitler ordered could not have been carried out. Nor should it be forgotten that the motivation and the success of that purge must be ascribed in part to religious and social prejudices against the Jews that had disfigured European history since the Middle Ages.

The two world wars of the twentieth century brought a deterioration in the moral sense of the nations and their leaders. The destruction of unfortified cities by explosive and incendiary bombs, the impressment of civilians in conquered countries for war work, the merciless treatment sometimes accorded prisoners of war, and the use of nuclear bombs at Hiroshima and Nagasaki, all reflected a growing disregard for human life. Under the pressure of war all nations resorted to expedients which they could not recall with pride. The secret shame they felt helps to explain why they preferred to forget disturbing truths rather than to keep the memory of the war atrocities alive. This policy enabled former enemies to work together with less bitterness. But it also meant that the postwar generation learned too little of the immediate past.

After the war, committees of investigation from the United States Congress and the British Parliament visited Europe to verify the conditions revealed by the Allied military reports and the dispatches of the newspaper correspondents. The true and terrible price which Europe had paid for submission to Hitler and his regime was now apparent; and the suicide of Hitler, Himmler, Goebbels, and other nazi leaders did not attenuate the crimes committed under their rule. For the most inexplicable fact in the monstrous story of human degradation was the attitude of the German people. They had acquiesced in conditions which no veil of official secrecy could have wholly hidden from their knowledge. This was their responsibility before the world and before history.

But the Germans were by no means unique in their barbaric oppression. There remained one category of prisoners in Germany to whom the Allied armies brought liberation but not a return to normalcy: some

[2] Leo Szilard, quoted in *Scientific Monthly* (March, 1954), p. 131.

500,000 Estonians, Latvians, Lithuanians, and Ukrainians as well as Russians, brought to Germany as prisoners or forced laborers, who preferred exile and an uncertain future in war-ravaged Germany to return under Soviet rule. These were victims of two totalitarianisms: the nazi and the communist. Their ranks were soon swollen by thousands of East Europeans who fled their native countries before or after the arrival of the Soviet army because of fear of punishment for collaboration with the Germans or because of hatred for communism. Nor did this end the exodus of victims of twentieth-century intolerance. There followed millions of other refugees, victims of the nefarious practice of expelling undesirable minorities to make ethnic borders coincide with national boundaries. From the territories annexed from Finland and Germany (in East Prussia) the Soviet government expelled the Finnish and German populations. It "exchanged" the Poles left in the territories annexed from Poland for some Russians still left in Poland. It further took upon itself to rid Rumania of its sizable German minority in Transylvania, which was deported not to Germany but to Siberia! Moreover, at the Potsdam conference, on Soviet insistence and with the reluctant approval of the western powers, Poland, Czechoslovakia, and Hungary were authorized to expel their large German minorities (altogether about 6,500,000 persons). Without troubling to obtain international sanction, Yugoslavia followed suit by expelling its relatively small German and Italian minorities, and Bulgaria later by expelling the remnants of its Turkish minority. Further millions were displaced by the partition of India in 1947 and by the Arab-Israeli war in 1948. Until the erection of an armed barrier in 1961, there continued to escape a steady stream of refugees from Soviet-occupied East Germany to West Germany through a chink in the Iron Curtain: Berlin. Altogether, for barbarism, cruelty, and disregard of human rights, sentiments, and needs, World War II and its aftermath have no precedent in European history.

2. THE DECLINE OF EUROPEAN AND THE GROWTH OF AMERICAN AND SOVIET INFLUENCE

The Allies had won a great victory in World War II — perhaps too great, for during its course they completely destroyed the balance of power in Europe which Britain and France had set out in 1939 to restore. Yet it would be an error to suppose that the destruction of the European balance was solely the result of World War II. The classical European balance of power, as it was maintained in the nineteenth century, had already been undermined in World War I. By 1918 the Russian, Austrian, and German empires of Central and Eastern Europe had collapsed, leaving the powers of the Atlantic seaboard, France and Britain, as masters of Europe. This unhinged the European balance, and incidentally created an illusion of French and British power which really did not exist. It was often forgotten, because of the voluntary withdrawal of the United States into a new isolationism, that it had been the American intervention in the war that made the Franco-British victory in 1918 possible.

In the 1930's Germany and Russia made a military comeback and the European balance was restored. The German-Italian alliance and the territorial annexations the Axis powers made in 1938–1939 tipped the balance in their favor. When Britain and France finally realized this and decided to go to war to prevent the further extension of German power at the expense of Poland, it was too late; within ten months France was crushed and British forces were driven off the continent. Yet the British refused to concede defeat and abandon their war aims. They refused Hitler's offer of peace and fought on bravely although they had little hope of defeating Germany and restoring the European balance with their forces alone. However, the British leaders sensed that the war was far from over, and that it would spread like a forest fire, engulfing all the major powers before it burned itself out. They calculated notably that the United States and the Soviet Union, which had held aloof from the conflict, would be involved sooner or later. Their calculations proved entirely correct; by 1941 both Russia and the United States were drawn into the conflict. By associating herself with the United States and Russia, Britain rode to victory. But it was a Britain considerably weakened and impoverished by six years of war. Although she was treated on a footing of equality by her two great allies, this was not a tribute to superior British power but to superior British diplomacy.

The aims of British diplomacy throughout the conflict had been first to safeguard their interests and those of their empire and secondly to restore the European balance. While they succeeded well enough in their first aim, they failed in the second one, largely because at the end of the conflict there was no force left in Europe with which to construct a balance. Germany and Italy lay trampled and prostrate. And France, which — at British insistence — was associated with the victors at the end of the conflict, was after two invasions in 1940 and 1944 hardly better off than Germany or Italy. For the first time in centuries the fate of Europe was not in her own hands. The European balance was held by two outsiders, the American and Soviet superpowers. Should the Soviet army choose to march to the Channel, no European power but only the American armies could stop it. Should the United States army choose to march to the Urals, no European power but only the Soviet army could hope to stop it.

Postwar events, moreover, were to prove that the American and Soviet influence in Europe, unlike American influence in Europe in 1917–1919, would not be a passing phenomenon, but a long-term one. As relations between the United States and Russia rapidly deteriorated after the war, neither power dared to withdraw from Europe for fear the other would organize and dominate that continent. The result of this development has been a division of Europe in twain and the organization of Western Europe under the American aegis and reduction of Eastern Europe into a Soviet security sphere. Thus, Europe, which for centuries had imposed her will on other parts of the world, found herself reduced not to one but to two spheres of influence. However, it would be an error to suppose that this dramatic reversal in relationship between Europe and the rest of the world resulted from any crippling loss of population or of productive forces of Europe during World War II; both were soon enough replaced. It resulted rather from the more rapid growth of the productive forces of other areas of the world, notably of the United States and the Soviet Union, which began before the war. The war simply brought this development to a dramatic culmination.

Under the whiplash of fear of defeat and of ambition for victory, nations are often capable in time of war of exertions that in time of peace would be inconceivable. Under the stimulus of war the United States, which already before the war was the leading industrial nation in the world, harnessed its productive forces and reached astonishing levels of production. Moreover, after the war it did not lose momentum but went on to further production records. From a low point of $56 billion in 1933 at the height of the depression the gross national product of the United States soared to $214 billion in 1944, the peak war year, and an astonishing $675 billion by 1965, a peak postwar year. Similarly, Russia laid the basis of her postwar industrial might before the war. During the war, owing to the temporary loss of her most industrialized areas in western Russia, the Soviet government was forced to develop industrial resources in eastern Russia and Siberia more rapidly than had been planned. As a result, after the recovery and reconstruction of the heavily damaged western areas, Russia found herself with a vastly expanded industrial plant. As often in the past, she showed an amazing vitality and recuperative ability after the war. By 1949 she had broken the American atomic monopoly, by 1951 reached her prewar levels of production, and thereafter went to new heights of production. Thus, to give but one illustration in a key sector of production, steel, Soviet output reached the prewar level of 31,000,000 metric tons of steel in 1951 and rose to 50,000,000 metric tons by 1957, which was only half the United States steel capacity but more than all of that of Western Europe put together.

It is this rapid growth of American and Soviet productive capacity that explains the reversal in the power relationship between Europe and other areas of the world. European productive capacity had been severely damaged but by no means destroyed by the war. In fact, Europe also showed an amazing recovery from the destruction of the war, but the growth of her production was not proportionate to that of the United States or Russia. Spurred by generous American aid (the Marshall Plan, 1948–1952), European production generally recovered its prewar levels by 1952 and thereafter went on surging to new heights. The most amazing was the rapid recovery of West German production from the ashes and rubble, in which the war had left German industries. By 1952 West German production reached 145 per cent of its prewar level. The recovery of Britain, France, Italy, and the smaller West European countries was less spectacular than the German *Wirtschaftwunder* (economic miracle) but nevertheless impressive. Britain not only reached and surpassed prewar levels of production but for the first time in two hundred years of her industrial history provided full employment. France and Italy, too, after a slower start, showed a vitality and energy, which no one had suspected still existed in their old bodies politic.

The European recovery from World War II completed the economic, social, and political transformation of Europe, which had begun in 1918. After World War I, in response to the noble vision of Woodrow Wilson of a democratic and peaceful world, European governments became generally more democratic or at least more responsive to the wishes of the people. But the European masses did not substantially improve their economic lot. Following World War II, perhaps as a result of revulsion to Hitlerism, there was a general swing to the left in Western Europe, as shown by the rise to power of the British Labor Party in 1945 and the emergence of Christian Socialist parties in Germany, Italy, and France and of strong communist parties in France and Italy. Only Spain and Portugal, always standing aloof from Europe, retained their authoritarian dictators.

The decline of old European ruling elites, which had begun after World War I, was greatly accelerated. The working class gained in political power and social advantages. Complete cradle-to-grave social services were widely consolidated. The European masses shared in the new European prosperity. In the 1960's they were to enjoy a living standard such as they had never dreamed of in the Victorian Golden Age of European glory. The automobile, which before World War II was strictly a toy and status symbol of the rich, became accessible to the common man. The ancient highways of Europe were soon to experience the baffling and exasperating traffic problems so familiar to American motorists. Despite this unwonted prosperity, European influence in other areas of the world continued to decline, for these were progressing at a faster rate.

3. REVOLT OF THE COLONIAL WORLD

Nowhere has the decline of European influence after World War II been so marked as in the colonial world. The causes of this decline have been many and complex. Colonial empires had been built and maintained by force. The humiliating defeats of colonial powers at the hands of Japan, an Asian nation only some eighty years out of oriental seclusion, revealed to Asians the essential weakness of colonial empires. American military prestige was restored by the end of the conflict by the spectacular defeat of Japan. But this was not the case with the European colonial powers; France and the Netherlands did not contribute to the defeat of Japan and the British contribution appeared to Asians as minor.

There were, moreover, other, less tangible causes of the decline of European influence in the colonial world. Nationalism and democracy, once the exclusive property of Western Europe and North America, had been projected by World War I into Eastern Europe. World War II projected them further, into the colonial world. Although Japanese wartime propaganda preaching "Asia for the Asians" failed to provoke any broad response among the Asian masses, it did find response among small groups of men who had been trained in western schools and had begun to think in western nationalistic and democratic terms. It was this new class of Asian intellectuals, some of whom also imbibed at the fountainheads of communism, rather than the old native elites, which provided the leadership of the colonial peoples in their struggle for emancipation from western tutelage. Although few of them rallied to the Japanese cause during the war, all of them were firmly opposed to western colonial rule after the war. On this point there was no difference between communists and nationalists. Such widely different leaders as Syngman Rhee, Chiang Kai-shek, Mao Tse-tung, Ho Chi Minh, Sukarno, U Nu, Nehru, and many Arab leaders agreed on little except that colonial control must not be restored where it had collapsed during the war and must disappear where it still held out.

The reaction of the colonial powers to the upsurge of nationalism among the colonial peoples varied. The United States, which had never felt comfortable in the role of a colonial power, began to liquidate its modest colonial possessions even before the war. After the war, although it alone among the colonial powers had the power to hold on to its possessions, it freed the Philippines. Although it was under no pressure from the Filipino people to leave, it hastened to implement its prewar pledge to grant independence to the Philippines. The British also showed an awareness of the transformation in the thinking of colonial peoples and began to liquidate their colonial empire and transform it into a commonwealth of independent nations. They generally anticipated movements to oust them and granted their colonial subjects a choice of complete freedom or association in the commonwealth. In this way they managed to preserve the good will of their former colonial subjects.

The French and Dutch, on the other hand, perhaps because of their isolation under German occupation and concentration on their own liberation, had lost touch with the trends in the colonial world. The French, whose revolutionary armies had once carried the gospel of nationalism and democracy as far as the Nile, showed a particular lack of understanding for the aspirations of colonial peoples. The Dutch and French efforts to reimpose colonial control in an undiluted form on their former possessions resulted in armed clashes. While the Dutch soon yielded and withdrew from their Indonesian empire, the French — extremely sensitive about their military prestige after their defeat at the hands of the Germans in 1940 — persisted in their efforts to reimpose their control by force. In this they showed a European parochial unawareness not only of the psychological transformation of the colonial peoples but also of their technological progress.

The European colonial empires were created in the eighteenth and nineteenth centuries, at a time when, because of the great discrepancy between the industrialized and non-industrialized nations, it took very little effort to conquer and subdue peoples lacking in modern technology, weapons, skills, and organization. Often actual use of force proved unnecessary. A mere display of it — for instance, dispatch of naval units to Alexandria, Saigon, or Shanghai — sufficed. However, by the mid-twentieth century this situation did not exist any more. The great masses of Asia and Africa were, indeed, still unaffected by industrialism. But in both continents there had grown up relatively large groups of men who had acquired technical and military skills in the service of Europeans. To them the rifle, machine gun, bazooka, grenade launcher, or mortar held no mystery any more. And weapons were easily available. After World War II, as after all great wars, there were stocks of surplus weapons all over the world which could be seized or purchased in the great illegal arms markets in Hongkong, Singapore, Naples, or Brussels. The colonial peoples were now able to meet the Europeans on more even terms.

As a result of these changes, the French encountered stiff resistance in their efforts to restore their colonial control or maintain it in areas where it had not been disturbed by the war. They were forced into a series of colonial wars from Indochina to Morocco, the last of which ended in 1962. Unlike the British, the French invariably overstayed their welcome. They withdrew usually only under pressure of superior force — and then with such poor grace that they forfeited any good will on the part of their former colonial subjects that they might have otherwise preserved. Their belated efforts to transform the French colonial empire into a French Community of Nations on the pattern of the British Commonwealth of Nations generally have not been successful. Long denied autonomy, the French colonial subjects, when given the choice of freedom or association in the French Community of Nations, have generally rushed into independence, often ill prepared for nationhood, and have cut abruptly their valuable cultural and economic ties to France and through her to the western world. The abrupt and panicky withdrawal of the Belgians from the Congo in 1960 has had similarly unfortunate results.

Only little Portugal, the first to enter the field of colonial enterprise, has shown no inclination to withdraw from it. But few observers doubt that the European colonial empires have had their day.

Section VIII: THE AFTERMATH OF THE WAR:

INTERNATIONAL AFFAIRS

46

THE PEACE SETTLEMENT: AN UNFINISHED BUSINESS

The mere conquest of our enemies is not enough. We must go on to do all in our power to conquer the doubts and fears, the ignorance and the greed, which made this horror possible . . .

FRANKLIN D. ROOSEVELT (1945)

1. THE UNITED NATIONS ORGANIZE

THE LEAGUE OF NATIONS, formed largely on American initiative in 1919 to promote world order and adjust international disputes, failed to avert the outbreak of a second world war twenty years later. Although it scored some successes in arbitrating disputes among smaller nations, it was powerless to restrain the major powers upon which the peace of the world depended. It was crippled from its origins by abstentions, defections, and the defiance of the major powers: the United States turned its back on the League as early as 1920; Japan withdrew in 1933 after the League criticized Japanese aggression in Manchuria; Germany followed in the same year when Hitler rose to power; Italy walked out in 1937 after the League instituted sanctions against Italy for her aggression against Ethiopia; and Russia, which was admitted to the League only in 1934, was expelled in 1939 for her aggression against Finland. The only major powers which were continuously represented in the League were France and Britain. This fact led many of its critics to regard it — not entirely without justice — as little more than a Franco-British syndicate. With the defeat of France and the humiliation of Britain at the hands of Germany in 1940 the League was deprived of even their support and passed into complete oblivion.

During the course of World War II the Americans once again took the initiative to form a new international association to maintain peace. Rather than revive the moribund and discredited League, President Roosevelt proposed to transform the United Nations war machinery into a United Nations peace machinery. Soviet and British concurrence was secured at the conference of the Allied foreign secretaries in Moscow (October 19–

30, 1943), when it was announced that the Allies intended to establish "at the earliest practicable date a general international organization, based on the principle of the sovereign equality of all peace-loving States, and open to membership by all such States, large and small, for the maintenance of international peace and security." A plan for the organization, to be known as the United Nations, was worked out by representatives of the major Allied powers at a conference at Dumbarton Oaks, an estate in Washington, D.C. (August 21–October 7, 1944). The plan, which was published, was approved by the Big Three at the Yalta conference (February 4–11, 1945). Roosevelt, Churchill, and Stalin further agreed at Yalta on the controversial voting procedure in the proposed Security Council of the United Nations, which provided that "substantive" (nonprocedural) decisions must be approved by seven of its eleven members, including all of its permanent members (i.e., the great powers). This "unanimity clause" meant in effect that the great powers would have a veto over the decisions of the Security Council. On the ground that the members of the British Empire would be separately represented in the proposed Assembly of the United Nations, as they had been in the League of Nations, and the British Empire would have several votes, Stalin demanded sixteen votes for the sixteen constituent republics of the Soviet Union. However, when it was pointed out to him that the United States could on the same ground demand forty-eight votes for the forty-eight states of the American Union, he contented himself with two extra votes, for the Ukrainian and Bielorussian (White Russian) constituent republics. The Big Three further agreed at Yalta to invite all Allied nations and such nations as might declare war on the Axis powers by March 1 to a general conference at San Francisco to draft the United Nations Charter. To meet this deadline and qualify as "peace-loving states," Turkey, Egypt, and several other smaller countries hastened to issue paper declarations of war on the Axis powers.

The fighting in Germany and Italy had reached its dramatic and terrible finale when the delegates of fifty Allied nations met in San Francisco to found the United Nations.[1] In two months (April 25–June 26) they completed a charter for the United Nations. The organizational structure of the new international association resembled closely that of the League of Nations. As in the League, its principal organs were the Security

[1] The nations represented at the San Francisco conference, which might be considered charter members of the United Nations were: Argentina, Australia, Belgium, Bolivia, Brazil, Bielorussia, Canada, Chile, Colombia, Costa Rica, Cuba, Czechoslovakia, Denmark, the Dominican Republic, Ecuador, Egypt, El Salvador, Ethiopia, France, Great Britain, Guatemala, Haiti, Honduras, India, Iran, Iraq, Lebanon, Liberia, Luxemburg, Mexico, the Netherlands, New Zealand, Nicaragua, Norway, Panama, Paraguay, Peru, the Philippines, Saudi Arabia, the South African Union, the Soviet Union, Turkey, the Ukraine, the United States, Uruguay, Venezuela, and Yugoslavia. Ironically, the oldest Allied nation, Poland, was not represented, because of disagreement between Soviet Russia and the western Allies as to whether the exiled Polish Government in London or the Communist-dominated Polish government in Warsaw should represent Poland.

Council, the Assembly, the International Court of Justice, and the Secretariat.

The Security Council, which was the executive organ of the United Nations, was composed of five permanent members (the United States, Great Britain, Russia, France, and China) and six nonpermanent members (elected for two-year terms from among the smaller nations with the tacit understanding that they should be representative at all times of the principal regions of the world). The second chamber, the Assembly, was to form a sort of international deliberative parliament in which all member states, whether large or small, had one vote. The third organ, the International Court of Justice, was to adjudicate international disputes, submitted to it voluntarily by sovereign states. Like the League, the United Nations disclaimed any right "to intervene in matters which are essentially within the domestic jurisdiction of any state" (Article 2). The Secretariat, with permanent headquarters in New York, consisted of a corps of international civil servants headed by a Secretary General. However, conscious of the weaknesses of the League of Nations, the Founding Fathers of the United Nations took steps to strengthen its organs analogous to those of the League, and created some new organs which the League did not have.

The Council of the League of Nations had no authority to employ armed force against an aggressor nation; it could only recommend various forms of diplomatic or economic pressure. Article 43 of the United Nations Charter provided that if such pressures failed, the Security Council could call upon member states to assist in restraining an unruly neighbor, if necessary, by armed force. To allay the fears — principally of Soviet Russia — lest this provision be misused by one group of members of the Security Council as a tool to coerce another one, it had been agreed already at the Yalta conference to give permanent members of the Security Council veto powers over its decisions. At the San Francisco conference this procedure came under sharp criticism of some spokesmen of the "little forty-five nations" who feared lest it provide the "Big Five" with a handy club over the smaller nations. But, even though the East-West tension was already apparent at the San Francisco conference, on this particular point the United States and Russia as well as the other larger powers saw eye to eye, and on their insistence the controversial voting procedure for the Security Council was adopted into the United Nations Charter (Article 27). On the other hand, to allay the fears of American isolationists lest the extension of the powers of the Security Council under Article 43 usurp the sovereign right of the United States Congress to declare war on behalf of the American nation, the provision was hedged with many conditions which made of it considerably less than a blind commitment to go to war at the summons of the Security Council. Believing that the roots of wars were often social and economic, the Founding Fathers of the United Nations created a new organ which the

League of Nations did not have: the Economic and Social Council, a body designed to function under the direction of the Assembly to promote economic stability, friendly intercourse, and general welfare among all peoples. To prevent the United Nations from becoming an exclusive club of the victors in World War II — as the League of Nations tended to be after World War I — the San Francisco conference provided that membership should be open to all "peace-loving States" on recommendation of the Security Council and a two-thirds vote of the Assembly (Article 5).[2]

The United Nations Charter was speedily ratified by the member governments. Unlike in 1919, the United States Senate did not balk but ratified the Charter by a vote of 89 to 2 (December 4, 1945), for this time the American people were in the majority unquestionably behind the new world organization. The ratification of Great Britain was deposited on October 20, and that of the Soviet Union on October 24. The latter date saw the total ratification reach 29, the number required to bring the Charter officially into effect. The United Nations thus became a historical reality on October 24, 1945. With this formal appearance of a new world league, the older League of Nations lost meaning. It was dissolved at a final session held at Geneva on April 18, 1946, after voting to hand over its property, such as its splendid Palace of Nations at Lake Geneva, to the United Nations.

While the function of the main organs of the United Nations has been to promote international peace and security, there has grown up around the United Nations a host of "specialized agencies" to promote international cooperation and good will in such fields as transportation and communications, health and nutrition, currencies and credit, labor standards and women's and children's rights, control of narcotics, etc. The origin and the relationship of these specialized agencies to the United Nations greatly vary. Some of them, like the International Telecommunications Union (1865), the Universal Postal Union (1874), or the International Meteorological Organization (1878), are quite old and are only loosely associated with the United Nations. Others, like the International Labor Office, whose concern is the improvement of labor conditions, have been inherited from the League of Nations. Other agencies have been founded since 1946 under the Economic and Social Council of the United Nations to attend to special economic, social, and cultural problems on an international scale: the United Nations Educational, Scientific, and Cultural Organization (UNESCO), with headquarters in Paris, to encourage exchange of useful cultural information and scientific discoveries;

[2] By 1966 the membership of the United Nations had grown to 117. A large portion of this number were the newly constituted Afro-Asian nations. The only nations of consequence which did not belong were Switzerland, which declined to join because of preference for complete neutrality, Red China, and the "Cold-War twins" — East and West Germany, North and South Korea, and North and South Viet Nam — which were excluded because of the East-West deadlock.

the Food and Agricultural Organization (FAO), to raise nutritional levels in the world; the International Civil Aviation Organization (ICAO), to codify the rules and reduce the risks of air traffic; the World Health Organization (WHO), to combat epidemics and disease; the International Bank for Reconstruction and Development (World Bank), to provide funds for reconstruction and development; the International Monetary Fund, to help regulate and stabilize currencies; the International Refugee Organization (IRO), to repatriate and resettle refugees and displaced persons; the International Children's Emergency Fund (UNICEF); etc.

Other agencies have been created to attend to a specific and temporary problem. This was notably the case of the United Nations Relief and Rehabilitation Administration (UNRRA), founded in 1943 to relieve the misery resulting from World War II. Before this body turned over its duties to other permanent agencies in 1947 it spent over $4,000,000,000 (provided mainly by the United States) to alleviate the suffering of the sick and hungry in many parts of the world, including White Russia and the Ukraine. It undoubtedly saved thousands, perhaps millions, of lives.

The special agencies of the United Nations have performed in a quiet and undramatic way yeoman service in promoting international cooperation and good will. With the steady "shrinking of the globe" few social and economic problems remain national in scope or can be solved by national means alone. In the future, new special agencies of the United Nations will no doubt be set up to help to solve them.

2. THE PARIS PEACE TREATIES OF 1947

History shows that wartime alliances seldom outlive victory. Alliances are based on a variety of political, economic, and ideological interests, but their most binding force is fear — fear of a common enemy. When this enemy is defeated and the fear of him disappears there is little reason left to continue the alliance. Moreover, fear of one of the members of the alliance often takes the place of fear of the former enemy. There was little reason why the alliance of Britain, the United States, and Russia in World War II should be an exception to this general rule. It was based on a solid community of political, economic, and cultural interests between Britain and the United States, but between the western powers and Russia it was based solely on fear of the Axis powers. When the Axis powers were defeated, the common political, economic, and cultural interests existing between Britain and the United States remained, and the two nations continued to cooperate, but nothing remained to hold the western powers and Russia together. On the contrary, there appeared many reasons why they should distrust and fear each other. Yet the alliance of Britain, the United States, and Russia did not break up at once, but instead, as do all alliances, it underwent an evolution. It was strongest when the danger from the Axis powers was most acute, weakened when victory came in sight, and died slowly after victory. Of the three wartime conferences of the Big Three, the Teheran conference was marked by great cordiality but little practical accomplishment; the Yalta conference by considerable practical accomplishment and a mood alternately strained and cordial; and the Potsdam conference by further accomplishment and an atmosphere of cold reserve but determination to "get along" — at least, until the conclusion of peace.

It was decided at Potsdam to hold no further Big Three conferences but to create the Council of Foreign Ministers and charge it with the task of preparing the peace treaties, first with the Axis satellites and later with Germany and Japan. The first meeting of the Council of Foreign Ministers was held in London (September 11–October 3, 1945) and proved a complete failure. The British Foreign Secretary, Ernest Bevin, and the United States Secretary of State, James Byrnes, insisted on inclusion of French and Chinese representatives. The Soviet Foreign Minister, Vyacheslav Molotov, reluctantly agreed, but when the French and Chinese voted with the western ministers he went back on his assent. The meeting broke up after weeks of acrid wrangling. The ministers were unable to agree even on the final communiqué registering their disagreement. Nevertheless, they left behind their deputies, who after months of toil produced draft treaties for peace with Italy, Hungary, Rumania, Bulgaria, and Finland. The Council of Foreign Ministers took up the discussion of the draft treaties at three meetings in Moscow, London, and Paris (December 16–26, 1945, April 25–May 16, 1946, and June 15–July 12, 1946). The ministers clashed on point after point: on the disposition of the Italian colonies, on reparations, on the status of Trieste, on the treatment of the Franco regime in Spain, on the freedom of elections in Rumania and Bulgaria, and other points. Twice they referred the draft treaties back to their deputies, but on adjourning for the third time on July 12 they issued a bland announcement that they were in substantial agreement on all essential issues.

On July 29, 1946, twenty-one Allied nations, which had "actively waged war with substantial military forces against European enemy states," [3] met in a peace conference at the Luxembourg Palace in Paris to approve the peace terms for Italy, Rumania, Hungary, Bulgaria, and Finland. In a purely formal way, the Paris Peace Conference of 1946 adhered to the Wilsonian ideal of "open covenants openly arrived at" more closely than the Paris Peace Conference of 1919; the proceedings were public and the defeated nations were given a chance to plead their cause. In reality,

[3] The twenty-one Allied nations which participated in the Paris conference were: Australia, Belgium, Bielorussia, Brazil, Canada, China, Czechoslovakia, Ethiopia, France, Great Britain, Greece, India, the Netherlands, New Zealand, Norway, Poland, the South African Union, the Soviet Union, the Ukraine, the United States, and Yugoslavia. Some thirty other Allied nations, which had issued only paper declarations of war on the Axis, were excluded from the conference.

however, the proceedings were scarcely democratic. The draft treaties had been prepared in advance by the Council of Foreign Ministers and had to be returned to it afterward for its approval. When some of the smaller nations of Western Europe and of the British Empire took issue with the terms submitted to the conference by the Council, the Big Three stuck together and imposed their solution. Although Russia and the western powers were by then scarcely on speaking terms, great-power solidarity outweighed other considerations. Unlike the smaller nations of Western Europe and of the British Empire, the smaller nations of Eastern Europe (Poland, Czechoslovakia, and Yugoslavia, which — together with Soviet Russia, the Ukraine, and White Russia — constituted the "Slavic Block") voted in a disciplined fashion according to the instructions of the Soviet delegation. The addition of the East-West hostility to the natural tension between the victors and vanquished confused and prolonged the debates for two months and a half.

Generally speaking, territorial questions figured less prominently in the deliberations of the Paris Peace Conference of 1946 than in those of the Paris Peace Conference of 1919. This was because many old territorial disputes in Europe had been "solved" by the evil principle of forced transfers and exchanges of minorities in the days immediately preceding and following the end of hostilities (see p. 534). The principal territorial changes in Europe resulting from World War II concerned the western border of Russia, the eastern border of Germany, and the Italian border with Yugoslavia. The question of Germany's boundary with Poland, however, did not come within the purview of the Paris Peace Conference which dealt only with Germany's satellites.

Russia was determined to keep the territories which she had gained from Finland, Poland, and Rumania, as well as the Baltic states she had absorbed, first partly in cooperation with Nazi Germany in 1939–1940, then lost during the German invasion, and finally reconquered in 1944–1945. The western powers concurred in the Soviet demands, in principle at the Teheran conference and more explicitly at the Yalta conference. The Paris Peace Conference was called on to confirm formally only the territorial losses of Finland and Rumania, since technically only they were "defeated" nations. Poland, which was technically a "victorious" nation, ceded her eastern territory to Russia, in theory voluntarily, by a treaty signed on April 22, 1945. Czechoslovakia, another "victorious" nation, was also called on to make a "voluntary" tribute of territory to her Big Slav Brother. By a treaty signed on June 29, 1945, she ceded to Russia her easternmost province, Ruthenia (known also as Subcarpathian Russia, Carpatho-Ukraine, or Transcarpathian Ukraine). Russia also seized, with the acquiescence of the western powers at Potsdam, a slice of East Prussia, including its capital Königsberg (renamed Kaliningrad). Most of the Soviet territorial annexations could be justified on historical or ethnic grounds; most of them had belonged to the Russian Empire

TERRITORIAL CHANGES IN EUROPE RESULTING FROM WORLD WAR II

before 1914 or were inhabited by White Russian and Ukrainian populations, or both. It may be legitimately doubted, however, whether their
populations, if freely consulted, would have voted to be included in Russia.
In making these annexations, the Soviet government was undoubtedly
motivated primarily by strategic and political considerations, since they
added about 200,000 square miles of territory and about 22,000,000 inhabitants to her territory and population and projected her border as much as
300 miles westward. This greatly improved the Soviet defense position.
The acquisition of Ruthenia put the Soviet army on the southern slopes
of the Carpathian Mountains, which the Russian armies had found difficult to penetrate in both world wars. It also gave Russia a common border
with Hungary and thus strengthened her hold on the Danubian plain.

The rectification of the Italo-Yugoslav border caused trouble at the
Paris Peace Conference in 1946, as it had in 1919. The advantage of force
this time was on the side of Yugoslavia. In the final stages of the war,
Yugoslav partisans seized all territories disputed with Italy since World
War I (the ports of Zara and Fiume, Istria, Gorizia, Venezia Giulia,
and the Adriatic islands). They briefly held also the great port of Trieste,
but were later displaced from it by American and British troops. At the
Paris Peace Conference, Yugoslavia refused to bargain over the former
Italian territories which she held (ethnically they were in the main Yugoslav), and with Soviet backing loudly demanded Trieste. Italy, in an
effort to limit her losses and to enlist the support of the United States,
based her claims on the proposals for an Italo-Yugoslav boundary made
in 1919 by President Wilson — which at that time the Italians had bitterly
resented. In the end, the Yugoslavs were confirmed in the possession of
all the territories which they held, and Trieste was set up as a free territory under the protection of the United Nations Security Council.[4] The
port was of primary economic importance neither to Italy nor to Yugoslavia but to the countries of the Central European hinterland — Austria,
Hungary, and Czechoslovakia — and these were best served by the solution adopted.

In addition to suffering losses to Yugoslavia in the Adriatic, Italy was
forced to yield the Dodecanese Islands in the Aegean to Greece. This,
too, was not a new problem but one left unsolved by World War I. At
the Paris Peace Conference in 1919 Italy had promised to cede to Greece
the Dodecanese Islands, inhabited mainly by Greeks, but later she had
backed out of her promise. Italy was also forced to cede some border
strips in the Alps to France. Finally, she was deprived of her colonial

---

[4] This sensible solution, which resembled the solution adopted for Danzig in 1919,
satisfied neither Italy nor Yugoslavia. Like Poland and Germany after 1919, they
continued to clamor for Trieste. Thus, Trieste in 1946 took the place of Fiume in
1919 as the source of international trouble in the Adriatic. In 1954 the great powers,
concerned by then only with the Cold War, agreed to abandon their earlier solution
and to partition the free territory. The city of Trieste, whose population was overwhelmingly Italian, was awarded to Italy, but the immediate countryside, which was
mainly Yugoslav in population, went to Yugoslavia.

empire. Because of disagreement among the Big Three on how to dispose of the Italian colonies (Russia had raised a claim to Libya), they (Libya, Eritrea, and Somaliland) were put under the authority of the United Nations Trusteeship Commission and temporarily left under the administration of the British army which had conquered them.[5] This decision did not apply to Ethiopia, which had been freed by British arms as early as 1941 and immediately restored to independence.

With the exception of the Italo-Yugoslav frontier, the territorial settlement in the Danubian region was, to a large extent, a return to the much criticized boundaries of the peace treaties of 1919–1920. Hungary came to Paris in 1946 with the hope of obtaining a rectification of her Trianon boundaries and found a champion in the Australian delegate, Herbert V. Evatt, but the western powers had had their fill of bargaining with Russia and were not prepared to help Hungary. On the other hand, Russia which in the past had often joined in pious invective against the inequities of the peace treaties of 1919–1920, having now satisfied her own appetite for territory, was not anxious to stir up a hornet's nest among the nations of Eastern Europe, all of which she regarded as her satellites. Hungary not only returned from Paris empty-handed, but was forced to cede to Czechoslovakia a small bridgehead on the right bank of the Danube opposite the Slovak capital of Bratislava. The only other territorial change in the Danubian region which the Paris Peace Conference approved, was to permit Bulgaria, the pivot of the Soviet Balkan policy, to retain southern Dobrudja, lost to Rumania in 1913 and recovered, with Hitler's aid, in 1940. Nevertheless, as a result of the various boundary rectifications and the forced transfers of population after World War II, the ethnic map of Eastern Europe became largely identical with its political map for the first time in modern history.

As with most territorial questions, so also the question of economic reparations had already been decided at the Paris Peace Conference by previous actions of the Soviet government. Russia had already exacted reparations from Finland, Rumania, and Hungary in the armistice treaties and had proceeded at once to collect them. It had also laid claim to all German external assets, not only in the territory of the former Axis satellites but in Allied countries of Eastern Europe as well. At the Paris Peace Conference Russia also determined to get something out of Italy. The former Axis satellites were assessed altogether $1,330,000,000 in reparations. Out of this sum Russia obtained the lion's share, $900,000,000 ($300,000,000 from Finland, $300,000,000 from Rumania, $200,000,000 from Hungary, and $100,000,000 from Italy). Yugoslavia was awarded the next largest sum, $200,000,000 ($125,000,000 from Italy, $50,000,000

---

[5] In 1950 the British handed the thankless task of administering Somaliland, which has little economic or strategic value, back to Italy. In 1960, during the general freeing of African colonies, it became independent. Libya became independent as early as 1951 and Eritrea was federated with Ethiopia in 1952.

from Hungary, and $25,000,000 from Bulgaria). Greece received $150,000,000 ($105,000,000 from Italy and $45,000,000 from Bulgaria). Czechoslovakia received $50,000,000 from Hungary. Ethiopia and Albania received $25,000,000 and $5,000,000, respectively, from Italy. While the reparations were to be paid in kind rather than in cash, they represented a heavy tribute from countries whose territory and economies had been ravaged by war. The former Axis satellites could, however, derive wry satisfaction from the fact that the Soviet "allies" in Eastern Europe — Poland, Czechoslovakia, and Yugoslavia — had to pay equally heavy tribute to Russia, disguised in a variety of ways. Russia was determined to get every possible assistance to restore her war-shattered economy and cared little where it came from.

The Paris peace treaties put strict limitations on the military, air, and naval establishments of the former Axis satellites. After World War I such limitations had proved unenforceable; after World War II they were soon rendered completely meaningless by the East-West split. Both Russia and the United States not only permitted, but actively assisted, the rearming of the ex-enemy countries drawn into their respective orbits.

The former Axis satellites were also forced to dissolve all fascist organizations and to extradite war criminals demanded for trial by their former enemies. They were also required to guarantee "the enjoyment of human rights and of fundamental freedoms" to all of their citizens — a provision, which in view of the contemporary communization of Eastern Europe and the persecution of anti-communists, proved a singularly hollow mockery.

On October 15, 1946, the delegates to the Paris Peace Conference finally approved the draft treaties and returned them to the Council of Foreign Ministers, which met in London (November 25–December 15, 1946) to put the finishing touches on them. On February 10, 1947, in the historic Clock Room of the French Foreign Ministry at the Quai d'Orsay in Paris, the peace treaties with Italy, Rumania, Hungary, Bulgaria, and Finland were signed.

3. ALLIED FAILURE TO DRAFT A GERMAN PEACE TREATY

After the conclusion of peace with Germany's former allies, the next task of the Council of Foreign Ministers was to draft peace treaties with Germany and Austria. The Council had considered the problem for some time, but made little headway because of increasing disagreements among the Allies over occupation policies in Germany. The Yalta conference had provided for joint occupation of Germany by the United States, Russia, Great Britain, and France and for the formation of the Allied Control Council to coordinate their policies. The Potsdam conference had laid down the broad principles and aims of Allied policy in Germany: Germany was to be demilitarized and deprived of ability to wage future wars by dismantling her war industries; she was to pay reparations for the destruction of Allied property by her armed forces; her public life was to be cleansed of Nazis and democratized; and German war criminals were to be tried.

In implementing these policies, the Allies agreed most readily on the punishing of war criminals. Hitler, Himmler, and Goebbels had committed suicide at the end of the war and Bormann had disappeared. But in November, 1945, twenty-two other top Nazis were indicted before the International Military Tribunal at Nürnberg for plots against peace and crimes against humanity. In September, 1946, after months of exhaustive hearings, nineteen were convicted and three acquitted. Of the condemned, ten were hanged, two committed suicide in prison, and seven were sentenced to various terms of imprisonment. The Allies also agreed on common denazification procedures, but differed widely on their application. The most zealous in trying to denazify their zone were the Americans. Eventually, however, after finding out that in a totalitarian state nearly all prominent personalities and innumerable lesser officials were compromised by the regime, they relented, and ultimately handed over the difficult task to German authorities. The Russians punished swiftly the conspicuous Nazis, but in dealing with lesser officials were guided by the person's usefulness and readiness to serve Soviet purposes. The British, who had the longest experience in ruling other peoples, were skeptical of the possibility of reforming the Germans and were moderate in their denazification efforts. The French tended to regard all Germans as evil and hopeless, whether they had been Nazis or not, and followed an opportunist course similar to that of the Russians.

On the methods by which to carry out their political and economic policies, the Allies clashed. The Potsdam declaration had called for "the decentralization of the political structure" of Germany and for the rapid restoration of self-government "on democratic principles." In implementing these principles the four occupants were guided by their respective national experience and their national interests. Each tried to refashion its zone according to its own image. The Americans set out with great enthusiasm and ultimately with considerable success to promote democratic self-government on a local and state (Land) level, on the federal principle. The British went along with the Americans, less out of conviction than out of a desire to cooperate with the United States, on which they were much dependent. The Russians formally abolished the state of Prussia, much of which they occupied, and restored various states (Länder) which had been merged into Prussia. They endowed these states with the ornamental autonomy enjoyed by the Soviet constituent republics, but they organized their whole zone along centralist and authoritarian lines. The French, following their historical policy of keeping Germany divided and weak, advocated a radical decentralization of Germany which would have reduced her to a loose confederation in the nature of the nineteenth-century German Confederation or the Holy Roman Empire. They controlled too small a portion of Germany to apply this policy effectively, but they detached the Saar district, rich in coal and iron, from Germany and attached it economically to France (December, 1946). Ultimately, they hoped to attach it to France politically.[6]

As the East-West conflict developed, the Allies became less concerned with reforming the Germans than with wooing them. Both Russia and the United States (supported by Britain and more hesitantly by France) sought to bring the whole of Germany under their influence. From the first the Russians had addressed themselves in their propaganda to all of Germany and they were the first of the occupants to permit formation of political parties, which they sought to infiltrate and use for their purposes. As the Communist Party had little appeal to the Germans, in their zone they engineered the merger of the Communist Party with the much larger Social Democratic Party into the Socialist Unity Party (April, 1946). However, the Social Democrats in the western zones repudiated this merger and foiled the Soviet attempts to infiltrate their ranks. The Americans were slower in developing political activity designed to influence all of Germany. However, in September, 1946, Secretary of State Byrnes, in an important address at Stuttgart, announced a new, lenient United States policy toward Germany. This represented the initial step in a vigorous American effort to win German support. Among the German parties the Americans favored the Christian Democratic Party.

The broad aim of the economic policy adopted at the Potsdam conference had been to strip Germany of heavy industry necessary to wage war, to revive light industries necessary to produce consumer goods, and to develop German agriculture to free Germany from dependence on food imports. German production was to be carefully regulated to cover the costs of the occupation armies, as well as to provide a surplus for reparations, thus making the Germans pay for the war. At the same time the German people were to be assured a reasonable minimum standard of living. Reparations were to be collected from Germany by the transfer of machinery and industrial equipment, the confiscation of the German merchant marine, the taking over of internal assets not needed for a minimum production, and the seizure of Germany's foreign assets. If this was insufficient to pay for reparations, the balance was to be provided from current production. At the Yalta conference the Soviet government demanded $10,000,000,000 in German reparations. At the Potsdam conference it repeated this demand, but agreed to satisfy from its share

[6] After the creation of the European Steel and Coal Community (1951), the Saar lost importance to France economically while it continued to create bad blood between France and West Germany — now both members of the western team — politically. As a result, France and West Germany signed an agreement (June 4, 1956), providing for the political reunion of the Saar with Germany in 1957 and its economic reintegration in 1960.

of reparations, the Polish claims against Germany, which in view of the frightful devastation of Poland were considerable. The Soviet demand was not unreasonable; the damages caused in Russia by the German armies certainly exceeded $10,000,000,000, even if the Soviet estimate of them — $128,000,000,000 — was exaggerated. In normal times Germany could have paid off the Soviet claim without straining her economy. At Yalta and Potsdam the United States and Britain evaded committing themselves on any specific figure, but they recognized that Russia had suffered in the war more than they and that she was entitled to a lion's share of the reparations. The Soviet occupation zone in Germany was largely agricultural and the western zones (especially the British zone which included the Ruhr district with its great complex of coal and steel industry) were more industrial. Therefore, it was decided at Potsdam that to supplement what she obtained from her zone, Russia was to be recompensed from the western zones by an additional ten per cent of the industrial equipment above normal German needs, with a further 15 per cent in exchange for food and commodities from the Soviet zone.

It would have been exceedingly difficult to implement this complex policy even by a single authority under normal peacetime conditions, let alone by four authorities, which failed to cooperate, and under conditions which were far from normal. The war and the accompanying destruction and dislocations had weakened and disorganized the German economy more than the Allies had anticipated, and it failed to produce enough to pay for the occupation and war reparations and at the same time maintain a minimum standard of living for the Germans.

Allied economic policy soon broke down completely. There were acute shortages of both industrial and agricultural products and the Allies found themselves in the position of having to import more goods than they took out of Germany — or of letting the Germans starve. As they faced deficits, each of the allies tried to keep the goods in short supply in their zones for their own use. In May, 1946, the British and the Americans discontinued reparations shipments to the Soviets, on the ground that the Russians had halted shipments of food into the western zones. To solve the problem the Americans reminded their allies that the Potsdam agreement had postulated the principle that Germany was to be treated as an "economic unit" and proposed to fuse the zones. On January 1, 1947, the British and American zones were merged into "Bizonia." Later France added her zone to form "Trizonia."

When the Council of Foreign Ministers met in Moscow (March 10–April 24, 1947) to consider the German and Austrian treaties the Russians still demanded $10,000,000,000 in German reparations and Four-Power administration of the Ruhr. The western ministers categorically refused the Soviet demands and the meeting broke up. The final meeting of the Council of Foreign Ministers in London (November 25–December 15, 1947) also ended in an East-West deadlock, and the Council adjourned *sine die.* Both Russia and the western powers came to the conclusion that an agreement over Germany was impossible and proceeded to consolidate their zones of occupation in Germany into their respective alliance systems. In September, 1949, the Western powers took the initiative to form the (Western) "Federal Republic of Germany"; in October Russia countered this move by organizing the (Eastern) "German Democratic Republic."

Austria was an innocent victim of the East-West deadlock in Germany. At the Moscow conference (October, 1943) the Allies had agreed to separate Austria from Germany and to treat her as a "liberated" rather than a defeated nation. When Soviet troops entered Vienna in April, 1945, Soviet authorities took the initiative in forming an Austrian government, and to head it summoned from retirement the veteran Austrian socialist Karl Renner, Chancellor of the first Austrian Republic in 1918. At Potsdam the Allies had agreed to recognize this government and also not to demand reparations from Austria. What stood in the way of peace with Austria was the question of German assets in Austria and Yugoslav territorial claims on Austria. After the *Anschluss* in 1938, the Germans, by questionable methods, had gained control of the major economic assets in Austria, and Russia now claimed these assets. A deadlock developed in the Council of Foreign Ministers over this question and the question of Yugoslav territorial claims. After the break between Yugoslavia and Russia in 1948, the Soviet government ceased to support the Yugoslav claims but held out on the question of the German assets in Austria. This relatively unimportant matter does not seem to have been the real reason why Russia held out so long against concluding peace with Austria. It was rather her desire to use Austria as a means to force the western Allies to make concessions in Germany.

In 1955, during a brief truce in the Cold War, Russia yielded to the western powers and agreed to the conclusion of a state treaty [7] with Austria, providing for Soviet evacuation and the restoration of Austrian sovereignty (see p. 652). But no peace treaty was concluded with Germany. The lines of demarcation separating the Soviet zone from the western zones, determined at Yalta, were intended to be temporary. They became frozen into an apparently permanent international frontier between the West German state associated with the western alliance and the East German state integrated into the Soviet Bloc.

[7] The Allies concluded a "state" treaty rather than a "peace" treaty with Austria because Austria was technically not an enemy but a liberated country.

47

THE SOVIET POLICY OF EXPANSION

. . . it is necessary that the anti-imperialist, democratic camp should close its ranks . . . against the forces of the imperialist camp, against American imperialism and its British and French allies.

FIRST MANIFESTO OF THE COMINFORM, WARSAW, OCTOBER, 1947

1. THE POSTWAR AIMS OF SOVIET RUSSIA

THE AIMS OF RUSSIA in World War II were clear and definite. For the most part they were historical Russian aims; in fact there was a remarkable similarity between the objectives of Tsarist Russia in World War I and the objectives of Soviet Russia in World War II. However, Tsarist Russia failed to achieve its objectives in World War I, whereas Soviet Russia succeeded in attaining most of its objectives in World War II. The most striking feature of Russian history has been expansion, although the motivation of and the justification for this expansion have varied: unification of Russian-inhabited lands, search for outlets to warm seas, considerations of national security, the logic of strategy, economic advantage — all of these have been involved. Historically, Russia has expanded in three directions: westward into Europe, southward into the lands adjoining the eastern Mediterranean, and eastward toward the Pacific. Beyond this immediate area of Russian expansion, Russia has long sought to exert an influence in the countries adjoining her borders on the ground that they have often been avenues for invasion. In World War II Soviet Russia followed the historical Russian trend toward expansion and by the end of the hostilities had attained considerable success: she had recovered the territorial losses which she had suffered in 1918; she had rounded out her borders to include (for the first time in history) all Russian-inhabited lands; she had won a broad sphere of influence in Eastern Europe; and she had retrieved the positions in the Far East, which Tsarist Russia had first gained and then lost in the Russo-Japanese War. She had failed, however, to attain the historical Russian objectives in the eastern Mediterranean.

The postwar objectives of Russia were to consolidate her gains, to try to achieve those objectives which she had hoped but had failed to attain during the war, and to exploit any opportunity that might present itself for strengthening and extending her influence in any part of the world. In sum, peace was to her only a continuation of war by other means — to paraphrase the famous maxim of Clausewitz. In this "war" in time of peace — popularly known as the "Cold War" — the Soviet army, since it remained the largest army in the world, continued to exert a powerful influence, although an indirect one. But Russia did not lack other weapons for the Cold War. Her diplomacy represented a formidable and disciplined weapon, and it had an advantage enjoyed by all dictatorial countries: it could maneuver swiftly without the necessity of consulting and preparing public opinion for its sudden tactical reversals. Soviet propaganda did not disdain such old-fashioned tools of Tsarist diplomacy as appeals to Slav and Greek Orthodox solidarity, but it also exploited to the full Soviet achievements in atomic science and missiles. Apart from diplomacy and propaganda, for some time Russia had at her disposal a weapon for which her opponents had no equivalent: the disciplined world-wide communist movement — groups of men ever ready to sow strife and dissension in their own countries or to rise against their own governments at a signal from Moscow. Later the Soviet-Yugoslav break, the Sino-Soviet conflict, and the emergence of "communist polycentrism" diminished the usefulness of this weapon. In 1949, impressed with the great political import of the United States' Marshall Plan in Western Europe, the Soviet government established the "Council for Mutual Economic Assistance" for Eastern Europe. In the immediate postwar years, however, Russia used the satellite economies for her own reconstruction. It was not until the 1950's, when its economy had recovered from the war, that Russia was able to exercise an economic influence in the world.

The multiple Soviet activities in Europe, the Near and Middle East, and the Far East caused alarm among the former allies of Russia and before long provoked resistance. The western world, led by the United States, began to organize to contain Soviet influence. As western policy stiffened, so also did Soviet policy. At first Soviet policy was relatively flexible. Since the Soviet leaders still hoped to obtain economic aid from the western powers to help restore their war-ravaged economy, they did not wish to break with them openly — at least not until conclusion of peace and international recognition of the gains they had made in the war. Later, however, after 1947 and the consummation of the East-West break, Soviet policy grew completely rigid in its unrelenting hostility to the western world at every point and level of contact. After the death of Stalin in 1953, his successors recognized that the rigid Soviet policy had ceased to pay dividends. They proclaimed their desire for "peaceful coexistence" between the communist and non-communist worlds and reverted to a more flexible policy. Western statesmen and observers, however, were generally agreed that the Soviet call for peaceful coexistence did not represent any basic change in Soviet aims and purposes, but only a change in tactics.

2. SOVIET SATELLIZATION OF EASTERN EUROPE

Perhaps the foremost postwar aim of Russia was the satellization of Eastern Europe. After World War I, when French influence was preponderant in Eastern Europe, France sought to organize its nations into a *cordon sanitaire* against the westward spread of communism. Later French influence was replaced with German influence, which was also hostile to Russia. During World War II the nations of Eastern Europe were forced to make a considerable contribution to the Axis war effort, especially against Russia. When victory for the Allies came into sight, Soviet leaders determined that this situation must not arise again after the war; there would be a *cordon sanitaire* again, but it would be one turned against the west. The prospect of the extension of Soviet influence over Eastern Europe — an area comprising some 560,000 square miles and a population of about 100,000,000 — disquieted British statesmen, but American leaders, except for some officials in the lower echelons of the United States government, were not alarmed. Failing to secure American support to limit the extension of Soviet influence in Eastern Europe, British statesmen sought to protect their Mediterranean lifeline by securing a sphere of influence at least in Southeastern Europe by agreement with Russia (see the Churchill-Stalin agreement of October, 1944, p. 520).

However, while American officials did not object to the extension of Soviet influence in Eastern Europe, they hoped that this would not preclude the establishment of truly democratic governments, enjoying genuine internal autonomy, even though aligned in foreign policy with Soviet Russia. It was on American insistence that the Big Three issued at Yalta the "Declaration on Liberated Europe," in which they pledged themselves to restore "sovereign rights and self-government to those peoples who have been forcibly deprived of them by aggressor nations." This noble declaration remained a dead letter in Eastern Europe, principally because — as Stalin frankly admitted at Potsdam — "any freely elected government would be anti-Soviet and that we cannot permit." Toward the end of the war, when American leaders became aware of the real Soviet intentions in Eastern Europe they were dismayed, but they were not prepared to challenge them. On April 23, 1945, President Truman summoned a conference of political and military officials at the White House to consider the Soviet violations of the Yalta agreement in Poland and elsewhere in Eastern Europe. The Secretary of War, the venerable Henry L. Stimson, President Hoover's former Secretary of State, counseled against action on the ground that "the Balkans and their troubles were beyond the sphere of proper United States action," and General Marshall warned that a break with Moscow might destroy the hope "for Soviet participation in the war against Japan at a time when it would be useful to us." It was decided to send Harry Hopkins, a confidant of former President Roosevelt, on a mission to Moscow to "talk things out" with the Soviet leaders. A few days later, as a sign of American displeasure over Soviet actions, it was decided to halt shipments of Lend-Lease supplies to the European Allies immediately upon conclusion of hostilities in Europe. This action produced no results; Stalin expressed disapproval of it to Hopkins, but proved no more amenable. Nothing more was done to save the countries of Eastern Europe from Soviet domination.

Therefore, it was with western acquiescence that Soviet Russia proceeded to satellize the nations of Eastern Europe, and her task was facilitated by the conditions which prevailed in the region after the war. Having been a battlefield, alternately occupied by the Germans and the Russians, Eastern Europe was physically and morally exhausted. Her political and intellectual leaders had been decimated by war, executions, and exile, and, except for Czechoslovakia (and that only the western, Czech, half), East European countries had no strong democratic traditions. Undoubtedly, Russia could have imposed on them without much difficulty full-blown communist regimes immediately after their occupation by the Soviet army, but out of regard for western opinion — at least, until the conclusion of the satellite peace treaties and the legalization of their international status — Russia preferred to move gradually and give the process the outward appearance of orderly, legal, and spontaneous changes. In the wake of the advance of the Soviet army in Eastern Europe in 1944–1945, Soviet security police rounded up all known anti-communists and sundry other "fascists" (most of the real fascists had already fled with the retreating Germans) and deported them to Siberia. Soviet authorities also saw to it that communists were represented in the East European governments formed after the collapse of the pro-German wartime regimes. Thereafter, however, they interfered only in exceptional cases and left matters in the hands of native communists.

However, while outwardly aloof, Russia exerted a continuous and strong pressure on the East European governments. The mere presence of Soviet troops on their soil was a deterrent to independent action. During their advance in 1944–1945, Soviet troops committed many outrages, which had left the population terrified. Although Soviet occupation troops were better disciplined, the fear of them remained; the squat figure of the Soviet soldier with a submachine gun slung across his chest became the dreaded symbol of the crude might of Russia. The Soviet government used several old but still serviceable imperialist methods of strengthening its control over the East European countries. The reparations, which had been inscribed in the armistice treaties and which the Soviet government proceeded to collect at once, provided it with a handy club to wield over the heads of the former Axis satellites. The Soviet claim to all German economic assets in Eastern Europe, recognized by the western powers at Potsdam, gave it unlimited possibilities of blackmailing East European governments, whether Allied or ex-enemy.

Another method by which the Soviet government strengthened its control over the East European countries was to exploit their old nationalist rivalries and their fear and hatred of Germany, engendered by Hitler's criminal policies. Native communists never tired of stressing that "only by loyal cooperation with Soviet Russia" could they hope to realize their national aspirations at the forthcoming peace conference, and communists often outdid old-fashioned nationalists in chauvinism. Thus, the Czech communists were the most vehement in demanding the complete expulsion of the Sudeten German minority — including the Sudeten German communists — from Czechoslovakia. Often communists in two East European countries advocated, with the seeming approval of the Soviet government, conflicting aspirations. This was notably the case of the Polish communists and the East German communists with regard to the Oder-Neisse border. At Teheran and Yalta the Big Three had agreed that Poland should be "compensated" for her territorial losses to Russia in the east at the expense of Germany in the west. But the western leaders evaded committing themselves on any specific cessions. In May, 1945, the Soviet government, without consulting the western governments, handed over to Poland the German territory up to the Oder and Neisse Rivers. Faced with this *fait accompli,* the western leaders reluctantly acquiesced in it at Potsdam, with the reservation that the question should be definitely decided at the peace conference with Germany. While the Polish communists assured their compatriots that only Russia would support this territorial acquisition at the peace conference, at the same time East German communists held out the hope to their compatriots that if they cooperated with Russia, she might yet restore the disputed territory to Germany. Angered by this double game, the United States decided to force Russia to make her stand clear. Bidding for German support and writing off East Europe as a loss, Secretary of State Byrnes in his Stuttgart address in September, 1946 (see p. 555), announced the reversal of United States support of the Oder-Neisse border. Molotov was then forced to come out and endorse unequivocally the Polish claim. This had the effect of weakening the communist cause in Germany but strengthening it in Eastern Europe. It gave substance to the allegation of East European communists that American policy was "pro-German," and that the East European countries could rely only on Soviet Russia to protect them against German revisionism.

After the conclusion of the Paris peace treaties in January, 1947, the formal distinction between Allied and enemy nations disappeared. Their former alignments were replaced with a series of bilateral treaties, tying them to Soviet Russia and to one another. With certain exceptions (Greece and Finland), all East European countries now became satellites of Russia.

3. SOVIET PRESSURE ON TURKEY, IRAN, GREECE, AND YUGOSLAVIA

By satellizing the nations of Eastern Europe, Russia succeeded in covering her western approaches against invasion, such as the Germans carried out in the two world wars. Another old invasion route of Russia was by way of the lands adjoining the eastern Mediterranean and the Persian Gulf: Greece, Turkey, and Iran. The central problem of Soviet defense against an invasion from the south was the question of the control of the Bosporus and Dardanelles Straits. The Soviet leaders discussed the problem with the western leaders at the wartime conferences of the Big Three. The western powers agreed at Yalta and reaffirmed at Potsdam that the Montreux Convention, which had regulated the status of the Straits since 1936 and was due to expire in 1946, "should be revised as failing to meet present-day conditions."

On February 23, 1945, in order not to be left out when the status of the Straits was decided, Turkey, which had until then remained steadfastly neutral, declared war on Germany and joined the United Nations coalition. This belated gesture, however, did not save her from Soviet pressures. On March 20, 1945, the Soviet government denounced the Soviet-Turkish friendship pact of 1925 and inaugurated a press campaign to secure bases in the Straits and to obtain Kars and Ardahan in eastern Turkey, which Imperial Russia had conquered from Turkey in 1878 and Soviet Russia had lost in 1918. However, the Turks do not frighten easily, nor did the Soviet government find in Turkey a built-in fifth column in the form of a communist party, ready to bring pressure to bear on its own government, as in some of the other neighbors of Russia. The Turkish government kept the Turkish army mobilized and in the negotiations with Moscow, which opened in June, 1945, firmly resisted the Soviet demands. It received at first little backing from the western powers. The United States suggested as a possible basis of a new status for the Straits the internationalization of all major European waterways. Later, however, when the Cold War broke out, the western powers firmly backed Turkey, and the Soviet-Turkish negotiations broke down definitely in October, 1946. Although Turkey's economy was nearly bankrupt from the strain of continued mobilization, she had not yielded anything.[1]

Soviet policy was equally unsuccessful in Iran, which, it will be re-

---

[1] Russia took revenge at the Danube Conference of ten nations, which met in Belgrade to determine the status of the Danube River (July 30–August 18, 1948). The conference, at which Russia and her satellites had a majority, voted down the United States proposal for internationalization and approved the Soviet proposal to create a Danube Commission limited to "riparian" nations (i.e., those touching the river).

called, was occupied in 1941 jointly by Soviet and British troops (see p. 476). Subsequently, American troops arrived to reorganize the country's railways and roads for shipping Lend-Lease supplies to Russia. At the Teheran conference the Big Three pledged to respect the sovereignty and independence of Iran and at the Potsdam conference to evacuate the country within six months after the conclusion of hostilities, that is, by March 2, 1946. However, during the war, the Soviet government encouraged the growth of a secret communist party, the Tudeh Party, in its zone of occupation and the growth of a secessionist movement in Iranian Azerbaydjan, which adjoined Soviet Azerbaydjan. After the war, American troops left Iran by January and British troops by February, 1946, but by March 2, 1946, Soviet troops had failed to leave. The Iranian government, with British and American backing, brought the matter before the United Nations Security Council. This case was the first international dispute brought before the Council, and the attendant unfavorable publicity apparently decided the Soviet government to back down. While the Soviet delegate in the United Nations stalled, the Soviet government entered into direct negotiations with the Iranian government, and on March 24, 1946, a deal was announced, under the terms of which the Iranian government granted Russia an oil concession in northern Iran to match the British oil concession in southern Iran. By May, Soviet troops were withdrawn from the country. After their withdrawal, Iranian troops re-entered Azerbaydjan, and the secessionist movement in the province collapsed. In September, 1947, the Iranian parliament refused to ratify the Soviet oil concession. The Soviet government loudly complained of Iranian duplicity, and there was fear that it might intervene in the country, but by then the Cold War was crackling on many fronts. The United States, which was already extending military and economic aid to Greece and Turkey under the "Truman Doctrine" (see below), granted Iran a military credit of $25,000,000 and promised to send a military mission to assist in reorganizing the Iranian army. The crisis passed away.

Meanwhile, Greece was in a more parlous situation. It has been seen how Churchill and Stalin agreed in Moscow in October, 1944, that Greece should be in the British sphere of influence (see p. 521). The Soviet government abided by this agreement until after the war when inter-Allied cooperation broke down. It made no protest when British troops landed in Greece in October, 1944, and prevented the Greek communist partisan forces (ELAS) from seizing Athens and installing a government of the communist-organized National Liberation Front (EAM). The communists, however, continued to thrive in the anarchy and civil strife which smoldered in the war-ravaged country. In March, 1946, elections were held, which the communists boycotted and which consequently resulted in a non-communist victory. In May, the communists reopened the civil war in full force. Their operations centered in the northern districts, adjoining the Soviet satellites — Albania, Yugoslavia, and Bulgaria

— which assisted them by providing military supplies, food, and refuge areas. On the other hand, the British continued to assist the Greek government. It was assumed in the West at the time that the Greek communists were acting on orders from Moscow. However, after the Soviet-Yugoslav break in 1948, it transpired from Yugoslav sources that the Soviet leaders had serious misgivings about the Greek civil war, and that the support it received from abroad came not from Soviet Russia but from communist Yugoslavia, Bulgaria, and Albania. Nevertheless, in February, 1947, when the British government, pleading financial stringency, asked the United States to take over the support of the Greek royalist government, President Truman decided to comply in the name of fighting international communism. Before long, under the "Truman Doctrine" (see next chapter), American aid began to flow into Greece, and an American military mission arrived to assist the Greek royal army. The communists denounced the Athens government as a tool of American imperialism and in September, 1947, formed a "Provisional Government of Free Greece" under "General" Marko Vafiades. However, after the Soviet-Yugoslav break in 1948, communist Yugoslavia, Bulgaria, and Albania closed their frontiers with Greece. In October, 1949, the Greek communists, left to their own devices, succumbed to the forces of the Greek royalist government, which was supported by the United States.

In September, 1947, as both East and West girded for the Cold War, representatives of communist parties from Eastern and Western Europe met in Poland and founded the Communist Information Bureau (Cominform), with permanent headquarters in Belgrade, to coordinate their activities. This revival, in a modified form, of the former Comintern represented an effort on the part of the Soviet government to strengthen, discipline, and revitalize the international communist movement as a tool of Soviet policy. Unexpectedly, however, it encountered resistance on the part of the Yugoslav Communist Party.

The Yugoslav Communist Party had been built up during the war by "Marshal Tito" (Josip Broz), a tough Croat communist and former Comintern agent. Until 1948 he was believed to be the favorite satrap of Moscow, but behind the scenes friction had developed between the Soviet and Yugoslav governments. Unlike other peoples of Eastern Europe, the Yugoslavs had a tradition of independence which affected even their communists. This trait was strengthened by the fact that they had liberated themselves from the Axis rule largely through their own efforts. During the war they received weapons and supplies from the Western powers but only very little help from Russia. After the war the Yugoslav communists were disenchanted with the Soviet failure — in Yugoslav eyes — to give strong support to the new communist nations of Eastern Europe and foreign communist movements (for instance, in Greece) against the Western "Imperialists." Friction also developed between the Soviet and Yugoslav governments over alleged Soviet attempts to exploit

Yugoslavia economically and to infiltrate the Yugoslav state and party apparatus with spies.

One of the subjects discussed at the founding congress of the Cominform in 1947 was the formation of a Balkan union under communist aegis. Generally speaking, the Soviet government did not favor regional organizations. It preferred to deal with its satellites singly rather than collectively. It had shown this by concluding with them a series of bilateral alliance treaties rather than a multilateral single treaty, in the nature of the North Atlantic Pact. Nevertheless, in the immediate postwar period the Soviet government had encouraged the formation of a Balkan union, apparently as a means of tying the Balkan states better to Russia. Following the Cominform congress, Tito discussed the project for a Balkan union with George Dimitrov, the veteran Bulgarian communist leader (November, 1947). Then, apparently without clearing the matter with Moscow, they set out on tours of the satellite capitals to secure support for the project. In a press interview in Bucharest in January, 1948, Dimitrov revealed that their hope was not only to form a Balkan union but also a general satellite federation from Poland to Greece. This proved too much for Moscow, which saw in it a satellite plot. A *Pravda* editorial (January 28, 1948) sharply condemned the project. Tito and Dimitrov were summoned to Moscow to justify themselves. Tito, sensing trouble, sent in his place his deputy Edvard Kardelj, but Dimitrov heeded the summons. In their interview with Stalin on February 10, 1948, Dimitrov and Kardelj were sharply disciplined; the union of Yugoslavia, Bulgaria, and Albania was approved but there was to be no general satellite federation; and the Greek communist cause was to be abandoned. Dimitrov hastened to submit, but Kardelj did so reluctantly.

The Yugoslav show of independence, added to Soviet-Yugoslav friction over Soviet economic exploitation and espionage in Yugoslavia, proved the last straw. The matter had become one of Soviet authority and satellite discipline. Stalin determined that Tito must be made to confess his errors, express regret, and promise to mend his ways. A prolonged and increasingly bitter correspondence followed between Moscow and Belgrade (March–June, 1948). When Tito failed to submit, Moscow decided on an open break. The Cominform moved its headquarters from Belgrade to Bucharest, pronounced a solemn anathema against Tito and his associates, and appealed to the rank-and-file of the Yugoslav Communist Party to overthrow their leaders. Moscow assumed that, in disciplined communist fashion, the Yugoslav communists would instantly depose their leaders. "I will shake my little finger — there will be no more Tito. Tito will fall," Stalin is supposed to have said (according to Nikita Khrushchev in 1956). But to the amazement of the world and consternation of Moscow, Tito did not fall. The Yugoslav communists remained loyal to him. Even noncommunists rallied to Tito's government when Soviet Russia and the satellites brought every means of pressure — short of war — to bring him down. Yugoslavia accepted military and economic aid from the United States and successfully resisted the Soviet pressure.

The breach in the seemingly solid, monolithic structure of the Soviet Bloc caused a great stir in the west. It raised hopes that Yugoslavia might discard communism and join the western camp. These hopes, however, were not borne out. Tito maintained, with certain modifications, communism at home and steered a carefully neutral course abroad.

By 1948 Russia had succeeded in securing her western approaches and (as will be seen in a following chapter) also her Far Eastern approaches. But she had failed to secure the routes to the south of her. Soviet diplomacy had been outmaneuvered in Iran and successfully defied in Turkey; communism had been defeated in Greece; and Yugoslavia had defected.

<h1 style="text-align:center">48</h1>

THE AMERICAN POLICY OF CONTAINMENT

. . . any United States policy towards the Soviet Union must be that of a long-term, patient but firm and vigilant containment of Russian expansive tendencies.[1]

GEORGE F. KENNAN

1. THE POSTWAR AMERICAN OUTLOOK

THE UNITED STATES emerged from World War II vastly strengthened in power, prestige, and wealth. Its armed forces had won brilliant victories, its territory was unscarred by war, and its productive capacity had reached unprecedented levels. Its adversaries, the former Axis powers, had been crushed. With the collapse of Germany and Italy, the balance of power in Europe, it appeared to the Americans, lay between Britain and France on one side and Russia on the other. Both were allies of the United States, grateful (the Americans thought) for the military and economic assistance given them during the war by the United States and still dependent on American economic aid to reconstruct their economies after the war. In Asia aggressive little Japan had been humbled and China, toward whom the United States had traditionally entertained friendly feelings, had been restored in her integrity under a nationalist government, which continued to look to the United States for support and guidance. As for the rest of Asia and for Africa, they were still under the colonial rule of the friendly Western European powers. The nations of Latin America were good neighbors and good customers of the United States of old standing. During the war European influence in Latin America had declined, and the dependence of Latin American countries on the United States had increased. An additional guarantee of American security was the United States monopoly of atomic power.

As the Americans surveyed the world scene on the morrow of victory, therefore, they felt confident that a long era of peace, prosperity, and progress was about to begin. In these happy circumstances it was natural

[1] "The Sources of Soviet Conduct," *Foreign Affairs*, July, 1947, p. 575.

that they should desire to return to normal conditions as soon as possible, but not to "normalcy" in the same isolationist sense as after World War I. This time, they were prepared to shoulder the responsibilities of a great nation under the United Nations, in whose creation they had played a decisive part. To hasten the restoration of normal and peaceful conditions in the world, they were prepared to give economic assistance to nations suffering from the ravages of war and technical assistance to those nations struggling along the path of progress. The generous American contributions to UNRRA and other agencies associated with the United Nations amply testified to that. In return, they demanded nothing, neither territory nor reparations, nor even — unlike after World War I — the repayment of war debts. They expected only to enjoy the blessings of peace and the fruits of their labor, undisturbed by international crises and emergencies. Feeling absolutely secure and as a token of American peaceful intentions, they wished to bring home the American forces overseas and demobilize them as soon as possible.

There were many prominent Americans, both within and without the government, who realized that there were serious flaws in this optimistic picture. They knew that some of the Allies were more envious than grateful and that gratitude, in any event, was not a factor in international politics; that Russia had been far less and Britain and France far more weakened by the war than was generally realized, and that the European balance was therefore seriously threatened; that China was in a serious crisis; and that conditions in the colonial world were far from settled. They feared that a too precipitous demobilization of the American forces might weaken American influence abroad when it was most needed to assure an orderly transition from war to peace. But the pressure of American public opinion to "bring the boys back home" was too strong. The American armies were hastily brought home and demobilized in a helter-skelter fashion, and vast quantities of arms, munitions, and supplies overseas were sold at bargain prices, given away, or simply abandoned. Only small occupation forces were left in Germany and Japan until the conclusion of peace, which the American public opinion expected to take place soon.

However, as difficulties and tensions grew up among the Allies over the treaty drafts in the Council of Foreign Ministers, occupation policies in Germany and Austria, the frequent Soviet use of the veto in the United Nations, the Soviet satellization of Eastern Europe and Soviet activities in the Near and Middle East, the control of atomic energy, and the outbreak of civil war in China, the prospects of peace waned and American public opinion began to change. On March 4, 1946, Churchill, then out of power and therefore free to speak his mind, in a speech at Fulton, Missouri, with President Truman in the audience, warned of the dangers ahead. "From Stettin in the Baltic to Trieste in the Adriatic, an iron curtain has descended across the Continent." Behind this curtain, he said,

Russia had subjected the nations of Eastern Europe to her control. To ward off further Soviet encroachments, he pleaded for a "special relationship between the British Commonwealth and the United States" "with all that such cooperation implies in the air, on the sea, and in science and industry." The address disconcerted some by reminding them of the propaganda of the late and unregretted Dr. Goebbels seeking to exploit the latent fears of the western powers of Soviet Russia.[2] Stalin promptly denounced Churchill as an "instigator of World War III." Nevertheless, the address served a useful purpose in awakening the American people to the realities of the European situation. However, the dream of peace died slowly. For some time, both in public opinion and in official policy, two trends, one still seeking to find an accommodation with Russia and another proposing to challenge her, coexisted. Thus, on September 12, 1946, former Vice-President Henry A. Wallace pleaded in a speech in New York: "The real peace we now need is between the United States and Russia. On our part we should recognize that we have no more business in the political affairs of Eastern Europe than Russia has in the political affairs of Latin America, Western Europe, and the United States." By coincidence, on the same day, John Steele, National Commander of the American Legion, urged in a speech in New Orleans: "We ought to aim an atomic bomb right at Moscow — and save one for Tito, too!" These were two extreme points of view. But by the beginning of 1947, the majority of the American public opinion had given up hope of an early peace with Germany, and reluctantly but firmly faced the prospect of a long test of strength with Russia.

The United States government determined upon the "policy of firm containment" of Soviet pressure, the aim of which was, according to George F. Kennan of the State Department's Policy Planning Staff, to bring counter-pressure "at a series of constantly shifting geographical and political points, corresponding to the shifts and manoeuvres of Soviet policy." The hope was that this policy would "promote tendencies (in Russia) which must eventually find their outlet in either the break-up or the gradual mellowing of Soviet power." The first concrete application of the policy of containment was to grant aid to Greece and Turkey. It has been seen (p. 564) that in February, 1947, Britain asked the United States to aid Greece where the communists had provoked civil war. During the war the United States had steadfastly refused to commit itself in the eastern Mediterranean, but by 1947 American opinion had changed. On March 12, 1947, President Truman requested Congress to appropriate $400 million to "defend" not only Greece but also Turkey, on the ground

---

[2] "If the German people should lay down their arms, the agreement between Roosevelt, Churchill, and Stalin (i.e., at Yalta) would allow the Soviets to occupy all Eastern and Southeastern Europe together with a major part of the Reich. An iron curtain would at once descend on this territory." Dr. Goebbels in *Das Reich*, February 23, 1945.

that "totalitarian regimes imposed on free peoples by direct or indirect aggression undermine the foundations of international peace and hence the security of the United States." Congress approved the request. It became known as the "Truman Doctrine" and represented a radical departure from traditional American policy. Never before in American history had the United States government admitted in time of formal peace that events in a distant area, like the eastern Mediterranean, constituted a threat to American security.

2. THE MARSHALL PLAN

While assuming the task of containing Soviet expansive energy, by force if necessary, the United States did not abandon efforts to promote a stable and orderly world through peaceful means. By 1947 Europe had shown little signs of recovering from the ravages of war. On June 5, 1947, General George C. Marshall, who had succeeded James Byrnes as Secretary of State, in a commencement address at Harvard University, made a momentous offer to aid Europe to recover economic health: "It is logical that the United States should do whatever it is able to do to assist in the return of normal economic health in the world, without which there can be no political stability and no assured peace. Our policy is directed not against any country or doctrine but against hunger, poverty, desperation, and chaos." General Marshall urged European nations to agree on a program for mutual reconstruction, which the United States would support with its resources so far as possible. In consequence, Britain and France took the initiative to summon a conference of European nations in Paris in June to draw up a program of economic cooperation and list their requirements for American aid. Russia participated in the conference, but the suspicious men of the Kremlin could not bring themselves to believe that "capitalist" America would aid Europe without some sinister ulterior motive. After much wrangling, the Soviet delegates withdrew from the conference, charging that the whole proposal was an American conspiracy to enslave Europe economically.. Russia thus deprived herself and her satellites of an opportunity to obtain American aid, which at the time they very much needed. The American offer, originally addressed to all European nations, was accepted by only sixteen west European nations. Inevitably, therefore, it took on an anti-Soviet character and contributed to the division of Europe. This had one advantage: it made the program more palatable to Congress, which originally had not been enthusiastic about it.

By September, the sixteen participating nations submitted plans requiring $19.33 billion in American assistance through 1951 when the program was to end. After carefully sifting through the European requirements and scaling them down to about $17 billion, the Administration submitted to Congress a "European Recovery Program" (ERP). With some hesitation and some reservations, Congress eventually appropriated about $13 billion for the implementation of ERP. The administration of the "Marshall Plan" — as ERP was popularly styled — was entrusted to a central agency, the Organization for European Economic Cooperation (OEEC) in Paris, while the Economic Cooperation Administration (ECA) in Washington handled the American funds. Shipments under the Marshall Plan included food, fuel, raw materials, as well as machinery, for Europe was then deficient even in items which it traditionally exported.

Another disinterested American effort to combat poverty and economic stagnation in the world was the "Point Four" program. This program, which President Truman announced in his inaugural address in 1949 and for which Congress appropriated funds (more modest than for ERP) in September, 1950, proposed to provide technical aid and raise production and living standards in the underdeveloped areas of the world, under the administration of the International Development Fund.

Within the relatively narrow limits of Western Europe to which it was reduced by Soviet obstructionism, the Marshall Plan was a striking success. By June 1, 1952, when it terminated, thanks to the enthusiasm of the participating nations, good planning, and American generosity, Western Europe was well on its way not only toward economic recovery but unprecedented prosperity. As a result of joint efforts toward recovery, West European economy became better integrated and more closely associated with the American economy than before, and in turn economic integration stimulated movements toward political integration (see Chapter 57).

3. THE NORTH ATLANTIC TREATY ORGANIZATION

Economic cooperation among the nations of Western Europe and the United States was accompanied by military cooperation. As the dream of peace receded and new threats to security appeared, the United States determined upon a strategy of containment of Soviet power. The implementation of this strategy was based on a modification and extension (to include the element of air) of the famed theories of Admiral Alfred T. Mahan (1840–1914), which held that the power (or group of powers) which controlled the seas could control the world, for in the event of war it (or they) would have access to the bulk of the world's resources.

After World War II the United States emerged as the largest sea and air power, controlling, either directly or through its allies, all the important sea and air routes of the world. On the other hand, Soviet Russia, together with Communist China (after 1949), controlled the Eurasian heartland. To contain the communist powers within this heartland, the

United States determined to form alliances with and to extend military and economic aid to those nations on the periphery of this heartland which were determined to resist communist pressure. The first and most important alliance that the United States formed after the war was the North Atlantic Treaty Organization.

The communist seizure of power in Czechoslovakia by the Prague coup (February, 1948) caused great uneasiness in Western Europe and the United States. Another cause for alarm was the Soviet siege of West Berlin (June 24, 1948–May 2, 1949). In June, 1948, the Western powers reformed the inflated German currency and introduced new bank notes into their zones of Berlin. Russia, which had not participated in the currency reform, closed all land and water routes to West Berlin. Although the immediate reason for the Soviet siege of West Berlin was economic, its purpose was political as well. West Berlin was an inconvenient gap in the Iron Curtain. Using the currency reform as a pretext, the Soviet government decided to squeeze the Western powers out of Berlin. However, the Western powers were determined to stay. They countered the Soviet siege of West Berlin with the famous Berlin "airlift," which caught the imagination of the world and deeply impressed the Soviet government with American technological prowess. The United States, supported by Britain and France, instituted a counter-blockade of the Soviet zone and supplied West Berlin with food, fuel, clothing, and raw materials for its industries by the only route left to them — the air. The siege of West Berlin provided the final impetus for the United States to conclude a formal military alliance with the nations of Western Europe — a step unprecedented in American history since the early days of the American Republic.

After the election of President Truman in November 1948, negotiations were opened in Washington among representatives of the United States, Britain, France, Canada, and the Benelux countries. In March, 1949, Denmark, Iceland, Norway, Italy, and Portugal joined in the discussions. On April 4, 1949, the twelve nations [3] signed the North Atlantic Pact. It was to be a "regional security arrangement" valid for twenty years to "maintain the security of the North Atlantic area." The signatories reaffirmed their allegiance to the United Nations and their desire to live in peace with other peoples, but declared that in the event of an attack upon any one of them all would immediately come to the assistance of the nation attacked.

The conclusion of the North Atlantic Pact was followed in September, 1949, by the formation of the North Atlantic Treaty Organization

[3] In 1951 Greece and Turkey were admitted to NATO. The United States wished to include also Spain, but the West European nations opposed it because of the pro-Axis policy of General Franco during World War II. The United States, therefore, concluded a separate treaty with Spain, providing for the use of Spanish aerial and naval bases by United States forces in return for American military and economic aid to Spain. (September 26, 1953)

(NATO) to plan joint defense, to determine the size and nature of the forces to be supplied by each member nation, and to allot funds necessary to carry out the plans of the organization. The main burden of the cost of NATO was assumed by the United States. In September, 1951, Congress created the Mutual Security Agency (MSA) in Washington to coordinate the administration of all the United States military, economic, and technical aid programs.

NATO has an elaborate, partly military and partly civilian, organization. The military organ of NATO is Supreme Allied Command Europe whose headquarters (SHAPE) were formerly in Paris and have recently moved to Belgium. The policy-making organ of NATO is the North Atlantic Council. It consists of the NATO foreign ministers, who meet regularly twice a year. The day-to-day work of the Council is carried on by permanent representatives with ambassadorial rank. The strategy-planning organ of NATO is the permanent Military Committee in Washington.

The Soviet government bitterly denounced the conclusion of the North Atlantic Pact for allegedly contributing to "the whipping up of war hysteria." But it at once took steps to raise the siege of Berlin, and a relaxation of international tensions followed. This bore out the belief of the architects of the policy of containment that Russia was impressed only with evidence of strength. However, the feeling of increased security, which the formation of NATO gave the western nations, proved short-lived. In September, 1949, President Truman revealed that Russia had produced and tested atomic bombs, and the Soviet government later confirmed the fact. The revelation that the American atomic monopoly was at an end, produced a panic and a "spy scare" in the United States (see p. 615). In October, 1949, the Chinese communists proclaimed the Chinese People's Republic, after defeating and driving the nationalists off mainland China. In June, 1950, communist North Korea attacked South Korea.

As the point of communist pressure shifted along the line of demarcation between the Soviet and American spheres of power, the United States kept extending its "defensive perimeter" along the rim of the Eurasian heartland, until it stretched from Norway through Europe, the Near and Middle East, Southeast Asia, and the Pacific islands to Alaska.

49

THE AFTERMATH OF THE WAR IN EAST ASIA

. . . the destruction of Japan destroyed the Far East as an "autonomous power zone" in international relations, i.e., as a base from which attempts at world mastery might be launched by combined naval, military, and air forces. A power vacuum has thus been created there which, as it re-fills, draws two of the Great Powers — the United States and the Soviet Union — into closer contact.[1]

1. THE AMERICAN OCCUPATION OF JAPAN

BY THEIR DEFEAT in 1945 the Japanese lost not only the gains which they had made in World War II but also all their colonial possessions which they had acquired since the nineteenth century. Pending a Japanese peace treaty, Allied armies took *de facto* possession of the Japanese overseas territories: the Caroline, Marshall, Mariana, Bonin, and Ryukyu islands remained under American occupation; Formosa and the Pescadores were occupied by the Chinese; Manchuria was occupied partly by Soviet and partly by Chinese forces; Korea was occupied jointly by American and Soviet forces, with the 38th parallel forming a line of demarcation between them; and southern Sakhalin and the Kurile Islands were occupied by Soviet forces. The Japanese islands, properly speaking, were occupied by American forces, with, until 1947, token participation by British and British Empire troops. Being under the sole authority of the United States proved to be of great advantage to Japan in that she was not divided and compartmentalized into several occupation zones like Germany, but was subject to a single authority and to uniform occupation policies. Another feature in which the occupation of Japan differed from that of Germany was that the Japanese government under the Emperor Hirohito had not been dissolved like the German government of Hitler's successor, Admiral Dönitz. The American occupation authorities ruled Japan indirectly through the Japanese government rather than directly as they did in Germany.

When Britain and Russia expressed dissatisfaction with the exclusively

---

[1] W. Gordon East and O. H. K. Spate, *The Changing Map of Asia* (New York: E. P. Dutton, 1950), p. 45.

American character of the occupation of Japan, the United States government moved to associate all Allied nations with interests in the Pacific in the formulation of Japanese occupation policies by creating the Far Eastern Commission in Washington, on which eleven Allied nations were represented, and the Allied Council in Tokyo, on which Britain, Russia, and China were represented (December, 1945). The influence of these bodies, however, remained limited. The Supreme Commander of Allied Powers (SCAP) in Japan, General Douglas MacArthur, was — despite his title — subject to the authority of the United States government alone. An able and strong-willed officer with political ambitions, General MacArthur not only paid scant attention to the wishes of the Allies but often clashed over policy with his superiors in Washington and was ultimately dismissed by President Truman for his independence (April, 1951).

The United States policy in Japan in the immediate postwar period was strongly influenced by the American indignation over Pearl Harbor. Its objective was to make certain that Japan would never again become a threat to the security of the United States or any other Pacific nation. The Japanese armed forces were completely dissolved and their arms and equipment scrapped. The Japanese statesmen responsible for the Japanese policy of aggression, as well as officials and officers responsible for crimes against Allied nationals, were arrested and tried before an International Military Tribunal in Tokyo. Of the major Japanese war criminals who were convicted, seven (including former Prime Minister General Tojo) were executed, while sixteen were given life sentences. At the same time, the Japanese bureaucracy, universities, and public life in general were thoroughly purged of men known for their ultranationalist views. Moreover, the American occupation authorities set out with great energy to transform the Japanese people into a "peace-loving" nation by democratic reforms.

The Emperor Hirohito was induced to disclaim the divinity attributed to him by the Japanese people, to emerge from the oriental seclusion in which he had lived, and to act like a democratic western monarch. The old authoritarian constitution of 1889 was replaced with a new democratic one (May, 1947). Drafted largely by American constitutional experts, it sought to transform Japan into a constitutional monarchy on the British pattern. Sovereignty was transferred from the Emperor to the people, civil freedoms were guaranteed, and suffrage (previously limited to men) was extended to women; in the Diet the upper House of Councillors became elective and made subordinate to the lower House of Representatives; the Cabinet was made "responsible" to the lower house; an independent judiciary was created with a Supreme Court which was to pass on all questions of constitutionality; a large measure of local self-government was introduced and the powers of the centralized and arrogant bureaucracy were limited. To guard against the revival of militarism, the constitution included the famous "renunciation-of-war" clause

(Article 9), which states that the "Japanese people forever renounce war as a sovereign right of the nation" and that "land, sea, or air forces, as well as other war potential, will never be maintained." Further reforms were showered on the bewildered Japanese people, designed to revamp their whole social, economic, and cultural life: a radical land reform, which was designed to weaken the feudalistic landowning class (it received only modest compensation for the expropriated lands) and to create a large, politically democratic, and socially conservative peasantry, was carried out; the great family-owned industrial and financial combines (*zaibatsu*), which controlled the Japanese economy, were dissolved and small business was encouraged; the rights of laborers to organize unions, bargain collectively, and strike were guaranteed; the social, legal, and political rights of women were safeguarded; and schools were reformed with a view to making them training grounds of democratic ideals.

Gradually, however, the United States policy in Japan changed, and the reforming zeal of the American occupation authorities declined. The reasons for this change were several. The American authorities faced in Japan a formidable task of economic reconstruction, which was not always well served by the democratic reforms. At the end of the war the Japanese economy was in a state of collapse: most of the large cities of Japan had been devastated by aerial bombardment and thousands of Japanese people were homeless; the Japanese industries and railways had suffered damage and their equipment was worn out; the Japanese agriculture was disorganized as a result of the mobilization of millions of peasants for military service; three-fourths of the merchant shipping was lost; the important fishing fleets were depleted; the loss of the overseas empire had deprived Japan of food for her population and of raw materials for her industries; the Japanese investments abroad were lost; five million soldiers, officials, and businessmen had to be repatriated from overseas, which swelled the population to about 76,500,000 in 1945 and further burdened the economy; and Japanese foreign trade was at a standstill. In these circumstances, the American taxpayer had to make up the Japanese deficits or the Japanese people would have starved. It was therefore important that the Japanese laborers should not use their newly granted rights to strike and demand wage raises and disrupt production; the *zaibatsu* were patently a violation of the American concept of free enterprise, but without them Japanese business was in a state of chaos; the end of Japanese competition in international trade was welcome to many American, British, and other businessmen, but Japan could not be suddenly thrown back to the self-sufficing, isolated, feudal-agrarian economy of a century earlier; since she emerged from her self-imposed isolation, Japan had become a great maritime and mercantile nation like Britain and had to trade or die. Consequently, the American authorities curbed the rights of labor, closed their eyes to the revival of the *zaibatsu*, and encouraged the revival of foreign trade.

In general elections for the House of Representatives in 1949 the Japanese Communist Party scored about 3,000,000 votes (about 10 per cent of the popular vote). Subsequently, the Japanese Communist Party declined, but at the time its growth warranted fears lest it endanger democracy in Japan. The American authorities did not abolish the Japanese Communist Party, but their ardor for promoting full democracy in Japan understandably cooled. The beginning of the Cold War in 1947 led the United States to view Japan less as an enemy to be kept in check than as a potential ally to be built up — against Russia and later against China. The outbreak of the Korean War in 1950 suggested to both the United States and Japanese policy-makers the desirability of a United States-Japanese alliance. After months of arduous negotiations, conducted on the American side largely by John Foster Dulles, the Americans and the Japanese agreed upon terms of a treaty of peace and a treaty of alliance.

On September 5, 1951, on the invitation of the United States, a peace conference met in San Francisco to discuss and conclude peace with Japan. Neither China nor Korea was represented at the conference, and India and Burma refused to attend it. Russia attended, but after vainly offering amendments to the draft treaty of peace refused to sign it. The Peace of San Francisco, signed by forty-nine nations on September 8, 1951, formally restored peace in the Pacific and sovereignty to Japan. It imposed no military or economic restrictions on Japan such as had been imposed on Italy and the Axis satellites in Europe. It left the question of reparations, demanded of Japan by such nations as the Philippines, to later negotiations. Japan, on her part, relinquished title to the Pacific mandates (the Mariana, Caroline, and Marshall islands and the Ryukus (including Okinawa), which were placed under United States trusteeship. She relinquished title also to Formosa (occupied by the nationalist Chinese) and southern Sakhalin and the Kurile Islands (occupied by Soviet forces). But since China and Russia were not parties to the treaty, the definite status of these possessions could not be determined. In 1952 Japan signed a separate treaty with India and one with nationalist China. The latter settled, at least as far as Japan was concerned, the status of Formosa. On October 19, 1956, Japan signed with Russia and her satellites a "Peace Declaration" (rather than a "peace treaty") and a "Trade Protocol" in Moscow, which restored normal diplomatic and trade relations between them but left the legal status of the Kurile Islands and southern Sakhalin in abeyance. The Moscow peace declaration, moreover, freed the way for the admission of Japan to the United Nations, which had been blocked until then by Russia.

On April 28, 1952, when the Peace of San Francisco went into effect, the American occupation of Japan formally came to an end. However, under the United States–Japanese Security Treaty, signed in San Francisco at the same time as the peace treaty, Japan granted the United

States bases and allowed United States forces to remain in Japan, not as occupation but as allied troops. The United States–Japanese alliance treaty gave impetus to the formation of an intricate network of alliances whereby the United States organized the defenses of the Pacific area against communist expansion. The United States' intention to rearm Japan caused apprehension in Australia and New Zealand, which had not forgotten the spectacular Japanese advance to their very threshold in 1941–1942. To reassure them, the United States concluded with Australia and New Zealand on the eve of the San Francisco conference a tripartite Pacific Security Pact (the ANZUS Treaty, September, 1951), providing for the creation of the Pacific Council to coordinate their defense policies. Similarly, the fear of the Philippines of a Japanese military revival was allayed by conclusion of the United States–Filipino Mutual Defense Treaty (August 30, 1951).

2. THE COMMUNIST VICTORY IN CHINA

For China the defeat of Japan in 1945 brought to an end eight years — or if one reckons from the Japanese invasion of Manchuria in 1931, fourteen years — of war. The Chinese people had suffered many privations and humiliations during this long conflict, but on the morrow of victory the future appeared bright for them. Not only did they recover all the territories seized from them by Japan since the Sino-Japanese War of 1894–1895, but during World War II the western powers had renounced all their privileges and concessions extorted from China during a century of imperialism. China was admitted to the United Nations as one of the great powers with a permanent seat in the Security Council. This bright picture was marred only by one setback; Russia, which had renounced after World War I her privileges and concessions in China, at the Yalta conference during World War II demanded the restoration of the privileges and concessions which Russia had lost as a result of her defeat in the Russo-Japanese War of 1904–1905. The Chinese nationalist government of General Chiang Kai-shek was indignant over the Soviet demands, but in view of the acquiescence of the western powers in them felt obliged to grant them. In the summer of 1945 a Chinese delegation arrived in Moscow and after weeks of negotiations signed on the day of Japanese surrender six Soviet-Chinese agreements, which substantially met the Soviet demands. Under these Soviet-Chinese agreements of August 14, 1945, China and Russia entered into a military alliance against Japan for thirty years. Russia promised moral and material support to the Chinese nationalist government. The two nations pledged to respect each other's sovereignty and territorial integrity and not to interfere in each other's internal affairs. Russia recognized China's title to Sinkiang and Manchuria and pledged to evacuate the latter within three months after the war. China accepted the Soviet demands for the use of Port Arthur as a joint Soviet-Chinese naval base, for making Dairen a free port, and for joint ownership and management of the Manchurian railroads (the Chinese Eastern Railway and the South Manchurian Railway, renamed "Chinese Chanchung Railway"). China further recognized the independence of Outer Mongolia, subject, theoretically, to a plebiscite.

It was galling for the Chinese nationalist leaders to have to make these concessions to Russia. But they hoped that the concessions would assure Soviet noninterference while they settled scores with the Chinese communists — a task which they regarded as most pressing after the war. With the end of the war with Japan, the uneasy and oft-broken truce which prevailed between the nationalists and communists during the war (see p. 522) came to an end. Clashes occurred as the nationalist and communist armies raced to fill in the vacuum left by the evacuation of the Japanese army. Both parties regarded the control of Manchuria as particularly important because it was industrially the most developed region in China. The Japanese, during their occupation of Manchuria after 1931, invested a sum equal to $1 billion to develop iron and coal mines, build railroads, develop steel, aluminum, machinery, and chemical industries, and make Dairen the second largest port in East Asia. However, the value of Manchuria as an industrial region declined greatly during the short Soviet occupation. In August, 1945, Soviet forces overran in their "one-week war" with Japan much of Manchuria, stripped it of all movable property as "war booty," and damaged or destroyed more. Because of their closer base at Yenan in northwestern China, the Chinese communists arrived in Manchuria before the nationalists and succeeded in occupying much of the territory, particularly in the north. The Soviet authorities apparently turned over to them much of the military equipment surrendered to them by the Japanese. When the nationalists arrived in Manchuria in November, 1945, from their distant bases in southwestern China, they found the communists well entrenched and well armed. Nevertheless, the nationalists, aided by American landing craft and transport planes, succeeded in seizing the principal cities in southern Manchuria. By the end of 1945 the nationalists held central and southern China and the cities in southern Manchuria, while the communists held northern China and the countryside in Manchuria. Early in 1946 Soviet forces were withdrawn from Manchuria, and the Chinese communists were left to their own devices. In 1945 the Soviet government had apparently assumed that the nationalists could maintain themselves and had advised the communists to seek an accommodation with the nationalist government.

The United States government also underestimated the strength of the communists and overestimated that of the nationalists. It continued to advance economic and military aid to the nationalist government, because it was the recognized government of China, but it scrupulously refrained from interfering militarily in the conflict, and by 1947 withdrew the slim United States forces from China. American public opinion was disturbed by the resumption of civil war in China, not because it anticipated the eventual debacle of the nationalists but because it felt a sympathy for the Chinese people as a whole. In December, 1945, President Truman sent General Marshall to China to attempt to mediate between the warring factions. His efforts appeared at first successful. Although both parties were determined to fight it out, neither party wished to assume the onus of being an obstacle to peace, which the war-weary Chinese people intensely desired. As a result, agreements were concluded to cease fire and to integrate the communist units into the nationalist army (January– February, 1946). The nationalist government also promised to convoke a constituent assembly. However, the military agreements were not lived up to, for neither party really wished a reconciliation. General Marshall, increasingly frustrated, continued his efforts for another year until recalled to Washington to become Secretary of State (January, 1947). The constituent assembly actually met, although the communists did not attend it, and drafted a constitution. It was to go into effect in December, 1947, but by then the civil war had gone too far for the constitution to have any effect.

In the civil war the nationalists appeared at first to have most of the advantages. The nationalist armies were more numerous and better equipped, and they controlled a larger portion of China. The nationalist government was recognized as the only government of China by all the Allied powers, including Russia. It received substantial economic and military aid from the United States (ultimately to the value of $2 billion). On the other hand, the nationalist regime had become corrupt and demoralized through long exercise of unrestrained power. Among government officials graft and embezzlement of state funds were common, and the mismanagement of finances resulted in a spiraling inflation. The nationalist armies were poorly disciplined, and their commanders often did not hesitate to make deals with the communists and sell them their American equipment. The communists, by contrast, proved more disciplined and efficient, both as soldiers and administrators, and they were more adept at propaganda. They apparently received no direct aid from Russia, which permitted them to pose as Chinese patriots and to stigmatize the nationalists as tools of predatory foreign imperialists.

Above all, the Chinese people were weary of war, inflation, and disorder; they yearned for peace and stability, which the nationalist government seemed unable to give them. Discontent with the nationalist regime steadily grew, and the loyalty of the nationalist armies began to waver. At the end of 1948, the nationalist troops in Manchuria, which were the best the nationalist government had, surrendered after little resistance. In January, 1949, the nationalist commanders in Peking and Tientsin defected to the communists, who then rapidly advanced to the Yangtze

River. The final collapse of the nationalist regime was an anticlimax. The conquest of southern China by the communists was little more than a military parade. By the end of 1949, all nationalist troops had either surrendered or had withdrawn to the island of Formosa. On October 1, 1949, the communist leaders proclaimed the People's Republic of China. The communist government under Mao Tse-tung in Peking was soon recognized by Russia and Great Britain. The United States, however, steadfastly continued to recognize the nationalist government under Chiang Kai-shek in Formosa as the rightful government of all of China.

The victory of the communists in China was the most important post-war event. By swinging China, with its 600 million inhabitants (almost a quarter of the world population) and considerable resources, to the communist side, it profoundly affected the balance between communist and noncommunist nations. For the United States it was a major set-back. The just indignation of the American people over this calamity, together with the "spy scare" engendered by the simultaneous revelation of the end of the American atomic monopoly, was exploited by Senator McCarthy and other demagogic politicians to launch a witchhunt against "traitors" supposedly responsible for the Chinese debacle. In retrospect, however, it seems certain that the only thing which could have saved the nationalist cause in China would have been direct American military inter-vention on a large scale. For such drastic action the American people were at the time psychologically unprepared. However, they had learned a lesson. When the communists struck in Korea in the summer of 1950, the Americans did not hesitate to resort to arms to stop communist aggression.

3. THE KOREAN WAR

To Korea the end of World War II brought independence after thirty-five years of Japanese servitude, but unfortunately also a completely artificial division, imposed at first inadvertently but later deliberately by Russia and the United States. At the Potsdam conference it was decided that Soviet and American troops should occupy Korea pending the estab-lishment of a Korean government. The 38th parallel — a completely arbi-trary line, corresponding to no real geographic, economic, or ethnic divi-sion — was to serve as the line of demarcation between the Soviet and American occupation zones. This arrangement was supposed to be strictly temporary, but with the deterioration in East-West relations it became permanent. Because of the complete lack of native administrators the occupants were forced to stay in Korea longer than they had originally intended. At its meeting in Moscow in December, 1945, the Council of Foreign Ministers decided to place Korea under a four-power (the United States, Russia, Britain, and China) trusteeship for five years. Meanwhile, a joint Soviet-American Commission was to find means to unite Korea, but, as in all joint Soviet-American councils, by 1947 a deadlock had been reached in the Commission. The United States then turned the matter over to the United Nations.

After due deliberation, the UN General Assembly recommended that elections be held to choose a national constituent assembly to draft a constitution and set up a government for all of Korea (November, 1947). Russia rejected this solution and when the UN Commission charged with supervision of the elections arrived in Korea, denied it admission to North Korea. The elections therefore could be held only in South Korea (May, 1948). The National Constituent Assembly at Seoul in South Korea, after vainly inviting delegates from North Korea to join it, went ahead and proclaimed the Republic of Korea under Dr. Syngman Rhee, an old Korean patriot who had lived for many years in exile in the United States and Europe (August 15, 1948). North Korea retorted by proclaiming at Pyongyang the People's Democratic Republic of Korea under Kim Il-sung, a veteran communist (September 9, 1948). Both governments claimed to represent all of Korea but in reality represented two distinct states. North Korea, patterned on Russia, was more industrial and had a population of some 9,000,000 and an area of 48,000 square miles. South Korea, patterned on the United States, was more agrarian and had a population of some 20,000,000 and an area of 37,000 square miles. Under Japanese rule the economy of Korea had been closely integrated with that of Japan, and the abrupt separation of Korea from Japan in 1945 caused severe economic dislocations, which were further aggravated by the artificial division into North and South Korea. After completing their work of division, Soviet forces retired from North Korea in 1948 and American forces from South Korea in 1949. This, however, did not diminish the rivalry between the two states.

On June 25, 1950, the Soviet-trained North Korean army suddenly crossed the 38th parallel with a view to reuniting Korea by force. The exact motivation of and the Soviet responsibility for this crass act of aggression remain uncertain. Perhaps Moscow or Pyongyang or both were encouraged to think that they could get away with it by an imprudent statement of Secretary of State Dean Acheson in January excluding Korea from the "defensive perimeter" of the United States. South Korea was, indeed, unimportant to the defense of the United States, but after the recent setback of United States policy in China the American leaders realized that to fail to respond to this challenge would completely destroy the confidence of the noncommunist world in United States leadership. On the same day, June 25, President Truman instructed General MacArthur to send United States troops from Japan to the aid of the South Koreans. By an extraordinary stroke of luck, the UN Security Council happened to be free of the Soviet veto because of a Soviet boycott of the Council over the question who should fill the seat of China, the nationalists or the communists. When the United States appealed to the Security Council, it promptly enjoined North Korea to retire behind the 38th parallel. When Pyongyang ignored the summons, it called on UN members to join the United States in defending South Korea. Fifteen nations responded to the appeal and sent token forces to Korea. The defense of South Korea thus took on the character of a UN campaign, although in practice it remained predominantly a United States military operation.

The fortunes of war in Korea swung wildly from one side to the other. At first, thanks to the element of surprise, the North Korean army overran most of South Korea and pinned the UN forces to a narrow perimeter around Pusan. But in September General MacArthur effected an amphibian landing at Inchon, far behind the North Korean lines, and forced them to flee for their lives. By October, South Korea had been cleared and the original objective of the campaign — the defense of South Korea — had been attained. But, as history shows, wars are more easily started than ended. The question then arose whether to halt operations or to continue them with a view to freeing North Korea and reuniting it with South Korea. Against the advice of India and the warning of China that she would not "stand idly by" if North Korea were invaded, the UN General Assembly endorsed the liberation of North Korea (October 7, 1950). When the UN forces crossed the 38th parallel and invaded North Korea, about 200,000 Chinese troops — officially styled "volunteers" — intervened and in November and December drove them back into South Korea. By the spring of 1951, the front was stabilized approximately along the 38th parallel.

The UN superiority in equipment and firepower was offset by Chinese numbers and toughness. The ruggedness of the Korean terrain and the lack of elbow room in the narrow, peninsular theater largely cancelled the use of armored vehicles. The operations were reduced to an exhausting struggle of foot soldiers. In these circumstances, General MacArthur proposed the strategic bombing of railroads, bridges, factories, and cities in China itself. However, this proposal provoked anguished cries from the United States' allies, many of whom feared that the bombing of China would result in Soviet intervention and that the limited Korean War would spread into World War III. Among the chief critics of MacArthur's strategy in the United States were Secretary of State, Dean Acheson and Chairman of the Joint Chiefs of Staff, General Omar Bradley. President Truman, in accord with his advisors, rejected this proposal which, in Bradley's words, would lead to "the wrong war, in the wrong place, at the wrong time." When MacArthur refused to carry out the decision of his superiors, Truman dismissed him and replaced him with General Matthew B. Ridgway (April, 1951). Although the American people accepted the necessity of the Korean War and American soldiers endured its rigors with great fortitude, the American character had little enthusiasm for this war without victory. In these circumstances, President Truman renounced the hope of liberating North Korea and responded to a Soviet suggestion for armistice talks (June, 1951).

The negotiations at Panmunjom, lasting for two dreary years, finally produced an armistice (July 26, 1953). It retained the existing front line as the permanent demarcation line between North and South Korea. The war thus ended in a stalemate. The attempt of the UN forces to liberate North Korea failed, but the communist attempt to expand by armed aggression had been contained and the confidence of the noncommunist world in the determination of the United States to back up its policy of communist containment by force if necessary was restored. As a token of its intention to defend South Korea against any future aggression, the United States concluded with it a Mutual Defense Treaty (October 1, 1953). The great victims of the irresponsible communist attempt to probe American strength were the unfortunate Korean people who suffered some 3,000,000 casualties and frightful devastation of their land.

4. THE PARTITION OF INDOCHINA

The postwar development in Indochina was much more complex than in Korea. Unlike Korea, which was a well-integrated nation, Indochina consisted of several units and peoples put together by the accidents of French colonial empire-building in the nineteenth century (see p. 372). Along the Pacific coast were Cochin China (a French colony) and Annam and Tonkin (both French protectorates). All three were inhabited in the majority by Annamese (Viet) people. Inland along the tortuous Mekong River were Cambodia and Laos (both French protectorates). Cambodia was inhabited by the Cambodians (Khmers) and Laos by the Laotians, both of whom were more closely related to the Siamese (Thais) to the west of them than to the Annamese to the east of them. The cities, of which Hanoi and Saigon were the most important, had — as was true in most East Asian cities — strong Chinese (500,000) and smaller European (42,000) minorities. While the Chinese were merchants (controlling, among other things, the important rice trade), the Europeans were officials, soldiers, and businessmen.

The deathblow to French colonial rule in Indochina was given by the Japanese as early as 1941 when they occupied Indochina. However, for reasons of expediency, the Japanese left the Vichy-appointed French officials and soldiers in charge until March, 1945, when they were interned. In a last-minute bid for Asian support the Japanese then encouraged the emperor of Annam, Bao Dai, and the kings of Laos and Cambodia to declare independence. However, the French were determined to reclaim Indochina after the war. During the war General de Gaulle, the Free French leader, promised Indochina "a new political

status within the French community" (December 8, 1943). Upon returning to France in 1944, he made preparations to send a French expeditionary corps to the Pacific theater of war to be in a position to reoccupy
Indochina upon the defeat of Japan. This plan, however, was frustrated
by President Roosevelt, who disliked de Gaulle and was opposed to
colonialism in general and French colonialism in particular. At the Potsdam conference the United States, Russia, and Britain decided upon an
arrangement similar to that adopted in Korea. Chinese (nationalist)
troops were to occupy the north and British troops the south of Indochina, with the 16th parallel forming a demarcation line between their
respective occupation zones.

The British, who had no interest in staying in Indochina, freed the
interned French officials and soldiers and restored them to power in their
zone. The French, strengthened by new arrivals from France, had no
difficulty in re-establishing their rule also in Cambodia and Laos, but they
encountered difficulty in the Chinese zone. During the war, in 1941, a
group of Viet exiles in nationalist China had formed the Vietminh, or
League for Independence of Vietnam (i.e., the "Land of the South,"
comprising Tonkin, Annam, and Cochin China). Its leader was Ho Chi
Minh, a French- and Soviet-trained Communist, but most of its members
were nationalists. On September 2, 1945, the Vietminh proclaimed the
Republic of Vietnam at Hanoi. The Emperor Bao Dai was induced to
abdicate and was sent into exile at Hongkong. The Vietminh government
received for some time the economic and political support of the United
States, on the theory that it was nationalist rather than communist. In
1946, to get rid of the Chinese who had looted the country and intrigued
against him, Ho Chi Minh decided to come to terms with the French. On
March 6, 1946, the French agreed to recognize the Vietnam Republic as "a
free state having its government, its parliament, its army, and its finances,
forming a part of the Indochinese Federation and of the French Union."
As a result of this agreement, the Chinese left north Vietnam and the
French reoccupied it. However, the agreement soon broke down, with
both sides placing the blame on each other, and in December, 1946, just
after returning from Paris where he supposedly had come to terms with
the French, Ho Chi Minh raised the banner of revolt.

The Indochinese War, which was to last almost eight years, at first
partook of the nature of diffuse guerrilla warfare. The Vietminh controlled
the countryside, while the French controlled the cities. In an effort to
split the ranks of the Vietnamese nationalists the French created at Saigon
a counter-government to Ho Chi Minh's government and brought back
the ex-Emperor Bao Dai to preside over it (June, 1949). The war took
a new turn with the communist victory in China late in 1949, at which
time China and Russia recognized Ho Chi Minh's government and provided it with military and economic aid, enabling it to wage conventional
as well as guerrilla warfare. On the other hand, the United States re-

versed its policy of aloofness toward the "colonial" war in Indochina. On June 25, 1950, in the same statement in which he announced the United States' intervention in Korea, President Truman announced also the United States' intention to send a military mission and military and economic aid to the French and Bao Dai's government in Indochina. Indochina was thus drawn into the sphere of the Cold War.

As the Indochinese war continued with no victory in sight, French public opinion became increasingly weary of the struggle, the cost of which was severely hampering French economic recovery. In 1954 the hopelessness of the French effort was dramatically shown when the Vietminh forces besieged Dien Bien Phu, a great fortified camp on the Laotian border, created and supplied by air by the French to harass their rear. In April the French government requested United States intervention to relieve Dien Bien Phu. Although Secretary of State Dulles and the Joint Chiefs of Staff were in favor of aerial operations against the Vietminh, President Eisenhower overruled them. On May 7 Dien Bien Phu surrendered. At a conference of French, British, Soviet, and Chinese (communist) foreign ministers in Geneva it was decided to end the war and to partition Vietnam along the 17th parallel between the communist government at Hanoi in the north and the pro-western government at Saigon in the south (July 21, 1954). Lip service was paid to Vietnamese unity by a provision to hold elections in 1956, but they were never held. This Geneva conference also confirmed the independence of Laos and Cambodia.

The Geneva agreement marked the end of French influence in Indochina. Bao Dai, who was discredited by his ineffectiveness and by his French associations, was replaced as head of South Vietnam by Ngo Dinh Diem, an American protégé. The United States, which had stood pointedly aloof from the Geneva agreement (although it stated its intention to "respect" it), then moved to plug the gap left by the French defeat in the western defenses of Southeast Asia. On September 8, 1954, the United States signed with Great Britain, France, Australia, New Zealand, Pakistan, the Philippines, and Thailand the Manila Pact, which provided for the creation of the Southeast Asia Treaty Organization (SEATO). This regional collective security organization resembled in structure its Atlantic counterpart but remained more limited in scope and effectiveness.

50

THE AFTERMATH OF THE WAR IN THE
NEAR AND MIDDLE EAST

Zionism originates in the simple truth that there are not only individual Jews, there is a Jewish nation.[1]

DAVID BEN-GURION

We cannot . . . ignore that there is an Arab circle surrounding us and that this circle is as much a part of us as we are a part of it . . .[2]

GAMAL ABDAL NASSER

1. THE DECLINE OF FRENCH AND BRITISH INFLUENCE

THE NEAR AND MIDDLE EAST was never an important theater of operations in World War II, as it had been in World War I. After the defeat of the Italians and the Germans in the North African deserts in 1942–1943, the Axis threat to the Allied control of the region waned. However, the Allied cause did not enjoy much sympathy among the native peoples, unlike in World War I when many of the Arabs rallied to it. Turkey feared Germany, but she also distrusted Russia. Therefore, Turkey steered a carefully neutral course until February, 1945, when it appeared safe to issue a paper declaration of war on the Axis to qualify for admission to the United Nations as a charter member. After the war, as already recounted, Soviet pressure forced Turkey firmly into the western camp (see p. 563). Iran disliked equally Russia and Britain and leaned toward the Axis until 1941 when she was jointly occupied by Soviet and British forces. Reza Shah was deposed and deported, and his son and successor, Mohammed Reza Shah, declared war on the Axis. After the war Iran, like Turkey, was forced by Soviet intrigue into the western camp (see p. 564). Afghanistan was neutral during the war and remained neutral after the war. Until the withdrawal of the British from India and an out-

---

[1] David Ben-Gurion, *Rebirth and Destiny of Israel* (New York: Philosophical Library, 1954), p. 108.
[2] Gamel Abdal Nasser, *The Philosophy of the Revolution* (Buffalo, N. Y.: Economics Books, 1959), pp. 59–60.

break of a border dispute with Pakistan, however, Afghanistan leaned toward the west; thereafter it began to lean toward Russia.

The Arabic people felt no fear of Russia, which had never exercised much influence among them. Moreover, Russia enjoyed a reputation for being a revolutionary, anticolonial power, because of its anticolonial policy after World War I, but hardly justified by its policy after World War II. The United States also enjoyed a reputation for being anticolonial. President Roosevelt gave great encouragement to Arab nationalism and dismayed French and British colonial officials by receiving the Sultan of Morocco, Sidi Mohammed Ben-Yusef, during the Casablanca conference in 1943 and King ibn-Saud after the Teheran conference in 1944, but the United States was a distant country and had never exercised any important influence over the Arabs. For the Arabs the Allied powers that counted were Britain and France, and with them — largely because of their contradictory promises to the Jews and Arabs in World War I — they had little sympathy. However, Britain had strong forces in the Near and Middle East during World War II and did not hesitate to use them to assert her authority. Although peninsular Arabia was unaffected by the war and remained quiescent, in 1941 a pro-Axis revolt broke out in Iraq. The British forces suppressed it energetically and installed a pro-Allied ministry at Bagdad, which declared war on the Axis. At the high tide of Rommel's drive in 1942 the loyalty of Egypt wavered, but by a show of force and a threat of deportation, the British forced King Faruk to appoint a pro-Allied ministry. When the Egyptian prime minister announced the declaration of war on the Axis in February, 1945, as a purely opportunist measure to qualify for admission to the United Nations, he was assassinated by an Arab fanatic.

While they disliked but feared Britain, the Arabs neither liked nor feared France after her defeat at the hands of Germany in 1940. In 1941, after Free French and British forces had entered Lebanon and Syria and had defeated the Vichy forces, General de Gaulle, the Free French leader, recognized their independence. Although the Lebanese and Syrians were not satisfied with the way the Free French implemented this recognition, they remained relatively quiescent until the end of the war. The presence of British troops, the recognition of their independence by the United States and Russia in 1944, and their admission to the United Nations (obtained by a paper declaration of war on the Axis in February, 1945) seemed to them sufficient guarantees that after the war they would be rid of French rule. However, in May, 1945, immediately after the conclusion of the war in Europe, French reinforcements began to arrive at Beirut. De Gaulle hoped to establish a relationship between France and Lebanon and Syria analogous to that between Britain and Iraq and Egypt, but this was unacceptable to the Arabs, for they felt that her weakness in World War II had disqualified France from exercis-

ing any influence over them. When disorders broke out in Beirut and Damascus, the French proceeded to put them down with great ferocity, and
in Damascus they repeated their feat of twenty years before of shelling
the city. The British, who were not disinclined to try to deflect the Arab
wrath from themselves by posing as their protectors against France, then
stepped in. In a stern ultimatum to the French they ordered them to
confine their troops to the barracks and assumed responsibility for maintaining order, on the ground that this was necessary for the safety of
Allied communications to the Far East where the war was still in progress.
Under British pressure, as well as the pressure of the United States and
Russia in the United Nations, France agreed to evacuate Syria and
Lebanon. Upon the completion of the evacuation in 1946, French influence in the Near and Middle East disappeared and Syria and Lebanon
gained full control of their own affairs.

While the Arabs were willing to use Britain as a counterweight to
France, they disliked her scarcely less than France, and after the war
when Britain, beset by economic problems at home, was forced to curtail
sharply her forces in the Near and Middle East, her influence among the
Arab people declined. However, it was not the Arabs but the Jewish
people in Palestine who first openly defied Britain.

2. THE ARAB-ISRAELI CONFLICT

The Jewish people of Palestine, alone among the peoples of the Near
and Middle East, rallied fully to the Allied cause in World War II. This
was, to be true, a tactical decision. They disliked Britain, whom they
accused of not living up fully to the Balfour Declaration of 1917, which
provided for the establishment of a Jewish "national home" in Palestine
(see p. 174). However, the Nazi slaughter of Jews made Germany their
primary enemy and they determined — more firmly than ever — to realize
their dream of creating in Palestine a Jewish national state and a haven.
Jews were urged to volunteer for service with the British forces to strike a
blow against Germany, and also to acquire military experience for a postwar showdown with the Arabs and with Britain herself. Jewish commandos took part in the destruction of the Italian empire in Ethiopia and in
the suppression of the pro-Axis revolt in Iraq, and a Jewish Legion fought
in the desert campaigns in North Africa, in Italy, and in Belgium.

In their efforts to establish a Jewish national state, the Jews of Palestine had the support of Zionist organizations in Allied countries, notably
the large and influential Zionist organization in the United States. In
1942 an American Zionist Congress met at the Biltmore Hotel in New York
and adopted a program calling for unlimited immigration of Jews into
Palestine and the transformation of all of Palestine into a Jewish state.

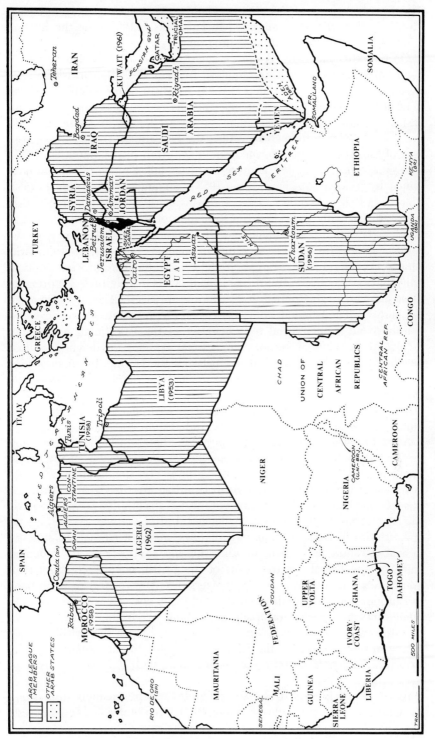

THE ARAB LEAGUE, 1967

The Jewish Agency in Palestine, under David Ben-Gurion, an energetic Zionist leader who had emigrated to Palestine in 1906 from the Russian Empire, endorsed this "Biltmore program."

On the other hand, the Arabs of Palestine were equally determined to keep Palestine a purely Arab country. In 1939, after the British had deposed their leader, Haj Amin al-Huseini, as Mufti of Jerusalem and President of the Moslem Council of Palestine, he fled to Germany and broadcast over Radio Berlin exhortations to the Arabs to rally to the Axis. In their determination to keep Palestine, the Palestinian Arabs had the support of the Arab League, formed under the Arab Pact (March 22, 1945) by Egypt, Syria, Lebanon, Transjordan, Iraq, and Saudi Arabia, and later joined by Yemen (1945), Libya (1953), Sudan (1956), Tunis (1958), Morocco (1958), Algeria (1959), and Kuwait (1961). While the British, who had originally suggested the formation of the Arab League, had in mind an Arab defensive alliance tied to Britain, the Arab leaders gave the Arab League entirely different aims: to emancipate the Arabs from British and French tutelage, to promote the Pan-Arabic ideal of Arab political unity, and to check the ambitions of the Zionists in Palestine. To promote these aims an Arab Council and a permanent Secretariat in Cairo were established. The Council, composed of one representative of each member state and a semiofficial representative of the Palestinian Arabs, met in regular semiannual sessions (or special sessions on demand of two members). Because of the jealousy between the Hashimite rulers of Iraq and Transjordan and King ibn-Saud on the one hand and between the Hashimites and King Faruk of Egypt on the other, the Arab League made little headway toward unification, but it proved effective enough in mobilizing Arab opinion against France and Britain and the Zionists.

After the war, Britain, caught between the irreconcilable Arab and Jewish nationalism in Palestine, stood pat on the provisions of the White Paper of 1939, which called for ending of Jewish immigration after five years and self-rule for a Jewish-Arab Palestine after ten years. Although this solution had been rejected by both the Arabs and the Jews before the war, it was the Jews who first challenged it after the war. With the end of hostilities in Europe, thousands of Jews, many of whom had suffered in concentration camps, sought admission to Palestine, only to be denied entry by the British. Patrol boats of the British navy intercepted emigrant ships and interned their passengers in Cyprus or turned them back to Europe. Jewish organizations devised ingenious ways of smuggling in immigrants, and Jewish terrorist organizations, the Irgun Zwei Leumi and the Stern gang, launched a terrorist campaign against the British, culminating in the wrecking of the King David Hotel, the headquarters of the British administration and army in Jerusalem, with the loss of a score of lives (July 22, 1946).

As the terror increased, the United States was increasingly drawn into the conflict. Until the end of the war, the United States had few interests in Palestine or in any part of the Near and Middle East, apart from a little trade and the cultural interests bequeathed by nineteenth-century American missionary efforts, such as the American University at Beirut. The United States was therefore generally content to leave matters in the hands of the British. After the war, however, the rapid development of the American oil interests in Arabia created an important American economic stake in the region. Above all, the outbreak of the Cold War forced the United States to abandon its previous aloofness toward this strategically vital area. The Truman Doctrine (1947) has already been mentioned (see p. 564). President Truman, sensitive to Jewish opinion in the United States, suggested in 1945 the modification of the White Paper to admit 100,000 Jewish immigrants into Palestine. The British regarded this suggestion as gratuitous meddling in a difficult situation and countered by suggesting that the United States share in the burden of policing Palestine. The United States demurred, but it did agree to participate in an Anglo-American commission to investigate conditions in Palestine and make recommendations for their solution. The recommendations were rejected by both the Jews and the Arabs, for they were based — like numerous previous British recommendations — on compromise, and both the Arabs and the Jews regarded their own cause as sacred and compromise as treason. The frustrated British then appealed to the United Nations (February, 1947).

After investigating the matter, a UN Palestinian Commission recommended the only solution left, namely, partition (August, 1947). With the support of the United States as well as of Russia, the UN General Assembly approved this solution (November 29, 1947). The Jews were jubilant but the Arabs were outraged. While the Arabs had held aloof during the Jewish terrorist campaign against the British, they now sprang into action. A confused three-corner struggle developed, and the country sank into anarchy. Appalled by this situation and also pressured by the American oil interests in Arabia, the United States government abruptly reversed its stand on partition (March, 1948) and urged Britain to stay on in Palestine. However, the British government refused to reconsider its decision to withdraw its troops from Palestine and to wash its hands of the whole matter. On May 14, 1948, the British terminated their mandate in Palestine. On the same day the Jews proclaimed the state of Israel, which was at once recognized by the United States and Russia. At the same time the armies of the Arab League crossed the Palestinian borders to save the country for the Arabs. To the general surprise, the Jewish Haganah, originally a militia organized to defend the Jewish agricultural settlements (*kibuz*) against Arab raids, proved to be an efficient fighting force. The Arabs, on the other hand, suffered from disunity of command and political jealousy. While Egypt sponsored a Palestinian Arab "government" at Gaza, Transjordan sponsored a Palestinian Arab meeting at Jericho which hailed King Abdullah as King of

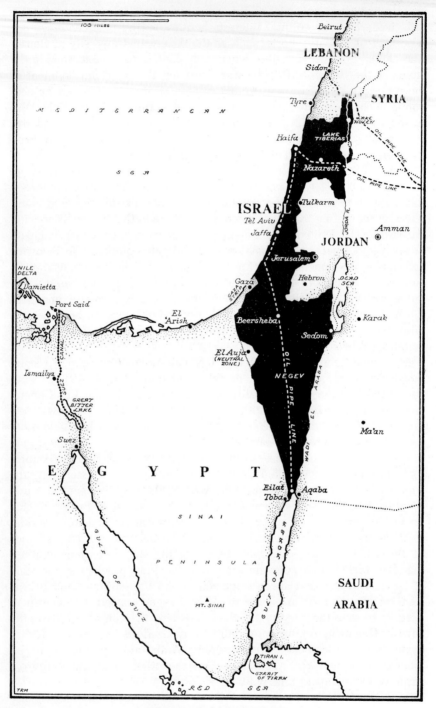

ISRAEL AND ITS NEIGHBORS

Palestine and Transjordan. With the advantage of "inner lines," the Haganah inflicted a series of humiliating defeats on the Lebanese, Syrian, and Egyptian armies, seized the New City of Jerusalem, and considerably broadened the area assigned to Israel by the UN partition. It found a match only in the British-trained Arab Legion of Transjordan, which held east-central Palestine and the Old City of Jerusalem. When the head of the UN Truce Commission, Count Folke Bernadotte of the Swedish royal family, ventured to suggest that the Jews should evacuate Jerusalem, he was ruthlessly murdered by a Jewish terrorist. The Israeli government profusely apologized, but the murderer was never arrested.

Thanks to the tact, firmness, and patience of Bernadotte's successor, Dr. Ralph Bunche, a distinguished American Negro, first Egypt and then the other Arab countries concluded armistice agreements with Israel, which froze the winding front lines into a permanent international border (February–August, 1949). The lion's share of Palestine went to Israel; the hilly east-central portion and the Old City of Jerusalem were annexed by Transjordan (renamed thereafter Jordan); and a narrow strip along the Mediterranean with the town of Gaza went to Egypt. The Arab states, however, stubbornly refused to conclude a regular peace treaty with Israel, for this would have implied their legal recognition of the state of Israel. In violation of the Convention of Constantinople of 1888, which provided for the freedom of navigation through the Suez Canal for all nations in time of war and peace, Egypt denied Israel the use of this waterway. And Egypt and Saudi Arabia blocked the egress of Israel to the eastern seas by the way of the Gulf of Aqaba.

By their victory over the Arabs the Jews, after almost 2000 years, realized their dream of ending the Diaspora and restoring a Jewish national state. On the other hand, by their defeat some 600,000 Palestinian Arabs, who had fled or had been expelled from Israel, lost their homes and lands which they had held for some 1300 years. Huddling in fetid camps on the Israeli borders, these Arab refugees were a turbulent element and a constant menace to the peace which uneasily reigned over the Holy Land.

3. THE SUEZ CANAL CRISIS

After the armistice of 1949 relations between Israel and her Arab neighbors were almost continuously disturbed by border incidents, some of them involving regular armed forces. In an effort to prevent an armament race and eventual resumption of war between them, the United States, Britain, and France agreed on May 25, 1950, to limit the sale of arms to Israel and the Arab states, which was fiercely resented by both countries. Partly to appease the Arabs and partly out of general concern for the security of the Near and Middle East, Britain and the United

States planned to re-establish the wartime Allied Middle East Command. By joining the command the Arab countries would qualify for western arms, but of course would be subject to a degree of western control in the use of them. When Britain and the United States made this proposal to Egypt (October, 1951), the Egyptian government not only scornfully rejected it but denounced the Anglo-Egyptian alliance treaty of 1936 and angrily clamored for British withdrawal from the Suez Canal and Sudan. At the same time relations between Britain and Iran were disturbed by the nationalization, in October, 1951, of the Anglo-Iranian Oil Company by Prime Minister Mossadeq (see pp. 811–812). The incidents revealed the growth of nationalism and the decline of British influence in the Near and Middle East since the war.

The Suez Canal had been the fulcrum of British defenses in the Near and Middle East since Gladstone ordered the "temporary" occupation of Egypt in 1882. The British withdrawal from India in 1947 had somewhat diminished the importance of the "Imperial lifeline" through Suez. On the other hand, not only Britain but all Western Europe received nearly all their oil from the Near and Middle East. About 60 per cent of this oil, which they vitally needed for their postwar recovery, was transported in tankers through the Suez Canal, while the rest was pumped through pipelines to Mediterranean ports. Therefore Britain was not prepared to leave the canal without some sort of agreement with Egypt about its defense and use. She denounced the unilateral repudiation of the Anglo-Egyptian treaty by Egypt and prepared to hold firm at Suez against provocation and violence, which occurred with increasing frequency. The situation improved somewhat after the fall of King Faruk of Egypt (July, 1952) and the rise of the revolutionary regime headed first by General Naguib and later by Colonel Nasser (see p. 803), because the revolutionary leaders, while no less nationalist than the fallen king, were at first preoccupied with internal problems. As a result, Britain succeeded in coming to terms with Egypt, first concerning Sudan and later the Suez Canal.

On February 12, 1953, an Anglo-Egyptian agreement was signed at Cairo, which provided for ending the Anglo-Egyptian condominium over Sudan (since 1899) and giving that country the right to choose in 1956 whether it wished to federate with Egypt or become independent.[3] On July 27, 1954, a preliminary Anglo-Egyptian agreement was signed in Cairo (a definite agreement was signed in October) which disposed of the Suez problem. The agreement, which replaced the Anglo-Egyptian treaty of 1936 and was valid for seven years, provided for: a phased British withdrawal from the canal zone to be completed by June 18, 1956; Britain's right to return to the canal zone in case of an attack (presumably by Russia) on any Arab country or Turkey; continued operation of the canal by the Suez Canal Company; and respect by both countries for

---

[3] In 1956 Sudan chose independence. See p. 783.

Border patrols of the Israel Defense Forces along the Gaza Strip. Camels are used where sand dunes prevent passage of wheeled vehicles, (Authenticated News International).

Salvage vessels clear the entrance of the Suez Canal of sunken ships, November, 1956 (International News Photo).

Construction site of the turbine power station of the Aswan Dam in Egypt,
(Authenticated News International).

the Convention of Constantinople of 1888 providing for freedom of navigation in the canal. Britain then began to transfer her defenses to the island of Cyprus only to encounter there the same kind of nationalist opposition that she had encountered in Egypt.

American diplomacy had facilitated the Anglo-Egyptian agreement, which was by no means popular among Arab nationalists, by offering Egypt a grant of $40,000,000 for her economic development. American diplomacy also assisted in composing the Anglo-Iranian oil dispute in August, 1954 (see p. 811). However, the United States was aware of the decline of British influence and popularity. Secretary of State Dulles, who assumed the direction of the United States foreign policy in 1953, was inclined to regard Britain as more of a liability than an asset in the Near and Middle East. Therefore, he tended to disassociate the United States from British policy and follow an independent course. The aim of his policy was to organize a regional defense arrangement analogous to NATO or SEATO to contain Soviet expansion by strengthening the "Northern Tier" of western defenses in the region. Among Arab states he favored building up Iraq rather than Egypt, and as between Israel and the Arab countries he was much more partial to the latter than his Democratic predecessors. His efforts were at first eminently successful. After a preliminary agreement between Iraq and Pakistan in April, 1954, which he regarded as a mere stopgap, Iraq and Turkey concluded ·on February 24, 1955, the Bagdad Pact. This was a firm military alliance in the nature of NATO, open to other parties. It was called Middle Eastern Treaty Organization (METO) until 1958 when Iraq withdrew from it and its headquarters were moved to Ankara. It was then renamed Central Treaty Organization (CENTO). Britain, which at first regarded the American efforts coolly, was glad to join METO (April 5) because her alliance treaty of 1930 with Iraq was due to expire in 1957 and there was little hope that Iraq would renew it. Pakistan joined on September 23 and Iran on November 3. Because of some opposition in Congress, the United States joined, for the moment, only the economic and military committees of METO. Nevertheless, since it undertook to pay most of the cost of the organization, it was assured of a strong voice in its direction. Since Turkey was a member of NATO and Pakistan a member of SEATO, METO closed the chain of interlocking alliances whereby the United States sought to contain Soviet expansion.

However, METO had serious defects. First, Pakistan joined it principally to qualify for American arms, which she needed not so much against Russia, which did not threaten her directly, as against India with which she had a quarrel in Kashmir. The arming of Pakistan by the United States was naturally resented by India and pushed her further along the road of neutralism. Secondly, METO incurred bitter Arab hostility. Egypt, which was coming forth increasingly as the spokesman of Arab neutralism, denounced it as an instrument of western imperialist enslavement of the Near and Middle East and castigated Iraq for breaking Arab solidarity. Egypt and Iraq had been rivals for Arab leadership for centuries and for the leadership in the Near and Middle East since the days of the Pharaohs, and the arming of Iraq by the United States increased this rivalry. Egypt desired weapons to settle scores with Israel and assert her influence over the Arab states. Under the Tripartite Agreement of 1950 the western powers refused to sell them to her. She could obtain them by joining the Bagdad Pact, but then she would have to submit to western control in using them. This was unacceptable to her.

The frustration of Egypt opened the arena of Arab politics to Russia, which had previously exercised no influence among the Arabs. Grasping this opportunity, she jettisoned her pro-Israel policy and assumed the posture of the protector of Arab nationalism. In September, 1955, it was announced that Russia and communist Czechoslovakia (the great arsenal of the Soviet Bloc) would supply Egypt with arms in exchange for cotton, the principal item of Egyptian export. This deal caused a sensation. By it Russia "leapfrogged" over the "Northern Tier" of western defenses in the Near and Middle East and established an influence among the Arab nations. On the other hand, Nasser by outmaneuvering the hated western "imperialist" powers became overnight the great hero not only of the Egyptian but of all Arab nationalists. The United States, greatly disconcerted, countered the Soviet move by offering to finance the construction of the High Aswan Dam – a project of great importance to the Egyptian economy. An agreement in principle was announced in December, 1955, under which the United States, Britain, and the World Bank were to finance the project jointly, but the Egyptian government delayed a definite agreement for months in an obvious effort to force the United States and Russia into further bidding for its favor. In June, 1956, Egypt, followed by other Arab states, recognized communist China. The Soviet Foreign Minister, Dimitry T. Shepilov, was invited to attend the celebration of the departure of the last British troops from the Suez Canal Zone on June 18. During his visit in Cairo the Egyptian government put out a rumor that he had offered to supplement an earlier Soviet offer of 400,000,000 pounds to build the Aswan Dam, "with no strings attached."

By this time Secretary of State Dulles had had enough of Egyptian blackmail and insults and on July 19 he abruptly withdrew the American offer to finance the project. Britain and the World Bank followed suit. Shepilov then revealed that he had made no commitment concerning the dam. The Egyptian bluff had been called. Nasser, left in a difficult position and casting about angrily for a way out, announced the nationalization of the Suez Canal Co. on July 26. This meant little to the United States or Russia, but much to Britain and France, who depended on the canal for their supply of oil, and both nations began to make military preparations to assert their rights by force if necessary. Fearing complications, Dulles flew to London to persuade the British to negotiate instead. They agreed on the assumption that if negotiations failed, the United States would back them up in the use of force. There followed a series of conferences (Conference of Twenty-two, Menzies Mission, Conference of Eighteen, the Suez Canal Users' Association, the UN Security Council), the proposals of each of which Nasser rejected or evaded. Only the use of force seemed to remain, but Dulles had renounced it in advance by stating during the negotiations that the western powers did not intend to "shoot our way through the canal." Britain and France felt keenly that the United States had let them down.

At this point Israel entered the picture. The Israelis were naturally greatly disturbed by the Soviet-Egyptian arms deal and by the withdrawal of the British troops from the Suez Canal, which removed a protective shield between them and Egypt. It seems from strong circumstantial evidence that Israel proposed to France, with which it had forged strong ties based on their common dislike of the Arabs, to "set up" the situation in the Suez Canal for western intervention: Israel would attack Egypt, whereupon France and Britain would intervene, ostensibly as impartial agents, to protect the canal. Whether the charge of collusion was true or not, this is indeed what happened. On October 29 Israel unleashed a lightning campaign, which sent the Egyptians reeling across the Sinai desert leaving behind their fine Soviet equipment. On the following day Britain and France addressed an ultimatum to Israel and Egypt to retire ten miles from the canal. Israel, which had not yet reached the ten-mile limit, at once complied. Egypt refused. Five days later an Anglo-French force landed in the canal zone. The Egyptians put up a plucky fight in Ismailia and blocked the canal by sinking ships in it, but otherwise their resistance was weak. Had the Anglo-French force moved more swiftly and seized the canal rapidly, the world might have acquiesced in the *fait accompli*. But its slowness and caution allowed world opinion to form and the United Nations to act. Russia threatened to send "volunteers" to the rescue of Egypt, but was probably glad of the Anglo-French intervention which diverted attention from her bloody suppression of the contemporary Hungarian Revolt. The United States, which had no advance information of the Anglo-French plan, was annoyed and disassociated itself completely from it. The world was treated to the unaccustomed spectacle of the United States and Russia voting together in the UN General Assembly to order a cease-fire and dispatch a UN Emergency Force to the canal to replace the Anglo-French force (November 7). The French were inclined to finish the job in defiance of the UN order, but the British, under heavy pressure from Canada and India, yielded. Israel, isolated, also yielded. The situation soon reverted to the *status quo ante*. The net result of the Suez adventure was the collapse of whatever influence Britain still had in the Near and Middle East and a great diplomatic victory for Nasser — after a stinging military defeat. The western alliance — and consequently also METO — was greatly shaken.

This development was clearly not to the interest of the United States. After riding the high horse of moral principle during the crisis, the American leaders had some pragmatic second thoughts. President Eisenhower requested of Congress a special fund of $200,000,000 for military and economic aid to the nations of the Near and Middle East and authorization "to employ the armed forces of the United States as he deems necessary to secure and protect the territorial integrity and political independence of any such nation or group of nations requesting such aid against overt armed aggression from any nation controlled by international communism." (January 5, 1957). With some hesitation Congress appropriated the requested funds and voted a resolution authorizing the President to use the armed forces of the United States as he saw fit in the Near and Middle East (March 9, 1957). This became known as the "Eisenhower Doctrine."

In the caustic words of former Secretary of State Dean Acheson the Eisenhower Doctrine proposed "to fight an enemy that is not going to attack with forces that do not exist to carry out a policy you have not yet decided upon." It postulated that Nasser was dominated by international communism and assumed that he was bent on armed aggression, for which there was little evidence. Actually, Nasser was an Arab nationalist, with whom Russia soon found it as difficult to deal as did the western powers. He was bent on uniting the Arabs, not by armed aggression but by propaganda and internal subversion. By its efforts to check his influence, the United States became deeply involved in the turbid and swiftly changing currents and countercurrents of Arab politics, in which it, no less than Russia, found it difficult to navigate (see Chapter 65).

Section IX: THE WESTERN NATIONS IN THE AFTERMATH OF THE WAR

51

THE UNITED STATES

. . . In the councils of government, we must guard against the acquisition of unwarranted power, whether sought or unsought, by the military-industrial complex. The potential for the disastrous rise of misplaced power exists and will persist.

DWIGHT D. EISENHOWER, FAREWELL ADDRESS, 1961

1. DEMOBILIZATION AND RECONVERSION

THE PEOPLE OF the United States emerged from the Second World War in a singularly fortunate position. They had suffered no armed invasion like those which devastated France, Italy, Russia, and Germany. Their cities had not been blasted to rubble in repeated air raids like the cities of Britain and Japan. Their population had endured no famine or epidemics; their factories had doubled their output within six years; their farms produced surpluses that were feeding hungry millions in Europe and Asia. The American army was the best equipped and the American navy the most powerful that the world had ever known. The contrast between American prosperity and world poverty had become even more striking than it was before the war. Although the 140,000,000 people in the United States in 1945 made up only 6 per cent of the global population, they enjoyed 40 per cent of the world's estimated income and controlled 50 per cent of the world's industrial machinery. Less fortunate nations, enemy or Allied, had watched with awe as the giant republic of the west gathered its resources and struck down its foes. When peace returned they waited with equal apprehension to learn what use the American people would make of their position of world leadership.

The American people themselves did not know the answer. Their first wish, in the exuberance of victory, was to have the millions of service men and women return and to relax the war restrictions on food, travel, consumers' goods, and luxuries. Despite warnings from military and naval experts that too-sudden demobilization might wreck an unsurpassed fighting machine and might leave the nation inadequately protected in a world still full of menace, the personnel of the armed forces was reduced from over 12 to under 3 million in less than a year. Fears that the release of so many active workers would bring on a wave of unemployment proved groundless. Although late in 1945 the Office of War Mobilization and Reconversion forecast a possible unemployment total of 8 million by the spring of 1946, the Bureau of Labor, when spring came, announced that only 2,310,000 eligible workers were unemployed. By December, 1946, all but 750,000 discharged veterans had found work and were being rapidly absorbed into the business life of the country.

Rising prices, fear of inflation, and a national debt that had increased fivefold in five years were the chief economic problems that disturbed the American people in the first postwar years. They could still recall the decade of expansion after World War I and the disastrous collapse of prosperity after 1929. In 1946 war savings and soldiers' pay, added to the swollen income of the war years, created a situation in which the demand for consumers' goods far exceeded the supply. The removal of government controls, which were blamed for the lack of goods, did not satisfy the impatience of the buying public because the problem was not so simple that the abolition of a few regulations would solve it. No shortage was more acute, for instance, than that of housing. For five years building materials had been diverted to essential factory construction, to new dwellings for 400,000 migrant workers summoned to war jobs, to barracks and offices for military and naval personnel. Old houses had fallen into disrepair and few new ones had been built to replace them. The lack of living quarters became a national scandal, but it did not prove feasible to speed new homes from an assembly line.

Thus the people of the United States after 1945 were forcibly reminded that their economy was partly out of joint. They were the richest people in the world. They had amazed other nations by their capacity for organization and production to meet the demands of war. Within six years they had doubled their industrial output, their available electric power, and their national income. They had tripled the amount of money in circulation within their borders and quadrupled their savings, which had soared from $13 billion to $50 billion. But they could not produce on demand the houses they needed to shelter millions of families crowded into tenements, rooming houses, shacks, and automobile camps. Despite the efforts of the federal bureaus — the National Housing Agency, the Federal Home Loan Bank, the Federal Housing Authority — lack of homes remained a major grievance of the people. There was also a lack of sufficient school buildings, and a need for better highways with safer intersections.

A generation later the cost of over-hasty industrialization began to dismay the American people as the air of their cities became increasingly contaminated by poisonous gases and many lakes and rivers were polluted by excess industrial wastes.

BUDGET EXPENDITURES OF THE UNITED STATES
FEDERAL GOVERNMENT

Total ———   For Defense ― ― ―

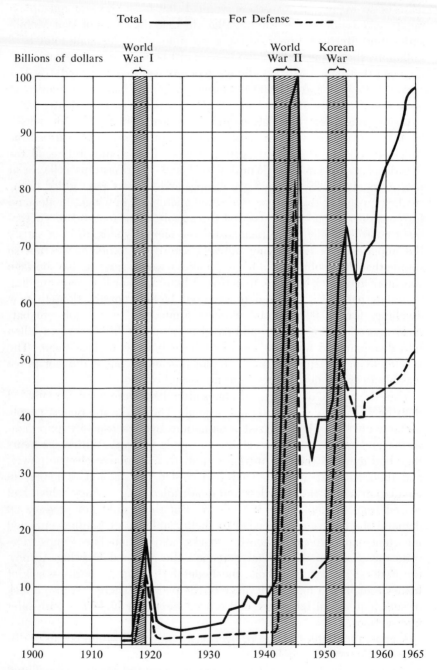

2. AMERICAN PROSPERITY AND PRODUCTION

Between 1900 and 1967 the population of the United States rose 166 per cent, from roughly 75 million to 200 million. During the same period the world population increased approximately 127 per cent, from about 1.5 billion to over 3 billion. Thus, in the first half of the twentieth century, the American people increased faster than the global population as a whole. In 1900 the United States held 5 percent of the human race; in 1967 it held 6 per cent. By 1967, however, this trend had been reversed and the world population had begun to increase faster than that of the United States.

Prosperity and progress not only brought the people of the United States richer, fuller lives, it brought them *longer* lives. Between 1900 and 1967 the average life expectancy in the United States rose from forty-eight to seventy years (see page 669). For comparisons it might be noted that, although the expectancy was increasing almost everywhere on the globe, three-fourths of the world population in 1967 still had a life expectancy of little more than thirty-five years, roughly half of the American total. Women in the United States had a higher life expectancy than men; by 1967 they outnumbered the men by nearly 3 million.

The care of the aged became an increasingly acute problem as their numbers increased. A Social Security Act, passed in 1935, and frequently amended, provided old age, survivors, and disability insurance. By 1966 most American workers were covered by this act. During their years of employment they contributed a percentage of their earnings and their employers contributed an equal amount. When insured workers reached sixty-five they became eligible for a retirement pension. If a worker died before retirement age his widow received a pension and an allowance for any children while these were under eighteen years. In 1966 the Social Security Act was further amended to increase the benefits and to provide hospital and medical insurance for the aged.

The production and prosperity of the American people increased more rapidly than their population. Nowhere in the world were the techniques of mass production developed so successfully. With more machines to help him, the hourly output of the American worker was three times that of a British worker, even though England had been the original home of the industrial revolution. This increased production brought the American worker higher wages and a higher standard of living. Within twenty-five years (1940–1965) the gross national product of the United States (the total value of goods and services produced) had climbed from $100 billion to $675 billion. Within a decade (1955–1965) the total personal income of the American people had risen from $310 billion to over $500 billion.

Farm output as well as factory output increased at an astonishing rate. One reason for this was the construction of irrigation dams which pro-

AGRICULTURE IN THE UNITED STATES, 1920-1965

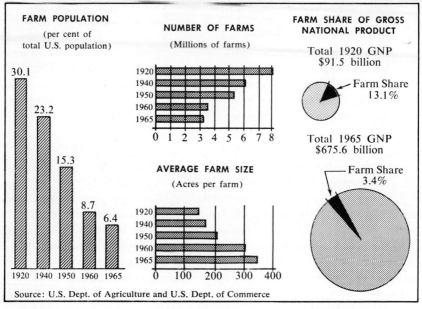

FARM POPULATION
(per cent of total U.S. population)

30.1

23.2

15.3

8.7

6.4

1920 1940 1950 1960 1965

NUMBER OF FARMS
(Millions of farms)

1920
1940
1950
1960
1965

0 1 2 3 4 5 6 7 8

AVERAGE FARM SIZE
(Acres per farm)

1920
1940
1950
1960
1965

0   100   200   300   400

FARM SHARE OF GROSS NATIONAL PRODUCT

Total 1920 GNP
$91.5 billion

Farm Share
13.1%

Total 1965 GNP
$675.6 billion

Farm Share
3.4%

Source: U.S. Dept. of Agriculture and U.S. Dept. of Commerce

vided water and electricity for rural areas. Although the initial cost of such dams was sometimes high, they paid for themselves more than ten times over by the value of the additional crops they made possible. A rapid rise in the use of chemical fertilizers, and of other chemicals that destroyed weeds, blights, and insect pests, further increased the farm output while reducing the farmer's labor. Within a century this "agricultural revolution" changed the American farmers from a majority to a minority group. In 1940 one farmer could produce enough food to feed ten people; by 1965 one farmer could produce enough food to feed thirty-two people. By 1965, farm population had dropped to 7 per cent of the total United States population. Yet the farmers not only fed the whole United States population but also produced vast surpluses which became increasingly difficult to dispose. The average size of the farms increased as improved equipment enabled a farmer to cultivate more land, but the farm population and the farmer's share of the national income declined. The "farm problem," the question of how to market the excess crops and assure the farmer a fair share in the national prosperity, became an acute political issue. In 1965, the Department of Agriculture paid the farmers $2.4 billion in subsidies, partly to support farm prices and partly to limit production.

In contrast to the farmers, the factory workers improved their income rapidly, especially after 1945. The average hourly wage of American factory workers after World War II was $1.25, but by 1965 this had risen to $2.60. In addition those workers received "fringe benefits" (social insurance, accident insurance, paid vacations, bonuses) that were equivalent to another fifty cents an hour.

Their higher incomes enabled American families to enjoy material benefits that most people in less affluent countries could not afford. In the United States one person in five owned an automobile, compared to one in twenty-four in Britain, one in forty-two in France, one in 300 in the Soviet Union. Almost half the world's tractors operated on American farms, and almost half the world's telephones, radios, and television sets were to be found in the United States.

Yet despite the increasing production and prosperity in the United States there were dark spots in the picture. Some areas and some groups did not profit adequately from the expanding economy. By 1965 the average income per capita was $2600, and in the wealthiest states (New York, Connecticut, Delaware, Illinois, Nevada, California) it was over $3000. But in the less fortunate states of the southeast it was less than $2000. This inequality of income imposed a serious handicap on such activities as education, for 90 per cent of the cost of educating the young was raised by state or local taxes. If a state or locality was poor this meant that its schools were likely to be inadequate and over-crowded. Such conditions tended to *keep* a community poor and economically retarded because the length and quality of a child's schooling largely decided his later earning capacity. Census returns for 1960 showed that if the head of a family had only elementary schooling the family income was likely to be about $4200. If the head of a family had finished high school the family income averaged $5500. For the one household in ten where the head of the family had college training the income was $7600.

In an age when the need for unskilled laborers was declining and the demand for skilled workers and professionally trained experts increasing, adequate provision for the education of the young was essential. Yet the American people, despite their unprecedented prosperity, showed a surprising indifference to this critical problem. At the opening of the twentieth century 17 per cent of all taxes raised had been devoted to education. By 1932 the quota had risen to 25 per cent of all taxes collected. But twenty-five years later the proportion had declined over one-half and only 12 per cent of the total taxes raised was expended on public education. In the decade after World War II the affluent American people spent $13 billion a year for recreation, and $15 billion a year for alcoholic beverages, tobacco, and cosmetics. But they spared less than eight billion dollars a year for their public elementary and secondary schools.

In the 1950's the fear that the Soviet Union would outstrip the United States in trained manpower began to awaken American leaders to the gravity of the educational problem. They noted, for example, that be-

EDUCATION IN THE UNITED STATES
ENROLLMENT, 1950-65

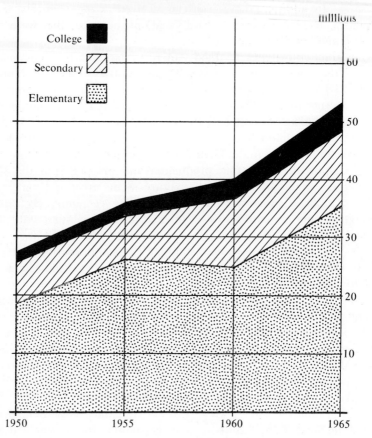

tween 1950 and 1955 the number of engineering graduates in Russia rose from 28,000 to 63,000, while during the same years the number of engineering graduates in the United States dropped from 52,000 to 23,000. The solution most frequently suggested was that the Federal Government should help the individual states by standardizing the quality of American education through legislation and grants. In 1953, in response to these suggestions, Congress created a new Department of Health, Education, and Welfare, which in 1965 distributed $7.6 billion in federal aid to education. In 1954 the United States Supreme Court ruled that the segregation of Negro children in separate schools was unconstitutional, but a number of states evaded or delayed desegregation. A double crisis — financial and racial — had developed in American education, but solutions lagged until the 1960's and will be discussed later in this chapter.

PUBLIC DEBT OF THE UNITED STATES — BEFORE AND AFTER THREE WARS

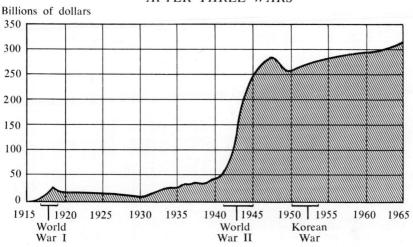

3. TAXATION, DEFENSE, AND FOREIGN AID

Two main factors accounted for the phenomenal rise in the annual budget and the public debt of the United States after 1940. The first, which may be distinguished as the domestic factor, resulted from the continued growth of "big government" the assignment to federal departments, bureaus, and regulatory agencies of ever-mounting responsibilities for supervising public affairs. This meant, inevitably, that as its duties increased the Federal Government needed a larger and larger staff, until by 1965 it employed 2.7 million civilian workers.

By 1965 the cost of national defense, past and future, amounted to $55 billion annually. This was greater than twice the cost of all other government services combined. The major items in this $55 billion outlay for national defense were the maintenance of the army, navy, and air force, the development of atomic weapons, the purchase and storing of essential materials, pensions and medical care for veterans of past wars, and military aid to nations whose defense was considered important for the defense of the United States. Five-eighths of the annual federal budget represented the price the American nation paid to preserve its position as the leader of the "free" peoples of the world.

The extraordinary increase in government spending had effects on American life that were not easy to estimate. By the 1950's more than half the scientific research and development in the United States was sponsored and financed by the Federal Government. It might seem, at first thought, that so long as the money was made available for research, where that money came from was not important. But there is an ancient proverb that he who pays the piper calls the tune. Many federal agencies,

UNITED STATES FOREIGN AID, 1946-1966

THE YEARLY TREND
Spending in billions of dollars

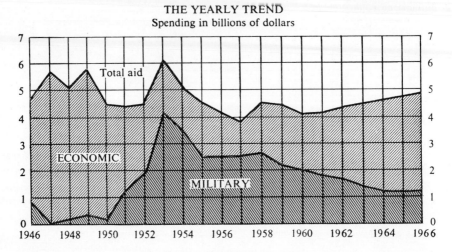

especially those concerned with national defense, stipulated what line the research should take. It was significant that the government allocated thirty times as much money for the physical and biological sciences as for the social sciences, and that some research projects were pursued in complete secrecy. Whether directed research was as valuable or creative as unrestricted and independent research raised further questions. One of the leading American scientists, Karl T. Compton, offered a thoughtful opinion on this point. He warned that:

Scientific discovery, in its very nature and as proved by experience, does not progress according to preconceived plan and is stifled if attempts are made to control the free initiative of the research workers or to limit the freedom of communication.[1]

Viscount Hailsham, British minister for science, expressed the same thought even more forcibly. ". . . The marriage between science and defence is corrupting," he declared, "and will at best turn science from a liberating to a destructive source, and at the worst ultimately dry up the wells of inventiveness in the scientist himself."

Another problem created by the rapid growth of "big government" was the danger that the vast organizations built up to handle the defense plans and expenditures might become unwieldy and unmanageable. Bureaucracies tend to grow and to perpetuate themselves, almost like living organisms. After 1945 the United States maintained a large defense force to meet its global commitments. In an attempt to reduce the rivalry between the army, navy, and air force, Congress approved a measure for

[1] John E. Burchard (ed.), *Mid-Century: The Social Implications of Scientific Progress* (Cambridge, Mass., 1950), p. 25.

unifying the armed forces (1947) but the rivalry continued. The Department of Defense, with its headquarters in the Pentagon building near Washington, exercised a broad influence in national affairs. To some foreign observers this military influence seemed disturbing and incalculable. A member of the British Parliament voiced the fear that "the military machine" in the United States would "become the dictator of political policy."

Three difficulties helped to explain the high cost and limited success of American defense efforts. One was the continuing rivalry between the army and the air force, both of which pursued rocket programs. A second difficulty arose from the scramble of business firms for defense contracts, which brought pressure groups and "lobbyists" to Washington. But perhaps the most serious threat to a sound allotment of defense funds resulted from the attempt to make them serve two purposes. The American people expected the Federal Government to reduce unemployment and aid areas where economic progress lagged. The readiest way the government at Washington could do this was to allot contracts for war materials, purchase excess commodities to "harden" prices, or establish defense installations or military airfields in retarded regions. These various difficulties that beset the defense effort were frankly summed up by a former head of the Army Ordnance Missile Command who wrote in 1960:

Varying and opposing pressures stemming from such considerations as the desire to receive the benefits of Government spending, to preserve the status quo, to support current employment levels in specific areas — such elements seem to me to do more to distort and upset proper decisions where national defense is concerned than any other group of factors.[2]

During the Second World War, as already explained in Chapter 42, the United States provided some fifty billion dollars in aid to its partners in the struggle. After the war ended this aid to foreign countries continued but took new forms. How American dollars financed a European Recovery Program, and helped to arm the nations that joined the North Atlantic Treaty Organization, has already been discussed in Chapter 48. Between 1946 and 1965 the United States provided over $100 billion in foreign aid, a total that exceeded the sum it expended under the wartime Lend-Lease activities. Most of this $100 billion was spent to help non-communist peoples improve their economy or to provide them with war material so that they might better resist communist pressure.

By 1960 there were signs that American generosity, or what some critics called American waste and extravagance, was straining the American economy. Foreign competition from nations which the United States had helped to strengthen became steadily more severe. The continual outflow

[2] Reprinted by permission of G. P. Putnam's Sons from *Countdown for Decision* by Major General John B. Medaris. Copyright © 1960 by Major General John B. Medaris.

of dollars in the form of economic and military aid, the expense of supporting American forces and bases overseas, the money spent by American tourists, and the capital exported by Americans for investment abroad where interest rates were higher caused an adverse balance of payments. One result was a reduction in the American gold reserve. A second was the slowing down in the rate of American economic growth. The need to spur American business to a more rapid development was recognized, but the best method for accomplishing this remained in doubt.

4. POLITICAL DEVELOPMENTS 1939–1961

The victory of the Democratic Party in the election of 1932 opened a fourteen-year period during which the Democrats controlled the Presidency, the Senate, and the House of Representatives. Franklin Delano Roosevelt, who received nearly twenty-three million popular votes in 1932, was re-elected in 1936 with his popular vote increased to more than 27 million. His decision to defy precedent and stand for a third term in 1940 was again endorsed by some twenty-seven million voters, against 22 million for his Republican Party opponent, Wendell Willkie. In 1944, in the midst of World War II, when Roosevelt ran for a fourth term, his popular vote declined slightly to 25 million, his opponent Thomas E. Dewey receiving 22 million. Roosevelt died in office on April 12, 1945, and was succeeded by the Vice President, Harry S. Truman.

With the election of the Eightieth Congress in 1946 the Republican party won the lead in both houses and anticipated a sweeping victory in 1948. Instead, Truman defeated Thomas E. Dewey, and the Democrats regained control of both houses in the Eighty-first Congress. For the presidential contest of 1952 the Republicans nominated Dwight D. Eisenhower, the popular general who had won fame by his leadership in the liberation of Europe in 1944–45 and his organization of the North Atlantic Treaty forces in 1951–52. Eisenhower won easily over his Democratic opponent, Adlai E. Stevenson, and the Republicans gained a small lead in the House but failed to control the Senate.

Eisenhower's eight years in the White House (he was re-elected for a second term in 1956) proved that his talent for cooperation and his desire to preserve harmony in domestic and international relationships were deep and genuine. He failed, however, to provide the vigorous leadership most Americans believed necessary in a time of critical developments. A heart attack (1955) and a mild stroke (1957) reduced his activities and made him increasingly dependent on his assistants. The fact, too, that during the eight years of his presidency his party never had a clear majority in both houses forced him to work as best he could with a critical Congress. American foreign policy was largely shaped by John Foster Dulles from 1953 until his death in 1959, whereupon Christian A. Herter succeeded him as secretary of state. The vice president, Richard M. Nixon, also relieved Eisenhower of some duties and was regarded as his logical successor when Eisenhower's second term ended in 1961. A constitutional amendment, ratified in 1951, provided that no president should serve more than two terms.

American policies, domestic as well as international, were profoundly influenced after World War II by the "Cold War" that developed between the "free nations" led by the United States and the Communist nations led by the Soviet Union. Russian success in developing nuclear weapons by 1949 ended the American monopoly of atomic power and alarmed the American people. The belief that the Russian success would not have been possible without the secret information obtained by Soviet spies made espionage a political issue. Suspicious legislators, notably Senator Joseph McCarthy, sought proof of subversive activities. The "spy scare" was intensified when several Soviet agents were brought to trial and some members of the State Department and other government agencies were convicted of copying secret documents for Communist use. Unfortunately, the listing of numerous organizations as pro-Communist and the theory of guilt by association led the investigating committees to darken the reputation of many innocent citizens without adequate evidence. Although McCarthy was finally rebuked by the Senate in 1954 and died three years later, the spirit of "McCarthyism" lingered. Foreign observers often viewed the hunt for "subversives" in the United States more seriously than most Americans did, and concluded that the democratic principles of freedom of speech, belief, and opinion had been curtailed in this country.

The basic cause of the "spy scare" was the growing sense of insecurity that oppressed the American people. The feeling that America was lagging in its efforts and that the prestige of the United States was declining while that of Russia was increasing, played a large part in deciding the election of 1960. The Republican party nominated Richard M. Nixon to succeed Eisenhower; the Democrats nominated John F. Kennedy. Kennedy, the first Roman Catholic to occupy the presidency, won by a narrow popular plurality, and the Democrats increased their lead in the Senate and the House of Representatives. The United States entered the decade of the 1960's under a Democratic regime that was pledged to increase American prestige and expand the national economy.

5. POLITICAL DEVELOPMENTS SINCE 1961

As President John F. Kennedy gained exceptional popularity and his tragic death from an assassin's bullet on November 22, 1963, shocked the nation profoundly. His youth (he was forty-three when he took office), his magnetic personality, and the advisors he chose gave his administration qualities of vigor and vision that quickened the popular imagination. "My fellow Americans," he urged in his Inaugural Address, "ask not what your country can do for you — ask what you can do for your country." His domestic program, identified with the phrase "the New Frontier," included aid and expansion for education at all levels, relief (medical and financial) for the aged, assistance for blighted areas, both urban and rural, conservation of natural resources, and a vigorous policy of space exploration. A further and novel element in his program was the stimulus and encouragement of American writers, musicians and artists, a venture in which he was assisted by his charming and talented wife, Jacqueline.

In foreign affairs Kennedy's successful combination of firmness, realism and idealism brought him an initial failure subsequently redressed by outstanding successes. The failure came in April, 1961, in a venture already prepared before he took office — a plan, encouraged by the United States Central Intelligence Agency, to equip and land an insurgent force in Cuba to overthrow the Communist dictator, Dr. Fidel Castro. The attempt failed catastrophically, to the discredit of the United States and the advantage of Castro. By October, 1962, at Castro's invitation, Russian engineers were equipping Cuban sites with ballistic missiles which threatened American cities. After alerting all the Latin American republics, Kennedy promptly announced a naval blockade of Cuba. The Soviet government agreed to withdraw all missiles (see p. 844).

In its final years the Eisenhower administration had sought to improve its relations with the Latin American republics through proposals for cooperation (Act of Bogotá, 1960). To increase and extend such aid, Kennedy proposed an "Alliance for Progress." The United States offered to provide financial aid and scientific advice and equipment to help the people of Latin America improve their social and economic condition and strengthen their democratic institutions. A further project initiated by Kennedy — the Peace Corps — provided "a pool of trained American men and women sent overseas . . . to help foreign countries meet their urgent needs for skilled manpower. . . ."

On Kennedy's assassination, Lyndon Baines Johnson succeeded him. Johnson's main interest lay in domestic affairs. His deep sympathy for the impoverished and underprivileged moved him to hasten legislation, already pending, to promote civil rights, and to recommend an intensified "war on poverty." His proposals to shape a "Great Society" won the approval of the Congress and the nation. In the presidential election of 1964 Johnson defeated the Republican party candidate, Barry Goldwater, by the largest popular majority and the largest popular margin in United States history.

After 1965, however, Johnson's popularity declined, despite his geniality, his skill in managing the Congress, and his eagerness to obtain a consensus on controversial issues. On the domestic front, the struggle to achieve civil rights and opportunities for Negro citizens — in the use of

BUDGET ESTIMATES, 1966

Defense, Space Exploration
(primarily for defensive aims)
Veterans Administration
Foreign Aid, partly economic,
partly military

66%

Other Budget Expenses — 11%

Education Health and Welfare — 11%

Interest on the Public Debt — 12%

public facilities, in education, in employment, and in housing — encountered persistent opposition and resulted in rioting, loss of life, and destruction of property. These riots proved particularly costly in cities where large discontented Negro majorities were crowded into decayed tenements and slum areas.

The rapid growth of American cities created a multitude of difficulties for which there could be no cheap or easy solution. By the 1960's only one-third of the American people still lived in rural areas. The remaining two-thirds, who lived under urban conditions, found the larger cities congested and beset with problems — problems of housing, transportation, water supply, waste disposal, air pollution, and crime. The Federal Government made increasing contributions to encourage plans for "urban renewal." In 1965, Congress created a new Department of Housing and Urban Development. As its head, President Johnson named and the Senate confirmed Robert C. Weaver, the first Negro ever to be appointed to the United States Cabinet. The continuing shift in population from rural to urban regions also created a political problem — an imbalance in legislative representation. In two historic decisions (1964) the Supreme Court ruled that a reapportionment of congressional districts and districts in both houses of the state legislatures was overdue. The Court affirmed that "as nearly as may be practicable," such districts should be made substantially equal in population.

Although the country continued to enjoy a prolonged period of economic prosperity, by 1966 the Stock Market declined while the cost of living rose. The main reason for the creeping inflation and the decline in Johnson's popularity, was a fateful and frustrating conflict in Southeast Asia, a war into which the American nation drifted slowly, reluctantly, and inextricably.

The origin, motivation, and escalation of the second Indochinese War will be discussed in Chapter 64. Its effects on American life were to stimulate defense industries through increased expenditures, reduce the funds available for the "Great Society," and increase the public debt through budget deficits. Despite Johnson's earnest efforts at economy in Federal spending, the national budget continued to rise. Opposition to the growing American involvement in the Vietnamese conflict led a vocal minority to denounce "Mr. Johnson's War" and the congressional elections of November, 1966 provided a test of sentiment on the war issue. The results indicated that a majority of the American people were prepared to continue the war despite the risk that it might lead to hostilities with China and possibly with Russia. The election did reveal, however, some change of mood on domestic issues. Discontent at the rising cost of living, and resentment among the whites in some areas at the programs for assuring equal rights for the Negroes, brought losses to the Democratic party. These and other influences enabled the Republicans to win back some of the ground their party had lost in 1964; they gained 4 seats in the Senate and 47 in the House of Representatives. Although the Democrats retained a 4–3 majority in the House and a 2–1 majority in the Senate, it seemed almost certain that President Johnson's policies would encounter increased legislative resistance in the new Congress.

52

GREAT BRITAIN

"If you overstrain your resources, you weaken the country's economic position and so become less influential in the world as a whole. That is the error we have got to avoid."

BRITISH FOREIGN SECRETARY MICHAEL STEWART, 1966

1. THE BRITISH BALANCE SHEET OF WAR

GREAT BRITAIN FOUGHT two great wars against Germany in the first half of the twentieth century and won both, but the cost in blood and treasure strained British resources. A comparison of the British losses in World War I and World War II illuminates the strange odds and vicissitudes of combat. In the four years of World War I (1914–1918) the toll for the embattled empire was almost one million dead. In the six years of World War II (1939–1945) its losses on the battlefronts reached about 545,000 dead. The lighter loss of life in the second struggle is surprising because it was the longer and more desperate of the two, an ordeal in which the people stood fast amid stranger perils than their ancestors had ever known.

British financial expenditure also appeared at first sight to be somewhat lighter in World War II, but this was a deceptive impression. In the earlier struggle the public debt climbed almost tenfold, but in the six years from 1939 to 1945 it increased only threefold. When World War II closed the British debt stood at 22 billion pounds (about $90 billion, or less than $2000 per capita). The postwar debt of the United States ($300 billion) was approximately $2050 for each American citizen. Such comparisons can be misleading. A debt burden of $2000 weighed more heavily on the average Briton with his smaller income, and Britain had no natural resources equivalent to those of the United States. The chief wealth of the British people lay in their tenacity, skill, and manufacturing techniques. Both America and Britain had learned that the cost of victory comes high, but for the British the cost was so high that it threatened to lower permanently their economy and their standards of living.

This gloomy economic prospect did not daunt the British: they assailed the tasks of reconstruction with dogged determination. During the war defense needs had overshadowed all others; but as victory neared, the nation turned to audit its resources, prepare a peacetime program, and organize the delayed drive for greater social justice. This shift of attention was already manifest in the general election of July, 1945. The war government headed by Winston Churchill was overthrown, and the Labor party, which won almost 400 seats in Parliament against 240 for all other parties combined, controlled the new cabinet. The Conservatives, with Churchill still at their head, now formed "His Majesty's Loyal Opposition." Thus, even before Japan capitulated in August, 1945, the British people were turning from total war to the equally exacting problems of peace. The triumph of the Labor party proved that planned production, full employment, adequate health protection, nationalization of basic industries, better housing, better schools, and other social aims were regarded as urgent and overdue. The British electors by a majority of almost 3 million had registered their conviction that Churchill, the dynamic wartime minister, had fulfilled his mission. For the social reforms of peace the Labor party, headed by the methodical, conscientious, and somewhat colorless Clement R. Attlee, seemed a more suitable agent of the national will. The British respect their statesmen and reward them, but they do not forget that excessive popularity and power confided to one man is a peril to democratic government. This chapter will describe how the British people met the problem of resources, the problem of social justice, and the problem of imperial defense after 1945.

The first step in national bookkeeping was to adjust debits and credits and prepare a peace budget and balance sheet. As in previous wars Great Britain had poured out subsidies to numerous allies, subsidies which totaled over $8 billion before the war ended. Of this sum, about 60 per cent, or $5 billion was credited to the United States (charged against American Lend-Lease credits of $30 billion); and 15 per cent, or over $1 billion, to Russia. Other belligerent states, war governments-in-exile, and neutral nations which received British financial aid, were Poland, France, Greece, Czechoslovakia, Belgium, the Netherlands, Yugoslavia, Norway and Denmark, and two nonbelligerents, Turkey and Portugal. The Turks received $128 million from London to help them arm against a possible German attack, a heavy outlay for the British but prudent because it helped to keep Turkey secure and neutral.

Few, if any, of the British loans to wartime allies were collectible. Like the American government, the British did not ask or expect a full or prompt settlement. Their chief concern was to see the world return to normal trading, for trade was essential to their survival and it is difficult to trade with insolvent debtors while berating them for nonpayment of old obligations. It seemed better to clear the board of as many old scores as possible, and this generous spirit determined the debt settlement (or more correctly debt cancellation) which the British concluded with the

BRITISH TRADE DILEMMA AFTER WORLD WAR II

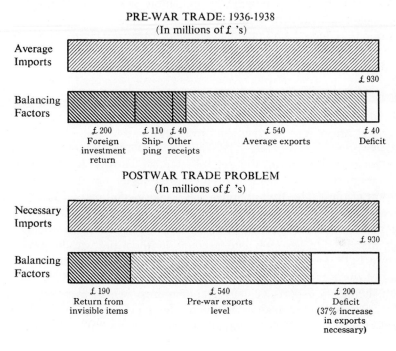

PRE-WAR TRADE: 1936-1938
(In millions of £ 's)

Average Imports — £ 930

Balancing Factors

£ 200 — Foreign investment return
£ 110 — Ship-ping
£ 40 — Other receipts
£ 540 — Average exports
£ 40 — Deficit

POSTWAR TRADE PROBLEM
(In millions of £ 's)

Necessary Imports — £ 930

Balancing Factors

£ 190 — Return from invisible items
£ 540 — Pre-war exports level
£ 200 — Deficit (37% increase in exports necessary)

United States. They agreed to modify their existing system which gave preference to states within their empire and to open their trade lanes more freely to all nations. In return the United States reduced British Lend-Lease debts to 650 million dollars to be repaid with 2 per cent interest over a period of fifty years. At the same time, however, the British government obtained a new loan of $3.75 billion so that their postwar obligations to the United States, after refunding, totaled about $4.5 billion.

How swiftly and how completely the British could restore their national prosperity was by no means clear, for their economy had suffered a drastic dislocation. The tripling of their public debt during World War II did not tell the full story of their indebtedness. Part of the war costs had been met by the liquidation of foreign investments. In 1939 British investors held title to an estimated $40 billion in foreign ventures and this "exported" capital brought them dividends of one billion dollars a year. The government, in contrast, was relatively free from foreign debt and owed the rest of the world the moderate sum of five hundred million pounds (one billion eight hundred million dollars). But the war inverted this balance. The curtailment of normal commerce, the increased armament burden, the ship losses and property destruction exhausted credit and transformed Great Britain from the leading lender to the leading borrower among the nations. By 1946 British international liabilities (omitting Lend-Lease debts to the United States) exceeded 3.5 billion pounds ($14 billion). These heavy obligations, which were termed "sterling balances," the British hoped to repay in time but they were in no position to reduce them immediately. They therefore invited the nations, including their own Dominions, which had built up these sterling balances by supplying British war needs, to accept British manufactures in repayment.

2. THE DRIVE FOR ECONOMIC RECOVERY

What many Americans did not fully realize was that the British drive for foreign trade was dictated by inexorable logic. Great Britain had to "export or die." The United States was a continental market in itself but Great Britain, for a century the "workshop of the world," would be a shop without customers if its overseas trade collapsed. This was the first fact that the British took into account in their postwar bookkeeping. Before 1939 the value of their yearly imports reached almost $5 billion. Half of these essential purchases of food and raw material they paid for with their own exports (chiefly manufactures) which averaged a little over $2.5 billion annually. Shipping, banking, insurance, and other services brought in $700 million additional. But this still left the balance of trade adverse by over a billion dollars, and they counted upon the billion a year which came from foreign investments to help rectify the balance. After 1945, with their shipping reduced to 24 per cent of the world total; with $5 billion of their foreign investments liquidated; with overseas liabilities increased sevenfold from $2 billion to $14 billion they faced a serious dilemma. To recover the living standards of prewar days they estimated that they would have to raise their export trade by 50 per cent. To improve living standards appreciably they would have to increase export volume 100 per cent, which meant they must double the 1938 figures.

To increase their exports and reduce their imports to achieve a trade balance was thus the key to British national recovery. Without increased trade there could be little social progress and no guarantee of full employment. The end of the war did not mean an end to the emergency, a fact which the new Labor Government recognized by asking (and obtaining) an extension of its wartime emergency powers for a five-year period. The government was to lead the economic battle for trade and direct all British subjects, as in wartime, in the cooperative effort demanded for survival.

British prosperity in the nineteenth century had been built on "coal, cotton, and cargoes" — that is, on the production, consumption, and export of coal, on an unrivalled leadership in the manufacture of textiles, and on the rewards that came from carrying a great part of the world's sea trade in British-built and British-owned ships. By the middle of the twentieth century British leadership in all three activities had passed. The best British coal mines were exhausted, and oil (which Britain did not produce) was replacing coal as a fuel. British leadership in the manufacture of textiles declined sharply as the United States, Japan, India, and other countries expanded their output. Britain's share of the world's mercantile marine also declined. In 1939 the British Empire, with some 24 million tons, had twice the tonnage of the United States which had less than 12 million; but by 1946, although the British Empire still had 24 million, the United States had 50 million tons of merchant shipping.

British trade was dependent upon British shipping. This dependence had increased as British mines became less productive and the minerals and raw materials ferried from other continents filled a larger part in feeding British factories. War losses cut the British share of world tonnage from 30 to 24 per cent between 1939 and 1945, while the registered merchant tonnage of the United States rose from 14 to 51 per cent and that of the Soviet Union from 2 to 3 per cent of the total. One year after peace returned the iron or steel ships of over 1000 tons burden registered for all countries still showed the destructive effects of the submarine warfare. Aside from the rise already noted for Russia and the United States, only the two neutrals, Spain and Sweden, had gained during the war. All other maritime powers had declined in total tonnage, several of them catastrophically. The increase in the world total, from about 80.5 million tons in 1939 to slightly over 99 million in 1946, was almost wholly the result of the extraordinary rise in United States shipping. The figures in the accompanying chart do not include army or navy vessels, small boats under one thousand tons, oil tankers, or shipping on inland waterways, but they suggest the position of the leading mercantile nations in 1939, 1946, and 1964.

Although the British Commonwealth, by 1946, had almost the same total tonnage in ships as in 1939, the 25 per cent rise in world shipping made the British share relatively less. The shipyards of the British Isles sped new ships down the ways to make good the war depletion and fill waiting orders from abroad. In 1946 Britain led the world in new ship construction, while the United States, unable to operate its 51 per cent of the world's shipping economically, allowed construction to lag, sold its surplus vessels at a loss, or tied them up in port with skeleton crews. This relative lethargy of the Americans offered Norway, Germany, Japan, and Italy a chance to restore their mercantile standing as the 1964 figures show.

The British did not manage to regain their lost lead in shipping, coal production or textile manufacture. They continued to produce sufficient coal for their own needs but reduced the number of miners by the use of more efficient mining methods. As they lacked large rivers and waterfalls for hydroelectric power they generated their electricity from coal, but

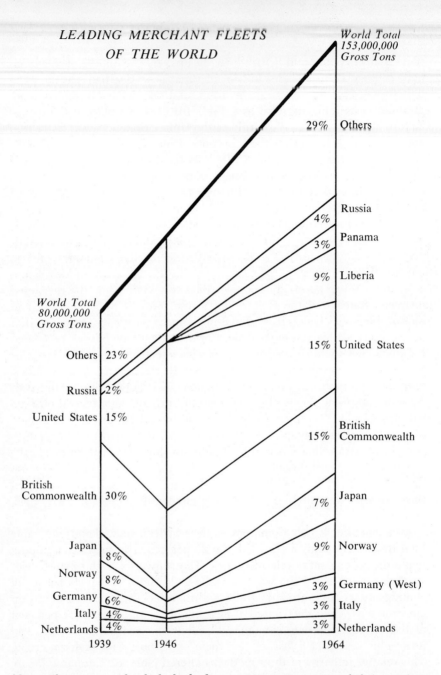

LEADING MERCHANT FLEETS
OF THE WORLD

World Total
153,000,000
Gross Tons

29% | Others

4% | Russia

3% | Panama

9% | Liberia

15% | United States

15% | British Commonwealth

7% | Japan

9% | Norway

3% | Germany (West)

3% | Italy

3% | Netherlands

World Total
80,000,000
Gross Tons

Others | 23%

Russia | 2%

United States | 15%

British Commonwealth | 30%

Japan | 8%

Norway | 8%

Germany | 6%

Italy | 4%

Netherlands | 4%

1939   1946   1964

NOTE: The success with which the leading maritime nations restored their merchant marines after World War II is evident from this graph, but one change calls for explanation. Two additional countries, Panama and Liberia, appear in the 1964 list. Both, though nominally sovereign republics, have long been under the protection of the United States. Shipping under Panamanian registry, relatively unimportant before World War II, climbed to 4,269,000 gross tons by 1964. Even more startling was the rise in Liberian registration, from 1000 tons in 1946 to 14,550,000 in 1964. The Liberian government charged only a small fee for registration and did not exercise any control over the operation of ships that flew the Liberian flag. Another postwar increase worth noting is that of Russia.

CHANGES IN BRITISH TRADE VOLUMES
1960-1965

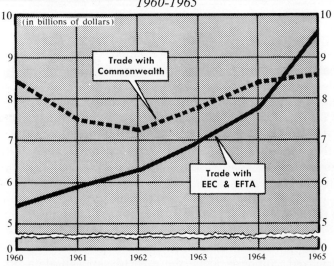

Trade between Great Britain and other members of the Commonwealth remained the same while British trade with members of the European Economic Community and the European Free Trade Association doubled.

they also developed nuclear power plants for this purpose. Textiles, once their major product, lost importance and by 1964 this item had shrunk to about 7 per cent of their export trade.

By deliberate planning the British attempted to transform their industries and to expand their output of such manufactured goods as they could still sell to the world markets. Machinery, motor vehicles, electrical equipment, chemicals and aircraft became their most successful exports in the 1950's. By reducing their imports of food and non-essentials they narrowed the "trade gap," but they could not recover their economic leadership. Despite attempts to strengthen their trade relations with other countries still adhering to the Commonwealth, the British found that by 1965 their trade with the countries of Western Europe had increased much more rapidly than had trade with their Commonwealth partners.[1] Despite this increase, however, their balance of trade turned seriously adverse; their trade deficit exceeded $2 billion; and their foreign liabilities rose to five times their reserves. The Labor Government, under the

---

[1] The Irish Republic withdrew from the Commonwealth in 1949, the Republic of South Africa in 1961. In 1965 the Commonwealth included the United Kingdom, Canada, Australia, New Zealand, India, Pakistan, Ceylon, Ghana, Nigeria, Cyprus, Sierra Leone, Jamaica, Trinidad and Tobago, Uganda, Kenya, Malaysia, Tanzania, Malawi, Malta, Zambia, Gambia, the Colonies and Protectorates, and the Territories under Trusteeship.

leadership of Harold Wilson, urged a new period of austerity and self-denial in an effort to cope with Britain's growing economic dilemma.

3. SOCIAL WELFARE

While waging World War II, for their national survival the British people accepted many strict regulations which in peacetime they would have resisted. Yet when peace came again they did not at once demand the abolition of such controls. Instead, a popular majority accepted the fact that increased social regimentation was a trend of the twentieth century. If the results justified the experiment, they were prepared to yield some of their cherished liberties for the common good. The war hastened a shift toward social control which had been developing since before 1900. This shift toward a socialized, or nationalized, economy, with all essential public facilities subject to state management, was the avowed program of the Labor party when its leaders took office in 1945.

The British people, however, prefer to make haste slowly and do not welcome rigid plans or ideological programs in politics. The Labor Government moved cautiously along the road to nationalization, for Prime Minister Attlee and his colleagues knew that of the 33 million eligible voters perhaps half had endorsed the Labor candidates, 10 million had favored the opposition groups, and 8 million had not voted at all. With only one-half the electorate behind them, the Labor candidates had no definite mandate to create a socialist state. Nevertheless, during the war years social planners had drawn up projects for improving the schools, guarding the health of the people, and raising the standard of living. When peace came, these plans were dusted off and some of them were carried into effect.

A new Education Act, one of the first reforms, actually went into operation on April 1, 1945, and was thus a measure of the wartime government. Its execution, however, rested with the Labor Cabinet after July, 1945. The Act provided that students in all grades were to have better schooling, better equipment, and better-paid teachers. From kindergarten to college, public education became one continuous process. Attendance at school was made compulsory for all normal children until they reached fifteen, and part-time instruction was required until they were eighteen. Children who showed exceptional ability were to receive scholarships so that they might complete their secondary school work and attend college. Adults whose education had remained incomplete were invited to renew their studies. The need for more trained technologists, for machinists, electricians, engineers, scientists, and research specialists had been evident in the war crisis. All this expansion meant that many new schools were needed, with more teachers and more taxes. While Oxford and Cambridge remained small schools for a privileged elite, thanks to government investment, the University of London and the thirteen provincial "Red-bricks" (so called because, until recently, they were housed mostly in dreary red-brick buildings) experienced a remarkable expansion. The cost of public instruction soon rose to double that of the prewar years, but the people hoped the outlay would prove a sound national investment. By 1965 some 140,000 students were attending British universities, more than three times the prewar total.

Care for the citizen's mind was not enough; it was also essential to care for his body. Many English men and women who sought to serve their country in the war had been rejected as unfit for duty because of poor health or physical defects. A National Health Service established in 1948 provided medical care for all through a system of socialized medicine. Many millions of citizens were already protected by some form of health insurance; now all were to be guaranteed medical attention, hospitalization, home nursing, drugs, and appliances as needed. The minister of health had general supervision over the entire program, the British Medical Association and College of Surgeons were to be invited to collaborate, and the cost was to be defrayed through insurance dues and national taxes.

Despite some criticism and opposition, the introduction of "socialized medicine" was carried through successfully. The great majority of physicians, surgeons, and dentists accepted it, and received an annual fee from the government based on the number of patients registered with each. Patients chose their own doctor, paid a flat rate (equal to fourteen cents) for each prescription, and were charged for dental plates, for spectacles, and some other appliances. But general medical fees, and expenses in hospitals, maternity homes, and mental institutions, were borne by the state. The annual cost of these services rose to $2 billion or nearly $40 a year per capita. Better working conditions, food, and medical care extended the average life span in Great Britain to sixty-eight years for men and seventy-three for women.

Other reforms that the government undertook for the national welfare affected housing and agriculture. Measures for the reduction of slum areas and the replacement of dwellings judged unfit for habitation proceeded steadily with the aid of government subsidies. Owners who undertook to improve dwelling units might receive up to half the cost of such improvements if they met certain standards. To encourage farming and reduce the need for imported food the government provided subsidies to farmers and maintained price supports. The number of farm tractors increased ten-fold between 1939 and 1966. Home-grown food, which had met less than one-third of British needs before the war, came to supply almost half the demand in the postwar period.

Government regulation of wages and salaries, and government benefit payments for sickness, maternity, widowhood, child care, unemployment, and old age, placed a heavy strain on the British taxpayer. From a total of roughly 335 million pounds in 1938 the cost of the social services rose by 1966 to more than 2900 million pounds. This was partly the result of inflation, partly a consequence of the rise in the British population from forty-six million in 1938 to 50 million in 1965. One effect of the income tax, and especially of the surtax imposed on higher incomes, was to reduce the gulf that once separated the rich and the poor. By 1960 only one Englishman in a hundred enjoyed an annual income (after taxes) of more than 2000 pounds, or $5600.

It was significant that the social and economic reforms introduced by the British Labor party during its period in office from 1945 to 1951 were retained almost in their entirety by the Conservative party which held office from 1951 to 1964. Britain had become a "welfare state," and both parties supported programs designed to promote full employment, a favorable balance of trade, and far-reaching social services at state expense. When the Labor party returned to power in 1964, and strengthened their lead in successive elections, they strove to solve the economic dilemma that confronted Britain by urging measures to increase production, combat inflation, and expand British exports. The enterprising Labor prime minister, Harold Wilson, tried various expedients, visiting the United States and Soviet Russia in efforts to improve the British position, and urging his countrymen to confront the problems of peace with the same courage and energy they had displayed in war.

The British, however, twenty years after the end of World War II, were not in a heroic mood. The imperial spirit that had driven them to create a world empire in earlier years waned as that empire dissolved. The business acumen and craftsmanship that had made Great Britain the "workshop of the world" in the early nineteenth century failed to keep Britain in the lead a century later. Even in decline, however, the British preserved many of their traditional loyalties and national characteristics. Their parliamentary democracy remained unchanged and their loyalty to their monarchy undiminished. George VI (1936–1952), though neither a brilliant nor colorful figure, was loved and respected by his subjects for his dignified and blameless character and his devotion to duty. On his death in 1952 he was succeeded by his older daughter Elizabeth II (1952–   ). Her husband and consort, formerly Prince Philip of Greece, was given the title Prince Philip, Duke of Edinburgh, in 1957. Their son Charles, born in 1948, is heir apparent to the British throne.

In a second respect — their class consciousness — the British have also remained true to tradition. The economic levelling that resulted from income and inheritance taxes and socialist policies did not eradicate the snobbery that had long held the "classes" and the "masses" apart. Malcolm Muggeridge, a distinguished writer and former editor of the London humorous weekly paper *Punch*, observed in 1966 that

The French have an obsession about money.
The Americans have an obsession about sex.
But we [British] have an obsession about social status.[1]

4. DEFENSE AND ARMAMENTS

The British people learned in World War II that their island kingdom, that "precious stone set in a silver sea," was no longer inviolable and that the silver sea no longer served (in Shakespeare's phrase) "as a moat defensive." War planes could cross the Channel in a few minutes; the cities of England were dangerously vulnerable; and the tentacles of British sea power could be severed.

Although Britain regained control of Hongkong and Singapore after World War II, still held Gibraltar, Malta, and Aden, and guarded the Suez Canal, its former system of imperial defense was rapidly dissolving. India and Burma, where one-fourth of the British imperial forces had been stationed, gained independence in 1947. British influence in Palestine, Jordan, and Iraq declined and British forces there were withdrawn. Egypt took over the Suez Canal in 1956. The revolt of Asian and African peoples against European domination (see Section XI) greatly reduced the British Empire which had included one-fourth of the land area and population of the world a generation earlier.

The nation that "rules the waves" can afford to "waive the rules" but by the middle of the twentieth century that nation no longer was the British. Their naval strength suffered a sharp decline as the empire contracted. Once the mistress of the seas, Great Britain sank to third place as a naval power after World War II, with the United States ranking first and Russia second. These facts led the British to place their hopes of security in a collective pact. They joined the North Atlantic Treaty Organization and granted the United States the privilege of establishing air bases and naval bases in the British Isles.

British expenditure for defense in the postwar period varied but in general it amounted to about one-fourth of the national budget and from 6 to 7 per cent of the gross national product. In the United States during the same period defense expenditures took more than half the national revenue and equaled some 10 per cent of the gross national product. For the British, however, with their smaller average income, defense costs equivalent to $100 per capita were as hard to bear as the $300 per capita that the people of the United States were paying for defense by 1966.

Despite the relative decline of British power Great Britain remained the center of a Commonwealth that exerted an important though intangible influence in world affairs. Yet the strength of the ties that held that Commonwealth together was difficult to estimate. After 1945 many of

[1] Quoted in *U.S. News and World Report,* 25 July 1966, p. 69.

these ties were transformed and appeared to be loosening. To make it clear that the self-governing dominions were truly autonomous, the British government came to be styled "Her Majesty's Government In the United Kingdom." Canadian nationals after 1946 were "Canadian citizens" not "British subjects." In 1949 Newfoundland (which had been ruled by a British royal commission since 1933) became the tenth province of Canada. Burma separated entirely from the Commonwealth in 1948 and Eire (the Irish Republic) dissolved its last political ties with Britain in 1949. The Union of India, independent after 1947, became a sovereign democratic republic in 1950 but remained a member of the Commonwealth and continued to accept the British monarch as "the symbol of the free association of its independent member nations and, as such, the head of the Commonwealth." Pakistan, which became an Islamic Republic in 1956, likewise remained a voluntary member of the Commonwealth. Ceylon, which obtained its independence in 1947, remained in the Commonwealth and allowed the British to retain air and naval bases in the island, but a subsequent agreement (1957) provided that these should be evacuated within three to five years.

For Great Britain, therefore, the question of defense depended in part on the vitality of the nebulous ties that still existed between the motherland and its former colonial possessions. One critical test of these ties came in 1956 when the British prime minister, Sir Anthony Eden (who succeeded Winston Churchill in 1955) risked military action against Egypt which had seized the Suez Canal. British and French forces attempted to regain the canal but were withdrawn when the United States, Russia, and a majority in the United Nations protested. In this sharp test of Commonwealth solidarity, public opinion in the self-governing dominions was divided and the Anglo-French attack was widely criticized as a mistake, badly conceived and badly executed.

The strain the Suez Canal episode imposed on Anglo-American friendship was eased when Eden resigned and the more diplomatic Harold Macmillan replaced him as prime minister. But the rebuff suffered by Britain and France had a wider import. It demonstrated that Britain had lost much of its freedom of action through its association with the United States. Anti-American feeling, though repressed, remained a force in British politics. The fact that Britain would almost certainly be involved if war broke out between the United States and Russia led the more radical spokesmen of the Labor party to denounce the American alliance and demand its cancellation.

When the Labor party returned to power in 1964, however, there was no change in the relationship between the United States and Britain. For the British needed American support in their efforts to maintain the value of the pound sterling which was strengthened at the close of 1964 by a $3 billion loan from the Bank for International Settlements. British critics continued to deplore British dependence on American aid, financial and military, and to condemn American military action in Vietnam, but the Anglo-British alliance remained firm.

5. THE IRISH REPUBLIC AND NORTHERN IRELAND

The Irish Republic (Eire) remained neutral during World War II and dissolved its remaining ties to the Commonwealth in 1949. The newly independent state had an area of 26,600 square miles and a population of 2,850,000 (1964) which had declined for over a century, mainly through emigration. In 1964 the birth rate was reasonably high at 22 per thousand, the death rate 12, the infant mortality 27, and the life expectancy 68 years.

In the hundred years from 1845 to 1945 nearly 6 million people left Ireland. After World War II this emigration continued at the rate of some 35,000 a year and Ireland continued to suffer a population loss. Only in the prosperous 1960's, when emigration slowed down, was a population balance achieved.

Emigration from Ireland was a consequence of continued poor socio-economic conditions in that country. After 1945, however, some foreign capital (American, British, German, and even Japanese) flowed into the country and resulted in the establishment of more small modern industries. Such investments were attracted by the prospect of cheap labor, a political climate favorable to capital and indifferent toward labor, by Ireland's insular position with easy access to the sea routes, and by her isolation from Europe and European wars.

Despite the growth of industry, Ireland remained predominantly an agrarian country. In 1955, industry accounted for only one-fourth of the national income and employed about one-fourth of the workers, but it increased steadily in importance over the next ten years. Half the population, however, continued to depend, directly or indirectly on the land for a living. Per capita income rose slowly after the war, reaching $900 annually in 1964, still low by West European standards. Ireland lacked mineral wealth, but its economic retardation was due not only to its lack of natural resources but also to the burden of its tragic past.

The Catholic Church in Ireland, which commanded the deep loyalty of 90 per cent of the population, exercised a strong influence in Irish national life, and Catholic Irishmen kept alive the memory of the wrongs they had suffered at the hands of British Protestants in the past. After winning independence, Irish nationalists concentrated on undoing the partition of Ireland which left one-fifth of the island still politically united with Britain. Despite continuous agitation and frequent resort to violence, however, their efforts to absorb the six "lost counties" of Northern Ireland into the Irish Republic proved unsuccessful. The people of Northern Ireland, who were predominantly Protestant (Presbyterian), remained deeply attached to the British monarchy and resolutely opposed the re-unification of Ireland. Another manifestation of Irish nationalism, the attempt to revive the ancient Gaelic (Celtic) language of Ireland, was also unsuccessful. Despite efforts to teach Gaelic in schools, it lost ground even in the western counties and off shore islands where it was still a living tongue. Excessive concern with national symbolism, which was psychologically understandable in a people long oppressed, led to an over-concentration on politics at the expense of economics and helped to explain Ireland's relative economic backwardness.

Under the constitution of 1937 Ireland became a republic with a president elected for a term of seven years. The Irish parliament at Dublin consisted of an appointed senate (*Seanad Eireann*) and a lower house (*Dail Eireann*) elected on the basis of proportionate representation. In 1959 Eamon de Valera, the grand old man of the Irish struggle for independence, was elected president, while his lieutenant, Sean F. Lemass, became prime minister. The two principal Irish political parties, the Fianna Fáil (de Valera's party) and the Fine Gael (the opposition party), represented two brands of competing nationalism. Only the small Labor party represented class and economic interests. In the elections of 1965 the Fianna Fáil won 72, the Fine Gael 47, and the Labor party 22 out of 144 seats in the lower house. In 1966 de Valera was re-elected to the presidency, while Lemass sought to improve the economy of Ireland by encouraging foreign investment and tourism and by maintaining good, workable, if not especially cordial, relations with Britain. In 1965 he took the unprecedented step of meeting in secret with the prime minister of Northern Ireland to discuss cooperation in such practical matters as tourism, transport, electric power, and tariffs. The touchy subject of the re-unification of Ireland, however, was not on their agenda.

Northern Ireland (Ulster) is smaller (5,451 square miles) but more highly industrialized, wealthier, and slightly healthier than the Irish Republic. In (1965) its birth rate was 23 per thousand, death rate 11, and infant mortality rate 28, while life expectancy was 69. In Northern Ireland there has been a small annual increase in the population, which reached 1,458,000 in 1964. In 1920 Northern Ireland became a self-governing unit of "the United Kingdom of Great Britain and *Northern* Ireland," with a parliament of its own at Belfast (see p. 253). The people of Northern Ireland, who were for the most part descendants of Scottish and English settlers in Ireland, have resolutely opposed union with the Irish Republic. Their opposition arose not only from the historical Catholic-Protestant enmity, but also from their fear that union with the Irish Republic would result in depressing their higher living standard and would deprive them of British markets for their products.

53

FRANCE

I do not think that I could in all conscience serve the nation well . . . by presiding in impotence over an impotent state.

CHARLES DE GAULLE (1946)

1. PROBLEMS OF RECONSTRUCTION AND ECONOMY

FRANCE EMERGED FROM the disasters and humiliations of World War II as "The Fourth French Republic." The First Republic had been proclaimed in 1792 in the midst of the great French Revolution. The Second Republic was born of the revolutionary ferment of 1848 and transformed within four years into the Second Empire under Napoleon III. The Third Republic was proclaimed in 1870 after the defeat and capture of Napoleon III by the Prussians, and it came to an end in 1940 when the German armies under Hitler were in Paris once again. The interim regime (1940–1944) of Marshal Henri Philippe Pétain, established at Vichy, collapsed when the Fighting French forces rose to aid the Anglo-American armies of liberation which invaded Normandy in June, 1944. General Charles de Gaulle, leader of the Fighting French and of the French government-in-exile, which had never acknowledged Pétain's Vichy regime, became the hero of liberated France and the temporary head of the newly proclaimed Fourth Republic.

Like all governments erected in the midst of turmoil and revolution, the provisory postwar regime of 1944–1946 was an unstable edifice. De Gaulle himself was a military man, conservative and somewhat authoritarian in temper. The political uncertainty and political divisions which weakened France under the Third Republic seemed likely to persist and weaken the Fourth Republic also. For several months after their liberation the French people disputed and voted and disputed again in their efforts to find the form of government which would divide them least. Their successive elections showed them to be split into three main political groups very nearly equal in strength. When they chose a National Constituent Assembly in October, 1945, the Communists led with 151 seats, the Popular Republican Movement (liberal Catholic) came second with 150, the Socialists won 139, and minor groups combined had 62. The constitution prepared by this Assembly (which was a provisory parliament as well as a constitutional convention) was submitted to the nation for a plebiscite in May, 1946. The French electors rejected it by some 10 million Noes against 9 million Yeas, the first time a proposed constitution had failed in France to win approval in a popular vote. In June, therefore, a new election was held to bring the Assembly into closer harmony with the will of the electorate. The results indicated a shift to the right. The Popular Republicans led with 165 seats, the Communists fell to second place with 145, and the Socialists dropped to 128. This reorganized Assembly then undertook to revise the constitutional draft, and the revised charter was accepted in October by 9,200,467 Yeas to 7,790,676 Noes, a not very enthusiastic popular majority. French women, newly granted equality before the law and the right to vote, participated in the plebiscite.

The constitution of the French Fourth Republic did not differ much from that of the Third Republic. The sovereignty of the people was exercised through a National Assembly elected by universal suffrage and a Council of the Republic (the former Senate) elected by indirect suffrage. The President of the Republic was to be chosen by the Assembly and Council, but in other matters the Assembly had a dominant role. It controlled the cabinet (Council of Ministers), and, as in the Third Republic, its multiplicity of parties made the successive cabinets dependent on shifting *blocs* that might dissolve with little warning, creating frequent cabinet crises that sometimes lasted for weeks.

The first election under the new constitution was held on November 10, 1946. The division of parties in the resulting National Assembly proved that France was still split into three dominant groups, for the Communists polled about 5.5 million votes, the Popular Republican Movement slightly over 5 million, and the Socialists 3.5 million. The Popular Republicans lost prestige. Furthermore General de Gaulle resigned as head of the provisional government early in 1946 as a protest against the factional strife and denounced the constitution on the ground that it set up an impotent head over an impotent government. He sought to organize an opposition party of his own (Rassemble du Peuple Français), but had little success and in 1953 withdrew from public life altogether. Despite his criticism, the new government was formed with the organization of a second chamber known as the Council of the Republic in December, 1946, and the election of Vincent Auriol as president of the republic in January, 1947.

The delay in settling political problems, and the great doubt as to how far leftward France might swing if the Communists and Socialists should combine to dominate the government, checked economic recovery. The nation had suffered heavily during five years of war and occupation, more heavily in lives lost and property damaged than Great Britain. It was estimated that half a million French citizens had lost their lives as a result of military casualties, air raids, the ceaseless strife and reprisals of the underground warfare, and the deportation and death of Frenchmen transferred to German prison camps. The total French population in 1946 was slightly over 39 million, a decline of over 1 million from the figure for 1936. Between 1900 and 1940 the French birth rate declined from 21 to 14 per thousand, and although it returned to 21 briefly after 1945, by 1950 it had dropped back to 19 and by 1960 to 17. The presence of 1,670,000 foreigners helped to disguise the falling French birth rate, and the Minister of Population not only encouraged this foreign influx but offered to allow the 700,000 German war prisoners to remain permanently if they so wished. The French leaders recognized that economic recovery would be retarded by the acute manpower shortage. More than 2 million buildings had been wrecked and 5 million people needed new or improved habitations. France had been an open battlefield not once but twice in World War II, and the struggle of the underground forces had multiplied the damage. Throughout France there were 7000 miles of ruined roads, 2300 fallen bridges or wrecked railway passes, buried mines to locate and destroy, and 1800 towns and cities to reconstruct.

Like other nations that had suffered in World War II the French recognized the need to restore and expand their economy. They still had the resources to preserve the status of a great power if those resources were wisely and energetically developed. France was blessed with unusually rich agricultural lands and could feed itself. One-fourth of the labor force worked at farming, and although the farms were small, the number of tractors in use rose thirty-fold between 1937 and 1965. The government subsidized agriculture and maintained farm price supports.

French industries, like French farms, tended to remain small units, often controlled by a single family. Ninety per cent of French firms employed fewer than ten workers. This individualism permitted more variety and inventiveness, and helped to explain why French wines, perfumes, cosmetics, and dress designs preserved a global reputation. Yet at a time when mass production methods were winning world markets with standardized goods, the French emphasis on the older traditions of handicrafts seemed anachronistic to some observers. After World War II a comprehensive economic program (the Monnet Plan) was introduced to increase French output. American aid helped in the development of hydroelectric power and the modernization of factories. By 1951 French industry had almost doubled its prewar levels; by 1965 the national income was 150 per cent higher than it had been in 1937.

In steel production postwar France ranked fifth among the nations and in aluminum and textile production it ranked fourth. Its share of the international trade of the world remained surprisingly stable at approximately 6 per cent. While other countries shifted their position France stayed fairly consistently in fourth place. In 1938 the rank of the five leading nations in terms of international trade was: Great Britain, the United States, Germany, France, Japan. In 1948 the revised order read: United States, Great Britain, German Federal Republic (West Germany), France, Soviet Russia. By 1963 the order had become: United States, German Federal Republic, Great Britain, France, Russia. Although France (unlike Britain) did not have to import half its food, the French trade balance remained unfavorable, largely because of its heavy imports of petroleum. The discovery in the postward period of important oil reserves under the sands of the Sahara Desert promised to relieve the French of this deficit and helps to explain why they were reluctant to let North Africa escape from their control.

The French national budget proved even more difficult to balance than French imports and exports. As a people the French were unfavorable to a personal income tax. The American government raised 55 per cent of its revenue, and the British government 45 per cent, by taxing personal incomes, but the French government had difficulty obtaining more than 25 per cent by this method. As an alternative it secured the larger part of its revenue indirectly through sales taxes. Another practice adopted by Frenchmen — that of hoarding gold or investing their savings abroad — made the work of the tax collector difficult. One of the reasons for the hoarding of gold and flight of capital abroad was the instability of the French currency, which depreciated steadily after the war. However, as the economic position of France improved in the 1950's, the government was able to stabilize the currency. On January 1, 1960, a "new" franc was issued, which was pegged at 5 francs to one dollar. Thereafter, French gold reserves steadily grew and the franc became a "hard" currency. In 1966 the government was so confident of its stability that it made the franc freely convertible, in an effort to make it a medium of international monetary transactions, like the dollar.

2. SOCIAL WELFARE

After World War II the various laws covering workmen's compensation, health insurance, and family allowances were broadened and unified in France, with a single Social Security Administration supervising the whole. All wage earners, regardless of their status or wages, were covered. Health insurance was enlarged, with cash benefit payments extending up to three years, and sometimes longer if necessary, to help rehabilitate and retrain the sick or injured. An insured worker, while sick, received monthly payments equal to half his salary, or two-thirds of it if he was the head of a family with three or more dependent children. Workers who incurred illness or accident through their professional activities received compensation. Physicians trained as "industrial health specialists" watched over working conditions. The unemployed received financial aid.

To encourage larger families the government undertook to pay family allowances of roughly one-fifth a worker's monthly salary if he had two children, one-third if he had three, with subsequent increases for larger families. Maternity insurance covered medical, surgical, and hospital costs for each child. Under this policy of state assistance the postwar birth rate rose, as already noted, but did not maintain the peak of 21 reached between 1945 and 1950. Other factors beside family allowances helped to encourage an increased birth rate, among them the reduction in maternal and infant mortality.

Old age pensions for workers were also supervised by the Social Security Administration. After 1947 aged citizens whose income proved insufficient were granted an extra allowance. The system was also extended to include agricultural workers, craftsmen, small businessmen, and members of some professions.

The costs of maintaining the Social Security Administration were met by an assessment of 18.5 per cent of payrolls, 12.5 per cent being contributed by employers and 6 per cent by employees. By 1965 public aid and welfare accounted for nearly one-fifth of the French national budget. The government also subsidized a program for repairing old houses and building new homes. Three-fourths of French dwellings were over forty years old, and as rents were fixed by law at a low level landlords had little incentive to improve their property. Permission was therefore granted to increase rents on older buildings; and firms with more than ten employees were required to invest a sum equal to one per cent of their payroll in housing programs.

French vital statistics after World War II reflected the effects of better living and working conditions and improved medical care. Hitherto, despite the notable work done by French scientists, the death rate had been higher in France and life expectancy at birth lower than in most neighboring countries. As late as 1949 the infant mortality rate in France (the children that died before they were one year old) was 60 in 1000, whereas the average for England, the Netherlands, Switzerland, and the Scandinavian countries had been cut to half that figure. By 1963, however, the French rate likewise had been sharply reduced and was down to 25 in 1000. This was a remarkable improvement, although the success of the Swedes, who cut their rate to 15, suggested what might still be achieved. The over-all death rate in France declined in less spectacular fashion, from 16 per 1000 in the 1930's to 11 per 1000 in the 1960's. The average life expectancy at birth of the French people, which was about 50 in 1914, climbed by 1964 to 67 for males and 74 for females. Thanks to improved health, the population of France rose — despite a modest birth rate — to 49 million in 1965.

3. POLITICAL PROBLEMS

De Gaulle's predictions that the Fourth Republic would reveal the same weaknesses and divisions that had characterized the Third Republic were unhappily verified. The first grave crisis that faced the Fourth French Republic was the outbreak of a revolt in Indochina. The French were not willing to grant independence and withdraw voluntarily, as the British did from India. Nor could they be driven out as quickly as the weaker Dutch forces were expelled from Indonesia. The French chose to reinforce their army units and to fight a costly seven-year war (1947–1954) in an effort to retain their control. An attempted solution (1949), whereby they recognized Cambodia, Laos, and Vietnam as independent self-governing states within a French Union, failed to end the fighting. Support from Communist China enabled the insurgents to continue the war until the French suffered defeat and agreed to an armistic in 1954. A conference held in Geneva, Switzerland, ended this First Indochinese War. Vietnam was divided into a northern and a southern half, and the United States began to aid the South Vietnamese to establish a stable government. Cambodia, Laos, and South Vietnam obtained complete sovereignty while Northern Vietnam became a communist republic.

Charges that the French military effort in Indochina had provided excessive dividends for war profiteers intensified the bitterness felt in France over the outcome of the struggle. At the same time (1954) the Fourth French Republic faced a new colonial conflict in north Africa, where Tunisia and Morocco gained independence in 1956, but Algeria became the scene of a long and bitter struggle. The million French settlers there were outnumbered eight to one by the Algerian Moslems, and fear that France might abandon the struggle led to a revolt of the French military forces in Algeria in 1958. The crisis found the shaky cabinet at Paris too uncertain of its authority to restore order. This was the situation that supporters of General de Gaulle had anticipated, and the French people turned to him in their uncertainty. On June 1, 1958, de Gaulle became prime minister, and undertook to strengthen the French government by a new constitution and a solution to the Algerian war.

The constitution of the Fifth French Republic was approved by a referendum held in France and the overseas departments and territories on September 28, 1958. Of 45,840,642 eligible voters, nearly four-fifths, or 36,486,251, cast valid ballots, with 31,066,502 Ayes and 5,419,749 Noes. A majority of almost six to one suggested the confidence de Gaulle's character inspired. Under the new constitution the parliament of the Republic was to consist of a National Assembly and a Senate (its name was restored). The important changes concerned the powers of the president of the Republic, a post to which de Gaulle was speedily elected. The president was to nominate and dismiss the ministers (who need not be members of parliament) and could dissolve the National Assembly.

Furthermore, in a crisis, he could "take the measures demanded by the circumstances," a provision that implied his right if necessary to rule by executive decree in an emergency. In 1960 the chambers voted de Gaulle's government special powers for one year.

From 1958 to 1962 the most pressing problem de Gaulle faced remained the tense Algerian struggle. In 1959 he offered the Algerian nationalists the hope of self-rule. To many Frenchmen, who had raised him to power a year earlier in the belief that he could find a solution that would assure French control, this offer to let Algeria go appeared a bitter betrayal. Several attempts were made on his life; and once again, as in 1958, French army leaders in Algeria raised a revolt. But they were no longer dealing with confused and divided politicians in Paris. De Gaulle took a firm stand and the revolt collapsed. But a secret army organization kept up a reign of terror and sabotage in a desperate effort to prevent or at least delay a Franco-Algerian settlement. The settlement came none the less. Algerian independence was approved by a referendum and became effective in 1962. The following year the new republic chose Ben Bella as president; but he was overthrown by Algerian army officers in 1965. A "Revolutionary Council" seized power under the leadership of Colonel Houari Boumédienne.

The French people, relieved to see the Algerian conflict, with its heavy drain on French lives and resources, finally at a close, acclaimed de Gaulle's leadership. Elections for the National Assembly at the end of 1962 gave de Gaulle's party (*Union pour la Nouvelle République*) control of the legislature. His prestige had never appeared more secure. However, soon the bloom began to wear off de Gaulle. The French people appreciated his efforts to restore to France order and stability at home and dignity abroad. But, being traditionally irreverent toward their leaders, they soon found his hauteur as insufferable as foreigners did. Activity of opposition political parties, virtually suspended after the collapse of the Fourth Republic in 1958, gradually revived. In 1965, when a presidential election returned de Gaulle to office for a second seven-year term, he obtained only 12,645,315 ballots against 10,557,480 cast for his chief opponent, François Mitterand.

4. FOREIGN RELATIONS

Although the French were defeated in the first year of World War II, and withdrew from the struggle, the British and Americans recognized the valuable and courageous services rendered by the "Free French" who escaped to fight with the Allied armies, and by the "underground" forces within France which harassed the German armies of occupation. After the defeat of Germany, Britain and the United States insisted that the French should have a part in the peacemaking and a share in occupying

German territory. The Russians were reluctant to concede this, but agreed when the British and Americans created a French occupation zone in western Germany from segments of the territory comprised in their own zones. Thus in 1945 France found itself one of the "Big Four" powers that undertook the problem of disarming Germany and bringing the German "war criminals" to justice.

France also became a charter member of the United Nations, when delegates from fifty countries signed the charter drafted at San Francisco in the spring of 1945. It won a place as one of the five permanent members of the Security Council, along with the United States, Great Britain, Soviet Russia, and China (then governed by the Nationalist regime of Chiang Kai-shek). This recognition of the importance of France in world affairs, despite the eclipse it had suffered between 1940 and 1944, was a tribute to the greatness of the French nation. Finally, France still possessed the second largest colonial empire in the world, 4.6 million square miles in area, with a population of 65 million. However, it was an empire threatened with unrest in Madagascar, Morocco, Algeria, and Indochina. To pacify the colonial peoples the French permitted them to elect 75 representatives to the National Assembly in Paris and recognized the protectorates of Morocco and Tunisia in North Africa and Cambodia, Laos, and Vietnam in Indochina as "associated states of the French Union."

The strength of the Communist movement in postwar France made its future uncertain. As noted earlier in this chapter, the Communists won 151 seats in the election of 1945. Communist influence declined, however, especially after 1949, when the European Recovery Program (Marshall Plan) strengthened the French economy. American aid in money and arms also helped France to pay for its military campaigns in Indochina, for the United States paid one-third of the $1.25 billion annually which the war there cost. This assistance from across the Atlantic did not seem adequate to the French — they were doing the actual fighting against Communist aggression — and by 1952 Franco-American relations grew strained. Franco-American relations were also strained by the different attitudes of the United States and France toward the problem of German reunification, the United Nations, and the revolt of the colonial peoples. The last named difference came into focus notably during the Suez crisis of 1956.

The return to power of General de Gaulle in 1958 brought about a passing improvement in Franco-American relations. However, soon friction developed between the two countries over French insistence on becoming a nuclear power, French demand for an equal voice in the formulation of NATO strategy, French opposition to Britain's admission to the Common Market, French recognition of Communist China, and finally French criticism of the American intervention in Vietnam. At the same time French policy toward the nations of Western Europe was one of the alternate snubs and blandishments, designed to wean them away from American influence. In this purpose, however, it failed. Although de Gaulle often had the satisfaction of causing a sensation by his rude rebuffs to the United States and France's West European partners, it was evident to all that the security of Western Europe, including that of France, still depended on the power of the United States.

From the early years of World War II onward both Frenchmen and foreigners agreed that De Gaulle was a most difficult man to deal with. He strained his popularity at home and abroad by arbitrary acts and by his proud and inflexible insistence on French grandeur. He made France a nuclear power by pressing forward the necessary experiments and authorizing atomic explosions in the atmosphere even after the American, British and Russian governments had agreed to avoid such tests because the radioactive fall-out could prove harmful to life. His relations with the German Federal Republic became less friendly after Ludwig Erhard succeeded Konrad Adenauer as chancellor (1963). He annoyed other members of the European Economic Community by his arbitrary emphasis on French interests and by rejecting a British application to join the Common Market (see p. 697). Even more significantly, he deliberately opposed American policy and withdrew French support from the North Atlantic Treaty Organization. Going further, he insisted (1966) that all NATO headquarters, communication centers, air fields and equipment be withdrawn from French territory. Yet this did not mean, the French government explained, that France was wholly severing its connections with the North Atlantic Treaty Alliance. De Gaulle's moves were designed to make France the master of military armaments on its own soil and to end a period in which decisions made in Washington could vitally affect French policies and the security of the French Nation.

While Americans were still pondering the cost and labor of relocating NATO installations in another European country, De Gaulle gave them further cause for concern by paying a state visit to the Soviet Union (1966) and by recommending that American forces should be withdrawn from Vietnam. At the same time, however, he displayed a desire to improve Franco-British relations. France provided aid to support the pound sterling in its recurrent difficulties, and French emissaries assured the Labor government of Prime Minister Wilson that France would no longer oppose British entry into the European Economic Community. Furthermore, approval was indicated for a joint plan to complete a tunnel under the English Channel to provide swifter communication between Dover and Calais. This project (promptly labeled "Chunnel") promised to draw France and Britain into closer contact. For the British, such contact had become highly important. Their trade with the continent had grown until it outweighed their trade with members of their dissolving Commonwealth, and they felt that they might also benefit through an exchange of electric power with northern European states during hours of peak consumption. De Gaulle, aware of these factors, hoped the moment would prove opportune to weaken the ties between Britain and the United States and strengthen the ties between Britain and Europe

54

WEST GERMANY

. . . There was and is no such thing as a "German economic miracle" . . . it was the purposeful use of economic means and strict adherence to the market economy program which brought success.

DR. LUDWIG ERHARD, MINISTER OF ECONOMIC AFFAIRS

1. POSTWAR RECONSTRUCTION

AFTER THE GERMAN ARMIES capitulated in May, 1945, the entire country was divided into zones and subjected to military occupation by the victors. In addition, some of the territories the Germans had conquered and annexed were taken from them. The Russians took northeast Prussia The Polish frontier was pushed westward to the Oder and Neisse rivers. Alsace and Lorraine, taken from France in 1871, regained in 1919, lost again in 1940, became French once more after World War II. At the opening of the twentieth century the German Empire had included 209,000 square miles; after World War I this declined to 181,000; by 1939 Hitler's "Greater Germany" had expanded to 235,000; and by 1945 the Germans were confined to an area of 137,000 square miles. The conquerors were determined to disarm and render powerless the dynamic and aggressive nation that had cost Europe two gigantic wars in thirty years.

The work of reconstruction in postwar Germany may be considered under three headings — economic, political, and social. As the economic program proved the most striking and successful achievement it will be considered first.

The four military zones, Russian, American, British, and French, into which postwar Germany was divided, split the country into two unequal parts. The Soviet zone (East Germany), some 41,000 square miles in area with a population of 17 million, became a satellite state of the Soviet Union: its development will be discussed in Chapter 61. The American, British, and French zones (West Germany), some 95,000 square miles in area with a population of 47 million (1946), were combined under the protection of the Western powers. In 1949 West Germany became the

German Federal Republic. The restrictions imposed in 1945 were gradually removed, and in 1955 West Germany regained the prerogatives of a sovereign state. The American, British, and French zones in Berlin, which were surrounded by East German territory, were declared a part of West Germany. The efforts of the Soviet and East German authorities to "absorb" West Berlin and its two million inhabitants were tenaciously resisted by the West German government with the resolute support of the Western powers.

With East Germany under Communist rule and West Germany a liberal democratic state, the two afforded a test by which the efficacy of the contrasting regimes might be compared. The Western democracies, anxious to see their protégé succeed, provided financial aid and encouragement. The results proved phenomenal. The Federal Republic established a stable currency, curbed inflation, and all but eliminated unemployment. Industries revived and income expanded. Between 1950 and 1960 the Gross National Product increased three-fold, growing at an annual rate of almost 8 per cent, but in the 1960's the rate of growth fell to 5 per cent. The merchant marine was rebuilt until it approached the prewar tonnage. Foreign trade increased until West Germany ranked third in the value of its imports and exports, being exceeded only by the United States and Great Britain. This business expansion continued even though, after 1955, defense costs mounted and the West Germans undertook to pay off much of Germany's prewar indebtedness. By 1960 they had repaid between $2 and $3 billion on outstanding obligations, one-third of the payments going to survivors of Jewish families whose wealth and property had been confiscated.

The business prosperity in West Germany was the more remarkable because the Federal Republic had to absorb and find occupations for a stream of refugees. Germans from the areas annexed to Russia and Poland, from Czechoslovakia, and other eastern European regions fled westward after the war. Fugitives who disliked the Communist regime in East Germany slipped across the dividing line. In all, some 12 or 13 million refugees sought new homes in West Germany. By 1965 the population of the German Federal Republic (including West Berlin) had risen to 58 million, while that of East Germany stood at 17 million, less than it had been in 1945.

The continued exodus to West Germany alarmed and angered the leaders in East Germany, for it advertised how many Germans preferred the greater liberty and prosperity the West offered. Between 1955 and 1961 over 2 million East Germans fled to the West, whereas only one-eighth that number migrated *to* East Germany *from* West Germany. In August, 1961, the East German government ordered a fortified wall constructed across divided Berlin to close the borderline. Discontented East Germans still attempted to cross, but the number who succeeded in making their escape declined sharply. Over 100 were killed between 1961 and

1966 as they attempted to elude the East German border guards and cross the wall.

2. POLITICAL REORGANIZATION

After World War I, the ill-starred attempt to create a democratic government in Germany ended fifteen years later with the transformation of the Weimar Republic into a one-party dictatorship under Hitler. After World War II the victors made a new effort to "democratize" German institutions and German society. They could conduct their experiment only in West Germany; in East Germany a Communist "German Democratic Republic" was set up with Russian aid in 1949. (See Chapter 61.)

The American, British, and French governments agreed in June, 1948, that the zones of Germany which they controlled should be united under a central government. A Basic Law (constitution) for the new regime was drafted later that year by a Constituent Assembly that met in Bonn. West Germany was composed of nine provinces (*Länder*), and when two-thirds of the provincial parliaments ratified the Basic Law it came into force in May, 1949. Subsequently the Americans, British, and French issued an Occupation Statute (September, 1949) which they promptly modified (November, 1949) by further concessions to the new German Federal Republic. They permitted it to join international organizations and appoint its own consuls to foreign countries. Two years later, as the East-West tension still delayed a formal peace settlement, the United States, Britain, and France declared the war with Germany ended; the Soviet Union delayed such action until January, 1955. Four months later the American, British, and French high commissioners announced that the Occupation Statute was revoked. The Federal Republic of Germany (West Germany) became a sovereign independent state on May 5, 1955, almost exactly ten years after the German surrender.

The government of the new republic, like that of the United States, was a federal union in which the component states relinquished certain specified powers to the central government. These powers included defense, foreign affairs, currency, weights and measures, customs and commercial agreements, control of the Post Office and communication systems, federal citizenship, passports, immigration and emigration.

The Federal Government consisted of a Diet (*Bundestag*), elected for a four-year term by universal suffrage and secret ballot. There was also an upper chamber, the Federal Council (*Bundesrat*), in which each province (*Land*) had at least three votes and the more populous had four or five. The deputies composing the Council were the members of the governments of the provinces. The Federal Diet, plus an equal number of delegates elected by the representative bodies of the *Länder*, chose a President for a five-year term (he could be re-elected once). This

Bundespräsident had considerably less executive power than the President of the United States.

The most important political figure in the government of the German Federal Republic was the Federal Chancellor. As head of the cabinet responsible to the Diet, the Chancellor held a position comparable to that of a prime minister. But German political traditions and respect for authority invested the Chancellor with more individual influence than most prime ministers exercised. In 1949, when the German Federal Republic was organized, the first Diet elected contained 139 Christian Democrats, 131 Social Democrats, 52 representatives of various liberal organizations, and 80 deputies from minor political parties. As the Christian Democrats constituted the largest group, the leader of the Christian Democratic Union, Konrad Adenauer, was proposed as Chancellor by the Federal President. After the Diet elected him to this post, Adenauer chose the other members of his cabinet. As Chancellor he could suggest the nomination or dismissal of ministers to the Federal President and this gave him a high degree of control over his "team." Among his ministers he was more than first among equals: he was the master.

Konrad Adenauer was seventy-three when he was elected Chancellor but age had not impaired his mind or energy. From 1917 to 1933 he had served as Mayor of Cologne, a position from which he was banished when the Nazis won control of Germany. Twice during Hitler's regime he was arrested. After the defeat of Germany he became zonal chairman of the Christian Democratic Union, and president of the parliamentary council that prepared the Basic Law for the German Federal Republic in 1948. As Chancellor he helped, by his resolute course and firm administration, to guide West Germany until he resigned the chancellorship to Ludwig Erhard in 1963. Erhard faced difficulties in both foreign and domestic affairs. The French and the Russians criticized him for working too closely with the Americans. His fellow countrymen were disappointed because the economic "miracle" which he had helped to plan did not maintain the same pace in the 1960's that had marked the 1950's. Nevertheless, the elections of 1965 gave Erhard's government a fresh vote of confidence. The Christian Democratic Union (CDU) and the Christian Social Union (CSU), the parties on which he leaned, received together 46.7 per cent of the vote, whereas they had received only 45.3 per cent in 1961. Late in 1966, however, Chancellor Erhard's cabinet fell. A new cabinet was formed, which was based on a "grand coalition" of the Christian Democrats and Social Democrats. The new Christian Democratic leader Kurt Kiesinger, a former member of the Nazi party and official of Dr. Goebbels' Propaganda Ministry, became Chancellor, while the Social Democratic leader Willy Brandt, who was mayor of West Berlin, became Vice Chancellor and Foreign Minister.

Outwardly, the course of events and expressions of opinion in the German Federal Republic indicated that the West Germans were satisfied with their new democratic experiment. But the division of Germany into two parts affronted the patriotic feelings of the German people. They clung to a deep, though frustrated, conviction that Germany must be reunited. Once such reunification occurred, it was certain to bring a conviction of strength and awaken in them a sense of grievance that part of Germany had been taken over by the Poles. The expedients adopted by the victors after World War II did not promise a better or more durable solution for "the German question" than the peace settlement of 1919 had provided. But the massive threat of the Soviet Union introduced a new factor into the situation. All the peoples of Europe were forced to recognize that further resort to war among themselves might leave them so weakened they could no longer hope to resist Soviet pressure. This new factor, coupled with the relative decline of Europe's world influence, made the concept of a European union or federation more attractive. Such a union could hardly be viable unless it included Germany, and if the Germans joined it their aggressive impulses might be curbed. The measures adopted in the postwar period to promote European cooperation afforded some hope that European union might prove an attainable ideal. What those measures were is discussed in Chapter 57.

3. SOCIAL PROBLEMS

As already noted the people of West Germany made a remarkable economic recovery after World War II. They doubled their per capita income in the 1950's, and by 1964 it was equal to that of France and Britain, and about one-half that in the United States. In the composition of their labor force and their economic activities the West Germans resembled the British more than they did the French. As in Britain, over 40 per cent of the workers were employed in industry, with less than 5 per cent in agriculture, and women comprised over one-third of the working force. In France manufacturing occupied only one-quarter of the workers while agriculture claimed approximately one-quarter also. Fewer Frenchwomen took jobs outside the home, and they constituted only 25 per cent of the French working force.

The birth rate in West Germany remained remarkably steady in the postwar years at 18 per thousand. The death rate also remained fairly constant at 10 to 11 per thousand. On the other hand infant mortality, which stood at 60 per thousand in 1938, climbed to 90 per thousand in 1946 (a reflection of war conditions and the German defeat). By 1963 infant mortality in West Germany had been reduced to 37. This reduction largely accounts for the increase in life expectancy there; it rose from 60 years at birth in 1946 to 68 in 1960.

Throughout most of the 1950's and 1960's the West German government devoted larger sums to social services and reconstruction than to

GROWTH OF THE GROSS NATIONAL PRODUCT
IN SEVEN COUNTRIES

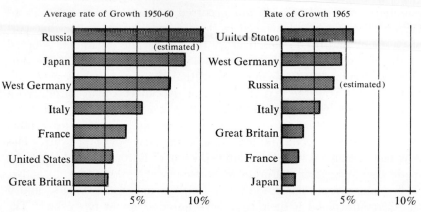

Average rate of Growth 1950-60   Rate of Growth 1965

defense, unlike the United States, where defense remained the largest single item in the budget. Nine-tenths of the West German workers were covered by compulsory sickness, unemployment, and old age insurance, with employers and employees contributing to the funds established for these purposes. In addition accident insurance was provided by a 2 per cent levy on wages and health insurance by a 7 per cent levy.

One of the most serious problems the West Germans had to meet was the assimilation of over 12 million immigrants and refugees, the great majority from Eastern Europe. Special funds were established to support people whose property and income had been destroyed as a consequence of the war. An acute housing shortage developed because one-fourth of the dwellings in West Germany had been wrecked through air raids and other causes. Within ten years, however, these wrecked homes were replaced, and by 1957 there were one-quarter more dwellings than there had been twenty years earlier.

In 1955, to encourage larger families, an allowance of thirty marks a month was granted toward the support of each child after the second. Maternity insurance and child care were also provided. A slight increase in the birth rate became perceptible after 1957, and the rate of population increase in West Germany remained higher than that of Britain, France or Italy.

Education in the German Federal Republic was compulsory for all children between six and fourteen and free up to the age of eighteen for those who continued their studies. Each of the federated states (*Länder*) retained responsibility for the direction and maintenance of its schools. After completing their primary education in an elementary school (*Volksschule*), children were directed, in accordance with their aptitudes, to a vocational school for three years or to a *Gymnasium* (high school) for nine years. The high schools were of three types: those that emphasized classical languages, modern languages, or the sciences. West Germany also had eighteen universities, as well as engineering colleges, scientific academies, and special institutions for training teachers. Those who wished to specialize in theology could study at the universities or attend religious seminaries.

The division of Germany into two republics after World War II left most German Catholics in the western segment. In 1933 less than one-third of the total German population was Roman Catholic, but after 1945 four-fifths of the inhabitants of East Germany were Protestant while in West Germany Protestants and Catholics were almost equal. This helped to explain why communism made little progress in West Germany. The strongest political group in the postwar period was the Christian Democratic Union (CDU), which joined forces with the Christian Socialist Union (CSU) to dominate the Federal Government and the republic.

The most noteworthy — and tragic — alteration in the religious composition of the German nation was the virtual disappearance of the Jewish minority. When Hitler came to power in 1933 the number of Jews in Germany was estimated at half-a-million. Although they comprised less than 1 per cent of the population the Jews had played an exceptionally important part in the artistic, economic, and scientific life of the nation. After World War II scarcely thirty thousand German Jews remained, the great majority having perished as a result of the deliberate policy of extermination for which Hitler bore the heaviest but by no means the exclusive blame.

When the enormity of the crimes authorized by Hitler's regime was officially documented after 1945 the revelations affronted the conscience of mankind but the German people felt no profound sense of guilt or responsibility. The very magnitude of the atrocities had a stunning and numbing effect. Amid the mounting problems of the postwar period their significance faded, and the inclination increased "to let bygones be bygones." The Western nations, which wanted German aid in their Cold War with Russia, found it convenient to forget, while rearming the German Federal Republic, that twice in the twentieth century German militarism had made all Europe tremble. In Germany itself a "conspiracy of silence" tended to enshroud the whole question of atrocities committed during the Hitler regime. Those who had helped to organize and operate the concentration camps were the most reticent about them and the most eager that the atrocities should be forgotten.

Yet when the government announced, in 1964, that a twenty-year Statute of Limitations would end the prosecution of Nazi criminals in 1965, there was widespread protest, and the Statute period was extended until 1969. Furthermore, prosecutions might continue after that date in cases where an indictment had been obtained before the expiration of the Statute.

4. GERMANY BETWEEN EAST AND WEST

The ambiguous status of the German Federal Republic complicated its foreign relations. Neither West Germany nor East Germany was willing to grant the other diplomatic recognition; both hoped in time to see all Germany reunited under its direction. In this competition West Germany, as the larger, more populous, and more prosperous segment of the divided realm, appeared to hold an advantage. But the failure to establish diplomatic relations between the German Federal Republic and the German Democratic Republic created numerous difficulties. On some urgent matters, such as trade, temporary accords were worked out. But the right of the West Germans to visit and transport goods to and from West Berlin remained as a subject of dispute.

The East Germans found West Berlin, an enclave of the Western powers located deep within their own territory, a source of irritation. With the support of their Russian allies (and masters) the Communist leaders of East Germany strove to absorb West Berlin. They obstructed and sometimes closed the road and rail routes by which travellers, food, and merchandise reached this isolated half of the city. In 1949 the Americans, British, and French were forced to fly in supplies for their sector of Berlin (see p. 575). But they would not give it up though the cost of maintaining it proved heavy. The United States advanced $600 million to the government of West Berlin in ten years, and the German Federal Republic provided large subsidies to balance West Berlin's budget and cover its unfavorable trade balance. This situation was not unpleasing to the Communist leaders in East Germany. They knew that the Federal Republic and its allies were paying heavily to hold West Berlin and that they gained little in return except the maintenance of their prestige.

Neither the German Federal Republic nor the German Democratic Republic was admitted to membership in the United Nations. But the Federal Republic joined the special UN organizations and other international bodies and made financial contributions to them. It also became a member of the North Atlantic Treaty Organization in 1955 and undertook to support the other NATO powers with military forces.

The German Federal Republic also joined the Western European Union, the Council of Europe, the European Coal and Steel Community, the European Atomic Energy Community, and the Common Market (see Chapter 57). This cooperation advanced the cause of European unity. As its prosperity increased the Federal Republic made loans to aid economically retarded countries, advancing nearly $200 million to India, $150 million to Turkey, some $80 million to Egypt, and $50 million to Greece. These credits helped to increase the foreign markets of the Federal Republic. Its exports by 1964 were valued at more than $16 billion, its imports at $14 billion, which gave it a very favorable trade balance.

In the earlier years of the postwar period one-third or more of the revenue raised in the American, British, and French zones of Germany was used to pay the costs of the allied occupation forces. After 1955, when the German Federal Republic had gained sovereign status, these expenditures were classed as defense, but they still included the cost of maintaining allied military forces as well as the cost of arming and training (West) German troops. The burden on the West German taxpayers declined however. From 1955 to 1959, defense (and occupation) costs amounted to only one-fifth of the budget, whereas from 1950 to 1955 occupation costs had amounted to one-third of it. In 1960, however, partly as a result of American insistence, the West German government increased its outlay for defense to 30 per cent of its budget. This was roughly proportionate to the budget percentage the French and British were allotting for military purposes, but it was far below the effort of the United States.

5. AUSTRIA

When the Austro-Hungarian Empire collapsed at the close of World War I, the victors refused to allow the German Austrians to unite with Germany. Consequently, the small Austrian Republic was created (see pp. 314–316). In 1938 Hitler annexed it to Germany, and for the next seven years Austria formed an integral part of Greater Germany.

In 1945 Austria was "liberated" by the Allies and then divided into American, British, French, and Soviet occupation zones. Vienna was also placed under four-power occupation, like Berlin. Unlike Germany, however, Austria was permitted to set up a provisional government under the veteran Socialist leader Dr. Karl Renner, who had also presided over the establishment of the first Austrian Republic in 1918 (see pp. 194–195). The constitution of 1920 was restored, with minor amendments. The attitude of the Austrians toward their state greatly changed after the war. In 1918, regretting the loss of their empire and resentful of the Allied prohibition to join Germany, they were indifferent to or openly scornful of the Austrian Republic. In 1945, however, disillusioned with *Anschluss* to Germany under Hitler, they rallied behind their government in support of the Republic. The principal Austrian political parties, the Socialist (formerly Social Democratic) party and the People's (formerly Christian Socialist) party, before the war maintained private armies and fought bloody battles. After the war, they overcame their ideological hostility and formed a coalition which endured until 1966. In that year the People's party won a clear majority in elections and formed a cabinet alone. The Austrian people presented a solid front to the occupying powers. Soviet efforts to foster a Communist movement were a complete failure, even in the Soviet occupation zone.

Originally it was expected that the Allied occupation of Austria would be of short duration. However, as a result of the East-West split, an impasse was reached over the Austrian question between the United States, Britain, and France on the one hand, and the Soviet Union on the other. The principal obstacle to the conclusion of a treaty between the former Allies and Austria was Soviet fear that if Austria were evacuated it might unite with Germany or join the Western alliance. It was not until 1955, during a thaw in the Cold War, that the Soviet government relaxed its opposition to the conclusion of an Austrian treaty. In return for guarantees of Austrian neutralization, it indicated its willingness to evacuate Austria. On May 15, 1955, the Austrian State Treaty was signed in Vienna between the former Allies and Austria. Austria promised not to form a political or economic union with Germany nor to join any alliance, and the Soviet government waived its claim to the German assets in Austria in return for an Austrian promise to pay $150 million in goods over a period of six years and 10 million metric tons of crude oil over a period of ten years. In September and October, amidst scenes of frenzied joy on the part of the Austrians, the Allied occupation forces were withdrawn. Austria recovered independence and sovereignty within her borders of 1938. Before the war, the Austrian economic position was perennially precarious. As a result of the war, the Austrian national income declined to one-third of what it had been in 1938. Gradually, however, despite the burden of "reparations" to Russia, Austria made a remarkable economic recovery. One reason for this was the generous financial assistance provided by the United States in the postwar period. Austria received over $1 billion in American aid. This was a higher subsidy per capita than the United States granted to any other European nation. The Austrians used the American funds to rebuild and improve their industries, modernize their agriculture, and increase their industrial and agricultural production. Particularly after the departure of the occupation armies in 1955, Austria made rapid economic strides. By 1964 the per capita income had reached $1,100 annually, placing the Austrians among the more prosperous nations of Europe. Like that of Switzerland, however, the Austrian balance of trade remained perennially adverse. Even more than Switzerland, Austria depended on tourism, which earned some $400 million annually.

The division of Western Europe into rival economic blocs (see Chapter 57) presented a serious threat to Austrian prosperity. Prevented by the Austrian State Treaty from joining the Common Market, with whose members it traded most (notably Germany and Italy), it was forced, as a second best choice, to join the Free Trade Association with whose members it traded little. As tariff barriers between the two blocs arose, Austria was caught in a trade squeeze. It sought to solve this dilemma by seeking "associate" membership in the Common Market. It hoped that this would give it the economic advantages of belonging to the Common Market, without prejudicing its neutrality.

The strain of war and occupation was reflected in Austrian vital statistics. In the postwar period, the birth rate averaged only 16 per thousand (despite the highest incidence of illegitimacy in Western Europe). At the same time the death rate stood at 12 to 13 per thousand, and infant mortality averaged an appalling 52 per thousand in the 1950's. Had it not been for the influx of refugees from Eastern Europe the population of Austria would have become almost stationary.

Because of the introduction of a comprehensive system of social welfare and health insurance, however, the situation improved markedly. By 1964 the birth rate rose to 19 per thousand, the death rate stood at 13, and infant mortality dropped to 31. The population of Austria rose to 7,195,000. Despite economic prosperity, however, Austria never recovered its former cultural brilliance. Under the empire and even under the First Republic, Vienna — the city of Mozart, Beethoven, Schubert, Brahms Grillparzer, Arthur Schnitzler, Max Reinhardt, Franz Werfel, Stefan Zweig, and Dr. Sigmund Freud — vied with Paris as a European cultural center. Since World War II, however, though still charming, gay, and *gemütlich*, it remained, culturally, a provincial town. Many attributed this mediocrity to the disappearance of the Jewish community of Vienna (once 300,000) into exile and the gas chambers of Dachau and other concentration camps. The Jewish minority had contributed in a disproportionately high degree to the cultural life of the Austrian capital.

55

EIGHT SMALL NATIONS OF WESTERN EUROPE

. . . We know of no reason in the nature of things why a state should be any better for being large . . .

SIR JOHN R. SEELEY

1. PROSPEROUS AND PROGRESSIVE LANDS

THIS CHAPTER WILL DISCUSS eight European states which have received in earlier chapters less attention than they merit. Some of the reasons for this neglect have already been explained (see p. 103). In a global survey small nations are eclipsed by the great powers and empires, much as small countries become dwarfed and difficult to find on a global map. The eight separate states discussed in this chapter, if it were possible to draw their territories together and unite their peoples, would be equivalent to a great power — a power with an area larger than France and Spain combined and a population of some 50 million inhabitants. But as individual countries, with an average area of some 60,000 square miles (roughly the size of Georgia or Florida), these eight states are too small to present in separate chapters.

It would be regrettable, however, to omit the lessons that may be learned from studying these small nations. They illustrate, sometimes more sharply and clearly than the great powers, the currents and forces that are shaping the world today. The eight nations appraised in this chapter differ in many respects — in geography, language, history, resources, density of population, prevailing religion, and forms of government and economy. But all have certain common attributes — they are prosperous and progressive; with two exceptions, they are monarchies, but all are model democracies; they enjoy a high degree of political and social stability; they have the best social services in the world; their administration and courts are noted for efficiency and honesty; they are marked by an absence of strong social contrasts and bitter social strife; their peoples are the most literate in the world and have low crime rates. They have many lessons to offer to larger and wealthier nations.

2. THE NETHERLANDS, BELGIUM, AND LUXEMBURG

The Netherlands, Belgium, and Luxemburg occupy a wealthy and strategic area of Europe, which gives them an importance out of proportion to their size, individual or collective. With a population of 12,042,000 (1965) and an area of 12,927 square miles, the Netherlands is the largest and most populous of them. As its name indicates, the Netherlands is low and flat. About two-fifths of it lies below the level of the sea, from which it is protected by dikes. For centuries the Dutch have waged a ceaseless struggle with the North Sea. They reclaimed land from it, drained this land with their famous wind mills, and brought it under cultivation to relieve the congestion of their country. With about 930 people to the square mile, the Netherlands is a densely populated country. Overcrowding and a housing shortage have been chronic Dutch problems. Yet slums are virtually unknown, because of careful planning and the Dutch aversion to the ugly and the squalid. The Dutch experimented with modern "functional" architecture and city planning long before these were taken up by more spacious countries, such as the United States.

From medieval times commerce has played an essential part in promoting Dutch prosperity. With excellent seaports and the navigable Rhine to carry goods deep into Europe, the Netherlands has always been naturally fitted to receive and transfer cargoes. Trade and transportation account for one-fourth of the gross national product. Rotterdam, which was heavily damaged in World War II, has been rebuilt and its port facilities improved and extended until it now surpasses both Amsterdam and London and has become the busiest port of Europe.

The great value of their imports and exports gave the Dutch one of the highest per capita rates of any nation in this respect. On the other hand, their mineral wealth was modest. Since they lacked coal or waterfalls to produce electricity, their consumption of electricity was comparatively low for a prosperous country. After World War II oil replaced coal as the main fuel, and laid the basis of a new petrochemical industry. Rotterdam now has the largest oil refineries in continental Europe. Oil, of course, has to be imported. This disadvantage has been partially offset by the recent discovery of large reserves of natural gas under the shallow North Sea.

In appreciating Dutch prosperity, one should note that the annual per capita income ($1,120 in 1964) seems lower than it is. One-sixth of the workers are employed in agriculture, and, as the Dutch are excellent scientific farmers, they obtain a high yield from their small cultivable area and farm families supply many of their own wants. Furthermore, they have a high birth rate (21 per thousand), a low death rate (8 per thousand), a rate of population increase of 1.3 per cent a year, and a life expectancy of 72 years. This reduces the per capita income *statistically*, for wives with numerous children are needed at home and a considerable fraction of the population (9 per cent) are over 64 years of age. These facts reduce what is termed the "economically active population" to two-fifths of the total population. But these wage earners, by working a forty-five hour week, provide a high standard of living for their families. The Dutch are a healthy and enterprising people. They like good food, spend nearly one-third of their income on it, and consume an average of 3000 calories a day. They are well educated (illiteracy is almost unknown), and many of them speak English, French, or German as well as their national language. Historically, the Netherlands was predominantly a Protestant country. But today slightly over two-fifths are Catholic, slightly under two-fifths are Calvinist, the remainder belonging to various faiths or none.

The government of the Netherlands, which has its seat at the Hague, has been a constitutional monarchy since 1814 when the country was liberated from Napoleonic occupation. Since that time the Dutch constitution has been amended several times. It now proclaims that "the king (or queen) is inviolable, the ministers are responsible." The cabinet, which is responsible to the parliament, actually exercises the sovereign's powers. The Dutch parliament (States General) is a bicameral legislature; members of the Upper House are elected for six years by the Representative Councils of the eleven historic provinces of the Netherlands; members of the Lower House are elected for four years by direct suffrage. All Dutch subjects in the Netherlands above the age of twenty-three may vote. Like most continental constitutions, the Dutch constitution provides for proportional representation. This has resulted in the growth of numerous political parties, the largest two of which are the Catholic party and the Socialist party. Since neither party is strong enough to form a cabinet alone, the two parties — though ideological adversaries — usually cooperate to form a coalition cabinet. Dutch politics, though often agitated, have been characterized by a pragmatic good sense and an aversion to extremes of any kind.

The Netherlands managed to stay neutral in World War I, but was overrun by the German armies in World War II. Queen Wilhelmina (1890–1948) fled to London, where she and her ministers maintained a "government in exile" and became the symbol of Dutch resistance to the Germans. After the war the Queen returned to her people, but, because of advanced age and failing health, abdicated in favor of her daughter Juliana (1948–   ). The Netherlands suffered considerable loss and damage from the four years of German occupation in World War II. Yet the most serious permanent loss the country endured came after the war when the Dutch surrendered their colonial empire in the East Indies. In 1949 they relinquished it to the newly constituted Republic of Indonesia — with the exception of West New Guinea, which they held on to until 1963. The Indonesians expelled the Dutch officials, traders, and plantation owners, then confiscated the huge Dutch investment in the islands (see Chapter

64). Of the once proud and profitable Dutch colonial empire there remain only Dutch Guiana (Surinam) in South America and a few islands in the Antilles.

Belgium is somewhat smaller (11,775 square miles) and less populous (9,428,000 in 1964) than the Netherlands. It is flat in the north, like the Netherlands, but hilly in the south where the Ardennes traverse it. Thanks to rich deposits of coal and iron ore, Belgium became a highly industrialized country early in the nineteenth century. Less than one-eighth of the people make a living from agriculture, which furnishes about one-fifteenth of the gross national product. Mining, manufacturing, construction, commerce, transport, and communication provide employment for seven-tenths of the economically active population. Foreign trade plays a very important part in the economy of Belgium, as it does in that of the Netherlands. Together with the small Grand Duchy of Luxemburg (with which it formed a customs union in 1922), Belgian imports and exports were valued at $11.5 billion in 1964. Half the exports from Belgium-Luxemburg are iron and steel, textiles, and machinery; the imports consist largely of raw materials for industry and food for the urban population. After World War II the large Belgian coal industry, like the coal industry of all Western Europe, suffered from the competition of cheaper American coal and the increasing use of oil as fuel. Many Belgian coal mines were forced to shut down, and the miners compelled to seek other employment.

The Belgian social services are not as effective as those of the Netherlands, a deficiency which is reflected in the Belgian vital statistics. The birth rate of 17 per thousand is lower than the Dutch rate, but the death rate of 14 per thousand is higher. The Belgian population increases about one-half per cent a year, and life expectancy in Belgium is 65 years. These facts help to explain why Belgium, which had a larger population and higher population density than the Netherlands before World War II, has fallen behind since the war. On the other hand, the per capita income in Belgium is about $1,300 a year (1964). Belgian workers are organized in strong labor unions; working hours and conditions are regulated by law; and there is unemployment insurance. But the national government has not expended large sums on pensions, medical care, and other social services as have the governments in most neighboring states. There has been more social tension in Belgium than in the Netherlands.

Another cause of tension is the perennial language question. Unlike the Dutch who are united in language but divided in religion, the Belgians are united in religion (they are overwhelmingly Catholic) but divided in language. About 60 per cent of the Belgians are Flemings whose language (Flemish) is closely related to Dutch, while the remainder are Walloons who speak French. Both languages enjoy legal equality, but since the nineteenth century, when the French language enjoyed great prestige, it has been the language of government, business, and intellectual intercourse in Belgium. A knowledge of French is indispensable for social advancement. Few Walloons bother to learn Flemish, but many Flemings are forced to learn French if they want to get ahead in life. This has given the Flemings a sense of inequality which has led them often to explode in riots and violence reminiscent of the struggle of nationalities in the old Hapsburg Empire (see Chapter 9). Belgian politics is more explosive than the Dutch.

Belgium is a constitutional monarchy, with a conventional West European nineteenth-century constitution. The Belgian parliament consists of a Senate and a Chamber of Deputies. The cabinet is responsible to the parliament. All Belgians (including women since 1949) over twenty not only have the right but the duty to vote (those who fail to vote are fined). Proportional representation prevails. As in the Netherlands, the Catholic (Christian Socialist) and Socialist parties attract a majority of the voters. Although divided by ideology, the two parties usually form a coalition cabinet.

The strategic location of Belgium has made it a battlefield in nearly every European war since Caesar. It was overrun by the Germans in both World Wars. In 1914 King Albert I (1909–34) retreated with his army into France and continued fighting until victory, but in 1940 his son Leopold III (1934–51) remained in Belgium and surrendered his army to avoid further bloodshed. The cabinet fled to London, and from there it directed the Belgian resistance to the Germans. Many Belgians felt that the king had brought dishonor on the country. After the war they opposed his return from Switzerland, in which he had taken up residence following his release from German internment. Although in a referendum held on the question in 1950 a slight majority voted in favor of recalling him, he abdicated in favor of his son, Baudouin I (1951–   ).

Belgium suffered great damage in World War II, as it had in World War I. While Brussels, the national capital, escaped extensive destruction, Mons, Tournai, Liège, and Louvain, with their ancient cathedrals and guild halls, suffered in both wars. The Library of the Catholic University of Louvain, burned in 1914, then restored with American aid, was burned again in 1940. After the war, Belgium, like the Netherlands, lost its colonial empire. The vast Belgian Congo in Africa, nearly one hundred times the area of Belgium, became independent in 1960. The former Belgian administrators and businessmen were expelled and the huge Belgian investment in the colony was lost (see Chapter 66).

The Grand Duchy of Luxemburg is a diminutive state of about 1000 square miles and a population of 329,000 (1964). In 1867, thanks to the jealousy of the European great powers, its independence and neutrality were guaranteed. Located entirely in the Ardennes, it is a hilly country dotted with bleak industrial towns and picturesque castles, the latter serving to remind the Luxemburgers of the days of their glory in the fourteenth century when their dynasty provided several German emperors as well as kings of Bohemia and Hungary. Luxemburg has rich iron ore deposits and a large steel industry, to which it owes its prosperity (its per capita income in 1964 was $1,900). It is the sixth largest steel producer in Western Europe. Steel constitutes 70 per cent of its exports, while coke — to make steel — is the largest item of import.

Luxemburg resembles Belgium closely in political, social, and economic structure. In 1940, when the Germans occupied the country as they had done in 1914, the Grand Duchess Charlotte (1919–64) escaped to London where she established a government in exile. In 1964 she abdicated in favor of her son, the present Grand Duke Jean. Under the Luxemburg constitution, the sovereign appoints the head of the cabinet as well as the members of the upper house of the parliament, the Council of State, while the members of the lower house, the Chamber of Deputies, are elected for five years by universal suffrage. As in Belgium, French is the language of government, business, and intellectual intercourse, although Luxemburg has a national language — *Letzeburgesch*. Fearful of German designs on their independence, the Luxemburgers deny the German claim that *Letzeburgesch* is but a west German dialect, and insist that it is a distinct Germanic tongue. Like the Belgians, the Luxemburgers are predominantly Catholic.

In 1944, while in exile in London, the governments of Belgium, the Netherlands, and Luxemburg agreed to form a customs union after the war. This plan was implemented in 1948 when the three countries adopted a schedule for progressively abolishing tariffs among themselves and erecting uniform tariffs against other countries. Despite some initial hardships to competing industries in the three countries, the customs union proved successful. In 1958 the three governments went one step further and signed an agreement to form the Benelux (BElgium, NEtherlands, LUXemburg) economic union. This meant adopting common economic and social policies, in order to strengthen their position in the European Common Market (see Chapter 57). Although once proponents of neutrality, Belgium, the Netherlands, and Luxemburg learned a bitter lesson in World War II when their neutrality was brutally violated. After the war they joined the NATO alliance and firmly aligned themselves with the West.

3. SWITZERLAND

The Swiss succeeded in keeping their small mountainous country (15,966 square miles) neutral in World War II, as they had done in all European wars since the Peace of Vienna (1815) which first internationally recognized their neutrality. The Swiss economy shows the blessings of a long period of peace. In the first years after 1945 they enjoyed the second highest per capita income among the nations, being exceeded only by the United States. Switzerland lacks both sufficient arable land and mineral wealth; but the industrious Swiss, who numbered only about 6 million in 1965, have made such good use of their talents and resources that they have become famous throughout the world for their products. Lacking coal and iron ore, they concentrated on developing small, clean, and highly decentralized industries, which do not disfigure their charming cities and lovely countryside. For power to operate their factories and railways they rely heavily on electricity generated from their mountain streams.

As the largest Swiss city, Zurich holds less than 500,000 inhabitants, the national capital, Bern, has 167,000 inhabitants, and two-thirds of the people live in centers of 10,000 or less, most Swiss citizens enjoy a rural or semirural existence. Their vital statistics show them to be healthier than the Belgians but not quite so healthy as the Dutch in the postwar years. Their life expectancy has risen to 70, their death rate fallen to less than 10 per thousand, their birth rate fluctuating between 18 and 19 per thousand. Their annual rate of increase is 1.3 per cent, almost as high as that of the Netherlands; but this is partly due to the fact that few Swiss choose to emigrate. On the contrary, in the prosperous early 1960's Switzerland had to import some 720,000 foreign seasonal laborers to do hard manual work, while the native Swiss concentrated on trades and professions requiring high skills. The labor force of Switzerland includes almost half the population, and half that force is engaged in manufacture.

Although Switzerland has no sea coast or harbors, the value of its foreign trade exceeds $4 billion a year and is equivalent per capita to that of the Dutch. More than half the exports are watches (50 per cent of the world's supply of watches is produced in Switzerland), precision instruments, electrical goods, complex machinery (e.g., high-speed rotary presses), and textiles. Dyes and chemicals, cheese and chocolates are likewise important Swiss products. Imports include food, petroleum products, and raw materials for manufacture or processing. The Swiss also prefer to import rather than to build automobiles; although with their sophisticated technology they could produce them if they so chose. Swiss prosperity (its per capita income in 1964 was $1,950) could not be guessed from the Swiss balance of trade, which is chronically adverse.

The explanation of this paradox is that the balance of trade does not indicate "invisible exports" — sources of income which are derived not from movement of goods across frontiers but from services. Of these the most important are tourism and banking. Tourism is a major industry in Switzerland, employing some 140,000 people to accommodate and entertain about 5 million foreign tourists who visit the country annually. Tourism brings in $300 million a year and helps to reduce the gap in the balance of trade. Banking is an important service because the stability of the Swiss franc makes it easily convertible into other currencies. Citizens of other countries who are anxious to keep their capital from depreciation, and some who have assets they wish to conceal, find Swiss banking facilities convenient. The laws of Switzerland guarantee secrecy to clients of Swiss banks and shareholders in Swiss companies. Foreigners who deposit funds in the banks for safeguarding do not receive interest; on the contrary, they pay fees for the privilege. This provides a profit for the Swiss bankers and capital for Swiss economic development. In the prosperous early 1960's the Swiss government was obliged to curb foreign investment, because — among other reasons — it threatened Swiss control of many of their enterprises and caused an alarming boom in Swiss real estate.

The Swiss place a high value on education and have seven universities, an Institute of Technology, and a School of Economics and Public Administration, as well as numerous specialized schools, including a famous school of hotel management. Swiss schools enjoy such a high reputation that many foreigners seek admission to them. About one-quarter of the students enrolled in Swiss institutions of higher learning are foreigners.

Switzerland is one of the oldest republics in the world. Organized as a loose federation of twenty-two cantons, with each canton reserving control over its local affairs, it is as diversified as the United States (see Chapter 10). Switzerland is one of the few countries that still relies for defense on a national militia. The Swiss army is a well organized and well equipped force. All male Swiss citizens between 20 and 50 are liable for service in it, first for regular training and then for summer exercises. All through World War II the Swiss kept their militia mobilized to fend off any possible encroachments against their neutrality. Although they were once known for their aggressiveness and export of mercenaries, since the nineteenth century they have become increasingly attached to neutrality. With the European wars becoming national in character, Switzerland, which includes elements of the language and culture of Germany, France, and Italy, could not join one group of belligerents against the other in either of the World Wars, without causing serious strains between its linguistic-cultural communities. Although Switzerland joined the League of Nations after World War I, it refused to join the United Nations after World War II. It also remained completely aloof from the East-West Cold War. It refused to join the European Common Market because the original program of this group included plans for political integration. Instead, Switzerland joined the looser Free Trade Association (see Chapter 57), even though it trades more with the members of the former than the latter.

4. THE SCANDINAVIAN STATES AND FINLAND

Geographically, only Sweden and Norway are Scandinavian countries, that is, are located in the Scandinavian Peninsula. Denmark is geographically a part of the European continent. However, because of their long and close historical, cultural, and economic ties, all three countries are commonly designated "Scandinavian." On the other hand, Finland, despite its long ties to Sweden, is generally considered a "Baltic" rather than a Scandinavian country — together with Estonia, Latvia, and Lithuania, now absorbed in the Soviet Union. If Finland is considered in this chapter it is because of its own efforts since World War II to attach itself to the Scandinavian bloc of nations in order to lessen its isolation and strengthen its resistance to its vast and intimidating neighbor — Soviet Russia.

The largest and wealthiest Scandinavian nation is Sweden. It is a fair-sized country in area (173,394 square miles) but relatively small in population (7,661,000 in 1964); its population density is only 44 persons to the square mile. Only the southern region of Sweden, called Götaland (the Land of the Goths), is suitable for agriculture — its arable land comprises 11.6 per cent of the area of Sweden. The central and northern regions, Svealand and Norrland, are covered with vast forests (55 per cent of the area of Sweden) and innumerable lakes or barren mountains. It is, however, in these regions that a main source of modern Sweden's prosperity lies — top-grade iron ore.

The combination of iron ore and timber have provided the basis of Sweden's iron industry since the Middle Ages. But lack of coal, which had to be imported from Germany, retarded the development of modern industry generally in Sweden. The Swedes are energetic and efficient, but as long as Sweden continued to depend on agriculture and forestry for its income it was a poor country. The Swedes emigrated in large numbers, principally to the United States. In the twentieth century, however, Sweden was partly relieved from its dependence on coal, first by electricity which it can produce cheaply from lakes and mountain streams, then by oil. As a result, Sweden has experienced remarkable industrial growth. Industry has succeeded agriculture as the major occupation and has expanded until it furnishes half the national income. Emigration has tapered off. In the prosperous early 1960's the unemployment rate dropped to a negligible 1 per cent of the labor force, and the per capita income climbed from $800 in 1948 to $2,000 in 1964. Sweden, once a land of emigration, became a land of immigration. It had to import seasonal laborers from Southern Europe to work in its expanding industries.

Iron ore, steel, ball bearings, automobiles, airplanes, electrical goods, and petrochemicals comprise two-thirds of Sweden's exports, forestry products (lumber, celulose, pulp, paper, and matches) one-third. Sweden imports food, coal, oil, and metals. Imports and exports combined attained a value of $7 billion in 1963. A merchant fleet exceeding $4 million tons carries the Swedish flag to all oceans.

Owing to the growth of industry, population has shifted from the rural areas to the cities. One-quarter of Sweden's population now lives in the three principal Swedish cities: Stockholm, Göteborg, and Malmö. Stockholm (the "Venice of the North"), the national capital, is built upon numerous granite islands, which provide spectacular views of its striking architecture (both old and ultra modern).

Sweden has long had a strong cooperative movement, both of producers and consumers. It has also been noted for the excellence of its social services, on which it spends 14 per cent of its national income compared to 6 per cent in the United States. These services include old age and disability pensions, medical care and benefits, allowances for all children below sixteen, and for widows and orphans. Because of its excellent social services, the Swedish death rate (10 per thousand) and infant mortality rate (15 per thousand) are both exceptionally low, and the life expectancy (72 years) is high. But as the birth rate is also unusually low (14 per thousand), the rate of population increase is only 0.7 per cent a year.

Like the Swiss, the Swedes place a high premium on education. Illiteracy is unknown. They display great originality in architecture, sculpture, and ceramics, and the Swedish theater and cinema have reached high esthetic standards. Unlike the Swiss, the Swedes are culturally and religiously a homogeneous people. The overwhelming majority of Swedes belong to the Lutheran Church, which is the state church of Sweden. Apart from a handful of Lapps, nomad herdsmen of reindeer in the far north, probably of Asian origin, there are no racial or national minorities in Sweden. Sweden is singularly free of slums and poverty, of social contrasts and social strife, and of racial or minority tensions. Paradoxically, despite the absence of problems which plague many greater and richer nations, Sweden has the highest known suicide rate in the world.

Sweden became a parliamentary monarchy after the Napoleonic Wars. The king originally had considerable powers, and in theory still does. However, King Gustaf V (1907–50) conducted himself as a model constitutional and democratic monarch during his long reign, and established a tradition which his son, the present King Gustaf VI, continues. The sovereign's powers are exercised by the cabinet, which is responsible to parliament. The Swedish parliament (*Riksdag*) has two chambers, the first of which is elected by indirect suffrage, one-eighth being replaced each year, and the second by universal suffrage. The Social Democratic party is the leading party. Despite its Marxist origins, it is a moderate, reformist, non-revolutionary party, deeply attached to the monarchy. It has been continuously in power since 1932.

Sweden, like Switzerland, has not been at war since the conclusion of the Napoleonic Wars. The aggressiveness of Germany during World War II and of Soviet Russia after the war alarmed the Swedes. They hesitated to place undue trust in international guarantees of their neutrality, and sought to protect it by strengthening their armed forces, which they equipped with the latest modern weapons. Sweden has declined to join NATO and remains carefully aloof from the East-West struggle. Unlike Switzerland, however, it has joined the United Nations.

Norway is a very rugged land, stretching along the Atlantic coast of the Scandinavian Peninsula for some 1,100 miles. The coast is mountainous and indented with fjords, the longest one of which, the Sogne Fjord, cuts 112 miles inland. Norway has an area of 125,181 square miles, which is approximately the size of New Mexico, but a population of only 3,700,000 (1964). Population density is thus about 30 to the square mile.

Some 70 per cent of Norway is little better than naked rock. Only about 2.7 per cent of its area is suitable for agriculture. Farming requires exceptionally hard work, and its rewards are modest. Agriculture, though it engages nearly one-fifth of the labor force, accounts for only 6 per cent of the national income. The sea, despite its dangers, is more rewarding; it provides one-fifth of the national income. Fishing, whaling, and shipping ranked as important activities for the Norwegians, who possessed the fourth largest merchant fleet in the world in 1964, reckoned in gross tonnage. Mining and manufacturing, however, took the lead after World War II, producing nearly one-third of the gross national product. Industrial development was speeded by an abundant supply of hydroelectric power. Lacking oil or sufficient coal, the Norwegians have harnessed their waterfalls. Their per capita consumption of electricity is the highest in the world, rising to double that of the United States (1965).

Although Norwegian imports and exports combined attained a value of more than $3 billion by 1964, the import total considerably exceeded the export total. The Norwegians offset this unfavorable balance by their income from shipping and other revenue from abroad. Their economy remains vulnerable, however, to changes in world conditions because of their dependence on foreign earnings. Norway suffered considerable damage in World War II when it was invaded by the Germans. This was reflected in its national income, which remained considerably smaller in the postwar years than that of Sweden or Denmark. However, by hard work and enterprise the Norwegians have reduced the gap. By 1964 their per capita income was about $1,300, which still fell short of that of the Swedes and even of the Danes but exceeded that of the Dutch.

Like Sweden, Norway has excellent social services, on which it spends 13 per cent of its national income. The Norwegians enjoy good national health. With a birth rate of 18 per thousand, a death rate of less than 9, and an infant mortality rate of 15, the Norwegians have achieved a life expectancy of 73, and an annual increase of 1 per cent in the population. This is a record few other nations can match. The school system of Norway is likewise an exemplary one. It faces a problem, however, which neither that of Sweden nor that of Denmark has to face. It has to give instruction in two languages. Although the Norwegians, like the Swedes and Danes, are a homogeneous people in religion (Lutheran) and race (apart from the Lapp minority in the far north), they use two languages: *riksmål* and *landsmål*. This is a product of historical circumstances. During Norway's long dependence on Denmark a version of the Danish tongue (*riksmål*) became the language of government, business, and literature in Norway. After the country separated from Denmark, the native idiom of Norway (*landsmål*) was elevated to the dignity of a literary tongue. Both languages continue to be used.

Norway has been a constitutional monarchy since 1814 when it entered into a personal union with Sweden. The first independent king of Norway, Haakon VII (1905–57), was a Danish prince. In 1940, when the Germans invaded Norway, he refused to surrender and retreated northward fighting with the army. When further resistance on Norwegian soil proved impossible, he escaped to London where he established a government in exile. During his long reign he always conducted himself as a democratic, constitutional monarch, establishing a tradition which his son, the present King Olav V, has continued. Under the Norwegian constitution, legislative power rests with a popular assembly (the *Storting*), which is elected by universal suffrage and controls the cabinet. After assembling, the *Storting* divides into two sections, one-fourth of the members being chosen to form the *Lagting*. This smaller body serves in part as the upper chamber, in part as a court of justice. As in Sweden, a Marxist but moderate and reformist party, the Norwegian Labor party, dominated Norwegian politics from 1935 until 1965 when it was defeated in elections and replaced with a right-of-center coalition.

Denmark resembles the Netherlands in its geography rather than its Scandinavian neighbors, from which it is separated by the Skagerrak and Kattegat straits. It is a level, low-lying country with productive farms (over 70 per cent of the soil is cultivable) but few mineral resources. It has an area of 16,619 square miles, a population of 4,773,000 (1964), and a population density of 280 to the square mile. One quarter of the Danish people derive a living from farming. The Danes have applied scientific methods to farming and have had remarkable results. Nethertheless farming accounted for only 13 per cent of their gross national product in 1961, while manufacturing accounted for 30 per cent and trade and transportation for about 25 per cent. Lacking coal, oil, and minerals, the Danes have to import these commodities, and also bring fertilizers and farm machinery. In return they exported dairy products, bacon, ham, fish, but also machinery, transport equipment, chemicals, and textiles. Total imports and exports had a value of about $4.5 billion (1964).

To get the maximum out of their modest resources, the Danes recognized early the value of cooperative effort. They pioneered in organizing cooperative societies, both producer and consumer, as early as the 1860's. Unemployment was the bane of the Danish laborers. During the Great Depression of the 1930's as much as 30 per cent of the Danish labor force was unemployed. Even after World War II unemployment was a serious problem. Only in the prosperous 1960's was full employment achieved. Danish workingmen therefore appreciate the social services of their country, on which about 13 per cent of the national income is spent. The

Danes likewise regard adequate schooling as a matter of utmost importance.

The intelligent manner in which the Danes have utilized their limited resources has made them a prosperous nation. Their per capita income rose from about $800 in 1948 to $1,440 by 1964. They are also a healthy nation, with a death rate of 11 per thousand and a life expectancy of 71 years. A moderate birth rate of 18 per thousand and limited emigration have kept the annual population increase below 1 per cent. About two-fifths of the Danish people live in cities, of which the largest is the capital, Copenhagen, a lovely, gay, and cosmopolitan city and the traditional gateway to the Baltic.

The government of Denmark is a constitutional monarchy, and the constitution was last revised in 1953. Executive power is exercised by the cabinet, which is responsible to the *Folketing* — a single-chamber legislature, elected for a term of four years by universal suffrage. As in Sweden and Norway, the Social Democratic party is the leading party. Denmark adjoins on land only one country — Germany. The frontier which separates them is not a natural one, and is, therefore, difficult to defend. In 1940 when the Germans invaded Denmark, the king and government recognized the futility of resistance and surrendered without a fight. Later the Danes developed an effective resistance to Germany. They saved their small Jewish minority by literally smuggling them out to the safety of neutral Sweden. King Christian X (1912–47), who remained with his people during the German occupation, died in 1947 and was succeeded by his son, Frederick IX.

The brutal violation of their neutrality during the war led both Denmark and Norway to join NATO and align themselves firmly with the West after the war. In the late 1940's when the formation of regional federations and unions was widely discussed in Europe, Denmark, Norway, and Sweden discussed the possibility of forming a Nordic economic union. However, on studying the matter, they found that they traded more with outsiders than with one another and that they might lose more by forming a customs union than they would gain. In the end, therefore, they limited themselves to the establishment of the Nordic Council (1952), which provided only for a common labor market. The division of Western Europe into rival economic blocs, the Common Market and the Free Trade Association, presented the Scandinavian nations with a serious dilemma, because they traded with members of both blocs. In the end, they joined the looser Free Trade Association.

Finland, the pre-war development of which was discussed in Chapter 28, emerged from World War II a diminished (by about 17,000 square miles of territory), impoverished, and exhausted land. The area of Finland was reduced after the war to 130,165 square miles. Under the terms of the Soviet-Finnish armistice of 1944 (see p. 513), which was confirmed by the Paris peace treaty of 1947 (see p. 553), Finland was forced to cede

— in addition to the territories lost in 1940 (see p. 456) — the area of Petsamo in the far north, thus depriving the Finns of access to the White Sea. They also had to grant Russia a fifty-year lease on the military base of Porkkala near Helsinki, and to pay Soviet Russia reparations valued at $300 million which were to be delivered in the form of goods and services over a period of six years. These provisions put in the hands of Soviet Russia a powerful club to wield over the head of Finland.

Finland's future appeared grim. Unlike Greece, Turkey, or Czechoslovakia, it was isolated from the West by neutral Sweden. It could depend only on its own resources to resist Soviet pressures. In these circumstances it seemed quite possible that it would not survive as an independent and democratic nation, but would be satellized and communized, perhaps even absorbed into the Soviet Union, as Estonia, Latvia, and Lithuania have been.

Such a grim future might have broken the spirit of a less determined people, but the Finns faced it courageously. They wasted no time on self-pity, as the Germans had done in 1919, but adopted what has since come to be known as the "Paasikivi-Kekkonen line," after President J. K. Paasikivi (1946–56) and President U. Kekkonen (1956–   ). They punctually fulfilled their international obligations to Soviet Russia but did not allow the destruction of their democratic institutions at home, either by overt or covert Soviet (Communist) action.

The Soviet demands for reparations included goods, such as ships, cables, and metal products, for the production of which Finland had little or no capacity. The Finns grimly resolved to create the capacity and satisfy the Soviet demands. By extreme exertions and with little outside help, they punctually paid the reparations by 1953. In the end, the ordeal brought some rewards. Finland found itself with an enlarged industrial capacity. It was less dependent on agriculture, fishing, and hunting for its income than it had been before the war. While in 1938 these activities accounted for one-fifth of the national income, by 1964 they accounted for only one-tenth. On the other hand, manufacturing increased from one-quarter to one-third. The repair of the war damage and the necessity to provide housing for 500,000 refugees doubled the importance of construction and building as a source of income. Exports and imports reached a value of $3.5 billion by 1964, and the Finns kept the balance between them remarkably close. Seventy per cent of Finnish exports consisted of forestry products: timber, pulp, and paper. But increasingly Finland exported also ships, metals, machinery, and textiles. The imports were mainly oil, metals, and machinery. The per capita income climbed from a modest $500 in 1948 to $1,180 by 1964.

The cooperative movement was as important in Finland as in the Scandinavian countries. The Finnish social services, while well organized, were less extensive, owing to the lower Finnish national income and the necessity to devote some 11 per cent of it to Soviet reparations in the postwar years. The population of Finland reached 4.6 million in 1964, and population density was 36 persons to the square mile. The death rate was 10 per thousand, the birth rate 16 per thousand, and life expectancy was 68 years. The rate of population increase was about 1 per cent annually. The Finns had always attached great importance to schools, and continued to do so after the war, despite pressing demands on their income. School attendance was required up to fifteen, and the labor force included half the population of fifteen and over.

In February, 1948, at the same time that Czechoslovakia lost her democratic constitution by a Communist coup (see p. 750), Stalin addressed a note to Paasikivi summoning Finland to sign a treaty of friendship and mutual assistance. Both inside and outside Finland this move was regarded as a prelude to Soviet attempts to satellize and communize the country. However, the Finns stood their ground, and the Soviet government hesitated to coerce them as it had done in 1940. This was probably out of fear lest it push neutral Sweden into the Western alliance. Had this happened it could have led to the establishment of American bases in Sweden, which was separated from Soviet territory only by the narrow Baltic Sea.

In April, 1948, a carefully worded Soviet-Finnish treaty of friendship and mutual assistance was signed, which was valid for ten years and provided for military cooperation in the event of aggression by Germany or a power allied with Germany (presumably the United States) against Finland. Since neither Germany nor the United States was likely to attack Finland, this left it in a different position than, for instance, Poland or Czechoslovakia. The Finnish government insisted that the treaty did not constitute alignment in the Cold War. In the following years it declined to join the military and economic organizations in Eastern Europe sponsored by the Soviet Union. This made its international position somewhat anomalous. A disgruntled Finn characterized it as that of a "cross between a neutral and a satellite." But apparently the Soviet government was content with it. In 1956 when the Soviet-Finnish treaty was renewed, it restored Porkkala to Finnish control. It also consented to Finland's joining the Nordic Council (1956) and the Free Trade Association (1961), the latter as an "associate" member.

Moreover, Finland kept her democratic constitution intact. As a result of proportionate representation, Finland had numerous parties. After the war the middle-of-the-road Agrarian party became the largest. It was around it that most of the postwar coalition cabinets were organized. The second largest party was the Finnish Communist party, which commanded between one-fifth and one-quarter of the electorate. After the war it was represented in the cabinet, in which it held the key post of minister of interior which controlled the police. However, in July, 1948, only three months after the conclusion of the Soviet-Finnish treaty, it suffered defeat in elections and was forced out of the cabinet. Contrary to general expectation, the Soviet government did not protest. In general elections in 1966, the Social Democrats, a moderate socialist party, displaced the Agrarians as the leading party. In consequence, the Social Democratic leader formed a coalition cabinet, to which the Communists were admitted. But by then the fear of absorption into the Soviet Union was gone. For the time being, at least, the Paasikivi-Kekkonen line apparently has succeeded.

5. FOUR CLUES TO PROGRESS

When the eight European countries described in this chapter are compared, they are seen to differ widely in geographic features, area, and population density. The Netherlands and Denmark are low and level, Switzerland and Norway largely elevated and mountainous. In area the eight countries likewise vary widely: Belgium has less than 12,000 square miles, Sweden more than 173,000. The population density in the Netherlands is 900 to the square mile; in Sweden it is under 30. Some of the countries (the Netherlands, Sweden) ranked as great or semi-great powers in earlier centuries. Some (Belgium, the Netherlands) have recently lost large and valuable empires overseas. Some (Switzerland, Luxemburg) never held colonial empires. The conclusion that appears to follow is that none of these variations and dissimilarities provide much aid in explaining why these eight countries have achieved high standards of income, health and welfare.

That they have achieved such standards is attested by their vital statistics. The average death rate for these eight nations in 1960 was 9.3 per thousand, the average life expectancy 70 years. These figures are considerably more favorable than the averages for Europe as a whole and agree almost exactly with the rates prevailing in the United States in 1960. A low death rate, and a life expectancy of "three score years and ten," are blessings every nation desires but very few have yet attained. Here, it seems safe to assume, is the first test one might apply in judging the welfare of a nation. *A low death rate and a high life expectancy mark a progressive nation.*

The eight countries under consideration had a combined population of 46 million people in 1960. The value of their external trade (exports and imports) reached a total equivalent to $27 billion. This was an exceptionally large total; it almost equaled the external trade of the United States, which held almost four times the population of the eight countries. Foreign commerce by itself, however, is an indication rather than a proof of prosperity. A more dependable index may be obtained by measuring the part played by mining and maufacture, commerce and transportation working together. In the eight countries, considered as a group, these activities accounted for three-fifths (60 per cent) of their collective income. As a contrast, one might note that agriculture accounted for only one-eighth (12 per cent) of it. Mining, manufacture, and transportation are activities that demand a considerable supply of mechanical energy, and this fact provides a further correlation. The energy consumed within the eight countries, per capita, was equal to that provided by 2700 kilograms of coal. This was higher than the average energy consumption per capita for Western Europe. These estimates suggest a second clue to economic progress. *Prosperous nations devote their major efforts to mining, manufacturing, trade, and transportation, and develop the energy needed for mechanization.*

Among the eight nations considered, the education of the young is regarded as a problem of the highest importance. The Scandinavian countries in particular were among the first European states to establish free schools and make education compulsory for all. This emphasis on education offers a third clue to progress. *The wealth and welfare of a state are closely related to its system of education and the quality of its schools.*

A fourth point to note is that — as the case of Switzerland most strikingly shows — neither mineral wealth nor abundance of fertile soil is indispensable for the prosperity and progress of a country, but the character of its people is. The eight nations reviewed in this chapter are, in general, well-trained, industrious, law-abiding, and politically mature. All have representative, responsible, democratic governments. None has been disturbed by a serious or destructive internal revolution in the twentieth century. On the average, their governments devote one-third of the national revenue to education and social services. Those that spend most on public health programs, maternity clinics, and child care have the lowest death and infant mortality rates and the highest life expectancy. These facts suggest a fourth clue to national progress. It is a confirmation of the proverb that "to be mature is to be responsible" and it might be expressed thus: *If the people are intelligent, prudent, and industrious the state is likely to be orderly and prosperous.*

56

SIX NATIONS OF SOUTHERN EUROPE

The sun-bleached lands of the Mediterranean were once Europe's most civilized and prosperous, but now are its poorest and most backward.

SIR GEOFFREY HAMILTON

1. OLD AND EXHAUSTED LANDS

IN THIS CHAPTER SIX less prosperous and less progressive countries will be considered: Italy, Spain, Portugal, Greece, Turkey, and Cyprus. They widely differ in size, population, history, and culture. Spain, with an area of some 195,000 square miles, is a sizeable country; Cyprus, with an area of only 3,572 square miles is a tiny one. Italy has a population of about 52 million; Cyprus of only about 587,000. Although all of the countries under study in this chapter once formed a part of the Roman empire and felt its civilizing influence, their subsequent development diverged. In Italy Roman influence is still everywhere in evidence; in Turkey it is felt only indirectly. In fact, Turkey is both in geography and culture an Asian land, although in the 1920's, by the will of its dictator Kemal Atatürk, it deliberately turned its back on its Asian past and set out to recast its institutions in the image of Europe.

Still there are certain similarities between the countries discussed in this chapter. These similarities have been imposed by geography. With the exception of Portugal, all the countries discussed in this chapter are Mediterranean lands. They have similar climatic conditions. They suffer from insufficient rainfall — a condition which was aggravated by deforestation centuries ago and consequent erosion of soil. All of them have long supported relatively dense populations. Their soil has been cultivated and their resources — never abundant — have been exploited continuously for thousands of years. They are old and exhausted lands.

In ancient times when Europe outside the boundaries of the Roman empire was largely covered with tracts of primeval forest and sparsely inhabited by primitive barbaric tribes, the lands of the Mediterranean were civilized and relatively prosperous. In modern times, however, they

671

have fallen behind other European countries in their social, economic, and cultural development. They have become Europe's poorhouse. While each has a wealthy and sophisticated elite, their masses are steeped in poverty and ignorance. Social welfare was, until recently, an exclusive concern of the Church. The governments of the countries under study in this chapter are not noted for honesty or efficiency; they tend to be dictatorial and are chronically unstable. Their standards of law and order are low. The notorious *Mafia* in Sicily arose originally as an organization for the self-protection of citizens, who could not obtain justice in courts. The well-known clannishness and strong family ties of the Mediterranean peoples are a result of the fact that society offered the individual no protection; he could rely only on his family. Although in the prosperous 1950's and 1960's all of the countries studied in this chapter have made progress, if compared to the countries studied in the previous chapter, they remain poor and backward.

2. ITALY

On June 10, 1940, Mussolini plunged Italy into World War II. He was confident that the imminent collapse of France would end the war and that Italy would share in the spoils of victory — without having to make any sacrifices (see p. 461). In 1943 when the fortunes of war inclined toward the Allies, Italy once again tried to "rush to the rescue of the victors." Mussolini was overthrown and under Marshal Badoglio Italy defected from the Axis and joined the Allies as a "co-belligerent" (see pp. 503–504). The maneuver misfired, however. Italy was trampled under the feet of the great combatants, who fought over the length of the country, from south to north. Italy suffered heavy losses in lives and property, was deprived of its empire, had to pay reparations, and was reduced in area to 116,246 square miles (see pp. 551–552).

The Italian people, who had paid a heavy price for the faithlessness and frivolity of their leaders, turned in wrath not only against fascism but also against the monarchy. Mussolini was killed and King Victor Emanuel III (1900–46) was forced to abdicate and go into exile. In a plebiscite in June, 1946, the Italian people voted by a majority of 54.3 per cent to abolish the monarchy altogether. On June 10, 1946, Italy was proclaimed a republic.

The National Constituent Assembly drafted a conventional West European constitution, which was similar to the pre-fascist constitution of 1848 (see p. 75). The new constitution, which went into effect on January 1, 1948, replaced the king with a president, who was to be elected for seven years by a two-thirds majority of the parliament. Legislative power rested with a bicameral legislature; members of the Senate were chosen by voters over twenty-five, members of the Chamber of Deputies by voters over twenty-one years of age. Like the French president under the Third or Fourth Republics, the Italian president was largely a figure-head. The real powers were vested in the cabinet, which was responsible to the parliament.

Proportionate representation was adopted. It resulted in the rise of numerous parties. The three dominant parties which emerged in the elections into the Constituent Assembly in 1946, were the Christian Demo-crats, the Communists, and the Socialists. The Christian Democratic party is a moderate Catholic party, which is descended from the Populist party of the 1920's (see p. 274). It is the largest Italian party, and has provided all the prime ministers of the Italian Republic. Under the able leadership of Alcide de Gasperi (1881–1954) it garnered 48 per cent of the electoral strength in the elections of 1948; but after his death it de-clined in strength to 38.3 per cent in 1963. The Communist party is the second largest Italian party and the largest Communist party in Western Europe. Under the leadership of the spell-binding orator Palmiro Togli-atti (1893–1964), who had spent many years in exile in Moscow, it rose from 20 per cent of the electoral vote in 1946 to 25.3 per cent in 1963. However, as it grew in numbers, it appeared to decline in revolutionary zeal. It was, in fact, Togliatti who coined the term "Communist polycen-trism" (see p. 847) to describe his belief that individual Communist par-ties should have the right to devise their own tactics, instead of following those dictated by Moscow. The Italian Socialist Party, the third largest Italian party, was weakened by a schism between its two principal lead-ers Pietro Nenni, who for some time favored a "People's bloc" with the Communists, and Guiseppe Sarragat, who was irreconcilably opposed to cooperation with the Communists. As a result, Sarragat withdrew from the Socialist party and established the Social Democratic party. In addi-tion to the three "mass" parties, three small parties arose, all on the po-litical right; the Liberal party under the leadership of the famous Italian philosopher Benedetto Croce, the Monarchist party, and the neo-fascist Italian Social Movement (MSI).

Under the leadership of de Gasperi, who was prime minister from 1945 to 1954 and who was an ardent proponent of Western unity, Italy worked her way out of the humiliation of defeat. She joined NATO and the various West European councils. Her rehabilitation was consummated in 1955 when she was admitted to the United Nations. De Gasperi's foreign policy won the sympathy of the United States, which poured some $3 billion in aid into Italy in the postwar years. This enabled Italy to repair the war damage and to expand notably the production of hydro-electric power, which reduced her dependence on imported coal. The Italian merchant marine, largely lost in World War II (see chart, p. 624), was rebuilt until it exceeded the prewar tonnage.

In domestic politics, however, de Gasperi was less successful. He belonged to the right wing of the Christian Democratic Party. To gain a majority in the parliament, he formed a coalition with the Liberal party, which prevented the government from carrying out needed social and economic reforms. A case in point was the land question. In 1948 the government announced a plan to expropriate and partition the large and inefficiently cultivated estates, but it did nothing to implement the announcement until 1950 — after it had been prodded into action by a wave of bloody peasant riots in the south. This *immobilismo* (do-nothing policy) in social and economic matters no doubt accounted for the decline in the electoral strength of the Christian Democratic Party. After de Gasperi's death left-wing leaders, who advocated an "opening to the left," gained control of the party. The Liberals were dropped from the government coalition, and first the Sarragat Social Democrats, then, in 1963, the Nenni Socialists joined it. This enabled the government to attend to social and economic matters more energetically.

Italian vital statistics showed the result of increasing attention to social welfare. The death rate remained fairly stable at 12 per thousand, but infant mortality declined from an appalling 88 in the postwar years to 39 by 1964. The birth rate, about 22 per thousand in the postwar years, declined to 20 by 1964. Life expectancy rose to 67 years. Italy remained a country of heavy emigration, but the nature and direction of emigration changed. It was seasonal rather than permanent, and was directed to the prosperous labor-short countries of Western Europe rather than to the Americas.

In 1957 Italy joined the Common Market, and shared in the growing prosperity of Europe. Production of automobiles, electrical supplies, ships, chemicals, glass, textiles, and ceramics steadily expanded. The Fiat automobiles became a trademark known all over the world. In 1960 a landmark was established when the Italian office-machines manufacturer Olivetti bought out the famous old American Underwood Typewriter Company. Italian manufacturers and engineering firms entered into numerous deals with the Communist countries of Eastern Europe as well as the new nations of Africa and Asia. Milan, the old commercial capital of Italy, became dotted with ultramodern skyscrapers.

Not all of Italy's economic expansion, however, was due to private enterprise. Under the fascist regime the Italian government had become the largest economic *entrepreneur* in Italy. It had secured a monopoly of mining and of rail, sea, and air transportation. It was also the largest producer of steel, ships, and radios. Under the Republic it not only continued the ownership of these enterprises but expanded into other fields. In fact, a larger share of business enterprise is under state ownership in Italy than in any other European country, except in Communist Eastern Europe. The Italian National Hydrocarbons Agency distributed natural gas found in the Po valley and built a large petrochemical industry, and entered into aggressive competition with the petroleum giants of the United States and Western Europe for a share of the world's oil.

As a result of this economic activity the Italian per capita income rose to $760 by 1964. This was gratifying to the Italians but modest by the standards of Western Europe. Moreover, the Italian national income is unevenly distributed, both socially and regionally. The middle class and even the industrial working class have improved their standards, but the peasants — especially landless peasants — have not. As before the war, Italy remained divided into the industrialized and relatively prosperous north and the agrarian and poor south. In fact, the contrast between the two regions has become more pronounced after the war, as the benefits of the postwar prosperity went almost exclusively to the north. The Italian government has sought to mitigate the problem by establishing the "Fund for the Development of the South," by extending to the south the ambitious Italian system of superhighways (*autostrade*), and by trying to divert to it a share of the huge ($900 million in 1965) Italian tourist business. But the *mezzogiorno* (south) still remains poor and backward.

The Italian culture, stifled under fascism, experienced a remarkable revival after the war. Italy's writers, artists, and motion-picture producers recovered an honorable place for Italy in European cultural life. However, as in the past, Italian culture was — with, perhaps, the exception of the cinema — one for the elite, not the masses.

Thanks to the domination of the Italian government by the Catholic Christian Democratic Party, relations between the Italian state and the Roman Catholic Church improved after the war. The moral prestige of the Catholic Church had suffered during World War II when Pope Pius XII (1939–58) failed to speak out against fascist excesses (especially the slaughter of the European Jews by the Nazis) and to forcefully urge peace. Under his conservative leadership the Church had also failed to cope with the many psychological and social problems besetting twentieth-century men.

His successor, Pope John XXIII (1958–1963), though an aged man at the time of his election (76), set out vigorously to recover the moral position of the Church. He summoned the Second Vatican Council, which met in four sessions from 1962 to 1965, for the purpose of "updating" (*aggiornamento*) the Church and promoting Christian unity and international peace. He was not able to see the Council complete its great work of modernizing the Church, but his successor, Pope Paul VI (1963–   ), a somewhat younger man (65), continued energetically to promote the Christian ecumenical movement, a more Christian attitude toward non-Christian faiths, and international peace. He broke papal precedent by undertaking strenuous trips to the Holy Land (January, 1964), India (December, 1964), and New York (October, 1965), the last trip to address the UN Assembly in behalf of peace. He was prepared even to travel behind the Iron Curtain to Poland, on the occasion of the millennium of its Christianization in 1966; but the Polish Communist government, fearful of the effect of the papal visit on its position in strongly Catholic Poland, would not invite him. After the war despite the communization of Eastern Europe and much of Asia and the growing secularization of the West, the Catholic Church showed that it was still a moral force to reckon with.

3. SPAIN AND PORTUGAL

In 1940 General Franco considered taking Spain into the war on the side of the Axis powers, but Hitler refused to pay the price that he asked (see p. 476). Spain remained neutral, although friendly to the Axis. After the war, Franco — unlike Hitler and Mussolini — remained in power. But the former Allied powers ostracized Spain for its pro-Axis policy during the war. Spain was excluded from the United Nations (until 1955), the Marshall Plan, NATO, and the various European councils. However, as the Cold War was intensified, the United States became anxious to effect a reconciliation with Spain and to enlist Spanish support in its anti-communist crusade. The European powers were less forgiving. Therefore, the United States offered to conclude a bilateral treaty with Spain. Franco, anxious to break out of the isolation imposed on Spain by European nations, readily agreed. Under the Spanish-American treaty of 1953 Spain allowed the United States the use of a number of aerial and naval bases, and the United States offered Spain military and economic aid.

In domestic politics Franco likewise trimmed his sails to the new winds. Since fascism was no longer fashionable, he quietly dropped most of its blatant trappings (mass rallies, banners, arm salutes, etc.), but retained its substance. The Falange remained the sole party of Spain. Civil rights, though guaranteed by law, were non-existent. The press was muzzled. Labor unions and strikes were forbidden. The Roman Catholic Church was the only recognized religion, and Protestants and Jews had no legal status. In 1947, to cover the nakedness of his dictatorial power, Franco had the appointive *Cortes* (parliament) pass six "fundamental laws," which became Spain's constitution. They defined Spain as a monarchy. However, Spain remained a kingdom without a king. No monarch was selected. Instead, Franco was proclaimed chief of state (*caudillo*) for life and a regency council was appointed. The legitimate claimant of the throne of Spain was a son of the late King Alfonso XIII (1886–1931), Prince Juan of Borbon, who still lives in exile in Portugal. Franco regards him as too liberal, but has permitted his son, Juan Carlos, to be educated in Spain. Whether father or son will ever mount the throne of Spain, however, remains uncertain.

Socially and economically, Spain remains a retarded country. Education and social welfare are regarded as concerns of the Catholic Church, not the state. Class divisions are sharply defined and social contrasts are pronounced. As in Italy, peasant proprietorship of the land predominates in the north, while in the south large estates are common. Industry too, is concentrated in the north, while the south is largely agrarian. Next to Portugal, Spain has the highest illiteracy rate in Europe. Health conditions improved after the war, though diphtheria and smallpox, largely conquered in more advanced countries, continue to exact a toll. The infant mortality rate — if Spanish statistics could be trusted — dropped from 75 per thousand in 1948 to 40 by 1964. The birth rate in 1964 was 22 per thousand and the death rate 11. The population had grown to 31,600,000 by 1965.

Despite American aid, the Spanish economy experienced serious diffi- culties after the war. Spain lacked capital and economic know-how. A rigidly protectionist policy and Spanish xenophobia discouraged foreign investment. An unenlightened, corrupt, and inefficient administration and the peculiarly Spanish attitude toward business activity (a tendency to regard money-making as sordid) stifled business enterprise. The major economic activity, which employed half the labor force, was agriculture. Wheat remained the most important crop; but although the wheat acre- age equaled that of France the yield was poor and Spain had to import food. Antiquated methods and dependence on manpower and draft ani- mals, as well as frequent drought, handicapped the Spanish farmers. It is estimated that about 12 million acres of potentially arable land remained uncultivated, because neither the government nor the landowners had the capital or interest to irrigate or improve it.

Despite considerable mineral wealth (coal and iron, copper, lead, zinc, mercury, and sulphur), industry was little developed in Spain. Mining, the second most important economic activity, was limited by lack of mod- ern methods and equipment. Manufacturing plants and transportation were repeatedly crippled by lack of electrical energy and lack of coal. The trade balance was consistently adverse. By 1959 Spain was on the verge of bankruptcy. Reserves of gold and foreign currencies were depleted, inflation was rife, production was falling off, and unemployment was rising. By July of that year, in desperation, the government adopted a stabilization plan, under which the peseta (the unit of Spanish currency) was first devalued to a realistic rate and then stabilized with the aid of an international loan of $400 million. At the same time, the budget was slashed, taxes raised, and trade policies liberalized.

The drastic reforms had salutary effects. The economy revived and entered into a period of rapid and continued expansion. Encouraged by liberal trade policies foreign capital entered the country. Another source of foreign currency, which Spain needed to buy equipment for her indus- tries, were foreign tourists. Until about 1950 tourism was little developed in Spain. But then, discouraged by high prices and overcrowding at tourist attractions elsewhere in Europe, foreign visitors "discovered" Spain. In 1951 about 1 million tourists visited Spain. By 1965 the tide reached 15 million, almost 1 million of them Americans, who funnelled in that year alone $1.1 billion into the Spanish economy. Still another source of foreign currency was the remittances of some 850,000 Spanish laborers who had gone to work in the prosperous countries of Western Europe. In addition to money, these Spaniards brought home new skills and new ideas, which was perhaps what Spain needed most.

Encouraged by an abundance of capital, in 1963 the government adopted an ambitious four-year plan for industrialization. Industrialists willing to establish new plants in six widely dispersed "development poles" (industrial areas) were offered exemption from taxation for five years and the right to import industrial equipment duty-free. The plan appears to be having considerable success. However, what Spain needs most are new markets for its industrial products. The closest and most logical markets are the countries of the European Common Market. Twice, Spain has applied for associate membership in it. But, largely because of the fears of Italy whose economy is similar to that of Spain, it has been turned down. Yet, despite this setback, Spain's industrialization has continued. This progress in turn, is spurring the disintegration of the medieval pattern of Spanish life. There has been a large exodus of population from the rural areas into the cities. This, and the necessity to accommodate the flood of tourists has resulted in a great construction boom and wild speculation in real estate. The lot of the peasants remains poor, but the middle class and the industrial working class are improving their status. In 1965 Spain reached in per capita income the mystical figure of $500, which is often taken to separate the "rich" from the "poor" nations. If the trend can be maintained, Spain might yet enter the twentieth century before that century is over.

The problems of Portugal are similar to those of Spain, except that they are perhaps more serious. Like Spain, Portugal is a fascist dictatorship. The long-time dictator of Portugal, however, is not a bemedaled general but an austere, self-effacing former economics professor, Dr. Antonio de Oliveira Salazar. Called to power in 1926 to save the country from bankruptcy (see p. 107), he was largely responsible for the drafting of the 1933 constitution, under which Portugal became a "corporate state." It has a president, elected for seven years by an electoral college, but the real executive power is held by the cabinet which has been presided over by Dr. Salazar from 1933 on. A national assembly elected by direct suffrage and a chamber of corporations, the members of which represent various corporative bodies, comprise the legislature. Only one political party exists. Civil rights, though guaranteed by law, are ignored. The Roman Catholic Church, to which most Portuguese belong, has a privileged position, but other faiths are allowed freedom of worship.

Though neutral in World War II, Portugal helped the Allied powers. After the war, therefore, unlike Spain, it was in the good graces of the victorious powers. It was admitted to the United Nations, shared in the Marshall Plan, and joined NATO. Portugal's association with the democratic powers encouraged the growth of a democratic opposition to the dictatorship of Salazar. At first this opposition was limited mainly to students and intellectuals. To ease its pressure, Salazar permitted an opposition candidate, General Humberto Delgado, to run for the figure-head presidency in 1958. However, when Delgado unexpectedly garnered one-quarter of the vote, the government became alarmed and suppressed the opposition. Delgado was forced to flee into exile, from which he continued to rouse opposition to Salazar. In 1965 his dead body was found near the Spanish-Portuguese frontier. It was assumed that he was murdered when he tried to enter Portugal secretly. There have been other signs of political unrest in Portugal; but, for the time being, the old dictator appears to have matters firmly in hand.

Socially and economically, Portugal is perhaps the most retrogressive country of Europe. It has the highest rate of illiteracy in Europe. In 1964 the reported birth rate was 24 per thousand, the death rate 12, and infant mortality 73. Some 25,000 Portuguese emigrated annually, the majority settling in Brazil. The per capita income in 1964 was barely $300. This was only three-fifths of that of Spain.

The population of Portugal, about 9,100,000 in 1964, is less than one-third that of Spain, and its area, 34,216 square miles, less than one-fifth the area of Spain. Density of population is therefore higher, the average being about 27 to the square mile. In Portugal, as in Spain, agriculture employs half the labor force. Since it depends on human and animal power, the yield remains mediocre. Portuguese industry is backward, employing less than one-fourth of the labor force, and is handicapped by lack of power development. Fishing holds an important place in Portuguese activities and the catch brought back by thousands of fishing boats helps to supplement the national food supply. Canned fish form the largest single export commodity, and with wine (the famous "port") and cork it helps to pay for coal, petroleum, machinery, and consumer goods. Portugal's balance of trade remains adverse. But tourism, which is of longer duration than in Spain, helps to keep Portugal solvent.

Portugal was the first European nation to build a large overseas colonial empire, and it is the last nation to retain one. Unlike Spain which retains of its former vast colonial empire only small remnants, Portugal still holds substantial overseas colonies. After World War II the Portuguese empire comprised (in addition to Madeira and the Azores which were regarded as parts of Portuguese home territory) the Cape Verde Islands, and the islands of Sao Tome and Principe in the Atlantic; Angola, Mozambique, and Portuguese Guinea in Africa; Diu and Goa on the Malabar coast of India; Timor in the Indonesian archipelago; and Macao near Canton in China. The Portuguese empire had an aggregate area of more than 800,000 square miles and an aggregate population of about 13,000,000.

While larger and richer European colonial powers freed their colonies or were forced out of them, Portugal grimly held on to its possessions. In 1961 India succeeded in expelling the Portuguese from Diu and Goa, which they had held for 400 years. But when native uprisings took place in Angola and Mozambique, the Portuguese ruthlessly suppressed them (see Chapter 66). In the United Nations, where their complaint against India for the seizure of Diu and Goa went unheeded, but their action in Africa was severely criticized by the new nations of Africa and Asia as well as Soviet Russia, they defiantly proclaimed their determination to stay on in Africa and their other possessions indefinitely. They became disillusioned with the value of the Western alliance when the United States and Britain refused to give them full support for their ruthless colonial policies. They, therefore, loosened their ties with NATO.

The Portuguese empire brings them little economic benefit. On the contrary, its defense and policing constitutes a severe drain on their slim resources. The reasons for their determination to hold on must not be sought in economics but in national psychology. The Portuguese regard their explorations and empire-building in the fifteenth and sixteenth centuries as one of the most glorious and constructive chapters, not only in their history, but in world history. And whatever the price of continuing this glory, they are determined to pay it.

4. GREECE, TURKEY, AND CYPRUS

Greece emerged from World War II and German occupation with a ruined economy and a starved population — only to have to face four more years of turmoil and civil war. Thanks to British and American help, the Communist insurrection was crushed and the monarchy saved (see p. 565). But interrogations, trials, and executions of real or suspect Communists went on for years, and the bitterness engendered by the civil war has not died yet.

In 1951 Greece adopted a new constitution. It provided for a single-chamber legislature, to be elected by universal secret ballot, and a council of state, the members of which were to be appointed by the king, with the consent of the cabinet. Civil liberties were guaranteed, but because of fear of communism not always observed. Most Greeks belong to the Greek Orthodox Church, which was accorded the status of the state church. However, the small Moslem community and other religions were assured freedom of worship.

As before the war (see p. 327), Greek politics has remained mercurial. However, until 1964 they were usually dominated by rightist coalitions. The relations between the parliament and King Paul (1947–64) were on the whole harmonious. In 1964, however, a left-of-center coalition came to power. In 1965 Greece was shaken by a severe and prolonged crisis when Prime Minister Papandreou attempted to purge the army of

rightist officers. The young King Constantine (1964–   ) regarded this
as an encroachment on his prerogative and resolutely opposed it. In the
end he had his way, but the crisis revealed a strong anti-monarchist undercurrent in Greece.

Helped by the infusion of massive American aid, Greece repaired the
damages of foreign and civil war relatively quickly. From 1947, when it
was first advanced under the "Truman Doctrine" to 1962 when it was
terminated, American aid to Greece amounted to a total of $3.4 billion.
Of that sum $1.7 billion was military aid, the rest economic. In 1962
Greece applied and was granted associate membership in the European
Common Market. The terms were quite generous. If the Greek economy
were thrown into open competition with, for instance, that of West Germany, it would be crushed. Therefore, the nations of the Common Market
allowed Greece a period of from twelve to twenty-two years to reduce its
tariffs to the levels prevailing within the Market.

Even with such advantages the Greek economy has remained precarious in the extreme, for the natural resources of Greece are pitifully few.
With an area of 51,145 square miles and a population of 8,482,000
(1964), Greece supports nearly 170 people to the square mile. This is a
dense population for a country in which only one-fourth of the land is
cultivable, and the rainfall inadequate during the dry summer season.
Half the people are tradition-bound peasants. Owing to their antiquated
methods of farming, as well as deforestation, soil erosion from winter
rains, and lack of fertilizer, the wheat yield of Greece is one of the lowest
in Europe. The most important crop as well as export commodity is tobacco. Greece has varied mineral resources but no coal or oil. Imports
of food, coal, oil, and consumer goods have resulted in a permanently unsatisfactory trade balance, in which imports usually double exports. Industry, though increasing, remains limited for lack of capital and power.

Greece has several "invisible" incomes, which helped to keep its foreign
payments in balance. First of all, there is shipping. Greece actually has
the third largest merchant marine in the world. In 1965 it totalled 18
million tons, but only 6.8 million tons was registered under the Greek
flag, the rest — to evade taxation and government regulation — was registered under "flags of convenience," such as those of Liberia or Panama.
Other sources of income are tourism and the remittances of Greek laborers in Western Europe, Australia, and elsewhere.

The economic dilemma of the Greeks is similar to that of the Spaniards
and Portuguese but more severe because of greater population pressure
and scantier resources. Yet they tackle them with greater energy. By
1964 their per capita income was $450, which was a little less than that of
the Spaniards but considerably more than that of the Portuguese. Greece,
unlike Spain and Portugal, has no hereditary aristocracy; but it has a
class of rich merchants. The contrasts between the sophisticated society
of Athens and Greek villagers are about as pronounced as those between

the fashionable society of Madrid or Lisbon and the Spanish or Portuguese peasants. But Greece is seeking to lessen them, not maintain them. A great deal of attention is paid to education. Social services are improving. Thanks to a health program to curb tuberculosis, malaria, and other diseases, the health of the Greeks, especially in the villages, is steadily improving. The vital statistics for 1964 indicated a birth rate of 18, a death rate of 8, and an infant mortality rate of 36 per thousand.

Turkey was prudently neutral in World War II until the final months of the conflict when she joined the Allies. Although spared the horrors of war, its fragile economy was strained by the necessity to keep its armed forces mobilized to resist German pressure during the war and Soviet pressure after the war.

Under the founder of the Turkish Republic, Kemal Atatürk, Turkey was formally a parliamentary democracy but in practice a dictatorship (see p. 352). Only one political party, the People's Republican party, was permitted. After the war, the faithful lieutenant and successor of Atatürk, President Ismet Inönü (1938–1950), decided that the time had come to realize Atatürk's hope of gradually introducing real democracy in Turkey. Formation of opposition parties was permitted, and in May, 1950, free and honest elections were held. When the opposition Democratic party won an overwhelming victory, Inönü gracefully resigned. The leader of the Democratic party, Adnan Menderes, became prime minister. He showed commendable energy in pushing economic development but proved increasingly intolerant of opposition. Civil liberties were suspended and critics of the government jailed. Runaway inflation, brought about by overambitious industrial expansion and a record foreign debt of $1.4 billion, contributed to political restlessness. In May, 1960, Menderes was overthrown by an army coup and later tried and executed for abuse of power. The Democratic party was dissolved. The leader of revolt, General Cemal Gürsel, pledged: "I have no intention, I repeat, no intention whatsoever of being dictator."

General Gürsel carried out his pledge literally. In 1961 a new constitution was drafted, which specifically provided for a civilian parliamentary government, protection of human rights, and safeguards against abuses of executive power. As for the organs of government, it provided for a parliament of two houses, a senate and a national assembly, to be elected by universal suffrage; a cabinet responsible to the parliament; and a president, to be elected by the parliament for seven years and to be ineligible for reelection. General Gürsel, who was unopposed, was the first president elected under the new constitution. Parliamentary elections produced, in addition to the old People's Republican party, four new parties. The most important of them was the Justice party, which it turned out, was the old Democratic party under a new name. Since none of the parties had a majority, a coalition government was formed under ex-President Inönü.

One of the reproaches made against Menderes was that he was erratic and had no plan in his economic policy. The new government, therefore, created a state planning board. In 1962 this board produced an enormously ambitious five-year economic plan, but, because of continued party bickering and two abortive army coups, little was done to implement it. The impassioned party debates, however, served one useful purpose — they forced the two principal parties to clearly define their aims. The Justice party emerged as a rightist party, which favored private enterprise, a greater role for Islam in national life, and continued close relations with the United States. The People's Republican party became a leftist party, which favored the old ideals of Atatürk — state participation in economic enterprise and a secular state — and a more "independent" course in foreign policy. In 1965 the Justice party won a sweeping victory in parliamentary elections and was able to form a cabinet alone. It should have been able then to tackle Turkey's economic problem energetically, but Turkish opinion was then distracted by the Cyprus question.

Turkey, with a population of 31,113,000 (1964) and an area of 296,500 square miles, has a population density of over 100 per square mile. The major activity is agriculture, which occupies four-fifths of the people, provides two-fifths of the national income, and four-fifths of the export earnings. Archaic farming methods, soil erosion, and a long dependence on human and animal power result in a low yield. Although Turkey contains varied and valuable mineral resources (coal, iron, copper, chrome, and others), mining, industry, and manufacture remain limited and retarded. Per capita income in 1964 was a modest $290.

Vital statistics for Turkey have to be accepted with caution but the general trends are discernable. A phenomenally high rate of increase in population (almost 3 per cent per year) indicates a remarkably high birth rate, but specific estimates of births, deaths, infant mortality, and life expectancy are unavailable. The fast growth of population without a corresponding growth of the economy has resulted in chronic unemployment. The Turks were not a nation of emigrants before World War II, but after the war increasing numbers of Turkish workers (some 200,000 by 1965) have gone to work in labor-short Western Europe. Their remittances, however, are not as important for Turkey's balance of payments as those of Greek immigrants for Greece, for Turkey's needs are far greater.

The trade problems the Turks face match or exceed those of other retarded nations. Their exports, predominantly tobacco, fruits, nuts, and cotton, are insufficient to pay for imports of machinery, petroleum, chemicals, wheat, and consumer goods. Turkey has needed continuous foreign aid and loans to survive. Soviet pressure in the postwar years moved the United States to provide Turkey with over $3 billion in aid, of which about two-thirds was military and one-third economic. Perhaps the greatest permanent benefit of this aid was the construction of a better system of roads, which, though intended for strategic purposes, proved of great economic value as well. It notably opened up eastern Turkey, previously virtually inaccessible.

In 1963, after the United States was forced to curtail its foreign aid, Turkey applied for associate membership in the European Common Market. It sought at the same time a loan of $1.5 billion to launch its five-year economic plan (1963–1967). The Common Market nations admitted Turkey and advanced it a loan of $175 million over a period of five years, during which it was to put its economy in order. This period was to be followed by a twelve-year period of grace, during which Turkey was to bring its tariffs down to the level of the Common Market. After that it would qualify for full membership in the Market. The loan fell far short of Turkey's needs. Its problem was that in order to feed its growing population it had to expand its economy, but the economy did not provide the surplus capital necessary for its own expansion.

The key to the solution of this dilemma lies perhaps in the field of education. The Kemalist revolution in the 1920's and 1930's resulted in the growth of a Western-trained, Western-thinking class of government officials and professionals; but it left the tradition-bound peasantry unaffected. It was estimated after the war that about 60 per cent of the Turks over nine years of age were still illiterate. American aid in the 1950's, notably the delivery of thousands of tractors, resulted in the expansion of land under cultivation, but it did not noticeably improve output per man and yield per acre. In the 1960's the limits of acreage expansion had been reached. What was then clearly necessary was to re-educate the tradition-bound peasantry to improve their methods of farming in order to increase farm production, reduce food imports, and save the capital necessary for industrial expansion.

In 1951 Turkey and Greece joined NATO, thus extending this alliance to the eastern Mediterranean. NATO was gravely shaken by the problem of Cyprus. The island, lying about forty miles off the southern coast of Turkey and having an area of 3,572 square miles, was a British crown colony. Of its population of some 587,000, 80 per cent are Christian Greeks, the rest Moslem Turks. The Greeks have always regarded the island as a part of "unredeemed" Greece, and for many years carried on agitation for its *enosis* (union) with the Greek motherland. The Turks, however, have strenuously opposed this on the ground that the island had for centuries (1570–1878) belonged to the Ottoman Empire and lay closer to Turkey than to Greece. The British, who had occupied the island at the time of the Congress of Berlin in 1878 and annexed it at the outbreak of World War I in 1914, were determined to hold on to it, especially after they withdrew from Palestine (1948) and from Suez (1956). They hoped to keep Cyprus as the fulcrum of their defenses in the Near and Middle East.

In 1955 a secret Greek organization (EOKA) under the command of a Greek officer, Colonel Grivas, launched a ruthless terrorist campaign against the British forces in Cyprus in an effort to oblige them to surrender the island. The British retaliated by suspending civil rights, instituting summary drumhead justice, encouraging the Turkish Cypriotes to attack their Greek fellow-islanders, and deporting the Greek spokesman, the Greek Orthodox Archbishop of Cyprus, Makarios. Scores of people, often innocent, fell victim to this pernicious triangular struggle. The Turkish and Greek governments, at first aloof, were forced by their nationalist opinion to intervene in the situation. In February, 1959, the Turkish and Greek prime ministers met in Switzerland. After coming to a preliminary agreement, they flew to London, where they worked out with the British government a joint Turkish-Greek-British agreement. It provided that Cyprus was to be an independent republic within the British Commonwealth under a joint guarantee of the three nations; that the British were to retain two bases in the island; that its president was always to be a Greek Cypriote and the vice-president a Turkish Cypriote; and that the two communities were to be represented in parliament on a fixed basis of 70 per cent Greeks to 30 per cent Turks. After prolonged negotiations to implement the agreement, Cyprus was launched as an independent nation on August 15, 1960. Archbishop Makarios, who had, in the meantime, been released by the British, became its first president.

The newly independent state was beset by serious economic difficulties. Without British and American aid it could scarcely have survived. But its economic difficulties were overshadowed by the conflict between the Greek and Turkish communities. It would have been difficult to operate under the rigid constitution of Cyprus even if the Greek and Turkish Cypriotes had had a democratic tradition and were filled with good will toward each other. This was hardly the case. The Greeks tended to abuse their majority to impose their will on the Turks, and the Turks tended to abuse their right of veto to obstruct the Greeks. The result was an impasse in the parliament and a breakdown in the functioning of the Cypriote government. In 1963 President Makarios proposed to break the impasse by amending the constitution to deprive the Turks of their veto. Naturally, the Turks rejected the solution. Tempers rose, and in December severe fighting broke out between the two communities. At first British forces entered; later a UN peace-keeping force intervened. During the course of 1964 they gradually halted the fighting. But life did not return to normal. The island remained in effect partitioned between two armed camps, with the UN force patroling a no-man's land between them.

The conflict brought Greece and Turkey to the verge of war. Perhaps only the presence of the American Sixth Fleet in the Mediterranean and the quiet intimation of the United States that it would not tolerate war, averted the conflict. Since both Turkey and Greece were NATO allies, the Cyprus conflict put the United States in a difficult situation. It saw only one way out: to maintain strict impartiality between Turkey and Greece and to try to mediate between them. However, under pressure of their nationalist opinion, both countries adopted intransigent positions: Greece insisted on outright *enosis* and Turkey on partition of the island and annexation of the Turkish share (generously defined).

The situation was not helped by the meddling of Soviet Russia or the tortuous, Byzantine maneuvers of President Makarios. Soviet diplomacy saw in the Cyprus conflict a golden opportunity to drive a wedge between Greece and Turkey and to weaken the Eastern anchor of NATO. Communist influence among Greek Cypriotes was strong. If Cyprus were completely freed from British ties it might become a Cuba in the Mediterranean. Therefore, Soviet diplomacy first supported Makarios' demand for the withdrawal of British forces from Cyprus, then for the withdrawal of Cyprus from the Commonwealth. It also offered the Greek Cypriotes arms and assistance in the event of a Turkish invasion. Later, after an exchange of visits between Turkish and Soviet officials, it shifted to a position close to that of Turkey. It supported, not outright partition of Cyprus, but a federation of two Cypriote states, Turkish and Greek, and withdrawal of UN and British forces. Makarios, abandoned by the Soviets, shifted back to his pre-1960 position of supporting *enosis*. The net result of all of these maneuvers was not to advance the solution of the Cyprus question one whit, but only to set Greece and Turkey irreconcilably at loggerheads and alienate both countries from the United States and the Atlantic alliance.

5. PROBLEMS OF HEALTH, WEALTH, AND EDUCATION

The six countries discussed in this chapter have a combined population of nearly 134 million, which is almost three times the combined population of the eight more prosperous nations (48,337,000) discussed in the preceding chapter. Although the statistics available should not be trusted implicitly, they provide sufficient information to permit some comparisons between the two groups and some generalizations on the factors that tend to promote or retard prosperity and social welfare.

In the matter of health the eight nations first discussed appear to have some definite advantages. Their citizens, on the average, live ten years longer than those in the six less prosperous countries. Their infant mortality rate is only half as high. They have been more successful in reducing debilitating illnesses and in curbing diphtheria, smallpox, and other diseases against which modern medicine has provided protection.

The more prosperous countries are more highly industrialized than the less prosperous. Yet the less prosperous nations, with one-half to three-fourths of their workers engaged in agriculture, are less efficient at farming and less adequately fed. As might be anticipated, since food is a prime necessity, people with a small income spend half or more of it for food, while people with larger incomes may spend one-quarter for food and use the remainder for other needs or luxuries or for investment. Savings provide capital for new enterprises and for expansion. Part of the vicious cycle that keeps poor nations poor is that their "subsistence econ-omy" makes it difficult for them to provide a surplus for expansion or for export. With nations as with individuals the Biblical text often holds true: "Unto every one that hath shall be given, and he shall have abun-dance; but from him that hath not shall be taken away even that which he hath."

The foreign commerce of the six less prosperous countries, taken as a group, has an annual value of about $150 per capita, whereas for the eight more prosperous countries it averages about $960 per capita. This reflects to some extent the higher prices that manufactured goods command in the world markets, compared to raw materials and agricultural products. But it also reflects the lower yield per man-hour in the poorer countries, where too little machinery was available to supplement human and ani-mal power.

A further comparison might be worked out to show that the level of education achieved by a nation offers a clue to its per capita income. The six less prosperous countries noted in this chapter all entered the twentieth century with high rates of illiteracy. Although resolute efforts are being made to correct this situation, there were probably 20 million adults in these countries as a group who were still illiterate in the middle of the twentieth century. With nations as with individuals, the duration and quality of their schooling largely determine their earning capacity and income. But a free and compulsory system of national education not only involves a large expenditure of revenue; it keeps the older children from going to work as early as possible to supplement the income of their elders. Here again it is easy to see why poverty tends to perpetuate it-self. A poor nation lacks the means to set in rapid motion the changes that would most surely enable it to overcome its deficiencies.

57

PLANS FOR WESTERN EUROPEAN INTEGRATION

It would be wrong for the Americans to turn away from Europe because they felt that the European countries were not advancing quickly and boldly toward integration. . . . The precondition of success is the awareness that this is a long-term undertaking.

PAUL-HENRI SPAAK (1950)

1. THE COUNCIL OF EUROPE

IT IS ONE OF THE ironies of their history that the Europeans, who created the greatest civilization the world has known, and linked all the continents of the globe by their conquests, their colonization, and their commerce, have remained disunited and frequently at war among themselves. From the collapse of the Roman Empire to the twentieth century the ideal of European unity was often invoked but never realized. Like the city states of ancient Greece, the nation states of modern Europe developed a high civilization that exerted a profound influence on the world around them. But, like the Greek city states, they weakened themselves by fierce local conflicts until their colonies revolted, their influence waned, and larger and more powerful non-European states threatened to absorb them. World War II engendered the latest and strongest movement for European integration.

The first plans for European integration originated in wartime London in the somber days after the fall of France in 1940. Winston Churchill, the wartime prime minister, took a keen personal interest in them. Just before the fall of France he made a dramatic but vain appeal for the merger of the British and French empires (see p. 461). Afterwards the British government availed itself of the presence of the exiled governments of the Netherlands, Belgium, Luxemburg, Norway, Poland, Czechoslovakia, Yugoslavia, and Greece and the Free French Committee in London to discuss projects for European unification. European integration went counter to the British historical policy of keeping Europe divided and carefully balanced against itself. However, under the impact of the debacle of France and its own armies on the continent, and with the realization that it had no more strength to play the arbiter between European alliances, the British government considered alternatives to its historical policy.

Churchill urged, among other projects, the federation of East Central Europe, in which both world wars originated. As early as 1940, with British encouragement, the exiled Polish and Czechoslovak governments concluded an agreement to form a confederation after the war. A little later the Yugoslav and Greek governments signed a similar agreement. The entry of the Soviet Union into the war in 1941 cast a shadow over these projects and ultimately doomed them. The Soviet government opposed all projects for federation of East Central Europe, not initiated by itself, as camouflaged attempts to create a new *cordon sanitaire* against Soviet influence in Europe. At the Teheran conference Stalin vigorously opposed Churchill's suggestions for a great Central European federation.

The entry of the United States into the war, on the other hand, gave Britain an alternative to European unification, namely, a close Anglo-American partnership. The British government did not for that reason abandon its interest in European integration. Rather, in Hamlet fashion, it began to oscillate between a desire for a partnership with Europe and a partnership with America — a tendency which it continued after the war. In 1944 the exiled governments of Belgium, the Netherlands, and Luxemburg concluded in London an agreement to form a customs union after the war. As was seen in Chapter 55, the Benelux customs union became a reality in 1948.

After the war, movements for integration mushroomed all over Europe. In 1946 Churchill, then out of office, added his powerful voice to the rising chorus in a memorable speech at Zürich: "We must build a kind of United States of Europe." Churchill had been worried by the rapid demobilization of the American army and withdrawal from Europe in 1945, while Soviet Russia continued to maintain a massive army on the Elbe. In 1947 his fears were borne out. The Iron Curtain had fallen across Europe, cutting it in two. Eastern Europe was forcibly integrated into the Soviet Bloc. This added urgency to integrate Western Europe, if not into a solid block, at least a close community. But even if integrated, Western Europe was then too weak to resist alone the might of the Soviet Bloc. But there were indications that the United States was reconsidering its policy and taking a new interest in Europe. Therefore, Churchill reverted to the alternative policy of seeking an Anglo-American partnership. In his famous Iron Curtain speech of March 4, 1947, he called for a "special relationship between the British Commonwealth and the United States" (see p. 570) to resist Soviet expansion.

The announcement of the "Truman Doctrine" a few days later (see p. 571) indicated that the thinking of American policy makers was moving along similar lines. However, it does not appear that American thinking was then definitely fixed. It too was groping for a solution which did not exclude European unification. The Marshall Plan in June, 1947, was offered to *all* European nations, not to those of Western Europe alone (see Chapter 48). It was by Soviet self-exclusion that it became limited to Western Europe. Though not so intended by the Americans, the Marshall Plan contributed to the close integration of Western Europe and the deepening of the chasm between it and Eastern Europe. Henceforth, all plans issued in the name of European unity were really meant for the unification of Western Europe.

In May, 1949, ten European nations meeting in London — Great Britain, France, Italy, the Irish Republic, the Netherlands, Belgium, Luxemburg, Denmark, Norway, and Sweden — agreed to form the Council of Europe. Later West Germany, Austria, Switzerland, Greece, Turkey, Cyprus, Iceland, and Malta joined it, bringing its membership to eighteen. "The aim of the Council of Europe," Article 1 of the Council's Statute stated, "is to achieve a greater unity between its members for the purpose of safeguarding and realizing the ideals and principles which are their common heritage and facilitating their economic and social progress." Article 3 stressed that "every member of the Council of Europe must accept the principles of the rule of law and of the enjoyment by all persons within its jurisdiction of human rights and fundamental freedoms," which was obviously intended to exclude dictatorships, whether communist or fascist (Spain and Portugal). The machinery of the new organization, the headquarters of which was at Strasbourg, France, consisted of a council of ministers (the foreign ministers of the member states) and a consultative assembly eventually of 147 delegates representing the member states roughly in proportion to their strength. The Council of Europe lacks authority, and its aims are vague. It has fallen short of the high hopes originally placed in it. Nevertheless, it has accomplished some useful work in advancing human rights and by providing a sounding board for European opinion.

2. THE ECONOMIC ORGANIZATIONS OF WESTERN EUROPE

The Americans, seeing Europe from a distance and therefore as a unit, often proved better Europeans than many Europeans. When the United States Congress voted over $5 billion in 1948 to launch the Marshall Plan, the Americans made it clear that they expected the European states that accepted this financial assistance to put the welfare of all Western Europe ahead of their separate and selfish interests. It was necessary, when distributing this American aid, to avoid the risk that grants might be used to increase national competition. For this purpose, the United States sponsored the formation of the Organization for European Economic Cooperation (O.E.E.C.), a multinational agency through which Marshall

Plan aid was funneled into Western Europe. In 1960, after the Marshall Plan was terminated, the O.E.E.C. was transformed into the O.E.C.D. (Organization for Economic Cooperation and Development), to utilize the experience and continue the cooperation obtained in launching the Marshall Plan. Meanwhile, several European regional economic organizations were formed.

The reconstruction of the German economy was deemed indispensable for West European recovery. The question arose how to restore the German economy without arousing the fears of France and other West European countries that a recovered Germany would become an aggressive Germany again. The answer was supplied by Jean Monnet, a French businessman and economist, who had conceived and brilliantly executed the plan for the modernization and re-equipment of French industry after the war. In 1950 he persuaded the French premier, Robert Schuman, to sponsor a proposal for the pooling and modernization of the French and German coal and steel industries under a supranational authority. Coal and steel are basic to the capacity to wage war. If France and Germany gave up control of their coal and steel industries to a supranational agency, they would lose their capacity to wage war on each other.

There was enthusiastic response to the Schuman proposal, not only in France and Germany but in Western Europe generally. The United States also heartily endorsed it. In consequence, on April 18, 1951, six European nations – France, Germany, Italy, Belgium, the Netherlands, and Luxemburg – signed an agreement establishing the European Coal and Steel Community (E.C.S.C.). The treaty placed the coal and steel industries of the member states under a "High Authority" of nine men (two each for France, West Germany, and Italy, and one for each of the Benelux countries) who were chosen by the six member states but thereafter were free of all national control. They had the right to levy or to cut taxes on coal and steel, and their decisions were binding on member nations. The High Authority, which had headquarters in Luxemburg, was responsible to a ministerial council, a parliament (chosen from and by the members of the parliaments of the six member states), and a court of justice with power to determine whether the High Authority was carrying out the provisions of E.C.S.C. treaty and to adjudicate conflicts between member states.

The Coal and Steel Community was a complete success, both in its political purpose and its economic objectives. The fact that Frenchmen and Germans, who had fought three bitter wars in less than a century, could agree to cooperate in such a critical field of industry was no mean achievement. Instead of competing for raw materials the nations that joined the Community became, as a group, the second greatest steel producing combination in the world, surpassed only by the United States. In 1961, after ten years of participation in the Coal and Steel Community, the combined steel production of the six nations was 73,000 metric tons compared to 89,000 metric tons for the United States. Because of the ability to import coal and iron ore cheaply, Italy was able to become an important steel producer, ranking third in the Community. Coal production did not rise comparably to steel production because of the general replacement of coal with oil as a fuel after World War II. But the High Authority was able to mitigate the hardships caused by this revolution in fuels. The Belgian coal miners, who suffered most from the competition of the German and French coal miners and the general decline of demand for coal were granted special relief.

The success of the Coal and Steel Community was encouragement to further integration of Western Europe. Monnet, who was chosen first president of the coal and steel High Authority, always regarded the Coal and Steel Community as only a stepping-stone to further integration. In 1955 he suggested the expansion of the Coal and Steel Community to embrace the total economic life of the six members. "Once a Common Market interest has been created," he said, "then political union will come naturally."

European economists had long recognized that one great advantage the United States enjoyed was the possession of a large tariff-free home market which permitted cheap mass production, while Western Europe was divided into a dozen states, with obstructive tariffs, different currencies, and competing policies. This division kept their production low, expensive, and often inefficient. But many European businessmen, especially small businessmen, feared that the establishment of the Common Market would cause economic dislocations and social hardships in the participating nations. There was fear, notably in France, that its tariff-sheltered industries might not survive in open competition with German industries. But such was the public enthusiasm for European integration that the governments of France, West Germany, Italy, and the Benelux countries were moved to accept economic integration.

On March 27, 1957, on the Capitoline Hill in Rome, representatives of the six nations signed two agreements, one to establish the European Economic Community (E.E.C.), popularly called the Common Market, and another to create the European Atomic Energy Community (Euratom). The machinery of the two new organizations, which began functioning officially on January 1, 1958, was similar to that of the Coal and Steel Community. The Common Market was placed under a nine-man European Economic Commission and Euratom under a five-man European Atomic Energy Commission. Both commissions had their headquarters in Brussels and were responsible to a ministerial council, parliament, and court of justice. In 1965 the Coal and Steel Community, the Common Market, and Euratom were placed under a common executive of the "European Community," making the whole apparatus of the Community uniform.

Euratom was established partly under the impact of the Suez crisis of 1956, which suddenly cut off Western Europe from its customary source of oil in the Near and Middle East. The need for energy of the six nations of Euratom was steadily rising, while their coal reserves were diminishing and their supply of oil was costly and insecure. It was hoped that the development of nuclear energy would eventually free them, partly or wholly, from their dependence on coal and oil. In 1959 the member states subscribed to a fund of over $200 million to establish nuclear research facilities and build reactors for generating energy. The Euratom Commission worked out agreements with the United States, Britain, and Canada for the sharing of information on nuclear research and cooperation on its peacetime application. Euratom may in time become the most important organization of the European Community. For the moment, however, it is eclipsed by the Common Market.

The Treaty of Rome called for the establishment of a customs union by the six members of the Common Market. This was to be effected by a gradual removal of tariffs among them on industrial goods and a gradual adoption of common tariffs toward non-members. A precise schedule of tariff cuts was adopted. It envisaged that the final cut would be effected in 1970. The first two cuts of 10 per cent each went into effect on January 1, 1958, and January 1, 1959. The hardships and dislocations caused by these cuts proved less painful than had been feared. Many small and inefficient enterprises were forced out of business, but the large and efficient ones prospered. Therefore, it was decided to advance the schedule of tariff reductions. The final cut was to be made on July 1, 1967. It was hoped that common external tariffs would by then be agreed upon, and that the Common Market would become a single-tariff area.

The combined population of the six member states of the Common Market is about 180 million (1964). This represents a mass market almost as large as that provided by the population of the United States (about 190 million in 1964). As the tariff cuts were effected, goods began to flow across the frontiers of the six member states. In the first three years of operation of the Common Market, trade among the six nations increased by 45 per cent. This had a stimulating effect on their industrial growth. In 1960, the third year of operation, the combined gross national product of the six nations increased 7 per cent as compared to 4.5 per cent in the United States in that year. The six nations' reserves of gold and foreign currencies speedily reached and then outstripped those of the United States. The Common Market has become the second largest exporter of industrial goods in the world, exceeded only by the United States, and the largest importer of all kinds of goods.

Already prosperous in the late 1950's, the six nations of the Common Market have achieved unprecedented prosperity in the 1960's. The biggest problems of the Common Market are an acute shortage of labor and a shortage of investment capital. The shortage of labor has been alleviated by importing hundreds of thousands of laborers from Southern Europe — Italians, Spaniards, Greeks, and Turks. The shortage of investment capital has been partially alleviated by the influx of American capital. Anxious to get in on a rapidly expanding market, many American firms have established branch offices or factories, or have bought out, modernized, and expanded old businesses in the Common Market. In the 1960's the influx of American capital into the Common Market has become such as to incite fears, especially in nationalistic France, of "Americanization" of their economy.

Another problem of the Common Market is the farm problem. The Treaty of Rome envisaged the removal among member states of tariffs not only on industrial goods but eventually also on agricultural products. But this proved more difficult to realize than the removal of tariffs on industrial products. European farmers are notably protection-minded. In 1965 this led to a severe crisis in the Common Market. France, which has abundant fertile soil and productive farms, was more anxious to remove tariffs on farm products than Germany, whose soil is less fertile and whose farms are less productive. The French felt that since they had gone along on cutting tariffs on industrial goods in the production of which the Germans have an advantage, the Germans should not mind cutting tariffs on agricultural products in the production of which France has an advantage. In July, 1965, after the Common Market negotiations over farm policy failed, the French representative walked out of the ministerial council and for seven months boycotted it. He returned in February, 1966, and negotiations were resumed. After five months of arduous bargaining, a compromise solution was agreed upon. It fixed the prices to be paid throughout the Common Market for certain farm products. The prices were higher than those prevailing in France and the Benelux countries whose farmers are more efficient, and lower than those in Germany and Italy whose farmers are less efficient. A system of price supports and export subsidies was also agreed upon.

France found itself at variance with the Common Market over other matters too. As conceived by Jean Monnet, the Common Market was to be a stepping-stone toward political integration of the six member states. Ultimately it was hoped to embrace all West European states and perhaps the United States in a great Atlantic Community. This was also the belief of the president of the Common Market Commission in Brussels, the German economist Walter Hallstein, and most of the Common Market civil servants (a large body of some 5,700 "Eurocrats"). "Make no mistake about it," Hallstein declared in 1961, "we are not in business, we are in politics. We are building the United States of Europe."

This aim ran counter to the policy of General de Gaulle, the president of France. The Common Market was created before he achieved power in 1958. Personally uninterested in economics ("What do I have a Minister of Finance for?"), he went along with it because it promised to benefit the French economy and perhaps free Europe from its economic dependence on the United States, which he greatly resented. However, a proponent of old-fashioned nationalism (the "Europe of fatherlands"), he opposed the supranational aims of the "Eurocrats." He also clashed repeatedly with them on how to deal with nonmembers.

When the Coal and Steel Community was established in 1951, Britain and other West European countries were invited to join. For different reasons, they declined. When the Common Market was formed in 1957, again Britain and other West European countries were invited to join, and again they declined. The reason for the British refusal to join the Common Market is more easily understood when their peculiar position and outlook are examined. Many British businessmen with business interests on the continent were not averse to some sort of economic accord with the nations of Western Europe. On the other hand, British laborers feared the competition of cheaper continental labor. Although there was not a clear-cut party division on the matter, the British Labor party was on the whole more opposed to economic integration with Western Europe than the Conservative party. On the other hand, the Conservative party was more mindful of British imperial interests.

Britain had worldwide trade commitments, among them the preferential accords whereby wheat, meat, fruit, and other food shipments from Canada, Australia, New Zealand, and other Commonwealth nations entered Britain free or almost free of duty. If, as the Treaty of Rome envisaged, the Common Market was to be agricultural as well as industrial, and farm products could enter Britain free of duty, Britain's agreements with the Commonwealth countries would be disrupted. In addition to these economic reasons, there were political and psychological reasons for Britain's reluctance to integrate with Western Europe. The architects of the Common Market had a *political* as well as *economic* program. The British people are an insular people, geographically and psychologically. They hesitated to merge with nations of Western Europe in a supranational community which would entail relinquishing some of their prized sovereignty and modification of their cherished institutions. Finally, they have a deep-seated mistrust of and a sense of superiority to the continental peoples. At that time, they did not believe that the Common Market without the British would work.

The British reaction to the formation of the Common Market was to organize seven other West European nations into a rival trade bloc. In January, 1960, at Stockholm, Britain, Denmark, Norway, Sweden, Austria, Switzerland, and Portugal signed an agreement to form the European Free Trade Association (E.F.T.A.), with headquarters in Geneva. Since the seven nations of the Free Trade Association lay scattered on the periphery of the "Inner Six" of the Common Market, they became popularly known as the "Outer Seven." From the beginning, the Free Trade Association appeared to be a defensive organization, designed not to last

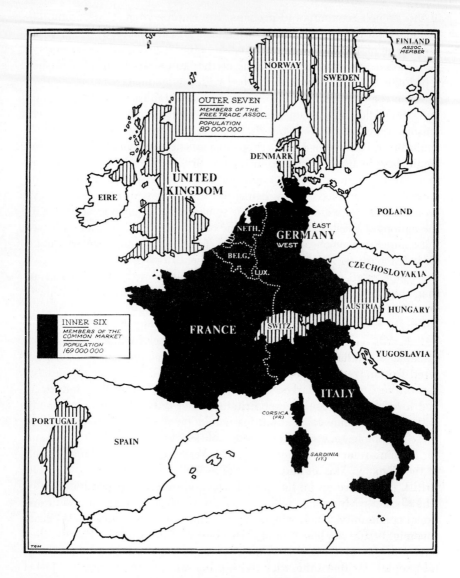

RIVAL TRADE BLOCS IN EUROPE, 1967

permanently but to give a better bargaining position to the Outer Seven
in their dealings with the Inner Six and to prepare the ground for a
merger. Most of the Outer Seven had traded more with the Inner Six
than among themselves. The formation of the Free Trade Association did
not significantly stimulate trade among its member nations nor production in them. To facilitate its dealings with the Common Market and pos-

sibly a merger, the Free Trade Association adopted the same schedule of tariff reductions on industrial goods among its members as those adopted in the Common Market. It did not, however, plan adoption of common tariffs toward non-members or a common agricultural policy.

As the external tariffs of the Common Market rose and it became closed to an increasing amount of British goods, and as the British trade with the Commonwealth remained about the same or even declined, Britain reconsidered its position toward the Common Market. In 1961 Britain applied for admission to it. The Benelux countries, which had previously traded heavily with Britain, favored its admission. Germany was also sympathetic. But France, more especially de Gaulle, was determined to exact a political price for it, namely, that Britain give up any "special relationship" with the United States and line up unconditionally with Western Europe. After seventeen months of arduous negotiations, Britain's entry into the Common Market appeared assured. Then, on January 14, 1963, de Gaulle peremptorily vetoed it. "Britain," he said, "is insular, maritime and linked by trade . . . to a great variety of nations, many of which are distant ones." But he left no doubt that he feared not so much Britain's entry into the Common Market as that of the United States — by proxy, as it were, through Britain. "In the end there would appear a colossal Atlantic community under American dependence and leadership which would soon completely swallow up the European community."

De Gaulle's move caused a sensation. From the exchange of recrimination which ensued between Britain and France, it appeared that de Gaulle's immediate motive for barring Britain's admission to the Common Market was not economic but political, namely, that it had yielded to the United States in a matter of nuclear strategy (see p. 851). Britain bitterly resented its exclusion from the Common Market. The United States also regretted it. "We are concerned at the failure of the British to secure admission to the Common Market," President Kennedy said. "We have supported the unification of Europe, economically and militarily. . . . We put over $50 billion worth of assistance in rebuilding Europe. . . . We felt that Britain would be an effective part of that Europe." De Gaulle's action was criticized also by the partners of France in the Common Market. But he refused to reconsider his position.

The United States had hailed the formation of the Common Market and at first had taken a paternal interest in it. Later, however, when the Common Market showed a tendency toward exclusiveness, when its rising tariffs barred an increasing amount of American goods from entering it, and when the rush of American investment capital began seriously to drain the American gold reserves and aggravate the American difficulties in balancing their foreign payments, the United States became alarmed over its growth and its effect on the American economy. In January, 1962, the United States concluded an agreement with the Common Market, which provided for a partially reciprocal reduction of tariffs to increase each side's chances of exporting to the other. The tariff reductions agreed upon were up to 20 per cent, which was all that could be achieved under existing American tariff legislation. This, the United States government felt, fell short of the needs. Therefore, shortly afterwards, President Kennedy submitted to Congress a draft of the Trade Expansion Act of 1962, which would give him general authority to reduce tariffs as much as 50 per cent in exchange for comparable reductions by other nations. Congress duly passed the act. Under its authority, which would expire on July 1, 1967, the United States opened the "Kennedy round" of negotiations with the Common Market and the Free Trade Association at Geneva. In 1966 the marathon negotiations were still in progress.

Although the Common Market had succeeded in its economic goals, it had failed in its ultimate objective, namely, to unite Western Europe politically. In 1966 Western Europe was still "at sixes and sevens."

3. MILITARY COOPERATION OF WESTERN EUROPE

On March 4, 1947, at Dunkirk, Britain and France signed a fifty-year alliance to insure that "Germany shall not again become a menace to peace." This was a classical case of closing the barn door after the horse had escaped, for by 1947 it was not Germany but Soviet Russia that appeared to threaten peace. Both Britain and France had contracted twenty-year alliance treaties with the Soviet Union during the war, Britain in 1942 and France in 1944. Although these treaties were still legally valid after the war, the great change in the balance of power which had been caused by the collapse of Germany, and the Soviet advance deep into Europe had voided them of all meaning. The realization of this fact on the part of British, French, and the West European public in general, took time. By 1948, however, West Europeans were aware of the Soviet danger. The ruthless satellization of Eastern Europe, especially the suppression of democracy in Czechoslovakia in February, 1948, made a deep impression. On March 17, 1948, at Brussels, Britain, France, and the Benelux countries signed a fifty-year alliance, styled the "Western Union." Unlike the Dunkirk treaty, aimed against Germany, the Brussels treaty provided against any "armed attack in Europe," that is, presumably, also by Soviet Russia.

The forces of the "Western Union" still appeared to be no match for the mighty divisions of Russia, augmented by the forces of her satellites — although the latter were regarded at the time as of dubious loyalty to Moscow. Only the United States, with its atomic monopoly and vast resources, appeared able to balance the vast manpower and resources of the Soviet Bloc. When Soviet Russia attempted to squeeze the Western powers out of West Berlin by blockading it (June, 1948 – May, 1949), only the United States had the resources to supply the West Berliners with food, fuel, clothing, and raw materials for their industries. During the Berlin siege, on April 4, 1949, the North Atlantic Treaty was signed. Under this treaty the United States undertook to contain Communist power in Europe. However, the United States had a vital interest in containing Communist power, not only in Europe but in Asia as well.

In its "defensive perimeter," which stretched from Norway to Alaska, Western Europe was a relatively small segment, albeit a most important one. The United States could not commit to the defense of Western Europe all or even the bulk of its forces. The function of the limited United States forces in Europe (five divisions in West Germany, plus communications and service troops, an air force, a fleet in the Mediterranean) was to serve as a "trip-wire" or "plate-glass window," the smashing of which would unleash "massive (thermonuclear) retaliation." Bombers of the United States Strategic Air Command (SAC) and of the United States Navy, taking off from bases or aircraft carriers on the periphery of the communist powers, would smash their production and communications centers and transportation lines, thus paralyzing their ability to wage war.

The weakness of this strategy — as the progress of the Korean War (1950–53) showed — was that it was ill-adapted to cope with limited, conventional ("brush-fire") conflicts. In case of Soviet — or even satellite — attack in Europe, many West Europeans feared that the small NATO forces might not be able to prevent the numerous Soviet or satellite forces from overrunning West Germany and possibly all of Western continental Europe. While the West Europeans did not doubt the ability of the United States to defeat Soviet Russia and Communist China in an all-out thermonuclear war and, thus, ultimately to liberate Western Europe, many wondered whether there would be then much left in Europe worth liberating. Therefore the West European governments insisted that the United States increase its forces in Europe. The United States government, however, maintained that it could not increase its commitments in Europe without risking its defenses in other parts of the world or — if it increased its whole defense establishment — without risking bankruptcy.

The logical solution to this dilemma seemed to be to rearm West Germany. But this suggestion, when it was first made by Secretary of State Dean Acheson, proved extremely distasteful to many West Europeans, especially to those who, like the French, had endured Nazi occupation. Even in West Germany there was little enthusiasm for rearmament, for the Germans, too, had experienced a strong reaction against their own militarism, which had brought them defeat and humiliation twice in the twentieth century.

In 1951, prodded by Secretary of State John Foster Dulles, the French premier René Pleven proposed the formation of the European Defense Community (EDC) with a supranational army in which German units, mainly infantry, would be carefully meshed with other European troops. The French hoped in this way to tap German manpower for West Euro-

pean defense without giving the West German government control of
German troops. The Germans were not enthusiastic about serving as
lowly foot soldiers under foreign officers, but the West German government agreed to go along with EDC. However, the British government,
showing the same aloofness toward the European Defense Community as
it had toward the European Coal and Steel Community, declined to join
EDC — except, like the United States, as one of its guarantors. The British expected to explode their first atomic bomb (which they accomplished
in October, 1952) and to join the United States as an atomic power. The
European Defense Community, therefore, was limited to France, West
Germany, Italy, and the Benelux countries — the same nations that formed
the Coal and Steel Community and were to form the Common Market.

As finally worked out, the EDC treaty differed substantially from the
original French proposal. On American insistence, provision was made
for a substantially larger German contingent in EDC than the French had
envisioned, and also for admission of the West German government to
EDC on a footing of complete equality. The six member states were to
have "common institutions, common armed forces, and a common budget."
Each partner was to place a contingent at the disposal of the Community;
the soldiers of this collective army would wear a common uniform and be
equipped, trained, and organized in a common pattern. Since all the members of EDC except West Germany were also members of NATO, the
EDC treaty included three protocols whereby NATO and EDC were to
be closely united in a common defense policy. Like the Coal and Steel
Community, the European Defense Community was to have a council
of ministers and a consultative committee, but a single court of justice
and a single parliamentary assembly would serve both organizations.

On May 26, 1952, the EDC treaty was signed in Paris by the six member nations and the United States and Britain, the latter two nations as
guarantors. When ratified, it was to be valid for fifty years. The British
Parliament and the United States Senate readily ratified it, but it encountered great difficulties in the French National Assembly. The French
were not only reluctant to accord West Germany equality, but also resented the special position of Britain. Since the United States and Britain
had atomic weapons and the EDC nations did not, this put the latter in
the position — as one French official put it — of humble foot soldiers to
American and English atomic knights. In August, 1954, after two years of
bitter debates and a threat by Secretary of State Dulles to make an "ago-
nizing reappraisal" of the United States policy if the EDC treaty were not
approved, it was put to a vote in the French National Assembly and defeated.

In Washington the defeat of the EDC treaty by the French National
Assembly excited anger and frustration. Secretary of State Dulles called
it "a shattering blow," and Congress, angered that a European nation
should accept American aid and then refuse to support American aims,

voted to deny Mutual Security funds to any country that failed to ratify the EDC treaty. But the European Defense Community was dead. The American policy of containment had to be pursued by other means. The British proposed a new formula. West Germany and Italy were to be admitted to the Western Union and to NATO. West Germany was to have a national army, limited to 500,000 men and a small air force and navy. A new draft treaty was worked out and signed in Paris on October 23, 1954. This treaty was duly ratified by all Western parliaments, including the French National Assembly.

The decision to rearm West Germany was not popular either in Germany or in Europe as a whole. The West German Social Democratic party, fearing that it might lead to a revival of German militarism, vigorously opposed it. In Western Europe, not only Communist but leftest opinion generally, opposed it. However, after a bitter, last-ditch struggle on the part of the Social Democrats, the West German Federal Council ratified the new Paris treaty in May, 1955.

NATO, of which West Germany became in time the most important European member, proved an effective shield of Western Europe against Soviet aggression. Despite continuous denunciation of NATO and occasional sabre-rattling, the Soviet Union never ventured to test its effectiveness by outright aggression.

58

CANADA, AUSTRALIA, NEW ZEALAND,
AND SOUTH AFRICA

In the circumstances I wish formally to withdraw a request for South Africa to remain a member of the Commonwealth . . .

H. F. VERWOERD, PRIME MINISTER OF THE
UNION OF SOUTH AFRICA (1961)

AT THE OPENING OF the twentieth century only one of the four dominions included in this chapter had more than five million inhabitants and their total white population was approximately ten million. By 1965 their combined white population exceeded 37 million and their total population had passed 51 million. Even more remarkable was the growth of their commerce. By 1965 the total exports and imports of these four countries had an estimated value of $28 billion. A hundred years earlier they had been relatively unimportant British colonies, ruled from London. Now all four had attained complete self-government; and the international trade of the four, taken as a group, exceeded that of Great Britain itself.

The development of these four dominions in the earlier part of the twentieth century was related in Chapters 11 and 30. The present chapter will describe their expansion after World War II and the circumstances that caused the Union of South Africa to withdraw from the Commonwealth.

1. CANADA

Canada entered World War II with Great Britain in September, 1939. Its armed forces reached a peak strength of 780,000 members, of whom 37,476 were killed in battle. The output from Canadian farms, factories, mines, and timberlands provided an important contribution to the cause of the Allied powers and wartime demands stimulated Canadian economic expansion. This expansion, particularly in mining, continued in the post-

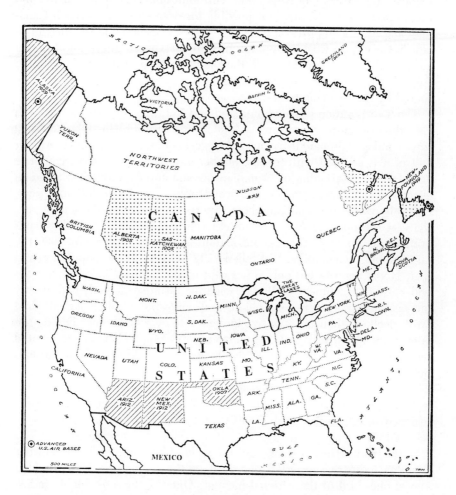

CANADA AND THE UNITED STATES, 1898–1967

war period — asbestos, nickel, platinum, and natural uranium, as well as gold, silver, copper, aluminum, cobalt, cadmium, magnesium, and zinc. Reserves of iron ore, petroleum, and natural gas were developed, and a 2300-mile pipeline constructed to carry the gas to the urban and industrial centers of Ontario and Quebec. Electric energy, nine-tenths of it developed from water power, reached 26 million Kilowatts in 1963. This production placed Canada sixth among the countries of the world in available electric energy and provided Canada with a surplus which it sold to the United States.

The St. Lawrence Power and Seaway Project opened in 1959, adding over 2 million horsepower, to be divided equally between the Province of

Ontario and the State of New York. This joint undertaking of Canada and the United States also made it possible for ocean vessels to reach Canadian and American ports on the Great Lakes, thus opening the interior of North America to world shipping. In 1961 the United States and Canada concluded a treaty providing for their joint development of the Columbia River basin, the cost and the advantages in power and irrigation to be shared by the two countries.

The incorporation of Newfoundland and Labrador in 1949 as the tenth Canadian province gave Canada a total area of approximately 3,850,000 square miles and made it the second largest country in the world. Almost half of it is covered with forests; lumber and wood derivatives comprise one-fifth the total value of Canadian manufactured products. Canadian exports of newsprint, timber, and wood pulp exceed $1.6 billion a year, twice the value of Canadian wheat exports. Agriculture, the leading activity at the opening of the twentieth century, declined steadily in importance as forestry, mining, and manufacturing increased. By 1960 the farmers and their families had fallen to 17 per cent of the population and their labors contributed only 6 per cent of the national income. But the wider use of machinery and more scientific farming methods had greatly increased the output per man-hour, and while the number of individual farms declined their average size increased to over 300 acres. During the later years of World War II, when twenty-two million acres were planted with wheat to meet wartime needs, the average yield was about 340 million bushels annually. Twenty years later, with acreage increased to 27 million, the average yield had risen to 723 million bushels. Wheat output per acre had nearly doubled, although the number of workers engaged in agriculture had declined and their hours of labor had been reduced.

In the twentieth century agriculture yielded its leading role to industry. By 1965 industry supported one-third of the population and provided almost one-third of the national income. Ontario, the most highly industrialized of the provinces, accounted for half the industrial output. This included the preparation of pulp and paper, the refining of petroleum and metals, the manufacture of automobiles, aircraft, industrial machinery, electrical devices, and food products.

In the postwar years Canadian imports and exports increased until Canada ranked fifth in foreign trade, following the United States, Britain, France, and West Germany. The United States absorbs almost 60 per cent of Canadian exports and furnishes 70 per cent of the imports, thus accounting for nearly two-thirds of Canada's external commerce. This excessive dependence on their powerful neighbor displeases many Canadians, who are concerned that their imports from the United States exceed their exports to that country by over half a billion dollars a year. In contrast, Canadian trade with Britain and other Commonwealth countries averages less than 20 per cent but produces a credit balance. Large investments of foreign capital in Canadian enterprises, and the half-billion dollars a year sent abroad in dividends and interest, are further causes of concern to Canadians, who need capital to develop their country but do not want to mortgage it too heavily.

The population of Canada increased at a rapid rate after World War II, reaching 14 million by 1951 and 20 million by 1966. Some 2.5 million immigrants arrived between 1945 and 1965, but many later re-emigrated, particularly to the United States. About 6 million Canadians were French-speaking. The Canadian birth rate averaged 28 per thousand in the 1950's, but declined to 25 in the 1960's. The death rate averaged between 8 and 9, slightly lower than the American average, but the infant mortality rate in Canada, though it fell from 41 to 30, remained higher than that of the United States.

The slight differences in the vital statistics of the two countries provided interesting comparisons. Despite a harsher climate and a lower per capita income of $1700, the Canadians attained much the same level of health as the population of the United States and a similar average life expectancy of about 70 years. But the higher birth rate and higher ratio of population increase in Canada (nearly three per cent annually) gave Canada a somewhat "younger" population. Children of fourteen years or less comprised over 33 per cent of the Canadian people, and the average age was 27. In the United States children fourteen or less comprised 31 per cent of the population and the average age was 29. The more rapid rate of increase of the Canadian people could be measured with each decennial census. In 1900 the population of Canada equaled only 7 per cent of the United States population but by 1965 it had climbed to 10 per cent. There was no likelihood, however, that Canada could overtake the United States. Four-fifths of the Canadian people lived within 200 miles of the border, and over a million Canadian-born citizens had crossed it to live in the United States, whereas only one-fourth as many people moved from the United States to Canada.

With a large area, thinly peopled, the Canadians realized in the postwar period that they must be prepared to defend their heritage. They devoted over one-fourth of their budget to defense measures, joined the North Atlantic Treaty Organization, and linked their radar warning system with that of the United States. Canada's northern frontier and arctic islands, which extend to within some 500 miles of the North Pole, face the northern frontier of Soviet Russia across the Arctic Ocean. The leading Canadian cities — Montreal, Toronto, Winnipeg, Vancouver — are as vulnerable to intercontinental missiles as the cities of the United States, and in both countries seven-tenths of the people had become urban dwellers by 1965.

Canada is a federation of ten provinces and two territories with its capital at Ottawa. The Parliament consists of a House of Commons elected by universal suffrage, and a Senate, the members of which are appointed by the governor-general on the advice of the prime minister.

The governor-general represents the British monarch, but he is selected
by the prime minister and his duties are limited. The leader of the political party that obtains the largest number of seats in the House of Commons heads the cabinet, the members of which he nominates, and the
cabinet holds the executive power so long as a majority of the Commons
supports it. Of the two leading political parties, the Liberals and Conservatives, the Liberals draw their main strength from Quebec and lean
toward the United States, the Conservatives draw more strength from the
British elements of the population and favor closer ties with the Commonwealth. The Liberals held power from 1935 to 1957, when the Conservatives took over. They obtained a large majority in a second election in
1958, but by 1964 their majority had declined to a minority. The Liberal
Prime Minister, Lester Pearson, clung to power with the aid of small
minority groups. The French-speaking and other non-British minorities
have always resented Canada's connection with Britain, which was symbolized by Canada's unofficial flag, a red ensign with a Union Jack in one
corner. In 1964, as a concession to these minorities, Prime Minister
Pearson sponsored a bill in the Parliament to adopt a national flag which
featured a maple leaf as Canada's emblem. The bill passed. An election
at the end of that year kept the Liberals in office though they still lacked
a majority.

2. AUSTRALIA

The development of Australia during and after World War II paralleled
that of Canada. Its area, 2,974,581 square miles including the island of
Tasmania, and its population were smaller than those of Canada. The
Australian birth rate (22 per thousand) and rate of annual increase (a
little over 2 per cent) were also smaller. Until World War II immigration
to Australia was severely limited. Trusting on one hand to British naval
power to protect them and wishing on the other to prevent unemployment and to keep wages high, the Australians excluded Asian and non-
white immigrants altogether and limited white immigrants, in practice,
to those from the British isles. However, the fall of the great bastions of
the empire, Hong Kong and Singapore, and the rapid advance of the
Japanese to the gates of Australia in 1941–1942 scared the Australians
and caused them to change their immigration policy after the war. Although non-whites were still excluded, immigration from Western Europe
and North America, as well as the British Isles, was encouraged. As a
result of the new immigration policy, the population rose from 7 million
in 1939 to 11 million in 1965, approximately half this growth being the
result of immigration. Six out of seven Australians were native-born at
the latter date and nine-tenths were of British ancestry. Less than one
per cent of the population was non-white. The primitive Australian

aborigines, whose numbers have declined to about seventy thousand, live mainly on government reservations.

Like the Canadians, the Australians are concentrated in a small segment of a vast country. Only one-fifth of Australia receives more than thirty inches of rain a year, and roughly half is almost uninhabitable desert. January temperatures (the southern summer) average over eighty degrees Fahrenheit throughout most of the country; July temperatures (the southern winter) range from forty to sixty except in the north where they remain higher. Nine-tenths of the population live in the southeastern section or other coastal areas, four-fifths are classified as urban, and half live in the six leading cities.

A high per capita income ($1400 a year) and an efficient public health service make Australia one of the healthiest countries in the world. The death rate has been reduced to 8.7 per thousand and the infant mortality rate to 19. Life expectancy at birth is 70 years. Children fourteen or less comprise 30 per cent of the population and the average age is 29 years. One Australian in twenty is 70 or older. The good general health of the Australians is reflected in their spectacular achievements in the field of sports. Social services, long a feature of Australian government, were further extended by a new Social Services Act in 1947. Men over 65 and women over 60 receive old age pensions if in need, and payments are also provided for those who become incapacitated. Allowances are provided for the birth of a child and weekly payments for each child under sixteen. An act of 1945 extended the benefit of weekly payments to the sick and the unemployed, and a National Health Act of 1953 provided a daily allowance for patients in public hospitals. Free care and allowances are granted victims of tuberculosis. Diseases of the heart and arteries are the leading causes of death.

The Australian economy is heavily dependent on animal products and considerable areas too dry for farming have sufficient forage for sheep or cattle. Australia holds roughly one-sixth of the billion sheep in the world; yet these flocks are supervised and sheared by only one-fortieth of the Australian population. Wool accounts for about one-third the value of Australian exports, and animal products other than wool account for another third. Imports consist largely of machinery and metals, petroleum, textiles, paper, and chemicals. One-third of the external trade is carried on with Great Britain, the United States holds second place, and Japan third. Cost of transportation to and from distant markets produces an adverse balance but Australia has built up reserves of credit overseas totaling $1 billion. In 1966 the Australians abandoned the British currency of pounds, shillings, and pence and adopted a decimal system with 100 cents to one (Australian) dollar.

The major problem — lack of water — has been met in part by drilling artesian wells, but these tend to exhaust the underground supply after a few years. A vast and costly project has been planned, to impound rain that falls on the mountains of the east coast, and divert it across the mountains to the interior for irrigation and stock raising. This program, when completed, will also provide additional electric energy. As most Australian rivers dry up entirely for part of the year little hydroelectric power can be generated, but coal reserves make steam generators serviceable. Per capita consumption of energy is high, being equivalent to 3800 kilograms of coal a year.

The loneliness and monotony of life in the "outback" causes a steady migration to the urban areas. Out of a labor force of four million, over one million have found employment in industry, and another million in commerce, retail trade, transportation, and communication. The Australian automobile industry produces a quarter million cars a year, and other industries supply most of the home market demand for radios, furniture, electrical appliances, and plastics.

High wages and high transportation cost make it difficult to sell Australian manufactures abroad. Even within the country itself transportation remains a problem. There are no inland waterways, the railroads have different gauges, and many of the highways are of poor quality. As most of the cities lie on or near the sea, coastal shipping affords a method of shipping heavy freight, and air travel has gained great importance in recent years.

Australia has a federal, parliamentary, democratic government. A governor-general representing the British sovereign, and an executive council, head the administration; but actual power resides with the prime minister and cabinet members, who are responsible to the Parliament. A Senate represents the states and an elected House of Representatives the people. Like Australia, New Zealand has pioneered in the field of social security. The leading political parties of Australia are the Liberal, Country, and Labor parties. Long under the dominance of the Labor party, in 1949 Australia passed under a Liberal-Country coalition, led by Sir Robert Menzies and (after his retirement in 1966) Harold E. Holt. All citizens twenty-one and over have the suffrage and voting is compulsory. Conscious of their remoteness from Europe and America, and their proximity to the densely populated regions of Asia and the East Indies, the Australians are active supporters of the United Nations and value their connection with Great Britain and the Commonwealth, but since World War II have trusted mainly to the United States for their defense. Australia is a member of the Southeast Asia Treaty Organization and has an alliance with New Zealand and the United States (ANZUS Treaty, 1951). It supported the American effort to protect South Vietnam and sent a small contingent to participate in that war. Australia has claimed a large segment of the Antarctic continent, administers part of New Guinea as a Trust Territory, and holds several small and scattered islands in the Pacific and Indian oceans.

3. NEW ZEALAND

The area of New Zealand, 103,736 square miles, is a little larger than that of Great Britain, which lies opposite it on the other side of the globe. Like the Australians, the New Zealanders are almost exclusively of British descent. The only significant non-British element in the country is the native Maoris, who are of Polynesian origin. They numbered about 194,000 out of a total population of 2.6 million in 1965. The New Zealanders treasure their ties with the Old Country, export large shipments of wool, meat, and dairy products, maintain a high per capita income ($1400), and enjoy exceptionally good health. In 1966 a limited free trade accord came into operation between the two dominions and they drew closer together on defense policies. The possibility that they might seek closer political ties awakened speculation.

The similarities between Australia and New Zealand are matched by some startling contrasts in climate and geography. Where two-thirds of Australia is arid or semiarid, two-thirds of New Zealand is suited to farming and stock raising. The blessings of an adequate rainfall and lush vegetation make it possible for New Zealand, which is about one-thirtieth the size of Australia, to export half as much wool and maintain an external commerce one-third as valuable as that of its huge neighbor. By exporting almost half their total production, and importing machinery, metals, textiles, and other items in exchange, the New Zealanders have achieved one of the highest per capita trade ratios in the world.

Most of Australia is level and lies only a few hundred feet above the ocean, but New Zealand is largely elevated and mountainous, with volcanic peaks over 6000 feet high in the North Island and the Southern Alps with peaks over 10,000 feet in the South Island. The New Zealand climate is moist and temperate with abundant sunshine, a rainfall of forty to fifty inches, and little seasonal variation in temperature.

Aware of their good fortune, the New Zealanders have sought to preserve it for themselves by a strict immigration policy, accepting British citizens but taking few applicants from other countries. Unlike Australia, New Zealand has not lifted restrictions on immigration since World War II. Between 1945 and 1965 the New Zealand population increased from 1.4 million to 2.6 million. In view of the relatively small immigration, this increase was a tribute to the high birth rate of the New Zealanders (26 per thousand) and their low death rate (between eight and nine per thousand). Their life expectancy is exceptionally high (71 years) and their infant mortality rate exceptionally low (19 per thousand). Approximately one-third of the population are under fifteen and one-half under twenty-eight.

With an adequate rainfall and mountainous terrain, New Zealand has waterfalls to provide plentiful hydroelectric power. It is available to 99 per cent of the population and the per capita consumption is equivalent to 2000 kilograms of coal. The same preference for urban living noted in the Australians marks the New Zealanders. Approximately one-fourth live in rural districts, and of the three-fourths who prefer town life the majority are crowded into the four leading cities.

Like Australia, New Zealand has developed its industries sufficiently to provide for many of its own requirements. But the home market is too limited to stimulate mass production methods to top efficiency, and high wages and transportation costs make it difficult for New Zealand to seek external markets. Although manufacturing and food processing increased after World War II until they claimed almost twice as many workers as agriculture, most of the factories were small, with ten or less employees.

Social services in New Zealand provide benefits and insurance for the people from the cradle to the grave. The old, the sick, the disabled, the unemployed, widows, and orphans — all receive aid. Families receive an allowance of sixteen shillings a week (about $2.25) for each child under sixteen. Medical and hospital care is provided for the sick and for mental patients. Expenditures for social services approximate 40 per cent of the budget, or about ten times as much as the outlay for defense. Compulsory military service was abolished in 1959.

The government of New Zealand differs from that of Australia only in that it is not federal. The Parliament consists of a single house, with 80 seats, 4 of which are reserved for the Maoris. The leading political parties are the National and Labor parties. Since 1949 the National party has been in power.

Like the Australians, the New Zealanders cherish their ties with Britain and the Commonwealth, have made an alliance with the United States, and have joined the Southeast Asia Treaty Organization. They administer the territory of Western Samoa, the Cook Islands and some other island groups in the Pacific Ocean, and they claim the Ross Dependency in the Antarctic continent. Their interest in Antarctica is understandable, for New Zealand is nearer to the South Pole than any other states except Chile and Argentina.

4. SOUTH AFRICA

The Union of South Africa has an area of 472,359 square miles, larger than Texas, Oklahoma, and Arizona combined. South West Africa, a former German-held territory, was entrusted to the Union as a mandate after World War I and as the population there has been granted representation in the South African Parliament it may be considered an adjunct of the Union. Their joint area is nearly 790,000 square miles and their joint population was 18 million in 1965. Of the total, Africans constituted approximately two-thirds, and the "Colored" (people of mixed descent) about one-tenth. There were also nearly half-a-million Asians. South

Africans of European blood comprised one-fifth of the population in South and South West Africa. About 60 per cent of the White population is descended from Dutch colonists in the seventeenth and eighteenth centuries and speaks "Afrikaans," a distorted version of the Dutch language. The rest of the White population is descended from British and other European settlers, who had come to Africa more recently. The "Afrikaners" nurtured memories of their defeat in the Boer War (1899–1902) and resented South Africa's connection to the British empire, even though it was economically advantageous to them. During World War II they were stoutly pro-German and professed admiration for the Nazi racial policies — even when Holland was occupied by the Germans. Out of deference to their opinion, South Africa remained neutral in the conflict.

The health and income of the white minority in South Africa are high. Their birth rate is 25 per thousand, their death rate below 9 per thousand, and their infant mortality rate 29 per thousand. The small Asian minority has also improved in health, with a birth rate of 29 and an infant mortality rate of 68, but the estimate of 8 for their death rate (lower than that for whites) is incongruous. The "Coloreds" are less fortunate; as their birth rate is nearly 50 and their infant mortality rate 132, their death rate is almost certainly higher than the 17 per thousand recorded for them. For the African two-thirds of the population a birth rate of 46 per thousand and a death rate of 15 have been cited, but poor housing, malnutrition, inadequate health service, and the prevalence of tuberculosis make a higher mortality rate appear more probable. Their life expectancy is only two-thirds that of the white population.

South Africa lies in the same latitudes as Australia and has a somewhat similar climate, with a little more rain and a lower range of temperature. The more moderate temperatures are due to the influence of the ocean and to the fact that most of South Africa is a tableland with an elevation of 3000 to 4000 feet. In July (the winter season) the thermometer ranges from 40 to 60 degrees Fahrenheit, except in the Drakensberg Mountains where it falls below 40. In January (the summer season) the average is 70 to 80 degress, giving a mean annual temperature of about 60 degrees. The average rainfall is 16–17 inches but most of it falls during the southern summer and it is unevenly distributed. Almost one-third of the country receives less than ten inches. The Kalahari Desert, lying north of the Orange River, is an arid plateau extending beyond the border of the Union into South West Africa and Bechuanaland. The most productive areas are the narrow coastal belt and the valleys of the eastern mountain slopes; the interior plateau is made up of steppes and prairie lands where grazing is more profitable than farming.

South Africa supports some forty million sheep, slightly less than New Zealand, and wool is one of its main exports. World War II stimulated the growth of industry, and the Union itself furnished most of the raw materials its factories required. Electric power, generated chiefly from low grade coal, provided the equivalent of 2450 kilowatts per capita. South African industries have begun to meet home market demands for textiles, footwear, furniture, electrical devices, processed foods, and oil (from coal), but motor vehicles and petroleum products are still prominent on the list of imports.

The extraordinary mineral wealth remains the most significant factor in the South African economy. Shipments of gold and specie, atomic energy materials (chiefly uranium), chromium, manganese, asbestos, and other minerals, together with diamonds, make up the most valuable part of South African exports. Great Britain and the rest of the Commonwealth play the largest part in the external trade of the Union; but while preserving and depending on these economic ties the South Africans have severed their political ties with Britain. In 1961 South Africa became a republic and withdrew from the Commonwealth.

The government of South Africa, as organized under the South Africa Act (1909), included a governor-general to represent the British monarch, a Senate, and a House of Assembly. The Senate was reconstituted in 1955, with 90 members, 19 appointed by the governor-general and the remainder elected. The House of Assembly was reorganized in 1957. The seats of four senators and three assemblymen, who had represented the African Bantu peoples, were abolished. In 1958 the franchise was extended to all white citizens over eighteen.

The policy adopted by the South African government toward the non-white majority became a subject of concern within and outside the Union. The Nationalist party, which represented the "Afrikaner" element and which came to power in 1948 under Daniel François Malan's program, on which he obtained the support of a parliamentary majority, aimed at a complete separation of Europeans and Africans. This proposed segregation (*apartheid*) of races was to be accomplished by providing separate areas for whites and nonwhites. The treatment accorded citizens of India resident in South Africa excited protests from India and a debate in the United Nations. Malan refused to place South West Africa, which South Africa had received as a mandate from the League of Nations, under the trusteeship of the United Nations, whereupon the General Assembly adopted a vote of censure and the South African delegation withdrew. Despite criticism, the Nationalist party increased its majority in successive elections and *apartheid* won the approval of a large majority of the voters (only Europeans retained the right to vote). Johannes Strijdom, who followed Malan as premier in 1954, and Hendrik F. Verwoerd, who succeeded to the office in 1958, extended the *apartheid* program while the United Nations reiterated annually its "regret and concern" but took no action. To enforce the *apartheid* policy, the South African government suspended civil rights, muzzled the press, and gave the police extraordinary powers. In fact, South Africa remained a democracy only in form. Though outwardly orderly, there was an undercurrent of violence in South African life.

The determination of the European minority in South Africa to maintain white supremacy was certain to encounter opposition as a rising tide of nationalism and anticolonialism swept Africa and newly liberated colonies there assumed sovereign status. The nonwhites in South Africa, without arms and lacking organization or cohesion, could not easily rebel, but they found other methods of protest. The government required them to carry passes under penalty of arrest if they were found to be without them. In March, 1960, thousands of Africans left their passes at home and converged on the police stations to surrender to arrest. At some points the police in alarm fired on the demonstrators, killing several score. Prime Minister Verwoerd proclaimed a state of emergency, ignored rebukes from the United States and other governments, and maintained control.

The determination of the Nationalist party in South Africa to maintain its racial policy had an unhappy result in 1961. The prime ministers of the British self-governing dominions, meeting in London, debated the question whether, if the Union of South Africa became a republic, its membership in the Commonwealth should be reaffirmed. Canada, Australia, New Zealand, and South Africa were no longer the only dominions — by March, 1961, they had been joined by India, Pakistan, Ceylon, Ghana, Malaya, Nigeria, and Cyprus. Not surprisingly, the prime ministers of the seven new Asian and African dominions took a critical view of South African racial policies. When Prime Minister Verwoerd realized the strength of the opposition he faced, he made a startling announcement.

In the circumstances, [he declared] I wish formally to withdraw a request for South Africa to remain a member of the Commonwealth after she becomes a republic on May 31.

In the same week that Verwoerd chose to leave the Commonwealth rather than yield to pressure and abandon or modify *apartheid,* the United Nations General Assembly, by a vote of 70 to 0, censored the South African government for its plans to incorporate South West Africa. The evidence of international disapproval did not shake the will of the South African white minority to maintain their policies and their ascendency. In 1966 Hendrik F. Verwoerd was assassinated by a mentally disordered white South African who believed, ironically, that Verwoerd was doing too much for the Negroes and too little for the poor whites. As successor, the South African Nationalist party chose Balthazar J. Vorster, who, as Minister of Justice, Police and Prisons, had been resolute in applying the laws and repressing opponents of the official policies. Vorster took office with the promise, "I will walk further along the road set by Hendrik Verwoerd."

Northeast of the Republic of South Africa another former British colony defied other members of the Commonwealth by its insistence on maintaining white supremacy. In 1953 Southern Rhodesia, Northern Rhodesia, and Nyasaland joined in a loose confederation (see page 823), but this union dissolved in 1963. In 1964 Nyasaland became independent as the state of Malawi and Northern Rhodesia as the Republic of Zambia. Southern Rhodesia reverted to the status of a self-governing member of the Commonwealth. But in 1965 the Rhodesian government, headed by Prime Minister Ian Smith, declared Rhodesia independent, a measure taken by the white minority (about 220,000) in their determination to resist the acquisition of political power by the non-European majority of more than 4 million. The British government imposed economic restraints on Rhodesia and the United Nations Security Council called on all United Nations members to break off economic relations with the defiant republic.

59

LATIN AMERICA

Violence has been an essential in Latin America because the governments have been unstable, and the governments have been unstable because violence is a traditional means of coming to office. And violence is traditional because there has generally been no other sure means of transferring political power from one administration to another.[1]

FRANK TANNENBAUM

1. THREE BASIC PROBLEMS

SOME OF THE HISTORIC contrasts that have distinguished the United States and Canada from the republics of Middle and South America were discussed in Chapter 31. These contrasts were the product of geographic, climatic, racial, cultural, and economic factors. They shaped Anglo-Saxon America and Latin America into separate societies with different temperaments and values, different aims and ideals. Absorbed in their own dynamic growth and progress, the people of the United States and Canada gave too little thought to the problems and the preferences of their Latin American neighbors. This neglect, though unwise and discourteous, raised no critical difficulties in the nineteenth century. But in the shrinking world of the twentieth century, when all parts of the globe became increasingly interdependent, the lack of a sympathetic understanding between the two Americas held grave implications. Some of these implications hardened into realities in the years after World War II.

The difficulties the Latin American people faced in the twentieth century were intensified by three unresolved problems. The first problem was *demographic* — it was the increasingly rapid growth of the Latin American population. The second problem was *economic* — how could resources be best developed and income increased to provide an adequate standard of living for the multiplying millions? The third problem was *administrative* — what form of political organization, what mode of government, could best protect and promote the welfare of impoverished

[1] From *Foreign Affairs* (April, 1960), p. 500; with the permission of *Foreign Affairs*.

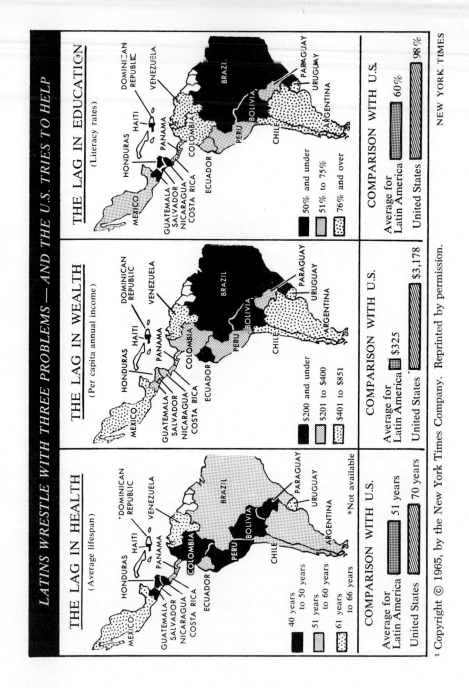

LATINS WRESTLE WITH THREE PROBLEMS — AND THE U.S. TRIES TO HELP

THE LAG IN HEALTH
(Average lifespan)

- 40 years to 50 years
- 51 years to 60 years
- 61 years to 66 years

*Not available

COMPARISON WITH U.S.

Average for Latin America — 51 years
United States — 70 years

THE LAG IN WEALTH
(Per capita annual income)

- $200 and under
- $201 to $400
- $401 to $851

COMPARISON WITH U.S.

Average for Latin America — $325
United States — $3,178

THE LAG IN EDUCATION
(Literacy rates)

- 50% and under
- 51% to 75%
- 76% and over

COMPARISON WITH U.S.

Average for Latin America — 60%
United States — 98%

NEW YORK TIMES

peoples struggling to survive in a harsh and competitive world? These three problems were not new. They were the familiar trio — resources, defense, and social justice — that no nation or government could long ignore. By the middle of the twentieth century, however, the phenomenal rate at which the population increased in Latin America made efficient government and effective use of resources issues of immediate urgency.

The demographic revolution, the rate of population increase in Middle and South America, is frequently attributed to a *rising* birth rate, but this misrepresents the problem. Actually, the number of births per thousand population declined slightly, from an estimated 42 in the 1950's to 40 in the early 1960's. The really dramatic change in recent decades has been the *decline* in the death rate, a result of better medical care and the use of antibiotics to control diseases formerly frequent and fatal. By 1966 the population of Middle and South America reached a quarter of a billion. It exceeded the population of the United States and Canada by 30 million and was increasing twice as fast.

If population increases more rapidly than food resources, the consequences are grim: either extra food must be imported or millions will suffer from slow starvation. But money sent abroad to buy food that is promptly consumed leaves the hungry nation poorer than before. This dilemma can be clearly illustrated from statistics on South America. Before World War II the South Americans *exported* 11 million tons of surplus grain, using the profit to buy machinery and other needed imports. By 1966, however, South America could no longer raise surplus grain for export; it was *importing* 25 million tons annually because its population had doubled in thirty years. It will double again, at prevailing rates, before the end of the twentieth century.

Could the Latin Americans develop their resources sufficiently within another forty years to support a population of 600 million people? The per capita income there in 1965 ranged from less than $100 to $900. In many of the republics a single product dominated the economy, and fluctuations of the world market, over which they had no control, could spell ruin. To diversify their activities and improve their techniques they needed capital to buy machinery, expand transportation, develop industries. But how could they accumulate capital on a subsistence economy, with the population rising as fast as the national income?

This combination of population pressure and limited income made it essential that the government should direct and stimulate the economy with the utmost vigilance and efficiency. But what was the most efficient type of administration? The richest nations of the world, the peoples who enjoyed the highest per capita incomes, lived in democracies. But some of the countries that were developing their resources and expanding their economies most rapidly were ruled by communist regimes. Did communism offer a quicker route to economic efficiency and an equitable distribution of income than democracy could assure? It was a question all the impoverished people of the world were asking, and two-thirds of the world's people were impoverished. It was a question the Latin Americans were certain to ask with increasing earnestness as they strove to cope with their problems.

Democracy, in the sense that the people of Anglo-Saxon America understood it, had never struck deep roots in Latin America. Throughout the colonial period authority emanated from a distant king, a monarch in Madrid (or, for Brazil, in Lisbon) who ruled by divine right. After a century and a half of independence the peoples of Latin America still lacked a deep democratic tradition. Their intellectual leaders, who had studied the working of democracy in the United States and Western Europe, drafted ideal constitutions. But the masses of the people could not read, nor could they grasp the abstract concept of a government of laws, not of men. For them, authority had to be symbolized by a leader, a *caudillo*, who was obeyed because he had the power to compel obedience. The theory that a president exercised powers delegated to him by their votes did not appeal to them because it belied the facts. They repeatedly saw duly elected presidents deposed by leaders who seized power by a successful coup and held it until another leader displaced them by violence. The conviction that authority belonged to the man or clique that had the will and the power to seize and exercise it remained strong because the realities of Latin American politics so often supported it.

The "strong man," the dictator, who controlled the police and the army and allowed no avowed opposition party to exist, was a familiar figure in Latin America. A centralized authoritarian regime was a familiar political model. The persistence of such concepts and such practices made the dictatorial methods of a Communist regime more comprehensible to many Latin Americans than the division of authority, the checks and balances and limitations, implicit in a democratic and responsible government. To argue that a constitution, and the right of civil liberty, free speech, and free elections which it guarantees, are stronger than a dictator is meaningless to people who think the dictator *is* the law and the constitution. The established traditions, the habits of thought, the legal precedents for an orderly transmission of authority had never developed strongly in Latin America or been firmly consolidated there. This absence of a broad and firm basis for democracy left most Latin American states open to the inroads of totalitarian creeds — fascism, Nazism, or communism.

2. MIDDLE AMERICA

The term "Middle America" is used here as a collective caption to describe the mainland states from Mexico to Panama and the islands of the West Indies. This region has the highest rate of population increase, and as it is the region closest to the United States, developments there have the most direct impact on the people of the United States. Some posses-sions in this area should not, in a strict sense, be listed as parts of *Latin America*. The British, French, and Dutch still hold a number of islands in the West Indies, and Guiana on the mainland of South America is divided among the three. Britain also controls a small area — British Honduras — adjoining the republics of Mexico and Guatemala. The United States is responsible for Puerto Rico, the Virgin Islands, and the Panama Canal Zone. In all these areas the problems that confront the Latin American peoples — a mounting population, a retarded economy, and agitation for a better standard of living — exist in a more or less criti-cal degree. It is not illogical, therefore, to ignore political and cultural affiliation, and to regard Middle America as a region where all the peoples are beset by similar problems and have developed similar grievances.

Mexico, with an area of 758,259 square miles and a population of 40 million in 1966, was the second largest nation of Latin America (Brazil ranking first). Its most essential problem in the postwar period was to increase the domestic food supply at a faster rate than 3 per cent a year, the approximate rate of population growth. Although one-eighth of the land area could be cultivated, four-fifths of this arable land had to be irrigated to assure regular crops. Roughly half the acreage was used for growing maize (Indian corn) which with beans comprised the major elements of Mexican diet. But insufficient rain limited the maize output per acre to one-third that of North American farms, and Mexico had to import corn from the United States. At the same time it exchanged "cash" crops (cotton, coffee, sugar, fruit, and sisal fibre) worth some 300 million dollars a year, and mineral products of equal value, for machinery, vehi-cles, electrical equipment, chemicals, fertilizers, and other essentials. Two-thirds of the external trade was conducted with the United States.

In addition to the program for increasing the food supply the Mexican government adopted a broad educational program. It was designed to reduce illiteracy and train the scientists, engineers, technicians, and medi-cal experts Mexico needed for its national development. In the 1950's federal expenditure for education steadily increased until it was almost double the sum expended on defense. This provided a striking contrast to the relative importance attached to the two activities in most countries. In the United States during the same decade defense costs outweighed the total spent on education at all levels by three to one. Mexico, however, because of the high birth rate there, had a larger proportion of its popu-lation (over 45 per cent) under fifteen years of age. About three-fourths of the Mexican children between six and fourteen attended school in 1965. A successful campaign was also in operation to reduce illiteracy in the adult population.

The per capita income in Mexico stood between $300 and $400 in 1965 and the per capita consumption of energy at the equivalent of 936 kilo-grams of coal. To the south of Mexico lay four smaller countries with lower incomes but higher rates of population increase that ranged from 3 to 3.4 per cent. These four republics, Guatemala, Honduras, El Salvador, and Nicaragua, had a total area of 150, 621 square miles and a total population of 11 million. Their per capita income averaged between $100 and $199, and their per capita consumption of energy was about one-sixth that of Mexico. These countries depended heavily on one or two commodities. Coffee constituted 75 per cent of the exports from Guatemala, 80 per cent of those from El Salvador. Exports from Honduras were 65 per cent bananas. For Nicaragua, where efforts were made to diversify the economy, coffee and cotton still accounted for half the exports in 1966.

Heavy dependence on a single crop involved high risks. Nicaragua, once a large exporter of bananas, suffered when a blight, the "Panama disease," appeared. Guatemala suffered when coffee prices declined. The Guatemalan government seized German-owned plantations during World War II, but found itself in difficulties ten years later when an "Agrarian Reform Law" was adopted. The law provided that landed estates which the owners neglected to cultivate would be taken over and developed. At this the United States protested and the law was modified. Guatemalan exports exceeded imports in value, but interest on foreign loans and payments to foreign companies operating in the republic turned the credit to a deficit. Radical political leaders, who considered Guatemala a victim of "capitalist exploitation," veered toward communism during the presidency of Jacobo Arbenz Guzmán (1951–1954). The United States replied by reducing its financial aid and by urging other American states to bring pressure to bear on Guatemala. Anticommunist elements led by Carlos Castillo Armas overthrew Arbenz in 1954 and received financial aid from Washington, but Armas was assassinated in 1957. His successor, Miguel Ydigoras Fuentes, preserved an anticommunist policy, but was deposed in 1963 when a military coup placed Colonel Enrique Azurdia in power.

The republic of Costa Rica had an area of 19,647 square miles and a population of 1,391,000 in 1965. The population, which was 97 per cent white or mestizo (native Indians comprised only one per cent), increased 4 per cent a year, but a per capita income of $200–299 made Costa Rica more prosperous than the four republics that lay between it and Mexico. After a civil war in 1949, a new republican government came to power which improved the financial condition of the country and encouraged private enterprise and foreign investment. Free primary education reduced illiteracy to a low figure. By 1965 Costa Rica had the highest living standard in Central America, justifying its name of "the rich coast." As early as 1960, Guatemala, Nicaragua, El Salvador and Honduras planned to form a Central American Common Market, with equalized tariffs and a central bank. These plans were brought closer by the San Salvador Charter, signed in 1962.

Panama, unlike Costa Rica, had a diverse population. Two-thirds were of white and Indian or white and Negro descent, one-eighth were Negro, one-ninth white, and one-tenth Indian. The total population was 1,210,000 in 1965 and the area (excluding the Canal Zone) was 28,745 square miles. Per capita income ranges between $200 and $299, but the third of the population in and around Panama City is considerably better off than the two-thirds in rural areas. The claim that Panama should exercise sovereignty over the Canal Zone has been resisted by the United States, but the latter raised its annual rental payment to about $2 million in 1956. Dissatisfaction continued among the Panamanians, and rioting occurred in 1964. The United States agreed to consider a further increase in payment; but, at the same time, American engineers explored other routes whereby a sea-level canal might be constructed in Panama, Columbia or Costa Rica.

Of the three independent states of the West Indies, Cuba ranked first in area, population, and per capita income, the Dominican Republic second, and Haiti third. With a population of 7,330,000 in 1965 the Cubans stood next to the Mexicans as the second largest nation of Middle America. The area of Cuba, however, was 44,128 square miles, about one-sixteenth the size of Mexico, which gave it a population density of more than 170 per square mile.

From 1934 to 1958 the strong man of Cuban politics was Fulgencio Batista but his regime collapsed at the opening of 1959. Fidel Castro, leader of a successful revolt, became head of the government amid widespread rejoicing. One serious weakness of the Cuban economy was the over-dependence on sugar which made up four-fifths of Cuban exports. During the grinding season the sugar industry employed half-a-million workers but most of these were laid off from May to December. Castro announced that his government would become proprietor of all the land in Cuba, would compensate owners of large estates, and set up farm cooperatives. The United States government protested and cut down imports of Cuban sugar (on which it had been paying more than the market price). Apprehension that Castro's regime was veering toward communism was borne out when Russia purchased Cuban sugar and supplied arms and petroleum (the main fuel used in Cuba). When American refineries there refused to refine the Russian oil shipments Castro seized more United States property but refrained from attacking the naval base at Guantánamo Bay which was held on lease by United States forces. In 1960 Russia pledged Cuba a hundred million dollars in aid, five times as much as the United States had provided in five years.

After 1960, relations between the United States and Cuba became increasingly tense and Castro looked toward Moscow and Peking for Communist aid. In 1961 the Central Intelligence Agency at Washington supervised the preparations for an invasion of Cuba by anti-Castro forces which had been trained in Florida and Guatemala. An expedition of more than 1,000 fighting men were put ashore at the Bay of Pigs in April, but the invasion proved a complete failure. No widespread uprising occurred; and the invaders were all killed or captured in a few days. Castro thereafter found the Russians more ready to assist him against "American imperialism" and Soviet missiles were promised to Cuba while Soviet engineers prepared sites from which they might be launched. The discovery of these sites and the prompt steps taken by President Kennedy and his advisers to check this threat is described elsewhere (see page 844). Despite continued economic aid from Russia and China, Cuba suffered from low crops, hurricane damage, and lack of industrial development. By 1966 a stream of refugees were seeking admittance to the United States, and Castro allowed many to obtain exit visas from his over-crowded island, where the per capita income averaged about $500 a year.

The Dominican Republic, with a population of 3,452,000 in 1965 and an area 19,332 square miles, has remained, like Cuba, a thickly populated country. Its people are predominantly (over 50 per cent) of mixed Spanish and Negro descent, with some 18 per cent Negro and 30 per cent white completing the total. Sugar, coffee, and cocoa comprise 85 per cent of Dominican exports while metal products, machinery, and fuel oil make up 70 per cent of the imports. The income per capita is less than $200. From 1930 until his assassination in 1961, Rafael Leonidas Trujillo Molina dominated the government. Thereafter, attempts to set up a stable regime proved unsuccessful and civil war broke out in 1965. The United States landed 23,000 marines and army troops to preserve order until an election could be held, and in 1966 the Dominican voters chose Joaquin Balaguer president.

Haiti, with an area of 10,700 square miles and a population of 4,551,000 in 1965 was the most densely populated of the three island republics, with 337 people per square mile. Negroes comprise 95 per cent of the population, mulattoes 5 per cent. The per capita income is less than $100 and the per capita energy consumption equivalent to only 30 kilograms of coal. Seven-eighths of the Haitians were illiterate in 1965. Their economy was too heavily dependent on coffee, which made up 70 per cent of their exports. The prevailing language in Haiti is French. The government of Haiti has rested since 1957 in the hands of Dr. François Duvalier whose rule has been fortified by ruthless police and secret informers. In 1961 Dr. Duvalier was declared president for a second term, and in 1964 president for life.

Puerto Rico, which was liberated from Spanish rule in 1898 at the same time as Cuba, was ceded to the United States, and in 1917 its inhabitants were granted United States citizenship. By 1965 nearly 2 million Puerto Ricans and children of Puerto Ricans were living in the United States. This exodus helped to ease the population pressure in the island, where in 1965, 2.6 million people were crowded into an area of 3423 square miles, a population density of over 700 per square mile. Puerto Rico provides a striking example of the leap in population that modern medical care

A section of the Pan
American Highway in
Chile (UPI).

*Plaza of the Three Powers, part of the government buildings in Brasilia, capital
of Brazil* (Ministerio Das Relacoes Exteriores).

Slum dwellings in Lima, Peru (Wide World Photos).

The University of Mexico library (Wide World Photos).

may precipitate. Before World War II a death rate of 20 per thousand and a birth rate of 40 per thousand meant that births outnumbered deaths two to one. A little over ten years later, in 1950, the death rate had been halved, while the birth rate remained the same, and births outnumbered deaths by four to one. By 1965 the death rate was reported as less than seven, and although the birth rate had declined to 31.2 it outnumbered the death rate by nearly five to one. A majority of the Puerto Rican people descended from Spanish and Negro ancestry, and one-eighth of those over ten years of age were illiterate in 1966. In 1952 Puerto Rico became a free Commonwealth associated with the United States. To improve the economy, Governor Luis Marín Muñoz (1948–1964) launched "Operation Bootstrap." It has had considerable success. By a promise of long-term exemptions from corporate taxes, Puerto Rico has attracted much American industry. The Puerto Rican economy has been freed from the dominance of sugar and has become diversified. Manufacturing now accounts for a larger share of income than agriculture. Tourism, which has grown especially after Cuba was closed to American tourists by the Castro revolution, comes third as a source of income. Per capita income rose to $900 in 1965 — the highest in Middle America.

3. THE ANDEAN REPUBLICS

Colombia, Ecuador, Peru, Bolivia, and Chile all lie on the western, or Pacific, side of South America, between the Isthmus of Panama and Cape Horn. As a group they supported 45 million people in 1966, roughly one-fifth of the total population of Latin America. Of these 45 million, about 35 million were mestizos or Indians and between 8 and 9 million were of European descent. Because the mountain regions proved less suited to African slaves, and these five countries lay farther from the Atlantic, relatively few Negroes were settled there. Negroes comprised one-twentieth of the population in Colombia and Ecuador, and a still smaller and diminishing fraction in Peru, Bolivia, and Chile. The most notable ethnic difference among the five countries lay in their proportion of Europeans. The percentage ranged from 30 per cent in Chile, and 20 per cent in Colombia, to 12 per cent in Peru, and about 10 per cent in Ecuador and Bolivia. The per capita income followed the same order, ranging from over $400 for Chile, to $128 for Bolivia. Energy consumption descended in approximately the same order, from the equivalent of 1025 kilograms per capita in Chile to 161 in Bolivia.

The Andean republics followed the pattern common to most of Latin America: high birth rate, declining death rate, rising population, and low income. The income, furthermore, was often very unequally distributed, agricultural workers receiving the lowest wages. In Colombia 5 per cent of the population received half the national income, and as coffee made up nearly four-fifths of the exports a general decline in world coffee prices in the 1950's had serious effects there. In Ecuador during the same decade a moderate rise in income was almost entirely offset by the rise in population. In Peru one-sixth of the population, in the Lima Department, produced two-fifths of the national income, and per capita income in that mining Department was three times the average for Peru as a whole. Although Peruvian wages rose in the 1950's the cost of living rose almost as fast. The Bolivians, with the lowest income of the five countries, failed to improve their economic status and the increase of population in the 1950's actually *reduced* the per capita income. Chile, the most advanced of the five countries, suffered a sharp inflation in the 1950's and 1960's. Although wages were increased to meet the rising cost of living, investment lagged and production declined. Copper and potash, which constituted two-thirds of Chilean exports, fell off; copper failed to regain its World War II peak of half a million tons and potash production declined by one-fourth in the 1950's. Like Bolivia, where sales of the main export, tin, fell sharply in the 1950's, Chile with its dependence on copper suffered the penalties to which a "one-commodity" country was exposed.

It was significant — and ominous — that none of these countries made any rapid or noteworthy gains in the postwar period except for their increase in population. This last, it is true, rose remarkably. Between 1939 and 1966 it more than doubled from a collective total of about 18 million to 45 million. High birth rates, which ranged from 46 per thousand in Ecuador to 33 in Chile, combined with declining death rates to produce this notable rise in numbers. But a population increase was not necessarily a blessing if production and income failed to rise fast enough to improve the standard of living at the same time. The discontent produced by low wages and inflation led to disorders and political coups in the postwar period, and communist agitation remained a constant threat to orderly government.

4. ARGENTINA, URUGUAY, AND VENEZUELA

The Argentine Republic, with an area of 1,072,700 square miles and a population of 22,044,000 in 1965, was the second largest Latin American country in size and third in population. Argentines differed from other Latin American peoples (except the Uruguayans) in being overwhelmingly of European descent, mainly Spanish and Italian. Indian and other non-Caucasian races accounted for only 3 per cent of the population. Buenos Aires, the capital, with over 2.9 million people, was one of the largest cities of Latin America. Steady improvements in health regulations and free medical clinics reduced the death rate to a figure announced as 8 per thousand and the infant mortality rate to 61. The birth rate, 23 per thousand, was moderate by Latin American standards, but together with immigration it assured a population growth of nearly 2 per cent a year.

Meat, wheat, hides, wool, and other animal agricultural products made up nine-tenth of Argentinian exports, while the largest import item was petroleum. During World War II and the early years of the postwar period foreign demands brought prosperity to Argentina. Per capita income reached a peak in 1948, but it then started to decline and averaged only $316 in 1962. Industries, stimulated during the war when Argentina could not obtain manufactures easily from abroad, filled many home demands but did not compete successfully in foreign markets.

The political history of Argentina proved turbulent during the war and postwar years. A group sympathetic to Germany and Italy seized power in 1943, and in 1946 Colonel Juan Domingo Perón became president. Perón enjoyed the support of the army and the labor unions but his policies undermined the economy. He was overthrown in 1955. After two civilian presidents, who were likewise overthrown, Argentina returned to military rule in 1966.

The smaller neighboring republic of Uruguay, like Argentina, had an economy almost wholly dependent on crops and herds. Its area, 72,172 square miles, and population, estimated at nearly 3 million in 1965, gave it a density of 40 per square mile. Nine-tenths of the people were of European birth or descent, and only 8 per cent were illiterate. Despite the fact that their republic was the smallest in South America, the Uruguayans maintained their independence between their two great neighbors, Brazil and Argentina. The realization that internal feuds might provide an excuse for intervention helped them to avoid disorders and develop their government along liberal constitutional lines in the twentieth century. The decline in food prices kept the per capita income between $300 and $400 in the 1960's. An extensive program of social welfare — health aid, maternity care, sickness, old age, and unemployment insurance — helped to reduce the death rate, reputedly to 8 per thousand, and the infant mortality rate from over 100 to 47, but these figures were not official. The announced birth rate of 20 per thousand was the lowest in Latin America.

In 1958 the Uruguayan electors ended the rule of the Colorado Party, which had controlled the government for nearly a century, and installed the Blanco Party. The motive for the change was apparently a growing dissatisfaction with the costs of the "welfare state." Taxation had come to absorb one-sixth of the average citizen's income. Although defense expenditures, necessary because of the vulnerability of the country, constituted the largest single item of the budget, education, health, and welfare combined had come to absorb a larger share of the revenue and the national debt had risen sharply. After experimenting with Swiss-style executive council and a rotating president, Uruguay returned to the presidential government in 1966.

Venezuela differed from other Latin American republics in its depend-ence on oil production, petroleum forming 92 per cent of its exports. Rich iron reserves, developed in the 1950's, added to the wealth of the country, and per capita income rose to $700 by 1965. This figure, the highest for any Latin American republic, should have made the Venezuelans a satis-fied nation, but the national income was largely concentrated in the hands of a small minority. Furthermore, a very high birth rate of 45 per thou-sand, and a death rate reputedly reduced to between 10 and 15 per thou-sand gave Venezuela a population growth of 3 per cent annually. Al-though the country had an area of 352,150 square miles, half of it was unoccupied and largely unexplored, and only 2 or 3 per cent of it was cultivated. The rapidly growing population, which reached 8,772,000 in 1966, could not find sufficient gainful employment. Before the oil de-velopment, Venezuela had been the world's second largest producer of coffee, but after World War II coffee exports declined in importance and in quantity. This economic dislocation helped to cause political disorders.

From 1945 to 1948 a liberal reform party held power under Romulo Betancourt. Then an army revolt installed Marcos Pérez Jiménez as dictator, and the conservative oligarchy regained control. Jiménez be-came intensely unpopular, and the belief that the United States approved and supported his repressive rule became stronger when Jiménez was driven out in 1958 and sought refuge in the United States. The anger of the Venezuelan populace led to scenes of violence when Vice President Nixon visited Caracas in May, 1958. His car was stoned and his life en-dangered. On his return to Washington he insisted that it was a mistake to blame the incident wholly on communist agitators. Many Latin Ameri-cans, he warned, thought the United States preferred to support a "gov-erning elite" or a dictator and that its policies were helping to "make the rich richer and the poor poorer." At the close of 1958 the Venezuelans restored Betancourt to power after a ten year interval and the new presi-dent announced a program of democratic reforms. These he endeavored to promote, despite attempted political and military coups. When his term expired in 1964, Dr. Raúl Leoni was elected for a five-year period.

5. BRAZIL AND PARAGUAY

The United States of Brazil had a troubled history in the postwar period. Getulio Vargas, president from 1934 to 1945, resigned under pressure in 1945 and a new constitution was adopted in 1946. It pro-vided for a Senate elected for eight years, a Chamber of Deputies elected for four years, and a president elected for five years who could not suc-ceed himself. Illiterates (over half the adult population) were denied a vote. In 1951 Getulio Vargas was chosen president but committed sui-cide in 1954 when his term neared its end. Of his successors one resigned and one was deposed, both in 1955. Juscelino Kubitschek, elected in 1956, pressed forward a project to construct a new federal capital, Brazilia, in the central Brazilian highlands. Brazilia was constructed on an impressive plan with imposing modernistic buildings but the expenditure overstrained the resources of the government. When Janio Quadros became president in 1961 Brazilian finances and the Brazilian economy were in a precarious condition. He resigned after a few months, and the Vice President, João Goulart, succeeded. Goulart lasted until 1964, when he was deposed and Marshal Castelo Branco assumed the presidential office. Branco altered the constitution to permit presidents to be elected by Congress rather than by popular vote. Under the new electoral law, Congress elected another soldier, Marshal Costa e Silva, in 1966.

Within its great area of 3,286,170 square miles Brazil possessed exceptional natural resources, some of them unexplored and most of them almost unexploited. Its population of 80 million (1965) increased 2.5 million a year but per capita income lagged at between $100 and $200 a year. A high birth rate (uncertain, but probably between 40 and 50 per thousand) and declining death rate (between 15 and 20) made possible a population growth of 2 to 3 per cent annually. Sufficient capital, wisely invested in schools, roads, machinery, factories, power plants, and sanitation could have made Brazil a major power if at the same time the Brazilians could achieve stable and efficient government.

Political instability resulted in part from economic confusion. Under President Kubitschek (1956–1961) the government stressed the need to protect agriculture, to promote power and transport facilities, and to encourage education. The plan proved overambitious and was mismanaged. By 1959 an adverse foreign trade balance, and mounting budget deficits that equaled $200 million a year, involved the government in the hazardous expedient of issuing extra currency to the amount of $180 million. A consequent rise in prices intensified the economic strain. The United States provided Brazil with over half-a-billion dollars in foreign aid between 1955 and 1960; but this did not deter the Brazilian government from concluding a hundred million dollar trade agreement with the Soviet Union in 1959 to exchange coffee for petroleum. All the Latin American nations resented their economic dependence on the United States, which absorbed a major share of their exports and could, by reducing prices or restricting its purchases, bring pressure to bear on regimes that earned its disfavor. The Alliance for Progress concept which President Kennedy promoted was designed to soften this resentment.

The small inland republic of Paraguay, with 157,047 square miles of territory, and a population of 2 million in 1966, endured nine changes in the presidency between 1939 and 1954. Most of the shifts resulted from military coups, violent and irregular; and General Alfredo Stroessner, who seized power with the aid of his cavalry in 1954, retained it grimly by terrorist methods. Half-a-million Paraguayans, more than one-fourth of

the population, were exiled or fled the country. Nevertheless, General
Stroessner was re-elected in 1958 and 1963.

The Paraguayan economy was dominated by farming and sheep-raising
and wool constituted over half the exports. Paraguay long suffered from
inflation. Under Stroessner's dictatorship loans to Paraguay, largely United
States funds, helped to stem the inflation and stabilize the currency. But
per capita income remained low, probably under $200 although no defi-
nite estimates were available. Energy consumption likewise remained
low. But the birth rate was high (40 to 50 per thousand) and the ratio
of increase averaged 2 to 3 per cent a year. The great majority of the
Paraguayans were of mixed Spanish and Indian descent and one-third
were still illiterate in 1960.

6. INTER-AMERICAN RELATIONS

The course of Latin American politics during the 1950's indicated a
widespread reaction against the conventional type of military dictatorship
long prevalent there. By 1960 the two most notable cases were the ruthless regimes of Stroessner in Paraguay and Trujillo in the Dominican
Republic. But the distinction between a dictator and a truly representative and popularly elected president was often far from clear because all
established governments claimed to be legal and constitutional and made
at least a pretense of consulting the electors from time to time. The
United States, which supported an insurrection that overthrew a pro-
communist regime in Guatemala in 1954, and helped to organize an unsuccessful invasion of Cuba by anti-Castro forces in 1961, refused aid to
insurgents who plotted against Stroessner or Trujillo. These dictators,
both of whom had outlawed the Communist party in their domains, enjoyed the recognition of the State Department at Washington. In 1958
John Foster Dulles explained that the government of the United States
preferred regimes that rested on the consent of the governed, "where the
governed are educated people able to carry the responsibilities of self-
government." His statement did not dispel the impression that the United
States policy was to support any government that was firmly anti-communist, regardless of its other qualifications.

In four years, from 1962 to 1966, the United States spent $600 million
constructing homes, providing educational materials, and improving the
land. These projects, under the authority of the Alliance for Progress, were
only the first steps in a long march against Latin American poverty and
economic instability. Nevertheless, the Alliance seemed to have inspired
each country to massive lifting by its own bootstraps. Since 1961, 1 million children have been provided with new classrooms and 10 million
textbooks were made available. Illiteracy, the most difficult fight of
all, has declined from 50 per cent to 43 per cent, whereas in the under-

developed regions of Asia and Africa, it actually has increased. Since 1955 the number of universities has grown from 160 to 196, and student enrollment is increasing at the rate of 6 per cent a year. Tax collections were 10 per cent higher in 1964 than in the financial year 1961. By 1965 there were 250,000 depositors in savings and loan associations.

The main difficulty has been changing stone into bread. Agriculture remains the chief problem of all Latin American countries and one that threatens to become more severe. In 1965 sugar was at a fourteen year low, coffee prices were down, and South America's share of world trade dropped from 11 per cent in 1955 to 6 per cent in 1965.

The desperate need for faster rural development is only beginning to be recognized. Farms and farmers seem to be resisting the trend toward mechanization. The result is a great lag in crop yields which threatens to put Latin America at an even greater disadvantage on the world market. The advances and the needs, then, are often at odds. New classrooms are not needed so much as more teachers. Universities do not affect nearly so many people as agricultural training centers which are, perhaps, more urgently needed. Efficient tax collection systems only burden the peasant with more financial woes. These problems affect every Latin American country to a greater or lesser degree; collectively and individually they demand solutions imperatively, and time is running short.

Section X: THE COMMUNIST STATES IN

THE AFTERMATH OF THE WAR

60

THE UNION OF SOVIET SOCIALIST REPUBLICS

It will probably take us another five years after completing the Seven-Year Plan (1959–1965) to catch up with and surpass the United States in per capita industrial output. By this time, or probably earlier, the Soviet Union will have advanced to first place in the world both in total volume of industrial output and in per capita production.

NIKITA KHRUSHCHEV, REPORT ON THE SEVEN-YEAR PLAN TO THE TWENTY-FIRST CONGRESS OF THE SOVIET COMMUNIST PARTY, JANUARY 27, 1959

1. DEMOBILIZATION AND RECONSTRUCTION

THE PROBLEMS WHICH Russia faced on the morrow of victory were formidable. In all of western Russia, portions of central Russia, the Ukraine, and the north Caucasus region as far as Stalingrad on the Volga hardly a hamlet had been left unscathed by the war. This area — about equal to the United States east of the Mississippi — was before the war the most populous, and industrially and agriculturally the most developed, one in Russia. According to official Soviet figures, 1700 towns, 70,000 villages, 84,000 schools, 40,000 miles of railroad track, and 800 bridges had been destroyed, and some 25 million people were homeless. Despite great efforts to save basic industries from the advancing Germans by removing them to safe regions in eastern or Asian Russia, production in key industries had greatly declined. In 1940 on the eve of the German invasion, production of steel was 18.3 million (metric) tons; of coal 160 million tons; of oil 31 million tons; and of electric power 11,300,000 kilowatts. By 1945 production of steel had declined to 11,200,000 tons; coal to 149 million tons; oil to 19.5 million tons; and electric power to 10.7 million kilowatts.

The Soviet government tackled the problems of reconstruction energetically. On March 15, 1946, it announced the Fourth Five-Year Plan (1946–1950), the purpose of which was not only to repair war damages but to expand Soviet production beyond prewar levels. To provide the necessary manpower for reconstruction the government decreed as early as June, 1945, while the war with Japan was still going on, the demobilization of 7 million men from the armed services, and followed this up by

733

releasing a further 4 million men in March, 1946. The Soviet veterans had no great difficulty in finding work in the civilian economy, for the demand for labor far exceeded its supply.

The financing of the Fourth Five-Year Plan presented greater difficulties. Russia, largely because of her own policies, could obtain little foreign aid. UNRRA, by the end of June, 1947, when its operations ended, had provided Russia $248 million worth of goods; but this aid, while helpful, fell far short of Soviet needs. The Soviet government counted heavily on reparations to aid Soviet reconstruction. At the Yalta conference the Soviet government demanded that Germany pay $10 billion worth of goods and services as reparations, and in the Paris peace treaties of 1947 it exacted from Germany's former allies a promise to pay $900 million worth of goods and services as reparations. The other East European countries were laid under equally heavy tribute. However, Germany and the East European countries had been ravaged by the war and were themselves in desperate need of outside assistance. Because of disagreements with the Western Allies Russia never collected much from West Germany, and the ruthless Soviet efforts to collect reparations or tribute from East Germany and the East European countries caused such restlessness that after the Soviet-Yugoslav break in 1948 they were gradually abandoned as politically inexpedient.

The only other source of foreign aid for Russia could have been the United States, but largely because of her own policies Russia, alone among the Allies, did not benefit from American postwar generosity. In 1945 Russia applied to the United States for a loan of $6 billion, but because of the growing tensions between the two countries over the sovietization of Eastern Europe and Soviet activities in the Near, Middle, and Far East, the negotiations came to nothing. And the Soviet government itself declined the benefits of the Marshall Plan in 1947. Soviet postwar reconstruction was therefore largely carried out by their own means. This meant more years of back-breaking labor and self-denial for the Soviet people after four years of privations during the war. In 1946 a drought and a disastrous crop failure further compounded their difficulties. Starvation was evaded by rigid rationing of food, but the rations were as lean as during the war.

In spite of many privations, however, the Soviet people showed, as many times in the past, an amazing recuperative power and vitality. They not only recovered from the war in a surprisingly short time but astounded the world by forging ahead to develop their country into a great industrial power.

2. ECONOMIC PLANNING AND EXPANSION

On February 9, 1946, on the eve of elections for the Supreme Soviet (the Soviet parliament), Stalin reviewed in an "electoral" speech the past policies of the Soviet government and took a look at the future. The outbreak of World War II, he said, was "an inevitable result" of "modern monopoly capitalism." Other conflicts bred by capitalism could be expected. The Soviet government therefore planned "a new mighty upsurge in the national economy" to guarantee the Soviet homeland "against all possible accidents." He envisioned that Soviet industry would have to produce annually up to 50 million tons of pig iron, 60 million tons of steel, 500 million tons of coal, and 60 million tons of oil. He estimated that it would take three or more five-year plans to accomplish these goals; that is, they could at best be achieved by 1960. "But," he said, "it can be done and we must do it."

At the time, Soviet citizens regarded these plans rather glumly, for they opened the prospect of fifteen years of unrewarding toil and privation. Foreign observers tended to regard the plans as overly ambitious. Yet by 1960, it appears, they were substantially attained. In 1959, according to the latest available Soviet figures, production of pig iron was 43 million tons, which fell short of the goal set. But production of steel (59 million tons) reached approximately the level set for 1960; coal (506 million tons) surpassed it; and oil (129 million tons) exceeded it by more than 100 per cent. Soviet figures further indicated that the pace of production had been greatly accelerated. According to the Soviet Central Statistical Board, the increase of over-all production in 1959 was 11 per cent over that of 1958 instead of the planned increase of 7.7 per cent. In some areas the sharp increase in production created problems. Thus Russia produced much more oil than she normally consumed, since there were few automobiles in the country and oil was not much used for heating. To dispose of the surplus Russia began to export oil and give serious competition to western oil companies.

On January 1, 1959, before the completion of the sixth Five-Year Plan, the Soviet government announced the adoption of the first Seven-Year Plan (1959–1965). In presenting the Seven-Year Plan to the Twenty-first Congress of the Communist party, Khrushchev confidently predicted that by about 1970 the Soviet Union would advance "to the first place in the world both in total volume of industrial output and in per capita production." In 1965 when the Seven-Year Plan ended and it was possible to analyze its results, it appeared that it had fallen somewhat short of its goals. Production of heavy industrial goods had risen 96 per cent above the 1958 level. The production of light consumer goods, however, had risen only 60 per cent above the 1958 level.

After its spectacular growth in the 1950's, the Soviet gross national product slowed down to an average annual growth of 9.1 per cent from 1959 to 1965. In February, 1966, when presenting a new Five-Year Plan for the years 1966–1970, Prime Minister Alexei Kosygin was less boastful than his predecessor. He expected that by 1970 the Soviet national income would rise 85 per cent above the 1960 level — only half of Khrushchev's goal. The new plan forecast that by 1970 the annual electric power capacity would rise to 840 billion kilowatts (Khrushchev had predicted 950 billion kilowatts), steel production to 124 million metric tons (Khrushchev: 145 million), and oil production to 355 million metric tons (Khrushchev: 380 million).

In the 1950's basic consumer goods — such as clothing, shoes, and household goods — became relatively abundant, although their quality often remained shoddy and their prices high. In the 1960's something like a buyers' resistance to shoddy goods developed. Hats, shoes, clothes, and other consumer goods stopped moving off the shelves of Soviet stores. This astonished the Soviet authorities, because for thirty years such had been the hunger of the Soviet public for all kinds of consumer goods that no matter how poor the article, everything had sold. In 1964, to cope with the new situation, the Soviet government allowed certain consumer goods industries to apply the ideas of the Soviet economist Yevsei Liberman. Liberman had urged that, instead of setting rigid production quotas for consumer goods industries, these industries should be allowed to gear their production to the market demand and also that they be allowed to keep part of the profits as an incentive.

The darkest spot in the Soviet economy remained agriculture. In spite of the much-touted collectivization and mechanization of agriculture in the 1930's, it remained primitive and inefficient. On the eve of World War II agricultural production was actually smaller than in 1928, when collectivization began. In the immediate postwar years the government gave little attention to improvement of agriculture, and it was only after the death of Stalin and the rise of Khrushchev to power that it sought seriously to improve farming. Even before his rise to power Khrushchev was associated with various schemes to reform agriculture. In 1950 he proposed the amalgamation of small kolkhozes into larger and more efficient ones. At the same time, the slovenly, tradition-bound villages were to be replaced with "agrarian towns" (agrogoroda). The amalgamation was carried out, but nothing came of the grandiose scheme for agrarian towns. In 1954 Khrushchev announced a grand scheme to increase acreage by plowing and cultivating 90 million acres of "virgin land" in Kazakhstan and southwestern Siberia. A great campaign was launched to induce young "pioneers" to go to the virgin land and develop it into prosperous settled farm country. Later the project had to be largely abandoned because the parched, thinly grassed soil had rapidly eroded; and dust storms, reminiscent of those in the American Mid West in the 1930's, had developed.

In 1958 Khrushchev announced that the state machine and tractor stations, which Soviet propaganda had elevated to a great symbol of socialism and progress, would be abolished and their machinery sold to the kolkhozes. In 1942 Stalin had said that to abolish the stations would be "a step away from communism." The announcement, therefore, caused considerable commotion in Russia and abroad.

Despite considerable attention and increased investment in agriculture, this continued to be the weakest sector of the Soviet economy. In 1963 and 1965 Russia, which once used to export grain, had to import virtually its whole wheat supply from Canada and pay for it in gold. The Five-Year Plan (1966–1970) projected a 4 per cent annual increase in grain production (as against an 8 per cent increase envisaged by Khrushchev) and an annual crop of 170 million tons of grain. Whether this will be achieved remains to be seen.

3. POLITICS: STALIN'S DEATH AND HIS SUCCESSORS

The highest organ of the Soviet Communist party is the party congress. It elects the Central Committee of the party, and the Central Committee in turn selects the Politbureau (Presidium). The last congress of the party held before the war was the Eighteenth Congress, held in 1939. During the war emergency no congress was held. At the conclusion of the war, it was generally expected that the communist leaders would summon a party congress, at which the new course for the country would be announced. It was also generally felt that a period of greater freedom and relaxation would follow. The Soviet people felt — with justice — that they had proved their courage and loyalty to the party and the country during the war and that they deserved a gentler treatment at the hands of the government. Instead, however, the government headed by Stalin offered them only more years of toil and privation. Discipline, somewhat relaxed during the confusion of the war, was generally tightened up, and Stalin continued to rule in a dictatorial fashion. According to subsequent revelations of his associates, in his final years Stalin's paranoia — his illusions of grandeur and morbid suspiciousness — reached psychopathic proportions. No party congress was summoned until October, 1952. In the meantime, the members of the Central Committee and the highest party and government officials were appointed or removed by Stalin's sole decision. The Communist party, within which in the early years of the Soviet Union a certain amount of democracy was practiced, had become a rigidly disciplined organization which carried out orders handed down from above without any discussion. In return for their loyalty and devotion, its members enjoyed many material advantages. The early idealistic Old Bolsheviks were almost all gone as a result of natural death or the purges in the 1930's. New membership was recruited increasingly from the Soviet elite of government officials, army officers, industrial managers, and favored intellectuals and artists. The highest organ of the government, the Supreme Soviet, functioned more regularly but hardly more effectively. It met periodically in brief sessions and approved by acclamation the decrees already promulgated by the government.

When at last, in October, 1952, the Nineteenth Party Congress met, no new departure but only a reorganization of the party machinery was announced. The compact Politbureau consisting of the top Soviet leaders who represented the broad interests of the country — Stalin (the *Vozhd* leader), Beria (police), Voroshilov (army), Kaganovich (industry), Malenkov (party bureaucracy), Molotov (foreign affairs), Mikoyan (trade), Andreyev (agriculture), Khrushchev (Stalin's general trouble shooter), and the alternates Bulganin, Kosygin, and Shvernik — was broadened to include twenty-five members and eleven alternates and re-named "Presidium."

In January, 1953, discovery of a sinister plot by a number of doctors, mostly bearing Jewish names, was announced. Allegedly, the doctors had poisoned Andrey A. Zhdanov, regarded until his death in 1948 as heir apparent to Stalin, and were conspiring to poison a number of high-rank-ing officers of the Soviet Army. The "Doctors' Plot" was followed by a "vigilance" campaign, a vicious witch hunt against "cosmopolites" (i.e., Jews), some minority groups suspected of lack of loyalty to the regime, and supposed traitors and spies. All of this reminded the Soviet citizens of another vigilance campaign following the assassination of Kirov in 1934, which became a prelude to the great purges of the 1930's. Was the present vigilance campaign a prelude to another wave of purges? In this atmo-sphere of tense and fearful expectation the death of Stalin on March 6, 1953, was announced.

Stalin's associates, who were apparently relieved at his death, closed their ranks and chose George M. Malenkov to assume both of Stalin's functions: premier of the government and first secretary of the party. This smooth transfer of power, it soon transpired, had by no means defi-nitely settled the question of succession. Behind the scenes there began a contest for power among Stalin's heirs, which was not unlike the contest for power among Lenin's heirs in 1924 (see pp. 294–5). At first there were several candidates for Stalin's mantle, but they soon narrowed to two: George Malenkov and Nikita Khrushchev. The Trotsky-Stalin contro-versy had been between "world revolution" and "socialism in one country." Malenkov and Khrushchev fought over the priority to be given to light or heavy industry. It was, in a sense, a guns or butter argument. Malenkov urged a higher priority for light industry and consumer goods. Khru-shchev continued to put emphasis on heavy industry and military strength, while blandly claiming that the Soviet standard of living could be im-proved at the same time. Within two weeks of his appointment, Malenkov surrendered the post of first secretary of the party to Nikita Khrushchev, who was then relatively little known abroad. The "Doctors' Plot" was de-nounced as a fabrication and the unfortunate suspects were exonerated. The membership of the party Presidium was again limited to the small number of Stalin's closest associates who had formed the old Politbureau. They loudly proclaimed the principle of "collective leadership," but be-hind the scenes the struggle for the sole possession of Stalin's mantle continued. In June, 1953, Beria was arrested and in December executed, presumably for plotting a coup with the aid of the police, whom he controlled. To insure that no one could abuse this dangerous power, the police were stripped of many of their powers and placed under the control of a committee (KGB). On February 8, 1955, Malenkov, pleading "inexperience," resigned and was appointed deputy premier and minister of electric power stations. His successor as prime minister became Nikolai A. Bulganin. Increasingly, however, Khrushchev made his weight felt in the "collective leadership."

At the Twentieth Party Congress in February, 1956, Khrushchev denounced in his famous "secret" speech the tyranny of Stalin, whom he condemned for encouraging a "cult of personality," that is, a fawning, Byzantine adulation. The speech caused a sensation not only in Russia, where it was read behind closed doors at party meetings, but also abroad, where it had "leaked." In Russia it accelerated the post-Stalinian "thaw" — a great relaxation of controls and tensions, curbing the arbitrary powers of the police, liquidation of the vast penal labor camps, amnesty and rehabilitation (in some instances posthumous) of the victims of Stalin's tyranny, and a new emphasis on "socialist legality." Abroad it caused disarray among communists, who had been taught to adulate Stalin as a demigod. In the Soviet East European satellites the "de-stalinization" caused deep tremors. In Poland almost and in Hungary actually it led to revolution.

The convulsions precipitated in Communist parties by de-stalinization, the Hungarian Revolution, the Soviet intervention to suppress it, the odium this intervention incurred, furnished arguments to Khrushchev's rivals who tried to oust him. According to a "leak" through Poland, Khrushchev was actually voted down in the party Presidium in June, 1957, by a vote of seven to four. But he refused to accept the decision. "In mathematics, two and two are indeed four," he is reported to have said, "but that does not apply to politics." And he proceeded to prove it. By using his prerogative as first secretary of the party, he summoned the Central Committee, which overruled the Presidium. His opponents, Malenkov, Molotov, Kaganovich, and Shepilov, were branded the "antiparty group," demoted to obscure or provincial posts, and later expelled from the party. Significantly, however, they were never arrested and executed as they probably would have been in Stalin's time.

Not much better was the fate of Marshal Zhukov, the popular war hero. He had been demoted by Stalin immediately after the war to the obscure post of commander of the southwestern military district at Odessa. After Stalin's death, he was brought back to prominence, elevated to the party Presidium, and appointed minister of defense. In the crucial party battle in June, 1957, he is reported to have sided with Khrushchev. But when he presumed to curb party interference in the army, he was stripped of his functions and banned again to oblivion in October, 1957. Bulganin, who apparently wavered in his loyalty to Khrushchev during the party fight, was kept on until March 27, 1958, when he resigned and, after several demotions, vanished into oblivion. His place as prime minister was taken by Khrushchev, who like Stalin combined the functions of head of the government and head of the party. With this act he clearly emerged as Stalin's successor, and the "collective leadership" came to an end.

Khrushchev was practically a dictator for seven years, but never a despot in the image of Stalin. The Twenty-first Party Congress (January, 1959), which was devoted mainly to economic affairs, marked the peak of his power. By the Twenty-second Party Congress (October, 1961) however, he was on the defensive. He found it necessary to attack the "antiparty group" again and to invoke the specter of Stalinism. The Congress passed a resolution to remove Stalin's embalmed body from the Lenin-Stalin Mausoleum in the Red Square in Moscow and bury it more modestly in the cemetery of Soviet notables under the Kremlin wall.

Although Soviet political life appeared outwardly placid, underneath, opposition to Khrushchev's rule was gathering. Failures in agriculture, setbacks abroad, and a conflict with Communist China had weakened his position. On October 15, 1964, the world was startled by a communiqué by Tass, the Soviet news agency, which announced that Khrushchev had asked, "in view of his advanced age and deterioration of his health" (he was then seventy years old), to be relieved of his duties as first secretary of the party, member of the party Presidium, and premier of the government, and that his request had been granted. An editorial in *Pravda*, the party organ, on October 17, listed a bill of particulars against him: "Hare-brained scheming, immature conclusions and hasty decisions and actions divorced from reality, bragging and phrasemongering, commandism, (and) unwillingness to take into account the achievements of science and practical experience." The editorial also condemned his "cult of personality" and reaffirmed the "Leninist principle of collective leadership." Although stripped of power, Khrushchev was permitted to retire with dignity.

Khrushchev's ouster had been prepared in complete secrecy by his associates, apparently while he was vacationing in the Crimea. His two functions were divided between two of his former associates, Leonid I. Brezhnev who became first secretary of the party, and Alexei N. Kosygin who became prime minister. Upon acceding to power, they carried out no basic changes in Soviet domestic or foreign policy. Their style, however, differed markedly from that of their predecessor. Unlike the ebullient, extroverted, and much-traveled Khrushchev, Brezhnev and Kosygin remained "faceless" men. They carefully cultivated an anonimity, which was reminiscent of that of Stalin before World War II. The Twenty-third Party Congress (April, 1966), which was the first one held under the duumvirate of Brezhnev and Kosygin, launched no radical departures from Khrushchev's policies. The party Presidium was again named Po-

May Day parade in Moscow (Alan Band Associates).

A frontier settlement in eastern Siberia, 1965 (Wide World).

Khrushchev visits Chinese leaders on the tenth anniversary of China's Communist regime, September, 1959. Left to right: Premier Chou En-lai, President Liu Shao-chi, Chairman Mao Tse-tung, Khrushchev (UPI).

litbureau, and Brezhnev was awarded Stalin's former title of secretary-general of the party. But there was no return to the cult or policies of Stalin.

4. SOCIAL AND CULTURAL CHANGES

The war had brought about no new social and cultural developments in Soviet Russia but rather accelerated the social and cultural tendencies which began to manifest themselves in the 1930's. Vital statistics would seem to be of special importance in a country in which the economy is planned and every phase of life is regulated. It is strange, therefore, that after the war the Soviet government did not have a census taken until January, 1959 — the first time since 1939. The census reported a population of 208,826,000, an increase of 38,226,000 over the population in 1939. Out of this increase about 18 million must be attributed to the annexations of the Baltic states, eastern Poland, Bessarabia, and the acquisitions in the Far East, which increased the area of the Soviet Union to about 8,600,000 square miles. That leaves a net increase for the area of prewar Soviet Russia of only about 20,000,000 over 1939, or 11.8 per cent. This figure revealed how severely the war had depleted Soviet manpower. It was, moreover, young, able-bodied males — the most productive element in any nation — who suffered most. It is estimated that at the end of the war Russia had only about 25 million able-bodied young men between the ages of twenty and forty-five left. The sex ratio already in 1939 was unfavorable to males: 48 per cent male to 52 per cent female. In 1959 it became 45 per cent male to 55 per cent female, which meant that Soviet Russia had an excess of 20 million women over men. This explained the large employment of women in Russia in many professions and trades traditionally reserved to men in western countries. For instance, over 60 per cent of Soviet doctors were women. Women were also employed in heavy manual labor on a wide scale.

The census revealed twelve marriages per 1000 of population per year, more than twenty births per 1000, and a remarkably low 7.5 death per 1000. Natural increase (excess of births over deaths) exceeded 3.5 million per year. The census also revealed an acceleration of the prewar tendency of the rural population to leave the villages, where life is drab, the work hard, and the rewards poor, for the urban centers, where the growing industries provide abundant employment and wages and social services are better. The urban population increased from 60.4 million in 1939 to 99.8 million in 1959, or about 48 per cent of the population. Regionally, the greatest increase in population was registered in Asian Russia, where population rose from about 48 million in 1939 to 63 million in 1959. Many of these people, however, were war refugees who stayed on after the war, or deportees whose residence in Asian Russia was involuntary. By

1965 there was an improvement in the Soviet labor supply. The postwar generation, swollen by the high birth rate immediately after the war, began to reach working age. The western areas of the Soviet Union experienced the almost forgotten phenomenon of unemployment. To alleviate it, the Soviet government encouraged young people to move to Siberia where there was still a labor shortage.

The social differentiation, based in part on a wide wage differential, which began before the war, continued afterwards at an accelerated pace. Although officially the Soviet society continued to be a classless one, in reality there was a clear tendency toward formation of classes along the traditional lines in industrial countries of Europe: a new "bourgeoisie," a working class, and the peasantry. The new bourgeoisie, consisting of industrial managers, government officials, army officers, and favored intellectuals and artists, began to consolidate its position as a new ruling class. Like any social elite, it eagerly sought and showed a pride in status symbols. It also showed a tendency to perpetuate itself. In Russia, perhaps more than in noncommunist countries, university education opens the way to social advancement; and members of the new social elite, like dutiful parents anywhere, go to extreme lengths to provide their children with this advantage. While social mobility continues to be great in Russia, and the expanding economy provides many opportunities for social advancement, complete equality of opportunity does not exist. In principle nothing bars the son of a Siberian tribesman from acquiring a university education and to begin to climb up the social ladder, but in practice his chances of doing so are much smaller than those of a son of a government official in Moscow.

As a part of revitalizing the ideologically moribund Communist party, Khrushchev ordered that its membership should include workers and peasants. After the Hungarian Revolution, during which some of the students at the University of Moscow showed a sympathy for the Hungarian revolutionaries, Khrushchev lectured them on the virtue of manual labor and ordered that university students should be employed in manual work for a time. But the demand of the growing industries for skilled personnel and the desire of the government for social stability largely nullify such fleeting democratizing tendencies. There appears to be a decline of interest in communist ideology among Soviet youth. This does not, however, necessarily mean — as it is often hopefully interpreted in the West — that young Soviet people are losing faith in communism, but only that after fifty years of its existence they take communism so much for granted that they do not feel compelled to profess their faith in it daily, as their fathers had done.

The war had greatly stimulated Soviet patriotism. In the early years of the Soviet regime any distinction between the various nationalities that constitute the Soviet Union was frowned upon. However, since the Great Russian people are the most numerous nationality in the Soviet Union, most readily identify themselves with the Soviet regime, and during the war most loyally defended it, the government has since the war officially recognized their special position in Soviet Russia as "the oldest brother in the family of Soviet peoples." The symbols of Great Russian nationalism have largely become the symbols of Soviet patriotism. On the other hand, the national minorities, although they remain legally equal and retain cultural autonomy, are in many ways treated as second-class citizens. During the war some of them showed a lack of enthusiasm for the struggle and some who came under German occupation openly collaborated with the occupants. For their lack of loyalty, fancied or real, the Crimean Tartars, Kalmyks, Chechen, and Karachai were collectively punished; they were bodily uprooted and dispersed in Siberia and their autonomous republics were abolished. A like fate befell the Volga Germans, except that in their case deportation was preventive rather than punitive; they were deported at the very beginning of the war before they had a chance to show whether they were loyal or not. Since the rise of Israel and especially since the Soviet government began to court the Arabs, the large Russian Jewish community came under a cloud. For their interest in Israel Jews were accused of "cosmopolitanism," and the government not only permitted but encouraged anti-Semitism.

During the war many Soviet citizens had been abroad and were exposed to the "corrupting" influences of alien bourgeois cultures. After the war, to restore the purity of their outlook and faith, the government launched a chauvinist campaign of denunciation of everything foreign and exaltation of everything Russian. In 1946 Zhdanov laid down the law to writers and artists. They were enjoined to adhere strictly to "socialist realism," the stultifying official doctrine which had reduced Russian arts and letters to crass propaganda. A like function among scientists was performed by Trofim D. Lysenko, a talented practical agronomist but no great theoretical scientist. His biological theories, which he foisted on Soviet scientists, were denounced by Western scientists as pure charlatanism.

After the death of Stalin a whiff of fresh air was permitted to penetrate the stale atmosphere of Russian arts and letters. The government permitted cultural exchanges with Western countries, opened Russia to foreign visitors, and permitted carefully selected Soviet citizens to make visits abroad. But the real "thaw" (so named after a 1954 novel by Ilya Ehrenburg) did not set in until after Khrushchev's denunciation of Stalin at the Twentieth Party Congress in 1956. Soviet writers and artists then joyfully cast off the straight jacket of socialist realism and gave vent to their real feelings. Under the guise of anti-Stalinism, they ventured to criticize conditions, not only under Stalin but under Khrushchev as well. A young writer, Vladimir Dudintsev, in a novel *Not by Bread Alone* condemned — in terms guarded by Western standards but bold by Soviet standards of freedom — the inhumanity of Soviet bureaucracy.

In the face of mounting boldness on the part of Soviet writers, the government vacillated in its policy on freedom of expression. Now it pulled in the reins and now it relaxed them again. Its attitude toward the Stalin cult at any given time was an indication also of its attitude toward artistic freedom. After the Hungarian Revolution in 1956, which had been precipitated indirectly by de-Stalinization in Russia and directly by a protest of the Hungarian writers, Khrushchev decided that Stalin had been a "good Marxist" after all, and affirmed that "when it comes to fighting imperialism we are all good Stalinists." In May, 1957, he summoned the leading Soviet writers to his villa and sternly warned them that if they abused the new freedom that they had been given they would be disciplined — by force if necessary. But there was no return to Stalinist terror.

The publication of the novel *Dr. Zhivago* by the distinguished Soviet lyrical poet Boris Pasternak, in 1957 in Italy (and later in all Western countries but never in Russia), caused a sensation. It condemned not only shortcomings in Soviet life but also the very idea of the Russian Revolution. Pasternak was severely condemned in Russia and forced to renounce the Nobel Prize awarded him for his novel, but he was not arrested as he probably would have been under Stalin. The success of Pasternak's novel abroad had deep reverberations in the Soviet world of letters. It broke the sense of complete isolation that Stalin had succeeded in imposing on Soviet writers. They realized now that that outside world had not forgotten them, and that they could appeal to outside opinion against their own government. If they were barred from publication at home, they smuggled manuscripts abroad.

Khrushchev's new attack on Stalin at the Twenty-second Party Congress in 1961 again emboldened the writers. In 1962 Alexander Sholzhenitsyn caused a sensation with a novel, *One Day in the Life of Ivan Denisovich*, in which he described with stark realism his experiences in a Stalin prison camp. The existence of prison camps was well known in Russia, but the novel marked the first time that they were publicly mentioned. By the end of the year Khrushchev felt compelled to pull in the reins again. He attacked Soviet abstract painters for boldly ignoring the canons of socialist realism. In March, 1963, at a meeting of some 500 Soviet writers and artists, he insisted that there must be no "peaceful coexistence between socialist and bourgeois ideologies," even though there might be peaceful coexistence in the relations between communist and noncommunist states. His successors, Brezhnev and Kosygin, pursued the same vacillating course.

5. DEFENSE AND ARMAMENTS

In World War II Russia won a great victory by conventional methods of land warfare. She emerged from the conflict with the largest land army in the world, but her manpower had been severely depleted. This presented the Soviet government with a difficult dilemma. On one hand, it needed all of the available Soviet manpower for the urgent task of reconstruction; on the other, it had to maintain a large army, because the war was not followed by a relaxation of tensions but by the increasingly bitter Cold War with the United States. Under the containment doctrine the United States began to encircle Russia and her allies with a chain of bases and interlocking alliances from Europe to Japan. In 1949 the United States organized the NATO alliance in Western Europe, which (without the United States) could match Russia and its European satellites in manpower. The solution to this dilemma was obviously to discard the traditional Russian reliance on massed infantry assaults and to develop more modern and scientific methods of warfare which would permit reduction of the personnel of the Soviet armed forces while increasing their firepower.

The Soviet government dedicated itself to this task with great energy. By employment of experienced German scientists, by intensive spying on western military developments, and by remarkably original and competent work of Soviet scientists Russia succeeded in breaking the American monopoly in atomic bombs in 1949 and in hydrogen bombs in 1955. At the same time Russia did not neglect older, more conventional arms. The army continued to receive careful attention, and its organization and equipment were constantly improved. A competent strategic air force — an arm which Soviet Russia did not have in World War II — was developed. In March, 1953, the First Lord of the British Admiralty startled the House of Commons and the world by reporting a great increase in Soviet naval construction, placing the Soviet navy in second place in the world, behind the United States Navy but ahead of the Royal Navy. Soviet military scientists, moreover, gave greater attention than their western counterparts to rockets and missiles — weapons developed by the Germans toward the end of World War II. Soviet progress in rockets and missiles, which made both air forces and navies somewhat obsolete, was spectacularly revealed when they placed in orbit the first earth satellite (Sputnik I) on October 4, 1957.

Success in the field of rockets and missiles permitted the Soviet government to cut down substantially its land army and expensive naval construction (except submarines). In 1965 Western authorities estimated that the Soviet armed forces consisted of about 3.3 million men. The Soviet army had about 2.2 million men who were distributed in 150 infantry divisions, 40 artillery divisions, and missiles and specialized units. The Soviet navy had about 750,000 men, who operated 35 cruisers, 180 destroyers, 1000 torpedo boats, patrol boats, minesweepers, and 465 submarines, some of which were nuclear-powered. The Soviet air force had about 800,000 men and some 20,000 operational aircraft. Whether these figures were correct or not, no one in the Western world doubted that the Soviet armed forces represented a powerful weapon.

61

EASTERN EUROPE

Giant of the Revolution, Comrade Stalin, you are the world's hope, the world's dream, the world's ambition.
You are another name for immortality.
Earth is grateful to you, Comrade Stalin; sunshine is grateful, since you have made it rush into the homes of millions once imprisoned in the dark.[1]

POEM READ OVER RADIO PRAGUE ON STALIN'S BIRTHDAY, DECEMBER 21, 1950

1. POSTWAR POLITICAL DEVELOPMENTS

THE SOVIETIZATION OF Eastern Europe after World War II has already been discussed in Chapter 47 as an aspect of Soviet foreign policy. It had, however, important domestic aspects in the East European countries. These varied from country to country, according to local circumstances, but the over-all pattern of communization was much the same in all of them. It is possible to discern in the communization of Eastern Europe definite phases, the length of which varied in individual countries, but the end result of which was the same in all of them.

In the first phase the Communists of Eastern Europe, following apparently a policy determined in Moscow, formed with all non-fascist parties spurious coalition governments. These were variously styled: Fatherland Front, People's Front, National Front, etc. There was only one exception to this rule, namely, Albania. Out of the total chaos into which Albania had fallen during the war, the Albanian Communists emerged as the sole organized party. Under the leadership of Enver Hoxha they formed from the first a frankly communist government, which was recognized by the Allied governments in November, 1945. In all other East European countries, however, noncommunist parties participated at first in power, and in most of them they nominally still do. The degree of their participation varied according to their strength and the strength of the Communists. Generally speaking, the strength of the Communists varied according to the historical attitude of the peoples of Eastern Europe toward Russia. In

[1] Dana Adams Schmidt, *Anatomy of a Satellite* (Boston: Little, Brown, 1952), p. 244.

746

Poland, Rumania, Hungary, and East Germany, all of which had had quarrels with the Russians, the Communists were essentially weak. In Bulgaria, Yugoslavia, and Czechoslovakia, whose peoples were traditionally Russophile, the Communists were much stronger.

In Yugoslavia, Tito, the leader of the Communist wartime resistance, assumed from the first the premiership and tolerated only briefly (until August, 1945) and with very ill grace the noncommunist foreign minister and former premier of the exiled Yugoslav government in London, Ivan Šubašić, who had been imposed on him by the Allied powers. In Bulgaria the strength of the Communists also grew very rapidly. In September, 1946, after a series of troubled ephemeral governments, the veteran Communist, hero of the Reichstag fire trial, and former secretary-general of the Comintern, George Dimitrov, assumed the premiership. In Rumania, the Communists delayed in openly assuming the leadership of the country. In February, 1945, as a result of direct Soviet intervention, the cabinet of General Radescu, who had ventured to defy the Communists, was removed and a Communist fellow traveler, Petru Groza, was installed as prime minister. In Hungary the Soviet occupation authorities committed the imprudence of permitting free elections to be held in November, 1945. The Smallholders' (agrarian) party won a great electoral victory, and its leader, Ferencz Nagy, became prime minister.

In Czechoslovakia the task of the Communists was facilitated by the eagerness of the exiled President Beneš to cooperate with them. A genuine democrat and originally pro-Western statesman, he was so embittered by the part France and Britain had played in the Munich conference that he turned to Russia during the war. In December, 1943, against British advice, he flew to Moscow and concluded a Soviet-Czechoslovak alliance. In 1945, he returned to Prague with the Red Army via Moscow. Zdeněk Fierlinger, an opportunist socialist fellow traveler, became prime minister. In the first parliamentary elections in May, 1946, which were generally conceded to be honest and free, the Communists made a good showing in the western (Czech) provinces but a poor one in the eastern province of Slovakia. Altogether, they won 38 per cent of the vote and emerged as the largest single party. In consequence, Klement Gottwald, the Communist party leader, became prime minister in a coalition government.

The exiled leaders of Poland proved less tractable than the Czechs. In 1943 the Soviet government broke off relations with the exiled Polish government in London, and in 1945 the Red Army imposed on Poland as a temporary government the "Polish Committee of National Liberation," which was composed of communists and fellow travelers. Western powers, however, protested, and after arduous negotiations between the Soviet and Western governments at Yalta and afterward the Committee was broadened in June, 1945, to include some members of the London government. In the new "Government of National Unity" a Moscow-

trained Communist, Boleslaw Bierut, became president; an obscure fellow
traveler, Edward Osóbka-Morawski, prime minister; and the former prime
minister of the London government and leader of the Polish Peasant
Party, Stanislaw Mikolajczyk, deputy premier. But the position of the
Communists long remained precarious in the country.

The advent of the Cold War produced accidentally a new satellite —
East Germany — which followed the general trends in East Europe. In
October, 1949, to counter the formation in the previous August of the
(West) "German Federal Republic" under Western protection, the Soviet
government took steps to form the (East) "German Democratic Republic." Like the East European countries, it had nominally a coalition government, but the leading party in the coalition was the "Social Unity
Party." This had already been formed in 1946 in the Soviet zone in Germany by the forced merger of the Communist and Social Democratic
parties. The new party was clearly Communist-dominated. The president
of East Germany became Wilhelm Pieck, a venerable old Communist
figurehead; the prime minister, Otto Grottewohl, a turncoat socialist; and
deputy premier, Walter Ulbricht, a dour Moscow-trained Communist and
the "Gray Eminence" of the regime. Berlin, in the middle of East Germany, remained divided into East and West Berlin and represented the
whole German problem in miniature.

Whether the Communists formally presided over the East European
governments or not, they always held firmly the levers of command by
entrenching themselves in such key ministries as interior, war, communications, and information, which gave them control over police, armed
forces, means of communication, and propaganda. Behind the scenes
they manipulated all the levers of command. Such positions of power
or influence as were held by noncommunists were subjected to a process
of attrition, imaginatively called "salami tactics" by the veteran Hungarian
Communist Mátyás Rákosi, and sliced away, sliver by sliver.

The task of the Communists was facilitated by the conditions prevailing
in the countries of Eastern Europe. They were morally and materially
exhausted after the war in which Eastern Europe had been a battlefield,
alternately occupied by the Germans and the Russians; their noncommunist leadership was decimated by the Germans or compromised by collaboration with them; with the exception of Czechoslovakia (and that only
the Western, Czech, half), they had no strong democratic traditions; with
the same exception, they were agrarian countries to whom the Soviet
example of power through forced industrialization held a certain appeal;
and they were disappointed with the equivocal Western policies toward
Eastern Europe and fearful lest the Western powers support a revival of
German power. The Communists opportunistically adjusted their policies
to these conditions and cleverly exploited the fears of the peoples of
Eastern Europe. The Communists took the initiative in abolishing the
discredited monarchies where these still existed (in Yugoslavia in 1945,

in Hungary and Bulgaria in 1946, and in Rumania in 1947). They demanded the partition of large estates among the peasants where estates still existed (principally in Hungary, Rumania, and Poland), but did not yet suggest collectivization of agriculture. They pressed for nationalization of heavy industry, which was generally foreign-owned, but not yet of small industry; and they adopted a posture of fervent patriotism, demanding most loudly the expulsion of German and other minorities. Finally, they insisted that the countries of Eastern Europe could trust only to Soviet Russia to protect them against a revival of Germany, supported by the Western powers. These Communist policies, which were not, properly speaking, marxist ones, undoubtedly enjoyed some popular support. Events, however, were to prove that these policies did not represent the ultimate aims of the Communists, but were adopted by them only for tactical reasons — until they gained a safe monopoly of power.

2. COMMUNIST SEIZURE OF POWER

After the completion of the East-West break in 1947, the Communists discarded the democratic facade and frankly claimed a monopoly of power. The policy of national fronts was ostensibly not abandoned. But the noncommunist parties, which the Communists regarded as real or potential fifth columns of Western influence, were effectively destroyed. Their real leaders were either jailed or driven into exile and replaced with Communist tools. To coordinate the moves of European Communist parties the Cominform was founded in September, 1947.

The Communist onslaught against the agrarian parties, their drive for a monopoly of power with which they began, marked the second phase in the communization of Eastern Europe.

In January, 1947, the long-deferred parliamentary elections were held in Poland. Amidst a crude campaign of police terrorism, directed by the dour Moscow-trained secretary-general of the Polish Workers' (Communist) party, Wladyslaw Gomulka, the Communist-dominated coalition rode to victory over Mikolajczyk's Peasant party by gaining about 9 million votes against the latter's 1 million. The cabinet was reconstituted under Joseph Cyrankiewicz, a socialist turncoat. Mikolajczyk was dropped and Gomulka added as deputy premier. The Peasant party was then subjected to such harassment that by September Mikolajczyk fled abroad to save his life and the party disintegrated. In Hungary the campaign was directed by the redoubtable "Muscovite" Mátyás Rákosi. In May, 1947, the premier and leader of the Smallholders' Party, Ferencz Nagy, was driven into exile and replaced with a dependable tool. Rigged elections in August gave the Communists the largest number of seats in parliament. They further consolidated their position by forcing the Social Democrats to merge with them in the United Workers' Party. Hungary

was proclaimed a "people's democracy" under a new, Soviet-styled constitution in August, 1949.

Bulgaria had formally been proclaimed a "People's Republic" in September, 1946, after the expulsion of the king. In 1947 Dimitrov had the
Peasant party leader, Nikola Petkov, arrested. He was tried and, amidst
world-wide protests, executed in September. In Rumania the leaders of
the National Peasant party, Iuliu Maniu and Ion Mihalache, were arrested and sentenced to life terms in November, the king was expelled
in December, and Rumania was formally transformed into a "people's
republic" by adoption of a Soviet-styled constitution in April, 1948. In
Yugoslavia the monarchy was abolished and a "federal people's republic"
proclaimed as early as November, 1945. The largest prewar agrarian
party, the Croat Peasant party, was not permitted to reconstitute itself in
1945 because of alleged treason during the war. But there remained the
Serb Peasant party. Its leader, Dragoljub Jovanović, was arrested and
sentenced to a long prison term in October, 1947.

In Czechoslovakia the Agrarian party, which was the largest party
before the war, was not permitted to reconstitute itself in 1945 because
of alleged treason on the part of some of its leaders. Instead, the Communists, led by Klement Gottwald, attacked the largest postwar non-
communist party, the Slovak Democratic party, which in the elections
of May, 1946, had won 61.43 per cent of the vote in Slovakia. The Czechs'
turn came next.

A protracted crisis broke out in November, which culminated on February 21, 1948, when all noncommunist ministers (except the Social Democrats, swayed by the turncoat Fierlinger) resigned from the cabinet in
Prague in protest against the packing of the police forces with Communists by the Communist minister of interior. Gottwald then demanded
that President Beneš replace the resigned ministers with fellow travelers
from a list made up by the Communists. For the eventuality that Beneš
might refuse and violence might break out, the Communists assembled in
Prague large police forces and workers' militias. Once again, as during
the Munich crisis ten years before, the fate of the Czechoslovak democracy was in the hands of Beneš. And once again, after a brief and feeble
show of defiance, Beneš yielded to the threat of force. On February 25 he
appointed the Communist-picked ministers. The vaunted "Masaryk's
democracy" expired without a shot being fired. The "Prague coup" was a
bloodless one; in characteristically Czech fashion all constitutional nice-
ties had been observed. The extent of their tragedy was brought home to
the Czech people when Jan Masaryk, foreign minister and son of the liberator and first president of Czechoslovakia, committed suicide on
March 10. Beneš resigned in May rather than sign the new constitution
formally transforming Czechoslovakia into a "people's democracy," and
died in September.

With the Communist victory in Czechoslovakia, their struggle for a political monopoly in Eastern Europe had come to a successful conclusion. But the Communists demand a total and undivided loyalty of the populations which they rule, and this they had not yet attained. The churches still could command some loyalty of the peoples of East Europe, and from 1945 on, but especially after 1947, the Communists attacked them. The Orthodox churches, to which the Bulgars, the Serbs, and most Rumanians adhered, as well as the small minority Protestant churches (Calvinist in Hungary, Lutheran in Slovakia, and Czech Brethren in Bohemia and Moravia), were not regarded by the Communists as too dangerous because they had traditionally recognized the supremacy of state over church. The Moslems of Albania and Bosnia also did not present too much of a problem. The Communist attack centered on the Roman Catholic Church and its Eastern branch — the Greek Catholic or Uniat Church (which preserved the Eastern rite but recognized the supremacy of the Pope). The Catholic Church was a well-disciplined, universal organization with headquarters in a Western country. It had never admitted the principle of supremacy of state over church and passionately opposed dialectical materialism (the Communist philosophic system) on religious grounds (it is atheist). The first to feel the ire of the Communists was the Greek Catholic Church, the strongholds of which were eastern Poland, Ruthenia, and Transylvania. Eastern Poland and Ruthenia were annexed by Russia in 1945 and the Uniats forced to rejoin at once the Greek Orthodox Church of Russia. Similar was the fate of the Rumanian Uniats in Transylvania, who were forced to join the Greek Orthodox Church of Rumania in 1945.

The Communist attack on the Roman Catholic Church, which was dominant in Poland, Czechoslovakia, Hungary, and the Croat half of Yugoslavia, came a little later. Their task was facilitated by the fact that the Roman Catholic clergy had identified themselves with the prewar non-democratic regimes in Poland and Hungary and the wartime quisling regimes in Slovakia and Croatia. In 1946 Archbishop (and later Cardinal) Aloisije Stepinac of Zagreb was tried for collaboration and sentenced to a long prison term (in 1951, three years after the Tito-Cominform break, he was released but until his death in 1960 not permitted to resume his functions). In 1948 the Primate of Hungary, Cardinal Archbishop Mindszenty, was arrested, tried, and sentenced for life (in 1956 during the Hungarian Revolution he escaped from prison and found refuge in the American Embassy in Budapest, where he continues to live). The Primate of Poland, Archbishop (later Cardinal) Wyszynski, was never arrested and formally tried but was kept in virtual internment until 1956. Archbishop (later Cardinal) Beran of Prague was protected by his wartime record (he had been an inmate of Nazi concentration camps) and the fact that the Czech Catholics (unlike the Slovak Catholics) are somewhat suspect to Rome of Hussitism and are consequently more acceptable to the Communists. But when Archbishop Beren vigorously resisted Communist efforts to induce the Czech Catholics to break with Rome and establish a national Czech Catholic Church, he too came under a cloud. In 1949 he was arrested and interned in a monastery until 1903. At the same time, martyrs among lesser clergy in all of Eastern Europe were legion. Church schools, organizations, and property were taken over by the state.

3. ECONOMIC PLANNING AND PURGES

Moscow had laid down as an immutable dogma for non-Soviet Communist parties that there was only "one road to socialism," namely, the road covered by the Soviet Communist party. This meant that the East European countries would have to imitate the Soviet plans for industrialization and collectivization of agriculture. There was much to be said for industrialization and reorganization of agriculture in Eastern Europe, for, with the exception of the western (Czech) provinces of Czechoslovakia, East European countries were underdeveloped agrarian countries, suffering from rural overpopulation. Their economies would benefit by a better balance between industry and agriculture. However, whether the Soviet example of industrialization was the best one for them to follow may be doubted. Soviet Russia is a large country with virtually unlimited resources. The East European countries are relatively small countries with limited resources. Similarly, there was a good case for reorganizing agriculture from extensive to intensive farming, but whether collectivization was the best way to do it is doubtful.

It may be also doubted whether the time was opportune for the effort. None of the satellites had yet recovered from the effects of the war. Under Soviet pressure they rejected Marshall Plan aid in 1947. In January, 1949, a "Council for Mutual Economic Assistance" (CEMA, COME-CON) was organized in Moscow, as a Soviet counterpart to the American-sponsored European Recovery Program. But at the time Russia was in no position to make up to the East European countries the loss of possible American economic aid and technical assistance. On the contrary, she depended to a large extent on looting the satellite economies to provide for her own postwar reconstruction. This was done by a variety of techniques, the most common of which was to set up joint Soviet-satellite companies in which Russia put up as assets the confiscated former "German" properties in Eastern Europe while the East European countries had to put up their own assets. Another was to calculate Soviet exports to the satellite countries on the basis of world prices in dollars, whereas satellite exports to Russia were calculated on a basis that was arbitrary but invariably advantageous to Russia.

Nevertheless, in 1947–1950, all satellite countries prepared Soviet-style plans for industrialization and collectivization of agriculture. Yugoslavia eagerly led the way with the most ambitious plan. As in Russia, a heavy emphasis was placed on developing basic heavy industries while light consumer industries were neglected. As in Russia, the drive was eventually to result in strengthening of the satellite economies, but initially it called for much unrewarding toil and misery. The plans were enforced in a rigid, dogmatic spirit with little regard for local conditions and needs. This caused much restlessness. Even Communists were not spared tensions and doubts as they saw the interests of their countries systematically subordinated to those of Soviet Russia. Yet any sort of remonstrance, even the most mild and loyal, was treated by Soviet representatives as inadmissible criticism of Russia, ingratitude, and even treason to the cause of communism. In Yugoslavia, which did not owe her liberation to Russia (nor did the Communist leaders owe their elevation to power to Soviet intervention), Soviet interference and domineering attitude led to the Tito-Cominform break in May, 1948. Yugoslavia was then subjected to military threats and a complete political and economic ostracism on the part of her Communist neighbors. When to the great amazement of the Soviet leaders this pressure failed to bring Yugoslavia into line, Moscow was seized with panic lest other satellite countries imitate the Yugoslavs and the Soviet East European empire disintegrate. "Titoism" — often called "national communism" in the West — became the worst heresy in the Moscow book. In 1949 orders went out of Moscow to satellite Communist parties to purge themselves of "Titoists." As a result, several top satellite Communist leaders as well as many lesser fry were purged. In many instances the purged were innocent of "Titoism" but were victims of the nasty infighting among satellite leaders for power. In the personal vendettas which raged among them, Moscow served as arbiter. Moscow-trained Communists generally had an advantage over Communists who had not imbibed at the Moscow fountainheads of communism.

In Albania, Enver Hoxha disposed of his rival, Koci Xoxe, the dreaded minister of interior, who was executed. In Bulgaria, where the Communist leaders were then struggling for the mantle of Dimitrov, who died in Moscow in July, the charge of "Titoism" provided a handy weapon against rivals. The most prominent victim of the purge was Traicho Kostov, a Communist of long standing, a veteran of the Spanish Civil War, who was executed. In Hungary, the principal victim was another veteran of the Spanish Civil War, László Rajk, who was tried secretly and hanged. In Czechoslovakia, Foreign Minister Vlado Clementis, a Slovak Communist who in 1939 had ventured to criticize the Nazi-Soviet Pact and then spent the war in exile in London rather than Moscow, was condemned as a Titoist but temporarily spared. In Poland, Gomulka, who had shown a certain independence of Moscow, was first banned and later imprisoned. In fact, the Soviet leaders appeared to lack confidence in all Poles. In November, 1949, they foisted on Poland a reliable watchdog, Konstantin Rokossovsky, a marshal of the Soviet army of Polish origin with a distinguished war record. Although he had left Poland as a young man and made a career in the Soviet army, he was now made Polish minister of defense, commander in chief of the Polish army, and member of the Polish Communist Politbureau.

The outbreak of the Korean War in 1950 increased international tensions. The East European governments were obliged to increase their armed forces, which their strained economies could ill afford. A vicious "vigilance" campaign against real or imaginary spies and traitors was launched, which reached its hysterical climax in 1951–1953. Police terrorism, arbitrary arrests, secret trials, and executions were the order of the day. The so-called "Doctors' Plot" in Russia (see p. 738) unleashed a wave of antisemitism in the satellite countries. In addition to "Titoism," "cosmopolitanism" (the Communist euphemism for an alien mentality, which was attributed principally to Jews) became a deadly sin. The most prominent victim of this pernicious antisemitic campaign was the Czechoslovak Communist party chief Rudolf Slánský, a Jew, like many satellite Communist leaders. In his public trial he was accused, among other things, of sympathy for Zionism. Illogically, the "Titoist" Clementis, previously spared, was tried along with the "cosmopolitan" Slánský. Both were hanged. In Rumania, the notorious Ana Pauker, daughter of a rabbi, was removed from the foreign ministry and her party functions, but apparently she was not tried.

4. DESTALINIZATION — POLAND AND HUNGARY, 1956

The death of Stalin in 1953 and the struggle of his lieutenants for his succession caused much confusion among the satellite Communist leaders. Stalin had exacted from them a personal, almost feudal, loyalty. Like a feudal overlord, he summoned them to Moscow (unlike his successors, he never condescended to visit the satellite leaders in their fiefs), to invest them in power — or to divest them of it. With Stalin gone and his lieutenants locked in combat over his succession, to which one of the contestants were the satellite leaders to pay homage? The policies of which one of the contestants were they to follow? The shifts in the Kremlin power struggle were followed by shifts in the satellite leadership, and the shifts in Soviet policy were followed by shifts in satellite policy.

The relaxation of controls in Soviet Russia after Stalin's death and Malenkov's policy of more consumer goods was reflected in a series of reforms adopted in the satellite countries in the summer of 1953, which were generally known as the "new course." Police surveillance and censorship were relaxed, a greater emphasis was placed on the production of consumer goods, and collectivization of agriculture was halted. When Malenkov fell from power in January, 1955, there was new confusion until Khrushchev's intentions were ascertained. These were at first far from clear. In the guns or butter argument with Malenkov, Khrushchev preached a complex guns *and* butter course, without specifying how much butter and how many guns. In foreign policy his many initiatives were likewise confusing.

On May 14, 1955, amidst much vituperation against the West for admitting West Germany to NATO (see p. 841), the Soviet government concluded with the East European governments a multilateral pact on "Friendship, Cooperation, and Mutual Aid" at Warsaw. Although billed as a counterpart to the Atlantic Pact, the Warsaw Pact was essentially political in purpose. It provided for a unified command of the satellite armies and the Soviet army units and satellite territory under a Soviet officer and for a Political Consultative Committee. The commander was appointed (the first one was Marshal Ivan Konev), the Political Consultative Committee met from time to time, but — presumably owing to the lack of confidence of the Soviet command in the satellite armies — these were not equipped with atomic weapons and no unified staff, analogous to the NATO staff, was ever created. The Warsaw Pact changed the form but not the substance of the Soviet military control of the satellites.

Shortly after the conclusion of the Warsaw Pact, in June, 1955, Bulganin and Khrushchev set out on a penitent trip to Belgrade to try to bring it back into the Soviet fold. After the Soviet-Yugoslav break in 1948, the development of the Yugoslav society and economy diverged considerably from that of the Soviet satellites. The harshness of the regime was moderated, peasants were permitted to withdraw from collective farms, industry was decentralized and given considerable autonomy under worker-management councils which were authorized to gear production to the demand of the market and retain part of the profits. Foreign trade was reoriented to the West. The standard of living improved. Yugoslavia was reluctant to give up these advantages and changes for the sake of conciliation with Soviet Russia. Although Khrushchev astonished the world by the manner in which he humbled himself in Belgrade, Tito remained wary. He declined to join the Warsaw Pact, reaffirmed Yugoslav neutrality, and continued Yugoslavia's profitable trade relations with the West.

In January, 1956, as another concession to Tito, the Cominform was abolished. In June he was invited to visit Moscow, where he was showered with honors. During his triumphant tour of Russia he elicited from Khrushchev recognition of the principle that "the roads and conditions of socialist development are different in different countries." This principle that there was not one (Soviet) road but many roads to socialism, was fraught with dangers for the unity of the Soviet satellite empire. If there could be a special "Yugoslav road to socialism," why could there not be also a Polish, Hungarian, and so on road to socialism?

Khrushchev's declaration of the principle of "peaceful coexistence" between socialist and capitalist countries and the destruction of the Stalin myth at the Twentieth Congress of the Soviet Communist party in February, 1956, completed the disarray of the satellite leaders. The Stalin cult had been an important element of cohesion in the Soviet satellite empire. Its destruction — presumably necessary for the advancement of Khrushchev in the Kremlin power struggle — had the unexpected effect of destroying Soviet authority over the satellites.

Alexis de Tocqueville, the nineteenth-century French political philosopher, observed that a tyranny is never in greater danger than when it begins to reform itself. As a result of the relaxation of controls in the satellite countries, matters almost got out of hand. In June, 1953, a violent strike broke out in Plzeň (Pilsen), the Czechoslovak industrial center, but the incident remained isolated and was easily suppressed. On June 17, the workers in East Berlin, dissatisfied with working conditions, went on a strike which spread over East Germany and rapidly took on the aspects of a revolt against the regime. The authority of the East German government collapsed and was restored only with the aid of Soviet tanks. But the most momentous events took place in 1956 in Poland and Hungary, where "nationalist" or "Titoist" Communist leaders, previously demoted or banned, sought to return to power in the name of rehabilitation of "victims of Stalinian terror."

In June a violent uprising of workers took place in Poznań. It was suppressed by force, but the Polish Communist leaders were deeply troubled. Their arguments over policies culminated in October at a meeting of the Central Committee of the Polish Workers' (Communist) Party in Warsaw. One faction demanded the restoration of the "Titoist" Wladyslaw Gomulka to the post of secretary-general of the party and the removal of the Soviet watchdog Rokossovsky. This was a challenge to Soviet authority. On October 19, Khrushchev, Mikoyan, Kaganovich, and Molotov, representing the then still existing "collective leadership," flew to Warsaw. A dramatic confrontation between them and the Polish Communists took place. Both sides made military preparations. But the storm blew over, as Gomulka apparently succeeded in convincing the Soviet leaders of his loyalty to Moscow. Restored to power, Gomulka made a number of concessions which won him considerable popularity among the Polish population: the peasants were permitted to withdraw from the collective farms, the persecution of the Catholic Church was halted, and the intellectuals were given an extraordinary freedom of expression for a Communist country.

In the long run, however, these measures proved to be only a series of tactical retreats which probably averted a genuine Polish revolution. Entrenched in power, Gomulka hastened to prove that he was a good Communist and that he was loyal to Moscow. Intellectual freedom was soon curtailed. Relations between the Polish government and the Catholic Church became strained again. In 1966, on the occasion of the thousandth anniversary of the Christianization of Poland, the festivities became a bitter test of strength between the government and the church. Of Gomulka's original program only one point remained: no attempt was made to force the peasants back into the hated collective farms. As seen in retrospect, the Polish revolt of 1956 represented only a victory of one Polish Communist faction (albeit supported in this instance, as a lesser evil, by the Polish population) over another. In Hungary matters took a more radical course. There a genuine (and temporarily successful) revolution of the Hungarian people against their government took place.

In July, 1953, the harsh Mátyás Rákosi relinquished the premiership, but retained the post of party chief. His successor as premier was Imre Nagy, another "Muscovite" but a more moderate one. He launched the "new course" in Hungary, which won him considerable popularity. The fall of Malenkov in 1955 was erroneously interpreted in Hungary as a return to Stalinism. In April Nagy was removed as premier, and Rákosi experienced a brief revival of influence. But his days were numbered, for he was a symbol of Stalinian brutality. When Khrushchev denounced Stalin in 1956, Rákosi's position became untenable. He was removed in July and replaced with another "Muscovite" and Stalinist, Ernö Gerö, which caused much discontent. The news of the events in Poland brought matters to a head. On October 23 students of Budapest staged a demonstration of sympathy for Poland and of hostility to Russia. Their ranks were swelled by workers and citizens. When the hated security police (A.V.O.) fired into the crowd, Budapest rose up in arms. Units of the Hungarian Army went over to the insurgents and the authority of the government in Budapest, and soon also in the countryside, collapsed. On October 24, in a desperate effort to stem the tide, the Communists announced the reappointment of Nagy to the office of prime minister. János Kádár, a victim of imprisonment and torture under Rákosi, replaced Gerö as party chief. Pressed by public opinion, Nagy formed a genuine coalition cabinet and suggested that Hungary should become a neutral country. By October 28, the security police had been disarmed and the small Soviet forces, which aided them, agreed to evacuate Budapest. With the Soviet government apparently. acquiescent, the Hungarian Revolution seemed to have triumphed, and Hungary appeared to be heading the way of Yugoslavia.

On October 30 the Anglo-French invasion of the Suez took place. Whether this determined the Soviet government to intervene in Hungary is not known, but it certainly provided an excuse for Soviet intervention and also diverted world opinion from Hungarian events. On November 4 large Soviet forces suddenly attacked Budapest and after several days of heavy fighting drowned the Hungarian Revolution in blood. The United States was unprepared to act, apart from filing resolutions in the United Nations, although hints of "liberation" of Eastern Europe in American propaganda had encouraged the Hungarians to defiance. Nor did the other Soviet satellites stir to help Hungary, which elicited from Warsaw students the caustic comment that "Hungarians acted like Poles, Poles like Czechs, and Czechs like swine." Kádár, who was a member of the Nagy cabinet, apparently agreed to betray him and form a Soviet-backed cabinet. Nagy found temporary refuge in the Yugoslav Embassy, but upon leaving it — despite a safe-conduct from the Kádár government — was arrested and later (1958) executed. During the confusion of revolution and intervention some 200,000 Hungarians fled the country.

The Soviet government propped up the weak Kádár government by providing considerable aid and credits, which permitted restoration of the shattered Hungarian economy and repairs of the damage suffered in Budapest during the revolution. Apparently on Soviet advice, the Kádár government punished sternly the active participants in the revolution, but sought to conciliate the Hungarian population as a whole. Later Kádár proclaimed the uncommunist principle that "those who are not against us, we take to be for us." On Krushchev's personal advice to pursue "goolash communism," the Hungarian government adopted an economic policy, which sought to raise the living standards of the people as rapidly as possible rather than to build ambitious projects which might bring benefits only much later. As Communist regimes go, the Kádár regime proved to be a moderate one.

5. THE WEAKENING OF SOVIET CONTROLS

Appalled by the unexpected repercussions of destalinization, the Soviet government sought to reverse the course, both in Russia and in the satellite countries. But Soviet authority over the satellites had been damaged beyond repair. Khrushchev would not and could not revive Stalinian methods, for both domestic and foreign reasons.

After the Polish Revolt and the Hungarian Revolution, the pendulum began to swing backward, but it never went all the way. In November, 1957, when the world Communist leaders assembled in Moscow to observe the fortieth anniversary of the Bolshevik Revolution, the ruling Communist parties were presented with a Soviet draft of a declaration, which paid homage to the complete equality of all Communist countries, but significantly said nothing about many roads to socialism. It implied Soviet superiority over the satellites by noting "the victory of socialism in the USSR" but only "progress of socialist construction in the people's democracies." With the exception of the Yugoslav Communists, representatives of all the ruling Communist parties signed the declaration. The Yugoslav refusal to sign the document was followed by a perceptible cooling of Soviet-Yugoslav relations, but it was the Chinese Communists who took upon themselves to cast the first stone against the Yugoslavs. In May, 1958, the Chinese Communist organ, the *People's Daily*, intemperately attacked the Yugoslav Communists for "sinking into bourgeois nationalism" and concluded that the Cominform condemnation of Yugoslavia in 1948 had been "basically correct." The Soviet government followed this attack by one in *Pravda* and cancelled a recent credit agreement with Yugoslavia. The Communist neighbors, especially Albania, which had strenuously opposed Soviet appeasement of Yugoslavia for fear lest it result in Yugoslav tutelage again, eagerly followed suit. The situation in 1958 appeared to have reverted to what it had been in 1948. The Soviet Bloc had weathered the post-Stalinian storm, its unity and discipline had been restored, and Yugoslavia had defected again. However, this was more apparent than real. The Soviet authority over the satellites could not be fully restored because, among other reasons, the Soviet leadership, not only in the satellites but in the whole Communist world, was presently challenged by the Chinese Communists.

Although no outsider realized it at the time, the Chinese attack on the Yugoslav Communists was also meant as oblique criticism of Soviet Communists. It marked the first public shot in the Sino-Soviet dispute. The Sino-Soviet conflict, which unfolded over several years, will be discussed in Chapter 68. Here, suffice it to say that Soviet Russia, faced with a conflict with Communist China, was forced to be cautious and accommodating in its treatment of the East European countries.

Among other steps, the Soviet government found it expedient to appease Yugoslavia again. This, however, alienated Albania. In 1960 Soviet representatives in Albania were implicated in an abortive conspiracy to unseat the staunchly Stalinist and violently anti-Tito government of Enver Hoxha. Thereafter, Soviet-Albanian relations rapidly deteriorated and, after the Twenty-second Party Congress in 1961, were broken off altogether. The Chinese government, however, not only continued its relations with Albania but encouraged and aided it in every possible way. In December, 1962, Tito was once again received with honors in Moscow, while Albanian representatives were welcomed in Peking.

In 1962, which marked a new high point in Soviet-Yugoslav relations, Soviet-Rumanian relations began to deteriorate. The Rumanian party chief, Gheorghe Gheorghiu-Dej, was as dour a Stalinist as Mátyás Rákosi. In 1956 the Rumanian government ruthlessly suppressed the incipient demonstrations of sympathy for the Hungarian Revolution among the large Hungarian minority in Rumania. The Rumanian Communist regime remained rigidly Stalinist. The cause for Rumania's estrangement from Soviet Russia was originally not political but economic. It had to do with the activities of CEMA (COMECON).

In 1957, when the Soviet government found itself in the position of having to aid the ailing Hungarian, Polish, and East German economies, it decided to revive CEMA, after years of inactivity, as a means of distributing the burden to the other East European countries, in the name of East European economic cooperation. There was room for greater economic cooperation among the East European countries, the economics of which were centrally planned and rigidly autarkic. Each was as self-sufficient and self-contained as possible. In 1957 CEMA drew up plans for a "socialist division of labor" among them. East Germany was to specialize in the production of precision machinery and chemicals; Poland in coal mining and transport equipment; Czechoslovakia in heavy machinery; Hungary in aluminum processing and agriculture; Rumania in agriculture and oil production; and Bulgaria in agriculture. This meant that East Germany, Poland, and Czechoslovakia would continue to develop industry, while Hungary, Bulgaria, and Rumania would revert to the position of agricultural countries or, at best, producers of raw materials and fuels. While Hungary and Bulgaria accepted the plans, Rumania rebelled.

Among the East European countries, Rumania is undoubtedly the most richly endowed in natural resources. For centuries, owing to alien and incompetent rule, its natural resources were little developed. However, the Rumanian Communists, at the cost of much toil and sacrifice, had made considerable progress in developing Rumanian industry. It was, therefore, not surprising that they should be reluctant to abandon their achievement and allow Rumania to revert to the position of an underdeveloped agrarian country.

In order to gain the backing of the Rumanian people to defy the Soviet government, the Rumanian government was forced to liberalize the regime. It also appealed to Rumanian nationalism. The hated forced russification of Rumanian culture was abandoned. Rumania again turned to France for cultural influence. Thanks to the support of the country and the long Rumanian experience in evading pressures, the Rumanian government successfully asserted its independence of Soviet Russia. In 1966 Nicolae Ceausescu, the successor of Gheorghiu-Dej as party chief, had the temerity to suggest the disbanding of the Warsaw Pact and Soviet withdrawal from Eastern Europe. The Soviet government did not heed the suggestion, but the mere fact that it had been made and that the Rumanians had not been instantly punished for impertinence, as they might have been in the days of Stalin, indicated how much Soviet influence in Eastern Europe had declined.

It would be, however, an error to discount Soviet influence in Eastern Europe altogether. The Rumanian case was an extreme one. Nevertheless, in the 1960's even the Stalinist governments of Walter Ulbricht in East Germany, of Antonín Novotný in Czechoslovakia, and of Todor Zhivkov in Bulgaria adopted somewhat more liberal policies at home and took a more independent position abroad. In fact, the old distinctions between Titoists and Stalinists became blurred. Nationalism reasserted itself throughout Eastern Europe. While this refuted the old marxian belief that once socialist revolutions took place nationalism would give way to "proletarian internationalism," it did not necessarily indicate the decline of communism in Eastern Europe. On the contrary, communism appeared to have set independent roots in Eastern Europe. The Communist governments of Eastern Europe did not need the support of Soviet Russia to prop them up any more. After twenty years of rule they had the voluntary support — or, at least, the tacit acceptance — of their peoples.

62

CHINA UNDER COMMUNISM

. . . The policy of the state toward capitalist industry and trade is to utilize, to restrict, and to reform them. The state gradually replaces capitalist ownership by ownership by the people.

CONSTITUTION OF THE PEOPLE'S REPUBLIC OF CHINA (1954)

1. THE INTELLECTUAL FRAMEWORK

IT WOULD BE A MISTAKE to assume that the triumph of the Chinese Communists in 1949 was an enslavement of the Chinese people achieved entirely through deceit, force, and ruthlessness. The long course of Chinese history has always been marked by periods of unity and stability divided by intervals of disorder and division. Over and over again, when an existing regime became inefficient and corrupt, it has been assailed by internal and external enemies. Its fall was usually followed by one or more generations of disorder. Then the longing for peace and unity moved the Chinese to support some leader or party that seemed capable of restoring peace. When order was achieved the new dynasty or regime was said to possess "the mandate of heaven" — that is, it proved its right to govern by governing successfully.

With the overthrow of the complacent and inept Manchu dynasty in 1911 China was plunged into nearly forty years of confusion and civil war. The revolutionary party, the Kuomintang, failed to carry through its promised reforms or to pacify and defend the country. From 1931 to 1945 China was invaded by the Japanese, who occupied a large part of it. The defeat and expulsion of the Japanese in 1945 left the Chinese people in a mood to support any government that could assure them a period of quiet and could reorganize their shattered economy. Confronted by a renewal of the civil war between the Kuomintang and the Communists, they allowed the Communists to gain control. The apparent ease with which the Chinese Communists triumphed took both the Americans and the Russians by surprise at the time. In the light of subsequent developments what reasons can be offered to account for it?

762

There are four major points to consider when weighing the success of the Chinese Communist movement. Like most Asian and African peoples in the twentieth century the Chinese were impressed by the triumphs of Western science and technology. Enlightened Chinese recognized that the wealthiest and most powerful nations were those which had become most highly industrialized, which had developed the most powerful machines. China had the territory, the resources, and the population to play the part of a great and independent power. What it lacked was a modernized economy, a coordinated system of factories, railroads, and generators whereby it could produce its own machines, fertilizers to increase the crops, power to link its scattered provinces through adequate transportation and communication. Looking abroad, observant Chinese saw that there were three nations that had pursued such a program in the twentieth century with phenomenal success — the United States, Japan, and Russia. The United States was ready to help; it supplied Chiang Kai-shek with arms and money; but many Chinese feared that the Americans wanted to exploit China, to control it by controlling its Kuomintang government. On the other hand, to take Japan as a model was unthinkable after 1945: one does not imitate a hated and defeated adversary. This left Soviet Russia as a pattern to imitate and Russia seemed an appropriate pattern. Like China it was a large country with vast resources. The Russians had modernized and industrialized their retarded economy at an astounding pace, with little aid or capital from abroad. The Chinese Communists promised that under their leadership China could do the same.

A second point to remember is that the Chinese had no state church and no national religion. Wherever communism spread in Europe and the Americas it found any firmly established religion its most stubborn and resilient opponent. In China, however, there were several faiths — Confucianism, Buddhism, Taoism, Islam, and a small minority of Christians. The Chinese were neither fanatical nor doctrinaire on religious issues; in fact they found some tenets of communism compatible with Confucian ethics. The Chinese Communists did not have to overthrow a single powerful entrenched priesthood that claimed a monoply on spiritual truth.

A third point to consider is that, historically, the Chinese system of government was closer to communism than to modern democracy. The Chinese had never enjoyed the right to vote or to govern themselves through elected representatives. Throughout their long history their successive emperors had been symbols — in theory at least — of benevolent despotism. The people, most of whom were illiterate, had been accustomed to leave the business of government to those who had the will and capacity to govern. They judged their rulers realistically and pragmatically; those who maintained internal order, promoted great works of irrigation and reclamation, defended and extended the frontiers, were capable rulers who deserved support. The Chinese Communists came to power at an opportune moment. After nearly forty years of division and foreign invasion, they enjoyed over a decade of relative calm in which to consolidate their gains and develop China's resources. Actually, China before 1949, like Russia before 1917, had already entered on a process of modernization, but in both countries the Communists belittled what their predecessors had done and claimed all the credit for themselves.

The fourth and final point to bear in mind is that the attitude adopted by the United States left the Chinese Communists no choice but to look toward Russia for support. The American government refused to recognize the government at Peking, refused to trade with Communist China, and urged all its allies and associates to follow the same policy. To the mainland Chinese, American hostility appeared a constant threat. The United States aided Chiang Kai-shek's forces in Taiwan (Formosa) and supplied them with arms and money. Chiang's hope that revolts in China would open the way for him to return to the mainland proved illusory; but his well-equipped forces, poised a few hundred miles from their coast, kept the Chinese Communists uneasy. American opposition also barred Communist China from membership in the United Nations, where an emissary of Chiang Kai-shek's exiled government continued to sit in the Security Council as the representative of China. This anomalous situation, which has endured for over twenty years after the Peking regime became the actual functioning government of China, enabled the Communist leaders to spur the Chinese masses to extraordinary efforts. China, they insisted, was in constant danger of an American attack. Only by unity, sacrifice, and rapid modernization could it defend itself against the hostility of the capitalist powers. By exaggerating the state of emergency the Communist leaders could excuse their ruthlessness and also maintain armed forces with which to subdue internal discontent.

2. THE POLITICAL FRAMEWORK

After World War II the Chinese Communists renewed their struggle against the Kuomintang regime headed by Chiang Kai-shek. Within four years, as already described in Chapter 49, the Communists achieved a sweeping triumph and gained control of all mainland China. Chiang Kai-shek withdrew the remnants of his forces to the island of Taiwan (Formosa) where he was protected by American naval power. Disregarding the realities of the situation, the United States continued to recognize Chiang's exiled regime as the government of China and refused diplomatic recognition to the Communist government at Peking.

On October 1, 1949, Mao Tse-tung, leader of the Chinese Communists, proclaimed the "People's Republic of China." In structure and organization the new regime resembled the pattern that had been developed in

Russia and imitated with variations by other Communist states. Although it underwent some changes in the decade that followed, the Chinese Communist government maintained effective control and functioned successfully. As in the case of Soviet Russia, however, foreigners found it difficult to penetrate behind the deceptive facades and to determine how important policies were decided and where the power of decision really lay.

In theory the People's Republic of China was a representative government resting on popular support. The constitution and organic laws provided for a National People's Congress, with over 1200 deputies, chosen to represent the provinces, the larger cities, the armed forces, national minorities, and other segments of the population. The Congress, elected for a four-year term, was defined as the supreme legislative authority, and was supposed to meet at least once a year. But its authority was really concentrated in a Standing Committee composed of about eighty of its members. This Standing Committee shared a joint authority with the "Chairman of the People's Republic," who was likewise elected by the Congress and was the chief executive and nominal head of the state. This elaborate parliamentary structure was designed to create the impression that the deputies and the Chairman represented the people and ruled the country, but this impression was deceptive. The mainspring of power and the officials who controlled it formed "a government within the government."

The Standing Committee of the Congress was too large to function as a cabinet or executive council. This role was filled by a State Council (comparable to the Council of Ministers in the Soviet Union) which consisted of a premier, a secretary-general, some sixteen vice-premiers, and the heads of various commissions. Chou En-lai, one of the outstanding Communist leaders in China, was chosen to fill the important position of premier. In addition to the State Council, a Defense Council was created to direct and coordinate the armed forces, defend the country, and repress revolts. There was also a department of justice, or Supreme People's Court, which supervised the administration of the laws.

The "government within the government" which operated behind the scenes was the Chinese Communist party. Although it expanded until it claimed over 12 million members, the Communist party remained a closely knit, well-disciplined body directed by an inner core of able and energetic leaders. Like the national administration, the government of the Chinese Communist party was representative and responsible in theory. From time to time the members were called upon to choose delegates for a National Congress. The Congress elected a Central Committee and the Committee elected a Political Bureau of some thirty to forty members. This Political Bureau not only directed the activities of the Communist party; it also exercised a powerful and sometimes a controlling influence over the national government.

The Political Bureau might make its influence felt through various channels. Its members could be counted upon, when they received the word, to stir up popular demonstrations in favor of measures the Party heads favored, and to denounce policies or officials the Party heads opposed. The newspapers and publishing houses it controlled could likewise influence public opinion. But the most effective method the Party used to shape decisions at every level was to place its members (sometimes secret members) in key positions. As the secretary or chairman of a council, board, or other cooperative group, a Party member could often shape the policy of the group and could report its activities to the Political Bureau.

How effective and far-reaching this method of control could be was clear from the composition of the Political Bureau. Its first seven members constituted a Standing Committee — the high command of the Chinese Communist party. The Chairman of this inner group was Mao Tse-tung, the most powerful man in China. Five of his associates were the five most influential officials of the "People's Government" — the "Chairman" of the Republic; the "Chairman" who headed the Standing Committee of the National Congress; the Premier (Chou En-lai), who directed the State Council; his next in command, the first deputy premier; and the minister who controlled the armed forces of the republic. The seventh member of this all-important inner group was the secretary-general of the Communist party.

When these seven men decided on a course of action they had the influence, the machinery, to force their decision through. Their subordinates in the Party — members of the Congress, of government commissions, of provincial or village councils — would obey instructions and follow their lead. In every country the great majority of the people have little time for politics, and this is particularly true in a large country like China, with over 700 million inhabitants. A small but active and energetic minority, well coordinated, firmly led, skilled in the tactics of persuasion and propaganda, proved that it could manipulate and control the inert and ignorant masses.

In 1966, however, the extraordinary discipline of the Chinese Communist party appeared to be breaking down. Early in the year a widespread purge of "antiparty" officials and intellectuals was launched. In August, what Premier Chou En-lai called "cultural revolution" began. The outside world was startled by reports, according to which thousands of teen-agers who called themselves Red Guards, took over Peking, apparently with official blessing, and started ordering people to rid themselves of their "Western ways." Further reports indicated that the rampaging of the teen-agers, which spread to other cities, encountered resistance on the part of citizens, often culminating in pitched battles. Gradually, it became clear that behind the so-called cultural revolution there was hidden a struggle for power between factions in the Chinese Communist party. It was not clear, however, what the issues in the struggle were or what the outcome might be.

3. ECONOMIC GROWTH

Dr. Sun Yat-sen, who was revered after his death in 1925 as the most unselfish and farsighted leader of the Chinese Revolution, declared that China must seek a government based on the "Three Principles of the People." (See Chapter 34.) These principles were nationalism, democracy, and social progress. In their struggle against Chiang Kai-shek and the Kuomintang party, the Chinese Communists insisted that Chiang had betrayed these three principles, particularly that of social progress, or "the People's Livelihood." The Kuomintang party was controlled by the wealthy landlords, who distrusted the masses and sometimes used the arms and subsidies furnished by the United States to strengthen and enrich themselves. The Communists, claiming to be friends of the people, promised that when they gained power they would divide up the land and free the peasants and farmers from their servitude. As four-fifths of the Chinese lived on the land it is not surprising that they decided to take the Communists at their word. Twenty years of Chiang Kai-shek's rule had failed to free them from their debts or gain them land of their own and they were tired of waiting. It was significant that the Kuomintang leaders feared the common people and would not give them arms even to fight the invading Japanese. The Communists gave them arms, and urged them, after the Japanese were expelled, to chase out the landlords who oppressed them.

It could be predicted that, once peace was restored, China would make remarkable economic progress. The Communists realized that the land question was the first and most pressing problem. "Those who work the land should own it," they announced, and their agents roused the villagers to take action. Landlords who lived entirely on rents, and wealthy farmers who employed landless workers to cultivate their property, were denounced as exploiters and usurers. The movement to confiscate their property spread so rapidly that the government at Peking strove at first to slow it down. But the outbreak of the Korean War in 1950 alarmed the Communist leaders, especially when the United Nations forces aiding the South Koreans advanced to the border of Manchuria. Fearing that the "capitalist" nations meant to invade China and restore the "capitalist" landlords to power, the Communist leaders unleashed a wave of terror. They not only sent a "volunteer" army to strengthen the North Korean communists in their resistance, they hastened to intimidate all suspected opponents of their regime in China itself. Their earlier caution forgotten, they filled the jails with "enemies of the people." No certain totals are available, but it is possible that two million Chinese were executed or died in captivity.

The distribution of confiscated lands among the poorer farmers did not at first bring an increase or improvement in the crops. Although up to half the cultivable land was taken over and divided up, many of the new owners lacked the experience, the tools, and the resources to work their new farms efficiently. Any decline in the food supply was certain to have grave consequences, for China had an enormous and rapidly increasing population. Estimates for 1949 — the year the communists gained power — gave the Chinese population as 536 million. An official census in 1953 raised this to 601 million, and estimates for 1965 reached 750 million. The Chinese had to increase their farm output, not only because their population was rising, but because millions of workers were needed for industry. Almost nine-tenths of the Chinese people lived in rural villages and most of them worked as farmers. The problem that faced the communist leaders was obvious. They must *reduce* the number of farmers but make those who continued to cultivate the land produce more food.

The Russians had attacked the same problem twenty-five years earlier by combining small farms into large "collective" farms, and introducing farm machinery to cultivate them. But Russia, before the Communists seized power, had already begun to feel the effects of the industrial revolution. It possessed some factories, railroads, and trained engineers and technicians. China, in 1949, had a more retarded and custom-bound economy than that of Russia had been in 1917. Nevertheless China's new masters adopted plans to improve Chinese agriculture and develop its industries simultaneously.

A First Five-Year Plan for China went into effect in 1953 and closed in 1957. It included changes in agricultural organization and production and the creation of "communes" that would force the farmers in each community to work together, share their tools and animals, and raise the crops the government ordered. In 1958 the First Five-Year Plan was declared a success and a Second Five-Year Plan (1958–1962) inaugurated. The year 1958 was to be marked by a "Great Leap Forward" with a phenomenal rise in food and factory output. By 1959 it became clear that something had gone wrong. Nature failed to cooperate in the agricultural program and serious floods occurred throughout China. The new communes were not popular with the farmers. The "Great Leap Forward" turned out to be a stumble, and the party leaders had to revise their estimates. Instead of the 375 million tons of grain promised for 1958 only 250 million were produced. The cotton crop fell by over one-third and steel production by over one-fourth below their quotas.

This setback forced the government to reduce its production goals for 1959. Instead of 525 million tons of grain, the figure was cut almost in half to 275 million tons. Instead of 5 million tons of cotton little more

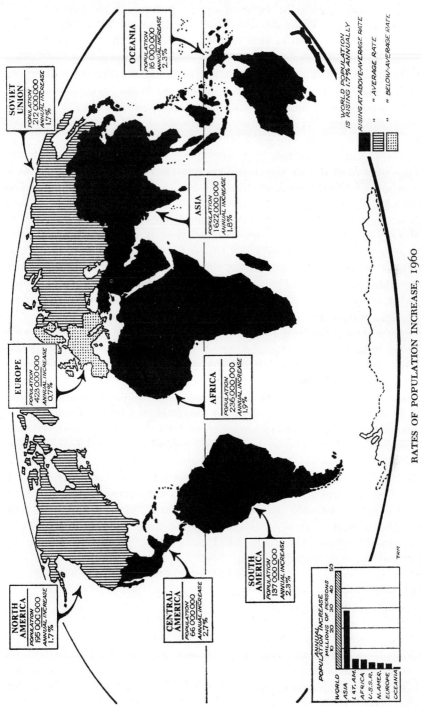

OCEANIA
POPULATION
16 000 000
ANNUAL INCREASE
2.3%

SOVIET
UNION
POPULATION
212 000 000
ANNUAL INCREASE
1.7%

ASIA
POPULATION
1 622 000 000
ANNUAL INCREASE
1.8%

EUROPE
POPULATION
423 000 000
ANNUAL INCREASE
0.7%

AFRICA
POPULATION
236 000 000
ANNUAL INCREASE
1.9%

NORTH
AMERICA
POPULATION
195 000 000
ANNUAL INCREASE
1.7%

CENTRAL
AMERICA
POPULATION
66 000 000
ANNUAL INCREASE
2.7%

SOUTH
AMERICA
POPULATION
137 000 000
ANNUAL INCREASE
2.3%

WORLD POPULATION
IS RISING 1.7% ANNUALLY
RISING AT ABOVE-AVERAGE RATE
"   " AVERAGE RATE
"   " BELOW-AVERAGE RATE

ANNUAL
POPULATION INCREASE
MILLIONS OF PERSONS
10   20   30   40   50
WORLD
ASIA
LAT. AM.
AFRICA
U.S.S.R.
N. AMER.
EUROPE
OCEANIA

RATES OF POPULATION INCREASE, 1960

TRM

than 2 million could be counted upon. Instead of 18 million tons of steel — the quota originally set — a smaller quota of 12 million tons was substituted. In countries that feared and opposed Red China these reverses were hailed as a proof that the Communist experiment was failing. "The imperialists count upon our not handling our economic problems well," Mao Tse-tung warned his followers in 1949. "They stand on the sidelines and wait for our failure." Fifteen years later the "imperialists" were still hoping for the failure of communism in China, but they were also watching China's progress with apprehension.

For Communist China, with the aid of loans, arms, equipment, and engineers from Russia, developed energetically in the 1950's. In 1960, as a result of the outbreak of the Sino-Soviet conflict (see Chapter 68), Soviet technicians were withdrawn from China, and Soviet aid to China was discontinued. Despite this handicap, the Chinese pressed on. Although all statistics were open to question, it appeared probable that during the years 1950–1965 the Chinese population increased by one-fourth, or roughly by 150 million. Production of wheat and rice rose by one-third, the supply of fish and tea doubled, the supply of sugar tripled. In other words, the Chinese succeeded in raising essential food commodities sufficiently fast to outpace their rising population.

After 1961 agriculture received more attention, and the pressure to develop industry first was eased, for industry proved easier to stimulate. The output of raw materials for industry rose faster than the output of food. Coal production tripled, tin production rose fourfold, antimony fivefold, pig iron tenfold, crude steel, cement, and petroleum twelvefold.

In research and development the progress of Chinese scientists took many Western observers by surprise. In 1964 the Chinese achieved their first successful atomic test. In 1965 they exploded a second, more sophisticated nuclear device. It appeared probable that by 1970 they would have developed hydrogen bombs. In biochemistry they succeeded, in 1966, in synthesizing insulin in the laboratory. This triumph of Chinese patience and ingenuity won the praise of European and American specialists who had been striving for years to create insulin artificially because of its indispensable role in the treatment of diabetes.

4.   EDUCATION

When the Communists gained control of China in 1949 four-fifths of the people were illiterate or semi-illiterate. One reason for this was the difficult and cumbersome form of Chinese writing which included some thirty thousand characters. For thousands of years higher learning had been confined to a relatively small group of scholars whose influence in the administration remained very great. Knowledge of European history, politics, science, and literature reached the Chinese largely through mis-

An aspect of Chinese village life untouched by Communist modernization (Wide World Photos).

Trainees for the militia of a commune near Canton (Wide World Photos).

Shanghai, Communist China's largest city, scene of riots by thousands of Red Guards in early spring, 1967 (Wide World Photos).

The sayings of Chairman Mao-Tse-tung on Red Guard wall posters in Peking (Wide World Photos).

sionary schools maintained by Catholics and Protestants and through Chinese students who were able to study abroad. With the triumph of communism the missionary schools were closed and the teachers imprisoned or expelled. Students who wished to study abroad were sent to Russia instead of to Western European or American universities.

The Communists realized that if education was to be extended to the masses it would have to be a simpler and more practical type of education than the literary and philosophical training the older Chinese scholars had admired. One major step, decreed in 1958, was the gradual substitution of the 26 letter Latin alphabet to replace the 30,000 characters of the older script. The adoption of the more simplified form of writing made the task of the student, the typist, and the typesetter much easier. It also enabled those Chinese who learned by the new methods to master books in European languages more easily. Meanwhile, a shortened system of some 4000 ideographs was utilized, and telegrams reproduced by an electro-facsimile method because the Morse code was not applicable.

Another source of confusion which the Communists sought to combat was the existence in China of many varying standards of weights and measures. It was essential, for machine technology and mass production, that these many discrepant modes of measurement be reduced to a single approved scale. Machines, their products, and their interchangeable parts have to be standardized, and this is particularly true of military weapons. If guns, shells, and instruments are made to various gauges endless loss and frustration can be the result. Knowing that it is difficult to change people's habits the new rulers of China began by introducing the metric system for official use, and extended it to factories, power plants and arsenals, before they attempted to convert the artisans and handicraftsmen. They also called in all the existing currency (which had depreciated until it had little value) and replaced it by a decimal currency in 1955. One "People's Bank Dollar" (worth about $2.40 in American funds) was divided into ten *chiao* and each *chiao* into ten *fen* so that each new dollar equaled 100 *fen*. In 1957 the government issued small aluminum coins of one, two, and five *fen* for everyday needs.

By 1960 the Chinese claimed to have 100 million children enrolled in their elementary schools, over 10 million in secondary schools, and over 1 million in colleges and universities. In addition some 10 thousand students were studying abroad, almost all of them in Russia. It was significant of the new spirit stirring the younger generation in China that nearly half the college students were registered in engineering courses. The Chinese Communists placed great emphasis on science. Their Academy of Science had 20 provincial branches by 1964. The emphasis on science and engineering was evident in the status and curriculum of the schools. By 1957 China had 48 engineering colleges, 43 teachers colleges, 37 medical schools, 31 agricultural and forestry colleges, but only five schools of economics and five devoted to law and political science. These totals increased in the 1960's, but figures were difficult to secure. It should not be forgotten that the half-million recruits called up annually for three, four, or five years of service also received some educational training. This was also true, in a lesser degree, of the 200 million men and women reputedly enrolled in the People's Militia. In adopting these various and far-reaching plans for popular education the Communists did not overlook the opportunities the plans provided for indoctrinating the masses with Communist principles. This was, indeed, one of the main reasons for the nation-wide educational program.

5. FOREIGN POLICY

The proclamation of the Chinese People's Republic in 1949 was followed within a few months by a treaty of "friendship, alliance and mutual aid" between Communist China and Soviet Russia. This thirty-year defense pact was worded to suggest that the Chinese and Russians regarded Japan as the possible enemy; but it also mentioned "other nations which may take aggressive action by collaborating with Japan." This accord, and the aid furnished by Russian scientists and engineers, proved valuable to the People's Republic of China in its first years of struggle and reorganization after 1949. But after 1953, the year in which the Korean War ended, and Joseph Stalin died, relations between China and Russia grew less friendly. Under Nikita Khrushchev's leadership (1956–64) the Russians sought a "relaxation of international tensions." The Chinese Communist leaders feared that this policy might lead to an accord between Soviet Russia and the United States at the expense of China. Mao Tsetung and Chou En-lai accused the Russians of abandoning true Marxist doctrine and declared the policy of "peaceful coexistence" between the Communist and capitalist worlds was a betrayal of Communist principles. When Moscow persisted in its stand and the Soviet regime endorsed Khrushchev's "revisionist" thinking and his denunciation of Stalin's policies, the Peking leaders insisted that Peking, not Moscow, had become the center of the world Communist movement. The Chinese sought to draw the Soviet satellites away from Moscow. China subsidized active pro-Peking groups in Albania, in Cuba, in Indonesia, and in several of the new African states. But in opposing Russia and the United States simultaneously, the Chinese Communist leaders overtaxed their resources and their influence. After 1964 they suffered a series of reverses in the international struggle. When a conference of Asian and African nations was planned in 1965, China endeavored to exclude Russia on the ground that Russia was a European power. When Russia was admitted, China withdrew and the conference was indefinitely postponed. In the same year the Communist party of Indonesia, which was linked to Peking in its policies, attempted to seize power and suffered virtual extermination when the coup failed (see page 796). In Africa the republics of Burundi, Kenya and Malawi turned against China. In Vietnam the United States forces were steadily increased despite Chinese warnings, and American raids were extended into North Vietnam without Chinese retaliation (see page 799).

Relations between China and India continued to be strained, and armed border clashes threatened to excite a more serious conflict. The Chinese occupation of Tibet in 1959 drove the Tibetan religious leader, the Dalai Lama, to flee to India, and 100,000 other Tibetan refugees likewise emigrated. Resistance persisted in Tibet. The Chinese found it difficult to pacify that mountainous realm, although half a million Chinese had settled there. In 1965 the exiled Dalai Lama was declared a traitor, and a Chinese-sponsored regime was installed. Tibet was declared an Autonomous Region associated with the Chinese People's Republic.

The United Nations continued to exclude China, largely through the consistent opposition of the United States.

In 1966 the question of admission of China in the United Nations was once again voted on in the General Assembly. The motion was soundly defeated, 56–47 with 17 abstentions. The issue had grave implications, for the Nationalist regime, headed by Chiang Kai-shek, still claimed to be the legitimate government of China although it had been limited to the island of Taiwan since 1949. The Communist government at Peking, which controlled mainland China, insisted that Taiwan should be part of China and that Chiang Kai-shek's regime should be abolished and his representative expelled from the Security Council of the United Nations. As China held one of the permanent seats on the Security Council, the United States could not agree to remove the Nationalist Chinese representative (who was friendly to America) and install a Peking representative (who would oppose American policy). But many nations felt that the impasse ought to be resolved and that the United Nations could not claim to be a world body if it continued to exclude nearly one-fourth of the global population from representation in the Assembly and the Council.

6. OUTER MONGOLIA AND NORTH KOREA

While Communist China reasserted Chinese control over Tibet, two other former Chinese dependencies — Outer Mongolia and North Korea — maintained their independence. Mongolia, the home of the great warrior and conqueror Genghiz Khan and his famous horsemen in the twelfth and thirteenth centuries, was in more recent times one of the outlying provinces of the Chinese Empire. It was a large province covered with forbidding mountains and thinly-grassed plains, which supported a sparse population of nomad herdsmen and Buddhist lamas (monks). Like the

Dalai Lama in Tibet, the chief lama at Urga (Ulan Bator) was considered to be a "Living Buddha" and was the highest spiritual, and, in effect, temporal authority in Mongolia.

In 1911, after the fall of the Manchu dynasty in China, the northern portion of Mongolia (Outer Mongolia) came under the influence of Imperial Russia, while its southern portion (Inner Mongolia) remained attached to China. During the Russian Civil War following World War I, a White Russian general and adventurer, Baron Ungern von Sternberg, seized Ulan Bator, the Mongolian capital, and used Outer Mongolia as a base for raids against the Russian Reds in Siberia. In 1921, pursuing Baron Sternberg, the Russian Red Army invaded Mongolia, seized Ulan Bator, and organized the Mongolian People's Republic. Despite Soviet withdrawal and recognition that Outer Mongolia constituted a part of China in the first Sino-Soviet Treaty of 1924, Nationalist China was too weak to assert its claim over the province. Thanks to modest Soviet military and economic aid, the Mongolian People's government at Ulan Bator under Choibalsan (the "Mongolian Stalin," 1923–1952) survived, thus winning the dubious distinction of being the oldest Soviet satellite. It remained, however, a very primitive land with an area of some 626,000 square miles and a population of about 1 million. Its development into a modern state did not begin until after World War II.

In 1945 the Soviet government obtained the explicit recognition of the independence of the Mongolian People's Republic from the Allies at the Yalta conference and from Nationalist China in the second Sino-Soviet Treaty, signed in Moscow (see p. 579). However, in the treaty of alliance between Soviet Russia and Communist China in 1950, the potentially divisive question of the status of Outer Mongolia was left in abeyance. The Communist fears that it would become a bone of contention between Soviet Russia and Communist China proved true. Even before the outbreak of the Sino-Soviet conflict, Outer Mongolia became an object of intense rivalry between the two Communist giants. Both the Russians and the Chinese poured lavish aid into the country. Ulan Bator was linked by railway to both the Soviet and the Chinese railroad systems, and was built up into a respectable capital of some 200,000 inhabitants. Because of Soviet and Chinese aid, the Mongolians were freed from exclusive dependence on herding for a living and were able to develop their agriculture and some industry.

In the 1950's it was difficult to say whose satellite Outer Mongolia was. Ultimately, however, because of their greater resources and ability to assist Outer Mongolia to obtain admission in the United Nations — a status symbol much coveted by the underdeveloped countries – the Russians succeeded in outbidding the Chinese. In 1962 the Mongolian premier and Communist party chief Tsedenbal (1952–   ) clearly sided with Moscow.

Little is known about the development of North Korea after the Korean War of 1950–1953. It appears, however, that its situation was similar to that of Outer Mongolia. Thanks to Soviet and Chinese aid, the frightful destruction of the war was rapidly repaired, and considerable industry developed. Pyongyang, the North Korean capital which had been completely destroyed in the war, was rebuilt and was reported to have a population of 1.2 million in 1962, while the country as a whole had a population of 11.8 million and an area of 46,768 square miles. In the Sino-Soviet dispute, the North Korean premier and Communist party chief Kim Il-sung (1948–   ) long sided with China, but in 1966 affirmed North Korean independence of both Russia and China.

Section XI: THE MARCH TOWARD INDEPENDENCE

IN ASIA AND AFRICA

63

INDIA: INDEPENDENCE AND DIVISION

We are pledged to end the alien domination of Asia.
JAWAHARLAL NEHRU

1. THE REPUBLIC OF INDIA

IN THE YEARS THAT followed World War II, the rivalry that developed between the Communist and anticommunist blocs made it difficult for any government to remain neutral. Yet there was an increasing number of nations that had no wish to align themselves with the Soviet Union and its satellites or with the United States and its associates. These nations preferred to remain uncommitted in the Cold War. In a divided world they constituted a third group, not formally allied with Russia or America, nor with one another. Many of them were states newly formed from the dissolving empires of the European powers. Having thrown off European imperialism they remained highly distrustful of all imperialistic influence, and they had no intention of exchanging one master for another, of winning independence from Europe only to fall under the control of the United States or the Soviet Union.

Among the Asian and African countries that emerged as independent states after World War II the largest and most populous was the Indian Union. As noted earlier, discontent with British rule grew rapidly in the British Indian Empire between the world wars (see Chapter 33). On the outbreak of World War II the British viceroy at New Delhi declared India was a belligerent, an arbitrary act that exasperated Indian leaders who had been working for independence. In 1942 the British government sent Sir Stafford Cripps to discuss plans for transferring authority to an Indian government but the "Cripps Mission" failed. Thereupon the India Congress, a national body that had been formed as early as 1885 to work for independence, adopted a resolution that the British must "Quit India." The leader of the Congress was Jawaharlal Nehru, but the most revered nationalist figure was Mohandas Karamchand Gandhi, known as the *Mahatma* or "great-souled" teacher. Gandhi's formula for

779

ending British rule was a campaign of noncooperation and nonviolence. The British refused to yield, however, and jailed the leaders of the Congress until the end of the war. Some Indian troops joined the Japanese in World War II, and organized a small Indian National Army to fight for independence. After the war the British brought some of the deserters to trial, thus unwisely calling attention to the fact that loyalty to India might be punished as disloyalty to Britain, an anomaly that stirred the Indians deeply.

Meanwhile the Moslem minority in the Indian Empire, who had formed a Moslem League, demanded that the segments of India where the Moslem population was most heavily concentrated should become a separate state when independence was attained. The Indian Congress opposed this plan.

After the British Labor party won control of Parliament in 1945, the new cabinet offered India independence. Lord Louis Mountbatten was sent to New Delhi as viceroy in 1947 and persuaded the leaders of the Congress to accept the idea of partition and to permit the Indian Moslems to organize a separate state to be known as Pakistan. The partition took place on August 15, 1947. Two years later, at a conference in London, India as an independent nation accepted membership in the (British) Commonwealth as an equal partner with Britain and the other dominions. The problem of the princely states — the domains of rajahs and maharajahs whom the British had left semi-independent rulers — was solved by organizing them within the political framework of the new union or absorbing them into neighboring provinces. By 1950 India had become a sovereign independent republic.

The new republic had an area of 1,266,210 square miles and a population of approximately 350 million in 1950. By 1967 the number of inhabitants had risen to 500 million. India was the second most populous country in the world after China. It had a high birth rate of 42 per thousand; the death rate was reported as 22 per thousand but was probably higher for the annual rate of increase was listed as 1.8 per cent. This was sufficient, however, to raise the population seven million a year in the 1950's and if maintained would give India a population of one billion by the year 2000. To feed these vast and increasing multitudes overtaxed Indian resources. Although 80 per cent of the population lived in rural areas and 70 per cent worked on the land, the food supply, chiefly cereals, was never adequate. Antiquated farming methods, low yield per acre, and lack of adequate fertilizers kept the Indian masses close to starvation.

A Five-Year Plan introduced in 1951 to improve economic conditions brought some improvements in agriculture, transportation, and the generation of electricity, but per capita income remained about $60 and per capita consumption of energy was equivalent to only 115 kilograms of coal when the five years ended. A second Five-Year Plan, aimed particularly at encouraging basic industries, proved disappointing and had to be curtailed. Between 1955 and 1965 the United States provided India with billions of dollars in aid, and the Soviet Union provided her with three-quarters of a billion, but the problems were so vast that progress remained slow.

The government of India, provided for in a constitution adopted in 1950, is a democratic republic. A Council of States represents the states and territories of the Union. A House of the People is elected by universal adult suffrage. The President of the Republic is chosen by an electoral college, and he in turn appoints a Council of Ministers. The first prime minister and most influential leader in India after it became independent was Jawaharlal Nehru. Mahatma Gandhi did not live to see the completion of Indian independence for he was assassinated by a religious fanatic in 1948.

The problem of creating a unified country out of some fourteen states and eight territories taxed the political skill of the Indian legislators. The peoples of India represent a complex mixture of races, with the Caucasian strain predominating, but there were also Mongoloid, Negroid, and Australoid elements. Only one-sixth of the population could read in 1950 and the multiplicity of languages was particularly baffling. The first census taken after independence listed 845 languages or dialects, two of which, Hindi and Urdu, were the most widely used. The government decided to make Hindi the national language because about half the population could understand it. For official purposes, however, it was judged necessary to use English until Hindi had been more widely established. A dozen other regional languages were recognized by the Constitution. As many of the spoken languages had their own type of script, and some included a notable body of literary and religious writings, the language problem defied any rapid solution. Yet so long as the population of India was split into many groups divided by language and custom, any genuine national unity would be difficult to achieve. The possibility that the union might be divided or rent by civil war remained a serious danger.

The foreign policy of the Republic of India was directed toward the easing of world tensions. As spokesman for the largest of the uncommitted nations, Nehru took the lead in urging these nations to form a third force in international affairs, holding the balance between the rival Communist and anticommunist blocs. Nehru also lent diplomatic support to colonial peoples who were seeking independence. Despite friction between India and China he favored recognition of the Chinese Communist government and the admission of China to the United Nations. This considerate attitude did not conciliate the Chinese who made several armed incursions into Indian territory. They were resisted by Indian border garrisons, and in 1963 Nehru threatened to sever diplomatic relations with China if the raids continued. After some dispute a cease-fire was arranged along the tense Sino-Indian border.

In 1965 the Indian defense forces became engaged in a more serious clash, this time with Pakistan. Both India and Pakistan claimed the province of Kashmir and, although the United Nations arranged a truce in the fighting there in 1948, the territory remained in dispute. New fighting occurred in 1965; both the Indian and the Pakistani forces conducted bombing raids; but neither had resources for a long struggle unless they received external supplies, and both the United States and the Soviet Union urged a peaceful settlement. This was arranged through the United Nations and a cease-fire was signed in the Soviet city of Tashkent in January, 1966. The United Nations prepared to furnish a new mission that would observe and report on the possibilities of an enduring settlement.

Jawaharlal Nehru, who served as the first prime minister of India after 1947, died in 1964, and the ruling Congress party selected Lal Bahadur Shastri, a cabinet minister who had served under Nehru, to succeed him. Shastri's humility, patience, and diplomacy appealed to the Indian masses, but unfortunately his health was frail. His journey to Tashkent to conclude a cease-fire with Pakistan a few months after he took office exhausted him and he died in Tashkent one day after the agreement was signed. In an effort to draw all factions together, the office of prime minister was then conferred on Mrs. Indira Gandhi, daughter of Nehru. Both Shastri and Mrs. Gandhi continued Nehru's policies, but they tended to draw closer to the Western powers, especially to the United States. On a visit to Washington in 1966, Mrs. Gandhi received a cordial welcome and obtained further aid to combat a severe food shortage that had brought millions in India to a state of famine. But India did not abandon its neutral position nor compromise its leadership of the unaligned nations of Asia and Africa.

2. THE DOMINION OF PAKISTAN

When the British granted independence to their Indian subjects in 1947 the ancient religious divisions of the subcontinent split India asunder. Approximately two-thirds of the population practiced the Hindu religion, while one-fourth were Moslems. The remainder, roughly one-tenth, included Sikhs, Buddhists, Christians, and minor sects. The Moslems feared that they would be mistreated if they remained in the Indian Union as a minority, and they insisted that the areas in northwestern and northeastern India, where they formed a majority of the local population, must be granted independence. Thus the departure of the British, who had established political union in India for the first time in its history, was followed by immediate division.

The Moslem areas were formed into the Dominion of Pakistan, a state composed of two segments that lay nearly a thousand miles apart. East and West Pakistan, though separated, were one Dominion with a total area of 365,907 square miles. As the census of 1951 listed some 76 million inhabitants, of whom possibly one-sixth were Hindu or Christian, it was apparent that only two-thirds of the Moslem population of the Indian peninsula had found refuge within the new state. If the division of territory had been planned in strict accordance with the relative numbers of Hindus and Moslems, Pakistan should have been larger.

The division of India on religious lines excited passionate demonstrations, rioting, and persecution. Six million Hindus fled from Pakistan to the Indian Republic. Millions of Moslems left India for Pakistan but those that remained still accounted for one-tenth of the Indian population. The turbulence and bloodshed that marked the first year of independence left a heritage of hostility between the two states of the divided peninsula. No peaceful solution could be worked out for delimiting their boundaries for both claimed the state of Kashmir and sought to occupy it by force. The United Nations ordered a cease-fire in 1948 and advised a plebiscite but, as already mentioned, the Indian and Pakistani forces continued to hold their disputed ground although a truce ended the fighting.

The leader who did most to achieve independence for Pakistan was Muhammad Ali Jinnah, president of the All-India Moslem League, but he died in 1948. The name Pakistan was coined for the occasion; it was formed by taking the initial letters of Punjab, Afghans, and Kashmir and adding the last five letters of Buluchistan. The new state remained a member of the Commonwealth but the plan to establish a constitutional representative government encountered difficulties. The flight of 6 million Hindus left too few trained officials with experience in administrative methods; four-fifths of the people were illiterate; and differences in language divided the Pakistani population. The first prime minister, Liaquat Ali, was assassinated in 1948. West Pakistan, which included six-sevenths of the territory, but less than half the population, was not consolidated until 1955. The following year a Constitution went into effect, defining Pakistan as an independent Moslem Republic with a president instead of a governor-general. In 1958 President Iskander Mirza proclaimed martial law, dismissed the parliament, dissolved all political parties, and suspended the constitution. The army commander, General Ayub Khan, became president, and his authority was confirmed by a ballot in 1960. In 1962 President Ayub Khan proclaimed the adoption of a new constitution under which he was head of the state and chief executive. A national assembly, representing East and West Pakistan, was to be elected by a limited electorate. Ministers and governors of the provinces were to be appointed by the president. In 1965 President Ayub Khan was reelected, but signs of opposition to his administration increased.

Pakistan remained a poor country of limited resources. The population

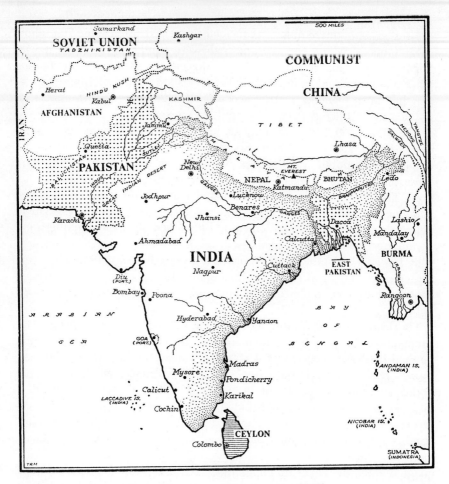

INDIA, PAKISTAN, AND CEYLON, 1967

reached 100 million by 1964. A high birth rate of 45 per thousand and a death rate of about 17, gave it a rate of increase of roughly 28 per thousand, or 2.8 per cent a year. The income per capita was estimated at $79 a year for 1964.

3. THE DOMINION OF CEYLON

The island of Ceylon at the foot of the Indian peninsula gained independence in 1947 at the same time as India and Pakistan. The inhabitants, of whom the Sinhalese formed a 70 per cent majority, also included Tamils, Moors, and Eurasians. There were also a few thousand primitive forest people, small, slender and dark, who were known as Veddas. Ceylon has an area of 24,332 square miles and a population of approximately

6.7 million in 1947. The dominant religion was Buddhism, but one-sixth of the inhabitants were Hindus, one-tenth Christians, and one-twelfth Moslems.

Ceylon is one of the more densely populated regions of Asia. As the birth rate remains high (between 35 and 40 per thousand) and the death rate has declined rapidly (it was cited as less than 11 by 1966) the population rose at a ratio of 2.5 per cent a year. By 1967 it exceeded 11 million, with an average of nearly 410 per square mile. Fortunately the island enjoyed an adequate rainfall, except in the central mountains, and the soil was fertile, permitting extensive cultivation. The main food crop was rice, the main export crops tea, rubber, and coconuts. The profits from these exports enabled the Ceylonese to purchase additional rice, wheat, sugar, fish, and dairy products, as well as petroleum and fertilizer. Per capita income in Ceylon was high by Asian standards, running about $125 a year.

During their first years of self-government the Ceylonese appeared satisfied with dominion status. A governor-general represented the British Crown, and a Senate and an elected House of Representatives formed the parliament. Great Britain retained an air and naval base and provided for the defense of the island. By 1956, however, a growing spirit of independence asserted itself. The People's United Front, which won control of the Assembly in that year, demanded the withdrawal of all British forces, and the air and naval bases were transferred to the control of the Sinhalese the following year. A measure was introduced to proclaim Ceylon a republic but it remained a member of the Commonwealth.

Like India and Pakistan, Ceylon needed capital to develop and diversify its economy, which depended too heavily on tea, rubber, and coconuts. Changes in the condition of the world market that reduced the price or quantity of its exports might have serious consequences, for by 1965 the Ceylonese were importing more than half the rice they consumed. This and other expenditures — for manufactured goods, machinery, oil, and coal — unsettled their balance of trade. Their industries lacked capital for expansion and power for operation, the energy consumption remaining less that 115 kilograms of coal per capita.

The advantage of being an "uncommitted" country permitted Ceylon to enjoy favors from both the Communist and the anticommunist blocs. Between 1955 and 1960 the United States provided some 50 million dollars in financial aid and the Soviet Union about $60 million. The government of Ceylon also negotiated an accord with the Chinese Communist regime to exchange 50,000 tons of rubber a year for 270,000 tons of rice. Other barter agreements with the Soviet Union and the Soviet satellites made it clear that Ceylon was ready to recognize and trade with the Communist world. In the 1960's the U.S. reduced its aid for this reason.

To emphasize their unwillingness to lean too far to either side in the Cold War, the Ceylonese adhered to the Colombo Plan, a project formed in 1951 whereby twenty-one governments agreed to consult on the development of Asian countries that needed aid. By 1960 over 6 billion dollars had been advanced under this plan, nine-tenths of this large sum being provided by the United States. But the government of Ceylon refused to join the Southeast Asia Collective Treaty Organization when that defense league was formed in 1954 (see p. 587). Like India, Burma, and Indonesia, Ceylon held to a policy of "non-alignment."

4. THE UNION OF BURMA

Burma, conquered by the British between 1824 and 1886, formed part of the British Indian Empire until 1937. The Burmese did not accept British rule willingly, nor were they placated when Burma was separated from India in 1937 and allowed a measure of self-government. During World War II a Burmese army of independence was organized and aided the Japanese invaders who "liberated" the country in 1942. Finding Japanese occupation no more to their liking than British rule had been, the Burmese nationalists turned against the Japanese and helped the British to expel them in 1945. In 1947, when the British granted their Indian subjects independence, they withdrew from Burma also. The Union of Burma, formally proclaimed in 1948, did not remain a member of the (British) Commonwealth but chose complete independence and separation.

The area of the Union, 261,789 square miles, was slightly smaller than that of Texas. The population before World War II was about 16 million and the majority were Buddhists in religion. About 30 per cent of the population consisted of minorities — Karens, Shoms, Mons, and Kachins. They were mostly primitive hill tribes. The total population had increased to approximately 18 million when independence was attained in 1947, and was approaching 25 million by 1966. This gave Burma an average of 80 inhabitants to the square mile. An exceptionally high birth rate, possibly as high as 50 per thousand, should have given Burma a high ration of population growth, had it not been offset by a high infant mortality rate of 195 and a high death rate of 35 per thousand. These estimates were approximations, for no recent census had been taken and outside of the cities little effort was made to keep vital statistics up to date. The World Health Organization and the United Nations Children's Fund helped the Burmese to improve their inadequate medical service and curb the ravages of malaria, tuberculosis, leprosy, and other diseases.

The form of government the Burmese established on winning independence was a parliamentary democracy. A Chamber of Nationalities and a Chamber of Deputies, elected by all citizens over eighteen, formed the legislature and chose the President. As in Pakistan, this system led to dissention and corruption and in 1958 the prime minister, U Nu, transferred the authority of the cabinet to the army commander. After two years of dictatorship an election was held and U Nu again headed a responsible cabinet. He was deposed, however, in 1962. A new dictatorship was established under Ne Win, who adopted a friendlier attitude toward the Western World and provided a more stable government.

The main factor in the Burmese economy was rice production before World War II and the postwar government labored to restore Burmese agricultural output. By 1965 rice exports were over the prewar level of three million tons, which helped to pay for the manufactured goods imported. Rice shipments were still dispatched to India, Ceylon, and Indonesia, the traditional markets, but Communist countries also bid for and secured an increasing share of Burmese foreign trade. Seventy-two million dollars in aid from the United States and twelve million dollars from Russia helped the Burmese, who also received financial assistance from Canada, Australia, and New Zealand. Despite this assistance, the per capita income remained very low, averaging about $56 per year.

In international affairs the Burmese government sought to maintain a neutral position. Its common frontier with China exposed it to communist pressure but it succeeded in maintaining its independence. Under the Colombo Plan it received part of the aid provided for the reconstruction of Asian countries, but it did not join the anticommunist bloc. The main problems the country faced were economic — low income, a limited and retarded industrial development, lack of road and transport facilities, and an unbalanced foreign trade.

5. FREE ENTERPRISE *vs.* COMMUNISM

When the British Indian Empire split up into four independent states after World War II many traces of British influence persisted. All four of the new republics remained within the "Sterling Area," that is, they relied on the British pound sterling as an international unit of currency. All save Burma remained members of the Commonwealth, and all adopted a form of representative government based on the British model of parliamentary democracy. The fact that half a billion people in the south of Asia chose to imitate Britain rather than Soviet Russia was a decision of great importance for Asia and for the world. Numerically, that half-billion people, if they had moved into the Communist bloc, would have changed the global balance and made over half the population of the world communists. Furthermore, as India, Pakistan, Ceylon, and Burma were the first large countries to escape from colonialism after the war, their example had a strong influence on other emerging states in Asia and Africa.

It was fortunate that the leaders of the British Labor party, which controlled the British Parliament from 1945 to 1951, granted independence to the Indian Empire promptly and generously. If Britain had delayed, or had attempted to preserve its control by force, a cruel and costly struggle might have resulted instead of a peaceful separation. India, Pakistan, Ceylon, and Burma were spared the years of warfare that rent French Indochina and the clashes that left the Indonesians embittered against their former Dutch masters, and this helps to explain why Britain's Indian subjects preserved friendly relations with Britain after they became independent. If they had been driven to fight for liberty they would have looked abroad for aid. If Russia had supplied it the new states would have been drawn into the orbit of communism.

The fact that none of the four new nations adopted a Communist form of government was therefore a victory for the Western powers in the Cold War. But it was not an irreversible decision. The severe economic problems that beset the new nations could not easily be solved. The rapid growth of Soviet power and prestige, and the reforms introduced in China after the Communists came to power there (see Chapter 62), created a powerful impression throughout Asia. If the Indians, Pakistanis, Ceylonese and Burmese found their progress too slow under democratic parliamentary regimes, they might turn to a more authoritarian type of government. Pakistan and Burma, as already noted, both resorted to military dictatorships in 1958. For all these new countries, the effort to raise and export agricultural surpluses in order to pay for imports of machinery, the struggle to obtain capital to develop their own industries and supply the energy to run them, proved a desperate and discouraging ordeal.

If their progress seemed too slow, or the cost of assistance from the Western powers too high, newly independent peoples had an alternate path they could follow. They knew that the Russians had expanded their economy and modernized their industries without foreign aid. They could observe the progress made by the Chinese Communists with the assistance of Russian technicians, while the Western powers remained indifferent or hostile. It often seemed, to neutral foreign observers, that the Russians and Chinese had found, through communism, a secret of inner strength, discipline, and efficiency that could help retarded nations to develop at remarkable speed. All Asia watched and compared the progress achieved in India, under its democratic government, with the gains in agricultural and industrial output, in the generation of power and growth of population claimed by the Chinese. These two great Asian countries, which together held over a billion people, were confronting similar problems under dissimilar modes of government. If either clearly outpaced the other in economic development, impoverished peoples in Asia, Africa, and Latin America would digest the lesson and regard the result as a vindication of free enterprise or of communism.

64

EAST AND SOUTHEAST ASIA

The United States light has grown dim. The other light is bright.
PRESIDENT SUKARNO OF INDONESIA (1958)

1. JAPAN

THE DEFEAT OF Japan and the reforms under American occupation (see Chapter 49) caused great confusion in the minds of the Japanese people. The young Japanese generation was notably affected by the clash between the authoritarian beliefs of their fathers and the democratic principles of the occupiers. This did not always produce happy results. There was an increase in juvenile delinquency. In their haste to accept the ideas of the successful, victorious United States, the young Japanese often missed the inner humanitarian spirit of the American civilization and absorbed only its outward tinsel. With the end of the American occupation in 1952, however, things gradually settled down and the Japanese began to find an equilibrium. With their keen intelligence and pragmatic sense, they kept of the American-inspired reforms that which best suited their needs, while in other respects they reverted to their time-honored ways.

To minimize the inevitable friction between two peoples with very different scales of value, the American authorities wisely limited American personnel in Japan, and kept their officers and men under strict discipline. As an important concession to Japanese self-esteem, the United States government concluded with the Japanese government an executive agreement placing American personnel in Japan under Japanese jurisdiction in cases of crimes committed off American bases and off duty. As a result, while the Japanese gradually reasserted their nationalism and independence they showed singularly little resentment against their erstwhile conquerors.

American fears that communism might spread in Japan proved largely unwarranted. The young Japanese democracy functioned reasonably well. The Liberal Democrats, a right-of-center party, dominated the Japanese political scene continuously in the postwar years. The Socialists were next in importance. The Communists gained 10 per cent of the vote in 1949, but thereafter dwindled to insignificance. In the 1060's a new force emerged in Japanese politics — the Komeito (clean government) party, which was the political arm of the militant Buddhist Soka Gakkai sect.

The Korean War stimulated the Japanese economy, and by the end of the 1950's the country had recovered considerable prosperity and direct United States aid to Japan was discontinued. Japanese goods reappeared in foreign markets. They were not only the "cheap" goods that characterized Japanese exports before the war: textiles (cotton, rayon, silk, and wool), toys, pottery, and metalware. Japan began to export many "solid" products: machine tools, rolling stock, ships, office machines, optical goods, textiles, and electronic equipment. In 1966 Japan was the leading ship builder and the third-ranking (after the United States and West Germany) automobile manufacturer in the world. Yet the balance of trade remained unfavorable, but American expenditures and tourism helped to adjust the balance. Per capita income in Japan was the highest in Asia, reaching $740 by 1966.

One-fifth of Japanese exports were directed toward the United States, a situation that made the Japanese economy unduly dependent on the American market and its fluctuations and created strains in both countries. Many American businessmen resented Japanese competition as unfair, because it was made possible by the substantially lower level of Japanese wages, and they brought pressure to bear on the United States government to raise tariffs on a variety of Japanese goods. On the other hand, many Japanese businessmen resented their dependence on the American market and looked increasingly to the resumption of exports to the "natural" market of Japan — China. By 1965 Japanese trade with China had risen to almost half-a-billion dollars a year.

Before World War II the Japanese islands, with an area of 147,611 square miles, already supported a population of 70 million, a density of 474 to the square mile. After 1945 the repatriation of 6 million Japanese from Japan's lost territories overseas raised the total, and a high birth rate added a million new mouths to feed each year. By 1950 the Japanese population had passed 83 million. The postwar birth rate of more than 30 per thousand, combined with a death rate that declined to 11 per thousand, created a serious problem. The Japanese islands could not provide food for such numbers. Cereals, vegetables, and sugar had come to form half the Japanese imports. Facing their dilemma in a realistic spirit the Japanese decided they must reduce their birth rate. By 1965 they had lowered it to 17 per thousand, and their death rate to about 7 per thousand, while life expectancy rose to 68 years. As a consequence, the Japanese population stood at 98 million in 1965 instead of exceeding 110 million as it might have done.

The Japanese peace treaty of 1951 removed international obstacles to

Japanese rearmament. There was, however, a "renunciation of war" clause in the Japanese postwar constitution. On the ground that renunciation of war did not imply renunciation of self-defense, the Japanese government was persuaded to disregard this limitation in 1954. It began to build a "Self-Defense Force," consisting of military, naval, and air reserves, which were to reach the modest total of 241,000 by 1966. As in Germany, there was no great enthusiasm for rearmament in Japan. Many Japanese felt a strong distrust of militarism, which had brought them defeat, humiliation and suffering. The Japanese, moreover, were the only people who had direct experience of the horrors of atomic war. In the event of war between the United States and Russia, Japan — as an ally of the United States — was likely to be a primary target of Soviet nuclear bombs. This terrifying thought fed a strong neutralist opinion in Japan, which was led by but was not limited to the Socialists.

At the same time other factors stimulated a revival of Japanese nationalism. The Japanese nationalists did not object to rearmament, but they criticized the supposed subservience of Japan to the United States. Yielding a little to both pressures, the Japanese government renegotiated its treaty with the United States, to limit the rights American forces exercised in Japan. In 1960, after months of bargaining, Prime Minister Nobusuke Kishi signed a new United States–Japanese Treaty of Mutual Cooperation and Security in Washington. The ratification of the treaty by the Japanese Diet in May, 1960, became an occasion for mass demonstrations in Tokyo by leftist students and other neutralists. The government was obliged to cancel a scheduled visit to Japan by President Eisenhower. Shortly afterward, an unsuccessful attempt was made on the life of Kishi by a fanatical nationalist. These incidents embarrassed both governments and raised some doubts in the United States about the future of Japan as a democracy and an ally, but they did not appear to impair American-Japanese relations seriously.

2. TAIWAN

The development of Nationalist China followed a somewhat similar course to that of Japan. After the collapse of the Nationalist regime in China (see Chapter 49), the Nationalist government, the remnants of the Nationalist army, and many civilians fled to the island of Taiwan (Formosa). The Nationalist government under General Chiang Kai-shek established its headquarters in the island's capital of Taipei. Since it claimed to represent all China, it maintained the constitution of 1946. The Nationalists experienced at first considerable difficulty in maintaining themselves in Taiwan. The resources of the island appeared too limited to support the population, suddenly swollen by the flood of refugees from the mainland (in 1966 the population of Taiwan was 12.8 million including about

1.5 million mainland Chinese). Friction developed between the newcomers and the indigenous population, which was Chinese, apart from the remnants of the head-hunting Malay aborigines. During fifty years of Japanese rule (1895–1945) the Taiwan Chinese developed a distinct, insular mentality, but they gradually came to accept and merge with the Nationalist influx. Thanks to the massive aid of the United States ($1.5 billion between 1951 and 1965), as well as their own commercial enterprise, the economic situation of the Taiwanese improved. Increase in the production of sugar, rice, and tea left surpluses, which accounted for three-fourths of the island's exports. The development of roads and hydroelectric power stimulated the growth of small-scale industry, especially textiles, machinery, and household goods. By 1965 exports were almost sufficient to pay for imports. Consequently, United States economic aid was terminated, although military aid continued.

The international position of the Nationalist regime of Chiang Kai-shek was also dependent on the policies of the United States. After the defeat of the Nationalist government, not only Russia but also Britain, India, and many other noncommunist nations recognized the Chinese Communist government at Peking. The United States, after a brief initial period of "waiting for the dust to settle" in China, adopted a policy of firm support of the Nationalist government in Taiwan. In the same statement (1950) in which he announced the United States' intervention in defense of Korea, President Truman made it known that he had ordered the United States Seventh Fleet to "neutralize" the Formosa Straits, that is, to interpose a protective shield between Nationalist-held Taiwan and Communist China. In the United Nations the United States successfully blocked the Soviet efforts to transfer the Chinese seat in the Security Council from the Nationalist government at Taiwan to the Communist government at Peking. To resolve the ensuing impasse, Britain proposed the "two-China" policy, that is, recognition of the Communist government as representing mainland China and the Nationalist government as representing Taiwan. This proposal, however, was rejected by both Chinese governments and their Soviet and American backers. The Nationalist government continued to insist that it alone spoke for China, and the Communist government continued to claim Taiwan.

In November, 1954, the Communists began to bombard some Nationalist-held, off-shore islands (Quemoy, Matsu, and Tachen), which raised the fear that they were preparing for an assault on Taiwan. The United States responded to this threat by concluding with the Nationalist government a Mutual Defense Treaty (December 1, 1954). At the request of President Eisenhower, Congress passed the "Formosa Resolution," authorizing him to use American forces "as he deems necessary for the specific purpose of securing and protecting Formosa and the Pescadores against armed attack, this authority to include securing and protection of such related positions and territories of that area now in friendly hands" (January 25, 1955). Whether this meant that the United States would defend the off-shore islands remained uncertain even as late as the presidential campaign of 1960, in which this issue figured prominently. In January, 1955, the United States persuaded the Nationalist government to evacuate the distant (200 miles) Tachen Islands. But in August, 1958, when the Communists renewed the bombardment of Matsu and Quemoy, the United States assisted in their defense.

Still hopeful that he might return to the mainland, Chiang Kai-shek proposed in 1965 that Communist China's nuclear power be destroyed, an insurrection incited there, and an invasion launched against the coastal provinces. The proposal was inspired, clearly, by hopes that the Americans might soon expand the Vietnam conflict.

3. THAILAND AND MALAYSIA

The kingdom of Thailand (Siam), lying between Burma and Indochina, was the only state in Southeast Asia that did not come under European control during the nineteenth century. In World War II the Thai government formed an alliance with the Japanese and declared war on Great Britain and the United States. When Japan was defeated the Thais made peace by restoring the territories they had annexed from British Malaya and French Indochina. Though nominally a kingdom, under King Bhumibol Adulyadej, Thailand was ruled in the postwar period by Marshal Pibul Songgram, who gained a commanding position through two military *coups d'état* in 1947 and 1951 and, after his overthrow, by General Thanom Kittikachorn.

With an area of 198,270 square miles and a population of 30 million in 1964, Thailand supported 150 inhabitants to the square mile. The religion of the great majority was Buddhism. Agriculture dominated the economy and rice, rubber, tin, and teak wood comprised the bulk of the exports. Imports consisted mainly of textiles, machinery, and petroleum. Per capita income was low but rose slowly to approximately $100 a year in 1965.

With long land frontiers, difficult to defend, the Thai government felt a need for allies. It joined the Southeast Asia Treaty Organization in 1954 and accepted financial and military aid from the United States. Thailand also participated in the Colombo Plan and received economic assistance from the United States. Excessive dependence on one commodity (rice), large expenditures for defense, a rising population, and low living standards intensified the problems common to underdeveloped countries. Medical care provided by the United Nations improved health and sanitation by curbing malaria and other diseases of the tropics, but expansion of the economy barely kept pace with the resulting rise in population.

The gravest danger that menaced Thailand after 1960 was the risk that it would become involved in the expanding war that ravaged its neighbor, Vietnam. As Thailand accepted American aid, financial and military, and provided bases for American planes, the Communist government of North Vietnam, and the Communist leaders at Peking, threatened to stir up civil war within Thailand as a method of retaliation. In 1965 two Communist-supported groups in the country, the Thailand Independent Movement and the Thailand Patriotic Front, joined forces with the avowed intention of driving all American forces out and establishing a new government in Thailand on communist lines.

The states of the Malay Peninsula, which came under British protection in the nineteenth century, were occupied by the Japanese in World War II after the fall of the British naval base at Singapore. After the war the British returned to Malaya but faced a bitter ten-year guerrilla struggle with Communist insurgents. Despite the resultant disturbances, plans for a peaceful transference of power to an independent Malayan government were carried out. The Malayan Federation of eleven states became an independent state in 1957 with a parliamentary government but remained a member of the (British) Commonwealth.

In 1963 an attempt was made to establish a union of four states, the Federation of Malaya, the State of Singapore, and the (British) colonies of North Borneo and Sarawak. The new union took the name Malaysia; it had an area of 128,654 square miles and a population approaching 11 million. But troubles beset it from the start. President Sukarno of Indonesia sought to wreck it by border attacks on Borneo. The four newly independent territories failed to work well together. In 1965 Singapore seceded from the union and became an independent state, and both Sarawak and North Borneo (renamed Sabah) threatened to withdraw. When the hostilities between Malaysia and Indonesia ended in 1966, Sabah and Sarawak became less dependent on Malaysian (and British) defense aid. Proposals were voiced that a new federation be formed to include Borneo, Sarawak, and the British protectorate of Brunei, but not the Federation of Malaya.

4. THE REPUBLIC OF INDONESIA

During World War II the Japanese occupied the Dutch East Indies, but after they withdrew the Dutch attempted to reassert control. The Indonesians wanted independence, and after four years of struggle and negotiation the United Nations intervened and the Dutch yielded. By a settlement worked out at The Hague in 1949 Indonesia became a sovereign state, and a constitution adopted in 1950 declared it a unitary republic. The Dutch hoped to keep Indonesia part of their empire as a self-governing member of the Netherlands Union, but the Indonesians felt too much resentment against their late masters to keep this plan alive.

In 1954 the Union was dissolved, and in 1957 the Indonesian government expelled Dutch citizens and took over most of their property. One reason for the strained relations was the refusal of the Netherlands government to cede its half of New Guinea to the new republic.

Indonesia had an area of 735,268 square miles and a population of 107 million in 1965. The dominant faith was Islam and nine-tenths of the people were Moslems. Two-thirds of the population lived on the crowded islands of Java and Madura, one-sixth on Sumatra, and the remainder was distributed throughout the three thousand islands of the archipelago. This diffusion made the ideal of a unitary republic difficult to achieve. An experiment with parliamentary democracy did not work well, and President Sukarno assumed increasing authority. Adopting a program which he described as "guided democracy," he dismissed the parliament in 1960.

The problems that confronted the Indonesians — low income, high birth rate, and an economy heavily dependent on exports of petroleum and rubber — were intensified by lack of capital. Distrusting the Western European powers and the United States, Sukarno hesitated to accept financial assistance from Washington. Between 1955 and 1960 Indonesia received some $200 million in American aid but balanced it by grants approximating $250 million from the Soviet Union. Like Prime Minister Nehru of India, Sukarno kept his government "uncommitted" in the Cold War.

With a birth rate of 43 per thousand and a death rate of 21, the Indonesian population rose rapidly. This created serious difficulties for a nation with a per capita income of less than $100, a nation that had to import millions of tons of rice. The government sought to make Indonesia self-supporting in food products by encouraging the use of better seed and fertilizer, and by urging a migration to the outer islands from the densely-peopled islands of Java and Madura. Java, with nearly 1000 inhabitants per square mile, was one of the most densely populated areas of the globe. This congestion was certain to increase, for the United Nations, through its World Health Organization and Children's Fund, aided the Indonesian Ministry of Health to combat prevalent diseases. Malaria, yaws, and trachoma were successfully reduced, but plague, venereal disease, and leprosy proved more difficult to curb.

The years of Japanese occupation, followed by the struggle for independence and the expulsion of many European officials and overseers, dislocated Indonesian life. Illiteracy remained high (estimates varied from 45 to 85 per cent) and the lack of teachers, physicians, engineers, and other trained personnel retarded the plans for economic and social improvement.

Independence did not solve the dilemma of the Indonesians. Like other Asian and African peoples, who attributed their poverty to the exploitation they had endured under European control, they faced the realization that political liberty did not bring prosperity. President Sukarno's administration mismanaged the finances, and the conflict he pursued with Malaysia increased government deficits. He denounced American imperialism, favored the Communists, and sought closer ties with Peking. But an attempted coup by the Indonesian Communists in 1965 brought swift retaliation. It is estimated that 300,000 people perished for suspected leftist sympathy. Although Sukarno who was suspected of playing a part in the attempted coup remained in office, a military group headed by General Suharto took control. The military junta blamed the former government officials for the chaotic state of the finances and the growing inflation; but it was not clear that the new masters had a workable plan for restoring Indonesian economic life to a sound condition.

5. THE REPUBLIC OF THE PHILIPPINES

The Philippine Islands, which the United States acquired from Spain in 1898, progressed steadily during the half-century that they remained under American control. The population, between 7 and 8 million at the opening of the twentieth century, was close to 19 million in 1946, when the Philippines became independent, and reached 32 million in 1965. The Philippine Archipelago included over seven thousand islands or islets with a total area of 115,600 square miles, but only 400 were permanently inhabited. About one-third of the Filipinos understood English, one-third Tagalog (adopted as the national tongue), and the remainder spoke various dialects. About 72% were literate by 1965. Though Spanish sank into disuse, a large majority of the people (over four-fifths) remained members of the Roman Catholic religion, to which their ancestors were converted during the centuries of Spanish rule.

In World War II the Philippines were occupied by the Japanese, and the complete independence which had been promised in a Congressional measure of 1934 was delayed. On the return of peace, the Republic of the Philippines was inaugurated (July 4, 1946), with a Senate and House of Representatives (chosen by literate citizens over twenty-one) and a president who was also elected by popular vote.

Recovery from the damage and devastation of the war years was delayed by Communist guerrillas, whose resistance was suppressed by the wise and energetic measures of Ramón Magsaysay, who was elected president in 1953 but was killed in an airplane accident in 1957. After years of negotiation a settlement on Japanese reparations for war damage was concluded in 1956. Japan undertook to pay over half-a-billion dollars in twenty years and to provide a quarter of a billion dollars in private loans. The United States supported the Philippine economy with financial assistance and its defense forces with military aid. Like most Asian countries the republic depended heavily on a few agricultural crops. Sugar and coconut products constituted half the exports; rice and corn were grown for food; and machinery, textiles, and petroleum were imported. The trade balance was heavily adverse, but American aid of more than $100 million a year helped to resolve this problem. Per capita income in the Philippines averaged $130 a year, a low figure but considerably better than most Asian people received.

Improvements in medical care and sanitation reduced the death rate, though infant mortality remained high. Life expectancy was about 49 years in 1965, twenty years less than in the United States. The birth rate, which had been 33 per thousand before World War II, rose to 50 per thousand in the 1950's, and the population continued to rise at a rapid rate.

Expenditures for economic and social development and for education formed the major items in the Philippine budget. The defense of the republic continued to rest very largely with the United States which maintained air and naval bases in the islands. A ninety-nine year mutual defense treaty between the two countries was concluded in 1947, and the Philippines joined the Southeast Asia Treaty Organization when it was formed in 1954. Years of discussion and friction over the rights of American personnel and the administration of American bases in the Philippines led to a new agreement in 1959 which limited the United States forces to four major bases and restricted their privileges. Despite such disputes, however, American-Philippine relations remained firm. As a charter member of the United Nations the Philippine Republic sent 6000 troops to support the United Nations forces in the Korean War, and also supported the United States forces in their efforts to expel communist invaders and to pacify South Vietnam.

6. THE SECOND INDOCHINESE WAR

The costly war that racked French Indochina from 1946 to 1954 has been described in Chapter 49. The defeat suffered by the French in this First Indochinese War, and the surrender of North Vietnam to Communist rule, left the states of Indochina in a precarious balance. Though South Vietnam became an independent republic and Cambodia and Laos independent monarchies, the Geneva armistice agreement of 1954 that ended the First Indochinese War denied these new states the right to join the Southeast Asia Treaty Organization or other military pacts. Cambodia and Laos were admitted to the United Nations but North and South Vietnam were not, for the armistice plans provided for a plebiscite in 1956 to determine their future. The plebiscite was not held.

It was a much more difficult task to prevent Communist infiltration across a land frontier than to guard seagirt islands such as the Philippines or Taiwan. The United States furnished $1 billion in financial and

SOUTHEAST ASIA, 1966

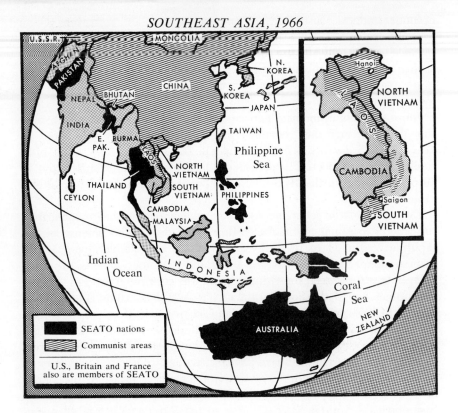

military assistance to South Vietnam between 1954 and 1960. It also provided some $200 million in aid to Laos, but its assistance to Cambodia was restricted to peaceful enterprises.

The regime established in the northern zone of Vietnam after 1954 was Communist. North Vietnam became a "People's Republic" with a constitution resembling that of the People's Republic of China, and Ho Chi Minh, who had led the resistance in the First Indochinese War and expelled the French, became president of the North Vietnamese government. North Vietnam had an area of 63,344 square miles and a population of 17 million by 1965.

In the southern zone of Vietnam a republic was set up, with a National Assembly, and a Christian Vietnamese, Ngo Dinh Diem as chief of state. South Vietnam had an area of 66,263 square miles and a population that reached about 16 million by 1965. Nearly 1 million refugees from North Vietnam sought refuge in the South, and hundreds of thousands of peasants, seeking to escape rough treatment by the Communists in their areas, migrated to the cities of South Vietnam. The civil war waged by the "National Liberation Front" as the insurgents (Viet Cong) styled themselves, increased the wretchedness and confusion in South Vietnam and intensified the discontent against President Diem's rule. In 1961 Diem proclaimed a state of emergency and the National Assembly voted him extraordinary powers. Unwisely, he used his authority to persecute his critics, particularly the Buddhist leaders. In 1963 a sudden insurrection overturned his government and he was taken prisoner and murdered.

For two years a succession of military and civilian groups attempted to set up a stable administration and restore order, but without success. The Viet Cong, profiting by the political confusion took over large sections of the country. The South Vietnamese army became discouraged in their efforts to resist the forays and ambushes of their guerrilla foes. In 1965 a young Air Vice Marshal, Nguyen Cao Ky, was chosen premier and the morale of the army began to improve.

Yet it appeared all but certain that, without more help from outside, the South Vietnamese Republic could not survive. It was already receiving American aid, both in money, food, and military supplies, and American advisers were helping to train the South Vietnamese forces. By 1963 it became apparent that such assistance would prove insufficient. After some hesitation the United States began, in 1964, to pledge reinforcements in the form of American troops. The purpose of the American expeditionary force was to aid the South Vietnamese in checking the infiltration of Communist reinforcements and supplies from North Vietnam, and the American government emphasized that its forces were in South Vietnam at the invitation of the South Vietnamese government to assist in repelling an armed invasion and subversion. The issue was not as clear and simple as this, however. The war in South Vietnam was in part a civil war, for the Viet Cong, or National Liberation Front, was composed of South Vietnamese as well as North Vietnamese Communist sympathizers. Ho Chi Minh and other Communist spokesmen protested that the Viet Cong were fighting the Americans for the same reason that they had fought the French — because the people of Vietnam wanted no alien and imperialistic nation to rule and exploit them.

By 1964 the United States had nearly 200,000 men in South Vietnam; by 1966 the number exceeded 400,000. In 1965 American bombing planes, from airfields and from aircraft carriers, began to raid military targets and supply depots in North Vietnam. The intent was to induce the North Vietnamese to halt the aid they were providing for the Viet Cong, or to check the flow of aid by destroying railroads, bridges, trucks, and ferries. But air power alone proved incapable of fulfilling this purpose. The Americans were also unsuccessful in preventing the theft and diversion to the Viet Cong of arms and supplies intended for their own troops.

As the fighting intensified and the casualties mounted, the risk grew that further "escalation" of the fighting might lead to a major war involving the United States with China and possibly other communist countries. In the Korean War (1950–53), the United States had the support and endorsement of the United Nations; but in the Second Vietnamese War, world opinion was critical of the American policy and American intentions. Of the forty two states around the globe with which the United States had treaties and accords for mutual security, few approved the American course and fewer still offered assistance. Australia and New Zealand sent several thousand troops to fight with the United States detachments in South Vietnam; South Korea dispatched 15,000 soldiers; and the Republic of the Philippines offered military aid. By 1966, when the tide began to turn against the Viet Cong, the electors of South Vietnam went to the polls and chose an assembly which would restore civilian rule and orderly government. But repeated appeals to North Vietnam and to China to halt the fighting and open peace discussions were scornfully rejected. The people of Vietnam, who had known two decades of conflict, continued to suffer and endure with fortitude; but plagues and epidemics spread increasingly through the stricken land and threatened to cause millions of deaths before they could be brought under control.

65

THE NEAR AND MIDDLE EAST

The idea that the Middle East as a whole is a region of extreme poverty can . . . no longer be accepted without major qualification.[1]

1. PROBLEMS AND PROSPECTS

IN THE NEAR AND MIDDLE EAST — as everywhere else — World War II stimulated nationalism and social discontent. Both forces were directed against the European powers which, directly or indirectly, had long exercised a dominating influence in the region. In the postwar years this influence rapidly declined (see Chapter 50). However, the withdrawal of the Europeans did not result in any quick improvement in the standards of living of the people of the region, since its resources were limited. Traditionally, agriculture and grazing provided the principal occupation for its people. Owing to a water shortage, cultivable land was at a premium, and it was generally owned by a class of landowners and tilled by peasants under a system of land tenure that was invariably grossly unfair to the tenants, who were generally ruthlessly exploited. Additional land was suitable for grazing, but it could sustain only a thin population of nomads, organized along ancient tribal lines.

Landowners, tribal chiefs, government officials, and army officers constituted a ruling elite in most of the countries of the Near and Middle East. Their record for honesty, justice, and social responsibility was not an edifying one. As long as it was possible to blame the Europeans for all the ills in the region, the system was not seriously challenged; but with the disappearance of the Europeans, it was necessary to come to grips with the real causes of the economic and social ills. As a result, in the postwar years efforts were made in all countries of the region to develop their resources, combat disease, and reduce illiteracy. These efforts were often halting and quite uneven in the various countries, but some progress was registered in all of them.

[1] Royal Institute of International Affairs, *The Middle East, A Political and Economic Survey* (3rd edition, New York: Oxford University Press, 1958), p. 53.

The spokesmen of progress were members of the *intelligentsia* — the small but growing class of men educated along Western lines. Reflecting a nineteenth-century European tradition, most of these men were trained for government service or as lawyers and professors. Engineers and doctors were less numerous. An education in liberal arts generally stimulates an interest in politics. Most of the intellectuals in the Near and Middle East were articulate, although politically inexperienced; often they contented themselves with criticism, which was frequently more demagogic than constructive. Nevertheless, there were some men who were anxious to do more than talk and criticize — junior army officers who had acquired in military colleges a smattering of Western culture. Intensely nationalistic and keenly aware of the backwardness and weakness of their countries, these "armed intellectuals" were impatient with the older generation of leaders. Possessing military skills, they were determined to hasten progress by seizing power through military coups. Outstanding examples of this pattern of evolution were the revolutions in Egypt in 1952 led by Colonel Gamal Abdul Nasser and in Iraq in 1958 led by Colonel Abdul Karim Kassim. Military dictatorships replaced pseudo-parliamentary monarchies in both countries. In some countries of the Near and Middle East pseudo-parliamentary regimes persisted, and in others feudal monarchies based on tribal and religious loyalties survived. But the general trend appeared to be toward authoritarian regimes based on armies. An exception was Israel.

The *intelligentsia* were receptive to Western ideas of social justice and economic progress, but they were undecided as to whether these should be attained by gradual evolution, as suggested by the Western democracies, or by radical revolutions, as suggested by the Communist countries, for the peoples of the Near and Middle East were caught in the East-West struggle not only on an international plane but also on an ideological one. The Cold War presented both dangers and opportunities: dangers of new foreign domination and opportunities to obtain from the competing power blocs economic and technical assistance necessary for economic development.

The development of oil promised the quickest rewards, but none of the countries in the Near and Middle East which possessed this resource (Saudi Arabia, Kuwait, Iran, Iraq, Bahrain, Trucial Oman, and Qatar), had the necessary capital and skill to develop it. Much as they resented it, they still had to depend on the capital and technical know-how of foreigners. In the immediate postwar years only British and American skill and money were available. Later Italian, German, and Japanese enterprise entered the field. By playing off the competing foreign oil interests against each other, the oil-producing countries of the Near and Middle East were able to get a better share of the profits of the industry. The 50:50 formula for sharing profits, prevalent in the oil-producing countries of Latin America for some time, became general also in the Near and Middle East.

The principal market for the Near Eastern oil was Western Europe but increasingly also the United States, which since World War II has become an importer of oil. While the income from oil made it possible to develop other resources in the oil-producing countries, the countries which did not produce oil had to depend on their traditional exports or on loans to finance their development. In 1955 Russia and later China entered the field of foreign aid. They were not interested in oil, of which Russia at least was an exporter, but in extending their political influence in the region. Thanks to the rivalry which developed between them and the Western countries, even the poorest of the Near and Middle Eastern countries were able to secure foreign aid on advantageous terms.

2. EGYPT, IRAQ, AND THE FERTILE CRESCENT

The postwar development of the Arab states was marked by many dramatic political events and less evident but still important social and economic progress. Owing to its large population and strategic location on the Suez Canal, the most important of the Arab states was Egypt. The population of Egypt was officially estimated in 1965 at 29.2 million. This indicated an increase of 3.1 million over 1960 when the last official census was taken, and represented an average annual increase of over 600,000. The fast growth of population created strains on the Egyptian economy, which was based on agriculture, with cotton its principal export. The resulting social restlessness vented itself first against the British and, after their withdrawal from the country (except the Canal area), against the government of King Faruk (1936–1952) which was corrupt to a degree shocking even in the Near and Middle East. The humiliating defeat of Egypt at the hands of Israel in 1948 completely discredited Faruk. On July 23, 1952, a junta of junior officers carried out a bloodless coup, which resulted in the exile of the king and a year later (June 18, 1953) in the proclamation of a republic under the presidency of General Mohammed Naguib. However, there soon developed a struggle for power between Naguib and a junior officer, Lt.-Colonel Nasser, who appeared to have been the real inspirer of the revolution. In April, 1954, Naguib was removed and Nasser succeeded him.

The Revolutionary Command Council, as the officers' junta styled itself, had a revolutionary program. The old political parties were suppressed and a single authoritarian political grouping, the Liberation Rally, organized. From 1952 on, a radical land reform was carried out which resulted in partitioning of the estates among peasants, but it failed to remedy the basic problems of land hunger and overpopulation. These could be solved only by increasing the irrigated area and by industrialization. The Egyptian government made plans for the construction of the Aswan High Dam, which was to increase arable land by some 2 million acres, but for this Egypt needed capital. As already seen (p. 596), Egyptian negotiations with the United States and Britain concerning the Dam broke down in June, 1956, followed by the nationalization of the Suez Canal and the Suez crisis. In 1958 Egypt received a large Soviet loan to carry out a five-year plan of industrialization. In the following year, after the Egyptian government came to an agreement with the Suez Canal Company on compensation for the nationalization of its property and with Sudan on the distribution of the Nile waters, the United States renewed financial and technical assistance to Egypt. As a result, work on the High Aswan Dam began in 1960.

Though badly mauled militarily during the Suez conflict, Egypt came out of the scrap diplomatically strengthened, and President Nasser used his increased prestige to advance the cause of Arab unification under Egyptian leadership. Leaders of other Arab states resented his tendency to arrogate to himself the exclusive right to speak for the Arabs, but they feared to challenge him openly, for the ideal of Arab unity which he came to symbolize was popular with the Arab masses. At the command of the shrill "Voice of the Arabs," broadcast over Radio Cairo, demonstrators poured into the streets of Amman, Beirut, Damascus, and Bagdad. The Egyptian-led Pan-Arab movement culminated in 1958. On February 1 Syria agreed to merge with Egypt into the United Arab Republic (UAR), and on March 8 Yemen federated with UAR, although this association remained a paper one. In July it appeared that Iraq, Jordan, and Lebanon would join UAR, but the landing of American troops in Lebanon and of British paratroopers in Jordan halted the movement. On September 30, 1961, Syria seceded from the United Arab Republic. Nevertheless, Egypt continued to style itself United Arab Republic. Thereafter Nasser's prestige with the Arabs declined. In addition to addressing itself to the Arabs, Egyptian propaganda turned to the inchoate nations of Africa. It assiduously preached to them the doctrine of "positive neutralism," which presumably meant a risky policy of playing off the great power blocs of East and West against each other and deriving benefits from both.

This propaganda was not without success, although it did not lead to particularly close relations between Egypt and the African nations. Sudan, the vast territory (967,500 square miles) on the upper Nile with a mixed Arab and Negro population (estimated in 1965 at about 13.2 million), which had long been associated with Egypt under British rule, voted to become an independent republic (proclaimed on January 1, 1956). Libya, the former Italian colony west of Egypt (679,350 square miles), for the most part a bleak desert with a thin Arab population (estimated in 1964 at 1.6 million) and still nomadic in the interior, became under UN auspices an independent monarchy (January 2, 1952). It showed little inclination to merge with Egypt, especially after the discovery of rich oil deposits in 1955.

The traditional rival of Egypt for the leadership of the Arab world was Iraq, a large (172,000 square miles), potentially rich, and rather thinly populated country estimated at 7.6 million in 1965 in the Tigris-Euphrates valley. In 1950 the Iraqi government established a Development Board to draw up and execute a series of five-year plans for the development of the country's considerable resources, the richest of which was oil in the Mosul and Kirkuk areas. The oil fields were owned by the government, but oil was extracted, refined, and marketed by the Iraq Petroleum Co., an international concern (British, American, French, and Dutch) under a concession granted in 1951 providing for the conventional 50:50 split of profits. The Board of Development was allocated 70 per cent of Iraq's oil revenues. The main development project was irrigation and flood control in the Tigris-Euphrates valley. Its aim was to extend the arable land of the valley to over 10 million acres and to make the country into a flourishing "Garden of Eden," as it had been in classical antiquity.

The political development of Iraq up to the Revolution of 1958 was marked by relative stability and a pro-Western orientation. In 1952, at the age of fourteen, King Faisal II (1939–1958) formally acceded to the throne. His uncle and former regent, Abdul Illah, continued to exercise a strong influence, but the real strong man of the regime was Nuri es-Said, a former Ottoman officer who had gone over to the British in World War I and thereafter always represented the pro-British and pro-Allied course in Iraqi politics. Said was instrumental in the formation of the Arab League in 1945 and sought to steer the whole Arab world into the western camp. He favored good relations with Turkey and Iran and in 1955 took the lead in the formation of the Bagdad Pact. To counter the formation of the United Arab Republic under the aegis of Egypt in 1958, he formed with Jordan (ruled by Faisal's Hashimite cousin, King Hussein) the Arab Union (AU) under aegis of Iraq (February 14, 1958). Said's rivalry and pro-Western course won him the bitter enmity of Nasser. Radio Cairo vilified him as "a stooge of Western imperialism" and undermined his position in Iraq, and on July 14, 1958, a junta of junior "Free Officers" led by Colonel Kassim carried out a swift coup against Said's government. King Faisal and his uncle were assassinated in their palace, and Said was lynched by a mob as he sought to escape from Bagdad. Kassim, who became premier in a new republican regime, withdrew Iraq from the Arab Union and declared it a "part of the Arab nation."

The coup was generally regarded as a preliminary step to the merger of Iraq and UAR, but once in power Kassim showed little inclination to surrender it to Nasser. Instead, he pursued a cagey and tortuous policy designed to perpetuate and consolidate his personal dictatorship. By reaffirming Iraq's international obligations he won speedy recognition from the Western powers, but to rid himself of the dangerous taint of being pro-Western, he withdrew Iraq from the Bagdad Pact and proclaimed

Iraq's neutrality (March, 1959).[2] He then concluded an arms deal with Russia. At the same time, to rid himself of his opponents at home, at first he gave free rein to Communists against the partisans of the fallen regime, then in 1959 suppressed his erstwhile comrades who were impatient to merge with Egypt, and finally in 1960 curbed the Communists, who were getting out of hand. On February 8, 1963, Colonel Kassim was overthrown and killed by pro-Nasser officers. But his rival and successor Colonel Abdul Salam Arif (1963–66), despite ardent support of Arab unity, was unwilling to accept Nasser's terms for union of Iraq and Egypt: complete subordination to his (Nasser's) direction. Iraq's political situation has remained extremely unstable. The problem of the Kurds who inhabited the northern districts of Iraq, adjoining the Kurdish-inhabited districts of Iran, Turkey, and Syria, likewise contributed to Iraqi instability. Under the leadership of Mustafa al-Barzani who had spent some time in the Soviet Union, the Iraqi Kurds were more or less in continuous revolt. Their objective was the establishment of an independent Kurdistan, or at least substantial autonomy in Iraq.

Jordan (Transjordan until 1949), the last of the Hashimite kingdoms, had to travel a difficult path after the war. It was an artificial state created by the British in 1921 out of their Palestinian mandate to accommodate their wartime Arab ally, Emir Abdullah (1921–1951). Until the Palestinian War in 1948, it was a desert kingdom peopled mainly by nomads. Since its resources were negligible, its administration and small but efficient British-trained army (the "Arab Legion") were supported by a modest British subsidy. As a result of the Palestinian War in 1948 Jordan acquired a portion of east-central Palestine (the area of Jordan after 1948 was about 37,500 square miles), and a horde of some 600,000 refugees, who had fled or had been expelled by the Israelis from Palestine. The population of the country more than tripled, from an estimated 400,000 to 1,420,000. This growth was far from a boon, since Jordan simply did not have the resources to take care of the refugees. The growth also had adverse political results. The original Jordanese had developed a feudal loyalty to King Abdullah, but the new, ex-Palestinian Jordanese considered him a British tool and bitterly reproached him for not continuing the war until the last Jew was driven from Palestine. In July, 1951, King Abdullah was assassinated by a disgruntled ex-Palestinian. He was succeeded briefly by his son, who, however, had to be removed for insanity, and then by his youthful grandson, King Hussein I (1951–   ).

The position of King Hussein was extremely precarious, for the ex-Palestinians were responsive to Egyptian Pan-Arab propaganda and favored a merger with Egypt and Syria. By inciting riots in Jordan, Egypt was able to prevent the king from joining the Bagdad Pact (December, 1955) and then to force him to expel the British military mission and

[2] Deprived of its headquarters in Bagdad, METO moved to Ankara and renamed itself CENTO (Central Treaty Organization) (October, 1959).

renounce the British subsidy (March, 1956). To forestall merger with the United Arab Republic, Jordan formed with Iraq the rival Arab Union (February, 1958). After the dissolution of this union as a result of the Kassim coup in Bagdad, King Hussein appealed to the British for help. At the same time that American marines landed in Lebanon, British paratroopers arrived in Jordan (July 17, 1958). Thereafter Egyptian influence declined and the king somewhat consolidated his position. Thanks to generous American economic aid, the economic situation of the country improved, but the future of Jordan remained doubtful.

Syria was the larger (72,234 square miles), richer, and most populous of the former French mandatory territories in the Near and Middle East. Its mineral wealth was relatively small, but its agriculture, small-scale industries, and handicrafts were able to support a population estimated in 1964 at 5.4 million. After the end of the French rule, Syria experienced great political instability. The nationalist politicians, who had won independence from France, showed little aptitude for governing. The Syrian fiasco in the Palestinian War in 1948 completely discredited them. In March, 1949, a young army colonel overthrew the republican regime at Damascus, and for five years Syria was ruled by a succession of three military dictators. These proved no more able to handle the situation than the old republican politicians. In February, 1954, a constitutional regime was restored. Four years later, in February, 1958, the pressure of Egyptian Pan-Arab propaganda and the fear of communism, which was making rapid gains, led President Shukri Quwatli to negotiate with Nasser the merger of Syria and Egypt in the United Arab Republic. Under the new government Syrian parties were abolished, the Communists suppressed, and a land reform launched. In September, 1961, the Baath (Arab Socialist Renaissance) party, which professed support for Arab unity but opposed Egyptian domination, engineered a successful coup and Syria seceded from the United Arab Republic. However, the new Baath government was unable to provide stability. Abortive coups by pro-Nasser elements, the conservative Moslem Brotherhood, and business interests dissatisfied with the Socialist policies of the government, followed one another with monotonous regularity, while the Syrian economy stagnated.

Perhaps the most evolved and certainly the most Westernized of the Arab states of the Near and Middle East was the little Republic of Lebanon (4000 square miles). Although most Lebanese are Arabs, only about half of them are Moslems, with the rest Christians. However, both religious communities, Moslem and Christian, are subdivided into a variety of mutually antagonistic sects. During the French mandatory rule an unwritten convention was established that the president of the republic should be a Christian, the prime minister a Sunni Moslem, and the president of the single-chamber parliament a Shii Moslem. Cabinet posts were distributed to give due representation to the various sects.

By another convention designed to preserve the delicate equilibrium among the religious communities, no census has been taken in Lebanon since the French rule. The population is estimated to number over 2 million, one-third of whom live in the capital, Beirut.

The Christian Lebanese traditionally looked to Christian Europe. These Western contacts were strengthened by large-scale emigration from Lebanon to the United States. Although Lebanon participated in the Palestinian War in 1948, it did so without fanaticism. The Egyptian Pan-Arab propaganda found ready response only among the Sunni Moslems. In the spring of 1958 a complicated civil war broke out over this issue, in which the Lebanese army refused to intervene. When the Kassim coup took place in Bagdad and it was generally thought that the Arab world was about to unite, President Chamoun invited the United States to land troops (July 17, 1958). Although the American marines did not intervene in the civil war, their presence had a sobering effect on Nasser's partisans and the civil strife died down. Chamoun's successor, General Fuad Chehab, paid lip service to the ideal of Arab unity and to neutralism, but Lebanese independence was maintained.

The resources of Lebanon are negligible. Still the country enjoyed relative prosperity because of its position as the "Switzerland of the Near and Middle East." Beirut became a great tourist and banking center and a clearing house for most business transactions in the Near and Middle East, and there were numerous small industries. Lebanon collected sizeable tolls because Tripoli and Sidon were terminals of oil pipelines from Iraq and Saudi Arabia.

3. PENINSULAR ARABIA

Until recent times, peninsular Arabia, or *Arabia Deserta*, as distinguished from the Fertile Crescent, was regarded as a worthless desert. It long remained isolated and only thinly populated by primitive nomads. Only in the coastal regions — in Hejaz adjoining the Red Sea, in Yemen in mountainous southern Arabia, in Aden, Hadramaut, and Oman facing the Arabian Sea, and in the Persian Gulf sheikdoms — was settled life possible. However, the discovery of oil in the area adjoining the Persian Gulf in the 1930's gave it great commercial importance, and oil revenues gave several Arab states unexpected means for economic, social, and cultural development.

The largest of the states of peninsular Arabia is Saudi Arabia (870,000 square miles, with a population estimated in 1965 at 6.8 million). Saudi Arabia was created by the remarkable exploits of the crafty desert warrior, ibn-Saud (see p. 359). To his people, who consisted mainly of adherents of the fanatical, puritanical sect of Wahabis, ibn-Saud was not only a worldly ruler (king) but also a spiritual leader (Imam). Originally, Saudi Arabia was a desert kingdom ruled in a paternalistic way by ibn-Saud and his numerous sons and relatives, who alone made up the "government." Its principal income came from the expenditures of pilgrims to the Holy Cities of Mecca and Medina. However, in 1938 American oil experts discovered oil in quantity at Dhahran, near the Persian Gulf. Although production could not be expanded until after World War II, the oil companies immediately advanced large sums of money, which permitted ibn-Saud to play an increasing role in Arab politics. In 1950 the Arabian-American Oil Company (ARAMCO), jointly owned by four American oil companies, was granted a concession based on a 50:50 split of profits — the first application of this formula in the Near and Middle East. Later the American-owned Getty Oil Company and the Japanese-owned Arabian Oil Company were granted concessions; and the Saudi government received a more advantageous split of profits. Thanks to the competition of the oil companies, production rose rapidly (102.3 million metric tons in 1965).

This horn of plenty wrought some visible changes in the country. Riyadh, the desert capital, became dotted with air-conditioned princely palaces and government buildings. It became linked to the modern port of Damman on the Persian Gulf by railway and to the old port of Jidda on the Red Sea by a paved highway. Dhahran, the headquarters of ARAMCO, became a bustling modern industrial city, with an oil refinery, modern hospitals, schools, and an airport. Thousands of former desert dwellers were transformed into city dwellers and salaried employees of the government or the oil companies; hundreds of students were sent abroad to study. Politically, however, the country remained an absolute monarchy, ruled by members of the Saud family who held all the high government offices. The flood of wealth had a demoralizing effect on some members of the family. An increasing share of the oil payments was used to satisfy their personal taste for luxury. King Saud (1953–1964) showed less political acumen than his father ibn-Saud. His policies were generally pro-Western. In Arab politics, at first he followed the lead of Nasser. In 1962, however, disturbed by the anti-monarchist propaganda of Nasser, he effected a reconciliation with King Hussein of Jordan. This caused some surprise in view of the old rivalry between the Saudi and Hashimite dynasties. In 1964 King Saud was deposed for incompetence by a family council. He was replaced with his half-brother Faisal. King Faisal (1964–   ) adopted a more neutralist foreign policy, but continued to defy Egypt.

Even richer were the oil profits of the little sheikdom of Kuwait (area: 5800 square miles, population in 1965: 468,000) at the head of the Persian Gulf. Oil was first discovered in Kuwait in 1938, but it was produced in quantity only after World War II. Under concessions granted British, American, and later Japanese companies, oil production rose so rapidly that Kuwait became the leading oil producer among the countries of the

Near and Middle East. In 1965 production was 125 million metric tons, and the oil payments to Kuwait topped $605 million.

Like other Persian Gulf sheikdoms, Kuwait was a British protectorate, ruled by members of the as-Sabah dynasty. In 1961, however, Britain changed its relationship to Kuwait from that of a protectorate to that of an alliance. Kuwait became independent and joined the Arab League. The oil payments to the Kuwaiti dynasty exceeded domestic investment possibilities and excited the envy of larger but poorer Arab countries. Sheik Abdullah as-Salim (1950–1965) agreed that about one-third of the income was to be used for development projects, one-third to build up a state reserve, and one-third to go to his privy purse. To keep his subjects happy, the sheik paid all current state expenses, which included free schooling, medical services, and old-age pensions. There were no taxes except customs duties. In 1963 the sheik granted a constitution. He established a foreign aid fund, out of which grants to other Arab nations were made.

Three other Persian Gulf sheikdoms shared in the oil boom, although on a much smaller scale: Qatar on the Qatar peninsula (estimated size: 8000 square miles; population: 60,000), Bahrain Island (estimated size: 250 square miles; population: 160,000), and Abu Dhabi which was one of the seven sheikdoms of the Trucial Coast (combined size: 32,000 square miles; population: 110,000). All were British protectorates. The Sultanate of Muscat and Oman and the sheikdoms of Hadramaut — once haunts of Arab pirates preying on the Eastern Trade — remained poor and primitive lands, dependent on fishing, pearling, and modest British subsidies to keep them going. In 1959, to counter Arab agitation for independence, Britain combined the sheikdoms of Hadramaut into the Federation of South Arabia and promised them independence by 1968. Aden, a British crown colony, retained importance as a naval and military base, refueling station on the Atlantic-Indian Ocean route, and growing industrial center. In 1963 it joined the Federation of South Arabia.

Yemen, a mountainous and isolated state in southern Arabia (estimated size: 75,000 square miles; population: 5 million), was independent. Feuding with Britain over Aden, it tended to lean on Italy before the war and on Russia after the war. However, it was guided in its "neutralist" policy not by any preference for communism but by a desire to play off the great power blocs against each other. In 1958 it nominally federated with the United Arab Republic; but internally it remained an extremely conservative theocratic (the ruler was also Imam) monarchy. In 1962, however, the Imam Ahmed was overthrown and killed by revolutionary officers, who proclaimed Yemen a republic. His heir, the Iman Mohammed al-Badr, fled to the mountains to seek the support of tribesmen. Civil war followed, in which Saudi Arabia intervened on the side of the Imam's forces and Egypt on the side of the Republican forces. In 1966 the conflict remained unresolved.

4. IRAN AND AFGHANISTAN

The postwar development of Iran and Afghanistan was deeply affected by the fact that they held the most exposed position in the Cold War, adjoining as they did the southern flank of the Soviet Union. However, neither country was a stranger to the pressures of the Cold War; for them it was simply a continuation of the old Anglo-Russian rivalry in the area. And just as they had resisted the dangers of this rivalry by playing off Britain and Russia against each other, so now they planned to weather the Cold War by playing off the United States and the Soviet Union. The unsuccessful Soviet attempts to satellize Iran in the immediate postwar period have already been reviewed in Chapter 47. The result of those Soviet attempts was to push Iran militarily into the Western bloc. In October, 1947, Iran concluded an agreement with the United States which provided for equipping the Iranian army with American arms and for its training by an American military mission.

Iran was also eager to obtain $650 million of American economic aid to implement her program of economic development worked out by the American Morrison-Knudsen International Company in 1946. However, this aid to Iran was delayed by more pressing calls on American generosity elsewhere. In 1949, during the visit of the Shah Mohammed Reza Pahlevi (1941–   ) to the United States, Iran was promised $25 million for Point Four projects, but even the grant of this modest sum was delayed until 1952. Meanwhile, the Iranian government cast about for other sources of income and fastened on the Anglo-Iranian Oil Company (AIOC), which extracted, refined, and marketed Iranian oil under a concession granted it after much controversy in 1933 (see p. 354). After the war the oil payments to the Iranian government declined because of development of oil elsewhere in the Near and Middle East and because of the policy of the British Labour government to restrict dividend payments. However, when the Iranian government broached the subject of revising the 1933 concession, the AIOC officials proved obdurate. They felt that the company was in a strong position because it was part owner of other oil companies in the Near and Middle East and could, if it wished to, curtail production in Iran and step up production in Iraq, Bahrain, and Qatar. The controversy soon became venomous, especially after ARAM-CO agreed (December, 1950) with the Saudi Arabian government on the 50:50 formula for splitting profits. The Iranian share of profits was considerably smaller than that. A nationalist leader, Mohammed Mossadeq, chairman of the oil committee in the Iranian parliament (Majlis), won wide popularity with a bill to nationalize the Iranian oil industry. In April, 1951, the bill passed the Majlis, and a few days later Mossadeq became prime minister. By the summer of 1951 the British employees of AIOC had left Iran, and the great refinery at Abadan had closed down.

The British government, which was the principal shareholder in AIOC, took up the cudgels for it. Paratroopers were alerted in Cyprus and British naval units sent to the Persian Gulf. The Iranian government broke off diplomatic relations with Britain, which took the controversy first to the International Court at the Hague and then to the UN Security Council. Mossadeq denied that either the Hague court or UN had jurisdiction in the controversy, which was one between a sovereign state and a private company. To show his independence, moreover, he abrogated a Soviet fishing concession in the Caspian Sea.

The loss of oil revenue meant little to the Iranian masses of peasants and nomads, but it did mean much to the ruling elite of government officials, army officers, and landowners. To check growing opposition to his policies, Mossadeq progressively assumed dictatorial powers. In August, 1953, he unconstitutionally dissolved parliament, whereupon the shah dismissed him and appointed General Fazullah Zahedi prime minister. Mossadeq, however, refused to resign. Amidst great disorders in Teheran, the shah fled abroad and Zahedi to the provinces. But then the situation abruptly changed. With troops from the provinces Zahedi suppressed Mossadeq's supporters, who included both fanatical Moslems and communists of the dissolved (since 1949) Tudeh Party. The shah returned to Iran and Mossadeq was tried and sentenced to three years of imprisonment. The new government of Zahedi resumed diplomatic relations with Britain and opened negotiations with British and American oil interests, resulting in an agreement (August, 1954) under which the oil industry remained the property of the National Iranian Oil Company, the AIOC was compensated for its loss, and an international consortium of eight oil companies (British, American, Dutch, and French) was granted a 25-year concession to extract, refine, and market Iranian oil on the basis of the conventional 50:50 spilt of profits.

The United States government facilitated the oil agreement with an initial grant of $45 million for development projects, followed by other grants and credits. Thanks to this aid and the oil payments, Iran launched a Seven-Year Plan (1956–1962) of economic development. Under this program transportation was improved. A number of small industries were opened up, mainly in Teheran, which grew to a sizable city of some 2.3 million inhabitants by 1964. In 1962, to secure financial support for a new five-and-a-half-year economic plan (1962–1968), the shah visited the United States. His visit was not a success because in 1962 the United States was forced by action of the Congress to curtail sharply its foreign economic and military aid. Thereafter, Iran began to seek better relations with the Soviet Union. It received Soviet aid for a number of minor economic projects. In 1965 the Iranian government granted five oil companies concessions to explore and exploit Iran's off-shore oil deposits. The companies paid $185 million for the concessions and agreed to a 75:25 split of profits (75 per cent for Iran, 25 per cent for the companies) if oil were found.

Meanwhile, the shah undertook to solve the most difficult social question of Iran — the land question. Of the total Iranian population of 22,860,000 in 1964, 60 per cent were peasants, 20 per cent were nomads, and the rest were city dwellers. Most of the land was owned by the crown and a small class of landowners. In 1949, to set an example, the shah began to distribute the crown lands to the peasants. The hope of the shah was to create by this "white revolution" a class of independent farmers who would give Iran much needed social stability. His example was not widely followed, however. In 1962, under the shah's pressure, the Majlis passed a land reform act. However, the government had to be careful in implementing it because the landowning class was politically powerful while the peasants had little political influence. Their social condition remained poor. Owing, however, to their traditional distrust of everything Russian, they remained impervious to Communist propaganda. Communism won adherents only among the growing city class of workers and intellectuals. The basis of the shah's power remained a narrow one. It rested mainly on the army and the police.

The remote monarchy of Afghanistan, in the towering Hindu Kush mountains to the east of Iran, made little progress after the war. Agriculture and sheep raising continued to be the principal occupation of its population, estimated at 14 million. Passionately jealous of its independence, Afghanistan pursued a policy of judicious neutrality in the East-West struggle. In the immediate postwar years it leaned to the West; but after quarreling with Pakistan over some Pushtu tribesmen in Pakistan which it claimed were Afghans, it tended to lean toward Russia. This policy won it foreign aid from both Russia and America for a number of minor development projects.

5. ISRAEL

Israel is geographically a part of the Near and Middle East, but in every other respect it is a foreign enclave in the region. The Jews are an ancient people but a new and unique nation. The form of the state of Israel, which was created in 1948, has remained provisional. The first *Knesset* (parliament), which was elected in 1948, was forced to postpone the task of drafting a constitution for the sake of attending to the task of defending the country against Arab invasion. In 1949 it proclaimed a temporary "small constitution," leaving the task of drafting a definite constitution to the indefinite future. The temporary constitution provided for a republic under a president, elected for five years; a single-chamber legislature (*Knesset*) of 120 members, elected by universal suffrage under the system of proportionate representation; and a cabinet, responsible to the *Knesset*.

What the ultimate form of the Israeli state would be was difficult to say. Before 1948 the Jewish immigrants came mainly from Europe, especially Eastern Europe. Whether they came from Western or Eastern Europe, they were invariably literate and often highly skilled. After 1948, the Jewish immigrants came mainly from the Arab states, Iran, and North Africa. They were often as primitive as the peoples among whom they had lived. It was natural that a certain amount of tension arose between the progressive European (Ashkenazy) Jews and the retarded oriental (Sephardic) Jews, especially when the latter outnumbered the former. The earliest Jewish immigrants in Palestine had come from the Russian empire, where they had been strongly influenced by the socialist and revolutionary thought that permeated Russian society before 1917. Russian Jews provided the leadership of the new state of Israel. Dr. Chaim Weizman, the first president of Israel (1949–1952), and David Ben-Gurion, the first prime minister (1948–1963), were born in the Russian empire. They desired to create a Western-style, secular state and a socialist, egalitarian society. Many oriental Jews were conservative orthodox believers, who would have preferred a theocratic state, run by the rabbis in strict accordance with the precepts of the Old Testament.

It was difficult to forge a single nation out of such disparate elements as the sophisticated Jews of Germany and primitive Jews of Yemen. Unlike a score of new nations established in modern times, the Israelis had no national identity, except for religion. During the two thousand years of their dispersal they had been culturally assimilated to a score of peoples among whom they lived. They had, for instance, no national language. The ancient Hebrew language was a dead tongue like Latin. It was used for liturgical purposes only. It was, therefore, necessary to create a national language and to teach it to the successive waves of immigrants. Using ancient Hebrew as a basis, Israeli scholars created modern Hebrew, a language endowed with a full modern technical vocabulary and suitable for modern usage. Old immigrants found it difficult to learn, but the young *sabras* (Jewish men and women born in Israel) learned it in schools and spoke it spontaneously. With no memory of other countries and cultures, they were, properly speaking, the only true Israelis.

Another problem of Israel were the minorities, which amounted to about 10 per cent of the population. Israel accorded the minorities full rights of citizenship; but it was only natural that the Jews, living under a constant threat of war with the Arab states, should look at the Arabs in Israel with suspicion. They represented a potential fifth column. On the other hand, it was equally natural that the Arabs, whether Moslem or Christian, should be disgruntled at being reduced to a minority in the land in which they once formed an overwhelming majority. Nor were they readily appeased by the fact that, owing to a higher living standard in Israel, they were on the whole economically better off than their kinsmen across the border in the Arab states. The Arab minority constituted the backbone of the Israeli Communist party.

Owing to proportional representation, the political parties of Israel were numerous. While the Communist party stood at the extreme left, the Herut party stood on the extreme right. It was a Nationalist party, the principal objective of which was to conquer those portions of Palestine still retained by the Arab states. In the center stood the Mapai party, a moderate Socialist party, which was headed by Ben-Gurion until his retirement in 1963.[3]

The Mapai were supported by the Histradut (General Federation of Labor), which was not only a protective association of laborers but also the largest employer in Israel. Its various industrial and agricultural enterprises accounted for 23 per cent of Israel's national income. The task of making Israel an economically viable state was a very difficult one in view of its small area (7,993 square miles) and population (2,563,000 in 1965), paucity of natural resources, unnatural frontiers, and constant threat of war with the Arab states. Before 1948 it had been a cardinal point of the Zionist movement that all Jews should not only return to the Land of Israel but should set deep roots in it by becoming farmers. Thanks to the enthusiasm of the Zionist immigrants, by 1965 about 1 million acres had been brought under cultivation. Of these, about 350,000 acres were irrigated. Most of the land belonged to the *kibbutzim,* the cooperative farms, some of which were organized along socialist lines. A thriving citrus industry had grown up. Citrus fruits constituted Israel's main item of export.

Israel, however, could not survive by farming alone. After 1948 a determined effort was made to develop industry. To secure capital, the Israeli government issued bonds for sale abroad. Sympathetic Jews abroad, especially in the United States, purchased $812 million worth of them by 1964. Another source of capital was West German reparations, which when completed in 1965, amounted to $860 million in cash and goods. The United States also helped. It made grants and shipped agricultural surpluses to Israel. Thanks to the flow of foreign capital, Israel, which was virtually devoid of industry before 1948, became dotted with factories, producing textiles and fashion goods, autos, building materials, tires, pharmaceutical goods, and polished diamonds. By 1964 Israel's per capita income had climbed to $970 — the highest in the Near and Middle East, except for Kuwait. Israel's exports, which by 1964, amounted to $340 million annually, were directed mainly to Europe, the United States, and to a lesser extent to Asia and Africa. Unfortunately, owing to the hostility of the Arab states which steadfastly boycotted Israel, no trade with them was possible. Israel is far from economically viable, however; its imports exceeded its exports by some $450 million in 1964. In part this is due to an extremely heavy burden of expenses for national defense.

In the East-West conflict, Israel sided with the West, especially after 1955 when the Soviet government established friendly relations with

[3] Subsequently, Ben-Gurion returned to political life and formed another party.

Egypt and other Arab states. But Israel trusts mainly in its own strength to defend itself against the ever present Arab threat. It maintains disproportionately large and well-equipped armed forces. Both men and women are subject to military service, first in the standing army and then in the reserves. As long as the Arab threat persists Israel feels that it can survive only by being a tough little Spartan state, always ready to repay the Arabs, an eye for an eye and a tooth for a tooth.

66

AFRICA ASTIR

Ex Africa semper aliquid novi — *Always something new out of Africa*
PLINY

1. A CHANGING CONTINENT

AFRICA, WITH AN AREA of 11,500,000 square miles, is the second largest continent, only Asia exceeding it in size. In shape, latitude, and in several other respects, Africa has much in common with South America. Both are linked in the north to a larger land mass by a narrow isthmus that has been cut by a man-made canal. Both are roughly triangular with the acute angle pointing toward the South Pole. Both are transected by the equator. Both have equatorial rain forests drained by large rivers — the Congo system in Africa and the Amazon system in South America. Both have the same density of population, roughly 25 inhabitants to the square mile. Both have great resources — minerals, petroleum, water power — that need capital for their development. In both the birth rate is high while the standard of living of the great majority of the population is low. Finally, both were subjugated by the Europeans and reduced to the status of colonies, and both rebelled. The peoples of South America freed themselves from Spanish and Portuguese rule early in the nineteenth century. The peoples of Africa, subjugated by various European nations in the nineteenth century, were rapidly asserting their independence by the middle of the twentieth century.

Africa and South America have still other features in common. Despite their large dimensions they contain relatively little arable land. Less than 7 per cent of Africa and less than 4 per cent of South America are under cultivation, compared to roughly 12 per cent for North America, 13 per cent for Asia and 30 per cent for Europe. This deficiency of cultivated land helps to explain the generally low living standards and the malnutrition from which millions of Africans and Latin Americans suffer. There is an urgent need in both continents for better farming methods to increase the food supply for a rapidly rising population. Between 1900 and

1965 the population of Africa increased from 120 million to 300 million, and the population of South America rose still more rapidly.

Historically, geographically, and economically Africa is a continent of paradoxes. It may have been the original cradle of the human race, for the most ancient traces of primitive man, probably over one million years old, have been uncovered there. It contains, in the Nile Valley, the ruins of one of the earliest civilizations known to history. Yet today Africa is economically the most retarded of the continents, although it is the most important source of gold and diamonds and produces a large fraction of the world's copper, manganese, chromium, and uranium. These facts make it easy to believe that the Africans are an exploited people, whose wealth is being plundered by imperialist powers while they themselves remain impoverished. This is a standard Communist interpretation. But it is an interpretation that ignores several relevant and important facts. For centuries Africa remained stationary and unprogressive, with a static population. Only in the last hundred years, since the Europeans explored the interior and carved the "Dark Continent" into colonies and protectorates, has Africa felt the stimulating effects of modern Western Civilization. By maintaining order, curbing tribal wars, establishing systems of transportation and communication, and reducing the toll of widespread diseases through the triumphs of modern medicine, the Europeans laid the foundation for an economic and social transformation. One result of European enterprise, of the capital invested to organize plantations, develop mines, construct roads and railways and power plants, and tap the continent's hidden resources, has been to draw Africa into the current of world trade. A second result has been to awaken the Africans to an awareness of world trends, to acquaint their leaders with the concepts of nationalism, independence, and self-government.

The "Revolution of Rising Expectations," that was stirring the impoverished and retarded peoples of the world by the middle of the twentieth century, struck Africa with sudden and surprising force. From Cairo to the Cape of Good Hope all Africa was astir. During the 1950's and 1960's one colony after another rose to sovereign status, threw off European rule, and emerged as an independent state. This rapid process of political emancipation is the central theme of the present chapter. The map of Africa changed so swiftly that the older division of the continent into French, British, Belgian, Italian, Portuguese, and Spanish Africa lost meaning. Africa (like South America when the colonial period ended) was changing into a patchwork of independent states.

In Latin America three centuries of intermingling between the European conquerors, the native Indians, and the imported African slaves produced a mixed society. Those of predominantly European blood, though a minority in most Latin American states, comprised about one-fifth of the total population, while the *mestizos* (people of mixed blood) comprised one-third. The Europeans remained and dominated the political and so-

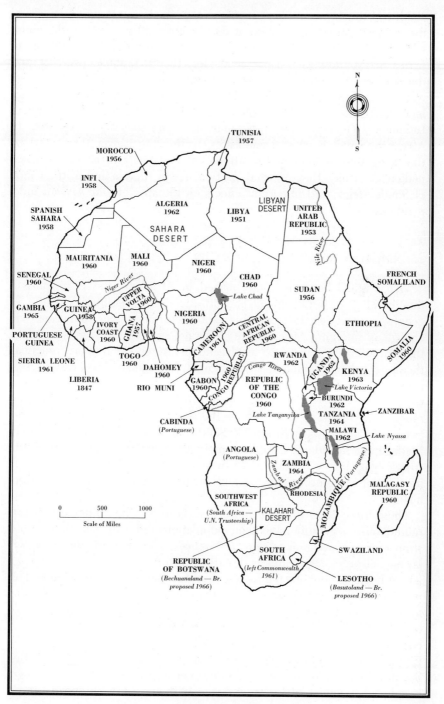

AFRICA IN 1967
(showing dates of independence)

cial life of the new republics. In Africa the situation was different. There the colonists of European descent did not form 20 per cent of the population, or 10 or even 5 per cent. Among the 300 million inhabitants of Africa in 1965 less than 3 per cent — less than 9 million — were of predominantly European blood. What might happen to this small minority was foreshadowed by the fate of the small Dutch minority in the Netherlands East Indies when these colonies became the independent republic of Indonesia. Their property was confiscated and they were expelled. In Africa the small European minorities, feeling themselves threatened by the rising tide of nationalism, attempted to hold it in check. The expedients to which they resorted, particularly in Algeria and in the Union of South Africa, had important effects on the struggle for African independence.

2. NORTH AFRICA

The political boundaries established in Africa by the Europeans as they divided up the continent had little relation to cultural, climatic, or geographic realities. It is probable, moreover, that former boundaries will change as emerging African states federate, split up, or otherwise adjust their frontiers to their new needs and pressures. It is more practical, therefore, when viewing the continent, to recognize three natural segments: North Africa, Tropical Africa, and South Africa. North Africa is roughly that quarter of the continent which extends from the Mediterranean and Red seas to 15° above the equator. Tropical Africa lies between 15° North Latitude and 15° South Latitude and (with the island of Madagascar included) comprises more than half the continent. South Africa, lying below 15° South Latitude, includes the area (approximately one-fifth of the continent) lying south of the Zambesi River and its tributaries.

These three areas differ in more than latitude: they differ in climate, rainfall, and vegetation, and their populations differ in density, in racial strains, and in religion. These differences, and their significance, will become clearer as each area is described in turn.

North Africa contains the largest desert in the world, the Sahara. This predominantly arid region of more than 3 million square miles is equal to the United States in area. In general it is very sparsely peopled except for the Nile Valley with its irrigated fields and the Mediterranean coast of North Africa. The peoples of North Africa belong to the Indo-European race, and the same racial strain predominates south of the Red Sea in Ethiopia and Somaliland. Since ancient times, however, the Negro peoples of Tropical Africa have mixed with the Indo-Europeans and a dividing line between the ethnic groups is not easy to draw. Nor are religious divisions clear-cut. In general, however, the North Africans are Moslems, while the Tropical Africans belong to various native cults.

The flag of the British Empire is lowered as Kenya attains independence, December, 1963 (Wide World Photos).

Shanties and highrise apartment buildings in Lagos, Nigeria (Wide World Photos).

All sections of North Africa had been reduced to the status of European colonies or protectorates by the twentieth century. The French extended their power over Algeria, Tunisia, and most of Morocco, and gradually annexed the vast desert hinterland until they linked up their north and central African domains. The British controlled Egypt and the Anglo-Egyptian Sudan. The Italians, entering the contest late, conquered Libya in 1911 and Ethiopia in 1936. All three nations claimed portions of the African coastal regions to the north and east of the Ethiopian highlands.

After World War II these North African conquests were rapidly lost. Egypt, indeed, as explained in Chapter 32, won virtual independence from Britain as early as 1936. Later developments, which led the Egyptians to seize the Suez Canal in 1956, were discussed in a preceding chapter. The Sudan gained independence from Britain the same year and became a republic. In 1960 the British government granted independence to British Somaliland, thus relinquishing control over its last possession in North Africa.

Italian conquests in North Africa at the outbreak of World War II included Libya, Ethiopia, Eritrea, and Italian Somaliland. All were lost to Italy during or after the war. Ethiopia was liberated early in the war, and Eritrea was joined to it in 1952 by a decision of the United Nations. Libya became an independent state in 1951 and Italian Somaliland in 1960.

The emancipation of the French North African empire proved a longer and more tumultuous process. The French protectorate over Tunisia was abandoned after some years of conflict and Tunisia became independent in 1956. Morocco, threatened by internal disorders, was likewise accorded independence in 1956, with Spanish Morocco and the international port of Tangier added to the new state. Morocco became a monarchy, with the former sultan assuming the title Muhammad V.

Between 1958 and 1960 some 12 million people inhabiting the hinterland of the Sahara indicated their desire for independence although at first they remained loosely joined to France as members of the French Union. As a result five new states came into existence — the republics of Mauritania, Senegal, Mali, Niger and Chad. The territories thus transformed into free republics stretched across Northern Africa from the Atlantic coast to the eastern border of the former Anglo-Egyptian Sudan, which had achieved independence in 1956.

This rapid liberation of North Africa had a disturbing effect on the Algerians. The French territory of Algeria lay between Tunisia and Morocco, but unlike these former French protectorates Algeria had been united politically with France itself and was ruled from Paris. Furthermore, although the Algerian population, estimated at about 9 million in 1954, was overwhelmingly Moslem and African, it included perhaps 1 million inhabitants of European birth or European descent. Nowhere else on the continent, except in the Union of South Africa, was there so large a group of Europeans. These French Algerians insisted that their home-land was a part of France itself and must not be surrendered. Many French people shared their sentiment. The French army, its pride still suffering from the defeat of 1940 and the more recent reverses in Indo-china, was ready to fight to hold Algeria. Unfortunately, after 1954 a small but desperate army of Algerian insurgents was also prepared to wage a guerrilla war for Algerian independence. This situation resulted in a prolonged and costly struggle.

The Algerian insurgents, organized as the *Front de Libération National* (FLN), resorted to acts of terrorism not only in Algeria but in France also. The French government built up its military forces in Algeria to half-a-million men but failed to suppress the revolt. After de Gaulle came to power in France in 1958, he labored to resolve the struggle. In 1962 Algeria became independent (see page 639). The new republic had an area of 919,590 square miles and a population that reached about 12.5 million by 1965. The average income per capita in that year was $220; but the Algerian economy suffered a deterioration after the Algerians won independence, despite French aid. Economic difficulties partly explained why the first president, Ben Bella, was overthrown by a group of army officers in 1965. Colonel Houari Boumédienne headed the new regime.

3. TROPICAL AFRICA

Approximately 15° above the equator the Sahara Desert changes from sandy wastes almost devoid of vegetation to grasslands dotted with occasional trees. A line drawn across a map of Africa, from Dakar on the Atlantic to the north of Lake Chad, extended to Khartoum on the upper Nile, and thence to the Red Sea coast will mark this division with fair accuracy. Below this line the annual rainfall (less than ten inches a year in the Sahara) increases rapidly. There is a belt between 100 and 200 miles wide which enjoys from ten to twenty-five to fifty inches; and finally, for several hundred miles above and below the equator, there is a region that is deluged with fifty to seventy-five inches and more of tropical precipitation. The eastern highlands, near the coast of the Indian Ocean, receive less, it is true. But virtually all Tropical Africa, from the southern limits of the Sahara to the Zambesi River, has an annual rainfall that varies from adequate to excessive. Much of this central segment of Africa is covered by heavy rain forests. Throughout most of it the mean annual temperature is 80° Fahrenheit and Europeans find the heat and humidity of the lowlands oppressive. Tropical Africa supports a population of nearly 200 million (1965), but less than 1 million of these are of European descent.

The numerical weakness of the European minority made it difficult for them to hold in check the rising tide of African nationalism. Between

1950 and 1965 most of the peoples of Tropical Africa gained political independence. The French possessions — French Equatorial Africa, the French Congo, the Ivory Coast, Dahomey, Gabon, the Upper Volta, and the island of Madagascar — all were transformed into independent republics in 1958 although they chose to remain members of the vaguely defined French Union. The former territory known as French Guinea, however, became a wholly independent republic in 1958 and left the French Community in 1959.

The vast extent of these African territories to which the French conceded independence is difficult to appreciate. Altogether they had an area of more than 3 million square miles, an area fifteen times the size of France itself. In the main, however, they were thinly peopled, their total population of some 50 million (1965) being only a little greater than that of the French Republic.

Great Britain likewise granted independence to some of its possessions in Tropical Africa during the 1950's. The most important of these liberated states was Nigeria, which had an area of 356,668 square miles, but a large population of 57 million (1965). This population, over 99 per cent African, agitated for self-government after World War II and Nigeria achieved full independence in 1960. Farther west on the Gulf of Guinea another state, named Ghana, had come into existence three years earlier. Ghana included the former British Gold Coast Colony, British Togoland, and Ashanti, giving it an area of 92,100 square miles and a population of 7.6 million (1965). Sierra Leone became independent in 1961 and remained a member of the Commonwealth. Its area was roughly 28,000 square miles and its population 2.25 million.

In eastern Africa, Great Britain controlled three contiguous territories, Tanganyika, Uganda, and Kenya, which had a total area of some 680,000 square miles and a population of 21 million. Tanganyika became independent in 1961, and in 1964 it joined with Zanzibar to form the Republic of Tanzania. Uganda became independent in 1962 and a republic in 1963. Kenya became independent in 1964. A fourth British territory, Nyasaland, likewise attained independence in 1964; it became the Republic of Malawi in 1966.

To the west of Malawi lay the former British protectorate of Northern Rhodesia. In 1964 this territory became independent as the Republic of Zambia. To the east and west of the new state stretched the Portuguese colonies of Mozambique and Angola. Despite growing discontent among their African subjects, the Portuguese showed no willingness to grant them independence. In Bechuanaland, to the south of Zambia, the British helped to set up a Legislative Assembly in 1965 and Bechuanaland became the independent Republic of Botswana in 1966.

Southern Rhodesia, renamed Rhodesia, pursued a course after 1964 that resulted in its withdrawal from the Commonwealth and the severance of its ties with Great Britain. As in the Union of South Africa, its small

European minority were determined to preserve their ascendency and became apprehensive as they saw most African states win freedom and establish their own governments. The steps which led the Prime Min ister of Rhodesia, Ian Smith, to proclaim Rhodesia independent in 1965, have been discussed earlier (see page 714).

The last large region of Tropical Africa not yet mentioned was the Belgian Congo. With an area of 905,380 square miles and a population of 14 million (1960) this colony provided Belgium with an impressive overseas empire. But the rising tide of African nationalism affected it after World War II, and the concessions the Belgian government finally offered in the late 1950's failed to placate the inhabitants. Attempts to repress the mounting disorders in 1959 failed and in 1960 the Congo gained independence.

No adequate provision had been made for a peaceful and orderly transfer of authority and the Congo was plunged into civil war when the Belgians withdrew. It is possible they hoped that the Africans, unable to hold the large country together and rule themselves, would ask the Belgians to return and preserve order. Instead, the newly created Congo government asked the United Nations for help. Mutinies among the African troops, secessionist movements in several provinces, and widespread disorder made it difficult for the United Nations personnel to move freely or make their authority felt. In the rich mining province of Katanga, a local leader, Moise Tshombe, set up a separate regime. United Nations troops tried but failed to disarm the Katanga forces. In 1961 the UN Secretary-General, Dag Hammarskjöld, flew to Africa to consult with Tshombe, but his plane crashed and he was killed. The Congo situation remained confused for several years. Democratic methods failed to work effectively, and in 1965 the commander in chief of the army, General Joseph Mobutu, set up a new government with himself as president.

Section XII: THE SEVENTH DECADE

67

THREE PERSISTENT QUESTIONS

. . . The question of general and complete disarmament is the most important one facing the world today . . .

UNANIMOUS RESOLUTION OF THE GENERAL ASSEMBLY
OF THE UNITED NATIONS (1959)

It is simply not possible for small oases of prosperity to continue to exist amidst vast deserts of poverty without engendering storms that might engulf those oases.

B. K. NEHRU, COMMISSIONER GENERAL FOR ECONOMIC AFFAIRS
SOVEREIGN DEMOCRATIC REPUBLIC OF INDIA (1961)

1. GLOBAL RESOURCES

EARLIER IN THIS TEXT, when individual nations were under discussion, it proved helpful to analyze their progress under three heads: resources, defense, and social justice. The history of each nation, and the welfare of its members, have always been determined very largely by the manner in which they met these three persistent problems: (1) The development and utilization of their resources; (2) the defense of their territory, wealth, and way of life against threatening neighbors; (3) their achievement of social justice and economic opportunity in sufficient measure to avert destructive class conflicts and civil wars. In the present chapter an attempt will be made to analyze the present condition of humanity as a whole under these same three heads.

Modern efforts to safeguard and prolong human life doubled the world population between 1900 and 1965. If maintained, these efforts promised to double it again before the end of the twentieth century. Never before had the world's most essential resource — humanity — been more numerous and never before had it multiplied so rapidly. But these gains involved a paradox. Never before had there been so many millions of undernourished people.

When World War II ended in 1945 the global population was estimated at 2300 million. Twenty years later, in 1965, it reached 3300 million. This increase did not result from a rise in the birth rate. On the contrary the available statistics indicate that the world birth rate declined slightly during these twenty years, from 36 or 37 per thousand to 34. The increase in population resulted from the fact that during these twenty years the death rate declined by one-third, from 24 per thousand to 16 per thousand. In 1945 the world population was rising by 12 per thousand per year (36–24), or 1.2 per cent annually. By 1965 it was rising by 18 per thousand per year (34–16), or 1.8 per cent annually. Stated as a mere difference in percentage this change makes no emotional impact: to be appreciated it must be translated into human terms. In 1965 an average of 6 people in a thousand stayed alive, people who would have died if the death rate of 1945 had still prevailed. This meant, in round numbers, that 20 million lives were saved in 1965; 20 million individuals survived who would otherwise have perished.

The "Population Explosion" is the most important development of twentieth-century history. Although it is a result of the progress made in medical knowledge, science, and technology, its effects are more pervasive, dynamic, and imperious than any other movement shaping the world today. For these multiplying millions must not only be fed; they must be better fed than most of them have been in the past. There is a "Revolution of Rising Expectations" stirring among the impoverished peoples of the globe. If their expectations are to be satisfied, food production, income, and education must expand faster than population. The Director of the United Nations Food and Agriculture Organization was forced to admit that "levels of income and food supply are barely keeping pace with population growth." The report of the Educational, Scientific, and Cultural Organization offered an equally serious warning. In the early 1950's the proportion of the world's children receiving some sort of school training was raised by prodigious efforts to 55 per cent. But as more and more children survived the ills of infancy, school expansion failed to keep pace. After 1955 the proportion of the world's children attending school declined to 53 per cent.

To augment the world's food supply, and make it rise faster than the rising population, the most essential step was to increase the quality of the crops and the yield per acre. In the advanced countries this had been done by the use of chemical fertilizers, by controlling blights and destructive insects, by developing better grains, fruits and vegetables, and by using machines to plough, harvest and process the crops. If these improved methods were adopted in underdeveloped areas the harvests there might be similarly increased.

To purchase chemical fertilizer and farm machinery costs money, and impoverished farmers, living on the verge of starvation, have no money to spare. Furthermore, the use of machinery, of chemical fertilizers and insecticides, required special knowledge that old-fashioned farmers lacked. The development of better seed, the breeding of better livestock, the manufacture of chemicals — all these called for the investment of capital in agricultural experiment stations, in power plants and factories; but poor countries lacked surplus capital. Finally, these newer and more productive methods had to be supervised by scientists and engineers, and to train them schools and colleges were needed. The dilemma of the economically retarded peoples was a cruel one. To increase their output they needed capital to invest. But only *after* they had increased their output could they accumulate the capital they needed. Finally, the irony of their situation was intensified by two further difficulties. In the economically retarded continents — Asia, Africa, and South America — the birth rate was high; these three continents produced four-fifths of the world's annual population increase. In 1965 they supported 71 per cent of the world's population. But they contained only 42 per cent of the world's naturally cultivable land.

To this dilemma there was one obvious solution. The advanced nations of the world, which possessed a larger share of the land suitable for agriculture, and had accumulated surplus wealth, might send food and lend money to less fortunate peoples to ease their hunger and speed their development. This duty most of the wealthier nations acknowledged. But they were slow to advance the enormous sums needed for the development of the economically retarded regions of the earth. Although they enjoyed a standard of living far above the world average, the wealthy nations were heavily taxed. A large share of their productive efforts, a large portion of the taxes they paid, were devoted to armaments.

THE POTENTIALS OF NUCLEAR WEAPONS, 1965

Countries that had nuclear arms in 1965	Countries capable of producing nuclear arms within a few years	Countries that might produce nuclear arms in a longer period
China	Canada	Brazil
France	India	Egypt
Great Britain	Israel	Spain
Soviet Union	Italy	Switzerland
United States	Japan	Yugoslavia
	West Germany	

2. DEFENSE

The great development of science and technology during and after World War II made weapons not only increasingly complex but increasingly costly. Impelled by mutual fear and distrust, the United States and the Soviet Union harnessed their vast resources and technology to the task of creating and maintaining a full arsenal of ever changing and more

complicated and destructive weapons. After the war they devoted themselves to the development of ever more powerful thermonuclear bombs,
until, by the 1050's, they reached a "balance of terror," that is, both sides
were held back by the knowledge that they had the capacity to destroy
each other — and perhaps the rest of the world — totally. The armament
race then shifted to the development of more efficient delivery and interception systems, in order to gain the advantage of being able to deliver
the first and perhaps decisive blow and to intercept the blow of the adversary.

In the immediate postwar years both powers relied on long-range
"strategic" bombers to deliver the thermonuclear bombs. At the time, the
United States appeared to possess an advantage in having better bombers
and in controlling, directly or through its allies, bases close to the Soviet
Union. However, on October 4, 1957, the Soviet Union astonished the
world, which had previously held Soviet science and technology in rather
low esteem, by successfully orbiting the first world satellite ("Sputnik I").
This success in probing outer space was followed by others; notably by
putting a satellite around the moon, which was able to take and relay
back to earth photographic pictures of the dark side of the moon (September, 1959), and by putting in orbit a manned spaceship and bringing
it safely back to earth (April, 1961). Apart from the scientific and propaganda advantage to the Soviet Union, the Soviet feats in missiles and
rocketry had an important bearing on national defense and the balance of
power. If the Soviets could successfully fire a rocket at the moon, then
undoubtedly they could also fire an intercontinental ballistics missile bearing a nuclear warhead at targets in the United States.

This possibility forced the United States to revise its strategy which had
hitherto relied on strategic bombing, and to adopt a crash program for
expediting its own missiles development. On January 31, 1958, American
scientists and technicians placed in orbit a world satellite ("Explorer I"),
which was followed by many others. On May 5, 1961, they, too, succeeded
in sending into the stratosphere and safely retrieving a manned spaceship.
The ultimate objective of the American space program was to put a
manned spaceship on the moon by about 1970. American scientists and
technicians also successfully experimented with short-range and inter-
mediate range missiles, intercontinental ballistics missiles (the first of
which was the "Atlas"), as well as the "Polaris" missiles which were fired
from submerged atomic-powered submarines. The Polaris submarines had
some advantages over strategic bombers, notably that they could operate
away from their bases for months at a time and approach enemy territory
silently and undetected.

In the 1960's, without abandoning strategic bombers or intercontinental
ballistics missiles, the United States began to rely heavily on nuclear-
powered, Polaris-equipped submarines for its front-line defense. The
United States, however, did not neglect conventional land forces. In 1961,

An electronic tape controls machine operation, (Courtesy of General Electric).

Operations of Shasta Dam in California are regulated by the small staff of a master control room (U. S. Bureau of Reclamation).

The first Apollo spacecraft, launched from Cape Kennedy in May 1964 (North American Aviation, Inc.).

faced with another limited war in Asia, the war in South Vietnam, President Kennedy ordered a study and reorganization of United States strategy. In view of the Soviet-American nuclear standoff, the concept of massive retaliation was de-emphasized but by no means abandoned. However, measures were taken to strengthen conventional forces and increase their mobility by building up fleets of aerial troop-carriers. Little was known about the development of conventional Soviet forces, but it seemed safe to assume that the Russians who had historically relied on massed infantry for defense would not neglect these forces.

The cost of maintaining both nuclear and conventional armaments proved a heavy burden. In 1965 the United States spent about $50 billion for its own defense and military aid to its allies. The Soviet Union probably spent $40 billion or more, Great Britain and France, about $4 billion each. For the world as a whole the cost of defense approached $150 billion. This crushing burden as well as the fear of nuclear war led to innumerable efforts to limit or abolish armaments. The UN Charter provided that the Security Council should have the responsibility of preparing plans "for the regulation of armaments." The General Assembly likewise had authority to consider "principles governing disarmament."

In 1946 the United States submitted to the UN Atomic Energy Commission a plan (known as the "Baruch Plan") for the control of atomic energy, in the production of which it then had a monopoly. It offered to put all atomic activities under strict control of an international authority, and when this was constituted, to destroy all of its existing stocks of atomic bombs. Understandably, it demanded a "foolproof" system of inspection to prevent violation of the agreement. The Soviet Union countered with a proposal to destroy the existing bombs first and consider inspection and controls later. If the United States had agreed to the Soviet counter-proposal, it would have been deprived of its advantage in possessing atomic bombs without any assurance that the Soviet Union would be likewise (when and if it succeeded in producing them) other than the word of the Soviet government. In view of the fact that the Soviet record of living up to their international pledges was far from perfect, the United States rejected the Soviet counter-proposal.

In the following years, while all nations busily armed, disarmament, both nuclear and conventional, was endlessly discussed in the UN Disarmament Commission, but no progress was made. The matter of inspection invariably proved to be a stumbling block in the negotiations. In view of the impasse in the UN, suggestions were made to try to reach an agreement on disarmament outside it. Before his retirement in 1955, Winston Churchill called for a meeting "at the summit," that is, of the top leaders of the Western powers and the Soviet Union, to try to resolve world problems. On July 18–23, 1955, President Eisenhower, Prime Minister Eden, and the French premier Edgar Faure met with the Soviet premier Bulganin, accompanied by the Communist Party chief Khrushchev, in the first "Summit" conference at Geneva. President Eisenhower availed himself of the opportunity to propose that the United States and the Soviet Union exchange information on their military installations and agree to aerial inspection of each other's territories. This bold and imaginative proposal was hailed all over the world, but the Soviet leaders to whom military secrecy was somewhat of a fetish shrank from accepting it.

In 1958 the disarmament delegates of the United States, Britain, and Soviet Russia began to discuss a limited objective; namely, to suspend thermo-nuclear test explosions. After the Cuban crisis in 1962 which added urgency to the matter, the American, British, and Soviet delegates reached a limited agreement to ban test explosions of nuclear devices, except under ground. France which had exploded a nuclear bomb in 1960 and Communist China which was to do so in 1964 were invited to adhere to the agreement, but they declined to do so. Although limited in kind and in the number of signatory nations, the test-ban treaty, which was signed in Moscow on August 4, 1963, produced a great relaxation of international tensions. However, in 1966, the fundamental question of disarmament remained unsolved.

3. SOCIAL JUSTICE

Throughout history the material wealth of this planet has always been unequally divided, with some peoples enjoying a more adequate source of supplies and higher standard of living than others. Before the twentieth century most of the poorer peoples of the world accepted their condition and were resigned to it. They had little opportunity to make effective comparisons or to observe how the wealthier nations lived. In recent times, however, the better transportation and communication, and the closer contacts between countries, have changed this situation. As the twentieth century advanced more people in retarded areas came to realize that the world was divided into rich countries and poor countries, rich continents and poor continents. A somber awareness that their income was far below the global average began to influence the thinking of impoverished peoples. They took note of the fact that the regions held by the Europeans, in Europe and North America, were in many respects the choicest areas of the globe. In comparison, the portions occupied predominantly by the colored races had in general a less stimulating climate, less cultivable land, and less adequate resources.

The countries with the highest living standards, at the opening of the twentieth century, were the countries of Western Europe, the United States, Canada, Australia, and New Zealand. By the middle of the century Russia too could be included in this list. In contrast, most of Asia, Africa, and Latin America were regions of low income and low living standards, often desperately low.

In 1900 the combined population of Asia, Africa, and Latin America constituted 70 per cent of the global total. By 1930, however, the figure had declined to 66 per cent. If this trend had continued, the discrepancy between the distribution of population and the distribution of cultivable land would gradually have corrected itself. But the trend did not continue: after 1930 it reversed itself. By 1940 Asia, Africa, and Latin America together held 67 per cent of the world population; by 1950 they held 69 per cent; by 1965 they held 71 per cent.

In Asia and Africa the rising population pressure helped to explain the revolt against colonialism which compelled the European powers to grant their Asian and African subjects independence. But independence did not solve the problem of economic inequality between the rich and poor regions of the world. On the contrary it intensified that problem. In 1938, on the eve of World War II, the Asians, Africans, and Latin Americans earned 24 per cent of the world income. Five years after the war ended, when they comprised 69 per cent of the world population, their share of the world income had fallen to 23 per cent. The weakening of European *political* control over millions of Asians and Africans did not alter the *economic* realities. By 1965, when the Asians, Africans, and Latin Americans made up 71 per cent of the global population their share of the global income had declined to 22 per cent.

In the Americas, the disparity between the rising per capita income in the United States and Canada and the low income in the poorer Latin American countries created increasing tensions. When Vice President Nixon visited South America in 1958 on a "good will" tour, angry crowds hurled stones at his car and agitators in Peru and Venezuela threatened his life. After Fidel Castro overthrew Fulgencio Batista and seized control of Cuba in 1959, relations between the United States and Cuba became acutely strained. Castro confiscated the wealth of United States citizens; the United States cancelled imports of Cuban sugar. Turning toward Moscow, Castro made a "trade and aid" deal with the Russians, purchased Russian arms, and adopted "socialist" policies. The United States Central Intelligence Agency secretly trained and equipped 1,200 Cubans opposed to Castro and helped them to invade Cuba in 1961 (see page 721). No uprising occurred to aid them, and Castro's forces defeated and captured them with ease. The incident shook the faith of the American people in the efficiency of their secret service and exposed them to world criticism for attacking a small neighbor.

The Cuban situation emphasized a fact that had already been demonstrated in Asia and Africa. Small nations that needed aid to develop their retarded economy might obtain this aid from Moscow or Peking if it was refused in Washington. But to accept financial aid, Russian, Chinese, or American, tended to draw a country into the Communist or the Western orbit. Small nations had become pawns in the global chess game waged between Communist and anticommunist forces. In the conflict between the United States and the Soviet Union the "uncommitted" countries had to endure pressure from both sides. This made them regard the aid they received, not as assistance generously offered, but as a bribe. Men are not grateful for bribes. Nor, as a rule, do they feel bound to fulfill the promises made in exchange for a bribe if those promises can be safely repudiated. Neither Russia, China, nor the United States could count upon the continued loyalty of the nations they subsidized.

In the five years from 1955 to 1960 the United States pledged some $8 billion and Russia about $5 billion to aid underdeveloped countries in Asia, Africa, and Latin America. Most of this aid went to twelve countries, and the source of the aid indicates whether the country concerned leaned toward the United States, toward Russia, or followed a middle-of-the-road policy. Data on Chinese aid are less readily available.

COUNTRY	AID FROM U.S.	AID FROM U.S.S.R.	TOTAL
(All estimates are expressed in millions of dollars)			
India	2,102	933	3,035
United Arab Republic	290	783	1,073
Pakistan	1,041	3	1,044
Turkey	818	17	835
Indonesia	272	509	781
Brazil	644	3	647
Argentina	375	104	479
Iran	352	6	358
Afghanistan	113	206	319
Cuba	20	215	235
Cambodia	173	55	228
Iraq	11	216	227

The total aid furnished impoverished countries during the decade 1950–1960 was impressive. Never before in history had the wealthier nations assisted the poorer nations more generously. But, as already noted, the gap separating the rich from the poor did not narrow; on the contrary it tended to widen. One important reason for this was the high birth rate in most underdeveloped regions. Unless income and food supply could be increased *faster* than the birth rate, the income *per capita* declined because there were more to share it, more mouths to feed. At the opening of the 1960's the question of making the impoverished countries more prosperous and more self-sufficient was a problem of vital importance. Armaments, and the danger of nuclear war, offered the most *immediate* threat to the future of mankind. But the poverty that beset two-thirds of the world population might, in the long run, lead to conflicts and disasters almost as tragic as war. It remained to be seen whether the conscience of mankind could triumph over both dilemmas.

68

INTERNATIONAL PROBLEMS

Finally, the reappearance of [France] . . . with its hands free — clearly modifies the world play of forces which, since Yalta, appeared to have been limited to two participants. Since the liberty, equality, and fraternity of peoples decidedly do not receive their fair share in this division of the world between two hegemonies and hence two camps, another order and another equilibrium are necessary for peace. Who can maintain these better than we, provided we remain ourselves.

CHARLES DE GAULLE,
BROADCAST, APRIL 27, 1965

1. DECLINE OF THE UNITED NATIONS

THE ESTABLISHMENT OF the United Nations after World War II raised perhaps greater hopes for peace than had the creation of the League of Nations after World War I. Regrettably, however, the United Nations was not notably more successful in maintaining international peace and order than had been the League of Nations. Like the League, the UN succeeded in appeasing a number of minor international conflicts.

The difficulty did not arise from any imperfection of the UN machinery, but from the refusal of the major powers to allow a limitation of their sovereignty when their basic interests were at stake. The UN Charter undoubtedly represented an advance in international organization over the League Covenant. But even the best machinery for international cooperation cannot function properly if its principal members do not want to cooperate. The proper functioning of the UN was predicated upon the continuance of inter-Allied cooperation after World War II. This, however, failed to materialize for reasons which were explained in Sections VII, IX and X.

From the first meeting of the UN Assembly in London in January, 1946, the world organization was caught in the East-West Cold War. Instead of becoming an agency to promote international peace and harmony, it became the principal arena for East-West propaganda battles. In the early postwar years the United States largely dominated the UN. The American public at the time showed great enthusiasm for the world organization. Thanks to the support of Britain, France, and Nationalist China, the United States had a majority in the UN Security Council. Thanks to the support of the countries of Western Europe, the British Commonwealth, and Latin America, all of which were at the time dependent on American economic and military aid, the United States also commanded a crushing majority in the UN Assembly. On the other hand, the Soviet Union was isolated in the Council and supported in the Assembly only by the small band of its East European satellites. Resolution after resolution, sponsored by the Soviet delegates in the Council and Assembly, were defeated by the "automatic" American majority. In these circumstances, the Soviet Union tended to rely on its right of veto in the Council. Time and time again it vetoed American-sponsored resolutions in the Council.

In 1950, after the Communist victory in China, the Soviet Union demanded that China's permanent seat in the Council be transferred from the Nationalist to the Communist government of China. When the United States blocked this move, the Soviet delegate imprudently walked out of the Council. During his absence, the Council voted the American-sponsored resolution to brand North Korea an aggressor for having attacked South Korea in June, 1950. The Soviet delegate then hastened to resume his seat in the Council and continued to veto American moves.

Frustrated by the repeated Soviet use of the veto in the Council, the United States began to build up the influence of the Assembly. In 1950 the Assembly approved the American-sponsored "Uniting for Peace" resolution, which empowered it (the Assembly) to vote peace-keeping operations when the Council was dead-locked. The Soviet Union vehemently protested this usurpation of the prerogatives of the Council, defied the Assembly's resolutions when they violated its interests, and refused to contribute to the cost of UN peace-keeping forces. Angered by its impotence in the UN, the Soviet Union vented its wrath on the first UN Secretary General Trigve Lie (1946–1952). By 1952 it had hounded the former Norwegian foreign minister into resigning. As his successor, the UN chose Dag Hammarskjöld (1952–1961), a cool, intellectual Swedish diplomat.

In the late 1950's the composition of the Assembly began to change as a result of the dissolution of the British and French colonial empires and the wholesale and instant admission to the UN [1] of these former colonies. Unlike the League, which was dominated by European nations, the UN became increasingly dominated by the new nations of the former colonial world. The United States and the Soviet Union eagerly bid for their support against each other. The West European nations on the other hand, began to lose interest in the UN. They felt it had fallen captive to the new Afro-Asian nations and victim to Soviet and American demagoguery.

[1] The League of Nations required a lengthy probationary period before admitting its mandates to membership.

In June, 1956, the former French premier Robert Schuman complained that the UN gave disproportionate strength to "prejudiced" and "fanatical" blocs "riding rough-shod" over "weak and divided" Europeans. Indeed, during the Suez Crisis in October, 1956, the United States and the Soviet Union, catering to the new nations of Asia and Africa, voted together against Britain and France.

The Soviet and American courting of the neutralist nations came to a climax at the 1960 meeting of the UN Assembly. The Soviet delegation was led by Premier Khrushchev in person. He was accompanied by all the top Communist leaders of Eastern Europe. Nehru of India, Nasser of Egypt, Castro of Cuba, and a host of less well-known heads of state were present. While President Eisenhower contented himself with address-ing the Assembly in a dignified manner, Premier Khrushchev caused a series of sensations by his rash statements and unorthodox behavior. But both the American and Soviet efforts to capture the neutralist "bloc" were a failure, for the neutralist nations constituted no bloc at all; they had nothing in common, except a distrust of all power blocs.

In 1961 the Assembly voted to send a UN peace-keeping force to the former Belgian Congo to thwart secessionist movements and preserve the unity of the Congo. This, strictly speaking, constituted intervention in the internal affairs of a member state rather than an attempt to preserve international peace. The United States supported the measure. On the other hand, the Soviet Union and France, for different reasons, opposed it and refused to contribute their share of the cost of the operation. In the same year Dag Hammarskjöld was killed in an airplane accident, while inspecting the UN forces in the Congo. The Soviet government, which blamed him for the Congo operation, proposed to replace him with the so-called *troika* — three secretaries instead of one, one to represent each, the Soviet bloc, the Western bloc, and the supposed neutralist bloc. The United States opposed the move, which, it insisted, would paralyze the UN. In the end, after much bargaining, U Thant, a citizen of neutralist Burma, was appointed UN Secretary General.

In 1964 the UN found itself in increasing financial difficulties, which re-sulted from the failure of several of its members to pay their share of the cost of the world organization. For some time the United States had helped it out by contributing more than its share of UN dues. However, in 1964 the United States invoked the UN Charter to deprive the Soviet Union of its vote in the Assembly for its refusal to pay its share of the cost of the UN peace-keeping forces. Although the United States had ceased to have an "automatic" majority in the Assembly, it probably could have mus-tered the necessary votes to deprive the Soviet Union of its vote in the Assembly. However, it had second thoughts on the matter. The American resolution, had it passed, would have given the Assembly and the small nations that it represented too much power. The day might come when they could use that power against the United States, for instance, to admit

Communist China to UN membership against American wishes. The United States decided, therefore, not to diminish the powers of the Security Council in which it had the right of veto, by augmenting those of the Assembly where its interests were not so clearly protected. Consequently, the United States did not press for a vote on its resolution to deprive the Soviet Union of a vote in the Assembly. The Assembly side-stepped the issue by taking no formal vote in its entire 1964 session. The storm passed away, but the inactivity of the Assembly further diminished UN prestige.

There were increasing indications of disenchantment with the UN, not only in the United States and Western Europe, but also in Soviet Russia and Eastern Europe. Only the new nations of Asia and Africa continued to appreciate it, for it provided them with a forum in which to voice their aspirations. In 1966 U Thant, frustrated over the growing difficulties of the UN, indicated a desire to relinquish his office. He was, however, persuaded to accept a second five-year term.

2. THE PASSING OF THE COLD WAR

During the American presidential campaign of 1952, John Foster Dulles, the principal Republican spokesman on foreign policy, took issue with the policy of containment which had been inaugurated by the Administration of President Truman. He argued that it was a passive policy, which accepted the *status quo* resulting from World War II. In the foreign policy plank of the Republican electoral platform he inserted a call to "roll back the Iron Curtain" and to "liberate" the "captive peoples" of Eastern Europe and China from Communist tyranny. However, on becoming Secretary of State in President Eisenhower's cabinet, he soon found out that this was easier said than done. In practice, he was unable to depart from the policy of containment. Indeed, propaganda addressed to the captive peoples through such media as the official "Voice of America" broadcasts or the unofficial "Radio Free Europe" was stepped up. But as the bloody suppression of the Hungarian Revolution in 1956 painfully showed, the Communists were determined to hold on to that which they had already gained and the United States could not actively help the captive peoples without risk of provoking World War III. The Republican electoral platform of 1956 said nothing more of rolling back the Iron Curtain or liberating the captive peoples.

Nevertheless, until his fatal illness (he died in 1959), Dulles provided vigorous and able leadership to the Western world. He labored hard and successfully to complete the ring of interlocking alliances with which his Democratic predecessors had begun to contain the Communist powers. He excoriated the Communists and exhorted the American allies in stern, moralistic terms, which — at times — obscured the continuously peaceful purpose of the American people but held the allies of the United States firmly together and its opponents at a respectful distance. After Dulles' death President Eisenhower took a more active part in the conduct of American foreign policy and managed to give it an air of greater reasonableness, but its premises did not change. Under President Kennedy (1961–1963) the *style* of American foreign policy again changed, but not its substance. Secretary of State Dean Rusk, who continued under President Johnson (1963–), stressed "quiet diplomacy" — that is, patient, plodding negotiations with the Communists, preferably behind closed doors, over concrete issues. But the aims of American foreign policy remained static. It did not seek to expand American influence into the Communist area, but would not tolerate the expansion of Communist influence into its area.

Meanwhile, after the death of Stalin in 1953, Soviet foreign policy became more flexible, but its aims likewise did not change. In his funeral oration over the bier of Stalin, George Malenkov affirmed that the Soviet government was guided by the "Leninist-Stalinist principle" of "coexistence and peaceful competition between the two systems, the capitalist and socialist." At the Twentieth Party Congress in 1956, Khrushchev elevated peaceful coexistence and competition to a fundamental Marxist doctrine. However, as his famous statement to the Western ambassadors in Moscow in November, 1956 — "History is on our side, whether you like it or not. We shall bury you." — indicated, the Soviet government had not abandoned its hope of seeing the world eventually united under communism, but the rigidity and simplicity of tactics that characterized Soviet foreign policy under Stalin gave way to a greater flexibility.

Khrushchev abandoned the simple Leninist-Stalinist concept of a world divided into two irreconcilable camps, Communist and capitalist, and recognized the emergence of a third, neutralist, camp, which he sought to capture for Soviet purposes. He was an innovator and a resourceful and agile tactician. Under his leadership, the Soviet government managed to give the *appearance* of greater reasonableness than under Stalin. It assiduously courted world opinion by putting forward innumerable disarmament plans and other peace proposals, which, however, were designed more to impress world opinion than to reach an agreement with the United States. He broke the precedent established by Stalin for Soviet leaders never to leave Soviet or Soviet-controlled territory, by launching innumerable good-will tours abroad. He made himself readily available to foreign visitors and showed none of the Stalinian reticence about Soviet aims. Under his successors, the style of Soviet foreign policy again changed but not its aims. Brezhnev and Kosygin (1964–) reverted in part to Stalinian reticence and inscrutability, but made no radical departure from Khrushchev's policy. Therefore, the Cold War continued after Stalin, but its grounds and tactics kept shifting.

In Europe, the Cold War centered around Germany in the 1950's. What the Germans hoped for most fervently was reunification. Both the United

States and the Soviet Union held out hope of reunification to them, each on its own terms. Actually, neither was in a position to effect German reunification because each was determined to hold on to its share of Germany. Consequently, German reunification could be achieved only by force, and both the United States and the Soviet Union were reluctant to resort to force, for fear of unleashing World War III. But the United States, thanks to its economic power, was in a position to unite at least the western zones of Germany. Germany — as, indeed, all of Europe — needed foreign economic aid for its postwar reconstruction. The Soviet government was not only unable to provide foreign aid, but counted on German reparations for its own postwar reconstruction. On the other hand, the United States, thanks to its economic power, was able first to tie the nations of Western Europe to its policy through the Marshall Plan (1947); then to unify the richer and more populous American, British, and French zones of Germany into Trizonia (1948); and, finally, to create the West German Federal Republic (1949).

The American initiative put the Soviet government on the defensive. Rather reluctantly, it followed suit by creating the East German Democratic Republic (1949). Impressed with the political import of the Marshall Plan, it created the Council for Mutual Economic Assistance (CEMA, COMECON) in Moscow (1949) as a counterpart to the American-sponsored Organization for European Economic Cooperation in Paris. Western newsmen dubbed it the "Molotov Plan," which was really an unearned compliment. Owing to Soviet poverty, there was no Molotov Plan; CEMA remained a purely paper organization until 1957. If the Soviet government had been able to offer an effective Molotov Plan in 1947, it is not inconceivable that not only Germany but also France and Italy, with their large and vocal Communist parties, would have been drawn into the Soviet orbit instead of the American one.

Because of American economic aid West Germany soon recovered its economic prosperity; while, owing to Soviet poverty, East Germany remained economically debilitated and politically discontented. This proved constantly embarassing to the Soviet government, but what was positively frightening to it was the American determination to rearm West Germany and admit it to NATO. Despite the fact that Soviet Russia shared in the Allied victory over Germany in World War II, the Soviet people retained a healthy respect for the German fighting qualities. The conclusion of the Treaty of Paris in 1954 (see p. 701) which provided for the admission of West Germany to NATO, caused genuine fear among the Soviet people.

Soviet diplomacy and propaganda exerted every ounce of pressure to prevent the ratification of the Treaty of Paris. The Soviet government loudly protested that the Treaty of Paris constituted a violation of the Potsdam agreement of 1945. It reminded Britain and France of their wartime alliance treaties with the Soviet Union, and threatened to denounce them if the Treaty of Paris went into effect. To the Germans it held out the hope, not of simple reunification but of confederation of the two Germanies. The confederation of East and West Germany was to be evacuated by all foreign armies and neutralized. To convince the Germans of its earnestness, suddenly, after years of stalling, the Soviet government agreed to the conclusion of the Austrian State Treaty (see p. 652).

West Germany, however, encouraged by the Western powers, insisted that free elections must be held throughout Germany under four-power supervision, to form an all-German government, which would conclude formal peace with the former Allies and determine whether Germany should side with the West, East, or remain neutral. On May 5, 1955, the West German Federal Council (parliament) ratified the Treaty of Paris and West Germany joined NATO. On May 14, as a counter-part to the Atlantic Pact, the Soviet government signed with its satellites the "Warsaw Pact," which placed the East European armies under Soviet command (see p. 755). It also solemnly denounced its alliance treaties with Britain of 1942 and with France of 1944.

These acts completed the division of Europe into two rigid military blocs. Both the Western and Soviet governments were reluctant to admit it, because world opinion had grown weary of the Cold War and yearned for a *détente*. Therefore, they went through the motions of negotiating, without much expectation of reaching an agreement. The following years were filled with much East-West diplomatic activity but with little concrete accomplishment.

With the rigid division of Europe into two military blocs, the Atlantic alliance and the Warsaw pact, the attention of the American and Soviet leaders began to shift to Asia and Africa. On April 18–27, 1955, representatives of twenty-nine former colonial or semi-colonial nations of Asia and Africa met at Bandung in Indonesia and loudly called for the liquidation of the remnants of colonialism and the independence, self-determination, and UN membership for all colonial peoples. The United States and the Soviet Union hastened to bid for their support, both within the UN (see p. 837) and outside of it. In September, 1955, the Soviet government surprised the Western governments by concluding an arms deal with Egypt (see p. 598). This opened the eyes of the emerging nations to the possibility of forcing the United States and the Soviet Union into a game of bidding for the honor of making them lavish presents. In November and December, 1955, Bulganin and Khrushchev made a triumphant tour of neutralist India, Burma, and Afghanistan, and made promises of generous aid to them. In December, 1959, President Eisenhower made a good-will tour of eleven nations (Italy, Turkey, Pakistan, India, Iran, Greece, Tunisia, France, Spain, Morocco). This brought Khrushchev back to South Asia (India, Burma, Indonesia, Afghanistan) in February and March, 1960. In speeches and impromptu remarks, he accused the Western powers of having grown rich by exploiting their colonies and promised Soviet aid "on most easy terms" with "no profit" to the Soviet

Union. In June, 1960, President Eisenhower visited the Philippines, Formosa, and South Korea.

Meanwhile, the Soviet Union and the United States did not neglect Europe. On April 18–28, 1956, Bulganin and Khrushchev visited Britain. This was the first visit by Soviet leaders to a major Western capital and old citadel of capitalism. Because of its novelty, it received a great deal of attention, but produced no agreement. Nevertheless, Khrushchev doggedly pursued the good will of the West Europeans by visiting nearly every one of their capitals in the following years.

The Polish and Hungarian revolts and the Suez Crisis in October, 1956, deeply disturbed the Eastern and Western camps. In 1957, the United States sought to repair the damage to its relations with Britain and France caused by the Suez Crisis. In that same year, the Soviet Union sought to repair the damage to its relations with the Communist countries caused by the Polish and Hungarian revolts.

The year of 1957 was uneventful for East-West relations. By contrast the year of 1958 was crowded with events. In April the Polish foreign minister, Adam Rapacki, no doubt with Soviet approval, put forward a plan for an atom-free zone in Central Europe. It was to comprise West and East Germany, Poland and Czechoslovakia. The Western governments brushed the plan aside as inconsequential. In July, East-West relations were disturbed by the landing of American troops in Lebanon, of British troops in Jordan (see p. 808), and by a new Chinese Communist attack on Matsu and Quemoy. In November, Khrushchev startled the world by announcing that the Soviet government intended to conclude peace with East Germany within six months and hand over to it the Soviet rights in Berlin. The Western powers did not recognize the East German regime and were determined not to deal with it. The growing tension over Berlin was broken when President Eisenhower invited Khrushchev to visit the United States.

Khrushchev toured the United States on September 15–27, 1959, and was cordially welcomed by the American people. President Eisenhower engaged him in confidential conversations at Camp David for three days. The conversations were apparently harmonious but produced no concrete results. Nevertheless, Khrushchev invited Eisenhower to reciprocate his visit by visiting the Soviet Union in 1960; and Soviet-American relations were briefly animated by the "spirit of Camp David." This came to an abrupt end when the Russians shot down a United States Lockheed U-2 high altitude reconnaissance plane over Sverdlovsk in the Urals on May 1, 1960. The ensuing Soviet-American quarrel also disrupted the second Summit conference in Paris (May 14–18, 1960). Khrushchev angrily denounced the American action as "thief-like," "piratical" and "cowardly." He called Eisenhower a "fishy" friend, but at once announced that he would seek an agreement with Eisenhower's successor, due to be elected in November.

The Soviet government was most anxious to get the Western armies out of West Berlin ("a bone in our throat," in Khrushchev's words) and to close this gap in the Iron Curtain. The continuous flight of East Germans through Berlin deprived East Germany of essential labor and delayed its economic recovery. As long as the East German people had the possibility of flight through Berlin it was difficult for the East German regime to get a firm grip on them. Khrushchev's meeting with President Kennedy in Vienna (June 3–4, 1961) produced no agreement.

Amidst growing tension, the Western powers fortified their garrisons in West Berlin and prepared for a showdown. But they were unprepared for the East German move when it came. On the night of August 12–13 the East German police closed the border between East and West Berlin, and proceeded to erect a wall along it. The Western powers protested against this action, but were powerless to undo it. The questions of Berlin and Germany passed from the active list of international problems. In the 1960's the peace of Europe appeared undisturbed, but the unsolved questions of Berlin and Germany remained potential causes of war.

In the late 1950's it became apparent that the Geneva agreement of 1954, which had provided for the partition of Vietnam and the neutralization of Laos and Cambodia, had not brought peace to these unhappy lands. In South Vietnam the Communists (the Vietcong), supported by Communist North Vietnam, continued to fight a guerrilla war against the government in Saigon. In 1959 the Communist-led Pathet Lao, aided by Communist North Vietnam, staged a revolt against the Laotian government. The United States, which was not a signatory to the Geneva agreement, offered military and economic aid to the South Vietnamese and Laotian governments. In 1961 the signatory powers of the Geneva agreement arranged a cease-fire in Laos and the Laotian crisis abated. In South Vietnam, however, the war continued.

In 1961 President Kennedy sent General Maxwell Taylor, the Chairman of the United States Joint Chiefs of Staff, to South Vietnam to study the situation. As a result of General Taylor's recommendations, United States aid to South Vietnam was increased and the United States Military Assistance Command (MAC) established in Saigon. MAC not only trained but assisted South Vietnamese troops in the field. Despite this assistance, however, the South Vietnamese army was unable to put down the Vietcong and their North Vietnamese helpers. In 1965 President Johnson committed large United States forces to take a direct part in the war. He also ordered the systematic bombardment of supply bases in North Vietnam and the routes over which the Vietcong and North Vietnamese troops in South Vietnam were supplied. On the other hand, Communist China and Soviet Russia supplied North Vietnam, but apparently committed no troops. In 1966 the war in Vietnam remained localized.

The Castro revolution in Cuba in 1959 provided the Soviet Union with an unexpected opportunity to extend its influence into the Western Hemisphere. Castro, a brave revolutionary and dilettante Marxist (a type particularly despised by the Communists), was driven by his lack of a program and of administrative skill to lean increasingly on the Communists who had a program and organizing ability. This provoked increasing American hostility to his regime, which in turn forced it deeper into the arms of the Soviet Union. The Soviet government handled Cuba at first gingerly. It provided Cuba with economic and military aid, but did not conclude with it an alliance treaty.

In 1962, however, the Soviet government encouraged perhaps by the American acceptance of the defeat of the Cuban exiles at the Bay of Pigs in 1961, determined to go further and transform Cuba into a Soviet military base equipped with rockets and missiles. On October 22 President Kennedy revealed that United States surveillance of Cuba (presumably, by high-flying reconnaissance planes) had detected that a series of Soviet "offensive missile sites" were being built on the island. He declared that the launching of nuclear missiles from Cuba against any Western Hemisphere nation would be considered "an attack by the Soviet Union on the United States, requiring a full retaliatory response upon the Soviet Union." He further stated that he had ordered a naval and air quarantine (blockade) on shipments of offensive weapons to Cuba. Other official spokesmen intimated the intention of the United States to remove the threat to American security in Cuba by invading the island or bombing the missile launching pads. On October 28, after an attempt to bargain, the Soviet government agreed to dismantle and remove the missile installations from Cuba. It was the most humiliating diplomatic defeat that the Soviet government had suffered since World War II. It seriously undermined Soviet leadership of the Communist world. Paradoxically, however, it was followed by a notable improvement in Soviet-American relations.

During the Cuban crisis neither the United States nor the Soviet Union thought of, or had time to, consult its respective allies. Although during the crisis the nations of Western Europe rallied around the United States, in the sobering aftermath of the crisis they realized that they might have been drawn, without being consulted, into a Soviet-American nuclear war, over an issue in the Western Hemisphere in which they were little interested. No official protests followed, but the crisis increased the desire, notably of France, to disassociate itself from the United States. The crisis likewise widened the Sino-Soviet rift.

3. TOWARD A NEW BALANCE OF WORLD POWER

The architects of the American policy of containment predicted that it would eventually bring about tendencies in the Communist world that would result in the "break-up" or "mellowing" of Communst power (see p. 570). Events proved this prophecy correct. In the late 1950's and in the 1960's the Communist world did, indeed, show a tendency to break up into mutually antagonistic groups, and in the Soviet Union, at least, if not in Communist China, Communist power did show a tendency to mellow. However, what the architects of the containment policy did not foresee was that, at the same time, as the danger of Communist aggression receded, the Western world likewise showed a tendency to break up.

This development was not an abrupt one but rather a gradual one. It was influenced by many internal and external factors as well as by the outlook of individual leaders in the Communist and Western worlds. The year of 1958 may be selected as a significant one in this development. It marked the opening of a public quarrel between the Soviet Union and Communist China and the return of General Charles de Gaulle to power in France.

Until 1958 relations between the Soviet Union and Communist China appeared to outsiders properly "fraternal" — to use the favorite phrase of the Communists to describe their relations. However, behind the scenes certain rifts had developed between them. In 1945 a Chinese Communist delegation arrived in Moscow to seek the advice of the Soviet leaders on a course to follow. At that time the Soviet government apparently believed that the Chinese Nationalist government of General Chiang Kaishek would survive in power. It concluded with the Chinese Nationalist government an alliance for thirty years (see p. 579) and advised the Chinese Communists to seek a *modus vivendi* with it. The Chinese Communists disregarded this advice, mustered their forces, and defeated the Chinese Nationalist government. Shortly after the formal proclamation of the Chinese People's Republic (October, 1949), the Chinese Communist leader Mao Tse-tung hastened to make his first pilgrimage to Moscow. After three months of leisurely, oriental negotiations with Stalin, they concluded a thirty-year treaty of "friendship, alliance, and mutual assistance" and two subsidiary agreements (February 14, 1950), which repudiated the 1945 Soviet treaty with Nationalist China.

Superficially, the position of Communist China resembled that of the Soviet satellites in Eastern Europe, especially Yugoslavia before 1948. In reality, however, by the very size of its area and population, Communist China escaped the character of a satellite. On the other hand, it did not become a full and equal partner of the Soviet Union. Its status in the Communist world was, in fact, unique. Whatever it was, superficially, relations between the two Communist giants appeared harmonious until 1958. The Soviet government provided a long-term loan to China and much needed technical assistance, and the Chinese Communists paid fulsome homage to the leadership of the Soviet Union in the Communist world.

Mao Tse-tung was present at the fateful Soviet Twentieth Party Congress in 1956, at which Khrushchev repudiated Stalin. The Chinese leader expressed misgivings over this policy and did not follow it in China. Outwardly, however, Sino-Soviet relations appeared undisturbed. The first indication of Soviet-Chinese disagreement came to the outside world in connection with the adoption of the ambitious Chinese program of industrialization (the "Great Leap Forward," May, 1958) and the launching of the rural communes (September, 1958). The latter were proclaimed a shortcut to communism. The Soviet leaders, who claimed that the Soviet Union had reached socialism but not yet communism, were apparently annoyed by the Chinese presumption to skip "historic stages" and reach the ultimate stage of communism before Russia. The Chinese showed increasing disapproval of the Soviet policy of peaceful coexistence with the "imperialists" and Soviet courting of the neutralists, especially India and Indonesia with which Chinese relations were not good.

Immediately after his visit to the United States in September, 1959, Khrushchev hastened to try to appease the Chinese. Apparently, however, he failed to reach an agreement with them. Khrushchev then decided on a coercive measure. In 1960 the Soviet government recalled all Soviet technicians from China, causing a disruption of Chinese industrialization plans. Far from "knuckling under," however, the Chinese Communists retaliated by challenging the Soviet monopoly to formulate ideology and determine strategy for the whole Communist world. They made a bold move to seize leadership. A public polemic broke out between the Soviet and Chinese Communist organs. The gist of the Chinese argument appeared to be that peaceful coexistence with the "imperialists" and the "neutralists" was admissible as a temporary tactic in the Cold War but not as a permanent doctrinal goal; that ultimately there would have to be a final reckoning with the " imperialists" to determine (as Lenin once put it) *kto kogo* — who would do in whom; that a third world war, therefore, could not be excluded *a priori*; that colonial wars (such as the war in Vietnam) were "just" wars of "national liberation," and that "class struggle" (that is, fomenting Communist revolutions) in the former colonial world must not be abandoned for the sake of wooing their new "bourgeois nationalist" governments (such as those of Nehru in India or Nasser in Egypt).

Impelled, however, by "proletarian solidarity" and above all by fear of "imperialist" America, the Soviet and Chinese Communists did not at first attack each other directly but used Tito of Yugoslavia and Hoxha of Albania as symbols of the sins of "revisionism" (a watering-down of Marxist ideology) and "dogmatism" (a literal, lifeless interpretation of Marxist scriptures), respectively, of which they accused each other. Like voodooist *hungans* sticking pins in dolls symbolic of their victims, Moscow attacked Hoxha "and other dogmatists" (that is Mao Tse-tung), while Peking attacked Tito "and other revisionists" (that is, Khrushchev).

After a heated discussion of the issues at the Congress of the Rumanian Communist party in Bucharest in June, 1960, the Soviet leaders agreed to submit them to a general discussion at a conference of all the Communist parties in Moscow in November. The conference was attended by 81 Communist parties and was the largest Communist conclave since the last Comintern congress in 1935. After weeks of arduous debate, the breach was papered over by an ambiguous declaration on December 6. Subsequent events, however, showed that the two parties had not changed their fundamental positions. The quarrel broke out again a year later at the Twenty-second Congress of the Soviet Communist party in Moscow (November, 1961), at which Khrushchev renewed his attacks on Stalin and, indirectly, on Mao Tse-tung. The conflict raged at congresses of the Bulgarian, Hungarian, Italian, Czechoslovak, and East German Communist parties (November, 1962–January, 1963). The substitution of Hoxha for Mao and Tito for Khrushchev was discarded. The Chinese and Soviet leaders now attacked each other directly.

The Sino-Soviet dispute led to what the Italian Communist leader Palmiro Togliatti called "Communist polycentrism" — a split between, and sometimes within, the Communist parties of the world, with one group looking to Moscow and another to Peking for leadership. Nor was the Sino-Soviet rivalry limited to Communist countries and parties. China entered the game of courting the former colonial and underdeveloped nations with foreign aid — a task for which it, an Asian nation and former victim of colonialism, felt better qualified than Russia, a former European "imperialist" power. But China could ill afford it, for by 1960 the Great Leap Forward had failed and China faced a protracted economic crisis. Because of its greater resources and experience, the Soviet Union not only kept the allegiance of the overwhelming number of the world's Communist parties, but won many more friends among the neutralists than China.

After the abject Soviet surrender in Cuba, which coincided with the spectacular Chinese victory over India on the Himalaya border (October, 1962), the Chinese leaders accused the Soviet leaders of first taking unnecessary risks ("adventurism") and then showing cowardice ("capitulationism"). Khrushchev retorted in December by pointing out that while the Indians had gotten rid of the Portuguese colonialists in Diu and Goa the Chinese had not yet rid themselves of the Portuguese in Macao and the British in Hong Kong.

After Khrushchev's dismissal, the Chinese leaders paused briefly in their attacks on the Soviet Union; but they soon decided that the policy of Brezhnev and Kosygin was nothing but "Khrushchevism without Khrushchev" and the Sino-Soviet conflict resumed. It had, however, changed grounds. In August, 1964, speaking to a delegation of Japanese Socialists in Peking, Mao Tse-tung replied to Khrushchev's barb about Macao and Hong Kong by hinting that China would not only reclaim them but also territory taken from it by Imperial Russia. "About a hundred years ago," he said, "the area to the east of Baikal became Russian territory, and since then Vladivostok, Khabarovsk, Kamchatka, and other areas have been Soviet territory. We have not yet presented our bill for this list." This was not a Communist quarrel over ideology or tactics, but an old fashioned nationalist quarrel over territory. The national interests of the Soviet Union and Communist China are not identical. Both are large land powers with a long common border, along which their imperial predecessors often clashed. Neither wishes to nor can repudiate its respective national history. The Soviet Union is the proud carrier of the old Russian civilization and Communist China the carrier of the ancient Chinese civilization, and these civilizations had little in common. Although it would be foolish to try to prophesy the future course of Sino-Soviet relations, in 1966 the divergent national interests of the two powers appeared to outweigh their Communist solidarity.

Meanwhile in the West, the divergent national interests of France and the United States likewise appeared to outweigh their traditional friendship and considerations of Western solidarity. Like the Sino-Soviet conflict, the Franco-American dispute had its roots in the period immediately after World War II. Having suffered a humiliating defeat in World War II, the French were unusually sensitive to slights, real or imaginary. A proud people, keenly aware of their historical role as the "grand nation" of Europe, they felt that they still had an important role to play after the war, both in Europe and the world at large. France is the largest country of Europe after Soviet Russia and, after the war, still possessed a large colonial empire. Owing to its strategic location in Western Europe, the French expected that the role of the fulcrum of the Western alliance would naturally fall to France. However, because of the chronic instability of the French government under the Fourth Republic (1944–1958), in Europe, the United States preferred to depend politically on Britain and militarily on West Germany.

In the colonial world French and American concepts and policies were likewise diametrically opposed. The Americans had traditionally regarded colonies as an evil. After World War II, moreover, they felt that the continued subjection of the colonial peoples made them susceptible to Communist subversion. It was better, therefore, to dissolve colonial empires and assist the colonial peoples to nationhood before they were swept over by Communist revolutions. To set an example, the United States freed the Philippines after World War II and looked with favor on the demand of British, French, Dutch, and Belgian colonial people for freedom.

The French, on the other hand, were determined to preserve their colonial empire, the peoples and resources of which would augment those of France and permit it to resume a position of a first-rate power, equal to that of the United States or the Soviet Union. They regarded North Africa as the equivalent of the American Great West or the Russian Siberia. Apart from these national considerations, the French tended to believe that the dissolution of colonial empires would open the colonial peoples to Communist influence. Therefore, the preservation of the French colonial empire was in the best interest not only of France but of the West as a whole. The Soviet Union — even while possessing a huge colonial empire in Asia — had been anti-colonialist ever since the Russian Revolution and the Allied Intervention after World War I. Therefore, it did not surprise the French when the Soviet government encouraged the revolt of the French colonial peoples. It did, however, surprise them and painfully disappoint them that the United States government carefully disassociated itself from the French struggle to suppress the revolt of their colonial peoples. The United States decision to line up with the Soviet Union against France and Britain in the Suez Crisis in 1956 was not only incomprehensible to the French but positively treasonous to common Western interests. After the Suez Crisis, Franco-American relations, already strained, became barely civil.

The return of General de Gaulle to power in France in 1958 tended at first to improve them. The Americans were glad to see him return to power, because they believed that he would end the internal instability of France and thus strengthen the Western alliance. They hoped that he had lived down the resentment against the memory of President Roosevelt, who had during World War II — unnecessarily, in the opinion of many Americans — snubbed De Gaulle personally and sought to thwart the Free French movement which De Gaulle had led. These hopes appeared at first to be borne out. De Gaulle, a conservative Catholic, appreciated the American efforts to stem the tide of Communism, both internationally by organizing the Western alliance and internally through the Marshall Plan and other economic assistance. He was also less resentful than other Frenchmen of the United States attitude toward colonies. Unlike most French army officers, De Gaulle had never served in the colonies and did not regard them as indispensable to the restoration of French greatness. It was he who made the decision to give up the struggle for the preservation of the French colonial empire and took the initiative to transform it into the loose French Community in 1958. It was also he who made the politically unpopular and personally dangerous decision to relinquish Algeria, which had the legal status not of a colony but of French metropolitan territory (1961).

On the other hand, De Gaulle regarded possession of nuclear power as indispensable to the restoration of France to the position of a first-rate European power. The United States and Britain possessed nuclear power, but France did not. Therefore, De Gaulle requested American and British assistance in the development of French nuclear power. Furthermore, he demanded a position of equality with the United States and Britain, but was reluctant to accord it to West Germany. Twice in 1958 he proposed to President Eisenhower the formation of a three-power (United States-Britain-France) directorate, which would determine jointly Western political and military strategy. However, the United States was reluctant to accord France equality for fear of alienating West Germany. It was also opposed to what the State Department called "proliferation" of nuclear power. De Gaulle's requests and suggestions were evaded, even while the United States and Britain continued to cooperate in the development of nuclear power. This intensified the old French suspicion of the existence of a tacit conspiracy between the "Anglo-Saxon" powers to dominate the European continent. Therefore, De Gaulle determined to develop a purely French nuclear *force de frappe* (striking force) with French resources only. He also began to revive the old concept of Europe stretching "from the Atlantic to the Urals," as opposed to the concept of Europe stretching from the Atlantic to the Elbe, held by the British and the Americans.

In February, 1960, France exploded its first thermonuclear device in the Sahara desert. Fortified by this success, De Gaulle visited the United States in April, in preparation for the second Summit conference which was due to meet in Paris in May. It was his first visit to the United States since his return to power, and he received full honors. He addressed a joint session of the two houses of Congress, but his conversations with President Eisenhower and other American officials were fruitless.

In 1961, De Gaulle renewed his suggestions to President Kennedy, but again they were evaded. Thereafter, Franco-American relations cooled. France took an increasingly independent course. French units were withdrawn from NATO command for service in Algeria, but were not restored to NATO command after the conclusion of the Algerian conflict.

In June, 1960, the United States and Britain concluded an agreement, under which the United States undertook to develop a new air-to-ground "Skybolt" missile for the use of the American and British air forces. The same offer does appear to have been made to France. In December, 1962, after several unsuccessful experiments with the missile, Secretary of Defense MacNamara recommended the abandonment of the Skybolt program as a part of his effort to reduce the cost of American defenses. There was great dismay in Britain, which had based its nuclear defense plans on the Skybolt, and had spent vast sums of money to adapt its otherwise obsolescent Vulcan II bombers to the Skybolt. In place of the Skybolt missiles, President Kennedy offered to sell Britain Polaris missiles to be mounted on British submarines.

The question was to be discussed at a conference between Prime Minister Macmillan and President Kennedy at Nassau later in December. Before going to Nassau, Macmillan visited De Gaulle at Rambouillet in France (December 15–16). A joint communiqué stated that they had discussed the Common Market, to which it was expected Britain would be admitted shortly, and nuclear strategy. However, later reports disagreed on exactly what happened at the meeting. According to French reports, which the British denied, De Gaulle proposed to Macmillan to form an Anglo-French nuclear partnership, in other words, that Britain throw in its lot with Europe, not only economically (in the Common Market) but militarily, instead of with the United States, which had just let it down on the Skybolt program. Allegedly, Macmillan agreed — or so De Gaulle thought. Be that as it may, at the Nassau conference (December 17–21) Macmillan not only agreed to abandon the Skybolt but to accept the American plan for a NATO multilateral force (MLF). According to this plan, which was designed to give the European members of NATO a sense of participation in nuclear strategy without surrendering American control of nuclear power, the European NATO members would create a multinational submarine force, equipped with Polaris missiles, but the Americans would keep the nuclear warheads for the missiles.

On January 14, 1963, De Gaulle vetoed Britain's admission to the Common Market (see p. 697) and scornfully rejected the MLF plan, on the ground that "it would be truly useless for us to buy Polaris missiles when we have neither the submarines to launch them nor the thermonuclear warheads to arm them." Bitter recriminations between Britain and France followed. Franco-American relations likewise reached a nadir. Thereafter, De Gaulle pursued a course completely independent of the United States. While he systematically sought to undercut American influence in Europe, the United States itself became increasingly aloof from Europe, being increasingly absorbed in the war in South Vietnam.

To strengthen its influence in Europe, on January 21, 1963, France signed an alliance treaty with West Germany. Chancellor Adenauer had likewise become increasingly disillusioned with the United States leadership because of its growing absorption in Asia and failure to press for German reunification. However, after his retirement in October, 1963, his successor, Chancellor Erhard, reoriented West German policy back to a dependence on the United States, which in part caused his downfall in 1966.

In January, 1964, France recognized Communist China. In September, 1965, De Gaulle announced that France would not renew the North Atlantic Treaty when it expired in 1969 (France would end "the subjection known as integration . . . which puts the destiny of France in the hands of foreigners"), and in March, 1966, asked NATO to move its headquarters out of France. All along, profiting from its surplus of dollars, France increased the American balance-of-payment problem by demanding payment of its claims in gold. De Gaulle was increasingly critical of the American involvement in South Vietnam. However, during his visit to the Soviet Union in July-August, 1966, he refused to curry favor with his Soviet hosts by joining them in attacks on the United States. Nor would he join them in attacks on the Germans — historically, the common enemy of France and Russia. He curtly rejected the Soviet suggestion that France recognize East Germany: "East Germany is only an artificial creation of yours." In short, he kept the Soviet leaders at arms length, much as he did the American leaders. On the other hand, by 1966 the United States and the Soviet Union, both annoyed by the ingratitude of

their respective allies and disappointed with the fickleness of the neutralists, appeared to form what the journalists called a "cold alliance" — a
tacit agreement not to embarrass each other unduly while each attended
to its own problems.

To sum up, in the first ten to fifteen years after World War II, international relations were characterized by bipolarization of power between
the United States and the Soviet Union, each with its cluster of Allies or
satellites around it. In the late 1950's and early 1960's the two power
blocks experienced internal strains and stresses and began to break up.
In 1966 there appeared to be a trend toward a return to a multiple balance of power in international relations. Whether this would safeguard
international peace better than the previous dual balance of power, remained to be seen.

SUGGESTIONS FOR FURTHER READING

It is encouraging to remember, no matter how elusive a research topic may appear, that thousands of experts are constantly at work making data available to the inquirer. One valuable aid to the historian, *A Guide to Historical Literature*, was revised and reissued under the auspices of the American Historical Association in 1961. *Foreign Affairs, An American Quarterly Review* (New York, 1922–) briefly evaluates books on recent history and international relations as they appear, and also lists new collections of source materials. For the years 1922–1962 these lists, with additions, have been republished in *Foreign Affairs Bibliography* (4 vols., New York, 1933–1965). *A Guide to Bibliographical Tools for Research in Foreign Affairs,* compiled by Helen Conover, has been prepared in the Reference Department of the Library of Congress (Washington, 1956). *Bibliographic Index: A Cumulative Bibliography of Bibliographies* issued semi-annually (New York, 1938–), is particularly helpful for finding bibliographies that appeared in books, pamphlets or periodical articles that might otherwise be overlooked. A new and useful aid in a more limited area is *America: History and Life, A Quarterly Guide to Periodical Literature* (Santa Barbara, California) of which Volume I, 1964–1965, appeared in 1966. For those seeking such information, *The World of Learning: A Standard Guide to Academic, Scientific and Cultural Life in Every Country* is a compendious reference work published annually in London, England.

These and other aids cited in the following pages provide a lesson and a warning. Before you undertake to prepare a list of books and articles on any subject it is well to remember that such a list is almost certainly in print already. The first step to take, if you wish to become an authority on a subject, is to learn how to find pertinent and trustworthy information about it without wasting time. Many practical guides have been prepared, and more are issued each year, to speed your research. To form an idea of how numerous and helpful these aids can be, consult Robert W. Murphey, *How and Where to Look It Up: A Guide to Standard Sources of Information* (New York, 1958).

SECTION I: THE CENTURY OF EUROPE'S APOGEE

R. ALBRECHT-CARRIÉ, *A Diplomatic History of Europe Since the Congress of Vienna* (New York, 1958). G. BRUUN, *Nineteenth Century European Civilization* (London, 1959). A. L. C. BULLOCK and A. J. P. TAYLOR, *Select List of Books on European History, 1815–1914* (2nd ed., Oxford, 1957). BENEDETTO CROCE, *History of Europe in the Nineteenth Century* (New York, 1933). K. S. LATOURETTE, *The Great Century, A.D. 1800–A.D. 1914*, Volume 4 of *A History of the Expansion of Christianity* (New York, 1941). J. B. Noss, *Man's Religions* (3rd ed., New York, 1963).

853

CHAPTER 1: INTRODUCTION: THE HISTORICAL BACKGROUND

W. C. Abbott, *The Expansion of Europe: A Social and Political History of the Modern World, 1415–1815* (New York, 1938). Sir Ernest Barker, *The Development of Public Services in Western Europe, 1660–1930* (Hamden, 1966). G. Bruun and H. S. Commager, *Europe and America Since 1492* (Boston, 1954). S. B. Clough and C. W. Cole, *Economic History of Europe* (3rd ed., Boston, 1952). W. L. Langer, ed., *The Rise of Modern Europe* (20 volumes planned, New York, 1934–). R. R. Palmer and Joel Colton, *A History of the Modern World* (New York, 1964). R. H. Powers, *Readings in European Civilization: Since 1500* (Boston, 1961). O. Spengler, *The Decline of the West*, (2 vols. New York, 1945). Abridged edition (New York, 1962). *The New Cambridge Modern History* (New York, 1957–). A. J. Toynbee, *A Study of History* (12 vols., New York, 1935–1961). Abridged edition by D. C. Somervell (2 vols., New York, 1947–1957).

CHAPTER 2: THE CHARACTER OF WESTERN CULTURE

S. E. Ayling, *Portraits of Power: An Introduction to Twentieth-Century History Through the Lives of Seventeen Great Political Leaders* (New York, 1963). I. Asimov, *The Intelligent Man's Guide to Science* (2 vols., New York, 1960). F. L. Berckelaers, *Sculpture of This Century* (New York, 1960). A. Brecht, *Political Theory: The Foundations of Twentieth-Century Political Thought* (Princeton, 1959). J. Cassou, N. Pevsner, and E. Langui, *Gateway to the Twentieth Century: Art and Culture in a Changing World* (New York, 1961). M. Colum, *From These Roots: The Ideas that Have Made Modern Literature* (New York, 1944). H. S. Hughes, *Consciousness and Society: The Reorientation of European Social Thought, 1890–1930* (New York, 1958). E. J. Jurji, ed., *The Great Religions of the Modern World* (Princeton, 1946). L. Mumford, *Technics and Civilization* (New York, 1934). H. Smith, ed., *Columbia Dictionary of Modern European Literature* (New York, 1947). A. P. Usher, *A History of Mechanical Inventions* (Boston, 1959). A. N. Wilder, *Theology and Modern Literature* (Cambridge, 1958).

CHAPTER 3: EUROPE IN THE AGE OF TECHNOLOGY

J. L. Hammond and B. Hammond, *Rise of Modern Industry* (3rd ed., New York, 1927). S. Hook, *Marx and the Marxists: The Ambiguous Legacy* (Princeton, 1955). H. Kohn, *The Idea of Nationalism* (New York, 1944). J. Kuczynski, *A Short History of Labor Conditions under Industrial Capitalism* (4 vols., London, 1942–1946). H. J. Laski, *The State in Theory and Practice* (New York, 1935). J. A. Schumpeter, *Capitalism, Socialism, and Democracy* (3rd ed., New York, 1950). L. S. Wolf, *Imperialism and Civilization* (New York, 1928).

CHAPTER 4: GREAT BRITAIN

M. Beer, *A History of British Socialism* (New York, 1942). E. A. Benians, J. Butler, and C. E. Carrington, *The Cambridge History of the British Empire*, Vol. III, *The Empire Commonwealth, 1870–1919* (New York, 1959). J. H. Clapham, *An Economic History of Modern Britain* (3 vols., New York, 1931–1938). G. D. H. Cole, *A Short History of the British Working Class*

Movement, 1789–1937 (rev. ed., New York, 1960). W. H. B. COURT, *British Economic History, 1870–1914* (New York, 1966). P. GUINN, *British and Politics, 1914–1918* (New York, 1965). R. J. S. HOFFMAN, *Great Britain and the German Trade Rivalry, 1875–1914* (Philadelphia, 1933). A. H. IMLAH, *Economic Elements in the Pax Britannica* (Cambridge, 1958). S. MACMANUS, *The Story of the Irish Race: A Popular History of Ireland* (New York, 1944). A. J. MARDER, *The Anatomy of British Sea Power: A History of British Naval Policy in the Pre-Dreadnought Era, 1880–1905* (New York, 1940), and *From the Dreadnought to Scapa Flow: The Royal Navy in the Fisher Era, 1904–1919* (New York, 1961). D. C. SOMERVELL, *British Politics Since 1900* (2nd ed., London, 1953).

CHAPTER 5: GERMANY

G. A. CRAIG, *From Bismarck to Adenauer: Aspects of German Statecraft* (Baltimore, 1958). L. DEHIO, *Germany and World Politics in the Twentieth Century* (New York, 1959). M. DILL, *Germany: A Modern History* (Ann Arbor, 1961). O. J. HALE, *Germany and the Diplomatic Revolution: A Study in Diplomacy and the Press* (Philadelphia, 1931). R. H. LUTZ, *The Fall of the German Empire, 1914–1918* (2 vols. Stanford, 1932). G. RITTER, *The Schlieffen Plan* (New York, 1958). A. ROSENBERG, *The Birth of the German Republic, 1871–1918* (New York, 1964). H. VOGT, *The Burden of Guilt: A Short History of Germany, 1914–1945* (New York, 1964).

CHAPTER 6: FRANCE

R. ALBRECHT-CARRIÉ, *France, Europe, and the Two World Wars* (New York, 1961). D. W. BROGAN, *France Under the Republic, 1870–1939* (New York, 1940). G. BRUUN, *Clemenceau* (Cambridge, 1943); reprint (Hamden, Conn., 1965). G. CHAPMAN, *The Dreyfus Case* (New York, 1955). W. M. FROHOCK, *Studies in French Fiction, 1925–1960* (Cambridge, 1966). A. GUÉRARD, *France: A Modern History* (Ann Arbor, 1959). J. H. JACKSON, *Jean Jaurès, His Life and Work* (New York, 1944). W. L. LANGER, *The Franco-Russian Alliance, 1890–1894* (Cambridge, 1929); *Reprint* (New York, 1966). C. W. PORTER, *The Career of Théophile Delcassé* (Philadelphia, 1936). T. F. POWER, JR., *Jules Ferry and the Renaissance of French Imperialism* (New York, 1966). H. I. PRIESTLEY, *France Overseas: A Study of Modern Imperialism* (New York, 1966). A. SILVERA, *Daniel Halévy and His Times: A Gentleman-Commoner in the Third Republic* (Ithaca, 1966). R. WOHL, *French Communism in the Making, 1914–1924* (Stanford, 1966).

CHAPTER 7: ITALY

R. ALBRECHT-CARRIÉ, *Italy from Napoleon to Mussolini* (New York, 1950). W. C. ASKEW, *Europe and Italy's Acquisition of Libya, 1911–1912* (Durham, 1942). S. B. CLOUGH, *The Economic History of Modern Italy* (New York, 1964). B. CROCE, *A History of Italy, 1871–1915* (Oxford, 1929). R. F. FOERSTER, *The Italian Emigration of Our Times* (Cambridge, 1919). H. L. GUALTIERI, *The Labor Movement in Italy* (New York, 1946). S. W. HALPERIN, *The Separation of Church and State in Italian Thought from Cavour to Mussolini* (Chicago, 1937). M. HENTZE, *Pre-Fascist Italy: The Rise and Fall of the Parliamentary Regime* (New York, 1939). C. PICHON, *The Vatican and Its Role in*

World Affairs (New York, 1950). W. A. SALOMONE, *Italian Democracy in the Making: The Political Scene in the Giolittian Era, 1900–1914* (Princeton, 1945). C. J. SPRIGGE, *The Development of Modern Italy* (New Haven, 1944). A. J. B. WHYTE, *The Evolution of Modern Italy, 1715–1920* (Oxford, 1944).

CHAPTER 8: IMPERIAL RUSSIA

J. D. CLARKSON, *A History of Russia* (New York, 1961). M. T. FLORINSKY, *Russia: A History and Interpretation* (2 vols., New York, 1947). SIR BERNARD PARES, *A History of Russia* (New York, 1953). S. PUSHKAREV, *The Emergence of Modern Russia, 1801–1917* (New York, 1963). H. SETON-WATSON, *The Decline of Imperial Russia, 1855–1914* (New York, 1956).

J. BLUM, *Lord and Peasant in Russia from the Ninth to Nineteenth Century* (Princeton, 1961). C. JELAVICH, *Tsarist Russia and Balkan Nationalism, 1879–1886* (Berkeley, 1958). A. MALOZEMOFF, *Russian Far Eastern Policy, 1881–1904* (Berkeley, 1958). W. E. MOSSE, *Alexander II and the Modernization of Russia* (New York, 1958). R. A. PIERCE, *Russian Central Asia, 1867–1917: A Study in Colonial Rule* (Berkeley, 1960). G. T. ROBINSON, *Rural Russia under the Old Regime* (New York, 1932). B. H. SUMNER, *Russia and the Balkans, 1870–1880* (London, 1937). T. H. VON LAUE, *Sergei Witte and the Industrialization of Russia* (New York, 1963). B. D. WOLFE, *Three Who Made a Revolution: A Biographical History* (Boston, 1948). A. YARMOLINSKY, *Road to Revolution: A Century of Russian Radicalism* (London, 1951).

CHAPTER 9: THE HAPSBURG AND OTTOMAN EMPIRES

O. JÁSZI, *The Dissolution of the Habsburg Monarchy* (Chicago, 1929). W. A. JENKS, *Austria under the Iron Ring, 1879–93* (Charlottesville, 1966) and *The Austrian Electoral Reform of 1907* (New York, 1950). R. A. KANN, *The Multinational Empire: Nationalism and National Reform in the Habsburg Monarchy, 1848–1918* (2 vols., New York, 1950). A. J. MAY, *The Hapsburg Monarchy, 1867–1914* (Cambridge, 1951). J. REDLICH, *Emperor Francis Joseph of Austria* (New York, 1929). B. E. SCHMITT, *The Annexation of Bosnia, 1908–1909* (New York, 1937). A. J. P. TAYLOR, *The Habsburg Monarchy, 1815–1918* (New York, 1941).

R. H. DAVISON, *Reform in the Ottoman Empire, 1856–1878* (Princeton, 1963). R. DEVREUX, *The First Ottoman Constitutional Period* (Baltimore, 1963). E. M. EARLE, *Turkey, the Great Powers and the Bagdad Railway: A Study in Imperialism* (New York, 1923). G. J. S. EVERSLEY and V. CHIROL, *The Turkish Empire* (London, 1923). J. A. R. MARRIOT, *The Eastern Question* (4th ed., New York, 1940). E. E. RAMSAUR, *The Young Turks: Prelude to the Revolution of 1908* (Princeton, 1957). J. T. SHOTWELL and F. DEAK, *Turkey at the Straits* (New York, 1940).

CHAPTER 10: THE SMALLER STATES OF EUROPE

B. A. ARNESON, *The Democratic Monarchies of Scandinavia* (New York, 1939). A. J. BARNOUW, *The Making of Modern Holland* (New York, 1944). GERALD BRENAN, *The Spanish Labyrinth: An Account of the Social and Political Background of the Civil War* (Cambridge, 1950). M. W. CHILDS, *Sweden: The Middle Way* (rev. ed., New Haven, 1960). E. S. FORSTER, *A Short History of Modern Greece, 1821–1945* (London, 1946). J. A. GORIS, ed., *Belgium* (Berkeley, 1945). SALVADOR DE MADARIAGA, *Spain* (New York, 1958).

A. C. O'Dell, *The Scandinavian World* (New York, 1957). Wilhelm Oechsli, *History of Switzerland, 1499–1914* (Cambridge, 1922). Riemens, *The Netherlands: Story of a Free People* (New York, 1944). R. W. Seton-Watson, *A History of the Roumanians* (Cambridge, 1934). L. S. Stavrianos, *The Balkans Since 1453* (New York, 1958). W. S. Vucinich, *Serbia between East and West: The Events of 1903–1908* (Stanford, 1954). J. H. Wuorinen, *History of Finland* (New York, 1965); and *Scandinavia* (Englewood Cliffs, 1965).

CHAPTER 11: NEWCOMERS ON THE WORLD STAGE

H. K. Beale, *Theodore Roosevelt and the Rise of America to World Power* (Baltimore, 1956). H. S. Commager, *Documents of American History* (7th ed., New York, 1963). F. R. Dulles, *America's Rise to World Power, 1898–1954* (New York, 1954). J.-B. Duroselle, *From Wilson to Roosevelt: Foreign Policy of the United States, 1913–1945* (Cambridge, 1963). N. A. Graebner, *An Uncertain Tradition: American Secretaries of State in the Twentieth Century* (New York, 1961). *Harvard Guide to American History* (Cambridge, 1954). C. L. and E. E. Lord, *Historical Atlas of the United States* (New York, 1956). S. E. Morison and H. S. Commager, *The Growth of the American Republic* (2 vols., 5th ed., New York, 1963). (*See also Chapters 21 and 51.*)

Cambridge History of the British Empire (8 vols., New York, 1929–1963). J. B. Condliffe and W. T. G. Airey, *A Short History of New Zealand* (Christchurch, 1953). D. G. Creighton, *Dominion of the North: A History of Canada* (Boston, 1958). B. Fitzpatrick, *The Australian Commonwealth: A Picture of the Community, 1901–1955* (Melbourne, 1956). (*See also Chapters 30 and 58.*)

I. H. Nish, *The Anglo-Japanese Alliance: The Diplomacy of Two Island Empires, 1894–1907* (New York, 1966). E. O. Reischauer, *Japan: Past and Present* (rev. ed., New York, 1964). T. C. Smith, *The Agrarian Origins of Modern Japan* (Stanford, 1959). (*See also Chapters 34, 49, and 64.*)

SECTION II: WORLD WAR I: 1914–1918

A. Baltzly and A. W. Salomone, *Readings in Twentieth Century European History* (New York, 1950). C. R. M. F. Cruttwell, *A History of the Great War, 1914–1918* (New York, 1936). G. L. Dickinson, *The International Anarchy, 1904–1914* (New York, 1926). E. M. Earle, ed., *Makers of Modern Strategy: Military Thought from Machiavelli to Hitler* (Princeton, 1943). T. C. Frothingham, *A Guide to the Military History of the World War, 1914–1918* (Boston, 1920). H. S. Hughes, *Contemporary Europe* (New York, 1960). S. King-Hall, *Our Times, 1900–1960* (London, 1961). *New Cambridge Modern History*, Vol. XII, *The Age of Violence, 1898–1945* (New York, 1960). R. J. Sontag, *European Diplomatic History, 1871–1932* (New York, 1933). D. Thompson, *World History from 1914 to 1950* (London, 1959).

CHAPTER 12: THE WAR ON LAND AND SEA, 1914–1916

L. Albertini, *The Origins of the War of 1914* (3 vols., New York, 1952–1957). V. Dedijer, *The Road to Sarajevo* (New York, 1966). S. B. Fay, *The Origins of the War* (2 vols., rev. ed., New York, 1930). J. Remak, *Sarajevo* (London, 1959). P. Renouvin, *The Immediate Origins of the War* (New

Haven, 1928). B. E. Schmitt, *The Coming of the War, 1914* (2 vols., New York, 1930).

J. Buchan, *A History of the Great War* (4 vols., New York, 1921–1922). W. S. Churchill, *The World Crisis, 1911–1918* (4 vols., New York, 1923–1927). C. H. Crutwell, *A History of the Great War, 1914–1918* (Oxford, 1934). C. Falls, *The Great War* (New York, 1959). A. Horne, *The Price of Glory* (New York, 1963). B. H. Liddell Hart, *A History of the World War, 1914–1918* (Boston, 1934). B. Tuchman, *The Guns of August* (New York, 1963).

T. G. Frothingham, *The Naval History of the World War* (3 vols., Cambridge, 1924–1926). R. Gilson and M. Prendergast, *The German Submarine War, 1914–1918* (London, 1931). L. Guichard, *The Naval Blockade, 1914–1918* (New York, 1930). H. Newbolt, *A Naval History of the War, 1914–1918* (London, 1920).

CHAPTER 13: THE WAR ON LAND AND SEA, 1917–1918

R. S. Baker, *Woodrow Wilson: Life and Letters* (vols. V–VIII, Garden City, N. Y., 1935–1939). J. G. Harbord, *The American Army in France, 1917–1918* (Boston, 1936). R. Lansing, *War Memoirs* (Indianapolis, 1935). A. S. Link, *Wilson* (vols. III–V, Princeton, 1961–1965). E. May, *The World and American Isolation, 1914–1917* (Cambridge, 1959). F. Palmer, *Newton D. Baker: America at War* (2 vols., New York, 1931). C. Seymour, *The Intimate Papers of Colonel House* (4 vols., Boston, 1926–1928). W. S. Sims and B. J. Hendricks, *The Victory at Sea* (New York, 1920). C. C. Tansill, *America Goes to War* (Boston, 1938).

M. T. Florinsky, *The End of the Russian Empire* (New Haven, 1931). G. Katkov, *Russia 1917: The February Revolution* (New York, 1966). A. F. Kerensky, *Russia and History's Turning Point* (New York, 1965). A. Moorehead, *The Russian Revolution* (New York, 1958). B. Pares, *The Fall of the Russian Monarchy* (New York, 1939). J. Reed, *Ten Days That Shook the World* (New York, 1919). N. N. Sukhanov, *The Russian Revolution, 1917: A Personal Record* (New York, 1955). L. Trotsky, *The History of the Russian Revolution* (3 vols., New York, 1932).

F. B. Maurice, *The Armistice of 1918* (New York, 1943). B. Pitt, *1918: The Last Act* (New York, 1963). H. B. Rudin, *Armistice, 1918* (New Haven, 1944). J. B. Scott, ed., *Preliminary History of the Armistice* (New York, 1924).

CHAPTER 14: THE WAR OF FINANCE, DIPLOMACY, AND PROPAGANDA

R. B. Armeson, *Total Warfare and Compulsory Labor: A Study of the Military-Industrial Complex in Germany during World War I* (The Hague, 1965). B. M. Baruch, *American Industry in the War* (New York, 1941). M. R. Dickson, *The Food Front in World War I* (Washington, 1944). C. E. Fayle, *The War and the Shipping Industry* (New Haven, 1927). G. D. Feldman, *Army, Industry, and Labor in Germany, 1914–1918* (Princeton, 1966). H. F. Grady, *British War Finance* (New York, 1927). G. Gratz and R. Schüller, *The Economic Policy of Austria-Hungary during the War* (New Haven, 1928). G. Jèze and H. Truchy, *The War Finance of France* (New Haven, 1927). A. M. Mikelson, *et al.*, *Russian Public Finance during the War* (New Haven, 1928).

G. G. Bruntz, *Allied Propaganda and the Collapse of the German Empire*

(Stanford, 1938). G. CREEL, *How We Advertized America* (New York, 1920). H. D. LASSWELL, *Propaganda Technique in the World War* (New York, 1927). H. C. PETERSON, *Propaganda for War: The Campaign against American Neutrality, 1914–1917* (Norman, 1939). J. M. READ, *Atrocity Propaganda, 1914–1918* (New Haven, 1941). J. D. SQUIRES, *British Propaganda at Home and in the United States, 1914–1917* (Cambridge, 1935). SIR CAMPBELL STUART, *Secrets of Crewe House* (New York, 1920).

K. FORSTER, *The Failures of Peace: The Search for a Negotiated Peace during the First World War* (Washington, 1941). H. W. GATZKE, *Germany's Drive to the West* (Baltimore, 1950). W. W. GOTTLIEB, *Studies in Secret Diplomacy during the First World War* (London, 1957). D. LLOYD GEORGE, *War Memoirs* (6 vols., Boston, 1933–1937). V. S. MAMATEY, *The United States and East Central Europe, 1914–1918: A Study in Wilsonian Diplomacy and Propaganda* (Princeton, 1957). J. B. SCOTT, ed., *Official Statements of War Aims and Peace Proposals, December 1916 to November 1918* (Washington, 1921). A. VAN DER SLICE, *International Labor, Diplomacy and Peace, 1914–1919* (Philadelphia, 1941). C. J. SMITH, *The Russian Struggle for Power, 1914–1917* (New York, 1956). J. W. WHEELER-BENNETT, *The Forgotten Peace: Brest-Litovsk, March, 1918* (New York, 1939).

CHAPTER 15: POLITICAL, SOCIAL, AND ECONOMIC RESULTS OF THE WAR

E. L. BOGART, *Direct and Indirect Costs of the Great World War* (New York, 1920). J. M. CLARK, *The Costs of the World War to the American People* (New Haven, 1931). S. DUMAS and K. O. VEDEL-PETERSEN, *Losses of Life Caused by War* (Oxford, 1923). H. FOLKS, *The Human Costs of the War* (New York, 1920). L. GREBLER and W. WINKLER, *The Costs of the World War to Germany and Austria* (New Haven, 1940). S. KOHN and A. F. MEYENDORFF, *The Cost of the War to Russia* (New Haven, 1934). F. W. HIRST, *The Consequences of the War to Great Britain* (New Haven, 1934). A. MARWICK, *The Deluge: British Society and the First World War* (Boston, 1966). D. MITRANY, *The Effects of the War in Southeastern Europe* (New Haven, 1936). J. T. SHOTWELL, *What Germany Forgot* (New York, 1940).

M. BAUMONT, *The Fall of the Kaiser* (New York, 1931). R. H. LUTZ, *The German Revolution of 1918–1919* (Stanford, 1922). B. MENNE, *Armistice and Germany's Food Supply, 1918–1919: A Study of Conditional Surrender* (London, 1944).

W. H. CHAMBERLIN, *The Russian Revolution, 1917–1921* (2 vols., New York, 1952). W. P. and Z. COATES, *Armed Intervention in Russia, 1918–1922* (London, 1935). D. FOOTMAN, *Civil War·in Russia* (New York, 1962). G. F. KENNAN, *Soviet-American Relations, 1917–1920* (Princeton, 1956–   ). J. W. MORLEY, *The Japanese Thrust into Siberia, 1918* (New York, 1957). R. H. ULLMANN, *Anglo-Soviet Relations, 1917–1921* (Princeton, 1961–   ). B. M. UNTERBERGER, *America's Siberian Expedition 1918–1920* (Durham, 1956). J. O. White, *The Siberian Intervention* (Princeton, 1950).

E. BENEŠ, *My War Memoirs* (New York, 1928). L. L. GERSON, *Woodrow Wilson and the Rebirth of Poland, 1914–1920* (New Haven, 1953). E. GLAISE VON HORSTENAU, *The Collapse of the Austro-Hungarian Empire* (London, 1924). O. JÁSZI, *Revolution and Counter-revolution in Hungary* (London, 1924). M. KÁROLYI, *Faith Without Illusion: Memoirs* (New York, 1956). T. G. MASARYK, *The Making of a State, 1914–1918: Memories and Observations* (New York, 1927). A. J. MAY, *The Passing of the Hapsburg Monarchy,*

1914–1918 (2 vols., Philadelphia, 1966). D. STRONG, *Austria, October 1918–March 1919: Transition from Empire to Republic* (New York, 1939). Z. A. B. ZEMAN, *The Break-up of the Habsburg Empire, 1914–1918* (New York, 1961).

G. ANTONIUS, *The Arab Awakening: The Story of the Arab National Movement* (New York, 1938). HALIDÉ EDIB, *The Turkish Ordeal* (New York, 1928). AHMED EMIN, *Turkey in the World War* (New Haven, 1930).

SECTION III: THE SEARCH FOR INTERNATIONAL STABILITY

P. BIRDSALL, *Versailles Twenty Years After* (New York, 1941). CARNEGIE ENDOWMENT FOR INTERNATIONAL PEACE, *The Treaties of Peace, 1919–1923* (2 vols., New York, 1924). WINSTON S. CHURCHILL, *The Aftermath, 1918–1928, The World Crisis* (vol. V, New York, 1929). H. M. CORY, *Compulsory Arbitration of International Disputes* (New York, 1932). W. E. STEPHENS, *Revisions of the Treaty of Versailles* (New York, 1939). H. W. V. TEMPERLEY, ed., *A History of the Peace Conference of Paris* (6 vols., London, 1920–1924). U. S. DEPARTMENT OF STATE, *Papers Relating to the Foreign Relations of the United States: The Paris Peace Conference* (13 vols., Washington, 1942–1947).

CHAPTER 16: THE PROBLEMS OF PEACEMAKING

R. S. BAKER, *Woodrow Wilson and the World Settlement* (3 vols., New York, 1922). T. A. BAILEY, *Wilson and the Peacemakers* (New York, 1947). H. HOOVER, *The Ordeal of Woodrow Wilson* (New York, 1958). J. M. KEYNES, *The Economic Consequences of the Peace* (New York, 1920). D. LLOYD GEORGE, *Memoirs of the Peace Conference* (2 vols. New Haven, 1939). E. MANTOUX, *The Carthaginian Peace: Or, the Economic Consequences of Mr. Keynes* (New York, 1946). F. S. MARSTON, *The Peace Conference of 1919: Organization and Procedure* (New York, 1944). H. NICOLSON, *Peacemaking 1919, Being Reminiscences of the Paris Peace Conference* (Boston, 1933). J. T. SHOTWELL, *At the Paris Peace Conference* (New York, 1937). S. P. TILLMAN, *Anglo-American Relations at the Paris Peace Conference of 1919* (Princeton, 1961). L. A. YATES, *United States and French Security, 1917–1921: A Study in American Diplomatic History* (New York, 1957).

CHAPTER 17: POLITICAL SETTLEMENTS, 1919–1924

A. M. LUCKAU, *The German Delegation at the Paris Peace Conference* (New York, 1941). H. I. NELSON, *Land and Power: British and Allied Policy on Germany's Frontiers, 1916–1919* (Toronto, 1963). G. B. NOBLE, *Policies and Opinions at Paris, 1919: Wilsonian Diplomacy, the Versailles Peace, and French Public* (New York, 1935).

R. ALBRECHT-CARRIÉ, *Italy at the Paris Peace Conference* (New York, 1938). N. ALMOND and R. H. LUTZ, eds., *The Treaty of St. Germain* (Stanford, 1935). F. DEAK, *Hungary at the Paris Peace Conference* (New York, 1942). G. P. GENOV, *Bulgaria and the Treaty of Neuilly* (Sofia, 1935). H. N. HOWARD, *The Partition of Turkey: A Diplomatic History, 1913–1923* (Norman, 1931). T. KOMARNICKI, *Rebirth of the Polish Republic, 1914–1920* (London, 1957). I. J. LEDERER, *Yugoslavia at the Paris Peace Conference* (New Haven, 1963). D. PERMAN, *The Shaping of the Czechoslovak State, 1914–1920* (Leiden, 1962). G. P. PINK, *The Conference of Ambassadors: Paris, 1920–1931* (New

York, 1942). S. D. SPECTOR, *Rumania at the Paris Peace Conference* (New York, 1963). S. WAMBAUGH, *Plebiscites Since the World War* (2 vols., Washington, 1933).

F. KAZEMZADEH, *The Struggle for Transcaucasia, 1917–1921* (New York, 1951). S. W. PAGE, *The Formation of the Baltic States* (Cambridge, 1959). R. PIPES, *The Formation of the Soviet Union: Communism and Nationalism, 1917–1923* (Cambridge, 1954). J. S. RESHETAR, *The Ukrainian Revolution, 1917–1920* (Princeton, 1952). A. E. SENN, *The Emergence of Modern Lithuania* (New York, 1959). C. J. SMITH, *Finland and the Russian Revolution, 1917–1922* (Athens, 1958). J. M. THOMPSON, *Russia, Bolshevism, and the Versailles Peace* (Princeton, 1966). (*See also Section III and Chapter 16.*)

CHAPTER 18: THE ECONOMIC SETTLEMENTS

P. M. BURNETT, ed., *Reparations at the Paris Peace Conference from the Standpoint of the American Delegation* (2 vols., New York, 1940). C. G. DAWES, *A Journal of Reparations* (New York, 1939). C. M. FRASURE, *British Policy on War Debts and Reparations* (Philadelphia, 1940). LEAGUE OF NATIONS, *International Currency Experience: Lessons of the Inter-War Period* (New York, 1944).

CHAPTER 19: THE ATTEMPT AT INTERNATIONAL ORGANIZATION

S. S. GOODSPEED, *The Nature and Function of International Organization* (New York, 1959). M. O. HUDSON, *The Permanent Court of International Justice, 1920–1942* (New York, 1942). S. S. JONES, *The Scandinavian States and the League of Nations* (New York, 1939). D. H. MILLER, *The Drafting of the Covenant* (2 vols., New York, 1928). E. F. RAMSHOFEN-WERTHEIMER, *The International Secretariat: A Great Experiment in International Administration* (New York, 1945). W. E. RAPPARD, *The Quest for Peace Since the World War* (Cambridge, 1940). F. P. WALTERS, *A History of the League of Nations* (New York, 1960).

SECTION IV: EXPERIMENTS IN GOVERNMENT

D. KIRK, *Europe's Population in the Interwar Years* (New York, 1947). W. E. RAPPARD and OTHERS, *Source Book on European Governments* (New York, 1939). B. E. SCHMITT, *From Versailles to Munich* (Chicago, 1938). J. T. SHOTWELL and OTHERS, *The Governments of Continental Europe* (New York, 1940). F. H. SIMONDS and B. EMENY, *The Great Powers in World Politics: International Relations and Economic Nationalism* (New York, 1939).

CHAPTER 20: DEMOCRACY ON TRIAL

F. BORKENAU, *The Totalitarian State* (London, 1940). A. COBDAN, *Dictatorship: Its History and Theory* (New York, 1939). F. GROSS, ed., *European Ideologies, A Survey of 20th Century Political Ideas* (New York, 1948). H. KOHN, *Force or Reason* (Cambridge, 1937). W. N. LOUCKS and J. W. HOOT, *Comparative Economic Systems* (New York, 1938). W. M. McGOVERN, *From Luther to Hitler: The History of Nazi Political Philosophy* (Boston, 1941). SIR JOHN A. R. MARRIOT, *Dictatorship and Democracy* (New York, 1935).

A. G. Meyer, *Marxism: The Unity of Theory and Practice* (Cambridge, 1954). M. F. Parmalee, *Bolshevism, Fascism, and the Liberal-Democratic State* (New York, 1934). W. E. Rappard, *The Crisis of Democracy* (Chicago, 1938). H. Rogger and E. Weber, eds., *The European Right: A Historical Profile* (Berkeley, 1965).

CHAPTER 21: THE UNITED STATES

S. F. Bemis, *A Diplomatic History of the United States* (5th ed., New York, 1965). J. K. Fairbank, *The United States and China* (rev. ed., Cambridge, 1958). F. Freidel, *Franklin D. Roosevelt* (3 vols., Boston, 1952–56). A. W. Griswold, *The Far Eastern Policy of the United States* (New York, 1938). J. D. Hicks, *Republican Ascendency, 1921–1933* (New York, 1960). R. W. Howard, *Two Billion Acre Farm: An Informal History of American Agriculture* (New York, 1945). M. Jonas, *Isolationism in America, 1935–1941* (Ithaca, 1966). A. S. Link, *Woodrow Wilson and the Progressive Era* (New York, 1954). G. B. Mowry, *The Era of Theodore Roosevelt* (New York, 1958). E. B. Potter, *The United States and World Sea Power* (Englewood Cliffs, 1955). B. Rauch, *The History of the New Deal* (New York, 1944). A. M. Schlesinger, Jr., *The Age of Roosevelt* (4 vols., Boston, 1957–). P. W. Slosson, *The Great Crusade and After, 1914–1928* (New York, 1930). H. and M. Sprout, *Foundations of National Power: Readings on World Politics and American Security* (Princeton, 1951). B. D. Zevin, ed., *Nothing to Fear: The Selected Addresses of Franklin Delano Roosevelt, 1932–1945* (Boston, 1946). (*See also Chapters 11 and 51.*)

CHAPTER 22: GREAT BRITAIN

C. Brinton, *The United States and Britain* (Cambridge, 1948). R. S. Churchill, *Winston S. Churchill* (5 vols., Boston, 1966–). W. M. Jordan, *Great Britain, France, and the German Problem, 1918–1939* (New York, 1944). C. L. Mowat, *Britain Between the Wars* (Chicago, 1955). W. E. Simnett, *The British Colonial Empire* (New York, 1949). J. H. Stembridge, *An Atlas of the British Commonwealth and Empire* (New York, 1944). A. J. P. Taylor, *English History, 1914–1945* (New York, 1965). E. A. Walker, *The British Empire* (New York, 1966). T. Wilson, *The Downfall of the Liberal Party* (Ithaca, 1966). (*See also Chapters 4 and 52.*)

CHAPTER 23: THE FRENCH REPUBLIC, 1919–1939

W. C. Baum, *The French Economy and the State* (Princeton, 1958). D. W. Brogan, *France under the Republic, 1870–1939* (New York, 1940). S. B. Clough, *France: A Study of National Economics, 1789–1939* (New York, 1939). M. Duverger, *The French Political System* (Chicago, 1958). V. Lorwin, *The French Labor Movement* (Cambridge, 1954). J. T. Marcus, *French Socialism in the Crisis Years, 1933–1939* (New York, 1958). C. Micaud, *The French Right and Nazi Germany, 1933–1939* (Durham, 1943). W. E. Scott, *Alliance against Hitler: The Origins of the Franco-Soviet Pact* (Durham, 1962). J. J. Spengler, *France Faces Depopulation* (Durham, 1939). D. Thomson, *Democracy in France: The Third Republic* (New York, 1946). P. S. Wandycz, *France and Her Eastern Allies, 1919–1925* (Minneapolis, 1962). A. Werth, *The Twilight of France, 1934–1940* (New York, 1942) and *France and Munich: Before and After the Surrender* (London, 1949). (*See also Chapter 6.*)

CHAPTER 24: ITALY

D. A. Binchy, *Church and State in Fascist Italy* (New York, 1942). G. A. Borgese, *Goliath: The March of Fascism* (New York, 1938). G. L. Field, *The Syndical and Corporative Institutions of Italian Fascism* (New York, 1938). D. Germino, *The Italian Fascist Party in Power: A Study in Totalitarian Rule* (Minneapolis, 1959). I. Kirkpatrick, *Mussolini: A Study in Power* (New York, 1964). M. H. M. Macartney and P. Cremona, *Italy's Foreign and Colonial Policy, 1914–1937* (New York, 1938). R. MacGregor-Hastie, *The Day of the Lion: The Life and Death of Fascist Italy, 1922–1945* (New York, 1964). L. Minio-Paluello, *Education in Fascist Italy* (New York, 1946). J. F. Meenan, *The Italian Corporative State* (Oxford, 1944). G. Megaro, *Mussolini in the Making* (Boston, 1938). C. T. Schmid, *The Plough and the Sword: Labor, Land, and Property in Fascist Italy* (New York, 1938). H. A. Steiner, *Government in Fascist Italy* (New York, 1938). W. G. Welk, *Fascist Economic Policy: An Analysis of Italy's Economic Experiment* (Cambridge, 1938). (*See also Chapter 7.*)

CHAPTER 25: GERMANY

A. L. Bullock, *Hitler: A Study in Tyranny* (rev. ed. New York, 1964). F. L. Carsten, *The Reichswehr and Politics, 1918–1933* (New York, 1966). H. L. Dyke, *Weimar Germany and Soviet Russia, 1926–1933* (New York, 1966). E. Eyck, *A History of the Weimar Republic* (2 vols., Cambridge, 1962–63). B. H. Klein, *Germany's Economic Preparations for War* (Cambridge, 1959). R. Manvell and H. Fraenkel, *Dr. Goebbels, His Life and Death* (New York, 1960). J. Parkes, *The Jewish Problem in the Modern World* (New York, 1946). G. Prange, ed., *Hitler's Words: Two Decades of National Socialism, 1923–1943* (Washington, 1944). K. Rosenbaum, *Community of Fate: German-Soviet Diplomatic Relations, 1922–1928* (Syracuse, 1965). W. L. Shirer, *The Rise and Fall of the Third Reich* (New York, 1960). J. W. Wheeler-Bennett, *Nemesis of Power: The German Army in Politics, 1918–1945* (London, 1953). (*See also Chapters 5, 37, and 54.*)

CHAPTER 26: THE SOVIET UNION: FORMATION
27: THE SOVIET UNION: GROWTH OF POWER

E. H. Carr, *A History of Soviet Russia* (New York, 1950–). G. von Rauch, *A History of Soviet Russia* (New York, 1957). F. L. Schuman, *Russia Since 1917* (New York, 1957). D. W. Treadgold, *Twentieth Century Russia* (Chicago, 1959).

I. Deutscher, *Stalin: A Political Biography* (New York, 1959) and *Trotsky* (3 vols., New York, 1954–1963). L. Fischer, *The Life of Lenin* (New York, 1964). R. Payne, *The Rise and Fall of Stalin* (1965).

R. R. Abramovitch, *The Soviet Revolution, 1917–1939* (New York, 1962). J. S. Curtiss, *The Russian Church and the Soviet State, 1917–1950* (Boston, 1953). D. J. Dallin and B. I. Nicolaevsky, *Forced Labor in Soviet Russia* (New Haven, 1947). M. Dobb, *Soviet Economic Development Since 1917* (New York, 1948). M. Fainsod, *How Russia Is Ruled* (rev. ed., Cambridge, 1963). J. M. Hazard, *The Soviet System of Government* (Chicago, 1957). N. Jasny, *Soviet Industrialization, 1928–1952* (Chicago, 1961). J. S. Reshetar, *A Concise History of the Communist Party of the Soviet Union* (New York,

1960). L. Schapiro, *The Communist Party of the Soviet Union* (New York, 1960). M. Slonim, *Modern Russian Literature from Chekhov to the Present* (New York, 1953).

M. Beloff, *The Foreign Policy of Soviet Russia, 1929–1941* (2 vols., New York, 1947–1949). E. H. Carr, *German-Soviet Relations Between the Two World Wars, 1919–1939* (Baltimore, 1951). L. Fischer, *The Soviets in World Affairs, 1917–1929* (2 vols., Princeton, 1951). G. Hilger and A. G. Meyer, *The Incompatible Allies: A Memoir History of German-Soviet Relations, 1918–1941* (New York, 1953). G. F. Kennan, *Russia and the West Under Lenin and Stalin* (New York, 1961). K. E. McKenzie, *Comintern and World Revolution, 1928–1943: The Shaping of Doctrine* (New York, 1964). H. Seton-Watson, *From Lenin to Khrushchev: A History of World Communism* (New York, 1960). (*See also Chapters 8, 15, and 17.*)

CHAPTER 28: THE BORDERLAND OF GERMANY AND RUSSIA
         29: SOUTHEASTERN EUROPE

A. Basch, *The Danube Basin and the German Economic Sphere* (New York, 1953). O. Halecki, *Borderlands of Western Civilization: A History of East Central Europe* (New York, 1952). W. Kolarz, *Myths and Realities in Eastern Europe* (London, 1946). C. A. Macartney and A. W. Palmer, *Independent Eastern Europe: A History* (New York, 1962). R. Mackray, *The Struggle for the Danube and the Little Entente, 1929–1938* (London, 1938). D. Mitrany, *Marx Against the Peasant: A Study in Social Dogmatism* (Chapel Hill, 1951). H. Seton-Watson, *Eastern Europe between the Wars, 1918–1941* (Cambridge, 1946). L. S. Stavrianos, *Balkan Federation: A History of the Movement toward Balkan Unity in Modern Times* (Northampton, 1944). D. Warriner, *Economics of Peasant Farming* (New York, 1939). R. L. Wolff, *The Balkans in Our Time* (Cambridge, 1956).

B. B. Budurowycz, *Polish-Soviet Relations, 1932–1939* (New York, 1963). J. Gehl, *Austria, Germany, and the Anschluss, 1931–1938* (New York, 1963). A. Gulick, *Austria from Habsburg to Hitler* (2 vols., Berkeley, 1948). J. B. Hoptner, *Yugoslavia in Crisis, 1934–1941* (New York, 1962). R. J. Kerner, ed., *Czechoslovakia* (Berkeley, 1945) and *Yugoslavia* (Berkeley, 1949). J. Korbel, *Poland Between East and West: Soviet and German Diplomacy Toward Poland, 1919–1933* (Princeton, 1963). C. A. Macartney, *Hungary and Her Successors: The Treaty of Trianon and Its Consequences, 1919–1937* (New York, 1937) and *A History of Hungary, 1929–1945* (2 vols., New York, 1957). R. Mackray, *The Poland of Pilsudski, 1914–1935* (New York, 1937). T. W. Pick, *The Baltic Nations: Estonia, Latvia, Lithuania* (London, 1945). H. L. Roberts, *Rumania: Political Problems of an Agrarian State* (New Haven, 1951). B. E. Schmitt, ed., *Poland* (Berkeley, 1945). J. Tomashevich, *Peasants, Politics, and Economic Change in Yugoslavia* (Stanford, 1955). J. H. Wuorinen, *A History of Finland* (New York, 1965). (*See also Chapters 15 and 17.*)

CHAPTER 30: THE CHANGING BRITISH COMMONWEALTH

J. B. Brebner, *North Atlantic Triangle: The Interplay of Canada, the United States, and Great Britain* (New Haven, 1945); and *Canada* (Ann Arbor, 1960). W. J. Cameron, *New Zealand* (Englewood Cliffs, 1964). R. A. Esthus, *From Enmity to Alliance: U.S.-Australian Relations, 1931–1941* (Washington, 1964). M. A. Fitzsimons, *Empire by Treaty: Britain and the Middle East in the Twen-*

tieth Century (Notre Dame, 1964). J. E. FLINT, *Books on the British Empire and Commonwealth* (New York, 1966). D. MACARDLE, *The Irish Republic* (New York, 1965). B. R. NANDA, *Mahatma Gandhi* (Boston, 1958). D. PIKE, ed., *Australian Dictionary of Biography*, Vol. 1 (New York, 1966). T. G. TAYLOR, *Australia: A Study of Warm Environments and Their Effects on British Settlement* (6th ed., London, 1955). M. C. URQUHART, *Historical Statistics of Canada* (New York, 1965). K. C. WHEARE, *The Statute of Westminster and Dominion Status* (New York, 1938). (*See also Chapters 11, 58, and 63.*)

CHAPTER 31: LATIN AMERICA

G. ARCINEGAS, *Latin America* (New York, 1966). J. M. BELLO, *A History of Modern Brazil, 1889–1964* (Stanford, 1966). H. BERNSTEIN, *Venezuela and Colombia* (Englewood Cliffs, 1964). J. C. CAREY, *Peru and the United States* (Notre Dame, 1964). H. F. CLINE, *The United States and Mexico* (rev. ed., Cambridge, 1963); and *Mexico: Revolution to Evolution, 1940–1960* (New York, 1962). W. R. CRAWFORD, *A Century of Latin American Thought* (rev. ed., Cambridge, 1961). G. FREYRE, *New World in the Tropics: The Culture of Modern Brazil* (New York, 1959). C. FURTADO, *Diagnosis of the Brazilian Crisis* (Berkeley, 1965). P. H. HISS, *Netherlands America: The Dutch Territories in the West* (New York, 1943). V. B. HOLMES, *A History of the Americas*, Vol. II, *From Nationhood to World Status* (New York, 1964). R. A. HUMPHREYS, *Latin American History: A Guide to the Literature in English* (New York, 1958). E. LIEUWEN, *Venezuela* (New York, 1962). *Pan-American Yearbook*, Annual (New York, 1945–   ). H. B. PARKES, *Mexico* (rev. ed., Boston, 1960). F. B. PIKE, *Chile and the United States* (Notre Dame, 1962). J. F. RIPPY, *Latin America: A Modern History* (Ann Arbor, 1958). J. R. SCOBIE, *Argentina: A City and a Nation* (New York, 1964). A. TORRES-RÍOSECO, *The Epic of Latin American Literature* (Berkeley, 1959). G. WYTHE, *The United States and Inter-American Relations* (Gainesville, 1964). (*See also Chapter 59.*)

SECTION V: ASIA AND THE COLONIAL WORLD

C. A. BUSS, *Asia in the Modern World* (New York, 1964). H. F. CONOVER, *Research and Information on Africa: Continuing Sources* (Washington, 1954). G. B. CRESSEY, *Asia's Lands and Peoples* (3rd ed., New York, 1963). C. A. FISHER, *Southeast Asia: A Social, Economic, and Political Geography* (London, 1964). W. FITZGERALD, *Africa: A Social, Economic, and Political Geography of its Major Regions* (London, 1955). W. M. HAILEY, *An African Survey: A Study of Problems Arising in Africa South of the Sahara* (rev. ed., London, 1957). D. G. E. HALL, *A History of South-east Asia* (New York, 1964). K. S. LATOURETTE, *Short History of the Far East* (3rd ed., New York, 1957). G. A. LENSEN, *The World Beyond Europe* (2nd ed., Boston, 1966). C. ROBEQUAIN, *Malaya, Indonesia, Borneo, and the Philippines: A Geographical, Economic, and Political Description* (rev. ed., New York, 1958). G. WINT, *Asia: A Handbook* (New York, 1966).

CHAPTER 32: THE NEAR AND MIDDLE EAST AND AFRICA

S. N. FISHER, *The Middle East* (New York, 1959). W. B. FISHER, *The Middle East* (New York, 1950). G. E. KIRK, *A Short History of the Middle East*

(London, 1952). G. LENCZOWSKI, *The Middle East in World Affairs* (3rd ed., Ithaca, 1962). W. YALE, *The Near East: A Modern History* (Ann Arbor, 1958). H. V. COOKE, *Challenge and Response in the Middle East: The Quest for Prosperity, 1919–1951* (New York, 1952). H. H. CUMMINGS, *Franco-British Rivalry in the Post-War Near East* (London, 1938). H. M. DAVIS, ed., *Constitutions, Electoral Laws, Treaties of State in the Near and Middle East* (Durham, 1947). J. C. HUREWITZ, ed., *Diplomacy in the Near and Middle East: A Documentary Record* (2 vols., Princeton, 1956). G. LENCZOWSKI, *Russia and the West in Iran, 1918–1948* (Ithaca, 1953). M. N. SETON-WATSON, *Britain and the Arab States, 1920–1948* (London, 1948). W. C. SMITH, *Islam in Modern History* (Princeton, 1957). D. WARRINER, *Land and Poverty in the Middle East* (New York, 1948).

A. BANANI, *The Modernization of Iran, 1921–1941* (Stanford, 1961). A. M. HYAMSON, *Palestine under the Mandate, 1920–1948* (London, 1950). MAJID KHADDURI, *Independent Iraq: A Study of Iraqi Politics since 1923* (New York, 1951). LORD KINROSS, *Atatürk* (London, 1965). S. H. LONGRIGG, *Syria and Lebanon under French Mandate* (London, 1958). H. MACMICHAEL, *The Sudan* (London, 1954). H. S. J. B. PHILBY, *Saudi Arabia* (London, 1955). R. D. ROBINSON, *The First Turkish Republic* (Cambridge, 1963). R. H. SANGER, *The Arabian Peninsula* (Ithaca, 1954).

H. L. HOSKINS, *European Imperialism in Africa* (New York, 1930). H. J. LIE-BESNY, *The Government of French North Africa* (Philadelphia, 1943). D. L. WIEDER, *A History of Africa South of the Sahara* (New York, 1962). H. A. WIESCHOFF, *Colonial Policies in Africa* (Philadelphia, 1944).

CHAPTER 33: INDIA, SOUTHEAST ASIA, AND THE PACIFIC ISLANDS

G. L. ABERNATHY, *Pakistan: A Selected, Annotated Bibliography* (New York, 1960). S. ARASARATNAM, *Ceylon* (Englewood Cliffs, 1965). W. N. BROWN, *The United States, India, and Pakistan* (Cambridge, 1963). F. DEBENHAM, *Antarctica: The Story of a Continent* (New York, 1961). J. S. FURNIVAL, *Colonial Policy and Practice: A Comparative Study of Burma and the Netherlands Indies* (New York, 1966). G. T. GARRATT, ed., *The Legacy of India* (New York, 1937). G. M. KAHIN, ed., *Major Governments of Asia* (Ithaca, 1958); and *Governments and Politics of Southeast Asia* (Ithaca, 1964). J. D. LEGGE, *Indonesia* (Englewood Cliffs, 1964). J. NEHRU, *The Discovery of India* (New York, 1960). P. SPEAR, *The Oxford History of India* (New York, 1958); and *India: A Modern History* (Ann Arbor, 1961). H. TINKER, *The Foundations of Local Self-Government in India, Pakistan, and Burma* (London, 1954). P. G. WILSON, *Government and Politics of India and Pakistan, 1885–1955: A Bibliography of Works in Western Languages* (Berkeley, 1956). (*See also Chapters 49 and 64.*)

CHAPTER 34: CHINA AND JAPAN

C. BRANDT, *Stalin's Failure in China, 1924–1927* (Cambridge, 1958). L. C. GOODRICH, *A Short History of the Chinese People* (3rd ed., New York, 1950). E. R. HUGHES, *The Invasion of China by the Western World* (London, 1937). K. S. LATOURETTE, *The Chinese: Their History and Culture* (4th ed., New York, 1964) and *A History of Modern China* (New York, 1951). W. LEVI, *Modern China's Foreign Relations* (Minneapolis, 1953). C. B. MCLANE, *Soviet*

Policy and the Chinese Communists, 1931–1946 (New York, 1958). E. Snow, *Red Star Over China* (New York, 1944). A. S. Whiting, *Soviet Policies in China, 1917–1924* (New York, 1953).

G. C. Allen, *Japanese Industry: Its Recent Development and Present Condition* (New York, 1940). W. A. Beasley, *The Modern History of Japan* (New York, 1963). H. Borton, *Japan's Modern Century* (New York, 1955). E. F. Penrose, *Population Theories and Their Application with Special Reference to Japan* (Stanford, 1934). E. O. Reischauer, *Japan: Past and Present* (2nd ed., New York, 1953) and *The United States and Japan* (rev. ed., Cambridge, 1957). G. B. Samson, *Japan: A Short Cultural History* (rev. ed., New York, 1962) and *The Western World and Japan* (New York, 1950). (*See also Chapter 11.*)

SECTION VI: THE FAILURE OF COLLECTIVE SECURITY

G. D. H. Cole, *A History of Socialist Thought*, Vol. V, *Socialism and Fascism, 1931–1939* (New York, 1960). H. F. Conover, *A Guide to Bibliographical Tools for Research in Foreign Affairs* (Washington, 1956). *Foreign Affairs*, published quarterly (New York, 1922–   ). A. Shonfield, *Modern Capitalism* (New York, 1965). A. P. Whitaker, ed., *Inter-American Affairs*, published annually (New York, 1941–   ).

CHAPTER 35: ECONOMIC INSECURITY AND THE GREAT DEPRESSION

J. K. Galbraith, *The Great Crash, 1929* (Boston, 1955). J. M. Keynes, *General Theory of Employment, Interest and Money* (New York, 1936). K. Mannheim, *Diagnosis of Our Time* (New York, 1944). B. Mitchell, *Depression Decade, 1929–1941* (New York, 1947). A. U. Romasco, *The Poverty of Abundance: Hoover, the Nation, the Depression* (New York, 1965). E. J. Russell, *World Population and World Food Supplies* (London, 1954). E. Staley, *The Future of Underdeveloped Countries* (New York, 1961).

CHAPTER 36: THE RESORT TO AGGRESSION

A. H. Furnia, *The Diplomacy of Appeasement: Anglo-French Relations and the Prelude to World War II* (Washington, 1960). F. C. Jones, *Japan's New Order in East Asia: Its Rise and Fall, 1937–1945* (London, 1954). D. E. Lee, *Ten Years: The World on the Way to War, 1930–1940* (Boston, 1942). H. Rothfels, *The German Opposition to Hitler* (Chicago, 1962). H. Thomas, *The Spanish Civil War* (New York, 1961). A. J. and M. Toynbee, *The Eve of War, 1939* (New York, 1958). United States Department of State, *Documents on German Foreign Policy, 1918–1945*, Series C, Vols. II and III (Washington, 1959); and *Papers Relating to the Foreign Relations of the United States: Japan, 1931–1941* (2 vols., Washington, 1943). A. Wolfers, *Britain and France Between Two Wars: Conflicting Strategies of Peace Since Versailles* (New York, 1940).

CHAPTER 37: THE ROAD TO THE SECOND WORLD WAR

W. S. Churchill, *The Second World War*, Vol. I, *The Gathering Storm* (Boston, 1948). Count Galeazzo Ciano, *Ciano's Hidden Diary, 1937–1938*

(New York, 1953), and *The Ciano Diaries, 1939–1943* (ed. by Hugh Gibson, New York, 1946). G. A. CRAIG and F. GILBERT, eds., *The Diplomats, 1919– 1939* (Princeton, 1953). A. EDEN, *Facing the Dictators* (Boston, 1962). K. FEILING, *Life of Neville Chamberlain* (New York, 1946). M. GILBERT and R. GOTT, *The Appeasers* (Boston, 1963). W. L. LANGER and S. E. GLEASON, *The Challenge to Isolation 1937–1940* (New York, 1952). L. B. NAMIER, *Diplomatic Prelude* (London, 1948) and *Europe in Decay, 1936–1940* (London, 1950). W. L. SHIRER, *The Rise and Fall of the Third Reich: A History of Nazi Germany* (New York, 1960). A. J. P. TAYLOR, *The Origins of the Second World War* (New York, 1962). E. WISKEMANN, *The Rome-Berlin Axis: A History of the Relations between Mussolini and Hitler* (New York, 1949).

G. BROOKE-SHEPHERD, *The Anschluss* (Philadelphia, 1963). K. EUBANKS, *Munich* (Norman, Okla., 1963). G. E. R. GEDYE, *Austria and Czechoslovakia: The Fallen Bastions* (New York, 1939). R. G. D. LAFFAN, *The Crisis over Czechoslovakia, January to September 1938* (London, 1951). H. RIPKA, *Munich; Before and After* (London, 1939). J. R. WHEELER-BENNETT, *Munich* (London, 1948). E. WISKEMANN, *Czechs and Germans* (London, 1938).

A. BALL, *The Last Day of the Old World* (Garden City, N. Y., 1963). J. BECK, *The Final Report* (New York, 1956). G. L. WEINBERG, *Germany and the Soviet Union, 1939–1941* (Leiden, 1954).

SECTION VII: WORLD WAR II, 1939–1945

COUNCIL ON FOREIGN RELATIONS, *Political Handbook of the World,* Annual (New York, 1927–   ). *Jane's All the World's Aircraft,* Annual (New York, 1909–   ). *Jane's Fighting Ships,* Annual (New York, 1898–   ). ROYAL INSTITUTE OF INTERNATIONAL AFFAIRS, *Chronology of the Second World War* (New York, 1947). *Science in Progress,* Annual (New Haven, 1941–   ). *Statesman's Year-Book,* Annual (New York, 1864–   ).

CHAPTER 38: INTRODUCTION: CONTEMPORARY CIVILIZATION

P. E. BALDRY, *The Battle Against Bacteria* (New York, 1966). F. BOR-KENAU, *World Communism* (Ann Arbor, 1962). C. S. BRADEN, *World's Religions* (Nashville, 1954). C. A. GLASRUD, *The Age of Anxiety* (Boston, 1960). T. F. HAMLIN, *Forms and Functions in Twentieth Century Architecture* (4 vols., New York, 1952). H. M. McLUHAN, *Understanding Media* (New York, 1964). H. D. SMYTH, *Atomic Energy for Military Purposes* (Princeton, 1945). C. P. SNOW, *The Two Cultures and the Scientific Revolution* (New York, 1959).

CHAPTER 39: BACKGROUND OF CONFLICT

J. W. GANTENBEIN, ed., *Documentary Background of World War II, 1931– 1941* (New York, 1948). J. C. GREW, *Ten Years in Japan* (New York, 1943). D. KIRK, *Europe's Population in the Interwar Years* (Princeton, N. J., 1946). W. L. LANGER and E. S. GLEASON, *Challenge to Isolation: The World Crisis of 1937–1940 and American Foreign Policy* (2 vols., New York, 1952–1953). K. LONDON, *How Foreign Policy is Made* (New York, 1950). P. W. SCHROE-DER, *The Axis Alliance and Japanese-American Relations, 1941* (Ithaca, 1958). G. SMITH, *American Diplomacy During the Second World War, 1941–1945*

(New York, 1965). W. S. and E. S. Woytinsky, *World Population and Production: Trends and Outlook* (New York, 1953), and *World Commerce and Governments: Trends and Outlook* (New York, 1955).

CHAPTER 40: THE WAR IN THE EAST AND THE WEST, 1939–1941

F. Brown and L. Manditch, eds., *The War in Maps: An Atlas of the New York Times Maps* (New York, 1946). W. S. Churchill, *The Second World War* (6 vols., 1948–1953). C. Falls, *The Second World War* (London, 1948). J. F. C. Fuller, *The Second World War, 1939–1945: A Strategical and Tactical History* (New York, 1949). W. C. Langsam, *Historic Documents of World War II* (New York, 1958). W. Millis, ed., *The War Reports of General Marshall, General Arnold, and Admiral King* (Philadelphia, 1947). S. E. Morison, *History of the United States Naval Operations in World War II* (14 vols., Boston, 1947–1960). L. L. Snyder, *The War: A Concise History, 1939–1945* (New York, 1960).

M. Jacobson, *The Diplomacy of the Winter War: An Account of the Russo-Finnish Conflict, 1939–1940* (Cambridge, Mass., 1960). V. A. Tanner, *The Winter War: Finland against Russia, 1939–1940* (Stanford, 1957). A. N. Tarulis, *Soviet Policy Toward the Baltic States, 1918–1940* (Notre Dame, 1959).

J. G. Benoit-Mechin, *Sixty Days That Shook the West: The Fall of France, 1940* (New York, 1963). B. Collier, *The Battle of Britain* (New York, 1962). A. Goutard, *The Battle of France, 1940* (New York, 1959). V. Rowe, *The Great Wall of France: The Triumph of the Maginot Line* (London, 1959). E. Spears, *Assignment to Catastrophe* (2 vols., New York, 1954–1955). T. Taylor, *The March of Conquest* (New York, 1958). R. Wheatley, *Operation Sea Lion* (New York, 1958).

CHAPTER 41: INVOLVEMENT OF SOVIET RUSSIA AND THE UNITED STATES, 1941–1943

A. Clark, *Barbarossa: The Russian-German Conflict, 1941–1945* (New York, 1965). V. I. Chuikov, *The Battle of Stalingrad* (New York, 1964). A. Dallin, *German Rule in Russia, 1941–1945: A Study of Occupation Policies* (New York, 1957). G. Gafencu, *Prelude to the Russian Campaign* (London, 1945). L. Goure, *The Siege of Leningrad* (Stanford, 1962). H. Guderian, *Panzer Leader* (New York, 1952). E. von Manstein, *Lost Victories* (Chicago, 1958). P. K. Schmidt, *Hitler Moves East, 1941–1943* (Boston, 1964). R. Seth, *Operation Barbarossa: The Battle for Moscow* (London, 1964). G. L. Weinberg, *Germany and the Soviet Union, 1939–1941* (Leyden, 1954). A. Werth, *Russia at War, 1941–1945* (New York, 1964).

C. A. Beard, *President Roosevelt and the Coming of the War, 1941* (New Haven, 1948). R. J. Butow, *Tojo and the Coming of the War* (Princeton, 1961). H. Feis, *The Road to Pearl Harbor: The Coming of the War between the United States and Japan* (Princeton, 1950). F. C. Jones, *Japan's New Order in East Asia, 1937–1945* (New York, 1954). W. L. Langer and S. E. Gleason, *The Undeclared War, 1940–1941* (New York, 1953). D. MacIntyre, *The Battle of the Atlantic* (New York, 1961). P. W. Schroeder, *The Axis Alliance and Japanese-American Relations, 1941* (Ithaca, 1958). C. C. Tansill, *Back Door to War* (New York, 1952). R. Wohlstetter, *Pearl Harbor* (Stanford, 1962). (*See also Chapter 40.*)

CHAPTER 42: RESOURCES AND PRODUCTION OF THE
ALLIED POWERS

R. E. ANDERSON, *The Merchant Marine and World Frontiers* (New York,
1945). P. AUPHAN, and J. MORDAL, *The French Navy in World War II*
(Annapolis, 1959). G. M. BARNES, *Weapons of World War II* (New York,
1947). J. P. BAXTER, *Scientists Against Time* (Boston, 1946). W. F. CRAVEN
and J. L. CATE, eds., *The Army Air Forces in World War II* (7 vols., Chicago,
1948–58). D. L. GORDON and R. DANGERFIELD, *The Hidden Weapon: The
Story of Economic Warfare* (New York, 1947). J. L. HODGSON, *British Mer-
chantmen at War: The Official Story of the Merchant Navy, 1939–1944* (New
York, 1945). D. M. NELSON, *Arsenal of Democracy: The Story of American
War Production* (New York, 1946). G. W. PAWLE, *The Secret War, 1939–
1945* (New York, 1957). W. RUNDLE, JR., *Black Market Money: The Collapse
of U. S. Military Currency Control in World War II* (Baton Rouge, 1964).
V. R. SILL, *American Miracle: The Story of War Construction Around the
World* (New York, 1947).

CHAPTER 43: THE ALLIED COUNTEROFFENSIVE, 1933–1944

A. ARMSTRONG, *Unconditional Surrender: The Impact of the Casablanca
Policy upon World War II* (New Brunswick, N. J., 1963). R. ARON, *The
Vichy Regime, 1940–1944* (New York, 1958). A. BRYANT, *The Turn of the
Tide* (New York, 1957). C. M. CIANFARRA, *The Vatican and the War* (New
York, 1944). M. CARVER, *El Alamein* (New York, 1962). F. W. DEAKIN, *The
Brutal Friendship: Mussolini, Hitler, and the Fall of Italian Fascism* (New
York, 1963). C. DELZELL, *Mussolini's Enemies: The Italian Anti-Fascist Re-
sistance* (Princeton, 1961). R. S. HARRIS, *Allied Military Administration of
Italy, 1943–1945* (London, 1957). N. KOGAN, *Italy and the Allies* (Cam-
bridge, Mass., 1956). W. L. LANGER, *Our Vichy Gamble* (New York, 1947).
D. MACINTYRE, *The Battle for the Mediterranean* (London, 1964). M. MAT-
LOFF and E. M. SNELL, *Strategic Planning for Coalition Warfare, 1941–1942*
(Washington, 1953). W. W. SMITH, *Midway: Turning Point of the Pacific
War* (New York, 1966). C. G. STARR, *From Salerno to the Alps: A History
of the Fifth Army, 1943–1945* (Washington, 1948). L. VILLARI, *The Libera-
tion of Italy, 1943–1947* (Appleton, Wis., 1959). D. S. WHITE, *Seeds of Dis-
cord: De Gaulle, Free France, and the Allies* (Syracuse, 1964). D. YOUNG.
Rommel: The Desert Fox (New York, 1950).

D. D. EISENHOWER, *Crusade in Europe* (New York, 1948). C. DE GAULLE,
War Memoirs (3 vols., New York, 1955–1960). D. MACARTHUR, *Reminis-
cences* (New York, 1964). B. L. MONTGOMERY, *Memoirs* (New York, 1950).
(*See also Chapters 40, 41, and 42.*)

CHAPTER 44: THE TRIUMPH OF THE ALLIES, 1944–1945

W. ANDERS, *Hitler's Defeat in Russia* (Chicago, 1953). M. BLUMENSON,
The Duel for France, 1944 (Boston, 1963). A. BRYANT, *Triumph in the West*
(New York, 1959). V. I. CHUIKOV, *The Battle for Berlin* (New York, 1966).
H. RUMPF, *The Bombing of Germany* (New York, 1963). H. SPEIDEL, *In-
vasion, 1944* (Chicago, 1950). C. WILMOT, *Struggle for Europe* (New York,
1952).

A. EDEN, *The Reckoning* (Boston, 1965). H. FEIS, *Churchill, Roosevelt,
Stalin: The War They Waged and the Peace They Sought* (Princeton, 1957),

and *Between War and Peace: The Potsdam Conference* (Princeton, 1960).
R. E. SHERWOOD, *Roosevelt and Hopkins: An Intimate History* (New York,
1948). J. L. SNELL, and OTHERS, *The Meaning of Yalta: Big Three Diplomacy
and the New Balance of Power* (Baton Rouge, 1956). J. L. SNELL, *Wartime
Origins of the East-West Dilemma over Germany* (New Orleans, 1959).
H. S. TRUMAN, *Memoirs*, Vol. I, *Year of Decision* (New York, 1955).

H. FEIS, *The China Tangle: The American Effort in China from Pearl Harbor
to the Marshall Mission* (Princeton, 1953). C. F. ROMANUS and R. SUNDER-
LAND, *Stillwell's Mission to China* (Washington, 1953).

R. ARON, *De Gaulle before Paris: The Liberation of France, June–August
1944* (London, 1962), and *De Gaulle Triumphant: The Liberation of France,
August 1944–May 1945* (London, 1964). E. BENEŠ, *Memoirs: From Munich to
New War and New Victory* (Boston, 1955). C. FOTICH, *The War We Lost:
Yugoslavia's Tragedy and the Failure of the West* (New York, 1948). S. D.
KERTESZ, *Diplomacy in a Whirlpool: Hungary between Nazi Germany and
Soviet Russia* (Notre Dame, 1953). J. A. LUKACS, *The Great Powers and East-
ern Europe* (New York, 1953). C. L. LUNDIN, *Finland in the Second World
War* (Bloomington, 1957). F. MacLEAN, *Eastern Approaches* (London, 1949).
E. J. ROZEK, *Allied Wartime Diplomacy: A Pattern in Poland* (New York,
1958). C. M. WOODHOUSE, *Apple of Discord: A Survey of Recent Greek Politics
in Their International Setting* (London, 1948).

R. J. BUTOW, *Japan's Decision to Surrender* (Stanford, 1954). R. L. EICHEL-
BERGER, *Our Jungle Road to Tokyo* (New York, 1950). H. FEIS, *Japan Subdued: The Atomic Bomb and the End of the War in the Pacific* (Princeton,
1961). M. KATO, *The Lost War* (New York, 1946). (*See also Chapters 41,
42, and 43.*)

CHAPTER 45: POLITICAL, SOCIAL, AND ECONOMIC RESULTS
            OF THE WAR

G. D. H. COLE, *World in Transition* (New York, 1949). S. C. EASTON, *The
Rise and Fall of Western Colonialism* (New York, 1964). H. HOLBORN, *The
Political Collapse of Europe* (New York, 1951). H. SETON-WATSON, *Neither
War nor Peace: The Struggle for Power in the Postwar World of Europe* (New
York, 1955). A. and V. TOYNBEE, eds., *The Realignment of Europe* (New
York, 1955). T. H. WHITE, *Fire in the Ashes: Europe in Mid-Century* (New
York, 1953).

The Black Book: The Nazi Crime against the Jewish People (New York,
1946). D. ROUSSET, *A World Apart* (London, 1951). J. PROUDFOOT, *European
Refugees, 1939–1952: A Study in Forced Population Movements* (Evanston,
1956).

SECTION VIII: THE AFTERMATH OF THE WAR:
               INTERNATIONAL AFFAIRS

C. BRANDT and others, *A Documentary History of Chinese Communism*
(Cambridge, Mass., 1952). H. W. GATZKE, *The Present in Perspective: A Look
at the World Since 1945* (2nd ed., Chicago, 1961). J. H. JACKSON, *The World
in the Postwar Decade, 1945–1955* (Boston, 1956). A. C. LEISS and R. DEN-
NETT, eds., *European Peace Treaties after World War II* (Boston, 1954).
W. REITZEL and others, *United States Foreign Policy, 1945–1955* (Washington, 1956). *United Nations Yearbook* (New York, 1947–   ).

CHAPTER 46: THE PEACE SETTLEMENT: AN UNFINISHED BUSINESS

S. ARNE, *United Nations Primer* (rev. ed., New York, 1948). N. BENTWICH, From Geneva to San Francisco (London, 1946). L. M. GOODRICH and E. I. HAMBRO, *Charter of the United Nations* (2nd rev. ed., Boston, 1949). R. B. RUSSELL and J. E. MUTHER, *A History of the United Nations Charter: The Role of the United States, 1940–1945* (Washington, 1958).

J. F. BYRNES, *Speaking Frankly* (New York, 1947). F. W. PICK, *Peacemaking in Perspective: From Potsdam to Paris* (New York, 1950). Z. M. SZAZ, *Germany's Eastern Frontiers: The Problem of the Oder-Neisse Line* (Chicago, 1960). E. WISKEMANN, *Germany's Eastern Neighbors: Problems Relating to the Oder-Neisse Line and the Czech Frontier Regions* (New York, 1956).

L. C. CLAY, *Decision in Germany* (Garden City, 1950). R. EBSWORTH, *Restoring Democracy in Germany: The British Contribution* (New York, 1961). W. G. FRIEDMANN, *The Allied Military Government of Germany* (London, 1947). J. L. HEYDECKER and J. LEEB, *The Nürnberg Trial* (New York, 1962). J. P. NETTL, *The Eastern Zone and Soviet Policy in Germany, 1945–1950* (New York, 1951). F. R. WILLIS, *The French in Germany, 1945–1949* (Stanford, 1961). H. ZINK, *American Military Government in Germany* (New York, 1947).

CHAPTER 47: THE SOVIET POLICY OF EXPANSION

E. D. CARMAN, *Soviet Imperialism: Russia's Drive Toward World Domination* (Washington, 1950). E. R. GOODMAN, *The Soviet Design for a World State* (New York, 1957). W. GURIAN, ed., *Soviet Imperialism: Its Origins and Tactics* (Notre Dame, 1953). V. S. MAMATEY, *Soviet Russian Imperialism* (Princeton, 1964). P. E. MOSELY, *The Kremlin and World Politics: Studies in Soviet Policy and Action* (New York, 1960). M. D. SHULMAN, *Stalin's Foreign Policy Reappraised* (Cambridge, Mass., 1963).

R. H. BASS and E. MARBURY, eds., *The Soviet-Yugoslav Controversy, 1948–1958: A Documentary Record* (New York, 1959). R. R. BETTS, ed., *Central and Southeastern Europe, 1945–1948* (New York, 1951). S. BORSODY, *The Triumph of Tyranny: The Nazi and Soviet Conquest of Central Europe* (New York, 1960). C. M. CIANFARRA, *The Vatican and the Kremlin* (New York, 1950). V. DEDIJER, *Tito* (New York, 1953). S. D. KERTESZ, ed., *The Fate of East Central Europe: Hopes and Failures of American Foreign Policy* (Notre Dame, 1956). J. KORBEL, *Communist Subversion of Czechoslovakia, 1938–1948* (Princeton, 1959). S. MIKOLAJCZYK, *The Rape of Poland* (New York, 1948). F. NAGY, *The Struggle Behind the Iron Curtain* (New York, 1948). H. RIPKA, *Czechoslovakia Enslaved* (London, 1950). H. SETON-WATSON, *The East European Revolution* (New York, 1952). L. S. STAVRIANOS, *Greece: American Dilemma and Opportunity* (Chicago, 1952). A. B. ULAM, *Tito and the Cominform* (Cambridge, Mass., 1956). R. L. WOLFF, *The Balkans in Our Time* (Cambridge, Mass., 1956).

CHAPTER 48: THE AMERICAN POLICY OF CONTAINMENT

W. P. DAVISON, *The Berlin Blockade: A Study in Cold War Politics* (Princeton, 1958). H. A. KISSINGER, *Nuclear Weapons and Foreign Policy* (New York, 1957), and *The Necessity for a Choice: Prospects of American Foreign Policy*

(New York, 1961). K. KNORR, ed., *NATO and American Security* (Princeton, 1959). W. LIPPMANN, *The Cold War: A Study in United States Foreign Policy* (New York, 1947). G. LISKA, *The New Statecraft: Foreign Aid in American Foreign Policy* (Chicago, 1960). B. T. MOORE, *NATO and the Future of Europe* (New York, 1958). H. J. MORGENTHAU, *In Defense of the National Interest: A Critical Examination of American Foreign Policy* (New York, 1951). P. PEETERS, *Massive Retaliation and its Critics* (Chicago, 1959). H. B. PRICE, *The Marshall Plan and Its Meaning* (Ithaca, 1955). J. W. SPANIER, *American Foreign Policy Since World War II* (2nd rev. ed., New York, 1965). H. S. TRUMAN, *Memoirs*, Vol. II, *Years of Trial and Hope, 1946–1952* (New York, 1956). A. WOLFERS, ed., *Alliance Policy in the Cold War* (Baltimore, 1959).

CHAPTER 49: THE AFTERMATH OF THE WAR IN EAST ASIA

M. BELOFF, *Soviet Policy in the Far East, 1944–1951* (London, 1953). M. D. KENNEDY, *A History of Communism in East Asia* (New York, 1957). SIR FRANCIS LOW, *Struggle for Asia* (New York, 1955). H. M. VINACKE, *The United States and the Far East, 1945–1951* (Stanford, 1952).

C. COHEN, *The Political Process and Foreign Policy: The Making of the Japanese Peace Settlement* (Princeton, 1957). KAZUO KAWAI, *Japan's American Interlude* (Chicago, 1960). J. D. MONTGOMERY, *Forced to Be Free* (Chicago, 1958).

J. K. FAIRBANK, *The United States and China* (Cambridge, Mass., 1958). C. P. FITZGERALD, *Revolution in China* (New York, 1952). R. C. NORTH, *Moscow and the Chinese Communists* (Stanford, 1953). B. J. SCHWARTZ, *Chinese Communism and the Rise of Mao* (Cambridge, Mass., 1951).

L. M. GOODRICH, *Korea: A Study of United States Policy in the United Nations* (New York, 1956). E. GRANT MEADE, *American Military Government in Korea* (New York, 1951). W. H. VATCHER, *Panmunjom: The Story of the Korean Military Armistice Negotiations* (New York, 1958). A. S. WHITING, *China Crosses the Yalu: The Decision to Enter the Korean War* (New York, 1960).

E. HAMMER, *The Struggle for Indo-China* (Stanford, 1954). J. ROY, *The Battle of Dienbienphu* (New York, 1965).

CHAPTER 50: THE AFTERMATH OF THE WAR IN THE NEAR AND MIDDLE EAST

M. ADAMS, *Suez and After: Year of Crisis* (Boston, 1958). A. J. BARKER, *Suez: The Seven-Day War* (New York, 1965). B. Y. BONTOS-GHALI, *The Arab League, 1945–1955* (New York, 1955). J. C. CAMPBELL, *Defense in the Middle East: Problems of American Policy* (New York, 1960). H. FINER, *Dulles over Suez: The Theory and Practice of his Diplomacy* (Chicago, 1964). J. C. HUREWITZ, *The Struggle for Palestine* (New York, 1950). G. E. KIRK, *Contemporary Arab Politics: A Concise History* (New York, 1961). W. Z. LAQUEUR, ed. *Communism and Nationalism in the Middle East* (New York, 1957). W. Z. LAQUEUR, *The Soviet Union and the Middle East* (New York, 1959). N. LORCH, *The Edge of the Sword: Israel's War of Independence, 1947–1949* (New York, 1961). J. MARLOWE, *Arab Nationalism and British Imperialism* (New York, 1961). J. MORRIS, *Islam Inflamed* (New York, 1957). D. WARRINER, *Land Reform and Development in the Middle East* (New York, 1957). G. LENCZOWSKI, *Oil and State in the Middle East* (Ithaca, 1959). S. H.

Longrigg, *Oil in the Middle East* (New York, 1954). B. Shwadran, *The Middle East, Oil, and the Great Powers* (New York, 1955). (*See also Chapter 32.*)

SECTION IX: THE WESTERN NATIONS IN THE AFTERMATH OF THE WAR

D. C. Coyle, *The United Nations and How It Works* (rev. ed., New York, 1965). J. F. Dewhurst, ed., *Europe's Needs and Resources* (New York, 1961). C. Eichelberger, *U.N.: The First Fifteen Years* (New York, 1960). M. Einaudi, J. M. Donenach, and A. Garosci, *Communism in Western Europe* (Ithaca, 1951). J. Gottman, *A Geography of Europe* (New York, 1954). J. Luka, *History of the Cold War* (Garden City, 1961). F. J. Monkhouse, *A Regional Geography of Western Europe* (New York, 1959), and *Geography of Northwestern Europe* (New York, 1966). A. Wolfers, *Changing East-West Relations and the Unity of the West* (Baltimore, 1966). P. L. Yates, *Food, Land and Manpower in Western Europe* (London, 1960).

CHAPTER 51: THE UNITED STATES

F. Broderick and A. Meier, *Negro Protest Thought in the Twentieth Century* (Indianapolis, 1965). H. S. Commager, *Freedom and Order: A Commentary on the American Political Scene* (New York, 1966). Council on Foreign Relations, *Documents on American Foreign Relations,* Annual (New York, 1939–). J. F. Dewhurst and associates, *America's Needs and Resources: A New Survey* (New York, 1955). J. K. Galbraith, *The Affluent Society* (Boston, 1958). E. F. Goldman, *The Crucial Decade, 1945–1955* (New York, 1956). S. D. Kertesz, *American Diplomacy in a New Era* (Notre Dame, 1961). E. Latham, *The Communist Controversy in Washington: From the New Deal to McCarthy* (Cambridge, Mass., 1966). M. Lerner, *America as a Civilization* (New York, 1957). H. H. Ransom, *Central Intelligence and National Security* (Cambridge, Mass., 1958). C. Rossiter, *Marxism: The View From America* (New York, 1960). W. W. Rostow, *The United States in the World Arena* (New York, 1960). T. C. Sorenson, *Kennedy* (New York, 1965).

CHAPTER 52: GREAT BRITAIN

H. Eckstein, *The English Health Service* (Cambridge, Mass., 1958). A. Eden, *Full Circle: The Memoirs of Anthony Eden* (Boston, 1960). M. Harrison, *Trade Unions and the Labour Party Since 1945* (Detroit, 1960). M. Kuczynski, *Demographic Survey of the British Colonial Empire* (3 vols., London, 1948–1953). J. D. B. Miller, *The Commonwealth in the World* (3rd ed., New York, 1965). B. R. Mitchell and P. Deane, *Abstract of British Historical Statistics* (New York, 1962). D. Taylor, *The Years of Challenge: The Commonwealth and the British Empire, 1945–1958* (New York, 1960). H. Thomas, ed., *The Establishment* (London, 1959). K. C. Wheare, *The Constitutional Structure of the Commonwealth* (New York, 1960). C. M. Woodhouse, *British Foreign Policy Since the Second World War* (New York, 1962). A. J. Youngson, *The British Economy, 1920–1957* (Cambridge, Mass., 1960).

CHAPTER 53: FRANCE

R. Aron, *France: Steadfast and Changing* (Cambridge, Mass., 1960). R. Barron, *Parties and Politics in Modern France* (Washington, 1959). S. C. Easten, *The Twilight of European Colonialism* (New York, 1960). A. L. Funk, *Charles de Gaulle: The Crucial Years, 1943–1944* (Norman, Okla., 1959). Charles de Gaulle, *War Memoirs* (New York, 1958–1960). J. A. Laponce, *Government of the Fifth Republic* (Berkeley, 1961). D. M. Pickles, *Fifth French Republic* (3rd. ed., New York, 1966). Francis de Tarr, *The French Radical Party from Herriot to Mendès-France* (New York, 1961). A. Werth, *The De Gaulle Revolution* (London, 1960).

CHAPTER 54: WEST GERMANY

W. A. Bader, *Austria Between East and West, 1945–1955* (Stanford, 1966). E. Davidson, *The Death and Life of Germany: An Account of the American Occupation* (New York, 1959). W. P. Davison, *The Berlin Blockade* (Princeton, 1958). G. Freund, *Germany Between Two Worlds* (New York, 1961). A. von Knieriem, *The Nuremberg Trials* (Chicago, 1959). E. McInnis and others, *The Shaping of Postwar Germany* (New York, 1960). J. L. Richardson, *Germany and the Atlantic Alliance* (New York, 1966). (*See also Chapters 46, 47, and 48.*)

CHAPTER 55: EIGHT SMALL NATIONS OF WESTERN EUROPE

F. G. Eyck, *The Benelux Countries: An Historical Survey* (Princeton, 1959). D. Loder, *Land and People of Belgium* (Philadelphia, 1957). A. de Meüs, *History of the Belgians* (New York, 1962). Organization for European Economic Cooperation, *Belgium-Luxemburg Economic Union* (Paris, 1960). C. Weststrate, *Economic Policy in Practice: The Netherlands, 1950–1957* (Leyden, 1957).

E. Bonjour, *Swiss Neutrality: Its History and Meaning* (London, 1946). G. A. Codding, *The Federal Government of Switzerland* (Boston, 1961). C. Gilliard, *A History of Switzerland* (London, 1955). J. C. Herold, *The Swiss without Halos* (New York, 1948). C. Hughes, *The Parliament of Switzerland* (London, 1962). G. Sauser-Hall, *The Political Institutions of Switzerland* (Bern, 1946).

I. Anderson, *A History of Sweden* (New York, 1956). B. E. Arneson, *The Democratic Monarchies of Scandinavia* (Princeton, 1949). P. J. Bjerve, *Planning in Norway, 1947–1956* (Amsterdam, 1959). E. F. Heckscher, *An Economic History of Sweden* (Cambridge, Mass., 1962). E. Jutikkala, *A History of Finland* (New York, 1962). K. Larsen, *A History of Norway* (New York, 1950). P. Lauring, *A History of the Kingdom of Denmark* (Copenhagen, 1960). W. R. Mead, *An Economic Geography of Scandinavian States and Finland* (London, 1959). F. Wendt, *The Nordic Council and Cooperation in Scandinavia* (Copenhagen, 1959). J. H. Wuorinen, *A History of Finland* (New York, 1965). (*See also Chapter 10.*)

CHAPTER 56: SIX NATIONS OF SOUTHERN EUROPE

J. C. Adams, *The Government of Republican Italy* (Boston, 1961). S. B. Clough, *The Economic History of Modern Italy* (New York, 1964). M. Grind-

ROD, *The Rebuilding of Italy: Politics and Economics, 1945–1955* (New York, 1955). N. KOGAN, *Italy and the Allies* (Cambridge, Mass., 1956), and *The Government of Italy* (New York, 1962), D. MACK SMITH, *Italy: A Modern History* (Ann Arbor, 1959).

J. CLEUGH, *Image of Spain* (London, 1961). J. C. CROW, *Spain: The Root and the Flower* (New York, 1963). H. V. LIVERMORE, *A History of Portugal* (London, 1947). R. M. SMITH, *Spain: A Modern History* (Ann Arbor, 1965). D. STANISLAWSKI, *The Individuality of Portugal* (Austin, Tex., 1959). B. WELLES, *Spain: The Gentle Anarchy* (New York, 1965). A. P. WHITAKER, *Spain and the Defense of the West* (New York, 1961).

F. W. FREY, *The Turkish Political Elite* (Cambridge, Mass., 1965). D. G. KOUSOULAS, *The Price of Freedom: Greece in World Affairs, 1939–1953* (Syracuse, 1953), and *Revolution and Defeat: The Story of the Greek Communist Party* (New York, 1965). Z. Y. HERSHLAG, *Turkey: An Economy in Transition* (The Hague, 1959). K. KARPAT, *Turkey's Politics: The Transition to a Multi-Party System* (Princeton, 1959). A. KILIC, *Turkey and the World* (Washington, 1959). C. A. MUNKMAN, *American Aid to Greece* (New York, 1958). W. F. WEIKER, *The Turkish Revolution, 1960–1961* (Washington, 1963). (*See also Chapters 10, 24, and 32.*)

CHAPTER 57: PLANS FOR WEST EUROPEAN INTEGRATION

E. B. HAAS, *The Uniting of Europe* (Stanford, 1958). G. LICHTHEIM, *The New Europe: Today and Tomorrow* (New York, 1963). R. MAYNE, *The Community of Europe* (New York, 1962). A. J. ZURCHER, *The Struggle to Unite Europe, 1940–1958* (New York, 1958).

E. BENOIT, *Europe at Sixes and Sevens* (New York, 1961). M. CAMPS, *Britain and the European Community, 1955–1963* (Princeton, 1964). C. A. CERAMI, *Alliance Born of Danger: America, the Common Market, and the Atlantic Partnership* (New York, 1963). W. DIEBOLD, *The Schuman Plan: A Study in Economic Cooperation, 1950–1959* (New York, 1959). S. N. FISHER, ed., *France and the European Community* (Columbus, 1964). D. D. HUMPHREY, *The United States and the Common Market* (New York, 1962). A. LAMFALUSSY, *The United Kingdom and Six* (Homewood, Ill., 1963). J. G. POLACH, *Euratom: Its Background, Issues, and Economic Implications* (Dobbs Ferry, N. Y., 1964). H. A. SCHMITT, *The Path to European Union: From the Marshall Plan to the Common Market* (Baton Rouge, 1962).

J. FREYMOND, *Western Europe Since the War* (New York, 1964). J. L. RICHARDSON, *Germany and the Atlantic Alliance: Interaction of Strategy and Politics* (Cambridge, Mass., 1966). F. ROY WILLIS, *France, Germany, and the New Europe, 1945–1963* (Stanford, 1965). (*See also Chapters 48 and 68.*)

CHAPTER 58: CANADA, AUSTRALIA, NEW ZEALAND, AND SOUTH AFRICA

H. G. J. AITKEN, *American Capital and Canadian Resources* (Cambridge, Mass., 1961). J. BARKER, *Good Fences Make Good Neighbors: Why the United States Provokes Canadians* (Indianapolis, 1958). J. B. CONDLIFFE, *The Welfare State in New Zealand* (London, 1959); and *Development of Australia* (New York, 1964). C. W. DE KIEWIET, *History of South Africa, Social and Economic* (New York, 1941). B. K. GORDON, *New Zealand Becomes a Pacific Power* (Chicago, 1960). H. L. KEENLEYSIDE, and others, *The Growth of Canadian Policies in External Affairs* (Durham, 1960). W. LEVI, *Australia's*

Outlook on Asia (East Lansing, 1958). R. A. MacKay, ed., *Newfoundland: Economic, Diplomatic and Strategic Studies* (New York, 1946). W. H. Oliver, *The Story of New Zealand* (New York, 1960). N. Phillips, *The Tragedy of Apartheid* (New York, 1960). W. Scott, *Australia and the Challenge of Change* (Sydney, 1957).

CHAPTER 59: LATIN AMERICA

R. N. Adam and D. B. Heath, eds., *Contemporary Cultures and Societies of Latin America* (New York, 1965). S. A. Bayitch, *Latin America: A Bibliographical Guide to Economy, History, Law, Politics and Society* (Coral Gables, Fla., 1961). C. T. Goodsell, *Administration of a Revolution: Executive Reform in Puerto Rico Under Governor Tugwell, 1941–1946* (Cambridge, Mass., 1965). R. Gruber, *Puerto Rico: Island of Promise* (New York, 1960). N. A. Havenstock, ed., *Handbook of Latin American Studies*, Annual (Gainsville, Fla., 1936–). J. D. Martz, *Dynamics of Change in Latin American Politics* (Englewood Cliffs, 1965), and *Central America: The Crisis and the Challenge* (Chapel Hill, 1959). D. Perkins, *The United States and Latin America* (Baton Rouge, 1961). F. B. Pike, *Conflict Between Church and State in Latin America* (New York, 1965). J. F. Rippy, *Globe and Hemisphere: Latin America's Place in the Postwar Foreign Relations of the United States* (Chicago, 1958). (*See also Chapter 31.*)

SECTION X: THE COMMUNIST STATES IN THE AFTERMATH OF THE WAR

American Universities Field Staff, *A Select Bibliography: Asia, Africa, Eastern Europe, Latin America* (New York, 1960). R. N. C. Hunt, ed., *Books on Communism* (New York, 1960). G. A. Lensen, *The World Beyond Europe: An Introduction to the History of Africa, India, Southeast Asia and the Far East* (Boston, 1960). John Plamenatz, *On Alien Rule and Self Government* (New York, 1960). L. D. Stamp, *Our Developing World* (London, 1960). World-mark Press, *The Worldmark Encyclopedia of the Nations* (New York, 1960).

CHAPTER 60: SOVIET RUSSIA

J. A. Armstrong, *The Politics of Totalitarianism: The Communist Party of the Soviet Union from 1934 to the Present* (New York, 1961). Z. K. Brzezinski, *The Permanent Purge: Politics in Soviet Totalitarianism* (Cambridge, Mass., 1956). G. S. Counts, *The Challenge of Soviet Education* (New York, 1957). E. Crankshaw, *Khrushchev: A Career* (New York, 1966). N. T. Dodge, *Women in the Soviet Economy* (Baltimore, 1966). W. Kolarz, *Russia and her Colonies* (New York, 1952), and *Religion in Soviet Russia* (New York, 1962). A. G. Korol, *Soviet Education for Science and Technology* (New York, 1957). R. D. Laird, ed., *Soviet Agriculture and Peasant Affairs* (Lawrence, Kan., 1964). B. I. Nicolaevsky, *Power and the Soviet Elite* (New York, 1965). R. Payne, *The Rise and Fall of Stalin* (New York, 1965). A. Parry, *The New Class Divided: Science and Technology versus Communism* (New York, 1966). R. W. Pethybridge, *A History of Postwar Russia* (New York, 1966). F. R. Randall, *Stalin's Russia* (New York, 1965). H. Schwartz, *The Red Phoenix: Russia since World War II* (New York, 1961), and *Soviet Economy since Stalin* (Philadelphia, 1965). A. B. Ulam, *The New*

Face of Soviet Totalitarianism (New York, 1963). (*See also Chapters 26, 27, 47, and 68.*)

CHAPTER 61: EASTERN EUROPE

Z. K. Brzezinski, *The Soviet Bloc: Unity and Conflict* (Cambridge, Mass., 1966). J. F. Brown, *The New Eastern Europe: The Khrushchev Era and After* (New York, 1966). R. V. Burks, *The Dynamics of Communism in Eastern Europe* (Princeton, 1961). K. Grzybowski, *The Socialist Commonwealth of Nations: Organizations and Institutions* (New Haven, 1964). M. Kaser, *COMECON: Integration Problems of the Planned Economies* (London, 1965). S. D. Kertesz, ed., *East Central Europe and the World: Developments in the Post Stalin Era* (Notre Dame, 1962). H. Ripka, *Eastern Europe in the Postwar World* (New York, 1961). H. Gordon Skilling, *Communism National and International: Eastern Europe after Stalin* (Toronto, 1964), and *The Governments of Communist Eastern Europe* (New York, 1966). N. Spulber, *The Economics of Communist Eastern Europe* (Cambridge, Mass., 1957). J. H. Wszelaki, *Communist Economic Strategy: The Role of East Central Europe* (Washington, 1959).

S. Brant, *The East German Rising* (New York, 1957). A. Cretzianu, ed., *Captive Rumania: A Decade of Soviet Rule, 1945–1955* (New York, 1956). M. Djilas, *The New Class: An Analysis of the Communist System* (New York, 1957). M. K. Dziewanowski, *The Communist Party of Poland* (Cambridge, Mass., 1958). F. Gibney, *The Frozen Revolution — Poland: A Study in Communist Decay* (New York, 1959). W. E. Griffith, *Albania and the Sino-Soviet Rift* (Cambridge, Mass., 1963). R. Hiscocks, *Poland: Bridge for the Abyss* (New York, 1963). G. W. Hoffman and F. W. Neal, *Yugoslavia and the New Communism* (New York, 1962). G. Ionescu, *Communism in Rumania, 1944–1962* (New York, 1964), and *The Break-up of the Soviet Empire in Eastern Europe* (Baltimore, 1965). P. Kecskemeti, *The Unexpected Revolution: Social Forces in the Hungarian Uprising* (Stanford, 1961). A. Korbonski, *Politics of Socialist Agriculture: Poland, 1945–1960* (New York, 1965). F. McLean, *The Heretic: The Life and Times of Josip Broz-Tito* (New York, 1957). R. F. Starr, *Poland, 1944–1962: The Sovietization of a Captive People* (Baton Rouge, La., 1962). F. Stolper, *The Structure of East German Economy* (Cambridge, Mass., 1960). K. Syrop, *Spring in October: The Polish Revolution of 1956* (New York, 1958). E. Taborsky, *Communism in Czechoslovakia, 1948–1960* (Princeton, 1961). F. A. Vali, *Rift and Revolt in Hungary: Nationalism versus Communism* (Cambridge, Mass., 1961). P. Zinner, ed., *National Communism and Popular Revolt in Eastern Europe: A Selection of Documents on Events in Poland and Hungary, February–November, 1956* (New York, 1956), and *Revolution in Hungary* (New York, 1962). (*See also Chapters 28, 29, and 47.*)

CHAPTER 62: CHINA UNDER COMMUNISM

G. M. Beckman, *The Modernization of China and Japan* (New York, 1962). Kuo-chün Chao, *Economic Planning and Organization in Mainland China: A Documentary Study* (2 vols., Cambridge, Mass., 1959–60). L. M. Chassin, *The Communist Conquest of China, 1945–1949* (Cambridge, Mass., 1965). O. E. Clubb, *Twentieth Century China* (New York, 1963). G. B. Endacott, *A History of Hong Kong* (New York, 1958). C. O. Hucker, *China: A Critical*

Bibliography (Tucson, Ariz., 1961). A. KUBEK, *How the Far East Was Lost: American Policy and the Creation of Communist China* (Chicago, 1963). O. LATTIMORE, *Nomads and Commissars: Mongolia Revisited* (New York, 1962). D. H.; PERKINS, *Market Control and Planning in Communist China* (Cambridge, Mass., 1966). PING-TI HO, *Studies on the Population of China, 1368–1953* (Cambridge, Mass., 1959). W. S. THOMPSON, *Population and Progress in the Far East* (Chicago, 1959). (*See also Chapters 44 and 49.*)

SECTION XI: THE MARCH TO INDEPENDENCE IN ASIA AND AFRICA

A. J. BROWN, *Introduction to the World Economy* (New York, 1960). A. M. CARR-SAUNDERS, *New Universities Overseas* (London, 1961). R. EMERSON, *From Empire to Nation: The Rise to Self-Assertion of Asian and African Peoples* (Cambridge, Mass., 1960). R. GRUBER, *Science and the New Nations* (New York, 1961). M. F. MILLIKAN and D. L. M. BLACKMER, *The Emerging Nations: Their Growth and United States Policy* (Boston, 1961). L. D. STAMP, *Regional Geography: Africa* (8th ed., New York, 1965); *Asia* (16th ed., New York, 1965). R. THEOBALD, *The Rich and the Poor: A Study of the Economics of Rising Expectations* (New York, 1960). W. E. F. WARD, *Educating Young Nations* (New York, 1960).

CHAPTER 63: INDIA: INDEPENDENCE AND DIVISION

N. AHMAD, *An Economic Geography of East Pakistan* (New York, 1958). A. J. COALE and E. M. HOOVER, *Population Growth and Economic Development in Low-Income Countries: A Case Study of India's Prospects* (Princeton, 1958). W. N. PEACE and others, *Basic Data of the Economy of Pakistan* (New York, 1959). G. D. OVERSTREET and M. WINDMILLER, *Communism in India* (Berkeley, 1959). H. TINKER, *India and Pakistan: A Political Analysis* (rev. ed., New York, 1966). B. WARD, *India and the West* (rev. ed., New York, 1964). W. S. WOYTINSKY, *India: The Awakening Giant* (New York, 1957). W. H. WRIGGINS, *Ceylon: Dilemmas of a New Nation* (Princeton, 1960).

CHAPTER 64: EAST AND SOUTHEAST ASIA

G. C. ALLEN, *A Short Economic History of Modern Japan* (New York, 1963). H. H. BAERWALD, *The Purge of Japanese Leaders Under the Occupation* (Berkeley, 1959). N. F. BUSCH, *Thailand: An Introduction to Modern Siam* (Princeton, 1959). J. F. CADY, *A History of Modern Burma* (Ithaca, N.Y., 1958). J. W. COULTER, *The Pacific Dependencies of the United States* (New York, 1957). F. H. GOLAY, *The Philippines: Public Policy and National Economic Development* (Ithaca, N.Y., 1961). C. H. GRATTAN, *The United States and the Southwest Pacific* (Cambridge, Mass., 1961). KAZUO KAWAI, *Japan's American Interlude* (Chicago, 1960). F. H. H. KING, *The New Malayan Nation* (New York, 1957). S. KLEIN, *The Pattern of Land Tenure Reform in East Asia and World War II* (New York, 1958). F. M. LEBAR and A. SUDDARD, *Laos: Its People, Its Society, Its Culture* (New Haven, 1960). I. B. TAEURNER, *The Population of Japan* (Princeton, 1958). H. TINKER, *Union of Burma* (3rd ed., New York, 1961). D. A. WILSON, *Politics in Thailand* (Ithaca, 1962). D. WOODMAN, *The Making of Burma* (London, 1962). S. YOSHIDA, *The Yoshida Memoirs* (London, 1961). (*See also Chapter 49.*)

CHAPTER 65: THE NEAR AND MIDDLE EAST

W. Z. LAQUEUR, ed., *The Middle East in Transition* (New York, 1958).
D. PERETZ, *The Middle East Today* (New York, 1963). W. SPENSER, *Political Evolution in the Middle East* (New York, 1962).
R. W. COTTAM, *Nationalism in Iran* (Pittsburgh, 1964). H. R. P. DICKSON, *Kuwait and Her Neighbors* (London, 1956). H. INGRAMS, *The Yemen: Imams, Rulers, and Revolutions* (New York, 1964). J. MORRIS, *The Hashemite Kings* (New York, 1959). B. SHWADRAN, *Jordan: A State of Tension* (New York, 1959). G. H. TORREY, *Syrian Politics and the Military, 1945–1958* (Columbus, 1963). J. M. UPTON, *The History of Modern Iran* (Cambridge, Mass., 1960). M. B. WATKINS, *Afghanistan: Land in Transition* (Princeton, 1963). L. WHEELOCK, *Nasser's New Egypt* (New York, 1960). W. WYNN, *Nasser of Egypt* (Cambridge, Mass., 1959). N. A. ZIADEH, *Syria and Lebanon* (New York, 1957).
A. BEIN, *The Return to the Soil: A History of Jewish Settlement in Israel* (Jerusalem, 1952). M. H. BERNSTEIN, *The Politics of Israel* (Princeton, 1957). R. H. S. CROSSMAN, *A Nation Reborn* (New York, 1960). B. HALPERN, *The Idea of the Jewish State* (Cambridge, Mass., 1961). O. I. JANOWSKY, *Foundations of Israel: Emergence of a Welfare State* (Princeton, 1959). O. KRAINES, *Government and Politics in Israel* (Boston, 1961). A. RUBNER, *Economy of Israel* (New York, 1960). H. M. SACHAR, *Aliyah: The Peoples of Israel* (New York, 1961). (*See also Chapters 32 and 50.*)

CHAPTER 66: AFRICA ASTIR

D. E. APTER, *The Political Kingdom in Uganda* (Princeton, 1961). D. E. ASHFORD, *Morocco-Tunisia: Politics and Planning* (Syracuse, 1965). N. BARBOUR, ed., *A Survey of North West Africa: The Maghrib* (2nd ed., New York, 1962). R. M. BRACE, *Morocco, Algeria, Tunisia* (Englewood Cliffs, 1964). Z. K. BRZEZINSKI, ed., *Africa and the Communist World* (Stanford, 1963). G. M. CARTER, *Independence for Africa* (New York, 1960). M. CROWDER, *A Short History of Nigeria* (rev. ed., New York, 1966). J. DUFFY, *Portuguese Africa* (Cambridge, Mass., 1959). R. EMERSON and M. KILSON, *The Political Awakening in Africa* (Englewood Cliffs, 1965). A. J. HANNA, *The Story of the Rhodesias and Nyasaland* (rev. ed., New York, 1961). J. HATCH, *Africa Today – and Tomorrow* (2nd ed., rev., New York, 1965). G. H. T. KIMBLE, *Tropical Africa* (2 vols., New York, 1960). C. LEGUM, ed., *Africa: A Handbook to the Continent* (New York, 1966). V. McKAY, *Africa in World Politics* (New York, 1963), and *African Diplomacy* (New York, 1966). P. PARTNER, *A Short Political Guide to the Arab World* (New York, 1960). R. I. ROTBERG, *Political History of Tropical Africa* (New York, 1965), and *The Rise of Nationalism in Central Africa: The Making of Malawi and Zambia, 1873–1964* (Cambridge, Mass., 1965). ROYAL INSTITUTE OF INTERNATIONAL AFFAIRS, *Nigeria: The Political and Economic Background* (New York, 1960). E. ULLENDORFF, *Ethiopians: An Introduction to Country and People* (London, 1960). UNITED NATIONS, *Economic Survey of Africa Since 1950* (New York, 1960).

SECTION XII: THE SEVENTH DECADE

C. E. BEEBY, *The Quality of Education in Developing Countries* (Cambridge, Mass., 1966). C. M. EICHELBERGER, *The United Nations: The First Twenty Years* (New York, 1965). W. GILMAN, *Science, U.S.A.* (New York,

1965). M. Greenberger, ed., *Computers and the World of the Future* (Cambridge, Mass., 1962). J. H. Herz, *International Politics in the Atomic Age* (New York, 1959). G. Piel, *Science in the Cause of Man* (New York, 1961). *Science in Progress,* Annual (New Haven, 1943–   ). B. D. Wolfe, *Marxism: One Hundred Years in the Life of a Doctrine* (New York, 1965). United Nations, *Statistical Yearbook, Demographic Yearbook, Yearbook of the United Nations,* Annual (New York, 1947–   ).

CHAPTER 67: THREE PERSISTENT QUESTIONS

P. E. Baldry, *The Battle Against Bacteria* (New York, 1966). E. R. Black, *The Diplomacy of Economic Development* (Cambridge, Mass., 1960). D. G. Brennan, *Arms Control, Disarmament, and National Security* (New York, 1961). K. Davis, *The World's Metropolitan Areas* (Berkeley, 1959). J. M. Fowler, ed., *Fallout: A Study of Superbombs, Strontium 90, and Survival* (New York, 1960). C. J. Hitch and R. N. McKean, *The Economics of Defense in a Nuclear Age* (Cambridge, Mass., 1960). H. Kahn, *On Thermonuclear War* (Princeton, 1960). G. Myrdal, *Rich Lands and Poor* (New York, 1958). G. I. Pokrovsky, *Science and Technology in Contemporary War* (New York, 1959). A. Shonfield, *The Attack on World Poverty* (New York, 1960). A. E. Sokol, *Seapower in the Nuclear Age* (Washington, 1961). R. Theobald, *The Rich and the Poor* (New York, 1960). United Nations: Food and Agriculture Organization, *Millions Still Go Hungry* (Rome, 1957). W. Vogt, *People: Challenge to Survival* (New York, 1960).

CHAPTER 68: INTERNATIONAL PROBLEMS

H. R. Alker and B. M. Russett, *World Politics in the General Assembly* (New Haven, 1965). L. P. Bloomfield, *The United Nations and the United States Foreign Policy* (Boston, 1960). J. Comay, *The UN in Action* (New York, 1965). A. Dallin, *The Soviet Union at the United Nations* (New York, 1962). C. M. Eichelberger, *UN: The First Twenty Years* (New York, 1965). E. E. Gross, *The United Nations* (New York, 1962). T. Hovet, *Bloc Politics in the United Nations* (New York, 1962). J. M. Jones, *The United Nations at Work* (London, 1965). G. Rosner, *The United Nations Emergency Force* (New York, 1963). J. G. Stoessinger, *The United Nations and the Superpowers: United States–Soviet Interaction at the United Nations* (New York, 1965).

D. G. Brennan, *Arms Control, Disarmament, and National Security* (New York, 1961). W. C. Clemens, *Soviet Disarmament Policy, 1917–1963* (Stanford, 1965). J. M. Goldsen, ed., *Outer Space in World Politics* (New York, 1963). R. A. Goldwin, ed., *Beyond the Cold War* (Chicago, 1963). J. H. Herz, *International Politics in the Atomic Age* (New York, 1959). J. B. Whitton, ed., *Propaganda and the Cold War: A Princeton University Symposium* (Washington, 1963).

R. L. Allen, *Soviet Economic Warfare* (Washington, 1960). H. L. Boorman, *Moscow-Peking Axis: Strengths and Strains* (New York, 1957). A. Bromke, *The Communist States at the Crossroads: Between Moscow and Peking* (New York, 1965). Z. K. Brzezinski, ed., *Africa and the Communist World* (Stanford, 1963). D. J. Dallin, *Soviet Foreign Policy after Stalin* (Philadelphia, 1961). H. S. Dinerstein, *War and the Soviet Union: Nuclear Weapons and the Revolution in Soviet Military and Political Thinking* (New York, 1959). D. J. Doolin, *Territorial Claims in the Sino-Soviet Conflict:*

Documents and Analysis (Stanford, 1965). R. L. GARTHOFF, *Soviet Strategy in the Nuclear Age* (New York, 1958). D. FLOYD, *Mao against Khrushchev: A Short History of the Sino-Soviet Conflict* (New York, 1964). W. E. GRIF-FITH, *The Sino-Soviet Rift* (Cambridge, Mass., 1964), and *Communism in Europe: Continuity and Change and the Sino-Soviet Dispute*, Vol. I (Cambridge, Mass., 1964). W. KOLARZ, *Communism and Colonialism* (New York, 1964). K. MENHERT, *Peking and Moscow* (New York, 1963). F. L. PRYOR, *The Communist Foreign Trade System* (Cambridge, Mass., 1963). D. S. ZAGORIA, *The Sino-Soviet Conflict, 1956–1961* (Princeton, 1962).

J. R. BEAL, *John Foster Dulles, 1888–1959* (2nd ed., New York, 1959). J. E. BLACK and K. W. THOMPSON, eds., *Foreign Policies in a World of Change* (New York, 1963). K. H. CERNY and H. W. BRIEF, eds., *NATO in Quest of Cohesion* (New York, 1965). A. J. COTTRELL and J. E. DOUGHERTY, *The Politics of the Atlantic Alliance* (New York, 1964). J. F. DULLES, *War or Peace* (New York, 1950). H. FEIS, *Foreign Aid and Foreign Policy* (New York, 1964). R. H. FIFIELD, *Southeast Asia in United States Policy* (New York, 1963). R. GOOLD-ADAMS, *John Foster Dulles* (New York, 1962). H. A. KISSINGER, *The Troubled Partnership* (New York, 1965). R. KLEIMAN, *Atlantic Crisis: American Diplomacy Confronts a Resurgent Europe* (New York, 1964). R. G. O'CONNOR, *American Defense Policy in Perspective* (New York, 1965). T. W. STANLEY, *NATO in Transition* (New York, 1965). (See also Chapters 46, 47, and 67.)

INDEX

Big Three (France, Britain, U.S.), at Peace Conference, Paris, 180–185; and the Fourteen Points, 185–188
Big Three (Churchill, Roosevelt, Stalin), 549; meet at Teheran (1943), 506–507; on the United Nations, at Yalta, 548
Birthrate, decline of during Depression, 400; a world problem, 828–834
Bishop, Billy, 452
Bismarck, Otto von, 60, 74, 82, 114; consolidates German nation, 44, 47, 190; quoted on blood and iron, 52; social legislation under, 54–55
Bismarck Archipelago, 140, 511
Bizerte, 478
Black Shirts, Italian Fascists, 270
Blanco Party, Uruguayan, 725
Blitzkrieg, technique of, 452
Bloc National, French, 259
Bloody Sunday (1905), 88
Blum, Léon, 264, 265
Boer War, 40, 126
Boers, 126, 333, 711
Bohemia, 95, 194, 196, 313, 314, 421, 422
Bolivia, 345–346, 348, 723, 724
Bolsheviks, 88–89, 149, 162, 196; opposition to, 169, 200; and democracy, 233; and Lenin, 288; trials of, under Stalin, 301; and China, 382
Bolshevism, as totalitarian system, 234–235
Bonin Islands, 511, 575
Bordeaux, 461
Boris, King of Bulgaria, 325, 328
Bormann, Martin, 554
Borneo, 373, 794
Bosnia, 83, 114, 115, 131, 323; Austria-Hungary annexes (1908), 84, 93, 97, 102; as World War I prize, 160, 172
Bosporus, struggle for, 82; route for invasion of Russia, 563
Boulanger, Georges, 65
Boumédienne, Colonel Houari, 822
Bourgeois, Léon, 217
Boxer Rebellion, 83, 381
Bradley, Gen. Omar N., 524, 584
Brandes, Georg, 111
Brătianu, Ionel, 318
Brazil, 106, 340, 347–348; after World War II, 726, 727
Brazilia, 727
Breslau, German cruiser, 140
Brest-Litovsk, peace of (1918), 151, 158–159, 162, 169, 186, 201, 288
Brezhnev, Leonid I., 740, 741, 744, 839, 847
Briand, Aristide, 138, 259, 260, 278
British Commonwealth of Nations, 254, 623–626; in World War I, 330–331; slackening of ties in, 330–333; Canada, 333–334, 702–705; Australia, 335–336, 706–708; New Zealand, 335–336, 709–710; South Africa, 336, 337, 710–713; trade commitments, 695; withdrawal from, 713; India, 780; Ceylon, 785; Burma, 786; Malayan Federation, 794
British East Africa, 798
British Honduras, 705

British North America Act (1867), 125
Brockdorff-Rantzau, Count, 193
Brown Shirts, Nazi militia, 285
Broz, Josip. *See* Tito, Marshal Josip Broz
Brusilov offensive (1916), 138
Brussels, 539, 698
Bryan, William Jennings, 145
Bucharest, 308
Bucharest, Peace of (1812), 112; (1913), 115
Bucharest, Treaty of (1916), 160, 194
Buchlau, 84
Budapest, 308, 514, 524; scene of revolt (1956), 757
Buddha, the, 436
Buddhists, in India, 369; in Burma, 371; in China, 379, 763; in Ceylon, 785; in Thailand, 793
Buenos Aires, 344, 346
Bukharin, Nikolai, 301
Bukovina, 92, 160, 172, 317, 469
Bulganin, Nikolai A., 738–740, 831, 841, 842
Bulgaria, 82, 102; prior to World War I, 114–115; enters World War I, 132, 137, 139, 147, 155, 160; after World War I, 168, 196, 220, 307, 318; between the wars, 324–325, 327, 328; in World War II, 470–471, 513; after World War II, 534, 564, 749, 750, 760; peace treaty, 548, 553
Bulge, Battle of (1944), 519–520
Bülow, Count Bernhard von, 55
Bunche, Ralph, 595
Burke, Edmund, 251–252
Burma, 30, 371, 381, 483, 521, 522, 578, 629, 786–787; leaves Commonwealth, 630, 786, 787
Burma Road, 479, 483, 522
Butcher, Captain Harry, 520
Byrnes, James Francis, 548, 555, 562, 571
Byron, George Gordon, Lord, 113
Byzantine Empire, 97–98

Cagoulards, 262
Cambodia, 59, 372, 587, 590, 797, 798, 843
Cameroons, 141, 192, 252
Campbell-Bannerman, Sir Henry, 41
Canada, becomes British Dominion, 124–125, 254; in World War I, 330–331; in League of Nations, 331; between the wars, 333–334; as part of Anglo-Saxon bloc, 340; after World War II, 630, 702–706
Canal Zone, Panama, 721, 722
Canberra, Australia, 336
Canton, 381, 384, 478
Cape Colony, 29, 30, 126
Cape of Good Hope, 108
Cape Town, 33, 126
Cape Verde Islands, 106
Caporetto, 151
Caprivi, Leo von, 55
Caribbean Islands, 342; Negroes in, 340
Carlos I, King of Portugal, 107
Carmona, Gen. Antonio Oscar de Fragoso, 107
Carol II, King of Rumania, 319, 469
Caroline Islands, 140, 376, 511, 575, 578

132, 139, 140–142, 153–155; war aims, 159; and Russian revolution, 169; in Near East, 174, 197–200; at Peace Conference, 180–193, 197; and war debt, 207–212, 397; in League of Nations, 222; on disarmament, 224–225; economic problems, 230–231, 248–250; and naval armament, 245, 405; abandons gold standard, 249, 401, 441; political genius, 250–252; slackening of imperial ties, 252–254, 330–333, 539; and Ireland, 253, 331; in East Central Europe, 321, 328; and Near and Middle East, 353–354, 357–358; Egypt, 360–361; in India, 365–370, 780; in Burma, 371; Pacific islands, 376; in Spanish Civil War, 412; policy of appeasement, 415, 418–421; takes lead in rebuilding alliances, 422; naval warfare in World War II, 457–458; battles of western Europe (1939–1940), 456–464; aerial blitz (1940–1941), 464–465; and lend-lease, 466-467, 494; in Mediterranean campaign, 475–478; and Far East, 478–480; struggle for control of sea and air, 489–494; invasion of France, 514–518; in Greece, 521, 564; and destruction of Germany, 523–536; after World War II, 534–537, 538, 587; in United Nations, 545; occupation of Germany, 553–557; in NATO, 545–547; and East Asia, 575; in Near East, 589, 590, 790; Suez Canal crisis, 595–599; balance sheet after the war, 619–622; economic recovery, 622–626; social welfare, 626–629; defense, 629–631; relations with Germany, 644, 645; and Cyprus, 685; plans for western European integration, 690; and the Common Market, 695–697; and European Free Trade Association, 695–697; and Western Union alliance, 698; and the European Defense Community (EDC), 699–701; in Africa, 711–713; and Rhodesia, 714

Great Depression, 237; background, 238–242; and laissez-faire, 242; New Deal, 243–245; worldwide influence, 398–400; programs for recovery, 400–403; resulting in resort to aggression, 403

Greece, and Balkan Wars, 102, 115; and Russo-Turkish Wars, 113; independence declared, 113; enters World War I, 133, 137, 160; after World War I, 196, 198, 200, 220, 321, 325; quarrel with Italy (1923), 268, 274, 327; exchange of minority groups, 307, 327; between the wars, 326–327; guarantee offered by Britain and France (1939), 423; invaded by Italy, (1940), 469; invaded by Germany (1941), 470; in World War II, 513–514, 521; after World War II, 551, 553, 564, 565, 680–682; in Council of Europe, 690

Greek Catholic Church, opposed by communism, 751

Greek Orthodox Church, 82, 111, 235, 322, 474, 559, 680, 751

Greenland, 111, 467,

Grévy, Jules, 64

Grey, Sir Edward, 38, 159n, 418

Grieg, Edvard, 111

Groningen, 108

Grottewohl, Otto, 748

Groza, Petru, 747

Guadalcanal Island, 483, 484

Guam, American protectorate, 105, 376; U.S. not to fortify, 247; falls to Japan, 483

Guantánamo Bay, 721

Guatemala, 720, 728

Gulflight, American freighter, 145

Gurion, David Ben, 814, 815

Gursel, Gen. Cemal, 682

Gustav V, King of Sweden, 663

Gustav VI, King of Sweden, 663

Haakon VII, King of Norway, 458, 665

Hácha, Emil, 421, 422

Hadramaut, 358, 808, 810

Hague Peace Conference (1899), 216; (1907), 216–217, 344

Haiti, 344, 722

Haj Amin al-Huseini, 592

Hamburg, 530

Hammarskjöld, Dag, 824, 836, 837

Hankow, 478

Hanoi, 585, 587

Hapsburg dynasty, 44, 90–97, 108, 317, 323; attempts to unify, 94; Austro-Hungarian Compromise, 95; breaking of, 161, 171–173, 193–195

Harding, Warren Gamaliel, 237

Hashimite dynasty, 358–359

Hatay, 356, 423

Have-not Powers, contrasted with Haves, 442–445

Hawaii, Territory of, annexed by U.S., 30, 122, 375

Hejaz, 174, 358–359, 808

Helen, Queen of Rumania, 319

Hemingway, Ernest, 153, 438

Henlein, Konrad, 314

Herter, Christian A., 614–615

Herzegovina, 83, 114; Austria-Hungary annexes (1908), 84, 93, 97, 102; as World War I prize, 160, 172

Himmler, Heinrich, 525, 533, 554

Hindenburg, Field Marshal Paul von, 136, 154; as President, 278, 280, 281

Hindus, and struggle for Indian independence, 368; worldwide numbers of 436; proportion of, in India, 783

Hirohito, Emperor of Japan, 387, 48? 528, 575, 576

Hiroshima, Americans bomb (1945? 528, 807

Hitler, Adolf, 265, 415; occupies Rhin land, 263; meets Mussolini, 275; r of, 279–283; revival of militarism, 2? 286, at Munich, 305; and Czecho? vakia, 314, 418–422; annexes Aus? (1938), 416–418; invades Pol? (1939), 453–454; invades Denm?rk and Norway (1940), 456–458; inv?es France (1940), 458–463; and B?tle of Britain (1940–1941), 463–465 occupies Italy (1943), 503; and F?nch liberation, 516–518; assassinatio? at- tempted, 519; death of, 524–525 533, 554; quoted, 277, 307, 413, 452, 468

Mossadeq, Mohammed, Prime Minister of Iran, 596, 811, 812
Mosul, 197, 200, 354, 357, 805
Mountbatten, Admiral Lord Louis, 528, 780
Mozambique, 106, 823
Muhammad V, Sultan of Morocco, 821
Munich Conference (1938), 265, 286, 305, 321, 328, 420
Munoz, Luis Marin, 723
Murmansk, 170, 492, 504
Muscat, 810
Music, development of modern, 20
Mussolini, Benito, 267, 269–270, 414; rise of, 270–273; foreign policy, 274–276, 413; at Munich, 305, 419–420; and Albania, 422; declares war on France (1940), 461, 672; overthrown (1943), 503; rescued by Germans, 504; death of, 525, 672
Mutsuhito, Emperor of Japan, 127

Nagasaki, 528
Naguib, General Mohammed, 596, 803
Nagy, Ferencz, 747, 749, 757, 758
Nagy, Imre, 757, 758
Nanking, Treaty of (1842), 381
Naples, 539
Napoleon I, 11, 44, 47, 72, 81, 99, 106, 445, 470
Napoleon III, Emperor of France, 64, 73, 114
Narkomindiel, 304
Narvik, 458
Nasser, Gamal Abdul, 596, 802, 803, 805–809, 837, 846; in Suez crisis, 598–600; relations with Jordan, 805; quoted, 588
Natal, 126
National Council of Corporations, in Fascist Italy, 273
National Socialist German Workers Party (National Socialists, Nazis), 279–281, 450
Nationalism, Italian, 269; German, 279–281; and communism, 308; in India, 368; in Indonesia, 373; European, after World War I, 450; growth of among colonial peoples, 537–540; fostered by Russia in other countries, 562; Arab, 589, 600
Naval limitation, Washington (1921–1922), 245; London Naval Conference (1930), 246–247
Naval Limitation Treaty (1935), Great Britain, Germany, 286, 415
Navarino, battle of (1827), 113
Nazism, as totalitarian system, 234–235; rise of, 279–283
Near and Middle East, problems of, 351–352; Turkey, Iran, and Afghanistan, 352–356; Arabia, 356–360; open to Hitler in 1941, 476; in Allied strategy, 500; after World War II, 588–590; problems and prospects, 801–803; Egypt, 803–805; Iraq, 805–806; Jordan, 806–807; Syria, 807; Lebanon, 807–808; Iran and Afghanistan, 808–810; Peninsular Arabia, 811–813; Israel, 813–816

Near Eastern question, in World War I, 197–200
Negroes, in Latin America, 721; in U.S. schools, 610; in South Africa, 820
Nehru, Jawaharlal, 538, 779, 781, 782, 837, 846; quoted, 779
Nejd, 174, 359
Nenni, Pietro, 673, 674
Netherlands, 108; seek control of sea, 10–11; as colonial power, 28; before World War I, 104, 108–109; in World War I, 141; after World War I, 245; in East Indies, 372–374, 479–480, 538, 539, 776–778; invaded, World War II, 458–460; Jews in, 533; description and history, 655–657, 690, 691, 794, 795
Netherlands East Indies, 108, 372–374, 479, 488, 794–796, 820
Neuilly, Treaty of (1919), 196, 325
Neutrality Act (1935), 465
New Britain, 376
New Caledonia, 483
New Deal, 242–245
New Economic Policy (NEP), Russian, 291–294
New Guinea, 140, 336, 373, 376, 511, 708, 795
New Hebrides, 483
New Ireland, 376
New Zealand, 125–126, 192, 253, 254; in World War I, 330–331; between wars, 335–336; and Pacific islands, 376; restrictions on immigration, 449; after World War II, 579, 587, 708–710, 800
Newfoundland, 630
Ngo Dinh Diem, 587, 798, 799
Nguyen Cao Ky, 799
Nicaragua, 720
Nicholas I, Tsar of Russia, 86, 99
Nicholas II, Tsar of Russia, 62; Bloody Sunday, 88; assumes command of army (1915), 148; abdicates, 148; and Hague Peace Conference, 216
Niger, Republic of, 821
Nigeria, 713, 823
Nine-Power Treaty, reaffirms independence of China, 245, 386, 407
Nivelle, General Robert, 151
Nixon, Richard M., 615, 726, 833
Nobel, Alfred, 111
North Africa, campaign in World War II, 475–478; French colonial struggle in, 638, 639; in the 1950's, 821, 822
North America, cultivable land in, 6, 8
North Atlantic Pact (1949), 573, 699
North Atlantic Treaty Organization (NATO), 573, 574, 613, 629, 650, 699–701, 705, 745, 755, 840, 850, 851
North German Confederation (1867), 44
North Korea, attacks South Korea (1950), 574, 582–585, 775, 800, 836. See also Korea
North Pole, 694; studied, 434
Northern Ireland, 253, 331
Norway, 444, 456; prior to World War I, 110–111; in World War I, 141; in World War II, 457–458; after World

Perón, Juan Domingo, 725
Perry, Commodore Matthew Calbraith, 127
Pershing, General John J., 154, 155, 499
Persia, German influence in, 51; Anglo-Russian friction in, 62, 83. *See also* Iran
Peru, 220, 345–346, 723, 724
Pescadores, 575, 792
Pétain, Marshal Henri Philippe, 151; Chief of State (1940), 461–462
Peter the Great, 81, 84–85, 303
Peter II, King of Yugoslavia, 324, 470
Peter V, King of Portugal, 107
Petkov, Nikola, 750
Petrovich, Michael Boro, 78
Philip II, King of Spain, 11, 108
Philippine Islands, 30; American protectorate, 105, 122–123, 374–375; in World War II, 510–511; granted independence, 539; after World War II, 538, 578, 579, 796, 797, 800, 848
Philippine Sea, Second Battle of (1944), 511
Philosophy, trends in modern, 20–21
Pieck, Wilhelm, 748
Pilsen, 525; strike (1953), 756
Pilsudski, Joseph, 171, 201–202, 263, 311; Dictator of Poland, 312
Pius IV, Pope, 73, 77
Pius XII, Pope, 675
Platt Amendment (1901), 123
Pleven, René, 699
Ploesti oil fields, 469
Plombières, 73
Poincaré, Raymond, President of France, 259, 260, 262
Point Four program, 572, 811
Poland, 81, 151; Germans occupy (1915), 137; in World War I, 158, 171; restoration after World War I, 188, 190, 194, 195, 307, 310–312; relations with Russia after World War I, 201–202, 223, 320; invaded by Germany (1939), 223, 286, 305, 422–424, 453–454; treaty with France (1921), 257, 260, 263, 319, 320; alliance with Rumania (1921), 320; refuses to join Little Entente, 320; non-aggression pact with Germany (1934), 320; and Czechoslovakia, 420; guaranteed by Britain and France (1939), 422; invaded by Russia, 454; in World War II, 505, 506–507, 512–513; after World War II, 534, 549, 553, 749, 751, 760; and effects of destalinization, 562, 756, 758
Polish Committee of National Liberation, 747
Polish Diet, 51
Polish-German non-aggression pact (1934), 263, 320; denounced by Hitler (1939), 423
Polish Workers' Party (communist), 749, 756
Politbureau, 291, 738
Poltava, 85
Popular Front, French, 263–264, 265
Popular Republican Movement, French, 634
Population, world distribution of, 6–8;

problem in France, 59; rise in, under reign of science, 100, pressures of, before World War II, 445–449; in United States after World War II, 607; problem in Latin America, 715–716; global, 828, 833–834
Populist Party, Italian, 274
Port Arthur, 83, 128, 522, 580
Portsmouth, Treaty of (1905), 83
Portugal, Oceanic Age in, 10–11; as colonial power, 28, 339, 364, 381, 823; prior to World War I, 105, 106–107; enters World War I, 133, 141; after World War I, 245; after World War II, 537, 540, 678–680, 695
Potsdam, Big Three Conference (1945), 526, 548, 554, 555, 557, 560, 562, 563, 582, 586, 840
Poznań, 312, 756
Prague, 308, 525, 750
Pribichevich, Stoyan, 322
Prince of Wales, British battleship, 492, 508.
Princip, Gavrilo, 131
Production, in World War II, 536; recovery in, 536–537; in postwar United States, 607, 608; in postwar France, 635, 636
Propaganda, in World War I, 161–163; and the totalitarian state, 235; in the Soviet Union, 293
Prussia, leads in unification of Germany, 44, 52–53; abolished, 554
Puerto Rico, American protectorate, 105, 344, 722, 723
Purges, Soviet (1934), 301, 302
Pu-yi, Emperor of China, 382
Pyongyang, 583, 775

Qatar, 358, 802, 810
Quadros, Janio, 727
Quadruple Alliance, Britain, Russia, Austria, Prussia, 216, 275
Quebec, Summit conference (1943), 503; second conference (1944), 520
Quemoy, 792, 793, 842
Quezon, Manuel, 375
Quisling, Vidkun, 458
Quwatli, Shukri, 807

Rackiewicz, President of Polish Government in exile, 454
Radar (Radio Directing and Ranging), in World War II, 486
Radić, Stepan, 324
Radical Socialist Party, French, 258, 264
Railroad War Board, World War I, 154
Rajk, Lászlo, 753
Rákosi, Mátyás, 748, 749, 757, 759
Rapallo, Treaty of (1920), 195, 304
Rasputin, Gregory, 148
Rathenau, Walther, 131, 304
Reconstruction Finance Corporation, 242
Red Cross, 110
Red Guards, 766, 767
Reform bills, British, 39, 250
Refugees, after World War II, 644, 645
Reichsrat, abolished by Hitler, 281
Reichstag, composition of, 53; building burned, 280
Reinsurance Treaty, Germany, Russia, 60

898

nish War, 454–456, 543, 666, 667; growing tension with Germany, 468–471; Germany attacks (1941), 471–475; difficulties of cooperating with, 496–497, 502, 503; westward drive (1943–1944), 504–507; conquest of Eastern Europe (1944), 512–514; and destruction of Germany, 523–526; declares war on Japan, 528; postwar influence, 534–537; in the United Nations, 545–548; territorial settlements, 548–549; occupation of Germany, 553–557; postwar aims, 558, 559; satellites in Eastern Europe, 560–562, 746–761; relations with China, 580–582, 763, 764, 772–775; Korean War, 582–585; in Indochina, 586; in Suez crisis, 598, 599; and East Germany, 643, 644; relations with Latin America, 721, 722; economic planning and expansion, 734–737; death of Stalin and struggle for succession, 737–741; social and cultural changes, 741–744; defense and armaments, 744, 745, 829–832; industrialization and collectivization of agriculture in Eastern Europe, 752–754; break with Tito, 753, 755; and revolt of Budapest, 758; weakening of controls over satellite countries, 758–761; relations with Albania, 759; revives CEMA, 759, 760; and India, 782; and Ceylon, 785; and Vietnam, 843; and Castro, 843, 844; rift between Communist Chinese and, 845–848; bipolarization of power between United States and, 852

Soviet-Chinese agreements (1945), 579, 580, 774; alliance (1950), 772

Space, exploration of, 830

Spaak, Paul-Henri, 688

Spain, Moorish civilization in, 5; Oceanic Age in, 10–11; as colonial power, 28, 339; prior to World War I, 62, 105–106, 122; in World War I, 141; civil war (1936), 223, 264, 286, 410–413; relations with Italy, 275; and Morocco, 362; republican revolution (1931), 411; World War II, 476, 623; after World War II, 537, 676–678

Spanish-American War (1898), 106, 122, 344

Spanish Civil War, 223, 264, 286, 410–413

Spartacists, German, 277

Spengler, Oswald, 438

Sputnik I, 830

Stalin, Joseph (Joseph Vissarionovich Djugashvili), 288, 291, 294–295, 560, 561, 570, 772; Purges of 1934, 301, 302; as despot, 302; China policy, 384; orders Russian counteroffensive, 474–475; attends Summit conferences, 497, 500, 502, 506–507, 520–521, 528; at Yalta, 522–523, 544; death of, 559, 738, 754; and Tito, 565–566; on reconstruction, 734, 735, 737; denounced by Khrushchev, 739

Stalingrad (Volgograd), siege of (1942–1943), 475, 505

Stamboliisky, Alexander, 168, 325

Standard of living, in post-war United

States, 607; and global population pressures, 832–834

Stanley, Henry Morton, 30, 362

Stauffenberg, Col. Count Claus von, 519

Stavisky case, 263

Stevenson, Adlai E., 614

Stilwell, General Joseph W., 521–522

Stimson, Henry L., 560

Stolypin, Peter A., 89

Straits Convention of 1923, 356

Straits Settlements (Malaya), 371

Stresemann, Gustav, 260, 278

Strijdom, Johannes, 712

Strindberg, August, 111

Stroessner, General Alfredo, 727, 728

Sturzo, Don Luigi, 273

Šubašić, Ivan, 747

Submarine warfare, in World War I, 143, 144–145, 151, 153; in World War II, 489–490, 491–492; in the Pacific, 508–509

Sudan, 361, 476, 592, 596, 804, 821

Sudeten Germans, 314

Suez, 33

Suez Canal, 101, 123, 253, 351, 361, 629; closed in World War II, 475; closed to Israel, 595; crisis over (1956), 595–600, 630, 757, 804, 837, 842, 844

Suez Canal Co., 596, 804

Sukarno, President Ahmed, of Indonesia, 538, 794, 795, 796

Sumatra, 221, 373, 795

Sun Yat-sen, 382, 384, 767

Supreme Commander of Allied Powers (SCAP), 576

Supreme Headquarters, Allied Powers, Europe (SHAPE), 574

Sverdlovsk, U-2 plane shot down near (1960), 842

Sweden, 444; prior to World War I, 80, 81, 110–111; in World War I, 141; after World War I, 220, 456; in World War II, 623; after World War II, 661–663, 695; in Council of Europe, 690

Switzerland, 444; prior to World War I, 104, 109–110; during World War I, 161; description and history, 659–661, 690; after World War II, 661, 690, 695

Sykes-Picot Treaty (1916), 174, 197

Syndicats, rise of, in France, 68

Syria, 174, 197; French mandate, 198, 356, 357, 358; in World War I, 476, 589, 590; in Arab League, 592, 804; after World War II, 804, 807

Szálasi, Ferencz, 317, 514

Szilard, Leo, quoted, 532–533

Taaffe, Count, 96

Tachen, 792, 793

Taff Vale Decision, 40, 41

Taft, William Howard, 237

Taiwan, 791–793. See also Formosa

Talaat Bey, 102

Tallin, 513

Tanganyika, 823

Tangier, 362, 821

Tanks, in warfare, 452–453

Tannenberg, Battle of (1914), 136

Taoism, 379, 763

Tariff, struggle for protective, in Britain,

673; and South Africa, 713; Communist China barred, 764, 773; on Kashmir, 782, 783; and "two-China" policy, 792; and Indonesia, 794; and the Philippines, 797; Cambodia and Laos admitted, 797; and the Congo, 824, 837; on problem of disarmament, 831, 832; decline of, 835–838; the Security Council and the Assembly, 836–838

United Nations Children's Fund (UNICEF), 547, 786, 795

United Nations Educational, Scientific and Cultural Organization (UNESCO), 546, 828

United Nations Relief and Rehabilitation Administration (UNRRA), 547, 569, 734

United Nations Trusteeship Commission, and Italian colonies, 552

United States of America, emergence of as world power, 12–13, 117–121, 424–425; Spanish-American War, 106, 122, 344; foreign poicy, 121–124; in World War I, 133, 144–147, 154–155; foreign loans in World War I, 157, 207; war aims, 160; use of propaganda, 162; as symbol of idealistic program, 179–180; and war debts, 207–213, 397; defers payment on international loans, 213–214; repudiates League of Nations, 219–220, 543; post-war mood, 236–237; events preceding Depression, 238–242; New Deal, 242–245; and world affairs, 245–247; trade with Canada, 334; as typical of Anglo-Saxon bloc, 340; relations with Latin America, 344, 728, 729; and China, 386, 407; material prosperity and emotional insecurity, 397–398; Depression, 398–399; abandons gold standard, 401, 442; and disarmament, 405; attitude toward World War II (1939–1941), 465–467; lend-lease, 467, 471; and North African campaign, 476–478; relations with Japan (1939–1941), 478–484; resources and production, 487–489; struggle for control of sea and air, 489–494; and invasion of Italy, 502–504; offensive in Pacific, 507–511; invasion of France, 514–518; destruction of Germany, 523–526; collapse of Japan, 526–528; post-war influence, 534–537; and the United Nations, 545–548; and peace treaties, 548–553; occupation of Germany, 554–557; Truman doctrine, 565; post-war outlook, 568–571; Cold War, 569, 570, 835–844; Marshall Plan, 571, 572; NATO, 572–574; occupation of Japan, 575–579; attitude toward China, 580–582, 791–793; Korean War, 582–585; relations with China, 582, 764, 791–793; and Indochina, 585–587; in Suez crisis, 595–600; demobilization and reconversion, 604–606; postwar prosperity and production, 607–610; finances, 611–614; political development (1939–1961), 614–615; political developments since 1961, 615–618; Soviet-American duel for world leadership, 698–701; and European Defense Community (EDC),

699–701; and Canadian economic projects, 703, 704; and ANZUS, 708, 710; and Cuba, 721, 722; and Brazil, 727; and Alliance for Progress, 727, 728; and India, 781; and Ceylon, 785, 786; and Indonesia, 795; and the Philippines, 796, 797; and Vietnam, 797–800, 843; on control of nuclear energy, 832; and the Franco-American dispute, 848–852; bipolarization of power between Soviet Union and, 852

United States-Japanese Treaty of Mutual Cooperation, 791

Uruguay, 346–347, 725

Vafiades, Marko, 565
Valera, Eamon de, 331
Vargas, Getulio, 726
Vasilevsky, Marshal Alexander M., 528
Vatican City, 275
Venetia, 93
Venezia Giulia, 551
Venezuela, 122, 346–347; after World War II, 726
Venizelos, Eleutherios, 160, 200, 326, 328
Verdun, Germans besiege, 138
Versailles, Treaty of (1919), making of, 181–185; Fourteen Points, 185–188; political settlements of, 189–202; War Guilt clause, 192; reparations, 193, 203–206; economic settlements, 206–214; rejected by U.S. Senate, 219; enforcement of, 259; violated by Germany, 263, 285; Chinese refuse to sign, 382; outmoded, 406, 414; defied by Germany, 410; France as upholder of, 415

Verwoerd, Hendrik F., 712, 713
Vichy, 462, 633
Victor Emmanuel III, King of Italy, 270; deposed, 672
Victoria, Queen of England, 36
Vienna, 308, 315; Turkish attempt to capture, 99; Russians capture (1945), 524, 525, 557; site of Kennedy-Khrushchev meeting (1961), 843
Vienna, Congress of, 90
Viet Cong, 798–800, 843
Vietminh, 587
Vietnam, North, 794, 797–800, 843; South, 586, 638, 708, 794, 797–800, 843, 851
Vilna, 320, 321
Virgin Islands, 111, 719
Vladivostok, 78, 170, 504
Vlassov, Andrey A., 525
Voltaire, François Marie Arouet de, 44
Voroshilov, Kliment, 738
Vorster, Balthazar J., 713

Wake Island, 376, 483
Wallachia, 113, 114, 139, 317
War debts, proposals to cancel, 397. *See also* Reparations
War Guilt Clause, of Versailles Treaty, 192
War guilt thesis, 177–180
Warsaw, 308, 312; rising of Polish underground, 512; captured by Russia, 523
Warsaw Pact, 755, 760, 841

34567890

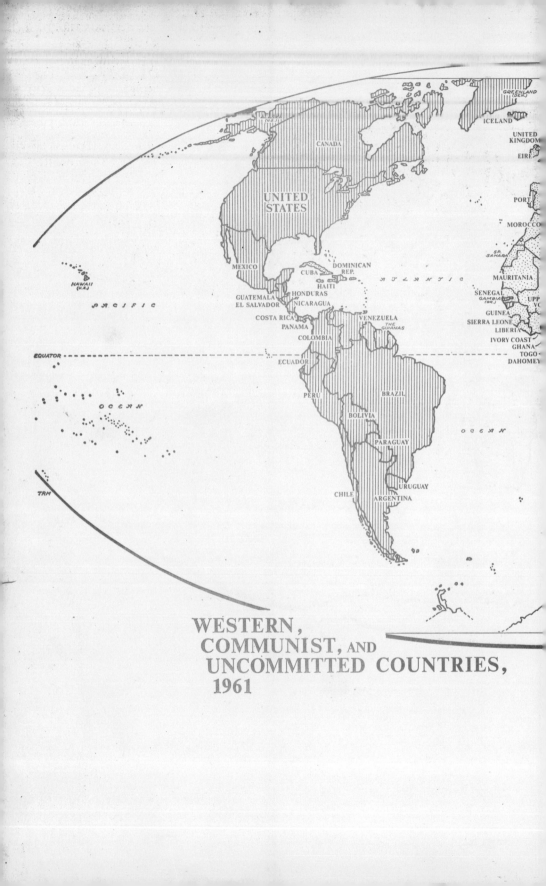

WESTERN,
COMMUNIST, AND
UNCOMMITTED COUNTRIES,
1961